Merriam-Webster's Concise Dictionary of English Usage

Merriam-Webster, Incorporated
Springfield, Massachusetts

A GENUINE MERRIAM-WEBSTER

The name *Webster* alone is no guarantee of excellence. It is
used by a number of publishers and may serve mainly to mislead an unwary buyer.
Merriam-Webster™ is the name you should look for when
you consider the purchase of dictionaries or other fine reference books. It carries the reputation of a company that has
been publishing since 1831 and is your assurance of quality and
authority.

Library of Congress Cataloging in Publication Data

Merriam-Webster's concise dictionary of English usage.
    p.   cm.
Includes bibliographical references.
ISBN 0-87779-633-5
    1. English language—Usage—Dictionaries. I. Title: Concise
dictionary of English usage II. Merriam-Webster, Inc.
PE1464.M47   2002
423'.1—dc21

               2002141587

Made in the United States of America

2 3 4 5 DF:RRD 050403

Contents

Preface

MERRIAM-WEBSTER'S CONCISE DICTIONARY OF ENGLISH USAGE is a guide to common problems of confused or disputed usage. It offers information and guidance about these problems by providing readers with the historical backgrounds of the usage and of the attitudes toward it, the current status of the usage, and recommendations for writers. Most of the topics treated have been selected from existing books on usage, primarily those published in the second half of the 20th century. We have also ranged freely over much earlier books, many of which contain the seeds of current concerns.

Besides dealing with the traditional concerns of usage, we have included entries illustrating idiomatic English usage, chiefly in the area of which prepositions go with nouns, verbs, and adjectives. Although, the listing of idioms here is not exhaustive, we believe that the approximately 500 idioms included are the ones most likely to raise questions, especially for people learning English as a second or foreign language. All of the entries for these idioms include quotations illustrating instances of varying usage.

A number of common spelling problems are also discussed briefly. While the emphasis of this work is on usage in writing, a small number of articles is devoted to problems of pronunciation.

Insofar as practicable, we have generously supplied the articles with illustrative quotations on the theory that examples of actual usage are more valuable to the person who is grappling with a problem of usage than are the made-up examples many commentators rely on. The bulk of these quotations have been taken from the Merriam-Webster files; however, we have occasionally included quotations taken from other published sources, such as historical dictionaries. The sources of all quotations taken from other sources are identified with parenthetical notes.

The preface is followed in the front matter by two sections which we recommend to all users of this work. The Explanatory Notes provides information about the conventions used in this dictionary. A Brief History of English Usage provides useful orientation for readers who wonder how these usage questions came

Explanatory Notes

Articles

Each article in this dictionary, like the entries in a general dictionary, is introduced by one or more boldface words indicating the subject for discussion:

media

glimpse, glance

reason is because

agreement: indefinite pronouns

Words that are homographs are distinguished by italic labels indicating part of speech:

hold, *verb*

hold, *noun*

An article that treats more than one aspect of its subject may be divided into sections, each section introduced by a boldface arabic numeral. Where it seems useful, the topic of the section is indicated with an introductory word or phrase:

locate . . .

1. *Locate* "settle." . . .

2. *Located* "situated." . . .

3. *Locate* "find." . . .

The articles in this dictionary are too diverse and many are too complex for all to be treated according to a single uniform pattern. The longer ones, however, usually contain all or most of the following elements: origin and development of the usage with examples, origin and development of criticism of the usage, the contemporary status of the usage with examples, review of alternatives, summary and recommendation. The order and proportion of the elements vary with the requirements of the topic, of course.

Citation of Sources

Sources cited within the text of an article—as distinct from illustrative quotations, discussed below—are handled in two different ways. Works cited infrequently are identified at each appearance by author, title, and date of publication. Works cited frequently are treated in a different way, in order to conserve space. References to these works—chiefly books of commentary on English usage, handbooks for writers of various kinds, grammars, and dictionaries—take a shortened form, most often the author's last name and the date of the book's publication (as Fowler 1926 or Bolinger 1980).

Handbooks and dictionaries cited as sources of usage opinion may instead be identified by an element of the title combined with the date (as Prentice Hall 1978 or Heritage 1969).

A dictionary referred to as a record of usage is usually given its title without a date on its first appearance in an article (as Dictionary of American Regional English) but is thereafter referred to by a customary abbreviation (as DARE). The exception to this last rule is the Oxford English Dictionary, which is consistently cited by the well-known abbreviation OED. Noah Webster's An American Dictionary of the English Language and its successor editions are cited in this way: editions from 1828 to 1909 appear as Webster and the year of publication. The two most recent (and most familiar) editions are simply called Webster's Second and Webster's Third, for the most part, but a date is sometimes added when it seems to be helpful in the context.

to take on such importance to teachers, writers, and others. Following the main A–Z section, there is a Bibliography, which serves the dual purpose of recording those dictionaries, grammars, commentaries on usage, and other works frequently consulted during the writing of this book and providing a source of suggestions for further reading.

Merriam-Webster's Concise Dictionary of English Usage is based on and abridged from *Merriam-Webster's Dictionary of English Usage,* which was prepared under the editorship of E. Ward Gilman and has drawn high praise from scholars, educators, and journalists. Articles for that book were written by Stephen J. Perrault, Kathleen M. Doherty, David B. Justice, Madeline L. Novak, and E. Ward Gilman, and the entire manuscript was reviewed by Frederick C. Mish, Editor in Chief of Merriam-Webster. E. Ward Gilman provided the updating and abridging necessary to produce the current volume, which was copyedited by John M. Morse. Quotations were verified by Kathleen M. Doherty, who also compiled the bibliography. Adrienne Scholtz and Jennifer N. Cislo connected the loose wires of cross-reference. Data entry was performed by Louise Johnson under the supervision of Veronica P. McLymont. Proofreading was done by Cynthia S. Ashby. Robert D. Copeland directed the book through editorial and typesetting stages.

As we said of our first *Dictionary of English Usage,* so can we say of this volume: We believe it contains a wealth of information, along with some quite practical advice, and we are confident that you will find it a useful, interesting, and sometimes entertaining work of reference.

Full references to all works cited in these ways appear in the Bibliography at the end of this volume.

Illustrative Quotations

This book includes thousands of illustrative quotations intended to clarify and to test the discussion. These may very occasionally be run in with the text but are usually indented and are always followed by an attribution, typically consisting of the author's name (if known), the title of the book or serial, and the date of publication. When the sources discussed in the last section are quoted, however, the usual shortened form of attribution is used.

We have not italicized the word or construction being illustrated in a quotation, so that the typographic conventions of each passage as we found it can be reproduced with reasonable accuracy. We have tried not to interfere with spelling. If the editor of an old work cited in a modern edition modernized the spelling, we have used it; if the editor preserved the old spelling, we have used that. We have only very rarely modernized spelling on our own and then only to make old words more easily recognizable. We have, however, silently corrected a few typographical errors irrelevant to the matter under discussion.

Quotations have been dated, insofar as possible, in order to establish the antiquity of a locution or its currency at some particular time or to show when an unfamiliar writer was working. As a reader you can generally assume that any quotation from the last fifty years or so represents current usage—editors have frequently preferred a clear older quotation to an ambiguous or unhelpful newer one.

The date given for a work that has passed through several editions is, in general, the date of the edition actually seen by us. Exceptions are made for famous works of earlier periods, for which the date is usually that of original publication, even though we may have consulted a modern edition.

We have taken a few liberties with the sources of quotations, generally omitting initial *the* when it is part of the title of a periodical, and abbreviating *supplement, magazine, journal,* and *review.* Short titles like *Robinson Crusoe* and *Tom Sawyer* are used for a few well-known works.

Cross-Reference

Directional cross-references to articles where relevant discussion may be found are employed liberally throughout the book. These may take any of several forms. If the term where the discussion is located is mentioned within the text, a parenthetical "(which see)" is placed immediately after the term. All other cross-references are in small capital letters; they may appear at the end of an article or section of an article, or they may receive separate entry:

good 1. *Feel good, feel well.* . . . See also FEEL BAD, FEEL BADLY.

under the circumstances See CIRCUMSTANCES.

No separate entry is made, however, if it would fall immediately before or after the article where the discussion is located. Thus, the misspelling *quandry* is discussed at **quandary**, but no entry for the former appears.

Pronunciation

Articles on problems of pronunciation necessarily include pronunciation respellings. The symbols used in these respellings are essentially those of Merriam-Webster's New Collegiate Dictionary, Tenth Edition, and are explained on the Pronunciation Symbols page, which faces the first page of the dictionary.

A Brief History of English Usage

English usage today is an area of discourse—sometimes it seems more like dispute—about the way words are used and ought to be used. This discourse makes up the subject matter of a large number of books that put the word *usage* in their titles. Behind usage as a subject lies a collection of opinions about what English grammar is or should be, about the propriety of using certain words and phrases, and about the social status of those who use certain words and constructions. A fairly large number of these opinions have been with us long enough to be regarded as rules or at least to be referred to as rules. In fact they are often regarded as rules of grammar, even if they concern only matters of social status or vocabulary selection. And many of these rules are widely believed to have universal application, even though they are far from universally observed.

Chancery English

To understand how these opinions and rules developed, we have to go back in history, at least as far back as the year 1417, when the official correspondence of Henry V suddenly and almost entirely stopped being written in French and started being written in English. By mid-century many government documents and even private letters were in English, and before 1500 even statutes were being recorded in the mother tongue. This restoration of English as the official language of the royal bureaucracy was one very important influence on the gradual emergence of a single standard dialect of English out of the many varied regional dialects that already existed. English now had to serve the functions formerly served by Latin and French, languages which had already assumed standard forms, and this new reality was a powerful spur to the formation of a standard in writing English that could be quite independent of variable speech.

The process was certainly not completed within the 15th century, but increasingly the written form of the language that modern scholars call Chancery English had its effect, in combination with other influences such as the newfangled process of printing from movable type.

The English Renaissance

But the rise of Standard English did not by itself generate concern over usage. There was no special interest in language as such at that time. Not until near the end of the 15th century did the intellectual ferment of the European Renaissance begin to be felt in England. By the middle of the 16th century the English Renaissance was in full flower, and the revival of learning and letters brought with it a conscious interest in the English language as a medium for literature and learned discourse. There were those who had their doubts about its suitability. Still, the desire to use the vernacular rather than Latin was strong, and some of the doubters sought to put flesh on the bare bones of English by importing words from Latin, Italian, and French—the European languages of learned and graceful discourse. Among those who enriched English from the word stock of Europe were Sir Thomas Elyot and Sir Thomas More. Opposed to these enrichers of the language were purists such as Roger Ascham and Sir John Cheke, who preferred their English, rude as it might be, untainted by foreign imports. The imported learned terms became known as *inkhorn terms*, and their use and misuse by the imperfectly educated became the subject of much lively satire—some of it written by Shakespeare, among many others.

In addition to the controversy over imported words there were other concerns, such as the state of English spelling. In those days people mostly spelled things the way they sounded, and there was little uniformity indeed. A number of people consequently became interested in spelling reform and in regularizing spelling as best they could. Among these was the schoolmaster Richard Mulcaster, who may have served as the model for Shakespeare's pedant Holofernes. There were more radical reformers, too—John Hart, Sir Thomas Smith, and William Bullokar are examples—who devised phonetic alphabets to better represent English speech sounds. Bullokar is worthy of note for another reason: in 1586 he published *Bref Grammar for English*—the first English grammar book. It was probably intended as an introduction to the subsequent study of Latin grammar.

So 16th-century interest in language produced two of the basic tools of the writer on usage. Bullokar, out of his interest in regularizing and reforming, had been moved to write a grammar of English. And the vocabulary controversy— the introduction of inkhorn terms by the enrichers and the revival of English archaisms by the purists (of whom the poet Edmund Spenser was one)—led another schoolmaster, Robert Cawdrey, to produce the first English dictionary in 1604.

The 17th Century

The 17th century provides several more signposts on the way to the treatment of usage as we know it. One of these is the expression of a desire for regulation of the language by an academy similar to the ones established in Italy in the 16th century and in France in 1635. Calls for the establishment of an English academy came as early as 1617; among the writers to urge one were John Dryden in 1664, John Evelyn in 1665, and Daniel Defoe in 1697.

More grammar books were also published at this time. Ben Jonson's appeared posthumously in 1640. It is short and sketchy and is intended for the use of foreigners. Its grammar is descriptive, but Jonson hung his observations on a Latin grammatical framework. It also seems to be the first English grammar book to quote the Roman rhetorician Quintilian's dictum "Custom is the most certain mistress of language."

John Wallis, a mathematician and member of the Royal Society, published in 1653 a grammar, written in Latin, for the use of foreigners who wanted to learn English. Wallis, according to George H. McKnight, abandoned much of the method of Latin grammar. Wallis's grammar is perhaps best remembered for being the source of the much discussed distinction between *shall* and *will*. Wallis's grammar is also the one referred to by Samuel Johnson in the front matter of his 1755 dictionary.

John Dryden deserves mention too. He defended the English of his time as an improvement over the English of Shakespeare and Jonson. He is the first person we know of who worried about the preposition at the end of a sentence. He eliminated many such from his own writings when revising his works for a collected edition. He seems to have decided the practice was wrong because it could not happen in Latin.

The 18th Century: Grammar

By the 18th century, grammars were being written predominantly for English speakers, and although they were written for the purpose of instructing, they seem to find more fun in correcting. A change in the underlying philosophy of grammar had occurred, and it is made explicit in perhaps the first 18th-century grammar, *A Key to the Art of Letters* . . . , published in 1700 by a schoolmaster named A. Lane. He thought it a mistake to view grammar simply as a means to learn a foreign language and asserted that "the true End and Use of Grammar is to teach how to speak and write well and learnedly in a language already known, according to the unalterable Rules of right Reason." Gone was Ben Jonson's appeal to custom.

There was evidently a considerable amount of general interest in things grammatical among men of letters, for Addison, Steele, and Swift all treated grammar in one way or another in *The Tatler* and *The Spectator* in 1710, 1711, and 1712. In 1712 Swift published yet another proposal for an English academy (it came within a whisker of succeeding); John Oldmixon attacked Swift's proposal in the same year. Public interest must have helped create a market for the grammar books which began appearing with some frequency about this same time. And if controversy fuels sales, grammarians knew it; they were perfectly willing to emphasize their own advantages by denigrating their predecessors, sometimes in abusive terms.

We need mention only a few of these productions here. Pride of place must go to Bishop Robert Lowth's *A Short Introduction to English Grammar,* 1762. Lowth's book is both brief and logical. Lowth was influenced by the theories of James Harris's *Hermes,* 1751, a curious disquisition about universal grammar. Lowth apparently derived his notions about the perfectibility of English grammar from Harris, and he did not doubt that he could reduce the language to a system of uniform rules. Lowth's approach was strictly prescriptive; he meant to improve and correct, not describe. He judged correctness by his own rules—mostly derived from Latin grammar—which frequently went against established usage. His favorite mode of illustration is what was known as "false syntax": examples of linguistic wrongdoing from the King James Bible, Shakespeare, Sidney, Donne, Milton, Swift, Addison, Pope—the most respected names in English literature. He was so sure of himself that he could permit himself a little joke; discussing the construction where a preposition comes at the end of a clause or sentence, he says, "This is an idiom, which our language is strongly inclined to."

Lowth's grammar was not written for children. But he did what he intended to so well that subsequent grammarians fairly fell over themselves in haste to get out versions of Lowth suitable for school use, and most subsequent grammars—including Noah Webster's first—were to some extent based upon Lowth's.

The older descriptive tradition of Jonson and Wallis was not quite dead, however. Joseph Priestley, whose grammar was first published in 1761, added a supplementary section in 1768 that used false syntax too. In the main Priestley was more tolerant of established usages than Lowth, and he disagreed with Lowth on specific points. Priestley's grammar enjoyed some success and his opinions were treated with

respect, but he was not imitated like Lowth.

The most successful of the Lowth adapters was Lindley Murray. Murray was an American living in England. Friends asked him to write a grammar for use in an English girls' school, and he obliged. Murray considered himself only a compiler, and that he was. He took over verbatim large patches from Lowth and teased them out with pieces taken from Priestley and a few other grammarians and rhetoricians. He removed the authors' names from the false syntax and stirred in a heavy dose of piety. He silently and primly corrected Lowth's jocular little clause to "to which our language is strongly inclined." The resulting mixture was one of the most successful grammar books ever, remaining a standard text in American schools for a half century.

George Campbell's *The Philosophy of Rhetoric,* 1776, is not a grammar book proper, but it contains a long discussion of grammatical proprieties. Campbell starts out sensibly enough; he says that grammar is based on usage, and he rejects notions of an abstract or universal grammar. But he then proceeds to examine usage, concluding that the usage that counts is reputable, national, and present use. He goes on to present nine canons of verbal criticism, by one or another of which he can reject any usage he chooses to. By the time all the discussions of barbarisms, solecisms, and improprieties are finished—the discussions are well supplied with examples from many of Bishop Lowth's favorite whipping boys—it is quite apparent that the reputable, national, and present use that passes all tests is simply whatever suits the taste of George Campbell.

The 18th Century: Commentary

The 18th century's new contribution to ways of writing about grammar and rhetoric was the book of unvarnished usage opinion, best exemplified by Robert Baker's anonymously published *Reflections on the English Language,* 1770. According to his preface, Baker left school at fifteen, learned no Greek and only the easiest Latin, had never seen the folio edition of Johnson's Dictionary, and owned no books. He fancied he had good taste, however, and he clearly understood French. His book is patterned on *Remarques sur la langue françoise,* 1659, written by Claude Faure de Vaugelas, a leading member of the French Academy.

Baker's *Reflections* is a random collection of comments, mostly about what he considers misuses, based chiefly on books that he has borrowed or read. He brings forward no authorities to support his *ipse dixit* pronouncements, many of which are on the order of "This is not good English" or "This does not make sense." Yet a surprising number of the locutions he questioned are still to be found as topics of discussion in current books on usage. It is less surprising, perhaps, that the moderns are still repeating Baker's conclusions.

The 19th Century

The 19th century is so rich in usage lore that it is hard to summarize. We find something new in the entrance of journalists into the usage field. Reviews had commented on grammatical matters throughout the 18th century, it is true, but in the 19th newspapers and magazines with wider popular appeal began to pronounce. One result of this activity was the usage book that consists of pieces first written for a newspaper or magazine and then collected into a book along with selected comments and suggestions by readers (this type of book is still common today). Perhaps the first of these was *A Plea for the Queen's English,* 1864, by Henry Alford, dean of Canterbury. Alford was vigorously attacked by George Washington Moon, a writer born in London of American parents, in a work that eventually became titled *The Dean's English.* The controversy fueled several editions of both books and seems to have entertained readers on both sides of the Atlantic.

On the American side of the Atlantic the puristic strictures of Edward S. Gould, originally newspaper and magazine contributions, were collected as *Good English* in 1867. Gould was apparently annoyed to find that Alford had anticipated him on several points, and devoted a section to belaboring the Dean, only to discover that

Moon had anticipated him there. He acknowledged the justness of Moon's criticisms and then appended a few parting shots at Moon's English, before tacking on an assault on the spelling reforms of Noah Webster and a series of lectures on pulpit oratory. Moon replied with *The Bad English of Lindley Murray and Other Writers on the English Language,* 1868. (Gould was one of the "other writers.") Language controversy sold books in America as well as in England.

The most popular of American 19th-century commentators was Richard Grant White, whose *Words and Their Uses,* 1870, was also compiled from previously published articles. He did not deign to mention earlier commentators except to take a solitary whack at Dean Alford for his sneer at American English. His chapters on "misused words" and "words that are not words" hit many of the same targets as Gould's chapters on "misused words" and "spurious words," but White's chapters are longer. Perhaps his most entertaining sections deal with his denial that English has a grammar, which is introduced by a Dickensian account of having been rapped over the knuckles at age five and a half for not understanding his grammar lesson. White, who was not without intellectual attainments—he had edited Shakespeare—was nevertheless given to frequent faulty etymologizing, and for some reason he was so upset by the progressive passive *is being built* that he devoted a whole chapter to excoriating it. These last two features caught the attention of the peppery Fitzedward Hall, an American teacher of Sanskrit living in England.

Hall produced a whole book—*Recent Exemplifications of False Philology,* 1872—exposing White's errors, and returned to the attack again with *Modern English* in 1873. Hall was a new breed of commentator, bringing a wealth of illustrative material from his collection of examples to bear on the various points of contention. Hall's evidence should have been more than enough to overwhelm White's unsupported assertions, but it was not. Partly to blame is the public's disdain of the scholarly, and partly to blame is Hall's style—he never makes a point succinctly, but lets his most trenchant observations dissipate in a cloud of sesquipedalian afterthoughts. White's books remained in print until the

1930s; Hall's collection of examples became part of the foundations of the *Oxford English Dictionary.*

Two other 19th-century innovations deserve mention. William Cullen Bryant's *Index Expurgatorius,* 1877, is the start of the American newspaper tradition in usage—works written by newspaper editors. Bryant was editor-in-chief and part owner of the *New York Evening Post.* His *Index* is simply a list of words not to be used in the *Post;* there was no explanatory matter. Lists of forbidden words were popular for a time afterward, but the fashion passed. The newspaper editor as usage arbiter has continued to the present, however. The pseudonymous Alfred Ayres in *The Verbalist,* 1881, seems to have been the first, or one of the first, of these to arrange his comments in alphabetical order, creating a sort of dictionary of usage.

We have said nothing about 19th-century grammars, and not much needs to be said about them. Some dissatisfaction with the older English traditions existed, but little seems to have resulted from it. One grammarian worthy of note is Goold Brown, whose *Grammar of English Grammars* was first published in 1851. He collected most of the grammars published up to his own time and used them for his examples of false grammar. He also exhibited at length their inconsistencies and disagreements. Goold Brown permitted himself one mild observation (most were rather tart): "Grammarians would perhaps differ less, if they read more."

American English

In the early decades of the Republic, many Americans patriotically supported the home-grown version of the language against the language of the vanquished British oppressors. There were proposals for a Federal English—Noah Webster was in the forefront of the movement—and for the establishment of an American academy to promote and regulate the language—John Adams made one such proposal.

The British, for their part, were not amused by the presumption of former colonials. Americanisms had been viewed askance as early as 1735, but the frequency and the ferocity of denunciation markedly increased in the 19th century, as British travelers, some of them literary folk like Captain Marryat, Mrs. Frances Trollope, and Charles Dickens, visited the United States and returned to England to publish books of their travels, almost always disparaging in tone. They seldom failed to work in a few criticisms of the language as well as the uncouth character and manners of Americans. British reviewers, too, were outspoken in their denunciation of things American, and especially Americanisms.

American writers put up a spirited defense for a time, but the writing class eventually began to wear down under the onslaught. By 1860, in an article extolling the virtues of Joseph Worcester's dictionary, the *Atlantic Monthly* could call American English "provincial." The general attitude after the Civil War seems to have been one of timidity rather than defiance. The timid attitude is of interest here because it was in the second half of the 19th century that Americanisms began to make their way silently into American usage books as errors. Many of these, such as *balance* for *remainder* and *loan* for *lend,* are still denigrated by American usage writers and their native origin passed over in silence.

By the end of the 19th century, differences had developed between the ways usage issues were being treated in England and in the United States. Except for the fruits of the Alford–Moon controversy, there seem to be very few British books concerned exclusively with usage problems. The most frequently reprinted of these few was one written by a Scot: William B. Hodgson's *Errors in the Use of English,* 1881. British literati were not indifferent to such issues, but they seem mainly to have put their comments in reviews and letters and works directed primarily to other subjects. Walter Savage Landor, for instance, delivered himself of a number of idiosyncratic views about language and usage in one or two of his *Imaginary Conversations.* John Stuart Mill put a few of his opinions into *A System of Logic.*

America, on the other hand, saw the growth of a small industry devoted to the cultivation of the linguistically insecure, who were being produced in increasing numbers by American public schools using the grammar of Lindley Murray combined with the opinions of Richard Grant White. After the Civil War little handbooks for the guidance of the perplexed appeared with some frequency. We have mentioned one of these, Alfred Ayres's *The Verbalist*. Others bear such titles as *Vulgarisms and Other Errors of Speech, Words: Their Use and Abuse, Some Common Errors of Speech,* and *Slips of Tongue and Pen.* The production of popular books on usage topics continues to be common to this day in the United States.

The 20th Century: The British View

The different approaches of the British and Americans to usage questions have continued along the lines evident in the last half of the 19th century. Fewer books devoted to usage issues have been produced in England, and the arena there has been dominated by two names: Fowler and Gowers. H. W. Fowler's best-known work is *Modern English Usage,* 1926, an expanded, updated, and alphabetized version of *The King's English,* which he had produced with one of his brothers in 1906. This book gained ready acceptance as an authority, and it is usually treated with considerable deference on both sides of the Atlantic. It is a thick book in small print, packed with a combination of good sense, traditional attitudes, pretension-pricking, minute distinctions, and a good deal of what Otto Jespersen, the Danish scholarly grammarian of the English language, called "language moralizing." Fowler, in the tradition of Alford and Richard Grant White, found much to dislike in the prose of contemporary newspapers. He had no gadfly like George Washington Moon to challenge his authority, although he did dispute a few constructions with Otto Jespersen in the pages of the tracts issued by the Society for Pure English. In some of these disputes a characteristic pattern emerges: the historical grammarian finds a construction in literature and wonders how it came to be; Fowler finds the same construction in the newspapers and condemns it.

Sir Ernest Gowers came into usage commentary from a different direction: he was asked to prepare a book for British civil servants to help them avoid the usual bureaucratic jargon of British official prose. The result was *Plain Words,* 1941. This slender book has gone through several editions, growing a bit each time. In 1965 a new edition of Fowler appeared, edited by Gowers, to which Gowers added a number of his own favorite topics.

A third edition of *Modern English Usage* was published in 1996. It was prepared by Robert Burchfield, former editor of the *Oxford English Dictionary,* and it is far more of a rewriting than a revision. Based on historical principles and on an examination of written sources from the 1980s and 1990s, Burchfield's edition is more open-minded than either the 1926 or the 1965 editions, which has left many of the hardcore Fowler fans more than a little annoyed.

In addition to Fowler, Gowers, and Burchfield, the work of Eric Partridge, particularly *Usage and Abusage,* 1942, has been influential.

The 20th Century: The American View

The treatment of usage in America over the past century has hewed steadfastly to the traditional line of linguistic etiquette. School grammars are elaborately graded and decked out with color printing, but the most successful are still solidly based on Lowth and Murray. College handbooks have proliferated since 1907, the date of the earliest one of which we've heard. The contents of these works have not changed greatly, however; the essential sameness of the "Glossaries of Usage" attached to them suggests that their contents are to some extent determined by a desire to carry over from the previous edition as much as possible and to cover what the competition covers. General-purpose guides for those whose schooling is complete are still produced regularly, and in a wider variety of shapes and sizes than in the 19th century. These have developed offshoots in the form of books aimed at business writers and others aimed at technical and scientific writers.

The newspaper tradition has also continued strong. Some usage questions are dealt with in house stylebooks (now often published for outsiders, as well), and newspaper editors have written usage guides for the general public, though these usually have a strong newspaper slant. Especially prominent among these are the several books of Theodore Bernstein, particularly *The Careful Writer,* 1965.

A characteristic of writing on usage has been, right from the beginning, disagreement among the writers on specific points. Various attempts at reconciling these differences have been made. One of the earliest dates from 1883. C. W. Bardeen, a schoolbook publisher, put out a little book in which he tried to discover a consensus by examining some thirty sources, including a number of current usage books, some grammars, some works on philology, some on synonymy, and Webster's and Worcester's dictionaries. Roy Copperud produced books on the same general plan in 1970 and 1980.

Another approach to the problem of varying opinion has been the survey of opinion. Sterling A. Leonard made the first in 1931. Leonard's survey was replicated in 1971 by Raymond D. Crisp, and a similar survey was conducted in England by G. H. Mittins and three colleagues and published in 1970. The results of these surveys are quantified, so that interested readers can discover the relative acceptability or obloquy of each tested item. Somewhat the same idea has also been tried with the usage panel, an assembled panel of experts to whom each individual item is submitted for approval or disapproval. Again, quantification of relative approval or disapproval is the aim.

Usage Scholarship

The 20th century was the first in which usage was been studied from a scholarly or historical point of view, although Fitzedward Hall's *Modern English* of 1873 should probably be acknowledged as a precursor. Thomas R. Lounsbury collected a number of his magazine articles into *The Standard of Usage in English,* 1908, which examined the background of attitudes and issues. J. Lesslie Hall's *English Usage,* 1917, checked 141 issues drawn from the work of Richard Grant White and from several college-level grammars and rhetorics against evidence from English and American literature. Sterling A. Leonard in *The Doctrine of Correctness in English Usage 1700-1800,* 1929, provided the first thorough examination of the origins of many attitudes about usage in the 18th century.

The 1920s and 1930s were a time of considerable interest in the examination and testing of attitudes and beliefs about usage and in a rationalization of the matter and methods of school grammar. Various publications written by Charles C. Fries and Robert C. Pooley, for example, seemed to point the way. They had relatively little influence in the following decades, however; the schoolbooks by and large follow the traditional lines, and the popular books of usage treat the traditional subjects. A notable exception is Bergen and Cornelia Evans's *A Dictionary of Contemporary American Usage,* 1957. The book takes the traditional view of many specific issues, but it is strong in insisting that actual usage, both historical and contemporary, must be weighed carefully in reaching usage opinions.

If the mainstream of usage commentary has continued to run in the same old channels, there have nonetheless been some undercurrents of importance. Serious examination of the received truths has continued. Margaret M. Bryant's *Current American Usage,* 1962, reported the results of the testing of many specific items against actual use as shown in current books, magazines, and newspapers. Articles in scholarly books and journals (like *American Speech*) evince continuing interest in real language and real usage in spite of a strong tendency in modern linguistics toward the study of language in more abstract ways. If the popular idea of usage is represented by the continuing series of books produced by the journalists Philip Howard (in England) and William Safire (in the United States) and by the continuing publication of traditionally oriented handbooks, there is also some countervailing critical opinion, as shown by such books as Dwight Bolinger's *Language—the Loaded Weapon,* Jim Quinn's *American Tongue and Cheek,* Dennis Baron's *Grammar and Good Taste,* and Harvey Daniels's *Famous Last Words,* all published in the early 1980s.

For Further Study

A historical sketch of this length necessarily must omit many deserving names and titles and pass over many interesting observers and observations. Much of the historical information herein draws heavily on materials available in Leonard's *Doctrine of Correctness*; Charles Carpenter Fries's *The Teaching of the English Language,* 1927; George H. McKnight's *Modern English in the Making,* 1928; H. L. Mencken's *The American Language,* 4th edition, 1936, and Supplement 1, 1945; Baron's *Grammar and Good Taste,* 1982; Daniels's *Famous Last Words,* 1983; and Sundby et al.'s *Dictionary of English Normative Grammar,* 1991. These books constitute a rich mine of information for the serious student of English usage and its history, to whom we also recommend a perusal of our bibliography.

Pronunciation Symbols

ə.......banana, collide, abut

ˈə, ˌə.......humdrum, abut

ᵊ.......immediately preceding \l\, \n\, \m\, \ŋ\, as in battle, mitten, eaten, and sometimes open \ˈō-pᵊm\, lock and key \-ᵊŋ-\; immediately following \l\, \m\, \r\, as often in French table, prisme, titre

ər.......further, merger, bird

ˈər-, ...as in two different pronunciations
ˈə-r.......of hurry \ˈhər-ē, ˈhə-rē\

a.......mat, map, mad, gag, snap, patch

ā.......day, fade, date, aorta, drape, cape

ä.......bother, cot, and with most American speakers, father, cart

ȧ.......father as pronounced by speakers who do not rhyme it with bother; French patte

au̇.......now, loud, out

b.......baby, rib

ch.......chin, nature \ˈnā-chər\ (actually, this sound is \t\ + \sh\)

d.......did, adder

e.......bet, bed, peck

ˈē, ˌē.......beat, nosebleed, evenly, easy

ē.......easy, mealy

f.......fifty, cuff

g.......go, big, gift

h.......hat, ahead

hw.......whale as pronounced by those who do not have the same pronunciation for both whale and wail

i.......tip, banish, active

ī.......site, side, buy, tripe (actually, this sound is \ä\ + \i\, or \ȧ\ + \i\)

j.......job, gem, edge, join, judge (actually, this sound is \d\ + \zh\)

k.......kin, cook, ache

k̲.......German ich, Buch; one pronunciation of loch

l.......lily, pool

m.......murmur, dim, nymph

n.......no, own

ⁿ.......indicates that a preceding vowel or diphthong is pronounced with the nasal passages open, as in French un bon vin blanc \œⁿ-bōⁿ-vaⁿ-bläⁿ\

ŋ.......sing \ˈsiŋ\, singer \ˈsiŋ-ər\, finger \ˈfiŋ-gər\, ink \ˈiŋk\

ō.......bone, know, beau

ȯ.......saw, all, gnaw, caught

œ.......French boeuf, German Hölle

œ̄.......French feu, German Höhle

ȯi.......coin, destroy

p.......pepper, lip

r.......red, car, rarity

s.......source, less

sh.......as in shy, mission, machine, special (actually, this is a single sound, not two); with a hyphen between, two sounds as in grasshopper \ˈgras-ˌhä-pər\

t.......tie, attack, late, later, latter

th.......as in thin, ether (actually, this is a single sound, not two); with a hyphen between, two sounds as in knighthood \ˈnīt-ˌhu̇d\

th̲.......then, either, this (actually, this is a single sound, not two)

ü.......rule, youth, union \ˈyün-yən\, few \ˈfyü\

u̇.......pull, wood, book, curable \ˈkyu̇r-ə-bəl\, fury \ˈfyu̇(ə)r-ē\

ᵫ.......German füllen, hübsch

ᵫ̄.......French rue, German fühlen

v.......vivid, give

w.......we, away; in some words having final \(ˌ)ō\, \(ˌ)yü\, or \(ˌ)ü\ a variant \ə-w\ occurs before vowels, as in \ˈfäl-ə-wiŋ\, covered by the variant \ə(-w)\ or \yə(-w)\ at the entry word

y.......yard, young, cue \ˈkyü\, mute \ˈmyüt\, union \ˈyün-yən\

ʸ.......indicates that during the articulation of the sound represented by the preceding character the front of the tongue has substantially the position it has for the articulation of the first sound of yard, as in French digne \dēnʸ\

z.......zone, raise

zh.......as in vision, azure \ˈa-zhər\ (actually, this is a single sound, not two); with hyphen between, two sounds as in hogshead \ˈhȯgz-ˌhed, ˈhägz-\

\.......slant line used in pairs to mark the beginning and end of a transcription: \ˈpen\

ˈ.......mark preceding a syllable with primary (strongest) stress: \ˈpen-mən-ˌship\

ˌ.......mark preceding a syllable with secondary (medium) stress: \ˈpen-mən-ˌship\

-.......mark of syllable division

( ).......indicate that what is symbolized between is present in some utterances but not in others: factory \ˈfak-t(ə-)rē\

A

a, an There is an article on the proper use of *a* and *an* in almost every usage book ever written, although hardly a native speaker of English has any difficulty with them—in fact one seldom thinks about them at all in speech.

The difficulty, when there is any, is to be found in writing. The basic rules are these: use *a* before a consonant sound; use *an* before a vowel sound. Before a letter or an acronym or before numerals, choose *a* or *an* according to the way the letter or numeral is pronounced: *an* FDA directive, *a* U.N. resolution, *a* $5.00 bill.

Actual usage, of course, is more complex than the simple rules would lead you to expect. Here is what actual usage shows:

1. Before words with an initial consonant sound, *a* is usual in speech and writing. This is in line with the basic rule.

2. Before *h* in an unstressed or weakly stressed syllable, *a* and *an* are both used in writing (*an* historic, *a* historic) but *an* is more usual in speech, whether the *h* is pronounced or not. This variation is the result of historical development; in unstressed and weakly stressed syllables, *h* was formerly not pronounced in many words where it is pronounced at the present time. A few words, such as *historic* and (especially in England) *hotel*, are in transition, and may be found with either *a* or *an*. You choose the article that suits your own pronunciation.

3. Occasionally in modern writing and speech and regularly in the King James Version of the Bible, *an* is used before *h* in a stressed syllable, as in *an* hundred. Again, we have the same historical change: many more words were pronounced with a silent initial *h* in the past than are at present. A few words, such as *heir, hour,* and *honest,* generally have silent initial *h*; some others, like *herb* or *humble* are pronounced both ways. Use *a* or *an* according to your own pronunciation.

4. Before words beginning with a consonant sound but an orthographic vowel, *an* is sometimes used in speech and writing (*an* unique, such *an* one). This use is less frequent now than in the past.

5. Before words with an initial vowel sound, *an* is usual in speech and writing. This is in line with the basic rule.

6. Occasionally, and more often in some dialects than others, *a* is used in speech before words beginning with a vowel sound. The Dictionary of American Regional English reports this to be frequent in the United States; some British observers have found it in public pronouncements, both British and American.

7. *A* is normally unstressed, and pronounced \ə\. When stressed, as in "It's *a* solution, but not the only solution," it is pronounced \'ā\ in the United States, but often \'a\ in Canada.

abbreviations Abbreviations have been receiving bad notices since the 18th century. Such writers as Addison and Swift satirized the fashionable practice of the time of using truncated or clipped forms of long words—such as *pozz, phizz, plenipo,* and *hippo* for *positively, physiognomy, plenipotentiary,* and *hypochondria*—in conversation. Ordinary contractions—*can't, haven't, shan't, isn't,* for instance—were likewise satirized. Usage books took up the cudgels from the satirists. MacCracken & Sandison 1917, for instance, lists several truncations disapprovingly—among them *auto, phone, photo, exam,* and *gym.* Guth 1985 continues the critical tradition but changes the truncations:

> Avoid informal abbreviations. Avoid clipped forms like *bike, prof, doc, fan mag, exec, econ.* (Other shortened forms, like *phone, ad,* and *exam* are now commonly used in serious writing.)

Aside from the social acceptability of clipped forms (Emily Post in 1927 disapproved *phone* and *photo*), there are other considerations to be taken into account. Handbooks in general recommend avoiding abbreviations in "formal" writing. Flesch 1964 disagrees, however:

> It's a superstition that abbreviations shouldn't be used in serious writing and that it's good style to spell everything out. Nonsense: use abbreviations whenever they are customary and won't attract the attention of the reader.

Flesch's advice seems sound; but care should be taken to observe what in fact is customary. It is obvious that what is customary in technical writing will be different from what is customary in journalism or in scholarly articles. If you are uncertain, you should consult an appropriate style manual or handbook.

General advice can be found in any of a number of composition handbooks and in general style manuals, such as *Merriam-Webster's Manual for Writers and Editors*.

See also ETC.; I.E., E.G.

abdomen This word may be pronounced with the main stress on the first syllable or on the second: \\'ab-də-mən\\ or \\ab-'dō-mən\\. The former version predominates among laypeople; physicians are more evenly divided.

abhorrence Bernstein 1965 notes that *abhorrence*, when followed by a preposition, takes *of*. This is true in a large majority of cases.

> . . . the public fear and abhorrence of a ground war —Ellen Goodman, *Springfield* (Mass.) *Union-News*, 15 Feb. 1991

> . . . my natural abhorrence of its sickening inhumanity —George Bernard Shaw, *Back to Methuselah*, 1921

The word has also been used with a few other prepositions, however, such as *to*, *against*, and *for*. These are less frequent by far, and are in the main to be found in older literature.

> He recognized her as "Goldy," famous in Hsi-Yu for her abhorrence to sleeping alone —*Sericana Quarterly*, April 1952

> . . . abhorrence against relationship with Wickham —Jane Austen, *Pride and Prejudice*, 1813

> . . . my unbounded abhorrence for this miserable wretch —P. B. Shelley, quoted by Matthew Arnold, *Essays in Criticism*, Second Series, 1888

abhorrent When used with a preposition, *abhorrent* is almost always followed by *to*:

> Not only was success abhorrent to their ethical prejudices —Lewis H. Lapham, *Harper's*, May 1971

> . . . words like "unfair" whose very sound is abhorrent to him —Joseph Conrad, *Chance*, 1913

abide 1. The original principal parts of *abide* are *abode*, past, and *abidden*, past participle. The OED notes that in time the past and past participle coalesced in *abode*, and *abidden* fell into disuse, although a few 19th-century writers tried to revive it. During the 19th century a regular past and past participle *abided* came into use. It is more likely to be used now than *abode* is. *Abode*, while not very much used by modern writers, is kept alive by its use in such familiar literary works as "The Legend of Sleepy Hollow."
2. Except for *can't abide* and *abide by*, which are in continuing vigorous use, most senses of *abide* have a rather literary or old-fashioned

flavor. They do, however, continue in reputable, if somewhat infrequent, use.

abjure, adjure A number of commentators warn that these words are confused with some frequency. Our files, however, show such confusion to be rare (we do have one citation for *adjure* used in place of *abjure*). *Abjure* means "to renounce, reject, avoid"; *adjure* "to urge or advise earnestly." Besides differing in meaning, the two words take different grammatical constructions. *Abjure* regularly takes a noun as direct object. The noun is rarely a personal noun.

> . . . it was easier to abjure allegiance to Philip II than to decide to whom or what sovereignty should be transferred —Simon Schama, *The Embarrassment of Riches*, 1988

> . . . finding what things can serve us and what we must avoid or abjure —Robertson Davies, *N.Y. Times Book Rev.*, 12 May 1991

Adjure, on the other hand, typically takes a personal noun or pronoun followed by *to* and an infinitive:

> . . . Isabella regarded the Rock of Gibraltar as the key to the future defense of Spain and Christianity; she adjured her countrymen to hold it at all costs —Timothy Foote, *Smithsonian*, September 1997

> Shawn had adjured her to come up with some other term —Roy Blount, Jr., *Atlantic*, December 1994

Adjure, incidentally, is used quite a bit less frequently than *abjure*.

ablative See INCOMPARABLE.

able to In constructions where *able* is followed by *to* and the infinitive, the infinitive is nearly always in the active voice.

> With this information the thieves are able to impersonate their victims —Beverly Molander, *Atlanta Jour.-Constitution*, 11 December 1995

> So far, I have been able to keep my enthusiasm . . . under control —John Fischer, *Harper's*, November 1970

> . . . a reader may eventually be able to download any of the 20 million volumes now in the Library of Congress —Martin Gardner, *Civilization*, October/November 1999

The passive infinitive is much less common. Some commentators (Longman 1984, Garner 1998) think the construction awkward and profitably revised. Awkwardness may account for its being fairly uncommon.

> The new yard is bigger, and it can hold ships twice as large as the ones able to be docked

in Jacksonville —Mark Gordon, *Florida Times-Union*, 20 Dec. 1999

Using this example for illustrative purposes, we can avoid the passive infinitive by revising it to include *can*:

. . . twice as large as the ones that can dock in Jacksonville.

abortive Safire 1982 seconds a correspondent's objection to the use of *abortive* to describe a failed mission to rescue U.S. hostages in Iran in 1979. Safire claims to see in the suffix *-ive* an implication of continuation or permanence, and he maintains that *abortive* must therefore "suggest a continuous process of aborting." This is a conclusion that could only be reached by ignoring the history of the use of the word in English in favor of speculating about what it might mean. Burchfield 1996 points out that the notion of continuity is not a necessary component of the word. No continuity is suggested by Shakespeare's line

Why should I joy in any abortive birth? —*Love's Labour's Lost*, 1595

Safire further asserts that " 'abortive efforts' should be used only when the emphasis is on a series of past failures." In actuality the word is often used to modify a plural noun, but emphasis on past failures may or may not be present:

Such abortive showers are called virga —Jonathan Weiner, *Planet Earth*, 1986

. . . a civil war in which Serbia . . . is killing thousands of Croats, despite 14 abortive cease-fires —Anthony Astrachan, *Manchester Guardian Weekly*, 19 Jan. 1992

. . . in the early Seventies he survived no fewer than three abortive coups —Robert Fox, *The Inner Sea*, 1993

Both of these are species of abortive attempts to retrieve a known word —M. F. Garrett, *Linguistics: The Cambridge Survey*, 1988

Moreover, many a writer from Shakespeare to the present has used the word of a single incident with no hint of continuation:

After the abortive Decembrist insurrection in 1825 —George F. Kennan, *New Yorker*, 1 May 1971

In describing her abortive visit —Margery Sharp, *Britannia Mews*, 1946

. . . in 1924, after the Nazis' abortive Beer Hall putsch —Istvan Deak, *New Republic*, 15 Dec. 1997

Only at the third did our visit prove abortive —Sir Arthur Conan Doyle, *The Return of Sherlock Holmes*, 1904

. . . Mr. Pickwick expressed a strong desire to recollect a song which he had heard in his infancy, and the attempt proving abortive, sought to stimulate his memory with more glasses of punch —Charles Dickens, *Pickwick Papers*, 1836–37

abound When a person, place, or thing abounds—that is, is copiously supplied—it usually abounds *in* or abounds *with*.

Literary men indulge in humbug only at a price, and Bancroft abounded in humbug —Van Wyck Brooks, *The Flowering of New England, 1815–1865*, rev. ed. 1946

. . . London abounds in public monuments —Max Beerbohm, *And Even Now*, 1920

Yet if life abounded in mysteries —Norman Mailer, *Harper's*, March 1971

. . . buoyed by the most personal of human hopes, he abounded with good nature —Francis Hackett, *Henry the Eighth*, 1929

. . . a school ostensibly abounding with fair-sized drips —J. D. Salinger, *Nine Stories*, 1953

Both prepositions are in frequent use; when the object is a relative pronoun, *with* appears to be more common:

. . . those ironies with which history abounds —John Dewey, *Freedom and Culture*, 1939

The pictures with which it abounds —Charles Lamb, *Essays of Elia*, 1823

about **1.** Perrin & Ebbitt 1972 say *around* is more common than *about* in reference to physical position; the assertion cannot be confirmed from the Merriam-Webster files. Both are very common. See AROUND 1.
2. A number of commentators point out that *about* can be used redundantly with figures when other signs of approximation, such as the mention of a span (150 to 200) or the words *estimate* or *guess* are present. If the evidence in the Merriam-Webster files is representative, this is a minor problem—we have nearly no evidence of its occurrence in edited prose.
3. Bernstein 1958, 1965 objects to the expression "about the head" as "police-blotter lingo." This is perhaps an expression used much less frequently than in the past. Here is a typical example, from a story in the *Saturday Evening Post* in 1954:

He slapped Mr. Norris heavily about the head several times —Harold H. Martin

Bernstein's objection was originally made in 1953. Since then we have continued to collect scattered evidence of its use. Some uses may be facetious; others seem serious: Copperud 1970 says it is standard, anyway.

> The Democratic negotiators . . . had resolved that they wouldn't put forward tax proposals only to have the Republicans beat them about the head as taxers —Elizabeth Drew, *New Yorker,* 6 Aug. 1990

> Sammy . . . suddenly began to hit his father about the head with both fists —Toni Morrison, *The Bluest Eye,* 1970

4. For two further current idiomatic uses of *about,* see AT ABOUT and NOT ABOUT TO.

above 1. Sometime during the later part of the 19th century, a number of critics began objecting to the use of *above* as an adjective and as a noun. The critics, except for being generally unhappy about both uses, are a bit uncertain of just what is so bad. Some disapprove the adjective while others find the adjective acceptable but not the noun. Some commentators object that such uses of *above* smack too much of commercial or legal lingo; on the other hand, writers on business writing recommend against its use.

The issue appears to be more long-lived than substantial. Most recent commentators find both noun and adjective unobjectionable, but Harper 1985 and Freeman 1983 still object.

The adjective *above* is not uncommon in writers on language and usage:

> The facts of the case being now sufficiently supplied by the above list —Robert Bridges, *S.P.E. Tract 2,* 1919

> . . . a few remarks on some of the above words may perhaps instil caution —Fowler 1926

> . . . for a comment on the above use of the word "claims," consult Chapter 1 —Bernstein 1958

> The above discussion gives us some idea about the complexity —Braj B. Kachru, in Greenbaum 1985

Other writers also have used it:

> I don't for a moment doubt that for daily purposes he feels to me as a friend—as certainly I do to him and without the above reserve —Oliver Wendell Holmes d. 1935, letter, 12 Jan. 1921

> "Fear God, Honour the Queen" . . . I was brought up on the above words —Sir Bernard Law Montgomery, *This Week Mag.,* 1 June 1952

The use of *above* as a noun is somewhat more lightly attested in our files. It too has been around a long time:

> . . . the above is Theseus's opinion —William Blake, *Annotations to Swedenborg's Of Heaven and Hell,* 2d ed., 1784

> It is not of pictures like the above that galleries, in Rome or elsewhere, are made up —Nathaniel Hawthorne (cited in Hall 1917)

> Let us pretend that the above is the original plot —Ring Lardner, preface, *How to Write Short Stories,* 1924

We judge that both adjective and noun uses of *above* are standard, notwithstanding the objections of a few holdouts for 19th-century opinion. Gowers's revision of Fowler 1965 sums the matter up:

> There is ample authority, going back several centuries, for this use of a[bove] as adverb, adjective, or noun, and no solid ground for the pedantic criticism of it sometimes heard.

2. "*Above* should not be used for 'more than.' " This curious statement from Vizetelly 1906 may have had its origin in William Cullen Bryant's 19th-century *Index Expurgatorius* for the *New York Evening Post,* which he edited. Bryant objected to the use of either *above* or *over* in this sense. It is an odd usage for any critic to pick on; it goes back to the 16th century and has good literary credentials:

> It was never acted; or, if it was, not above once —Shakespeare, *Hamlet,* 1601

> After that, he was seen of above five hundred brethren at once —1 Corinthians 15:6 (AV), 1611

> "It is above a week since I saw Miss Crawford." —Jane Austen, *Mansfield Park,* 1814

> . . . telling Aubrey that he cannot remember being drunk above a hundred times —Harold J. Laski, letter, 19 Mar. 1928

> He doesn't look above forty —*The Journals of Arnold Bennett,* ed. Frank Swinnerton, 1954

> . . . and it took above 10 minutes to get the police —Edward Dahlberg, *Prose,* Spring 1972

Burchfield 1996 calls these objections "out of order." We agree. See also OVER.

absent Bernstein 1977 and Copperud 1980 both comment on the appearance of *absent* as a preposition in constructions such as this:

> Absent such a direct threat, Mr. Carter professes to feel no pressure —William Safire, *N.Y. Times,* 20 Dec. 1976

Both of these commentators note that the preposition is entered in Webster's Third, and neither condemns it. Copperud concludes by saying, "Whether *absent* as a preposition will win any wide acceptance only time will tell."

Evidence we have accumulated since Copperud wrote his remark indicates that the prepositional use has gained acceptance, though perhaps grudgingly. Safire 1984 discusses it; unsurprisingly, he approves it but notes some opposition. Harper 1985 puts the prepositional use, which the editors ascribe to "a few rather pretentious columnists," to a vote of their usage panel; unsurprisingly the panel rejects it by a thumping 92 percent in writing, and 95 percent in speech.

What is the background of this use? It is not as new as these commentators think. Garner 1998 has an example from a 1919 law case. We found it in 1945:

> We think it clear, continued the Supreme Court, that under this definition, absent any other facts, there arises an implied contract —*JAMA*, 24 Feb. 1945

The preposition pretty clearly had its origin in legal language. Up until the early 1970s all of our evidence for it came from published judicial decisions or reports of such decisions. In the 70s we began to see a spread of the preposition into quasi-legal contexts and into the reported speech of lawyers and politicians:

> A program of unconditional amnesty, absent some accommodation on the part of the beneficiaries would be a disservice to the memory of those who fought and died in Vietnam —Hubert H. Humphrey, quoted by James A. Wechsler, *N.Y. Post* (undated citation received from a correspondent 15 Dec. 1975)

But by the late 1970s and the 1980s, the use of the prepositional *absent* had broadened, and we now find it in many general publications:

> Absent any demands for uniformity chip designs can often end up as hodgepodge —Seth Lubove, *Forbes,* 20 Sept. 1999

> . . . a child who (absent a compensating source of love and attention) shuts down emotionally —Sharon Begley, *Newsweek,* 3 May 1999

> Absent nuclear war or a comet striking the planet, at least one more generation of increasing human population is a certainty —Gregg Easterbrook, *New Republic,* 11 Oct. 1999

absolute adjectives *Absolute adjective* is one of the terms used by usage writers to refer to adjectives that are not, or (more often) should not in the view of the writer, be compared or intensified (other terms applied to these words include *incomparables* and *uncomparable adjectives*).

How many words belong to this class? Here is one commentator's answer:

> Our language contains perhaps a score of words that may be described as *absolute words*. These are words that properly admit of no comparison or intensification —Kilpatrick 1984

A score, perhaps? In one column of a page chosen at random from a recent edition of Merriam-Webster's Collegiate Dictionary we find *ultrashort, ultrasonic, ultrasonographic, ultrastructural, ultraviolet, ululant, umbellate, umbelliferous, umber, umbilical, umbilicate, umbonal, umbral*—a baker's dozen of adjectives most persons would be hard put to use in the comparative or superlative. It takes no great effort to fill out our score—how about *ancillary, residual, aliphatic, Triassic, epoxy, diocesan, diphthongal?* The plain fact is that a majority of adjectives in English admit of no comparison—they are of too narrow an application, or too technical, to be so used, or they simply name a quality that cannot exist in degrees (Quirk et al. 1985 calls them nongradable).

Then why, you may ask, is there a question at all? The reason is simple: the absolute adjectives that concern the usage writers have, almost without exception, actually been used in the comparative, in the superlative, or with an intensifier. But commentators, ever since Lindley Murray in 1795 raised the earlier speculative footnotes of Lowth and Priestly into a rule, have set their own ratiocinations against actual usage. Several commentators have compiled lists of absolute adjectives. Sometimes one commentator will make fun of another's list; Bernstein 1971, for instance, gently derides the selection of Partridge 1942. But Bernstein has his own treasured list. It seems to be traditional to list as words not susceptible of comparison words that have, in fact, been compared.

The reason for the mismatch between actual usage and the writers' expressed preference is simple: the lists are wish lists. The reason such words are compared was succinctly summed up as long ago as 1946:

> Adjectives expressing some quality that does not admit of degrees are not compared when used in their strict or full sense; as, *square, perpendicular, circular, absolute, eternal, illimitable, complete, perfect,* etc.

But such adjectives are often used in a modified or approximate sense, and when so used admit of comparison.

If we say, "This is *more perfect* than that," we do not mean that either is perfect without limitation, but that "this" has "more" of the qualities that go to make up perfection than "that"; it is *more nearly* perfect. Such usage has high literary authority —Fernald 1946

To summarize, a majority of adjectives, perhaps a substantial majority, do not admit of comparison simply because they are too technical or have a meaning that truly does not allow such modification. Most of the adjectives called uncomparable by usage writers have, in fact, been compared or modified by adverbs of degree other than *more* and *most,* for two reasons. First, they tend to be common words with more than one meaning and are liable to comparison in some senses, if not all. Second, the comparative degree is commonly used to mean "more nearly," as Fernald explains.

     See also COMPLETE, COMPLETELY; CORRECT; EQUAL 2; ESSENTIAL, *adjective*; PARAMOUNT; PERFECT; PREFERABLE; UNIQUE.

absolute constructions, absolute clauses
See ABSOLUTE PHRASES.

absolutely   At least since the 1920s commentators have been disparaging the intensive use of *absolutely.* I. A. Richards, in *Basic English and Its Uses,* 1943, says

> In all but a few contexts *absolutely* is an absolutely (completely) meaningless intensifier. . . .

There are two separate uses here. The first is use as what Quirk et al. 1985 terms a "maximizer"—it indicates the greatest degree of something. Here are a few typical instances:

> Unwilling to make myself disagreeable . . . , I absolutely refused —Benjamin Franklin, *Autobiography,* 1788

> And where else but in England can one find three expensive but flourishing weeklies devoted to absolutely nothing but the life of the rich and the titled? —Aldous Huxley, *The Olive Tree,* 1937

> If absolutely ripe, damsons can be eaten raw, but they are much better cooked —Joanna Morris, *The Encyclopedia of Cooking,* 1985

> . . . neither disavowal nor avowal seemed absolutely essential —John Kenneth Galbraith, *Harper's,* February 1971

> Scientifically testable? Absolutely not —Jerry A. Coyne, *New Republic,* 3 Apr. 2000

Although it can be argued that the adverb might have been omitted in some of these instances without great loss, its intensifying or maximizing purpose is clear. We have another set of instances, however, in which the intensity of the adverb is much diminished. Such use is not especially modern:

> She grew absolutely ashamed of herself —Jane Austen, *Pride and Prejudice,* 1813

> Of course, it is absolutely okay to use family or other connections to get a job —Helen Gurley Brown, *Cosmopolitan,* February 2000

> John McClain of the New York *Journal-American* (March 19, 1965) described the sets as "absolutely magnificent beige and pastel etchings" —*Current Biography,* December 1967

> Markel had been absolutely shattered when he had not been invited —Gay Talese, *Harper's,* February 1969

> . . . my piano playing was absolutely terrible —Rosemary Brown, *Ladies' Home Jour.,* September 1971

> This book . . . is absolutely vital for pop culture collections —Mike Tribby, *Booklist,* 15 Nov. 1999

This second use is more open to criticism as unnecessary or meaningless than the first. The weakened use, however, does have literary authority. If it is a fault, it is, to paraphrase the 18th-century grammarian Joseph Priestley, but a venial fault.

absolute phrases   A participial phrase that is not overtly connected to the rest of the sentence is called an *absolute phrase* or *absolute construction.* Absolute phrases may contain either a past or present participle. An absolute phrase has a head, usually a noun or pronoun, which the participle modifies. We may think of it as the subject of the phrase.

     The subject of the absolute phrase and that of the sentence are always different:

> The scholars increasing fast, the house was soon found too small —Benjamin Franklin, *Autobiography,* 1788

> Miss Ward's match, indeed . . . was not contemptible, Sir Thomas being happily able to give his friend an income —Jane Austen, *Mansfield Park,* 1814

> But I don't believe that any writer under thirty—geniuses excepted—can stay writing in the attic forever without drying up —Joan Aiken, *The Writer,* May 1968

If the subject of what would otherwise be an absolute phrase is suppressed as though it were the same as that of the main clause, a dangling participle may result. Here are two excerpts from a speech of Richard M. Nixon (quoted by William Safire, *N.Y. Times Mag.,* 19 June 1983) that illustrate the problem. In the first example, both subjects are the same—*I*—and the phrase is properly attached to the clause; in the second, they are different

—I and *tendency*—and connection is not made: the phrase dangles:

> Speaking candidly, I believe some of our Chinese friends have misunderstood and misjudged President Reagan's position on the Taiwan issue.

> Speaking as an old friend, there has been a disturbing tendency in statements emanating from Peking to question the good faith of President Reagan. . . .

See DANGLING MODIFIERS.

Perrin & Ebbitt 1972 point out that absolute phrases, when short, are direct and economical; and that when they follow the main clause, they are a convenient way to add details. Reader's Digest 1983 warns that absolute phrases with a pronoun subject (as "he having gone on ahead") are often felt to be awkward or old-fashioned.

A number of absolute phrases have been so frequently used that they are now fixed phrases:

> No, my friends, I go (always, other things being equal) for the man who inherits family traditions —Oliver Wendell Holmes d. 1894, *The Autocrat of the Breakfast-Table,* 1858

> I suggest that the university's most feasible function, all things considered, is essentially what it has been for nearly a millennium now —Robert A. Nisbet, *Psychology Today,* March 1971

> So, beyond the damage to the front end, the valves had to be reground. It came to $350 all told —Garrison Keillor, *Lake Wobegon Days,* 1985

absolve Bernstein 1965 observes that when *absolve* is followed by a preposition, the choice is *from* or sometimes of. Before 1965 *from* was certainly more frequent than *of*, but since then the proportion of *of* to *from* has increased noticeably. Both prepositions are in current good use.

> By this device I am absolved from reading much of what is published in a given year —Lewis H. Lapham, *Harper's,* May 1984

> . . . establishing more than 100 new public schools that are absolved from certain red tape —*Detroit News,* 15 June 1998

> . . . in order to establish their independence and absolve the guide of any responsibility —Jeremy Bernstein, *New Yorker,* 30 Oct. 1971

> . . . the hospital was absolved of any wrongdoing —Clare Ansberry, *Wall Street Jour.,* 29 Nov. 1988

A less frequent, but still current, construction uses *for*:

> . . . the manner in which Chicago police were absolved for the brutality they visited on the young —Donald McDonald, *Center Mag.,* July/August 1970

> We may perhaps absolve Ford for the language of the article—it seems somewhat too academic for his unassisted pen —Roger Burlingame, *Backgrounds of Power,* 1949

abstain When abstain is followed by a preposition, it is regularly *from*.

> They seemed careful to abstain from rich, extravagant, or passionate language —Norman Mailer, *Harper's,* November 1968

> She has abstained from ecstasy for more than a year —Mary Ann Marshall, *Cosmopolitan,* August 2000

In reference to voting, *abstain* usually takes no preposition. *From* may be used, and rarely *in* appears:

> No less than 213 Diet members abstained in the final vote —*Collier's Year Book,* 1949

abstract The verb *abstract,* in most of its senses, takes the preposition *from,* if it takes one at all. The usual pattern is to "abstract a thing from something else." Occasionally we find that "something is abstracted by something else" or "something is abstracted into something else." These last two patterns are much less frequent than constructions with *from.* Here are some examples of the usual construction:

> With the nail of his right forefinger he abstracted a string of meat from between two teeth —Liam O'Flaherty, *The Informer,* 1925

> . . . artists in the group put the emphasis on geometric abstraction rather than images abstracted from nature —Robert Atkins, *Art Spoke,* 1993

> . . . the Romantic project was to abstract from religion its essential "feeling" and leave contemptuously behind its traditional formulations —Theodore Roszak, *The Making of a Counter Culture,* 1969

> . . . basic esthetic criteria and standards he has abstracted from long intimacy with time-tested masterpieces —Aline B. Saarinen, *N.Y. Times Book Rev.,* 7 Nov. 1954

> . . . the large illustrated Rabelais which she had abstracted from the library —Robertson Davies, *Tempest-tost,* 1951

And an example of each of the rarer constructions:

... these together do not supply more material to the soil than is annually abstracted by the extensive roots of trees, of bushes, and by the fern —Richard Jefferies, *The Open Air,* 1885

... conscientiously and with great purity made the uncompromising effort to abstract his view of life into an art work —Norman Mailer, *Advertisements for Myself,* 1959

abut Bernstein 1965 opines that the intransitive verb *abut* takes *against* for a wall and *on* for a line; Krapp 1927 allows *upon* or *against* for Bernstein's walls and *upon* for his line. Both of these commentators are partly right. Evidence in the Merriam-Webster files shows that *on* is the preposition of choice when something conceived of as having chiefly lateral extension is in mind:

The England of the later Middle Ages ... abutted on Scotland —G. M. Trevelyan, *A Shortened History of England,* 1942

The northeast and southeast arms of this cross abut on Ninth Avenue —Lewis Mumford, *New Yorker,* 19 Apr. 1952

Upon is occasionally used:

... a lot which abuts upon a public or private alley —*Zoning for Truck-Loading Facilities,* 1952

When the thing abutted is conceived of as having a vertical as well as lateral extension, *against* and *on* are both used:

... the Nechako Plateau, which abuts against the Rocky Mountains —*Canadian Geographical Jour.,* September 1952

The Whitney abuts at right angles on the Modern Museum —Lewis Mumford, *New Yorker,* 15 Oct. 1955

Other prepositions are occasionally used:

Here a retaining wall is to abut into a rocky hillside —Clarence W. Dunham, *Foundations of Structures,* 1950

On the Soviet side of Potsdamer Platz, which abuts on to West Berlin —*Time,* 29 June 1953

abysm Reader's Digest 1983 adverts to *abysm* as an old variant of *abyss* that is now archaic or obsolete. This is not quite correct, though it is close. Both *abysm* and *abyss* were in use in the 14th century for the void believed in the old cosmography to exist below the earth. *Abyss* has continued in vigorous use; *abysm* might well have become obsolete except for Shakespeare. In *The Tempest* (1612) he wrote this line:

What seest thou else
In the dark backward and abysm of time?

This line has continued to echo in later writers:

As an Italian, Alessandra has grown up aware of the dark backward and abysm of time —John Simon, *Connoisseur,* June 1990

'Soul,' in the dark backward and abysm of linguistic time, is another universal European word —John Fowles, *Island,* 1978

The baby was born famous ... for her arrival was broadcast by a world-known columnist from the dark backward and abysm of journalism —Karl Shapiro, *American Scholar,* Winter 1985/86

... the Cherry Lane Theatre, which is located somewhere in the dark backward and abysm of Greenwich Village —Wolcott Gibbs, *New Yorker,* 19 Feb. 1955

Other modern use of *abysm* also exists but is rare.

... the great man's own frosty tones send "poor Shelley" abseiling off into the Ravine of Arve, or whatever absym he happened to be contemplating when the blow was struck —Iain McGilchrist, *Times Literary Supp.,* 5 Nov. 1982

abysmal, abyssal Oddly enough, *abysmal,* derived from *abysm,* a relatively little used word, is the more commonly used adjective of this pair; *abyssal,* derived from *abyss,* which continues in vigorous use, is limited mostly to technical contexts. *Abysmal* has some use of actual depths:

... he tosses off the abysmal Royal Gorge of the Arkansas with the phrase "perpendicular precipices" —David Lavender, *N.Y. Times Book Rev.,* 25 Sept. 1966

... only a few miles from the beach the bottom breaks off into the abysmal depths of the ocean —Thomas Barbour, *That Vanishing Eden,* 1944

But it is usually used figuratively:

... right now, as we sway on a rickety suspension bridge over abysmal uncertainty —Sandra M. Gilbert, *PMLA,* May 1997

The difference between the sweet-smelling farm-house and the room where he lived was abysmal —John Cheever, *The Wapshot Chronicle,* 1957

Most often *abysmal* denotes wretchedness or low quality or sometimes quantity:

... gritty memoirs about abysmal poverty —Richard Alleva, *Commonweal,* 7 Apr. 2000

Churchill's character assassination did contribute to Chamberlain's abysmal historical reputation —Gaddis Smith, *N.Y. Times Book Rev.*, 29 Aug. 1993

. . . had an abysmal season in 1983—a .194 average —Roger Angell, *New Yorker*, 7 May 1984

. . . the season's worst sitcom, an abysmal show in which he plays a callous and cynical grade-school teacher —David Hiltbrand, *People*, 21 Oct. 1991

Abyssal is found chiefly in contexts referring to the bottom of the sea:

. . . the steep descent from the American continental shelf down onto a broad abyssal plain —Robert Kunzig, *The Restless Sea*, 1999

. . . the abyssal depths of the seas —Gregory McNamee, *Outside*, March 1993

Rarely, it is used figuratively:

. . . the dungeon of American slavery, and its abyssal night of the body and spirit —William Styron, *American Heritage*, October 1992

academe, academia   Copperud 1970 reports that both Fowler 1926, 1965 and Evans 1957 disapprove of *academe* as applied to a place of learning, an academy. Fowler maintains that *Academe* properly means *Academus*, a hero of Greek mythology: an olive grove in Athens sacred to his memory was near the place where Plato established his philosophical school, and it gave the name, Academy, to Plato's school. Fowler therefore opines that the "grove of Academe," mentioned by Milton, is correct in reference to Plato's Academy, and that the use of the phrase in Shakespeare to mean 'a seat of learning" is wrong. Evans says that *Academe* properly refers to Plato's academy; he censures its use otherwise as a pomposity, instancing the title of Mary McCarthy's novel *Groves of Academe* (1952).

These notions need to be disentangled and examined. First, we have *academe* used to mean a place of learning. As far as we can tell, this use was invented by Shakespeare, who needed a three-syllable word for *academy*:

From women's eyes this doctrine I derive:
They are the ground, the books, the academes,
From whence doth spring the true
   Promethean fire.
                        —*Love's Labour's Lost*, 1595

What Shakespeare has done here is to establish a literary expression—he used it both literally and figuratively in the same play—that would be echoed by later writers. Fowler's objection came 330 years too late.

Milton put *grove* and *Academe* together. In the fourth book of *Paradise Regained* (1671) Satan is lecturing the Son of God on the literature and culture of the gentiles. He mentions Athens:

See there the olive-grove of Academe,
Plato's retirement, where the Attic bird
Trills . . .

Here *Academe* means *Academus*; like Shakespeare before him, Milton changed the usual word for the sake of his meter. The phrase *grove of Academe* has stayed with us, eventually becoming plural by the mid-19th century.

. . . his studious frequentation of that Hercynian forest, which takes the place of the groves of Academe in German philosophical writing —George Saintsbury, *A History of Nineteenth Century Literature*, 1896

By the early 20th century the phrase came to be used to refer to the academic world or academic community:

Out of the groves of Academe comes a voice of lamentation for the political sins of New York. It is that of Arthur Twining Hadley, president of Yale University —*N.Y. Herald*, 24 Jan. 1904

This sense can also be found without the groves:

He lived within a stone's throw of Academe, and he threw the stone —*American Mercury*, November 1928

The sense relating to the academic world or community grew in use (with and without *groves*), while reference to Plato's Academy receded. Burchfield 1996 thinks Mary McCarthy's *Groves of Academe* helped establish the phrase in popular use.

Here are some examples of how *academe* is actually used. Shakespeare's original figurative sense is still alive, although the contexts are not so elevated:

. . . splendid new texts from two doyennes of Manhattan's Chinese cooking academe —Ellen Stern, *New York*, 9 June 1975

. . . people who lived far from the groves of any literary academe —Roger Sale, *On Not Being Good Enough*, 1979

But by far the most common use is to indicate the academic environment, community, or world:

. . . a predictable dispute in English Academe: It was said that all Cambridge scholars call the cipher aught and all Oxford scholars call it nought —John D. Barrow, *Pi in the Sky*, 1992

He had a real bee in his bonnet about being accepted and respected by the halls of academe —*Newsweek,* 28 June 1999

He deliberately lived outside Detroit and away from the other auto people, in the Ann Arbor groves of academe —David Halberstam, *Harper's,* February 1971

They have hardly conquered the high citadels of academe —James C. Turner, *Commonweal,* 15 Jan. 1999

. . . deep in the thickets of academe where feminism trysts with sociology —Anne Crutcher, *Wall Street Jour.,* 3 Feb. 1982

. . . the monsters of pretension and ambition that lurk in the groves of academe —Scott Veale, *N.Y. Times Book Rev.,* 21 June 1998

Academia is a more recent word. It has been filtered through Latin from the Greek. In 1946 it turned up as a synonym for the most popular sense of *academe*:

. . . beyond the complacent paddocks of academia, clubdom, or social status —Lucien Price, *Atlantic,* June 1946

It has stuck:

Instead of drawing adherents from academia, like the socialists, anarchism has tapped a different vein: the youth culture —Franklin Foer, *New Republic,* 1 May 2000

In theory, Academia functions on the principle of collegiality —M. Lee Goff, *A Fly for the Prosecution,* 2000

. . . students . . . itchy to close their notebooks and break out of the halls of academia —Susan McDonald, *Hampshire Life,* 7 Feb. 1986

So he entered academia, landing at the University of Utah —Roger Parloff, *N.Y. Times Mag.,* 26 Sept. 1999

The modern traffic from academia to public life can show nothing to its medieval counterpart —Gordon Leff, *Times Literary Supp.,* 20 Nov. 1981

Both *academe* and *academia* are in current good usage in American and British English meaning "academic life, environment, community, world." They appear to be used with about equal frequency at the present. They are usually but not always lowercased.

accede Janis 1984 points out that this word is spelled *-cede* not *-ceed*. The Oxford American Dictionary notes that it is also a homophone of *exceed* and so subject to being confused (Garner 1998 has an example of *exceed* for *accede*).

Accede is regularly followed by *to*:

. . . for the purpose of forcing employers to accede to their demands —Eugene J. McCarthy, *Dictionary of American Politics,* 1968

I don't want to accede to persistent demands to repeat myself —Susan Sontag, quoted in *Vogue,* 1 Aug. 1971

Pacifism acceded to the place of belligerency in the British heart —Michael Straight, *New Republic,* 18 Apr. 1955

accent, accentuate Fowler 1926 notes that *accentuate* is being used for figurative senses and *accent* for literal and technical ones and that he approves and encourages the differentiation. Fowler would be pleased to learn that in the years since his writing the differentiation has continued. *Accent* has more meanings, mainly technical, but *accentuate* has more usage.

The Merriam-Webster files show that when *accent* is used in a nontechnical way, it may be used to mean "to give prominence or emphasis to":

. . . skirts, pants, culottes and shorts that zero in on the fanny—and accent the belly —*Women's Wear Daily,* 27 Oct. 1975

The slightly starched atmosphere is accented by the stark design of the restaurant —Thomas Matthews, *Wine Spectator,* 15 & 31 Mar. 1995

Accentuate, however, is more common in such use:

. . . suggested a number of fantastic creatures and shapes, which he then accentuated by outlining them —David Gascoyne, *Times Literary Supp.,* 8 Mar. 1991

. . . bodysuits with an Op Art pattern that accentuated curves —Rose La Ferla, *N.Y. Times Mag.,* 16 Dec. 1990

Grayish daylight seeping into the tunnel accentuated the rough texture of the walls —Joseph Wechsberg, *New Yorker,* 12 May 1956

Whereas the ceremony of anointment was becoming a mere formality in Germany and in England, the religious and emotional qualities of this ceremony were still accentuated in France —Norman F. Cantor, *The Civilization of the Middle Ages,* 1993

Accent may emphasize a setting off by contrast; *accentuate* is seldom used thus:

. . . lavishly planted flower gardens accented with rugged, native plants —Marcia Tatroe, *Fine Gardening,* April 1999

The chassis is made of solid cherry, accented with brushed aluminum —*Newsweek,* 27 Mar. 2000

. . . work in silver, brass, and copper, accented by colored stones —Fran White, *Lapidary Jour.*, January 1992

. . . a pasty complexion and a wide, even smile accented by a rather pointy nose —Jack Falla, *Sports Illustrated*, 23 Jan. 1984

Accent is also used when the writer wants to single out or stress some particular:

Gunther's account of his record at SHAPE accents the General's deep belief in working toward a European Federation —Charles J. Rolo, *Atlantic*, March 1952

. . . thirty regional dramas, the more recent ones accenting Texas —Richard L. Coe, *Holiday*, May/June 1973

Accentuate is seldom used in this way, except in the phrase *accentuate the positive*, which has been reinforced by a popular song with that title.

We would rather accentuate the positive —Gerard Onisa, *Media & Methods*, March 1969

In the course of some missionary work . . . Whitehead stoutly accentuated the positive —Russell Watson, *Newsweek*, 15 Jan. 1973

Accentuate has developed an additional meaning, approximately "to intensify or increase," that is not shared by *accent*:

. . . pasty complexion accentuated by a taste for orange shirts —J. Hoberman, *Village Voice*, 1 Oct. 1991

. . . the Bank's operations would tend to accentuate rather than to moderate the cycle —*Proceedings of the Academy of Political Science*, January 1947

. . . a land always partly foreign—a factor accentuated by the dialogue's frequent departure into Greek —Randall Stevenson & Tom Morris, *Times Literary Supp.*, 24–30 Aug. 1990

Milwaukee's precipitous decline in the American League East was accentuated by a 10-game losing streak —Herm Weiskopf, *Sports Illustrated*, 3 Oct. 1983

So the differentiation between *accent* and *accentuate* noticed and encouraged by Fowler 1926 has continued. Except for the two general uses mentioned above where *accent* still predominates, *accentuate* holds the field for most general and figurative uses, and has developed a use of its own not shared by *accent*.

accept, except Nearly every handbook published between 1917 and the present carries a warning against confusing *accept* and *except*. A good half of these unnecessarily distinguish the preposition or conjunction *except* from *ac-*

cept, which is only a verb. The verb *except* is, however, sometimes written in place of *accept*:

Still excepting bookings for 1984 —advt., *Morgan Horse*, December 1983

This confusion must be due entirely to similarity of sound, for the meanings of the two verbs are so dissimilar as to obviate confusion on that score. Even though Queen Elizabeth I wrote *except* for *accept* in one of her own letters (noted in McKnight 1928), the 1983 use must be accounted an error. Queen Elizabeth I spelled as she pronounced, and she spelled before there were such amenities as spelling books and dictionaries for reference.

acceptance, acceptation Fowler 1926 proclaims *acceptance* and *acceptation* "fully differentiated" in meaning. The differentiation is not quite complete even now, however, although it characterizes most use of these words. *Acceptation* is the less frequently used word, and its usual meaning is "a generally understood meaning of a word or understanding of a concept":

Simon's relationship to such raw materials can in any case be said to be more realistic, on any acceptation of the word, than Robbe-Grillet's —Frederick James, *Postmodernism*, 1992

And it is in this spirit that they [authors of a work on French grammar] make use of such terms as punctual in their usual acceptation —Howard B. Garey, *Language*, April–June 1957

Occasionally it is used like *acceptance*:

His record is plainly true and worthy of all acceptation —*Times Literary Supp.*, 16 Nov. 1951

"All right, then!" he cried bitterly, with sudden acceptation of the other's story —Thomas Wolfe, *Of Time and the River*, 1935

Acceptance is much the more frequent word. It occasionally is used much like *acceptation*:

There is also a common acceptance among far too many teachers that the field trip is a device for exposing youngsters to museum facilities without any particular preparation or use of their experience upon return to the classroom —Gilbert Hagerty, *New-England Galaxy*, Fall 1970

But mostly it does duty as the noun for *accept*:

. . . uncritical acceptance of sense experience —Iris Murdoch, *The Fire and the Sun*, 1977

The first public high school had opened in Boston in 1821, but secondary education was very slow to win acceptance among working-class families that counted on their children's incomes for survival —Thomas Hine, *American Heritage,* September 1999

. . . a fine indifference to things that did not interest him, and an acceptance of those that did —Osbert Sitwell, *Noble Essences,* 1950

. . . the Nordic-model welfare state, which has wide acceptance in Finland —Ailli Mari Tripp, *The Nation,* 10 Apr. 2000

. . . in spite of their acceptance into the new structure —Martin Bernal, *N.Y. Rev. of Books,* 23 Oct. 1969

access 1. *Access, excess.* The Oxford American Dictionary 1980, Shaw 1962, and Garner 1998 warn against the confusion of these two words, which sound very much alike. The OED notes that *access* was used quite a bit in the past for *excess.* We have no clear-cut evidence of confusion, but Garner has found a couple of instances in which *access* replaced *excess* in the phrase *in excess of.* This is an error which will elude a spelling checker.

2. The most commonly used senses of *access,* when followed by a preposition, take *to:*

"Will that restrict your access to information?" —Upton Sinclair, *A World to Win,* 1946

. . . a man with access to the President —David Halberstam, *Harper's,* July 1969

. . . to provide poor citizens with access to the nation's courts —Donald McDonald, *Center Mag.,* March/April 1971

. . . the difficulty of gaining access to complete copies of such vital sources —*Times Literary Supp.,* 19 Feb. 1971

accessorize Popular writers on language enjoy lampooning advertising copy, which tends to make a target about as elusive as the proverbial side of a barn. Here is a typical instance:

As it happened, I did not have time to sparkle my table because I was busy following instructions given in another advertisement and was accessorizing my spacious master bedroom with oil paintings —Edwin Newman, *Esquire,* December 1975

One object of Newman's scorn here is the verb *accessorize,* which seems to have been discovered by usage commentators in 1975. Here is Harper 1975 on the subject:

Accessorize is a bastard offshoot of the noun *accessory.* It has appeared in advertising copy like the following: "The new kitchen range is *accessorized* with stainless steel." This says nothing that "trimmed" doesn't

say better and more simply. Avoid *accessorize.*

The advice implied here—that *trim* is preferable to *accessorize*—shows the weakness of relying on a single example. Try using *trim* in place of *accessorize* in these examples and see what the effect is in each case:

For a famous wearer of big diamonds, she is discreetly accessorized with bracelets and hoop earrings —Raymond Sokolov, *Wall Street Jour.,* 6 July 1993

. . . introduced her fall fashion presentation with models accessorized in the home-boy style with quilted baseball caps and big pendants —Woody Hochswender, *N.Y. Times,* 10 Apr. 1991

And even toy horses are now accessorized. Among the additional items you are at liberty to buy for them is a blacksmith set —*New Yorker,* 11 Dec. 1965

. . . herringbone jackets accessorized with long silk aviator scarves —Richard Natale, *Cosmopolitan,* April 1975

Accessorize is a relatively new word—it has been around since 1939—and it is found almost entirely in contexts dealing with fashion and interior decoration, where it is well established.

See -IZE 2.

accident See MISHAP.

accidently, accidentally Numerous commentators from the 1960s through the 1990s have disparaged *accidently* as a misspelling, a solecism, or a nonexistent word.

The OED shows that *accidently* was in occasional use as a variant of *accidentally* by the 17th century and it has continued to appear sporadically up until the present time. Its continued use is undoubtedly encouraged by its more closely representing the usual pronunciation of *accidentally* than the predominant spelling does. A few examples:

And I even question whether any tender virgin, who was accidently and unaccountably enriched with a bantling, would save her character —Washington Irving, *A History of New York,* 1809

"He asked me if it were true that it was accidently that you were locked up in the museum. . . ." —Oliver St. John Gogarty, *Mourning Became Mrs. Spendlove,* 1948

In early August, Shaka was accidently stabbed —Harry A. Gailey, Jr., *History of Africa,* 1970

During childhood a brother had accidently shot an arrow into his right eye —*Australian Dictionary of Biography,* 1966

. . . when he was accidently electrocuted by a high-voltage wire —Robert I. Friedman, *Village Voice*, 5 Nov. 1991

One policeman accidently shot another last night —*N.Y. Times*, 6 July 1971

. . . the serendipity that occurs when a user accidently discovers information —W. David Penniman, *Library Jour.* 15 Oct. 1992

The spelling *accidently* is not, strictly speaking, a misspelling, but it is a decidedly secondary form. We recommend *accidentally*.

accommodate 1. Several commentators warn that this word is often misspelled with one *m: accomodate*. It certainly is. And it has been so misspelled for some time:

We were accomodated in Henrietta St. —Jane Austen, letter, 25 Sept. 1813

It even sneaks into schoolbooks:

The lens in your eye changes quickly (a doctor would say it *accomodates*) —*You and Science* (9th-grade text), Paul F. Brandwein et al., 1960 ed.

The example of Jane Austen and many, many others notwithstanding, you should remember to double that *m*. The same warning goes for *accommodation*.

2. Bernstein 1965 says that *accommodate* can take either *to* or *with* as a preposition. Our files show that when a preposition is used, *to* predominates. It is used with the intransitive:

. . . she accommodated quickly to the traditional bisexuality of the British theatre and the British upper classes —Brendan Gill, *Harper's Bazaar*, November 1972

. . . emblematic of the artist's struggle to accommodate to our present age of celebrity —Barbara Goldsmith, *N.Y. Times Book Rev.*, 21 June 1987

. . . learn how to live together and to accommodate to each other —Ramsey Clark, *Center Mag.*, July/August 1970

The transitive verb may take *to* after a reflexive pronoun or after another direct object:

. . . political authority depended on tribal leadership, and the scholars had to accommodate themselves to it —Ernest Gellner, *Culture, Identity, and Politics*, 1987

. . . a secular morality . . . that accommodates itself to what man will actually do —Daniel P. Moynihan, *American Scholar*, Autumn 1969

A bride, to help take care of such a creature,
And accommodate her young life to his
        —Robert Frost, *North of Boston*, 1914

. . . he had to accommodate his step to hers —Michael Arlen, *These Charming People*, 1924

With is much less frequently used, though not rare:

. . . to accommodate them with valuable jobs —James Gould Cozzens, *Guard of Honor*, 1948

. . . we were determined to accommodate our basic interests with those of other powers —Dean Acheson, in *The Pattern of Responsibility*, ed. McGeorge Bundy, 1951

When the transitive *accommodate* is used in the passive, it is used with whatever preposition seems most appropriate according to sense. Here, again, *to* is the most frequent.

It was completely accommodated to their culture —John Kenneth Galbraith, *The Scotch*, 1964

. . . while the latter is covertly accommodated to events —John Dewey, *Freedom and Culture*, 1939

. . . then congratulates himself on being accommodated with a machine —Thomas Love Peacock, *Headlong Hall*, 1816

. . . careers of the "movie brats," each of whom is accommodated by a full chapter —Robert F. Moss, *Saturday Rev.*, 23 June 1979

Brummell's cravat was twelve inches broad, and had to be accommodated between his chin and his shoulders —*English Digest*, December 1952

The girl was accommodated at the station for the night —*Springfield* (Mass.) *Union*, 22 Aug. 1953

About seventy of them were accommodated in wards —Nevil Shute, *Most Secret*, 1945

It is not easily accommodated among the peculiarities of our constitutional system —Dean Rusk, in *Fifty Years of Foreign Affairs*, ed. Hamilton Fish Armstrong, 1972

accompanist See PIANIST.

accompany When *accompany* is used in the passive voice, Bernstein 1965 specifies "*with* (things), *by* (persons)." Several later commentators echo him. Garner 1998, on the other hand, insists on *by* in all cases. Our evidence shows that *accompanied by* is used in most cases, whether persons or things are involved. *Accompanied with* is limited to things; it is still in use but is much less frequent than *accompanied by*. Here are some typical examples:

. . . on foot and accompanied by one or another slimly identified friend —George Packer, *Civilization,* February/March 2000

Accompanied by a motley crew of friends —*Publishers Weekly,* 24 Apr. 2000

The use of violence is accompanied by anger, hatred and fear, or by exultant malice and conscious cruelty —Aldous Huxley, *Ends and Means,* 1937

It may be accompanied by vision, hearing, learning and eating problems —Darrell E. Ward, *Chicago Tribune,* 2 July 2000

But all this free-wheeling fun is accompanied by an almost desperate effort to entertain —Alexander Star, *New Republic,* 14 Aug. 2000

. . . splutterings about "trendies," accompanied with barks of approval for robust old-fashioned attitudes —Peter Kemp, *Times Literary Supp.,* 5–11 Oct. 1990

Usually such a reminder was accompanied with a sneer —Peter Hamill, *National Rev.,* 31 Dec. 1999

. . . a risotto made with veal stock and zucchini and accompanied with fried zucchini flowers —James Suckling, *Wine Spectator,* 31 Aug. 1995

account, *noun*   See ON ACCOUNT OF.

account, *verb*   When *account* is used as an intransitive verb, it is regularly followed by the preposition *for*:

. . . won twenty-seven games while losing ten, thereby accounting for nearly half of his team's total victories for the year —Roger Angell, *New Yorker,* 11 Nov. 1972

. . . still incapable of accounting for facts that are obvious to introspection —Noam Chomsky, *Columbia Forum,* Spring 1968

. . . the Humour definition quite fails to account for the total effect produced —T. S. Eliot, "Ben Jonson," in *Selected Essays,* 1932

accountable   One is accountable *to* someone who is due an explanation *for* something done or not done.

. . . public officials are agents of the people and accountable to them for their public acts —Hyman G. Rickover, *Center Mag.,* September 1969

The F.B.I. has not been forced to address such issues in public because it has never been accountable to the public —Victor S. Navasky, *N.Y. Times Book Rev.,* 14 Mar. 1976

They would, finally, make the schools accountable for results —Peter Janssen, *Saturday Rev.,* 5 Feb. 1972

accuse   The usual preposition used with *accuse,* to indicate the charge, is *of;* it has been the usual one at least since John Gower in the late 14th century. But from time to time other prepositions have come into use with *accuse,* and grammarians and commentators have been at pains to correct them. In 1762 Bishop Lowth corrected these two well-known writers for using *for*:

Ovid, whom you accuse for luxuriancy of verse —John Dryden, "Essay on Dramatic Poesy," 1668

Accused the ministers for betraying the Dutch —Jonathan Swift, *The History of the Four Last Years of the Queen,* 1758

Evidence in the OED shows *for* with *accuse* to have come in around the middle of the 17th century; the latest citation with *for* is dated 1809; the OED calls it obsolete.

The occasional use of *with* seems to have originated in the 20th century. Our earliest evidence is from Lurie 1927, who corrects this example from an unnamed newspaper:

Jeremiah Jenks, having sold butter for more than the market price, was accused with being a profiteer.

Lurie supposes *with* to have come from confusion of *charged with* and *accused of* (see SYNTACTIC BLEND). Bernstein 1965, 1977 and Garner 1998 also criticize the use of *with,* and concur in Lurie's theory of its origin. Aside from the examples provided by Lurie, Bernstein, and Garner, we have found only one other example:

In 1947, the FTC accused Monarch and Stolkin with "misrepresentation. . . ." —*Newsweek,* 3 Nov. 1952

Most examples are from journalistic sources (one is quoted speech, however, and Reader's Digest 1983 cites Louis Nizer's autobiography). *Accuse with* seems to appear seldom and sporadically.

The usual constructions are *accuse* + object (noun or pronoun) + *of* + noun, which is the older one, and *accuse* + object + *of* + gerund. Evidence in the Merriam-Webster files suggests that the gerund construction is somewhat more common in current use. Here are a couple of examples of each:

. . . two Negroes who had been accused by a federal grand jury in Jackson, Mississippi of perjury —*Current Biography,* July 1965

Niebuhr accuses secular social thinkers of these erroneous beliefs —Ralph Gilbert Ross, *Partisan Rev.,* January–February 1954

If you accuse me of being a gross optimist —Melvin M. Belli, *Los Angeles Times Book Rev.,* 23 May 1971

Carlyle has been accused of making a habit of this shifting of the phrase modifier in his writings —Margaret M. Bryant, *Modern English and Its Heritage,* 1948

accused No one quibbles over uses of the adjective *accused* like this:

. . . the accused teacher should be informed before the hearing . . . of the charges —*AAUP Bulletin,* December 1967

But several commentators note that *accused* is also used in such combinations as *the accused spy, the accused assassin, the accused murderer:*

Previously, accused shoplifters had been disciplined by an administration committee —Glynn Mapes, *Security World,* May 1968

Copperud 1970 advises avoiding these because they imply guilt before it is established; Reader's Digest 1983 calls the use an error; *Winners & Sinners* (19 Apr. 1985) finds it "journalese"; Bernstein 1971 finds the meaning of *accused* "distorted" but "accepted" and advises avoiding it as ambiguous. While many commentators say such uses of *accused* are quite common, our files hold few examples other than those held up as bad examples. Reader's Digest prefers and approves *alleged* in place of *accused* in such combinations. See ALLEGED, which has had its share of detractors, too.

This is, perhaps, more of a problem for journalists than for other writers.

Achilles' heel The majority of people who use this term in print retain the terminal apostrophe. The variant without the apostrophe may have been introduced by George Bernard Shaw, a notable contemner of the mark. Some British publications follow Shaw's lead. Either form is perfectly acceptable.

acid test Back in 1920 when H. W. Fowler was compiling his magnum opus (Fowler 1926), he noted that *acid test* had the greatest vogue of all the popularized technicalities he was listing. He attributed the popularity of the phrase to Woodrow Wilson's conspicuous use of it during World War I. The OED Supplement cites Wilson:

The treatment accorded Russia by her sister nations in the months to come will be the acid test of their good will —*The Times,* 9 Jan. 1918

The same statement was paraphrased just a couple of weeks later:

He said the attitude of other nations toward revolutionary Russia was the acid test of

their democracy and good faith —*Saturday Evening Post,* 25 Jan. 1918

The OED Supplement shows that the figurative sense of acid test—"a crucial test"—had actually been in use as early as 1912, but Fowler was probably right in attributing its sudden popularity to Wilson. The *Saturday Evening Post* report is the earliest citation in the Merriam-Webster files. It was soon followed by more evidence from 1918, 1919, and the early 1920s, and the term was entered in the 1923 Addenda section of Webster 1909.

As is often the case with a phrase that has become popular in a relatively short time, *acid test* was soon disparaged as a cliché—as early as 1929. Several commentators, right into the 1990s, have repeated the 1929 judgment. But well over eighty years of use have established it as standard. We do note that the phrase seems not to be much used in literary contexts.

Will Sandler's young male fans sit still for his bourgeois transformation? This may be the acid test for the '90's most unexpected superstar —David Ansen, *Newsweek,* 5 July 1999

A museum show is the acid test for photojournalism —Richard Lacayo, *Time,* 19 Aug. 1985

But this kid was the acid test, because this kid knew cool —Malcolm Gladwell, *New Yorker,* 17 Mar. 1997

He passed the brothers' acid test for tailors by spotting immediately that each twin has an arm that's a quarter inch longer than the other —Ben Brantley, *N.Y. Times Mag.,* 7 Sept. 1986

Even when all these acid tests are ruthlessly applied, however, the inventory of probable Scandinavian phonic and lexical influences in English remains impressive —John Geipel, *The Viking Legacy,* 1971

. . . Sawyer has devised an acid test for friendship: take a job that requires getting up at 5:30 in the afternoon —Margo Howard, *People,* 5 Nov. 1984

acoustics *Acoustics* takes a singular verb when it refers to the science, and a plural verb when it applies to the characteristics (as of an auditorium) that enable distinct hearing.

Acoustics is the science of sound —*Acoustical Terminology,* 1951

The acoustics of the place are not very good —Virgil Thomson, *The Musical Scene,* 1947

acquaint Two sources—Bernstein 1965 and Chambers 1985—remind us that *acquaint* should be followed by *with.* It was not always so. Johnson's Dictionary (1798 ed.) for the sense Johnson defined "To inform" carries this note: "*With* is more in use before the object, than *of.*" He includes a quotation from Shakespeare using *of.* Actually, the construction *acquaint someone* could also be used with a clause introduced by *that* or even a contact clause. Shakespeare uses all four possibilities, but even with him *with* is the most common. The OED shows the construction with *that* from Fielding and Sir Walter Scott but calls the construction with *of* obsolete. The *of* construction is not quite obsolete, but we have no evidence of it since the 1930s. *With* predominates, from Shakespeare's time to our own:

> Misery acquaints a man with strange bedfellows —Shakespeare, *The Tempest,* 1612

> Any young gentlemen and ladies, who wish to acquaint themselves with the English language —Noah Webster, quoted in Horace E. Scudder, *Noah Webster,* 1882

> . . . not very well acquainted with our Parliamentary or political affairs —Sir Winston Churchill, *The Unrelenting Struggle,* 1942

> . . . it will appeal equally to readers already acquainted with this engaging cast of characters —Patricia Cline Cohen, *N.Y. Times Book Rev.,* 18 June 2000

> The football player was acquainted with the drug dealers —Leigh Montville, *Sports Illustrated,* 6 Dec. 1999

> His interest in modern writers acquainted him with such philosophers as Pascal, Voltaire and Rousseau —Edmund White, *N.Y. Times Book Rev.,* 19 June 1983

acquaintanceship *Acquaintanceship* was created in the early 19th century, apparently on analogy with *friendship* and *friend,* to distinguish the meaning "the state of being acquainted" from *acquaintance,* "a person with whom one is acquainted." Its extra syllable found it employment in the poetry of Robert Browning and various lesser-known 19th-century poets. Toward the end of the century its use was recommended to preserve the distinction. But after World War I the spirit of 19th-century poetry was dead, and in 1926 H. W. Fowler condemned it as "a needless long variant" (an opinion still repeated as recently as 1998). Fowler was heedless of the distinction *acquaintanceship* was supposed to preserve, and so were most people, who had been using *acquaintance* for both meanings all along. *Acquaintanceship* is not widely used, but is not rare. It is still primarily used in literary contexts.

> . . . in contravention of received notions of good taste and of the protocols of acquain-

tanceship —John Melmoth, *Times Literary Supp.,* 5 Dec. 1986

> . . . our progressive acquaintanceship with one kind of person—what one might call the illustrative rather than the functional character —Elizabeth Bowen, *The Mulberry Tree,* 1986

> The author's acquaintanceship with Romanov history was evident in his previous book —Francine du Plessix Gray, *N.Y. Times Book Rev.,* 29 Oct. 1995

acquiesce   Around the beginning of the 20th century *acquiesce* began to receive attention from usage commentators. Vizetelly 1906 seems to have begun things with a prohibition of *with* after the word; he prescribes *in.* Numerous commentors since have prescribed *in,* disparaged *with,* and sometimes disparaged *to* as well.

The OED shows that *acquiesce* has been used with several prepositions—*from* and *under* in senses now obsolete, and *in, to,* and *with* in the current sense. *In* and *to* are of equal antiquity, both having been used by Thomas Hobbes 1651, who is the earliest user of the modern sense cited in the dictionary. The OED marks *to* and *with* obsolete, but in fact *to* has continued in reputable use:

> . . . to have Carrie acquiesce to an arrangement —Theodore Dreiser, *Sister Carrie,* 1900

> He passively acquired the reputation of being a snob, and acquiesced to it —George V. Higgins, *Harper's,* September 1984

> . . . the tender understanding with which he had acquiesced to her wish not to consummate their relationship out of wedlock —Dorothy West, *The Wedding,* 1995

> . . . they acquiesced to arguments by public officials that they should bank on the "magic" of the name Miami —Mirey Navarro, *N.Y. Times,* 29 Nov. 1997

But *acquiesce in* is the more common construction:

> . . . no organism acquiesces in its own destruction —H. L. Mencken, *Prejudices: Second Series,* 1920

> Her "shopkeeper's prejudices" . . . went unnoticed as she acquiesced in supporting the welfare state and trade unions —*Wilson Quarterly,* Spring 1990

> He discreetly acquiesced in the election of one of the principal assassins —John Buchan, *Augustus,* 1937

> The main body of Shi'is, in and around Iraq, accepted 'Abbasid rule, or at least acqui-

esced in it —Albert Hourani, *A History of the Arab Peoples,* 1991

. . . the general intellectual tendency is to acquiesce in what one no longer feels able to change —Irving Howe, *Partisan Rev.,* January–February 1954

. . . he seems to have acquiesced in his Christian Scientist wife's refusal to provide medical care —Joyce Carol Oates, *N.Y. Times Book Rev.,* 17 Dec. 1995

acquit When *acquit* means "to discharge completely," it is often used in the construction *acquit* (a person) *of* (something charged):

. . . was acquitted of robbery on an alibi —*Time,* 30 Oct. 1950

. . . cannot therefore be acquitted of being out of touch in some respects —*Times Literary Supp.,* 23 Apr. 1971

. . . neither pamphlet nor book could acquit him of indecency —Henry Seidel Canby, *Walt Whitman,* 1943

For may substitute for *of* in this construction but is rare:

In the end, Mary Todd Lincoln stands acquitted for any evil intent —Gerald W. Johnson, *New Republic,* 23 Feb. 1953

From was formerly in use, but is no longer:

If I sin, then thou markest me, and thou wilt not acquit me from mine iniquity —Job 10:14 (AV), 1611

When the person is not present in the sentence, other constructions may be found:

The military "jury" . . . voted 3-1 to acquit on the charges of failure to report for duty and resisting arrest —Steve Wise, *Great Speckled Bird,* 24 Jan. 1972

acronyms A number of commentators (as Copperud 1970, Janis 1984, Howard 1984) believe that acronyms can be differentiated from other abbreviations in being pronounceable as words. Dictionaries, however, do not make this distinction, and Burchfield 1996 observes that the general public does not either. Pyles & Algeo 1970 divide acronyms into "initialisms," which consist of initial letters pronounced with the letter names, and "word acronyms," which are pronounced as words. *Initialism,* an older word than *acronym,* seems to be too little known to the general public to serve as the customary term standing in contrast with *acronym.*

A number of commentators warn against the indiscriminate use of acronyms that may not be familiar to the reader of general text—sound common sense. Of course, if you are writing for a technical audience, you have more leeway in the use of acronyms. But even in technical articles, many authors gloss new acronyms for their readers' information at least upon their first appearance in the text.

act, action Both *act* and *action* can be similarly used to denote something done. In theory, an act is conceived of as individual and momentary or instantaneous; an action involves discrete stages or steps and is conceived of as occupying more time than an act. However, even though many writers and speakers give little thought to the theory, in most cases, as we shall see, the two words tend to fall into different patterns of use.

When *act* is modified by something descriptive, for example, it tends to be followed by *of* and a noun:

. . . performing numerous acts of kindness to those in need —*Times Literary Supp.,* 8 Feb. 1968

. . . they could never catch Reston in an act of arrogance or selfishness —Gay Talese, *Harper's,* January 1969

. . . sit down to commit an act of literature —William Zinsser, 1975

Once the act of reading has begun —Joe Flaherty, *N.Y. Times Book Rev.,* 27 Mar. 1977

One phrase is a notable exception:

The sex act has to do more for humans than for other creatures —Robert Jay Lifton, *N.Y. Times Book Rev.,* 19 Aug. 1979

Action tends to be preceded by its modifier:

. . . a similar CNVA protest action —*Current Biography,* October 1965

. . . his occasional political actions . . . seem unrelated to any other aspect of his character —*Times Literary Supp.,* 14 Mar. 1968

There are squatter actions going on all the time —Philip St. George, quoted in *N.Y. Times,* 23 Mar. 1930

When a prepositional phrase introduced by *of* follows *action,* it usually functions as a genitive:

It is the actions of men and not their sentiments which make history —Norman Mailer, *Advertisements for Myself,* 1959

. . . the future of our children depends in great measure on the actions of our political leaders —Lena L. Gitter, *Children's House,* Fall 1968

Action has a collective use that *act* does not:

. . . the only time in which it took decisive action —*Times Literary Supp.,* 16 Jan. 1969

... after the Socialists' April triumph, action against them was indicated —John Paton Davies, *N.Y. Times Mag.*, 13 July 1975

Action is also used attributively, while *act* is not:

... scrutiny by ... environmental action groups —*Annual Report, Owens-Illinois,* 1970

... lots of exciting action photographs —C. H. Simonds, *National Rev.*, 17 Dec. 1971

In addition, both *act* and *action* fit into characteristic idiomatic constructions where no native speaker of English would be tempted to interchange them: for instance, *caught in the act, a piece of the action*. Here is a sampling:

"She had a class act going there." —Cyra McFadden, *The Serial*, 1977 (*class action* is a legal term)

... Washington must get its act together —Wassily Leontief, *N.Y. Times Mag.*, 30 Dec. 1979

"... to try to clean up his act." —John Maher, quoted in *Harper's Weekly*, 20 Oct. 1975

... a bulletin on how the hairdressers are getting into the act —Lois Long, *New Yorker*, 8 Sept. 1956

... no action has yet been taken —Hugh Thomas, *Times Literary Supp.*, 11 Apr. 1968

"... tomorrow they swing into action. ..." —unnamed announcer, WTIC radio, 23 Feb. 1975

... a general program that ... was not put into action at first —*Current Biography,* May 1965

Its editorial offices are in Manhattan, near the action —Herbert Mitgang, *N.Y. Times Book Rev.*, 13 Jan. 1980

activate, actuate   Past commentary about these words is mostly beside the point here at the beginning of the 21st century. Both words are mostly used of mechanical, electronic, or physiological mechanisms in both general and technical writing. *Activate* is more commonly used, especially in general writing, but *actuate* is not at all rare.

The electronically actuated robots used in most applications —Harry H. Pook, *Fundamentals of Robotic Engineering*, 1989

... an alarm may be actuated if any measurement exceeds a safe value —*Dutton's Navigation & Piloting*, 1985

The door ... is secured by an electronically activated dead bolt —Paul Roberts, *Harper's*, June 1997

When the infected application is run, the virus code is activated —J. D. Biersdorfer, *N.Y. Times*, 3 Sept. 1998

When the words are used in reference to persons, they are usually distinguished. *Actuate*, which has a long background of literary use, almost always indicates an interior cause for the action:

Yet Oswald ... was not actuated by the atmosphere —Christopher Hitchens, *The Nation*, 22 May 1995

... that very British spirit of freedom which has actuated them throughout —Osbert Sitwell, *Triple Fugue*, 1924

... the man who is actuated by love of power is more apt to inflict pain than to permit pleasure —Bertrand Russell, *Atlantic,* March 1952

When *activate* is applied to individuals, it almost always implies an external force:

... her life in art is closely related to the places where she has lived and visited, to the natural phenomena that have activated her —Katharine Kuh, *Saturday Rev.*, 22 Jan. 1977

The politics of abortion rights, she says, "gives us an issue that activates people. ..." —Ellen Goodman, *Springfield* (Mass.) *Union-News*, 11 Aug. 1989

... he lacked the force to control his party and the personality and leadership to activate the public —Sidney Warren, *Current History*, May 1952

Activate is, in general, the more likely word to be used of something that is compared to or conceived of as machinery:

The federal government finally was activated —Donald Canty, *City*, March–April 1972

Economists are accordingly much more interested in societies activated by command than in those run by tradition —Robert L. Heilbroner, *The World of Economics*, 1963

American men rarely compliment a woman on her looks for fear of activating her suspicions about their motives —Holly Brubach, *New Yorker*, 30 Apr. 1996

active voice   See PASSIVE VOICE.

actual, actually   Both words are tarred with the brush of meaninglessness by Copperud 1970, who cites Fowler 1965 and Evans 1957 in support of his view, although Evans and Fowler (actually Gowers, since Fowler 1926 does not mention it) condemn only *actually*. We will examine the words separately.

Copperud's objection to *actual* lies in a single quoted sentence: "The stocks were sold at prices above actual market prices." The trouble with this example is that it lacks its preceding context. In a majority of instances of the use of *actual* in our files, it contrasts with some other adjective, either stated or implied. Combined with *price, actual* is usually so contrasted:

> . . . market participants' expectations may differ in a systematic manner from actual prices —George Soros, *New Republic,* 12 Apr. 1999

In Copperud's example, the contrasting price may have been mentioned or implied in an earlier sentence in such a way as to make the use of *actual* entirely apposite. Here are some other examples of *actual* in its contrastive use:

> I had enjoyed my actual sins, those I had committed rather than those I had been accused of —Ernest Hemingway, "Miss Mary's Lion," 1956

> . . . how would he set out to make any actual person a character in a novel? —Bernard DeVoto, *The World of Fiction,* 1950

> . . . space is not simply a backdrop in which we move, but an actual thing that can be measured —Jim Bell, *Astronomy,* March 1999

Phythian 1979 and Garner 1998 object to the phrase *in actual fact*. The phrase does not turn up in our files often enough to suggest that it is much of a problem. It seems to be used contrastively, and is simply an alternative to *actually*:

> Penrose and Hawking's work did not rule out oscillating universes —Alan Lightman, *Ancient Light,* 1991

> The canard that a mule needs less to eat than a horse. . . . In actual fact, the working mule requires pound for pound the same calories as a draft horse —Maxine Kumin, *In Deep,* 1987

Actual has, besides its use in pointing up a contrast, an intensive function sometimes meant to stress authenticity:

> Descriptivism involves the objective description of the way a language works as observed in actual examples of the language —Jesse Sheidlower, *Atlantic,* December 1996

> . . . some of his suits have actual whalebone up the ribs —Lois Long, *New Yorker,* 27 Mar. 1954

It is also used as a simple intensive:

> . . . their more resilient Internet and technology brethren that have been able to show—

ta-da!—actual profits —John Greenwald, *Time,* 17 Apr. 2000

> . . . many heavy leatherites will think twice about confronting an actual well-dressed lady —Blair Sabol, *Vogue,* November 1976

The intensive *actual* can reasonably be challenged as unnecessary in many instances.

Actually is a more difficult subject. The usages that seem to have excited the criticism are primarily spoken rather than written usages, so that printed evidence of the disputed usages is not as abundant as one would like it to be. We will first examine typical written usage before passing on to the spoken.

It should not be surprising to find *actually* used in adverbial functions corresponding to the adjective functions of *actual*. It is used to point up a contrast:

> . . . the two traditions on justification are actually complementary, not contradictory —Margaret O'Gara, *Commonweal,* 14 Jan. 2000

> What do you call xenophobia when it's actually the opposite —Adam Goodheart, *N.Y. Times Book Rev.,* 18 June 2000

> Sea anemones may resemble pretty flowers, but actually they are deadly animals —Murray T. Pringle, *Boy's Life,* April 1968

But the most common use is to stress the reality or factuality of something. In this use, *actually* is not necessarily emphatic:

> . . . could not even find out how many airplanes there actually were —David Halberstam, *Harper's,* February 1971

> . . . an imaginative reconstruction of ancient culture as it was actually lived —G. W. Bowersock, *New Republic,* 7 Feb. 2000

> . . . showing the picture that was actually on the air —Denis Johnston, *Irish Digest,* June 1954

> . . . what working ecologists actually do is mainly narrow, technical, and dreary —Robert M. Solow, *New Republic,* 15 May 2000

> ". . . but as I have actually paid the visit, we cannot escape the acquaintance now." —Jane Austen, *Pride and Prejudice,* 1813

It may be used to suggest something unexpected:

> When I was a senior in high school, I sent him some jokes I'd written, and he actually hired me —*UTNE Reader,* March/April 2000

> I had been actually invited —F. Scott Fitzgerald, *The Great Gatsby,* 1925

Of course any of these uses would be normal in speech, too. But in conversation the sense may be weakened or even absent, and it is presumably this use that has occasioned censure of *actually* as unnecessary. When its semantic content is low, *actually* may be serving as a filler (see FILLERS) as Phythian 1979 and Bremner 1980 observe (in different terms). "*Actually* is usually used to give the speaker a moment in which to think," says Phythian. The filler *actually* is likely to be syntactically a sentence adverb.

> I sometimes wonder what would happen if I lost it. I'd be pretty screwed, actually —Michael Stroh, quoted in *mediainfo.com*, November 1998

> Actually, the people who truly are Mrs. Lieberman's dearest friends are a great deal like her —John Corry, *Harper's*, February 1971

> Because I've seen some of the recent criticisms—the continuing criticism, actually—of the statistics —William Ruckelshaus, quoted in *N.Y. Times Mag.*, 19 Aug. 1973

> . . . he didn't fall about laughing, he helped me a lot actually —Saffron Summerfield, quoted in *Spare Rib* (London), December 1974

> As much a Wykeham Diary as a Langham Diary, actually —Alan Ryan, *The Listener*, 28 Mar. 1974

Conclusion: criticism of *actual* and *actually* as unnecessary is of very limited value in a usage handbook. The usages criticized are primarily spoken, and few people trouble to chasten their speech in accordance with the pronouncements found in usage books addressed to writers. Both *actual* and *actually* have legitimate uses in writing, which have been illustrated here.

actuate See ACTIVATE, ACTUATE.

ad After more than 80 years of disapproval, the clipped form *ad* has finally established itself. In the early days *ad* was disparaged not only by the handbooks but also by the advertising fraternity itself. H. L. Mencken, *The American Language, Supplement I,* 1945, gives the history:

> The American advertising men, in the glorious days when the more forward-looking of them hoped to lift their art and mystery to the level of dogmatic theology, astronomy, ophthalmology and military science, carried on a crusade against the clipped form *ad,* but it came, alas, to nothing.

Mencken says that nothing has been heard of the campaign since 1933. If the admen have given up the campaign themselves, a few writers of college handbooks are still carrying the old banner. Even so, a large majority find *ad* acceptable in general and informal writing.

A.D., B.C. *B.C.* is here for the record—there is no dispute about it and never has been. *B.C.* follows the year and follows the word century:

> . . . sometime before 2000 B.C., corn was introduced —Katherine Hinds, *Brown Alumni Monthly,* October 1982

> We have Panini's analysis of Sanskrit from the fourth century B.C. —Edward Finegan, *Attitudes Toward English Usage,* 1980

A.D. is a different story. It presents three problems: Does it go before or after the year? Can it be used with *in?* Can it be used after *century?*

The traditional and still most frequently used styling places *A.D.* before the year:

> A.D. 1942 was the year —*Time,* 28 Dec. 1942

> . . . objects, which date from A.D. 200 —*Newsweek,* 10 July 1944

> Until A.D. 1200 the Great Plains were virtually unpopulated —Albert H. Johnston, *Publishers Weekly,* 29 Dec. 1975

Some writers and publishers, however, place *A.D.* after the date like *B.C.*:

> Strictly speaking, we should use *A.D.* only with numbers indicating particular years (43 *A.D.,* 8–10 *A.D.*) —MacCracken & Sandison 1917

> Lucian flourished approximately 125–190 A.D. —*Insect Enemies of Books,* 1937

> . . . the vast platform that before 70 A.D. had supported the Temple —John Updike, *Bech is Back,* 1982

MacCracken & Sandison 1917 finds that usage justifies placing *A.D.* either before or after the year; Reader's Digest 1983 also finds placement after the date acceptable.

MacCracken & Sandison brings up the question of *in*: "Though purists insist on 'He died 48 A.D.' [not *in* 48 A.D.], usage allows *in*. . . ." The objection to *in* is based on insistence on the literal translation of the Latin *anno Domini* "in the year of the Lord." Bremner 1980 is still defending the position of the 1917 purists, but no one else mentions it.

Insistence on the literal "in the year of the Lord" is also the basis for the objection to using *A.D.* after *century*; the use is illogical if you insist on the literal interpretation. Bremner 1980 does. But many people will agree with Johnson 1982 when he terms the etymological objection to *A.D.* after century "rather a fussy point." There is plenty of evidence that writers and publishers have found *A.D.* convenient to use after *century*:

> . . . no parallels can be found before the mid-first century A.D. —G. W. Bowersock, *Fiction as History,* 1994

> . . . how the Torah . . . was interpreted . . . from the third century B.C. through the first century A.D. —Phyllis Trible, *N.Y. Times Book Rev.,* 21 Dec. 1997

> . . . During the fourth century AD —Bernard F. Reilly, *The Medieval Spains,* 1993

Perhaps if the abbreviations *C.E.* (common era) and *B.C.E.* (before the common era) catch on, these disputes will all be forgotten. Both of these routinely follow the date or century:

> In the fourth century C.E., it was observed on the Sunday after Pentecost —*Publishers Weekly,* 17 Aug. 1998

> . . . after the destruction of the Jewish temple (70 CE) —Garry Wills, *Under God,* 1990

> . . . texts of the second or first centuries B.C.E. —John E. Wills, Jr., *Mountain of Fame,* 1994

> The Romans, who initially celebrated the new year on March 1, were the first to move the date to Jan. 1, after 153 BCE —Jim Wilson, *Popular Mechanics,* January 2000

You may have noted that the styling of *A.D.* and *B.C.* and other abbreviated era designations varies in regard to type style and punctuation. In books and journals, they usually (but not always) appear as small capitals; in typed or keyboarded material they usually appear as full capitals. The punctuated styling is more prevalent in all kinds of publications.

adage   See OLD ADAGE.

adapter, adaptor   Phythian 1979 wants us to distinguish *adaptor* "an electrical device" from *adapter* "a person who adapts." Even for British English he is only partly right. Both *adapter* and *adaptor* are used in British English for devices (and not only electrical ones), and *adapter* is used for a person, while *adaptor* is not. In American English *adapter* is usual for both persons and devices; *adaptor* is relatively infrequent.

addicted   Some commentators, such as Bernstein 1965, dislike *addicted* being used of things that are not harmful. But evidence in the OED shows neutral use to have existed from the 17th century at least:

> He was much addicted to civil Affairs —Thomas Stanley, *The History of Philosophy,* 1660 (OED)

> His majesty is much addicted to useful reading —'Junius,' *Letters,* 1771 (OED)

Such use has continued undiminished:

> . . . rich sportsmen addicted to deer shooting —George Bernard Shaw, *Everybody's Political What's What,* 1944

> She was addicted to gaudy shawls and the most God-awful hats —*The Autobiography of William Allen White,* 1946

> . . . armchair degenerates addicted to reading tales of louche junkie glamour —David Gates, *N.Y. Times Book Rev.,* 21 Nov. 1999

> . . . addicted to watching pro wrestling on cable —William Finnegan, *New Yorker,* 16 Sept. 1997

> . . . the symptoms of a company dangerously addicted to discounting —*Wall Street Jour.,* 16 Sept. 1997

> Catherine Morland, having become addicted to novels of terror —Lionel Trilling, *Encounter,* September 1954

> He was hopelessly addicted to the Senators, a team of monumental incompetence on the baseball diamond —Russell Baker, *Growing Up,* 1982

There is a British tradition (starting with Fowler 1926) of warning writers not to follow *addicted* by an infinitive, although the regular preposition is *to*. OED remarks that the infinitive was formerly used in this way but shows no example of it later than the 16th century.

adequate   Follett 1966 touches on most of the points about *adequate* that others (Copperud 1964, 1970, 1980, Evans 1957, Partridge 1942) comment upon. He deals with idiom, first noting that *adequate* is normally followed by *to*:

> . . . occasions when school textbooks are not adequate to the purpose —Albert H. Marckwardt, *Linguistics and the Teaching of English,* 1966

> . . . his resources weren't adequate to the ambition —F. R. Leavis, *Revaluation,* 1947

> . . . even his dizzying command of the piano was not entirely adequate to the richness of the piece —George Steiner, *New Yorker,* 23 Nov. 1992

However, he does not note that it is also followed by *for*:

> . . . they are adequate for almost any computing need —Michael Meyer, *Newsweek,* 26 Oct. 1998

> One cup of seed per gallon of sand should be adequate for 1,000 square feet —Elizabeth Pennisi, *National Wildlife,* April–May 1990

And the nobility was not much more adequate for the role attributed to it by Montesquieu —*Times Literary Supp.*, 21 Sept. 1951

Follett says that idiom requires the gerund rather than the infinitive after *to*:

. . . mind . . . is not always adequate to mastering the forms of rage, horror, and disgust —Norman Mailer, *Advertisements for Myself*, 1959

However, the construction with the infinitive is considerably more common:

. . . bank funds have been adequate to meet loan demand in a strong economy —*Wall Street Jour.*, 18 Sept. 1997

. . . they are not adequate to bring man to any sense of the world as a whole —Robert Penn Warren, *Democracy and Poetry*, 1975

Psychological explanations alone are not adequate to understand today's student radicals —Kenneth Kenniston, *Change*, November–December 1969

Follett does acknowledge use without any complement, and in the Merriam-Webster files, *adequate* appears most frequently without a complement:

A rat has to have a protected home and an adequate food supply —Victor Heiser, *An American Doctor's Odyssey*, 1936

. . . simple causes which did not seem to him adequate —Joseph Conrad, *Chance*, 1913

It may be that there is nothing more demoralizing than a small but adequate income —Edmund Wilson, *Memoirs of Hecate County*, 1946

Follett calls *adequate enough* "too familiar" and "nonsense" (Evans, Partridge, Bremner 1980, and Garner 1998 find it redundant). We have but a single example in our files; the phrase does not seem frequent enough to be worth worrying about.

Follett also mentions *more adequate, less adequate, insufficiently adequate* with disapproval; he believes *adequate* "resistant to comparison." Like other adjectives usage commentators call "uncomparable" or "absolute," *adequate* is an adjective with which *more* patently means "more nearly":

. . . would regret the lack of a more adequate formal education —*Current Biography*, September 1966

The future of civilization depends on our having a more adequate supply of both —Robert M. Hutchins, *Center Mag.*, September 1968

Until there is a more adequate historical record from the Soviet side —Marshall D. Shulman, *N.Y. Times Book Rev.*, 1 Mar. 1987

In what areas is this support most adequate? —*ACLS Newsletter*, Winter/Spring 1995

. . . the government would have to bail out any bidder with less adequate resources —*The Economist*, 30 Aug.–5 Sept. 1986

The intensifier *very* is occasionally found:

. . . some very adequate salaries are given to a few —*American Guide Series: New Jersey*, 1939

. . . a very adequate summary of it was made by T. E. Hulme in a lecture —Herbert Read, *The Philosophy of Modern Art*, 1952

Copperud and Follett both observe that *adequate* is used in a conventional way by reviewers to convey faint praise or faint derogation. The sense is generally recorded in dictionaries.

. . . not particularly inspired. An adequate performance —Henry Barnard Stafford, *Saturday Rev.*, 30 Mar. 1940

. . . is at best adequate as the slight, brooding producer and moonstruck lover —Judith Crist, *Saturday Rev.*, 11 Dec. 1976

The sense is not limited to use by reviewers:

". . . After all, in any other walk in life it doesn't matter if you're not very good; you can get along quite comfortably if you're just adequate. . . ." —W. Somerset Maugham, *The Moon and Sixpence*, 1919

adherence, adhesion A number of theorists comment on the distinction between *adherence* and *adhesion* from Vizetelly 1906 to Garner 1998. The thrust of all these is the same: *adherence* is generally used figuratively, *adhesion* literally. This analysis is only partly correct. *Adherence* is mostly used figuratively:

. . . a few people's adherence to an obviously wacko creed —Walter Kendrick, *N.Y. Times Book Rev.*, 21 Sept. 1997

. . . their coverage is contingent on adherence to state licensing laws —Anita Hamilton, *Time*, 24 May 1999

Donald's adherence to the firm of Middleton was now the topic —Angus Wilson, *Anglo-Saxon Attitudes*, 1956

But it is also used literally:

. . . results in imperfect adherence of rubber to the fabric —*Industrial Improvement*, January 1946

. . . molecule important in the adherence of the epidermis to the underlying dermis

—Jack L. Strominger, M.D., et al., *JAMA*, 4 Oct. 1995

Adhesion is a bit more complex. Its various technical and literal senses account for more than half of the citations in our files. But figurative use is not at all uncommon. It falls into two varieties—political and general. (There is also a technical legal use, "adhesion contract.") President Harding's use of "adhesion to a treaty" was criticized, but his use seems to have been in line with standard use:

... the terms of this Convention which is open to adhesion by all countries of the world —*UNESCO Copyright Bulletin*, No. 3, 1951

... a France ... which was neutral and possessed a navy whose adhesion to Hitler would seriously threaten . . . Britain —D. Cameron Watt, *History Today*, December 1986

. . . the Communist International won at first the adhesion of several powerful and well-established labor organizations —H. B. Parkes, *Marxism—an Autopsy*, 1939

. . . his ardent attachment to Washington, and his adhesion generally to the federal party —Horace E. Scudder, *Noah Webster*, 1882

General figurative use seems a bit less frequent than the political:

. . . a too strict adhesion to those so-called 'laws' —Eric Partridge, "Imagination and Good Sense in Etymology," 1952

. . . to speak of the Visigoths . . . as Christian here implies merely a formal and legal adhesion —Bernard F. Reilly, *The Medieval Spains*, 1993

Our files, then, show that *adherence* is more often figurative than literal, while *adhesion* is more often used literally and technically, but its figurative use is perfectly standard.

adjacent   *Adjacent* is often followed by *to*:

. . . the border region below the Bolovens Plateau and adjacent to the Highlands —Robert Shaplen, *New Yorker*, 24 Apr. 1971

All I knew was the state—one adjacent to the state Beardsley was in —Vladimir Nabokov, *Lolita*, 1958

". . . something adjacent to your talents and interests—commercial art, perhaps." —Lore Segal, *New Yorker*, 25 July 1964

adjectives   **1.** Under the heading *adjective* most commentators on usage place a miscellaneous collection of faults they are intent on exposing and eradicating. Some include general observations on matters of grammar and rhetoric, as well. In this book, most of the usage issues that adjectives are involved in are treated under separate headings. See, for instance, ABSOLUTE ADJECTIVES; DOUBLE COMPARISON; FLAT ADVERBS; IMPLICIT COMPARATIVE; SENTENCE ADJECTIVE; SUPERLATIVE OF TWO; VERY 1.
2. *Idiomatic placement of adjectives.* Harper 1975, 1985 points out that some "nit-pickers" object to the illogical placement of adjectives in such expressions as "a hot cup of coffee," "a brand-new pair of shoes." The argument is that it's the coffee that's hot, the shoes that are brand-new. Harper points out that the placement of these adjectives is idiomatically correct, so the nitpickers may be ignored.
3. *Adjectives as nouns.* Adjectives are used as nouns essentially in two ways: as noncount nouns to indicate a quality or a number of a group having a quality—the *beautiful*, the *sublime*, the *just*, the *unemployed*—and as count nouns—*moderns*, an all-time *high*, the *ancients*, big-city *dailies*. Evans 1957 has a long article discussing these. The noncount use, which some grammarians refer to as "the absolute use of the adjective," seems to have excited little discussion in usage books. The count nouns, however, have drawn the attention of Harper 1985, which devotes a usage panel question to the propriety of a handful of advertising uses such as a toothpaste that leaves a "clean in your mouth" and a washing machine with a special device for washing "your delicates." There is no principle involved in this sort of discussion; the strained syntax of advertising is used solely to catch attention and evoke a predictable response.

adjectives as nouns   See ADJECTIVES 3.

adjure   See ABJURE, ADJURE.

adjust, adjusted   **1.** Copperud 1970 notes that prices are "adjusted"—upwards, as a rule—in his discussion of euphemisms. See EUPHEMISMS.
2. Bernstein 1965 says *adjusted* takes *to*. This is true, as far as it goes, but the participial adjective is more often used without a complement than with one. When there is a complement, *to* is the most common preposition:

. . . a program . . . as dramatic and as sound and as adjusted to today and tomorrow as the programs of 1933 —Leon H. Keyserling, *New Republic*, 8 Feb. 1954

. . . factory in which the workers are perfectly adjusted to the machines —Aldous Huxley, *Brave New World Revisited*, 1958

This characteristic of the participial adjective merely reflects the behavior of the verb:

. . . account of one man's addled efforts to adjust to his own obsolescence —Jane Clapperton, *Cosmopolitan,* March 1976

. . . a delightful girl who could adjust to any confusion —James A. Michener, *Report of the County Chairman,* 1961

. . . was trying to adjust to being the head of my family —Mrs. Medgar Evers, *Ladies' Home Jour.,* September 1971

. . . had no difficulty in adjusting to more than a million dollars —Hamilton Basso, *The View from Pompey's Head,* 1954

Adjust is also used with *for*;

. . . is altered when we adjust for the predisposition —Stanley L. Payne, *The Art of Asking Questions,* 1951

Adjust for tends to occur in financial contexts. Thus it would not be out of the ordinary to read of figures "adjusted for inflation."

administer 1. As late as 1942 Eric Partridge was expressing disapproval of *administer* when used of a blow. Several earlier handbooks also censured the use. But, as Burchfield 1996 observes, this criticism belongs to the past, and is no longer an issue.

The spider descends, embraces its victim while administering a paralyzing bite, then slowly wraps it securely in silk —William G. Eberhard, *Natural History,* January 1980

. . . criminal law, . . . whose violation results in publicly administered punishment —Norman F. Cantor, *Imagining the Law,* 1997

2. The Oxford American Dictionary tells us that "nurses do not administer to the wounded," echoing a sentiment expressed in Follett 1966 and F. K. Ball's *Constructive English,* 1923. Longman 1984 also notes that some disapprove of this intransitive use of *administer.* The OED traces the sense to *The Spectator* in 1712. No definite reason seems to be adduced by objectors as a basis of their objection. This use is entirely standard but not especially frequent:

Some also viewed it as an indictment of the medical profession's ineptitude in administering to the dying —Beverly Merz, *American Medical News,* 2 Sept. 1991

. . . physicians who served at hospitals administering to yellow fever victims —Gary W. Shannon, *Professional Geographer,* May 1981

As a man of dedication rather than a man of faith, Lionel Epsy is trying to administer to those suffering from the policies of the

1980s —Carol Homden, *Times Literary Supp.,* 15 Oct. 1993

3. See ADMINISTRATE.

administrate Usage writers will sometimes pass along misinformation because they have not used important resources such as the historical dictionaries. Copperud 1970, 1980 tells us *administrate* is an Americanism. It is not; it was first used in British English in the 17th century. Nickles 1974 and Garner 1998 call it a back-formation; it is not, having been coined out of pure Latin. Fisher 1996 would have us believe there is no such word. Nickles further informs us it is overused. As a matter of fact it is a much less frequently used word than its synonym *administer.* Jerry Adler, writing in *Newsweek* (8 Dec. 1980), quotes William Safire to the effect that administrators no longer administer, but administrate. Our files contain abundant evidence that they administer. Sometimes they do both:

I'm a good administrator when I have something to administer. I mean, I really think I administered the Civil Aeronautics Board very effectively, and the Public Service Commission. But I don't have anything to administrate here —Alfred E. Kahn, quoted in *N.Y. Times,* 9 Nov. 1980

Administrate is an unstigmatized entry in OED, Webster's Second, and Webster's Third. It might not have been noticed at all had not H. W. Fowler put it in his list of long variants in 1926. It is standard but infrequently used.

admission, admittance "*Admittance* is usu[ally] applied to mere physical entrance to a locality or a building: *admission* applies to entrance or formal acceptance (as into a club) that carries with it rights, privileges, standing, or membership." This discrimination appears in Merriam-Webster's Collegiate Dictionary, Tenth Edition, and others like it can be found in usage books from Vizetelly 1906 to Harper 1985.

The distinction is one you can certainly make in your writing if you want to. Most people do. But the words have a long history of being interchanged.

Physical entrance:

. . . somebody must gain admittance to his cell —George Meredith, *The Ordeal of Richard Feverel,* 1859

Tom lifted him in his arms, and got admission to the Inn —George Meredith, *The Ordeal of Richard Feverel,* 1859

Permission to enter an academic institution:

. . . the parental demand that their offspring obtain admittance to a four-year college

—James B. Conant, *Slums and Suburbs,* 1961

. . . the attempt of James Meredith, a Negro, to obtain admission to the University of Mississippi —*Current Biography,* July 1965

Permission to join the union as a state:

. . . a constitutional provision . . . it had to eliminate from its constitution as a condition of admittance in 1912 —Thomas P. Neill, *The Common Good* (12th-grade text), 1956

. . . until the size of the population warranted the territory's admission as a state —John H. Haefner et al., *Our Living Government* (12th-grade text), 1960

Entrance to society:

. . . a very accessible and, at the same time, highly enviable society. Whatever the quality that gained you admittance —Virginia Woolf, *The Death of the Moth,* 1942

. . . all the nice men she knew of moved in circles into which an obscure governess had no chance of admission —George Bernard Shaw, *Cashel Byron's Profession,* 1886

For a fee paid to gain entrance, *admission* is much more common, but *admittance* is not unknown:

. . . open to anyone with 500 yuan to spare, which at 3,000 yuan to the dollar, is not a ruinous admittance —James Cameron, *N.Y. Times Mag.,* 9 Jan. 1955

. . . there is no admission fee —*Village Voice,* 28 Feb. 1968

. . . the price of admission is starkly prohibitive —Norman Cousins, *Saturday Rev.,* 21 Feb. 1976

These last two examples show contexts in which *admittance* is no longer used—in the attributive position, and in the phrase "price of _____."

There is a distinction between the two words when preceded by *no.* The sign "No Admittance" refers to physical entrance, but *no admission* is likely to mean no admission fee:

Documentary film . . . shown several times daily. No admission —*Where Mag.,* 15 Mar. 1975

The persons who deal with the entrance of students to educational institutions regularly use *admission,* often in the plural:

. . . college admissions officers —Robert L. Foose, *NEA Jour.,* January 1965

Admission is the usual word for the granting of something not proven or an acknowledgment that something is true:

To ask for a pardon was, he said, an admission of guilt —Robert Penn Warren, *Jefferson Davis Gets His Citizenship Back,* 1980

Although many authors have used *admission* and *admittance* synonymously, there is no harm in your making the distinction outlined in the Collegiate Dictionary if you want to. Except for the sign "No Admittance" and the use of *admittance* as a technical term in electricity, *admission* is the more frequent word in all uses in current English.

admit   1. *Admit to.* Numerous commentators have found fault with intransitive *admit* followed by *to.* This objection seems to have its origin in some edition of Fowler published after World War II; it is in Gowers's 1965 revision but was cited as early as 1960. The basis for the objection is the assertion that *confess* can be followed idiomatically by *to,* but *admit* cannot. But the assertion is wrong. When *admit* is used as an intransitive verb meaning "to make acknowledgment," it is regularly followed by *to:*

The acquaintance of a lady very much misjudged and ill used by the world, Richard admitted to —George Meredith, *The Ordeal of Richard Feverel,* 1859

. . . in these cultures it is shameful to admit to emotional distress —Abraham Verghese, *N.Y. Times Book Rev.,* 2 July 2000

Even Noam Chomsky . . . had to admit to a need to modify his theories so as to accommodate the language of the deaf —Anthony Burgess, *Times Literary Supp.,* 19–25 Jan. 1990

. . . in some respects, I admit to being arrested in the Age of Eliot, a permanent member of it —Cynthia Ozick, *New Yorker,* 20 Nov. 1989

I admit to language limitations —Russell Baker, *N.Y. Times,* 2 Apr. 1994

Yet even those who admit to admiring Garland temper their enthusiasm —Michael Joseph Gross, *Atlantic,* August 2000

To admit to a taste for the sagas . . . might seem a bit like slumming —Nicholas Howe, *New Republic,* 28 Aug. & 4 Sept. 2000

. . . we just like it when stock prices fall. This is not the sort of thing you want to admit to in public —Jonathan Clements, *Wall Street Jour.,* 21 July 1998

. . . she admitted to occasionally making up stories out of whole cloth on slow news days —Stephen W. Byers, *N.Y. Times Mag.,* 3 Jan. 1999

This idiom is well established indeed.
2. As a transitive verb *admit* takes *to* in several common uses:

> The maid admitted him to the living room —Irving Stone, *McCall's,* March 1971

> . . . one of the first non-Communist journalists admitted to China —*Harper's,* February 1969

> . . . they have admitted to their pages execrable examples of English prose —J. Donald Adams, *N.Y. Times Book Rev.,* 7 Mar. 1954

> In 1962 Trinidad and Tobago was admitted to the United Nations —*Current Biography,* February 1966

> . . . was subsequently admitted to practice both before the New York bar and the U.S. Supreme Court —*Psychology Today,* February 1969

Admit is also used with *into*:

> . . . the process of admitting a new state into the Union —Stanley E. Dimond & Elmer F. Pflieger, *Our American Government,* 1961

> . . . she regretted admitting sorrow into their lives —Jean Stafford, *Children Are Bored on Sunday,* 1953

> . . . he is prepared to admit into history the irrational and the unconscious —Peter Stansky, *N.Y. Times Book Rev.,* 25 July 1976

None of these uses is the subject of criticism.
3. *Admit of.* Fowler 1926 points out that the combination *admit of* is more limited in application than it once was and that it usually takes a nonhuman subject. Numerous later commentators echo the same sentiment. The commentators are, in the main, correct.

> . . . questions which, by their very nature, admit of no satisfactory answer —Richard A. Posner, *New Republic,* 21 Aug. 2000

> They contend that many words are absolutes that do not admit of comparison —Bernstein 1971

> That rule . . . admitted of some justification —William Raspberry, *Springfield* (Mass.) *Union-News,* 20 Jan. 1989

> The problems of ecology . . . admit of a rational solution —Aldous Huxley, *Center Mag.,* September 1969

> It is a judgment that admits of no excuses —Barbara Ehrenreich, *N.Y. Times Book Rev.,* 14 Oct. 1990

Use with a personal subject in modern prose is rare:

> But even they will admit of a number of amusing eccentricities —Simon Winchester, *The Professor and the Madman,* 1998

See also PERMIT OF.

admittance See ADMISSION, ADMITTANCE.

ad nauseam This phrase from the Latin has been at work in English since the 17th century, when writers regularly learned to read and write Latin. Writers today are less familiar with Latin, and more likely to spell the phrase wrong when they trot it out to show off with. "If you are determined to use this poor old thing," says Kilpatrick 1984, "at least spell it right." Somebody goofed in these examples:

> As Brendan becomes the Horatio Alger of porn, we trace, ad nauseum, his rise to wealth and power —*Publishers Weekly,* 5 Sept. 1977

> . . . the motherlode of Yogi-isms is mined ad nauseum in this account of his life —*Booklist,* 15 Apr. 1989

> . . . discussing Wedtech's status ad nauseum —*N.Y. Times Book Rev.,* 29 July 1990

Even if these particular examples are typos, as they may well be, it behooves the writer to be careful.

adopted, adoptive Usage writers since Fowler 1926 and Krapp 1927 have been telling us that the rule is *adopted* children, *adoptive* parents. And it usually is so in practice. *Adopted* formerly had a fair amount of use applied to parents. It has dwindled, but can still occasionally be found:

> Good as his real father and his adopted father were —Garry Wills, *Under God,* 1990

> In the end, Mr. Baker evinces compassion for his adopted mother —Mindy Aloff, *N.Y. Times Book Rev.,* 30 Jan. 1994

Adoptive, too, crosses the usage boundary and is sometimes applied to children (Johnson's 1755 Dictionary has a citation from Francis Bacon for "adoptive son"):

> The Stein menage also included Mme. Gabrielle Osorio and her adoptive daughter —Edward T. Cone, *American Scholar,* Summer 1973

But most writers follow the pattern suggested in the usage books.

adult 1. Both the end-stressed pronunciation, \ə-ˈdəlt\, and the fore-stressed version, \ˈad-ˌəlt\, are perfectly acceptable, whether the word is used as an adjective or as a noun. \ə-ˈdəlt\ seems somewhat more prevalent in the U.S., and especially so as an adjective; \ˈad-ˌəlt\ is the form currently recommended in England.

2. Copperud 1980 describes *adu't* as "the current euphemism for *pornograpaic*." Howard 1977 writes "what seedy cinemas and pornographic publishers describe as 'adult' is in fact childishly prurient." The sense has been recognized in dictionaries.

adumbrate *Adumbrate* is a learned word, commonly found in works of literary and art criticism. The American commentators who mention it agree that it is a formal word and hence inappropriate for everyday contexts. This observaton pretty well reflects current usage.

> . . . after the great Reform Bill of 1332 had adumbrated the gradual democratization of England —Geoffrey Wheatcroft, *Atlantic*, January 1997

> . . . a travesty of translation sickeningly adumbrated by the tone of the preceding prose —Brian Phillips, *New Republic*, 8 May 2000

In his analysis of the parabolic path of projectiles, Galileo adumbrated an early stage in the formulation of the principle of inertial motion —I. Bernard Cohen, *Revolution in Science*, 1985

The presiding image of Lolita, so often missed by the first-time reader (I know I missed it, years ago) is adumbrated in its foreword —Martin Amis, *Atlantic*, September 1992

advance **1.** *Advance, advanced.* As adjectives these words are seldom used of the same things, and why usage writers, who treat them frequently, believe they are a problem is not clear. There is a little evidence that *advanced* is sometimes used in place of *advance* in such combinations as *advanced planning* and *advanced guard*. Here are some examples of the usual use of the words:

> Some people receive dramatic advance warning that they're headed for a stroke —*Consumer Reports*, July 1999

> Be prepared for a TV interview because you will receive little or no advance notice —Karen Hyman, *Library Jour.*, 1 Nov. 1996

> . . . advisors had already reviewed advance copies of Northeast's plan —Homer Page, *Not Man Apart*, July 1971

> . . . modernizing their building regulations to allow the advanced systems of construction —Harold Howe II, *Saturday Rev.*, 20 Nov. 1971

> . . . the education of those less gifted or less advanced —Jerome S. Bruner, *Saturday Rev.*, 15 Jan. 1972

> . . . recently the company has been hiring applicants who combine an MBA with an advanced degree in science —Jennifer Reese, *Fortune*, 8 Feb. 1993

> . . . his distinguished grandfather who got his first position at the advanced age of 36 —Cathleen S. Morawetz, *American Mathematical Monthly*, November 1992

2. The phrases *advance warning, advance planning*, and *advance preparations* are sometimes censured as redundant (see REDUNDANCY). We have little evidence of their use in print. In the first example in section 1 above, *advance warning* is roughly synonymous with *advance notice*, which has not been called redundant. Janis 1984 defends *advance planning*, judging that it is not redundant when *advance* means "early."

advantage In the sense of "superiority of position or condition," *advantage* was formerly followed by *of*:

> Lest Satan should get an advantage of us —2 Corinthians 2:11 (AV), 1611

> We undoubtedly have the advantage of England, in promoting a comparative purity in language among the entire mass of our population —William S. Cardell, circular issued in the name of The American Academy of Language and Belles Lettres, 1821 (in Baron 1982)

The phrase "have the advantage of" with personal subject and object at one time was used in polite conversation to admit not remembering having been introduced before:

> "You have the advantage of me; I don't remember ever to have had the honour." —Richard Brinsley Sheridan, *The Rivals*, 1775

The usual preposition in modern use is *over*:

> The exacting life of the sea has this advantage over the life of the earth, that its claims are simple and cannot be evaded —Joseph Conrad, *Chance*, 1913

> . . . it is generally conceded that Soviet chess players hold an advantage over competitors of other nationalities —*Current Biography*, July 1967

Of still prevails in *take advantage of*:

> . . . bullying or taking an unfair advantage of the other person —Margaret Mead, *And Keep Your Powder Dry*, 1942

In modern use *of* most often denotes a simple genitive relationship:

> . . . personal favoritism or the advantage of a family name —Charles Frankel, *Columbia Forum*, Summer 1970

The author of the second poem has the advantage of dealing with a more unusual death —Florence Trefethen, *The Writer,* May 1968

The advantages to an economy of this sort of literacy are apparent —Robert Pattison, *On Literacy,* 1982

Here are a few other idiomatic phrases with *advantage*:

. . . restaurateurs are more and more finding it in their advantage to tinker with menus —Dave Rank, *Cooking for Profit,* July 1982

She wears clothes from them all—and wears them to advantage —Gail Cameron, *Ladies' Home Jour.,* August 1971

A miner will learn . . . to use his body to best advantage —Laurence Leamer, *Harper's,* December 1971

What we should do is make it to everyone's advantage to reach environmental goals —Peter F. Drucker, *Harper's,* January 1972

adverbial disjunct   See SENTENCE ADVERB.

adverbial genitive   Bryant 1962 and Evans 1957 tell us that in Old English the genitive of some nouns could be used adverbially. For instance, the genitive of the Old English word for *day* could be used to mean "by day." Evans notes that many of our adverbs that end in an \s\ or \z\ sound—*nowadays, always*—are survivals of this form.

One survival of the old adverbial genitive is in certain adverbs of time: "He works *evenings* and *Saturdays.*" The propriety of this construction seems to have been questioned at some time in the past but is no longer. Here are a few typical examples:

During his college days at Harvard he taught days and studied nights —*Dictionary of American Biography,* 1929

. . . he sold cars, mowed lawns, sang nights and weekends whenever he could get bookings —*Current Biography,* July 1967

. . . waking up mornings in my own vomit —Conrad Rooks, quoted in *Evergreen,* December 1967

I got to thinking that I went to work nights and Saturdays in a paper mill when I was a boy —Bergen Evans, address at Marshall University, June 1968

Many commentators (Evans 1957, Fowler 1926, Mittins et al. 1970, Quirk et al. 1985, for example) observe that this adverbial genitive of time is better established in American English than in British English. It is not, however, dead in British English, as Evans thought in 1957. The OED Supplement under *nights* lists Australian and Canadian examples. It also can be found in spoken British English:

. . . but I don't stay up nights worrying —John Lennon, quoted in *Current Biography,* December 1965

Burchfield 1996 has New Zealand and U.S. examples, but says it is no longer found in edited English in Britain.

adverbial nouns   One of the charming and infuriating aspects of English is that English nouns may upon occasion function as adverbs. Some handbooks and other textbooks refer to these as *adverbial nouns.* A couple of examples:

Every night she runs four *miles.* (Clark et al. 1981)

Other grammarians would analyze the examples above as noun phrases (*every night, four miles*) used as adverbs. Adverbial nouns are one member of the larger class of *adverbials.*

See ADVERBIAL GENITIVE for another kind of adverbial noun.

adverbials   A noun, noun phrase, prepositional phrase, verbal phrase, or clause that functions in a sentence in the same way as an adverb would is called by many grammarians an *adverbial.* A few typical examples might include these:

They arrived *Monday.*

I finished the book *last week.*

We left *on a chartered bus.*

She entered the competition *hoping to set a new record.*

You must make a greater effort *to achieve your goals.*

His house was broken into *while he was away on vacation.*

It is only fair to warn you that different grammarians may put different limitations on the class of adverbials. If you are interested in learning more about the adverbial, you will find considerable detail in Sledd 1959 or Quirk et al. 1985 (nearly 175 pages in the latter). Adverbials are not mentioned very often in this book, but the term is frequently used in discussing matters of usage by the authors of composition handbooks.

adverbs   **1.** An adverb is a member of one of the traditional part-of-speech classes. The class of adverbs is highly useful to grammarians and lexicographers, for into it they toss many terms otherwise resistant to classification. Adverbs are versatile. Besides having the usual adverbial functions, they can be freely attached to other words as modifiers. Adverbs can premodify adjectives (*awfully* hot), participles (a *well*-acted play), adverbs (a *fairly* well acted play), particles (woke *right* up), propositional phrases (*almost* over the hill), indefinite pronouns (*nearly* everyone), predeterminers (*about* half the time), cardinal numbers (*over* 200 guests), prepositions (*nowhere* near what it should be), and noun phrases preceded by a determiner (that was *quite* a party). Adverbs also postmodify nouns (a view of the city *beyond*) and some—usually adverbs of time or place—can function as the object of a preposition (since *then*, came from *behind*, before *long*, from *whence*).

Some interesting aspects of the usage of adverbs can be found under these headings: FLAT ADVERBS; SENTENCE ADVERB.

2. Copperud 1970, 1980 talks about an erroneous idea widespread among newspaper journalists that adverbs should not separate auxiliaries from their main verbs (as in "you can easily see" or "they must be heartily congratulated"). This bugaboo, commentators agree, seems to have sprung from fear of the dread split infinitive (see SPLIT INFINITIVE). Copperud cites five commentators who see no harm in placing an adverb between the parts of a verb, and Garner 1998 cites authorities going back as far as Bishop Lowth in 1762 who approve such placement. Fowler 1926, 1965 prescribes it.

Comments in the 18th-century grammars of Priestley, Lowth, and Murray indicate a considerable interest in the placement of adverbs. Murray, for instance, rejects "We always find them ready when we want them," correcting the placement to "We find them always ready. . . ." For more discussion of this sort of adverb placement, see EVEN and ONLY 1.

3. Copperud 1970, 1980 states flatly that "an adverb should not intervene between a verb and its object," citing Fowler, himself, Evans, and Follett as being of that opinion. The statement is oversimplified. For instance, the sentence

He claimed quickly the victory

is certainly more awkward than

He claimed the victory quickly.

But if we change the object to a clause,

He claimed quickly that he had won

means one thing, and

He claimed that he had won quickly

something else. Thus, you as writer have to think the problem of meaning through for yourself in each case, and not just rely on a simple rule of thumb.

Another exception can occur with those phrasal verbs—verbs followed by particles—where the close connection of the ad-

verbial particle to the verb may keep it comfortably before the direct object:

Clemens struck out the side in the seventh inning.

This question, then, is partly a matter of grammar, partly of style, and partly of idiom. You will need to rely on your common sense and your ear for the language rather than on a rule.

adverse, averse 1. Many commentators warn us against confusing *adverse* and *averse* in such sentences as

He is not adverse to an occasional brandy —*The Observer*, cited in Bryson 1984

The word in such a sentence should be *averse*, we are told. Beyond that specific judgment, little help is given us, for the most part. Here is some information we think will be more helpful.

The two words are only close in meaning in the combination *adverse/averse to*. *Adverse*, however, is usually used attributively:

On more then one occasion his decrees provoked riots, and there were those who voiced adverse opinions on the Duke in public —Alison Weir, *The Princes in the Tower*, 1992

Some people can be exposed to pollen without having any adverse reaction —Donald J. Frederick, *Springfield* (Mass.) *Union-News*, 24 May 1994

But adverse winds looked like delaying the start of the expedition —Michael Wood, *In Search of the Dark Ages*, 1987

The plant tolerates adverse conditions —Dave Dunn, *Fine Gardening*, January/February 1991

Averse, on the other hand, is rare as an attributive adjective:

. . . he was on his way to fame despite the averse crew —Jane Ross, *Early American Life*, April 1977

It is most often a thing, rather than a person, that is said to be adverse, even when *adverse* is followed by *to*:

The Bankruptcy Code requires that debtor's counsel be disinterested and not have an interest adverse to the estate —*Lawyers Weekly*, 4 Oct. 1999

But it is really almost completely adverse to the very interests which it pretends to protect —Leland Olds, *New Republic*, 14 Sept. 1953

. . . private enterprise is not immune from, or adverse to, the pleasures of the buffered life —Robert Heilbroner, *N.Y. Times Book Rev.*, 17 Dec. 1989

. . . the whole Parliamentary tradition as built up in this country . . . is adverse to it —Sir Winston Churchill, *The Unrelenting Struggle*, 1942

When used of people, *adverse* and *averse* are essentially synonymous, but *adverse* chiefly refers to opinion or intention, *averse* to feeling or inclination. Or, as it was put in the *Literary Digest* of 10 Feb. 1934, "We are *adverse* to that which we disapprove, but *averse* to that which we dislike."

I . . . hope that our periodical judges will not be very adverse to me —William Cowper (in Webster 1909)

Protestants . . . adverse to all implicit submission of mind and opinion —Edmund Burke (in Webster 1909)

Mr. Camperdown had been very adverse to all the circumstances of Sir Florian's marriage —Anthony Trollope, *The Eustace Diamonds*, 1873

. . . Lizzie's mind was, upon the whole, averse to matrimony —Anthony Trollope, *The Eustace Diamonds*, 1873

The Roosevelts are, as you may suspect, not averse to travel; we thrive on it —Franklin D. Roosevelt, address to Congress, 1 Mar. 1945, in *Nothing to Fear*, ed. B. D. Zevin, 1946

He was never a Whig, being temperamentally averse to that patrician cousinage — Geoffrey Wheatcroft, *Atlantic*, January 1997

Under certain circumstances, to be explained later, I am not averse to pillorying the innocent —John Barth, *The Floating Opera*, 1956

But the distinction is a subtle one and not observed universally, even by respected writers:

. . . for Leonora Penderton was a person who liked to settle herself and was adverse to complications —Carson McCullers, *Reflections in a Golden Eye*, 1941

Her Majesty, as I have said, was by no means averse to reforms —Edith Sitwell, *Victoria of England*, 1936

The criticized uses of *adverse to* all occur in negative sentences. It is in such contexts that it is most difficult to distinguish opinion or intention from feeling or inclination. In the sentence about brandy at the beginning of this discussion, one suspects inclination, as one does in this:

. . . a man of honor who is not adverse to cutting a deal with the government —Tere-

sa Carpenter, *N.Y. Times Book Rev.*, 11 Sept. 1988

But either nuance may be plausibly inferred in these instances:

Aside from his desire to see the natives come out on top, Jarel was not at all adverse to the idea of a trick being played on Dulard —Sylvia Louise Engdahl, "Enchantress from the Stars," 1970, in *Literature*, Carl B. Smith et al., 1980

. . . Holbrook would not be adverse to a regular TV series —*N.Y. Times*, cited in Bernstein 1977

In summary, *adverse* and *averse* are only synonymous when used of persons and with *to*. *Adverse* is most often used as an attributive adjective and of things; *averse* is extremely rare as an attributive and is regularly used of persons. When used with *to* and of persons a subtle distinction can be drawn, but it is not universally observed, and in negative contexts it is hard to make out whether the distinction is being observed or ignored. Our evidence suggests *averse to* is more frequently used than *adverse to*.

2. See AVERSE TO, FROM.

advert Fowler 1965 and Flesch 1964 are reported in Copperud 1970 to consider *advert to* as obsolete for *refer to*. Burchfield 1996 thinks it may be slipping into obsolescence; Garner 1998 finds it formal. *Advert to*, however, is alive and well. It is not an expression of high frequency and tends to be found in learned or literary contexts.

So let us escape from all this for a while and advert to a fascinating subject —Simon 1980

. . . it will not be enough to advert to the dignity of man, the connectedness among things —A. Bartlett Giamatti, *Profession 79*, 1979

. . . a number of minor caveats and corrections should at least be adverted to —Steven Marcus, *N.Y. Times Book Rev.*, 16 Feb. 1997

. . . I talk about it often, but only to revile; just as Mrs. Whitehouse frequently adverts to sexual matters —Eric Korn, *Times Literary Supp.*, 30 Nov.–6 Dec. 1990

Encasing these names in his memory, adverting to them on occasion, he imagined he was practising something like the Jewish rite of Kaddish —George Steiner, *Granta*, Summer 1991

advice See ADVISE 1.

advise **1.** *Advise, advice.* Numerous commentators and handbooks, from grade school on up, warn us not to confuse *advise* and *ad-*

vice: advise is a verb, *advice* is a noun. Still, the spellings are mixed up:

> She can spot creative genius in a stick-figure drawing, pack a mean lunch and give great advise —advt., *N.Y. Times Mag.,* 27 Apr. 1980

> . . . honor bound to advice prospective students of the dismal prospects for employment —*Biographical Dictionary of the Phonetic Sciences,* 1977

2. A considerable number of commentators object to the use of *advise* to mean "inform." They chiefly object to its use in business correspondence, where it is of course long established. Reader's Digest 1983 notes that the sense is fully established "in its own sphere." It is not limited to business correspondence. It sometimes carries the sense of "to inform officially":

> The Immigration and Naturalization Service advised Krips that he must either depart voluntarily or be detained —*Current Biography,* June 1965

> They advised him of his rights and he agreed to talk to them without a lawyer —Ed McBain, *Fuzz,* 1968

But more often it simply means "inform":

> Los Angeles Center advised me of a Boeing 747 at my one o'clock position and 500 feet below —Barbara Cushman Rowell, *Plane & Pilot,* February 1994

> An internist . . . advised me of an experimental drug —Robert E. Neger, M.D., *American Medical News,* 2 Sept. 1991

> He had not advised his friends of his marriage —Willa Cather, *The Old Beauty and Others,* 1948

adviser, advisor Both of these spellings are in current good use. Copperud 1970 and Reader's Digest 1983 note *adviser* as being the spelling preferred by journalists; Garner 1998 calls *advisor* a variant, we have more evidence for *adviser.* For what it's worth, Reader's Digest tells us that *advisor* is the preferred spelling of fortune tellers.

> . . . appointed to the five-man panel of advisers —*Current Biography,* July 1965

> A chief advisor in the administrations of Franklin D. Roosevelt and of succeeding presidents —*Current Biography,* February 1966

The military euphemism of the Vietnam war era was spelled *adviser:*

> . . . though the Marines are "advisers," a Vietnamese seldom questions a U.S.

sergeant's advice —Sherwood Dickerman, *The Reporter,* 6 Apr. 1967

advocate Bernstein 1965 tells us the noun *advocate* takes the preposition *of,* the verb *for.* Both these generalizations are off the mark.

Advocate the verb is used almost entirely as a transitive verb and usually takes no preposition at all. When a prepositional phrase does happen to follow the direct object, the preposition can be *for* but can just as easily be *in, on,* or *by,* among others:

> While Henry advocates federal loan programs for individual needy students —*Current Biography,* June 1966

The use of *for* is seen when *advocate* is intransitive, but the intransitive is fairly rare.

The noun *advocate* most usually takes *of* to show what is being advocated:

> . . . advocates of our disastrous military-oriented policies in Asia —Chester Bowles, *Saturday Rev.,* 6 Nov. 1971

> . . . wrong if he takes me as an advocate of amorality in the conduct of foreign policy —Arthur M. Schlesinger, Jr., *Harper's,* October 1971

> . . . as an advocate of probity and thrift he could be seen splitting wood in front of his house each morning —John Cheever, *The Wapshot Chronicle,* 1957

For is also used sometimes to indicate what is being advocated:

> . . . is an advocate for the extended use of psychiatry in the field of law —Morris L. Ernst, *New Republic,* 8 June 1953

> I am certainly not an advocate for frequent and untried changes in laws and constitutions —John Morley, in *The Practical Cogitator,* ed. Charles P. Curtis, Jr., & Ferris Greenslet, 1945

More often, though, *for* indicates on whose behalf one advocates:

> Let them . . . be advocates for their organizations —Leslie H. Gelb & Morton H. Halperin, *Harper's,* June 1972

> . . . the responsibility of acting as a personal advocate for his chief —McGeorge Bundy, ed., in preface to *The Pattern of Responsibility,* 1951

> Young Heinrich became a sort of advocate for his people before the tribunal of Mr. Britling's mind —H. G. Wells, *Mr. Britling Sees It Through,* 1916

With may be used for the authority to whom one advocates a cause:

And if any man sin, we have an advocate with the Father, Jesus Christ the righteous: And he is the propitiation for our sins —1 John 2:1–2 (AV), 1611

. . . promising to act as his advocate with Katherine —James Sutherland, *English Literature of the Late Seventeenth Century,* 1969

We are their advocate with the credit company —unidentified spokesperson, NBC Radio News, 9 June 1974

aegis Back in 1939 the editors of Webster's Second (1934) added a new sense of *aegis* in the New Words Section: "Patronage; sponsorship; auspices; as, under the *aegis* of the Liberal Club." Bernstein 1965 criticizes this sense of *aegis.* The new definition had been occasioned by uses like this one:

It is improper to pass from the questions of Seneca's influence upon the Tragedy of Blood and upon the language of the Elizabethans without mentioning the group of "Senecal" plays, largely produced under the aegis of the Countess of Pembroke —T. S. Eliot, "Seneca in Elizabethan Translation," in *Selected Essays,* 1932

The history of *aegis* up to the development of the 1939 sense is fairly straightforward. Its earliest meaning was a shield or breastplate originally associated in classical mythology with Zeus and Athena. This meaning has had some use in literary English:

Where was thine Ægis, Pallas, that appalled Stern Alaric? —Lord Byron, *Childe Harold's Pilgrimage,* 1812 (OED)

From the shield or breastplate, the transition to a sense meaning "protection" is plain enough:

". . . now that the Imperial ægis protects me. . . ." —Raphael Sabatini, *The Strolling Saint,* 1924

Had they come to Philippi to preach the tidings of the Messiah under the aegis of their Roman citizenship? Their aegis was God —Sholem Asch, *The Apostle,* 1943

It is urged that motion pictures do not fall within the First Amendment's aegis —*Joseph Burstyn, Inc.* v. *Wilson,* 72 S. Ct. 777, 1952

. . . we witnessed the power of the people, and even now our bodies are wrapped in the magic aegis of their love —William Crain, *East Village Other,* 10 Nov. 1970

This sense of *aegis* does not necessarily come in the phrase *under the aegis of.* That phrase is not attested until 1910. A sharp-eyed reader for the OED Supplement found it

in the 11th edition of the *Encyclopaedia Britannica* in the article on billiards:

Under the aegis of the Billiard Association a tacit understanding was arrived at. . . .

The sense here is the new sense "patronage, sponsorship, auspices" recorded in Webster's Second; it is easy enough to see how this meaning developed from that of "protection." It is this meaning, especially used with *under,* that has produced, in its various subsenses, the predominant uses in 20th-century English.

In addition to T. S. Eliot and the encyclopedia, here are some examples of "sponsorship, patronage, auspices":

. . . a benefit album to be done under the aegis of the Red Hot Organization and the AIDS Music Project —Ted Sinclair, *Rolling Stone,* 11 Nov. 1993

A year or so later he surfaces as part of a new intelligence network, set up under the aegis of the Earl of Essex —Charles Nicholl, *The Reckoning,* 1992

. . . uninhabited Sint Eustatius was settled in 1636 by entrepreneurs under the aegis of the distant Dutch West India Company —Tony Gibbs, *Islands,* November/December 1997

Often the word carries the notion of direction, supervision, guidance, or control:

. . . the Spanish Inquisition . . . operated directly under the aegis of the Spanish crown —Norman F. Cantor, *The Civilization of the Middle Ages,* 1993

Yet even Apollo brought the prospect of long-term advantage, in the rockets and spacecraft developed under its aegis —T. A. Heppenheimer, *American Heritage,* November 1992

That was not our fault, however, but that of the Holy Alliance under the aegis of Metternich —A. L. Rowse, *Britain To-Day,* September 1944

This sense is sometimes used in the context of the theater and films to connote the functions of producer, director, or distributor:

. . . last done on film so satisfyingly by Joe Mankiewicz in 1953 under the star-studded aegis of M-G-M —Judith Crist, *New York,* 8 Feb. 1971

When used of individuals, the meaning may sometimes be close to "leadership":

. . . gave Guber and Peters free rein, and under their aegis Columbia became notorious for its profligacy —Connie Bruck, *New Yorker,* 9 Sept. 1991

. . . the nontonalists, relatively weak, but united under the aegis of Schoenberg —Robert Evett, *Atlantic,* July 1971

Aegis is also used in a sense of "a strong or guiding influence":

Indeed, whenever national origins were celebrated under the aegis of the Romantic movement, with its passion for the primitive and antiquarian, there the fairies . . . would be —Robert Hughes, *Time,* 23 Nov. 1998

. . . little was added to the requirements of notice and hearing developed by the courts under the aegis of the due process clause —Nathaniel L. Nathanson, *American Political Science Rev.,* June 1951

Without realizing it, many American mothers, under the aegis of benevolent permissiveness . . . actually neglect their children —*Time,* 28 Dec. 1970

Another use carries a notion of an identifying name or label:

. . . she became part of the contemporary canon, whether you construct it under the aegis of "postmodernism" or "feminism" —Lorna Sage, *Manchester Guardian Weekly,* 23 Feb. 1992

. . . Fawcett Crest reports that nearly 19 million softcover copies of 16 Taylor Caldwell novels are in print under its aegis alone —Nan Robertson, *N.Y. Times,* 11 Dec. 1976

These examples show the main areas of expansion that *aegis* is occupying in present-day English prose.

aerate Bryson 1984 reminds us not to misspell this word *aereate,* as is sometimes done:

. . . kept the water aereated —*Scouting,* April 1953

This is a case of minding your *a*'s and *e*'s.

affect See EFFECT, AFFECT.

affiliate *Affiliate* is used with both *with* and *to. Affiliate with* is usually but not always American; *affiliate to* is usually but not always British. We have Canadian evidence for both combinations:

. . . which will be affiliated with the University of Alaska —Michael A. Pollock, *Change,* October 1971

. . . it was affiliated with the University of Glasgow —Sir James Mountford, *British Universities,* 1966

. . . to affiliate it with a prevailing approach to the lyric stage —Irving Kolodin, *Saturday Rev.,* 26 Sept. 1964

. . . loose national federations with which the local bodies affiliated —Oscar Handlin, *The American People in the Twentieth Century,* 1954

. . . which is not affiliated with a university —John E. Robbins, *Institutions of Higher Education in Canada,* ca. 1944

. . . it was affiliated to the University of Edinburgh in 1933 —Sir James Mountford, *British Universities,* 1966

. . . said his organisation was affiliated to a world-wide body —*The Guardian,* 28 Nov. 1973

. . . socially it was advisable that everyone should be affiliated to the religious customs prevalent in his country —George Santayana, *Persons and Places,* 1944

. . . 150 colleges, many affiliated to the universities —*Canada Today,* 1953

affinity In modern use, *affinity* is used with *for* and *with* most often, with *to* and *between* somewhat less often, and with a few other prepositions occasionally. Perhaps it will be most helpful to show a few illustrations of the important general meanings of *affinity* and the prepositions used with each.

We find *to* with the original meaning:

In a few months it was announced that he was closely related by affinity to the royal house. His daughter had become, by a secret marriage, Duchess of York —T. B. Macaulay, *The History of England,* vol. I, 1849

And also when used of family relationships, both literal and figurative:

Every creature that bears any affinity to my mother is dear to me, and you, the daughter of her brother —William Cowper, letter, 27 Feb. 1790

. . . its degree of affinity with any other language or dialect —Mario Pei, *Word,* August 1949

". . . Whatever bears affinity to cunning is despicable." —Jane Austen, *Pride and Prejudice,* 1813

When close in meaning to "resemblance" or "similarity," we find *with, between,* and *to:*

. . . it is likely his Elvish language shows some affinities with Finnish —*Current Biography,* October 1967

. . . affirms a general affinity between the police and the military—both refer to outsiders as 'civilians' —Allen Young, quoted in *Playboy,* September 1968

. . . something in the English character, something mystical, tough and fierce, has a special affinity to Hebrew —Edmund Wilson, *A Piece of My Mind,* 1956

In the common figurative sense of "a feeling of kinship, sympathy, rapport," we find various prepositions:

. . . I feel a certain affinity to the situation and to the institution —Keith M. Cottam, *Library Jour.,* 1 Feb. 1967

. . . there is an affinity between them and their African friends —Michael Blundell, *London Calling,* 3 Feb. 1955

. . . I have always felt a real affinity with Havel's point of view —Tom Stoppard, quoted in *N.Y. Times,* 25 Oct. 1979

. . . the passion of Giovanni and Annabella is not shown as an affinity of temperament —T. S. Eliot, "John Ford," in *Selected Essays,* 1932

. . . the man who on the out-of-town hustings makes much of his affinity for "the street people, *my* people, the workers of my city" —Andy Logan, *New Yorker,* 30 Oct. 1971

The sympathy extended to foods to suggest that things go well together usually takes *for*:

. . . new crackers that have a true affinity for cheese —*New Yorker,* 12 Dec. 1953

Rum also has an amazing affinity for foods we love —Marilyn Kayter, *American Way,* December 1971

The use of *affinity* to denote an attraction to or liking for something usually takes *for*:

What an affinity for Christianity had this persecutor of the Christians! —Matthew Arnold, *Essays in Criticism,* First Series, 1865

. . . revels in Macaulay, who has a special affinity for the eternal schoolboy —W. R. Inge, *The Church in the World,* 1928

If you have no affinity for verse, better skip this —Oliver St. John Gogarty, *It Isn't This Time of Year At All!,* 1954

His affinity for controversy got him into further trouble —Michael & Sheila Cole, *Psychology Today,* March 1971

. . . this affinity for exotica made itself felt in St. Denis's repertory —Anna Kisselgoff, *N.Y. Times Book Rev.,* 10 Oct. 1976

Sometimes affinity suggests a natural or sympathetic aptitude or liking for something, a natural talent, a flair; here we find *for* and *with*:

. . . Weingartner had a close affinity with this style, and I recall some Haydn symphonies . . . that are well-nigh unsurpassable —Paul Henry Lang, *Saturday Rev.,* 26 June 1954

Gifted with an affinity for the art song —*Current Biography,* November 1966

. . . Irishmen, who seem to have an affinity for politics —Green Peyton, *San Antonio: City in the Sun,* 1946

. . . early displayed an affinity for finance and bookkeeping —*Current Biography,* April 1966

You may note in these examples what many commentators point out: when *affinity* suggests a mutual relationship, *between* and *for* are usual; when the relationship is one-sided, *with* and *to* are usual.

affirmative, negative A number of commentators have found the phrases *in the affirmative* and *in the negative* pompous or pretentious. They are following a line apparently begun in 1913 by Sir Arthur Quiller-Couch. But as one commentator reminds, the context in which the phrases occur should be taken into account. In a context like "the Circuit Court answered in the affirmative" the phrase fits comfortably; if one wrote "the Circuit Court answered yes," eyebrows might be raised. And it is in such formal and even fusty surroundings as judicial opinions and parliamentary proceedings that these phrases are most likely to be found. They turn up occasionally in ordinary prose where a simple *yes* or *no* might not be desirable:

. . . a question that can't be answered in the affirmative—for if it could, there would be no need to ask it —Jon Landau, *Rolling Stone,* 2 Mar. 1972

afflict See INFLICT, AFFLICT.

affluent There are several reasons for preferring the pronunciation with main stress on the initial syllable: \\'af-ˌlü-ənt\\. The variant with main stress on the second syllable, \\ə-'flü-ənt\\, is disapproved by usage writers, is less common among educated speakers (though certainly in respectable use), and could be confused with *effluent,* which is also sometimes pronounced with main stress on the second syllable. Confusion is far less likely when main stress falls on the contrasting initial vowels.

afraid Chambers 1985 and Evans 1957 discuss the constructions *afraid* is found in. It is derived from a past participle in Middle English and is used now as a predicate adjective, not as an attributive adjective. *Afraid* can be followed by a clause:

Afraid that any precipitous action on his part might well cost him his position. —*NEA Jour.*, January 1965

He seemed afraid, if he were kind, he might be ridiculed —Edwin A. Peeples, *Saturday Evening Post*, 25 Dec. 1954

It can be followed by an infinitive:

. . . ready to say bluntly what every one else is afraid to say —T. S. Eliot, "Charles Whibley," in *Selected Essays*, 1932

. . . is not afraid to go out and ask a playwright or a director just what he thinks he's doing —Richard Schickel, *Harper's*, November 1970

The usual preposition after *afraid* is *of*, which can be followed by a noun or a gerund:

We have been much too much afraid of the Russians —Edmund Wilson, *A Piece of My Mind*, 1956

". . . She told me she was afraid of him. He had threatened to kill her." —Dashiell Hammett, *Red Harvest*, 1929

". . . were you so afraid of a man like Keegan, you wouldn't step forward . . . ?" —Anthony Trollope, *The Macdermots of Ballycloran*, 1847

Some of us are afraid of dying —Thomas Pynchon, *V.*, 1963

But I am now as much afraid of drinking as of bathing —Tobias Smollett, *Humphry Clinker*, 1771

Afraid is also followed by *for*; in this construction the object is not the source of the threat but rather what is threatened:

. . . clerks, who had come early because they were afraid for their jobs —Wirt Williams, *The Enemy*, 1951

The men aren't afraid for their jobs, either, because unemployment is negligible —John Fischer, *Harper's*, January 1969

. . . once or twice she is in real physical danger and genuinely afraid for herself —*Times Literary Supp.*, February 1969

after In Irish dialect *after* is used in a construction *to be after doing something* about whose meaning there seems to have been some confusion. P. W. Joyce in *English As We Speak It in Ireland* (1910) explains it as an idiom by which the Irish get round the perfect tense—instead of "I have finished my work" they use "I am after finishing my work." Some older American dictionaries seem to have thought it to mean "to be about to" rather than "to have just done"; Gowers (in Fowler 1965) notes that some English novelists have made the same mistake. Here are a few genuine Irish examples:

'Listen to me,' says I, 'do you think I did this on purpose? I'm after having two punctures. . . .' —Rex MacGall, *Irish Digest*, November 1955

Cracked Mary it is, that is after coming back this day from the asylum —Lady Gregory, *The Full Moon*, in *New Comedies*, 1913

I'm after thinking of something good, something very good unless I'm very much mistaken, said Furriskey —Flann O'Brien, *At Swim-Two-Birds*, 1939

African-American, Afro-American See BLACK.

afterward, afterwards Copperud 1970 says that both forms are used in the U.S. while *afterwards* prevails in British English; Watt 1967 opines that *afterward* is more common in the U.S. Standard reference works and our evidence confirm these observations.

against The pronunciation \ə-'gin\ represented by the spelling *agin* is generally treated as dialectal or rural (the Dictionary of American Regional English covers it generously under *again*). Lounsbury 1908 points out that this form, like others that survive among the less educated, represents the original form of the preposition in Middle English.

agenda 1. Everybody agrees, according to Copperud 1970, 1980, that *agenda* is standard in English as a singular, with *agendas* as its plural. We have about a dozen commentators—both English and American—who are also in agreement.

Singular *agenda* is in standard use:

The ultimate assessment of the candidate's suitability will be made by persons whose primary agenda is not academic —John Langan, *Commonweal*, 21 Apr. 2000

They are not racists per se, though their basic agenda is virtually indistinguishable from that of white supremacists —Gary Cartwright, *GQ*, November 1998

But many have another agenda as well —Elizabeth Drew, *New Yorker*, 6 Dec. 1982

In those instances where a plural is necessary, *agendas* is the standard form.

. . . a rivalry fueled by personal differences and conflicting agendas —Nicholas Wade, *N.Y. Times*, 27 June 2000

Politicians look to use your name and your story to gain public attention, to advance their agendas —*Ms.*, June/July 2000

Agendum, usually in the form *agenda,* has some relatively infrequent use to mean "an item on the agenda":

> They should have the right to initiate agenda, to discuss the entire range of university concerns —William M. Roth, *Saturday Rev.,* 10 Jan. 1970

It is sometimes used like singular *agenda:*

> . . . has its own agendum: Outside marriage, no sex of any kind for the lower classes and a policing of everyone —Gore Vidal, *The Nation,* 21 July 1997

For other foreign plurals, see LATIN PLURALS.
2. William Safire (*N.Y. Times Mag.,* 16 Sept. 1984) tries to trace the development of the expression *hidden agenda.* He finds its roots in the use of *agenda* for a political program. Our earliest citation for *hidden agenda* suggests that the term may have already been familiar when the author used it:

> The schooling process has a hidden agenda—an invisible curriculum—that sorts knowledge into packages . . . ; that categorizes persons as successes or failures with a fixed criterion; that mistakes conformity for allegiance —John Gagnon, *Change,* October 1971

The phrase continues to be popular:

> . . . they charge that he had a hidden agenda hostile to Christianity —Merrill D. Peterson, *Atlantic,* December 1994

> . . . concludes that Kinsey was promoting a hidden agenda of sexual liberation —Richard Rhodes, *N.Y. Times Book Rev.,* 2 Nov. 1997

Burchfield 1996 notes that *hidden agenda* has somewhat sinister connotations; its meaning is somewhat similar to *ulterior motive.*

aggravate, aggravation, aggravating *Aggravate* has been used to mean "to rouse to displeasure, irritate, exasperate, annoy" since 1611, when one Randle Cotgrave used it (along with *exasperate*) to gloss a French word in his French-English dictionary. Some two and a half centuries later two amateurs of words—Richard Grant White 1870 in America and John Stuart Mill in 1872 in England—condemned the usage, apparently in reaction to increased use of the sense in the 19th century. Subsequent critics by the dozens have jumped on the White–Mills bandwagon, and it still has riders—right up to Garner 1998. Not one of this numerous clan of critics has adduced a single cogent reason for their condemnation; they are satisfied by simply calling names: incorrect, childish, vulgar, colloquial, misuse, confusion. Such commentators seem unable to realize that writers and speakers using a nearly 400-year-old extended sense of a word are not necessarily uneducated or confused or careless. Gowers in Fowler 1965 noted that writers have ignored admonitions to avoid the use, "refusing to be trammeled." Here are some examples:

> 'I'm very much obliged to you, Misses Brown,' said the unfortunate youth, greatly aggravated —Charles Dickens, *Dombey and Son,* 1848 (OED)

> . . . no doubt our two countries *aggravate* each other from time to time —Oliver Wendell Holmes d. 1935, letter to Sir Frederick Pollock, 27 Dec. 1895

> . . . & a thing once in the printer's hands is such a good riddance I never care to aggravate myself or him with any but the simplest corrections —Louisa May Alcott, letter, 28 Aug. 1863

> I am exhausted and the petty tribulations and crum people I have surrounding me aggravate me more than they help me —Fred Allen, letter, 3 Apr. 1932

> There are times when the French get aggravated and displeased by us —Jimmy Carter, quoted in *N.Y. Times,* 14 Feb. 1980

> She noticed his pleasant and contented manner . . . and it merely aggravated her the more —Theodore Dreiser, *Sister Carrie,* 1900

> He ate with good appetite, as he always did, even when aggravated—and he'd been plenty aggravated lately —T. Coraghessan Boyle, *The Road to Wellville,* 1993

> But the book chain especially aggravated them recently when it announced a 40 percent discount on hardcover best sellers —Edwin McDowell, *N.Y. Times,* 25 June 1990

> The man's lack of friends amazed and then began to aggravate and trouble Clancy —John Cheever, *New Yorker,* 24 Mar. 1951

> Nothing so aggravates an earnest person as a passive resistance —Herman Melville, "Bartleby the Scrivener," 1856

> . . . the celebrated incident of Mr. Yarborough's declining to participate directly in the motorcade, . . . greatly aggravating the President —William F. Buckley, Jr., *National Rev.,* 19 Nov. 1971

> Keitel . . . was aggravated at the delay —William L. Shirer, *The Rise and Fall of the Third Reich,* 1960

> . . . when his silly conceit and his youthful pomposity about his not-very-good early work has begun to aggravate us —William

Styron, *This Quiet Dust and Other Writings,* 1982

These examples show the disputed sense in expository prose, journalism, fiction, and letters. It seems to be more common in informal surroundings. Still, the "make worse" sense continues in vigorous use today and remains the primary meaning of the verb. The case with the derivatives *aggravation* and *aggravating* is somewhat different, however.

The noun *aggravation* has been used in the sense "irritation" at least since the end of the 17th century:

> In this respect the stage is faulty to a scandalous degree of nauseousness and aggravation —Jeremy Collier, *A Short View of the Immorality and Profaneness of the English Stage,* 1698

> . . . and to have Miss Crawford's liveliness repeated to her at such a moment, and on such a subject, was a bigger aggravation —Jane Austen, *Mansfield Park,* 1814

> Aggravations between people South and North were getting worse —Carl Sandburg, *Abraham Lincoln,* 1926

> Are foreign stocks worth the aggravation? —Michael R. Sesit, *Wall Street Jour.,* 22 Mar. 1996

> She is a holy terror, a predictable aggravation, runs his life for him —Denis Donoghue, *N.Y. Times Book Rev.,* 26 Mar. 2000

> . . . argues a consistent theme, but without the polemical aggravation —Hugo Young, *Manchester Guardian Weekly,* 4 Oct. 1992

> That too was perhaps an aggravation to Chuchu—that she could be sure of him —Graham Greene, *Getting to Know the General,* 1984

> They can't pay you enough for the aggravation you take —Art Buchwald, *You Can Fool All of the People All the Time,* 1983

The "irritation" sense is a bit more common than the earlier senses.

The participial adjective *aggravating* has seldom been used to mean anything except "annoying" since the middle third of the 19th century; it may have been, in fact, what set the critics off (it is the form cited by Mill). It is certainly well attested:

> . . . its grievances had become so numerous and aggravating —Diedrich Knickerbocker (Washington Irving), *A History of New York,* 1832

> . . . kicking pupils with his nailed boots, pulling the hair of some of the smaller boys,

pinching the others in aggravating places —Charles Dickens, *Nicholas Nickleby,* 1839

> Have called 3 times at the Tribune Bureau, but always missed the staff by some five aggravating minutes —Mark Twain, letter, 22 Nov. 1867

> Among the many boys . . . was one more aggravating than the rest —Rudyard Kipling, "Baa Baa, Black Sheep," 1888

> . . . only it is aggravating to have you talking about so small a business —George Bernard Shaw, letter to Ellen Terry, 16 Sept. 1896

> But Archbishop Tenison, though much out of favour with the Queen, outlived her in a most aggravating manner —G. M. Trevelyan, *Blenheim,* 1930 (Gowers 1948)

> This made the whole trip one of the most annoying and aggravating experiences in my life —F. Scott Fitzgerald, letter, 7 Apr. 1938

> . . . he can be extremely aggravating and silly —Cyril Connolly, *The Condemned Playground,* 1946

> . . . all the funny papers and Coca-Cola pictures plastering the walls were, he complained, crooked and aggravating —Truman Capote, *Other Voices, Other Rooms,* 1948

> This learned, eloquent, agile, aggravating and sometimes magical book —Michael Gorra, *N.Y. Times Book Rev.,* 5 Nov. 1995

> . . . this most stimulating, original, aggravating writer —*Times Literary Supp.,* 28 Sept. 1967

> But first a word about the tendentious word "bourgeois." It is abusive, aggravating, inexact, and unavoidable —Robert Darnton, *The Great Cat Massacre,* 1984

> Aggravating as they were to Flaubert —William Styron, *This Quiet Dust and Other Writings,* 1982

Conclusion: the senses of *aggravate, aggravation,* and *aggravating* involving annoyance were strongly established well before John Stuart Mill and Richard Grant White found fault with them. They are standard. *Aggravate* in this sense is considerably less frequent in edited prose than in the "make worse" sense; *aggravation* is more likely to mean "irritation" than not; *aggravating* is seldom used except to express annoyance.

ago   See SINCE 2.

agree   1. Numerous handbooks from as long ago as 1917 to the 1980s tell us that *agree* takes various prepositions idiomatically in various senses. The prepositions *to, on,* and *with* are most frequently mentioned, but some sources—chiefly older ones—mention others. Here is a selection of typical constructions with various prepositions; of all these only *in* seems to be showing signs of age.

. . . the company agreed to mediation —*Current Biography,* June 1953

. . . members of the Swedish Academy failed to agree on a candidate —*Current Biography 1951*

. . . they were always agreed on what movie they should see —Katherine Anne Porter, *Ladies' Home Jour.,* August 1971

In 1831 the payment by France of outstanding claims . . . was agreed upon by treaty —Francis D. Wormuth, "The Vietnam War: The President versus the Constitution," 1968

Christ, the boondocks of Oregon must agree with you, Stan —Lee Marvin, quoted in *Rolling Stone,* 21 Dec. 1972

. . . it is difficult not to agree with Byron that Pope was profoundly moved when he wrote this poem —Bonamy Dobrée, *English Literature in the Early Eighteenth Century, 1700–1740,* 1959

. . . he agreed with Lowell's opposition to the war —Eric F. Goldman, *Harper's,* January 1969

This agrees with seismic evidence —C. A. Cotton, *Geographical Jour.,* June 1953

Four of the nation's leading white urbanologists . . . were agreed about the nature of the urban crisis —Allen B. Ballard, *Change,* March 1973

. . . they agreed as to the unreadiness of Italian Somaliland for political independence —*Collier's Year Book,* 1949

. . . no two of his admirers would be likely to agree in their selection —Bliss Perry, *The Pocket University,* 1924

We agreed in our estimate of Beecham —*The Journals of Arnold Bennett,* ed. Frank Swinnerton, 1954

. . . as so often in morals and in motivation, the upper and lower classes agree against the middle —Basil Cottle, in Michaels & Ricks 1980

Evans 1957 reminds us that *agree* is also commonly followed by a clause or an infinitive phrase:

Traditional theories of esthetics agreed that coherent form emerges from the basic principle of fused elements —Frederick Gold-

man & Linda R. Burnett, *Need Johnny Read?,* 1971

. . . Deerslayer agrees to surrender his claims —Richard Poirier, *A World Elsewhere,* 1966

2. In British use, the transitive *agree* often replaces the *agree on* or *agree to* of American English. Longman 1984, Chambers 1985, and Burchfield 1981, 1996 find these uses acceptable; Gowers (in Fowler 1965) accepts *agree* "agree on" but not *agree* "agree to." Here are some examples:

". . . since this has to be, in its small way, a combined operation, we should want to agree the commander with you people." —Nevil Shute, *Most Secret,* 1945

. . . and after much discussion the following articles were agreed —Sir Winston Churchill, *Closing the Ring,* 1951

The price has yet to be agreed —*Times Literary Supp.,* 21 May 1970

On a small job you will probably have to agree a set fee with your architect —John Bath, *Australian Home Beautiful,* June 1975

As the awaited seed catalogues arrive there are long discussions . . . with the housekeeper to agree vegetable and herb varieties —*This England,* Winter 1983

This use is rare but not unknown in the U.S.:

But as happens so often with U.S.-Japan conversations, the parties departed with different impressions of what had been agreed —Sol W. Sanders, *Business Week,* 23 Mar. 1981

agreement In this book *agreement* usually refers to either the agreement in number between the subject and verb of a sentence, or to the agreement in number between a pronoun and its antecedent. The term *concord,* used by some American and many British writers, can be considered a synonym; it turns up here and there in various articles, especially in the terms *notional concord* and *formal* (or *grammatical) concord.* There are, in fact, two kinds of agreement in English:

There are two kinds of concord: *formal concord,* in which there is harmony of form, and *notional concord,* in which there is harmony of meaning. In such a sentence as "Two boys were in the room," we have both formal and notional concord, the subject and the verb both being plural in both form and meaning. But sometimes we have notional concord only, as "None were left," where the subject, though singular in form, takes a plural verb because it is plural in meaning; and sometimes we have formal concord only, as "Everybody was late," where the subject, though plural in meaning, takes a singular verb because it is singular in form —Paul Roberts, *Understanding Grammar,* 1954

The tug-of-war between notional and formal agreement underlies most of the agreement problems we deal with. There is one additional contributor to these problems. It is what Quirk et al. 1985 calls the *principle of proximity* (it is also called *attraction* and *blind agreement*)—the agreement of the verb with a noun or pronoun intervening between it and the subject. Quirk remarks that conflict between formal concord and attraction through proximity tends to increase with the distance between the noun head (true subject) and the verb, and that proximity agreement is more often found in unplanned discourse than in writing.

Fries 1940 notes that gross violations of concord—use of a number-distinctive form that matches neither the formal nor the notional number of the subject—are found only in uneducated English. Sentences like

And them bass fiddles that's electrified, they're so loud, and the average man that plays 'em don't know how to turn 'em down —Birch Monroe, quoted in *Bluegrass Unlimited,* September 1982

that are typical of the speech of uneducated people, are seldom treated in books on usage and grammar, simply because everyone recognizes them as nonstandard. They will not receive much attention in this book either, even though they turn up now and then in newspapers:

Orangemen misses coach —subhead, *Springfield* (Mass.) *Union-News,* 5 Dec. 2001

In the articles immediately following, we have broken the large subject of agreement into several smaller sections, which we hope you will find easier to refer to than one long treatment would be. In addition, many specific problems that usage writers treat separately have been put at their own places. See, for instance, AS WELL AS; EACH; MANY A; NONE; ONE OF THOSE WHO; THERE IS, THERE ARE; THEY, THEIR, THEM.

agreement: collective nouns See COLLECTIVE NOUNS.

agreement: indefinite pronouns The indefinite pronouns *anybody, anyone, each, either, everybody, everyone, neither, nobody, somebody, someone* share an interesting and often perplexing characteristic: they are usually grammatically singular and often notionally plural. The result is mixed usage with respect

to number agreement with verbs and pronouns.

Bryant 1962 reports 25 studies of verb agreement with indefinite pronouns and finds both singular and plural verbs in use, but with the singular outnumbering the plural in the ratio of six to one. Curme 1931 and Quirk et al. 1985 both say the singular verb is usual; the singular verb also predominates in the Merriam-Webster files. You are safe in assuming that the singular verb will be right.

Pronoun agreement has been more problematical. Conflict here revolves around the use of the pronouns *they, their, them, themselves* to refer to the indefinite pronouns. Such use, OED evidence shows, goes back to the 14th century. It has been disparaged as improper since the 18th century, however, when such grammarians as Lowth and Lindley Murray decreed the indefinite pronouns singular. Two considerations have strengthened the use of the plural pronoun in reference to a preceding indefinite. The first is notional concord; the indefinite pronouns are often notionally plural—some, indeed, more often than others—and in early modern English (before the 18th century) agreement is largely governed by notional concord. The other is the much-touted lack of a common-gender third person singular pronoun in English. How early *they, their, them* begins to be used as a common-gender singular is uncertain; perhaps Sir Kenelm Digby's use of *their* referring back to *one* in the middle of the 17th century (cited in the OED) represents such a use.

Let us look at a few examples from the letters of Thomas Gray, written in the second quarter of the 18th century, nearly a quarter century before Lowth and a half century before Murray. In the first he speaks of "People of high quality" in Paris and of their devotion to gambling:

Another thing is, there is not a House where they don't play, nor is any one at all acceptable, unless they do so too —21 Apr. 1739

Notional agreement seems to explain *they* in this instance, as it does in the next:

. . . if any body don't like their Commons, they send down into the Kitchen —31 Oct. 1734

In this letter Gray is complaining of not being written to; *them* might be interpreted here as a common-gender singular:

What! to let any body reside three months at Rheims, and write but once to them? —18 Sept. 1739

At any rate the plural pronouns, whether through notional agreement or through being used as common-gender singulars, were well entrenched when Lowth issued his opinion, as his footnote attests; in it he corrects the translators of the King James Bible, Addison in *The Spectator,* and Richard Bentley, the scholar and critic. Lindley Murray has even more passages to correct, but their authors are unidentified. Lowth's tradition continued deep into the 19th century. Hodgson 1889, for instance, corrects the grammar of such seasoned practitioners as Elizabeth Gaskell, Jane Austen, Sydney Smith, John Ruskin, Charles Reade, and Leslie Stephen. (Our latter-day critics satisfy themselves with smaller game, reproving anonymous journalists, media personalities, and a mixed bag of educators and bureaucrats.) Hodgson also notes the problem of the common-gender singular; he cites a 19th-century grammarian named Bain, who approved the plural use. "Grammarians," writes Bain, "frequently call this construction an error, not reflecting that it is equally an error to apply 'his' to feminine subjects. The best writers (Defoe, Paley, Byron, Miss Austen, &c.) furnish examples of the use of the plural as a mode of getting out of the difficulty." The professor's tolerant attitude toward the plural did not satisfy Hodgson, however; he insisted that the gender difficulty should be removed by revision (the same advice set forth in many recent sources).

Curme 1931 found the use of the plural to be typical of older literature and to have survived in popular speech; Bryant 1962 considers *they, their, them* established as the third person common-gender singular in all but the most formal usage.

The howls of the spiritual descendents of Lowth and Lindley Murray notwithstanding, the plural *they, their, them* with an indefinite pronoun as referent is in common standard use, both as common-gender singular and to reflect notional agreement. We give you a few examples below. Since many of the individual indefinite pronouns have received considerable comment, they have been treated separately (see ANYBODY, ANYONE; EACH; EVERYBODY, EVERYONE, for instance), and more examples of each will appear at those entries.

> . . . nothing was done without a clatter, nobody sat still, and nobody could command attention when they spoke —Jane Austen, *Mansfield Park,* 1814

> You talked to someone who didn't like this book—I don't know who, or why they didn't —F. Scott Fitzgerald, letter, Fall 1935

> . . . always look around . . . to see if any of the girls playing in the street was her, but they never were —Bernard Malamud, *The Magic Barrel,* 1958

Whenever anyone uses the pressure of usage to force you to accept the nonsensical and swallow the solecism, here's what to tell them —Safire 1984

agreement, notional   See NOTIONAL AGREEMENT, NOTIONAL CONCORD.

agreement: organizations considered as collective nouns   Quirk et al. 1985 says that collective nouns "differ from other nouns in taking as pronoun coreferents either singular *it* and relative *which* or plural *they* and relative *who* without change of number in the noun. . . ." Copperud 1970 (under *collective nouns*) asserts, "Ordinarily, nouns for organizations considered as an entity, like *company,* are referred to by *it,* not *they.* . . ."

Copperud is too dogmatic. Our evidence shows that names of companies and other organizations function like other collective nouns, being sometimes singular and sometimes plural (see also COLLECTIVE NOUNS). A few examples of the singular construction:

> Ratners, which embraces H. Samuel, Ernest Jones, Watches of Switzerland and Salisburys —Ben Laurance, *Manchester Guardian Weekly,* 19 Jan. 1992

> . . . until GM was tooling up for its 1940 models —*American Mercury,* May 1953

Some examples of the plural:

> The D.A.R. are going to do another pageant —Sinclair Lewis, *Dodsworth,* 1929

> The NBS now admit that they can confirm —*New Republic,* 11 May 1953

> I can see no use of changing publishers anyhow—Collins are established and, moreover, they are darn good —F. Scott Fitzgerald, letter, October 1921

> Frank Cass are interested in publishing scholarly journals —advt., *Times Literary Supp.,* 2–8 Nov. 1990

And like other collective nouns, organizations sometimes appear with a singular verb but a plural pronoun in reference:

> . . . M-G-M . . . hopes to sell their records in 5,000 key stores —*Time,* 24 Feb. 1947

> . . . the National Bureau of Standards has not been sufficiently objective, because they discount entirely the play of the market place —*New Republic,* 13 Apr. 1953

> CBS claims they were originally offered Qadcafi for five thousand dollars —Art Buchwald, *You Can Fool All of the People All the Time,* 1983

It seems reasonable to expect that use of the plural pronoun, even after the singular verb, will continue to flourish as large corporations try to present a more human and less monolithic face to the public.

**agreement, pronoun: nouns joined by *and,*
or**   When the 18th-century grammarians were
laying down the law of grammatical agreement, Lowth 1775—in a footnote—made the
statement that the "conjunction disjunctive,"
or, requires agreement in the singular number.
To illustrate his point, he reprinted this sentence:

> A man may see a metaphor, or an allegory,
> in a picture, as well as read them (it) in a de-
> scription —Joseph Addison, *Dialogues upon
> the Usefulness of Ancient Medals,* 1702

Lowth, of course, was correcting Addison's
them to *it.* It was a general practice of the
18th-century grammarians to give examples
that contravened their rules, for purposes of
correction; the practice has for us moderns
the weakness of leaving us wondering whether
anybody did, in fact, follow the rules the
grammarians laid down. Addison, one of the
master stylists of English prose who died in
1719, was simply following notional agreement, as everyone did before the middle of the
18th century. Notional agreement did not disappear with the preachments of Lowth and his
contemporaries, moreover, as you will see in
this book.

When singular nouns are joined by *and,* notional agreement will not often clash with
grammatical agreement (but see some of the
examples at EACH):

> One goaded professor once denied that two
> & two make four, merely because a pro-
> Adler student said they did —*Time,* 17 Feb.
> 1952

> . . . in a gentle stupefaction of mind, & very
> tolerable health of body hitherto. If they
> last, I shall not much complain —Thomas
> Gray, letter, 5 Mar. 1766

But singular nouns joined by *or* are more
likely to be affected by notional agreement at
the expense of grammatical agreement (as
Lowth well knew but would not accept):

> If the short or second baseman are tough
> (and they always are) —Ernest Hemingway,
> letter, 28 July 1948

> . . . no lady or gentleman would so far forget
> themselves —George Bernard Shaw, *Plays
> Pleasant and Unpleasant,* 1898 (in Jes-
> persen)

> How quickly the American student makes
> friends with a book or a man and treats
> them as if they were his contemporaries
> —*Time,* 2 Aug. 1954

> . . . a man or a woman would come in here,
> glance around, find smiles and pleasant
> looks waiting for them, then wave and sit

> down by themselves —Doris Lessing (in
> Reader's Digest 1983)

In the next example the author starts out
with the *him or her* prescribed by grammatical
agreement, but then abandons it for the less
unwieldy plural pronouns of notional agreement:

> If you have a young brother or sister of, say,
> fifteen years old or so, think that you have
> him or her before you and that you are try-
> ing to explain the point of your article to
> them and at the same time to prevent them
> from thinking what an ass you are to be
> wasting their time —R. B. McKerrow, *Rev.
> of English Studies,* XVI, 1940

> No man or woman can hesitate to give what
> they have —Woodrow Wilson, speech, 17
> Sept. 1918 (in H. L. Mencken, *The American
> Language,* abridged, 1963)

Mencken notes that this is the line as Wilson
spoke it, according to the papers reporting it.
But when it was published in his *Selected . . .
Addresses,* the professional Wilson emended
"they have" to "he or she has."

In our view, singular nouns joined by *and*
will seldom present a problem; notional and
grammatical agreement will join to call for a
plural pronoun. When singular nouns are
joined by *or,* notional and grammatical agreement will likely conflict. It would appear that
the farther the pronoun is from the set of
nouns referred to, the more likely it is to be
plural in accordance with notional agreement.
And the farther the pronoun is from its referent, the less likely it is to be noticed. You
should feel free to use a plural pronoun where
it sounds right and natural to you, even
though some stickler for grammatical agreement may spot it. Where it does not seem natural, stick to the singular. Ask yourself who
was the greater writer—Addison or Lowth?

**agreement, pronoun: singular nouns with
plural pronouns**   See THEY, THEIR, THEM.

**agreement, subject-verb: a bunch of the
boys**

> A bunch of the boys were whooping it up in
> the Malamute saloon —Robert W. Service,
> "The Shooting of Dan McGrew," 1907

The usage question is this: should the verb be
were or *was* whooping it up? The answer, say
the experts (Kilpatrick in *Pittsburgh Press,* 11
Aug. 1985, Jacques Barzun in Safire 1982,
Winners & Sinners, 5 Aug. 1983), is *were.*
Why? There are several reasons. First, we can
see two of the three forces that chiefly determine agreement—proximity and notional
agreement—pulling in the direction of the
plural. Second, we have the plain sense of the
subject-verb relation: the boys whoop, not the

bunch. And if *boys* is the real subject of the sentence, then the phrase *a bunch of* is functioning essentially as a modifier—it is, in fact, very similar to what many modern grammarians call a *predeterminer*. Here are a few more examples:

A rash of stories in the Chicago media have reported —cited by James J. Kilpatrick, *Pittsburgh Press Sunday Mag.,* 11 Aug. 1985

Yet the flock of acolytes surrounding each *jefe* are not expected to justify their servility —Alan Riding, *Distant Neighbors: A Portrait of the Mexicans,* 1985

A crew of Pyrates are driven —Jonathan Swift, *Gulliver's Travels,* 1726 (in McKnight 1928)

. . . a host of people who are interested in language —Charlton Laird, Foreword to Finegan 1980

A trio of genies are —Bryant Gumble, cited from a television broadcast in *Counterforce,* June 1983

. . . a class of sentences which are superficially parallel —Brian Joseph, *Language,* June 1980

Thus, only a fraction of such deposits are actually insured —*Consumer Reports,* January 1983

A large part of the Jewish communities were Arabic-speaking by this time —Albert Hourani, *A History of the Arab Peoples,* 1991

Though experts and common sense agree that the plural verb is natural and correct, actual usage still shows a few holdouts for the singular verb. The examples below may be the result of nervous copy editors or indecision on the part of the writers:

. . . a set of numbered rods, developed by John Napier, which was used for calculating —Ellen Richman, *Spotlight on Computer Literacy,* 1982

. . . a neat, little package of words that describes Bird's play —Gerry Finn, *Springfield* (Mass.) *Morning Union,* 29 Jan. 1985 (but the words describe, not the package)

. . . are run through a set of computer algorithms that rearranges them —*The Economist,* 17 May 1986 (the algorithms rearrange)

When you have a collecting noun phrase (*a bunch of*) before a plural noun (*the boys*), the sense will normally be plural and so should the verb.

See also NUMBER 1; ONE OF THOSE WHO.

agreement, subject-verb: compound subjects **1.** *Joined by "and."* Before the 18th-century grammarians undertook to prune the exuberant growth of English, no one seems to have worried whether two or more singular nouns joined by *and* took a plural or a singular verb. Writers of the 16th and 17th centuries used whatever verb sounded best and did not trouble themselves about grammatical agreement. "Scoffing and girding is their daily bread," wrote Gabriel Harvey in his 16th-century dispute with Thomas Nashe and Robert Greene (cited in McKnight 1928). Shakespeare could write "art and practice hath enriched" in *Measure for Measure* and in *Much Ado About Nothing* "All disquiet, horror, and perturbation follows her" (both cited in McKnight). The King James Bible at Daniel 5:14 has "light and understanding and excellent wisdom is found in thee" (cited in Hall 1917).

So when Lowth 1763 set his rule down, he was well aware of mixed usage. He favored the plural but allowed for the singular "sometimes," using James Greenwood's earlier analysis that the singular verb "is understood as applied to each of the preceding terms"; thus, we find in the Bible:

Sand, and salt, and a mass of iron, is easier to bear, than a man without understanding —Ecclesiasticus 22:18 (Douay), 1609

Priestley 1798 takes a different approach but reaches a similar conclusion:

It is a rule, that two distinct subjects of an affirmation require the verb to be in the plural number. . . . But, notwithstanding this, if the subject of the affirmation be nearly related, the verb is rather better in the singular number. *Nothing but the* marvellous and supernatural hath *any charms for them.*

Priestley's approach is reflected in some 20th-century commentators (as Barzun 1975 and Burchfield 1996) but where our moderns allow the singular verb with compound singular nouns close in thought, Priestley rather insisted on it.

The insistence that only the plural verb is correct seems to have begun with a writer named Philip Withers in 1788 (cited in Leonard 1929); his attack on the singular verb was based entirely on logic. He appears to have influenced several later grammarians including Lindley Murray 1795. Murray assembled his grammar largely from Lowth and Priestley, but in this instance he insists on the plural verb, mentioning Lowth's exceptions but finding them "evidently contrary to the first principles of grammar."

Modern grammarians are not so insistent. Curme 1931 and Quirk et al. 1985 agree that in modern practice the plural verb prevails after coordinate singular nouns with *and:*

While Keats and Chapman were at Heidelberg —Myles na gCopaleen (Flann O'Brien), *The Best of Myles,* 1968

The diversity and division . . . dominate Mr. Sheehan's portrayal —Thomas Childers, *N.Y. Times Book Rev.,* 11 Nov. 1990

. . . the streak of sentimentality and the lack of true originality which mark much of his creative writing —*New Yorker,* 18 Nov. 1985

. . . the bitterness and heartache that fill the world —Frank Sullivan, *A Rock in Every Snowball,* 1946

If the Arab and Israeli left are to develop a common program —Noam Chomsky, *Columbia Forum,* Winter 1969

But both recognize that when the nouns form "a collective idea" or "a oneness of idea" (the terms are Curme's; Burchfield uses "a single theme"), the singular verb is appropriate—notional agreement prevails.

. . . the end of all the privacy and propriety which was talked about at first —Jane Austen, *Mansfield Park,* 1814

The strange learning and arcane knowledge of James Joyce was already legend —Michael Reynolds, *Hemingway: The Paris Years,* 1989

Brinsley, whose education and maintenance was a charge on the rates of his native county —Flann O'Brien, *At Swim-Two-Birds,* 1939

The name and address of the grocery was painted on the slats —E. L. Doctorow, *Loon Lake,* 1979

. . . until American power and prestige was engaged —George F. Will, *Newsweek,* 22 May 1989

Curme also notes an exception to the required plural verb in a way that sounds much like Greenwood and Lowth: "when each of a number of singular noun subjects is considered separately, the verb is in the singular." He cites Emerson:

A fever, a mutilation, a cruel disappointment, a loss of wealth, a loss of friends, seems at the moment untold loss.

The same principle operates in these cases:

Every legislator, every doctor, and every citizen needs to recognize —Ronald Reagan, *Abortion and the Conscience of the Nation,* 1984

Linguistics and psychology has each brought its own approach to the subject —David Crystal, *The Cambridge Encyclopedia of Language,* 1987

We have seen so far that in present-day English coordinate singular nouns compounded by *and* (or *and* understood) usually are followed by a plural verb. The singular verb is appropriate when the nouns form a unitary notion or when they refer to a single person (as in "My friend and colleague says"). It is also possible to intend that the singular verb be construed with each noun separately; when such a construction is intended, it should perhaps be accentuated by distributive adjectives (as *each, every*) or punctuation. You should not forget that some people who evaluate other people's language have no idea the singular verb can ever be used, and even those whose understanding does encompass this possibility can disagree over what is a single idea—Burchfield 1996 did not like "the extent and severity of drug use . . . has" and Safire in 1983 did not like "The News Service's depth and scope represents. . . ."

2. *Joined by "or" (or "nor").* Lowth 1762 says that singular nouns joined by *or* take the singular verb; Priestley 1761 agrees; Quirk et al. 1985 notes that *or* is notionally disjunctive and that the singular verb is the rule.

. . . if the average man or woman was not endowed with courage —Harrison Smith, *Saturday Rev.,* 30 Jan. 1954

. . . neither she nor any other of the book's characters has endurance —E. L. Doctorow, *N.Y. Times Book Rev.,* 25 Aug. 1985

In English, neither chicken nor beef nor soup has formal gender —William Safire, *N.Y. Times Mag.,* 10 Aug. 1986

Quirk further notes that when plural nouns are so joined, the plural verb is used, and when nouns of different number are so joined, the principle of proximity tends to be called in, and the verb usually agrees with the nearest noun. Freeman 1983 makes the same point.

However strong the disjunctive notion that Quirk finds attached to *or* (and *nor*) may be, there is abundant evidence from the past— and some from modern writers—that the notion of plurality of the subjects can at times overbalance that of disjunctiveness. Lindley Murray 1795 accompanied his rule with several counterexamples using the plural, their authors tastefully suppressed. Curme 1931 notes that the negative *neither . . . nor* often contains a plural idea under the negative; he cites several instances from the 15th century to the 20th, including these:

Neither search nor labor are necessary —Samuel Johnson, *The Idler,* No. 44

Neither he nor his lady were at home — George Washington, diary, 2 Dec. 1789

. . . neither the friendship nor the sorrow seem so profound —Robert Bridges, *Forum,* May 1923

We have a couple of examples:

. . . neither Spencer nor Van Ness were renominated —*The Autobiography of Martin Van Buren,* begun 1854

If neither Marty nor me are there to meet them —Ernest Hemingway, letter, 23 Aug. 1940

Curme also finds examples with *or* with no negative attached; these, he opines, probably come from the author's feeling that the statement applies in all cases, even though applicable to only one or two at a time. He instances these extracts:

My life or death are equal both to me —John Dryden

A drama or an epic fill the mind —Matthew Arnold, *Essays in Criticism*

Acting, singing, or reciting are forbidden them —H. G. Wells

What are honor or dishonor to her? —Henry James

The notion determining the agreement in these examples often seems to be "this or that or both (or all)." We have similar instances among our citations:

But it's when sex or scurrility are used for their own sakes that they are in bad taste —Flannery O'Connor, letter, 10 Mar. 1956

In summary, compound singular nouns with *or* or *nor* are supposed to take a singular verb and in current use usually do. The plural verb is most likely to appear where the notion of plurality is suggested by negative construction or when the writer is thinking of "this or that or both."

3. *Quasi-coordination by words like "with," "along with," "together with" or by punctuation.* Quirk et al. 1985 points out that when a singular noun is joined to another by a quasi-coordinator (the term is Quirk's) like *with, rather than, as well as,* etc., grammatical concord calls for the singular verb. Here are some examples:

. . . that tale in prose . . . which was published at Christmas, with nine others, by us, has reached a second edition —Charles Lamb, letter, 7 June 1809

. . . the Petterell with the rest of the Egyptian Squadron was off the Isle of Cyprus —Jane Austen, letter, 1 Nov. 1800

And preceded by a comma can also take a singular verb:

There is no longer any doubt that your uncle Abraham, and my father was the same man —Abraham Lincoln, letter, 2 Apr. 1848

Quasi-coordinators are semantically equivalent to coordinators (as *and*), notes Quirk, and thus notional concord can interfere with grammatical concord:

This word, with all those of the same race, are of uncertain etymology —Samuel Johnson, *A Dictionary of the English Language,* 1755

Miss Macnulty, with the heir and the nurses, were to remain at Portray —Anthony Trollope, *The Eustace Diamonds,* 1873

. . . *A piece of cake,* along with *cakewalk,* were expressions used by Royal Air Force Pilots —Safire 1984

Parenthetical insertions are also separate in theory and should not affect grammatical agreement. Parenthetical insertions may be set off by commas, dashes, or parentheses:

. . . their management—and their companies' balance sheets—has suffered —Margaret Yao, *Wall Street Jour.,* 11 June 1980

Commas are the weakest way of setting off a parenthetical element that is not otherwise signaled; consequently, they may be thought not to be setting off a parenthesis at all:

They suggest that it is not just the world, and civilization as we know it, that are going to the dogs —Howard 1984

You would think, however, that actual parentheses would clearly remind a writer that the material included is not to affect the number agreement of the sentence. But real writers forget—even writers on language and grammar.

Southern Black English (and some white dialects influenced by it) have *bossman* as an elaboration on *boss* —J. L. Dillard, *American Talk,* 1976

The occurrence of *phenomena, criteria, strata* with *is* or *was* shows up the careless writer, even though *agenda* (and *data* for some) have achieved the singular number —Barzun 1975

The very complex gravity field of Mars (and the simple one of Venus) have been mapped —John S. Lewis, in *The New Solar System,* ed. J. Kelly Beatty et al., 1982

See also AS WELL AS.

agreement, subject-verb: miscellaneous problems 1. *Titles.* Curme 1931 notes that titles of written works are treated as singular even if the title is plural. Our evidence generally confirms this:

> . . . Shakespeare's *Sonnets* has remained the exception —A. Kent Hieatt, *PMLA,* October 1983

Pronoun reference, however, may be plural in notional agreement:

> I have been reading the *Lives of the Poets* for thirty years, and can testify that in all that time I have never known the day or the hour when I failed to find interest, instruction, amusement, somewhere in their pages —John Wain, *Samuel Johnson,* 1974

2. *Amounts of money, periods of time, etc.* "The principle of notional concord accounts for the common use of a singular with subjects that are plural noun phrases of quantity or measure. The entity expressed by the noun phrase is viewed as a single unit . . . ," says Quirk et al. 1985.   Quirk appends such examples as

Ten dollars is all I have left.

Two miles is as far as they can walk.

Two thirds of the area is under water.

Quirk's observations are consistent with the evidence in Curme 1931.

3. *Subject and complement of different number.* People are often uncertain about the number of a linking verb in sentences like "Potatoes are a vegetable." The uncertainty lies, says Curme 1931, in the uncertainty a copula (linking verb) creates about whether the noun before or the noun after is the true subject. Curme goes on to say, "The present tendency is to avoid a decision on this perplexing point by regulating the number of the copula by a mere formal principle—namely, as the nominative before the copula is often the subject, it has become the rule to place the copula in accord with it, whether it be a subject or a predicate." Copperud 1970, 1980 cites several of his sources as agreeing to what Curme observes to have become customary—to treat the first noun as the subject. The custom seems not to have changed over the last 50 years and more: the noun before the verb governs it.

agreement, subject-verb: one or more, one in (out of)____. **1.** Bernstein 1962, 1977, Freeman 1983, and Bryson 1984 remind us that the phrase *one or more* is plural in meaning and should take a plural verb; Bernstein 1958 asserts the same of *one or two.* What relevant evidence of these constructions we have in our files agrees with the commentators:

> One or two of the red brick and green copper pavilions . . . still remain —Gerald Weissman, *The Woods Hole Cantata,* 1975

> . . . scenes in which one or more actors take part —M. C. Howatson, *The Oxford Companion to Classical Literature,* 1989

In a majority of our instances, however, those phrases do not govern a verb.

2. Chambers 1985, Heritage 1969, 1982, Longman 1984, and Simon 1980 agree that the phrase *one in* (a larger number) or *one out of* (a larger number) should take the singular verb. Our evidence for this construction shows both singular and plural verbs used. A few examples of the plural verb:

> One out of ten soldiers, he reported, are unable to recognize an enemy on a dark starlit night at a distance of only ten yards —*Science News Letter,* 14 Oct. 1944

> Nationwide, an estimated one in four adults are functionally illiterate —Gannett Foundation news release, cited in *New Yorker,* 22 July 1985

> . . . straw polls reported that 1 in 4 of her own party's M.P.s want her to step aside —Daniel Pedersen, *Newsweek,* 2 Apr. 1990

While our citations are not numerous enough to be certain, the singular verb seems to be more common. Our earliest is from Benjamin Franklin:

> . . . about one citizen in 500 . . . has acquired a tolerable stile as to grammar and construction so as to bear printing —"Court of the Press," 12 Sept. 1789

Here are a few more recent ones:

> One of every five residents lives below the poverty line —Mary Anne Weaver, *New England Monthly,* February 1989

> . . . it is estimated that one in four Australians at present is not a native speaker of English —Robert B. Kaplan, *Linguistic Reporter,* February 1980

> One out of every eight small business in the country is in California —David J. Jefferson, *Wall Street Jour.,* 24 Apr. 1990

> One of every four Africans is a Nigerian —Blaine Hardin, *Wilson Quarterly,* Winter 1991

agreement, subject-verb: the principle of proximity Quirk et al. 1985 describes the principle of proximity (also called *attraction* and *blind agreement*) as the tendency of a verb to agree with a closely preceding noun or noun phrase rather than with the subject. Quirk further observes:

> Conflict between grammatical concord and attraction through proximity tends to increase with the distance between the noun phrase head of the subject and the verb, for

example when the postmodifier is lengthy or when an adverbial or a parenthesis intervenes between the subject and the verb. Proximity concord occurs mainly in unplanned discourse. In writing it will be corrected to grammatical concord if it is noticed.

Here are a few examples from unplanned discourse:

The fact is, the fertility of the plains are wonderful —Lord Byron, letter, 12 Nov. 1809

The difference of Religion & government are all that can make any man hesitate in his choice —George Washington, diary, 25 Jan. 1790

The filing of the false, fraudulent charges are a complete contradiction —Joseph McCarthy, 1953, at Army-McCarthy hearings (in Pyles 1979)

The reaction that I have taken to these steps are appropriate —Jimmy Carter, quoted in *N.Y. Times,* 14 Feb. 1980

Quirk's observations that proximity concord will be corrected if it is noticed is doubtless correct. But it seems to escape notice more often than you would expect:

. . . the word *regards* have no Nominative —Baker 1770

An event, or a series of events, which oppose success or desire —*Imperial Dict.,* 1882, s.v. *adversity*

And now everybody except the Germans were passing through —Gertrude Stein, *The Autobiography of Alice B. Toklas,* 1933

His system of citing examples of the best authorities, of indicating etymology, and pronunciation, are still followed by lexicographers —Howard 1984

News of Arthur's grandiose ambitions were sure to leak out —Robertson Davies, *The Lyre of Orpheus,* 1988

. . . a thermal beam of cesium atoms were prepared —David Golden, *Physics Today,* January 1986

The evidence required for affirmative answers to these two questions are enormously different —Thomas D. Gilovich, *Wilson Quarterly,* Spring 1991

It should be noted that proximity does not always influence a singular verb to be plural; sometimes the proximate noun is singular and the subject plural:

And the words that close the last story in the book has the music of a requiem —Padraic

Colum, Introduction to James Joyce, *Dubliners* (Modern Library edition), 1926

. . . the ease with which nice clothes and a pleasant address, with rank, imposes on everybody —George Bernard Shaw, letter, 9 Jan. 1930

The borders of Gaul was overwhelmed —John Davies, *A History of Wales,* 1990

Proximity agreement may pass in speech and other forms of unplanned discourse; in print it will be considered an error. And it is one that is probably easier to fall into than you might expect—let the examples above be a warning.

agreement, subject-verb: *what*-clauses

What is frightening is to discover how easily we can be misled —Alden Whitman, *Harper's,* April 1972

What officials have done is essentially this —Frederick N. Robinson, *General Electric Investor,* Summer 1971

The two clauses beginning with *what* in the examples are the subjects of their sentences. The pronoun *what* in the first example is the subject of the clause; in the second, it is the object. The usage problem with these *what*-clauses is primarily the number of the verb in the main sentence, and, when *what* is the subject of the clause, the number of the verb in the clause. Copperud 1970, 1980 reports various long discussions of the subject, mostly from different perspectives. From the welter of analysis and opinions he discerns one clear point of agreement: *what* is not necessarily singular in construction but can be plural. Commentators not covered by Copperud tend to agree. The best discussion of this question is in Bryant 1962; the citations in the Merriam-Webster files gathered since 1962 generally confirm the findings of the studies she reports.

The first point to observe is that mixed usage occurs in only a limited number of cases, namely when the complement of the verb of the main sentence is plural. In the great majority of *what*-clause sentences in our files, everything is singular, and there are no problems.

When the *what* in the *what*-clause is the object of the clause and when the predicate noun following the main verb is plural, it tends to pull the verb with it. Bryant reports the plural verb favored by about three to one over the singular. Here are examples of both kinds:

What we need and crave is shows as handsomely preposterous as . . . the kind George Edwards used to put on at Max's Gaiety —George Jean Nathan, *The Theatre Book of the Year, 1946–1947*

What we need in government, in education, in business . . . are men who seek to understand issues in all their complexity —J. W. McSwiney, *Annual Report, The Mead Corp.,* 1970

What we are getting is old answers to old questions —Daniel Boorstin, *Look,* 20 Aug. 1968 (Perrin & Ebbitt 1972)

When *what* is the subject of the clause, and the *what*-clause is the subject of the sentence, things get a bit more complicated. Perrin & Ebbitt 1972 points out that usage is consistent when the *what*-clause, linking verb, and predicate nominative agree in number—being either all singular or all plural. Bernstein 1958, 1962, 1965 and Johnson 1982 concur and urge writers to try for such a consistency. Simon 1980, however, wants only the singular and reproduces the following sentence for criticism, though it illustrates the consistent plural:

What *have* [Rubins's italics] surfaced are similes, viscous streams of them —Josh Rubins, *Harvard Mag.*

The consistent singular is actually the most common case:

What is absent from the present book is any attempt to think in terms of practical problems —*Times Literary Supp.,* 22 Oct. 1971

Mixed usage occurs when the subject *what* in the clause is singular but the predicate nominative is plural. In such cases the main verb tends to be plural:

What bothers Professor Teeter most are the guesses, hunches, speculations, and fancies in which many language shamans like me indulge —Safire 1984

What is needed from the left wing of university reform are programs that begin to specify the steps of change —John Gagnon, *Change,* October 1971

Bryant further points out that when the complement consists of two or more predicate nouns, the verb is plural if the nouns are plural and singular if the nouns are singular:

What impresses them are planes and divisions and ships —Harry S. Truman, radio address, 26 June 1953 (in Bryant)

What is most striking about Johnson is the vigor of his ideas, the variety of his knowledge, the forcefulness of his conversation —J. C. Mendenhall, *English Literature, 1650–1800,* 1940 (in Bryant)

When the complement of the main verb is a *that*-clause the verb is singular:

What does follow is that the issue is susceptible to rational methods —Phillip H. Scribner, *AAUP Bulletin,* September 1971

Clearly usage is mixed in these complex sentences, but you need not regard *what* as inflexibly singular. Dwight Bolinger notes in a letter reprinted in Safire 1984 that in the influence of the plural predicate noun over the main verb English is similar to French and Spanish. It is desirable to be consistent, but, in an area where notional agreement appears to hold absolute sway, it is perhaps even more desirable to be natural.

a half, a half a   See HALF 2.

ahold   Commentators from Bernstein 1958 to Garner 1998 call *ahold* dialectal (as do several dictionaries) and discourage its use in standard prose. The Dictionary of American Regional English shows examples from several states: Florida, Arkansas, Georgia, Maryland, West Virginia, Kentucky, Missouri, New York, New Jersey, Ohio, Illinois. Citations in Merriam-Webster files suggest Michigan, Wisconsin, Massachusetts, Alabama, Texas, and California as well. If it is indeed dialectal, it is well spread around (we have it in a few British sources also).

The idiom we are discussing here most often follows *get* (*catch, have, seize, take, lay,* and *grasp* as well) and is regularly followed by *of.* When *hold* is followed by a different preposition—*on, upon, over*—it always takes the indefinite article; only with *of* is the article idiomatically omitted. The majority idiom, then, is (to take the most common verb) *get hold of*; the minority or dialectal idiom is *get ahold of,* with the article separate from or attached to *hold.* The OED (under *get* 13b) shows the idiom as *to get (a) hold of*; no nonstandard label is appended. Its earliest citations, however, lack the article.

Part of the difficulty with *ahold* is simply the way it is styled in writing or print. When the article is separated from *hold,* the expression is not especially noticeable, as in these examples (the first two British):

. . . signal-towers improved the east coast defences; a stronger hold was taken of Wales —Jacquetta & Christopher Hawkes, *Prehistoric Britain,* 1949

. . . until you can get a hold of the splinter —Peter Heaton, *Cruising,* 1952

A reporter got a hold of this tax business —Sally Rand, quoted in Studs Terkel, *Hard Times,* 1970

But when *a* is attached to *hold,* with or without a hyphen, the expression calls more attention to itself:

If you can't get ahold of a voltmeter —Len Feldman, *Rolling Stone,* 6 June 1974

Ross took ahold of the stall rail —Susan M. Watkins, *Seventeen,* June 1993

We found this export control business was a nasty nettle to grasp ahold of —Gerald C. Smith, quoted in *Wall Street Jour.,* 30 Nov. 1984

The pronunciation spelling *aholt* is also used:

One spring-hatted Augusta lovely finally . . . said "Lookie here now, the Spanish boy has get aholt of the lead." —Rick Reilly, *Sports Illustrated,* 18 Apr. 1994

I must admit some of the birds tried to get aholt of me —Colin MacInnes, *Absolute Beginners,* 1959

. . . Jacob, who actually grabbed aholt of God. . . . Grabbed aholt? A Louisiana expression —Walker Percy, *Signposts in a Strange Land,* 1991

We find that *ahold* turns up in edited prose:

Sometimes, if you could get ahold of a representative who was a regular guy —Norman Mailer, *The Naked and the Dead,* 1948

An eleven-year-old boy . . . gets ahold of a million dollars in laundered money and goes on a spending spree —movie capsule, *New Yorker,* 14 Feb. 1994

. . . have become collectors' items to New Yorkers lucky enough to get ahold of them —Helen Antrobus, *UTNE Reader,* March/April 1993

Some bozo got ahold of my word processor —Bill Mandel, *San Francisco Chronicle,* 14 Apr. 1987

Better hope the Globe doesn't get ahold of this one —William Powers, *New Republic,* 9 June 1997

But it is primarily a spoken construction, and its most frequent appearance is in the transcription of speech:

I would kill to get ahold of her hairdresser —unidentified woman, quoted by Gail Sheehy, *Vanity Fair,* June 2000

As soon as Lyndon got ahold of the damn thang —Sam Houston Johnson, quoted by Larry L. King, *Harper's,* April 1970

When Rosalynn gets ahold of you, it's going to be even worse —Jimmy Carter, quoted by B. Drummond Ayres, Jr., *N.Y. Times Mag.,* 3 June 1979

I couldn't get ahold of my regular psychologist or coach —B. J. Bedford, quoted by

Leigh Montville, *Sports Illustrated,* 21 Aug. 2000

I got ahold of Eddie Condon and I said, "Eddie. I want to make a record" —Milt Gabler, quoted by Joe Smith, *Off the Record,* 1988

aim 1. *Aim to, aim at.* Fowler 1926 plumps for the *aim at* construction, but does not disparage *aim to,* calling it good American even though not good English. Fowler's reviser, Sir Ernest Gowers, notes (in Fowler 1965) that *aim to* has become established in British English. Burchfield 1996 notes that *aim* followed by *at* and a gerund was normal until about the end of the 19th century; *aim* with a *to*-infinitive was much less common, except in American English. Since then *aim to* has largely replaced *aim at* in British English except in passive constructions. His analysis of present-day British English pretty well describes American English as well.

. . . a format aimed to give pleasure to hand and eye —*Times Literary Supp.,* 19 Feb. 1971

. . . these programs aim to detect violence-prone kids —Jodie Morse, *Time,* 24 Apr. 2000

. . . hung out near Army bases aiming to create deserters out of recent inductees —Peter Collier, *National Rev.,* 17 July 2000

Or he may be aiming to further destabilize Kosovo —Elizabeth Rubin, *New Republic,* 13 Mar. 2000

. . . are aiming to revise the image it has acquired —Corby Kummer, *Atlantic,* December 1996

He aims to be a celebrity chef —Richard Eder, *N.Y. Times Book Rev.,* 2 Apr. 2000

. . . a long and well documented book, but it is parti pris and aims to redress the usual balance of Mozart studies —Peter Porter, *Times Literary Supp.,* 19 June 1998

. . . aims to produce a public database of genetic markers —Clive Cookson, *Financial Times* (London), 28 Oct. 1999

. . . gym in Wellington aims to cater for the fitness needs of women —advt., *The Dominion* (Wellington, NZ), 23 Sept. 1997

Aim at is usually found in passive constructions:

But advice on sexual matters was also available in literature aimed at promoting conception —Dr. Ruth Westheimer, *Civilization,* April/May 1999

. . . an endless number of talks aimed at generating the right trades —Murray Chass, *N.Y. Times,* 19 Dec. 1999

. . . a politics aimed at significantly reducing inequality —Paul Starr, *New Republic,* 14 Aug. 2000

. . . a talking tour aimed at defusing bombs and getting good press —Peggy Noonan, *Wall Street Jour.,* 8 July 1999

2. *Aim at, aim for* with a noun. Colter 1981 thinks only *at* and not *for* should be used with *aim,* but he is alone in his belief; Chambers 1985 and Janis 1984 say either may be used, and in fact both are widely used:

. . . Mr. Trudeau aims for the jugular —Herbert Mitgang, *N.Y. Times Book Rev.,* 12 July 1981

. . . climbed down a bank, aiming for a promontory —Edward Hoagland, *Harper's,* February 1971

. . . when Mr. Causley neglects this rare gift and aims specifically for children —*Times Literary Supp.,* 2 Apr. 1971

The thing to aim for in posture —James Hewitt, *Irish Digest,* April 1955

. . . to keep the antennas aimed at the earth —Henry S. F. Cooper, Jr., *New Yorker,* 11 Nov. 1972

. . . one sometimes wonders what effect their creator is aiming at —Edmund Wilson, *New Yorker,* 18 Sept. 1971

. . . we cannot even be sure what Hamlet is aiming at —William Empson, *Sewanee Rev.,* January–March 1953

. . . aim at results which the other sciences can neither prove nor disprove —Bertrand Russell, *Selected Papers,* 1927

Occasionally *toward(s)* may be used:

. . . products, systems and services aimed toward better living —*Annual Report, American Home Products Corp.,* 1970

It is towards London that touring companies aim —Peter Forster, *London Calling,* 11 Nov. 1954

ain't Everybody knows *ain't,* but few are familiar with where it came from. It is hard to see from its spelling how it is related to the verb *be.*

The connection of the spelling *ain't* with *be* goes back to the 17th century, when a number of contracted speech forms began to appear in print, chiefly in published plays. Some of these contractions—*ben't, an't, en't, han't*—have either been replaced by other contractions, or have simply dropped out of use. But several

others—*can't, shan't, don't, won't*—are still in use.

The one we are interested in is *an't* (sometimes spelled *a'n't*). It was used for *am not:*

MISS PRUE. You need not sit so near one, if you have any thing to say, I can hear you farther off, I an't deaf —William Congreve, *Love for Love,* 1695

and for *are not:*

LORD FOPPINGTON. . . .these shoes a'n't ugly, but they don't fit me —Sir John Vanbrugh, *The Relapse,* 1696

An't came to represent *am not* via the contraction *amn't* (still used in Scottish and Irish English); it is easy to see how it came to represent *are not* when we remember that in the principal British dialects *r* would not have been pronounced. It is also instructive to remember that the *a* of *are* was not pronounced the same then as it is now. For instance, John Donne (who died in 1631) rhymed *are* with *bare, starre,* and *warre,* which do not all rhyme in present-day English.

An't came to be used for *is not,* too, although we don't know quite how. But Jonathan Swift was so using it in his *Journal to Stella* as early as 1710.

There is also another line of derivation in which *an't* and *ain't* are used for *has not* and *have not.* It seems to be a later development, apparently occurring in the 19th century. The derivation itself is fairly straightforward: 18th-century *ha'n't,* for both *has not* and *have not,* becomes *an't* by loss of the *h* (in American English the *h* will sometimes be restored to produce *hain't*).

So by the early 18th century we find *an't* used for *am not, are not,* and *is not.* The spelling *ain't* is not found until later; our earliest evidence is from Fanny Burney's *Evelina* (1778), where it represents the speech of a countryman. How this spelling came to be the predominant one is not clear. In the U.S. both *an't* and *ain't* were in use in the late 18th century. The variables of pronunciation were present here too—some 19th-century American humorists used the spelling *air* for *are.* But during the 19th century *ain't* began to displace *an't,* for reasons we do not understand. We do have one possible hint from a story published in 1845 by the humorist Johnson J. Hooper. In it the rascally boy hero Simon Suggs regularly says *ain't* but his father says *a'n't.* Perhaps it was one of those generational differences. Hooper's story was set in the South; *an't* seems to have persisted longer to the north (we have Emily Dickinson in 1851 and the elder Oliver Wendell Holmes in 1860). But after the 1870s, even New England writers were spelling it *ain't.*

We also have to note *ain't*'s loss of prestige.

Linguists have observed a division in usage, particularly in Great Britain, where the pronunciation spelled *an't* (which would later be spelled *aren't*, with the *r* not pronounced) retained status, while the pronunciation spelled *ain't* lost it, to be associated with lower-class and uneducated speakers. It became a regular feature of Cockney speech.

In America it is not certain that the social status of *an't* speakers versus *ain't* speakers was important. American pedagogy chose rather to disapprove all contracted forms, and as the slight connection of *ain't* to *be* became less apparent, *ain't* became the most commonly condemned of all (*won't*, whose connection with *will* was equally obscure, was similarly vilified for a time).

But a century and a half of steady disapproval has not succeeded in eradicating *ain't*. On the contrary, it is in as frequent use as ever. It is part of the normal habitual speech of people from rural, working class, and inner city backgrounds—just the sort of people that teachers and other elders don't want the rest of us to sound like. But many persons from those backgrounds have become highly paid professional athletes whose interviews on television and in the print media keep habitual *ain't* conspicuously on display.

The improper odor of *ain't* makes it useful in speech and writing to catch attention or to gain emphasis. Thus we find it used in headlines and in the titles of articles: "Tara It Ain't" (*N.Y. Times Book Rev.*, 19 July 1998), "You Ain't Seen Nuthin' Yet" (*Astronomy*, October 1997), "This Ain't No Party" (*Riverfront Times* [St. Louis, Mo.], 19 July 2000). Here are some examples besides headings:

. . . everybody assumes I know where every train line goes, when it goes there, why it goes there. And that ain't the case at all —Marc Eichen, *Focus,* Winter 1991

He is surely an important writer and very much worth reading, but it helps to keep it in mind that the stuff ain't Shakespeare —Lawrence Block, *American Heritage,* July/August 1993

But NASA this ain't. Nothing at the offices seemed to work —Jason DeParle, *N.Y. Times Mag.,* 20 Dec. 1998

Next up for the man who claims he ain't misbehavin'—a round of appeals —*Time,* 19 June 2000

It is also used as a marker of an informal style:

. . . the mindless, gossip-driven culture of celebrity (which happens to put food on my table, so I, for one, ain't complaining) —A. J. Jacobs, *Entertainment Weekly,* 22/29 Jan. 1999

Bill Clinton is on Martha's Vineyard taking a three-week vacation . . . he's one hard workin' sumbitch, ain't he? —David Letterman, quoted in *The Bulletin's Frontrunner,* 20 Aug. 1997

Great claims will be made for "Road Hog," which ain't bad, and "Bold Rat," which ain't good —Robert Christgau, *Village Voice,* 22 Mar. 1994

This informal *ain't* is commonly distinguished from the habitual *ain't* by its frequent occurrence in fixed phrases like the old "and that ain't hay," or "Ain't America grand?" Some of the more common current ones:

. . . he suddenly popped up on my television screen and laid it on real heavy for a tire company. For money? Say it ain't so, Jimmy —*And More By Andy Rooney,* 1982

. . . Yogi Berra . . . was only partly right when he said, "It ain't over till it's over" —Matthew Jaffe, *Sunset,* June 1992

We're told that in opera it ain't over till the fat lady sings —Brad Leithauser, *N.Y. Times Book Rev.,* 30 Aug. 1998

"It ain't brain surgery," says one Pac-10 coach —Bruce Feldman, *ESPN,* 21 Feb. 2000

Violating the old "if it ain't broke, don't fix it" dictum —*TV Guide,* 14–20 Mar. 1992

Chaos? You ain't seen nothing yet —David Newnham, *Manchester Guardian Weekly,* 6 Sept. 1992

Glamour! Excitement! Entertainment! Well, one out of three ain't bad —Andy Meisler, *TV Guide,* 7–13 Dec. 1985

In fiction *ain't* is used for purposes of characterization. We also find it used in familiar letters, where it tends to be a sign of a close personal relationship:

Thence to Dresden. Ain't I glad, though the weather is no better —Henry Adams, letter, 6 Apr. 1859

No litrry news. Ain't seen nothing but Wilson's verdict that 'emotionally and intellectually Mr. MacLeish talks through his hat' —Archibald MacLeish, letter, 19 June 1927

Ain't it hell to have a head of the State in the family? —Harry S. Truman, letter, 11 May 1952

I trust you find my handwriting as bad as yr own. I ain't strong enough to hit a key tonight —Flannery O'Connor, letter, 26 Mar. 1957

Another use of *ain't,* seldom mentioned though often heard, is in popular music. In songs with lines like "It ain't necessarily so," "The old gray mare, she ain't what she used to be," "Ain't she sweet?" *ain't* is used for metrical purposes; it is also more clearly heard and more easily enunciated than the *isn't* it usually replaces.

Now an aside for the tag question "ain't I?": Fowler 1926 regretted its being considered indicative of low breeding, and H. L. Mencken in *The American Mercury* wondered what is the matter with it. The tag question was used by linguistic geographers to elicit oral uses of *ain't;* their results influenced the statement in Webster's Third that caused much controversy. A few commentators approve it, but they have not carried much weight with the general run of handbooks and teachers. And we do not have enough evidence to show that the tag question is actually in frequent use, although we know it turns up in inverted expressions, such as questions.

To conclude: *ain't* is a stigmatized word in general use; its habitual use in speech and writing tends to mark the speaker or writer as socially or educationally inferior. It is, however, frequently used in a few fixed contexts, and its controversial status lends its use in ordinary discourse a piquancy that many writers have found useful in gaining attention or increasing emphasis.

à la This imported preposition has its grave accent over the *a* printed often enough, even in American use, that the unaccented form is considered a secondary variant. And although it has been used in English contexts since the end of the 16th century, some writers still feel that it is French and italicize it. It is widely used in English outside the field of cookery as well as within. Longman 1984, Fowler 1965, and Burchfield 1996 note that its form is fixed in English; the preposition is often followed by a proper name, and even when the name is clearly masculine the feminine article *la* is retained. Here are a few examples:

Clinton and Gore will meet briefly on Tuesday for a symbolic, off-site torch-passing à la Ronald Reagan to Bush père —Michelle Cottle, *New Republic,* 31 July 2000

. . . eating up the keyboard *à la* Horowitz —Harold C. Schonberg, *Harper's,* April 1971

. . . is more user friendly and includes instant messaging à la AOL —Catherine Yang, *Business Week,* 7 Dec. 1998

I was filling in with my drumsticks all kinds of complicated rhythmical riffs *a la* castanet parts —Michael Tilson Thomas, quoted in *Rolling Stone,* 14 Sept. 1972

. . . will now try to ignore the flap and get the renominations over with, a la politics-as-usual —*Wall Street Jour.,* 3 June 1980

albeit Copperud 1970, 1980 observes that "a generation ago" *albeit* was considered archaic but is "now being revived." The source of the notice of revival is Gowers (in Fowler 1965). This is a most curious business, since *albeit* seems never to have gone out of use, though it may have faded somewhat in the later 19th century. If it did, the revival began decades before the commentators noticed. The brothers Fowler 1907 found it to be an archaism, citing two contemporary sources for censure. The opinion of 1907 was carried over to Fowler 1926. The word has considerably increased in use since the 1930s, to judge by our evidence.

The wind was new albeit it was the same that had blown before the time of man —Elizabeth Madox Roberts, *The Time of Man,* 1926

. . . living a modest life as an editor wasn't as appealing as living in the grand style, albeit as someone else's valet —Leslie Bennetts, *Vanity Fair,* 18 Sept. 2000

. . . he throws (albeit sparingly) a nice ball —Austin Murphy, *Sports Illustrated,* 18 Sept. 2000

. . . I watched the trees and the rain with increasing interest albeit with no radio support —E. B. White, *New Yorker,* 25 Sept. 1954

. . . conversation might have found its natural level, albeit low —Mary McCarthy, *Atlantic,* August 1970

. . . customers seemed generally cheery, albeit some were more cautious than others —Cynthia Clark, *Publishers Weekly,* 26 Jan. 1998

. . . they had treated me as a pal, albeit a junior one —Anthony Bailey, *New Yorker,* 29 July 1985

alibi **1.** *noun.* The extended sense of *alibi* meaning any excuse is an Americanism that is first attested in the years just before World War I. Its popularity is shown by its conspicuous use by Ring Lardner in 1915 in the title of one of his best-known stories, "Alibi Ike." The sense seems to have first been popularized in sports:

Among the countless alibis that go hand in hand with bad golf —*Vanity Fair,* December 1919

But writers for American newspapers and magazines used it in other contexts, too—especially politics.

They want an alibi to gouge the public —*Time,* 18 Jan. 1926

As soon as any new expression becomes widespread and popular enough, it is bound to draw unfavorable comment. The extended sense of *alibi* had only to wait until 1925 for disapproval, and by the end of the 1920s it had been roundly disparaged as far away as Australia (they blamed it on Americans).

British disapproval apparently began with Partridge 1942, and the Brits have remained in the forefront of the critics, although Howard 1980, who doesn't like it, considers it established and Burchfield 1996, ruefully perhaps, accepts it as inevitable.

There is a bit of a British–American split here. While some American handbooks and commentators follow the early condemnation, others are neutral, and Bernstein 1971 and William Safire (*New York Magazine,* 24 July 1983) defend it.

The use, therefore, seems to be regarded with considerably less disfavor in the U.S. than in the U.K. The examples in British usage books suggest that *alibi* is established in British use. In American use, it is still found in sports contexts:

A few players admit . . . that they have used bugs as an alibi for bad play —John Garrity, *Sports Illustrated,* 18 Aug. 1986

. . . in these days of handy athletic alibis —Peter King, *Sports Illustrated,* 16 Mar. 1998

And still in politics:

Structure is an alibi for policy failure — Arthur M. Schlesinger, Jr., *The Cycles of American History,* 1986

. . . that great alibi of modern Arab politics: Israel and the Palestinians —Fouad Ajami, *N.Y. Times Book Rev.,* 3 Mar. 1991

It also appears in more general contexts:

But the increasing pedantry was not merely devoid of grace and graciousness; all too often it proved to be an alibi for not taking any artistic or intellectual risks —Victor Brombert, *PMLA,* May 1990

. . . offers a typically winking alibi for such combinations of candor and calculation —Alexander Star, *New Republic,* 14 Aug. 2000

2. *verb.* The American Heritage 1969, 1982, 2000 usage panel, almost half of which accepted the extended sense of *alibi* as a noun, rejected intransitive use of the verb in writing; so does Garner 1998. The OED Supplement shows that the verb has been in use since 1909. It too was establishing itself by the

1920s and is now fully established in general prose:

. . . wherein he endeavors to alibi reversal, surprise, and defeat —S. L. A. Marshall, *Saturday Rev.,* 9 Oct. 1954

. . . to walk through life bitter, to alibi, to rationalize churlish behavior —Claire Smith, *N.Y. Times,* 25 Apr. 1996

After agreeing to an interview . . . Phillips canceled, alibiing through a harried secretary that he was "very busy" —Seth Lubove, *Forbes,* 1 June 1998

. . . he didn't alibi. He took the blame for his four interceptions —Dave Anderson, *N.Y. Times,* 8 Sept. 1980

alien When *alien* is used with a preposition, the current choice is most often *to:*

. . . the contempt he felt for a quality so alien to the traditions of his calling —W. Somerset Maugham, *The Moon and Sixpence,* 1919

Are such relationships alien to the principles of UNO? —Sir Winston Churchill, quoted in *Time,* 18 Mar. 1946

. . . an acrid empty home with everyone growing alien to one another —Norman Mailer, *The Naked and the Dead,* 1948

At one time, *alien* was also commonly used with *from,* especially in literary contexts. While still found occasionally, *alien from* is much less frequent now than *alien to:*

. . . to become a moral nihilist was to papa unthinkable, so alien was it from all his habits —Rose Macaulay, *Told by an Idiot,* 1923

I felt somewhat alien from this company because of my experience with would-be Communists —Katherine Anne Porter, *The Never-Ending Wrong,* 1977

all 1. See ALL OF; ALL THAT; ALL READY, ALREADY; ALL TOGETHER, ALTOGETHER.
2. In the worrisome world of pronoun agreement with indefinite pronoun referents (see, for instance: EACH; EVERY; EVERYBODY, EVERYONE; THEY, THEIR, THEM), some textbooks have recommended substituting constructions with *all* in place of constructions with *each* or *every* in order to make both pronoun and referent grammatically and notionally plural.
3. *All . . . not.* In conversation, a sentence with *all* and a negative (*not*), the negative element is often postponed so that it follows the verb, instead of preceding *all.* Such sentences go back at least as far as this well-known example:

All that glisters is not gold —Shakespeare, *The Merchant of Venice,* 1597

While they present no problem in speech, they can prove ambiguous in prose:

> . . . all seventy-four hospitals did not report every month —*Washington Post* (in Kilpatrick 1984)

Does this mean that none of the hospitals reported? Or did only some fail to report? Writers can avoid this possible ambiguity by simply placing the *not* before the *all.*

all-around, all-round Copperud 1970, 1980 cites a few commentators as worrying about which of these synonyms is more logical or otherwise preferable. This culminates in O'Connor 1996 expressing a preference for *all-around;* this is probably the preferred house style at the *New York Times.* Garner 1998 brings up the only thing of real interest: *all-around* is American and has little British use; *all-round* has both British and American use. Here are a few examples of each:

> . . . the best all-around athlete in U.S. college sports —John Gustafson, *ESPN,* 27 Dec. 1999

> . . . former member of Parliament and all-around good guy —R. W. Apple, Jr., *N.Y. Times,* 28 June 1998

> . . . has been a very common species and is the all-around best plant of the genus — George Elbert, *House Plant Mag.,* Summer 1993

> . . . the French have always been keen on giving pupils an all-around general knowledge —*The Economist,* 3–9 Dec. 1988

> . . . women constitute the great bulk of the world's weavers, basketry makers and all-around mistresses of plant goods —Natalie Angier, *N.Y. Times,* 14 Dec. 1999

> . . . disdains their sloppy handling, poor fuel economy and all-round "tiresome" feel —Daniel McGinn, *Newsweek,* 26 Oct. 1998

> . . . it needs that double layer . . . to make an all-round weatherproof —*Geographical Mag.,* November 1989

> . . . an all-round duffer moving in far from exalted circles —E. S. Turner, *Times Literary Supp.,* 20 Mar. 1987

alleged 1. *Alleged* is a fixture of both print and broadcast journalism. Its use is approved by Reader's Digest 1983 (in preference to *accused*). Other commentators accept its inevitability but point out that it is sometimes carelessly applied; they warn against such examples as "the alleged suspect."

> . . . is seeking three quarters of a million dollars in alleged libel damages —"Morning Edition," National Public Radio, 22 May 1986

Occasional careless use occurs outside straight reporting, too:

> This alleged account of sexual ambidexterity in high life —*Times Literary Supp.,* 18 Dec. 1969

We find that *alleged* is applied both to persons and to actions and things.

> . . . never compromised national security in his alleged computerized trespassing —Jose Martinez, *Boston Herald,* 24 Feb. 2000

> . . . has refused to cooperate with HUAC by naming names of alleged Communists —Patricia Bosworth, *Vanity Fair,* September 1999

One result of the frequency of the word in journalistic use has been the development of a humorous application:

> The only thing we could find was a bottle of alleged brandy —George S. Patton, Jr., *War as I Knew It,* 1947

> . . . a round tin of alleged pork and egg, ground up together and worked to a consistency like the inside of a sick lobster's claw —A. J. Liebling, *New Yorker,* 19 May 1956

2. When *alleged* is used as an adjective (as in "the alleged arsonist"), it is often pronounced as three syllables, though not as often as the adjective *learned* meaning "erudite" (as in "learned counsel") is pronounced as two. In the case of *learned,* the extra syllable helps to underscore the sharp difference in meaning between *learned* in "learned counsel" and *learned* in "learned and innate behavior patterns." By comparison, the semantic split between the adjective *alleged* and past participial uses of the verb *allege* is not so sharp, and the extra syllable is not as consistently used. Both pronunciations are acceptable, however.

all of Copperud 1970, 1980 reports "a morass of conflicting opinion" about the propriety of whether *all* should be followed by *of* where *of* is unnecessary, as in "All of the percussion instruments" (*American Mercury,* January 1935). Copperud goes on to say, "The point is hardly an important one, since the choice has no effect on meaning and is unlikely to be noticed by the reader."

Copperud is right. Since there is no practical importance to this question, it is a wonder that so many commentators bother with it. But bother with it they do, and they have been bothering with it since at least 1864. We can tell you this: *all of* is usual before a personal pronoun and is also common before an indefinite pronoun:

I do forgive thy rankest fault—all of them —Shakespeare, *The Tempest,* 1612

. . . her isolation . . . with this counselor—as all of us can foresee—is not going to be entirely clinical —Stanley Kauffmann, *New Republic,* 7 Feb. 2000

. . . all of whom fought to keep lavish spending for the program alive —Alan Brinkley, *N.Y. Times Book Rev.,* 16 Apr. 2000

All of which reveals a central truth —Ryan Lizza, *New Republic,* 3 Apr. 2000

. . . the capper to all this —Bruce Kluger, *Newsweek,* 31 Jan. 2000

Garner 1998 notes *all of* is preferable before a possessive noun, as in "all of Bob's money is gone." But this is preference; *of* can be omitted: "all Bob's money is gone." Occasionally a fixed phrase will require *all of*:

. . . but all of a sudden I just got mad —Elizabeth Berg, *The Pull of the Moon,* 1996

Before nouns *all* or *all of* may be used:

I got mad for all the times I've had these snobby people work on me and not see me —Elizabeth Berg, *The Pull of the Moon,* 1996

. . . you have all the time in the world to focus on looking drop-dead gorgeous —*Cosmopolitan,* June 2000

. . . writes at top volume almost all of the time —Adam Kirsch, *Atlantic,* July 2000

All of these yearbooks . . . were in Anglo-French —Peter M. Tiersma, *Legal Language,* 1999

I cannot remember, in all of my years, ever having the extreme displeasure of listening to an album as awful —Evgenia Peretz, *Vanity Fair,* September 2000

Except where idiom requires *of* you can use either *all* or *all of*—whichever sounds better in the sentence. It won't matter to the reader.

See also BOTH 4.

allow 1. From Vizetelly 1906 and Bierce 1909 to Garner 1998 critics make an issue of distinguishing between *allow* and *permit;* they say that *permit* is better for the giving of express consent or authorization and that *allow* is better where there is no objection or prevention. But writers do what seems best to them, and while some observe the distinction, others do not. Here are some examples of *allow* in its senses that are close to *permit.* Note that they are frequently found in negative contexts.

I tried to leave, but they wouldn't allow it —E. L. Doctorow, *Loon Lake,* 1979

The trial judge allowed testimony by the . . . officer —*Security World,* November 1969

She didn't allow stores to order specific patterns —Larissa MacFarquhar, *New Yorker,* 4 Sept. 2000

A South Carolina coastal development agency today refused to allow the construction of a private bridge to Sandy Island —Ronald Smothers, *N.Y. Times,* 13 Dec. 1995

The center's rules didn't allow children under 14 to train for that sensitive position —Susan Hauser, *People Weekly Extra,* Fall 1991

. . . the Kennedys would never have allowed her to act in the movies —Gore Vidal, *New Yorker,* 25 Oct. 1995

. . . rejected a referendum that would have allowed them to carry concealed weapons —Matt Bai, *Newsweek,* 2 Aug. 1999

2. The Dictionary of American Regional English lists four senses of *allow* with regional connections, some of which have come under attack as misuses, vulgarisms, or provincialisms. We will take them up in order of increasing complexity.

"To plan, intend" (DARE sense 4). The DARE labels this sense chiefly Southern and Midland. They cite examples from Mark Twain, Bret Harte, Edward Eggleston. In this sense, *allow* is regularly followed by *to* and the infinitive:

"I allowed to go back and help," Ellen said —Elizabeth Madox Roberts (born in Kentucky), *The Time of Man,* 1926

"To admit, concede" (DARE sense 3). This sense is mostly mainstream; it is not labeled in Webster's Third or in the OED. It has a considerable literary background:

Those were your words. . . . it was some time, I confess, before I was reasonable enough to allow their justice —Jane Austen, *Pride and Prejudice,* 1813

. . . I flatter myself, that it will be allowed that I, at least, am a moral man —W. M. Thackeray, *The Book of Snobs,* 1846

. . . one must allow that Pierre's promise of allegiance was kept —Henry Adams, *Mont-Saint-Michel and Chartres,* 1904

This sense continues to be used in mainstream English, usually followed by a clause:

He allowed that Erasmus was an instrument of God, but only up to a point —Hugh

Trevor-Roper, *Times Literary Supp.,* 12 Feb. 1993

Epstein allows that the priest was on the right track —*Time,* 14 Mar. 1955

Do ordinary people have more sense than professionals ordinarily allow? —*Nature,* 20 Sept. 1969

We must . . . allow that economic pressure in itself can be generally disruptive —Elizabeth Janeway, *Atlantic,* March 1970

The DARE remarks that its senses 1 ("to suppose, think, consider") and 2 ("to assert, remark, opine, declare") are often hard to distinguish; some books, like the OED and Reader's Digest 1983, do not try to distinguish them. Sense 1 is marked chiefly Southern and Midland; 2 is not labeled, indicating widespread dialectal use.

But the verb is frequently used as if the person speaking has an opinion and is expressing it, combining the two DARE senses. This use of *allow* is seeing increased use in general prose—that is, books, magazines, and newspapers intended for a general rather than a local readership. It is most often followed by a clause introduced by *that*:

They allowed that she would be shaken for a time by their divorce —Barbara S. Cain, *N.Y. Times Mag.,* 18 Feb. 1990

He allowed that "yes, I do have a very good time doing it" —John McPhee, quoted by Philip Shabecoff, *N.Y. Times Book Rev.,* 6 Aug. 1989

All allowed that they liked it all right —John Fischer, *Harper's,* November 1972

. . . the manual allowed that about a third of affected kids continued to show signs in adulthood —Anne Glusker, *Washington Post Mag.,* 30 Mar. 1997

I allowed that . . . I found the future boring, the present pleasant, and the past best of all —Joseph Epstein, *The Middle of My Tether,* 1983

He allowed that he was a musical ignoramus but his wife . . . could play anything —John Updike, *New Yorker,* 26 Dec. 1988

Reader's Digest 1983 quotes William Safire using the folksier conjunction *as how*:

Nixon allowed as how the best way to knock Romney down in the polls was to remove his winner status by beating him in New Hampshire —*Before the Fall*

The conjunction turns out to be quite commonly used:

. . . he allowed as how he was laboring under some kind of ailment —Bryan Di Salvatore, *New Yorker,* 12 Feb. 1990

Later Sam allowed as how he meant the media had barely laid a glove on the Great Communicator through 37 minutes and 25 questions —Hugh Sidey, *Time,* 30 Sept. 1985

Mr. Price allowed as how he, too, was available for help —Lorene Cary, *Black Ice,* 1991

. . . he allowed as how he appreciated my taste in art —Barbara Goldsmith, *Architectural Digest,* November 1989

The senses of *allow* that are not regionally limited seem to be a sign that general prose is more informal than it used to be. We can find *allow* "concede" in very serious writing:

It is allowed that Hegel may have propounded individual doctrines which could be of some interest: in aesthetics, in political philosophy, perhaps even in philosophy of religion —*Times Literary Supp.,* 19 June 1969

But *allow* "state as an opinion or concession" especially with *as how* tends to be found in informal surroundings.

See also AS HOW.

all ready, already The distinction between *all ready* and *already* no longer needs explanation except perhaps for school children. It is primarily a spelling problem now, one only rarely muffed by grown-ups:

A few of these have been sold for breeding purposes all ready —*Holstein-Friesian World,* 1 Mar. 1952

All ready is two words. When they occur together as a fixed phrase rather than a coincidence (as in "We are all ready to leave"), they mean *ready, all* is merely an intensive. The phrase exists chiefly in speech, and is seldom to be found in edited prose except transcribed speech. It is therefore seldom a problem.

Already is an adverb. It is used in sentences like this:

The train had already left when we got to the station —Corder 1981

all right See ALRIGHT, ALL RIGHT.

all-round See ALL-AROUND, ALL-ROUND.

all that The usage in question here is simply the adverbial *that* (see THAT 5) with the intensifier *all* added to it; it is almost always found in negative constructions:

Scarlet runners are huge—well, huge for beans—so you don't have to peel all that many —Leslie Land, *Yankee,* March 1999

. . . urban life has not changed all that much —Wilborn Hampton, *N.Y. Times,* 17 May 1998

A number of critics, from the 1960s to the 1980s, found fault with the expression; some even disputed whether it was a Briticism or an Americanism. Such disagreement means that *not all that* is common on both sides of the Atlantic.

A large tomcat came along the gutter and found a fish head; he spurred it once or twice with his claws and then moved on: he wasn't all that hungry —Graham Greene, *The Confidential Agent,* 1939

He likes to act country, but he don't have all that far to go—he *is* country —Eudora Welty, *The Ponder Heart,* 1954

. . . anything that it takes a computer to work out is not going to be checked all that quickly —*Times Literary Supp.,* 8 Sept. 1966

It was not that he would find life there dangerous or even, at the time, all that expensive —John Kenneth Galbraith, *New York,* 15 Nov. 1971

I know that Canadian films are not all that popular —Greg Preece, letter to the editor, *Entertainment Weekly,* 16 Oct. 1998

There is not all that much work by the young British artists . . . in the initial installation at Tate Modern —Jed Perl, *New Republic,* 19 June 2000

. . . but Latin American cuisine isn't all that strange to North American tastes —Jerry Adler, *Newsweek,* 7 June 1999

This is established as standard; Burchfield 1996 concurs.

all the   1. *All the* plus a comparative adverb (or sometimes adjective) is an English idiom that occurs in standard written English; in it *all the* functions as a simple intensifier:

. . . the omission found by me was an all the deadlier record of poor Soames' failure to impress himself on his decade —Max Beerbohm, *Seven Men,* 1920

. . . hating their clean white shiny faces and loving the Johnsons all the more —Morley Callaghan, *The Loved and the Lost,* 1951

That makes it all the more reprehensible that governments have dragged their feet —Katha Pollitt, *The Nation,* 26 June 2000

All the more reason to press on —Robert Lipsyte, *N.Y. Times,* 9 May 1999

. . . even James Joyce said she'd be all the better for a spot of correction —Eric Korn, *Times Literary Supp.,* 5 Sept. 1997

2. *All the* followed by a comparative (as in "that's all the farther I can go") and meaning "as . . . as" belongs to the spoken language. Surveys made for the Dictionary of American Regional English found the construction in 40 of the 50 states, but it is especially common in inland Northern and North Midland speech. Followed by an uninflected adjective it occurs in Midland and South Midland areas.

That's all the fast this horse can run. (DARE)

all together, altogether   Copperud 1970, 1980 warns us that these expressions are often confused: a score of books or more from 1907 to the present warn us not to confuse them.

The problem is perhaps exacerbated by the sense of the adverb *altogether* that means "in all, in sum, in toto":

Altogether, about 1,500 insects died in the Harvard laboratories —Isaac Asimov, *Think,* May–June 1967

. . . altogether she has recorded twelve discs for this label —*Current Biography,* June 1967

This sense is sometimes converted to *all together*:

Kazanski batted in five runs all together —*N.Y. Times,* 9 Aug. 1956 (cited in *Winners & Sinners* 15 Aug. 1956)

It is, however, the opposite error that the handbooks seem mostly interested in. The OED Supplement takes notice, with examples from 1765 to 1930. The Merriam-Webster files contain a few examples too:

Put it altogether, and it added up to a tragic Labor Day weekend —*Deerfield* (Wisc.) *Independent,* 2 Sept. 1954

. . . designs these three pieces with enough panache to be worn with basic black, or altogether as an ensemble —*Boston Proper Catalog,* Spring/Summer 1982

These should have been written *all together*.

all told   Bernstein 1965, who is perhaps more aware of etymology than most of us, is alone in objecting to the use of this phrase when enumeration is not involved. The phrase is derived from the sense of *tell* that means "count." But the phrase is used in general summation too; Burchfield 1996 notes this as standard. Here are a couple of examples of each kind of summation. The numerical is more frequent:

All told, half of the eight . . . lost money in '99 —Margaret Boitano, *Fortune,* 21 Feb. 2000

All told, the cost of modifying systems in Europe . . . will run between $150 billion and $400 billion —Alden M. Hayashi, *Scientific American,* August 1998

. . . but all told an incredibly compelling expression of American vigor —*Ski,* October 1994

All told, a bad and boring book —Joseph W. Bishop, *Trans-Action,* February 1970

allude   **1.** *Allude* is a 16th-century word that was used in many senses in its early years, but by the end of the 17th century many of these had dropped out of literary use (literary use is the chief medium through which we know the language of the past). The senses that have survived are all close in meaning to *refer;* the reference could be (to quote Burchfield 1996) "ambiguously direct or indirect or just plainly direct." The plainly direct use, which began in the 1580s, began to draw critical fire as a misuse in the 1860s. The first seems to have been Alford 1866, who found the "new" use in journals and in the prose of a post office official. Had he thought to look in older literature he would have discovered that the use was not so new, but he did not. Neither have most of the usage writers following Alford, some of whom are still dancing to the 1866 tune at the beginning of the 21st century. To put it as plainly as possible: *allude* has not been restricted to indirect reference since the latter part of the 16th century, and it is not now so restricted.

What we have in reality is a word with three interrelated uses—indirect, ambiguously direct, and direct—that can shade into one another imperceptibly. Here is a selection of examples from the past two centuries:

> She alluded once or twice to her husband but her tone was not such as to make the allusion a warning —James Joyce, *Dubliners,* 1914

> Hazlitt has written a *grammar* for Godwin; Godwin sells it bound up with a treatise of his own on language, but the *grey mare is the better horse.* I don't allude to Mrs. Godwin, but to the word *grammar* —Charles Lamb, letter, 2 Jan. 1810

> He never alluded so directly to his story again —E. E. Hale, *The Man Without A Country,* 1863

> . . . that intense mental collectedness and concentration to which I have previously alluded as observable only in particular moments —Edgar Allan Poe, "The Fall of the House of Usher," 1839

> "Wait Till Next Year" is a revisionist "Memories of a Catholic Girlhood" (Goodwin explicitly alluded to Mary McCarthy's book in a subtitle she later discarded, "Recollections of a 50's Girlhood") —Ann Hulbert, *N.Y. Times Book Rev.,* 26 Oct. 1997

> Adams had alluded to slavery in 1816, when he confided to Jefferson that "there will be greater difficulties to preserve our Union, than You and I, our Fathers Brothers Friends Disciples and Sons have had to form it" —Joseph J. Ellis, *American Heritage,* May/June 1993

> At one of the plenary sessions, Churchill alluded obliquely to his idea —*New Statesman & Nation,* 19 Dec. 1953

> As alluded to previously, the entire universe may actually exist in a higher-dimensional space —Clifford A. Pickover, *Surfing Through Hyperspace,* 1999

> . . . proposals, which were never called proposals, but always alluded to slightingly as innovations —Compton Mackenzie, *The Parson's Progress,* 1923

> At the same time, she's also alluded to . . . as just plain Hillary —Richard Goldstein, *Village Voice,* 12 Apr. 1994

> The more challenging problems, in fact— ones that the optimists rarely allude to—will be the problems of success —Charles R. Morris, *Atlantic,* October 1989

> . . . the records of the colony allude to beer as one of its commodities —*Dictionary of American History,* 1940

> . . . serves as a kind of fable, to which the rest of the novel will repeatedly allude in one way or another —*Times Literary Supp.,* 7 Nov. 1968

> . . . Mr. Greenspan alluded to the wealth effect when he remarked upon the "expanding net worth of households relative to income" —Gretchen Morgenson, *N.Y. Times,* 17 Nov. 1999

By now you will have a good enough sense of how *allude* is actually used to be able to ignore with safety the blinkered directions of the handbooks.

2. *Allude, elude.* MacCracken & Sandison 1917 warn against confusing *allude* and *elude.* The verbs sound about the same, but differ considerably in meaning, as a glance at your dictionary will demonstrate. We do have evidence that they are occasionally confused:

> To peek between the covers means to be confronted by a reality designed ever to allude me —Karen Sandstrom, *Plain Dealer* (Cleveland, Ohio), 15 Dec. 1996

If you are doubtful, get out that dictionary.

allusion   Fowler 1926 and a few other commentators discuss their disapproval of the sense development of *allude* under this heading. See ALLUDE 1.

ally *Ally* is used about equally with *to* or *with* when it requires a preposition:

> Closely allied to his pride was his very strict sense of justice —Robert A. Hall, Jr., *A Short History of Italian Literature,* 1951

> Allied to this general problem is the need in many cases to retrain teachers —James B. Conant, *Slums and Suburbs,* 1961

> It is to ally you with the events of the page —Bernard DeVoto, *The World of Fiction,* 1950

> John Dewey and Thorstein Veblen were allied in his mind with the Chicago sociologist George Herbert Mead —Alfred Kazin, *N.Y. Times Book Rev.,* 16 Sept. 1979

Our files show that when *ally* is used with *to,* the verb is usually in the past tense or in the past participle; when *ally* is used with *with,* a greater variety of tenses appears.

Ally is also used with *against* sometimes:

> . . . the great resources and wealth of the Arab states should be allied against the temptations . . . of godless communism —David L. Lawrence, *Land Reborn,* November–December 1953

almost 1. See MOST, ALMOST.
2. Copperud 1970, 1980 and Johnson 1982 object to *almost* before comparatives like *more, less,* and *better* on the grounds that it violates logic. The logic must be their own, because *almost more* appears in standard sources:

> To moosh is to shove in the face, and is almost more demeaning than a slap —Marcus Laffey, *New Yorker,* 10 Aug. 1998

> . . . in a purple satin dress and sequin mittens, the ultimate effect almost more exotic than if she had remained in the costume of the play —Anthony Powell, *Casanova's Chinese Restaurant,* 1960

> The near unanimity among reviewers in heaping execrations on the Whitney Museum of American Art for its Biennial exhibition . . . is almost more dispiriting than the exhibition itself —James Bowman, *Times Literary Supp.,* 2 Apr. 1993

At the present time we have no evidence for *almost less* and almost none for *almost better.*

alone From Ayres 1881 to Jensen 1935 a modest amount of objection was entered to *alone* meaning "only," as in

> It is written, That man shall not live by bread alone —Luke 4:4 (AV), 1611

Jensen explains that the sense is not current; but in fact the sense was current in the 19th century when Ayres wrote, and is still current in edited standard prose:

> He alone lynches in cold blood —G. Legman, *Love and Death,* 1949

> . . . not all of whom had their minds on baseball alone —Al Hirshberg, quoted in *Current Biography,* March 1965

> . . . decided that fur trading alone would never make New Netherland a proper colony —Samuel Eliot Morison, *Oxford History of the American People,* 1965

Burchfield 1996 points out that *alone* correlated with *but* has dropped out of use, but has remained alive in other constructions, as the examples above show.

alongside of, alongside Longman 1984 tells us *alongside of* is widely disliked, but little evidence of widespread dislike has reached our files. The Oxford American Dictionary, Shaw 1962, Harper 1975, 1985, and Garner 1998 mention it. It is perfectly proper, and historically antecedent to the single word preposition, *alongside,* recommended by the commentators. The adverb *alongside* came first, was then used as a preposition with *of,* and later the *of* was dropped. (For a counter case where the commentators object to dropping *of,* see COUPLE, *adjective.*) Burchfield 1996 says that both *alongside* and *alongside of* are in reputable use.

Our files show that *alongside* has been more frequently used in the modern era than *alongside of,* and that *alongside* is much more common in our most recent evidence. Our evidence also suggests that figurative use is at least as common as the literal use that refers to physical position. We will give you a sampling of uses of *alongside of* and then a few examples of the single-word preposition.

> Alongside of your last letter a day or two ago came a dear little note from your daughter —Oliver Wendell Holmes d. 1935, letter, 5 Nov. 1923

> . . . now engaged alongside of us in the battle —Dwight D. Eisenhower, *Britain To-Day,* September 1944

> They also use them alongside of the ideograms —Mario Pei, *The Story of Language,* 1949

> . . . postulate a second substance whose essence is thought, alongside of body —Noam Chomsky, *Columbia Forum,* Spring 1968

> This work had to be carried forward alongside the first —Harry S. Truman, State of the Union Address, 7 Jan. 1953

> Should it, in a draft . . . , have been published alongside the flawless final writing of *The Great Gatsby?* —James Thurber, *New Republic,* 22 Nov. 1954

. . . bring the launch alongside the Lamb Island dock —Daphne du Maurier, *Ladies' Home Jour.,* September 1971

Did the novel grow out of the critical study, or alongside it . . . ? —J. M. Cocking, *Times Literary Supp.,* 21 May 1982

. . . ever since she graduated (alongside Nancy Davis Reagan) from Smith College —William F. Buckley, Jr., *New Yorker,* 31 Jan. 1983

aloof The usual preposition following *aloof* is *from*:

. . . morbidly aloof from reality —William Styron, *Lie Down in Darkness,* 1951

I felt curiously aloof from my own self —Vladimir Nabokov, *Lolita,* 1958

. . . remain resolutely aloof from the Vietnam war —Norman Cousins, *Saturday Rev.,* 28 June 1975

Occasionally *to* is used:

. . . the United States remained coldly aloof to the suggestion —*Collier's Year Book,* 1949

. . . respectful but aloof to Marx, Engels, and Lenin —Lucien Price, *Dialogues of Alfred North Whitehead,* 1954

Other prepositions may be used to indicate somewhat different relationships:

He is terse, cool-headed in a crisis, inclined to be aloof with strangers —Tris Coffin, *Nation's Business,* April 1954

. . . holding herself aloof in chosen loneliness of passion —Paul Elmer More, *Selected Shelburne Essays,* 1921

alot, a lot *A lot* is apparently often written as one word—perhaps by people in a hurry—for we have numerous handbooks reminding their readers to write it as two words. Two words is the accepted norm:

Each of these writers had plainly worried about my Nat Turner a lot —William Styron, *This Quiet Dust and Other Writings,* 1982

The Kremlin must be a lot like this —Jay McInerney, *Bright Lights, Big City,* 1984

Our evidence for the one-word spelling *alot* comes mostly from memos, drafts, and private letters. It occasionally sees the light of day in newspapers where proofreading has not been careful enough:

"When I was in junior, I was on the power-play alot," Turgeon said —*Springfield* (Mass.) *Morning Union,* 3 Nov. 1983

See also LOTS, A LOT.

aloud See OUT LOUD.

already See ALL READY, ALREADY.

alright, all right Is *alright* all right? The answer is a qualified yes, with these cautions. First, *all right* is much more common in print than *alright.* Second, many people, including the authors of just about every writer's handbook, think *alright* is all wrong. Third, *alright* is more likely to be found in print in comic strips (like "Doonesbury"), trade journals, and newspapers and magazines than in more literary sources.

The one-word spelling first turns up around the end of the 19th century (the two-word adjective dates to the 18th century and the adverb to the early 19th).

The general was civil enough to him, and she was alright to mother —Edith Somerville, letter, 2 June 1887

Soon it would appear in print:

I think I shall pass alright —*Durham University Jour.,* November 1893 (OED Supplement)

Alright did not appear in a Merriam-Webster dictionary until 1934, but several dictionary users had spotted its omission earlier and had written to us to urge its inclusion. The earliest of these were businessmen who preferred the one-word form in order to save telegraph and cable charges.

Another influence on the use of the one-word form is analogy: words like *altogether, already,* and *although* had been formed as two words but had come into modern English as solid words. When *alright* came to be a matter of dispute, many commentators recognized the force of analogy and then had to devise reasons to deny its applicability.

The controversy over *alright* began as early as 1909 but received most of its impetus from Fowler 1926. After that nearly all usage commentators fall into line. We have recorded forty or so commentators, both British and American, expressing disapproval; only one or two dissent. It should be noted, however, that the usual way of disapproving *alright* is to append a pejorative label (as *illiterate* or *colloquial*) to it or to deny it exists; no very cogent reasons are presented for its being considered wrong.

Even the critics of *alright* admit it is found more often in manuscript than in print; undoubtedly it would be even more frequent in print than it is if copy editors were less hostile. Our evidence shows that it is used in letters, real and fictional:

He's alright, though —Fred Allen, letter, 10 Dec. 1931

. . . and strangely one thinks of her as coming together alright —Robert Graves, undated letter

Yes, I did get your letter alright —Margaret Kennedy, *The Feast*, 1950

He told Regina that he had told me and she said that was alright —Flannery O'Connor, letter, July 1952

One of the points involved in the discussion of *alright* hinges on the assertion that *all right* represents one stress pattern in speech, and *alright* another. Evans 1962 alludes to this point when he says, "My own—dissenting—opinion is that most people who write *alright* instead of *all right* (when they mean "alright" and not "all right") are not slovenly. They are simply asking for the privilege of making a distinction in writing which is accepted in speech." This argument is difficult to evaluate because stress patterns are observable only in speech, whereas *alright* is purely a spelling variant. But it may be relevant that when *alright* is used in fiction, it is very often used in representing the speech of the characters:

"My briefing alright, First Sergeant?" —Josiah Bunting, *The Lionheads*, 1972

"Alright, which one of you guys shot him. . . ." —W. P. Kinsella, *The Moccasin Telegraph and Other Stories*, 1985

". . . It's goin' to be alright. . . ." —Waldo Frank, *Not Heaven*, 1953

"Alright, wait a minute," —Langston Hughes, *Laughing to Keep from Crying*, 1952

Alright, already! I'll turn on the grill! —Gary B. Trudeau, *Guilty, Guilty, Guilty*, 1973

It appears in Molly Bloom's soliloquy:

. . . however alright well seen then let him go to her —James Joyce, *Ulysses*, 1922

It is also used in other transcribed speech.

"I'm alright!" Donny shouts from the wings —John Lahr, *New Yorker*, 1 Aug. 1994

"It's alright now, they've gone for milking" —a farmer quoted by Roger A. Redfern, *Manchester Guardian Weekly*, 6 Sept. 1992

. . . so let's look at Bittman. Bittman says he is trying to blackmail the White House. Alright you called Bittman —Richard M. Nixon, in *The White House Transcripts*, 1974

"Okay honey, I've ironed your blue ensemble if that's alright. . . ." —Jim Guzzo, *Springfield* (Mass.) *Republican*, 30 Dec. 1984

And it turns up in the titles of songs like "Don't Think Twice It's Alright" and "It's Alright with Me." Other titles, too, such as "The Kids Are Alright," a 1979 British-made TV movie.

From the beginning *alright* seems to have reached print primarily in journalistic and business publications. We have plenty of evidence that it continues to appear in these publications:

There's plenty of luxury here alright —*Variety*, 28 Jan. 1942

The first batch of aquatic ovines will get by alright —T. J. McManus, *Tasmanian Jour. of Agriculture*, May 1962

And that's alright —Richard Gehr, *Village Voice*, 15 Mar. 1994

. . . came out alright in the end —*National Jeweler*, January 1942

Berkeley is a weird city, alright —Ralph J. Gleason, *Rolling Stone*, 13 May 1971

. . . why the kids aren't alright —Mike Flaherty, *Entertainment Weekly*, 5 Nov. 1999

We got through it alright —Avery Corman, *Cosmopolitan*, October 1974

Alright, it might be fun to hunt tigers —*Newsweek*, 20 Oct. 1986

Gutenberg's movable type was alright for the middle ages —*British Printer*, February 1976

If I just acted OK, I'd feel alright —Joyce Maynard, *Parenting*, September 1995

Finally, we have a little evidence from books where speech is not being re-created.

Men don't want a woman to wilt on them. That was alright in Mother's time —Vivian Ellis, *Faint Harmony*, 1934

The first two years of the medical school were alright —Gertrude Stein, *The Autobiography of Alice B. Toklas*, 1933

Trying to decide if it is alright to say *anxious* when you mean *eager* —Quinn 1980

Summary: in its modern use *alright* has reached print primarily through journalistic and business publication and is still to be found in those sources. It has appeared now and again in literature, at least from the mid-1920s, though mostly in fictional dialogue. It is more often to be found in manuscript than in print; it would likely be much more nearly as frequent as *all right* if it were not so regularly suppressed by copy editors. It seems to have some acceptance in British English; the OED Supplement calls it simply "a frequent spelling of *all right*." It remains a commonly written but less often printed variant of *all right*. It is clearly standard in general prose, but is widely condemned nonetheless by writers on usage.

also   This word raises two related problems for usage commentators.

First we have the matter of *also* used as a loose connective roughly equivalent to *and*. This problem was first mentioned in Fowler 1907, where Richard Grant White and a couple of others were shown using the conjunctive *also*:

> 'Special' is a much overworked word, it being used to mean great in degree, also peculiar in kind —*Words and their Uses,* 1870

Since 1907 this construction has picked up considerable unfavorable notice, especially in handbooks. Criticism is strongest when the elements joined by *also* are words or phrases (as in the example from White), but some commentators extend it to the joining of clauses. The curious thing is that no one since 1907 has an attributed example to bring forward. The question is, then, who uses this construction, and where? The college handbooks suggest it turns up in student papers, and it apparently occurs in speech—Reader's Digest 1983 finds it acceptable in speech and most of the handbooks disapprove it only in writing. Margaret M. Bryant says in *English in the Law Courts* (1930) that it is common in speech. Her examples show it to have been common also in 19th-century American wills. It continues to occur in wills, and judges are still having to decide what *also* means in disputed cases.

It can also be found in literature and general published prose:

> . . . these are the only eels I have heard of here;—also, I have a faint recollection of a little fish some five inches long, with silvery sides and a greenish back —Henry David Thoreau, *Walden,* 1854

> Accompanying it were two accessories, also bits of pottery —Herman Melville, *The Confidence Man,* 1857

> . . . and they occasionally go to galleries together; also Mitterand fancies old books, and occasionally they browse together in bookshops —John Newhouse, *New Yorker,* 30 Dec. 1985

Our examples are not numerous, however, so it is hard to be sure just how common this use is outside of speech and student papers.

The handbooks' approach to the conjunctive *also* is to recommend conversion to *and* or *and also*. (Some commentators call *and also* redundant.) *And also* is common in all kinds of writing:

> By October of 1983, the CNN Headline News Service . . . was going out to six hundred and seventy-five cable systems, . . . and

also to a hundred and forty-three commercial television stations —Thomas Whiteside, *New Yorker,* 3 June 1985

> . . . a lifelong favorite of Borges and also frequently alluded to —Ambrose Gordon, Jr., *Jour. of Modern Literature,* 1st issue, 1970

> . . . a devout empiricist and also something of a visionary —Sam Tanenhaus, *Vanity Fair,* November 1999

> . . . slices of liver and also of kidney —*Annual Rev. of Biochemistry,* 1946

As mentioned earlier, Reader's Digest 1983 finds the conjunctive *also* acceptable in speech and informal writing, but would avoid it in formal writing. The rest tend to disapprove it in writing, period, although Fowler 1926 will allow it when the writer needs to emphasize that what follows is an afterthought. Our unabundant evidence for its use strongly suggests that we have here much ado over very little.

The second problem involves beginning a sentence with *also*. Several commentators suggest avoiding *also* at the beginning of a sentence. Bernstein 1971 allows some sentences to begin with *also*; his example turns out to be an inverted sentence of a kind also approved by the other commentators. Two examples:

> Also accurately interpreted are logos —*Editor & Publisher,* 10 Apr. 2000

> Also old are the words from Old English and Middle English —W. F. Bolton, *A Short History of Literary English,* 1967

Many of the sentences beginning with *also* in our files are of the straightforward type the commentators seem to disapprove:

> Also, at the mouth of the Nile, fish in the Mediterranean used to feed on organisms conveyed by the silt —William Styron, *This Quiet Dust and Other Writings,* 1982

> Also, certain even-numbered groups of protons and neutrons are particularly stable —*Current Biography,* June 1964

> Also, it was in itself, as I have said, a period of depressed spirits —Sacheverell Sitwell, *All Summer in a Day,* 1926

> Also, during the summer, so-called interim disciplinary rules were promulgated —Sylvan Fox, *N.Y. Times,* 9 Jan. 1969

The objections to this use of *also* are not usually stated clearly; it is simply described as "weak." The objection seems about as soundly based as the widely believed notion that you should never begin a sentence with *and.* Our evidence agrees with the statement in Perrin & Ebbitt that *also* usually stands within the sentence. But some writers do use it as an opener, and you can too, when you think it appropriate.

alternate, *verb* Bernstein 1965 tells us this verb takes *with*, but that is only half the story. One person or one thing may alternate *with* another or others; one person or thing may alternate *between* (usually) two things.

Some examples of *with*:

The plan enabled Robertson to alternate seven weeks of study with seven weeks of work —*Current Biography,* January 1966

Basso Norman Scott, who this season alternates with Moscona and three others in the part —*Time,* 28 Mar. 1955

. . . dark green alternating with light green stripes, bluish green, bluish or yellowish gray, light cream, yellowish brown, etc. —Jane Nickerson, *N.Y. Times Mag.,* 4 July 1954

Some examples of *between*:

The reader alternates between admiration . . . and irritation —*Times Literary Supp.,* 5 Mar. 1970

. . . alternating perpetually between physical and mental activity —Agnes Repplier, *The Fireside Sphinx,* 1901

The weather alternated between blinding sand-storms and brilliant sunlight —Willa Cather, *Death Comes for the Archbishop,* 1927

. . . the rest of the spectators continued to alternate between maddening immobility and creeping movement —Irving Wallace, *The Plot,* 1967

We have one citation with *among*, which may be a copy editor's doing:

. . . the author alternates among mod slang, clichés and quotes from literary giants —Albert H. Johnston, *Publishers Weekly,* 24 July 1978

alternate, alternative, *adjectives* The adjectives *alternate* and *alternative,* say many commentators, are often confused; they advise keeping them separate. The senses recommended are "occurring or succeeding by turns" for *alternate,* and "offering or expressing a choice" for *alternative.*

First, let's look at the use of *alternative* where *alternate* might be expected. This use seems to be the oldest sense of the adjective *alternative,* attested in 1540. Robert Herrick used it in a poem:

That Happines do's still the longest thrive
Where Joye and Griefs have Turns Alternative.
—*Hesperides,* 1648

This sense of the adjective is now quite rare, and it survives chiefly in the form of its derived adverb:

In one hand she held a peeled hard-boiled egg and a thick slice of bread and butter in the other, and between her sentences she bit at them alternatively —Aldous Huxley, *Antic Hay,* 1923

There are two courses open to them, which can be taken alternatively, sequentially or together —Margaret Mead, *Saturday Evening Post,* 3 Mar. 1962

The second use—that of *alternate* where *alternative* might be expected—is hard to trace. The OED marks the sense obsolete, citing only Robert Greene (1590). But it seems to have had a revival in the second third of the 20th century. Our earliest citations for this revival do not, unfortunately, include much in the way of context; they supply more in the way of opinion than information. The revival was not strictly an American phenomenon; Gowers 1948 complains of its occurrence in official British writing.

American citations begin to show up in some numbers in the 1940s and early 1950s. Among these there are three new uses where *alternative* had not been (and would not be) used—book clubs:

His *Collected Stories,* a Book-of-the-Month Club alternate selection —*Time,* 18 Dec. 1950

politics:

. . . was named alternate United States delegate to the fifth General Assembly of the United Nations —*Current Biography 1950*

and highways:

. . . an alternate route, built by the Federal Government in 1932 —*American Guide Series: Virginia,* 1941

These three uses continue to the present, with no competition from *alternative,* at least in American usage.

More general uses also appeared about the same time:

Right now, the U.N. weighs the advantage of having Russia at its conference table against the alternate advantage of having a set of basic principles on which members are agreed —*New Yorker,* 31 Mar. 1951

Early copper shortages stimulated manufacturers to investigate alumnium as an alternate material —*Bulletin, American Institute of Architects,* March 1952

But they found an alternate, and very free-trade, way of expressing themselves—the smuggling of opium —Christopher Rand, *New Yorker,* 29 Mar. 1952

Such uses as these, from much the same kinds of sources, continue unabated in current use, at least in the U.S. In addition, the antiestablishment use of the 1960s—alternative schools and the like—is expressed by both adjectives.

If we limit ourselves to the senses commented upon, we may point out that both adjectives appear to be losing ground to their relatives. *Alternative* is becoming more and more a noun, and *alternate* is being pushed aside by the verb *alternate* and its participle *alternating.*

alternative, *noun*   Garner 1998 notes that etymological purists have argued that *alternative* should be confined to contexts involving two choices. The writing of usage commentators shows that such a limitation is not observed:

> . . . two or more alternatives —Longman 1984

> . . . the number of alternatives should be definite —Bryson 1984

> . . . anyone who doesn't like the other alternatives —Reader's Digest 1983

Copperud 1970, 1980 says "The idea that *alternative* may apply to a choice between two and no more is a pedantry." Howard 1980 and Gowers in Fowler 1965 call it "a fetish."

alternatively, alternately   See ALTERNATE, ALTERNATIVE, *adjectives.*

altho   Garner 1998 notes that *altho* is an old-fashioned truncated spelling. The spelling was one of those simplified spellings urged on the public by spelling reformers (see SPELLING REFORM). It may still be common in personal communications, but its use in print pretty much died out by the 1950s. People who write for publication use *although* nowadays.

although, though   Although these conjunctions have been essentially interchangeable since about 1400 (according to the OED), usage books seldom fail to include them, apparently because people keep wondering whether one or the other is preferable. And no matter how much detail a study might contain, the results always come out the same: the conjunctions are interchangeable. *Though* is more frequently used than *although,* perhaps because it is shorter. Assertions of delicate shades of difference in formality made by some commentators cannot be confirmed by the citations in Merriam-Webster files. The difference seems merely to be a matter of personal choice.

Though is used as an adverb; *although* is not.

> A fine book though —W. H. Auden, *N.Y. Rev. of Books,* 27 Jan. 1972

altogether   See ALL TOGETHER, ALTOGETHER.

alum   See ALUMNUS, ALUMNA.

alumnus, alumna   1. As any dictionary will tell you, *alumna* is pluralized *alumnae; alumnus* is pluralized *alumni.* These words have not developed English plurals. *Alumna* is used for female graduates and *alumnus* for males, although it is sometimes used also of women. *Alumni* is the form usually used for a mixed bag of graduates of both sexes. Janis 1984 points out that the clipped form *alum* is available to those who feel that *alumni* is not sufficiently asexual:

> . . . second-guessing from undergrads and die-hard alums —Edwin McDowell, *Wall Street Jour.,* 5 Dec. 1972

> . . . join the 951 alums who have put, or are planning to put, Randolph-Macon in their wills —Carolyn Morrison Barton, *Randolph-Macon Woman's College Alumnae Bulletin,* Winter 1971

Alumnus is also used for a former member, employee, inmate, or contributor of any of a number of institutions:

> In fact, I still get the 69th Division alumni bulletin or whatever it's called —Frank Mankiewicz, quoted in *The Washingtonian,* October 1978

> . . . *Saturday Night Live* alumnus Michael O'Donoghue —Timothy White, *Rolling Stone* 24 July 1980

Alumna is not unknown in this use, but is fairly rare:

> . . . another debutante, albeit a Lee Strasberg alumna, whose Cecilia is teary-eyed vapidity —Judith Crist, *Saturday Rev.,* 11 Dec. 1976

2. The use of *alumni* as a singular is disapproved by various commentators. About our only genuine evidence of straightforward use is from speech:

> . . . another UCLA alumni —Frank Gifford, football telecast, 12 Nov. 1984

It has also been used facetiously:

> As a loyal alumni, you'll be aghast to know that the head football coach has to get by on just $96,000 a year —Jeff Millar & Bill Hinds, "Tank McNamara" (cartoon), *Boston Globe* 24 Jan. 1982

a.m., p.m.   These abbreviations are usually used with the hour as a short substitute for "before noon" and "after noon" (or whatever phrase you may use for the same idea). Copperud 1970 tells us that he and Evans 1957 agree that expressions like "6 a.m. in the morning" are redundant; our files show little evidence of such expressions, a fact which may mean that they exist mainly in speech.

amalgam *Amalgam* in its nontechnical senses takes *of* when it needs a preposition:

> . . . synthetic new genres that are amalgams of the old —Peter Winn, *N.Y. Times Book Rev.,* 10 June 1979

> The average reader imagines him as a rather Byronic, darkly brooding individual, an amalgam of Baudelaire, Robinson Jeffers, and MacKinlay Kantor —S. J. Perelman, *New Yorker,* 1 Jan. 1972

> . . . the British Walker Cup team, traditionally an amalgam of the top amateurs from England, Scotland, Wales, and Ireland —Herbert Warren Wind, *New Yorker,* 10 Apr. 1971

amalgamate When *amalgamate,* in its nontechnical uses, requires a preposition, *into* and *with* are used:

> Indian, African, and Portuguese ingredients and cooking techniques began to amalgamate into the rich Brazilian cuisine of today —Elizabeth Lambert Ortiz, *Gourmet,* October 1975

> Dirac amalgamated the varied equations into one —*Current Biography,* October 1967

> . . . the Workers' Union was amalgamated with it —*Current Biography 1948*

> . . . a chance to size me up, test me out by my reaction to his sallies, amalgamate me with his previous audience —Edmund Wilson, *Memoirs of Hecate County,* 1946

amateur Bernstein 1965 presents us with the choice of *of, in,* or (sometimes) *at* for a preposition with which to follow the noun *amateur.* Our files indicate that *of* and *at* are most frequently used. Some of *of*'s use can be accounted for by its being the only preposition used when *amateur* is used in its earliest sense—"devotee, admirer"—or in a use close to that meaning:

> "No, seriously," he said, in his quality of an amateur of dogs —Arnold Bennett, *The Old Wives' Tale,* 1908

> They are *amateurs* of Horace in the best sense of that word —Edward Townsend Booth, *Saturday Rev.,* 4 Oct. 1947

> As all amateurs of marzipan must agree —*New Yorker,* 8 Dec. 1956

> He was an amateur of gadgets, but he was not even an engineer on the model of Watt or Fulton —O. B. Hardison, Jr., *Entering the Maze,* 1981

When used in the sense of "one not a professional," *amateur* followed by *of* tends to have a bookish tang that probably favors its selection in such contexts:

> . . . edition of Donne is intended, I expect, for the university student and the advanced amateur of English letters —D. C. Allen, *Modern Language Notes,* May 1957

> . . . I must co-opt for our profession one or two amateurs of the discipline —John Kenneth Galbraith, *Esquire,* May 1977

> . . . a simplistic amateur of letters, boring students with one's own enthusiasm —John Bayley, *N.Y. Times Book Rev.,* 27 Feb. 1983

Amateur with *at* is more neutral in tone:

> In the shade of the trees two blacksmiths were shoeing mules. This interested me because I'm an amateur at shoeing —Christina Dodwell, *A Traveller in China,* 1985

> . . . there is nothing more difficult than making the transition from being an amateur at something to becoming a professional —Jeremy Bernstein, *American Scholar,* Winter 1987

> . . . Columbus is a man weighed down with human foibles, an able sailor, but an amateur at everything else —David Ewing Duncan, *Manchester Guardian Weekly,* 22 Dec. 1991

The prepositions *of, in,* or *at* serve to connect *amateur* with the name of some activity, profession, discipline, or field of study or interest. Our citations show that in recent time the indication of such a relationship has been more and more taken over by the adjective *amateur:* when in the past you might have been an amateur of, in, or at photography, nowadays you are much more likely to be an amateur photographer. The prepositions, of course, are still likely to be used where no fully appropriate agent noun is available, or where the writer simply chooses not to use the agent noun.

ambiguous See AMBIVALENT, AMBIGUOUS.

ambition Both the prepositions *for* and *of* are in use with *ambition,* but the most common construction (in our evidence) is *to* and the infinitive. Here's a sample:

> . . . developed an ambition to become a writer —*Current Biography,* February 1967

> . . . carrying out his ambition to reform the map of the world —Benjamin Farrington, *Greek Science,* 1953

> Dvořák had a great ambition for special success in his D minor symphony —John

Burk, *Boston Symphony Orchestra Program,*
5 Feb. 1972

He had nursed the ambition of becoming a
foreign correspondent —*Times Literary
Supp.,* 29 Feb. 1968

With *in* a somewhat different relationship is
suggested:

> . . . my brother Philip, who had ambitions in
> this direction —C. P. Snow, *The Conscience
> of the Rich,* 1958

ambivalent, ambiguous *Ambivalent* is a
much newer word than *ambiguous*; while the
latter has been in the language since the 16th
century, *ambivalent* is not attested until 1916,
and its earliest citations are from translations
of Jung and Freud. Its first use in English,
then, was as a technical term in psychology,
but it seems to have spread to popular usage
fairly quickly. *Ambiguous* had earlier been
used for analogous situations; consequently,
the words sometimes are used in similar contexts.

> My attitude toward the plan . . . will be
> called by some of my friends ambiguous, or
> perhaps—since the word is now in fash-
> ion—"ambivalent." —Albert Guérard, *Edu-
> cation of a Humanist,* 1949

> . . . her frustrating and ambiguous role—ac-
> knowledged neither as wife nor as mistress
> —William L. Shirer, *The Rise and Fall of the
> Third Reich,* 1960

> The 1960s have an ambivalent reputation
> —Harold Perkin, *Times Literary Supp.,* 18
> Dec. 1998

But they are seldom really confused, because *ambiguous* tends to stress uncertainty
and is usually applied to external things while
ambivalent tends to stress duality and is usually applied to internal things:

> English fleets and armies forced the am-
> biguous benefits of modern civilization on
> the reluctant Chinese —D. W. Brogan, *The
> English People,* 1943

> . . . the social standing of singleness remains
> an ambiguous one —Howard P. Chudacoff,
> *The Age of the Bachelor,* 1999

> . . . journalists were placed in the ambiguous
> and slightly comic position of constantly in-
> sisting on the gravitas of the news that they
> and their organizations were playing as
> scandal and smut —Katha Pollitt, *New Re-
> public,* 7 June 1999

> . . . his ambivalent feelings toward an audi-
> ence he both disdained and longed to win
> —Alfred Bendixen, *N.Y. Times Book Rev.,*
> 30 Nov. 1986

He has Thackeray's fruitfully ambivalent attitude toward his own class —Clifton Fadiman, *Holiday,* October 1954

That Americans harbor an ambivalent attitude toward risk is almost a truism —Cullen
Murphy, *Atlantic,* September 1999

Ambivalent may be followed by the prepositions *toward(s)* and *about*:

> In an era when Americans were not yet am-
> bivalent about the fruits of science —Harri-
> et Zuckerman, *Trans-Action,* March 1968

> . . . if its author had been a little less am-
> bivalent about its potential audience
> —*Times Literary Supp.,* 9 Dec. 1965

> . . . I'm a trifle ambivalent toward "Room
> Service" —John McCarten, *New Yorker,* 18
> Apr. 1953

> American woman, ambivalent towards
> fighting —Margaret Mead, *And Keep Your
> Powder Dry,* 1942

amenable *Amenable* is regularly followed by
to:

> As an idea "circle" is amenable to punning
> applications —Roger Greenspun, in *The
> Film,* 1968

> I am both submissive to facts and amenable
> to argument —Virgil Thomson, *The Musical
> Scene,* 1947

> Ever amenable to party demands, the Presi-
> dent responded —Samuel Hopkins Adams,
> *Incredible Era,* 1939

amend, emend A number of usage commentators feel the need to distinguish the sel-
dom-used *emend* from the much more common *amend*. *Amend* usually means "to put
right; change, improve."

> . . . I honestly thought Goldwater would also
> amend the error of his ways —Karl Hess,
> quoted in *Playboy,* July 1976

> Unless yours is a mature woods . . . you'll
> probably have to amend the soil —Elisabeth
> Sheldon, *Fine Gardening,* July/August 1990

> California law was amended last year, and
> prospective charter operators can now ap-
> peal to the state Board of Education
> —David Osborne, *New Republic,* 4 Oct.
> 1999

> Then in 1987 . . . the name was amended to
> "attention-deficit hyperactivity disorder"
> —Anne Glusker, *Washington Post Mag.,* 30
> Mar. 1997

> I remember my parents telling me that Dos-
> toevsky could not really be understood until
> one was forty, a figure that was amended

upward as they got older —Arthur Krystal, *Harper's,* March 1996

Emend is much the less common word and is usually applied to the correction of a text:

... has inserted an elegant fix, sent me back the emended version —Hugh Kenner, *Harper's,* November 1989

It is rarely used with a somewhat broader application:

Not especially gifted with literary originality, the Roman Paul borrowed Plato's image and emended it to suit his needs —Henry Silverstein, *Accent,* Winter 1947

... what he called his "aristocratic egotism," a description that Gertrude Stein emended by converting the adjective "aristocratic" to "brutal" —Bernard Denvir, *N.Y. Times Book Rev.,* 10 Oct. 1993

American Indian See NATIVE AMERICAN.

amid, amidst 1. Some commentators feel *amid* and *amidst* to be bookish, literary, or quaint; *among* or *in* are the recommended substitutes. But the words are in frequent current use. *Amid* is by far more frequent than *amidst*. 2. *Amid, amidst, among.* A curious belief is expressed in variant terms by Evans 1957, Copperud 1970, Bernstein 1962, Bryson 1984, and Simon 1980 that *amid* and *amidst* should go with singular nouns and *among* with plural nouns. The origin of this belief is obscure, but it is nonsense. *Amid* and *amidst* are used with both singular and plural nouns.

Singular nouns with *amid*:

... and amid a babble of goodnights the ladies came forward —Allen Tate, *Prose,* Fall 1971

... a major measure and as near to a final settlement as is ever possible amid the impermanence of politics —Roy Jenkins, *Gladstone,* 1995

... describing what it is like growing up amid urban decay —Mike Tribby, *Booklist,* 15 Nov. 1999

Amidst with singular nouns:

... she fled Cambodia amidst gunfire —Cable Neuhaus, *People,* 11 Mar. 1985

Amidst the junk mail and the hate mail and the crank mail —Aristides, *American Scholar,* Autumn 1979

... and I asked her how it felt to spend day after day amidst all this beauty —Stanley Kauffmann, *New Republic,* 2 Aug. 1999

Amid with plural nouns:

Amid the more elaborate constructions are numerous lovingly tended websites —Paul Quinn, *Times Literary Supp.,* 30 June 2000

Amid the partygoers at Luchow's restaurant —*People,* 20 Sept. 1982

Amid accusations of fraud and thuggery —*Time,* 12 June 2000

Amidst with plural nouns:

... floating amidst the planets and stars —Evan Thomas, *Time,* 26 Nov. 1984

Mexico once disdained its northward migrants as "pochos" whose culture had been coarsened by residence amidst the Anglos —Scott McConnell, *National Rev.,* 31 Dec. 1997

... amidst all the proposed new subsidies —Michael Kinsley, *Harper's,* January 1983

See also AMONG 2.

amidst See AMID, AMIDST.

amn't See AIN'T; AREN'T I.

amok See AMUCK, AMOK.

among 1. See BETWEEN 1.
2. Several commentators have brought *among* into the discussion of *amid* and *amidst*. These commentators would restrict *among* to use with plural nouns. The question of the propriety of using *among* with a singular noun or an indefinite pronoun is an old one, going back at least to Priestley, who, in his 1768 edition objected to Hume's "among every species of liberty."

Somewhere along the way Priestley's reference to *every* was lost, and the question became simply whether *among* could be used with a singular noun. The answer is a qualified yes: Burchfield 1996 notes that *among* can be used with a noun denoting something widespread, scattered, or diffuse:

Among the smoke and fog of a December afternoon —T. S. Eliot, "Portrait of a Lady," 1917

Often, I think, he slept in our barn among the hay —Adrian Bell, *The Cherry Tree,* 1932

... some land animals hibernate among the vegetation —W. H. Dowdeswell, *Animal Ecology,* 2d ed., 1959

It is more commonly used with other mass or collective nouns:

... he is clearly among the elite of America's blue-collar workers —Aaron Lucchetti, *Wall Street Jour.,* 1 Aug. 1996

... and show the remarkable diversity among even this small sample —Scott Bravmann, *Jour. of American History,* June 2000

... was being discussed among the faculty —Harvey Cox, *Atlantic,* November 1995

. . . to sign two free agents from among the cream of this year's crop —Ian Thomsen, *Sports Illustrated,* 17 July 2000

. . . nothing could happen, among a certain class of society, without the cognizance of some philanthropic agency —Arnold Bennett, 1899, in *The Journals of Arnold Bennett,* ed. Frank Swinnerton, 1954

. . . who was raised among the goat-herding Sianis family in a suburb of Tripoli —John Husar, *Chicago Tribune,* 14 June 1997

. . . to explain . . . the STI epidemic among the young —John Stoltenberg, *Ms.,* August/September 2000

Collective nouns are notionally plural, which is why they fit with *among. Among* is also used with notionally plural pronouns:

People with religious training were among the few who could write in those days —Peter M. Tiersma, *Legal Language,* 1999

3. *Among, amongst.* Most of the commentators who mention these words note that *amongst* is less common but both are correct. Our evidence confirms this; it also shows *amongst* a bit more common in British use than American. Nothing else need be said.

amongst See AMONG 3.

amount **1.** *Amount, number.* Many commentators explain the difference between *amount* and *number.* The general rule seems first to have been stated in more or less contemporary terms by Vizetelly 1906:

Amount is used of substances in mass; *number* refers to the individuals of which such mass is constituted.

Almost all modern commentators echo Vizetelly. They are only partly right, because the flat distinction does not account for all standard usage.

Number is regularly used with plural count nouns to indicate an indefinite number of individuals or items; its use is not disputed.

Amount is most frequently used with singular mass nouns:

. . . the amount of energy generated one second after the big bang —Atief Heermance, *Merlyn's Pen,* October/November 1992

He lived in a time and a place in which Jews enjoyed an extraordinary amount of political autonomy —David Novak, *New Republic,* 31 July 2000

. . . it took a certain amount of faith —Hollis Alpert, *Saturday Rev.,* 13 Nov. 1971

A megawatt is the amount of electricity being supplied to 1,000 average American

homes at any moment —Reena Jana, *N.Y. Times Mag.,* 20 Aug. 2000

Charged a fee for the amount of data they send —Irene M. Kunii, *Business Week,* 29 May 2000

. . . to assess the amount of dark matter in the universe —Marcia Bartusiak, *Astronomy,* August 1997

. . . spent any amount of money on him —*Times Literary Supp.,* 20 Feb. 1969

. . . the amount of snow that we usually have —Richard Joseph, *Your Trip to Britain,* 1954

Amount is also used with plural count nouns when they are thought of as an aggregate:

. . . who wrote the U.N. that he'd be glad to furnish any amount of black pebbles —*New Yorker,* 20 Sept. 1952

. . . the high amount of taxes —*Harper's Weekly,* 29 Sept. 1975

$6.5 billion: Amount of advertising dollars spent on pre-buys for the fall season —*Time,* 7 June 1999

. . . the beautiful Olympic Stadium that holds 110,000 spectators and accommodates a fair amount of oversized moths —Harvey Araton, *N Y. Times,* 24 Sept. 2000

No matter how skillful and conscientious she was, a midwife was really only of help in normal delivery. No amount of magic stones or herbal syrups could correct a serious problem —Karen Cushman, *The Midwife's Apprentice,* 1995

. . . an Eighth Avenue saloon that had become known affectionately as the Tavern of the Bite, in deference to the unique amount of worthless IOUs collected during each day's business —Robert Lewis Taylor, *New Yorker,* 12 Nov. 1955

This less common use of *amount* is sometimes called incorrect, but the critics bring forward no cogent reason for condemning it. The use is well established in general prose.

2. The verb *amount* is regularly followed by *to:*

Probably the population never amounted to more than a few hundred souls —Jacquetta & Christopher Hawkes, *Prehistoric Britain,* 1949

. . . a cumulative cheerfulness, which soon amounted to delight —Thomas Hardy, *The Return of the Native,* 1878

And according to my uncle, the scrapes he was always getting into didn't really amount to much —Peter Taylor, *The Old Forest and Other Stories,* 1985

amuck, amok The notice in Copperud 1970 that *amuck* is the preferred spelling is now out of date; the disparaging remarks about the spelling *amok* by various commentators have not influenced writers to reject it. *Amok* is currently the more common spelling; Burchfield 1996 recommends it.

amuse The verb *amuse* (and its past participle *amused* used adjectivally) commonly occurs with the prepositions *at*, *by*, and *with*. *At* is somewhat less common than the others, in part because it follows no form of the verb but the past participle.

> . . . at first surprised, then cynical, and eventually amused at this procession —David Halberstam, *Harper's*, January 1969

> . . . it was a private satisfaction . . . to see people occupied and amused at this pecuniary expense —Henry James, *The American*, 1877

> To be amused by what you read —C. E. Montague, *A Writer's Notes on His Trade*, 1930

> A small mob . . . amused itself by cheering —Joseph Conrad, *Chance*, 1913

> . . . amused the citizens by issuing a series of fancy proclamations —Green Peyton, *San Antonio: City in the Sun*, 1946

> A King may be pardoned for amusing his leisure with wine, wit, and beauty —T. B. Macaulay, *The History of England*, vol. I, 1849

> . . . a witness who was seen amusing himself with a lady on a haycock —Oliver Wendell Holmes d. 1935, letter, 20 May 1920

> . . . adult thumb-suckers, amusing themselves with comic strips, TV, cars —Elmer V. McCollum, *Johns Hopkins Mag.*, Winter 1966

Amuse can also be followed by *to* and an infinitive:

> . . . I had been amused to note that . . . —O. S. Nock, *The Railways of Britain*, 1947

analogous When it is followed by a complementary prepositional phrase, *analogous* almost always takes *to*:

> . . . gluons, force particles analogous to the photons of electromagnetism —Andrew Watson, *Science*, 22 Jan. 1999

> . . . great stretches of algae, analogous to terrestrial woodlands, in which kelp fills the role of trees —William K. Stevens, *N.Y. Times*, 5 Jan. 1999

> . . . the doctrines of Symbolism were in some ways closely analogous to the doctrines of Romanticism —Edmund Wilson, *Axel's Castle*, 1931

With is also idiomatic but seems always to have been much less frequent than *to*.

> . . . a hyperbolic presence is given that is analogous with and sometimes identical to dreams and madness —Charles E. Winquist, *Epiphanies of Darkness*, 1986

> Ferroelectricity . . . is analogous with ferromagnetism —*The Optical Industry & System Directory*, 1977

> . . . not by means superior to, though analogous with, human reason —Charles Darwin, *On the Origin of Species by Means of Natural Selection*, 1859

analogy Bernstein 1965 mentions only *between* or *with* as being used with this noun; Follett 1966, only *with*. They seem to have missed such other prepositions as *to*, *of*, and *among*. The examples below also incidentally illustrate many of the typical constructions in which *analogy* may be found.

> . . . tracing the analogies between star and metal or herb and element —Maurice Evans, *Essays in Criticism*, July 1953

> . . . those who would draw any kind of facile analogy between the situation in Vietnam today and Munich —Arthur M. Schlesinger, Jr., *N.Y. Times Mag.*, 6 Feb. 1966

> Analogies between sex manuals and cookbooks are being made in all literary quarters —Marcia Seligson, *McCall's*, March 1971

> Then *k* is said to determine or to measure the state of analogy among the things —Georg Henrik Von Wright, *A Treatise on Induction and Probability*, 1951

> . . . the sash, door, sheathing, chimney-top, and pendills are restored on analogy with examples elsewhere —Fiske Kimball, *Domestic Architecture of the American Colonies and of the Early Republic*, 1922

> A certain analogy with spherical Geometry . . . is also proved —Bertrand Russell, *Foundations of Geometry*, 1897

> Like other popular views, this one follows the analogy of the most usual experience —William James, *Pragmatism*, 1907

> . . . an impatience with all distinctions of kind created on the analogy of a class-structured society —Leslie A. Fiedler, *Los Angeles Times Book Rev.*, 23 May 1971

> . . . utters them *on the analogy* of similar forms which he has heard —Leonard Bloomfield, *Language*, 1933

> He preferred a more solemn analogy of himself as a *medico politico* —Irving Kristol, *Encounter*, December 1954

. . . uses the image of intensive husbandry as an analogy of the human situation — *Times Literary Supp.,* 9 Mar. 1951

. . . he went on, thoroughly mesmerized, it seemed, by the analogy he was drawing to his experiences —Joseph Lelyveld, *N.Y. Times Mag.,* 26 Feb. 1967

. . . the analogy of these societies to human and insect communities is quite superficial —Alexis Carrel, *Man, the Unknown,* 1935

. . . women in prison build a society on an analogy to the family —Paul Bohannan, *Science 80,* May/June 1980

analyzation Although Macmillan 1982 thinks this word does not exist, it does, and has since the 18th century. It is formed, perfectly regularly, from the verb *analyze.* It is a rarely used alternative to *analysis*—so rare that it is scarcely worth the space taken to disparage it in Macmillan, McMahan & Day 1980, Janis 1984, and Garner 1998. You need not use it, of course. Few writers do use it, in fact.

anchorperson See PERSON 2.

and 1. Everybody agrees that it's all right to begin a sentence with *and,* and nearly everybody admits to having been taught at some past time that the practice was wrong. Most of us think the prohibition goes back to our early school days. Bailey 1984 points out that the prohibition is probably meant to correct the tendency of children to string together independent clauses or simple declarative sentences with *ands*: "We got in the car and we went to the movie and I bought some popcorn and. . . ." As children grow older and master the more sophisticated technique of subordinating clauses, the prohibition of *and* becomes unnecessary. But apparently our teachers fail to tell us when we may forget about the prohibition. Consequently, many of us go through life thinking it wrong to begin a sentence with *and.*

Here are two examples of initial *and.* In the second example, it even begins a paragraph:

He didn't believe I found the cart abandoned at a tilt in an alley. And then I turned over into his hands the cash receipts. To the penny —E. L. Doctorow, *Loon Lake,* 1979

"Now, boys," he said, "I want to read you an essay. This is titled 'The Art of Eating Spaghetti.' "

And he started to read. My words! He was reading *my words* out loud to the entire class —Russell Baker, *Growing Up,* 1982

2. There are several other usage problems involving *and.* These are covered at such entries as AND WHICH, AND WHO; AGREEMENT, SUB-

JECT-VERB: COMPOUND SUBJECTS 1; FAULTY PARALLELISM; GOOD AND; and TRY AND.

and etc. See ETC.

and/or *And/or,* says Janis 1984, is "a formal expression used in law and commerce. . . ." It is, in fact, more widely used than that, but Janis has aptly described its origin. David Mellinkoff shows us in *The Language of the Law* (1963) that *and/or* was used first in maritime shipping contracts (of a kind called *charter party*) in the middle of the 19th century. Who first used the device we do not know, but no doubt the first user thought it a convenient way to indicate some limited variability in the contract. The trouble was, however, that one party to the contract might take one view of the matter and the other party a different view. So the interpretation of *and/or* became a matter of litigation.

Most of the criticism in our files is likewise aesthetic—*ugly* is the usual epithet—although a few consider it confusing or ambiguous. Mellinkoff says the term has both defenders and disparagers in the legal profession. A number of commentators recommend replacing "A and/or B" with "A or B or both."

While most of the handbooks refer to legal, commercial, technical, or bureaucratic contexts, none of them provides much in the way of illustrative material. Our evidence shows that it has a wider use; we present some examples of that here.

. . . and read aloud extracts therefrom for the general benefit and or diversion of the company —Flann O'Brien, *At Swim-Two-Birds,* 1939

. . . will deduce that the speaker is poorly educated and/or stupid —Robert Claiborne, *Our Marvelous Native Tongue,* 1983

The award . . . goes to a trade-book editor under 40 who has shown special talent in discovering and/or getting the best work out of his authors —Victor S. Navasky, *N.Y. Times Book Rev.,* 15 Apr. 1973

. . . discriminatory laws were passed almost everywhere to make certain women were treated as slaves and/or children —Pete Hamill, *Cosmopolitan,* April 1976

In the public mind it is generally considered to be carried out by priests and/or ministers — *Times Literary Supp.,* 19 Mar. 1970

These examples are fairly typical of the general uses of *and/or.* You may have observed that in each of these *and/or* is used between only two options and that it can readily be understood in the sense "A or B or both." But if the number of options is increased, the number of possibilities multiplies, and the chance for ambiguity likewise increases.

If you have a need to use *and/or*, we recommend that you use it only between two alternatives, where the meaning will obviously be "A or B or both." In longer series *and/or* will likely be either vague or unnecessary.

and which, and who   These headings cover a number of constructions marked by faulty parallelism (which see) in the use of conjunctions and relative pronouns (and sometimes other connectives). The problem is better exemplified than described:

> . . . a lady very learned in stones, ferns, plants, and vermin, and who had written a book about petals —Anthony Trollope, *Barchester Towers,* 1857 (in A. S. Hill 1895)

In the example *and* joins a clause ("who had written a book . . .") with an adjective phrase ("learned in stones . . .") not structurally parallel to it. The usual corrective measure would be to insert *who was* after *lady* and, perhaps, then omit the *who* after *and*.

Several commentators and handbooks discuss the question, a few at considerable length. There is no doubt that this construction is a fault. It is an offense against elegance or precision. It is a minor offense, however; the examples we have are readily understandable notwithstanding the fault; one third of the Heritage 1969 usage panel even found it acceptable. Here are a few samples:

> . . . Stephen, with a glance serious but which indicated intimacy, caught the eye of a comely lady —Benjamin Disraeli, *Sybil,* 1845 (in Hill)

> . . . preserve for him his Highland garb and accoutrements, particularly the arms, curious in themselves, and to which the friendship of the donors gave additional value —Sir Walter Scott, *Waverly,* 1814 (in Hill)

> . . . the hold he exerted over the friend of his youth, and which lasted until her death, is here, rather tragically, revealed — *Times Literary Supp.,* 31 Aug. 1951

> Declarations made under Article 36 of the Statute of the Permanent Court of International Justice and which are still in force shall be deemed . . . to be acceptances — *Charter of the United Nations,* 1945

The *and which* construction, in its various guises, is a fault that can be found, at least occasionally, in the work of good writers. It is most likely simply an inadvertency. Since it generally does not seem to interfere with the reader's understanding of the passage it appears in, it probably goes unnoticed for the most part. It is therefore a venial sin. We suggest that you try to avoid it, however, for when it is spotted, it distracts the reader's attention from more important matters—namely, what you are saying.

anent   The old preposition *anent* "concerning, about" underwent a revival of sorts in the 19th century—that is, it began to revive in England; it seems to have been in use in Scotland all along. Sir Walter Scott may have helped spread the use among English men of letters: Byron, Thomas Love Peacock, Dante Gabriel Rossetti, and W. S. Gilbert are some who found the word useful. Early in the 20th century the word was discovered by usage commentators (Utter 1913 seems to have been the first)—probably not in literary contexts—and was pronounced either bookish, archaic, or affected. While the usage commentators (as recently as Garner 1998) have contented themselves with repeating their predecessors' pronouncements, users of the language have established *anent* as a standard, if somewhat specialized, term.

Anent is an odd word. It does have a bookish air about it—you rarely (or perhaps never) hear it used in ordinary conversation—but it seems to pop up in contexts that are not at all bookish (along with some that are). Fowler 1926 noted the frequency with which it is met in letters to the press. It is still found in letters to the editor:

> Anent your editorial with its "Go ahead and gripe" message —letter to the editor, *InfoWorld,* 19 Sept. 1983

> Anent your allusion to the military predilection for the noun-comma-adjective format —letter reprinted in Safire 1982

The combined usage of letter-to-the-editor writers and literary as well as nonliterary people has brought *anent* back to life. Here is a sample of such usage. It is clearly not archaic, nor in most cases does the level of affectation seem especially high.

> . . . I should snarl again, anent "half-tones," which I abhor —Ambrose Bierce, letter, 14 Feb. 1893

> . . . a remark anent the advancement of the spring —George Moore, *The Brook Kerith,* 1916

> . . . a brief note from Felix anent some hostile review in the *New Republic* of my last book —Harold J. Laski, letter, 28 Nov. 1920

> . . . dispute over the dying wartime President's remarks anent the League of Nations —*Newsweek,* 11 June 1944

There is another marvelously wacky correspondence between Mr. Thurber and both customs officials and the Connecticut State Tax Commission, anent a small bottle of wine sent as a gift —Irwin Edman, *N.Y. Herald Tribune Book Rev.*, 1 Nov. 1953

. . . and saying, anent the rumors of my going to India, that perhaps a word might go to Ellsworth Bunker —John Kenneth Galbraith, *Ambassador's Journal,* 1969

"A middle-class white son-of-a-bitch without goals will usually break your heart," a trainer remarks, anent fighters —Judith Crist, *New York*, 29 Oct. 1973

A line from his 'Prologue to *Macbeth',* anent the apparition of Banquo —D. J. Enright, *The Listener,* 22 May 1975

Anent such superficial seductions —Marilyn Stasio, *N.Y. Times Book Rev.,* 28 May 1989

. . . the legal and moral arguments, pro and con, anent the several changes in U.S. abortion law —Ray Olson, *Booklist,* 1 May 1990

Anglo *Anglo* is an ethnic term used to distinguish those of English ethnic or English-speaking background from others.

There are at present two chief uses. The first is Canadian; it distinguishes the Canadian of English ethnic and language background from one whose background is French.

. . . the language we Anglos have all been speaking unwittingly—*Canajan* —Val Clery, *Books in Canada,* July–September 1973

We all know Quebec isn't entirely French . . . . there are still nearly a million Anglos in the province —Sonia Day, letter to the editor, *Word Watching,* June 1983

The second arose in the southwestern U.S. and originally distinguished the American of English-speaking background from one of Spanish-speaking background.

Early Anglo visitors to San Antonio —Donna R. Gabaccia, *We Are What We Eat,* 1998

The Spanish-speaking also are still about. They dress for the most part like Anglos now —Conrad Richter, *Holiday,* December 1953

Anglo is also used to distinguish white English-speakers from other ethinic groups:

Its mix of black, Hispanic, Asian and Anglo foreshadows population trends elsewhere —Howard Fineman, *Newsweek,* 1 Jan. 2000

. . . certain real Anglos on the nonfictional Navajo reservation —Verlyn Klinkenborg, *N.Y. Times Book Rev.,* 17 Oct. 1993

. . . the descendants of Old European immigrant groups are now seen by new waves of immigrants as thoroughly "Anglo"

—Michael Lewis, *N.Y. Times Mag.,* 31 May 1998

angry From Vizetelly 1906 to Chambers 1985 much advice and prescription has been written about the prepositions that can be used with *angry.* Much of the discussion deals with whether the object of the anger is human, animal, or inanimate; often particular prepositions are prescribed for particular objects. Much of the prescription is in conflict with actual usage, such as Shaw 1970's "Idiomatically, one is angry *with,* not *at,* a person." *Angry at* (a person) has been around since Shakespeare's time and is still in use.

The chief prepositions are *with, at,* and *about. With* is the most frequently used preposition when the object is a person:

I am sorry to be angry with you —Samuel Johnson (1776), in James Boswell, *Life of Samuel Johnson,* 1791

Be not angry with me, Coleridge —Charles Lamb, letter, 24 Oct. 1796

. . . I hope she isn't angry with me for talking nonsense about her name —Lewis Carroll, letter, 28 Nov. 1867

You have often made me angry with you, poor little innocent —George Bernard Shaw, *Cashel Byron's Profession,* 1886

The author is very angry with anyone who dislikes the cockney manner of speech — *Times Literary Supp.,* 20 Feb. 1953

On this day Mary was angry with me —Ernest Hemingway, "Miss Mary's Lion," 1956

He was angry with himself, still more angry with Rose —C. P. Snow, *The New Men,* 1954

". . . I get that it's okay to be angry with you." —R. D. Rosen, *Psychobabble,* 1977

With is sometimes used with inanimate or abstract objects:

. . . angry also with the change of fortune which was reshaping the world about him —James Joyce, *A Portrait of the Artist as a Young Man,* 1916

I think I was all the angrier with my own ineffectiveness because I knew the streets —*The Autobiography of Malcolm X,* 1966

At is used with objects that are persons and objects that are actions or things:

I find no considerable Man angry at the Book —Alexander Pope, letter, 16 Nov. 1726

"I do not see, Sir, that it is reasonable for a man to be angry at another. . . ." —Samuel

Johnson (1775), in James Boswell, *Life of Samuel Johnson,* 1791

I became angry at him and I went after him —Henry Clark, quoted in *Sports Illustrated,* 15 July 1968

They might be angry at him —Gay Talese, *Harper's,* January 1969

About is used of persons or actions or things:

. . . they are so angry about the affair of Duke Hamilton —Jonathan Swift, *Journal to Stella,* 2 Feb. 1712

Still it's better to have Mr. L. angry about her than about other topics —C. P. Snow, *The Conscience of the Rich,* 1958

Mr. Reed is angry about what he perceives to be negative characterizations of black men in fiction and drama —Brent Staples, *N.Y. Times Book Rev.,* 23 Mar. 1986

Other prepositions are also possible:

. . . he feels angry towards your community —Fred Sharpe, *6th Annual Report, Peace Officers Training School,* 1952

She said, 'I was only angry for my sweet little baby.' —Angus Wilson, *Anglo-Saxon Attitudes,* 1956

It does not seem reasonable, on the basis of the evidence here and in the OED, to make rigid distinctions about which prepositions are proper in which uses.

animadversion, animadvert Of these hard words Bernstein 1965 observes that the verb takes *upon.* Actually, both the noun and verb are followed by *on* or *upon,* as Simon 1980 says. The instance of *animadversion to* that he detected probably resulted from the writer's confusing *animadversion* with *aversion,* which usually takes *to.* A few examples of the usual prepositions:

There are quite a few animadversions, for example, on the plight of women —Anatole Broyard, *N.Y. Times,* 28 Aug. 1980

I refrain from further animadversions on the quality of tone —Richard Franko Goldman, *The Concert Band,* 1946

. . . animadversions upon the shortcomings of his fellow biographers —*Times Literary Supp.,* 21 Dec. 1973

. . . the justice of his animadversion upon his old acquaintance and pupil —James Boswell, *Life of Samuel Johnson,* 1791

. . . let us notice and animadvert on the vogue use of *reiterate* —Howard 1977

. . . had wearied of animadverting upon the late King's devotion to duty —Malcolm

Muggeridge, *Saturday Evening Post,* 19 Oct. 1957

. . . to the extent of our animadverting upon his economics or his politics —John Crowe Ransom, *Sewanee Rev.,* Spring 1953

annoy Since early in this century, some commentators have been trying to help us with the prepositions that go with *annoyed,* the past participle of this verb. Their distinctions are various and are based on such considerations as whether one *is* or *feels* annoyed, whether the annoyer is an action, thing, or person, and whether *annoyed* means "pestered." As is usual with such attempts, actual usage proves more complex than the proffered distinctions. Here are some examples of the common prepositions, *with, at,* and *by,* and the less common *about:*

. . . annoyed the British in Philadelphia with a satirical ballad — *American Guide Series: Pennsylvania,* 1940

. . . get greatly annoyed with anything in it that happens to interfere —Elmer Davis, *But We Were Born Free,* 1954

. . . annoyed about a trembling hand —*Current Biography,* December 1964

. . . annoyed at the waste of it all —Alan Rich, *New York,* 8 Feb. 1971

. . . became annoyed at newspaper reports —John Barkham, *Saturday Rev.,* 13 Feb. 1954

My hostess was annoyed at me —Maude Phelps Hutchins, *Epoch,* Fall 1947

. . . are often puzzled and sometimes annoyed by the ways of other peoples —William A. Parker, *Understanding Other Cultures,* 1954

. . . she was disturbed and next annoyed by the silence —Jean Stafford, *Children Are Bored on Sunday,* 1953

. . . much annoyed by the wolves that still existed in Florida then —Marjory Stoneman Douglas, *The Everglades: River of Grass,* 1947

He was annoyed by the cold, the starvation, and chiefly by the coarseness of the dying soldiers —Morris Bishop, *Saturday Rev.,* 11 Dec. 1954

Though annoyed by the tone of the Tringsbys' letters —Elizabeth Bowen, *The Heat of the Day,* 1949

Annoy and *annoyed* are followed by constructions other than those consisting of preposition and noun. A sample:

It annoys me to have smokers blow smoke in my face —H. Thompson Fillmer et al., *Patterns of Language,* Level F (textbook), 1977

. . . I was annoyed to lose it —Nora Waln, *The House of Exile,* 1933

Some of his friends were annoyed to recognize themselves in the latter book — *Dictionary of American Biography,* 1929

Annoyed that the university administrators had publicly aired their views —*Current Biography,* January 1966

"It's annoying that we have to rush. . . ." —*Adventures Here and There* (5th-grade textbook), 1950

an't, a'n't This is the original contraction that eventually gave us *ain't.* It may possibly have originated as an Irishism; at least the earliest evidence we have found so far occurs in the writing of Congreve, Farquhar, and Swift. The contraction seems to have dropped out of use in the U.S. around the middle of the 19th century and in England a bit later. In America it was replaced by *ain't*; in England it seems to have been replaced by *aren't,* although a few writers use *ain't.* See AIN'T, AREN'T I. Here are a few examples from the past:

CHERRY. . . . I hope, Sir, you an't affronted —George Farquhar, *The Beaux Stratagem,* 1707

. . . an't I a reasonable creature? —Jonathan Swift, *Journal to Stella,* 18 Feb. 1711

SIR PETER. Two hundred pounds! what, a'n't I to be in a good humor without paying for it? —Richard Brinsley Sheridan, *A School for Scandal,* 1783

It is thought he has gone sick upon them. He a'n't well, that's certain —Charles Lamb, letter, 26 Feb. 1808

An a'n't I a woman? —Sojourner Truth, recorded by Frances D. Gage, May 1851 (in J. L. Dillard, *American Talk,* 1976)

ante-, anti- Several handbooks warn against confusing these prefixes. *Ante-* means "earlier, before," and *anti-* (sometimes found as *ant-* or *anth-*) "opposite, opposed, against." See a good dictionary for fuller definitions. There was an *anti-* in use as a variant of *ante-* at one time, but it seems to have become disused because of the possibility of confusion with the "against" *anti-.* So there is now no excuse for a mistake with these prefixes.

antecedent The adjective *antecedent* is less attested in our files than the noun; as an adjective it is not usually placed in a construction requiring a preposition, but when it is, the preposition is *to.*

For him, character and society are antecedent to talk —Richard Poirier, *A World Elsewhere,* 1966

If we believe that we have rights antecedent to government —*Time,* 26 Sept. 1955

anterior Our evidence of *anterior* as an attributive adjective runs pretty heavily to technical contexts. As a predicate adjective it usually takes *to.* It tends to be found in rather learned or at least elevated styles.

In political theory, even a constitutional system entails powers anterior to those specified in the Constitution —*National Rev.,* 17 Nov. 1970

. . . the Babylonian epic *Gilgamesh,* which is a genuine epic by any definition and is not only anterior to the Bible but may also have influenced both the Greek and the Indian epics —Moses Hadas, *Commentary,* October 1957

. . . a parallel liberation which Croce seeks in his presentation of Art as ideally anterior to Thought —Cecil Sprigge, *Benedetto Croce,* 1952

anti- See ANTE-, ANTI-.

anticipate Usage writers decide for themselves how many meanings a word has. Chambers 1985 notes two for *anticipate,* Garner 1998 three (the OED lists nine, and Merriam-Webster's Collegiate Dictionary, 10th Edition, lists six transitive and one intransitive). What most of the commentators agree on is that the sense meaning "expect" is wrong. This opinion dates from 1881 and has been frequently repeated since, without gathering anything resembling a cogent reason for the disapproval. The "expect" sense has been around since the 18th century, and is now well established, as Burchfield 1996 (an earlier disapprover) admits.

Here are some examples:

He became more dependent on her; and she anticipated that he would become more exacting in his demands on her time —George Bernard Shaw, *Cashel Byron's Profession,* 1886

She certainly had not anticipated taking a whole day to get through a belt of reeds a mile wide —C. S. Forester, *The African Queen,* 1935

At last my studiously dropped aitches were paying dividends, although not in the way that I had at one stage anticipated —Nick Hornby, *Fever Pitch,* 1992

. . . said he anticipates offering as many as 100 courses —Bob Summer, *Publishers Weekly,* 10 Jan. 2000

The company anticipates stronger demand for copier and publishing papers —Lucinda Harper, *Wall Street Jour.*, 12 Oct. 1993

If earnings come in at the anticipated $3.55 per share —Christopher Palmeri, *Forbes*, 24 Jan. 2000

These are all standard.

antidote The OED and other dictionaries note that *antidote* can be followed by *against*, *for*. or *to*. Evidence in our files shows that all three are in use for both literal and figurative senses. Of the three, *to* is the most commonly used at the present time, *for* next, and *against* the least. A few examples:

An antidote against nerve gases —*Time*, 19 Mar. 1956

. . . no surer antidote against the dull monotony of travel —Douglas Carruthers, *Beyond the Caspian*, 1949

. . . the first effective antidote for PCP —*N.Y. Times*, 11 Feb. 1980

. . . hate may be the only antidote for despair —David Black, *New Times*, 11 July 1975

. . . an antidote to the arsenical blister gases —Russell L. Cecil & Robert F. Loeb, *Textbook of Medicine*, 8th ed., 1951

. . . the grim reality of life in Kiev acted as a strong antidote to romantic notions —Glenn Plaskin, *N.Y. Times*, 6 Feb. 1983

antipathy Bernstein 1965 says that *antipathy* takes *to*, *toward*, or *against*; Lincoln Library 1924 says *to*, sometimes *for* or *against*, and *between*; Krapp 1927 says *to* but not *for* or *against*; Webster 1909 says *to*, *against*, *between*, sometimes *for*. We had better straighten this out.

Although Garner 1998 says *against* is used, we have no recent evidence for it. It was once current:

What a strange antipathy I have taken against these creatures! —George Farquhar, *The Inconstant*, 1702

. . . nothing is more essential than that permanent inveterate antipathies against particular nations . . . should be excluded —George Washington, *Farewell Address*, 1796

The use of *between* (two persons or things), while not common, is still current:

. . . there was a marked antipathy between their radicalism or liberalism and the conservative peasant ideas of the mass of Italian immigrants —Oscar Handlin, *The American People in the Twentieth Century*, 1954

The antipathy between Mr. Barbieri and Mr. Lee has grown —William Borders, *N.Y. Times*, 15 Oct. 1967

The antipathy between the groups is deep —Renata Adler, *Pitch Dark*, 1983

To has been and continues to be the most common preposition:

. . . perceived above a dozen large bugs. You must know I have the same kind of antipathy to these vermin —Tobias Smollett, *Travels Through France and Italy*, 1766

Hogarth's antipathy to France —Agnes Repplier, *In Pursuit of Laughter*, 1936

. . . who shares this antipathy to the indefiniteness of aesthetic morality —Havelock Ellis, *The Dance of Life*, 1923

. . . a definite antipathy to permitting outside doctors to come into their home communities and take over their practice —*JAMA*, 3 Apr. 1943

. . . Grandmother's belief that the medical profession needed informed lay augmentation was the basis for her implacable antipathy to hospitals —James A. Maxwell, *New Yorker*, 24 Nov. 1951

. . . the growing sensibility cult with its antipathy to the generic explicitness of the novel —Anthony J. Hassall, *Novel*, Spring 1972

Both *for* and *toward* are also in regular use:

The antipathy Lessing felt for the French wit —Irving Babbitt, *The New Laokoon*, 1910

. . . both species knew instinctively of his pronounced antipathy for them —Osbert Sitwell, *Noble Essences*, 1950

Her one antipathy is for Schrader, whose work she has never liked —Robert F. Moss, *Saturday Rev.*, October 1980

Little remains of the Puritanical antipathy toward them as immoral —Thomas Munro, *The Arts and Their Interrelations*, 1949

And the American antipathy toward a preventive nuclear strike —Stephen A. Garrett, *Center Mag.*, July–August 1971

anxious The discovery that *anxious* should not be used to mean "eager" seems to have been made in the U.S. in the early 20th century. It has since risen rapidly to become a shibboleth in American usage, appearing in books from Bierce 1909 to Garner 1998. Although Garner uses Fowler's term *slipshod extension* to describe the sense, Fowler himself (1926) called it a natural development.

The disputed use began in the 18th century

(Burchfield 1996 cites a 1743 poem of Robert Blair containing the phrase "anxious to please") and has been in regular use ever since. It should be noted that the sense often includes both the notion of eagerness and anxiety. Here is Dr. Johnson holding forth:

> . . . there must always be some degree of care and anxiety. The master of the house is anxious to entertain his guests; the guests are anxious to be agreeable —in James Boswell, *Life of Samuel Johnson,* 1791

A few more examples that suggest a mixture of eagerness and anxiety are these:

> Even without his books, Don Quixote set forth once again, anxious as before not to lose any time, "for he could not but blame himself for what the world was losing by his delay. . . ." —Malcolm Muggeridge, *Punch,* 8 Apr. 1953

> The individual states—fearful of losing industry and richer residents to lower-tax rivals and anxious to minimize their burden of needy citizens —*Atlantic,* May 1997

> Most spiders are shy and far more anxious to avoid than to attack man —Katherine W. Moseley, *Massachusetts Audubon,* June 1971

> . . . aims at readers who are suffering from a degenerative disease or anxious to forestall one —*Publishers Weekly,* 6 Oct. 1997

> . . . and visibly anxious that his wife should be on easy terms with us all —Agnes Repplier, *Eight Decades,* 1937

The notion of anxiety is, however, often absent:

> . . . intellectual highbrows who are naturally anxious to impress British labor with the fact that they learned Latin at Winchester —Sir Winston Churchill, quoted by William Safire, *N.Y. Times Mag.,* 10 Oct. 1982

> I feel no hesitation in saying, I was more anxious to hear your critique, however severe, than the praises of the *million* —Lord Byron, letter, 6 Mar. 1807

> Thanks so much for the comments which I'll always be anxious to get, good or bad —Flannery O'Connor, letter, 30 Apr. 1952

> . . . the men looked hard at him, anxious to see what sort of a looking "cove" he was —Herman Melville, *Omoo,* 1847

> Punch was always anxious to oblige everybody —Rudyard Kipling, *Wee Willie Winkie and Other Child Stories,* 1888

> . . . city bankers anxious to furnish him capital —Sherwood Anderson, *Poor White,* 1920

> . . . many firms are anxious to employ their cash profitably —*Manchester Guardian Weekly,* 19 Jan. 1940

> . . . information which our enemies are desperately anxious to obtain —Franklin D. Roosevelt, fireside chat, 9 Dec. 1941, in *Nothing to Fear,* ed. B. D. Zevin, 1946

> . . . Paris, where there are a great many young writers anxious to experiment in literary form —Cyril Connolly, *The Condemned Playground,* 1946

> He was so anxious to get a fly into the water that he had to reproach himself for haste —John Cheever, *The Wapshot Chronicle,* 1957

> He was exhausted yet exhilarated, anxious . . . about getting on the ice with a team that had a chance to win —Michael Farber, *Sports Illustrated,* 20 Mar. 2000

> . . . welcome news for the Government which is anxious to see the skill levels of Britain's work-force improve —Paul Marston, *Daily Telegraph* (London), 30 May 1990

> . . . to the eye anxious for reform in the city and forgetful of conditions in the countryside —Joseph A. Amato, *Dust,* 2000

The objection to *anxious* in its "eager" sense is an invention; the sense has long been standard.

any 1. The pronoun *any* can be either singular or plural in construction. Bernstein 1977 believes the plural construction to be more common, but we cannot confirm his belief from the evidence in our files, in which the two constructions are roughly equal:

> . . . had reached its final shape before any of his volumes of poems were published — *The Tiger's Eye,* December 1947

> . . . nor is any of his novels purely a novel of ideas —Frederick J. Hoffman, in *Forms of Modern Fiction,* ed. William Van O'Connor, 1948

2. Longman 1984 notes that *any* with a singular noun may be referred to by a plural pronoun.

> . . . he would at no time be a willing party to any artist breaking their contract —*The Times* (in Longman)

> . . . he kept his door wide open so that any one of his 12,000 employees could walk in and spill their troubles —*Time,* 17 Nov. 1952

Notional agreement is the principle in operation here. It is a long-established construction:

Any man that has a Humour is under no restraint or fear of giving it a vent; they have a proverb among them which, maybe, will show the bent and genius of the people as well as a longer discourse —William Congreve, "Concerning Humour in Comedy," 1695

Congreve's use shows the typical singular-verb-plural-pronoun agreement of many indefinite pronouns and adjectives.

See THEY, THEIR, THEM and the articles under AGREEMENT.

3. *Of any, than any* (illogical comparison). In 1705 Joseph Addison, in the preface to a book of travels in Italy written by someone else, noted that the author

. . . has wrote a more correct Account of Italy than any before him. (OED)

Two centuries later Vizetelly 1906 calls the construction incorrect, objecting to "the finest of any I have seen." Bryant 1962 reports that the construction with a superlative (or, less often, a comparative) and *of* or *than* has been in use since the time of Chaucer. The handbooks and commentators following Vizetelly's lead are engaged in the ex post facto application of logical analysis to a long-established idiom—with entirely predictable results.

Here are a few examples of the idiom from writers more recent than Addison:

We boast that we belong to the nineteenth century and are making the most rapid strides of any nation —Henry David Thoreau, *Walden,* 1854 (in Reader's Digest 1983)

Its population would have remained the most carefully screened of any body of settlers ever to have come to America —*N.Y. Times Book Rev.,* 20 Apr. 1947 (in Bryant)

Although its coverage of the government, Capitol Hill and the world is more complete than any paper in the city —*Time,* 29 Dec. 1952

Why does Jennifer House sell more convertible sofabeds in Manhattan than the convertible department in any Manhattan department store? —advt., *N.Y. Times Mag.,* 18 Apr. 1982

The studies cited in Bryant suggest that the more logical constructions—"of any other" and "of all"—prescribed by the handbooks are more commonly met in print nowadays than the older *any* idiom.

anybody, anyone 1. These indefinite pronouns share with other indefinite pronouns the characteristic of taking a singular verb and, more often than not, a plural pronoun in reference. See AGREEMENT: INDEFINITE PRO-

NOUNS; THEY, THEIR, THEM; NOTIONAL AGREEMENT, NOTIONAL CONCORD. This use of the plural pronoun—*they, their, them*—has traditionally been disapproved by grammarians who do not recognize the existence of notional agreement, but the use is winning greater acceptance. Copperud 1970 records Bryant, Evans, and Flesch as finding the plural pronoun acceptable, and the four commentators he cites as disapproving it in writing are said to be "indulgent" of it in speech. Reader's Digest 1983 finds it acceptable.

Usage is, of course, not uniform; some occurrences follow notional agreement, and others formal agreement. Here are a few samples of each.

Formal agreement:

. . . before releasing a child to anyone except his parents —J. Edgar Hoover, *NEA Jour.,* January 1965

Anyone who thinks he's pure is surely not —Flannery O'Connor, letter, 1 Jan. 1956

Anyone who wishes to find his bearings —H. B. Parkes, *Marxism—An Autopsy,* 1939

. . . when anybody was condemned to be impaled, or knouted, or beheaded, he or she promptly retained the Empress as intercessor at a handsome fee —George Bernard Shaw, letter, 31 Dec. 1897

Notional agreement:

. . . as anybody in their senses would have done —Jane Austen, *Mansfield Park,* 1814

It is fatal to anyone who writes to think of their sex —Virginia Woolf, *A Room of One's Own,* 1929

. . . it will then be open for anyone to take up the quarrel, if they think there is any public advantage in so doing —Sir Winston Churchill, *The Unrelenting Struggle,* 1942

. . . anyone may progress to these better posts if they have the required qualifications —*Employment Opportunities in the Civil Service* (Canada), 1953

. . . it may be difficult for anyone to find their path through what may be a sort of maze —Ford Madox Ford, quoted in Graham Greene, *Collected Essays,* 1969

You haven't told anyone at work. When they ask about Amanda you say she's fine —Jay McInerney, *Bright Lights, Big City,* 1984

2. Both *anybody* and *anyone* were formerly spelled as two words, but the open styling is now reserved for instances in which *any* is a separate adjective.

3. *Anybody else's.* See ELSE 1.

anymore 1. Both *anymore* and *any more* are found in current written use. Although usage prescribers disagree about which form to use, the one-word styling is the more common. Feel free to write it as two words, if you prefer.

2. *Anymore* is regularly used in negative contexts ("we never go there anymore"), in questions ("do you listen to the radio anymore?"), and in conditional contexts ("if you do that anymore, I'll leave"). It is used in a number of positive statements in which the implication is negative:

> There's only one woman for him any more —Owen Wister, *The Virginian*, 1902

> . . . thought about whether such a profession as merely *pork* butcher exists any more —*Times Literary Supp.*, 13 Mar. 1969

> . . . she found it harder and harder to sort out anymore what was worth saving and how best to save it —Russell Baker, *Growing Up*, 1982

> But relatively few people buy word-processing software alone anymore —Fred Langan, *Christian Science Monitor*, 20 June 1996

None of these uses draws comment. But *anymore* is also used in contexts with no negative implication, much to the consternation and perplexity of some usage writers:

> Every time I even smile at a man any more the papers have me practically married to him —Betty Grable, quoted in *Time*, 25 Nov. 1940

> In a way he almost felt sorry for him, any more —James Jones, *From Here to Eternity*, 1951

> It sometimes seems to me that all I do anymore is go to funerals —Harry S. Truman, quoted in Merle Miller, *Plain Speaking*, 1973

> Every time we leave the house anymore, I play a game called "Stump the Housebreaker" —Erma Bombeck, syndicated column, 24 Jan. 1973

> Yasunari Kawabata was awarded the Nobel Prize in 1968. At the time, playwright Eugene Ionesco sniffed that anymore, they'd give the prize to almost anybody —Philip Gingerich, *N.Y. Times Book Rev.*, 12 Oct. 1997

> It seems I only know myself, anymore, by your attendance in my soul —Barbara Kingsolver, *The Poisonwood Bible*, 1998

This usage is dialectal. It has been discovered anew almost every year since 1931 and has been abundantly documented. The Dictionary of American Regional English reports it to be widespread in all dialect areas of the U.S. except New England. Both the older American Dialect Dictionary and the new DARE note that it is used by persons of all educational levels; it is not substandard, and it is not a feature of speech that is considered indicative of social standing.

Although many who encounter the usage for the first time think it is new, it is not: the earliest attestation cited in the DARE is dated 1859.

anyone 1. See ANYBODY, ANYONE.

2. The usage panel of Heritage 1969, 1982 objects to the use of *anyone* in the sentence "She is the most thrifty person of anyone I know." This is the same construction as the one discussed at ANY 3, with *anyone* in place of *any*.

any other See ANY 3.

anyplace For a word as recent as *anyplace*, it might seem a bit surprising that we know so little of its origins. It first came to the attention of Merriam-Webster editors through its mention in handbooks, and those handbooks, from 1916 to 1998, don't like it. We did not begin to find it in print with any frequency until the 1940s:

> . . . the minister never went any place in the house but the parlor and the diningroom —*New Republic*, 29 July 1940

> . . . if you just quit, you found yourself on a sort of a black list and they wouldn't let you work anyplace else —Edmund Wilson, *Memoirs of Hecate County*, 1946

Anyplace has been gaining in frequency of use in print since the 1940s, and is long since established as standard. The one-word form has gradually replaced the two-word form that was earliest attested. Here is a sample of use:

> Italian women dress more elaborately during the Venice season than they do anyplace else any time in the year —Janet Flanner, *New Yorker*, 23 Sept. 1950

> . . . it was worse in Poland than anyplace else —William L. Shirer, *The Rise and Fall of the Third Reich*, 1960

> He wants us to look at what we can see everyday, anyplace, here —Robert Coles, *Trans-Action*, May 1968

> Now there just aren't that many men among us who could go anyplace, never mind to work, after five pints —Malcolm S. Forbes, *Forbes*, 15 Sept. 1970

> Anyplace north of the Potomac was unthinkable —William Styron, *This Quiet Dust and Other Writings*, 1982

> No matter how similar its houses may be to others in Charleston or the rural Carolinas,

or anyplace else —Anne Rice, *N.Y. Times Book Rev.,* 31 Dec. 1989

. . . examined the double quasar and its surroundings with a sensitivity unmatched by surveys anyplace else in the sky —*Science News,* 29 Oct. 1994

San Jose . . . has the biggest single-man surplus of anyplace in America —Michelle Conlin, *Business Week,* 6 Mar. 2000

It is much less frequent than *anywhere.* See also EVERYPLACE, NOPLACE, SOMEPLACE.

anytime This adverb is generally spelled as one word. Johnson 1982 tells us that the one-word spelling is all right when it can be replaced by the phrase "at any time" but when it cannot be so replaced, it should be spelled as two words. Johnson's rule of thumb is a sensible one, though occasionally it is not observed:

"The old handkerchief-head didn't waste anytime, did he?" —Debbie Chocolate, *Neate to the Rescue,* 1992

Burchfield 1996 describes *anytime* as a characteristically American adverb. Some examples:

But such a rollback won't be enacted into law anytime soon —Ben Gerson, *Civilization,* April/May 2000

In fact, you can buy or rent it anytime, day or night —Joshua Quittner et al., *Time,* 6 Sept. 1999

Anytime they need him, he tells them, just call him —Gary Smith, *Sports Illustrated,* 10 Aug. 1998

anyways None of the senses of *anyways* are standard contemporary English, but you should not conclude that they are substandard. When *anyways* means "anywise," it is archaic:

And if the people of the land do any ways hide their eyes —Leviticus 20:4 (AV), 1611

. . . who have no places, nor are anyways dependent on the King —Thomas Gray, letter, 24 May 1742

The other uses—"to any degree at all" and "in any case, anyway, anyhow"—are mostly dialectal. The Dictionary of American Regional English marks both senses now chiefly South and South Midland. It turns up in fictional dialogue, in personal letters, in speech, and only occasionally in general prose, where it is probably the normal idiom of the writer. Some examples:

"What is a grit anyways?" Pesci asks the cook —Tim Warren, *Smithsonian,* October 1999

. . . continue to insist that he is our only hope and that, anyways, the worst is over —Stephen F. Cohen, *The Nation,* 10 Oct. 1994

. . . I think I will go to New York anyways sometime next summer —Flannery O'Connor, letter, 25 Jan. 1953

The "anyway" use exists in some British dialects, too. It is found in fictional dialogue from Dickens and Trollope to this more recent writer:

"Anyways," said the other man, "she's safe enough now. . . ." —Catherine Aird, *Last Respects,* 1982

anywheres *Anywheres* is an Americanism that has been censured ever since MacCracken & Sandison put out their handbook of language etiquette for Vassar girls in 1917. Subsequent handbooks treat it much like a social disease. Bryant 1962 believes it to be a receding form; our evidence would tend to bear her out, but the Dictionary of American Regional English has evidence as recent as 1981. The word is not quite dead yet. Here are a few samples from our less fastidious past (remember that *anywheres* is primarily a speech form and seldom appears in print outside of fiction):

"Anywheres in this country, sir?" —Herman Melville, *Pierre,* 1852

. . . if you are anywheres where it won't do for you to scratch, why you will itch all over in upwards of a thousand places —Mark Twain, *Huckleberry Finn,* 1884

. . . I would rather live in Detroit than anywheres else —Ring Lardner, *You Know Me Al,* 1916

Now instead of trees we have parking meters on Main Street . . . and very few trees anywheres else —John O'Hara, *Collier's,* 2 Mar. 1956

Our current evidence suggests it may occur more often in handbooks than even in fictional dialogue.

See also NOWHERES; SOMEWHERES.

apart from *Apart from* is a fixed two-word preposition in English. Some commentators believe it to be the British equivalent of American *aside from,* but in fact it is used on both sides of the Atlantic:

But 'ain't' will always be facetious in British English, apart from cockney —Anthony Burgess, in Harper 1985

Apart from a few sporadic digs, archaeology was left in the hands of half-demented amateurs —Tony Perrottet, *Civilization,* April/May 1999

So, apart from minor discontents . . . Americans were satisfied —Samuel Eliot Morison, *Oxford History of the American People*, 1965

But apart from that, it's hard to see how it's his fault —Carl Sagan, *The Demon-Haunted World*, 1996

The sheer efflux of time . . . quite apart from the dismissive nature of the reply had severely tried Gladstone's patience —Roy Jenkins, *Gladstone*, 1995

See also ASIDE FROM.

apathy   *Apathy* is not very frequently used in a context in which a preposition connects it to its object. When it is, *toward* and *towards* are most common.

. . . the American apathy toward the struggles of colonial peoples —*New Republic*, 28 Mar. 1955

Their apathy toward course designing borders on ignorance —William Johnson, *Sports Illustrated*, 15 July 1968

. . . apathy towards the Hindu-Moslem question —*Manchester Guardian Weekly*, 21 May 1937

About, to, and *regarding* are also in use:

. . . professional and public apathy about Australian drama —Leslie Rees, *Towards an Australian Drama*, 1953

Apathy of audience to all the good things —*The Journals of Arnold Bennett*, ed. Frank Swinnerton, 1954

. . . general apathy still prevailed regarding the potential of conventional agriculture —*Rockefeller Foundation: President's Five-Year Rev. & Annual Report*, 1968

apostrophe   1. The original use of the apostrophe in English appears to have been as a mark used to indicate in writing and printing the omission of a letter—usually a vowel—that was not pronounced. The plays of Restoration dramatists abound in such contractions. A great many of them are still familiar: *she'll, I'll, 'em, can't, 'tis, e'en, e'er, he's, I've*, among others. And some are no longer familiar: *i'fac, 'ygad, to't, in't, an't, on't, i'faith, 'zbud, wo't, dar'st*, for example.

The apostrophe was used to mark omission of silent *e* in the -*ed* ending of verbs as in *borrow'd, deform'd, refus'd, expung'd, banish'd, squar'd*. The convention of spelling -*ed* as -'*d* when the *e* was not pronounced was more common in verse than in prose for the purpose of emphasizing scansion. At any rate, the convention of marking the unpronounced *e* of the -*ed* ending by an apostrophe gradually died out.

Also gone are such early 18th-century apostrophized spellings as Defoe's *cou'd, shou'd, wou'd*—showing that the *l* was not pronounced.

The chief modern uses of the apostrophe are about the same as those of the late 17th century, with certain old conventions having been discarded. We still use the apostrophe to show contractions (*didn't, I'll*) and to mark features of speech (*singin', N'Orleans*). In addition, the apostrophe is used to mark the omission of numerals:

class of '86   politics during the '60s

Some words or their variants are consistently spelled with apostrophes:

fo'c'sle   bos'n   rock 'n' roll

2. The apostrophe is used to mark the possessive case of nouns and indefinite pronouns.

The chief variation in current use is in the case of nouns ending in an \s\ or \z\ sound, such as *audience, waitress, index*. Even with these -'*s* is usual: *audience's, waitress's, index's*. Some writers prefer the apostrophe alone, especially if the word is followed immediately by a word beginning with the same sound: for *convenience'* sake (see SAKE).

For other questions relating to the use of the possessive, see GENITIVE.

3. The apostrophe is sometimes used with -*s* to form the plural of letters, numerals, abbreviations, symbols, and words used as words.

Letters are usually pluralized with -'*s*:

mind your p's and q's

although capital letters are sometimes pluralized with -*s* alone.

The use of -'*s* to form the plurals of numerals, abbreviations, and symbols is not now as common as pluralization with simple -*s*; 1970s, CPUs, &s are more likely to be found than their apostrophized counterparts.

Words used as words—such as might be given as examples from a text: too many *howsoever's*—are usually pluralized with -'*s*. But words representing sounds or words used as words in common phrases are pluralized with -*s* alone:

the oohs and aahs of the crowd

the whys and wherefores of the issue

Theodore Bernstein's *Dos, Don'ts & Maybes of English Usage*

4. *Her's, our's, your's, their's.* Lowth 1762 notes that these pronouns "have evidently the form of the possessive case"; Baker 1770 likewise spells them with the apostrophe. But even then usage was mixed and today all these pronouns are regularly written without the apostrophe: *hers, ours, yours, theirs, its*.

5. Simon 1980 speaks of ". . . the Great Apostrophe Plague: the newfangled insertion of

apostrophes in ordinary plurals." The phenomenon is probably older than many writers think, but older evidence is scarce. It has certainly become more noticed in recent years by writers of English texts and writers on usage. Bernstein 1977, Simon 1980, Harper 1975, 1985, and Janis 1984 all notice 's plurals in the U.S.; Howard 1984 and Longman 1984 note them in Britain. No one has an explanation for the practice, but it is widely assumed to be practiced chiefly by the less well educated—handwritten signs offering "Fresh Strawberry's" or "Auto Repair's" are often cited. Such plurals also turn up in handwritten letters sent to this office: ". . . these type of dictionary's." Bernstein and Janis mention their appearing in ads; several such have been noticed here too:

> . . . the finest Tibetan Mastiff's —*Dog World*, May 1984

> The floating mover judge's look for —*Chronicle of the Horse*, 25 May 1984

Apostrophized plurals also turn up in other text:

> . . . by using *he* to refer to all people, she's and he's alike —Carol Tavris, *Vogue*, June 1984

> The buyback's included Texaco's purchase —*N.Y. Times*, 13 June 1984

> I thought we kept the weirdo's locked up —"Brock" (cartoon), *Springfield* (Mass.) *Morning Union*, 25 July 1984

No apostrophe is necessary or wanted in any of the above examples.

6. Words formed from abnormal elements, such as numerals, abbreviations, and the like, are often provided with an apostrophe before the addition of a suffix:

> OD'd on heroin
> 86'd our party
> 4-H'ers

7. If you need any further evidence that the apostrophe has not been universally understood, a correspondent of Simon's sent in as an example a sign reading "Larr'y 66 Service." To this gem we can add only

> T'was not always so —*Southwest Art*, May 1984

Commenting on the apostrophe, Robert Burchfield, editor of the OED Supplement, has said:

> The apostrophe was only a moderately successful device, and it is probably coming to the end of its usefulness, certainly for forming plurals and marking possession. It may only be retained for contractions —quoted in *Boston Sunday Globe*, 12 May 1985

8. Burchfield 1996 notes that since about 1900 many institutions, businesses, and journals have dropped the apostrophe from their titles: *Barclays Bank, teachers college, Publishers Weekly*. He expects this trend to continue.

append   *Append* regularly takes *to*:

> . . . failed to append the sticker to the windshield —*Springfield* (Mass.) *Republican*, 3 Jan. 1954

> This entitles him to append the letters "S.C." . . . to his name —*Current Biography 1950*

> To this is appended a calendar —Benjamin Farrington, *Greek Science*, 1953

> . . . stories, orderly set down, with the objection appended to each story —Charles Lamb, *Essays of Elia*, 1823

appendix   A generous number of commentators assure us that both *appendixes* and *appendices* are standard and acceptable plurals for *appendix*. Despite the pronouncements and preferences of various commentators —Garner 1998 prefers *appendixes* in nontechnical contexts, Burchfield 1996 the opposite—our evidence shows both plurals used about equally often. It is not unusual to find both spellings in the same publications.

> . . . 100 pages of exceedingly miscellaneous appendixes —*N.Y. Times Book Rev.*, 5 Aug. 1984

> The appendixes are particularly valuable —*Times Literary Supp.*, 21 May 1982

> . . . 30 pages of appendices —*N.Y. Times Book Rev.*, 9 Aug. 1981

> . . . study of the appendices to the working timetables —*Times Literary Supp.*, 15 July 1983

Take your pick.

apportion   The verb *apportion* may idiomatically take the prepositions *among, to*, and *between* when a complementary prepositional phrase is required.

Among has a certain cachet in writings on American government because of its use in the U.S. Constitution:

> Representatives and direct taxes shall be apportioned among the several States —Article I, Section 2

> . . . apportion the expenses among the member states —Frank Abbott Magruder, *National Governments and International Relations*, 1950

> It is left to the reader to apportion compassion . . . among those who suffer in the novel —Frances Gaither, *N.Y. Times Book Rev.*, 2 May 1954

To is about as frequent as *among, between* somewhat less frequent:

> . . . the roles are apportioned rather to episodes than to character —Richard Ellmann, *Times Literary Supp.*, 21 May 1971

> Nietzsche . . . urges that the law should apportion special privileges to a cultural elite —Arthur Pap, *Elements of Analytic Philosophy,* 1949

> But he will be a brave man who will apportion responsibility for Britain's attitude between parties and classes —Roy Lewis & Angus Maude, *The English Middle Classes,* 1950

> . . . to apportion the judicial power between the supreme and inferior courts —John Marshall, *Marbury* v. *Madison,* 1803

appositives Several commentators and handbooks are at some pains to distinguish restrictive and nonrestrictive appositives especially for purposes of punctuation. Our comments are based on Quirk et al. 1985, wherein the subject is dealt with in considerable detail.

An appositive is defined in school grammar books as

> . . . a noun or pronoun—often with modifiers—set beside another noun or pronoun to explain or identify it —*Warriner's English Grammar and Composition, Complete Course,* 1986

Quirk distinguishes three sets of characteristics of appositives. First, there is full and partial apposition. In full apposition, either of the nouns can be omitted from the sentence, and what remains will still be an acceptable English sentence. In the resultant sentence, each noun will have the same grammatical function, such as the subject or direct object. In addition, the sentences made by omitting one or other of the nouns will have the same meaning in the real world—"in extralinguistic reference," to use Quirk's term. Thus, in this sentence

> A cousin of mine, Leonard Davis, has been elected to Congress.

we can omit either noun

> A cousin of mine has been elected to Congress.

> Leonard Davis has been elected to Congress.

and still have acceptable English sentences with the remaining noun as subject. And the nouns are coreferential—they both stand for Leonard Davis, the new congressman, in the extralinguistic world. Appositives that do not meet all three criteria are said to be in partial apposition.

Quirk next notes strict and weak apposition. In strict apposition the appositives belong to the same syntactic class:

> Journalism, her choice of a career, has brought her great happiness.

In the example sentence, both *journalism* and *her choice of a career* fall into the class of noun phrases.

In weak apposition, they are from different syntactic classes:

> Her choice of a career, reporting the news, has brought her great happiness.

Here we have a noun phrase in apposition with a gerund phrase (or "-ing-clause" in Quirk's terminology); they are members of different syntactic classes.

Then Quirk discusses restrictive and nonrestrictive apposition. In nonrestrictive apposition (our examples so far are all nonrestrictive) the appositives are in different units of information which in writing are signaled by punctuation—usually commas. The two nonrestrictive appositive units contribute relatively independent information, with the first unit usually acting as the defined expression and the second as the defining expression. Because the appositives are distinctly separate units, the defining and defined roles can be switched by merely reversing their order:

> Sally Williams, the coach of the visiting team, predicted victory.

> The coach of the visiting team, Sally Williams, predicted victory.

In restrictive apposition the two units are not separated by punctuation in writing:

> I wish I could shimmy like my sister Kate.

One thing Quirk does not mention is the rule-of-thumb inference that Copperud, Safire, and Janis expound upon about the number of items in the class to which the appositives refer based on the restrictive or nonrestrictive status of the appositives. Their theory is that a nonrestrictive appositive signals but a single one of the items in the extralinguistic world, while a restrictive appositive means that one out of a group of more than one in the extralinguistic world is being identified. Thus, "His wife, Helen, attended the ceremony" would mean but one wife, and "He sent his daughter Cicely to college" would suggest more than one daughter. The inference will be valid in most cases but is not necessarily trustworthy. In this nonrestrictive example

> He sent the older daughter, Kathleen, to a good convent —James Joyce, *Dubliners,* 1914

older signals two daughters, in spite of the nonrestrictive appositive. Quirk says only that "restrictiveness . . . indicates a limitation on the possible reference of the head"; no numbers are given. This numbers game may be a favorite of American commentators, but it is hard to see what practical value it has.

appraise, apprise Several sources warn us against using *appraise* for *apprise*. The examples given suggest that the confusion occurs chiefly in speech; our files yield but a single example of the mistake in print:

. . . had not properly appraised herself of Mrs. Macduff's nature —Rex Ingamells, *Of Us Now Living,* 1952

Even if you did not know the difference in meaning between these two words, you could tell them apart by their typical constructions. *Apprise,* which means "give notice to," usually occurs in the construction *apprise (someone)* of *(something)*:

. . . Hitler . . . had not bothered to apprise them of his thoughts —William L. Shirer, *The Rise and Fall of the Third Reich,* 1960

. . . had kept him apprised of the high regard in which he is held —Hollis Alpert, in *The Film,* 1968

Sometimes the *of* phrase is replaced by a *that* clause:

. . . in a guarded way which apprised him that she had been in touch with Renata —Marcia Davenport, *My Brother's Keeper,* 1954

Appraise, which means "evaluate," is used in neither of those constructions. The object of *appraise* is usually inanimate or abstract:

. . . made it difficult for friends and foes alike to appraise his performance —Ronald P. Kriss, *Saturday Rev.,* 11 Mar. 1972

Less often the object is a person:

John was conscious that Jabez Winkleman had been studying him with shrewd eyes, appraising him —Clarence Budington Kelland, *Saturday Evening Post,* 25 Dec. 1954

appreciate Ever since Ayres 1881 various critics have felt it necessary to find fault with one sense or another of *appreciate*. Not infrequently one critic approves the very sense another disparages. More than a century of criticism has produced no clear, consistent, and legitimate concern. Reader's Digest 1983 lists the senses found in most dictionaries and declares them all acceptable. So they are. Trust your dictionary.

apprehensive When the object of concern is a person, *apprehensive* takes *for*:

Watching these contests, I could not help feeling apprehensive for Fitzgerald, whose physical condition was precarious at best —Andrew W. Turnbull, *New Yorker,* 7 Apr. 1956

More frequently the preposition links *apprehensive* to a usually impersonal cause of concern. In such cases, a selection of prepositions is available. *Of* is the most common:

. . . no sooner would they stow themselves away . . . than they would rush out again, as if apprehensive of some approaching danger —John Burroughs, *Wake-Robin,* 1871

The violence of his temper and his reputation for cruelty had made the City apprehensive of what would happen if he succeeded his father —Robert Graves, *I, Claudius,* 1934

. . . made a great many people apprehensive of aggregations of more than one or two birds —Deborah Howard, *Massachusetts Audubon Newsletter,* December 1970

About is also quite common:

The child with an infection of the bone will probably refuse to have the arm or leg examined and will be apprehensive about having it touched —Morris Fishbein, *The Popular Medical Encyclopedia,* 1946

He was apprehensive about the increase of China's influence inside the Communist world —Norman Cousins, *Saturday Rev.,* 30 Oct. 1971

Regarding is sometimes chosen:

. . . were outspokenly apprehensive regarding its full significance —*Collier's Year Book,* 1949

. . . was perhaps apprehensive regarding the ultimate effect in Japan —Rodger Swearingen, *Current History,* July 1952

Sometimes a clause will be used instead of a phrase:

As I stood aside to let that carriage pass, apprehensive that it might otherwise run me down —Charles Dickens, *A Tale of Two Cities,* 1859

. . . apprehensive lest this evacuation inspire the extreme Left to become even bolder —*Collier's Year Book,* 1949

apprise See APPRAISE, APPRISE.

approve When used as an intransitive verb with the meaning "to take a favorable view," *approve* takes the preposition *of*:

. . . she doesn't approve of fighting —Margaret Mead, *And Keep Your Powder Dry,* 1942

... does not mean that it favors it or even always approves of it —Roger Angell, *Holiday,* November 1953

The New York critics generally approved of the way she handled the part —*Current Biography,* June 1964

When used as a transitive verb—usually in the sense of "to sanction officially"—it can take *by* to indicate the agent of approval:

... magic hath been publicly professed in former times, ... maintained and excused, and so far approved by some princes —Robert Burton, *The Anatomy of Melancholy,* 1621

... the plan must be approved by state legislators —Peter Janssen, *Saturday Rev.,* 5 Feb. 1972

approximate   As an intransitive verb, *approximate* can take *to:*

... the result approximates more to fantasy than to science fiction —John Christopher, *The Writer,* November 1968

A study of medieval delinquency that rests principally on gaol delivery records can only approximate to veracity —R. B. Pugh, *Times Literary Supp.,* 15 Feb. 1980

... its guying of upper class English must have approximated to the real thing —Howard 1984

approximation   Follett 1966 says that *approximate* (presumably the verb) takes no preposition (see APPROXIMATE, where its use with *to* is illustrated) and that *approximation* takes *to.* This latter statement is partly true, but will not fully bear comparison with actual usage.

In mathematics we find *approximation* used with *to, of,* and *for:*

... successively better approximations to L —School Mathematics Study Group, *Calculus, Part I,* 1965

To get a better approximation of the mathematical idea of a point —School Mathematics Study Group, *Geometry, Part I,* 1965

... rational approximations for irrational numbers —Chuan C. Feng et al., *A Course in Algebra and Trigonometry with Computer Programming,* 1969

In other contexts we find both *to* and *of,* with more recent nontechnical writing favoring *of:*

... the second approximation to the vertical pressure gradient —E. V. Laitone, *Bulletin of the American Physical Society,* 2 Sept. 1965

... a first approximation to the data which would be thus obtained —James B. Conant, *Slums and Suburbs,* 1961

... an extremely simple mechanism requiring only an approximation to accuracy —Roger Burlingame, *Backgrounds of Power,* 1949

... a terrifyingly close approximation of her own situation —Richard Poirier, *A World Elsewhere,* 1966

... in which the common language will be English, or some approximation of it —Herbert A. Simon, *Think,* May–June 1967

... the early accounts and estimates ... are often cruelly inadequate approximations of the historic truth —Max Lerner, *Saturday Rev.,* 29 May 1976

... every effort should be made to achieve the closest approximation of it that is possible —Robert M. Hutchins, *Center Mag.,* January 1968

apropos, apropos of, apropos to   *Apropos* is a word taken into English from the French phrase *à propos* in the second half of the 17th century. It has functioned variously as an adjective, adverb, noun, and preposition. No one would have given it a second thought, perhaps, had not Fowler 1926 written

apropos is so clearly marked by its pronunciation as French, & the French construction is, owing to *à propos de bottes,* so familiar, that it is better always to use *of* rather than *to* after it. ...

Fowler gives no further elucidation, but presumably he felt *of* to be better because it translates the French *de* of the longer phrase. At any rate, later commentators take Fowler's recommendation to be a virtual commandment to use *of* and not to use *to.*

Apropos of functions in English as a compound preposition; it has been functioning as a compound preposition in English since the middle of the 18th century.

... tell you a story apropos of two noble instances of fidelity and generosity —Horace Walpole, letter, 1750 (in *Stanford Dictionary of Anglicised Words and Phrases,* 1892)

It was such an odd expression, coming *apropos* of nothing, that it quite startled me —Bram Stoker, *Dracula,* 1897

... apropos of the election of 1900, when McKinley ran against Bryan —Edmund Wilson, *New Yorker,* 20 Oct. 1951

Apropos of the Congressional vote to terminate action in Cambodia ... he writes —Barbara W. Tuchman, *N.Y. Times Book Rev.,* 11 Nov. 1979

Early in the 20th century it began to be used without *of* as a preposition having the same meaning:

> . . . remarked the other day, apropos the formal ending of the censorship —Dorothy Thompson, *Saturday Rev.,* 20 May 1939

> One of Oscar Wilde's characters made, apropos another character, the famous remark, "He always behaves like a gentleman—a thing no gentleman ever does" —Joseph Wood Krutch, *Saturday Rev.,* 30 Jan. 1954

> "The subject is unpleasant to dwell on," he writes primly, apropos the "life-denying nihilism" in Conrad's "Heart of Darkness" —Dwight Macdonald, *New Yorker,* 13 Oct. 1956

> A propos the exclusively female consciousness —John Bayley, *Times Literary Supp.,* 22 Aug. 1980

The use of *to* with *apropos* is not so much wrong (even Fowler did not call it wrong) as rare. The combination has been used in two ways. First, we find *to* used when *apropos* is a predicate adjective meaning "appropriate":

> . . . the remark was particularly apropos to the large wisdom of the stranger's tone and air —Nathaniel Hawthorne, *American Notebooks,* 1838 (in *Stanford Dictionary of Anglicised Words and Phrases,* 1892)

> Mudrick quotes a fan letter apropos of the *Life,* and apropos to his argument —D. J. Enright, *Times Literary Supp.,* January 1980

The combination was also formerly used as a preposition equivalent to *apropos of*:

> . . . it was, I think, apropos to some zoological discussion —John Gibson Lockhart, *Memoirs of the Life of Sir Walter Scott,* 1838

> Apropos to this, you ask me what my plans are —Henry Adams, letter, 3 Nov. 1858

> . . . the excellent and uplifted of all lands would write me, *apropos* to each new piece of broad-minded folly —Rudyard Kipling, excerpt from his *Autobiography,* reprinted in *N.Y. Times,* 10 Feb. 1937

As prepositions, *apropos of* and *apropos* are usual. *Apropos to* is rare but not wrong.

apt see LIABLE 2.

Arab See ETHNIC DESIGNATIONS: PRONUNCIATION.

area Copperud 1970, 1980 reports a few members of his consensus as objecting in a rather general way to *area* used as a vague or faddish term in place of *field, problem, issue,* or *question*—themselves no great shakes in respect to specific application. Copperud's critics are echoed by Nickles 1974 and Janis 1984.

The objection to vagueness is not compelling—you use *area* (or *field* or *problem,* etc.) in a vague and imprecise way when you do not want a more precise term, or when there is no such term. The vagueness is not inadvertent. Garner 1998 finds *area* sometimes used as what he calls a space-filler. In his examples, which are of the patterns "in the area of x" and "in the x area," he suggests that the first is better omitted and the second revised to "in x." Here are some similar examples:

> . . . the Company's development in the area of consumer products and services —Thomas E. Hanigan, Jr., in *Annual Report, W. R. Grace & Co.,* 1970

> In the area of international relations he has upheld military assistance —*Current Biography,* January 1966

> . . . shot in the stomach area . . . the knee area . . . the chest area —Springfield, Mass., police spokesman, television news, 13 Aug. 1984

This last use is typical of those who speak for public officials and, when interviewed, wish to avoid being too specific. You can see that *area* could be omitted in these instances, but how big an improvement would result you may well question.

aren't I It is a widely noted phenomenon of modern English that there is no satisfactory filler for the blank in sentences like this: "I'm a little late,____I?" *Ain't,* which several commentators approve in this construction, has been cried down successfully by the pedagogues (see AIN'T). *An't* (or *a'n't*), which had fairly considerable use beginning in the 17th century, dropped out of use as a printed form in the 19th century. *Amn't,* a logically formed contraction, is pretty much limited to dialectal use (in Scottish and Irish speech, according to Burchfield 1996; it is not substandard as Garner 1998 says). *Aren't I* began appearing in the work of British writers early in the 20th century. It is a pronunciation spelling in origin—British speakers don't pronounce the *r*. The subtlety of pronunciation was lost on American critics, to whom the construction looked glaringly incorrect. Those who did not damn it as bad grammar condemned it as a too-nice usage affected by women. But the acceptability of the phrase has been growing. It has never been a problem for British critics, who understand the reason for the spelling. (Amis 1998, however, thinks that its use in writing outside of fictional dialogue would mark the writer as vulgar.) Recent American critcs concede that it is respectable and standard.

argot   *Argot* is a vocabulary and idiom that is peculiar to a certain group. It is sometimes more or less secret, but perhaps its most important function is to identify the user as a member of the group. Fowler 1965, Burchfield 1996, and Garner 1998 discuss *argot* and other similar language terms under *jargon*; Bernstein 1965, under *Inside Talk*. See also JARGON.

argument from etymology   See ETYMOLOGICAL FALLACY.

aroma   *Aroma,* as many commentators tell us, is most often used of pleasant smells:

> . . . spiced among these odors was the sultry aroma of strong boiling coffee —Thomas Wolfe, *You Can't Go Home Again,* 1940

> . . . the pleasing aroma of fresh produce — *The Lamp,* Summer 1971

It may have, in technical contexts, an entirely neutral use:

> The aroma of a loaf should not be strong, sour, or gassy as a result of underbaking —Frank J. Gruber, *Baker's Digest,* February 1955

It also has euphemistic and humorous uses; they are not as frequent as the pleasant smell uses:

> . . . the critical scene in the comedy is set off by the gruesomely strong aroma of the old dog, who has eaten . . . too much fish —Christopher Morley, *Book-of-the-Month Club News,* May 1948

> . . . the particular meadows smell for which Secaucus is celebrated—a blend dominated by the pungent aroma of pigs —John Brooks, *New Yorker,* 16 Mar. 1957

The foregoing examples all refer to real odors. Unremarked by the commentators is the considerable figurative use of *aroma* for a distinctive quality or atmosphere. In this use *aroma* is pleasant, unpleasant, or neutral as the context dictates:

> . . . an atmosphere, impalpable as a perfume yet as real, rose above the heads of the laughing guests. It was the aroma of enjoyment and gaiety —Stella Gibbons, *Cold Comfort Farm,* 1932

> " . . . And by now it is all beginning to lose its eccentric charm, Nathan, and is taking on a decidedly paranoic aroma. . . ." —Philip Roth, *Atlantic,* April 1981

> The aroma of the continental tradition hangs about the sayings —John Dewey, *Freedom and Culture,* 1939

Figurative use is at least as common as use for an actual smell.

around   1. *Around, about.* The propriety of using *around* in senses and constructions that it shares with *about* has been the subject of much—and essentially pointless—comment since the 1870s. By the time the subject reached the 1970s and 1980s the grounds of dispute had entirely changed. But the more things change, the more they stay the same. All of the various uses of *around* that were criticized are American, and are, of course, standard for Americans. The most recent sense to come under fire is that of "approximately" or "near." Here are a few examples of that sense used by American writers:

> Around ten o'clock the little five-piece band got tired of messing around with a rhumba —Raymond Chandler, *The Simple Art of Murder,* 1950

> He was a bullet-headed man of around sixty —John Cheever, *The Reporter,* 29 Dec. 1955

> . . . overhung the rim of the bench at an angle of around thirty degrees —John Updike, *New Yorker,* 3 Dec. 1955

> My father, for around half a century, was the leading Liberal of the community —John Kenneth Galbraith, *The Scotch,* 1964

> Around the turn of the century, grammarians adjured writers not to use *people* for persons individually —Bernstein 1971

> . . . the planet's average temperature hovers around a paralyzing –67 F —Jeffrey Kluger, *Time,* 3 July 2000

The OED marks this sense *U.S.,* but British commentators recognize its existence in British English; everybody agrees that *about* is much more common there. Here are a few samples from writers of British English:

> Leopoldina Terminal debentures were also better at 86 and the ordinary units changed hands around 1s. 6d. —*Railway Gazette,* 15 Dec. 1950

> . . . at around the same price —*The Bulletin* (Sydney, Australia), 10 Feb. 1954

> . . . around and before the beginning of the Christian era —Stuart Piggott, *London Calling,* 10 June 1954

> Around fourteen per cent. of students —Sir James Mountford, *British Universities,* 1966

In sum, you can use *around* in senses it shares with *about* without apologizing or feeling diffident—especially if you are an American.
   See also ABOUT.
2. *Around, round.* Everybody knows that *around* is more common in American English and *round* more common in British English.

"More common" does not imply exclusiveness, however; both words are in use on both sides of the Atlantic and have been for a good while.

arrant See ERRANT, ARRANT.

array The verb *array* is used with many prepositions. When used in the sense of "dress," it usually takes *in*:

... the subsequent arraying of their persons in the poppy-colored jerseys that she considered suitable to the gloom of the day —Elizabeth Goudge, *Pilgrim's Inn*, 1948

... arrayed in gaudy attire —Walter Pater, *Marius the Epicurean*, 1885

... had arrayed herself in lipstick, rouge, perfume —Herman Wouk, *Marjorie Morningstar*, 1955

If the sense is close to "equip," *in* or *with* may be used:

... almost every county of England arrayed in arms against the throne —T. B. Macaulay, *The History of England*, vol. I, 1849

... arrayed with the most advanced equipment —*General Electric Investor*, Summer 1972

Many prepositions are used when the meaning is "to get or place in order":

... had his students arrayed on the stage —Gilbert Rogin, *New Yorker*, 5 June 1971

They arrayed themselves before us —Leon Uris, *Battle Cry*, 1953

... chairs were rounded up and arrayed in front of the Muller platform —John Brooks, *New Yorker*, 27 Apr. 1957

... chairs arrayed before a platform —Clifton Daniel, *N.Y. Times Mag.*, 12 Dec. 1954

Food was his material; his life's art was to array it upon mahogany and damask —*British Books of the Month*, March 1953

... scarcely had time to array his men at the townward wall —A. C. Whitehead, *The Standard Bearer*, 1915

... four brass buttons arrayed in a hollow square —Lois Long, *New Yorker*, 30 Oct. 1954

When there is a notion of drawing up forces, *against* is usual:

... arraying formidable resources against persons who gather and disseminate news —*Playboy*, April 1973

... the French encyclopedists, who were arrayed against the church —Harry S. Ash-more, *Center Occasional Papers*, February 1971

... each group is arrayed against one or more other groups —Margaret Mead, in *Personality in Nature, Society, and Culture*, ed. Clyde Kluckhohn & Henry A. Murray, 1948

arrive The question of what prepositions to use with *arrive* has been a matter of comment since 1770. Baker 1770 prescribes *at*, rather than *to*, for literal senses; either *at* or *to* for figurative senses. The figurative senses do not seem to occur to later commentators: Raub 1897 says "*at* a place, *in* a vehicle, *from* a place," and Bernstein 1965 says only *at* or *in* without explanation. We will take up literal and figurative senses separately, the literal first.

When the place of arrival is the object, we find *in* and *at*:

... arrived in the United States —*Current Biography*, April 1968

Ninety per cent of the emigrants arrive in New York City —*Geographical Rev.*, January 1954

Safely arrived at the capital —*Christian Herald*, October 1967

... members arrived at the classroom with arms full of books —Marel Brown, *Christian Herald*, March 1954

Either may be used of birth:

When Harley Johnston came into the world, he arrived at a small manor house —Donn Byrne, *A Daughter of the Medici*, 1935

Late that autumn a boy baby arrived in their home —Irving Bacheller, *A Man for the Ages*, 1919

On or *upon* may be used in some instances:

... by early morning the uniformed youngsters began to arrive on the dock —Frank Oliver, *The Reporter*, 6 July 1954

Two policemen at length arrived upon the scene —OED

Into is also sometimes used:

Neighbors arrive into what is already a madhouse scene —Elizabeth Bowen, *New Republic*, 9 Mar. 1953

... with which persons may arrive into the world at birth —*Psychiatry*, May 1945

When things—material or immaterial—arrive, we find *in*, *at*, or *on*:

... a just appreciation of Baudelaire has been slow to arrive in England —T. S. Eliot, "Baudelaire," in *Selected Essays*, 1932

. . . was safe when Allen's lob to Johnson arrived at the bag too late —Joseph Durso, *N.Y. Times,* 7 Sept. 1969

Swift's words arrive on the page with the regular tap of a day's rain —V. S. Pritchett, *Books In General,* 1953

If the object is the point of departure, *from* is the most common, with *out of* finding a little use:

. . . many of them recently arrived from the hill country —Cabell Phillips, *N.Y. Times Mag.,* 30 May 1954

When material aid arrived from the Soviet Union —*Current Biography,* June 1967

. . . a lost begrimed dark burnt army abruptly arrived out of some holocaust —Marshall Frady, *Harper's,* November 1970

. . . belches begin arriving out of your body —Richard Brautigan, *A Confederate General from Big Sur,* 1964

When the object is the means of arrival, we find *by, on,* and occasionally *in:*

. . . the visitor who arrives, as I did, by air —George Lichtheim, *Commentary,* October 1957

Francis Cooke, who arrived on the *Mayflower* —*Current Biography,* February 1967

. . . other invisible persons arriving in close carriages —Herman Melville, *Pierre,* 1852

In figurative use, the object in mind is almost always the point of arrival and the preposition in modern use is overwhelmingly *at.* The OED recognizes the use of *to,* which it labels obsolete. *To* is perhaps not quite obsolete, but it was more common in the 18th century (when Baker took note of it) than it is now.

I have arrived to vast courage and skill that way —Lady Mary Wortley Montagu, reprinted in *Encore,* November 1944

. . . power arrives to them accidentally and late in their careers —Hilaire Belloc, *Richelieu,* 1930

. . . he had at least arrived at what he considered a reasonable point —Norman Mailer, *Harper's,* March 1971

The investigator arrives at a list of units —W. F. Bolton, *A Short History of Literary English,* 1967

. . . want to do considerable exploring in college before arriving at a career decision —Milton S. Eisenhower, *Johns Hopkins Mag.,* February 1966

. . . each in his own way, suddenly arrived at inventing twentieth-century art —Janet Flanner, *New Yorker,* 6 Oct. 1956

. . . the deepest secret of the universe at which we can arrive —John Cowper Powys, *The Meaning of Culture,* 1939

It's restful to arrive at a decision —Robert Frost, *New Hampshire,* 1923

. . . began to arrive at a certain importance —Osbert Sitwell, *Triple Fugue,* 1924

From may indicate a figurative as well as a literal source:

. . . a century in which totalitarianism arrives as easily from the Right as from the Left —Barbara Ward, *N.Y. Times Mag.,* 20 June 1954

as There are a number of questions involving the little word *as*—"one of the most overworked words in the English language," according to Shaw 1970. Overwork is a fate shared by most small function words in English; Mr. Shaw himself works *as* as hard as anyone else. (*As* is the fourteenth most frequent word in the Brown University Corpus, according to Kučera & Francis 1967.)

We will treat at this entry several uses of *as* that tend to be lumped together in handbooks. When *as* forms part of a compound, correlative, or phrase whose use is questioned, the whole construction will be found at its own alphabetical place. See also LIKE, AS, AS IF.

1. *Causal "as."* Bryant 1962 reports that causal *as* appears in standard contexts but is quite a bit less frequent than *because* and *since.* Many other commentators object to the use; the most frequent objection is the possibility of ambiguity in the uncertainty, in certain made-up sentences, whether *as* signifies "because" or "while."

Actually, cases where causal *as* is clearly ambiguous are hard to find; the objection seems somewhat flimsy. Here are some genuine examples of causal *as*; you can judge whether they are ambiguous:

The class of '24's valedictorian did not make it from Southern California this year, for instance, as his wife had died —Tom Gavin, *Sunday Denver Post,* 7 Oct. 1984

THESEUS. Oh! then as I'm a respectable man, and rather particular about the company I keep, I think I'll go —W. S. Gilbert, *Thespis,* 1871

". . . I shall prepare my most plaintive airs against his return, in compassion to his feelings, as I know his horse will lose." —Jane Austen, *Mansfield Park,* 1814

. . . in cases of doubt I often leave them out, but I am apt to put them in, as they help the reader —Oliver Wendell Holmes d. 1935, letter, 27 July 1931

. . . I accepted at once as I like to make trips by plane —Flannery O'Connor, letter, 11 Sept. 1955

At the last possible minute, John carefully polishes all the brass, as it tarnishes so easily —Suzy Lucine, *Morgan Horse,* April 1983

As this chapter had no observable merits it did not seem worth reprinting here —Robert Burchfield, Note on the Text, 1984 reprint of Cobbett 1823

Causal *as* is a standard and acceptable alternative to *because* and *since,* but it is less frequently used than either. Objection to it on grounds of ambiguity seems dubious at best, since ambiguous examples in published writing are hard to come by.

See also SINCE 1.

2. *Relative pronoun.* The relative pronoun *as,* preceded by *such* or *same,* is perfectly standard:

Therefore let Princes, or States, choose such Servants, as have not this marke —Francis Bacon, *Essays,* 1625

Each house shall keep a journal of its proceedings, and from time to time publish the same, excepting such parts as may in their judgment require secrecy —*Constitution of the United States,* 1787

. . . appreciation of and interest in such fine, pleasant, and funny things as may still be around —James Thurber, letter, 20 Jan. 1938

. . . with such poor things as are our own —Leacock 1943

. . . faced by the same sort of problem as confronts many local housing committees —*Times Literary Supp.,* 1 Oct. 1954

. . . such innovations as they actually have made —James Sledd, in *Essays on Language and Usage,* 2d ed., ed. Leonard F. Dean & Kenneth G. Wilson, 1963

The same people as objected to "Inkhorn terms" . . . poured derision upon those who "peppered their talk with oversea language" —David C. Brazil, *The True Book about Our Language,* 1965

. . . a tarred timber barn, behind which such of the young as fancied and some as didn't used to box —Benedict Kiely, *New Yorker,* 20 Aug. 1973

In this construction *as* cannot be easily replaced by another relative pronoun like *that* or *which.*

Other uses of the relative pronoun are, as

Burchfield 1996 observes, regional or substandard in both British and American English.

She said to me: 'There's a lot of old maids in this village, sir, as wants men. . . .' —*The Journals of Arnold Bennett,* ed. Frank Swinnerton, 1954

. . . we was goin to tell the Gospel to them as had ears —Robert Penn Warren, in *New Directions,* 1947

. . . a lot of things happened inside of you as never ought to —Richard Llewellyn, *None But the Lonely Heart,* 1943

"Never trust a bloke as says that," Bert said —Alan Sillitoe, *Saturday Night and Sunday Morning,* 1958

I had me a little spell and took some pills as cost 60¢ a throw —Flannery O'Connor, letter, 4 Aug. 1957

Among these uses is a fixed phrase beginning "them as" followed by a third-person present singular verb. In the first of the examples below, the phrase is represented as the speech of an unlettered character. In the other two the fixed phrase is used—as are many fixed phrases with *ain't*—in such a way as to disinfect it of the suspicion of illiteracy and make it a leavening agent in the writing.

'Them as looks down their nose don't see far beyond it,' said Laffin —Robert Gibbings, *Lovely Is the Lee,* 1945

I'll stick to my casualty page; them as likes that kind of thing can have their newsworthy floozies —Alan Villiers, *Ships and the Sea,* January 1953

In literature, for example, it is often said that "the novel is dead," or that "the sentence is obsolete". All right for them as thinks so —Clancy Sigal, *Times Literary Supp.,* 6 Aug. 1964

It looks to us as if the plain relative pronoun *as* would be a little tricky to use if it is not part of your natural idiom. You need not, of course, avoid its survival in this proverb:

Handsome is as handsome does.

3. *Conjunction.* The use of *as* as a conjunction where *that,* or sometimes *if* or *whether,* could be substituted has been attacked by various commentators since 1881, but none of them gives a reason for the disapproval.

This use is a survival of an older one. The OED notes its existence from Caxton's time in the 15th century. Lowth 1763 lists it in a footnote of old-fashioned or out-of-date uses. It had high literary use in the 17th and early 18th centuries:

And certainly, it is the Nature of Extreme *Selfe-Lovers;* As they will set an House on

Fire, and it were but to roast their Egges
—Francis Bacon, *Essays,* 1625

I gain'd a son;
And such a son, as all men hail'd me happy
—John Milton, *Samson Agonistes,*
1671 (in Lowth)

. . . disposed to conclude a peace upon such
conditions, as it was not worth the life of a
grenadier to refuse them —Jonathan Swift,
*The [History of the] Four Last Years of the
Queen* (in Lowth)

These literary uses have dropped away. The
OED notes survival in southern British dialects; the Dictionary of American Regional
English notes American dialect use. It remains
almost entirely an oral use in American English. It can occasionally be found in positive
constructions:

Billy Sessions asked me if I thought you all
would read his play & I allowed as I thot you
would —Flannery O'Connor, letter, 1 July
1959

But usually it is followed in negative constructions, usually after the verbs *know, see,* or *say:*

I don't know as it makes any difference in
respect to danger —Walt Whitman, letter, 9
Feb. 1863

"Just as you say," returned the rejected. "I
ain't sure as you'd be exactly the one. . . ."
—Francis Lee Pratt, "Captain Ben's Choice,"
in *Mark Twain's Library of Humor,* 1888

I don't see as it's been any use —Edith
Wharton, *Ethan Frome,* 1911 (in American
Dialect Dictionary)

I didn't know as I'd go —Thornton Wilder,
Our Town, 1938 (in ADD)

But the last five years anyway we've managed to market it all in retail containers. I
don't know as I should say all, but the majority of it —Mac Joslyn, quoted in *New England Farmer,* October 1984

This use of the conjunction *as* is not ungrammatical, erroneous, or illiterate, but you
must remember that it is now a speech form
and is not found in ordinary expository prose.
See also AS HOW.

4. *Preposition.* Phythian 1979 believes that
"correct grammar" does not accept *as* as a
preposition, but that is not the case. *As* has a
few prepositional uses no one quibbles about:

When I sailed as a boy, yachting was confined to relatively few centers —Carleton
Mitchell, *Boating,* January 1984

. . . language is primarily learned as speech
—William Stafford, *Writing the Australian
Crawl,* 1978

He acted as her manager —E. L. Doctorow,
Ragtime, 1975

. . . they respect every man as a man —J.
Bronowski, *American Scholar,* Autumn
1969

Here's a good Ph.D. thesis for somebody:
Weber as a literary man —Harold C. Schonberg, *N.Y. Times,* 16 July 1967

There is another sense of the preposition *as*
that means the same as *like:*

. . . each of them, as their predecessors,
neatly tailored to the pocket —*Times Literary Supp.,* 26 Jan. 1967

Then I said, "Do you think that he is not as
other men?" —Jim Henderson, *Open Country Muster,* 1974

. . . that grimness is as nothing compared to
what was to come —Robert Penn Warren,
Democracy and Poetry, 1975

Because of the propensity of conjunctional *as*
to be used with what are called truncated
clauses, it is sometimes hard to tell whether
the conjunction or preposition was intended:

Comeau was thin and Adams was fat, but
after years of association they moved as
matched planets —John Updike, *Couples,*
1968

It sounds and reads as a forced word —John
O. Barbour, quoted in Harper 1985

Some writers choose *as* automatically out of
fear of misusing *like;* such uses are often ambiguous because the *as* can be understood in
its "like" sense or in its "in the character or capacity of" sense. In the E. L. Doctorow quotation above, "He acted as her manager," *as* reflects the latter sense; it is easy to see how "He
acted like her manager" would mean something quite different. Copperud 1964, Freeman 1983, and others warn against using *as* in
its "like" sense when it can be taken for the
other. Here is an example:

. . . convicted of assaulting a security guard
. . . and breaking up the hotel's furniture.
Said the judge to the defendants upon sen-
tencing them: "You acted as buffoons."
—*TV Guide,* 4 Jan. 1985

If the judge had used *like,* his meaning would
have been apparent at once.

5. Copperud 1970 and one or two others raise
an objection to the preposition *as* used after
what they term "designating verbs": *name, appoint, elect,* and the like. Verbs like *elect* and
appoint are complex transitive verbs—they
take a complement and a direct object:

We elected Helene president.

He was appointed vicar.

They named her their trade representative.

The problem with a blanket objection to the insertion of *as* between the object and the complement is that some similar verbs, such as *install,* are not complex transitives:

He was installed as vicar last week.

If the occasional insertion of an unnecessary but harmless *as* in

He was appointed as vicar.

avoids the unidiomatic

He was installed vicar.

it is a minor fault indeed.

as . . . as   **1.** *As . . . as, so . . . as.* Burchfield 1996 puts it succinctly: "In simple comparisons, the normal construction in standard English is clearly *as . . . as.* . . . Quite commonly, however, in the 19c. and earlier, the antecedent could also be *so,* esp[ecially], but not only, in negative sentences." It is the association of *so . . . as* with negative statements that has caused a usage issue. An obscure grammarian named J. Mennye started it in 1785 by insisting on *so . . . as* in negative statements. Mennye was probably doing his duty as a defender of the language against the use of *as . . . as* in negative statements; *as . . . as* seems to have begun to establish itself in negative contexts during the 18th century.

Leonard 1929 says that Mennye had a large number of followers in the authors of 19th-century grammars and handbooks. Handbooks continued to carry his insistence on *so . . . as* in negative statements well into the 20th century (it was still found as late as 1977).

In the meantime, writers went their own merry way, disregarding the handbook writers. Studies have shown that in the middle of the 19th century only 11 percent or so of writers used negative *as . . . as,* but by the middle of the 20th century, more than half were using it. By the end of the 20th century, Burchfield reports, *as . . . as* is the overwhelming choice. But *so . . . as* is far from extinct.

We should mention *so . . . as* in positive contexts. While it does not appear to have been especially common at any time, neither does it appear to have been rare. The OED has examples from the 15th century to the 19th century. It survives especially in a few expressions concerned with time. H. L. Mencken used one:

. . . so late as 1870 —*The American Language, Supplement II,* 1948

More often, however, we find positive *so . . . as* when the writer appears to want the additional emphasis of *so* that comes from its use as a degree word:

Super-duper profs even go so far as to try to enter real politics —Anthony Lambeth, *Change,* Summer 1971

To conclude: both *as . . . as* and *so . . . as* are used in negative constructions; you can choose the one that sounds better in any given instance. In positive constructions *as . . . as* is the prevalent form; positive *so . . . as* is not wrong but simply much less common.

2. Copperud 1970 notes a couple of commentators who object to *as . . . as* constructions with the first *as* omitted; he also notes that Evans 1957 considers it acceptable. The OED records it without stigma and lists citations from about 1200 on, including ones from such writers as Wyclif, Shakespeare, Spenser, Milton, and Richardson. Here are a couple of more modern instances:

It was jolly as could be —Henry Adams, letter, 22 Apr. 1859

He's hooked bad as I am —Robert Strauss, quoted in *N.Y. Times Mag.,* 20 May 1984

3. If a pronoun follows an *as . . . as* comparison, is it to be in the nominative case or the objective case? Is it "She is as tall as I" or "She is as tall as me"? Commentators differ: some prefer the nominative; some allow both but think traditionalists prefer the nominative; others prefer the objective.

Our evidence is of little help in this instance, because the typical "Is Mary as tall as I (or me)" construction is very rare in the sort of discursive prose most of our evidence comes from. What is more, *as* is often omitted from concordances of prose works because its great frequency of occurrence would add to the bulk of the work. Grammarians and commentators have their opinions, but hard evidence seems difficult to come by. Burchfield 1996 says that the objective is more common in speech and informal prose.

See also IT'S ME; THAN 1.

4. See AS GOOD OR BETTER THAN.

as bad or worse than   See AS GOOD OR BETTER THAN.

as best   James J. Kilpatrick, in a column printed in the *Portland Oregonian* of 2 Nov. 1985, worries about his use of "we must do as best we can"—several of his readers had written in to chide him about it. Kilpatrick believes "as best we can" to be a respectable idiom but concedes that it might be a Southern regionalism and wonders if anyone else uses it. The answer is yes, other people use it, and no, it is not a Southern regionalism. Bernstein 1977 specifically approves it:

It is perfectly proper to say, "He did the job as best he could."

Our evidence shows that *as best* has been around at least since the early 19th century:

. . . blow 'em up as best suits our convenience —Washington Irving, *Salmagundi,* 14 Aug. 1807

It is in widespread use:

The cops had to get the sick and injured to hospital as best they could —H. L. Mencken, *Happy Days,* 1940

. . . to where, or where as best he could see in the dark, she had gone through her rites —John Cheever, *The Wapshot Chronicle,* 1957

. . . to answer all questions that arise, as best I can —Robert Graves, *The Greek Myths,* Vol. I, 1955

. . . labour as best he might in the old vineyard —Flann O'Brien, *The Dalkey Archive,* 1964

They are trying, as best they can, to exercise responsible stewardship —Glenn C. Loury, *New Republic,* 27 Dec. 1999

. . . leaving the spectators to make out as best they could what was going on —Robertson Davies, *The Lyre of Orpheus,* 1988

It looks like a perfectly respectable idiom to us.

ascent, assent   One of the 8th-grade English texts in our collection warns students not to confuse *ascent* and *assent*—a quick check in your dictionary will show you that although they sound the same, they are not at all related. Whoever wrote the following should have checked a dictionary:

He analyzes the course of Russia's assent to superpower status —Advance Book Information, Oxford University Press, July 1983

as far as, so far as   **1.** In the October 1962 issue of *American Speech,* Paul Faris commented on the prepositional use of *as far as.* Although he had recorded a great many instances of the construction in speech and in writing, he found that dictionaries and usage books in general seemed unaware of the construction. He found only Fowler 1926 dealing with the subject.

Fowler disapproved figurative use of the preposition; literal use—"he went as far as New York"—was not disputed. But *as far as* in "As far as getting the money he asked for, Mr. Churchill had little difficulty" (among other instances) was condemned. The subject was not taken up again until Bernstein 1962. Since then many commentators have condemned the construction.

Let's us begin our review of the matter with a few examples from print:

The cabin . . . was in perfect condition so far as frame and covering until 1868 —Henry Seidel Canby, *Thoreau,* 1939 (in Faris)

As far as disturbing a writer at his work, this hotel bedroom might just as well have been filled with howling monkeys this past week, for all the work I've been able to get done —E. B. White, letter, 8 Feb. 1942

Pauls would be taken seriously, they felt, and as far as doing business with Germany this was the most important long-range consideration —James Feron, *N.Y. Times Mag.,* 31 Oct. 1965

As far as being mentioned in the Ten Commandments, I think it is —Billy Graham, newspaper column, 1974

As far as your transmission's health, this is a tough call —Mike Allen, *Popular Mechanics,* February 1999

Although these examples are characteristic of the construction, they are not exactly typical of our evidence. Most of our citations are from speech, either recorded off the air or reproduced in newspapers and magazines:

But as far as whether I could attend this sort of a function in your church . . . then I could attend —John F. Kennedy, quoted in *U.S. News & World Report,* 1960 (in Faris)

Not only was she a great actress, she was the Carole Lombard of her time, as far as being able to do comedy —Jack Lemmon, quoted in *Playboy,* June 1981

It was probably one of the worst, if not the worst, conditions I've played in as far as wind —John McEnroe, quoted in *Springfield* (Mass.) *Republican,* 8 May 1983

As far as raising kids, he didn't have a clue —Gary Crosby, quoted in *People,* 21 Mar. 1983

. . . but as one NBA owner says, "As far as staying in Vancouver, I think they're toast" —Jon Wertheim, *Sports Illustrated,* 1 Nov. 1999

Citations taken directly from broadcasts do not differ from the printed reports:

I wonder if he's got a physical problem as far as running —Earl Weaver, *ABC Game of the Week,* 15 Aug. 1983

. . . as far as bringing this sort of thing to a halt —Ara Parseghian, CBS football telecast, 25 Dec. 1986

We should note that this prepositional use can be identified only by the absence of a following verb (as *is concerned*). All a speaker or writer has to do is omit (or forget) the following verb, and the conjunctional *as far as* becomes a preposition. This is an odd state of affairs, but it is a price we pay for using Latin part-of-speech categories to describe English. Forgetfulness may have caused our earliest example:

> Then the king don Peter answered the prince and said; 'Right dear cousin, as far as the gold, silver and treasure that I have brought hither, which is not the thirtieth part so much as I have left behind me, as long as that will endure, I shall give and part therewith to your people.' —Lord Berners, translation of Froissart's *Chronicles,* 1523

In spite of this example prepositional *as far as* must be considered essentially a 20th-century form on the basis of what we now know. While we have by no means exhausted the possibilities, we have not yet found a 19th-century example.

There can be no question, after more than three quarters of a century, that prepositional *as far as* is established in speech; it was clearly established in 1962 when Faris published his findings. Reference books have been slow to catch up in this instance. But speech and reports of speech aside, the expression has made little inroad into ordinary prose. Our most recent evidence shows it still primarily a speech form.

2. Copperud 1970, Nickles 1974, and Garner 1998 object to *as far as* in any use as wordy or long-winded. *As far as* may indeed be long-winded in some instances, but it cannot be easily replaced by a shorter formula in many others. The examples that follow are from letters, where conciseness of expression is usually not of prime importance. We suspect that in these examples at least, it would not be easy to replace *as far as* with something shorter and better:

> I endeavour as far as I can to supply your place & be useful —Jane Austen, letter, 14 Sept. 1804

> We are in a state of anarchy so far as the President goes —Henry Adams, letter, 22 Dec. 1860

> . . . but, so far as I can see, I shall be in town on or before the 20th —Lewis Carroll, letter, 10 June 1864

> Those two seem to me achievements as far as the writing goes —Flannery O'Connor, letter, 2 Aug. 1958

as follows If you are really interested, *as follows* regularly has the singular form of the verb—*follows*—even if preceded by a plural.

> The principal parts of *lay* are as follows: —Macmillan 1982

All the experts agree—Copperud 1970, 1980, Harper 1975, 1985, Longman 1984, Freeman 1983, Phythian 1979, Bremner 1980, Johnson 1982, Heritage 1969, Bernstein 1977, Garner 1998, and undoubtedly many others.

The only interesting thing about this subject is its longevity—it was first discussed in Baker 1770.

as good or better than Under this heading we will discuss a construction involving both the positive and comparative of several adjectives (*good* seems to be the most common of them) that has been the subject of corrective efforts since the 18th century. Correction begins with Campbell 1776, who exhibits this sentence:

> Will it be urged that the four Gospels are as old, or even older, than tradition? —Bolingbroke, *Philosophical Essays*

What exercises Campbell is that *than,* which goes with *older,* does not go with *old.* Insert *as* after *old,* says Campbell, and everything will be put right. Lindley Murray 1795 picked up the example and the solution and passed both on to the 20th century, where we can find them in numerous commentators and handbooks right down to the end of the 20th century.

This issue arises from the 18th-century grammarians' concern with developing a perfectly logical language and eliminating as many untidy English idioms as possible. If Campbell had not noticed it, this locution might now be considered simply another idiomatic usage. It certainly is a venial fault, since no reader is confused by the construction.

Let us look at a few examples:

> . . . other slums, as bad or worse than those marked for obliteration —*N.Y. Times,* 1 Apr. 1954

> You will observe that I admire my own work as much if not more than anybody else does —Flannery O'Connor, letter, 4 May 1955

> . . . a rate it said was as good or better than conventional trains —*N.Y. Times,* 9 Apr. 1970

> . . . but the mayors have as good if not a better point —Glenn A. Briere, *Springfield* (Mass.) *Sunday Republican,* 1 Dec. 1985

These are the simple unpunctuated variety of the expression. You can see that they are readily understandable; the *as* that would follow the positive adjective if it were used alone has been omitted and the *than* that would normally follow the comparative has been retained—the proximate adjective has determined the choice of conjunction. This is a linguistic shortcut—an idiom.

We think that the *as good or better than* construction is probably simply a long-lived English idiom; it need not be routinely revised out of general writing that does not strive for elevation. If you prefer the more logical approach, there are at least two things you can do. We will use an example from Bernstein 1977 for illustration:

> . . . a giant rocket with lifting power as great or greater than the Saturn 5's.

The time-honored suggestion is to supply the missing *as*; supplying it will require two commas:

> . . . a giant rocket with lifting power as great as, or greater than, the Saturn 5's.

Bernstein thinks this solution a bit "on the prissy side." He suggests as an alternative putting the *or greater* at the end; it will need to be set off with a comma.

> . . . a giant rocket with lifting power as great as the Saturn 5's, or greater.

He finds this solution more graceful than the first. He also suggests that the following revision is a way out, if you don't like all the commas:

> . . . a giant rocket with lifting power at least as great as the Saturn 5's.

as great or greater than   See AS GOOD OR BETTER THAN.

as how   *As how* is aspersed by Phythian 1979 as incorrect and by Copperud 1970 as substandard for *that*. It is neither, however. It is simply dialectal: the OED characterizes it as southern (English) dialect; the Dictionary of American Regional English calls it chiefly Southern and Midland. It has had some literary use by figures like Tobias Smollett, Captain Marryat, and Anthony Trollope, who have put it in the mouths of characters not noted for elegant speech.

It is found in the combinations *being as how* and *seeing as how,* and is also fairly common after *allow*:

> She didn't know I had sent it to her . . . but she allowed as how she liked the book —Flannery O'Connor, letter, 24 Jan. 1962

This expression has current use in mainstream journalism to provide an air of studied informality:

> Nixon allowed as how the best way to knock Romney down in the polls was to remove his winner status by beating him in New Hampshire —William Safire, *Before The Fall* (cited in Reader's Digest 1983)

> Former French President Valery Giscard d'Estaing allowed as how he "regretted" the situation —Scott Sullivan, *Newsweek,* 28 Apr. 1986

> . . . also allowed as how it drove her crazy if some helpful friend tries to clean up while she is cooking —Enid Nemy, *N.Y. Times,* 14 Sept. 1983

> At the end of the tour I allowed as how I was interested in Quantrill and asked if the society had anything else of his —Edward E. Leslie, *American Heritage,* July/August 1995

It is also used to ascribe a certain lack of sophistication to someone indirectly quoted:

> He was a sad-eyed man of about forty-five, who allowed as how he was turning the store into an antique shop —Wade Roberts, *Cuisine,* October 1984

> Even the nurseryman was uncertain of its exact origin, although he did allow as how it was a local product —Michael Olmert, *Horticulture,* February 1983

These uses are neither regional nor nonstandard.

Asian, Asiatic, Oriental   As we move into the 21st century, *Asian* is the preferred word, noun or adjective, especially for ethnic purposes; *Asiatic* is held to be mildly offensive.

Some dictionaries and commentators have noted that *Oriental* as a noun designating a person is often taken to be offensive. Our citations indicate that there has been increasing sensitivity about this word in recent years and that many publications avoid this use of *Oriental,* preferring *Asian* or a more specific term in its place.

aside from   *Aside from* is a compound preposition found in American English; some writers hold it to be the American equivalent of *apart from* (which see), but both British and American writers use *apart from.*

> Aside from bending into a stance, which is good for most waistlines, there is considerable walking in our game —Willie Mosconi, *Winning Pocket Billiards,* 1965

> Aside from the members of the society, millions read the magazines involved in the debate —Georgie Anne Geyer, *Saturday Rev.,* 25 Dec. 1971

> . . . but aside from these two teachers there was no great offering of courses at the graduate level —Samuel Flagg Bemis, *New-England Galaxy,* Fall 1969

> Aside from being six feet tall, my image seemed inappropriate —Robben W. Fleming, *Michigan Business Rev.,* July 1968

You will note that in the first two examples *aside from* means "besides" and in the second two "except for."

as if, as though 1. At one time the propriety of *as though* used for *as if* was considered dubious. But nowadays commentators who mention the matter find *as though* and *as if* interchangeable.
2. Several commentators insist on a verb in the subjunctive mood following the conjunction, Fowler 1926 and Simon 1980 among them. Flesch 1964 says the subjunctive is extinct after *as if* and *as though*. A number of other commentators allow either the indicative or the subjunctive, reserving the subjunctive for formal occasions.

Evidence in our files shows both subjunctive and indicative in frequent respectable use. There seems to be little difference in formality. Some examples:

. . . there's not one moment in this too-long film when Quek looks as if she gets any pleasure from sex —Jill Nelson, *Ms.,* October/November 1999

It was as if she were prom queen —David Nyhan, quoted in *New Republic,* 3 Apr. 2000

It was as though this was not the land of room enough —John Hope Franklin, *Race and History,* 1989

. . . certain things grated on Schueler as though he were a wedge of parmesan regianno —Jeff Pearlman, *Sports Illustrated,* 12 June 2000

3. See also LIKE, AS, AS IF.

as is Harper 1985 reminds us that *as is,* most frequently used of goods to be sold, is always singular, regardless of the number of items, and Garner 1998 notes it is always in the present tense.

. . . sold on an "as is" basis —Diana Shaman, *N.Y. Times,* 20 Apr. 1980

. . . made up of odds and ends; sold as is —Henry M. Ellis, *Stamps for Fun and Profit,* 1953

ask Evans 1957 notes that *ask* may be followed by an infinitive or a clause:

. . . was asked to arrange and perform the music for the sound track —*Current Biography,* October 1966

. . . sent my brother upstairs to ask that I switch to the news —Otto Friedrich, *Harper's,* May 1971

. . . asks whether the appointment of chaplains to the two Houses of Congress is "consistent with the Constitution. . . ." —Joseph L. Blau, *Rev. of Religion,* No. 3, 1950

Raub 1897 prescribes as follows: "Ask *of* a person, *for* what is wanted, *after* one's health."

. . . if you ask it of him, he returns a hasty negative —Henry Fairlie, *N.Y. Times Mag.,* 11 July 1965

. . . the two or three people of whom I asked his whereabouts —F. Scott Fitzgerald, *The Great Gatsby,* 1925

Of may also be used with inanimate objects:

Comfort, beauty, and spacesaving efficiency are the three big things we ask of our rooms —*Better Homes and Gardens,* June 1954

From may be similarly used:

. . . an increasing number were asking many things from philosophy —Henry O. Taylor, *The Mediaeval Mind,* 4th ed., 1925

For does indeed take what is wanted as its object:

. . . getting a reasonable portion of what it was asking for —Philip D. Lang, quoted in *Change,* January–February, 1971

Just yesterday a letter came in from a girl your age in South Carolina asking for biographical material —James Thurber, letter, 4 Jan. 1958

Ask for is often used idiomatically with *trouble* or *it* in a figurative sense:

Dili had been asking for trouble ever since she left school —Richard Vaughan, *Moulded in Earth,* 1951

"You certainly made an ass of me today, Eloise. But I kept reminding myself that I was the one who had asked for it. . . ." —Louis Auchincloss, *A Law for the Lion,* 1953

After is indeed for health:

You ask after my health —Lord Byron, letter, 9 Sept. 1811

Another time a friend asked after King George VI's health —H. Durant Osborne, *Springfield* (Mass.) *Union,* 24 Mar. 1955

When information is sought, *ask* is often used with the preposition *about*:

The truck driver would have asked about me in the drugstore —Phil Stong, *New England Journeys,* No. 3, 1955

When *ask* means "invite" it may be used with the adverb *out* or the preposition *to*:

. . . the other young men in Sargentville asked Ann out —Charles Bracelen Flood, *Omnibook,* June 1954

. . . they were known collectively as the Grateful Hearts but seldom asked to the house —Osbert Lancaster, *All Done From Memory,* 1953

as much or more than See AS GOOD OR BETTER THAN.

as of It is a bit surprising how often you scratch a disapproved locution and find an Americanism that some British commentator has castigated. *As of* appears to be such a one:

Let me now turn to the strange American delusion that the words "as of" can always be used before a date as if they were a temporal preposition. . . . An additional illiteracy is introduced when the words "as of" precede not a date, but the adverb "now." "As of now" is a barbarism which only a love of illiteracy for its own sake can explain. What is generally meant is "at present." —Lord Conesford, *Saturday Evening Post,* 13 July 1957

American commentators soon appeared in support of Lord Conesford's view.

The first thing we must point out about *as of* is that it is used when something in a letter or other writing carries a different date than that of the document itself.

Statistics as of June 30, 1943 —*Britannica Book of the Year 1944*

This article was written and published by the Center in 1957. In the present version I have revised the figures as of the end of 1967 —Adolf A. Berle, *Center Mag.,* January 1969

The function of *as of* in these examples was explained by a Merriam-Webster editor in 1939 as "indicating an arbitrary, often official, designation for record or convenience. . . ."

This use of *as of* need never be avoided; it constitutes the bulk of our printed evidence for the phrase. You should be aware that most of our evidence comes from business sources—annual reports and such—and from reference sources—*Current Biography, Britannica Book of the Year,* etc.—with occasional evidence from the news media.

There is another use, chiefly oral, of *as of.* In this use *as of* occurs with words relating to time other than dates, including the *now* Lord Conesford found illiterate.

. . . an almost morbid resemblance to the Roosevelt–Landon figures as of about this time in 1936 —Elmo Roper, quoted in *Time,* 13 Sept. 1948

I am saying, as of now anyway, that Ross never knew of Fleischmann's offer of his job to you —James Thurber, letter, 7 Aug. 1958

Dr. Edward Teller announced that "the best scientists as of this moment are not in the

United States but in Moscow." —*Current Biography,* November 1964

Notwithstanding Lord Conesford's easy generalization, Roper and Thurber and Teller are not showing a love of illiteracy for its own sake—they are simply using an ordinary idiom. The idiom seems to be American. Garner 1998 notes that *as of now* is today unobjectionable in American English.

as per *As per* is a compound preposition that appears to have originated sometime during the 19th century, probably in that area of life where business and law intersect: contracts, bills of exchange, and the like. No one seems to have paid any attention to the phrase until the 1920s, when several commentators announced it was a term to be avoided. There is no consensus about what is wrong with *as per,* but one factor seems to be that it is a redundancy.

Our evidence shows that *as per* is still used in business and legal contexts and in straightforward but somewhat stiff prose similar to business correspondence:

The computer justifies and hyphenates the copy as per typographical specifications —John Markus, *American Documentation,* April 1966

. . . perform a few moves with this as per the sleight of hand section in this book —Ian Adair, *Conjuring as a Craft,* 1970

Just pre-heat or pre-chill as per directions on the bottom —mail order catalog, Spring 1980

We also find it in contexts quite unlike business letters or "how-to" prose. Sometimes the business-letter style is used for fun:

I note, as per your esteemed letter, that you cannot beg —George Bernard Shaw, letter, 2 Apr. 1913

When we say we do not like big girls, as per our letter of yesterday, we do not mean . . . —H. L. Mencken, in *The Intimate Notebooks of George Jean Nathan,* 1932

If only one little thing goes wrong—and as per Murphy's Law it usually does —David Larsen, *Los Angeles Times,* 24 Mar. 1988

. . . and, as per ritual, he is doing yoga in his dressing room —Chris Mundy, *Rolling Stone,* 27 May 1993

Sometimes the context is not facetious:

Was the Emperor head substantive in the way that the Pope is . . .? Was he a nominal head, as per Elizabeth II and the Church of England? —Edward N. Luttwak, *Times Literary Supp.,* 19 June 1998

Shactman's Third Camp was the anti-fascist and anti-capitalist resistance, as per Macdonald's wartime ideal —Paul Berman, *New Republic,* 12 Sept. 1994

It is also used in the phrase *as per usual:*

. . . in the third half hour, I strolled out and told a story as per usual —Garrison Keillor, *Leaving Home,* 1987

Duke, as per usual, refuses to choose —David Nyhan, *Boston Sunday Globe,* 19 Nov. 1989

I went to Finvara. . . . It was raining as per usual —Nina FitzPatrick, *Fables of the Irish Intelligentsia,* 1991

As per usual is not found in elevated contexts. See also PER.

aspiration *Aspiration,* says Bernstein 1965, takes *toward* or sometimes *after.* He is apparently talking about older literary, rather than modern, use. *Aspiration* is usually not used with a preposition now, except the expected *of* that shows whose aspirations are being talked about. When a preposition is used, it will most likely be *for:*

. . . the aspirations of Alexander for the Bosporus —*Times Literary Supp.,* 4 Jan. 1952

. . . those who have no power aspirations for themselves —Harry Levinson, *Think,* May–June 1967

. . . the aspiration of decent Americans for a just and lasting peace —Bruce Bliven, *New Republic,* 22 Nov. 1954

Of is used, followed by a gerund:

. . . with logical aspirations of getting there —William H. Whyte, Jr., *Is Anybody Listening?,* 1952

. . . Oak Ridge's aspiration of becoming an ordinary place —Daniel Lang, *New Yorker,* 31 Oct. 1953

We had aspirations of winning the NCAA championship this year —Wayne Vandenburg, quoted in *Sports Illustrated,* 15 July 1968

To may be used followed by either a noun or an infinitive:

. . . wide-eyed aspirations to become a television star —Richard Corbin, *The Teaching of Writing in Our Schools,* 1966

. . . aspirations to objectivity —*Times Literary Supp.,* 19 Feb. 1971

. . . the aspiration to touch the superlative in one's work —Oliver Wendell Holmes d. 1935, letter, 12 July 1921

Aspiration may be followed by a clause:

'. . . the aspiration that gainful activities should be socially serviceable —J. M. Clark, *Yale Rev.,* Autumn 1953

Toward is also found:

The aspiration of America is still upward, toward a better job —Bernard DeVoto, *The World of Fiction,* 1950

aspire Bernstein 1965 will allow us *to, after,* and *toward* as prepositions; Raub 1897, *to* and *after;* Evans 1957, the infinitive. All are in use except for *after,* of which we have no evidence in the Merriam-Webster files and which is unattested after 1794 in the OED. *At* is attested a bit later:

. . . others aspired at nothing beyond his remembering the catchword, and the first line of his speech —Jane Austen, *Mansfield Park,* 1814

To is the predominant preposition:

. . . the social class to which they aspire —James Sledd, in *The English Language Today,* ed. Sidney Greenbaum, 1985

. . . aspire to prestigious cultural properties —Pauline Kael, *Harper's,* February 1969

. . . the Russian aspires to hard, materialist, dialectically sound explanations —Arthur Miller, *Harper's,* September 1969

Bots are autonomous software programs . . . while some bots are mundane drones, others aspire to artificial intelligence —Jonathan Bing, *Publishers Weekly,* 11 Aug. 1997

To followed by the infinitive is also common:

Aspiring to be the leader of a nation of third-rate men —H. L. Mencken, *Prejudices: Second Series,* 1920

. . . aspired to become a professional breeder of ferrets —Sherwood Anderson, *Winesburg, Ohio,* 1919

. . . those who merely aspire to clean up a mess —Aldous Huxley, *Brave New World Revisited,* 1958

Toward and *towards* are both found:

. . . it aspires toward a ritualization of conflict —Irving Howe, *Harper's,* April 1970

. . . the literary values towards which he aspired —*Times Literary Supp.,* 25 Jan. 1968

For is sometimes used:

The Administration still seems to aspire for what is vaguely called an honorable agreement —J. William Fulbright, *The Progressive,* June 1969

as regards　See REGARD 1.

assay, essay　Copperud 1970, 1980 tells us these verbs are sometimes confused; the Oxford American Dictionary warns us against confusing them; Shaw 1975 exhibits the differences. Fowler 1926 says that the two verbs tend to be differentiated, and we think his summing-up of the situation comes very close to the truth. *Assay* is usually used in the sense of "test, evaluate" and *essay* in the sense "try, attempt." The differentiation, to use Fowler's word, is not complete, however.

The two verbs are etymologically the same; an early sense of *assay* was "try, attempt":

> And when Saul was come to Jerusalem, he assayed to join himself to the disciples —Acts 9:26 (AV), 1611

> . . . assayed
> To stanch the blood
> —John Dryden, *Stanzas on Oliver Cromwell*, 1658

This older variant is still occasionally used:

> . . . has assayed to penetrate a field that by its very nature requires consummate skill —John W. Chase, *N.Y. Times Book Rev.,* 25 July 1954

> How they accomplished this was a mystery, for they would draw the canvas curtains about his bed before they assayed such a task —Bette Howland, *Commentary,* August 1972

But *essay* is the more usual spelling for the "try" sense. We would suggest that you use *essay* to avoid puzzling your readers. Here are a couple of the more usual uses of *assay* in its figurative application:

> . . . she would walk to the full-length mirror and assay herself —Mary McCarthy, *New Yorker*, 23 Mar. 1957

> . . . I try to assay the man's or woman's importance —Alden Whitman, *Saturday Rev.,* 11 Dec. 1971

assent　When the verb *assent* takes a preposition, it is *to*:

> They did not readily assent to the selection —Irving Louis Horowitz, *Change,* January–February 1970

> It is difficult now to assent to Lamb's words —T. S. Eliot, "John Ford," in *Selected Essays,* 1932

> . . . in assenting to dance she had made a mistake of some kind —Thomas Hardy, *The Mayor of Casterbridge,* 1886

assimilate　Bernstein 1965 says that *assimilate* takes *to* and infrequently with *with*; this is true

as far as it goes. However, *into* is the most frequent preposition:

> Jews who had assimilated into German, Russian and other cultures —Elenore Lester, *N.Y. Times Mag.,* 2 Dec. 1979

> In order to be assimilated into a collective medium a person has to be stripped of his individual distinctness —Eric Hoffer, *The True Believer,* 1951

> Those groups were eagerly assimilating into the larger culture and rejecting their own cuisine —Corby Kummer, *N.Y. Times Book Rev.,* 16 Aug. 1998

> The mistaken attempts to assimilate Lindner's paintings into the Pop Art movement in the 1960s —Hilton Kramer, *Arts & Antiques,* 1 Jan. 1997

To is the next most frequently used preposition:

> . . . expounding a science, or a body of truth which he seeks to assimilate to a science —*Selected Writings Of Benjamin N. Cardozo,* ed. Margaret E. Hall, 1947

> Our manufacturing class was assimilated in no time to the conservative classes —H. G. Wells, *Mr. Britling Sees It Through,* 1916

> But Mr. Eliot was the one who assimilated the French achievement to English literature —H. Marshall McLuhan, *Sewanee Rev.,* Winter 1947

> Over time, most of the inhabitants of the "Little Italies" . . . assimilated rapidly to the society —Stephan Thernstrom, *Times Literary Supp.,* 26 May 2000

By, as you would expect, indicates the agent:

> . . . I was educated in, and assimilated by, the very bosom of the Yankee motherland —James Fallows, *Harper's,* February 1976

> . . . conquered and forcibly assimilated by the West —Arnold J. Toynbee, *Horizon,* August 1947

With, in, and *as* are quite infrequent:

> As the matured area assimilated itself with the region just to the east —Ray Allen Billington, *Westward Expansion,* 1949

> Some of the present hard-core unemployed can be assimilated in industry —Henry Ford II, *Michigan Business Rev.,* July 1968

> Countless Chinese have truly been assimilated as Americans —Mary Ellen Leary, *Atlantic,* March 1970

assist　1. When *assist* means "to be present," it regularly takes *at*:

> The picture of a saint being slowly flayed alive . . . will not produce the same physical

sensations of sickening disgust that a modern man would feel if he could assist at the actual event —Roger Fry, *Vision and Design,* 1920

She waited there, hesitant, not exactly on the watch, not exactly unwilling to assist at an interview between Amy and Amy's mistress —Arnold Bennett, *The Old Wives' Tale,* 1908

. . . compare the ugly, grinning peasant bystanders surrounding an Adoration or a Nativity in northern painting with the ideal figures assisting at Italian holy scenes —Mary McCarthy, *Occasional Prose,* 1985

It is not certain that every *assist at* means no more than "to be present at":

The Russian party moves through the streets at a clip that suggests they have been called to assist at a rather serious fire —Mollie Panter-Downes, *New Yorker,* 5 May 1956

. . . invited me to assist at the burning of a huge pile of manuscripts —Henry Miller, *The Air-Conditioned Nightmare,* 1945

My conscience stirs as if, in my impulse to do violence to my enemy, I had assisted at his crime —Katherine Anne Porter, *The Never-Ending Wrong,* 1977

When *assist* clearly means "help," however, *in* and *with* are usual. *In* can be used before a noun or a gerund:

The teacher, college students, and seventh-grade students all assist in the project —Rexine A. Langen, *The Instructor,* March 1968

. . . was assisted in the preparation of a manual —*Annual Report, National Bureau of Standards,* 1950

. . . have assisted in making plans —Robert M. Hutchins, *Center Mag.,* September 1969

. . . turned to stage design in 1948, when he assisted Salvador Dali with the extraordinary sets —*Current Biography,* December 1964

The Captain and the cook was playing a duet on the mouth harp while your correspondent assisted with the vocals —Richard Bissell, *Atlantic,* December 1954

A few other prepositions—*to, into, by* (+ gerund)—are found occasionally:

. . . the artist could assist all humanity to a similar flight —Thomas Munro, *The Arts and Their Interrelations,* 1949

. . . a fetish used to assist a childless woman to fertility —R. E. Kirk, *Introduction to Zuni Fetishism,* 1943

. . . 120 (24 per cent) were assisted into the world by instrumental and other operative methods —Ira S. Wile & Rose Davis, in *Personality in Nature, Society, and Culture,* ed. Clyde Kluckhohn & Henry A. Murray, 1948

. . . assisted the war effort by broadcasting messages —*Current Biography 1947*

Towards was formerly used:

He never . . . heard a circumstance, which might assist towards her moral instruction that he did not haste to tell it her —Mrs. Elizabeth Inchbald, *Nature and Art,* 1796

2. Most of the quibbles about the propriety of this or that sense of *assist* have receded into the past. The propriety of *assist at* meaning "be present at" was an issue in the 1920s —Fowler 1926 discussed it—but no one seems to care any more. In the 1940s it was fashionable to call *assist* overworked and recommend *help* instead (Garner 1998 still prefers *help*). Since *help* appears more than 15 times as often as *assist* in Merriam-Webster's database of citation text, that recommendation need give you no pause.

as such Copperud 1970 notes a couple of his sources find *as such* sometimes used meaninglessly. "The test of its utility," says Copperud, "is to leave the expression out and decide whether anything is lost." Here are a few samples that you can judge for yourself:

In fact, cannibalism as such has nothing to do with the law —Claude Rawson, *N.Y. Times Book Rev.,* 16 Apr. 2000

"We've come to the common conclusion that the war as such, is over on the territory of Chechnya," said General Gennady Troshev —*USA Today,* 26 June 2000

. . . are sympathetic to the difficulties gay couples face but do not approve of gay marriages as such —Andrew Sullivan, *New Republic,* 8 May 2000

. . . the corollary assumption that anyone not dark in hue is therefore white and measurable as such —Christopher Hitchins, *N.Y. Times Book Rev.,* 7 May 2000

Garner 1998 worries that the antecedent of *such* may not be clear. Although the antecedent may be unclear in these next two examples, the reader may still not be puzzled:

The strict settlement was therefore a prenuptial agreement that placed lands in a kind of entail, at least for one generation, and as such it can still be entered into today —Norman F. Cantor, *Imagining the Law,* 1997

Though the word anarchist seldom appears in the names of groups that claim responsibility for these actions, anarchist principles are behind them, and many members interviewed identify themselves as such —Evan Wright, *Rolling Stone,* 30 Mar. 2000

assume, presume   Many commentators are at pains to distinguish these two words. The two words are generally synonymous in one sense of each. Here are the definitions from Merriam-Webster's Collegiate Dictionary, Tenth Edition:

> **assume** . . . 5: to take as granted or true : SUPPOSE

> **presume** . . . 2: to expect or assume esp. with confidence

The idea is that *presume* tends to be more positive in its supposition than *assume.* Most commentators make this point.

Here are a few examples of *assume* and *presume* used in the shared sense.

> He assumed that he could negotiate with Mitterrand, the way he would have negotiated with a sharp investment banker —Jane Kramer, *New Yorker,* 18 Jan. 1982

> . . . the conversation implicitly assumes that Oxford is the centre of the universe —Harold J. Laski, letter, 1 May 1932

> As long as people assumed that learning a language was the product of an advanced intelligence, scholars were reluctant to place the birth of language too far in the past —Edmund Blair Bolles, *Saturday Rev.,* 18 Mar. 1972

> . . . had always assumed that the last volumes would be distinctive simply because of their sources —*Times Literary Supp.,* 19 Feb. 1971

> Because of her intransigent radicalism, many Catholic reformers assume she is on their side when they press for drastic changes inside the Church —Dwight Macdonald, *N.Y. Rev. of Books,* 28 Jan. 1971

> Nobody in Baskul had known much about him except that he had arrived from Persia, where it was presumed he had something to do with oil —James Hilton, *Lost Horizon,* 1933

> . . . the reading public, who might be presumed to know that dynamite and poison have a certain deadly quality —Sir Norman Birkett, *Books of the Month,* June–July 1953

> Of course, Eloise would never presume that they could still be friends —Louis Auchincloss, *A Law for the Lion,* 1953

> Granite shot was used for guns in Plymouth in the sixteenth century, and it may be pre-

sumed that these are of similar date —E. Estyn Evans, *Irish Digest,* June 1954

You can see that the two words would be interchangeable in some of the examples in this way: *assume* could have been used in every instance for *presume,* but something would have been lost in so doing. However, *presume* could not very easily be substituted in the examples of *assume.* Interchange would appear to be easier in one direction than the other—the less specific word can more readily replace the more specific than the other way round.

assure   See ENSURE, INSURE, ASSURE.

as though   See AS IF, AS THOUGH.

as to   1. For a phrase consisting of four letters with a space in the middle, *as to* has generated a surprising amount of criticism. The initial objection was made around 1907, when the Fowler brothers discovered that it was a compound preposition, a host of which were inundating the language, much to the detriment of clarity, precision, etc. The Fowlers were a bit behindhand here, because *as to* had been in use since the 14th century. The Fowlers' objection was in due time forgotten, to be replaced by others. The silliest of these, frequently repeated, was that *as to* is "wordy." Other objectors find it vague and imprecise. We can put a positive spin on this characterization by using Garner 1998's term, all-purpose. Its all-purpose, imprecise character may be one of the greatest virtues of *as to:*

> They keep a puppy tied up which is insignificant as to size, but formidable as to yelp —Mark Twain, 21 Aug. 1864, in *Early Tales and Sketches,* 1981

The truth is that none of the objections will stand up to comparison with evidence of actual use. *As to* is used in literary and general expository prose, in formal and informal settings, and in print and in speech. Some examples from across the years:

> It is the nature of Republicans, who are nearly in a state of equality, to be extremely jealous as to the disposal of all honorary or lucrative appointments —George Washington, 21 Mar. 1789, in W. W. Abbot, *The Papers of George Washington,* 1987

> And now as to the Dred Scott decision —Abraham Lincoln, speech on the Dred Scott Decision, 26 June 1857

> As to my home run hitting —*Babe Ruth's Own Book of Baseball,* 1928

> I was silent as to the need of giving old themes a new setting of words —Robert Frost, letter, 12 Mar. 1936

. . . she remembered the purport of her note, and was not less sanguine as to its effect than she had been the night before —Jane Austen, *Mansfield Park,* 1814

The opinions of relatives as to a man's powers are very commonly of little value —Oliver Wendell Holmes d. 1894, *The Autocrat of the Breakfast-Table,* 1858

. . . there were no special constitutional principles as to strong drink —Oliver Wendell Holmes d. 1935, letter, 20 May 1920

. . . my relation with the reader, which was another affair altogether and as to which I felt no one to be trusted but myself —Henry James, *The Art of the Novel,* 1934

Mr. Wilcox was positive as to the name Clyde —Theodore Dreiser, *An American Tragedy,* 1925

There have been a great many false rumors as to what actually happened —James Thurber, letter, 2 May 1946

One can, of course, instruct that eye as to what to see —James Baldwin, *Playboy* interview, January 1985

. . . but as to plain good sense the character of his mind is not reassuring —E. L. Doctorow, *Loon Lake,* 1979

I could not help speculating as to the possibility of my filling the vacancy —George Bernard Shaw, preface, *The Shaw–Terry letters,* 1931

. . . counted up a phantom savings of $6 billion from rooting out fraud, waste and abuse without any serious recommendations as to how —David A. Stockman, *Newsweek,* 28 Apr. 1986

. . . a jolly pantomime in which the bloodthirsty audience guessed along with the cast as to when the next jack-in-the-box death-blow would be struck —James Wolcott, *Vanity Fair,* September 1999

. . . begs the question as to how the Triple Entente would have reacted —Michael Howard, *Times Literary Supp.,* 13 Nov. 1998

Physicists call this point a singularity and tend not to talk about it because they have no clue as to what happens to matter at these densities —Ann K. Finkbeiner, *Air & Space,* August/September 1993

2. One of the chief complaints made about *as to* is its superfluity when used in front of such conjunctions as *how, why,* and *whether:*

. . . the question as to how they should be referred to —H. L. Mencken, in *Essays on Language and Usage,* ed. Leonard F. Dean & Kenneth G. Wilson, 2d ed., 1963

They gave the royal stamp of approval to a work, and in doing so they provided clues as to how it might be read —Robert Darnton, *The Kiss of Lamourette,* 1990

. . . it should be clear as to why Joyce could find no inspiration in a cultural renaissance that found so much of theme and subject in a legendary Irish past —James T. Farrell, *The League of Frightened Philistines,* 1945

The most frequent of these constructions is with *whether:*

. . . or he is almost indifferent as to whether his words mean anything or not —George Orwell, "Politics and the English Language," in D. Hall, *The Modern Stylists,* 1968

. . . there ensued a long conversation as they walked as to whether waiters made more in actual wages than in tips —F. Scott Fitzgerald, "May Day," in *The Portable F. Scott Fitzgerald,* 1945

Testimony as to whether this flag . . . was carried at Trenton and Brandywine and other land battles is elusive —Barbara W. Tuchman, *The First Salute,* 1988

The whole question as to whether we win or lose the war —Robert Graves, letter, 15 May 1940

Queried as to whether this was the guide whose name we had the old man admitted he was not —Ernest Hemingway, *Green Hills of Africa,* 1935

I never felt any desperation as to whether I could think of one more book to write —*An Autobiography/Agatha Christie,* 1977

. . . the condition has always been controversial, doctors disagreeing as to whether it even existed —Peter D. Kramer, *N.Y. Times Book Rev.,* 21 Nov. 1999

As to whether is a particular bugbear of the handbooks. Harper 1975, 1985 says this:

This formulation occurs frequently in the speech and writing of those who will never use a single word where three can be found. Example: "There is some question *as to whether* the bill will pass." The *as to* can simply be deleted. *Whether* says it all.

Sometime after Harper 1975 was published, an item in the *New Yorker* pointed out that the 1975 edition of Harper used *as to whether* at least three times, as here, under *excellent:*

A reader raises the question as to whether "very excellent" is acceptable . . .

The 1985 edition emended the passage to:

A reader raises the question whether "very excellent" is acceptable . . .

The emendation shows that *as to* can be omitted but does not prove that it must be omitted. It is clear that many writers find that their sentences sound better with *as to* retained.

astonished   *Astonished* can be used with either *at* or *by*.
Astonished was formerly used with *with*:

... astonish'd with surprize —John Dryden, 1697 (OED)

... his wits astonished with sorrow —Sir Philip Sidney, 1580 (OED)

We have somewhat more evidence for *at* than for *by*:

He opened his eyes wide, astonished at her denseness —Colleen McCullough, *The First Man in Rome,* 1990

Out-of-towners were often astonished at what they heard —John McDonough, *American Heritage,* February/March 1992

At first Ted was astonished at his wife's downplaying of his scholarship —Erich Segal, *The Class,* 1985

... dismayed and astonished at how the state organization has been struggling —James Dao, *N.Y. Times,* 5 Sept. 1995

They were astonished at the force of the discontent that welled up from the working classes —Robert Darnton, *The Kiss of Lamourette,* 1990

Yancey was astonished by the speed with which his parents and the priest responded —James A. Michener, *Texas,* 1985

... you would be astonished by his stamina —*Harper's,* April 1999

Roosevelt was astonished by the smokeless Mausers —Michael Blow, *MHQ,* Summer 1995

He was still astonished by his very presence in such a place that day —William Wilson, *American Heritage,* February 1990

as well as   *As well as* is mentioned in usage books chiefly in regard to its effect on the number of the verb following two nouns or pronouns between which it appears. These discussions typically betray some uncertainty about whether *as well as* is a conjunction or a preposition, and not infrequently they depend on examples which have been made up and bear little resemblance to actual usage. We will try to make matters clearer with examples of actual use.

We first take note of literal use, in which the phrase is the simple sum of its three words. Irmscher 1976 finds this literal use likely to be ambiguous by being confusable with the conjunction. A made-up example is presented to

prove the point. Real examples, however, are not ambiguous:

If Vick plays as well as he did last year, will he . . . declare for the NFL draft. . . ? —John Ed Bradley, *Sports Illustrated,* 14 Aug. 2000

Abercrombie-Smith's eyes went flinty. He knew when someone was taking the mickey as well as the next man —Desmond Bagley, *Windfall,* 1982

As well as is also used as a preposition. In this function it is usually followed by a gerund:

. . . a 42-foot . . . ketch. As well as having an exotic name, she boasted traditional lines —Tony Farrington, *Cruising World,* July 1999

. . . makes use of a variety of papers as well as providing a better jacket —*Times Literary Supp.,* 14 May 1970

An ordinary noun is sometimes the object of the preposition:

As well as a new dress, Pam will be wearing another family present, a . . . necklace, when she receives her guests —Jill Gray, *The Age* (Melbourne), 2 May 1975

Prepositional use of *as well as* is not as common as conjunctive use; indeed, the most common use of the phrase is as a conjunction. It joins nouns and noun phrases:

. . . an impressive array of arrowheads, used in hunting as well as combat —Doug Stewart, *Smithsonian,* March 2000

Words for him must become objects in themselves, as well as automatic signallers of meaning —Barzun 1985

. . . a virtuosic literary carpetbagger, as well as one of the freshest new voices in American short fiction —Donovan Hohn, *Civilization,* October/November 1999

It joins prepositional phrases:

. . . as it may have appeared from Versailles, as well as from Paris —*Times Literary Supp.,* 27 Aug. 1971

. . . caught fish for supper as well as for sport —Tom & Lucia Taylor, *Center Mag.,* July–August 1971

. . . in the United States as well as in Mexico —Sarah Kerr, *N.Y. Times Book Rev.,* 17 Jan. 1999

It joins verbs and verbal phrases:

. . . who acted the role as well as sang it —Leighton Kerner, *Village Voice,* 28 Feb. 1968

. . . was directed as well as written by Valdez —Thomas Thompson, *N.Y. Times Mag.,* 11 Mar. 1979

. . . were responsible for building roads as well as running the courthouse —Margaret Truman, *Harry S. Truman,* 1972

. . . adding that surgery can ease many of these difficulties, as well as improve the child's appearance —Darrell E. Ward, *Chicago Tribune,* 2 July 2000

It joins adjectives:

His conservatism is cultural and aesthetic, as well as political —Ian Buruma, *New Republic,* 31 Jan. 2000

. . . looked quite good, as well as understandably happy —Elizabeth Drew, *New Yorker,* 3 Dec. 1984

. . . has become so firmly established, in written as well as spoken English —Howard 1984

It also joins pronouns. Several handbooks recommend that the pronoun following *as well as* be in the same case as the pronoun preceding. Our evidence is sparse, but seems to indicate that the second pronoun does tend to match the case of the first.

You see I have a spirit, as well as yourself —Jane Austen, letter, 8 Feb. 1807

. . . and I want to see them again, as well as you —James Thurber, letter, 1 Aug. 1958

. . . headlines that hurt us as well as them —Len Morgan, *Flying,* March 1984

Sometimes *as well as* joins two words or phrases that are the subject of the same verb. While this is the function that gets most of the attention of the commentators, it is less frequent in our citations than the conjunctive functions just illustrated. In many of the instances in our files the first subject is plural, and the verb must likewise be plural, and in many other instances the verb is in the past tense, and shows no number. In the instances where the first subject is singular, usage is mixed.

Descriptive grammarians from Poutsma 1904–26 to Quirk et al. 1985 all say that the singular verb is more common, but that the plural is used. Evans 1957, Ebbitt & Ebbitt 1982, and Janis 1984 also recognize mixed usage. The rest of the handbooks that we have seen insist on the singular verb.

The root of this disagreement lies in the fact that *as well as* is what Quirk calls a quasi-coordinator: it is often felt to be adding something of a parenthetical nature. This characteristic is usually signaled by the use of commas. Ebbitt & Ebbitt observes that in gen-

eral when a writer considers the *as well as* segment part of the subject (and hence uses a plural verb), he or she does not set it off with commas. This is a general, but not an iron-clad rule; Bernstein 1962 shows this example, complete with commas:

He, as well as the producer, Jack H. Silverman, are Broadway newcomers —*N.Y. Times*

But more typical are these examples with plural verbs and no commas:

But the vocalism as well as the identity of the signs impose caution upon us —Cyrus H. Gordon, *Antiquity,* September 1957

Narcoanalysis (narcosynthesis) as well as psychoanalytically oriented psychotherapy (psychoanalytic psychotherapy) are both, in my opinion, practical and useful short-term methods of therapy —G. S. Philippopoulo, *Behavioral Neuropsychiatry 1976,* 1977

We find the singular verb with and without commas:

There's a Family Fun Zone where cursing, as well as alcohol, is prohibited —Adam Bryant, *Newsweek,* 22 Nov. 1999

. . . and available evidence as well as past experience suggests that the Soviet will attempt to mobilize maximum diplomatic, political and military force —Gene Gregory, *Atlas,* October 1969

These examples will, we hope, dispel any notion that in the real world *as well as* is used in simple sentences like "John as well as Jane was late for dinner."

Our advice to you is that if you join singular subjects with *as well as,* you should follow your instinctive feeling for the singular or plural verb, but it will help your readers if you omit the commas with the plural verb and insert them with the singular verb. If your instinct does not lead you to prefer one approach over the other, choose commas and a singular verb. That will offend no one.

at Handbook writers from Vizetelly 1906 to Harper 1985 have been concerned over the use of the preposition *at* somewhere in the vicinity of and especially after the adverb *where.* This combination is evidently chiefly an Americanism (attested by the OED Supplement and entered in the Dictionary of American Regional English), but not entirely unknown in British dialects. It is first attested as an American idiom in Bartlett's 1859 *Dictionary of Americanisms;* the DARE calls it chiefly Southern and Midland. It is, of course, entirely futile to attempt to eradicate a speech form by denouncing it in books on writing.

And a more harmless idiom would be hard to imagine.

Our evidence shows the idiom to be nearly nonexistent in discursive prose, although it occurs in letters and transcriptions of speech:

> 'Fore you begins for to wipe your eyes 'bout Br' Rabbit, you wait and see where 'bouts Br' Rabbit gwine to fetch up at —Joel Chandler Harris, *Uncle Remus: His Songs and Sayings,* 1880, in *The Mirth of a Nation,* ed. Walter Blair & Raven I. McDavid, Jr., 1983

> In half the stories I felt he didn't know himself where he was coming out at —Flannery O'Connor, letter, 2 Aug. 1958

In current speech, the *at* serves to provide a word at the end of the sentence that can be given stress. It tends to follow a noun or pronoun to which the verb has been elided, as in this utterance by an editor here at the dictionary factory:

> Have any idea where Kathy's at?

You will note that *at* cannot simply be omitted; the *'s* must be expanded to *is* to produce an idiomatic sentence if the *at* is to be avoided.

For a particular mid-20th-century use of this idiom, see WHERE . . . AT.

at about This two-word, three-syllable phrase has been the subject of an unlikely amount of discussion at least since the middle 1930s. The standard objection is that the phrase is redundant. Evans 1957 points out that redundancy is not a reasonable claim, since *at,* a preposition, is frequently followed by adverbs (such as *almost, approximately, nearly, exactly*), and *about,* an adverb in this construction, is frequently used with other prepositions (Evans instances *for about an hour, in about a week, by about Christmas*).

The basis for the assertion that *at about* is redundant is that *about* can be a preposition as well as an adverb, and as a preposition has nearly the same meaning as *at about.* It is not reasonable, of course, to require a writer to use *about* as a preposition where it works (or only sounds) better as an adverb, but handbooks tend to overlook this point. "*At about* can be reduced to either *at* or *about,*" says Ebbitt & Ebbitt 1982. But consider this sentence:

> Another leading librarian wrote at about the same time that it was the considered judgment of . . . —Eva Goldschmidt, *College & Research Libraries,* January 1969

If only *at* is used, the intended notion of approximate time is removed; if only *about* is used, ambiguity is introduced by the uncertainty whether *about* "approximately" or *about* "concerning" is intended. Obviously *at*

about is the proper choice. Here are some other examples in which neither *at* nor *about* can be omitted:

> . . . *With a Bare Bodkin* . . . is Mr. Hare at about his best —M. R. Ridley, *London Calling,* 6 Jan. 1955

> At about 60 pages, the story seemed perfect —David Gates et al., *Newsweek,* 27 Mar. 2000

> This overhang has been estimated at about $50 billion —R. S. Salomon, *Forbes,* 15 July 1996

> . . . the hottest lunar lavas . . . were produced at about 1700 K —A. S. McEwan et al., *Science,* 3 July 1998

At about is another instance in which the usage writers appear not to know of literary use. Edward C. Fletcher, in *American Speech,* October 1947, defended *at about* as reputable and established. He presented more than fifty examples from literary sources.

We have a few literary examples too:

> . . . and at about half after twelve . . . we separated —Henry Adams, letter, 17 May 1859

> But at about this time —Edmund Wilson, *Axel's Castle,* 1931

> A careful examination of Mr. Pound's work shows two very obvious changes at about this time —*Times Literary Supp.,* 13 Jan. 1950

> At about this time, she took me on as a kind of secretary —Louis Bromfield, "The Big Smash," 1952

At about is most frequently used with expressions of time, according to our evidence. In many of these cases, *about* can be used alone. But it need not be. When *at about* makes better sense or simply sounds better, use it without fear and with the encouragement of one contemporary commentator:

> June Guilford of Cleveland challenges a sentence in which I said "at about the same time. . . ." She wanted to know what that "at" was doing in there. Darned if I know. I suppose that "about the same time" would have sufficed, but "at about" just sounds better to me —James J. Kilpatrick, *Portland Oregonian* (syndicated column), 2 Nov. 1985

at present, at the present time Copperud 1964, Bernstein 1965, Garner 1998 discourage the use of these phrases in place of *now, nowadays, today,* or *currently.* It is difficult to see why. An examination of actual evidence shows that substitution of the shorter words will not always be desirable:

The courts' abortion jurisprudence makes their status unclear at present —*National Rev.*, 14 Aug. 2000

At present cladistics firmly nests birds within the category of theropod dinosaurs —Jennifer Ackerman, *National Geographic*, July 1998

Few of the drawings he mentions are at present known —*Times Literary Supp.*, 6 June 1980

. . . the prospects for civilianization at the present time seem to be reasonably good —Bernard Lewis, *Islam in History*, 1993

The argument can be used to explain why the conditions happen to be just right for the existence of (intelligent) life on the earth at the present time —Roger Penrose, *The Emperor's New Mind*, 1989

Which of the shorter words substituted well in these examples? It seems to us that these phrases are generally useful when they are chosen, and are not to be despised as somehow inferior. Our evidence shows that they often are used to begin a statement. You should feel free to use them when they sound right.

See also PRESENTLY.

attain The intransitive *attain* is usually used with *to*:

. . . Gulliver's impulse to self-advantage is such that he can attain only to a fantasy of political power —Paul Fussell, *Samuel Johnson and the Life of Writing*, 1971

Some writers of this sort of verse have even attained to something like celebrity —Leacock 1943

A not dissimilar kind of childlike Latin could attain to a remarkable symmetry and balance —Henry O. Taylor, *The Mediaeval Mind*, 4th ed., 1925

attempt The noun *attempt*, Bernstein 1965 tells us, takes *at*. It does, but it takes other prepositions too. Here we have *at*:

. . . the first attempt at a broad outline —*Times Literary Supp.*, 9 Apr. 1970

. . . inspired him to make his first attempts at writing —*Current Biography*, November 1967

This figure swung a silver tray in an attempt at careless grace —Kingsley Amis, *Lucky Jim*, 1954

On is the usual preposition when *attempt* means "an attempt to kill"; it is also used in other contexts.

. . . the Orsini attempt on the life of Napoleon III —*Times Literary Supp.*, 18 Apr. 1968

. . . believe the state to be so constituted that attempts on its authority are not easily justified —Michael Walzer, *Dissent*, September-October 1969

Before we could make an attempt on the summit —Sir John Hunt & Sir Edmund Hillary, *Geographical Jour.*, December 1953

Against and *upon* are also used:

. . . assassination attempt against President Ford —radio newscast, 22 Sept. 1975

. . . any attempt . . . against the integrity . . . of the territory —Vera Micheles Dean, *The Four Cornerstones of Peace*, 1946

. . . the four attempts upon Mussolini's life —*Times Literary Supp.*, 3 Apr. 1969

A very common construction is *to* and the infinitive:

. . . plunged into the water in an attempt to escape —*Current Biography*, July 1965

. . . to record with special sympathy the attempts of others to deal with like situations —Alice P. Kenney, *New-England Galaxy*, Fall 1970

. . . any attempt to offer evidence in the place of conjecture is welcome —*Times Literary Supp.*, 26 Mar. 1970

attend 1. When *attend* suggests application of the mind, the attention, or care, the intransitive regularly takes *to*:

You must attend to words when you read, when you speak, when others speak —Barzun 1985

. . . Sarah Shepard had always attended to the buying of his clothes —Sherwood Anderson, *Poor White*, 1920

How difficult it is to attend to the argument —F. R. Leavis, *Revaluation*, 1947

. . . has business to attend to outside —Martin Levin, *Saturday Rev.*, 8 Jan. 1972

When *attend* is used to mean "to be ready for service" or "to be present," *upon* is most common, while *on* and *at* are occasionally used.

The Nemesis that attends upon human pride —G. Lowes Dickinson, *The Greek View of Life*, 7th ed., 1925

. . . how he attended upon Wishart when the latter preached in Haddington —Kenneth Scott Latourette, *A History of Christianity*, 1953

Byron, George Eliot, Tolstoy—did the valet attend on them? —*Times Literary Supp.*, 22 Oct. 1971

After all, we constantly attend at music that is presented second-rate or worse —Stark Young, *New Republic,* 26 Jan. 1942

2. In the past participle, says Bernstein 1965, *attend* takes *with* for things and *by* for persons. The real world is not so tidy. While *with* is indeed used for things, it is not so frequent as it may have been in the past, and *by* is now being used for both persons and things.

. . . always attended with a certain degree of risk —George Fielding Eliot, *Harper's,* November 1939

. . . the qualification which enables him to do so may be attended with a disadvantage —F. R. Leavis, *The Common Pursuit,* 1952

He was attended by a half-dozen servants —Lloyd C. Douglas, *The Big Fisherman,* 1948

. . . battalions, attended by all their baggage and artillery —T. B. Macaulay, *The History of England,* vol. I, 1849

Attended by heron, tern, cormorant, and gull, these adorable mammals . . . —Doone Beal, *Gourmet,* August 1980

. . . any resolution of it is bound to be attended by risks —Charles Frankel, *Columbia Forum,* Summer 1970

. . . this may become inflamed and be attended by pain —W. A. D. Anderson, ed., *Pathology,* 1948

. . . his few efforts have been attended by instant failure —John Buchan, *Castle Gay,* 1930

at the present time   See AT PRESENT, AT THE PRESENT TIME.

at this point in time   See POINT IN TIME.

attitude   *Attitude* is generally followed by the prepositions *toward, towards,* and *to. Toward* is the most frequent in American English:

. . . corporate attitudes toward day care —Anita Shreve, *N.Y. Times Mag.,* 21 Nov. 1982

. . . a new attitude toward sex —Marcia Seligson, *McCall's,* March 1971

. . . his attitude toward almost all of his close collaborators —William L. Shirer, *The Rise and Fall of the Third Reich,* 1960

Towards is found chiefly in British English:

. . . a mental attitude towards the quality —George Bernard Shaw, *Harper's,* October 1971

. . . this cavalier attitude towards the established practices of his profession —*The Ob-*

server, 29 Sept. 1963 (in *Current Biography,* July 1965)

. . . his pugnacious attitude towards other geckos —Gerald Durrell, *My Family and Other Animals,* 1956

To is more common in British than in American English.

. . . similar attitudes to the Middle East crisis —*The Times* (London), 17 Nov. 1973

. . . the attitude of these boys to everyday honesty —*Times Literary Supp.,* 26 Mar. 1970

His intensely ambivalent attitude to his father —Anne Fremantle, *Commonweal,* 6 Dec. 1946

About has some use, usually spoken, in American English:

Some of them have an attitude about it —Janiece Walters, quoted in *Fortune,* 11 Nov. 1985

I'll tell you his attitude about those dangers —Joe Garagiola, radio broadcast, 14 Feb. 1974

Compound prepositions are sometimes used in what we may call wordier contexts:

. . . compensate for the failure of the inventionistic approach to justify anticipation by taking up a conventionalist attitude as regards the universal truth of inductive conclusions —Georg Henrik Von Wright, *A Treatise on Induction and Probability,* 1951

The fear of a specific object is an affect. The attitude with respect to this affect. . . . —Abram Kardiner, *The Individual and His Society,* 1939

attraction   See AGREEMENT, SUBJECT-VERB: THE PRINCIPLE OF PROXIMITY.

attributive   *Attributive* describes the position of a modifier directly in front of the word it modifies: *black* tie, *silly* remark, *big* toe, *kitchen* sink, *lobster* salad, *computer* terminal. That nouns can function like adjectives in this position is a feature of English noticed as long ago as Lindley Murray 1795. He mentions two-word compounds of which the first element is a noun.

John Simon, in Michaels & Ricks 1980, objects to the combination *language deterioration;* Simon says *deterioration of language* would be better. A combination like *language deterioration* is not the same thing that Lindley Murray was talking about in 1795; Murray's combinations we would call compound nouns. Combinations like *language deterioration* represent simply the free modification of one noun by another. Burchfield 1996 notes that the language permits more than one noun in an attributive series; sometimes a series can reach considerable length. Quinn 1980 gives some long strings of attributive nouns from a single picture caption in a 1980 Philadelphia newspaper: "the Chapel of the Four Chaplains Annual Awards Banquet" at which "the Rabbi Louis Paris Hall of Heroes Gold Medallion" was awarded to "Former NATO commander Alexander M. Haig Jr."

Burchfield also notes that plural nouns used attributively, formerly rather unusual, are now more common. Thus such combinations as *weapons system, singles bar, awards banquet, systems analyst* no longer raise eyebrows.

In "Former NATO commander Alexander M. Haig Jr.," the attributive descriptor "former NATO commander" is a journalistic device probably intended to compress information into a minimum amount of space. It is common in picture captions and in news articles. There are various objections to the practice. You will find a brief, more general discussion under FALSE TITLES.

audience It is not uncommon in the usage business for a specific usage to cause a broad general principle to be erected to correct it. When the movies became popular in the early years of the 20th century, the people who sat in front of the silent screen watching the action were designated by the name used for the people who sat in front of a stage watching the action: *audience*. Amateurs of Latin were appalled: an audience listens; spectators look. After all, *audience* is derived from the Latin verb for "to hear." Numerous handbooks from 1916 to 1965 lent their weight to the opinion.

But the battle had been lost before it began; *audience* had over a century earlier been transferred to seeing in reference to books by Ben Franklin. By the time movies came along, it had been fairly common for several decades at least. In spite of the etymology, the application of *audience* to movie and TV watchers, as well as readers, is standard. The issue of propriety is dead.

auger, augur Reader's Digest 1983 notes that these similar-sounding and similarly spelled words are sometimes confused. *Auger* as a noun refers to various boring tools, and as a verb to boring holes. *Augur*, noun and verb, deals with foretelling future events from omens. The verb *augur* is often used in the phrase *augur well for*. With words as disparate as these in meaning, any confusion is purely a matter of spelling. If in doubt, check your dictionary. We have found the confusion in unexpected places:

In the event, these appetizers auger well for the rest of the menu —*Notes and Queries,* December 1984

aught A number of commentators feel that *aught,* meaning "anything, all," is an archaism. While use in phrases such as "for aught I know" has not disappeared, it is quite rare in current American English (it is probably more common in British English). Here are a few examples, all of them 30 years old or more:

For aught we know they were a faithful and loving couple —Samuel Eliot Morison, *The European Discovery of America,* 1971

For aught he knew to the contrary, it might have been some quack —Gerald W. Johnson, *New Republic,* 20 June 1955

But it is a rare evening when the breeze carries the odor of aught but blossoms —Melvin R. Ellis, *National Geographic,* August 1955

. . . nor even in the Andes has this onlooker ever beheld aught to match it —Irvin S. Cobb, *Arizona Highways,* July 1971

augment *Augment,* often in the form of its past participle *augmented,* is used frequently with the preposition *by* and less frequently with *with.*

. . . in subfreezing temperatures augmented by a 35-mph wind —David Brudnoy, *National Rev.,* 29 Dec. 1970

. . . has twice augmented a couponing blitz by pledging to give a nickel to the Special Olympics for retarded children each time a coupon was redeemed —*Wall Street Jour.,* 25 Mar. 1982

Augmented at times of downpour by spillover from the great central lake, the water penetrated gradually into the peat beds —Fred Ward, *National Geographic,* January 1972

. . . skillfully augment the melodramatics of modern crime detection with these terrors inherent in our metropolises —Arthur Knight, *Saturday Rev.,* 6 Nov. 1971

To the north and east the forms descend from Anglian, as these have been altered, corrupted, and augmented with influence from Old Norse —Charlton Laird, *The Miracle of Language,* 1953

augur 1. See AUGER, AUGUR.
2. Finegan 1980 cites Newman 1974 as saying "Augur does not take for after it. It cannot take for after it." But in modern English *augur* very frequently takes *for,* and after the phrase *augur well* (or sometimes *ill*), *for* is usual:

. . . the book sets a standard that augurs well for the future —R. D. Martin, *Nature,* 29 Aug. 1984

... his very survival augurs well for his future mastery —Robert Coles, *Harper's,* November 1971

The record augurs well for the prospects of Britain's girls —*Illustrated London News,* 31 Aug. 1968

... felt that the hopefuls now in the field augur well for the party —*Time,* 7 Apr. 1952

... this is the significant message of his song that augurs bright for the working class —*Indian Rev.,* January 1946

... greater facility in negotiating with each other, which augurs well for the peace of the world —Franklin D. Roosevelt, report to Congress, 1 Mar. 1945, *in Voices of History 1945–46,* ed. Nathan Ausubel, 1946

Of is less frequently used now than formerly, but it too is standard:

This seemed to augur ill of Christianity —Kenneth Scott Latourette, *A History of Christianity,* 1953

We might augur more hopefully of Spain's attempt —Irving Babbitt, *Spanish Character and Other Essays,* 1940

... an unloved brother, of whom worse things had been augured —George Eliot, *Silas Marner,* 1861

Fletcher, from the beginning had augured ill of the enterprise —T. B. Macaulay, *The History of England,* vol. I, 1849

To seems to be no longer in use:

One vote, which augurs ill to the rights of the people —Thomas Jefferson, *Writings,* 1788 (OED)

author The transitive *author* is standard, but all manner of usage commentators, from the 1940s to the 1990s, despise it. We owe the verb to one of those Elizabethan poets who, like Shakespeare, were always turning nouns into verbs. In this case it was George Chapman, who used it ten times in his 1596 translation of Homer's *Iliad.* Chapman's use did not set off an avalanche of popularity—the verb is very sparsely attested until around World War II. Its critics consider it an unnecessary synonym for *write, compose, create, originate, draft, frame,* or, of legislation, *sponsor.* That it can replace so many words suggests *author's* versatility. Here are a few early examples of that versatility:

The edition on painting is authored by a number of leading authorities on the subject —*Birmingham* (Mich.) *Eccentric,* 10 Sept. 1936

He authored a saying, oft repeated among dairymen, "Treat the cow kindly, boys; re-

member she's a lady—and a mother." —*American Guide Series: Minnesota,* 1938

Samuel Hopkins Adams authored the screen success called "It Happened One Night" —*N.Y. Herald Tribune Book Rev.,* 26 Feb. 1939

... Volume I of this series, published in 1937 and authored by Dorothy Garrod and Dorothea Bate —*Science,* 3 May 1940

As the Princess Sapieha, she authored two best sellers of her own —Bennett Cerf, *Saturday Rev.,* 23 Aug. 1947

These examples reveal that *author* is not limited to books. Much of the evidence in our files is for something other than a literary production. The nonliterary writings that are authored are legislative bills, legal opinions, and such:

... authored a postal pay reclassification bill —*Current Biography,* February 1964

Bishops Isidore of Seville and Fructuosus of Braga also authored monastic rules —Bernard F. Reilly, *The Medieval Spains,* 1993

... an opinion authored by Justice Ruth Bader Ginsburg —Linda S. Mullenix, *National Law Jour.,* 11 Aug. 1997

... his ecology group authored some of the new report's more controversial policy recommendations —Janet Raloff, *Science News,* 3 Nov. 1990

... a compromise version, along the lines of the House bill, will be quickly substituted. Who authors this substitute will bear heavily on the final vote —*New Republic,* 15 May 1950

Quite a wide variety of things can be authored:

... uses a microcomputer game he authored to teach high-ranking managers how to make decisions —William W. Gunn, *InfoWorld,* 16 May 1983

... the young Godard made movies seemingly authored by a combination of all previous movies —J. Hoberman, *Village Voice,* 22 Mar. 1994

... the dynamic/age allowance (DAA), largely authored by U.S. designer Dave Pedrick —Malcolm McKeag, *Sail,* January 1997

And, of course, the usual suspects:

... the final Bond novel authored by Fleming —Gerald Early, *New Letters,* 1999

... she has authored numerous essays on these subjects —Susan W. Fair, *Professional Geographer,* November 1997

He authored countless articles and more than 20 books —Ellis Cose, *Newsweek,* 29 Nov. 1993

You may have noticed that *author* is used of things in which more than one hand is likely to have been involved. It is often used when joint effort is explicitly indicated:

A description of Latin syntax, authored by two scholars —Ernst Pulgram, *Word,* April 1954

. . . the successful textbook authored by David Halliday and Robert Resnick —John S. Rigden et al., *Physics Today,* April 1993

. . . as stressed in the jointly authored document —Paul E. Fenlon, *AAUP Bulletin,* December 1967

Author is used chiefly in journalism and is not a literary word. It is easily avoided by those who dislike it. The most useful function of *author* would seem to be in connection with joint effort in production of a piece, and in connection with things like computer games that are not regularly associated with writing.

authoress It is hard to generalize about the status of *authoress.* Some commentators find it a sexist term offensive to women, and others find it condescending. We do not really know what women think of it, because nearly all the commentators are men. It has been stated that *authoress* is used chiefly when sex is being emphasized:

. . . the illustrated sex-manuals of Elephantis (a late-Alexandrian authoress . . .) —Erich Segal, *Times Literary Supp.,* 26 June 1992

. . . & this work of which I am myself the Authoress —Jane Austen, letter, 5 Apr. 1809 (she signed this letter M.A.D.)

. . . the playwright, a distinguished authoress who shall also here be nameless —Cornelia Otis Skinner, *New Yorker,* 19 Mar. 1949

. . . the reputation that was to label her for all time to come: the first professional English authoress —Robert Phelps, introduction, *Selected Writings of the Ingenious Mrs. Aphra Behn,* 1950

But it is perhaps more commonly used in contexts where there is no reason to stress the sex, since it perfectly obvious:

. . . protected by the king and his sister Marguerite de Navarre, authoress of the Heptaméron —Samuel Eliot Morison, *The European Discovery of America,* 1971

The lady authoress goes on, too, to warn against 'exposure to the ray of the sun in summer . . .' —John Fowles, *Island,* 1978

Like many aspiring Victorian authoresses, she used a male pseudonym —Wendy Steiner, *N.Y. Times Book Rev.,* 17 Oct. 1993

Miss Rebecca West, the authoress, has made a special study —*London Calling,* 15 July 1954

Their mother, the famous authoress, seems to have had great charm —W. H. Auden, *New Yorker,* 1 Apr. 1972

Elizabeth Carter's reply has not survived, but the clear-headed young authoress evidently accused him of bad faith —Richard Holmes, *Dr. Johnson & Mr. Savage,* 1993

. . . the newspaper self-justification of the authoress, Elizabeth Furlong Shipton Harris, attempting to distinguish her own position from that advocated in the novel —Alan Horsman, *The Victorian Novel,* 1990

In a few instances the word seems somewhat pejorative:

. . . my wife, and the women in her consciousness-raising group, and the authoresses in *Ms.* magazine . . . have decided it's all my fault —John Updike, *Playboy,* January 1975

Murdoch cares too much to play the authoress paring her fingernails —Linda Kuehl, *Saturday Rev.,* 8 Jan. 1977

To summarize: *Authoress* is not a heavily used word, and it is one that you can easily avoid if the risk of giving offense seems great. Still, writers find it useful on occasion. It appears as if it will go on being used as it has been in the past.

authority When *authority* refers to a person, it is most often followed by *on,* but several other prepositions are possible:

I'm not an authority on civil rights —Johnny Mathis, quoted in *Globe and Mail* (Toronto), 18 May 1964

. . . who was an authority upon mushrooms —Eric Partridge, *From Sanskrit to Brazil,* 1952

He has attained identification as an authority in a certain vein of knowledge —Paul Horgan, *Ladies' Home Jour.,* January 1971

Man is the final authority of what he wants —James B. Coulter, quoted in *Johns Hopkins Mag.,* Summer 1971

When *authority* refers to a cited source, *for* is usual:

. . . one never knows the exact authority for any one statement —*Times Literary Supp.,* 29 May 1969

When it refers to a power or convincing force, several prepositions may be used:

> . . . the central government had no real authority over the states —Leon H. Canfield & Howard B. Wilder, *The Making of Modern America,* 1962

> . . . local-government units are created by, or on authority of, the state in which they are situated —Frederic A. Ogg & P. Orman Ray, *Introduction to American Government,* 8th ed., 1945

> . . . that formal authority under which . . . he was able to record some part of life —John Malcolm Brinnin, *New Republic,* 17 Nov. 1952

> . . . his similar constructions of the 1960's have the authority to mock the avant-garde as conservative —*Current Biography,* December 1965

> . . . is close enough to college to have authority about campus life —Walter Havighurst, *Saturday Rev.,* 13 Feb. 1954

> . . . a fantasist's pose of authority on such matters —Theodore Sturgeon, *E Pluribus Unicorn,* 1953

avenge, revenge   Watt 1967 puts the distinction between these two words this way: "*Avenge* . . . suggests an act of just retribution, often for wrongs done to others. *Revenge* . . . suggests malice or resentment rather than justice and usually applies to an injury, real or fancied, against oneself." Several commentators from Utter 1916 to Garner 1998 generally agree. It is a nice distinction, which we commend to your attention. Our evidence shows, however, that the distinction is only sometimes observed.

Here are a few examples of *avenge* that observe the distinction:

> During his second term he was impeached and removed from office. His wife . . . in 1924 entered the gubernatorial campaign to avenge her husband —*American Guide Series: Texas,* 1940

> . . . it was a son who would some day avenge his father —Charles Dickens, *A Tale of Two Cities,* 1859

But here we find *revenge* used in the same way:

> . . . has left little doubt that she is out to revenge her father's death —Geoffrey Godsell, *Christian Science Monitor,* 14 Sept. 1979

> . . . bands of Maryland men set out to revenge the deaths of their comrades —Howard Fast, *The Unvanquished,* 1942

The special use of *revenge* is to indicate a getting even on one's own account:

> Since then, the Administration has been revenging itself on the Post —Russell Watson, *Newsweek,* 15 Jan. 1973

> . . . revenging himself in a most devilish manner upon his greatest enemies —Roald Dahl, *Someone Like You,* 1953

> . . . the hope of revenging himself on me was a strong inducement —Jane Austen, *Pride and Prejudice,* 1813

But *avenge* is also used in the same fashion:

> . . . its outraged victim finally avenged himself —John Hohenberg, *Saturday Rev.,* 13 Nov. 1971

> He had an insult to avenge, a dishonor to be washed off his imaginary escutcheon —James T. Farrell, *What Time Collects,* 1964

> . . . thought he always avenged an injury, he never bore malice for one —Charles Kingsley, *Hereward the Wake,* 1866

> . . . boastful of what he would do to avenge himself on the rascal-people —Charles Dickens, *A Tale of Two Cities,* 1859

Although the distinction described above is a useful one which we would advise you to follow, it is actually ignored almost as often as it is observed.

aver   Copperud 1970, 1980 calls *aver* objectionable when it means "say." Garner 1998 and Burchfield 1996 think it formal, and Burchfield finds it stronger than the neutral *say.* You will find that *declare* will substitute for *aver* in many of these examples, but in others it seems merely to be a synonym of *say.*

> . . . grudgingly admits that the pot originated in France but avers that its true home is Naples —Corby Kummer, *Atlantic,* June 1990

> Catnapper, she cried. You can't catnap your own cat, I averred —William H. Gass, *Harper's,* February 1988

> Creationists feverishly averred that species arose fully realized at the hand of God —Natalie Angier, *N.Y. Times Book Rev.,* 6 Nov. 1988

> . . . fell in with many of Kael's past critics by calling her intelligence "quirky" and averring that she "thought quite highly of herself and her judgment" —Roy Blount, Jr., *Atlantic,* December 1994

> . . . another uplifting editorial deploring bias against the oldies, averring that age is really

quite subjective —Daniel Seligman, *Fortune,* 17 Dec. 1990

. . . I should begin by averring that I have never met her. But I should like to! —Suzanne Keen, *Commonweal,* 26 Sept. 1997

If, as some people aver, animals are not talking when they make noises, what is it they are doing? —Emily Hahn, *New Yorker,* 24 Apr. 1971

. . . a fussy English parson named William Butler who averred in 1599 that it was "unreasonable and unwholesome" to ingest oysters in months lacking an R —Donald Dale Jackson, *Smithsonian,* January 1988

averse to, from Samuel Johnson, in his Dictionary of 1755, preferred *averse from* to *averse to.* Some 18th-century grammarians, such as Lowth 1762, agreed; others, such as Priestley 1768 and Campbell 1776, did not. Burchfield 1996 points out that both *from* and *to* were in use, often by the same authors, but now *averse to* is by far the more common.

Averse from is still in good, albeit predominantly British, usage.

. . . Democratic senators from the East were no less averse from free trade than their Republican colleagues —Samuel Eliot Morison, *Oxford History of the American People,* 1965

. . . was not at all averse from a spice of gossip —Bonamy Dobrée, *English Literature in the Early Eighteenth Century, 1700–1740,* 1959

. . . averse from killing, he just tells the . . . bank staff that this is the greatest day in their lives —Dilys Powell, *The Sunday Times* (London), 2 June 1974

Here are a few examples of *averse to:*

A tiger is a semisolitary cat, living and hunting alone most of the time, but not averse to occasional congregations —Natalie Angier, *N.Y. Times,* 12 Oct. 1999

. . . naturally he was not totally averse to the promotion he got from the defenders of the peculiar institution —*Times Literary Supp.,* 12 Feb. 1970

Evans was not averse to the pleasures of a kind of exclusive bohemian anonymity —Jed Perl, *New Republic,* 14 Feb. 2000

He was never a Whig, being temperamentally averse to that patrician cousinage — Geoffrey Wheatcroft, *Atlantic,* January 1997

. . . a horror of cruelty which made me very averse to war —Bertrand Russell, *London Calling,* 24 Mar. 1955

See also ADVERSE, AVERSE.

aversion There has been less controversy over the years about the prepositions that go with *aversion* than about the ones that go with *averse.* Reader's Digest 1983 will admit *to* or *for,* Phythian 1979 *to, from,* and *for,* with *to* more common than *from* and *for.* Our files bear out Phythian's observation.

There are a few prepositions of which we have in our files but a single example. Phythian singles out for censure a British public speaker's *aversion of;* we have no other examples with *of.* We do have a single *against:*

. . . some particular word or expression against which he cherishes a special aversion —Lounsbury 1908

Lounsbury elsewhere uses *to.* And Boswell seems to have used *at* at least once:

He said that mankind had a great aversion at intellectual employment —James Boswell, *London Journal, 1762–1763,* ed. Frederick A. Pottle, 1950

When Boswell reconstructed Johnson's words for the *Life,* however, they came out this way:

Mankind have a great aversion to intellectual labour —*Life of Samuel Johnson,* 1791

To is, as Phythian observed, the most common preposition:

But I have no aversion to the issues being discussed —Jimmy Carter, quoted in *N.Y. Times,* 14 Feb. 1980

. . . had an aversion to makeup —Garson Kanin, *Cosmopolitan,* March 1972

And all aversions to ordinary humanity have this general character —G. K. Chesterton, in *A Century of the Essay,* ed. David Daiches, 1951

. . . their aversion to the split infinitive springs not from instinctive good taste, but from tame acceptance of the misinterpreted opinion of others —H. W. Fowler, *S.P.E. Tract 15,* 1923

Nonetheless, I believe that my aversion to Studio 54 has deeper wellsprings —Carll Tucker, *Saturday Rev.,* 28 Apr. 1979

From has the next greatest amount of use:

He felt an aversion from expressing his views —Angus Wilson, *The Middle Age of Mrs. Eliot,* 1958

My aversion from the word "teach" —F. R. Leavis, *Times Literary Supp.,* 29 May 1969

. . . she had an instinctive aversion from the past —Elizabeth Bowen, *A World of Love,* 1955

... his aversion from pipes and increasing affection for after-dinner cigars —Howard Nemerov, *Federigo, or, The Power of Love,* 1954

The use of *for* goes back quite a ways, but seems to be less common now than either *to* or *from*:

> But, of all the names in the universe, he had the most unconquerable aversion for Tristram —Laurence Sterne, *Tristram Shandy,* 1762

> For society indeed of all sorts ... he had an unconquerable aversion —Samuel Butler, *The Way of All Flesh,* 1903

> The aversion for boiled milk may be older than certain beliefs —Morris R. Cohen, *The Faith of a Liberal,* 1946

Besides these, the OED shows that Bacon used *towards* in the 17th century (we have no modern examples with *towards*) and also has an example from Addison with *against* (like the use by Lounsbury quoted above). But in the 20th century, *to*, *from*, and to a lesser extent *for* hold sway.

avid 1. Amis 1998 opines that *avid* means "greedy" and ought not be used to mean "eager, enthusiastic." This opinion, found also in Barzun 1985, is based on etymology. But Burchfield 1996 points out that the Latin original from which *avid* was borrowed in the 11th century also had the "eager" sense. Hence there is no foundation to the objection.

Avid can suggest greed:

> ... what Henry James ... called the "avid and gluttonous eye" —*Harper's,* May 1996

> ... every month hundreds of millions of dollars in new securities were snapped up by avid investors —Allan Nevins & Henry Steele Commager, *The Pocket History of the U.S.,* 1942

> ... you are almost snatched inside the shops by avid proprietors —Claudia Cassidy, *Europe—On the Aisle,* 1954

> ... a lifestyle devoted to rampant promiscuity and avid, recreational drug use —Peter Braunstein, *American Heritage,* November 1999

> ... avid consumers of the culture of convenience —*Time,* 26 Apr. 1999

But most often it connotes eagerness or enthusiasm:

> O'Connor, by contrast, is an avid golfer —*Sports Illustrated,* 12 June 2000

> ... named for President Theodore Roosevelt ... an avid supporter of environmental conservation —*Decisions on Geographic Names,* 1999

> A student and an avid reader with an interest in existentialist philosophy —Judith Dunford, *N.Y. Times Book Rev.,* 15 Feb. 1998

> His avid thirst for knowledge —*Times Literary Supp.,* 21 Jan. 1955

> What characterizes them as fads is the wave of avid fascination and sudden loss of interest —Roger G. Newton, *The Truth of Science,* 1997

2. When *avid* is used as a predicate adjective it tends to be followed by *for*, by *to* and an infinitive, or less often by *of*.

> Counter-Reformation popes were no less avid for lucre than Calvinist bankers in Geneva —Simon Schama, *The Embarrassment of Riches,* 1988

> Even as a reader, you grow avid for anecdote —Anthony Lane, *New Yorker,* 12 Apr. 1999

> Students and intellectuals at the time were avid for more quotables from Brecht —Ronald Speirs, *N.Y. Times Book Rev.,* 7 Aug. 1994

> The press, always avid for personality clashes —I. F. Stone's *Bi-Weekly,* 22 Mar. 1971

> A powerful will grown to manhood, avid of glory —H. A. Overstreet, *About Ourselves,* 1927

> Sinclair Lewis is close akin to his own Babbitt; avid of quick effects and immediate rewards —Ben Ray Redman, *Saturday Rev.,* 15 Feb. 1947

> The two cultures are equally avid of message —Edmund White, *Saturday Rev.,* 6 Jan. 1973

> ... Doc is so avid to know her every thought, movement, dream and aspiration, he's driving her nuts —Richard Freedman, *Springfield* (Mass.) *Union-News,* 29 Mar. 1988

> ... avid to spend such spare time as they possessed reading better things —Anthony Powell, *Punch,* 30 Dec. 1953

> ... crowded with journalists, avid to cover the Taliban takeover —Michael Ignatieff, *New Yorker,* 24 Mar. 1997

awake, awaken *Awake* is a verb that has not yet settled down from its long and tangled history. It, like *wake* (see WAKE, WAKEN), is a blend of two older verbs, one transitive (or causative) and the other intransitive. These two verbs had different principal parts—one

awaken

set being irregular and the other regular. The OED says that one of these inflected forms in Old English became used as a separate verb with regular inflections added; this verb became our modern *awaken*. *Awaken* is still regular, with *awakened* as its past and past participle.

Awake, on the other hand, still has its mixture of regular (*awaked*) and irregular (*awoke, awoken*) principal parts. The frequency with which these are employed has varied over the years. The OED points out that Shakespeare used only *awaked*. Fowler 1926 found *awoke* commoner than *awaked* in the past and *awaked* commoner than *awoke* in the past participle. Fowler does not mention *awoken*. Gowers in Fowler 1965 keeps the original note on the past (*awoke* rarely *awaked*) but changes the note on the past participle to "*awaked* sometimes *awoken* and rarely *awoke*."

Awoken presents a special problem. The OED notes that the past participle of the Old English equivalent of *awake* was (in modern spelling) *awaken*, but by the 13th century the *-n* had been lost, leaving a past participle *awake*, which survives now only as an adjective. As *awake* fell into adjectival use, a new past participle *awoken* was formed from the irregular past *awoke*. *Awoken* was so little attested that Webster 1909 listed both it and the original *awaken* as obsolete.

British commentators have disagreed about the status of *awoken*, but recent commentators (as Burchfield 1996) recognize that *awoken* is now the usual past participle.

Awoken staged a strong comeback in the 20th century. The evidence in our files begins during World War I and comes primarily from British sources:

. . . I was awoken by a very persistent lark —Robert Graves, letter, 22 May 1915

. . . his sense of insecurity was awoken —E. M. Forster, *A Passage to India*, 1924

. . . the householder spirit had awoken in me —P. G. Wodehouse, *Joy in the Morning*, 1946

He had awoken in this rare mood —Evelyn Waugh, *Scott-King's Modern Europe*, 1947

. . . should not have awoken to the truth —Arnold J. Toynbee, *Saturday Rev.*, 16 Aug. 1947

. . . the town was awoken by a wild yelling —Alan Moorehead, *The White Nile*, 1960

He had awoken early for once, rising before dawn —Salman Rushdie, *The Satanic Verses*, 1989

. . . Pepsi's Frito-Lay Inc. has awoken from a slumber and is poised to serve up a platter full of new munchies —Amy Dunkin, *Business Week*, 10 Feb. 1986

. . . Grandview Heights, a part of Columbus that has awoken in recent years —John Mutter, *Publishers Weekly*, 3 May 1993

. . . the historical nightmare from which Europe had finally awoken —David Armitage, *Lingua Franca*, April 2000

We do not have a great deal of American printed evidence, possibly because the verb itself is less common in American English than British English.

awaken See AWAKE, AWAKEN.

awesome The use of *awesome* as a generalized term of approval is relatively recent and has not received much comment in usage books, although Garner 1998 labels it a vogue word.

Awesome has been part of the standard hyperbole of sports broadcasting and writing for several years. It is not quite so recent as you might imagine, although our earliest citation appears to be sarcastic:

After this awesome exhibition the Yanks settled down and played baseball —*N.Y. Times*, 21 June 1925

A couple of more recent examples:

. . . finished his season in awesome fashion, winning eight of his last nine decisions and posting a 1.07 earned-run average for that span —Roger Angell, *New Yorker*, 3 Dec. 1984

In both games the younger kids played the second half and were awesome —Julie Foudy, *Women's Sports & Fitness*, July/August 1999

Such use is far from limited to the world of sports. We have evidence of its use in the speech and writing of young people:

The article on Henry Thomas of E.T. was totally awesome —letter to the editor, *People*, 13 Sept. 1982

"It's like they are saying to us 'If you play as a team, you too can be the best in the world,' " Julie Scovill says. "That's an awesome feeling." —David Hirshey, *ESPN*, 26 July 1999

"It's totally awesome," said 9-year-old Robin Meisner of Newton —Bella English & Patricia Currier, *Boston Globe*, 1 Jan. 1986

Marge Piercy, a Harper 1985 panelist, wrote "We lost 'awful' so then we needed 'awesome'. . . ." It is quite possible that her summary of the situation helps account for the growth in the use of *awesome*. The OED marks *awesome*

"Chiefly Scotch." Its introduction into present-day English seems to have come from Sir Walter Scott early in the 19th century, at approximately the same time that the weakened sense, "disagreeable, objectionable," of *awful* was developing. This sense, and the simple intensive sense that developed later may well have influenced some writers to choose *awesome* for "inspiring awe." Here are a few representative older examples:

> To harness its power in peaceful and productive service was even then our hope and our goal, but its awesome destructiveness overshadowed its potential for good —Dwight D. Eisenhower, message on atomic energy, 17 Feb. 1954

> Your nomination, awesome as I find it, has not enlarged my capacities —Adlai E. Stevenson, *Speeches,* ed. Richard Harrity, 1952

> One night this week, the flood reached its awesome crest —*Time,* 7 July 1947

> It was an awesome sight to watch the great seas piling in —Charles Nordhoff & James Norman Hall, *Pitcairn's Island,* 1934

Here are some more recent examples:

> The product of . . . the decidedly uncozy Windsor household, Charles suffered from self-doubt and appeared hesitant and distracted in the face of the burdensome demands of his awesome inheritance —Warren Hoge, *N.Y. Times Mag.,* 22 Nov. 1998

> Some cancers seem to erupt out of ordinary breast tissue with awesome virulence —David Plotkin, M.D., *Atlantic,* June 1996

> The awesome sight led Sella to believe the mountain would never be climbed —Mirella Tenderini et al., *The Duke of the Abruzzi,* 1997

> The dinosaurs of Como Bluff are so awesome that they win converts even among evolution's skeptics —Robert T. Bakker, *Lingua Franca,* April 2000

> . . . some of the more awesome vintages of Bordeaux and Burgundy —Jay Jacobs, *Gourmet,* March 1980

Awesome has not lost its primary meanings, but it seems to be a generalized intensive most of the time.

awful, awfully

> The word *awful* should however be used with caution, and a due sense of its importance; I have heard even well-bred ladies now and then attribute that term too lightly in their common conversation, connecting it with substances beneath its dignity — Hester Lynch Piozzi, *British Synonymy,* 1794

Mrs. Piozzi appears to have been the first person to remark in print on the weakened sense of *awful* that was developing in spoken English toward the end of the 18th century. It is more than a decade before written examples are found.

> It is an awful while since you have heard from me —John Keats, letter, 27 Apr. 1818 (OED Supplement)

> . . . there was an awful crowd —Sir Walter Scott, letter, 20 Feb. 1827 (in George Loane, *A Thousand and One Notes on A New English Dictionary,* 1920)

The sense became well established during the 19th century:

> . . . the awful chandeliers and dreary blank mirrors —W. M. Thackeray, *Vanity Fair,* 1848

> What an awful blunder that Preston Brooks business was! —Jefferson Davis, quoted by Mary Chesnut, diary, 27 June 1861

> It is awful to be in the hands of the wholesale professional dealers in misfortune — Oliver Wendell Holmes d. 1894, *The Autocrat of the Breakfast-Table,* 1857

Although Joseph Hervey Hull's *English Grammar* of 1829 put "the weather is awful" in a list of "incorrect phrases," there seem not to have been a great many decriers of the use before the 20th century, although Bardeen 1883 mentioned two 19th-century commentators as critics. But in the first quarter of the 20th century or so the use was roundly thumped by numerous commentators. It continued to flourish in the 20th century, in two distinct senses, "extremely disagreeable or objectionable" and "exceedingly great":

> He had rented a pretty awful house —Edmund Wilson, *Memoirs of Hecate County,* 1946

> On this last we all had an awful time with Hull —Sir Winston Churchill, *Closing the Ring,* 1951

> But his is the hand closest to the interest-rate lever, which gives him an awful lot of influence —*Time,* 14 Apr. 1997

> The weather has been awful —Janet Flanner, *New Yorker,* 27 June 1953

> When confronted with grits, most people take a nibble, think they're awful, and never try them again —Tim Warren, *Smithsonian,* October 1999

> The speech is beyond bad. It is awful, terrible —Michelle Cottle, *New Republic,* 14 Aug. 2000

Vulgar and awful, but useful —James Mac-Gregor Burns, in Harper 1985

After all, an awful lot of people learn American English —Janet Whitcut, in Greenbaum 1985

Awful is also used as an intensive adverb, like *awfully,* but in our evidence is not as common in writing as *awfully* is:

"It's awful hard for me to endure reality," he once said —Truman Capote, quoted in *People,* 10 Sept. 1984

. . . and an awful little is too much —Joseph Wood Krutch, *Saturday Rev.,* 24 July 1954

While the weakened senses were developing, the original senses continued in use:

She had not been used to feel alarm from wind, but now every blast seemed fraught with awful intelligence —Jane Austen, *Northanger Abbey,* 1818

. . . the awful striking of the church clock so terrified Young Jerry, that he made off —Charles Dickens, *A Tale of Two Cities,* 1859

. . . a vivid reminder that, the pen being mightier than the sword, ink is an awful weapon —Pamela White, *Editor & Publisher,* 17 Apr. 2000

The awful arithmetic of the atomic bomb —Dwight D. Eisenhower, address to U.N., 8 Dec. 1953

. . . in the half-light it had an awful majesty, so vast, so high, and so silent —Edward Weeks, *Atlantic,* July 1956

. . . she ends up being incinerated by Allied firebombs, another example . . . of the awful consequences of the lex talionis —Adam Kirsch, *New Republic,* 12 June 2000

The intensive adverb *awfully* was attacked as a Briticism by Richard Grant White in 1870. The Oxford American Dictionary as recently as 1980 continues the depreciation of the intensive with the remarkable claim that "careful writers" avoid it. Perhaps so, but good writers have certainly not avoided it since it became established in the mid-19th century.

". . . Would you think it awfully rude of me if I asked you to go away?" —Oscar Wilde, *The Picture of Dorian Gray,* 1891

. . . and they like it awfully —Rudyard Kipling, *The Day's Work,* 1898

. . . the awfully rich young American —Henry James, *The Wings of the Dove,* 1902

. . . who seemed so awfully afraid of anything that wasn't usual —John Galsworthy, *The Dark Flower,* 1913

. . . one of those awfully nice, well-brought-up, uneducated young creatures —Aldous Huxley, *Those Barren Leaves,* 1925

It's most awfully nice of you to think of it —Willa Cather, *The Professor's House,* 1925

. . . was something more than an awfully nice girl —*The Autobiography of William Allen White,* 1946

. . . suddenly all the frocks in size fourteen seem awfully girlish —Phyllis McGinley, *Saturday Rev.,* 21 Feb. 1953

. . . a masterpiece of its kind, and if the kind is not awfully profound . . . —*Times Literary Supp.,* 30 June 1966

I said it was awfully nice of her —Elizabeth Berg, *The Pull of the Moon,* 1996

Awfully has other uses than just that of intensifier; however, these are not so frequently met:

I should have been asleep instantly, but he of the red nightcap now commenced snoring awfully —George Borrow, *The Bible in Spain,* 1843

They sat, awfully gazing into the distance —Ford Madox Ford, *It Was the Nightingale,* 1933

. . . paused, to direct his eyeglass awfully upon a small boy sitting just beneath the lectern —Dorothy L. Sayers, *Busman's Honeymoon,* 1937

The history of *awful* and *awfully* is not unique; *dreadful, dreadfully, frightful, frightfully, horrid, horridly, terrible,* and *terribly,* for instance, had all undergone similar weakening to become used in intensive function earlier than *awful* and *awfully.* The process seems to be a normal one in English. Some writers have turned to *awesome* to avoid having their *awfuls* misunderstood, but even *awesome* now seems to be undergoing a similar change.

awhile, a while For a word that has been in use in English since before the 12th century, *awhile* has taken a long time to achieve a final form, and there is good evidence that the process is not yet complete. The underlying problem is etymology: *awhile* is compounded from the article *a* and the noun *while* and has been written as one word in adverbial function since the 14th century.

Now the usual prescription, propounded at least as early as Krapp 1927, is that when *awhile* is an adverb, it should be written as one word and when it functions as a noun phrase, it should be written as two words. Here are two examples that fit the theory:

. . . it gives him a chance to chat awhile —Edward Hoagland, *Harper's,* February 1971

". . . and I'll stay outside for a while . . ."
—James Stephens, *The Crock of Gold,* 1912

The prescription is neat and it seems sensible enough, but there are two problems with it. First, *awhile* is often written or printed as one word after a preposition, such as *for, in,* or *after,* where theory holds it should be two words, and second, *a while* is often written or printed as two words after a verb where theory holds it should be one word. Our evidence indicates that neither of these floutings of the prescription has shown the least tendency to abate. Let us look at them in turn.

It is the use of the one-word *awhile* after a preposition that attracts the most attention, for it is the easier of the two problems to be dogmatic about. A very large number of commentators from 1927 to 1998 discuss it. They all think *awhile* should be two words after a preposition. But grammarians such as Curme 1931 and Quirk et al. 1985 note that some adverbs of time and place do occur after prepositions. *Awhile* seems to be one of these:

. . . code-talkers would switch from one Navajo dialect to another every once in awhile —Bob Davis, *Wall Street Jour.,* 16 June 1994

He had a German girlfriend for awhile —Robert D. Kaplan, *The Arabists,* 1993

. . . I stood for awhile looking at what was left —Elizabeth Berg, *The Pull of the Moon,* 1996

. . . a time-delay switch that keeps it shining for awhile —*Consumer Reports,* November 1978

The price of gold has been at $500 for awhile —Barbara Ettorre, *N.Y. Times,* 29 May 1980

. . . he had dosed it for awhile with an elm compress soaked in whiskey —Garrison Keillor, *WLT: A Radio Romance,* 1991

He joins her act for awhile —Richard Schickel, *Video Rev.,* June 1991

He had to suspend publication of the Weekly for awhile —Thomas Powers, *Rolling Stone,* 17 Feb. 1972

. . . became friends and lived together for awhile —William M. McGovern, Jr., *Wills, Trusts, and Estates,* 1988

. . . I got better for awhile —Randall Jarrell, letter, March 1965

All she needs is a little guiding once in awhile —Katie Whitmore, quoted in *Christian Herald,* June 1967

After awhile, even the professors. . . . —Paul Potter, *Johns Hopkins Mag.,* October 1965

. . . for awhile the stuff was feared to be carcinogenic —Larry Martz et al., *Newsweek,* 13 Apr. 1987

And these examples are from just the last few decades; we have many others—Thomas Jefferson, Louisa Mary Alcott, Anthony Trollope—going back to the 19th century.

Now let's look briefly at the opposite side of the coin: the two-word *a while* where *awhile* might be expected. Some commentators believe in a strict dichotomy of style: two words after a preposition, one word after a verb, while others would allow either one or two words after a verb. Consider, for instance, these variant stylings:

. . . the commitments you mentioned awhile back —Cynthia Lofsness, quoted in William Stafford, *Writing the Australian Crawl,* 1978

. . . used a while back to dispose of cooking grease —*New Yorker,* 3 Dec. 1984

. . . and it will take a while —Flannery O'Connor, letter, 9 Nov. 1962

"And that's going to take awhile." —Martin Karpiscak, quoted in *Christian Science Monitor,* 21 Oct. 1980

. . . it has taken me awhile to read it —Jerome Beatty, Jr., *Saturday Rev.,* 11 Feb. 1967

What conclusion can we reach? It is obvious that both *awhile* and *a while* are in wide use in places where some commentators believe the opposite form belongs. It is also obvious that your using *awhile* or *a while* makes no great difference to the reader. You can choose whatever seems right to you.

B

back For use with *return, refer,* etc., see RE-DUNDANCY.

back-formations *Back-formation* is a term used by linguists, lexicographers, and etymologists to describe a word formed by removing an affix—real or supposed—from an already existing word. Back-formation is and has been an active process of word-formation; it has given us *burgle* (1870) from *burglar, peddle* (1532) from *peddler, grovel* (1593) from *groveling, enthuse* (1827) from *enthusiasm, diagnose* (ca. 1859) from *diagnosis, donate* (1785) from *donation, televise* (1927) from *television,* and *typewrite* (1887) from *typewriter.* Verbs are not the only kinds of words produced by back-formation. Another fairly numerous group consists of singular nouns formed from real or supposed plurals. Among these are *statistic* (1880) from *statistics, pea* (1611) from *pease,* and *kudo* (1926) from *kudos.*

Back-formations are mentioned here because a number of them have irritated commentators on usage from time to time. Some—for instance *burgle, donate,* and *enthuse*—have been carried from book to book for years, while others, such as *kudo,* are of more recent vintage. You will find several of these treated at their own alphabetical places.

back of, in back of Ambrose Bierce started it all in 1909 when he included *back of* in his book of words and expressions to be banned. He did not mention *in back of.* But by the 1920s, both *back of* and *in back of* were being condemned in American handbooks; the three-word phrase generally was considered worse. A typical example:

Back of is colloquial only. *In back of* is a vulgarism —J. C. French, *Writing,* 1924

This sort of criticism has continued right up to the present, but no one really says what's wrong. The longevity of the issue has left some commentators in a quandary—there must be something wrong (it wouldn't be in those other books if there weren't something wrong), but they are not sure quite what, so they settle for "wordy." Another recent commentator, unsure of the issue, calls *back of* informal for *in back of.* Some commentators, such as Evans 1957, Reader's Digest 1983, and Bernstein 1965, 1971, find both standard.

So what was wrong with these phrases? Nothing really. They are Americanisms, as far

as we know now; perhaps the native nervousness of American usageasters toward Americanisms is to blame.

Back of is traced by the OED Supplement to 1694. Here are a few examples:

Whether it is not a great Disadvantage to the French, . . . that from the Mouth of Mississippi to St. Lawrence they have no Ports to the Sea . . . tho' they possess a fine Country back of the same Extent? —Benjamin Franklin, "Queries on . . . Militia," 6 Mar. 1733/4

. . . and we may fairly infer that Mr. Volney did not ascend the height back of the tavern —Thomas Jefferson, letter, 14 May 1809

If he misstated, he asked his friends from Georgia, back of him, to correct him —John C. Calhoun, *Works,* 1840 (in Thornton, 1939)

Back of the bluffs extends a fine agricultural region —William Cullen Bryant, *Letters of A Traveller,* 1850

To be vested with enormous authority is a fine thing. . . . There was nothing back of me that could approach it —Mark Twain, *A Connecticut Yankee in King Arthur's Court,* 1889 (*A Mark Twain Lexicon,* 1938)

Bill placed it on the wall back of the bar —Joseph Mitchell, *McSorley's Wonderful Saloon,* 1938

. . . back of every exquisite dinner stands a temperamental chef —*Time,* 16 June 1952

Franklin stood back of me in everything I wanted to do —Eleanor Roosevelt, quoted by Catherine Drinker Bowen, *Atlantic,* March 1970

Back of the glittering facade of new office buildings is, perhaps, the most angry and unpleasant ghetto in all the country —John Kenneth Galbraith, *New York,* 15 Nov. 1971

. . . but back of the façades . . . there was wreckage and ashes and debris —George F. Kennan, *Atlantic,* April 1989

In back of is more recent. Garner 1998 says it is now more common than *back of;* our evidence suggests that the two forms are used with about the same frequency. A few examples:

The picture represents a burning martyr. He is in back of the smoke —Mark Twain, "How to Make History Dates Stick," 1899 (*A Mark Twain Lexicon,* 1938)

. . . the little window, with its beautiful view of the elm-studded "interval" in back of us —Elizabeth Bishop, *The Collected Prose,* 1984

Without a major employer in back of him, he felt he was only as hot as his last column —Wilfrid Sheed, *N.Y. Times Book Rev.,* 8 June 1986

. . . we stand on the promontory in back of the house —Diane Ackerman, *New Yorker,* 26 Feb. 1990

I made my first ski turns in the field in back of our house —Ed Pitoniak, *Ski,* February 1995

Heat rising off this collision zone builds the arc of volcanic islands, but it also cracks the crust in back of the arc —Robert Kunzig, *The Restless Sea,* 1999

Both *back of* and *in back of* are standard in American English.

bacteria *Bacteria* is regularly a plural in scientific and pedagogical use. In speech and in journalism it is also used as a singular to mean "a variety or strain of bacteria":

. . . the first authorized outdoor release of a genetically-altered bacteria —Neil Strassman, *The News-Dispatch* (Michigan City, Ind.), 11 Mar. 1987

In this use a plural *bacterias* is sometimes found:

. . . more resistant to chlorine and elevated water temperatures than other bacterias —Allan Bruckheim, M.D., *Chicago Tribune,* 8 Feb. 1990

These are acceptable uses in journalism, and were first accurately described in Evans 1957.
　For other foreign plurals, see LATIN PLURALS.

bad, badly　1. The adverb *bad* is not as old as the adverb *badly*. The OED notes a couple of instances of it from the 17th century; the OED Supplement picks it up from the early 19th century, calling it "chiefly U.S." But it must have existed in 18th-century British English, because Baker 1770 complains about it:

Some writers employ the word *bad* as an Adverb, and would not scruple to say *That was done very bad*: which is not English. . . . *bad* is only an Adjective. The Adverb is *badly*.

In modern use the adverb *bad* falls into two general areas of use, one of which is standard, and the other of which sounds more like a mistake and is usually considered less than standard.
　The standard use of the adverb *bad* is equivalent in meaning to *badly*. It often occurs with *off*:

The Americans didn't know how bad off they were until daylight —E. J. Kahn, Jr., *New Yorker,* 13 June 1953

I left Philadelphia not knowing how bad off she was —Lorene Cary, *Black Ice,* 1991

Just how bad off are the Hunts? Nobody really knows —Daniel Shapiro et al., *Newsweek,* 8 Sept. 1986

After *do* and a few other verbs, *bad* is interchangeable with *badly*:

. . . so I didn't do too bad —Denny McLain, quoted in *Sports Illustrated,* 29 July 1968

Politically Balkanized curricula will only ensure that our schools continue to do bad —Charles Krauthammer, *Time,* 5 Feb. 1990

Republicans gained two late upsets to go with a win in California and claimed, "we didn't do too bad" —*Springfield* (Mass.) *Union-News,* 8 Nov. 1990

Bad is also interchangeable with *badly* after *want* or *need*:

. . . the war which he says will surely come, though Prussia wants bad to dodge it —Henry Adams, letter, 9 Apr. 1859

Ard said . . . "We wanted it bad. Thirteen yards last time, that's an embarrassment" —Paul Zimmerman, *Sports Illustrated,* 12 Jan. 1987

. . . he added, "Goddamnit, I need it tonight. I need it bad. . . . " —Norman Mailer, *Rolling Stone,* 11–25 July 1991

I wanted to get a mandolin real bad —Bill Holt, quoted in *Bluegrass Unlimited,* May 1982

You should note that most of these examples are from speech and that the usage is not uncommon in the context of sports.
　When *bad* functions in an intensive sense, more or less equivalent to *severely,* it sounds wrong to more people and is less likely to be considered standard. Here are some examples:

"Justin is in the side yard, hurt bad," she told him —Deborah Morris, *Reader's Digest,* January 1992

. . . was only a Trotskyist, and hated Communists bad —G. Legman, *The Fake Revolt,* 1967

He has had frozen feet pretty bad —Walt Whitman, *Brooklyn Eagle,* 19 Mar. 1863

... he warned: 'Héctor, if you go ahead with this, you're goin' to get hurt, bad hurt' —James A. Michener, *Texas,* 1985

If the ratings fall a point or two, how bad can you hurt? —Jerry Solomon, quoted in *Forbes,* 14 Feb. 1983

2. Early in the 20th century many commentators warned against using *badly* after *want* in the sense of "very much." But now it is considered standard.

I wanted that boat, badly —Bill Lindsey, *Boating,* April 1998

As we have seen, *bad* also appears after *want,* but most of our evidence for it is from speech. Similar use of *badly* in the expressions "badly in need of" and "need badly" was criticized by commentators in the past, but it is standard.

... an early endorsement. Gore needed it badly —Bill Turque et al., *Newsweek,* 15 May 2000

... a rundown area of stores and apartments badly in need of renovation —Karen De Witt, *N.Y. Times,* 6 Sept. 1994

3. The use of *badly* after a copula (or linking verb) is widely discussed, with many handbooks warning of divided usage or warning against the use of *badly. Badly* comes most frequently after the verb *feel,* and for the subtleties of that usage, you should see FEEL BAD, FEEL BADLY.

Our evidence shows *badly* less common after other linking verbs.

Henry looked badly —Francis Hackett, *Henry the Eighth,* 1929

If a body of water is muddy, or otherwise discolored, or smells badly ... we can regard it as polluted —George S. Hunt, *Bioscience,* March 1965

The stuff tasted badly —Stephen Nemo, *Avant-Garde,* March 1968

Even though dictionaries recognize this standard use of *badly* as an adjective, our relatively spare evidence suggests that most writers use *bad* instead.
4. See also FLAT ADVERBS.

bail, bale The verb *bail,* derived ultimately from Middle English *baille* "bucket," is often spelled *bale* in British English. Gowers in Fowler 1965 and Chambers 1985 both comment on the fact, and the OED Supplement shows corroborating evidence. When *bail out* means "to dip and throw water" or "jump from an airplane with a parachute," Americans use the *bail* spelling and many Britons use *bale.*

... had no sooner bailed out than he was hit on the head by a piece of falling engine —Edwards Park, *Smithsonian,* June 1982

The British airman who baled out —*London Calling,* 23 Feb. 1956

Our evidence shows that the *bale* spelling was used in the U.S. as recently as 1939, and the OED Supplement shows that the *bail* spelling is sometimes used in British English. You can always check your dictionary if you are unsure.

baited, bated A few commentators point out that in the phrase "with bated breath" the *bated* is sometimes misspelled *baited:*

... we wait and wait with baited breath —*N.Y. Times,* 15 June 1980

balance The extension of the meaning of this word to the remainder or rest of something other than money is an Americanism. It seems to have been first noticed in John Pickering's *Vocabulary* of 1816. Noah Webster in a letter to Pickering in 1817 found the usage forced and unwarranted; he left it out of his 1828 dictionary.

Subsequently, the expression was damned in a number of 19th-century books. The chorus of objection continued unabated into the 20th century and lasted at least as late as 1984. But by the 1970s other commentators had found the expression acceptable.

The sense has now been in use for more than two centuries, and has been carped at—to no avail—for more than a century and a half. It would never have excited disapproval were it not an Americanism. Uses like the following are entirely standard:

About the balance of the book ... one can only say that it is so bad ... —William F. Buckley, Jr., *N.Y. Times Book Rev.,* 6 June 1976

The balance of the party was turned around and sent home —E. L. Doctorow, *Ragtime,* 1975

bale See BAIL, BALE.

baleful, baneful These two words are somewhat similar in meaning as well as appearance and are sometimes used in quite similar contexts, but in the main they differ in emphasis. *Baleful,* the older and more frequently used word, typically describes what threatens or portends evil:

... has baleful eyebrows, X-ray vision for other people's weak spots —James Wolcott, *Vanity Fair,* September 1998

"Pest!" he said sharply and gave Waldo a baleful look —Jean Stafford, *Children Are Bored on Sunday,* 1953

Men! Her gaze rested upon her husband with baleful intensity —Katherine Anne Porter, *Accent,* Summer 1946

Images like these interrogate the observer across 400 years with a baleful intensity —Hilary Spurling, *N.Y. Times Book Rev.,* 5 Mar. 2000

But *baleful* is also used of what has an evil or pernicious influence or effect:

The word "story" is one that, like "desire," has recently enjoyed a baleful vogue —Adam Kirsch, *New Republic,* 22 Mar. 1999

The pressure of the low-wage economy on all workers is . . . far greater than the blind and baleful forces the economists always talk about —John McDermott, *The Nation,* 14 Nov. 1994

. . . the baleful power of fanaticisms and superstitions —Edmund Wilson, *New Yorker,* 14 May 1955

Baneful applies typically to what causes evil or destruction:

He felt that some baneful secret in his life might be exposed —John Cheever, *The Wapshot Chronicle,* 1957

. . . mathematics could be a retreat from the baneful intrusions of politics —Charles C. Gillispie, *N.Y. Times Book Rev.,* 21 Mar. 1993

It was alchemy at last, an alchemy that changed metals rarer than gold into elements more baneful than lead —James Gleick, *Genius: The Life & Science of Richard Feynman,* 1992

Both words are used to modify terms like *influence, effect, result*; in such use there is little to choose between them:

From this dismal malady he never afterwards was perfectly relieved; and all his labours, and all his enjoyments, were but temporary interruptions of its baleful influence —James Boswell, *Life of Samuel Johnson,* 1791

The baneful influence of this narrow construction on all the operations of the government —John Marshall, *McCulloch* v. *Maryland,* 1819

balmy, barmy Around the middle of the 19th century *balmy* developed a sense suggesting weakness or unbalance of mind. It is used in contexts like these:

". . . I think I'd have gone balmy if it weren't for Walt Whitman. . . . —Christopher Morley, *The Haunted Bookshop,* 1919

"Two breakfasts? Wanting to let the child bathe? The man's balmy." —Evelyn Waugh, *A Handful of Dust,* 1934

Gowers in Fowler 1965 considers this later sense of *balmy* a misspelling of *barmy,* which has the same meaning:

. . . He knew He had to get out of it or go barmy —Richard Llewellyn, *None But the Lonely Heart,* 1943

But the OED Supplement shows that *barmy* in this sense is an alteration of the earlier *balmy.* Both *barmy* and *balmy* are originally British. Our files show *balmy* to be more common in American English than *barmy.* Burchfield 1996 says only *barmy* is used nowadays in British English.

baneful See BALEFUL, BANEFUL.

barbiturate The prevailing pronunciation today stresses the second syllable, \bär-'bi-chə-rət\ and minor variants. A version stressing the third syllable, as \ˌbär-bə-'tyür-ət\, may still be heard, especially among doctors. Increasingly common among ordinary educated speakers, and going against the spelling, is a version that does not reflect the second *r* in the spelling: \bär-'bi-chə-wət\. In accordance with this pronunciation, one sometimes finds the misspelling *barbituate* in print.

barely A couple of our more recent usage guides warn against following *barely* with *than* (as in "had barely arrived than . . .") and against using it with a negative (as in "couldn't barely see"). Our evidence shows that neither of these constructions occurs in normal edited prose. See HARDLY.

bargain The verb *bargain,* says Raub 1897, takes *with* a person, *for* a thing. Since 1897 a few prepositions have joined this pair, as the following examples show.

With a person or group of persons:

The employer must not bargain with any group other than the one which has gained the majority vote —Horace Kidger & William E. Dunwiddie, *Problems Facing America and You,* 1959

Judges bargain about reality with defendants —*Trans-Action,* March 1970

With may also be used with something considered as a helpful tool:

I didn't have much to bargain with when they presented me with my 1965 figures at contract time —baseball player, quoted in *Sporting News,* 26 Mar. 1966

For something:

We had to bargain for everything, live on a shoestring —Lenora Slaughter, quoted in *Ladies' Home Jour.,* September 1971

All you bargained for was a little music
—Howard Taubman, *N.Y. Times Mag.*, 14
Mar. 1954

The Wise Youth had not bargained for personal servitude —George Meredith, *The Ordeal of Richard Feverel*, 1859

About or *on* something or some subject:

. . . right to organize into unions and to bargain about wages —Marshall Smelser &
Harry W. Kirwin, *Conceived in Liberty*, 1955

It ruled unanimously that management
must bargain on pensions —*Time*, 4 Oct.
1948

To can also be used, when *bargain* is transitive:

. . . the right to bargain his services to the
highest bidder —*Springfield* (Mass.) *Daily
News*, 26 May 1953

Bargain may also be used with a number of
handy little adverbs. A sample:

We bargained out our differences —*Wall
Street Jour.*, 19 May 1955

. . . unwilling to bargain away the twelve
West German divisions —*Time*, 8 May 1954

. . . you can sometimes bargain the price
down —Izak Haber, *Rolling Stone*, 8 June
1972

barmy   See BALMY, BARMY.

bar sinister In 1903 the prolific writer
Richard Harding Davis published a novel titled *The Bar Sinister*. Its publication created a
bit of controversy in the press over the correctness of the term *bar sinister*. The press
clippings in our file concerning this affair are
lengthy explanations of heraldic terminology.
Bierce 1909 put it much more succinctly:
"There is no such thing in heraldry as a bar
sinister."

Maybe there is not one in heraldry, but
there is one in English literature. *Bar sinister*
seems to have been introduced by Sir Walter
Scott in *Quentin Durward*, 1823, as a heraldic
charge that was a mark of bastardy. A couple
of sources opine that Scott might have picked
up the term from French, in which language
barre means "bend sinister," which is a band
running from the lower left to the upper right
on a coat of arms.

Bierce assumed that the *bar* in *bar sinister*
was a misuse for *bend*—a bar is a horizontal
line in heraldry and a bend a diagonal one.
Bend sinister is indeed a heraldic term, sometimes used to denote bastardy.

But Scott's *bar sinister* caught the imagination of the public and the novel writer, and it
has stayed in use since. As early as 1926
Fowler dismissed its controversial aspects,

calling its correction "pedantry" except in
technical contexts (and it is not found in technical contexts). Copperud 1980 calls Fowler's
advice sensible. So do we. Here are a few examples:

. . . two who claimed a royal bar sinister
—*Time*, 1 Aug. 1955

. . . the destinies of an estate and a fortune
are decided by the intervention of a stranger
whose connexion with the family is by a bar
sinister —*Times Literary Supp.*, 27 Nov.
1969

In later years [T. E.] Lawrence treated his
bastard status lightly, remarking that "bars
sinister are rather jolly ornaments." In fact,
the bar sinister was a tall hurdle to overcome —James C. Simmons, *Passionate Pilgrims*, 1987

In a society in which landed property and
title descended by primogeniture and in
which illegitimacy was the bar sinister to inheritance —Norman F. Cantor, *The Civilization of the Middle Ages*, 1993

based When used to mean "established,
founded" and when followed by a preposition,
based is most often used with *on*:

As the university tradition came to America, it was based on four ultimate sources of
strength —James B. Conant, *Atlantic*, May
1946

Less often, *based* is used with *upon*:

. . . perhaps only in the end based upon a
complication in economics and machinery
—T. S. Eliot, "Tradition and the Individual
Talent," 1917

And least often, it is used with *in*:

. . . the non-denominational religion based
in the hope of progress —Reinhold
Niebuhr, *New Republic*, 23 Oct. 1953

Based, when used to mean "stationed or located at a base," is most often followed by the
prepositions *at* or *in*: "a fleet based at the island," "She was based in California."

From 1781 to 1788 he was based in Leeds,
touring in other north country towns —
George Metcalfe, *Country Quest* (Wrexham,
Wales), June 1974

. . . a couple of young Australian lawyers
who were based at the hotel —David
Butwin, *Saturday Rev.*, 13 Nov. 1971

Use of this sense with the preposition *on* is
chiefly British:

. . . the roving correspondent of a leading
Dutch newspaper, who has been based on

London for the past twenty years —*London Calling*, 17 June 1954

Only occasionally is *on* found in American usage:

General Benjamin Lincoln, after failing to recapture Savannah, was now based on Charleston —Samuel Eliot Morison, *Oxford History of the American People*, 1965

based on, based upon When *based on* begins a sentence, language commentators get worried. The problem is that in such a position, the phrase tends to be a dangling modifier:

Based on how galaxies rotate, astronomers infer that there is something like 10 times more matter in them than can be seen —*Newsweek*, 29 Jan. 1996

Based on signage alone, one does not get the impression that this is the friendliest of islands —*Islands Mag.*, March/April 1997

Based upon is occasionally used in the same way:

And based upon an overwhelming number of requests from past Maho Bay guests . . . , Selengut has created new "ecotents" at Estate Concordia —*Vogue*, January 1995

The sin here is a venial one. Some of the commentators on the use of *based on* (for instance, Barzun 1985, Freeman 1983, Bernstein 1965) readily admit that there are other fixed participial phrases used similarly—*owing to, strictly speaking, given, speaking of, according to*, for example—and never questioned. These writers feel that *based on* simply has not yet become established in the function of an absolute participle. Grammatically it works in the same way as the others, however, and the sentences given above as examples are prefectly understandable at first reading. Note that when a *based on* phrase clearly modifies an element later in the sentence, it is not dangling and is fully acceptable:

Based on one of the oldest concepts in war, strategic hamlets employed the fortified defense for protection —Archer Jones, *Elements of Military Strategy*, 1996

basic Both *basic* and *basal* are relatively recent words formed in the 19th century. Fowler 1926 comments on them; his notion is that both adjectives were formed for use in scientific texts where *fundamental* might have been misleading. But Fowler notes *basic* being used in general contexts in place of *fundamental*, and of this he disapproves. Fowler's disapproval has been echoed by later British commentators such as Phythian 1979 and Longman 1984.

Howard 1978, however, notes that *basic* has

won its place and that one would be pedantic to grumble about it. Burchfield 1996 also finds it established. Probably few modern users of *basic* are aware of the word's origin in scientific writing.

The combination *your basic* is apparently intended to be humorous:

Madison, New Jersey . . . is your basic polyester suburbia —Alan Rich, *New York*, 6 Oct. 1975

In both versions, Allegra Clayton, your basic blonde heroine, is cool, . . . accomplished —Eden Ross Lipson, *N.Y. Times Book Rev.*, 23 Dec. 1984

basically 1. Copperud 1970 notes that what he calls the "correct form" of the adverb—*basicly*—although sometimes seen in print, is unrecognized by dictionaries. Our evidence for the spelling is very slight. Correspondents wrote in to us in 1921 and 1927 suggesting the word be entered in our dictionaries. For some reason the spelling simply has not caught on, even though it is etymologically impeccable. Since dictionaries do not enter what is not used, *basicly* seems doomed to continue unrecognized.
2. Several British commentators—Burchfield 1996, Phythian 1979, Longman 1984, and Howard 1978—voice objections to *basically* used as a sentence adverb. Basically, they think it is overused.

The construction in question seems to be primarily a spoken one:

"Basically all the companies that have won, are run by bloodthirsty killers," says Mitchell Kertzman, a three-time technology CEO —Gary Revlin, *New Republic*, 15 May 2000

Shock basically means that your legs and arms are getting no circulating blood anymore —Dr. Thomas E. Root, quoted in *N.Y. Times Mag.*, 19 Sept. 1982

This construction is common in edited prose too:

Basically, it is an index of names and topics; it is not a concordance —*Times Literary Supp.*, 14 Nov. 1968

Basically, it was Christie's, now Sotheby's great rival, that created the auction world as we know it —Carol Vogel, *N.Y. Times Book Rev.*, 5 July 1998

Basically, the rest of their book is a variation on this theme —Bruce Mazlish, *Nature*, 8 Apr. 1999

Basically, USB is a hardware interface for low-speed peripheral devices —Michael R. Zimmerman, *Newsweek*, 25 Oct. 1999

"Nineteen sentences out of twenty in which *basically* appears would be sharpened by its deletion," says Howard. Well, maybe so. But the rigorous pursuit of excising *basically* does not look like an important path to better prose. *Basically* is not used in highfalutin prose. In general prose, however, its occasional use will not be harmful.

basis   1. *Basis* figures in two somewhat long-winded phrases that are just the sort of thing to make usage writers foam at the mouth. The first of these phrases is *on the basis of* (or sometimes *on a basis of*), which is often made a candidate for replacement. However, when your geometry book says

> . . . this cannot be proved on the basis of the postulates that we have stated so far —School Mathematics Study Group, *Geometry, Part 1*, 1965

you cannot improve the sentence by substituting *on, by, after,* or *because of,* as suggested by Copperud 1970. The periphrastic preposition is right for the geometrical statement, and no simple substitution will improve it. But this is not to say that it can never be replaced without improvement or reduction in long-windedness. In this sentence, for instance,

> Hence, we find that a primary characteristic of propaganda is the effort to gain the acceptance of a view not on the basis of the merits of that view but, instead, by appealing to other motives. —Herbert Blumer, in *Principles of Sociology*, rev. ed., 1951

you could well replace "on the basis of the merits of that view" with "on its own merits," but that involves more than a simple replacement of *on the basis of* with *on*. Let us draw a hasty conclusion: when you meet your *on the basis of* in revising, consider how it fits the whole context of your piece and how it fits the rhythm and sense of the sentence. A mechanical replacement will not necessarily make your text more readable.

The more challenging phrase is *on a ____ basis*. This phrase functions as an adverb. It is a phrase which looks and sounds awkward and which is found quite often in less-than-elegant writing. Its awkwardness seems to be its chief virtue, for it allows a writer to write what might otherwise not be easily expressible:

> Baseball as at present conducted is a gigantic monopoly intolerant of opposition and run on a grab-all-that-there-is-in-sight basis —Cap Anson, 1897, quoted in *The Ultimate Baseball Book*, ed. Daniel Okrent & Harris Lewine, 1984

Routine and remedial maintenance are available via resident engineers, single or multi-shift maintenance contracts, or on a per call basis —computer advt., May 1969

> . . . one lithographer announced commercial availability of continuous tone lithography on a production basis —Wallace B. Sadauskas, *Book Production Industry*, June 1967

In each of these examples the writer used the *basis* phrase to say something that would have been difficult to express in a less cumbersome way. You will note that the last two are of a technical nature; the phrase is not uncommon in technical contexts.

In these next examples the phrase is used in somewhat simpler contexts but in each case is not readily replaced by a plain adverb:

> . . . they're on a first-name basis with the agents —Joe Eszterhas, *Rolling Stone*, 17 Feb. 1972

> . . . transfer them to authorities which could handle them on a permanent peacetime basis —C. E. Black & E. C. Helmreich, *Twentieth Century Europe*, 1950

> . . . operates on a contract basis —*Current Biography 1948*

> . . . an appropriation of $7.5 million a year for a five-year period, allotted to the states on a matching basis —*Saturday Rev.*, 26 June 1954

> . . . will be run on a non-profit-making basis —Hardiman Scott, *London Calling*, 13 Jan. 1955

In the next example, *on a daily basis* means something different than *daily*:

> The accountants work on a daily basis in management's offices, plants and board rooms —*Forbes*, 15 May 1967

Now do not jump to the conclusion that we are recommending *on a ____ basis* as an all-purpose tool. It is awkward, and it can often be revised to advantage. But the revision will not always be simple. Safire 1984 reprints a sentence of his own using the phrase:

> . . . my cap is reverently doffed to Executive Editor A. M. Rosenthal, whose idea it was to thrust me into the language dodge on a weekly basis.

A correspondent of Safire's objects to the *basis* phrase and asks why *weekly* or *every week* wouldn't do. The question answers itself. If the sentence is changed to "thrust me into the language dodge weekly" or "thrust me into the language dodge every week," it does not mean the same thing as what was written. The simple substitution simply does not work. In order to avoid *on a weekly basis* Safire would have to rewrite, perhaps coming up with the starchier "whose idea it was to have me write a weekly column on language." Safire did better the first time.

The conclusion to be reached here is that *on a ____ basis*, while generally awkward, can sometimes be useful. It is not a phrase found in very formal writing. But care and judgment are required in revising it out of your text; it may be better left alone than hastily revised.
2. When used with a preposition, *basis* usually takes *of* or *for*:

> The basis of optimism is sheer terror —Oscar Wilde, *The Picture of Dorian Gray*, 1891

> . . . the frustrating task of putting international affairs on a permanent basis of law and order —Adlai E. Stevenson, *Speeches*, ed. Richard Harrity, 1952

> . . . Indian trails . . . were the basis for many of their roads —*American Guide Series: North Carolina*, 1939

> . . . his theory of synthetic cubism involves abstraction as a basis for painting —Herbert Read, *The Philosophy of Modern Art*, 1952

When *basis* is used with *in*, the phrase *basis in fact* is usual:

> . . . the common . . . rationalization . . . has no real basis in fact —William Styron, *This Quiet Dust and Other Writings*, 1982

Basis may also be followed by an infinitive:

> . . . three-man committee which was studying a basis to arrange a cease-fire plan —*Current Biography 1951*

bated See BAITED, BATED.

B.C. See A.D., B.C.

B.C.E. See A.D., B.C.

be 1. The history of this verb is long and complex, as anyone who looks at its entry in the OED will see plainly. Our present verb is made up of bits and pieces of three older verbs. In the 16th century, Strang 1970 tells us, *be* was regularly used for the second person singular and plural and the first and third persons plural in the present tense: we be, you be, they be. About this same time, *are*, a form surviving in northern dialects of English, began to stage a comeback. Eventually *are* ousted *be* from all its present indicative uses in standard English, and *be* was reduced in standard English to its subjunctive function. It has kept its older indicative uses in various dialects and in a few fossilized expressions such as "the powers that be."

The OED notes that *are* has even begun to drive *be* out of its subjunctive uses. This process may still be going on, but our evidence shows *be* continuing in its subjunctive

uses; only the first of these constructions seems to be falling out of use.

> If that be good fortune, it has recently become better —Vermont Royster, *Wall Street Jour.* 21 July 1982

> . . . although the basic shape is familiar, almost all the skin is new, be it ferrous or nonferrous —Tony Swan, *Car and Driver*, February 1999

> The father's reconciliation with his son, figurative though it be, pays tribute to the myth of the eleventh-hour reconciliation —Molly Haskell, *Vogue*, March 1982

> . . . I find it hard to say that any of them is overrated in public recognition, unless it be in the silly judicial quest for their "original intent" —Edmund S. Morgan, *American Heritage*, May/June 1999

> If there's going to be a fight, I'd rather it be with this government —Jean Guisnel, *Cyberwars*, 1997

The subjunctive *be* is especially strong in a few fixed phrases:

> Be that as it may, this work is as important —Martin Bookspan, *Consumer Reports*, September 1980

> If I'm accused of male chauvinism, so be it! —William C. Vergara, quoted in Harper 1985

2. A good deal has been written about the use of *be* in Black English to indicate habitual or continued action, as it does in these examples:

> Just before the post bar closed, the black custodian stepped out into the street. . . . "No telling how long any American Legion post can keep going, the way the members be getting older and older," he remarks —Jon Nordheimer, *N.Y. Times*, 27 Oct. 1974

> . . . even though he only sings in church now, Little Richard still knows how to work a crowd. "People be leapin' outta their seats," he says —Vicki Jo Radovsky, *US*, 19 Nov. 1984

Monroe K. Spears in Michaels & Ricks 1980 points out that use of *be* is known in other dialects of English as well as in Black English. Here are a couple of Irish examples:

> "Let me sit here for a while and play with the little dog, sir," said she, "sure the roads do be lonesome —" —James Stephens, *The Crock of Gold*, 1912

> The Government does be callin the brother in for consultations —Myles na gCopaleen (Flann O'Brien), *The Best of Myles*, 1968

The ability of a verb form or auxiliary to indicate continuation or duration of an action is called by grammarians and linguists *aspect*. Since English is somewhat deficient in aspect, compared to some other languages, these dialectal forms do constitute an enrichment of the language. But they are not yet available to the writer of ordinary standard English, and no one knows if they ever will be.

There is a great deal more on the dialectal uses of *be* to be found in the Dictionary of American Regional English.

beat, beaten "The use of *beat* where *beaten* is called for . . . is illiterate," says Harper 1985. Don't you believe it. It has a literary background:

He had beat the Romans in a pitched battle —Sir Richard Steele, *The Spectator,* No. 180, 1711 (OED)

They were beat . . . and turned out of doors —Dr. Arbuthnot, *The History of John Bull,* 1712

I have beat many a fellow, but the rest have had the wit to hold their tongues —Samuel Johnson, letter to Mrs. Thrale, in John Wain, *Samuel Johnson,* 1974

Sir, a game of jokes is composed partly of skill, partly of chance; a man may be beat at times by one who has not a tenth part of his wit —Samuel Johnson, in James Boswell, *Life of Samuel Johnson,* 1791

Reader's Digest 1983 calls *beat* "the old variant participle" and notes that it remains in "good, though slightly informal, use, especially in the sense 'defeated.' " This is much closer to the mark than Harper's casual damnation. Here are some examples:

I could have beat Kennedy —Richard Nixon, quoted in *Harper's,* August 1984

. . . would help lure high-tech talent who have beat a path to Web start-ups —Jared Sandberg, *Newsweek,* 13 Dec. 1999

I had beat up on a weak old man —Andrew M. Greeley, *Happy Are Those Who Thirst for Justice,* 1987

What was unforeseeable is now known: Johnson can be beat —*New Republic,* 23 Mar. 1968

He ran for the Senate and was beat —Harry S. Truman, quoted in Merle Miller, *Plain Speaking,* 1973

Narrowly but decisively John Lennon had beat those odds —*People,* 5 Mar. 1984

There are two constructions in which *beat* rather than *beaten* seems to turn up with regularity. One occurs when the verb *get* replaces the usual auxiliary *have;* it is fairly common in sports contexts.

Whatever happens, don't get beat deep —Peter King, *Sports Illustrated,* 10 Oct. 1994

The teams that complained about distractions got beat —John Madden, quoted by Michael Leahy, *TV Guide,* 24–30 Jan. 1987

. . . wondering if a cartoon me would be the only creature in history who ever got beat up by Elmer Fudd —Tim Redmond, *San Francisco Bay Guardian,* 1 Sept. 1993

The second is the phrase "can't be beat." *Beaten* does not seem to be used in this phrase.

The weather couldn't be beat —Audax Minor, *New Yorker,* 31 Oct. 1953

. . . the dry temperate summers can't be beat —Andrea Chambers, *People,* 16 Aug. 1982

Our conclusion is that *beaten* is by far the more common form of the past participle. *Beat* is found in older writing, but is still used in respectable circles. It is common after *get* and usual in *can't be beat.*

beau Both *beaux* and *beaus* are used as the plural of *beau.* Garner 1998 says *beaus* is more common, but our evidence shows *beaux* used a bit more often.

. . . her willingness to put up with assorted nasty and condescending high school beaux —Katha Pollitt, *New Republic,* 7 June 1999

. . . then, before her marriage to Onassis, became one of her beaux —*New Yorker,* 30 May 1994

She could remember the number of beaux she had —Darryl Pinckney, *High Cotton,* 1992

. . . none of these beaus lasted long enough to even be called relationships —Julia Alvarez, *How the García Girls Lost Their Accents,* 1991

. . . the once popular radio series about two girls and their beaus —*TV Guide,* 30 Apr.–6 May 1988

beauteous You wouldn't think that this little-used synonym of *beautiful* would excite comment by usage writers, but it does. Fowler 1926 considers it a poeticism; Krapp 1927 says it is "archaic and poetical"; Flesch 1964 calls it "an ugly, barbaric word"; Copperud 1970, 1980 thinks it may have a derogatory tinge; Harper 1985 says it is used chiefly by people trying for a bit of elegance; Garner 1998 says it means beautiful and sexy.

If you suspect that some of these commentators are shooting in the dark, you may be right. *Beauteous* is a word that has greatly decreased in literary use during the last couple of centuries. The OED shows that *beauteous* is an older word than *beautiful,* by nearly a century. A check into the concordances of several poets shows that in the 16th, 17th, and 18th centuries, *beauteous* was more frequently used than *beautiful.* But sometime around the beginning of the 19th century *beautiful* surpassed *beauteous* as the literary word of choice, and the use of the older word has dwindled considerably since. About the only generalization that can be made confidently is Garner's observation that it is usually applied to women. But, as you will note, not always:

> Today the beauteous Julia is a study in beige and brown —Joanne Chan, *Vogue,* November 1997

> . . . and the scenes in which a beauteous techie . . . shows how the stuff works are a nerd's wet dream —Peter Travers, *Rolling Stone,* 2 Sept. 1993

> . . . while the beauteous young heroine waits, as beauteous young heroines are wont —Erica Jong, *N.Y. Times Book Rev.,* 7 Sept. 1986

> . . . a dialogue of extended and unadorned smut concerning the beauteous Theoria —Jeffrey Henderson, *The Maculate Muse,* 1991

> . . . the smile of that beauteous being Billy Budd —Gary Schmidgall, *Opera News,* 28 Mar. 1992

> But just when Howard seems a touch overbearing, a beauteous smile comes forth —Sally Jenkins, *Sports Illustrated,* 9 Dec. 1991

> . . . makes beauteous Quebec City seem like the Black Hole of Calcutta —Stan Fischler, *Inside Sports,* November 1992

> . . . out on Rhode Island Sound 10 beauteous 12-meter yachts raced —Sarah Pileggi, *Sports Illustrated,* 8 Aug. 1983

You can see that the connotation "beautiful and sexy" is right for some of these examples, but not for all of them.

because 1. *Is because.* Someone—we do not know precisely who—decided that *because* could only be used to introduce an adverbial clause; it could not introduce a noun clause. This rule was devised, presumably, for the purpose of finding another weapon to attack *the reason is because* (see REASON IS BECAUSE). However, *because* has been used to introduce noun clauses for centuries. Here is a selection of examples:

> For to know much of other Mens Matters, cannot be, because all that Adoe may concern his owne Estate —Francis Bacon, *Essays,* 1625

> . . . but it's only because she doesn't know what she ought to be at —Anthony Trollope, *The Eustace Diamonds,* 1873

> . . . I don't know why I am surprised unless it is because I base my expectation on what I have observed of our Presidents at Washington —Robert Frost, letter, 7 July 1921

> And it is because you want engagements as a film actress that you live within half an hour of Hollywood —George Bernard Shaw, letter, 17 Mar. 1935

> However, it is not because he was a bad general that you should avoid claiming descent from him. It is because he was a bachelor —Alexander Woollcott, letter, 18 Nov. 1940

> There is indeed no mystery about why people go wrong; it is because, if the thing had to be said without the use of the verb *like, would* & not *should* is the form to use —Fowler 1926

> And so every Southern household when they bought books they bought Scott. That was because you got more words for your money —William Faulkner, 13 May 1957, in *Faulkner in the University,* 1959

> This is largely because they take care of each other —Herbert Hoover, *Memoirs,* 1951

> So if at that connubial dinner they seemed like strangers it was because they were —Connie Bruck, *New Yorker,* 9 Sept. 1991

> . . . Chappie theorized that it was because they grew up in Mississippi —Ishmael Reed, *Japanese by Spring,* 1993

> . . . it was because they had a larger, more generous view —Gertrude Himmelfarb, *Times Literary Supp.,* 15 Mar. 1991

> That is because the first key I punched on my computer keyboard has an arrow pointing upward on it —William Safire, *N.Y. Times Mag.,* 30 June 1991

> And this is because on these awful programs the whole studio is rigged against the dialectic —Christopher Hitchins, *The Nation,* 27 Dec. 1999

When *is because* is used without *reason,* it is so ordinary as to quite escape notice; you see that Fowler, who condemned *reason is because,* used *it is because* himself without thinking. The construction is common, and it is entirely standard.
2. Muriel Harris of Purdue University in an article in the May 1979 *College Composition and Communication* reported surveying several hundred incoming freshmen to find out what they had been taught about writing before they came to college. Seventy-five percent of

them said they had been told never to begin a sentence with *because*. This rule is a myth. *Because* is frequently used to begin sentences, particularly in magazine and newspaper writing.

> Because the detail being removed was such a telling illustration of his meticulousness, I put up a small brief argument for keeping it in —George F. Will, *Sports Illustrated,* 12 Mar. 1990

> Because of feminism, they say, America has been so focused on girls that we've forgotten about the boys —Michael Kimmel, *Ms.,* October/November 1999

3. A number of handbooks along with Longman 1984 and Garner 1998 point out that there can be ambiguity when *because* follows a negative verb in a sentence. A typical illustrative sentence might be

> He didn't leave because he was afraid.

The question is, did he leave or did he stay? The usual advice is to solve the ambiguity with a comma:

> He didn't leave, because he was afraid.

In this case he stayed; he was afraid to leave. If the comma is omitted

> He didn't leave because he was afraid.

the sentence presumably means he left, but not because he was afraid. What should be obvious to you by now is that sentences like the example are better rewritten than merely given or left without a comma.

4. See AS 1; SINCE 1.

beg the question 1. The phrase *beg the question* seems to have been coined in the 16th century. Aristotle is to blame for it. In his *Prior Analytics,* book II, chapter 16, he discusses a particular kind of false reasoning that an unknown translator rendered in English as *beg the question* (the Latin translation is *petitio principii*). Aristotle's verb does literally mean "to beg, ask for," but modern Greek dictionaries translate it as "assume" when used in logic. *Assume* comes much closer to describing the actual fault than *beg* does, but our 16th-century translator did not have the advantage of a modern dictionary. Consequently *beg the question* became established in English as the phrase to describe the false reasoning—unfortunately, because the phrase gives no clue whatever as to what the fault is. Little wonder, then, that people unschooled in syllogisms and the finer points of logical argument began to understand the phrase to mean "to evade or sidestep the issue," which is the result of the false reasoning—the point is assumed but not proved, and hence avoided. The result of these people's use of the phrase is a new

meaning of *beg*: "to evade, sidestep." This sense of *beg* is used not only with *question* but also with other words. It is fully established as standard.

> I may well be accused of begging the question of dictatorship by saying that the American system simply would not permit it —Clinton Rossiter, *The American Presidency,* 1956

> Maynard begs the difficulties set by the *Utopia* for a medievalist by designating its principles as "simply Christian" —Charles T. Harrison, *Sewanee Rev.,* 1949

> Pentagon and State Department officials beg the point when they suggest that sturdier barriers might have forced the terrorists to resort to aerial bombardment —*Time,* 8 Oct. 1984

2. In a more recent development we find *beg* being used literally in the phrase. The use appears to be increasingly common, but we cannot predict how long it will last. Some examples:

> Which begs the question: What happens to the children of these unconventional unions? —Elizabeth Larsen, *UTNE Reader,* November 1998

> . . . 38% of us fearful fliers are afraid the plane will go down, which begs a question: What the hell are the other 62% afraid of? —Al Hunt, *Wall Street Jour.,* 9 July 1999

> The discovery of extrasolar planets begs the question of how planetary systems form —Ray Jayawardhana, *Astronomy,* November 1998

> . . . its slogan: "One of the World's Six Great Newspapers" (begging the question of what the other five are) —Jacob Weisberg, *New Republic,* 3 Feb. 1992

behalf 1. Numerous commentators, from Utter 1916 to Garner 1998, insist on a distinction between *in behalf of* and *on behalf of. In behalf of,* they say, means "for the benefit or advantage of," while *on behalf of* means "as the agent, representative, or spokesman for." Reader's Digest 1983, Einstein 1985, and Copperud 1970, 1980 believe that the phrases are interchangeable; Johnson 1982 also notes that the distinction is no longer observed.

James A. H. Murray in the OED (1887) at *behalf* noted that *on* was being used where he thought *in* should be; he opined that a useful distinction was being lost. Murray may indeed have noticed a trend developing; a recent British dictionary, Longman 1984, says that only *on* is used in current British English.

Murray seems to have been the first to notice a distinction between *in behalf of* and *on behalf of.* He gives "in the name of" as the first sense of *in behalf of* (*behalf,* 2a) and marks it obsolete with a cross-reference to *on behalf of,* suggesting that the *on* phrase had replaced the *in* phrase in that function. At sense 2b Murray cites Shakespeare as the earliest user:

> Let me have thy voice in my behalf —*The Merry Wives of Windsor* (spelling modernized)

Bartlett's *Concordance to Shakespeare,* although begun in 1876, was not published until 1894, seven years later than the part of the OED that includes *behalf.* The first citation for *behalf* in the concordance is the same one given by Murray. A little farther down the list we find this:

> I come to whet your thoughts On his behalf —*Twelfth Night*

And toward the end of the list this:

> . . . good Cassio, I will do All my abilities in thy behalf —*Othello,* act 3, scene 3

> Tell him I have mov'd my lord on his behalf and hope all will be well —*Othello,* act 3, scene 4

It seems likely that if Murray had had the concordance, he would have realized that there never was such a distinction in the first place.

Modern American usage continues the interchanging of the *in* and *on* phrases that obtained in Shakespeare's time:

> . . . I am certainly much obliged to you and Mavis for all your effort in my behalf —Flannery O'Connor, letter, 26 Oct. 1949

> . . . let me thank you again . . . for everything you have tried to do on my behalf —Archibald MacLeish, letter, 15 Dec. 1944

> . . . mailed to Einstein a paper describing his calculations, and Einstein presented it in his behalf at a meeting —Kip S. Thorne, *Black Holes and Time Warps,* 1994

> "On behalf of every workingman who has gone down under the club or been shot in the back, I consign you to that place. . . ." —E. L. Doctorow, *Loon Lake,* 1979

> . . . saw parliament accept his museum on behalf of the nation —Martin Filler, *New Republic,* 7 Feb. 2000

Our 20th-century British evidence is all for *on behalf of*:

> She was "insignificant and undistinguished" and, being devoted to Shaw, would exercise all her energies on his behalf —Michael Holroyd, *Bernard Shaw,* 1988

> . . . research on behalf of the authors by an Arab scholar —*Times Literary Supp.,* 2 Oct. 1969

Our evidence appears to support the contention of Longman 1984 (and Burchfield 1996) that modern British writers use only *on.*

Conclusion: Some American writers preserve the distinction proposed by Murray and seconded by many American commentators, but many do not. Modern British usage routinely uses *on.* Our most recent evidence shows *on* more frequently used than *in.*

2. Burchfield 1996 notes with distaste the revival of an obsolete sense of *behalf* in which *on behalf of* means "on the part of." Dwight Bollinger has noticed the use too:

> . . . an utterance like the one produced by a company official trying to explain the death of an employee: His death was largely due to panic on his behalf —Dwight Bollinger, *English Today,* April 1990

behest Reader's Digest 1983 calls this an old word now used as a fancy synonym for *command* and for *urging* or *strong suggestion.* Flesch 1964 thinks it old-fashioned. *Behest* is indeed an old word, but it is still in current use. It suggests a stronger urging than *request* does. These examples don't look too fancy:

> . . . charges that he shaved points at the behest of gamblers —Jerry Kirshenbaum, *Sports Illustrated,* 15 Feb. 1982

> . . . Rock Creek Park . . . preserved at the behest of Teddy Roosevelt —Bill Gifford, *Outside,* September 1993

> . . . campaigned, at the behest of agribusiness, to allow undocumented farmworkers to remain in the United States —Michael Lind, *New Yorker,* 24 Apr. 1995

> A cookie is a file created at the behest of a Web server and stored on the user's PC —Zina Moukheiber, *Forbes,* 4 Nov. 1996

behoove, behove Those commentators who bring up the subject—Evans 1957, Bryson 1984—agree with the OED Supplement that *behoove* is the usual spelling in the U.S. and *behove* is the usual spelling in the U.K. Our evidence confirms the observation, our last British *behoove* and our last American *behove* both dating from the 1940s.

Behoove and *behove* are usually found in impersonal constructions beginning with *it*:

> . . . it behooves us to conform to it out of deference to public opinion —Geoffrey Nunberg, *Atlantic,* December 1983

> It would behoove sports fans to get used to Master P —Michael Silver, *Sports Illustrated,* 19 July 1999

> In an illiquid market, it behooves both buyer and seller to carefully arrive at a value —Bruce Upbin, *Forbes,* 6 July 1998

The commentators who say *beho(o)ve* can take only *it* for a subject, however, are wrong. *It* is the usual subject, not the only possible one.

> The creature comes wrapped in demonic myths of every sort, as behooves the largest and creepiest . . . wild animal on the island —Chet Raymo, *Boston Globe,* 22 Mar. 1999

> . . . one sees It so seldom one is behooved to be impressed —Liz Smith, *Cosmopolitan,* February 1972

Such uses are fairly uncommon, but are not wrong.

being, being as, being as how, being that If your regional dialect or personal vocabulary does not include the conjunction *being* or its compound forms, you might very well wonder at the wide coverage these terms receive in handbooks. The epithets usually applied to the terms are "nonstandard," "substandard," "barbarian," and "illiterate." Only two of the many handbooks correctly identify these as dialectal.

The conjunctions *being, being as,* and *being that* had at least some literary use in the 16th and 17th centuries:

> Sir John, you loiter here too long, being you are to take soldiers up in counties as you go —Shakespeare, *2 Henry IV,* 1598

> Being that I flow in grief,
> The smallest twine may lead me
> —Shakespeare, *Much Ado About Nothing,* 1599

> And being you have
> Declined his means, you have increased his malice
> —Beaumont and Fletcher (Webster 1909)

The Dictionary of American Regional English notes that currently these forms are chiefly Southern, South Midland, and New England.

Our current evidence shows that these forms turn up from time to time in print, chiefly in the indicated dialect areas. The media in which they appear are essentially informal—letters, transcribed speech, newspaper articles. Here are a few samples:

> Being she isn't about to mingle with other domestics in the servants' mess, Bobo's meals are brought to her suite —Fred Sparks, *Springfield* (Mass.) *Union,* 30 Mar. 1971

> Being as the exploitation began at the same time [in] almost every watershed there was simply not enough people —Warren Wright, quoted in *Our Appalachia,* 1977

> While I was in NC I heard somebody recite a barroom ballad. I don't remember any-thing but the end but beinst you all are poets I will give it to you —Flannery O'Connor, letter, 1 Apr. 1955

> That is when the kids get up early—naturally they get up early on Saturday mornings, being as how that is one of the two days in the week they do not have to get up early —George V. Higgins, *Boston Globe Mag.,* 21 Oct. 1979

> I was appreciative that any woman would come onstage in that state, being that it was the state of California —Martin Mull, quoted in *Rolling Stone,* 17 July 1975

The people quoted are two New Englanders, a Kentuckian, a Georgian, and the anomalous Martin Mull, who was born in Chicago. Flannery O'Connor's *beinst* is a variant spelling based on pronunciation (she spelled it *beingst* once, too).

The conjunction *being* survives dialectally in current English. If it—or its compounds—is part of your dialect, there is no reason you should avoid it. You should be aware, however, that when you use it in writing it is likely to be noticed by those who do not have it in their dialects.

belabor, labor A few commentators object to the use of *belabor* instead of *labor* in such expressions as "belabor a point." Copperud 1980 and Garner 1998 note that dictionaries agree the two words are interchangeable. Garner also notes that the figurative use of *belabor* so predominates over the literal that it has to be accepted as standard. Here are a few examples of each word:

> . . . and for that reason I needn't belabor here the question —Brendan Gill, *New Yorker,* 1 Jan. 1972

> We hardly need labor the point that Columbus's appreciation of the beauties of nature was . . . unique among pioneers in the age of discovery —Samuel Eliot Morison, *The European Discovery of America,* 1974

> . . . it does not . . . belabor an argument —Edward Weeks, *Atlantic,* August 1954

> . . . has a tendency to labor his points —John Kenneth Galbraith, *Atlantic,* November 1982

> It belabors the obvious to say that Nixon is a complex man —Caryn James, *Vogue,* September 1984

> . . . which made champions of English respectability so anxious to labor the obvious differences between them —Joseph Wood Krutch, *Samuel Johnson,* 1944

> I do not wish to belabor this ancestor theme —Alben W. Barkley, *Saturday Evening Post,* 17 Apr. 1954

I have labored a slight example —Allen Tate, *New Republic,* 2 Mar. 1953

belie A correspondent of William Safire, in Safire 1982, produced two examples of *belie* used to mean "betray" or "reveal," one from a newspaper story which read "Slight twitches in his eyes and hands belied his nervousness." Garner 1998 has a similar example. This does not appear to be a common mistake, but we do have this example:

I've noticed you have a deep affection for the word "hip." . . . I get the feeling that you secretly mean "hep"—something about the way you use the word belies a kind of nostalgia for hepness —Richard Corliss et al., *Time,* 21 Dec. 1998

Here are a couple of examples of the more usual use of *belie,* meaning "to give a false impression of":

His charm and ease of manner belied a difficult upbringing —Robert Fox, *The Inner Sea,* 1993

. . . and Malaysian durians, whose putrid smell belies their sweetness —Stanley Karnow, *Smithsonian,* August 1992

bemuse The OED cites a 1705 letter by Alexander Pope:

When those incorrigible things, Poets, are once irrecoverably Be-mus'd. . . .

Murray defines this use as "*humorously,* To devote entirely to the Muses." He defines the main sense as "To make utterly confused or muddled, as with intoxicating liquor . . . to stupefy." The earliest citation is also from Pope, dated 1735. It is shown thus:

A parson much be-mus'd in beer.

Dr. Johnson in his 1755 dictionary entered the word as an adjective *bemused.* He defined it "Overcome with musing; dreaming: a word of contempt." Johnson quotes Pope, too, but more fully:

Is there a parson much bemus'd in beer,
   A maudlin poetess, a rhiming peer?

Noah Webster in 1828 picked up Johnson word for word but omitted the quotation. There is no question that Pope's 1735 usage is the springboard from which our modern use starts. Webster 1864, Webster 1890, and Webster 1909 all used the Pope quotation, truncated as it is in the OED. But it seems likely that the interpretation that has given us our modern meaning comes from taking Pope's line out of context. Here are the first 22 lines of *An Epistle to Dr. Arbuthnot,* from which it comes:

Shut, shut the door, good John! fatigu'd, I said.
Tie up the knocker, say I'm sick, I'm dead.
The Dog-star rages! nay 'tis past a doubt,
All Bedlam, or Parnassus, is let out:
Fire in each eye, and papers in each hand,
They rave, recite, and madden round the land.
   What walls can guard me, or what shades can hide?
They pierce my thickets, thro' my Grot they glide;
By land, by water, they renew the charge;
They stop the chariot, and they board the barge.
No place is sacred, not the Church is free;
Ev'n Sunday shines no Sabbath-day to me;
Then from the Mint walks forth the Man of rhyme,
Happy to catch me just at Dinner-time.
   Is there a Parson, much bemus'd in beer,
A maudlin Poetess, a rhyming Peer,
A Clerk, foredoom'd his father's soul to cross,
Who pens a Stanza, when he should *en-gross?*
Is there, who, lock'd from ink and paper, scrawls
With desp'rate charcoal round his darken'd walls?
All fly to TWIT'NAM, and in humble strain
Apply to me, to keep them mad or vain.

In this context, where Pope is besieged by would-be poets who want him to read their verses, it seems quite likely that Pope is suggesting that the parson found his muse in beer—in other words, he is using *bemused* in much the same way he had in 1705. A parson who is simply muddled by beer would not make much sense in the larger context of the poem.

Harper 1985 says that centuries ago *amuse* and *bemuse* were synonyms, but that they are no longer. This is not quite accurate. The OED shows that the usual senses of *amuse* in the 17th and 18th centuries were approximately "distract, mislead, deceive." These senses have fallen into disuse and during the 19th century seem to have been transferred to a certain extent to *bemuse.*

Bemuse, then, is a somewhat slippery word. Harper 1975, 1985, Freeman 1983, Bernstein 1977, and Garner 1998 warn against using *bemuse* as a synonym for *amuse.* Our evidence shows little or no American use that clearly equates *bemuse* with *amuse.* But many of our examples do not really equate to the definitions given in dictionaries. Let us start with two examples that clearly match the definitions given in dictionaries:

We know that the commission salesman will, if we let him into our homes, dazzle and bemuse us with the beauty, durability, unexcelled value of his product —Jessica Mitford, *Atlantic,* July 1970

. . . he, bemused in his Neoplatonism and rapt . . . in the "egotistical sublime" —Robert Penn Warren, *Democracy and Poetry,* 1975

But we have many of these ambiguous uses:

Americans who take the trouble to examine exotic fruits like horned melons . . . typically respond with the bemused bafflement of zoo-goers encountering an aardvark or wombat —David Karp, *N.Y. Times,* 12 Jan. 1994

The senior Cuomo admits he's bemused by his son's tabloid apotheosis as New York's most eligible bachelor —Ruth Shalit, *GQ,* August 1997

. . . bemused college fund-raisers have received such donations as a malfunctioning dinosaur model, an unreachable island . . . and a passel of animals and cemetery plots —Claudia H. Deutsch, *Education Life,* 8 Jan. 1995

Answers to questions are often accompanied by a serene and at times almost bemused smile —Claire Smith, *N.Y. Times,* 5 May 1991

Phil Tufnell, in his bemused Stan Laurel fashion, was bowled first ball —Mike Selvey, *Manchester Guardian Weekly,* 16 Aug. 1992

British usage may be a bit closer to *amuse* (but the use of *bemuse* is not a subject in British usage books). In the first example, an Irish singer is quoted:

But walking into the Oval Office in my combat jeans and a T shirt, I noticed the president's secretary looking at me bemused. And even the president smiled when he saw the big boots —Paul Hewson Bono, quoted by John Leland, *Newsweek,* 24 Jan. 2000

The only serious fight that could be picked . . . was within the sisterhood, with men as bemused bystanders —Ferdinand Mount, *Times Literary Supp.,* 19 Mar. 1999

The problem for American users (the Brits don't seem to care) appears to lie in the fact that lexicographers have not yet succeeded in accurately describing the use of *bemuse,* which often seems to vary between mild bewilderment and inward amusement. We will

merely advise you to note that the word is a bit slippery to handle.

bereaved, bereft The variant past participles of *bereave—bereaved* and *bereft*—have developed somewhat separate adjectival uses. *Bereaved* is the word most frequently chosen to mean "suffering the death of a loved one":

At the front of the line, visitors signed their names in books for the bereaved families —James Bennet, *N.Y. Times,* 29 July 1998

When *bereaved* is followed by a preposition, it is *by* or *of*:

. . . he was bereaved by his partner's death —Susan Antilla, *N.Y. Times,* 7 May 1995

. . . orphans, spinsters and bachelors bereaved of their other relatives —Alice P. Kenney, *New-England Galaxy,* Fall 1970

Bereft usually denotes the loss, lack, or deprivation of something and is almost always used with the preposition *of*:

It's not that the country was completely bereft of humor —Joseph Contreras, *Newsweek,* 6 June 1994

When the theory made its debut . . . it lacked the Gell-Mann touch: bereft of a clever name, it was dully called the V-minus-A model —George Johnson, *Atlantic,* July 2000

. . . written in rococo sentences charmingly bereft of grammar, punctuation and spelling —Arthur Cooper, *GQ,* August 1997

. . . one of four novels that Mr. Clinton picked up (on blind credit, having been short of cash and bereft of plastic) —Marilyn Stasio, *N.Y. Times Book Rev.,* 22 Feb. 1994

Bereft is also used, although less frequently than *bereaved,* in the sense "suffering the death of a loved one":

. . . to enact so-called widows' pensions, so that women bereft of husbands would not have to place their children in institutions —Lawrence Mead, *Wall Street Jour.,* 2 Nov. 1994

She finds the child's mother, alone, who has apparently gone into the woods just to cry. The bereft mother is played by Julianne Moore —Stanley Kauffmann, *New Republic,* 31 Jan. 2000

It can also be used for a loss likened to death:

. . . made the tabloids when his wife ran off to France with her dentist and the bereft realtor placed a newspaper ad for a girl —Neal Gabler, *Life: the Movie,* 1998

beseech Since *beseech* is related to *seek,* you would think *besought* would be the form for the past and past participle. But both *besought* and *beseeched* are used. *Beseeched* has been around since the 16th century. Shakespeare used *beseeched* but not *besought*; on the other hand, Spenser, Sidney, Milton, and Pope used *besought* but not *beseeched*. From 1870 to 1998 opinions as to which is the better form have been expressed. Commentators differ, but both forms continue in use.

> On the left, pundits beseeched us to look beyond the tawdry theatrics —James Wolcott, *New Yorker*, 1 Apr. 1996

> . . . herdmen galloped to the top of a holy mountain . . . and beseeched the gods to protect the wild horse —Suzanne Possehl, *N.Y. Times*, 4 Oct. 1994

> He then beseeched assistant coach Michael Holton to corroborate his fictional account —L. Jon Wertheim, *Sports Illustrated*, 15 Nov. 1999

> . . . unpretentious, altogether delightful, and frenziedly besought Italian restaurant —Jay Jacobs, *Gourmet*, May 1980

> . . . the American Secretary of State . . . is besought by local authorities to send some American forensic experts —Francine du Plessix Gray, *N.Y. Times Book Rev.*, 29 Oct. 1995

> But Columbus felt . . . defrauded and repeatedly besought his son to obtain confirmation of what he called his tithes, eighths, and thirds —Samuel Eliot Morison, *The European Discovery of America*, 1974

You can use *beseeched*, like Shakepeare, or *besought*, like Spenser, Milton, and Pope.

beside, besides As a number of commentators remark and all conscientious dictionaries show, there is a certain amount of overlap between these two words. The OED shows that historically there was even more than there is now.

A few commentators try to reduce *beside* to a single sense and *besides* to one sense for the preposition and one for the adverb. Consultation of a dictionary will disabuse anyone misled by such oversimplification.

Besides is the easier word to deal with. It has the adverbial action all to itself; *beside*, the older adverb, is archaic.

> . . . lost her social position, job, and husband, and was broke besides —Sally Quinn, *Cosmopolitan*, November 1972

As a preposition, *besides* usually means "except, other than, together with":

> There were other irritations, besides the voice —Martha Gellhorn, *Atlantic*, March 1953

> Besides historic charm, narrow boats hold a less tangible appeal —Susan Hornik, *Smithsonian*, June 2000

> You wish you could remember something about Spinoza, besides the fact that he was excommunicated —Jay McInerney, *Bright Lights, Big City*, 1984

Beside is always approved in prepositional uses like these:

> . . . a sputtering old Model T . . . coughed and died right beside the schoolyard —Russell Baker, *Growing Up*, 1982

> But in a sense my feelings are beside the point —Nick Hornby, *Fever Pitch*, 1992

> All the 19th- and 20th-century scholarship and research upon Samuel Johnson are nugatory beside Boswell's account —Peter Ackroyd, *N.Y. Times Book Rev.*, 10 Jan. 1999

The only question arises when *beside* is used in the preposition sense of *besides*. Commentators have either disapproved it or ignored it. Although it is not nearly as frequent as *besides*, it is well attested. It has been in use since the 14th century and appears in the King James version of the Bible. Here are some more modern examples:

> . . . would become the only baseball club beside the Yankees to three-peat —Steve Rushin, *Sports Illustrated*, 6 Sept. 1999

> Beside the resident members, other members dropped in and out during the day —*The Autobiography of William Butler Yeats*, 1953

> Beside being taken into a world of escapist literature a thoughtful reader can go somewhat further —John P. Marquand, *Book-of-the-Month-Club News*, April 1946

> . . . his other mythical theme beside the South —Leslie A. Fiedler, *New Republic*, 23 Aug. 1954

While this use of *beside* is not wrong, nor rare, nor nonstandard, *besides* is the word most people use.

best foot forward Evans 1961 and Bernstein 1971 remind everyone that this ancient idiom is perfectly all right in spite of applying the superlative degree to only two. See also SUPERLATIVE OF TWO.

bestow Back in the 18th century the grammarian Lowth corrected a Swiftian *bestow to* to *bestow upon*; Lindley Murray corrected a *bestow of* to *bestow upon*. Lowth and Murray seem to have had an accurate feel for what idiomatic usage would be: in modern use *upon* and *on* are the usual prepositions.

> . . . the Queen is the fountain of honours and when she bestows a peerage upon a sub-

ject . . . —Nancy Mitford, *Noblesse Oblige,* 1956

. . . bestowing half-abstracted nods of greeting from time to time on passing acquaintances —Thomas Wolfe, *You Can't Go Home Again,* 1940

. . . the instant hero status that the press bestowed on these first seven astronauts —C. D. B. Bryan, *N.Y. Times Book Rev.,* 23 Sept. 1979

This example with *at* is probably influenced by *glance:*

But if you are to understand the new Oxford you must bestow a glance at the old —S. P. B. Mais, *The English Scene To-day,* 2d ed., 1949

When *bestow* means "to put in a place, stow," however, it often takes *in:*

Instead of bestowing the envelope safely in his pocket —Dorothy L. Sayers, *Murder Must Advertise,* 1933

. . . parcels which she bestowed in the corners of the vehicle —Arnold Bennett, *The Old Wives' Tale,* 1908

be sure and   See TRY AND.

bet   The verb *bet* has two forms of the past and past participle: *bet* and *betted.* A couple of American commentators insist that *betted* is the only correct form; another insists *betted* is wrong. They are all wrong. Both *bet* and *betted* are used, but *bet* is much more common.

. . . he hasn't bet on a single race —Anthony J. Aliberti, *Hub Rail,* January/February 1987

. . . has been helped by the fact that she bet on a writer who was becoming a new cult figure —*N.Y. Times Book Rev.,* 26 Sept. 1976

He bet basketball, baseball, football and . . . hockey games —Pat Jordan, *Sports Illustrated,* 9 Feb. 1987

Betted is pretty rare in American English but is more common in British English, where *bet* is about equally used.

better   1. The use of *better* for *had better* (see also HAD BETTER, HAD BEST) is rejected by a couple of critics, but Copperud 1970 says that the consensus is that it is not open to serious criticism. Longman 1984 notes that it is also used in informal British English, but Burchfield 1996 says it is much more common in American use than in British use. Our examples here suggest that it is not found in very formal surroundings.

. . . an internist, which is what you ought to see. You better listen to me —Flannery O'Connor, letter, 9 Oct. 1962

. . . a stubblehead German with an accent you better not laugh at —E. L. Doctorow, *Loon Lake,* 1979

You better buy it too —Pete Carey, *Popular Computing,* January 1985

. . . they're going to be awfully mad at me, and we better figure that in, too —John F. Kennedy, quoted in *Harper's,* February 1971

2. The idiom *better than* used to mean "more than" has been disliked by various commentators from as far back as Noah Webster in 1790, who deemed it "improper." Not one of these sources brings forth a better reason for questioning the expression than that more is not necessarily better, a truism irrelevant to a matter of idiomatic English. Burchfield 1996 notes that it is used but not common in British English. *Better than* is primarily a spoken idiom and like many spoken idioms it is not generally found in the more formal kinds of writing.

. . . it would take better than a fifty-degree incline to flip the moon car —Henry S. F. Cooper, Jr., *New Yorker,* 17 July 1971

. . . who has hit better than .300 for the last 14 seasons —Bill Lyon, *Hartford* (Conn.) *Courant,* 12 July 1983

We were whistling along at slightly better than Mach 2 —Horace Sutton, *Saturday Rev.,* 23 June 1979

. . . added up to better than 16 percent of consumer expenditures for health care —*American Labor,* July–August 1969

between   1. *Between, among.* James A. H. Murray in the OED says it as clearly and succinctly as anyone: "It *[between]* is still the only word available to express the relation of a thing to many surrounding things severally and individually, *among* expressing a relation to them collectively and vaguely." Still, the unfounded notion that *between* can be used of only two items persists, most perniciously, perhaps, in schoolbooks. The notion has its origin in the etymology of *between*—the *-tween* derives from an Old English form related to the Old English word for "two"; Samuel Johnson in his Dictionary (1755) took note of it. "*Between* is properly used of two, and *among* of more," he wrote, but being aware of actual use he added "but perhaps this accuracy is not always preserved." He himself did not always preserve this accuracy:

. . . and sincerely hope, that between public business, improving studies, and domestic pleasures, neither melancholy nor caprice will find any place for entrance —Samuel

Johnson, letter to James Boswell, 20 June 1771

Noah Webster in 1828 included in his definition of *between*: "We observe that *between* is not restricted to *two*." The originators of the restriction to two, then, ignored the evidence of the two most famous dictionaries of that time. Our earliest evidence for the prescribed restriction to two comes from Goold Brown 1851. We can still find a few holdouts for Goold Brown's position: the Harper 1975 usage panel, Simon 1980, Einstein 1985, Sellers 1975, Safire 1982, Bander 1978, and an occasional schoolbook (*Building English Skills*, orange level, 1982) among them.

Actually, the enormous amount of ink spilled in the explication of the subtleties of *between* and *among* has been largely a waste; it is difficult for a native speaker of English who is not distracted by irrelevant considerations to misuse the two words.

Here is a generous handful of examples of *between* used idiomatically of three or more or used with a plural noun, often of indeterminate number. Some are old and some are more recent.

> *Phœbus* was Judge betweene *Jove, Mars,* and *Love* —Sir Philip Sidney, *Astrophel and Stella*, 1591

> This, of course, is between our three discreet selves —Jane Austen, letter, 11 Oct. 1813

> Of course that's between you and me and Jack Mum —Myles na gCopaleen (Flann O'Brien), *The Best of Myles*, 1968

> . . . a choice between more than two things or decisions —Partridge 1942

> All the difference in the world, Dinny, between the 'buck,' the 'dandy,' the 'swell,' the 'masher,' the 'blood,' the 'nut,' and what's the last variety called —John Galsworthy, *Flowering Wilderness*, 1932

> . . . those who have not time to choose between *possession, gain, advantage, resource,* & other synonyms —Fowler 1926 (s.v. *asset*)

> Undoubtedly there is something in common between the three (Dante, Chaucer, Villon) —T. S. Eliot, "Dante," in *Selected Essays*, 1932

> . . . the relation between grammar, Latin, and social power —Robert Pattison, *On Literacy*, 1982

> The real basis for distinguishing between levels of usage —Barnard 1979

> Between doing all these things I read an advertisement that amused me —Randall Jarrell, letter, May 1952

> Between the mountains that cradled the yard there seemed to be thousands of freight cars —Russell Baker, *Growing Up*, 1982

Here a few examples of *among*:

> Also, could the children be *let alone* while I talk to them, and *not* have (. . .) people going about among them, stirring up the inattentive ones —Lewis Carroll, letter, 2 Sept. 1897

> My mother came home with that [joke] the other day. She circulates among all and sundry —Flannery O'Connor, letter, 1 Dec. 1957

> . . . the tribes of north-west Germany were continuously on the move; such movements probably contributed to the diminution of racial distinctions among them —D. J. V. Fisher, *The Anglo-Saxon Age*, 1973

> . . . it is no mere happenstance that Dilsey, alone among the four central figures . . . is seen from the outside —William Styron, *This Quiet Dust and Other Writings*, 1982

Between is not a possibility in any of these except perhaps the Fisher example, where *among* nonetheless does not seem at all forced. In the following example, note how *between* emphasizes differences between one person and each of a number of others, or the whole of them collectively, while *among* shows an indefinite relationship within the group:

> . . . it is doubtful whether the differences between Burchfield and the Americans are greater than the differences among the Americans themselves —Robert F. Ilson, in Greenbaum 1985

The following examples of *among* show signs of its having been chosen strictly on the basis of referring to more than two. The first was criticized by Theodore Bernstein in *Winners & Sinners*:

> The psychiatrist said under cross-examination . . . that he would include simultaneous intercourse among two men and a woman—a scene shown in the film—in the category of normal —*N.Y. Times*, 30 Dec. 1972

> . . . is a worthy book that nevertheless falls among many stools —John Simon, *N.Y. Times Book Rev.*, 14 Oct. 1979

> . . . the author alternates among mod slang, clichés and quotes from literary giants —Albert H Johnston, *Publishers Weekly*, 24 July 1978

We suggest that in choosing between *among* and *between* you are going to be better off fol-

lowing your own instincts than trying to follow someone else's theory of what is correct.
2. *Between each, between every.* Another cherished superstition of the commentators is that *between* should not be used with a singular noun preceded by *each* or *every.* Logic is given as the reason for the objection, but it does not take too deep thinking to realize that the "logical" reason is not logical. For an example we will use the phrase "with windows between each stall," which is taken from a 1790 diary of George Washington, describing a new stable he was having built. The *each* here has a distributive function: it refers to an individual only as a member of a group of similar individuals. So *each* implies plurality, and is not illogical. The construction does go back as far as Shakespeare:

> Between each kiss her oaths of true love swearing —*The Passionate Pilgrim,* 1599

Volume 2 of Jespersen's *Modern English Grammar* quotes Dickens:

> . . . with a shake of her head between every rapid sentence —*A Tale of Two Cities*

Here are some more recent examples:

> Stopping for ten seconds between every word —George Bernard Shaw, letter, 22 Oct. 1942

> The fortnights between each meeting tormented him with delicious anguish —A. N. Wilson, *Scandal or Priscilla's Kindness,* 1983

> . . . expiate a string of crimes he didn't know he had committed until they were thoughtfully explained to him between each stroke —John le Carré, *A Perfect Spy,* 1986

> . . . process in which nuclei capture successive neutrons slowly enough to undergo beta decay between each capture —Lawrence A. Marschall, *The Supernova Story,* 1988

> . . . cases where an extra vowel or consonant is inserted between each syllable —David Crystal, *The Cambridge Encyclopedia of Language,* 1987

> . . . tunable connections between every input and output —Steven Pinker, *Nature,* 5 June 1997

> Cookies can be frozen in an airtight container, with wax paper between each layer —Molly O'Neill, *N.Y. Times Mag.,* 13 Dec. 1992

> Layered between each bird is a choice of seasoned stuffing —Mark Robichaux, *Wall Street Jour.,* 27 Nov. 1996

Between each is very common; *between every* less so.

between you and I Of all the theories advanced to explain the existence of *between you and I,* the most popular one (invoked as recently as Amis 1998) is that the phrase is the result of children being taught to avoid *me* in "it is me," with the result that *I* is substituted for *me* in places where it should not be. The technical term for avoiding one grammatical trap only to fall in another is *hypercorrection.* Barnard 1979 will not accept hypercorrection as the cause, however:

> But in the Stratford Grammar School where Shakespeare was a pupil, it had not occurred to anybody that English grammar needed to be taught—only Latin. Yet the Bard has one of his heroes, Antonio in *The Merchant of Venice,* tell his friend Bassanio: "all debts are cleared between you and I." And this is not in light conversation, but in a letter written in the face of death.

A different explanation is offered by Henry Sweet, in his *New English Grammar* (1892). Sweet suggests that the early modern English *between you and I* resulted from *you and I* being so frequently joined together as the subject of a sentence that the words formed a sort of group compound with an invariable last element. The invariable last element is also mentioned by Anthony Burgess (in a book review collected in *Homage to Qwert Yuiop,* 1986), who notes that in some West Country dialects of England *I* is the invariable first person pronoun.

Another possible explanation (unnoticed by the commentators) comes from the linguist Noam Chomsky. In his *Barriers,* 1986, he says that compound phrases like *you and I* are barriers to the assignment of grammatical case. This means that *between* can assign case only to the whole phrase and not to the individual words that make it up. Thus the individual pronouns are free to be nominative or objective or even reflexives. Chomsky's theory would also explain some other irregularities in pronoun use (see PRONOUNS); it's the best that has been offered so far.

If the origin of the phrase is somewhat obscure, what about the usage? We should first note the existence of two varieties of the phrase. One we might call "confidential":

> LADY FROTH. . . . For between you and I, I had Whymsies and Vapours —William Congreve, *The Double-Dealer,* 1694

> BELINDA. Between you and I, it must all light upon Heartfree and I —Sir John Vanbrugh, *The Provok'd Wife,* 1697 (cited in OED, Wyld, and in *Literary Digest,* 27 June 1925)

> CLINCHER. . . . for, hark ye, captain, between you and I, there's a fine Lady in the

wind —George Farquhar, *Sir Harry Wildair,* 1701

As these examples suggest, the confidential *between you and I* is primarily a spoken usage. It also occurs in letters:

> . . . without speaking disrespectfully of the sweet town; (which between you and I; I wish was swallowed up by an Earthquake . . . .) —Lord Byron, letter, 23 Apr. 1805

> Between you and I, I believe that the secret of Ma's willingness to allow me to go to South America lies in the fact that she is afraid I am going to get married —Samuel Clemens, letter, 5 Aug. 1856

This "confidential" use occurs with *me* as well:

> Between you and me, the *Lyrical Ballads* are but drowsy performances —Charles Lamb, letter, February 1801

> . . . but privately between you and me, I was most confoundedly well pleased —Abraham Lincoln, letter, 1 Apr. 1838

> Bunny Wilson says that it's without a doubt the best American comedy to date (that's just between you and me.) —F. Scott Fitzgerald, letter, July 1922

The "confidential" *between you and I* is still in use, but mostly in spoken English; we have very little evidence of it in print.

Shakespeare's *between you and I* was not of the "confidential" type; it simply indicated some sort of transaction between two people. Farquhar gives us another example:

> YOUNG MIRABEL. . . . I tell thee, child, there is not the least occasion for morals in any business between you and I —*The Inconstant,* 1702

The transactional phrase occurs occasionally in our evidence, but in current use it is almost always *between you and me.*

We should note that *between you and I* is only the most commonly commented-upon variety of a general phrase *between x and y* in which *x* or *y* or both are pronouns. Shakespeare, in such constructions, almost invariably used the objective case of the pronoun, although he has one of the merry wives of Windsor say "There is such a league between my good man and he!" When the *x* is a proper name we sometimes find *I* in the second spot:

> . . . and many high words between Mr. Povy and I —Samuel Pepys, diary, 31 Mar. 1664

> There was nothing between Mr. Robert and I —Daniel Defoe, *Moll Flanders,* 1722

Evidence for such constructions is sparse, and sometimes *he* appears in the *x* slot:

> The principal difference between he and I is

stamina —Tennessee Williams, quoted in *Esquire,* 5 June 1979 (in Simon 1980)

> Rhonda's assessment of Darrin's casual attitude . . . seemed to be borne out by an "interview" with him. This consisted of interrupting a game of catch between he and Brian in Opryland's parking lot —Brett F. Devan, *Bluegrass Unlimited,* September 1983

> . . . relations between he and the two bosses are acrimonious as usual —Greg Gumbel, television broadcast, ESPN, 21 Oct. 1985

Such examples as there are seem to confirm Chomsky's theory.

Conclusion: *between you and I* seems now to be primarily a spoken form which no amount of correction by commentators aiming to improve written English will extinguish. Neither it nor the prescribed *between you and me* appears very often in print. Our little current evidence almost invariably uses *me.* For more instances of the anomalous use of pronouns, SEE MYSELF; PRONOUNS; WHO, WHOM 1.

betwixt James A. H. Murray in the OED considered *betwixt* to be archaic, and *between* to be the living word.

Betwixt has not yet fallen into disuse. Evidence in the Merriam-Webster files and in the Dictionary of American Regional English show its survival in American dialectal use, especially in the Southern and South Midland areas:

> Did you see him betwixt us & the light? —Jesse Stuart, "Uncle Joe's Boys," 1936 (American Dialect Dictionary)

> Well, betwixt us two, I do not identify myself with St. Catherine —Flannery O'Connor, letter, 16 Dec. 1955

It turns up now and then in literary surroundings:

> . . . the wild path betwixt printed word and word —Conrad Aiken, letter, 6 Feb. 1923

> . . . gliding betwixt the cakestands and antimacassared sofas —Salman Rushdie, *The Satanic Verses,* 1989

And it is also established in the fixed phrase *betwixt and between*:

> . . . robots. They lie betwixt and between, neither human nor machine —Daniel McNeill et al., *Fuzzy Logic,* 1903

> His Greeks are not Trobriand Islanders, nor yet are they Fellows of Balliol: they are betwixt and between —Jonathan Barnes, *Times Literary Supp.,* 23 Apr. 1993

> Even the pros are betwixt and between

—Robert D. Hof et al., *Business Week,* 21 Feb. 2000

Except in dialect and the fixed phrase *betwixt and between, betwixt* is uncommon enough nowadays to call attention to itself. It seems to be used for that very purpose:

Betwixt the neon bedizenments, general sleaze, and shops selling unlabeled clothes —C. P. Reynolds, *Gourmet,* January 1988

. . . the prosthetic bean bag she wore betwixt the thighs to pass as a man in the movie —David Hochman, *Entertainment Weekly,* 8 Jan. 1999

bi- Dictionary editors receive a lot of letters about time words formed with the prefix *bi-,* especially *bimonthly* and *biweekly.* The typical letter writer is outraged or distressed that *bimonthly,* for example, may mean either "every two months" or "twice a month." Many of our correspondents accuse us of abdicating our responsibility by not setting things straight. The trouble is that it is much too late to set things straight. People have been using these words in two different meanings for quite some time, and now we all simply have to live with that fact.

Perhaps the most irritating thing of all is that the writers who use these words almost always assume you know exactly what they mean. In the publishing world, for instance, everyone assumes you know *bimonthly* means "every two months." Only once in a while are you given a clue:

. . . there will now be 6 issues a year. Each bimonthly issue will have 48 pages —*Scouting,* January–February 1970

On the other hand, we have evidence that in the world of education *bimonthly* usually means "twice a month," as in this passage from a novel with an academic setting:

"Please listen," O'Connor said. "None of us has time to meet twice a week. The casebooks have grown like tapeworms. We simply have to get organized. I propose we shift to bi-monthly meetings." —John Jay Osborne, Jr., *The Paper Chase,* 1971

We find the same situation with *biweekly.* Writers assume that their meaning is your meaning:

. . . turns in a bi-weekly column —Jerome J. Shestack, *N.Y. Times,* 26 June 1973

What's your guess? Twice a week? Every other week? The writer does not tell us. Sometimes the context helps us:

They are repaid by weekly, biweekly, or monthly payments —McKee Fisk & James

C. Snapp, *Applied Business Law,* 8th ed., 1960

. . . is living in the house herself and giving bi-weekly square dances. . . . Many guests were told at the beginning of the season that they would be expected every Thursday and Sunday —Millie Considine, *The Diplomat,* April 1965

In a few cases there are contrasting words. For instance, we have *biannual* for "twice a year" and *biennial* for "every two years." But unfortunately *biannual* has sometimes been used to mean *biennial.* Here a solution is easy: skip *biannual* altogether and use in its place the common *semiannual.*

Semiannual reminds us of one possible general solution: use a *semi-* compound for "twice a" and a *bi-* compound for "every two." Apparently many writers do so, for a majority of our citations for *bimonthly, biweekly,* etc. seem to be for "every two." The trouble is that there are just enough of the other uses to leave the reader uncertain. Another solution is to avoid the *bi-* compounds altogether and come right out with it: "twice a week" or "every other month."

biannual, biennial See BI-.

bid *Bid* has irregular inflected forms. When it means "to make a bid" it usually has the unchanged *bid* as both past and past participle:

. . . was pleased when Betty Franklin, one of his black material handlers, bid for the job —Stephen Sahlein, *The Affirmative Action Handbook,* 1978

Wall Street has bid up the stocks of these young companies —Rita Koselka & Christopher Palmeri, *Forbes,* 1 Mar. 1993

Bidded can be found but is unusual:

. . . specified other particular suppliers on other bidded contracts —Jonathan Kwitny, *Wall Street Jour.,* 21 Jan. 1975

In other senses the most common past is *bade*:

. . . bade his marshals make the scene as lavish as possible —S. J. Perelman, *New Yorker,* 1 Jan. 1972

. . . the rabbi bade everyone rise to pray —Erich Segal, *The Class,* 1985

Bid is sometimes also found:

The outgoing Truman bid a similar farewell eight years ago —*Trends,* 24 Nov. 1960

In the phrase *bid fair to, bid* is more frequent as past, though *bade* is also used:

. . . first appeared in 1953 and together bid fair to become an institution —Martin James, *Saturday Rev.,* 10 July 1954

The summer of 1885 bid fair to be one of more than ordinary interest —*Dictionary of American Biography*, 1928

. . . what with the sweat and Indeharu's exertions it bade fair to disintegrate —C. S. Forester, *The Sky and the Forest*, 1948

As past participle, *bid* and *bidden* are the most usual:

. . . those manuscripts that he had once bid Max Brod to dispose of —Philip Roth, *Reading Myself and Others*, 1975

. . . was bid a hasty adieu by her millionaire common-law husband —Kathleen Parker, *Orlando Sentinel*, 3 June 1998

. . . thinking that I was a stray tourist rather than the guest he had bidden to lunch —Martin Gilbert, *N.Y. Times Book Rev.*, 14 Dec. 1986

. . . was bidden to listen to brief prayers —Lady Bird Johnson, *McCall's*, November 1970

Bade is a less frequent past participle:

. . . friends were bade farewell —*Dartmouth Alumni Mag.*, May 1954

billion Copperud 1970, Reader's Digest 1983, and others comment on the fact that in American English *billion* means "a thousand million" and in British English "a million million." Our latest British source, Burchfield 1996, notes that the American sense of *billion* is increasingly being used in British English; he suggests that in a British context the American sense be assumed unless there is evidence to the contrary.

bimonthly See BI-.

bite *Bite* has two past participles, *bitten* and *bit*. *Bitten* is by far the more common—it is the usual form of the past participle. *Bit*, the less common form, was thought archaic when the OED was edited. The Dictionary of American Regional English reports several dialect surveys on the subject that have established that *bit* as past participle is alive and well in speech. How does it fare in print? Our evidence shows that it still occurs, and in standard English contexts, but not nearly as often as *bitten*.

I have bit off more than I can chew —Flannery O'Conner, letter, 9 Nov. 1962

. . . hoping not to get bit by mosquitoes —Robert Coover, *Harper's*, January 1972

Emmett was bit on the throat and perished on the spot —Garrison Keillor, *Lake Wobegon Days*, 1985

Now Compaq has bit the bullet and includ-

ed the screen —Don Steinberg, *GQ*, November 1997

Conclusion: these citations are not evidence that *bit* is beginning to rival *bitten* in frequency, but only that *bit* continues to be used now and then, especially in various fixed phrases. *Bitten* is the usual past participle.

biweekly See BI-.

black Quite a few commentators mention the use of *black* in the sense of *Negro*, a revival of an old use that seems to have begun with the civil rights movement in the 1960s. The OED reports instances of *black* in the sense from the 17th century; evidently it began as a translation of the Spanish *Negro*, which had earlier been used in English. The term seems to have been neutral in the 18th century:

The negro case is not yet decided. . . . Maclaurin is made happy by your approbation of his memorial for the black —James Boswell, letter to Samuel Johnson, 14 Feb. 1777

Reader's Digest 1983 says that *black*, *Negro*, and *colored* were all in neutral use during the time of slavery; after the Civil War *colored* was the preferred term, with *Negro* replacing it in favor around the turn of the century. After *black* (sometimes capitalized) had its period of ascendancy, it began to be replaced as the preferred term by *Afro-American* (a 19th-century term, usually an adjective) and then by *African-American* (1984, both adjective and noun). Burchfield 1996 points out that when one is uncertain, *black* is the term least likely to give offense to anyone.

See also COLORED.

blame, *noun* The noun *blame* may be followed by the prepositions *for*, *with*, or *on*:

I take all the blame for not seeing further than my nose —C. P. Snow, *The Conscience of the Rich*, 1958

She could not bear any implied blame of him —Angus Wilson, *The Middle Age of Mrs. Eliot*, 1958

. . . and just as vaguely puts the blame on downtown businessmen —Jack Olsen, *Sports Illustrated*, 15 July 1968

blame on, blame for The real difference between "blame someone for" and "blame something on" is the direct object; in the first the direct object is the cause—usually a person —of the problem, and in the second the direct object is the problem. The first construction is older; the second is not attested in the OED until 1835.

In 1881 the pseudonymous Alfred Ayres in *The Verbalist* took note of the newer construction. *Blame on*, said Ayres, "is a gross vulgarism which we sometimes hear from persons of considerable culture." Ayres does not stop to explain why it is a vulgarism or how such cultured persons are capable of using such a vulgarism—or even to prescribe *blame for*. It is a simple ex cathedra pronouncement. From Ayres it spread rapidly into other usage books, textbooks, and dictionaries; it is being repeated as recently as Garner 1998. Others along the way had found the construction standard, as indeed it had been all the time.

> I am tempted to blame this on my own codgerly impatience —John Graves, *National Geographic*, April 1999

> One more facile copout, like blaming failure on not having a mentor —Patricia O'Toole, *Vogue*, March 1984

> . . . admitted to having physically abused his longtime girlfriend and blamed it on steroids —William Nack, *Sports Illustrated*, 18 May 1998

> She blamed herself for relying too much on the advice of aides —Donatella Lorch, *Newsweek*, 24 Apr. 2000

> O.K., so baseball has been so dull . . . for so long, can you blame America for getting excited? —Rick Reilly, *Sports Illustrated*, 7 Sept. 1998

> The mayor's flamboyantly gelid and authoritarian character makes it easy to blame him for this situation —Katha Pollitt, *The Nation*, 15 Mar. 1999

A few other prepositions are used with *blame*, but less often:

> . . . not to blame onto Latin the results of sloppy teaching —Marion Friedmann, in *Verbatim*, December 1974

> . . . tended to blame the evasion of such subject-matter . . . to the persistence of the romantic tradition —*Times Literary Supp.*, 21 July 1966

> . . . she blamed us with killing the canary birds, too —*New Yorker*, 25 Sept. 1926

blasé   When *blasé* is followed by a preposition, it is usually *about*:

> Twelve years ago it was still considered a tremendous journalistic coup to discover . . . a single dissenter. Now our correspondents have grown somewhat blasé about the breed —Adam B. Ulam, *Saturday Rev.*, 7 Feb. 1976

> . . . has been less blasé about the activities of the Sandinist National Liberation Front —Alan Riding, *Saturday Rev.*, 12 Nov. 1977

There is also evidence for *with* and *at*:

> . . . but in time, we became jaded and blase with ordinary heiresses with American for-

tunes —Eve Babitz, *Rolling Stone*, 3 Feb. 1972

> . . . to act a bit blasé at the prospect of yet another famous . . . customer holding forth —Allan Ripp, *Avenue*, March 1984

blatant, flagrant   Several commentators note that these words are confused or misused for each other, which is merely a judgmental way of saying that they have senses that overlap.

Blatant is usually the point of the comment. One matter that draws notice is the extension of *blatant* from its earliest "noisy" senses to a sense "glaringly conspicuous or obtrusive"— a shift from the ear to the eye, so to speak. The OED Supplement dates this development from the end of the 19th century. The sense was given in Webster 1909 but was deleted by a short-sighted editor working on Webster's Second (1934). It has become the predominant sense in modern use.

The conspicuousness denoted by both *blatant* and *flagrant* is almost always of an undesirable kind. Several commentators from Evans and Bernstein on note that *flagrant* stresses scandalous or wicked behavior. This is its most common use, and it commonly modifies such nouns as *violation* and *abuse*.

> Where lawyers and some Federal officials see a flagrant violation of law —Seth Faison, *N.Y. Times*, 20 Feb. 1999

> . . . such a flagrant discrimination against Negroes . . . that the United States Supreme Court in 1915 declared the "grandfather clause" unconstitutional —John Hope Franklin, *Race and History*, 1989

> Stretching accounting rules . . . is a flagrant trespass —Robert J. Samuelson, *Newsweek*, 3 Apr. 2000

Blatant is sometimes used similarly:

> Blatant racial and gender discrimination is just about over —Gregg Easterbrook, *New Republic*, 20 Dec. 1999

> . . . have refused to convict despite blatant transgressions of the "hard rule" —Lawrence O. Gostin, *National Law Jour.*, 11 Aug. 1997

> The surcharges are particularly galling . . . because they seem to amount to blatant double-dipping —John Greenwald, *Time*, 29 Nov. 1999

Blatant, in general, carries less moral freight than *flagrant*:

> Witness the Seinfeld gang's blatant contempt for family life—and for their married friends —Ken Tucker, *Entertainment Weekly*, 13 Nov. 1998

Still, *flagrant* is not limited to expressions of moral outrage. It can mean merely "conspicuous." In such use it is more or less interchangeable with *blatant*:

> . . . his son is a flagrant homosexual —*Saturday Rev.,* 8 Jan. 1955

> . . . let's say a blatant homosexual —Merle Miller, *Saturday Rev.,* 2 Jan. 1971

> . . . the coy gavotte of flagrant self-praise and blushing modesty —Fintan O'Toole, *New Republic,* 11 Oct. 1999

> . . . a song he'd written in blatant emulation of one of his favorite groups —David Fricke, *Rolling Stone,* 2 June 1994

In summary, while *blatant* and *flagrant* may both mean merely "conspicuous," *blatant* is usually used of someone, some action, or something that attracts disapproving attention:

> The most blatant instance is provided by the recent colloquial use of *like* whenever the speaker halts for an idea —Barzun 1985

Flagrant is used in the same way but usually carries a heavier weight of violated morality:

> . . . lands, honours, and titles . . . to which they were not entitled but had gained through flagrant disregard of the laws of England —Alison Weir, *The Princes in the Tower,* 1992

bleeding A euphemism for *bloody,* which see.

blend Bernstein 1965 and Partridge 1942 say that blend is followed by *with*:

> . . . blending the cadences of the liturgy with those of perplexed brooding thought —Edmund Wilson, *Axel's Castle,* 1931

> . . . whose life had been so strangely blended with hers —Winston Churchill, *The Crisis,* 1901

> . . . elation which comes when man feels himself blended with nature —Walter Prescott Webb, *The Great Frontier,* 1952

Partridge disapproves *blend* with *into,* but it is quite common and standard:

> The painting would blend into nature —Harold Rosenberg, *New Yorker,* 20 Nov. 1971

> . . . ordering their cadres to blend themselves into the government landscape —Robert Shaplen, *New Yorker,* 24 Apr. 1971

Sometimes we find *blend in* followed by *with*:

> . . . how well he blends in with the background —Andrew Sarris, in *The Film,* 1968

> . . . more imaginative sets, which are unfortunately blended in with others that are pretty poor —Henry Hewes, *Saturday Rev.,* 28 Feb. 1953

And in cookery, *blend* is followed by *in*:

> Blend in four tablespoons flour —Jane Nickerson, *N.Y. Times Mag.,* 10 Oct. 1954

blind agreement See AGREEMENT, SUBJECT-VERB: THE PRINCIPLE OF PROXIMITY.

bloc, block The spelling *bloc* is usual for the sense of a political combination.

blond, blonde As an adjective, the spellings *blond* and *blonde* are more often applied to females than to males. The noun *blonde* is used only of females, but the noun *blond* is used of persons of either sex. Either spelling is used when the word is applied to nonhuman objects such as wood.

See also BRUNET, BRUNETTE.

bloody *Bloody* is first attested as an intensifier in the second half of the 17th century:

> Not without he will promise to be bloody drunk. —George Etherege, *The Man of Mode,* 1676

The phrase *bloody drunk* may have been popular at the time; it also turns up in a prologue written by John Dryden in 1684 for a play of Thomas Southerne.

James A. H. Murray in the OED says that *bloody* was in "general colloquial use" from the Restoration to the middle of the 18th century. During that time it seems to have had no particular offensive taint:

> It was bloody hot walking to-day —Jonathan Swift, *Journal to Stella,* 8 May 1711

But by the middle of the 18th century it had gone out of fashionable use and had been left to the lower orders of society. Samuel Johnson characterized it as "very vulgar" in the second edition of his dictionary.

Still the word could be found occasionally in print. Byron put the word into the mouth of an English highwayman shot by his hero Don Juan:

> 'Oh Jack! I'm floor'd by that 'ere bloody Frenchman!' —*Don Juan,* Canto xi, 1823

But as the 19th century went along, the word acquired such loathsome connotations as to be unprintable and unmentionable by polite people. Nobody really knows why this happened—it seems to have been one of those Victorian things. Toward the end of the century it began to be replaced by euphemisms like *blooming* and *ruddy. Ruddy* began to be perceived as a bit tainted itself: in 1887 Gilbert and Sullivan created such an outcry with their operetta *Ruddygore* that they changed the spelling to *Ruddigore* after the fourth performance.

George Bernard Shaw created a sensation in 1914 by putting it in the mouth of Eliza Doolittle in *Pygmalion* and having it spoken in public on the stage. James Joyce had to delete it from some of his stories when he was trying to get *Dubliners* published in 1906.

After World War I the word began to creep into respectable literature again, appearing in works by such writers as W. Somerset Maugham, John Masefield, and Aldous Huxley. Still, the feeling against it in British English was very strong until after World War II. British newspapers were still printing it as b____ as late as 1946. *Bloody* never acquired much stigma in Australian English, where it was used a lot, or in American English, where it was not especially common. Burchfield 1996 says that it no longer creates much adverse reaction when used in TV plays, but that it is still not a word to use in polite society.

blooming   See BLOODY.

blow   *Blow* belongs to a class of verbs some of whose members have regular inflected forms and some irregular. The usual inflected forms of *blow* are irregular: *blew* and *blown*. The regular variant of these, *blowed*, says Burchfield 1996, is used only in expressions like "I'll be blowed." The OED also shows *blowed* only in that sense. Lamberts 1972 notes, however, that the regular forms are common in nonstandard English. The Dictionary of American Regional English narrows this observation, finding *blowed* to be chiefly Southern and South Midland with some scattered use in Northern areas. The DARE additionally notes that *blowed* occurs especially frequently among less educated male speakers.

Blowed does not seem to have had much literary use. Shakespeare puts it into the mouth of his Irish captain Macmorris in *Henry V*:

I would have blowed up the town. . . .

Defoe gave it to Robinson Crusoe:

May 16. It had blowed hard in the night. . . .

Our American citations of recent vintage are all from speech and fall within the dialect areas described by the DARE.

boast   When *boast* is used as an intransitive with a preposition, *of* and *about* are usual:

. . . this world of Capitalism, with its astonishing spread of ignorance and helplessness, boasting . . . of its spread of education and enlightenment —George Bernard Shaw, *The Intelligent Woman's Guide to Socialism and Capitalism*, 1928

. . . the magazine could boast of a critic . . . whose interest in the theatre was exceeded only by his interest in the living human drama —*Saturday Rev.*, 23 Apr. 1955

. . . he allows environmental pollution . . . at the same time that he boasts about playground facilities and law and order —Henry Hewes, *Saturday Rev.*, 3 June 1972

boggle   When a usage writer is determined to find something wrong with an expression, he will disapprove no matter how difficult constructing a rationale for the disapproval turns out to be. Both Barzun 1985 and Bremner 1980 dislike the expression "(something) boggles the mind." Bremner says it is an example of the error of making a transitive out of an intransitive. Presumably this means that if "the water boils" is earlier in standard use, then "boil the water" must be an error. Of course it isn't. Barzun thinks that making a transitive out of *boggle* is contrary to usage. If it were truly contrary to usage, however, he would not have had to write about it.

What really irks these writers is that the transitive use of *boggle* in this sense is quite recent. Our evidence for it began to appear in the mid-1950s, and in our early examples it is not the mind but the imagination that is boggled:

Efforts to capture the atmosphere of a European musical center come off on the whole far better than might be expected, but not without several moments that boggle the imagination —Arthur Knight, *Saturday Rev.*, 20 Mar. 1954

The amount of litigation that would be set off . . . boggles the imagination —*The Reporter*, 6 Apr. 1967

It also used with a personal direct object:

What boggled her, though, was why her uptight husband . . . was suddenly a sex symbol —Cyra McFadden, *The Serial*, 1977

What boggles the human parser is not the amount of memory needed but the kind of memory —Steven Pinker, *The Language Instinct*, 1994

Our files do not hold any evidence for "boggle the mind" before 1970. It is still in use:

. . . even good small claims courts tend to impose procedural requirements that boggle the mind of most laymen —Philip C. Schrag, *Columbia Forum*, Summer 1970

It boggles the mind that survival of the fittest can terminate in such wimphood —*National Rev.*, 20 June 1986

. . . geneticists can now do, almost routinely, an experiment so incredible that it boggles the mind —Matt Ridley, *Genome,* 1999

The intransitive uses have not been pushed aside by the transitive:

> . . . so much for a movie sale, so much for a major book club selection, and so on until even the statistical mind boggles —Robert Stein, *New York,* 30 Aug. 1971

> The mind boggles at what Lardner might have done with such a scene —Daniel Okrent, *N.Y. Times Book Rev.,* 6 Apr. 1986

> The mind boggles to learn that the No. 1 nonfiction best seller . . . is Marcia Clark's apologia —James Brady, *Advertising Age,* 16 June 1997

And the old *boggle at* construction is still in use:

> . . . who, however, might boggle at the chef's inclusion of butter —Jay Jacobs, *Gourmet,* June 1982

In summary, you can either have your mind boggle at something or have something boggle your mind—both are standard and common in American English.

bona fides *Bona fides* came into English from law Latin in the 19th century and subsequent users of English have not hesitated to make free with it. A number of commentators have pointed out that it is a singular noun in Latin, and should be singular in English. But that old devil *-s,* the usual sign of a plural in English, was edging *bona fides* into use as a plural noun.

While the commentators worried about construction, they failed to notice that a new meaning, roughly "evidences or proofs of good faith or genuineness," was developing. The intelligence community contributed to this development. A correspondent of William Safire, reprinted in Safire 1982, comments on the terminology used in the intelligence and counterintelligence business and notes among other things that there are people who volunteer information to intelligence services "whose 'bona fides' must be ascertained in order to establish their credibility." Is this, then, an established usage in the cloak-and-dagger business? Evidently so:

> My bona fides in this extraordinary case are known to the Turks, to the British and to security officers of JAMMAT (Joint Allied Military Mission to Aid Turkey) —Ray Brock, letter to editor of *Time,* 31 Mar. 1952

> When the war ended German intelligence archives were captured . . . and Fritz Kolbe's bona fides were unambiguously established —Edward Jay Epstein, *N.Y. Times Book Rev.,* 16 Jan. 1983

> . . . cases where the bona fides of a Soviet defector have been called into question —Philip G. Ryan (in Safire 1986)

It would thus seem that the plural use is an established one in the intelligence world. But it is not limited to that milieu:

> . . . his bona fides on this issue are still to be proven —Elizabeth Drew, *N.Y. Times Mag.,* 14 Mar. 1993

> It would also seem soulless even if Aretha's bona fides weren't in exactly that area —*People,* 15 Aug. 1983

> . . . flyers from companies . . . bent on publicizing both their wares and their social bona fides by displaying black and white models at cordial ease with one another —Benjamin DeMott, *Harper's,* September 1995

> He makes something of a try at the authentic, but he keeps letting his literary bona fides leak in —Stanley Kauffmann, *Before My Eyes,* 1980

This now-established new meaning, as the last two examples show, very often occurs in contexts where it does not govern a verb. But when it does, the verb is usually plural, though the singular is not unknown:

> There was very simple bona fides to the work —Robin D. G. Kelley, *The Nation,* 14 Dec. 1998

A singular made by pruning off the *-s,* first noticed by Fowler 1926, does exist, but is still not well established:

> . . . to the conspirators, arrest was a credential, a bona fide —Charles Nicholl, *The Reckoning,* 1992

border When *border* is used to mean "to approach the nature of a specific thing" and is followed by a preposition, *on* is usually the choice:

> . . . a passionate dedication that borders on fanaticism —Michael Novak, *Center Mag.,* September 1969

> . . . a waste of intellect bordering on the absurd —Joseph Conrad, *Chance,* 1913

> . . . she did nothing but walk up and down . . . in a state bordering on stupefaction —Thomas Hardy, *The Return of the Native,* 1878

When the literal sense of *border* is used in the passive, the preposition most often used is *by; with* is less frequent:

> . . . rice paddies bordered by earthen dikes —E. J. Kahn, Jr., *New Yorker,* 12 May 1951

. . . the river bordered with wild flags and mottled plane trees —Louis Bromfield, *The Man Who Had Everything*, 1935

born, borne When George Farquhar wrote in 1707

But I must tell you, Sir, that this is not to be born —*The Beaux Stratagem*

the conventions of English spelling were not as firmly established as they are today. Today we have a dozen or more handbooks and commentators to tell us that *bear* has two past participles, *born* and *borne*. As a verb *born* is used only in the passive of the literal or figurative act of birth:

I was born in his second-floor bedroom —Russell Baker, *Growing Up*, 1982

Some are born whole; others must seek this blessed state —Bernard Malamud, *N.Y. Times Book Rev.*, 28 Aug. 1983

The active past participle for giving birth is *borne*:

. . . a younger woman who had borne an illegitimate child —Russell Baker, *Growing Up*, 1982

Borne is used for all other senses:

Critics . . . charge that the Americans were borne to Paris on ideological wings —Walter Goodman, *N.Y. Times Book Rev.*, 17 Apr. 1983

. . . luxury almost too rich to be borne —Russell Baker, *Growing Up*, 1982

A modest revelation indeed, and not one fully borne out by the text —Noel Perrin, *N.Y. Times Book Rev.*, 6 Sept. 1981

The principal problem, and one which should be borne in mind by facility planners —E. M. Hargreaves, *Area Development*, August 1970

Our collection of errors shows that *born* is used in place of *borne* about twice as often as *borne* for *born*. The errors are both British and American.

borrow 1. The usual preposition linking *borrow* to the person or source is *from*:

. . . consents to borrow money from a usurer —Moody E. Prior, *American Scholar*, Autumn 1981

. . . borrowed a scene from another play —*Current Biography*, September 1965

"I like him because I have not read the books from which he has borrowed his opinions. . . ." —George Bernard Shaw, *Cashel Byron's Profession*, 1886

Of is used, but seems old-fashioned:

. . . my desire to borrow them of their parents —Henry Miller, *The Air-Conditioned Nightmare*, 1945

. . . what? not one single book? Oh, but . . . you can borrow of the parson —Jonathan Swift, *Journal to Stella*, 15 July 1711

On may also be used:

. . . borrowing heavily on the ideas of their European colleagues —*Dictionary of American History*, 1940

The prepositions *off* and *off of* appear to be limited to speech. Occasionally they may turn up in fiction:

. . . she even used to borrow books off me sometimes —Margaret Drabble, *The Needle's Eye*, 1972

Of is also used sometimes to link *borrow* with the object borrowed:

A few decades ago, songwriters borrowed freely of these words —*Phoenix Flame*, 1954

Mr. Jim had a lantern to peer out the ruts of the road. . . . Effie Turpin walked behind him to borrow of his light —Elizabeth Madox Roberts, *The Time of Man*, 1926

A preposition may likewise be used with *borrow* to indicate the collateral put up for a loan. *On* seems to have been used first and is still current:

". . . One time I borrowed on my saddle from the fella that was promotin' the show. . . ." —Richard Wormser, *The Lonesome Quarter*, 1951

. . . lived on what he could borrow on his expectations —John Fulton, quoted in *Sports Illustrated*, 29 July 1968

The present favorite in financial circles is *against*:

. . . policyholders who can borrow against the cash value of their life insurance policies —*Changing Times*, May 1981

2. The use of *borrow* to mean "lend" is dialectal. The Dictionary of American Regional English finds it most prevalent in the Northern area west of the Great Lakes.

both *Both* is used in a number of idiomatic constructions that have come under attack by usage experts from the 18th century to the 20th. Most of these criticisms occur between 1870 and the 1920s, but a surprising number of them have been repeated into the 1980s. Here is a representative selection.

1. Redundant (or, in the old days, pleonastic) uses: the censure of uses of *both*—primarily in

mild emphasis—that are held to be redundant is a favorite game of usage writers going back to Baker 1770. Hodgson 1889, for instance, finds fault with this:

> "I'm sure I would if I could," agreed both of the literary ladies.

To correct the redundancy of *both,* he revises to "the two literary ladies." What makes *two* acceptable and *both* wrong is not explained. And to bring these exercises up to date, we find Garner 1998 objecting to the redundancy of "both sides blamed each other." He corrects it to "each side blamed the other." Again we get no explanation of why the revision is an improvement.

Many of Hodgson's examples combine *both* with *agree.* This combination echoes down the ages. Here we have Copperud 1980: "Since *both* indicates duality, it is redundant with such words as *equal, alike, agree, together:* . . . 'Both agreed.' *They agreed.*" But who has limited *agree* to an implication of duality that makes *both* redundant? Not users of English, certainly.

Copperud mentions the combinations *both alike* and *both together.* These are great favorites; they have been given particular attention from the 1870s on. Why this is such an important issue is uncertain. We know that a writer named Shakespeare used these combinations:

> That very hour, and in the selfsame inn,
> A meaner woman was delivered
> Of such a burthen, male twins, both alike
> —*The Comedy of Errors,* 1593

A look into a Shakespeare concordance will show that he used *both alike* six times in the plays and *both together* three times. *Both alike* belongs more to poetry than prose (besides Shakespeare, Spenser, Marlowe, Dryden, Pope, Swift, Byron, Browning, Coleridge, Tennyson, and many others used it). We have very little contemporary evidence for *both alike,* but *both together* appears a bit more in modern prose. It is hard to see what great problem a use like this has:

> . . . most of these have to do with sex or violence and sometimes with both together —Joseph Epstein, *N.Y. Times Book Rev.,* 5 Feb. 1984

In the end, after more than two centuries of comment, this molehill is still a molehill. It is a trivial matter and not worth worrying about.

2. *Both . . . as well as.* Copperud 1970, 1980 tells us that "*Both* is also redundant with *as well as,*" whatever that may mean. He then compounds the confusion by recommending that *as well as* be changed to *and.* How does that cure redundancy? Chambers 1985 and

Garner 1998 say that *as well as* is incorrect after *both;* of course they don't tell us why. *As well as* is used as a correlative in a manner somewhat like *and* (see AS WELL AS), but how that fact is relevant to either of the foregoing comments is obscure at best. In our files the use of *both . . . as well as* is uncommon, but it does occur:

> . . . for fear such an impression might produce ill will both in the United States as well as in Formosa and Seoul —*N.Y. Times,* 9 Aug. 1955

> At later stages in my life, I had opportunity to eat both the presumably very best food in the world, as well as the very worst —Herbert Hoover, *Memoirs,* 1951

The worst that can be said of these is that they are not very elegant. Since the construction is fairly rare, it doesn't seem worth fussing about.

3. *Both . . . and.* Bernstein 1977, Phythian 1979, Bryson 1984, and Chambers 1985 all stress the necessity of placing the same construction after *both* and after *and* for the most pleasingly well-balanced results. This seems sensible enough. Bernstein pulls an example from the *N.Y. Times:*

> The Senator said that both from the viewpoint of economics and morality the nation must practice self-denial.

He points out that *From the viewpoint of economics* follows *both* but only *morality* follows *and.* He shows two ways to correct the problem and adds "Logical tidiness is always an asset in the use of language." The point to note here is that the quotation begins with "The Senator said." Presumably the reporter is transcribing very nearly what was said. What is said is spoken English, not written English, a distinction that in this case Bernstein does not take into account.

Dean Alford in 1866 had heard all of this before; he traces it back to Lindley Murray's *English Grammar* of 1795 (there's not much new in the usage game). Alford believes that a statement of the same form as the Senator's is "plain colloquial English"; he finds a revised and entirely parallel construction "harsh and cramped."

The sensible conclusion would seem to be this: when transcribing speech, even indirectly, leave the rhythms and constructions of speech undisturbed. In writing discursive prose, you might do well to seek out parallel constructions.

4. *Both of.* We still get correspondents wondering whether it is acceptable to use *both of,* as in "both of the books," or whether "both books" must be used. This is a fairly old issue, going back to the 19th century.

Both of is just like *all of* (which see). The *of* after *both* can be omitted before a plural noun (although it need not be), but it must be kept before a pronoun in the objective case.

5. *The both.* Correspondents have written to ask about the propriety of such expressions as *the both of you* which, they aver, are in constant use on television. It now and then appears in print:

> Mr. Epstein has two choice offerings to himself, 'Mack the Knife' and 'September Song,' lovely the both of them, in the writing and the doing —*N.Y. Times,* 17 June 1969

> He found it impossible to earn a living, and Alice's private income could not support the both of them —Andrew Raeburn, *Boston Symphony Orchestra Program,* 21 Oct. 1972

> You would sit across the dinner table from each other in bondage, in terrible bondage to what you thought was love. The both of you —E. L. Doctorow, *Ragtime,* 1975

A few commentators have disparaged the use. No reason has been given, but perhaps it has been perceived as an Irishism (we have no evidence that it is). Perrin & Ebbitt 1972 and Burchfield 1996 note that it is common in speech but usually avoided in print. This may well be true; we have little evidence of it in print. There is no reason you should avoid it if it is your normal idiom.

6. *Possessive.* A couple of dictionaries, Longman 1984 and Heritage 1982, 2000, mention the formation of the possessive with *both.* Evans 1957 notes that the *'s* genitive can be used but that the *of* genitive is more common: "the fault of both of us" being more common than either "both our faults" or "both's faults."

7. *Both* of more than two. Chaucer in *The Knight's Tale* has these lines:

> O chaste goddesse of the wodes grene,
> To whom bothe hevene and erthe and see
> is sene.

The lines were reprinted in more modern spelling in one of the editions of Richard Grant White's *Words and Their Uses* (apparently not the 1870 edition), and they appear to have upset him, because he says "it is impossible that the same word can mean two and three." Fitzedward Hall in *Modern English* (1873) solved the problem. White, he said, had befuddled himself by confounding the conjunction *both* with the pronoun *both.* Hall goes on to point out that the pronoun is not used of three, but the conjunction, which is used in much the same way as *either, neither,* and *whether* are, can be used of two or more. Here are three examples from the OED:

> . . . they answered that they would take better advice and so return again, both prelates, bishops, abbots, barons and knights —Lord Berners, translation of Froissart's *Chronicles,* 1523

> My dwelling is but melancholy. Both Williams and Desmoulins and myself, are very sickly —Samuel Johnson, letter, 2 Mar. 1782

> He prayeth well, who loveth well
> Both man and bird and beast
> —Samuel Taylor Coleridge, "The Rime of the Ancient Mariner," 1798

Our recent evidence for *both* with three or more comes primarily from literary sources, and is fairly old. Current evidence shows the conjunction used of two.

boughten Although Chaucer used *boughten* a couple of times as a past-tense form, it is usually employed as an adjective. Samuel Taylor Coleridge seems to have begun it in 1793. He, and a bit later Southey, used it of what was purchased rather than freely given or volunteered. This use still exists:

> Better to go down dignified
> With boughten friendship at your side
> —Robert Frost, *Complete Poems,* 1949

> . . . the good will of boughten allies —Garet Garrett, *Rise of Empire,* 1952

> . . . hatred of plastic posh, boughten elegance, empty sophistication —Benjamin DeMott, *Saturday Rev.,* 11 Dec. 1971

The usual American use, however, contrasts *boughten* with *homemade*:

> And even premade boughten biscuits from a tube can be good —M. F. K. Fisher, *With Bold Knife and Fork,* 1969

> . . . he did stop eating so much potato chips and pork skins and boughten popcorn —Ursula K. LeGuin, *New Yorker,* 2 Nov. 1987

> . . . a very passable imitation of boughten ice-cream —H. L. Mencken, *Happy Days,* 1940

> . . . for this reason homemade and frozen pies often do not come up to the quality of boughten ones —Dennis E. Baron, *American Speech,* Summer 1981

> Both "boughten" foods and local products . . . provided ample room for the development of a satisfying sense of expertise and culinary competence —Donna R. Garbaccia, *We Are What We Eat,* 1998

The quotation above shows that some writers are conscious that *boughten* is primarily dialectal. The Dictionary of American Regional English shows it to be mostly a Northern term.

breach, breech Copperud 1970, 1980, Bryson 1984, and Garner 1998 say that these two words are frequently confused. If you have any doubts about which word to choose, a dictionary will put you straight.

break The usual principal parts of *break* are *broke* for the past and *broken* for the past participle. The variant past participle *broke,* the OED tells us, was formed from *broken* in the 14th century and was in widespread use in the 17th and 18th centuries. By the 19th century its use was receding, but the OED notes that it was still used in poetry—by Tennyson, for instance—for metrical purposes. McKnight 1928 points out that Jane Austen in *Mansfield Park* (1814) put *broke* in the mouths of her upper-class Bertrams and their friends like Miss Crawford:

> If your Miss Bertrams do not like to have their hearts broke. . . .

But the middle-class Mrs. Norris uses *broken*:

> . . . a poor, helpless, forlorn widow, unfit for anything, my spirits quite broken down. . . .

This presumably illustrates the fact that older forms, forms going out of fashion in the use of the middle classes, often persist longer in the upper and lower classes. Jane Austen herself used *broke*:

> . . . the Maypole bearing the weathercock was broke in two —letter, 8 Nov. 1800

The Dictionary of American Regional English reports that the past participle *broke* is found chiefly in the speech of less educated Americans. It may also be found in the informal use of others:

> . . . turnip green potliquor with cornbread broke up in it —Flannery O'Connor, letter, fall 1952

It is also the current past participle among those who train horses:

> If you do a good job of driving a colt, you can have him broke well enough so that. . . . —Oscar Crigler, quoted in *Western Horseman,* May 1980

> . . . where he had been broke as a yearling —Mary Fleming, *Western Horseman,* October 1981

> Both colts were broke to drive singly —*Morgan Horse,* April 1983

This usage has been standard in the horse-training business for many years (citations in the Dictionary of American English go back to 1833). A correspondent in 1937 made this point: "A *broken* horse, they say, is infirm,

weak, aged; a *broke* horse, tamed and disciplined." In view of this distinction, it is easy to understand the preference for *broke*.

breakdown The fuss over the use of *breakdown* in the sense of "division into categories" or "something analyzed by categories" was apparently started by one Lord Conesford, who commented on usage issues in the late 1940s. Conesford's remarks were picked up by Sir Ernest Gowers in his 1954 *Complete Plain Words,* from where it found its way into a few American books. But Garner 1998 finds it acceptable.

The gist of the problem seems to have been that *breakdown* is too frequently used in this sense. If it was faddish for awhile, that time has long passed. You need not worry about it.

> . . . ratings services issue the individual breakdowns for 203 cities —Les Brown, *N.Y. Times,* 1 Dec. 1979

> It includes a breakdown of who sang what on every Drifters' single —Jon Landau, *Rolling Stone,* 20 Jan. 1972

> . . . published a country-by-country breakdown of born-again Christians —Marshall Sella, *N.Y. Times Mag.,* 7 Dec. 1997

breech See BREACH, BREECH.

bring 1. *Bring, take.* Although almost all native speakers of English have mastered the directional complexities of *bring* and *take* before they are old enough for school, a surprisingly large number of usage commentators have felt it necessary to explain the distinction to adults. Their basic points are these: *bring* implies movement toward the speaker or writer, and *take* implies movement away. These points are well taken, and they hold for all cases to which they apply. Unfortunately, they do not apply to all cases in the real world. There is a third point to be made that few commentators have noticed: either verb can be used when the point of view is irrelevant. This can be easily shown:

> Copies will be given to pupils to bring home to their parents —*N.Y. Times,* 5 Mar. 1970

The readers of the newspaper won't be misled by either *bring* or *take* in this sentence because they know that the writer is not a school administrator expecting copies to be taken home nor a parent expecting them to be brought home. When the direction of movement does not matter to the reader or hearer, it need not matter to the writer or speaker. Either verb will do. Such cases are common, and have been at least since Shakespeare's time. But usage writers cannot, it seems, forbear imposing their own point of view on something written by someone else and correcting it. The problem is that usage writers have formulated incomplete rules for the use of *bring* and *take*. Native speakers rarely misuse the words.

2. The Dictionary of American Regional English notes a widespread occurrence of the secondary variant past and past participle *brung*. It is used in the fixed phrase "dance with the one what brung me." While the DARE information suggests no educational level for users of *brung,* it is widely perceived as a form used by less educated persons:

> ". . . guess what? I brung along me new boyfriend. . . ." —David French, *Leaving Home,* 1972

It is used for humorous effect too:

> "Well, Mr. Ambassador," drawled South Carolina Democratic Sen. Ernest (Fritz) Hollings . . . , "we brung you a half." —Albert R. Hunt, *Wall Street Jour.,* 8 Aug. 1983

bring up See RAISE, REAR.

Brit *Brit* is a relatively modern word, unattested before 1901, that is a shortening of *Briton, Britisher,* or *British.* It is used to designate a native of England, and its use has been accelerating rapidly since the 1970s. It has several virtues that undoubtedly have helped foster its use: it is short, it can be made plural (as *British* cannot), it is not easily confused in speech (as *Briton* and *Britain* can be), and it is unmarked for gender (as *Englishman, Englishwoman* are not). Its usage is, however, a bit tricky. Reader's Digest 1983 says *Brit* is used by Australians and Americans, but is not liked by the British. Safire 1986 uses it but says it is a term not used by the British although it is not especially derogatory. It appears in the OED Supplement with no usage label.

Burchfield 1996 notes that the term has been used with a certain edge of derogation in some of the English-speaking nations, and our evidence suggests that *Brit* has had at least some coloration of disdain in Australia, New Zealand, Ireland, Scotland, and Canada. Recent American use, which is on the increase, does not, as Safire observes, seem especially derogatory:

> You see, I've become what the Brits call "keen about green" —Steve Silk, *Fine Gardening,* March/April 2000

> But Brits still tune in to the BBC radio soap "The Archers" —Kenneth Klee, *Newsweek,* 13 Sept. 1999

> . . . sells the foods that expatriate Brits most crave —Philip E. Ross, *Forbes,* 19 Apr. 1999

> Cleese narrowly wins our Funny Brit award over Peter Cook —*People,* 11 June 1984

The Brits themselves use the term. Burchfield notes it is used for its brevity and casual informality.

> No doubt young Brits, influenced by television, films, and magazines, will pick up the slang —Howard 1980

> . . . has learned something about dialogue. . . . His Hong Kong Chinese sound like the real thing, as do his Americans—the Cousins, as the Brits call them —Anthony Burgess, *N.Y. Times Book Rev.,* 25 Sept. 1977

> Talking to Dutch people is always a mortifying experience for us Brits because of their alarmingly good command of 'our' language —Michael Rundell, *English Today,* July 1995

The trend of American and British usage seems to suggest that *Brit* is on its way to becoming a relatively neutral, informal term used in place of the longer *Briton, Britisher,* or *Englishman.* See BRITON, BRITISHER.

Briton, Britisher While the recently popular term *Brit* is making some inroads into the use of these two words in informal contexts, both *Briton* and *Britisher* are in reputable use for "a native of England, Great Britain, or the United Kingdom"—and they are sometimes taken to include people from the Commonwealth nations—often in contrast to *American.*

Briton, the OED tells us, was extremely popular in the 18th century; it is more used in the U.K. than in the U.S.:

> . . . we Britons by our situation —James Harris, *Hermes,* 1751

> . . . I had the inalienable right of a freeborn Briton to make a morning call —Lewis Carroll, letter, 11 May 1859

> It was deep in Alabama that a fellow Briton persuaded me to change my ways —Vincent Mulchrone, *Punch,* 2 June 1976

> A MORI poll taken in Britain in February found that, although two-thirds of Britons said they liked Americans, over half did not trust Mr. Reagan's judgment —*The Economist,* 26 Apr. 1986

> . . . difference between the speech of Americans and Britons —Baron 1982

Britisher is more common in American than in British English:

> . . . it is naturally favored by Britishers on holiday —*Town & Country,* January 1983

> . . . no more intriguing . . . than any number of other pleasant Britishers might have been —Ethan Mordden, *N.Y. Times Book Rev.,* 23 Dec. 1984

> "I am a Britisher," May cheerfully tells everyone in the accent of her native Yorkshire —Giovanna Breu, *People,* 2 July 1984

While both of these terms appear to be in current good use, both have been and perhaps still are involved in some controversy:

> . . . are we Britons or Britishers? I don't like either very much —Hardcastle, *Punch,* 20 May 1975

> Nobody likes to be called a *Briton,* though it saves space in journalism. . . . *Britisher* is an Americanism —Longman 1984

> . . . we beg him to avoid in future the odious and meaningless word "Britisher" —Anthony Powell, *Punch,* 8 July 1953

The OED says that *Britisher* is apparently of American origin (as does the Dictionary of American English)—a point disputed by some 19th-century American commentators. Fowler 1926 noted that many dictionaries attached pejorative or other warning labels to the term. Fowler, however, doubted the accuracy of the labels in American dictionaries, and commented that if *Britisher* was used by Americans in reference to the English, the English had no right to object. The controversy, if it ever amounted to much, has died down. Burchfield 1996 notes that some Brits may register surprise or even be slightly affronted by *Britisher; Briton* is usual in British English.

See BRIT.

broke There is some disagreement over the status of the participial adjective *broke* meaning "without funds, penniless." Harper 1985 calls it "informal," Phythian 1979 "slang," Bell & Cohn 1980 and Macmillan 1982 "colloquial," Vizetelly 1906 "misused," and Bryant 1962 "standard formal English." Our evidence shows that Bryant is closest to the mark.

> There he went broke, and became harassed by creditors —Samuel Eliot Morison, *The European Discovery of America,* 1974

> Continuing cycles of boom and bust had their impact as freshly minted millionaires went broke —Anne Rice, *N.Y. Times Book Rev.,* 31 Dec. 1989

> The company went broke, owing its 401(k) more than $192,000 —Jane Bryant Quinn, *Newsweek,* 11 Dec. 1995

> No one ever went broke overestimating America's appetite for the lurid, the sensational, the morbid —Robert Goldberg, *Wall Street Jour.,* 10 June 1991

> We gleefully imagine our rivals going broke —Michael Krantz, *Time,* 17 Apr. 2000

> A lot of folks have gone broke mistaking a Southern accent for a lack of smarts —Kenneth Labich, *Fortune,* 16 Dec. 1991

brunet, brunette It would be nice to be able to say that these words are used in a way ex-

actly parallel to *blond* and *blonde* (which see). Such, however, is not the case. These words are much less frequently used than *blond* and *blonde.* Our evidence shows that *brunette* is used of females; *brunet* is applied to both males and females (but more often to females). *Brunet* is used somewhat more frequently as an adjective than as a noun and *brunette* somewhat more frequently as a noun.

bulk Bryson 1984 notes that "a few authorities"—among them Copperud 1970, Longman 1984, Phythian 1979, Janis 1984, Shaw 1975—object to the use of *the bulk of* when it means "the greater part of, the majority of" and would restrict it to contexts involving volume and mass. He discounts this criticism, noting that Gowers in Fowler 1965 says the usage is more than 200 years old (the OED cites it from Addison in 1711) and that Bernstein 1965 thinks no other word conveys quite the same idea of generalized and unquantified assessment. "So use it as you will," he recommends. Burchfield 1996 does not like *the bulk of* followed by a plural count noun. Our evidence shows that this is a common practice:

> . . . women constitute the great bulk of the world's weavers —Natalie Angier, *N.Y. Times,* 14 Dec. 1999

> . . . at which point they will have recovered the bulk of their so-called stranded costs —Steve Forbes, *Forbes,* 6 July 1998

Garner 1998 notes that when *the bulk of* plus a plural noun governs a verb, the verb is plural:

> In most American states, the bulk of the instructions are no longer drafted individually for each case —Peter M. Tiersma, *Legal Language,* 1999

> The bulk of BPI's customers . . . were aerospace and defense contractors —Emily Esterson, *The Inc. 500,* 1998

> . . . the bulk of the tracks are vintage AM-radio snarl —David Fricke, *Rolling Stone,* 16 June 1994

> The overwhelming bulk of new books with serious merit fall into a category euphemistically dubbed "mid-list" —Leonard Garment, *Forbes,* 20 Oct. 1997

> . . . the bulk of the Qumran nonbiblical texts date from the last two pre-Christian centuries —Joseph A. Fitzmyer, *N.Y. Times Book Rev.,* 21 Sept. 1997

All of these uses are perfectly standard.

bunch Whatever it is that seems to be wrong with *bunch* appears to be mostly an American problem, and one commented upon chiefly by writers of college handbooks. It seems to have begun in response to a sharp increase in the use of *bunch* early in the 20th century, both as a generalized collective and as a word for a group of people.

Objections were first to its application to a group of people, then switched to its use as a generalized collective. Along the way an objection to its use before a mass noun sprang up. This latter was a particularly bad idea, as the use goes back to Dr. Johnson:

> I am glad the Ministry is removed. Such a bunch of imbecility never disgraced a country —in Boswell's *Life,* 1791 (OED)

Our evidence shows that nearly a century of objection has had no ostensible effect on actual usage—except perhaps on papers written for college courses. About the only obvious characteristic of *bunch* in the following examples is that it does not turn up in especially formal surroundings.

> . . . a swimming pool ballet with a bunch of pretty girls —Stanley Kauffmann, *New Republic,* 10 & 17 July 2000

> These dogfaces who freed the world were a bunch of decent guys —Steven Spielberg, *Newsweek Extra,* Summer 1998

> The developers are so paranoid nowadays, they just make their efforts look as much like a bunch of early Victorian buildings as possible —Hugo Williams, *Times Literary Supp.,* 14 July 2000

> . . . Ketterle's group merged a bunch of atoms into a single mega-atom —*Discover,* July 1998

> But now they're irritating the wrong bunch of frequent flyers: members of Congress —Anne Wilde Mathews, *Wall Street Jour.,* 10 Mar. 1999

> Here's somebody, surely, who'd never try to tell you a bunch of hooey —David Gates, *N.Y. Times Book Rev.,* 21 Nov. 1999

bunk into Harper 1975, 1985 and Safire 1982 note that *bunk into* is used for *bump into* in New York City. The Dictionary of American Regional English confirms their observation, labeling it "N[ew] Y[ork] C[ity], esp[ecial-ly] Brooklyn."

burgeon, burgeoning It appears that no one was concerned about the figurative uses of *burgeon* until the 1960s, when Theodore Bernstein (in *Winners & Sinners* at least as early as 1964), Flesch 1964, and Follett 1966 discovered it. The recommendation of Flesch is short and to the point: "*burgeon* is a fancy word that can easily be replaced." And in fact it is a fancy word—you have to learn it, and if you learn it from an older dictionary, as Bernstein and Follett did, you learn that it means

"to send forth buds or shoots"—Webster's Second defines it simply as "to bud, sprout."

There is a perfectly sound reason for this brief 1934 dictionary treatment. At the time the book was edited, there was but little evidence of figurative use. The OED lists some, from the 14th century to the 19th, but the editors of Webster's Second had no recent evidence and omitted a definition to cover figurative use (notes in the file show that the need for a figurative sense occurred to at least one editor).

As a result, Bernstein and Follett, knowing from the Second that *burgeon* meant "to bud, sprout," were shocked to discover that it was being used in a much broader way in the public prints. And a usage problem was born.

The evidence in our files suggests that the use of *burgeon* and especially the participial adjective *burgeoning* in a broader sense connoting rapid and flourishing growth began to increase in frequency in the late 1930s. Here it is, for instance, used in a book review:

> With 1933 the focus takes in the Reichstag fire and burgeoning Hitlerism —*N.Y. Times,* 29 Jan. 1937

Widespread popular use began around the end of World War II.

> Quebec's burgeoning industries —*Time,* 16 Sept. 1946

> . . . who learns that the little stitch in the side is cancer and that he is carrying around inside himself that mysterious, apocalyptic, burgeoning thing which is part of himself but is, at the same time, not part of himself but the enemy —Robert Penn Warren, *All the King's Men,* 1946

> . . . one could go on at length listing the burgeoning varieties of periodicals —Frederick Lewis Allen. *Atlantic,* November 1947

By the 1950s the extended senses were firmly established:

> . . . what may well be the most difficult period of the burgeoning Western alliance —Richard H. Rovere, *New Yorker,* 10 Nov. 1951

> Suburban towns with burgeoning populations need more police and fire protection —*N.Y. Times,* 28 Feb. 1954

> . . . not one of those feminizing Faulknerians, who via Katherine Anne Porter and Eudora Welty have burgeoned into the full-blown epicene school —Leslie A. Fiedler, *New Republic,* 26 Sept. 1955

> . . . the high walls of the Kremlin were burgeoning with new mysteries —Harrison E. Salisbury, *N.Y. Times Mag.,* 21 Aug. 1955

The evidence makes the point. The extended uses of *burgeon* had been appearing in the august pages of the *New York Times* for more than a quarter century before Theodore Bernstein looked up a dated entry in Webster's Second and made an issue out of it. It still appears:

And women were at the forefront of the burgeoning temperance movement —Amy Waldman, *N.Y. Times*, 28 June 1998

The budding connotation has not been lost, but it is now a less frequent use:

I weighed this. It sounded promising. Hope began to burgeon —P. G. Wodehouse, *Joy in the Morning*, 1946

. . . zizyphus, acacia and mesquite were burgeoning out of the dunes —Michael Asher, *Geographical Mag.*, August 1990

Unless you are a lover of causes that were lost before they were begun, do not trouble yourself to limit *burgeon* to "to bud, sprout." There is no essential difference between current usage and that of the 1940s and 1950s with this word.

burglarize, burgle Apparently somebody about 1870 felt that a verb was needed to express the meaning "to commit burglary." We don't know why—*rob* had always served the purpose—but *burgle* (1870) and *burglarize* (1871) were coined at about the same time to supply the felt need. Both *burgle* and *burglarize* seem to be Americanisms, but they must either have crossed the Atlantic quickly or have been independently coined in England at about the same time.

Both *burgle* and *burglarize* were attacked by 19th-century commentators. American commentators in the first half of the 20th century disparaged *burgle* because it is a backformation. Later commentators, such as Bernstein 1971 and Kilpatrick 1984, find it funny. British usage differs. Fowler 1926 looked at both words and said "it is to be hoped that *burgle* may outgrow its present facetiousness & become generally current." Fowler's wish has come true in British English:

There was a story that he had once been caught burgling a house —H. G. Wells, *Joan and Peter*, 1918

In 1617 his house was burgled by Henry Baldwin and others —E. K. Chambers, *The Elizabethan Stage*, 1923

. . . in spite of having his cabin burgled by an enterprising gentleman —*Times Literary Supp.*, 19 Feb. 1971

Cars are broken into, handbags snatched, and premises burgled with depressing regularity —Robert Fox, *The Inner Sea*, 1993

Both *burgle* and *burglarize* are in current standard American use:

. . . he set up a secret White House posse to burgle offices —Arthur M. Schlesinger, Jr., *The Cycles of American History*, 1986

. . . allegedly killed a police officer while trying to burgle his father's apartment —Patricia J. Williams, *The Nation*, 16 June 1997

. . . everyone knows someone whose home has been burgled —Vic Sussman, *U.S. News & World Report*, 30 Mar. 1992

. . . a gang of unscrupulous ruffians who would stop at nothing to burglarize the Dutch warehouse —Simon Schama, *The Embarrassment of Riches*, 1988

. . . had planned to burglarize Matthew's house, but they got distracted —Melanie Thernstrom, *Vanity Fair*, March 1999

So why do people buy alarms after they've been burglarized? —Beth Wilson, *PC Computing*, January 1999

Garner 1998 says *burglarize* appears about 30 times as often as *burgle*. Our evidence suggests that use is much more evenly divided.

burglary, robbery The distinction between these words is spelled out in Kilpatrick 1984, Harper 1975, 1985, and Copperud 1970, 1980, and no doubt in countless law texts. If you really feel uncertainty on the point, check any conscientious dictionary, where you will find everything made clear. *Robbery* (13th century) is older and more general than *burglary* (16th century).

burgle See BURGLARIZE, BURGLE.

burn *Burn* has variants in both past and past participle—*burned* and *burnt*. Longman 1984 tells us that *burned* is commoner than *burnt* for intransitive uses and *burnt* commoner than *burned* for transitive uses, but Burchfield 1996 finds the evidence unconvincing.

In American English *burned* is the more common:

. . . a star, called a white dwarf, which has burned out and contracted —Ann Finkbeiner, *Science*, 24 Nov. 1995

The juke, a mecca for blues hounds from all over, burned down last April —Eric Pooley, *Time*, 10 June 2000

Burnt is also used in American English:

It burnt his tongue —Mary Karr, *The Liar's Club*, 1995

. . . the house, which burnt down last November —Susan Salter Reynolds, *Publishers Weekly*, 10 Nov. 1997

Burnt is the usual form in British English:

> . . . late in life when his carnal flame had burnt down —Roy Jenkins, *Gladstone*, 1995

> The school is closed now. The inn burnt down —Jan Morris, *Locations*, 1992

In American English both *burnt* and *burned* are used as adjectives:

> . . . blue sky showed through the charred skeleton of the burnt church —John Updike, *Couples*, 1968

> . . . a large, sun-scorched, burned section —Nathaniel Nitkin, *New-England Galaxy*, Fall 1967

> . . . had to make do with a blend of burnt barley and chicory —Josef Joffe, *Time*, 6 Dec. 1999

> . . . coquina rock, a concrete made with burned shells —Sue Miller, *Historic Traveler*, March 1999

burst The usual past and past participle is *burst*:

> Tuesday about 400 persons burst into a Santa Barbara city council meeting —*Berkeley Barb*, 17 Apr. 1969

> . . . and then to her shame she burst into tears —Daphne du Maurier, *Ladies' Home Jour.*, September 1971

The past and past participle *bursted* is not wrong, as some handbooks suggest, but it is old-fashioned in writing and dialectal in speech.

> . . . the night of a semi-serious earthquake (like in 1935) a few days after the opening of the story. It has been a very full day even for Stahr—the bursted water mains —F. Scott Fitzgerald, letter, 29 Sept. 1939

We have no recent evidence for *bursted* in print; the Dictionary of American Regional English records recent evidence in speech.

See also BUST.

bus The controversy over the propriety of the verb *bus* has long since died away. Note that both *-s-* and *-ss-* are in use in spelling the inflected forms:

> . . . supporters bused up from New York City —Max Boot, *Wall Street Jour.*, 17 Feb. 1998

> The school bussed the entire student body to a recent game —Phil Taylor, *Sports Illustrated*, 18 Feb. 1991

> In the 1970s, school busing became the leading civil rights issue —Michael L. Levine, *African Americans and Civil Rights*, 1996

> . . . ever since he was a prep legend, bussing it out of inner Detroit to suburban, private Country Day —*ESPN*, 29 Nov. 1999

Although some people prefer the double *-s* spellings because they better indicate the pronunciation, our most recent evidence shows that the single *-s* spellings are used considerably more often.

bust, *verb* The verb *bust* originated in an \r\-less pronunciation of *burst* that seems to have been widespread in many dialect areas in the 19th century and earlier. It became a pronunciation spelling and early in the 19th century began to take on a life of its own, gradually being used in senses separate from *burst*. Its separateness was emphasized by the fact that its past and past participle is regularly *busted* (less often *bust*) while that of *burst* is *burst* (rarely *bursted*). Handbooks from at least the 1920s have disapproved *bust*, mostly calling it wrong for *burst* or *break*, but they completely overlooked the independent senses *bust* was developing. By the time of World War II it was becoming established in general prose—newspapers and magazine articles, fiction and nonfiction. *Bust* has not reached the higher levels of formality, nor has it been seen in the prose of the bureaucrat. Our most recent handbooks have begun to drop their strictures on the word. Here is a sampling of some of the ways it is used:

> In winter they blame him when hungry elk and deer are busting their fences and devouring their haystacks —Robert C. Wurmstedt, *Time*, 5 Nov. 1984

> . . . police officers searching for a gasoline bomb factory busted their way with sledgehammers into 11 houses —*N.Y. Times*, 19 July 1981

> Courts enjoined them, police busted their heads —E. L. Doctorow, *Ragtime*, 1975

> James boxes—or did, until his jaw was busted —*New Yorker*, 17 Oct. 1983

> Naturally, all hell busted loose again. The GSA quickly tore down the huts —Jim Fain, *Atlanta Jour.-Constitution*, 23 Sept. 1984

> . . . Grant, a convinced Union partisan, joined the 21st Illinois Regiment to replace a colonel busted for overdrinking —Alden Whitman, *Atlanta Jour.-Constitution*, 16 Sept. 1984

> With a blast of electric guitars, a new generation busted loose and leapt onstage —Kenneth Auchincloss, *Newsweek*, 20 Dec. 1999

You may wonder if the appearance of *bust* in publications like these is recent. The answer is no. The same usages can be found from a quarter century or so earlier:

> We approach the scullery window. He busts in. I raise the alarm —P. G. Wodehouse, *Joy in the Morning*, 1946

> . . . unable to bust the tradition —*Newsweek*, 5 July 1948

> . . . were busting out all over with their own ideas —*Investor's Reader*, 9 Feb. 1955

> . . . but suddenly the Nazis bust loose and the captain's cowardice is revealed —John McCarten, *New Yorker*, 29 Sept. 1956

In addition, there are other uses in which *bust* is the verb of choice:

> . . . but most union-busting activities—such as the permanent replacement of striking workers—are within the law —Richard J. Barnet, *The Nation*, 19 Dec. 1994

> You have to draw a line and say: "If you want to be a cop . . . you can't be a bad guy, busting heads" —Don Terry, *N.Y. Times*, 10 Sept. 1991

> The Northern Securities trust was busted, and Morgan could do nothing but writhe —*Business Week*, 20 Apr. 1981

> And a real danger is that a partisan bidding war could cause that tax cut to grow into a budget-busting fiasco —Jackie Calmes, *Wall Street Jour.*, 30 Jan. 1992

> Over the last thirty years or so, it has become almost a Parliamentary rule that disgrace visits the two main parties in different ways. Tories are busted for sex, and Labourites are busted for graft —Julian Barnes, *New Yorker*, 5 Mar. 1990

> . . . in 1997 he was busted in Austin for soliciting a prostitute —Molly Ivins et al., *Time*, 13 Mar. 2000

See also BURST.

bust, busted, *adjective* Although handbooks warned against *bust* and *busted* for "broke" into the 1980s, we find the subject beginning to vanish from the most recent handbooks. Like the verb *bust,* the adjective is established in general prose. The two forms are used a bit differently. *Bust* is usually a predicate adjective and is most often found with the verb *go:*

> During the '90s, Donald Trump was flush, then went bust, then returned to form —Steve Hirdt, *ESPN*, 14 June 1999

> As the second largest owner of real estate in Britain . . . the church is not about to go bust —Madelaine Drohan, *Globe and Mail* (Toronto), 27 June 1995

Busted is used as both an attributive and a predicate adjective:

> Touring the campground is a walk on the dire side of the U.S. economy: busted farmers from Nebraska, laid-off factory workers from Wisconsin —Tony Horwitz, *Wall Street Jour.*, 16 June 1994

> Zell wasn't busted, but he was strapped for cash —Bruce Upbin, *Forbes*, 2 June 1997

but 1. Part of the folklore of usage is the belief that there is something wrong in beginning a sentence with *but*:

> Many of us were taught that no sentence should begin with "but." If that's what you learned, unlearn it—there is no stronger word at the start. It announces total contrast with what has gone before, and the reader is primed for the change —Zinsser 1976

Everybody who mentions this question agrees with Zinsser. The only generally expressed warning is not to follow the *but* with a comma, as in this example:

> But, hasty, ill-considered and emotional prohibitions can seriously threaten individual industries —*Annual Report, Owens-Illinois*, 1970

The argument is that the force of the *but* is weakened by the unneeded comma. Such commas are not common in the materials in our files. This example is more typical:

> . . . performing-arts organizations in this country are in desperate straits. But that is not for lack of public support —Harold C. Schonberg, *Harper's*, February 1971

2. One of the more vexatious questions that 19th-century commentators (and some of their 20th-century followers) wrangled over was the question of the case of the pronoun after *but* in passages like this:

> The boy stood on the burning deck,
> Whence all but he had fled; . . .

These lines are from a poem named "Casabianca" (1829) by the English poet Felicia D. Hemans (1794–1835). It appears that Mrs. Hemans originally wrote "but him," but someone seems to have persuaded her to change it—or perhaps some editor changed it without asking. *Bartlett's Familiar Quotations* now carries the version with *he,* and that is the form of the line most people remember.

The question boils down to whether *but* is a conjunction or a preposition. Those plumping for the conjunction have been the noisiest. Their standard approach is to invoke the "understood clause" that you have to imagine in sentences like Mrs. Hemans' and this:

No man but I has right to do her justice —Aphra Behn, *The Dutch Lover,* 1673

The nominative after *but* is supposed to be the subject of the nonexistent clause. If you don't "understand" the clause, you would use an objective pronoun, like Mrs. Hemans orginally did. The nominative pronoun is still used in such constructions:

. . . none but he can have seen them all —*Times Literary Supp.,* 16 June 1966

. . . it carried him farther than anyone but he dared dream —R. W. Apple, Jr., *N.Y. Times Mag.,* 3 Dec. 1978

But can also be interpreted as a conjunction followed by the objective case when the pronoun stands in a position normally calling for the objective:

Abuse everybody but me —Jane Austen, letter, 7 Jan. 1807

. . . I didn't even know of anyone else but him —Bill Holt, quoted in *Bluegrass Unlimited,* May 1982

Of course, one can equally well argue that *but* in each of these examples is a preposition. In the next two examples, *but* is clearly a preposition. Note that the style is more nearly conversational than it was in the examples with the nominative pronouns. The first is fictional speech.

. . . it was his misfortune to save her from a passel of raiding enemy in a situation that everybody but her is trying to forget —"My Grandmother Millard," in *The Collected Stories of William Faulkner,* 1950

Everybody but me among us old codgers proudly insists that he and his wife were married just like the kids of today —James Thurber, letter, 22 Dec. 1952

Our conclusion is that the absolutists who insist that *but* is only a conjunction or only a preposition are wrong. *But* has functioned in both capacities since Old English and still does. You are correct in choosing to use it either way. Bear in mind, however, that conjunctive *but* followed by a nominative pronoun seems rather more literary than the preposition.

3. *Except for* functions as a compound preposition. Although it is found less often, *but* works with *for* in exactly the same way:

But for the name of its author . . . it would not have had a hope of publication —*Times Literary Supp.,* 22 Oct. 1971

He liked to think of himself as Fitzgerald's mentor but for whom Scott's talents might never have fully matured —Norman Cousins, *Saturday Rev.,* April 1981

4. Otto Jespersen, in *Negation in English and Other Languages* (1917), wrote: "By a curious transition *but* has come to mean the same thing as 'only'; at first it required a preceding negative: *I will not say but one word,* i.e., 'not except (save) one word'. . . ." He points out that eventually the negative came to be dropped, creating one of those curious expressions we have in English in which a negative construction and a positive one mean the same thing (see also COULD CARE LESS, COULDN'T CARE LESS). The positive form came to be considered normal:

. . . with an urgency which differed from his but in being more gentle —Jane Austen, *Mansfield Park,* 1814

. . . which in all probability, had he but picked it up and carried it openly away, nobody would have remarked or cared —"Centaur in Brass," in *The Collected Stories of William Faulkner,* 1950

I saw Jonathan but one more time —Joseph Heller, *God Knows,* 1984

It is a turn-of-the-century brick building, and had but two large rooms —Robert Morrison, *Language Arts,* March 1989

The original form with the negative, however, did not disappear. It kept right on being used, chiefly in speech (see NOT . . . BUT). This has led several commentators (among them Bernstein 1977, Prentice Hall 1978, Little, Brown 1980, Johnson 1982) to label it a double negative—in ignorance of the origin of the use. Here are a few samples of the older construction:

At the Holler House, they haven't had but two 300 games in 80 years —Frank Deford, *Sports Illustrated,* 25 Jan. 1988

I never heard of but one skipper who did not arrive at the quarter deck by way of the hawsepipe —Captain Harry Allen Chippendale, *Sails and Whales,* 1951

. . . the other tenant who, bless his heart, isn't but two months behind in his rent —Flannery O'Connor, letter, 25 Apr. 1959

I'd be right there with him—I didn't lack but three lengths of the hoe —Gloria Naylor, *People,* 11 Mar. 1985

5. *But that, but what.* These phrases have troubled commentators since Lindley Murray in the late 18th century. Their use is governed by idiom, so it is no surprise that grammarians and usage commentators have found them worrisome. French idioms generally do not trouble the teacher of French, but English idioms seldom fail to perplex English teachers and commentators on English usage—or so it seems at times. The advice tendered is usually muddled and occasionally self-contradictory.

But that. It should be noted that when *but that* introduces a clause, it is usually found in negative constructions, but not always:

> I waited upon him accordingly, and should have taken Collins with me, but that he was not sober —Benjamin Franklin, *Autobiography,* 1771

> . . . there is little question but that Pound said a number of things which were at best extremely stupid —Archibald MacLeish, letter, 6 Dec. 1945

One of the problems that usage commentators find with *but that* comes from the fact that in some contexts *but* alone could be used:

> I don't see but that sheet has become as frankly partisan as any party paper —Oliver Wendell Holmes d. 1935, letter, 11 Oct. 1928

> . . . the words of E. B. White, who once wrote: "I'm sure there isn't a humorist alive but can recall the day when. . . ." —Kathleen Fury, *TV Guide,* 30 Dec. 1984

And sometimes *that* alone could be used:

> There's no question but that in the movie's terms what she has learned has made her more desirable —Pauline Kael, *New Yorker,* 27 June 1988

> . . . there is no doubt that Jewison's use of his camera and his fluid editing make for superior entertainment —Hollis Alpert, *Saturday Rev.,* 13 Nov. 1971

As a result, some commentators find *but that* wordy. The two-word idiom, however, has impressive literary credentials extending (in Jespersen's examples) back to Caxton in the 15th century. Here are a handful of examples, old and modern:

> I cannot be persuaded but that marriage is one of the means of happiness —Samuel Johnson, *Rambler,* 1752 (in Jespersen 1917)

> . . . I never see such a performance but that I later go out of the theatre and . . . become just such another —Sherwood Anderson (1923), cited in *New Yorker,* 12 Nov. 1984

> There can be no question but that the play gives Mr. Muni a rare opportunity —Wolcott Gibbs, *New Yorker,* 26 Feb. 1949

> Nothing is so absurd but that some philosopher has said it, Cicero told them —David Brudnoy, *National Rev.,* 19 Nov. 1971

The common use of *but that* with *doubt* has been questioned, but without much reason.

> I do not doubt but that I shall set many a reader's teeth on edge —John Ruskin, *Time*

and Tide by Weare and Tyne, 1867 (in Jespersen 1917)

> There can be no doubt but that economic disorders are fundamental —*Times Literary Supp.,* 5 Oct. 1940

> There is no doubt but that Congress was impressed —*New Republic,* 7 Feb. 1944

> There is no doubt but that Communists will associate themselves with it —Stanley K. Sheinbaum, in *Johns Hopkins Mag.,* December 1965

> . . . little doubt but that "Erewhon" has provided the guidelines for the "opportunity society" of conformity and evasion —William Gaddis, *N.Y. Times Book Rev.,* 5 Mar. 1995

These usages are all standard, as even some handbooks recognize.

But what. This is a more recent combination; it is attested as early as the 17th century, but most of the evidence for it comes from the 19th and 20th. Evidence in Jespersen and later dictionaries shows it to have been in good literary use:

> . . . scarce a farmer's daughter within ten miles round but what had found him successful —Oliver Goldsmith, *The Vicar of Wakefield,* 1766 (in Jespersen 1917)

> . . . not that I think Mr. M. would ever marry any body but what had had some education —Jane Austen, *Emma,* 1815 (in Jespersen 1917)

> I don't know but what it would —Charles Dickens, *Nicholas Nickleby,* 1838 (in Jespersen 1917)

> Her needle is not so absolutely perfect . . . but what my superintendence is advisable —Sir Walter Scott (Webster 1909)

> I don't see but what he'll have to be impeached —Henry Adams, letter, 29 Dec. 1860

> I did not know but what he was altogether 'conscientious' in that matter —Abraham Lincoln, debate with Douglas, 27 Aug. 1858

> He said they didn't know but what their writing was fine —Mark Twain, "Important Correspondence," 6 May 1865

And use continues, as these 20th-century examples testify:

> I don't doubt but what she could do it —Flannery O'Connor, letter, 1952

> There were, to be sure, a few motorcars, but not so many but what I could pretend not to see them —James Norman Hall, *Atlantic,* December 1952

> Not but what that could have been a blessing in disguise —W. J. Burley, *Wycliffe and the Schoolgirls,* 1976

Some moderates in his own party are not sure but what he has been fatally wounded already —Hedley Donovan, *Fortune*, 7 Mar. 1983

. . . and I'm not sure but what she could also accept the expressive view —Richard Fulkerson, *College Composition and Communication*, December 1990

But what was declared standard by Whitford & Foster, *American Standards of Writing* (1931) and Bryant 1962; Perrin & Ebbitt 1972 offers the same view but the authors find it less common than *but that* in print. Denigration of the phrase began with Murray 1795 and is still repeated by some modern commentators. Our more recent evidence suggests that *but what* is a standard idiom, but one more likely to be found in the less formal kinds of writing than in elevated prose.

but which, but who See AND WHICH, AND WHO.

by means of This phrase is commonly attacked as verbose or redundant for *by* or *with*. This assertion is often accompanied by a simple example in which the simple preposition is suggested as a substitute.

But of course *by means of* did not come into use to vex editors pressed for space. *By means of* is, in fact, seldom used in very simple sentences and is often used precisely to avoid a simpler preposition when the simpler one might be ambiguous—*by,* for instance, has ten or a dozen meanings shown in Merriam-Webster's Collegiate Dictionary, Tenth Edition. Consider these examples:

. . . the exploration of Palestine's rich past by means of material remains left behind by the Jews of Biblical times —*Current Biography,* February 1966

. . . on the . . . mosaic two scenes are telescoped into one by means of an awkwardly posed single figure doing double duty —*Times Literary Supp.,* 18 Dec. 1969

Jeff Bridges got zapped into it in Tron. Keanu Reeves reached it by means of a red pill in The Matrix —Chris Taylor, *Time,* 19 June 2000

It may be generally true that shorter is better, but longer can be clearer, especially if the shorter preposition is capable of several interpretations and the longer of only one.

by the same token See TOKEN.

C

cache See HYPERFOREIGNISMS.

caesarean See CESAREAN, CAESAREAN.

calculate There is more fuss about this word than is warranted in recent handbooks, which hasten to point out that when *calculate* is used to mean "to judge to be true or probable, suppose, think" and sometimes "to intend," it is dialectal, colloquial, or informal. Burchfield 1996 notes it has never been standard in American English. The Dictionary of American Regional English says it is somewhat old-fashioned. A few examples:

It is probable that the hospital poison has affected my system, and I find it worse than I calculated —Walt Whitman, letter, 14 June 1864

He ketched a frog one day, and took him home, and said he cal'lated to educate him —Mark Twain, "The Notorious Jumping Frog of Calaveras County," 1865

calculated On etymological grounds Richard Grant White 1870 belabored the use of *calculated* in the sense of "apt, likely" as an error. He brought forth a quotation from Oliver Goldsmith as an example of the error. His objection, however, was entirely factitious; the participial adjective had been used in that sense for a century and a half before he decided it must be wrong. Still, White had a number of followers, and the word is still considered a "debasement" as recently as Garner 1998. The sense is standard:

. . . the way in which this Debate came about was calculated to give one the feeling of a challenge —Sir Winston Churchill, *The Unrelenting Struggle,* 1942

What they found was not calculated to encourage an optimistic report —*Time,* 7 June 1954

Note that *calculated* can also be used in a sense "intended," which must be related to the dialectal sense of *calculate* meaning "intend." The participial adjective in this sense is not dialectal:

. . . forms of evasion calculated precisely to prevent me from getting information —Walker Gibson, in *The Hues of Modern English,* 1969

callous, callus The main point on which usage writers agree about these words is that *callus* is a noun and *callous* is an adjective.

As a noun, *callus* is the predominant spelling, and physical meanings are the predominant ones:

> . . . connecting cambium in the callus —H. J. Fuller & O. Tippo, *College Botany,* 1950

> . . . a combination of asteatosis (inherited dryness) and hyperkeratosis (callus formation) —Donald E. Baxter, M.D., *Runner's World,* January 1995

The spelling *callous* is an infrequent one (at least in edited prose) for the physical sense of the noun:

> . . . a callous formed there large as a bowl —Pearl Buck, *The Good Earth,* 1931

Extended uses of the noun occur with either spelling but are quite rare.

> . . . these moral callouses which she simply could not understand —Gilbert Knox, *The Land of Afternoon,* 1924

> . . . a protective callus of cynicism —Martin Levin, *N.Y. Times Book Rev.,* 17 Aug. 1975

Now for the adjective: *callous* is the spelling used, almost exclusively with emotional meaning.

> . . . a callous disregard for human rights —William O. Douglas, *Being an American,* 1948

> . . . shamed a callous Time Warner into dropping out of the gangsta-rap business —*Forbes,* 29 July 1996

Callus is not used as an adjective, but both *calloused* and *callused* are. *Calloused* usually has emotional connotations, and *callused* always has physical ones.

> . . . had become so stupid and calloused about the birds —Ernest Hemingway, "Miss Mary's Lion," 1956

> His hands were rough, callused, competent —Russell Baker, *Growing Up,* 1982

In summary, emotional meanings are almost entirely confined to *callous,* regardless of part of speech. Physical meanings are usually spelled *callus,* sometimes spelled *callous.*

calvary, cavalry The word *cavalry* refers to a component of the army traditionally mounted on horseback, while *Calvary* is the hill near Jerusalem where Jesus was crucified and *calvary* (lowercase) refers either to an open-air representation of the Crucifixion or to an experience of intense mental suffering. Don't confuse the spellings of these two words, usually *calvary* for *cavalry,* as is occasionally done.

can, may *Can* and *may* are most frequently interchangeable in senses denoting possibility. Here *can* denotes not power nor permission but possibility:

> Can we, with manners, ask what was the difference —Shakespeare, *Cymbeline,* 1610

It's not much of a stretch of meaning from the use in *Cymbeline* to

> "Can I come in, Frank?" —Anthony Trollope, *Dr. Thorne,* 1858

If our files are reasonably accurate reflections of present-day use, the "possibility" sense of *can* is the one most frequently used in edited prose:

> Naturally, we are always asking: Can I marry the girl I love? Can I sell my house? —W H. Auden, *Columbia Forum,* Winter 1970

> . . . an infinite number of lines . . . can be drawn through a point —Robert W. Marks, *The New Mathematics Dictionary and Handbook* 1964

The transition from "possibility" to "permission" is subtler than the handbooks think. Noah Webster's 1828 dictionary contained this as part of his definition 5:

> . . . to be free from any restraint of moral, civil or political obligation, or from any positive prohibition.

This sense involves nothing more than permission given by not prohibiting. It constitutes the most common "permission" sense we find written:

> . . . took off from her [the bride's] head the myrtle wreath, which only maidens can wear —Henry Adams, letter, 17 May 1859

> The new prayers are not compulsory, and vicars can use the old forms if they like —*N.Y. Times,* 11 Nov. 1979

> You cannot enter, but you can walk round part of the thick white walls —Nadine Gordimer, *Atlantic,* November 1971

The *cannot* in the last example distinctly implies a denial of permission. Lamberts 1972 and Garner 1998 point out that for negative uses in which permission is denied, *cannot* and *can't* have largely replaced *may not* and *mayn't.*

The use of *can* in a direct question to request permission is basically an oral use. These examples come from recorded speech or fictional speech:

> Can I proceed without interruption? —Senator Stuart Symington, at the 1953 Army–McCarthy hearings (Pyles 1979)

"Can I speak to Detective-Sergeant Sparrow?" I asked —Graham Greene, *Travels with My Aunt,* 1969

If this is almost exclusively an oral use, why should we find it so often mentioned in books on writing? The reason we find it in handbooks meant for college and graduate-school students, such as Cook 1985, seems to be that it has simply been carried forward from books aimed at schoolchildren. The *can/may* distinction is a traditional part of the American school curriculum. The fact that the distinction is largely ignored by people once out of school is also a tradition.

Conclusion: The uses of *can* which request permission are seldom found in edited prose. In general, this use of *can* belongs to speech, reported or fictional. In negative statements, *cannot* and *can't* are much more frequently used than *may not* and *mayn't*; use in negative contexts is seldom noticed or criticized. *May* is still used, of course:

And I said, 'Mr. President, I want to talk to you. If I may, I'll come right up there and see you.' —Harry S. Truman, quoted in Merle Miller, *Plain Speaking,* 1973

cancel out A number of commentators, such as Harper 1985, Freeman 1983, and Shaw 1987, object to *cancel out* as redundant, which is their way of telling you that some people use *out* idiomatically with *cancel* and others do not. Here are some completely acceptable examples of the senses in which *cancel out* is used.

As an intransitive, *cancel out* is used chiefly in the sense "to neutralize each other's effect":

. . . the various pressure groups to a large degree canceled out —James B. Conant, *Atlantic,* May 1946

It also occurs in technical contexts, such as mathematics:

The units "cancel out," and the ratio remains 4:5 —William L. Schaaf, *Mathematics For Everyday Use,* 1942

And it is used in the intransitive equivalent of "to call off an event":

. . . a little rain wouldn't make people cancel out —Jeff Brown, *Holiday,* June 1966

The most frequent use, however, is the transitive sense that means "to match in force or effect, offset":

. . . just as his irritability cancelled out his natural kindness —Osbert Sitwell, *Horizon,* July 1947

. . . every definite piece of advice he gives is cancelled out by another, equally definite,

contrary piece of advice —*Times Literary Supp.,* 29 Apr. 1955

candelabra Originally the plural of *candelabrum, candelabra* has been used as a singular with the plural *candelabras* since at least 1815:

Four silver candelabras, holding great waxen torches —Sir Walter Scott, *Ivanhoe,* 1819 (OED)

Surrounded by gauzy nymphs and staglike men with candelabras, Zorina appeared barefoot —Arlene Croce, *New Yorker,* 12 July 1982

Even though Fowler 1926 and Garner 1998 dislike the usage, it is so well established (unlike, for instance, the singular use of *criteria*) that it goes almost entirely unnoticed.

Candelabra is also still used as a plural of *candelabrum*:

There were white peacocks (stuffed) on the lawn, a tent hung with chandeliers and decorated with candelabra —Jody Jacobs, *Los Angeles Times,* 23 Sept. 1984

For other foreign plurals, see LATIN PLURALS.

cannot *Cannot, can not.* Both spellings are acceptable, but *cannot* is more frequent in current use. Chambers 1985 insists that *cannot* must be used in British English unless the *not* is to receive particular emphasis. A couple of American sources (Oxford American Dictionary 1980, Trimble 1975) mention that the two-word form can be used to indicate special emphasis, although Irmscher 1976 warns that publishing-house style may prevail over your emphasis. Emphasis on *not* appears to be intended in this passage:

You said a while ago, says your man, that you were a better man than any man here. Can you jump?

I can not, says the sergeant, but I'm no worse than the next man —Flann O'Brien, *At Swim-Two-Birds,* 1939

In general, however, the one-word form is used:

Dr Bourne cannot yet call her out of danger —Jane Austen, letter, 10 Jan. 1809

. . . a simple fact that . . . the C.C.C.C.'er cannot admit —Simon 1980

cannot but, cannot help, cannot help but A lot has been written about these phrases. To put as charitable a light on the matter as possible, most of what you may read is out of date. We have hundreds of citations for these phrases, and we can tell you two things for certain: these phrases all mean the same thing—"to be unable to do otherwise than"—and they are all standard. Our evidence is much heavier for *cannot but* and *cannot help but* than it is for *cannot help*.

Cannot help is grammatically the odd one. It is followed by a present participle, whereas the others are followed by the bare infinitive. It has been in use quite a long time:

> . . . yet I cannot help thinking, that . . . our Conversation hath very much degenerated —Jonathan Swift, "A Proposal for Correcting, Improving and Ascertaining the English Tongue," 1712

> In my grimmest imaginings I could not help thinking that he might have raped my daughter instead —William Styron, *This Quiet Dust and Other Writings*, 1982

Cannot but is an old established idiom.

> I cannot but applaud your zeal —Benjamin Franklin, letter, 26 Dec. 1789

> The outsider cannot but be struck by the frequent reluctance of the learned world —Edmund Wilson, *New Yorker,* 14 May 1955

> One cannot but wonder if the image . . . flashed before the mind of Davis —Robert Penn Warren, *Jefferson Davis Gets His Citizenship Back,* 1980

Cannot help but, which may have been formed as a syntactic blend of *cannot but* and *cannot help,* is the most recent of the phrases. It appears to have arisen just before the turn of the 20th century. We began to acquire citations in the 1920s, and a great many from 1940 on. Here is a sample:

> . . . I could not help but reflect that if I hadn't been so noble . . . —Robert Penn Warren, *All the King's Men,* 1946

> . . . could not help but be a little impressed by what Dottie disclosed —Mary McCarthy, *The Group,* 1963

> One cannot help but rejoice for those who escaped —Margaret Drabble, *N.Y. Times Book Rev.,* 14 Nov. 1982

> The single currency cannot help but pose a financial and economic challenge to Washington —William Pfaff, *Commonweal,* 15 Jan. 1999

Only *cannot but* and *cannot help but* have been the subject of much criticism. A great many commentators have had their say, many of them finding fault with one or the other by resorting to logic—their own brand—but of course logic cannot measure idioms. Degree of formality appears to be determined not by the phrase but by the choice of *cannot* or *can't* in the phrase. You can use whichever one seems most natural to you; all are standard.

cannot help, cannot help but See CANNOT BUT, CANNOT HELP, CANNOT HELP BUT.

can't but See CANNOT BUT, CANNOT HELP, CANNOT HELP BUT.

can't hardly See HARDLY.

can't help, can't help but See CANNOT BUT, CANNOT HELP, CANNOT HELP BUT.

can't seem

> I must be nervous this afternoon. I can't seem to settle down to anything —Kathleen Norris, *The Passing Show,* 6 Dec. 1933 (in Partridge 1942)

The expression *can't seem* is an idiom that came under critical scrutiny during the last quarter of the 19th century. The chief criticism is that the expression is illogical or involves, as Partridge 1942 puts it, "misplacement of words." Partridge has correctly identified the process, but it is not an error. Bolinger 1980 calls it "raising"—a name linguists use for the process by which a negative (or sometimes another element) gets moved from a subordinate clause to the main clause. Another well-known example of raising is "I don't think it'll rain today" for "I think it won't rain today." Negatives often tend to be raised in conjunction with *seem.* Look at these examples:

> My problem is that I cannot seem to remember this —Kilpatrick 1984

> . . . they do not seem to be seriously engaged in anything other than being oppressed —John Corry, *Harper's,* November 1970

> Senate members don't seem to recall any such understanding —*Time,* 23 Mar. 1953

The unraised negative with *seem* is also in use, but not so frequently as the *can't seem, don't seem* constructions.

> It is surprising how many otherwise quite rational people seem not to know this —Rexford G. Tugwell, *Center Mag.,* July/August 1970

Conclusion: while *can't seem* itself appears to be mostly used in speech, its cousins *cannot seem, don't seem, did not seem,* etc., are common enough in print. All are formed by negative-raising, and are standard idioms. The more logical construction, with the negative in the subordinate part of the sentence, can be used, but it is less frequent. See RAISING.

canvas, canvass Usage books tell you that the noun *canvas* refers to cloth, and the verb and noun *canvass* usually refer to the soliciting of votes or opinions. You will certainly not go wrong in making this division a rule of thumb. Actual usage, however, is not quite so clear-cut. These two words are closely related etymologically and from their earliest occurrences both words, to varying degrees, have been spelled both ways. Here is a summary of modern usage:

The noun which the usage books say is only *canvas* is occasionally spelled *canvass*.

> . . . for the painter to transfer his imaginative conception to canvass —John Dewey, *Art as Experience,* 1934

The verb meaning "to cover, line, or furnish with canvas" is spelled *canvas* but may be inflected with either a single or double *s.*

> An over-canvassed craft would be a liability —Bill Wallace, *Sailing,* rev. ed., 1966

> . . . the one hundred-foot-long Gallery, canvased from floor to ceiling with dozens of masterpieces by Reubens, Sir Joshua Reynolds . . . —*Town & Country,* April 1984

The much more common verb discussed in usage books has several senses (including "to examine in detail" and "to solicit support or determine opinions") and is usually spelled *canvass* but occasionally *canvas.*

> . . . the tendency of some of the members of the Advisory Council to canvas their government's interests not only at the Council table —Ann Dearden, *Middle East Jour.,* October 1950

The noun derived from this verb is also usually *canvass* but occasionally *canvas.*

> Funds for the bridge were raised by a house-to-house canvas —*American Guide Series: Maryland,* 1940

Except for the verb inflections of *canvas,* the secondary spellings are currently much less used than the primary spellings.

capability *Capability* is commonly followed by *of* or *for* when it is used with a preposition:

> They were viewing the country with the eyes of persons accustomed to drawing; and decided on its capability of being formed into pictures —Jane Austen, *Northanger Abbey,* 1818

> With childish faith in the capabilities of science —I. I. Rabi, *Atlantic,* October 1945

> Their ignorance of Man's capabilities for mischief —J. Stevenson-Hamilton, *Wild Life in South Africa,* 1947

> Today's student constituency has shown a thirst and capability for serious responsibility —Jean-Louis D'Heilly, *Change,* December 1970

It is also commonly followed by *to* and an infinitive:

> The capability of a great state to expand its influence —*New Republic,* 27 Jan. 1968

> . . . our capability to stop these bombers —Stuart Symington, *New Republic,* 13 July 1953

capable When followed by a preposition, *capable* nearly always appears with *of*:

> . . . when those muscles and joints were rendered capable of motion —Mary Shelley, *Frankenstein,* 1818

> . . . individually so capable of charm —Edmund Wilson, *A Piece of My Mind,* 1956

> . . . I became myself capable of bestowing animation upon lifeless matter —Mary Shelley, *Frankenstein,* 1818

> . . . people who valued machines more than men were capable under these conditions of governing men —Lewis Mumford, *Technics and Civilization,* 1934

The last two illustrations above show *capable of* used with a gerund in the active voice. *Capable of* may also be found used with a verb in the passive voice. Some commentators decry this construction, but it has been used by careful writers:

> An ideal so expansive is no longer capable of being compressed —*Selected Writings of Benjamin N. Cardozo,* ed. Margaret E. Hall, 1947

> . . . your language wardrobe is capable of being enlarged many times over —Jerome Martin & Dorothy Carnahan Olson, *Patterns of Language,* Level G (textbook), 1977

capacity *Capacity,* when it refers to ability, potential, facility, or power, may be followed by *to* and the infinitive:

> . . . has the capacity . . . to experiment with a variety of novelistic techniques —John W. Aldridge, *Saturday Rev.,* 6 Sept. 1975

> . . . the Pentagon thinks the capacity to make yourself invisible has huge military potential —Richard Schickel, *Time,* 7 Aug. 2000

It may also be followed by the preposition *for* and a noun:

> It is Mrs. Bush's own capacity for reassurance that was an invaluable asset to the campaign —Julia Reed, *Vogue,* June 2001

> . . . she developed a fine capacity for mischief —George Eliot, *Silas Marner,* 1861

A gerund phrase may follow the preposition when *capacity* is used with *for*:

> . . . demonstrate a capacity for solving the critical problems in our own society —James M. Gavin, "On Post Cold War Strategy," *Center Report,* June 1972

. . . his capacity for feeling snubbed by those whose superiority he recognized —Van Wyck Brooks, *The Flowering of New England, 1815–1865*, rev. ed., 1946

Capacity in this sense may even be found with *of* and a noun, although this combination is less frequent:

. . . bold adventurous people without nerves, minds, or the capacity of observation —Archibald MacLeish, *Yale Rev.*, Autumn 1941

Of may also be followed by a gerund phrase, but this use is infrequent:

David Lloyd George in England also had the capacity of glamorizing himself —Victor L. Albjerg, *Current History*, September 1952

When *capacity* is used to designate volume, the preposition *of* follows it:

One modern cement elevator has a storage capacity of 114,000 barrels —*American Guide Series: Minnesota*, 1938

When denoting a position or role, *capacity* is used a little more often in the construction *in his* (*her, our*, etc.) *capacity as,* than in the construction *in the* (*his, her,* etc.) *capacity of*:

. . . in their capacity as historians they have pointed out the effect of specific economic factors —John Dewey, *Freedom and Culture*, 1939

capital, capitol There are a number of things the spelling *capital* is used for—letters, money, cities—but *capitol* always refers to a building, even when used figuratively:

Not going to my grandmother's side of the road was an impossibility . . . for Ida Rebecca's house was the capitol of Morrisonville —Russell Baker, *Growing Up*, 1982

caption Copperud 1970, 1980 notes that Fowler 1926 did not like *caption* used for a title or heading. He was echoing an old complaint that probably started with Richard Grant White 1870. But this complaint is all but forgotten, more recently replaced by that of Partridge 1942, who says that *caption* is being misused for "a legend underneath (instead of above, as it should be). . . ." The meaning "heading" seems to come from legal use, where *caption* signifies a particular kind of heading.

All this criticism notwithstanding, *caption* is established in British and American use for a heading and for the legend under a picture or cartoon or the subtitle in a movie or television broadcast.

. . . an editorial which appeared in your issue of December 9th under the caption

"The Woollcott Menace" —Alexander Woollcott, letter, 19 Dec. 1935

He soon became a regular contributor to various comic periodicals and turned out quips, cartoon captions, and sketches —Marc Slonim, *Saturday Rev.*, 12 June 1954

carat, karat, caret *Carat* is a unit of weight for precious stones; *karat* (also spelled *carat* sometimes) is a unit of fineness for gold; *caret* is a wedge-shaped mark used by copy editors and proofreaders to mark a place in text where something is to be inserted. It is really unlikely that you will confuse these, let alone fuddle them with Bugs Bunny's old favorite *carrot*, as Shaw 1975 worries. If in doubt, check a good dictionary. We do have an instance of *carat* wrongly spelled with two *r*'s in a direct-mail advertisement for precious gems available "directly from those fabled mines in India"—an offer probably as dubious as the spelling.

care 1. Chambers 1985 and Raub 1897 remind us that the verb *care* is often followed by *for* and *about*; Chambers also mentions *to* and the infinitive.

. . . have always cared for patients beyond customary norms —Leonard Gross, *McCall's,* March 1971

. . . to prove that the rest of the country really cares about their problems —Henry Ford II, *Michigan Business Rev.*, July 1968

. . . spent more time in church on Sundays than I care to remember —Mrs. Medgar Evers, *Ladies' Home Jour.*, September 1971

2. The noun *care* is commonly followed by *for* or *of*:

. . . to provide medical care for the aged —*Current Biography*, October 1965

. . . the care of the aged and care of the insane —Paul Goodman, quoted in *Psychology Today*, November 1971

careen, career *Careen* began to be used to suggest some sort of irregular or erratic forward motion sometime around the end of the 19th century. The word had earlier been used to denote the side-to-side rolling or heeling over of a sailing ship:

She careened over so that her lee channels were under the water —Frederick Marryat, *Peter Simple*, 1834

This motion was brought ashore—perhaps first in a poem by George Meredith—and when the automobile made its appearance, it quickly took over the word.

. . . a great black car came careening down the road —Edgar Rice Burroughs, *Tarzan of the Apes*, 1914

. . . careening down the road comes a loaded ambulance —*N.Y. Times,* 8 Sept. 1918

You will notice that automobiles tend to move forward, often rapidly, while rocking from side to side, and thus the use of *careen* to describe such movement began to impinge on the territory of *career,* which had long denoted rapid headlong movement, often blending in the notion of swaying:

. . . sightseers had gathered in clumps to watch the cars careering homeward —James Joyce, *Dubliners,* 1914

The ambulance came careering toward us —Robert Rice, *New Yorker,* 20 Oct. 1956

The new use of *careen,* which is evidently an Americanism (Burchfield 1996 says it is little used in British English), spread rapidly from automobiles into figurative use. *Career* had similarly moved from the concrete to the figurative, much earlier than *careen.* Thus you will find both words used in similar contexts, almost interchangeably:

. . . the birds career wildly —Claudia Cassidy, *Europe—On the Aisle,* 1954

. . . and birds career through its open space —Ward Just, *Atlantic,* June 1975

. . . huge flying saucers, careening planets —Jack Kroll, *Newsweek,* 30 Mar. 1987

. . . careering asteroids and meteorites slammed into moons —Sharon Begley & Mary Hager, *Newsweek,* 4 Sept. 1989

By the 1930s the new usage of *careen* had come to the attention of usage writers, and it troubled them. They decided that *careen* must mean "to sway from side to side," *career* must denote headlong speed, and they disapproved those careening cars and ambulances that were by then firmly established in use. American writers have paid little attention to their strictures, leaving the critics bewildered— some holding out for their distinction, some approving the use, and some wondering if *career* is still in use (it certainly is).

The American use of *careen* is well established, and you can choose to use it or choose to use *career.* Nothing is wrong with either one.

careful, careless 1. *Careful,* when used with a complement, is most often followed by the preposition *of* and a noun or a pronoun, or by *to* and an infinitive:

At first she had been careful . . . of him —Hugh MacLennan, *Two Solitudes,* 1945

. . . in most cases the savages were careful to leave Quaker families unmolested —W. R. Inge, *The Church in the World,* 1928

When *careful* is used to mean "exercising prudence," however, it may be followed by *about* or *with*:

It is true that they generally are careful about money —John Fischer, *Harper's,* January 1969

The thrifty Scot, ordinarily so careful with a dollar —W. A. Swanberg, *True,* June 1954

2. *Careless,* according to our evidence, is most often used with *of* when it takes a complement:

Careless of all his advice, she swung at it . . . and poled it far over the fence —E. L. Doctorow, *Loon Lake,* 1979

. . . he was careless of facts, misty in principles —J. H. Plumb, *N.Y. Times Mag.,* 11 Feb. 1973

3. Both *careful* and *careless* are also used with *in* followed by a noun or gerund. This use is less frequent than use with the other prepositions or with an infinitive dealt with above:

. . . was short in stature, deep-chested, careful in dress —*Dictionary of American Biography,* 1929

Congreve's plays were deplorably careless in construction —Peter Forster, *London Calling,* 7 Apr. 1955

. . . who was as careless in handling his own money —*Dictionary of American Biography,* 1936

careful writer The careful writer is a fiction often invoked by usage commentators. Conveniently, the careful writer follows whatever precept the commentator is laying down at the moment. When you meet the careful writer in usage books, you should be careful to distinguish him from the good writer.

careless See CAREFUL, CARELESS.

care less See COULD CARE LESS, COULDN'T CARE LESS.

caret See CARAT, KARAT, CARET.

case Sir Arthur Quiller-Couch in his book *On the Art of Writing* (1916)—a collection of lectures delivered at Cambridge in 1914 and 1915—includes a lecture in which he has a little fun with the jargon of bureaucrats, some of whom were evidently employed at Cambridge. The word that is the chief butt of the lecture is *case* in a few of its typical phrases. Although Copperud 1970 says that the use of *case* is "unforgettably ridiculed," the actual humor of the lecture depends first on the audacity of tweaking the noses of the university examiners and second on the deliberate misconstrual of some harmlessly stodgy formula used by the poor clerk of a local board. If you are looking for unforgettable ridicule, you would do better to read Mark Twain on Fenimore Cooper.

In any case—to use one of the aspersed phrases—Quiller-Couch, once committed to print, became the source of a copious flow of imitation, from MacCracken & Sandison 1917 to Garner 1998. The usual criticism picks out one or two phrases and appends some comment like "wordy and usually unnecessary."

Copperud notes with some surprise that "these expressions seem immune to attack"—which simply means that writers regularly use the offending phrases without paying attention to the critics. So here—perhaps for the first time anywhere—you may see how real writers use some of the offending expressions.

In any case:

In any case, it would take a genealogist some days clambering around a man's family tree to determine whether he was entitled to the suffix of esquire —Howard 1980

The devastating reviews, in any case, have hardly hurt the book at the cash registers —Stephen Kinzer, *N.Y. Times Book Rev.,* 22 Oct. 1995

In case:

. . . and taking into consideration the vagaries of the English climate, I like to take some woollens just in case —Graham Greene, *Travels with My Aunt,* 1969

And in case the President still thinks law and order and Vietnam are what count —Anne Chamberlin, *McCall's,* March 1971

In case of:

They learned how to roll out of their cars in case of a shooting —Isabel Wilkerson, *Essence,* May 1998

The roof must be completed in case of rain —Thomas J. Smith, *Yankee,* July 1968

In that case:

He told me that he was not at the Writers' Workshop and in fact had no connection at all with the university. When I asked why in that case he was here, he looked at me with perplexity —Laurence Lafore, *Harper's,* October 1971

In that case, however, conquistadores contributed nothing directly to the societies' destruction —Jared Diamond, *Guns, Germs, and Steel,* 1997

The foregoing phrases are not easily removed, although sometimes they may be replaced by another phrase. *In the case of,* however, is a phrase that several handbooks believe can readily be done without or, as Copperud suggests, replaced by *concerning.* You will see in these next examples that you cannot always make the suggested expedients work. You may well be able to think of different, more workable revisions, though.

In the case of cancer or heart disease the only person who literally gets hurt is the one who failed to get to his doctor in time —Glenn V. Carmichael, *Ford Times,* September 1966

. . . asked if he would, in the case of an emergency, be willing to lend me some money —Jane Harriman, *Atlantic,* March 1970

Posterity, if she doesn't ignore him altogether, is far more likely to confirm and even to emphasize the vulgar judgment of his contemporaries, as she has done in the case of Doyle and Holmes —*New Yorker,* 12 Feb. 1949

In these last examples, the expression containing *case* can probably be revised for the better. If you try, remember that you are looking for an improvement, not just a substitution.

There are quite a number of so-called "magnetic hills" . . . located wherever the configuration of the landscape presents the illusion of nonexistent grades. It is usually a case of a slope of moderate steepness occurring between two steeper slopes —Donald A. Whiting, *Ford Times,* February 1968

If it is a truism that the quality of every college depends chiefly upon its faculty, it was even more the case at the Wyandanch College Center —Jerome M. Ziegler, *Change,* June 1972

Conclusion: sometimes phrases with *case* are superfluous, sometimes they are long-winded, and sometimes they are neither. You have to decide each case on its merits.

casket, coffin It is perhaps a bit surprising to see comment on the use of the all-American euphemism *casket,* which was first aspersed by Nathaniel Hawthorne in 1863, is still being published.

From around the turn of the century, the adoption of *casket* in preference to *coffin* was being urged by the undertaking trade. Although usage commentators disparaged the term, and although the suspicion that a casket was more expensive than a coffin received public expression, the term nevertheless seems to have reached acceptance. Burchfield 1996 points out that in many American newspapers, *casket* and *coffin* are used interchangeably. *Coffin* is the standard term in British English.

catachresis *Catachresis* is a term from classical rhetoric for "the use of a wrong word for the context." We present first a couple of examples of the thing:

There was quite an ecliptic collection of whale artifacts —*Antiques and the Arts Weekly,* 29 Oct. 1982

The Royals made three errors in the first five innings, but the Orioles failed to materialize on the mistakes —*Springfield* (Mass.) *Morning Union* (AP), 17 Mar. 1987

The catachreses are the use of *ecliptic* for *eclectic* and *materialize* for *capitalize.*

Catachresis has become part of the jargon of contemporary usage writers. They tend to apply the term loosely, using it as a sesquipedalian term of disparagement for whatever usage they choose not to approve. It has been pointed out at least once that usage writers themselves are not immune to the fault:

Catachresis for instance is grammarians' jargon for using a word in a wrong sense. When grammarians call writing jargon merely because it is verbose, circumlocutory and flabby, they themselves commit the sin of catachresis —Gowers 1948

The derivative adjective is *catachrestic.*

catastrophe, catastrophes Copperud 1970, 1980 notes that these are sometimes misspelled *catastrophy* and *catastrophies.* Our files contain one example of the first and four of the second. Watch out.

catchup See CATSUP, KETCHUP, CATCHUP.

cater In current American usage, the predominant preposition after *cater* is *to*:

So, our government, always on the alert to cater to the peace of mind of its citizens . . . —Goodman Ace, *Saturday Rev.,* 6 Mar. 1971

Both were in any case catering to a great appetite for self-expression —Marya Mannes, *The Reporter,* 28 Apr. 1953

In British usage the predominant preposition is *for*:

The pulps catered for a large audience, literate but not literary —Julian Symons, *Bloody Murder,* 1985

Australia's large public hospitals are operating to capacity catering for road accident victims —James E. Breheny, *The Age* (Melbourne), 14 Apr. 1975

To is also found in British English, perhaps a bit more often than *for* is found in American:

. . . when most British companies had not even thought seriously about catering to French tastes —*The Economist,* 16 Mar. 1974

. . . the plutocratic St. Moritzers for whom our popular dramatists cater —T. S. Eliot, "A Dialogue on Dramatic Poetry" (1928), in *Selected Essays,* 1932

catsup, ketchup, catchup The spellings *catsup* and *ketchup* are used with about equal frequency; *catchup* is not as common as the other two but it is used; all three spellings are standard. You can accept this statement as given or, if you feel contentious, you can advocate one of these spellings over the others. Your choice might be based on the brand you eat (Del Monte calls it *catsup,* Heinz and Hunts call it *ketchup*), the writers you read (J. D. Salinger and John Dos Passos used the spelling *catsup,* Eudora Welty and Norman Mailer used *ketchup,* William Faulkner used both, and Ernest Hemingway used *catchup*), or just personal preference.

causal *as* See AS 1.

cause The noun *cause* may be followed by the prepositions *of* and *for*:

. . . used his fame to champion the cause of the handicapped —*Current Biography,* January 1966

. . . New Englanders realize that the cause for land preservation is not yet hopeless —Eleanor Sterling, *Yankee,* July 1968

. . . admitted that recent bank failures were a cause of concern —*Current Biography,* July 1965

. . . there would be little cause for apprehension at the present time —Robert A. Nisbet, *Psychology Today,* March 1971

caution When the verb *caution* is used with a preposition, it is generally followed by *against*:

. . . I intend directly to introduce myself, caution you against certain possible interpretations of my name —John Barth, *The Floating Opera,* 1956

Less often, *caution* is used with *about*:

. . . Mother had cautioned them more than once about saying things like that —Mary Austin, *Starry Adventure,* 1931

Infrequently, *caution* is found with *of*:

. . . Professor Hay cautioned of a great debate on how far we should look on the spread of Renaissance values —*Times Literary Supp.,* 21 Mar. 1968

Caution is also used with *to* in both positive and negative constructions:

. . . encouraged her in this plan but cautioned her to involve Dr. Taylor in any reassignments —*AAUP Bulletin,* December 1967

She cautioned Miss Pollitzer not to show them to anyone else —*Current Biography,* February 1964

cavalry See CALVARY, CAVALRY.

C.E. See A.D., B.C.

celebrant, celebrator *Celebrant* is a 19th-century word that was originally applied to one who celebrates a Mass or some other religious rite. *Celebrater* is a 17th-century word for a person who celebrates anything; the spelling *celebrator* superseded *celebrater* in the 19th century. Sometime in the 1930s *celebrant* began to be used in the more general sense. Our earliest citation is from 1937:

Half a million celebrants tramped the streets from dawn to dusk today when New Orleans cast aside everyday cares to observe the century-old Mardi Gras —*N.Y. Times* (AP), 10 Feb. 1937

The broader sense is almost entirely American.

The use established itself quickly enough:

Some of the celebrants had been flown in by a former R.C.A.F. flying instructor —*Time,* 11 Feb. 1946

Printing took Walt from a Long Island farm to Brooklyn and to New York, whose celebrant he became —Henry Seidel Canby, *Turn West, Turn East,* 1951

Whitman was also a celebrant of the West as natural innocence —*Times Literary Supp.,* 17 Sept. 1954

The highlight for all, however, is the monthly party for members whose birthdays occur that month. After a program and just before the cake, each celebrant speaks briefly —Howard A. Rusk, M.D., *N.Y. Times,* 19 Dec. 1954

All of these examples (and others in our files) have one thing in common—they were printed before Theodore Bernstein discovered that this use was an error (*Winners & Sinners,* 19 Jan. 1955). Of course, it is not an error. *Celebrator,* the word recommended as a replacement for the broadened *celebrant,* is still in use but is not quite as frequent as *celebrant*:

. . . still others consider him the celebrator of a Third Sex —Leslie A. Fiedler, *Encounter,* January 1955

. . . as facile celebrators of Vatican II thought their church could do —Garry Wills, *New York,* 2 Aug. 1971

No difference in the level of formality between *celebrant* and *celebrator* is detectable from our citations. Both are in reputable use, with *celebrant* slightly more frequent.

. . . women have been America's chief celebrants of the art —Nancy Goldner, *Dance News,* May 1982

. . . gaily garbed celebrators parading through the streets —James Kelly, *Time,* 13 May 1985

Celtic As part of the name of a sports team, such as the Boston Celtics, this is pronounced \'sel-tik\. You will also hear this pronunciation in other contexts, and at times from very well-educated speakers. But the closer you get to circles substantively concerned with Celtic lore and languages, the more likely you are to hear \'kel-tik\.

cement, concrete Some time around the year 1300, according to the OED, a writer described a certain kind of clay as being strong as iron, stone, or cement. This writer was not sent a corrective letter pointing out that he must have meant concrete, since cement is only one ingredient of concrete—because the word *concrete* had not yet entered the language. Modern writers are not so lucky. Let a writer in the *Wall Street Journal* mention dragging a carton "across the cement floor," and someone will send a letter to the editor, giving the information above and (odds are) adding a recipe for concrete into the bargain.

The first thing to realize here is that if confusion exists, it lies solely in the realm of words, not things. The contractor who laid the floor had no difficulty in distinguishing the material cement from the material concrete. And once the floor is laid, what you call it is of little consequence. You can call it "cement," as our ancestors did, or "concrete," as the letter writer does; the floor remains unaffected.

As a term for a mixture of ingredients that sets hard when combined with water, *cement* is a term some 500 years older than *concrete*. *Concrete* began as an adjective, and was not used as a noun of the building material until the 19th century. But in current use *concrete* is more frequent than *cement,* quite possibly because of the increased use of concrete as a building material. Both words are still used of some familiar things:

The cement floors and sheetrock walls ring with industry and joy —Judson Jerome, *Change,* September 1971

. . . ochre-stained concrete floors —*Southern Living,* November 1971

Tap . . . tap . . . tap.
Heels on the cement walk
—John Rechy, *Evergreen,* December 1967

. . . garden apartments situated on a hilly mound, with a pond and concrete paths —John Coyne & Thomas Herbert, *Change,* Winter 1971–1972

But in some combinations only *concrete* is found:

> The white beams crossing white beams, all of prestressed concrete —Horace Sutton, *Saturday Rev.,* December 1978

Conclusion: the use of *cement* to refer to various building materials now mostly known as *concrete* has been around for some 600 years. Objection to its use, in other than technical contexts, in such combinations as "cement floors" or "cement walks" is pedantic. However, more people are using *concrete* than *cement* to describe such things these days, and there is certainly nothing wrong with maintaining the technical distinction in general writing.

censor, censure, censer We have in our collection a great many handbooks, from 1917 to 1998, warning against confusing *censor* with *censure.* A few toss in *censer* for good measure. A couple say the confusion is common but not where it is common. We have not a single example of such confusion in our files. Maybe students muddle them by poor spelling. If adults confuse them, however, they seem to be smart enough to look in a dictionary before committing to print. You should do the same if you have doubts.

center The intransitive verb *center* is idiomatically used with the prepositions *on, upon, around, round, about, in,* and *at:*

> . . . the town was a close-built brick huddle centered on a black river —John Updike, *Bech is Back,* 1982

> By May her thoughts were centered on him —Garrison Keillor, *Lake Wobegon Days,* 1985

> . . . the play centers upon the death of an eight-year-old flute-playing shepherd boy —*Current Biography,* March 1967

> The attack, slanderous and vile, centered around her prison story —Iris Noble, "First Woman Reporter," in *Dreams and Decisions,* ed. Carl B. Smith et al., 1983

> The novel itself is centered around a Norwegian village hostelry —Maxwell Geismar, *N.Y. Herald Tribune Book Rev.,* 7 Apr. 1940

> One group of apparent ironies, we noted, centred round the deflation of emotional considerations by practical ones —Ian Watt, *The Rise of the Novel,* 1957

> His delusions centered about money —John Updike, *Couples,* 1968

> . . . every literary movement centers about a political program —George Orwell, *New Republic,* 14 July 1941

> . . . over 70 per cent of our expanding population continuing to center in the nation's major metropolitan areas —Sylvia Porter, *Springfield* (Mass.) *Daily News,* 13 Aug. 1969

> . . . the love interest centers in Henry's chronic courtship of Beatrix —John E. Tilford, Jr., *PMLA,* September 1952

> . . . for any interval [–a,a] centered at the origin —School Mathematics Study Group, *Calculus, Part II,* 1965

> Then *I* is simply an interval in *S* centered at 0 —Casper Goffman, *Mathematics Mag.,* January 1974

The OED evidence, from the 17th century to the 19th century, shows primarily *center in* but includes some citations with *upon, on,* and *around.* Current American usage favors *on* and *around. About* has strong literary backing but is not as frequent as *around. Upon* is occasional; *round* is British. *In* seems to be less used than it was in the past. *At* is primarily mathematical.

Sometime before 1931 some person in England (as yet unknown; not H. W. Fowler) decided that *center round* was incorrect. He presumably invoked logic, as that has been the focus of most subsequent comment. The issue had crossed the Atlantic by 1935 and has been a staple of American commentators ever since. The most common "logical" argument involves *center* as a geometric point—an argument that loses its cogency once you realize that the geometric *center* is a noun, and the question involves a verb phrase, not used, it may be added, in geometry. Another commentator bases his logic on the assumption the verb means exactly what his argument says it does; this is a classic example of begging the question. A more inventive critic asserts that "it is physically impossible to *center around,*' as if the use of the verb phrase were something three-dimensional. The fallaciousness of these arguments has been pointed out by a few commentators, but the mainstream flows unabated onward in the same old channel—at least as recently as 1998.

Center around is a standard idiom, as commentators increasingly concede, even when they prefer another combination. You can use it freely if you want to. *Center on,* however, is more common in current American use and is also standard. In addition, *revolve* and similar verbs will combine satisfactorily with *around* in many contexts where *center* and a particle typically appear. There is no lack of alternatives here.

centimeter See HYPERFOREIGNISMS; KILOMETER.

ceremonial, ceremonious *Ceremonious* is a word brought in from the French in the 16th century. It was first used as a synonym for *ceremonial,* which had been brought in from the French in the 14th century. George Campbell, in his 1776 *Philosophy of Rhetoric,* seems to have been the first person to try to distinguish the two, but he seems to have had no followers.

Fowler 1926 revived the question. He begins with a distinction that initially seems clear enough, relating *ceremonial* to the countable use of *ceremony* ("a piece of ritual") and *ceremonious* to the use that is not countable ("attention to forms"), but the following discussion and example are not entirely transparent.

Later commentators, including Copperud 1970, 1980, Longman 1984, Harper 1985, Shaw 1975, and Reader's Digest 1983, have concentrated primarily on trying to make Fowler's treatment clear. Sometimes they have oversimplified, as Shaw 1975 and Garner 1998 do by saying *ceremonial* applies to things and *ceremonious* to people and things. Both adjectives are applied to persons and to things.

Without trying to discuss and exemplify all the distinctions of meaning that dictionaries show, let us look at the general tendencies of the two words. *Ceremonious* tends to be used in a way that suggests behavior while *ceremonial* tends to be used so as to suggest compliance or involvement with a ritual, which may be civil or personal as well as religious. This distinction is perhaps easiest to see in the application of the words to people:

> A large percent of the poultry products in the large cities must be ceremonially butchered. It is a matter of record that many of these ceremonial butchers . . . —Thurman W. Arnold, *The Bottlenecks of Business,* 1940

> He was not a very ceremonious beau; he never sent her flowers or whispered silly things in her ear —Louis Auchincloss, *Atlantic,* December 1949

The same distinction can be seen when the words are applied to a person's speech:

> He read in a synthetic ceremonial tone of voice that sounded preposterous as well as insincere, but he was conducting the marriage ceremony precisely as he had conducted countless previous ones —James T. Farrell, *What Time Collects,* 1964

> . . . his ceremonious diction wore the aspect of pomposity —Sir Winston Churchill, *Maxims and Reflections,* 1949

As generally applied, *ceremonial* tends to be the everyday adjective relating to any ceremony:

> True ceremonial centers sprang up all over central and north-central Peru —Edward P. Lanning, *Peru Before the Incas,* 1967

> . . . the ceremonial role of flowers at weddings and funerals —Genevieve Stuttaford, *Publishers Weekly,* 6 Sept. 1976

> . . . an Administration which seems to conceive its role as a ceremonial one —Haynes Johnson, *The Progressive,* December 1969

Ceremonious tends to emphasize actions and behavior:

> . . . just as a priest kneels before an altar piled with oranges and bread and performs some ceremonious hand flourishes —Robert Craft, *Stravinsky,* 1972

> . . . the cold and ceremonious politeness of her curtsey and address to his friend —Jane Austen, *Pride and Prejudice,* 1813

> . . . the ceremonious extinguishing of the candles —Logan Pearsall Smith, *All Trivia,* 1934

> He left her on her doorstep with a ceremonious little bow —Louis Auchincloss, *A Law for the Lion,* 1953

Ceremonious is sometimes used to emphasize the meaninglessness of the ritual performed:

> The cold bath that he took each morning was ceremonious—it was sometimes nothing else since he almost never used soap —John Cheever, *The Wapshot Chronicle,* 1957

In broad terms, then, *ceremonious* tends to stress a way of acting, doing, or behaving while *ceremonial* serves as the simple adjective for *ceremony.*

There are, however, a couple of complications. First we have instances in which perhaps either word might have been chosen, and some people would no doubt have chosen the one that the author did not:

> . . . Owner Fleitz marched off with the three-foot silver trophy, after a ceremonious ducking in the refuse-filled Almendares River —*Time,* 9 Dec. 1946

> Napoleon rarely appeared in public. . . . When he did emerge, it was in a ceremonial manner, with an escort of six dogs — George Orwell, *Animal Farm,* 1945

The second complication is frequency of use. Our files show *ceremonial* to be used more often than *ceremonious. Ceremonial* may possibly be spreading into areas where *ceremonious* would ordinarily have been used until recently. Only time will tell. You will be perfectly safe if your usage is in general accord with the broad outlines of use described and illustrated here.

certain Cook 1985 notes that *certain* can be used ambiguously. All the same, the "uncertain" use of *certain* is one of its chief uses:

... "average" American men, fairly good-looking, of a certain height —Joyce Carol Oates, *Harper's,* April 1972

... as a result of the acceptance of certain miracles —*Times Literary Supp.,* 2 Apr. 1971

New York's nightpeople of a certain age and condition indulged themselves —Judith Crist, *New York,* 15 Nov. 1971

The OED Supplement traces "of a certain age" back to the middle of the 18th century and notes that this use of *certain* was popular in euphemistic phrases, such as "in a certain condition" for *pregnant* and "a certain disease" for *venereal disease.* Euphemistic use has declined. The "specific but unspecified" notion, however, continues in vigorous use, and it is very popular in such places as annual reports:

... problems that had been creating strains in certain areas of manufacturing —*Annual Report, American Can Co.,* 1970

In addition, certain other companies were acquired —*Annual Report, Borden Co.,* 1970

certificated A correspondent whose letter is printed in Safire 1984 expresses dismay at the participial adjective *certificated* applied to a person who has been given a certificate. This correspondent is a bit late coming to the discovery of the term:

... they enter the normal school where they remain two years as with us, and then become certificated teachers —*Jour. of Education,* vol. 18, 1883

Certificated does not appear to compete much with *certified;* its use is largely limited to education and air transportation. A few examples of use:

... the certificated airlines have carried more cargo —*Air Transportation,* December 1948

... the steel-nosed Captain Morgan (pirate and certificated teacher) —*Times Literary Supp.,* 30 Nov. 1967

... moved to England, where she studied ballet for 11 years, actually becoming a certificated teacher —Vincent Canby, *N.Y. Times,* 11 Mar. 1973

Since *certificated* has been in use for at least a century, there is little point in complaining about it. It is the correct term in a small number of applications and can otherwise be ignored.

cesarean, caesarean The first spelling, *cesarean,* is the one now most frequently used in medical writing; *caesarean* is also acceptable. The spellings with an *-ian* termination are considerably less frequent but not wrong. The *c* is not usually capitalized.

chaff, chafe Copperud 1970, 1980 and Bryson 1984 warn against confusing *chaff* with *chafe.* Since, in the senses cited, *chaff* means "to tease good-naturedly" and *chafe* "to irritate, vex," you might well wonder how the words could be confused. Copperud gives us an example: "The mayor was chaffing at his confinement. . . ." The example makes things clearer—this is an intransitive sense we are dealing with, not the transitive ones cited. And, in fact, this problem does not involve the 19th-century verb *chaff* that means "tease, banter" at all.

It appears from evidence in the OED that back in the bad old days before printers—and schoolmasters in their wake—had normalized English spelling, the verb we now know as *chafe* was also spelled *chaff,* among many other ways. The OED says the spelling was fairly common from the 16th to the 19th century, and Webster's Third lists it as an archaic variant.

The sense of *chafe* in which the *chaff* spelling seems to turn up occasionally is the one that means "to feel or show irritation or discontent." Here are a couple of examples of it in the usual spelling:

There are scientists, however, who chafe at such restrictions —Otto Friedrich, *Time,* 10 Sept. 1984

... who for years has chafed under the burden of a WASP culture —Alfred Kazin, *Atlantic,* January 1983

Here are a couple of examples with the double *-f* spelling:

With much of Europe chaffing under the growing U.S. economic domination —Charles A. Wells, *Between the Lines,* 1 Jan. 1967

... and he is chaffing today because of the 26 per cent service charge on his hotel bill —Robert Craft, *Stravinsky,* 1972

These occasional occurrences suggest that the old spelling is still used once in a great while, that it is not so much archaic as just quite rare. If you use it, do so with the knowledge that it is rare and is likely to be thought a misspelling or a confusion.

chair 1. *Verb. Chair* is a verb formed by functional shift from the noun. On this basis Bernstein 1958, 1965 denounces the use of the verb *chair* in the meaning "to preside as chairman of"; Copperud 1970, 1980 calls it journalese. The sense objected to has been in use at least since 1921. Both Copperud and Bryson 1984 note that dictionaries accept the term without comment. It is standard.

. . . he willingly chaired committees and gave his energies selflessly —John Kenneth Galbraith, *The Scotch,* 1964

. . . opposition in the committee hearings, chaired by Senator Sam Ervin —*N.Y. Times,* 1 Feb. 1972

2. *Noun.* It has been fashionable for a few years for persons unacquainted with the forms of parliamentary procedure to disparage the use of *chair* in the sense "chairman, chairwoman" as an ugly creation of the Women's Liberation movement. There is, of course, no law that requires people to know anything about the history of what they disparage, but we can tell those who are curious that *chair* has been used in this sense since the middle of the 17th century. Its earliest citation in the OED is dated 1658–9; it is only four years more recent than *chairman.* It is, moreover, a standard term of parliamentary procedure:

> Sometimes the chair "appoints," in which case he names the members of the committee —*Robert's Rules of Order,* 2nd ed., 1893

Our evidence suggests that this sense of *chair* may perhaps be more often encountered in programs, directions for the submission of papers, and the like, than it is in running context. It is not, however, unusual in running context.

> The Conservative chairwoman . . . was far more liberal than the Labour chair had been in calling speakers who opposed the motion —Mollie Panter-Downes, *New Yorker,* 30 Oct. 1971

Harper 1985 and Reader's Digest 1983 recommend the use of *chair* in place of *chairperson.* See also CHAIRMAN, CHAIRWOMAN, CHAIRPERSON, CHAIRLADY.

chairman, chairwoman, chairperson, chairlady A fair amount of ink has been spilled in the discussion of the propriety and appropriateness of these terms. Usage writers who venture an opinion on the subject tend to dislike *chairperson* and recommend *chairman, chairman* or *chairwoman,* or *chair* (see CHAIR).

Chairman is the oldest of these words (1654) and the most widely used. It has been and still is used of women:

> Many doctors refrain from balance billing . . . , says Dr. Nancy Dickey, chairman of the American Medical Association —Nancy Ann Jeffrey, *Wall Street Jour.,* 26 Jan. 1996

> As chairman of Harpo Entertainment Group, as well as host, star, and supervising producer of *The Oprah Show,* Winfrey is the most successful woman ever to enter the

field of television —Harry Allen, *Vibe,* September 1997

> Pat Benjamin, running for party chairman, distributes pamphlets stating that she's "got the resources" —Dana Milbank, *New Republic,* 16 Aug. 1999

Because *chairman* is used of both men and women, some commentators claim that its *-man* element is not masculine, buttressing their arguments with reference to the Anglo-Saxon. However, the 17th-century origin of the term vitiates the Anglo-Saxon argument, and the fact that *chairwoman* appeared as early as 1699 suggests that *chairman* was not entirely gender-neutral even in the 17th century. But there is ample precedent for using *chairman* of both men and women.

Chairwoman is an entirely respectable word dating from 1699, but it seems not to have been used as often as it might, probably because it has long competed with *chairman* in application to women and has recently had competition from *chairperson.*

Chairperson is a recent coinage (1971) as a gender-neutral term to be used in place of *chairman* and *chairwoman,* one of several such gender-neutral coinages containing *-person* (see PERSON 2). It was greeted with much resistance by usage writers and others resistant to neologism, but seems to have quickly gained acceptance in a wide variety of publications. A number of commentators have noted that although *chairperson* was intended to be gender-neutral, it is chiefly used of vacant posts (in advertisements) and of women. Our evidence shows this to be generally true. Thus *chairperson* tends to be truly neutral when the position is vacant or when no name is associated with the office. But when a name is mentioned, *chairperson* is still more likely to stand for a woman than for a man.

Clearly all three of these words (or four, if you count *chair*) are in standard use, and you can use whichever you like best.

A curious term that is not really a contender for favor here is *chairlady.* This is an infrequent alternative to *chairwoman* that we have found mostly in American use. Leo Rosten in *The Joys of Yiddish* (1968) associates the term with American Jewish culture, and we have a little evidence supporting his observation. But our evidence also suggests that at one time *chairlady* might have been best established in labor-union usage:

> This is when we had the union. I was the chairlady —Evelyn Finn, quoted in Studs Terkel, *Hard Times,* 1970

> . . . she's union chairlady in her section —Richard Bissell, *7½ Cents,* 1953

We have no current evidence of such use. It has perhaps been supplanted by *chairperson*:

> Teresa works in a textile factory and, as her union's chairperson . . . —Judith Crist, *Saturday Rev.,* August 1980

We have scattered evidence for *chairlady* through the 1970s, but none since. It is not a serious contender with *chairman, chairwoman,* and *chairperson.*

chaise lounge, chaise longue   *Chaise-longue* is a French word that was brought into English around 1800. It designated a kind of elongated chair, and the word probably followed the piece of furniture to England. *Chaise lounge* is formed from the French word by a process known as folk etymology, in which words or word elements are transformed in such a way as to make them closer to more familiar or better understood words or word elements. In the case of *chaise longue, longue* is not an English word, but *lounge,* spelled with the same letters, is. In addition, a 19th-century American noun *lounge* that designated a similar piece of furniture (this *lounge* appears in *Uncle Tom's Cabin,* for instance) seems to have influenced the development of *chaise lounge.*

Chaise-longue (it seems to have been regularly hyphenated during the 19th century) seems not to have been entered in an English dictionary until it appeared in a section of the OED in 1889. It did not appear in one of our dictionaries until Webster 1909. In both the OED and Webster 1909 it was marked with double bars, indicating that the editors considered it a foreign word.

The OED mentions that Ogilvie's dictionary enters the word in the form *chaise-lounge,* a spelling not recognized in the OED, all of whose citations were for the French spelling. The Ogilvie's dictionary referred to turns out to be the 1855 Supplement to *The Imperial Dictionary,* edited by John Ogilvie and published in Edinburgh and London. *Chaise-lounge* is so marked we know Ogilvie intended the second part to be pronounced like English *lounge.* That he entered the term suggests that it was probably current in Edinburgh at the time he was editing the supplement. Unfortunately he gives us no citation of its use in print.

The American *chaise lounge* began to appear in print in the 1920s. As a printed term it seems to have become established first in the trade; many of our early citations are from manufacturers' catalogs and newspaper advertisements. When the spelling began to appear in both the Montgomery Ward and the Sears and Roebuck catalogs, it could no longer be ignored—millions of people would be familiar with it. *Chaise lounge* did have some general and literary use too, but the bulk of such use

belonged to the French spelling. The current situation is not much different. *Chaise lounge* is still most common in commercial use. It also continues in general and literary use to some extent, but there *chaise longue* predominates. The latter is usual in British use of all kinds.

chance   **1.** *Noun.* The preposition used most commonly after *chance* is *of*:

> . . . would have only a small chance of hitting us —Thomas C. Butler, *Johns Hopkins Mag.,* Summer 1971

> We must take him on if there was any chance of success —Ernest Hemingway, "Miss Mary's Lion," 1956

Chance is also used, in varying senses, with *at, for,* and *on*:

> . . . historians, who will get their chance at it . . . in the future —Jonathan Daniels, *N.Y. Times Book Rev.,* 9 May 1954

> . . . Italy's best chance for progress —*N.Y. Times,* 10 Dec. 1963

> . . . took advantage of a free chance on a set of 10 storm windows —*Springfield* (Mass.) *Union,* 21 Sept. 1955

And it is used with *to* and the infinitive:

> Even if we have the happy chance to fall in love —Graham Greene, *Travels with My Aunt,* 1969

2. *Verb.* The verb *chance* may be followed by the prepositions *on* or *upon*:

> . . . unless one chances on him while he is already laughing —Hiram Haydn, *American Scholar,* Summer 1964

> We chanced upon a pocket air-pollution indicator —*McCall's,* October 1971

It is also frequently followed by *to* and the infinitive:

> Chancing to pick up a copy —L. N. Wright, *CEA Critic,* May 1971

> Arnvid chances to rescue a young woman —Edmund Fuller, *Saturday Rev.,* 16 Oct. 1954

Other prepositions are occasionally used:

> . . . 24 Bewick . . . swans chanced into Slimbridge from their breeding grounds 2,600 miles away —Sophy Burnham, *N.Y. Times Mag.,* 27 Apr. 1980

> . . . I chanced by a bookstall —Deedee Moore, *Cosmopolitan,* January 1972

character   Copperud 1970, 1980, Strunk & White 1959, 1972, 1979, Watt 1967, and Prentice-Hall 1978 all point out that *character* is often used for unneeded padding. How often, we cannot judge; we know it happens at least now and then:

. . . that were partly economic and partly political in character —*Collier's Year Book,* 1949

But in the bulk of our citations the vagueness of the word seems to be useful, and it cannot easily be replaced:

> . . . wanted the furnishings to be mostly a traditional counterpoint to the open contemporary character of the house —Gary E. McCalla, *Southern Living,* November 1971

> But the character of these changes differed from one age to the next —W. F. Bolton, *A Short History of Literary English,* 1967

If *character* is sometimes used unnecessarily, it would seem to be a small matter and certainly no reason to forego use of the word entirely.

characteristic In general, when the adjective *characteristic* is followed by a preposition, the preposition is *of*:

> It's particularly characteristic of the Western industrialized society —Margaret Mead, *Barnard Alumnae,* Winter 1971

> . . . are related in different ways from those which are characteristic of the comprehensive high school —James B. Conant, *Slums and Suburbs,* 1961

Less frequently, *characteristic* may be used with *in* or *for*:

> The cough is so characteristic in whooping cough —Morris Fishbein, *The Popular Medical Encyclopedia,* 1946

> . . . which seem to be characteristic for the different organic groups —S. S. Tomkins, ed., *Contemporary Psychopathology,* 1943

charisma *Charisma* is an originally theological term that was first appropriated for secular use by the German sociologist Max Weber. The work of Weber's in which he uses the term was not translated into English until 1947, but it was known to people who were familiar with his thought:

> Charisma is, then, a quality of things and persons by virtue of which they are specifically set apart from the ordinary, the everyday, the routine —Talcott Parsons, *The Structure of Social Action,* 1937

Thus, the earliest uses of the word in English are elucidations of Weber's theories or applications to Germany:

> . . . the strange German conception of the leader's "charisma," a combination of manliness, recklessness, and intellectualism —Louis L. Snyder, *Annals of the American Academy of Political and Social Science,* July 1947

It was not long before *charisma* turned up in literary criticism:

> . . . for Paul radiates what the sociologists, borrowing the name from theology, call *charisma,* the charm of power, the gift of leadership —Lionel Trilling, *The Liberal Imagination,* 1950

So the word was current in some intellectual circles when John F. Kennedy was elected president in 1960. The frequent application of *charisma* to Kennedy seems to have been in large measure responsible for the popularity of the word in the press. By the end of the 1960s, *charisma* was busting out all over:

> Beauty, wealth, birth—where could you find a better summary of what gives the Kennedys . . . their charisma? —Max Lerner, *N.Y. Post,* 28 June 1968

> . . . Jesse Jackson, who has been described as being closer than anyone else to Dr. King in charisma —Charlayne A. Hunter, *Trans-Action,* October 1968

The boom has continued:

> Of all the world's capitals, this city seems to be the *most* gifted with charisma —Patrick McGivern. *Cosmopolitan,* March 1972

> Autumn is Libra's special season, and through Thanksgiving, the private you is blessed with extra sparkle and charisma —Lila Spencer, *Cosmopolitan,* October 1976

> . . . whose acting in *Sunday Too Far Away* and *Caddie* leaves no doubt of his intelligence and charisma —S. S. Prawer, *Times Literary Supp.,* 18 July 1980

> Clothes confer charisma, separating the slob from the snob —Ruth La Ferla, *N.Y. Times Mag.,* 17 Feb. 1991

> Café Pasqual's is a small, funky place that is chock-full of charisma and charm —*Wine Spectator,* 15 Nov. 1997

You can perhaps detect here—as several commentators have—a certain devaluation or trivialization of the word from its early application to national leaders. Commentators such as Howard 1977, Phythian 1979, Bremner 1980, and Harper 1985 object mildly to the trend. The word may have descended in application from the definition Weber gave it, but Parsons had already deflated it somewhat in 1937, and its spread to literary criticism also sowed the seeds for most current use. If the coin is somewhat devalued, it is nonetheless in wide circulation.

chary *Chary* is often followed by *of* and somewhat less often by *about*:

My business experience has taught me to be chary of committing anything of a confidential nature to any more concrete medium than speech —William Faulkner, *The Sound and the Fury,* 1929

I wanted my father's good opinion because he was chary of his compliments —*The Autobiography of William Allen White,* 1946

Nor are men merely chary of expressing pain and neediness —Susan Faludi, *Newsweek,* 13 Sept. 1999

. . . he himself was chary about the psychoanalytical technique in serious mental illness —Alfred Kazin, *N.Y. Times Mag.,* 6 May 1956

China watchers have become chary about pronouncing on the future —Orville Schell, *N.Y. Times Book Rev.,* 29 June 1997

Occasionally, *chary* may be found with *as to, in,* or *with*:

. . . the cautious and taciturn Yankees were sometimes very chary as to their answers —F. Eliot, *Atlantic,* July 1953

Such persons are usually expected to be chary in the exercise of their real power —Ralph Linton, *The Cultural Background of Personality,* 1945

I am always very chary with percentages . . . I like short words and vulgar fractions —Sir Winston Churchill, quoted in *Time,* 19 Oct. 1953

chastened By and large, when *chastened* is used with a preposition, it is *by*:

. . . were chastened but not defeated by the New Left experience —Michael Harrington, *N.Y. Times Book Rev.,* 11 Mar. 1973

. . . the process by which what is private is chastened and socialized by being made to enter public life —Charles Frankel, *Antioch Rev.,* Fall 1955

However, when *chastened* is used with a preposition, the choice of the preposition is dictated not by the meaning of the word, but rather by the meaning of the prepositional phrase. Thus, *by* denotes the agent doing the chastening and, among other prepositions that are used, *for* indicates the reason for the chastening and *to,* the state into which something is chastened or the extent of the chastening, while *in* may signify the circumstances that do the chastening:

. . . the proud have been chastened for their manifest sins —Albert Guérard, *Education of a Humanist,* 1949

. . . his character chastened to a Christ-like degree —James D. Hart, *The Popular Book: A History of America's Literary Taste,* 1950

. . . had been chastened in two marriages —*Time,* 29 Aug. 1955

cheap **1.** Copperud 1980 warns of the derogatory connotations of *cheap* meaning "inexpensive," and Reader's Digest 1983 worries that the pejorative uses are driving the "inexpensive" sense out of use. The neutral sense, however, is not being driven out of use:

If there is a cheaper hobby in the world than the collection of homonyms, I have yet to find it —James J. Kilpatrick, *Smithsonian,* April 1984

The initial purposes of the public development of the St. Lawrence . . . had been to supply home consumers . . . with cheap power —*Current Biography,* May 1967

. . . a new segment of the population that wouldn't travel at all without cheap group rates —Barbara Johnson, *Saturday Rev.,* 4 Mar. 1972

Pejorative senses can easily be told from the context, in most cases:

I won't tell you the brand name, but I bought it cheap, because it doesn't get used very much. And you know what I got? A cheap stove —Betty Furness, quoted in *Money,* December 1980

. . . motivated by insatiable vanity and a desire for cheap thrills —Barbara Tritel, *N.Y. Times Book Rev.,* 23 Feb. 1986

You probably need not worry about the neutral sense being taken as pejorative except when *cheap* is used attributively—directly ahead of the noun it modifies. In the next example *cheap* connotes shoddiness as well as low price:

. . . a desk, good but battered . . . , a bed serving also as a sofa, a cheap carpet —Janice Elliott, *Angels Falling,* 1969

The likelihood of the pejorative connotation creeping in is greatest when the noun denotes a physical object—no one is confused about *cheap electric power* or *cheap travel rates.* If you mean to say that an object is not expensive by using *cheap,* you had better take care to make your meaning unmistakable in context.
2. Bernstein 1971 reminds us that *cheap* is an adverb as well as *cheaply.* The adverb *cheap* is most frequently found in contexts of buying and selling, and it regularly follows the word it modifies:

. . . if there is an abandoned shed in your neighborhood that you can buy cheap —Daniel B. Weems, *Raising Goats,* 1983

. . . the multinationals got the licences cheap —Neal Ascherson, *Observer Rev.,* 3 Mar. 1974

Cheaply is used in a wider range of meanings and may either precede or follow the word it modifies:

> . . . which diminish his capacity to produce efficiently and cheaply —Ivar Berg, *Change,* September 1971

> . . . sell their cheaply made goods to America —Goodman Ace, *Saturday Rev.,* 25 Mar. 1972

> . . . real estate speculators blockbusted their West Side neighborhoods, snapping up homes cheaply —John Saar, *People,* 11 Apr. 1983

There are people who believe that all adverbs end in *-ly* and who avoid flat adverbs like *cheap* (see FLAT ADVERBS). It is therefore pretty common to see *cheaply* in a context where *cheap* would also have been perfectly idiomatic:

> For this reason, the Lutzes get the house cheaply —Stephen King, *Playboy,* January 1981

The adverb *cheaply* sometimes replaces the adjective *cheap* after a copulative verb. This is a phenomenon of fairly long standing; the OED has examples of the phrase *to hold cheap* "to think little of"—which dates from Shakespeare's time—written as *to hold cheaply* in the 19th century. This sort of substitution is one kind of hypercorrection. Here are a couple of more recent examples, first the adjective and then the hypercorrect adverb:

> . . . he needed money to acquire Old Masters, which never come cheap —Robert Wernick, *Smithsonian,* September 1979

> Quality, as one might expect, does not exactly come cheaply —G. Bruce Boyer, *Town & Country,* February 1983

check   The common English particles—*up, on, over, into,* for instance—are a frequent irritation to the usage commentator, who tends to suspect that they are often superfluous. But they are idiomatic and cannot simply be wished away. *Check* as a verb is used with a number of these.

Copperud 1970, 1980 comments especially on the use of *check into,* which seems to have been a particular bugbear of Theodore Bernstein. Bernstein, in *Winners & Sinners* (23 June 1954), disapproved of these two examples:

> . . . is kept busy checking into developments —*N.Y. Times,* 11 June 1954

> He said he also had asked Mr. Carr to check into such rumors —*N.Y. Times,* 12 June 1954 (proof)

Copperud points out that the *into* in each of these examples serves the purpose of disam-

biguation; without it *check* could be understood in the sense of "to slow or bring to a stop." This seems to be a reasonable point, and it is likely that the use of such idiomatic and "superfluous" particles often has the singling out of one sense of a multisense word as a main function.

Let us, then, not worry about alleged superfluity or redundancy in these idiomatic combinations of *check,* but look at those that are in current use and see by example what sorts of contexts they are found in.

Out seems to be the particle in most frequent use at the present time. You will note in these examples that *check* with *out* is not reserved to a single meaning:

> . . . try something on a small scale and check out the result —Richard M. Brett, *Blair & Ketchum's Country Jour.,* February 1980

> . . . they stop visitors and question them, and check out parked cars —B. J. Phillips, *Ms.,* March 1973

> Instead, he began to check out Donohue's story —Anatole Broyard, *N.Y. Times,* 23 Feb. 1972

> Be sure to check out the prettily embroidered place mats —Merrie A. Leeds, *Town & Country,* May 1980

> . . . so we might as well go check out that crowd to see who we're going to be hanging out with —Carolyn Becknell Mann, *Harper's Weekly,* 16 May 1975

On is also common:

> Through the monitoring center, physicians can check on a patient from anywhere inside or outside the hospital —*Psychology Today,* March 1971

> Wilbur G. Kurtz, an artist and historian of the South, was retained to check on every matter of detail —Gavin Lambert, *Atlantic,* March 1973

Check up and *check up on* can also be found. *Check up* followed by a clause appears to be British; *check up on* is predominantly American:

> Check up that the child has the means of obtaining any materials or books she may need —Ailsa Brambleby et al., *A Handbook for Guiders,* 1968

> . . . I had got up to look out of the window to check up if there was going to be a frost —Ian Cross, *The God Boy,* 1957

> . . . she planted herself in the front row of the House visitors' gallery to check up on the vote —James Egan, *McCall's,* March 1971

One may work his head off or just think and loaf. No one checks up on you —Albert Halper, *American Scholar*, Winter 1981–1982

And there are also *over* and *around*:

They asked for volunteers to check over the registration lists —*Boy's Life*, August 1952

. . . mothers who brought their babies in to be checked over by a city doctor —*The Lamp*, September 1953

The White House people had quietly checked around and found . . . —David Halberstam, *Harper's*, February 1971

cherub *Cherub* has had its problems with plurals. Some commentators say that the plural *cherubims* is wrong, since *cherubim* is itself a plural. Others concentrate on assigning the plural *cherubim* to angels, and *cherubs* to children. The history of these forms is curious. The original plural in English was *cherubins*. This was the popular form through the 16th century. Shakespeare used it, as did his contemporaries Marlowe, Lyly, Sidney, Spenser, and Donne. During the 17th century it was gradually displaced by *cherubims* (used in the King James Bible). By the 18th century *cherubins* had virtually disappeared. *Cherubim* was adopted by more scholarly writers during the 17th century. Bacon used it, and Milton used it in *Paradise Lost* (he also used *cherubins* and *cherubims* in his prose). *Cherubims* held on, though dwindling in use, through the 18th and 19th centuries, sustained by the 1611 Bible and hymns. It survived at least as late as 1930 in poetry:

. . . throng'd their heav'n with *cherubims* —Robert Bridges, *The Testament of Beauty*, 1930

Cherubims does not seem to be used anymore. In present-day use *cherubim* is usual for angels, *cherubs* and less often *cherubim* are used in reference to art and decoration. *Cherubs* is found in reference to children, but only infrequently.

Chicano The remarks on this term in Copperud 1980, Bremner 1980, and Harper 1985 suggest that there is some misapprehension about this word. It is a word, as Copperud notes, applied by some Mexican-Americans to themselves. It seems to have been introduced into American English in the late 1940s or early 1950s. It was first used by politically active groups and hence is a term considered offensive by those Mexican-Americans of different or opposed political views. Our evidence for objection to *Chicano* suggests that the objection is primarily political; we have no evidence from printed sources that *Chicano* has

been used as a pejorative term by either Mexican-Americans or other Americans.

Chicano has been frequently used in the Anglo press since 1968 or 1969 and is still in frequent use. With wider application the term has become less politicized, and objection to it has largely subsided, although there are probably still some Mexican-Americans who find it offensive; objectors have been noted as recently as 1991. Most of our citations are neutral or positive. The word is almost always capitalized.

chide When used with a preposition, *chide* is usually used with *for* to designate what has provoked the chiding:

. . . his wife . . . was forever chiding him for his grammatical lapses —William Styron, *Lie Down in Darkness*, 1951

Always the schoolmarm when it came to words, my mother chided him for ignorance —Russell Baker, *Growing Up*, 1982

There also is evidence for the use of *chide* with other prepositions—*with, on, as,* and *about*:

. . . is chided with the fact that he, while declaring himself inimical to everything the Festival represents, still uses it —Irwin Shaw, *Harper's*, September 1970

. . . chided the administration on farm . . . policies —*Wall Street Jour.*, 2 Sept. 1954

. . . chided advertisers and their agencies as being "the arch-conservatives of the contemporary world" —Tom Donlon, *Advertising Age*, 6 Apr. 1970

The last fellow who chided me about Southern ancestry was a Westerner —James Street, *Holiday*, October 1954

The past tense and past participle of *chide* have yet to settle in form. As you can see from the last three illustrations, *chided* is usual in active constructions in American English, while *chid* is more often used in British English:

I chid her for this unnecessary demonstration —Augustus John, *Chiaroscuro*, 1952

. . . chid them for drinking —Elizabeth Taylor, *A Game of Hide-and-Seek*, 1951

When the passive voice is used, the choice of past participle is not so clear-cut: *chidden* is found in both American and British writing, while *chided* seems to occur mainly in American English:

. . . [she] is chidden for continuing to write novels in her original mode —Frances Taliaferro, *Harper's*, February 1983

. . . the disturbers glanced round . . . as though chidden by an intruder in their own home —Vita Sackville-West, *The Edwardians,* 1930

. . . the Cardinal was chided for his words —Gay Talese, *Harper's,* January 1969

Less frequent is the form *chid*:

"Ah, no!" she sighs, and is chid —George Meredith, *The Ordeal of Richard Feverel,* 1859

chief justice Copperud 1970, 1980 says the proper title is *chief justice of the United States,* not *chief justice of the Supreme Court;* Harper 1985 says there is a distinction between the terms; Garner 1998 says *Chief Justice of the United States* is preferred over *Chief Justice of the Supreme Court* and *Chief Justice of the Supreme Court of the United States.* This appears to have little or no bearing on the usage of the ordinary person. We find all three terms in good use:

. . . never realize they are speaking with the Chief Justice of the United States —Joseph J. Ellis, *N.Y. Times Book Rev.,* 1 Dec. 1996

The Chief Justice of the Supreme Court presides over the Senate during the impeachment trial —Stanley E. Dimond & Elmer F. Pflieger, *Our American Government,* 1961

. . . to the position of Chief Justice of the Supreme Court of the United States —Lewis Paul Todd et al., *Rise of the American Nation,* 1961

We also have ample evidence for *Supreme Court Chief Justice*:

. . . limits on federal review of state death sentences even more stringent than those proposed by U.S. Supreme Court Chief Justice William H. Renquist —*National Law Jour.,* 16 July 1990

childish, childlike The conventional wisdom holds that *childlike* has positive or neutral connotations while *childish* has negative connotations. As a general guideline, this is true. *Childlike* usually connotes some good quality such as innocence, trustfulness, or ingenuousness; it is also used in neutral description. *Childish* usually implies a quality such as immaturity or lack of complexity, especially in an adult.

He was a devout man, with a childlike trust in God —Charles Nordhoff & James Norman Hall, *Men Against the Sea,* 1934

. . . an adult should be an adult, occasionally childlike perhaps, but never childish —John R. Silber, *Center Mag.,* September/October 1971

Nodding, for it would have been childish to cut him, I walked on quickly —W. Somerset Maugham, *The Moon and Sixpence,* 1919

. . . she was living a childish fantasy —Herman Wouk, *Marjorie Morningstar,* 1955

. . . shaking their fists and calling childish phrases —Katherine Anne Porter, *The Never-Ending Wrong,* 1977

Fowler 1926 says that *childlike* should always be used of adults or their qualities, and the evidence agrees. *Childish,* not *childlike,* is used as a neutral adjective to refer to children. In this way writers avoid saying that something is *like* a child's when it *is* a child's.

. . . a light, airy, childish laugh, in which . . . he recognized the tones of little Pearl —Nathaniel Hawthorne, *The Scarlet Letter,* 1850

. . . the clear, childish accents of the little children —Charles Nordhoff & James Norman Hall, *Pitcairn's Island,* 1934

When something other than children is being referred to, *childish* is sometimes used in a neutral or positive context, whereas *childlike* is only rarely used in a negative context. These are the uses for which you may find yourself criticized.

. . . those memories had indeed made this day poignantly perfect, childish in its brazen delight —William Styron, *Lie Down in Darkness,* 1951

She is a woman of beauty, very small, with childish wrists and ankles —Joyce Carol Oates, *Harper's,* August 1971

. . . assumptions that workers are basically lazy, conniving and childlike —John R. Coleman, *N.Y. Times Book Rev.,* 5 Oct. 1975

Chinaman Most dictionaries and usage commentators note that *Chinaman* meaning "a Chinese" is considered offensive. The term is originally an Americanism and dates from the middle of the 19th century when Chinese immigrants encountered the Gold Rush boom on the West Coast. From American English the term found its way into British English, where, according to our most recent sources, it is also considered offensive.

Current usage is a bit hard to describe. Our American evidence shows little use in reference to persons of Chinese ancestry; when used it tends to appear in old slang phrases like *a Chinaman's chance.* Recent British use is somewhat puzzling: the term is used in literary contexts of fictional figures and in humorous contexts in *Punch,* but it is hard for an American to understand the intent of such use. It is also used of a bowling delivery in cricket; this use is usually not capitalized.

chord, cord Everyone agrees that *chord* is used for a group of musical tones, and *cord* for a string. Beyond this there is some disagreement and some misinformation. Copperud 1970, 1980 says that *cord* and *chord* come from the same ancestor, which is only partly true. The musical *chord* is derived ultimately from *accord*, and is not related to the string *cord*. There is, however, another noun *chord* which is related to *cord*; it was originally spelled *cord*, but its spelling was altered in the 16th century to conform to Latin *chorda* or perhaps the Latin's Greek original. This *chord* has a few regular uses: technical (truss chord, the chord of an airplane wing), mathematical (the chord of a circle), and emotional:

> John's work has always awakened responsive chords in a large and loyal body of admirers —David Piper, *Times Literary Supp.*, 1 Feb. 1980

> During his interview he struck exactly the right chord —E. M. Swift, *Sports Illustrated*, 7 Mar. 1983

The emotional uses frequently suggest some musical influence.

Then we have anatomical use, in which both spellings can be found:

> Chordates are defined by the presence of three features. One is the nerve chord in the spinal cord —Chet Raymo, *Boston Globe*, 21 July 1986

> . . . *foramen magnum* (hole at the base of the skull where the spinal chord enters) —C. Loring Brace, *The Stages of Human Evolution*, 1967

American commentators (Copperud 1970, 1980, Bernstein 1958, 1965, 1977, Bremner 1980, Kilpatrick 1984, Garner 1998) insist on the *cord* spelling in such combinations as *vocal cords, spinal cord,* and reject the *chord* spelling as an error. British commentators (Fowler 1926, 1965, Treble & Vallins 1937, Longman 1984, Chambers 1985) are more perceptive; they recognize both spellings. OED evidence shows that *chord* was perhaps somewhat more common than *cord* in the 19th century; Fowler thought *chord* was predominant in the first quarter of the 20th. Longman recognizes both spellings; so does Chambers, but Chambers says that *cord* has become more common. Burchfield 1996 recommends *cord. Cord* seems to predominate in American use.

The *chord* spelling can still be found in American sources in combination with *spinal* and more frequently with *vocal*, where the unrelated musical *chord* may affect people's spelling:

> . . . whose spinal chord was severed in a mugging incident —Barry Schatz, *Springfield* (Mass.) *Union*, 13 May 1985

> . . . making my living by my pen and on occasion by agitating my vocal chords —Clifton Fadiman, *Holiday*, April 1957

Conclusion: even though the *chord* spelling with adjectives like *vocal* and *spinal* is historically justified and considered acceptable by a number of British authorities, it is widely understood to be a misspelling in American usage. While it is not really a misspelling, we recommend that you use the commoner *cord* spelling.

chronic Copperud 1970, 1980 warns against misuse of *chronic* to mean "severe." This is a puzzling adjuration on the surface; we can find no evidence in our files of such use in edited prose. Two British sources, Phythian 1979 and Chambers 1985, mention a sense "bad, very bad, deplorable, intense, severe" that they describe as slangy or informal. This sense, it appears, is primarily British oral usage. Webster's Third describes it as British slang and the OED Supplement as "used colloq[ually] as a vague expression of disapproval."

The evidence in the OED Supplement suggests that even this use is not especially common in written sources; its most common use seems to be in the adverbial combination *something chronic*:

> It's made my eyes water something chronic —H. G. Wells, *Mr. Polly*, 1910 (OED Supplement)

> But that blasted curvilinear geometry of theirs, it stirred you up something chronic —Donald Jack, *That's Me in the Middle*, 1973

If there really is a usage problem here, it appears to be British.

circle There are some language commentators who decry the use of the verb *circle* with *around* or *round* as redundant. The OED evidence shows that these words, along with *about,* have been used with *circle* for a long time:

> So cerclith it the welle aboute —[Geoffrey Chaucer,] *The Romaunt of the Rose*, ca. 1400 (OED)

> The Sea which circles us around —Abraham Cowley, *Works*, ca. 1667 (OED)

> That proud ring Of peers who circled round the King —Sir Walter Scott, *The Lady of the Lake*, 1810 (OED)

Although it is true that *circle* in this sense is now most frequently used by itself, there is contemporary evidence for its still taking *around, round,* or *about* in a complement:

> . . . hired a sound truck that circled around the home —Theodore H. White, *The Reporter*, 8 June 1954

> . . . he circled mentally round and round the core of the matter —Marcia Davenport, *My Brother's Keeper*, 1954

. . . reminds me of some Druidic ritual, and I see the monuments as the ancients themselves circled about —John Sedgwick, *New England Monthly*, September 1989

Note that in the example from Marcia Davenport *round* suggests cautious avoidance of or a failing to come to grips with something. *Around* is similarly used:

. . . after circling around the problem for years, finally took the plunge and committed itself —George W. Bonham, *Change*, Winter 1971–1972

. . . they circle warily around the resulting void at the centre of popular humanistic thought —Joan Fox, in *The Film*, 1968

There seems to be no compelling reason to avoid *around, round*, or *about*.

These are not the only particles in use with *circle*. Here are the adverbs *back, up*, and *in*, usually in conjunction with a preposition:

. . . thinks of his life as being a sort of long, boring, nonstop flight from Cuba that will eventually circle back there —Vincent Canby, *N.Y. Times*, 29 Apr. 1979

I can circle up behind him, she thought —Bill Pronzini, *The Stalker*, 1971

As they begin, first slowly, then with increasing cold certainty, to circle in on each other —Barbara A. Bannon, *Publishers Weekly*, 4 Aug. 1975

circumstances There has been a fairly long-lived dispute as to the propriety of the use of the preposition *under* as opposed to the preposition *in* with *circumstances*. The list of commentators from Fowler 1926 on who specifically approve *under* is quite impressive, and you can be assured that both constructions are in good odor and in standard use.

. . . men have written good verses under the inspiration of passion, who cannot write well under any other circumstances —Ralph Waldo Emerson, "Love," 1841

. . . died in 1944 under circumstances that indicated "his departure from this earth may have been somewhat accelerated." —Norman Cousins, *Saturday Rev.*, 30 Oct. 1971

With as benign a smile as I could under the circumstances manage I suggested that the general ask the President that question —Dean Acheson, quoted in Merle Miller, *Plain Speaking*, 1973

. . . and others who are Snobs only in certain circumstances and relations of life —W. M. Thackeray, *The Book of Snobs*, 1846

. . . some you see in bright canvas deck chairs on green lawns in country circum-

stances —E. B. White, in *Perspectives USA*, Summer 1953

In no circumstances will the Chinese leadership allow the country to become dependent on one major trading partner —Alastair Buchan, *The Listener*, 6 Dec. 1973

In seems to be more common than *under* in British usage, while both are in frequent use in the U.S. When *circumstances* means "financial situation," *in* is the preposition of choice; *under* is rare:

. . . living useful lives in reduced circumstances —Norman Stone, *N.Y. Times Book Rev.*, 28 Oct. 1984

While growing up in comfortable circumstances in Pasadena —*Current Biography*, February 1967

She lived at Nice in very modest circumstances —*Dictionary of American Biography*, 1936

You should not think, however, that *under* and *in* are the only prepositions to go with *circumstances*; others are used when the situation dictates. Here are just two others, but the selection is hardly exhaustive:

. . . it may be the right one for the circumstances of that nation —Donald McLachlan, *London Calling*, 24 June 1954

Life may be good or bad according to circumstances —Bertrand Russell, *Education and the Good Life*, 1926

The controversy over *in* and *under* seems to have had its origin in one of Walter Savage Landor's *Imaginary Conversations* (1824) in which Horne Tooke talks with, or perhaps at, Dr. Johnson. Landor's reason for reprehending *under* is etymological: *circum* means "round or around" in Latin and therefore *in* is appropriate and *under* is not. Many of you will recognize this sort of reasoning as the etymological fallacy. Fowler demolished Landor's logic, dismissing it as "puerile."

The etymological fallacy dies hard, however. Evans 1962 notes that Harold Ickes refused to sign letters containing *under the circumstances*. Gowers 1948 rejected *under* on logical grounds, but he recanted in his 1954 book and left the choice to the reader's own taste, while continuing to express his preference for *in*. And as recently as 1984 a correspondent has written to this company to inveigh against *under* on etymological grounds. You, we know, will not be taken in by the etymological fallacy.

cite, site, sight A number of handbooks, primarily those aimed at college and high-school students, point out that these three homophones (or any pair of them) should not be confused. That the meanings are entirely distinct you can confirm by a glance at your dictionary; substitution of *site* or *sight* for one of the others (we have no examples of *cite* wrongly applied) is made on the basis of sound alone—and presumably little or no forethought. You would think this never happens except in the writing of careless students, but it does.

> I have sighted only two examples —letter from an irate correspondent to Merriam-Webster, February 1980

> Set your sites on the future —advt., *Morgan Horse,* April 1983

> . . . a policeman who claims to have sited UFOs —*TV Guide,* 2 Sept. 1981

All together now: the first should have been *cited,* the second *sights,* the third *sighted.* Pay attention when you write, seems to be the appropriate motto here.

civilian Copperud 1970, 1980 complains that Merriam-Webster dictionaries are the only ones that recognize a use of *civilian* in which the word distinguishes the civilian from a member of a uniformed force such as a police force or fire department, as well as from a member of the military. Copperud does not like the extension beyond the military, and while Bernstein 1965 will accept extension to police and firefighting forces, he draws the line there.

A check of some recent desk-sized dictionaries shows that at least one recognizes the extension to police and fire-fighting units and another recognizes extension to police forces. Small wonder. The use has been around since the late 1940s or early 1950s, and here are a couple of examples:

> Until the fall of 1954 New York was the only city with a population of more than 1,000,000 that shunned the use of civilians as school-crossing guards —Joseph C. Ingraham, *Modern Traffic Control,* 1954

> Police forces of the stature of the Royal Canadian Mounted Police must have a proper concern for the traditions that make membership in the force something different from holding down a nine-to-five civilian job —*Globe and Mail* (Toronto), 30 Apr. 1975

The extension of *civilian* to distinguish ordinary people from members of any group, regardless of whether the group is uniformed or not, is what Bernstein objects to. This use is not especially new; our files show that the meaning was listed as new in the 1948 *Britannica Book of the Year.* It has become well established. Here are some representative examples:

> While a civilian girl will often try a new haircut at whim, for a model a haircut is serious business —Richard Natale, *Cosmopolitan,* April 1974

> We could only conclude that either belly dancers have vastly bigger navels than civilians or that inflation has had some queer effects —Betsy Wade, *N.Y. Times Book Rev.,* 2 Mar. 1975

> . . . Ellen Schwamm's second novel. . . . In civilian life, Schwamm is married to the fiction writer Harold Brodkey —James Wolcott, *Harper's,* August 1983

It appears that you can safely ignore the strictures of Bernstein and Copperud, who are looking backward. These extended uses of *civilian* are common, well established, and standard.

claim The disapproval of the verb *claim* used in a meaning close to "assert, contend, maintain" is a hoary American newspaper tradition stretching from William Cullen Bryant's *Index Expurgatorius* and James Gordon Bennett's *Don't List,* both dating from the later 19th century, and Bierce 1909 to Bernstein 1958, 1965, Copperud 1964, 1970, 1980, Bremner 1980, and Kilpatrick 1984. There have been defectors: Utter 1916 reports that the *New York Evening Post,* the paper for which Bryant compiled his *Index,* approved the use of *claim* as an alternative to *assert.*

Bryant's *Index* was reprinted in Ayres 1881 and probably from that source found its way into American usage books early in the 20th century. The subject seems to have become a favorite from Vizetelly 1906 to Strunk & White 1959, 1972, 1979. But comment in usage books outside the newspaper field was more varied and not uniformly disapproving, though most did express disapproval.

The subject reached British readers through the attention of the Fowler brothers, who discovered it in their 1907 *The King's English.* H. W. Fowler revised and expanded his treatment in 1926, and most subsequent British commentators have been mindful of his remarks. Fowler found the use first, a vulgarism, and second, a violation of English idiom. However, his rejected examples seem perfectly ordinary today.

The unmentioned secret behind the Fowlers' detection of a violation of English idiom in this use is that the use is of American origin. The OED included the sense, without illustrations, on the authority of Fitzedward Hall, an American philologist and controversialist living in England, who contributed to the dictionary. The Supplement to the OED supplies the examples, and they come from mid-19th-century America. The Dictionary of American English quotes Mark Twain:

. . . it is claimed that they were accepted gospel twelve or fifteen centuries ago —*Innocents Abroad,* 1869 (DAE)

The Fowler brothers found it in Richard Grant White:

Usage, therefore, is not, as it is often claimed to be, the absolute law of language —*Words and Their Uses,* 1870 (Fowler 1907)

Just how the usage reached Great Britain from the U.S. is uncertain. Perhaps transatlantic passage was not necessary, for the uses cited with distaste in Fowler 1907 are not very far removed from the more recent of the citations given in the OED under one of its unstigmatized senses. Here are examples from the Fowlers and from the OED:

The constant failure to live up to what we claim to be our most serious convictions —*Daily Telegraph* (Fowler 1907)

It is claimed, then, on behalf of Christianity, that there is a Holy Ghost —Joseph Parker, *The Paraclete,* 1874 (OED)

As you will see from the following examples, the Fowlers' examples are not what would now be considered violations of English idiom. Our examples are from both British and American sources.

He had always claimed that he was working for the glory of British Art —Aldous Huxley, *The Olive Tree,* 1937

He will claim that he has not only kept the country out of war . . . —*New Republic,* 1 June 1938

. . . Henry James, an old friend, who claimed perhaps a little too often that he was an artist and nothing else —W. Somerset Maugham, *Saturday Rev.,* 11 Apr. 1953

This volume's dust jacket claims that the mighty Argentine fantasist "has come into English in haphazard fashion. . . ." —John Updike, *New Yorker,* 24 May 1982

In reading the examples, you will have probably noticed the advantage *claim* can have over any of the words—*contend, assert, maintain,* etc.—proposed as superior. It regularly introduces a connotation of doubt or skepticism—the notion that what is claimed may well be disputed. Thus *claim* is seldom—perhaps never—used where *assert, maintain,* or *say* would work better. *Claim* does its job so well that it seems to have been in standard use almost from the beginning, and it continues in standard use in spite of the opposition of the newspaper stylists and many other commentators.

It is, therefore, useful to remember that *claim* followed by an infinitive phrase or a clause regularly introduces an element of doubt. In its other meanings, *claim* regularly takes a noun phrase as object.

classic, classical These two adjectives began life as variants in the early 17th century, and it is not surprising that they share several senses. But over the course of three centuries some differentiation has occurred, so that *classic* is the usual choice in some situations and *classical* in others. Usage writers have often noted this differentiation, but many of them tend to believe differentiation complete where it is not and others bog themselves down in trying to define the terms—for definitions we suggest you look in a good desk dictionary.

Classic is used in preference to *classical* in two rather recently established applications that usage writers tend to disparage rather than to recognize—sports and fashion:

The five classic races are . . . —*The Oxford Companion to Sports and Games,* ed. John Arlott, 1975

. . . the classic pure jump-shooting guard —Bruce Newman, *Sports Illustrated,* 20 Nov. 1985

. . . these classic khaki trousers are the best —*Banana Republic Catalog,* Summer 1984

Classical is the scientific choice:

According to classical electrodynamics, the electrons should radiate energy continually —Dietrick E. Thomsen, *Science News,* 11 Jan. 1986

. . . Pavlovian conditioning—also known as classical conditioning —Gerald Jonas, *New Yorker,* 26 Aug. 1972

Classical is also usual in music:

. . . have recorded everything baroque from Albinoni to Zelenka but have rarely invaded the classical period —Stephen Wadsworth, *Saturday Rev.,* November 1980

The records were mostly classical, Mozart, Haydn, Bach, stacks of them —Daphne du Maurier, *Ladies' Home Jour.,* September 1971

In reference to the language, art, and civilization of the ancient Greeks and Romans, *classical* is usual but *classic* is not unknown:

Where English designers . . . had interpreted Classical decorative elements . . . Napoleon wanted to follow, as closely as possible, true Greek and Roman forms —William C. Ketchum, Jr., *Antique Monthly,* October 1981

. . . the transition from the stiffer archaic style to the freer classical period —James A. Blachowicz, *N.Y. Times,* 27 Feb. 1983

. . . from back in the old classic times. It might have fauns and satyrs and the gods and—from Greece, from Olympus in it somewhere —William Faulkner, 30 May 1957, in *Faulkner in the University,* 1959

In the senses of "serving as a standard of excellence," "memorable," and "typical," *classic* is more commonly used and is the form prescribed by most usage writers, but in fact *classical* is also used quite frequently:

Far from being the classic period of explosion and tempestuous growth, my adolescence was more or less a period of suspended animation —Philip Roth, *Reading Myself and Others,* 1975

. . . I knew that long before his father's time the buffalo had found their classic habitat on the Great Plains —Robert Penn Warren, *Jefferson Davis Gets His Citizenship Back,* 1980

He was a classic sales go-getter —William Oscar Johnson, *Sports Illustrated,* 20 Sept. 1982

The Orioles won the thing in the eighth, in equally classical style —Roger Angell, *New Yorker,* 7 May 1984

. . . would be one response to such a classical Oedipal situation —Norman MacKenzie, *The Listener,* 25 April 1974

classifying genitive   See GENITIVE 1.

clean, cleanse   According to the OED, *cleanse,* the older of these two words, was originally the common word for both the literal and figurative senses of "to make clean." *Clean* was formed by functional shift from the adjective in the 15th century and gradually took on most of the everyday dirt, with *cleanse* becoming the more elevated word. Consequently *cleanse* became more frequent in figurative use.

Although *clean* remains the more common verb, *cleanse* has never lost its literal meaning. It tends to be used most often of the human body:

. . . if your skin feels "tight" cleanse it with a liquid cleansing lotion or a soft cream —*American Girl,* December 1952

Transplant candidates require dialysis to cleanse their blood —Neil A. Martin, *Dun's,* October 1971

Sometimes its use carries a whiff of ritual:

. . . he plunged the knife into the earth and so cleansed it —John Steinbeck, *The Pearl,* 1947

It is occasionally called in to do duty for the environment:

The rivers and the air need to be cleansed —Fred M. Hechinger, *Saturday Rev.,* 7 Aug. 1976

It also serves for the taste buds:

Throw in a crisp lemon sorbet after a rich dish to cleanse the palate —Shirley Lowe, *Sunday Mirror* (London), 30 June 1968

But mostly *cleanse* is used figuratively:

. . . Bowdler scoured Shakespeare word by word to cleanse him of every last smudge of impropriety —Richard Hanser, *Saturday Rev.,* 23 Apr. 1955

For at least 10 days I was possessed by fury, at everyone. One morning I awoke and felt for the first time cleansed and filled with hope —Nan Robertson, *N.Y. Times Mag.,* 19 Sept. 1982

clear, clearly   Both *clear* and *clearly* are adverbs, but in recent use they do not overlap. *Clear* is most often used in the sense "all the way":

. . . my ticket from San Francisco clear to New York City —Jack Kerouac, *Esquire,* March 1970

. . . with his shirt soaked clear through —Robert Greenfield, *Rolling Stone,* 20 July 1972

Clearly is used in the sense "in a clear manner":

. . . writes clearly and helpfully —*Times Literary Supp.,* 16 Apr. 1970

. . . looked clearly at their country and set it down freshly —*Smithsonian,* November 1982

It is also used to mean "without doubt or question":

He clearly knows his way about the complex and abstruse issues —*Times Literary Supp.,* 2 Oct. 1970

. . . except when national security is clearly involved —John Fischer, *Harper's,* October 1970

In this second sense *clearly* appears also as a sentence adverb, a use that is criticized by Howard 1980 and Safire 1980 as a vogue use. Both commentators seem a bit tardy in discovering this use, which has been around quite a few years and is established:

Clearly, we must look further and find a rational test —Zechariah Chafee, Jr., *Free Speech in the United States,* 1941

Clearly some literalist recourses to law are offensive to the sense of justice —Alexander Comfort, *Center Mag.,* May 1970

clew, clue In the detective sense and its derivative uses, the usual spelling is *clue*:

> The discovery of the crime, by the clues left behind —H. A. L. Craig, *London Calling,* 17 Mar. 1955

> . . . the Russians don't have a clue about making shock absorbers, so their cars hop and bobble down the road —P. J. O'Rourke, *Car and Driver,* August 1983

The original spelling was *clew.* An early meaning of *clew* was "ball of thread, yarn, or string." Because of the use of a ball of thread to effect an escape from a labyrinth in various mythological stories—that of Theseus in the labyrinth of Crete, most notably—*clew* came to be used of anything that could guide you through a difficult place and, eventually, to be used of bits and pieces of evidence. The variant spelling *clue,* says the OED, began to be used in the 15th century, became frequent in the 17th, and in the late 19th became predominant in the "evidence" sense.

> . . . I'll follow up the clue (Clew? my stylograph won't spell) —Ellen Terry, letter, 4 July 1892

Partridge 1942 calls *clew* an American spelling. We do have fairly frequent evidence of it in the 1940s and early 1950s, but it has largely dropped out of use since then.

The nautical use is always *clew.*

cliché *Cliché* is in origin a French word for a stereotyped printing surface. The *C* volume of the OED (1893) recognized it only as a foreign word with this meaning. Its use to mean "a trite phrase or expression" is only attested in the OED Supplement from 1892. It seems to have caught on very quickly; by the 1920s it was already being disparaged as "worn":

> The word *'cliche'* itself, we have seen, is a cliche, a worn counter of a word —Havelock Ellis, *The Dance of Life,* 1923

1. *The word.* Reader's Digest 1983 notes that *cliché* is regularly used as a term of disparagement, which should surprise no one. From the following examples you can see that it has been extended semantically from words to ideas to visual images to things of various kinds:

> The dialog is largely cliches decked out in current jargon —Howard Kissel, *Women's Wear Daily,* 27 Dec. 1976

> . . . "investing in human capital" is the cliche for this —Leonard Silk, *Saturday Rev.,* 22 Jan. 1972

A recurring media cliché is the "human interest" story about the grandmother graduating from college —Fred M. Hechinger, *Saturday Rev.,* 20 Sept. 1975

> Some of the illustrations for this volume are so familiar they have become clichés —Michael Kammen, *N.Y. Times Book Rev.,* 4 July 1976

> . . . tired and disconnected routines that drew on little more than the clichés of modern dance —Alan Rich, *New York,* 24 Apr. 1972

> The Georgetown cocktail party, by now, is as much of a political cliché as the rubber-chicken dinner —Linda Charlton, *N.Y. Times,* 19 Apr. 1976

> . . . an anthology of threadbare clichés of *haute* and bistro cuisine —Jay Jacobs, *Gourmet,* December 1980

Copperud 1970, 1980 notes that *cliché* is used redundantly with *old* and *usual.* Such qualifiers seem to go naturally with *cliché* much as *old* seems to go with *adage* and *maxim.* Our evidence suggests that such combinations are not preponderant, but also not uncommon. See OLD ADAGE.

> . . . the weary old cliché that man is "inherently" a religious creature —Irving Howe, *Harper's,* August 1970

> . . . them thar warmed-over cliches —*Winners & Sinners,* 28 Nov. 1955

Using the superlative presumably removes the taint of redundancy:

> . . . two of the oldest clichés in science fiction —Gerald Jonas, *N.Y. Times Book Rev.,* 30 Dec. 1979

> . . . what may be the hoariest cliché of all —John Simon, *New York,* 6 Sept. 1976

You may also have noted that the unaccented *cliche* is sometimes used but the accented *cliché* is much more common.

2. *The thing.* Although many commentators and handbooks discuss clichés, there is not a great deal to be learned from reading their discussions. You will be advised in most instances simply to avoid clichés.

You will also not learn much about what is and what is not a cliché. Oh, everybody agrees on a definition, but there is little agreement about what fits the description. The editors of Reader's Digest 1983 raise several questions (similar ones can also be found in Copperud 1970, 1980 and Harper's 1975, 1985) about what distinguishes a cliché from any number of other frequently used stock phrases and expressions such as *how do you do* or *thank you.* The questions have a serious point, but no one seems to know the answer.

Many writers seem to consider any word or

expression they encounter often enough to find annoying a cliché. Here, for instance, is a book reviewer:

> He doles out his ghoulish clichés to the exorcists with equal largesse: the priest's panic "was marinated in a tide of sullenness"; "Slivers of agony jabbed and pierced through his buttocks and groins." —Francine Du Plessix Gray, *N.Y. Times Book Rev.,* 14 Mar. 1976

Now those expressions may be clichés to the reviewer of exorcism novels, but there are plenty of nonreaders of the genre who have never seen them before. Indeed, you are likely to find, when you read anyone's list of clichés, at least a few that you have never seen or heard before.

Many of our commentators conclude that the utter avoidance of clichés is impossible for one reason or another. Therefore, they advise, if you come to a situation where a cliché is the best way to express an idea, go ahead and use it. "The most overworked cliché is better than an extravagant phrase that does not come off," says Howard 1984. Several other commentators concur. The advice seems sound to us.

3. If you suspect that *one-way ticket to oblivion* in "This is one of the many hoary newspaper clichés that have long since earned one-way tickets to oblivion" (Harper 1985) is a bit of a cliché, you may then realize that writers on usage and compilers of handbooks are not immune to the attraction of clichés in their own writing. Such frequently invoked terms as *the careful writer, strictly speaking, a more precise term, formal speech and writing, casual speech, anything goes, permissive linguist,* and the like, and such descriptive terms as *colloquial, overworked, wordy, awkward, illiterate,* and *overused,* certainly qualify as clichés. Some of these that present particular problems will receive separate treatment in this book.

client A few commentators—Copperud 1970, 1980, Shaw 1975, Chambers 1985, Janis 1984—comment on *client* and *customer.* The gist of their comments is that a customer buys goods while a client buys services from a professional and especially a lawyer. As a general rule this observation is true, even if some stores catering to high-class trade prefer to think of their customers as clients, as Janis observes. If you remember to construe *professional* broadly, most of the following examples are not out of line:

> It is not so bad for a client and architect to serve a common public purpose —Roger G. Kennedy, *Smithsonian,* November 1982

> Hoteliers are reluctant to disclose the extent to which their light-fingered guests help

themselves, not wanting to brand their clients as pilferers —Michael S. Lasky, *N.Y. Times,* 27 Jan. 1974

> ... like a client in a brothel maintaining his dignity during a police raid —Robert J. Clements, *Saturday Rev.,* 17 July 1971

> ... a fine meal tastes infinitely better to a cold client than to a hot one —Richard Eder, *Saturday Rev.,* 8 Jan. 1977

> With the growing importance of institutional clients stockbrokers have invested heavily in research departments —Jack Revell, *The British Financial System,* 1973

The distinction between goods and services, may, however, be blurred occasionally, as you can see.

Janis 1984 remarks on the euphemistic use of *client* for the recipient of social services; this use dates back to the 1920s and seems to be a true euphemism—the agencies did not think people wanted to be referred to as *cases.* Over the years the social-service use has been extended in various directions to other government agencies—police, tax collectors, urban renewal specialists. Much of this seems to have occurred in British usage.

climactic, climatic When nine or ten handbooks make haste to tell you that *climactic* relates to *climax* and *climatic* to *climate* and you should not confuse the two, you might suppose that there is some insidious tendency for the words to be muddled in somewhat similar contexts. Not so. This is a simple matter of spelling, and from what we can find in our files the error is more often mentioned in handbooks than it occurs in edited prose. *Climactic* is the rather more frequent word; it is useful to book and movie reviewers, among others. *Climatic* is used mostly in technical contexts, but occasionally creeps into ordinary public view in articles on ice ages, global warming, and such. Our scanty evidence suggests that when the spelling or the typesetting goes wrong, it is *climatic* that turns up in the place of *climactic.*

climax Theodore Bernstein knew the etymology of *climax*—it comes from a Greek word meaning "ladder"—and from his knowledge of the Greek he reached the conclusion that the English word could not properly mean "highest point, culmination, acme, apex," which is, of course, precisely what it means to most people.

The issue seems to have been first discovered by Hodgson 1889; it is repeated in Allbutt, *Notes on the Composition of Scientific Papers* (1923), F. K. Ball, *Constructive English* (1923), and G. M. Hyde, *Handbook for Newspaper Workers* (1926). Perhaps Bernstein picked up the topic from Hyde.

Allbutt calls the use "a modern abuse unknown to Samuel Johnson." Unknown to Johnson it certainly was; the earliest OED citation for the "acme" sense is dated 1789. The date, however, suggests that the use was not especially modern even in 1923. Copperud 1970, 1980 and Bryson 1984 tend to think Bernstein a little far-out; they go along with the recognition of the meaning in Evans 1957, Fowler 1965, and all dictionaries. You need not give *climax* a second thought. The etymologically pure meaning exists only as a technical term in rhetoric.

climb 1. *Climb* was originally an irregular verb of the same class as *sing* and *begin*. It began to be used with regular inflections around the 16th century. Webster's Third shows three surviving forms of the old strong inflections for both past and past participle: *clim, clomb, clum*. All are marked as dialectal. The Dictionary of American Regional English shows *clum* (also spelled *clumb*) to be fairly widespread; *clim* is found in the Atlantic states and New England; *clomb* is chiefly Midland. It also reports *clam* as a Southern form used chiefly by blacks. A recent survey of Canadian English (Scargill 1974) found *clumb* still in occasional use there.

Johnson's 1755 dictionary showed *clomb* as the first variant for both past and past participle; *clomb* was used as a rhyme word by both Coleridge and Wordsworth; it turns up in the journals of Lewis and Clark at about the same period (1805). But by the latter part of the 20th century, it dwindled to dialectal use, along with *clim* and *clum(b)*.

> . . . in the night sometime he got powerful thirsty and clumb out on to the porch-roof —Mark Twain, *Huckleberry Finn*, 1884

2. *Climb down, climb up*. Several 20th-century commentators, including Vizetelly 1906, Bierce 1909, and Einstein 1985, have decided that the use of *down* with *climb* (which has been going on since about 1300) must be wrong since *climb* means "to go up." These same writers, along with Bryson 1984, Partridge 1942, and Bernstein 1965, also censure *climb up* (which has been around since 1123) as redundant. But both *climb down* and *climb up* are perfectly idiomatic.

> . . . she began to smile, and MacIver climbed down off the stool —Robert Murphy, *Saturday Evening Post*, 4 Dec. 1954

> . . . the embarrassment . . . to the United States of climbing down from the perch from which we denounced all deals —Michael Straight, *New Republic*, 11 July 1955

> . . . the hills that climb dizzily up from Bernkastel's narrow cobblestone streets —Frank J. Prial, *N.Y. Times*, 3 Nov. 1976

> A major who climbed up to take a look —Burtt Evans, in *The Best from Yank*, 1945

The fact is that *climb* is very frequently used with adverbs, prepositions, and combinations of both, like *down from* and *up from*. Here is a selection of other adverbs and prepositions that the usage experts do not bother to mention:

> West of Iron River US 2 climbs steadily upward —*American Guide Series: Michigan*, 1941

> They exchanged glares and he climbed reluctantly out of the car —Mary Jane Rolfs, *No Vacancy*, 1951

> . . . let me climb out on a limb and tell you what the general sales outlook seems to be —Richard C. Bond, *Toys and Novelties*, March 1954

> . . . has no hesitation about climbing in & out of her filmy clothes —*Time*, 22 June 1953

> . . . temperatures will climb into the upper 70s —*Atlanta Jour.-Constitution*, 19 Sept. 1984

> . . . ivy climbs over the thick white porch columns —*American Guide Series: Louisiana*, 1941

> But after considering, the bear climbed back up —Edward Hoagland, *Harper's*, February 1971

> . . . the world population might climb to the 10,000 million mark —Lord Boyd Orr, *Books of the Month*, April 1953

> . . . climb on a plane in New York —Horace Sutton, *Saturday Rev.*, 2 Jan. 1954

> . . . has been unable to climb above third place —Joel Colton, *Yale Rev.*, March 1954

Those selections should give you a good idea of the adverbs and prepositions that regularly go with *climb*. It is not, however, an exhaustive list. Our advice is to use any of the ones that seem appropriate in a given context.

cling *Cling* is an irregular verb of the same class that *climb* formerly belonged to. It had principal parts analogous to those of *ring: clang, clung. Clang* was the singular form of the past tense; it has dropped out of standard use, although the OED notes it continuing in northern dialect through the 19th century. Presumably people from the northern areas of Great Britain brought it to this country. The Dictionary of American Regional English calls it *archaic*, but it is still around, although it is rare:

> I clang to it —University of Massachusetts undergraduate, in conversation, 19 Nov. 1979

The OED notes some use of the regular inflection *clinged* in the 17th and 18th centuries; by the 19th the OED considered the form dialectal. It, too, is rare but not obsolete:

> Bryant, once up 7–3, clinged . . . to a 7–6 margin —Dick Baker, *Springfield* (Mass.) *Daily News*, 24 Apr. 1980

The majority of us use *clung*:

> He clung to the railing —E. L. Doctorow, *Ragtime*, 1975

> They clung to what gave their status meaning in a desperate embrace of the past —Barbara W. Tuchman, in *The Contemporary Essay*, ed. Donald Hall, 1984

clipped forms See ABBREVIATIONS.

clique The only dispute over *clique* seems to be the appropriateness of the anglicized pronunciation \'klik\ for this word imported from French in the 18th century. By now the anglicized pronunciation must be judged acceptable, even if it is less frequent than \'klēk\.

close proximity This phrase is called redundant by a number of recent commentators such as Harper 1985, Bryson 1984, Macmillan 1982, and Garner 1998. The difficulty is not really a recent discovery: it can be found as far back as Krapp 1927 and Vizetelly 1920. What is interesting is that both the older books recognize that there are degrees of nearness, an idea that recent commentators neglect to mention. *Close proximity* simply emphasizes the closeness. Here are a few examples:

> But then the prospect of a lot
> Of dull M.P.'s in close proximity,
> All thinking for themselves, is what
> No man can face with equanimity
> —W. S. Gilbert, *Iolanthe*, 1882

> Swallow means porch-bird, and for centuries and centuries their nests have been placed in the closest proximity to man —Richard Jefferies, *The Open Air*, 1885

> I'm ever and still amazed that any artist considers himself God or in close proximity thereof —Nikki Giovanni, *Sacred Cows . . . and Other Edibles*, 1988

> In lieu of garages they boasted . . . carports . . . in close proximity to the front door —Brendan Gill, *Architectural Digest*, June 1990

> . . . signing seems to depend on Broca's and Wernicke's areas, which are in close proximity to vocal and auditory areas in the cortex —Steven Pinker, *The Language Instinct*, 1994

cloture Bernstein 1965 disparages *cloture* as an unnecessary word imported from French;

he prefers the more general term *closure*. Bremner 1980 disagrees: "The word is not a fancy word for *closure*. *Cloture* is a parliamentary term for ending debate and voting on a measure." Usage and dictionaries agree with Bremner.

clue See CLEW, CLUE.

coalesce When *coalesce* is used with a preposition, *into* is the one used most often, whatever the sense of the verb:

> Eventually they will coalesce into a single metropolitan area —John Fischer, *Harper's*, April 1972

Less frequently, *coalesce* may be followed by *with* or *in*:

> It was in this way that it coalesced so readily with the anti-rationalistic bias of the historical revolt —Alfred North Whitehead, *Science and the Modern World*, 1925

> . . . hardly soluble problems have coalesced in one problem which solves itself —George Bernard Shaw, *Back to Methuselah*, 1921

When *coalesce* is used to mean "to unite for a common end," it may be also used with *around* or, occasionally, *on*:

> . . . causing a sizable number of party faithful to coalesce around Kennedy —Godfrey Sperling, Jr., *Christian Science Monitor*, 11 Feb. 1980

> . . . the Republican, Democratic, and Liberal Parties coalesced on a candidate —Gus Tyler, *New Republic*, 23 Aug. 1954

coarse, course Chambers 1985 and a couple of schoolbooks discriminate between these two words. Since *coarse* is an adjective and *course* a noun and a verb, there is no serious chance of confusing them in use. This is merely a matter of spelling or careless handwriting that makes *a* and *u* indistinguishable.

coed Bremner 1980 notes that this word was formerly an acceptable word for a female student at a coeducational institution, but is now in disfavor. Our evidence suggests he may be right; at least we have gathered fewer and fewer citations for its use in recent years. This example tends to corroborate Bremner's view:

> At that time it was customary to locate a suitable female spectator (then known as a "coed") —Philip G. Howlett, *Sports Illustrated*, 31 Aug. 1981

The adjective *coed* continues to be used, most often in the sense "open to or used by both men and women."

coequal Bryson 1984 disparages this word as "a fatuous addition to the language." But *coequal* was actually added to the language in the 14th century and has been found useful now for about 600 years.

> A confederacy of coequal, sovereign states had been tried and found wanting —Samuel Eliot Morison & Henry Steele Commager, *The Growth of the American Republic*, 3d ed., 1942

> At one time botany and zoology were roughly coequal in biology at universities —Philip H. Abelson, *Science*, 18 June 1971

> Just as the President and Attorney General did not consider the Court a coequal branch of government —Laura Kalman, *N.Y. Times Book Rev.*, 23 Aug. 1998

It's used as a noun, too:

> By 1970 he had eclipsed Prime Minister Aleksei N. Kosygin, his coequal at the beginning —Craig R. Whitney, *N.Y. Times Mag.*, 10 June 1979

You can use the word without fear. As the examples suggest, *coequal* tends to be used in contexts where the equality is established on some formal basis, and it is frequent in political contexts.

coffin   See CASKET, COFFIN.

cohort   About 1950 people began to notice a new sense of *cohort*, one meaning "companion, colleague, follower." Since then it has spread into a large number of usage books, many of which assert that *cohort* does not mean "companion, colleague, follower" but means rather some subdivision of a Roman legion or "band, company."
How the new sense developed is a bit mysterious. Everybody agrees that it happened in America. From its original meaning of a subdivision of a Roman legion, *cohort* developed a sense "band, company."

> When the day came for Rabbi Silver to be inducted, Harry, with a loyal cohort of adherents, forcibly barred his entrance —S. N. Behrman, *New Yorker*, 1 May 1954

This sense was also used in the plural:

> If the Wood cohorts captured the Ohio delegation for their man, it would follow that Wood's adherents in the state would take over the party machinery —Samuel Hopkins Adams, *Incredible Era*, 1939

The problem with plural use is that it could be understood either as "groups"—as presumably the writer intended—or as "followers, colleagues"—understood as referring to a number of individuals forming one group rather than to a number of groups. Presumably the "companion, colleague, follower" sense developed from people's taking the plural use as referring to individuals.

The new sense was establishing itself by the 1940s. It is too firmly established in American English to be eradicated by commentators demonstrating their knowledge of Roman military organization. Here is a selection of examples from the 1940s to the present:

> With Dickinson and his cohorts perusing it in the meanwhile with critical eyes, it is not difficult to imagine the suffering of the too sensitive author —Claude G. Bowers, *The Young Jefferson, 1743–1789*, 1945

> He also enlisted in the café cohorts of Pablo Picasso —*Time*, 4 Apr. 1949

> It was on the night of Jan. 16, 1938, that Benny Goodman and his now-illustrious cohorts took over Carnegie Hall —*Newsweek*, 18 Dec. 1950

> He was on the phone, talking to Henry Cabot Lodge or Tex McCrary or some such cohort —*New Yorker*, 5 Apr. 1952

> . . . and my special, only technically unassigned cohort grinned up at me —J. D. Salinger, *New Yorker*, 19 Nov. 1955

> Nixon and his cohorts remain targets, not subjects —Max Lerner, *Saturday Rev.*, 29 May 1976

> . . . centralizing the power in the hands of Stalin and his cohorts —Richard Lowenthal, *N.Y. Times Book Rev.*, 3 Feb. 1985

> It falls upon an ex-con and his preening psychotic cohort to execute the caper —Sybil S. Steinberg, *Publishers Weekly*, 20 Mar. 1995

It is possible that the *New Yorker* may have been influential in establishing this sense in sophisticated writing. The use seems to have spread even to British English:

> It is more the pity then that he should use the new American vulgarism of "cohort" meaning "partner" —*Times Literary Supp.*, 25 Nov. 1965

The "new American vulgarism" has firmly established itself in standard use in the past fifty or so years.

coiffeur, coiffure   Both of these words were imported into English from French, *coiffure* in 1631 and *coiffeur* in 1847. They are not new; people should be used to them by now. *Coiffure* is the hairdo; *coiffeur* the hairdresser. All the same, they are sometimes muddled, and we get the hairdresser for the hairdo:

> . . . to model a most un-Beatle-like coiffeur —*People*, 11 June 1984

> . . . that little bounce of hair over the forehead that was the required *coiffeur* of Party

functionaries —Anne McElvoy, *New Republic,* 4 & 11 Jan. 1993

cold slaw, coleslaw Evans 1962 and Reader's Digest 1983 comment on the form *cold slaw* used for *coleslaw. Cold slaw* is an American folk etymology based on the Dutch *kool-sla.* It dates back to 1794 and is about a half century older than the presently much more common and etymologically more accurate *coleslaw.*

Our files show relatively little recent evidence of *cold slaw*'s use in print. It undoubtedly still appears on menus, however, and Garner 1998 has an example from as recently as 1990.

collaborate Einstein 1985 calls *collaborate together* redundant (see REDUNDANCY). We have extremely little evidence that *collaborate* is used with *together.* What we do find is that *collaborate* is frequently used with *in, on,* and *with*:

. . . unless the best minds of its time have collaborated in its construction —T. S. Eliot, "Lancelot Andrewes," *Selected Essays,* 1932

. . . American and Soviet scientists have already collaborated on studies of pollution —Anthony Wolff, *Saturday Rev.,* 17 Apr. 1976

. . . the mere suspicion that they are collaborating with their clients in activities of a criminal gang nature —John Dornberg, *Saturday Rev.,* 10 June 1978

With is often used with either *in* or *on* in the pattern "collaborate with someone in (or on) something":

. . . to collaborate with his old friend Howard Hawks on a screenplay —Bennett Cerf, *Saturday Rev.,* 26 Dec. 1953

At is also possible:

. . . repudiated Nixon's suggestion that they were collaborating at the job in the last months of 1968 —Garry Wills, *Harper's,* January 1972

collectable, collectible Janis 1984 reports a tendency toward differentiation between these spellings. He says that *collectable* is being used more as an adjective in relation to bills, while *collectible* is being used as a noun for things like glassware, furniture, political campaign buttons, and posters that are collected. Our evidence does not corroborate his observation. We find that both *collectible* and *collectable* are used as nouns for items to be collected, with *collectible* the more frequent spelling. We find both spellings used for the adjective, again with *collectible* more frequent. You can use whichever spelling you prefer.

collective Copperud 1964, 1970, 1980 cocks an individual snook at the use of the adjective *collective* in such uses as "industry has its collective eye on Washington" and "experts cocked their collective eyebrow at the prediction." This use of *collective* in the sense "shared by all members of a group" is owing to the writer's intention of extending a figure of speech normally associated with an individual to a group. It is in frequent and unnoticed use with many nonanatomical nouns:

. . . the most fantastic outburst of collective insanity —Noam Chomsky, *Columbia Forum,* Winter 1969

. . . a collective shudder swept across the city —Robert Bloch, *Cosmopolitan,* November 1972

. . . we can almost hear the bobby-soxers in the listening audience offer a collective swoon —Mel Gussow, *N.Y. Times,* 30 Nov. 1979

. . . good for our collective health —Albert Rosenfeld, *Saturday Rev.,* 14 Oct. 1978

When the figure of speech involves an anatomical noun, Copperud takes disapproving notice, but the usage is not really different.

The effulgent reality is in the collective brain —Anthony Burgess, *Saturday Rev.,* 2 Sept. 1978

. . . or even to scratch their collective head —Stringfellow Barr, *Center Mag.,* May 1968

If you feel the urge to use this sort of figurative expression, we advise you to keep the noun modified by *collective* in the singular. Notice that the plural noun in the following two examples makes *collective* unnecessary:

. . . if we hide our collective heads in the sand —James V. McConnell, *Psychology Today,* April 1970

. . . the promises . . . that flowed so trippingly off their collective tongues —*Women's Wear Daily,* 26 Mar. 1973

collective nouns 1. *Subject-verb agreement.* Collective nouns—singular nouns that stand for a number of persons or things considered as a group—have had the characteristic of being used with both singular and plural verbs since Middle English. The principle involved—referred to elsewhere in this book as notional agreement—is simple: when the group is considered as a unit, the singular verb is used; when it is thought of as a collection of individuals, the plural verb is used. All grammarians and usage commentators agree on the basic principle.

Chambers 1985 points out that one class of collective nouns—those like *baggage, cutlery, dinnerware* that stand for a collection of inanimate objects—can be omitted from consideration; they are regularly singular:

> Your luggage has been sent to Kansas City by mistake.

Those commentators who mention British–American differences agree in general that singular verbs are more common in American English and plural verbs more common in British English. Beyond this generality it can be unsafe to venture; where notional agreement operates, there are no absolutes. For instance, Bryant 1962 states that British usage employs the plural verb with *government*:

> In effect the Government are facing three distinct crises —David Basnett, *The Times* (London), 17 Dec. 1973

But though the plural verb with *government* is usual, it is not universal:

> . . . the Government has already made it clear —*The Economist,* 15 Feb. 1975

The difference in British and American usage may be illustrated by the word *family.* While Mittins et al. 1970 report a surprising amount of resistance in their survey to "his family are in Bournemouth," our evidence suggests that the plural verb is quite a bit more common in British English:

> I hope all the family are in a convalescent State —Lord Byron, letter, 12 Nov. 1805

> The family were not consumptive —Jane Austen, *Mansfield Park,* 1814

> . . . the Royal Family take the train —Carol Wright, *In Britain,* June 1974

> My family are nearly all gone —Sir John Gielgud, quoted in *People,* 19 Oct. 1981

But there is also singular use:

> . . . to determine where, for legal purposes, a family ends —Edward Jenks, *The Book of English Law,* 5th ed., 1953

> The modern family is increasingly to be viewed as the family of procreation —Peter G. Hollowell, *The Lorry Driver,* 1968

Quirk et al. 1985 say that in British English the plural verb is more frequently used with collective nouns in speaking than in writing. In American English, the singular verb is more common:

> The family includes a poodle —*TV Guide,* 23 Apr. 1954

> The family was a closely-knit one —*Current Biography,* September 1964

> A last family is leaving —Alice Mattison, *New Yorker,* 10 June 1985

But the plural verb is not at all rare:

> His family were enormously wealthy —F. Scott Fitzgerald, *The Great Gatsby,* 1925

> . . . checked with her family, who prefer the latter spelling —Erich Segal, *N.Y. Times Book Rev.,* 3 June 1984

Two areas often singled out to illustrate British–American differences are politics and sports: Quirk and Harper 1985, for instance, mention both. In British English terms like *Parliament, public, government, committee* are frequently used with plural verbs; the same (and similar) terms in American English are more likely to be used with singular verbs. The contrast in sports comes when the name of a city (or country) is used as the name of a team. A British headline might read

> Liverpool triumph over Swansea

while its American counterpart might read

> Oakland defeats Baltimore

2. *Pronoun agreement.* Collective nouns are often referred to by plural pronouns, though singular in form. This characteristic, too, is ascribable to the operation of notional agreement. A handful of examples:

> . . . Laurel's government moved to northern Luzon and in March they were flown to Tokyo —*Current Biography,* June 1953

> . . . the party, who at his suggestion, now seated themselves —Jane Austen, *Mansfield Park,* 1814

> The main difficulty with the South is that they are living eighty years behind the times —Harry S. Truman, letter, 18 Aug. 1948

Copperud 1970 lists a half dozen commentators who agree that writers should take care to match their pronouns and verbs, singular with singular, plural with plural. Evidence shows that writers have sometimes adhered to this policy and sometimes ignored it. Here are some examples of the approved practice.
Plural verb, plural pronoun:

> The Norton family have featured some of the greatest entertainers of all time at their park —Thomas J. Smith, *Yankee,* July 1968

> One thing the God-fearing Scandinavian and German stock of Wisconsin obviously like about their senior senator —Peter Ross Range, *Cosmopolitan,* December 1978

Singular verb, singular pronoun:

> . . . the majority does not necessarily trust in the correctness of its own language —Finegan 1980

. . . an enemy which is as pitiful as it is vicious —*N.Y. Herald Tribune Book Rev.,* 28 Sept. 1952

When verb and pronouns do not match, it is usually that a plural pronoun is being used after a singular verb; the reverse mismatch is highly unlikely. A collective noun with singular verb and plural pronoun exhibits the same pattern as many indefinite pronouns (see AGREEMENT, INDEFINITE PRONOUNS):

. . . no example of a nation that has preserved their words and phrases from mutability —Samuel Johnson, preface to the Dictionary, 1755

The entire diplomatic class has, in my forty years of acquaintance with them —Henry Adams, letter, 1 Feb. 1900

. . . a cross-section of the public is interviewed each day about their listening —*BBC Year Book 1952*

What industry now fears is that the government will move into their plants —*Newsweek,* 18 Aug. 1952

3. A collective noun followed by *of* and a plural noun (Curme 1931 calls this a "partitive group") follows the same notional agreement as collective nouns in general. Thus we find James J. Kilpatrick (*Pittsburgh Press Sunday Mag.,* 11 Aug. 1985) expressing approval of the use of a plural verb in a sentence beginning "A rash of stories"—the notion is clearly plural. Here are a few other examples:

Whether the higher order of seraphim illuminati ever *sneer?* —Charles Lamb, letter, 28 July 1798

. . . the only lodge of Christians who never try to get us barred off the newsstands —H. L. Mencken, letter, in *The Intimate Notebooks of George Jean Nathan,* 1932

The great majority of marriages that go on the rocks are those contracted in earlier years —George Jean Nathan, *Testament of a Critic,* 1931

When the idea of oneness or wholeness is stressed, the verb is singular:

The bulk of the stories by new writers is fairly dull —Valentine Cunningham, *Times Literary Supp.,* 13 Aug. 1976

4. See also AGREEMENT: ORGANIZATIONS CONSIDERED AS COLLECTIVE NOUNS; AGREEMENT, SUBJECT-VERB: A BUNCH OF THE BOYS; NOTIONAL AGREEMENT, NOTIONAL CONCORD.

collide It is a tradition for newspaper editors—or at least those who write usage books—to believe that *collide* can only be used when both objects in the encounter are moving. The notion can be found in Bryson 1984, who probably got it from Bernstein 1958, 1965, or 1977, or from various *Winners & Sinners* going back at least to 1955, and Bernstein may well have gotten it from G. M. Hyde's *Handbook for Newspaper Workers* (1926). Hyde may have picked it up from William Cullen Bryant; *collided* appears without explanation in his *Index Expurgatorius,* compiled during his years as a newspaper editor in New York and first published in 1877.

The OED notes that when *collide* came to be used of train and ship accidents the usage was widely disparaged as an Americanism. Schele de Vere, *Americanisms* (1872), is aware of this criticism, but says *collide* is a good English word. (He also says the British prefer *to collision,* a verb not attested in the OED.) Schele de Vere includes the notion of two bodies in motion in his definition of the word. Where he got the notion is uncertain; it is not implicit in the etymology of the word, and most 19th-century dictionaries did not include it. There seems to be little historical basis for the insistence and Burchfield 1996 says flatly that there is no basis for it.

Our citations for the literal sense of *collide* that come from sources other than newspaper accounts of plane, train, ship, or automobile accidents show that it is usually celestial objects, particles, vehicles, and people that tend to collide. In some instances—as with celestial objects and particles—it is clear that all bodies are in motion. In some instances it is not clear, and in others one object appears to be stationary. Here are two examples of the last type:

. . . short time it took Mr. Phelps to dodge inside the library, skid into the librarian, upset a stack of books, wreck a fernery and collide with The Mudhen at a table —*Boy's Life,* March 1953

The hawk turned and stooped, only to collide with some bushes under which the duck had managed to find shelter —Edward A. Armstrong, *Bird Display and Behaviour,* 2d ed., 1947

By far the greatest number of our citations for *collide* are figurative, in which ideologies, politicians, nations, searing glances, and the like collide. In these uses relative motion is not a consideration. We thus suspect that you will seldom have to worry about this matter. If you do, you may be assured that *collide* is standard, even when only one body is in motion.

colloquial *Colloquial* is an adjective evidently introduced into English by Samuel Johnson, even though he did not enter the word in his 1755 dictionary. Its first meaning is "conversational":

> . . . I found him highly satisfied with his colloquial prowess the preceding evening. "Well," said he, "we had a good talk." BOSWELL. "Yes, sir; you tossed and gored several persons." —James Boswell, *Life of Samuel Johnson,* 1791

According to OED evidence, Johnson introduced this sense in a paper in *The Rambler* in 1751; in 1752 he used the now more familiar sense "characteristic of familiar conversation" in another number of *The Rambler*. Boswell again echoes Johnson's use:

> But Johnson was at all times jealous of infractions upon the genuine English language, and prompt to repress colloquial barbarisms —*Life of Samuel Johnson,* 1791

It is this sense that has come to be used as a label by writers on language and by dictionaries.

One early combination involving *colloquial* that is found in the writings of grammarians is the phrase *colloquial speech*. The phrase designated ordinary conversational speech—the sort of talk you would engage in as part of any gathering—at a party, on the street corner, at the country store, or at the dinner table. It was contrasted with what was sometimes called *platform speech*. Platform speech was an artificially articulated version of English intended to make a speaker understood at a distance; it was the customary form of English for politicians and preachers addressing large audiences. The development of electronic public-address systems and radio and television has essentially eliminated the need for platform speech. We hear our preachers and politicians today speaking in a more ordinary—colloquial—way.

Colloquial, however, was probably a poor choice of term for describing ordinary everyday speech. It is a learned term and, especially in its abbreviated form *colloq.,* removed from everyday connotations. It is not surprising, really, that it was misunderstood as a pejorative label, in spite of the fact that dictionaries using the label were at pains to explain that it was not pejorative. The misunderstanding became so widespread that many dictionaries and handbooks abandoned the label altogether. The editors of Webster's Third decided not to try to distinguish the standard written from the standard spoken language. Other dictionaries and handbooks replaced *colloquial* with other labels, of which *informal* is the most common.

That *colloquial* is widely assumed to be pejorative is amply attested:

> All colloquial expressions are little foxes that spoil the grapes of perfect diction —Emily Post, *Etiquette,* 1927

> . . . the use of *like* as a conjunction. It *was* colloquial; it is now correct —Clifton Fadiman, *Holiday,* March 1957

> The tone is informal but not colloquial or condescending —Delores McColm, *Library Jour.* 15 May 1966

> I'm glad we took into full membership all sorts of robust words that previous dictionaries had derided as "colloquial" —Zinsser 1976

It would have been bad enough that the general public and schoolteachers misinterpreted *colloquial,* but there is abundant evidence that it was likewise misinterpreted by writers on usage—sometimes in spite of their explanations to the contrary. Here is one example:

> COLLOQUIAL Commonly used in speech but inappropriate in all but the most informal writing —Prentice Hall 1978

> **anyplace** Colloquial for *any place* —Prentice Hall 1978

Since the blank space between *any* and *place* has no sound, it cannot be detected in speech, and therefore it is meaningless to say that *anyplace* is "commonly used in speech"; *anyplace* and *any place* simply sound the same in the same environment. As applied to *anyplace,* therefore, *colloquial* is being used as some sort of stigmatizing label, and the intention is that the reader of the book avoid *anyplace* and use *any place*.

The use of *colloquial* with pejorative overtones is fairly common with usage writers:

> . . . must be considered at best colloquial —Bryson 1984

> **as.** (1) Highly colloquial when used in place of *that* or *whether* —Macmillan 1982

> Whether "plenty" is being used here as an adjective or an adverb, it is colloquial —Bernstein 1958

> *Out loud* is thought to be both unidiomatic and colloquial —Shaw 1970

> **prepositions often criticized.** . . . . *Back of* for *behind* . . . , *inside of* for *within* . . . , and *over with* for *over* . . . are colloquial —Guth 1985

> *Aggravate* should not be used in its colloquial meaning of "irritate" or "exasperate" —Little, Brown 1986

> *So* for *True* . . . . "Is that so?" Colloquial and worse —Bierce 1909

Perhaps some of the taint of Dr. Johnson's "colloquial barbarisms" has rubbed off on *colloquial*. If you see the term used regularly in a handbook or other book on usage, you can be reasonably sure it is thought of as disparaging by the author, no matter what explanation is attached to it when (and if) the term is explained.

collusion From the time of Samuel Johnson's 1755 dictionary and even before, *collusion* has been defined to show that it involves practices that are underhanded, deceptive, dishonest, or illegal. Typical uses look like these:

> He knew that every bill for gasoline, oil, tires, and overhauling was padded, that the chauffeur was in collusion with the garage owner for this purpose —Thomas Wolfe, *You Can't Go Home Again,* 1940

> They suspected with some justification . . . collusion between the French and British and the internal enemies of Bolshevism —George F. Kennan, *Soviet Foreign Policy, 1917–1941,* 1960

From Fowler 1926 to Bryson 1984 usage commentators have warned against the use of *collusion* in a weakened sense where *cooperation, concert,* or *collaboration* might do. Such use is typically labeled "confusion," but from our evidence it is clear that there is usually no confusion. *Collusion* seems to have been chosen for its effect:

> By collusion of nature and riotous living he was an extremely ugly man —Florette Henri, *Kings Mountain,* 1950

> . . . this escapade, achieved with the unwitting collusion of their grandmother —*Current Biography 1948*

> Probably it is blowing the whistle to reveal collusion between these competitors, but they did achieve a happy arrangement —Red Smith, *N.Y. Times,* 17 Mar. 1978

> . . . one of those authors who seem to write almost in collusion with their audience —Anatole Broyard, *N.Y. Times Book Rev.,* 9 Mar. 1986

In these examples, where nothing really underhanded or dishonest is going on, *collusion* has been chosen for an effect, such as irony or humor. But examples like these are not especially frequent; most writers use *collusion* in a straightforward way. Our suggestion to you is not to use *collusion* for effect unless you are certain that the effect will be perfectly plain to everybody. If your context allows the understanding that you simply avoided *collaboration* or *cooperation,* some readers will think you have made a mistake.

colored Janis 1984 notes that *black* and *Negro* are preferred to *colored* and the Oxford American Dictionary suggests that *colored* is sometimes offensive. The term was, some years ago, a common, relatively neutral term used to refer to black Americans. The reasons for its falling into relative disuse are not entirely clear, but there is no question that it has happened:

> I was "colored" until I was 14, a Negro until I was 21 and a black man ever since —Reggie Jackson, quoted in *Sports Illustrated,* 11 May 1987

Aside from specialized references to South Africa, most of our evidence for *colored* as a term of racial reference refers to a time in the past:

> White Morrisonville's hog-meat diet hadn't prepared me for terrapin soup. I hurried back across the road giggling to my mother that colored people ate turtles —Russell Baker, *Growing Up,* 1982

Once in a while it may be still found in neutral reference:

> She reminds people of the beauty of being colored. Katoucha is African —*Vogue,* February 1985

Presently, however, you are more likely to find *persons of color* than *colored persons.*

See also BLACK.

come and See TRY AND.

comic, comical A number of commentators hasten to distinguish between these words, generally on the grounds that *comic* applies to what is intentionally funny and *comical* to what is unintentionally funny. Most of these commentators also note some interchangeability of the two; Chambers 1985, for instance, notes some usurping of *comical*'s territory by *comic.* Copperud 1970 notes that dictionaries do not make the same distinction. The dictionaries are closer to reality than the commentators, whose analysis fails in two points. First, *comic* is a much more common word than *comical.* Being more familiar, *comic* tends to be used in places where *comical* might have been chosen. And second, the distinction the commentators draw is somewhat off base. Such distinction as there is rests on the fact that while *comic* can be used of anything that is funny, *comical* tends to be used of what is funny by reason of being unexpected or startling. *Comic* is the all-purpose adjective for comedy; *comical* is not used in that way. *Comic* may stress thoughtful amusement; *comical* spontaneous, unrestrained hilarity. Here are examples of each:

> . . . with but the smallest twist, Gladstone's words and actions can be transformed from Victorian gold into comic lead —Sheldon Rothblatt, *N.Y. Times Book Rev.,* 5 Aug. 1984

> . . . a constant sad and funny picture too. It is the knight that goes out to defend some-

body who don't want to be defended. . . . It is comical and a little sad —William Faulkner, 13 May 1957, in *Faulkner in the University,* 1959

These aren't cheerful tales, though they're often sharp and grotesquely comic —*Times Literary Supp.,* 23 Apr. 1970

. . . he looked so comical that some of the natives laughed —*Boy's Life,* June 1953

comma A great deal of space is devoted in many handbooks to the various standard uses of the comma. Since this information is so widely available—in Merriam-Webster's Collegiate Dictionary, *Merriam-Webster's Manual for Writers and Editors,* among other sound guides—we will not repeat it here. There is also a good deal of comment on the use or nonuse of a comma before the coordinating conjunction in a series of three or more. In spite of all the discussion, practice boils down to the writer's personal preference, or sometimes a house or organizational style. Additional comment is not needed. There are, however, a few other issues involving the comma.

1. See COMMA FAULT.

2. Comma between subject and predicate. It is no longer cricket to separate the subject and predicate with punctuation. "How," asks Simon 1980 rhetorically, "can one possibly separate the subject . . . from the predicate . . . by a comma?" The comma between subject and predicate is an old convention that has fallen into disuse and disfavor. It was common in the 18th century:

What Methods they will take, is not for me to prescribe —Jonathan Swift, "A Proposal for Correcting, Improving and Ascertaining the English Tongue," 1712

The first thing to be studied here, is grammatical propriety —Murray 1795

This comma is now universally frowned on and tends to be found only as a vice of comic-strip writers, advertisers, and others who are not on their guard. You should avoid the practice.

comma blunder, comma error See COMMA FAULT.

comma fault Comma fault is one of the names (others are *comma splice, comma blunder, comma error*) that composition teachers give to the joining of two independent clauses by a comma alone. It is one species of run-on sentence and has been denounced as an error at least since MacCracken & Sandison 1917. The modern comma fault seems to be a survivor from an older, looser form of punctuation:

As to the old one, I knew not what to do with him, he was so fierce I durst not go into the pit to him —Daniel Defoe, *Robinson Crusoe,* 1719

Why, sure *Betty,* thou art bewitcht, this cream is burnt too —Jonathan Swift, *Polite Conversation,* 1738

The New Jersey job was obtained, I contrived a copperplate press for it —Benjamin Franklin, *Autobiography,* 1771

These examples were not considered faulty when they were written, as 18th-century punctuation did not follow the conventions that we practice today. But even as the standards of punctuation were evolving during the 19th century to those we are familiar with, the older, looser punctuation continued to be employed in personal letters:

I have found your white mittens, they were folded up within my clean nightcap —Jane Austen, letter, 24 Aug. 1805

It is not necessary for Miss M. to be an authoress, indeed I do not think publishing at all creditable either to men or women —Lord Byron, letter, 1 May 1812

Well, I won't talk about myself, it is not a healthy topic —Lewis Carroll, letter, 29(?) July 1885

The epistolary comma fault continued into the 20th century:

This is a big picture as it has a million dollar budget and I think it is going to be a good one, it will be some time before it is finished —Ronald Reagan, letter, 2 Aug. 1938

Tell Johnny to read Santayana for a little while, it will improve his sentence structure —E. B. White, letter, 11 Mar. 1963

It seems most probable that the origin of the comma splice is the use of the comma to represent a relatively brief pause in speech. Further evidence for this hypothesis can be found in modern transcriptions of speech. In the next example, the speech is fictitious:

The Ambassador . . . responded with a blast of enthusiasm. "Those weren't tough questions, those were kid-glove questions. . . ." —John Updike, *Bech Is Back,* 1982

The two independent clauses beginning with *those* would have been spoken so rapidly that any punctuation other than a comma would hardly have been possible. The comma similarly turns up in transcriptions of actual speech:

The Encyclopaedia Britannica lives off installment buying, this is our whole business

—William Benton, quoted in Studs Terkel, *Hard Times,* 1970

And I thought, 'Oh my God, my bosoms are being seen for God's sake, I can't stand it!' —Jacqueline Bisset, quoted in *Cosmopolitan* (London), October 1974

Composition teachers, however, are rather more concerned with inadvertent comma faults that creep into student papers in ordinary expository prose. It is probably a tribute to these teachers that uncorrected examples are so hard to find in print. The example we show you below comes from a specialized journal more concerned with the dissemination of information than with literary values. It also, the sharp-eyed will note, contains a misspelling.

An unusual and beautiful coiffeur is not all that embellishes Daisy, she also has very long thick eye lashes and thin, flat, elongated nostrils —*Chronicle of the Horse,* 16 Mar. 1984

The comma fault in discursive prose is sometimes purposely used by writers for stylistic effect. As a device it can be found in the fiction of William Faulkner, Edna Ferber, E. L. Doctorow, and many others. You probably should not try the device unless you are very sure of what you want it to accomplish. Here are three examples:

Orvie was being very helpful, he organized dances and games, he had passed plates of chicken and ice cream, he danced with some of the more awful wives —Edna Ferber, *Come and Get It,* 1935

If I came in early I distracted them, if I came in late I enraged them, it was my life they resented, the juicy fullness of being they couldn't abide —E. L. Doctorow, *Loon Lake,* 1979

Her face is intelligent. The hair is somewhere between strawberry and gold, you can't tell in this light —Jay McInerney, *Bright Lights, Big City,* 1984

comma splice See COMMA FAULT.

commence *Commence* has come in for various kinds of criticism since the middle of the 19th century. There were originally three objections, of which only one survives. That objection was started by Alford 1866. He objected to the frequent use in the newspapers of *commence* where *begin* might have served. He was also plagued by printers changing his *begin*s in church announcements to *commence*s. Apparently *commence* was popular with journalists and printers at the time, but the Dean preferred *begin*. Ayres 1881 also opted for *begin,* as did Bierce 1909 and many subsequent commentators down to Janis 1984, Einstein 1985, and Garner 1998. A few distinguish *commence* and *begin* and often *start.* The consensus of those who compare is that *commence* is more formal. Other commentators supply other labels: Janis 1984 calls it "pretentious," Bryson 1984 "an unnecessary genteelism," Copperud 1970, 1980 "old-fashioned and inappropriate." Longman 1984 "bookish or pedantic."

There is a grain of truth in all these comments, but they should not be too insistently urged. The word has, after all, been in regular use in English since the 14th century, and it is not surprising that it has been used by writers of every stripe, from the artless to the humorous to the pedantic. It has been used to make fun of stuffed shirts:

MOCKMODE. . . . our friendship commenced in the college-cellar, and we loved one another like two brothers, till we unluckily fell out afterwards at a game at tables —George Farquhar, *Love and a Bottle,* 1698

. . . things never began with Mr. Borthrop Trumbull; they always commenced —George Eliot (in Longman 1984)

How to begin—or, as we professionals would say, "how to commence" —Ring Lardner, preface, *How to Write Short Stories,* 1924

It was part of the arsenal of 19th-century American humorists:

Directly I spy the heathens they commence takin' on, and the spirit it begin to move 'em, they gin to kinda groan and whine —William C. Hall, "How Sally Hooter Got Snakebit," 1850, in *The Mirth of a Nation,* ed. Walter Blair & Raven I. McDavid, Jr., 1983

. . . after she commenced her miserable gift of the gab —Frances Lee Pratt, "Captain Ben's Choice," in *Mark Twain's Library of Humor,* 1888

It is also used by writers in a serious vein:

His friendship with Arbuthnot was just now commencing —Sir Walter Scott, footnote in Swift's *Journal to Stella,* 1824

Before Webster commenced his tinkering, the spelling of those two hundred words, however irregular to his apprehension, was more uniform than probably it will ever be again —Gould 1870

The Report was an aid to my stopping a two-pack-a-day habit which commenced in early infancy —William Styron, *This Quiet Dust and Other Writings,* 1982

And in ordinary fiction:

> The ruggedness vanishes as quickly as it commenced in the east —Ernest K. Gann, *Fate Is the Hunter*, 1961

> At eleven-thirty he would dash through the city room to commence drinking his lunch —Gregory McDonald, *Fletch*, 1974

Some of our recent evidence shows that *begin* is used almost fifty times as often as *commence*; there is no danger of *commence* being overused. You need not routinely change it to *begin* or *start*.

commend When *commend* means "praise," it is usually used in the pattern "commend someone for" or "commend someone on":

> . . . his wife seriously commended Mr Collins for having spoken so sensibly —Jane Austen, *Pride and Prejudice*, 1813

> . . . commended her for her beautiful grasp and projection of the role —*Current Biography*, April 1966

> . . . commended the membership on carrying on a half-million dollar operation with a quarter-million dollar budget —George W. Corrigan, *Connecticut Teacher*, April 1963

When it means "entrust" or "recommend," the pattern is usually "commend someone or something to":

> Richard had commended her to the care of Lord Mountfalcon —George Meredith, *The Ordeal of Richard Feverel*, 1859

> . . . a university don . . . who had ventured to commend "Leaves of Grass" to the young gentlemen of his seminary —H. L. Mencken, *Prejudices: Second Series*, 1920

> These two counts alone are sufficient to commend the authors to the wise and wary —Oscar Cargill, *CEA Critic*, March 1971

commensurate *Commensurate*, when followed by a preposition, usually takes *with*:

> They say only gracious things, commensurate with the gratitude and exaltation they feel —John Updike, *Harper's*, July 1972

> . . . to project their voices at a volume commensurate with the music —Molly Haskell, *Saturday Rev.*, 30 Oct. 1971

It is sometimes also used with *to*:

> . . . face to face for the last time in history with something commensurate to his capacity for wonder —Richard Poirier, *A World Elsewhere*, 1966

commentate *Commentate* is a back-formation from *commentator*; it was first used as a transitive verb in the late 18th century and then as an intransitive verb in the early 19th. A number of American writers on usage over the past half century have taken umbrage at its use. We have Shaw 1970, Bremner 1980, Janis 1984, and Harper 1985, all registering their disapproval. Garner 1998 differentiates between *commentate* and *comment*, but finds it grandiose applied to journalists who cover sporting events. We know of no British denigration of the word, however.

Commentate is generally not used in quite the same way as *comment*, which is often recommended in its place; it tends to refer to the making of an extended, even systematic commentary or to the presentation of commentary on a regular basis rather than to scattered briefer comments. Some examples:

> Commentate upon it, and return it enriched —Charles Lamb (in Webster 1909)

> Raymond Moley, after seven months of professorial commentating, decided to call it quits —*Time*, 1 Oct. 1945

> . . . Weekend's Helen Gougeon commentated at yesterday's Fur Fashion Award Show —Harriet Hill, *The Gazette* (Montreal), 15 Apr. 1953

> . . . Stanley Marcus . . . will commentate the winning citations —Arnold Gingrich, *Esquire*, January 1974

> There is a very true blue and pukka British centaur called Dorian Williams who always commentates on horsefests —Philip Howard, *Verbatim*, Autumn 1980

> Bradley branched out into TV land, commentating on basketball and producing essays for CBS —Matt Bai, *Newsweek*, 15 Nov. 1999

> . . . Boomer Esiason decided that Monday-night commentating was healthier than Cincinnati Bengals quarterbacking —*Sports Illustrated*, 26 Jan. 1998

commiserate At one time language commentators warned against using a preposition with *commiserate*. While the transitive use of *commiserate* is still in evidence, the intransitive use followed by *with* is now somewhat more common:

> . . . conjoin to commiserate as well as to promote the teaching assistant's cause —Ann M. Heiss, *AAUP Bulletin*, December 1969

> . . . before my trip New Yorkers commiserated with me —David Butwin, *Saturday Rev.*, 3 Apr. 1971.

> . . . I commiserated with her once about the great lost fortune —Russell Baker, *Growing Up*, 1982

Commiserate is also used with *over*:

> . . . white liberals, who commiserate today over being excluded from the "Movement" —Harvey Wheeler, *Saturday Rev.*, 11 May 1968

committee *Committee* is one of those collective nouns that are much more often used with a plural verb in British English than in American English. See COLLECTIVE NOUNS.

common See MUTUAL, COMMON.

commune The verb *commune*, in modern use, is almost always intransitive and followed by *with*:

> His very capacity to commune with peasant villagers —John K. Fairbank, *N.Y. Times Book Rev.*, 28 Aug. 1977

> . . . they commune briefly with their only child —Winthrop Sargeant, *New Yorker*, 1 Apr. 1972

An older combination may be seen in the following:

> They had much earnest conversation, freely communing on the highest matters —Thomas Carlyle, *The Life of John Sterling*, 1851

communicate One of our older handbooks, Raub 1897, says that *communicate* should be followed by *to* for a singular noun and by *with* for a plural. Our evidence shows *with* in most cases, singular or plural, but *to* is still in idiomatic use.

> . . . how could Moses communicate to him that the thread of a woman's life might depend on his consideration? —John Cheever, *The Wapshot Chronicle*, 1957

> . . . Cynthia forced Cabot to communicate with her entirely through the keyhole —James Purdy, *Cabot Wright Begins*, 1964

> Now if you wish to communicate with someone —Huntington Hartford, *American Mercury*, March 1955

> Suppose . . . that there are actually human beings existing in our midst who are able to communicate with each other in this spin-off of the mother tongue —Thomas H. Middleton, *Saturday Rev.*, 16 Oct. 1976

comparable See INCOMPARABLE.

comparative See DOUBLE COMPARISON; IMPLICIT COMPARATIVE; SUPERLATIVE OF TWO.

comparatively The question raised about this adverb by commentators is whether it should be used when no comparison is stated or implied:

> I went into the Plymouth Theatre a comparatively young woman, and I staggered out of it, three hours later, twenty years older —Dorothy Parker, *Vanity Fair*, December 1918

> Condoling with the mourners for the dead, and sympathizing with the severely wounded, I congratulate you that the number of both is comparatively small —Abraham Lincoln, "Message to the Army of the Potomac," 22 Dec. 1862

The realization that a question exists does not seem to have come until Gowers 1948, some 30 years after Dorothy Parker wrote and 86 after Lincoln. As these venerable quotations show, the disapproved use was established long before Gowers supposed it to be a problem Gowers inserted his 1948 discussion into Fowler 1965, from where it got into numerous other usage books. Burchfield 1996, revising Fowler again, doesn't understand why Gowers thought anything was wrong with the use. Neither do we. This use of *comparatively* is standard, and you need not worry about it. See also RELATIVELY, similarly treated by the same critics.

compare to, compare with Our files contain slips from about 50 commentators who are all eager to explain the difference between *compare to* and *compare with*. Their basic rule is easy to state: when you mean "to liken," use *compare to*; when you mean "to examine so as to discover the resemblances and differences," use *compare with*. Raub 1897 put it more succinctly: "Compare *with* in quality, *to* for illustration." The real world of discourse, however, is not as tidy as the rule. Part of the problem can be seen in the initial summing up: how different is "liken" from "examine to discover resemblances"? Not very, and in practice *compare* is frequently used in such a way as to make the distinction between senses uncertain, a fact commented upon as long ago as Fowler 1926.

Back in 1947 a Mr. Bernstein wrote a letter to the editor of *Word Study*, published by Merriam-Webster, objecting to a *compare to* that he thought should, on the basis of Fowler and Webster's Second, be *compare with*. The editor undertook an examination of the evidence then in the files and discovered considerable variance from the prescribed rule. He found no more than 55% observing the rule for the "liken" sense and an even split between *with* and *to* in the "examine" sense. (He also discovered that the basic distinction was first set down in the 1847 Webster unabridged.)

How do things stand some 50 years later? Without attempting statistics, we think we can give you a clear notion by examining the citations a little differently than the *Word Study* editor did in 1947.

First we will look at the active verb. For the

"liken" sense, the basic rule prescribes *compare to*. Shakespeare's Sonnet XVIII is frequently set forth as an example:

Shall I compare thee to a summer's day? —1609

Modern speakers and writers have not abandoned the rule:

I know Patrick doesn't care about being compared to anybody. He's his own self —Moses Malone, quoted in *Springfield* (Mass.) *Sunday Republican,* 1 Dec. 1985

Mr. Ridley is surely not just to compare what Henry did to convicted felons in 38 years of rule to what Hitler did to innocent civilians —Maureen Quilligan, *N.Y. Times Book Rev.,* 11 Aug. 1985

. . . to be compared to Homer passed the time pleasantly —William Butler Yeats, *The Trembling of the Veil,* 1922

Some writers—they are a minority—use *with*:

Though Irwin is often compared with both Chaplin and Keaton as a silent clown, he is actually closer in attitude to Harold Lloyd —Mel Gussow, *New Yorker,* 11 Nov. 1985

. . . the first poem in which images seen are compared with sounds heard —Stephen Spender, *New Republic,* 2 Feb. 1953

So when *compare* is an active verb used in the "liken" sense, the basic rule is more often observed than not.

When *compare* is an active verb and used in the sense "examine so as to discover resemblances and differences," there is more variation in practice. Our citations show that more writers use *with* (as the basic rule prescribes) than use *to,* but the numerical difference between the majority and the minority is not as great as for the "liken" sense. Here are some examples from both groups:

Comparing himself physically with Keaton, he said, "My body is this sort of long spaghetti noodle and his was like a whippet." —Mel Gussow, *New Yorker,* 11 Nov. 1985

. . . of the other three only Susana could be compared to her ancestors in vital fiber —George Santayana, *Persons and Places,* 1944

We can conclude, then, that when *compare* is used as an active verb in the "examine" sense, the basic rule calling for *with* is more often observed than not, but quite a few writers use *to.* One other point should be mentioned: the possibility of uncertainty as to which sense of *compare* a writer has intended. Look at this example:

Mr. Eliot compares them in their possible wide effectiveness with the present body of segregated intellectuals who now write only for each other —Lionel Trilling, *Partisan Rev.,* September–October 1940

If *compare* can be used as an active verb in such a way that we cannot be sure which sense is intended, when *compared* is used as a detached past participle, sometimes introduced by *as,* it is much harder to try to distinguish between the prescribed *to* and *with* senses. Fowler 1926 was the first to take note of this fact. He puts it this way:

Compared with, or *to, him I am a bungler* (this is a common type in which either sense is applicable).

More recently we find James J. Kilpatrick observing:

I will never in my life comprehend the distinction between *compared to* and *compared with.* My ear hears nothing amiss in "This year's corn crop, compared *to* last year's," or in "This year's corn crop, compared *with* last year's." —Kilpatrick 1984

Our files show that *with* and *to* are used about equally after the past participle.

American text treatments are conservative, compared with ours —Allen Hutt, *Newspaper Design,* 2d ed., 1971

So much of the action of hockey was freewheeling, imaginative, instinctive, as compared to football with its precise routes and exact assignments —George Plimpton, *Sports Illustrated,* 30 Jan. 1978

. . . political thinking in the United States is skewed sharply to the right as compared with the other Western democracies —Noam Chomsky, *Columbia Forum,* Winter 1969

. . . the house is luxurious compared to some of the cabins up the hollow —Robert Coles, *Harper's,* November 1971

Compared with the fables, my own work is insignificant —Marianne Moore, quoted in *Time,* 24 May 1954

. . . you always seemed so firm to me compared to myself —E. B. White, letter, 13 Feb. 1972

We can conclude that in current practice, the general rule of the handbooks is followed more often than not when *compare* is used as an active verb, but both *with* and *to* are used equally with the past participle. The rule can be looked upon as a guide that you may choose to observe if you wish to. Many writers obviously do not.

There is one more point of interest. Fowler

says that with the intransitive verb, only *with* is possible. The construction he gives as an example is a negative one. In modern practice, both *with* and *to* are used:

And while Mr. Wilson doesn't compare with Miss Murdoch, the metaphysical playfulness in his book reminds us of her —Anatole Broyard, *N.Y. Times Book Rev.,* 9 Mar. 1986

. . . ham and bamboo shoots did not compare to those made at Ying's —Mimi Sheraton, *N.Y. Times,* 16 Dec. 1977

comparison 1. See ABSOLUTE ADJECTIVES; DOUBLE COMPARISON; IMPLICIT COMPARATIVE; SUPERLATIVE OF TWO.
2. Illogical comparison. Copperud 1970, 1980 notes that some people object to constructions like "the finback has the tallest spout of any whale" (R. C. Murphy, *Logbook for Grace,* 1947, cited in Bryant 1962) on the grounds that *any* includes the thing being compared in the group it is being compared with. This is rather subtle reasoning for everyday use, and it is little wonder that it is often ignored or unthought of. Bryant notes that such constructions have been used since Chaucer's time and can be found in informal and sometimes in formal prose. The one statistical study she mentions found the superlative with *any* about 30 percent of the time and the superlative with *all*—which is held to be more logical—about 70 percent of the time.

. . . 13 years in that high office—the longest of any President —*Boy's Life,* May 1968

. . . the tallest of all the girls —Patricia Browning Griffith, *Harper's,* March 1969

Bryant also notes the occasional use of the comparative in this construction—"a more intolerable wrong of nature than any which man has devised" (*Reader's Digest,* November 1957, cited in Bryant)—but finds it much less common than the same construction with *any other* in place of *any.* Most commentators who mention the problem recommend the use of *any other.*

Your father would probably remember Franklin Delano Roosevelt, the 32nd President, better than any other —*Boy's Life,* May 1968

3. Phythian 1979 says that the word *comparison* should be followed by *with* and not by *to. Comparison* is indeed followed by *with:*

. . . minor projects in comparison with the work he was doing —*Current Biography,* December 1967

Poor in comparison with rich relatives on either side —*Times Literary Supp.,* 22 Oct. 1971

It is also, but somewhat less frequently, followed by *to:*

. . . waspish by comparison to the cars he was accustomed to —Terry Southern, *Flash and Filigree,* 1958

. . . sales so pale and unpromising in comparison to those of the thirties —John Brooks, *New Yorker,* 27 Apr. 1957

Formerly *of* was used:

They who think everything, in comparison of that honor, to be dust and ashes —Edmund Burke, speech, 1780

. . . would be frail and light in comparison of ourselves —Thomas De Quincey, "The Vision of Sudden Death," 1849

Between is also used in constructions where both items being compared appear after *comparison:*

. . . draws an interesting comparison between Marcion's rejection of the Old Testament and Bultmann's existential approach —*Times Literary Supp.,* 18 Jan. 1968

. . . there is little comparison between Michelangelo's *Sonnets* and his sculpture and paintings —René Wellek & Austin Warren, *Theory of Literature,* 1949

compatible When *compatible* is used with a preposition, it is usually *with:*

. . . how to make full employment compatible with reasonable price stability —Charles L. Schultze, *Saturday Rev.,* 22 Jan. 1972

. . . forms of adventure and danger . . . which are compatible with the civilized way of life —Bertrand Russell, *Authority and the Individual,* 1949

If *compatible* is applied to devices, again the choice is usually *with.* However, there is evidence that *to* is sometimes used:

The system also will be compatible with cable television, and can provide 20 channels —*Wall Street Jour.,* 31 Mar. 1982

It seems like a tragic waste, if quad records are compatible to ordinary stereo systems, that more records aren't being made —Alan Rich, *New York,* 16 Aug. 1976

compendious In 1806 Noah Webster published *A Compendious Dictionary of the English Language.* Its vocabulary runs to 355 pages, and, when back matter and front matter are added in, the book amounts to more than 400 pages. It is not a slim volume. What is most noticeable about the book is that most of its 37,000 words are defined in a single line each. The *Compendious Dictionary* is tightly packed and its definitions are concise; it illustrates the definition of *compendious* that is found in Webster's Collegiate Dictionary, Tenth Edition: "marked by brief expression of a comprehensive matter."

Compendious has another salient characteristic: it sounds big. Many people, when they first read or hear the word, get the notion that it means "big and comprehensive" or simply "comprehensive." Probably most of them have to learn that it is also supposed to connote conciseness, compactness, brevity. Some never do learn this, and thus usage writers gain another topic for discussion.

And here is where the trouble begins. Evans 1957 says that the word "means concise, or containing the substance of a subject in brief form. . . ." His definition adequately covers Noah Webster's title and uses like this:

> For readers too anemic to face up to the 868 double-column pages . . . Twitchell gives a compendious summary in an appendix —S. Schoenbaum, *N.Y. Rev. of Books,* 30 Jan. 1986

But Evans goes on to say "A *compendious* work may be large or small, but its compendiousness has nothing to do with its size." Now let us assume he is right. Let us further suppose that a reader to whom the word is unfamiliar sees this passage:

> Goold Brown . . . in his compendious, and bulky, *Grammar of English Grammars* —Julia P. Stanley, *College English,* March 1978

If Evans is right, this book can be both compendious in its treatment and bulky in size. But how can the reader know that Goold Brown has treated his matter concisely? There is no way, unless he or she is already familiar with the book. The natural inclination of the reader seeing *compendious* linked with *bulky* is to think of comprehensiveness.

And to judge from our evidence, comprehensiveness is the usual connotation that readers pick up and, apparently, is also what writers intend. Our evidence runs from 1798 to the present. In our earliest example, Jane Austen is commenting on a one-sentence description:

> A short and compendious history of Miss Debarry! —letter, 25 Nov. 1798

The combining of *short* with *compendious* suggests that comprehensiveness was in Miss Austen's mind. She is not the only writer to use the combination:

> Such looseness cannot be afforded in a short and compendious book —*Times Literary Supp.,* 7 Dec. 1951

In this second example, the writer may have been following Evans's definition, but the reader has no way of knowing it for certain. And the same may be said for a few of the following examples. But we believe that not only is comprehensiveness the connotation the reader will take from these examples, it is in most cases clearly what the writer had in mind too:

> . . . Miss Mainwaring's achievement is, so far as my fairly compendious memory stretches, unmatched —Anthony Boucher, *N.Y. Times Book Rev.,* 15 Aug. 1954

> In times of violent action and rapid change, compendious treatises of political philosophy can scarcely be expected —W. L. Renwick, *English Literature 1789–1815,* 1963

> As for the writing of our more extreme, compendious, sociological novelists —Glenway Wescott, *Images of Truth,* 1962

> . . . which stocks what must be one of the most compendious collections of jackknives in the known universe —Jay Jacobs, *Gourmet,* December 1982

> It is doubtful that even the most compendious traditional or teaching grammar notes such simple facts —Noam Chomsky, *Knowledge of Language,* 1986

> This hefty, superslick Dutch quarterly's recent theme issue monumentalizes Yves Saint Laurent. Lavish, compendious, the 40-year retrospective provides . . . portraits of the master —Guy Trebay, *N.Y. Times Mag.,* 22 Feb. 1998

It appears to us that *compendious* tends to be generally understood as and frequently used for the "comprehensive" half of its older "concise and comprehensive" meaning. This understanding probably results from learning the word by reading it in contexts where, if Evans's analysis is correct, the "conciseness" half of its meaning can be ascertained only by acquaintance with the thing being described. Consequently, most of us are aware only of the "comprehensive" idea. Dictionaries have been slow to recognize this development, but they will inevitably have to do so.

compendium Bernstein 1962, 1965 and Copperud 1964, 1970, 1980 assert that a compendium must be an abridgment or something brief—something little, not big. Bryson 1984 says size has nothing to do with it—the point is the concise treatment. All three have unfortunately fixed on one use of a multipurpose word and assumed that their use is the only correct use. *Compendium* is not a narrowly or precisely applied word. It has been used of items as diverse as books, people, packages of stationery, periodicals, buildings, and collections of several kinds. The plurals *compendia* and *compendiums,* by the way, are both acceptable.

Polio victims are a compendium of all the virtues —Wilfrid Sheed, *People Will Always Be Kind,* 1973

Changing Climate, a compendium of reviews, original contributions, and synthesis —John S. Perry, *Nature,* 24 Oct. 1984

His compendia of shibboleths run for scores of pages —Harvey A. Daniels, *Famous Last Words,* 1983

. . . stationery in a wide choice of colors, ready-packaged in compendiums whose boxes are a stately form of gift wrap in themselves —*New Yorker,* 21 Nov. 1983

She suddenly became a compendium of knowledge about Maoris and kiwi birds and sheep dipping —Cynthia Heimel, *Playboy,* November 1983

From the administration's point of view, the direct subsidy to the Russians is a drop in the bucket compared with the full compendium of direct and indirect subsidies —*Wall Street Jour.,* 13 Aug. 1986

That music—a rich, chronological compendium of African-American song . . . —also is collected on a must-have double CD —Phil Kloer, *Atlanta Jour.-Constitution,* 18 Feb. 1995

. . . the film is feverish in its desire to reduce his experiences to a compendium of clichés —Richard Schickel, *Time,* 13 Nov. 2000

competence, competency Copperud 1970, 1980 finds the two forms interchangeable in American usage, with *competence* the predominant form. Fowler 1926 also says the forms are interchangeable, a statement repeated by Gowers in Fowler 1965.

The variants are not quite as interchangeable as the usage writers would suggest, as Garner 1998 points out, and dictionaries seldom have the space to spell out preferences in much detail. We can tell you that *competence* is much more frequently used in general than *competency*; *competence* seems to be the only form used in the linguistic sense (where it contrasts with *performance*); and *competency* seems to be most frequently used in the fields of education and law.

complacent, complaisant **1.** A number of commentators (Kilpatrick 1984, Bryson 1984, and Copperud 1970, 1980 among them) warn against the confusion of these words. If the words were used only in the senses assigned by these gentlemen, they would never be confused, of course. Conveniently overlooked in their defining is the fact that *complacent* has been and is used to mean "marked by an inclination to please or oblige"—the first sense of *complaisant* in Merriam-Webster's Collegiate

Dictionary, Tenth Edition. This is, in fact, the only meaning Johnson's 1755 dictionary gives *complacent.* Johnson's biographer Boswell also used this sense:

> Though for several years her temper had not been complacent, she had valuable qualities —James Boswell, *Life of Samuel Johnson,* 1791

Perhaps part of the problem was precipitated by the publication of the OED, which enters this sense of *complacent* but also wonders if it is obsolete. Despite the speculation, the OED cites three sources: Burke from 1790, Scott from 1821, and Charlotte Brontë from 1849. This evidence notwithstanding, language critics at the turn of the century began labeling this use of *complacent* as an error. But the sense has seen occasional use in the 20th century:

> . . . the man of feeling, the man of action and the man of thought. The one is tolerant, complacent, easy going, convivial, loving —*Horizon,* December 1946

> The University of Colorado courteously released me from my contract, but the Garrett Biblical Institute was less complacent —Robert Morss Lovett, *All Our Years,* 1948

On the whole, however, modern writers regularly spell this meaning *complaisant.* *Complacent* in its modern senses is used more commonly than *complaisant.* If you are doubtful about the meaning of either word, a good dictionary will solve your problem.

2. When *complacent* is used with a preposition, it is most likely to be *about*:

> She's not very complacent about having done that —Robert Penn Warren, *All the King's Men,* 1946

Less frequently used are *with, of,* or *to*:

> . . . with my office building paid for, is it any wonder that I grew complacent with the status quo —*The Autobiography of William Allen White,* 1946

> For several years, the U.S., complacent of its ability to stay ahead of Russia in all things technological —*Time,* 10 Jan. 1955

> But then, as she quickly reminded herself, she had been no more complacent to him . . . than she had been to half-a-dozen others. Men were so stupid! —*The Strand,* December 1913

Unlike *complacent, complaisant* hardly ever is used with a preposition:

> . . . who is known in history largely as the complaisant husband of his wife —Claude G. Bowers, *The Young Jefferson, 1743–1789,* 1945

compleat Labeled an obsolete spelling of *complete* in the OED, *compleat* is entered in the OED Supplement with the notation "Revived in imitation of its 17th-cent. use. . . ." The spelling seems to have made its comeback chiefly by means of titles such as *The Compleat Bachelor, The Compleat Pediatrician, The Compleat Strategyst,* titles modeled on Izaak Walton's *The Compleat Angler.* Use in titles has continued unabated. Since the middle of the 20th century, *compleat* has been turning up in running text as well, where it often has echoes of Walton's title:

> The compleat idler is a recurrent American dream —*Time,* 24 June 1957

> . . . one gazed on the compleat politician, accepted him as such, and did not much consider the man —Henry Fairlie, *Harper's,* January 1973

> . . . clarion calls for the compleat physician —*JAMA,* 29 Aug. 1980

> . . . the last of the compleat print journalists—energetic reporter, fine stylist, lofty thinker —*Newsweek,* 20 Jan. 1986

> . . . someone whose life has been spent building the kind of relationships that define what Americans call "insider" politics—the compleat Washington networker —Jeffrey A. Frank, *Washington Post,* 16–22 Dec. 1991

complected Not an error, nor a dialectal term, nor an illiteracy, nor nonstandard—all of which it has been labeled—*complected* is simply an Americanism, and apparently a 19th-century Americanism. It seems to be nonexistent in British English. It is attested as early as 1806 in the *Journals of Lewis & Clark,* used by Meriwether Lewis. Until the early 20th century it excited no notice except from compilers of Americanisms and regional terms. (Those who subscribe to the opinion that it is regional dialect—such as Harper 1985—should know that the Dictionary of American Regional English reports it "widespread.") Beginning with Vizetelly 1906, however, it began to raise hackles, and it has been variously aspersed in nearly every American handbook and usage book published from that time to the present. No British book mentions it.

There seems to be no very substantial objection to the term, other than the considerable diffidence American usage writers feel about Americanisms. It is irregularly formed, to be sure, but so are many other words. It has been used by some of our better-known authors:

> You look lots like yer mother: Purty much same in size;
> And about the same complected —James Whitcomb Riley, *Love-Lyrics,* 1883

> Here is the dark-complected hand with a potato on its fork . . . there the light-complected head's got it —Mark Twain, *Those Extraordinary Twins,* 1894 (*A Mark Twain Lexicon,* 1938)

> A heavy-sot man, sandy complected —O. Henry, *The Trimmed Lamp,* 1916 (OED Supplement)

> . . . the man they meant wasn't dark complected —William Faulkner, *Light in August,* 1932 (OED Supplement)

> . . . a blue-eyed, fair-complected man —A. B. Guthrie, Jr., *The Way West,* 1949

> . . . a tall, thin man, fairly dark complected —E. J. Kahn, Jr., *The Peculiar War,* 1952

> . . . his face, though lined a little, was fresh and well complected —Robert Penn Warren, *Band of Angels,* 1955

> . . . a stocky man with a red-complected shining brown face —E. L. Doctorow, *Ragtime,* 1975

Complexioned, universally recommended as a substitute for *complected,* has less literary use than *complected:*

> . . . all look too coarse complexioned and dowdy —Henry Adams, letter, 17 May 1859

> . . . a red-complexioned man of medium height —Santha Rama Rau, *The Reporter,* 16 Mar. 1954

> . . . the pale-complexioned women —Alan Moorehead, *New Yorker,* 1 May 1954

> A heavy-set, swarthy-complexioned man —Vern E. Smith, *The Jones Men,* 1974

> . . . Gallegos . . . are fair-haired and light complexioned —Penelope Casas, *N.Y. Times,* 27 Apr. 1997

Literary use slightly favors *complected,* current journalistic use favors *complexioned.*

complement, compliment A very large number of usage books and handbooks, from the grade-school level up, warn against confusing *complement* and *compliment.* This is really a spelling problem, as your dictionary will demonstrate, since the two words share no meanings whatsoever, as either noun or verb. The evidence we have of the misspelling tends to be the use of the commoner *compliment* in place of *complement:*

> To compliment the butter campaign, American Dairy Association has created new butter point-of-purchase materials —*Eastern Milk Producer,* April 1985

> . . . a knowledge of the possibilities of their branching pattern, complimented by nerve

dissection with fine instruments —*Biological Abstracts*, July 1954

A quick check of your dictionary should clear up any doubts about which spelling you need. The same caution applies to the adjectives *complementary* and *complimentary*.

complete, completely *Complete* is one of those words some people think are absolute adjectives—adjectives that cannot be logically modified by *more, most,* or *less*. It is, for instance, on lists of such adjectives in Partridge 1942 and Garner 1998. For a discussion of these, see ABSOLUTE ADJECTIVES.

Complete itself does not upset many commentators when modified; the usage panel of Heritage 1969, 1982, 2000 finds it acceptable, as do Harper 1985 and Bryson 1984. The pointlessness of worrying about the modification of *complete* can perhaps be illustrated by these quite ordinary examples:

His technical ignorance had proved even more complete than he thought —Norman Mailer, *Harper's*, March 1971

The composer with whom he was in closest and most complete sympathy —*Times Literary Supp.*, 16 Apr. 1970

. . . taking special pains to give an impression of completest normalcy —Saul Bellow, *Herzog*, 1964

The adverb *completely* is similarly modified, despite occasional objection (as by Sellers 1975):

But if Swift was . . . let in to all their secrets (more completely than has usually been thought) —Bonamy Dobrée, *English Literature in the Early Eighteenth Century, 1700–1740*, 1959

complexioned See COMPLECTED.

compliment, complimentary See COMPLEMENT, COMPLIMENT.

comply A couple of handbooks insist on *comply with* and reject *comply to,* but they fail to make an important distinction. When the agent is human, the preposition is *with*. When it is mechanical, however, either *with* or *to* may be used.

. . . should you think ill of that person for complying with the desire —Jane Austen, *Pride and Prejudice*, 1813

Rather than comply with various rulings of the Supreme Court, he . . . —E. J. Kahn, Jr., *New Yorker*, 10 Apr. 1971

In 1969, 10 percent of the automobile parts tested . . . failed to comply with federal safety standards —Philip G. Schrag, *Columbia Forum*, Summer 1970

. . . has softer front rubber insulators, and allows front wheels to comply to road shocks —*Motor Trend*, November 1967

compose See COMPRISE.

compound subjects See AGREEMENT, SUBJECT-VERB: COMPOUND SUBJECTS.

comprise Between thirty and forty commentators are represented in our files as subscribing to this dictum (from Copperud 1970): "The whole *comprises* the parts; thus *is comprised of* is wrong." Our commentators are both British and American, and as far as we can discover, all made their comments in the past hundred years. We have not yet discovered any 19th-century comment. The earliest we have found is in an American printers' trade journal, the *Inland Printer*, March 1903. Our earliest British source is Fowler 1907.

Copperud's brief summary is a bit too succinct. There are actually two constructions involved in the disputed usage: the passive one Copperud mentions and an active one that is most easily spotted when a plural noun is the subject of *comprise*:

The words they found comprise, if not the language of enormity, a language for enormity —David Reid, in Michaels & Ricks 1980

The active construction is the older of the two. The OED records it in the late 18th century, but the editors did not have much evidence and labeled the use *rare*. The OED Supplement has collected many later examples. The most noteworthy characteristic of the construction is that from the beginning into the early 20th century, it seems to have been rather more frequent in technical and scientific writing than in belles lettres. Its use in nontechnical contexts increased during the 20th century:

. . . each number . . . carries our names up in the corner as comprising the editorial staff —Alexander Woollcott, letter, Spring 1918

. . . the ceremonies which comprise the abdication —Sir James G. Frazer, *Aftermath*, 1937

. . . they comprise the only repertory that is unique to it —Virgil Thomson, *The Musical Scene*, 1947

The receipts . . . comprised the fifth-largest gate in boxing history —John Lardner, *New Yorker*, 17 Mar. 1951

. . . individuals who comprised the planting aristocracy —Oscar Handlin, *The American People in the Twentieth Century*, 1954

The buildings that comprise the Nunnery quadrangle —Katharine Kuh, *Saturday Rev.*, 28 June 1969

. . . the sixty or so scowling citizens who comprised the forward section of the line —T. Coraghessan Boyle, *Atlantic*, January 1982

Seven boys comprised the choir —Garrison Keillor, *Lake Wobegon Days*, 1985

It invited readers to sign a "statement of principles" whose initial signatories comprise a who's who of neo-family values crusaders —Judith Stacy, *The Nation*, 9 July 2001

This sense—"compose, constitute"—can be found from time to time with a singular subject:

Miss Sally Fagg has a pretty figure, & that comprises all the good looks of the family —Jane Austen, letter, 14 Oct. 1813

For too long there has existed a misconception as to what comprises a literary generation —William Styron, *N.Y. Times Book Rev.*, 6 May 1973

The active construction, we can see, is flourishing and is found in quite a wide range of writing.

The passive construction is the one that caught the eye of the Fowler brothers in 1907. They reproduced this example:

A few companies, comprised mainly of militiamen —*Times*

The passive construction is not as old as the active; the OED Supplement dates it from 1874. H. W. Fowler intended to give it extended treatment in his 1926 book, but the paragraph was accidentally omitted, and he had to content himself with publishing it five years later in *S.P.E.* (Society for Pure English) *Tract 36*. The passive construction too appears to be in a flourishing condition today, as does the detached past participle:

. . . it was universally believed that mankind was comprised of a single species —Ashley Montagu, *Man's Most Dangerous Myth: The Fallacy of Race*, 2d ed., 1945

. . . his vision of environment as comprised of chemic, economic, and natural force —Richard Poirier, *A World Elsewhere*, 1966

Like any other system comprised of complex feedback cycles —Barry Commoner, *Columbia Forum*, Spring 1968

. . . a great many of the present-day centers are comprised of militant groups —Irving Louis Horowitz, *Center Mag.*, May 1969

The audience, comprised mainly of undergraduates in sneakers and denim —William Kucewicz, *Wall Street Jour.*, 19 Jan 1981

. . . a series of 30 gates comprised of red and green poles —Patrick Strickler, *Sports Illustrated*, 10 Dec. 1984

The typical amber liquid in the plain bottle . . . may be comprised of 100 or more ingredients —*Consumer Reports*, December 1993

Her CD collection is comprised of Otis Redding, Sam Cooke, B.B. King and Mahalia Jackson —Betsy Peoples, *Emerge*, October 1998

But the vigorous condition of the disputed constructions has not crowded the older senses out of use. *Comprise* seems to have increased in overall use enough so that all the senses current within the last 200 years are still in good health. Here is a small sample of the two most common older senses. You should notice that they come from many of the same sources as the disputed constructions:

Three months comprised thirteen weeks —Jane Austen, *Mansfield Park*, 1814

. . . civilization as Lenin used the term would then certainly have comprised the changes that are now associated in our minds with "developed" rather than "developing" states —*Times Literary Supp.*, 5 Mar. 1970

. . . a series . . . that eventually comprised more than 200 titles —Judith Appelbaum, *N.Y. Times Book Rev.*, 2 Jan. 1983

Originally the Hogs comprised only the Skins' offensive linemen —Jack McCallum, *Sports Illustrated*, 6 June 1983

. . . a Senate comprising free-lance egos —*Wall Street Jour.*, 8 Nov. 1984

The course of studies comprised Classics, Theology, and Commercial —Garrison Keillor, *Lake Wobegon Days*, 1985

The midsized, midtown firm I worked for comprised a dozen lawyers —Lorrie Moore, *New Yorker*, 23 & 30 Apr. 2001

Conclusion: the aspersed active construction of *comprise* has been in use for nearly two centuries; the passive construction for more than a century. It is a little hard to understand why these constructions that are so obviously established are still the source of so much discontent. (They have been defined in Merriam-Webster dictionaries since 1934.) Perhaps the critics are worried about the older senses:

Unlike all but a few modern writers, Mrs. Spark uses the verb "comprise" correctly —John Updike, *New Yorker*, 23 July 1984

But our evidence shows no diminution of vitality in the older senses—"include" and "be made up of." Even sportswriters use them. Our advice to you is to realize that the disputed sense is established and standard, but nevertheless liable to criticism. If such criticism concerns you, you can probably avoid *comprise* by using *compose, constitute,* or *make up,* whichever fits your sentence best.

concensus See CONSENSUS 3.

concept Bryson 1984, Janis 1984, Ebbitt 1982, Macmillan 1982, and Copperud 1970, 1980 are among those who complain of a fad use of *concept* in a sense approximating *idea* (or any of a number of other words trotted out to suit the need). College handbooks may be trying to eliminate this from the writing of students in Freshman English, but the real problem here is that the commentators are all criticizing business and advertising use without saying so. Our files are full of examples of *concept* from the annual reports of U.S. corporations. And we have this sort of thing:

> . . . they perceive their roles as selling merchandise when they should be marketing a concept —Joel B. Portugal, *N.Y. Times,* 7 Dec. 1980

And this:

> . . . weaknesses come to the fore on this concept album about the songwriting team's scuffling days —Jon Landau, *Rolling Stone,* 17 July 1975

The language of business and showbiz is not especially amenable to correction by those who write college English handbooks.

Still more important is the fact that these commentators start from the wrong basic premise: they assume that *concept* is originally and basically a word from philosophy meaning "an abstract or generic idea generalized from specific instances." The OED shows that *concept* is a Latinized form of *conceit* introduced in the 16th century; its earliest meaning was, in fact, "idea, notion." The philosophers then came along in the 17th century and made a narrower application of the earlier general term. The general sense "idea, notion" has been used all along.

Our evidence suggests that *concept* is currently not in extensive use for literary purposes. We have, however, found some examples in which "notion, idea" is the prevalent meaning yet which are not specialized uses. You can judge for yourself how faddish these examples are.

> . . . "honor"—a word . . . of which they had such a curious concept —William L. Shirer, *The Rise and Fall of the Third Reich,* 1960

> . . . we must expand the concept of conservation to meet the imperious problems of the new age —John F. Kennedy, Introduction to Stewart L. Udall, *The Quiet Crisis,* 1963

> Were there two human minds functioning separately from each other in the same

brain? The concept was shattering —Irving Stone, *McCall's,* March 1971

> . . . the Falstaff who simply and fully enjoyed life and wasn't about to sacrifice it to some idiot concept of battlefield honor —Martin Gottfried, *Saturday Rev.,* 23 June 1979

concern When *concern* means "an uneasy state of blended interest, uncertainty, and apprehension," it is used especially with the prepositions *over, for,* and *about*:

> . . . their concern over issues of racism, poverty, war and ecology —Israel Kugler, *Change,* October 1971

> Their militant concern for the environment —Donald Gould, *Smithsonian,* May 1972

> . . . growing concerns about the environment —Fred J. Borch, *General Electric Investor,* Winter 1970

With is also used with this sense:

> . . . concern with fallout and nuclear war —Barry Commoner, *Columbia Forum,* Spring 1968

When *concern* denotes interest or involvement, the usual preposition is *with* or *in*:

> . . . concern with the nature and transmutability of matter —*Times Literary Supp.,* 17 July 1969

> Much of the concern of . . . Doxiadis in the problems of human settlements —*Current Biography,* September 1964

concerned When *concerned* suggests worry or anxiety, it can be followed by any of several prepositions. The most frequent are *about* and *for*:

> . . . were concerned about both their children —Eileen Hughes, *Ladies' Home Jour.,* September 1971

> . . . young people of today are concerned for others —Elisabeth Elliot, *Christian Herald,* June 1967

Over, at, and *by* are also used:

> . . . educators have been greatly concerned over the reading program in the elementary grades —Catherine Zimmer & Marjorie Pratt, *Quarterly Jour. of Speech,* April 1941

> . . . was concerned at the mounting indignation of the people against Americans —Robert Payne, *Saturday Rev.,* 27 June 1953

> The Kremlin was getting increasingly concerned by the stubborn survival of . . . Christianity, inside the Soviet Union —*Time,* 23 Aug. 1954

When *concerned* conveys the notion of interested engagement, *with* is the most common preposition:

> This book is more concerned with the earlier peoples than with the Incas —Edward P. Lanning, *Peru Before the Incas,* 1967

> They are concerned with the way individual human situations snowball into political situations —Erica Jong, *Barnard Alumnae,* Winter 1971

In is also used. It tends to suggest involvement:

> The British have been deeply concerned in foreign relations for a thousand years —Joyce Cary, *Holiday,* November 1954

In is used especially when something criminal is suggested:

> Was Mary Thoday . . . really after all concerned in the theft? —Dorothy L. Sayers, *The Nine Tailors,* 1934

> . . . accused of being concerned in murdering Thomas Smithson —*The Times* (London), 24 Jan. 1974

Concerned in the following three examples rather blends the notions of worry and interest:

> . . . not particularly interested in perspective, but he was much concerned about techniques of painting —*Current Biography,* May 1967

> . . . he has always been concerned for the relevance of philosophy —*Times Literary Supp.,* 19 Feb. 1970

> . . . is as concerned with status and prestige as the businessman is —Stephanie Dudek, *Psychology Today,* May 1971

When *concerned* suggests interest or care, it can also be followed by *to* and an infinitive. Our evidence shows this practice currently more common in British English than in American:

> . . . is concerned only to present one side of the case —*Times Literary Supp.,* 26 June 1969

> . . . a single department concerned to carry out a single policy —E. H. Carr, *Foreign Affairs,* October 1946

conciseness, concision *Conciseness* is a 17th-century word still in use. *Concision* is an even older word, but its original senses are now archaic or obsolete; it began to be used as a synonym of *conciseness* in the 18th century. *Concision* was used in some piece written by Henry James and noticed by the Fowler brothers (Fowler 1907) who thought it a bit exotic

for *conciseness.* Fowler 1926 took up the subject again, this time recommending *conciseness* and calling *concision* a "literary critics' word"; Sir Ernest Gowers left the remarks in his revision, Fowler 1965. In spite of Fowler's preference for *conciseness, concision* seems to be the word of choice in reviews. *Concision* is somewhat more frequently used than *conciseness.* Some examples of each follow:

> The first six volumes set a high standard for conciseness —*Times Literary Supp.,* 31 Oct. 1968

> His best poems make haiku seem wasteful. Their conciseness is such that the only legitimate way of reading them is by Talmudic and Cabalistic methods —George Steiner, *New Yorker,* 28 Aug. 1989

> Manuscripts are accepted on the understanding that the editors may revise them for greater conciseness, clarity, and conformity with the Journal's style —*Computer Music Jour.,* Winter 1992

> Though Seneca is long-winded, he is not diffuse; he is capable of great concision —T. S. Eliot, "Seneca in Elizabethan Translation," in *Selected Essays,* 1932

> His prose style is noticeable for its concision, luminous completeness —Edgar Allen Poe, *Godey's Lady's Book,* October 1846

> . . . forced upon me a concision that my practice as a dramatist had made grateful to me —W. Somerset Maugham, *The Summing Up,* 1938

> . . . the writing of the "Memoirs" is perfect in concision and clearness —Edmund Wilson, *New Yorker,* 4 Apr. 1953

> The guarded tone of earlier letters steadily eases, while concision and style are undiminished —Francis Steegmuller, *Times Literary Supp.,* 3 Dec. 1993

> With remarkable concision and insight, Mamet has mapped out the dynamics of a soul murder —John Lahr, *New Yorker,* 1 Aug. 1994

concord See the articles beginning with AGREEMENT.

concord, notional See NOTIONAL AGREEMENT, NOTIONAL CONCORD.

concrete See CEMENT, CONCRETE.

concur *Concur* may be used with various prepositions, chief among them being *with, in,* and *to:*

> . . . I asked him whether he concurs with the opinion of most psychiatrists that the cre-

ative impulse is a kind of neurosis —Jim Gaines, *Saturday Rev.*, 29 Apr. 1972

This recommendation, concurred in by all members of the Department —*AAUP Bulletin,* September 1971

Physical and moral causes had concurred to prevent civilisation from spreading to that region —T. B. Macaulay, *The History of England,* vol. I, 1849

Less frequently *concur* may be found with *on*:

We all concurred on the argument that when you have news, you have to print it —Katharine Graham, quoted in *McCall's,* September 1971

condemn, contemn Two or three commentators warn us not to confuse *condemn* and *contemn.* Likely no one has any trouble with *condemn*; the problem is *contemn,* which is a rather bookish word and is not much used. Your dictionary defines *contemn* as "to view or treat with contempt; scorn." Keep the definition in mind as you read the examples.

The real difficulty seems to be that a writer who chooses *contemn* instead of *scorn, sneer at,* or *despise* runs a certain risk of being thought to have spelled *condemn* wrong or to have otherwise been mistaken, when the context does not rule out the sense of *condemn.* We have no examples of confusion in our files, but we do have examples in which a reader unfamiliar with this relatively rare word could easily read *condemn* for *contemn.*

The priestly function transcended the individual, and an unworthy priest was contemned, not for performing service when unfit to do so, but for neglecting to do it at all —James A. Williamson, *The Tudor Age,* 1964

. . . his own early drawings of moss-roses and picturesque castles—things that he now mercilessly contemned —Arnold Bennett, *The Old Wives' Tale,* 1908

Much of the out-of-state press, with which Wallace had carried on a running feud for years, contemned Mrs. Wallace's candidacy —*Current Biography,* September 1967

Theirs would be a decidedly leftish antihumanist movement rejecting traditional Western "discourse," contemning Western "anthropological" values, and refusing to engage in the reasoned argument that the West claimed to prize —Mark Lilla, *Commentary,* January 1990

In these examples the unwary reader might read *condemn.* So the real problem, we think, is not that writers confuse the two words, but that some readers may mistake *contemn* as *condemn.*

condition Copperud 1970 states that his earlier (1964) characterization of *condition* used in *heart condition* as a "faceless euphemism for *ailment, disease*" is a common criticism in newspaper circles. The criticism may be widespread, but this use of *condition* is not usually a euphemism.

Condition has been used euphemistically in such time-honored combinations as in *an interesting* (or *delicate* or *certain*) *condition* to avoid *pregnant.* It can refer to pregnancy without euphemism:

Unwilling to face the stigma attached to unwed mothers in her own country or to reveal her condition to her elderly parents, Olga Scarpetta left Colombia and came to New York . . . to have her child in secrecy —Eileen Hughes, *Ladies' Home Jour.,* September 1971

Condition in the sense Copperud objects to is, as Harper 1985 remarks, "hardly a precise term." Its very imprecision is its chief virtue, for it is often used when the precise ailment is unknown or not understood. As a generalized term, its usefulness can be seen in these examples:

One of the major factors in his reversal of fortune was a series of physical ailments, the worst of which was a painful chest condition that beset him in 1962. The condition, apparently caused by a muscle spasm or pinched nerve, evaded specific medical diagnosis —*Current Biography,* April 1966

. . . in treating Paget's disease, which is a condition characterized by excessive bone formation —*Annual Report, Pfizer,* 1970

If newspaper editors want to fret over this use of *condition,* let them. You needn't worry about it at all.

conducive It is hard to understand why language commentators persist in reminding us that *conducive* is used with *to* and not *of.* The evidence in the Merriam-Webster citation files is unmistakable: *conducive* is almost always used with *to*:

Thus a feeling of apprehensiveness, conducive to attention, is aroused in the reader —T. S. Eliot, "Charles Whibley," in *Selected Essays,* 1932

The language critics insist that *of* should never be used with *conducive* and it is not so used in contemporary English. We have no citations for this combination. The OED mentions it but labels it obsolete and shows just one citation, that from 1793. The OED also labels as obsolete the construction *conducive for.* The evidence is overwhelming for *conducive to.*

conferencing Harper 1975, under the heading *educationese,* reports receiving a letter asking about the propriety of the word *conferencing,* used in the phrase "from much conferencing experience" by a junior high school principal in a letter to a parent. The Harper editors conclude by recommending the use of *conferring,* which would sound very strange indeed in the construction the principal used.

Thomas H. Middleton encountered the word in 1978:

> One of my prime candidates for quick death is *conferencing —Saturday Rev.,* 7 Jan. 1978

He too found it in an educational context, but the reference—"Clearly, conferencing is a booming business"—is not to parent-teacher conferences, but to large-scale meetings. In both cases, however, the meaning is "the holding of conferences."

"*Conferencing* may be getting entrenched, though," says Middleton in conclusion. He is right, but for reasons he did not suspect. A later use of *conferencing* has developed in the world of computers and business. It appears mainly in trade sources, often in combinations like *computer conferencing* and *video conferencing.* It can be found in Merriam-Webster's Collegiate Dictionary, Tenth Edition, along with its compound form *teleconferencing.*

confess For reasons that are hard to guess, Copperud 1970 finds the intransitive *confess* followed by the preposition *to* "clumsy" and unidiomatic. He even invokes Evans 1957 as support, but he has misread Evans, who rejects *confess to* only when it is followed by a perfect infinitive (*"I confess to have heard . . ."*). Evans and Shaw 1987 both note that *confess to* is often followed by a gerund:

> . . . I must confess to having done some flagrant cheating —Cornelia Otis Skinner, *N.Y. Times Mag.,* 23 Jan. 1955

> . . . will confess to having had at least one spontaneous apparently telepathic or clairvoyant experience —Antony Flew, *A New Approach to Psychical Research,* 1953

> We must confess to being somewhat conservative —*ita bulletin,* Spring 1965

George Bernard Shaw even used *of* with the gerund:

> . . . no Irishman ever again confessed of being Irish —*Back to Methuselah,* 1921

Confess to is also often followed by a noun:

> . . . and then confessed to the crime under the urgent moral persuasion of the company's chairman —C. R. Hewitt & Jenifer Wayne, *London Calling,* 19 Aug. 1954

> . . . I confess to a certain reluctance —Herbert Read, *The Philosophy of Modern Art,* 1952

> Let me begin by confessing to prejudice —Dudley Fitts, *N.Y. Times Book Rev.,* 4 July 1954

In short, there seems to be no real problem here. All of the examples are idiomatic and only GBS's is unusual.

confidant, confidante The usage books seem to present only a partial picture of the usage of these words: Fowler 1926 calls *confidant* masculine and *confidante* feminine; Copperud 1970, citing other commentators for support, agrees on *confidante* but says *confidant* is bisexual. In actual usage, *confidant* usually refers to a male:

> . . . had him as a confidant and friend —Gay Talese, *Harper's,* January 1969

> . . . the same detective and his friend and confidant, Dr. Watson —A. C. Ward, *British Book News,* May 1954

It is also used of females:

> . . . shows her caliber in permitting Miss Alice Marriott to be her confidant —Elizabeth S. Sergeant, *Saturday Rev.,* 24 July 1948

> She had specialized as the confidant and friend —Osbert Sitwell, *Horizon,* July 1947

Confidante is usually applied to females:

> . . . Emma moved from kitchen maid to royal confidante —Charles Lee, *Saturday Rev.,* 12 Mar. 1955

> . . . if he would be thoughtful, considerate, and treat her as a partner and confidante —Joseph P. Lash, *McCall's,* October 1971

But it is also used of males:

> . . . the minister, assumed to be a confidante of Eisenhower, reported his findings to the President —*Current Biography,* November 1967

> The informer, Douglass Durham, was the chief aide and confidante —John Kifner, *N.Y. Times,* 13 Mar. 1975

confide In its intransitive senses *confide* is often used with *in:*

> ". . . I have been so nearly caught once or twice already, that I cannot confide any longer in my own ingenuity" —Thomas Love Peacock, *Nightmare Abbey,* 1818

> . . . patients too awed by the doctor to confide in him —Leonard Gross, *McCall's,* March 1971

Confide may also be followed by a dependent clause:

> One husband confided that his wife buys an extra supply of cards —Goodman Ace, *Saturday Rev.,* 13 Nov. 1971

In its transitive senses, *confide* may be followed by *to* and the indirect object, which may be found before or after the direct object:

. . . began confiding to her all the daily twists and turns in her affair with a waiter —Herman Wouk, *Marjorie Morningstar,* 1955

. . . do not confide your children to strangers —Mavis Gallant, *New Yorker,* 1 Feb. 1964

confident When this adjective is followed by a preposition, *in* and *of* are the ones most likely to be used—they occur with equal frequency:

Why should he not walk confident in his own high purpose —Vernon Louis Parrington, *Main Currents in American Thought,* 1930

. . . people were confident of a golden future —Thomas Wolfe, *You Can't Go Home Again,* 1940

Less frequently, *about* or *at* may be found:

. . . make him more confident about speaking at length —Bernard H. & Charles D. McKenna, *American School Board Jour.,* June 1968

. . . but few would be at all confident at assigning him a particular place in the history of English writing —*Times Literary Supp.,* 17 Apr. 1969

And still less frequently, but nevertheless idiomatically, *confident* is used with *as to* or *on*:

. . . who were clear as to their goal and confident as to their victory —Lewis Mumford, *Technics and Civilization,* 1934

. . . the Democrats were confident on the point and the Republicans fearful —*Wall Street Jour.,* 4 Nov. 1954

Very often, of course, *confident* is followed not by a prepositional phrase but by a dependent clause:

We are confident that the budget . . . will permit both major segments of higher education to meet California's education needs . . . —Ronald Reagan, quoted in *Change,* September 1971

conform When *conform* is followed by a preposition, it is most likely to be either *to* or *with.* According to our evidence, the use of *to* is more frequent by a considerable margin:

. . . unwilling to conform to American ways —Oscar Handlin, *The American People in the Twentieth Century,* 1954

. . . in *1984,* the members of the Party are compelled to conform to a sexual ethic of

more than Puritan severity —Aldous Huxley, *Brave New World Revisited,* 1958

. . . have modified my views of conduct to conform with what seem to me the implications of my beliefs —T. S. Eliot, "Thoughts After Lambeth," in *Selected Essays,* 1932

Another adverbial prepositional phrase may sometimes intervene between *conform* and the phrase with *to* or *with*:

. . . provided they conform in dimensions to those publicly owned —Charlton Ogburn, *Harper's,* October 1971

conformity When followed by a preposition, *conformity* usually takes *to* or *with.* *With* is slightly more common, especially in the phrase *in conformity with*:

In conformity with his father's wishes —*Current Biography,* April 1967

. . . in conformity with international law —*Foreign Affairs,* July 1940

Conformity to the discipline of a small society had become almost his second nature —Edith Wharton, *The Age of Innocence,* 1920

Ideas are tested not in give and take, but in their conformity to doctrine —Ward Just, *Atlantic,* October 1970

Several special constructions should also be noted. When the things between which the relationship exists are both named after *conformity,* the preposition may be *between* or *of*:

. . . this is conformity between the old and the new —T. S. Eliot, "Tradition and the Individual Talent," 1917, in *Selected Essays,* 1932

. . . the close conformity of many of the tortuous veins with relic structures —*Jour. of Geology,* September 1948

When the prepositional phrase specifies, instead, the area of thought or experience where the conformity exists, *of* or *in* may be found:

. . . such grants encourage a conformity of approach to scientific problems —Henry T. Yost, Jr., *AAUP Bulletin,* September 1969

Conformity in habit of growth should be maintained even more than conformity in texture —M. E. Bottomley, *New Designs of Small Properties,* rev. ed., 1948

congenial By and large, when *congenial* is used with a preposition, it is *to*:

. . . such things are common here, and congenial to the Persian character —Elinor Wylie, *Jennifer Lorn,* 1923

. . . our earth is becoming less congenial to life with each passing year —Norman Cousins, *Saturday Rev.,* 27 Nov. 1976

Congenial used with *with* may also be found, but far less frequently:

> By temperament Decter is congenial with static law —Muriel Haynes, *Saturday Rev.,* 13 Nov. 1971

When the word modified by *congenial* is inanimate, there is a possibility that *for* may be used:

> . . . when the climate was much more congenial for such enterprise —Henry Ladd Smith, *New Republic,* 22 Nov. 1954

congruence See INFLUENCE 2.

conjunctive adverb See ALSO.

connect *Connect* is regularly used with the prepositions *with* and *to.* Some commentators have tried to limit the use of *with* to figurative senses and of *to* to concrete senses; this restriction is generally but not always followed in practice. There is a tendency for *with* to go with figurative senses and *to* to go with literal senses, but fully idiomatic exceptions are not hard to find. Some examples of *with:*

> His policy was identical with Lincoln's, but he was unable to connect with Northern sentiment —Samuel Eliot Morison, *Oxford History of the American People,* 1965

> The alleged message . . . simply does not connect with the plot of the film —Arthur M. Schlesinger, Jr., *Saturday Rev.,* 15 Apr. 1978

> . . . the trading centers which connect Finland with the outside world —Samuel Van Valkenburg & Ellsworth Huntington, *Europe,* 1935

> . . . built roads connecting the Fezzan with Tunisia —*Collier's Year Book,* 1949

Here are a few examples of *to:*

> . . . to measure people's responsiveness by connecting them to wires and laboratory devices —Marcia Seligson, *McCall's,* March 1971

> . . . long staircases that connect to the road —*Ford Truck Times,* Summer 1970

> None of Thaw's impressive series of five Goyas overtly connects to death —Thomas B. Hess, *New York,* 26 Jan. 1976

> The draft is what connects Kansas Wesleyan to the war —Calvin Trillin, *New Yorker,* 22 Apr. 1967

Two things may also be connected *by* still another thing:

> . . . we connect the points by a smooth curve —School Mathematics Study Group, *Elementary Functions,* 1965

The world of sports has its own set of prepositions:

> . . . connected for his first home run since Aug. 19 —Jim Fox, *Springfield* (Mass.) *Union,* 25 Sept. 1967

> Finding Morris Bradshaw free, he connected with him on a 50-yard scoring pass —Ron Reid, *Sports Illustrated,* 6 Aug. 1979

> . . . Sipe connected on a 45-yard bomb to Reggie Rucker —Gerald Eskenazi, *N.Y. Times,* 8 Dec. 1980

connection See IN CONNECTION WITH.

consensus 1. The consensus of opinion among writers on usage since the 1940s is that the phrase *consensus of opinion* is redundant. We have added "of opinion" advisedly; this is indeed a matter of opinion and not of fact, as will appear in what follows.

Consensus, it appears from OED evidence, developed at least three different new uses around the middle of the 19th century. The OED suggests the word itself first insinuated its way into the language through a physiological meaning introduced in a 16th-century book on physiology apparently written in Latin. In 1854 we have a "consensus of forces," in 1858 a "consensus of . . . evidence," in 1861 a "consensus of the Protestant missionaries," and in 1874 a "consensus of opinion."

The early citations suggest that *consensus* was not then limited to opinion, and indeed it has not been since. The Merriam-Webster files have instances of "consensus of views," "consensus of preference," "consensus of support," "consensus of political comments," "consensus of advanced thinking," "consensus of experts," "consensus of agreement," "consensus of behavior," "consensus of values," "consensus of belief," "consensus of readings," "consensus of dissent," "consensus of conscience," "consensus of scholarship," and "consensus of usage." Thus, the cautious writer might well be tempted to write *consensus of opinion,* being aware that *consensus* can be used of other things. This is the point made in the following passage, probably written by Frank H. Vizetelly:

> The accepted meaning of *consensus* is "general agreement." It is commonly defined as "a collective unanimous opinion of a number of persons," and on this account the phrase "consensus of opinion" appears to be tautological. But as there may be consensus of thought, of functions, of forces, etc., it is not tautological to speak of a "consensus of

opinion." Besides, the phrase is an English idiom —*Literary Digest*, 1 May 1926

The opinion that *consensus of opinion* is redundant appears to have begun with James Gordon Bennett the younger, who ran the New York *Herald* from 1867 until 1918. A list of his Don'ts for use by editors of the paper is reprinted in an appendix in Bernstein 1971. The list is not dated, but *consensus of opinion* was probably added to the list toward the end of Bennett's tenure; none of our late-19th-century or early-20th-century usage books mention it. Even Fowler 1926 notes *consensus* only because he found it confused with *census*. Although the question must have been in the air in 1926, as the excerpt from the *Literary Digest* above indicates, we find little discussion of it in books until the 1940s. Since that time nearly every writer on usage has clambered onto the bandwagon.

Of all our recent writers on usage, only Freeman 1983 seems to be aware of the issues discussed in the *Literary Digest*. He has also read Webster's Second, which has this note: "The expression *consensus of opinion*, although objected to by some, is now generally accepted as in good use."

> Such is the consensus of opinion of the leading authorities on international law —Thomas F. Bayard (U.S. Secretary of State), dispatch, 1 Nov. 1887

> The following comments are indicative of the present consensus of opinion —Mac-Cracken & Sandison 1917

> We made a systematic attempt to ascertain the consensus of usage throughout the English-speaking world —Frank H. Vizetelly, *N.Y. Times*, 2 Jan. 1927

> . . . the consensus of scholarship . . . assigns the two plays to Tourneur —T. S. Eliot, "Cyril Tourneur," in *Selected Essays*, 1932

> Tennyson's reaction to the consensus of critical opinion —*PMLA*, September 1951

> This language, according to a consensus of scholarly opinion —W. K. Matthews, *Languages of the U.S.S.R.*, 1951

> In the end, without a vote, but because it seemed to be the consensus of opinion —*The Autobiography of William Allen White*, 1946

> In place of authority in science, we have and we need to have only the consensus of informed opinion —J. Robert Oppenheimer, *New Republic*, 26 Apr. 1954

> The consensus of their opinion, based on reports that had drifted back from the border —John Hersey, *New Yorker*, 2 Mar. 1957

> . . . in a manner that maintains a consensus of public opinion—avoiding disruptive attack from Right and Left —Gaddis Smith, *N.Y. Times Book Rev.*, 3 June 1973

> . . . if the southern neighbours of the Iceni . . . were in some matter Belgic, it is the consensus of opinion that the Iceni in their geographic isolation remained 'Celtic' —Antonia Fraser, *The Warrior Queens*, 1988

The decision for you is whether you want to use *consensus of opinion*, and make your meaning perfectly clear while running the risk of being wrongly censured for redundancy, or use *consensus* alone and risk less than full clarity, perhaps. Technically, *consensus of opinion* is not a redundancy, but many nonetheless believe it is. You are safe using *consensus* alone when it is clear that you mean consensus of opinion, and most writers in fact do so.

2. *General consensus.* Some of the writers who condemn *consensus of opinion* as a redundancy do the same for *general consensus.* Their argument in this case is on a better footing, for generality is indeed part of the meaning of *consensus*. The added *general* is probably felt by the writers who use it to have an intensive effect:

> There is a general consensus that some social plan of production for the needs of the community, rather than for individual profit, is necessary if the routine of civilized life is to continue —Morris R. Cohen, *The Faith of a Liberal*, 1946

> Yet despite this and other dust-ups during the convention, the general consensus is that Episcopalians weathered this one with their customary civility intact —Antonio Ramirez, *Commonweal*, 12 Sept. 1997

General is sometimes added to *consensus of opinion*, though perhaps more often formerly than nowadays.

> . . . the general consensus of opinion in the City —*The Spectator*, 3 Jan. 1925

3. *Concensus.* Freeman 1983, Reader's Digest 1983, Howard 1977, and Copperud 1970 all note *concensus* as a frequent misspelling of *consensus*. We have a fair amount of evidence of its turning up in publications where it should have been detected. The OED notes the spelling as an obsolete variant of *consensus*. It is no longer acceptable.

consequent   When *consequent* is used with a preposition, the preposition is usually *on* or *upon*:

> The stillness consequent on the cessation of the rumbling and labouring of the coach —Charles Dickens, *A Tale of Two Cities*, 1859

The false perceptions of Mussolini . . . were consequent upon Pound's wanting his epic to be actively engaged in the process of history —A. D. Moody, *Times Literary Supp.*, 15 Aug. 1980

Consequent may also be followed by *to*, but far less frequently:

. . . the subsequent disorders consequent to the diverse demands of internal factions —*Current History*, March 1937

consequential Here we have a most curious case. The sense of *consequential* meaning "important" was rejected by some two-thirds of the Heritage 1969 usage panel, for reasons that are not given. (Later editions of Heritage have no comment on this subject.) Harper 1975, 1985 notes that the sense is disputed, but finds it logical and predicts eventual acceptance. Earlier American objection we have not found, and therefore we assume the Heritage question was based on H. W. Fowler's 1926 comment that "*c.* does not mean of consequence." "Of consequence" is part of the definition in the OED at *consequential* 5; but Fowler selected as an example an OED citation at sense 6a "having social consequence." Of course both of these senses mean the same thing; the OED separated uses of the adjective applied to nonhuman things from uses of the adjective applied to humans. The OED marks the earlier, nonhuman sense obsolete, but not the human sense. So it is not clear which sense Fowler had in mind.

Our files show almost no use of the human sense he gave as an example. (We do have evidence of the "self-important" sense—OED 6b—that Fowler said was still alive.) But if the example given by Copperud 1970, 1980 in reporting Heritage 1969 is accurate, the Heritage panel was objecting to the nonhuman sense (OED 5). This sense has a curious history too.

The OED shows it to start with Henry Fielding in 1728. In a comedy called *Love in Several Masques*, Fielding put the word into the mouth of Lord Formal, an updated Restoration fop with a taste for fancy language. Lord Formal takes the adjective, based till then on other senses of *consequence*, and bases it on the sense meaning "importance." These are his words as he takes leave of another character:

For the sweetness of your conversation has perfumed my senses to the forgetfulness of an affair, which being of consequential essence, obliges me to assure you that I am your humble servant.

If this sense started out as part of the fancy talk of Fielding's fop, it was also in serious use; the OED shows later and straight-faced citations from the mid-18th century to the

early 19th. But its last quotation is dated 1821, and the editor thought the sense obsolete.

Nevertheless, the use reappeared in the middle of the 20th century. We do not know whether the sense had continued all along, and the OED simply lacked citations, or whether it was re-formed from the same elements Fielding had used. In either case there is none of Fielding's playing with words in these examples:

Impressionism has proved itself the most consequential of the efforts of the nineteenth-century painters to reorganize the data of vision —Wylie Sypher, *Partisan Rev.*, March–April 1947

The social effects were more consequential —Oscar Handlin, *N.Y. Times Book Rev.*, 11 Apr. 1954

. . . so severely indifferent to the events the rest of us think consequential in our politics —Murray Kempton, *N.Y. Rev. of Books*, 23 Oct. 1969

Separately, none of these responsibilities seems very consequential —Albert R. Hunt, *Wall Street Jour.*, 24 July 1972

. . . provocative, constantly interesting, and in some regards profoundly consequential —Rodney Needham, *Times Literary Supp.*, 25 Jan. 1980

These examples, as you can see, are perfectly standard.

consider **1.** As far back as MacCracken & Sandison 1917 the use of *consider* followed by *as* was disapproved; it is still being viewed askance as recently as Barzun 1985 and Garner 1998. But constructions with *as* have been in use for a long time:

It was one of the Employments of these Secondary Authors, to distinguish the several kinds of Wit by Terms of Art, and to consider them as more or less perfect, according as they were founded in Truth —Joseph Addison, *The Spectator*, 10 May 1711

. . . the "bastard-wing" in birds may be safely considered as a digit in a rudimentary state —Charles Darwin, *On the Origin of Species by Means of Natural Selection*, 1859

. . . that metal, which was peculiarly considered as the standard or measure of value —Adam Smith, *The Wealth of Nations*, 1776

. . . consider him as on a par with the cart that follows at the heels of the horse —Washington Irving, *Salmagundi*, 4 Feb. 1807

. . . could not but consider it as absolutely unnecessary —Jane Austen, *Mansfield Park*, 1814

All Kentucky was still considered as a part of Fincastle County, and the inhabitants were therefore unrepresented at the capital —Theodore Roosevelt, *The Winning of the West,* 1889

. . . we have considered science as a steadily advancing army of ascertained facts —W. R. Inge, *The Church in the World,* 1928

Use of *consider* with *as* has continued unabated:

. . . the Calvinist clergy insisted that the Dutch should consider themselves as reborn into a fresh life —Simon Schama, *The Embarrassment of Riches,* 1988

Theology was still considered as the master science of which all other sciences were the servants —John A. Crow, *Spain: The Root and the Flower,* 1985

. . . argues that Chianti Classico is so much larger than the other Chianti districts that it deserves to be considered as a separate entity —James Suckling, *Wine Spectator,* 15 & 31 Mar. 1995

Evidence of fire and extended coverage insurance may be required by the lender of the borrower and the premium shall not be considered as a charge —*Code of Virginia Annotated,* 1994

Whether implies "or not" so saying "whether or not" is usually unnecessary, though it has been considered as acceptable idiom for more than 300 years —*New York Public Library Writer's Guide to Style and Usage,* 1994

You will have noted some older writers used above. Our evidence suggests that the *as* constructions are perfectly idiomatic but are not as common in recent use as they have been in the past. Nonetheless, they are still in use and are standard. *Consider* followed by *as* is a common and standard construction.

2. *Consider* can also be used with *for:*

. . . considered for an official position —*Dictionary of American Biography,* 1929

. . . was being considered for a new and rather difficult assignment —*Current Biography,* July 1965

3. The construction *consider of* is called by the OED "somewhat archaic." It does seem a bit old-fashioned:

She took three days to consider of his proposals —Jane Austen, *Mansfield Park,* 1814

"I will consider of her punishment." —Mark Twain, *The Prince and The Pauper,* 1881 (*A Mark Twain Lexicon,* 1938)

. . . they were to consider of their verdict —*Selected Writings of Benjamin N. Cardozo,* ed. Margaret E. Hall, 1947

considerable *Considerable* is involved in issues as an adjective, adverb, and noun. We will take them up separately.

1. *Adjective.* When *considerable* modifies a mass noun, with no determiner like *an* or *our,* Fowler 1926, 1965 notes a difference between British and American usage. Fowler says that in British usage *considerable* is used only with nouns for immaterial things, while in American usage it is used of nouns for material things. Evans 1957 also makes much the same statement without mentioning any use as specifically British. In fact Fowler's British use is both British and American:

. . . scenes of considerable crime —Robert Shaplen, *New Yorker,* 6 Sept. 1982

. . . a time of corruption, hatreds, sadism and considerable hysteria —Ernest Hemingway, "Miss Mary's Lion," 1956

. . . good wages, with considerable social prestige —Aldous Huxley, *The Olive Tree,* 1937

This use is standard and universal. The use with mass nouns of material does seem to be American. It occurs in standard English, but in works of a general and not a literary nature.

. . . has room for considerable luggage —Burgess H. Scott, *Ford Times,* September 1966

The product contains considerable salt —Raymond E. Kirk & Donald F. Othmer, eds., *Encyclopedia of Chemical Technology,* 1950

The Japanese . . . were equipped with considerable radio equipment —Herbert L. Merillat, *The Island,* 1944

Fore Shank—Rich in flavor, considerable bone —*Meat and Meat Cookery,* 1942

2. *Adverb.* The most ink has been spilled in the attempt to stamp out the old flat adverb *considerable* used to mean "to a considerable extent or degree; quite a bit." This use is not an Americanism in origin, but it seems to have survived chiefly in this country. Like most flat adverbs it seems to be primarily a speech form and like most flat adverbs, more common formerly than now. (See FLAT ADVERBS.) We have plenty of evidence of its currency in 19th-century American English, especially from the humorists.

"What air you here for?" I continued, warmin up considerable. "Can't you give Abe a minute's peace?" —Artemus Ward, "Interview with President Lincoln," 1861, in *The Mirth of a Nation,* ed. Walter Blair & Raven I. McDavid, Jr., 1983

... considerable many warts —Mark Twain, *Tom Sawyer,* 1876

In 20th-century use the adverb is found chiefly in speech, fictional and genuine, and in letters and similar speechlike prose.

My two new swans ... have high voices and use them considerable —Flannery O'Connor, letter, 15 Feb. 1964

... I bought my first professional mixer, one with a dough hook that kneaded the dough for me. That speeded things up considerable —Everett Burton, quoted in *American Way,* July 1984

Burchfield 1996 and Garner 1998 call the usage dialectal, but the Dictionary of American Regional English gives no regional limitation to the adverb, nor do our other citations suggest one. Only occasionally does the adverb appear in edited prose; Garner has a few citations from journalistic sources.

... the children of the upper and middle classes received the best schooling available with considerable greater frequency —Charles Frankel, *Columbia Forum,* Summer 1970

3. *Noun.* The noun use of *considerable* is evidently American. There is some disagreement among dictionaries as to which constructions are the adjective used absolutely and which are the noun. There is a construction "a considerable of (a)" which everyone calls a noun. It is, however, somewhat old-fashioned and may be going out of use.

It was a kind of mixed hound, with a little bird dog & some collie & maybe a considerable of almost anything else —William Faulkner, "Shingles," 1943 (American Dialect Dictionary)

This Faulkner quotation also appears in the OED Supplement and the Dictionary of American Regional English.

The following examples are felt to be adjectives by some dictionary editors and nouns by others. In either case they are standard usages, but they are perhaps passing out of use in edited prose.

... considerable is known concerning the literature of the Babylonians —*The Encyclopedia Americana,* 1943

... Arnold Shaw, who reputedly knows considerable about the business —*Saturday Rev.,* 21 Feb. 1953

... *The McGill News* apparently caused considerable of a furore by printing a "top secret" picture of the famous fence —*McGill News,* Spring 1954

... and that is considerable of an understatement —Rolfe Humphries, ed., *New Poems by American Poets,* 1953

... Robert Hunter, who at that time was considerable of a Socialist —*The Autobiography of William Allen White,* 1946

consistent When *consistent* is used with a preposition, *with* is by far the most common:

Father John did not think it to be consistent with his dignity to answer this sally —Anthony Trollope, *The Macdermots of Ballycloran,* 1847

consist in, consist of The world of usage writers tends to be tidier than the real world, and in drawing the customary distinction between *consist in* "lie, reside (in)" and *consist of* "to be composed or made up (of)" they take advantage of that artificial tidiness. The distinction is, in fact, usual—most writers observe it and so should you—but the OED shows that historical practice has not been consistent, and our evidence shows that current practice, while more consistent than in the past, is still not perfectly so. Here is one example each of mainstream use:

The skill ... consists in making them talk like little fishes —Oliver Goldsmith, quoted in Boswell's *Life of Samuel Johnson,* 1791

The committee ... consists of a baker's dozen of academics —Simon 1980

It is easy to see that when the subject is singular and the noun following is plural, *of* is the right preposition:

The remaining two-thirds consists of extracts of speeches —*Times Literary Supp.,* 5 Mar. 1970

But when *consist* appears with a singular noun on each side, there can be uncertainty. Sometimes the context is not sufficient to make it clear which meaning is intended:

... a new look at what Shaw's "reality" consisted in —*Times Literary Supp.,* 18 June 1971

Garner 1998 says *consist of* wrongly used for *consist in* is more common than the opposite mistake, but most of the ambiguous or uncertain examples in our files are uses of *consist in* where *consist of* might have made more sense:

Hypallage may consist in simple jumbling of the words in a sentence —John Dirckx, *The Language of Medicine,* 2d ed., 1983

Poe's reply consisted in a series of five articles —Nelson F. Adkins, *Papers of the Bibliographical Society of America,* 3d quarter, 1948

... a religious course that does not consist in memory work alone —Paul F. Klenke,

Bulletin of the National Catholic Education Association, August 1949

Chambers 1985 says that *consist in* is more formal than *consist of*; this may account for some writers' being uncertain in handling it since it is likely to be less familiar. At any rate our evidence indicates that writers are more likely to stray from the usual and recommended idiom with *consist in* than with *consist of*.

consonant When used with a preposition in contemporary English idiom, the adjective *consonant* is almost always followed by *with*:

> . . . he regarded his photography as an entirely wholesome pastime, consonant with his religious principles —Richard Ellmann, *N.Y. Times Book Rev.,* 17 June 1979

In earlier English (as far back as the 15th century, the OED attests), *consonant* was also used with *to*. This usage seems to have disappeared during the early part of the 20th century: our last citation is this:

> This, being consonant to tradition, need have done no harm —G. K. Chesterton, reprinted in *The Pocket Book of Father Brown,* 1946

constitute See COMPRISE.

consul See COUNCIL, COUNSEL, CONSUL.

consummate Bryson 1984 complains that *consummate* is used too much as an adjective, and Copperud 1970, 1980 complains that it is used too loosely by music critics. Copperud, however, is able to reach his conclusion because he arbitrarily restricts *consummate* to the single narrow sense "perfect." This is the sort of use he objects to:

> Victoria de los Angeles' consummate artistry is again evinced . . . —*Cambridge Rev.,* 22 Apr. 1950

Consummate here means "of the highest degree," a different sense from Copperud's and one recognized by most dictionaries. This sense is not always used flatteringly:

> . . . the only reason that anyone would buy things of such consummate ugliness —John Corry, *Harper's,* November 1970

Applied to a person, it suggests great skill and proficiency:

> . . . a reputation as a consummate professional —Don Heckman, *Stereo Rev.,* September 1971

> Onstage she is brash . . . the consummate hussy —Richard Grenier, *Cosmopolitan,* May 1973

These uses are not recent developments, as evidence in the OED shows. They are established beyond cavil.

contact The noun *contact* was turned into a verb about 1834. Its use was primarily technical, and it was noted by the OED in 1891. Sometime in the 1920s a nontechnical use of *contact* as a transitive verb began in the United States. The earliest citation in the OED Supplement is also, so far as we know, the earliest complaint about the use. It is from a 1927 review in *The Spectator,* a British periodical, of Theodore Dreiser's *An American Tragedy.* Here's what Dreiser wrote:

> . . . he was animated by a feverish desire to make use of this brief occasion which might cause her to think favorably about him—perhaps, who knows—lead to some faint desire on her part to contact him again —Theodore Dreiser, *An American Tragedy,* 1925

It is unlikely that Dreiser invented the use. In all probability he simply used something that was in the air. The earliest citation to come to our files does not suggest that this *contact* was suspected to be anything unusual:

> Men are divided in thought and feeling. They are no longer satisfied to be either churchmen or atheists, but are beginning to contact God vaguely, uncertainly, in many ways —*Springfield* (Mass.) *Union,* 14 Jan. 1926

Another early citation shows a use that helps explain why *contact* has remained alive; the substitutes usually recommended as "more precise" will not work very well here. Try *consult, talk with, telephone, write to* (the list from Little, Brown 1986) in this context:

> Bourne said he had been unable to contact Santo Domingo since the last weather report was received here at 2:12 p.m. —*Springfield* (Mass.) *Republican,* 14 Sept. 1930

Although the earliest objection to the use was published in England, our files show no direct British influence on the earliest American objectors. Reader's Digest 1983 opines that "the anglophile literary establishment" was a prime force in the controversy, but our evidence suggests that it started in the newspapers. Two events in the early 1930s seem to have fueled the controversy. On 1 Dec. 1931 several newspapers (we have clippings from the *New York Times* and the *Boston Post*) carried a story about one F. W. Lienau, a high official of Western Union, who denounced the verb *contact* and tried to get other officials of the company to forbid its use. The ensuing publicity lasted into 1932. Then in March 1932 the Lindbergh baby was kidnapped. There was intense publicity about the case, and *contact* cropped up often in the reporting of it, as in this news summary from an edition of the *Los Angeles Times*: "Lindbergh twice contacts kidnappers."

A 1935 clipping duly notes the presence of the literary establishment. A columnist in the *Brooklyn Times-Union* quotes Yale English professor William Lyon Phelps, who had a column in *Scribner's*, as denouncing the word. In 1938 the *New Republic* decided to campaign against the word. Opdyke 1939 is the first of the commentators in our library to express disapproval. From the 1940s on there is quite a lot of negative comment, and subsequently *contact* has become part of the standard furniture of usage books and college handbooks.

The assault on *contact* seems to have been based on two factors: the verb was formed from the noun by functional shift, and the use is supposed to have originated in business jargon. The first objection has been made for many other words of similar origin; yet, no objection has been raised to an even larger number of words formed in the same way. Functional shift has been an increasingly common method of word-formation in our language since Middle English. And the original functional shift of *contact* had taken place nearly a century earlier than the emergence of the disputed usage. It does not appear to be a strong basis for objection.

Of the ascribed origin in business jargon we cannot be certain. Early evidence is too sparse to support a judgment, even though there is plenty of later evidence of business use. Further doubt is cast by the speculations of a 1935 Brooklyn newspaper columnist, who claims a telegrapher told him that telegraphers had been using it for years. The same columnist also mentions army use in World War I. No evidence has yet appeared to confirm these speculations. Our present knowledge of the origin of the use, then, is still incomplete.

The objection in Great Britain to *contact* as an Americanism is on sounder ground, but it has proved so useful there, according to Longman 1984, that it is commonly used in all but the most formal contexts. The OED Supplement gives no warning label.

The real reason for the American objection is most likely popularity, as Safire 1982 observes. Sudden popularity underlies many a usage problem—see, for instance, HOPEFULLY and SPLIT INFINITIVE. Safire goes on to comment that *contact* "has fought its way into standard usage."

One of the interesting features of the dispute over *contact* is the growing number of commentators who have thrown in the towel. Copperud 1970 lists several commentators who find it acceptable, and Bernstein 1971, Kilpatrick 1984, Reader's Digest 1983, Burchfield 1996, and Garner 1998 can be added to his list. Geoffrey Nunberg, writing in *The At-

lantic (December 1983), wonders why anyone bothered to object. While Copperud claims the consensus of commentators to approve the usage, it has curiously become a fixture in the lists of disapproved usages reproduced in college handbooks. Thus we find that the newspaper writers who first raised the hue and cry have come to terms with usage, but the college English teachers, who came late into the game, are still fighting it.

All the fuss seems to have had no effect on actual use. The verb's usefulness seems to lie in the two characteristics mentioned by Bernstein when he came to accept it. It is short, usually replacing a longer phrase like "get in touch with." It is also not specific and for that reason is especially useful in such expressions—common in advertising—as "contact your local dealer." Such contact could be made by telephone, by mail, or simply by walking in. The writer does not need to speculate on how it might happen.

> . . . more people are using a computer at home to contact information services —Erik Sandberg-Diment, *N.Y. Times*, 15 Feb. 1983

> Alumnae interested in attending should contact the Public Relations Office —Erica Jong, *Barnard Alumnae*, Winter 1971

> What do you believe would be the effect on humanity if the earth were contacted by a race of such ungodlike but technologically superior beings? —*Playboy*, September 1968

Our evidence indicates that the verb *contact* is standard. It is not much used in literary contexts nor in the most elevated style. It is all right virtually anywhere else, however, with the probable exception of freshman English papers, where the instructors are likely to be observing the continuing opposition of the handbooks.

contact clauses   *Contact clause* is one of several terms grammarians use for a dependent clause attached to its antecedent without benefit of a relative pronoun. Some dictionaries and usage commentators discuss contact clauses under the heading *that, omission of*; in practice, however, any relative pronoun (as *who, whom,* or *which*) may be felt to be missing in a given instance.

Here are a few samples of contact clauses, all taken from the third volume of Jespersen 1909–49:

> Where is the thousand markes ∧ I gaue thee, villaine? —Shakespeare

> Here she set up the same trade ∧ she had followed in Ireland —Daniel Defoe

> The seed ∧ ye sow, another reaps —Shelley

> This wind ∧ you talke of —Shakespeare

Those nice people ∧ I stayed in Manchester with —Mrs. Humphrey Ward

I am not the man ∧ I was —Dickens

In each of these examples a relative pronoun could be inserted at the caret but is clearly not needed. Constructions such as these are appropriate in any variety of writing.

Historically the contact clause is the result of a paratactic construction of two independent clauses, not a relative clause with the relative pronoun omitted. Jespersen conjectures that contact clauses have been common in everyday speech for some six or seven hundred years; they seem to have come into literature as the forms of everyday speech came into it. In the 18th century, when the first influential grammars of English were written, English was analyzed by analogy with Latin. In Latin, relative clauses require the relative pronoun; English grammarians analyzing English in terms of Latin grammar decided that contact clauses must be relative clauses with the relative pronoun omitted. Their analysis has come down to the present day and may even be found in grammars not following Latin outlines:

In this transform the relative pronoun *which* replaces the noun phrase *the street*. If we wish, we may delete the relative pronoun and have a contact clause. . . . The transform is "The street we live on is quiet." —Harold B. Allen et al., *New Dimensions in English*, 1968

Since contact clauses did not exist in Latin, the 18th-century grammarians looked at them askance. Lindley Murray 1795 termed the construction "omitting the relative" and stated that "in all writings of a serious and dignified kind, it ought to be avoided." Jespersen quotes Samuel Johnson as calling the omission of the relative "a colloquial barbarism" (and also notes that examples can be found in Johnson's letters).

Burchfield 1996 notes that a clause lacking the conjunction *that* is also a contact clause:

Would you believe some reprocessing firms do not even remove the labels from old stock —Henry Hunt, *Houston Post*, 9 Sept. 1984

This construction is often included in treatments headed *that, omission of*. It is as long and well established in English as the contact clause and is appropriate in any variety of writing.

contagious, infectious Several usage books, including Bryson 1984, Phythian 1979, Bremner 1980, Copperud 1970, 1980, Shaw 1975, and Garner 1998, inform us that contagious diseases are spread by contact and infectious diseases by infectious agents. All contagious diseases are also infectious, but not all infectious diseases are contagious. Not many writers are likely to need to worry about the medical distinction, but if they do, they can always consult a good dictionary, where the distinction will be made clear.

Shaw, however, goes beyond the technical to the figurative uses. *Contagious,* he says, emphasizes speed while *infectious* emphasizes irresistible force. Bremner likes this distinction; on the other hand, Bryson sees no difference between the two when used figuratively. Our evidence from the past 20 or 30 years suggests that Bryson is closer to the mark. If there is a distinction in recent use, it is this: *contagious* can be used of pleasant and unpleasant things, but *infectious* is almost always used of pleasant things.

. . . European leaders felt terrorism could become contagious —Edward Girardet, *Christian Science Monitor,* 3 Apr. 1980

. . . put an end to contagious ideological heresy —John Darnton, *N.Y. Times Mag.,* 13 Apr. 1980

. . . the women's enthusiasm so contagious, that I for one could not keep my heart from beating faster —Germaine Greer, *Harper's,* October 1972

. . . radiating energy and vitality, a magnetic, irresistible current of warmth and contagious good humor —Tad Szulc, *N.Y. Times Mag.,* 27 May 1979

Here's the question . . . : Is this wild bout of "risk aversion" contagious, spreading from the markets to businesses and consumers? —Bernard Wysocki, Jr., *Wall Street Jour.,* 5 Oct. 1998

. . . a languid lyricism and elegance which proved highly infectious —*Times Literary Supp.,* 18 June 1971

. . . a freckled, impish face whose infectious grin reveals widely spaced teeth —Patrick O'Higgins, *Cosmopolitan,* July 1972

. . . with an enthusiasm that can be infectious —Tony Schwartz, *N.Y. Times Book Rev.,* 9 Dec. 1979

. . . the New York-based company . . . manages to get a surprising number of its projects built. This probably has something to do with the infectious zeal and canny determination with which the firm's partners . . . pursue their "investigations" —John Seabrook, *New Yorker,* 12 Feb. 2001

contemn See CONDEMN, CONTEMN.

contemporaneous See CONTEMPORARY.

contemporary 1. Back in the 1960s Theodore Bernstein was denouncing in *Win-*

ners & Sinners uses of contemporary in the sense "present-day, modern" that he had observed in the New York Times. He may, in part, have condemned the sense because he could not find it in his Webster's Second. Gowers in Fowler 1965 has a similar problem: he cannot find the meaning in the OED.

Webster's Second might well have served Mr. Bernstein better. Evidence in the OED Supplement and our own files shows that our editors simply missed the meaning. The oldest Supplement citation is the title of The Contemporary Review, which goes back to 1866. That title was known to the editors of Webster's Second, as was Contemporary American Literature, the title of a book from which citations for the dictionary were taken. And the use existed in other books marked for citations. For instance, here is George Bernard Shaw using the word in a way that illustrates the transition from "existing at the same time" to "present-day":

> In the preface to my Plays for Puritans I explained the predicament of our contemporary English drama —preface, Man and Superman, 1903

A little later in the same preface Shaw uses the word in the new sense:

> . . . what we call education and culture is for the most part nothing but the substitution of reading for experience, of literature for life, of the obsolete fictitious for the contemporary real . . .

These passages had been marked by our editors for other words than contemporary, as had this one:

> . . . very high in the waist, very full and long in the skirt; a frock that was at once old-fashioned and tremendously contemporary —Aldous Huxley, Those Barren Leaves, 1925

So our editors missed the sense and thereby contributed to the creation of a usage issue.

The new sense had become fully established by the late 1940s:

> The first of these, characteristic of the 1920's, was known to its adepts as Contemporary Music —Virgil Thomson, The Musical Scene, 1947

> . . . whose work is quite as contemporary as that of Austin Clarke even if he is no longer among the living —Babette Deutsch, New Republic, 21 Mar. 1949

Since this meaning is to be found in all recent American dictionaries as well as the OED Supplement, and is even part of the title of Evans 1957 and Harper 1975, 1985, you can assume that it is entirely standard.

The establishment of the "present-day" sense has led to a warning—in Cook 1985 and a couple of other books—about the likelihood of ambiguity in sentences like this:

> . . . but no one would consider Byron's poetry licentious by contemporary standards —N.Y. Times, 7 May 1968

The argument is that contemporary might refer either to Byron's time or to the present. While the possibility of ambiguity does exist, it seems remote unless the context has been deliberately removed. Even in the New York Times excerpt (cited in an issue of Winners & Sinners), the intent is made quite plain by "would consider"; if the writer had meant to refer to Byron's time the verb probably would have been "considered" or "would have considered." It is not very likely that a reader will be misled with the complete context to read.

2. Einstein 1985 recommends the use of contemporaneous for "existing at the same time" if the use of contemporary might cause confusion. Contemporary and contemporaneous have been synonymous since the 17th century. For many years the synonymy discriminations in Merriam-Webster dictionaries noted that contemporary was likely to be applied to people and contemporaneous to events. This distinction was only broadly true; contemporaneous was less frequently applied to people than contemporary and more often to things or events. But the development of the newer sense of contemporary has altered the relationship between the two words. Since the late 1940s the "modern, present-day" meaning of contemporary has become its predominant use. Contemporaneous, has essentially retained its original sense. What we are beginning to see is what H. W. Fowler called "differentiation": contemporary is being used chiefly in its most recent sense, and contemporaneous is being used for "existing at the same time"—more or less replacing contemporary in that sense. While this differentiation is not complete, it does permit writers to contrast the two words in a single sentence:

> But now that we have not merely contemporary but almost contemporaneous history, putting events in their place almost as they roll off the production line —Times Literary Supp., 9 Jan. 1964

So the "present-day, modern" sense of contemporary has become fully established, and contemporaneous appears to be replacing contemporary in its older sense. You will be able to observe whether this differentiation develops so completely that the sense Bernstein and Follett and Gowers thought to be the only correct one actually becomes old-fashioned. Do not expect the result to be too tidy, however; a countervailing force exists in the noun *contemporary,* for which the older meaning remains in vigorous use.

contemptible See CONTEMPTUOUS 1.

contemptuous **1.** *Contemptible, contemptuous.* In the 16th, 17th, and 18th centuries these two words were used interchangeably, as the citations in the OED show. Shakespeare, in particular, provides a good example of the practice of those times: the four Shakespearean citations listed in the OED at *contemptible* and *contemptuous* are the only ones listed in Bartlett's *Concordance to Shakespeare* (1894), and these four citations constitute one use of each word with each meaning.

By 1770, however, at least one person was voicing dissatisfaction over the ambiguity of the adverbial forms of these words:

> If I hear it said that one Man treats another contemptibly, I hardly know whether the Meaning is that he treats him with Contempt, or that his own Behaviour is contemptible —Baker 1770

The ambiguity is of the kind that can become a springboard for wit. Bache 1869 relates an anecdote about "Dr. Parr" (possibly Dr. Samuel Parr 1747–1825, an English pedagogue known as a vastly learned but dogmatic conversationalist):

> A man once said to Dr. Parr:—"Sir, I have a contemptible opinion of you." "Sir," replied the Doctor, "that does not surprise me: all your opinions are contemptible."

This riposte caught the fancy of Ayres 1881, who took the anecdote for his own book, and Lurie 1927, who did likewise.

Baker's complaint and Parr's retort were probably reflections of the attitudes and usage developing around them. The date of the last citation in the OED for *contemptuous* meaning "worthy of contempt" is 1796, for *contemptible* meaning "full of contempt" is 1816, and for *contemptibly* meaning "with contempt" is 1827. The evidence we have for later uses of these meanings is scanty.

Though we have little direct evidence for the continued use of the older meanings, there is plenty of indirect evidence in the form of injunctions against such uses. We know of more than twenty sources from the past century or so which advise readers not to confuse *contemptible* and *contemptuous.* No doubt some of these commentators include this topic simply because a predecessor did.

2. When *contemptuous* is used in the predicate and followed by a prepositional-phrase complement, the preposition is always *of:*

> . . . I have been indifferent to, if not indeed contemptuous of, blame —Havelock Ellis, *My Life,* 1939

> . . . they seem to grow more sullen, sloppy, and contemptuous of the public they are supposed to serve —John Fischer, *Harper's,* November 1971

contend The word *contend* is very commonly found followed by a clause:

> . . . contending that he will be editing the one journal no one could damage —John Kenneth Galbraith, *New York,* 15 Nov. 1971

Contend is also used with prepositions, and *with* is the one most often found:

> We must constantly—in an infinite variety of ways—be contending with one another —Edmund Wilson, *A Piece of My Mind,* 1956

> . . . they had contended first with wind and sandstorms, and now with cold —Willa Cather, *Death Comes for the Archbishop,* 1927

Less frequently, *contend* is used with *against* in this same relation:

> . . . some of the difficulties against which the French business man had to contend —Paul Johnson, *New Statesman & Nation,* 19 Sept. 1953

When the object of the preposition is the source of contention, *for* is the choice:

> . . . a gray stone castle, for whose keep Bruces and Comyns and Macdowalls contended seven centuries ago —John Buchan, *Castle Gay,* 1930

Earlier in this century, some usage books mention that *contend* may also be used with *about.* Our citation files, however, have no evidence for this use in running text.

continual, continuous As far as we can tell, the first person to draw a distinction between *continual* and *continuous* was Elizabeth Jane Whately, in her book *A Collection of English Synonyms,* published under her father's name in 1851.

> A 'continuous' action is one which is uninterrupted, and goes on unceasingly *as long as it lasts,* though that time may be longer or shorter. 'Continual' is that which is constantly renewed and recurring, though it may be interrupted as frequently as it is renewed.

Miss Whately's distinction has been repeated with some frequency since; our files hold examples from about 50 handbooks and usage guides published between the turn of the 20th century and 1998.

You may well wonder why this distinction needs such frequent repeating. Margaret M.

Bryant, writing in *Word Study* (May 1956) seems to have found the reason:

> As explicit as all handbooks for writing are, they have not succeeded in establishing a definite difference in *continual* and *continuous* in the minds of many.

The reasons for this failure are, as we shall see, historical. *Continual* is the older word, dating from the 14th century. The definition given first in the OED encompasses both the sense Miss Whately prescribes for *continuous* and the one she prescribes for *continual*; the latter is marked "less strictly" in the OED. *Continuous* came along in the 17th century and was first applied to continuity in space. The earliest distinction between the two words may be the one made by Dr. Johnson in his 1755 dictionary: "*Continual* is used of time, and *continuous* of place." The meaning of *continuous* prescribed by Miss Whately did not become established until her own time—from the 1830s on.

It is quite possible that Miss Whately was basing her discrimination on what she believed to be the cultivated practice of her time, although she gives us no actual examples nor does she cite any author who makes the distinction. She seems to have been entirely unaware of the earlier use of either word and of the fact that the original sense of *continual* had not died. When the first example below was written, *continuous* hardly existed in English:

> . . . the plot being busy (though I think not intricate) and so requiring a continual attention —Aphra Behn, epistle to the reader, *The Dutch Lover*, 1673

> . . . a continual supply of the most amiable and innocent enjoyments —Jane Austen, *Mansfield Park*, 1814

> . . . the waves, which poured in one continual torrent from the forecastle down upon the decks below —Captain Frederick Marryat, *Peter Simple*, 1834

> The cold evening breeze . . . sprinkled the floor with a continual rain of fine sand —Robert Louis Stevenson, *Treasure Island*, 1883

So this sense of *continual* persisted in use, while at the same time *continuous* was developing a new sense to compete with it. And in spite of the inroads of *continuous*, this sense of *continual* is still used now:

> . . . the continual dread of falling into poverty —George Bernard Shaw, *The Intelligent Woman's Guide to Socialism and Capitalism*, 1928

> We live in a country where His Majesty's Cabinet governs subject to the continual superintendence, correction and authority of Parliament —Sir Winston Churchill, *The Unrelenting Struggle*, 1942

> Or will the continual presence of abstraction in man's thought dry up . . . the old springs of poetry? —Robert Penn Warren, *Democracy and Poetry*, 1975

> During the long aging the two kinds of fermentation . . . take place, and continual evaporation thickens the liquid —Corby Kummer, *Atlantic*, September 1994

Miss Whately missed one genuine distinction, the one noted by Dr. Johnson. *Continuous* and not *continual* is used of continuity in space:

> Small windows, too, are pierced through the whole line of ancient wall, so that it seems a row of dwellings with one continuous front —Nathaniel Hawthorne, *The Marble Faun*, 1860

> . . . the horses and chariots alone . . . extended in a continuous line for more than six English miles —Sir James G. Frazer, *The Golden Bough*, 1935

> Paper tape is a continuous medium —Susan Artandi, *An Introduction to Computers in Information Science*, 1968

But something must be conceded to Miss Whately's observation: *continual* is more likely than *continuous* to be used for repetition of something that may be interrupted.

> There were continual quarrels —William Butler Yeats, *Dramatis Personae*, 1936

> What happens is a continual surrender of himself —T. S. Eliot, "Tradition and the Individual Talent," 1917

> You will also have to get used to continual visits from all the unbalanced people on the island, who love to plague editors —James Thurber, letter, 21 May 1954

And only *continuous* is used in a construction with *with* that emphasizes unbroken connection:

> He believed that the former was continuous with the Middle Ages and the world of antiquity —J. M. Cameron, *N.Y. Rev. of Books*, 6 Nov. 1969

> Some claim that the animals acquired the essentials of human language and, in so doing, revealed capacities continuous with human cognition —Colin Beer, *Natural History*, May 1986

But we have many instances where both words are used in similar contexts:

> . . . though it was a mild night on the sea, there was a continual chorus of the creak-

ing timbers and bulkheads —Jack London, *The Sea-Wolf,* 1904

. . . the continuous thunder of the surf —Robert Louis Stevenson, *Treasure Island,* 1883

. . . the air was full of a continual din of horns —Leslie C. Stevens, *Atlantic,* August 1953

There was a continuous rumble and grumble of bombardment —Siegfried Sassoon, *Memoirs of a Fox-Hunting Man,* 1928

. . . as if some deep continual laughter was repressed —Hallam Tennyson, *Encounter,* December 1954

. . . the irrepressible and continuous crying which her happiness caused here —E. L. Doctorow, *Ragtime,* 1975

Part of the seeming indifference on the part of writers to a distinction so often repeated is to be explained by the writer's point of view—whether the writer perceives the subject as uninterrupted or not over time. This is obvious in the next two examples: clearly the wars and the trials had some actual breaks between them, but the writer views them as an ongoing and uninterrupted sequence.

. . . the subcontinent will be rent by innumerable and continuous local wars —Hyman P. Minsky, *Trans-Action,* February 1970

From 1948 on, purges and trials have been continuous —Wayne S. Vucinich, *Current History,* February 1952

To summarize the discussion thus far: many factors enter into the choice between *continual* and *continuous*. As we have seen, *continuous* is the usual word when the application is to physical continuation, continuation in space; nobody uses *continual* in this way. And it is true (though we have not tried to illustrate) that *continuous* is the only choice in a large number of technical applications, in mathematics, construction, manufacturing, biology, and more; *continual* has almost no technical applications. And because it has a much broader spectrum of application, *continuous* is the more common word. Yet, *continual* has been used since the 14th century in its primary sense of "continuing indefinitely in time without interruption" and is still used in that sense. *Continuous* is more recent in this application, and it is very frequently so used in current English. *Continual* is the word most often chosen when the meaning is "recurring."

If you are a person who likes careful distinctions, H. W. Fowler's may lie closer to the actual use of *continual* and *continuous* in the areas in which they actually compete. Fowler

1926 says that that which is *continual* "either is always going on or recurs at short intervals & never comes (or is regarded as never coming) to an end." That which is *continuous* is that "in which no break occurs between the beginning & the (not necessarily or even presumably long-deferred) end." Here are two examples illustrating Fowler's distinction, and you may also wish to test it against the examples given above:

The promised visit from "her friend" . . . was a formidable threat to Fanny, and she lived in continual terror of it —Jane Austen, *Mansfield Park,* 1814

. . . that, for 100 days or more, during the primary season, his life could be in continuous jeopardy —James MacGregor Burns, *N.Y. Times,* 14 Sept. 1979

continually, continuously The first thing that needs to be said about these adverbs is that they are used in similar contexts so much of the time that it is very difficult to discern a marked difference between them. For the record, *continually* had a 350-year head start on *continuously,* which in its early uses was found principally in technical contexts. *Continuously* is currently used about as frequently as *continually* and for the most part in essentially the same contexts. However, two specific kinds of uses (which constitute only a small minority of all the uses in our files) are handled by *continuously* alone. It is the adverb used when something continues in space rather than time:

The hand binding will show a sewing thread running continuously from the first needle hole to the last —Edith Diehl, *Bookbinding,* 1946

. . . the frieze decorated continuously with mythical battle scenes —*Antiques and the Arts Weekly,* 3 Dec. 1982

And *continuously* does all the technical work:

Let *f* and *g* map *B* continuously into itself —Simeon Reich, *American Mathematical Monthly,* January 1974

. . . compare the amount . . . when interest is compounded continuously —School Mathematics Study Group, *Calculus of Elementary Functions,* 1969

A few commentators from Bierce 1909 to Bremner 1980 have tried to extend to these adverbs the distinction between the adjectives *continual* and *continuous* (see CONTINUAL, CONTINUOUS). Unfortunately, that distinction has even less to do with the way the adverbs are used in standard English than it does with the adjectives.

If *continuously* and *continually* are to be distinguished, they must be distinguished by criteria other than those advanced for the adjectives. We can do this best by pointing out the typical uses of each. *Continuously* has the two unshared uses mentioned above. It is also used to contrast with adverbs other than *continually* for the purpose of stressing that something happens steadily and imperceptibly without discrete stages or episodes:

Its proponents think that species evolve episodically, not continuously —*N.Y. Times Book Rev.,* 5 Dec. 1982

. . . the seatback angle can be adjusted continuously, rather than in steps —*Consumer Reports,* May 1979

Continuously is also used where stress is laid on an unbroken succession of discrete time periods:

The mayor . . . , elected continuously since 1945 —*Current Biography,* September 1965

After holding the international chess title continuously for nine years —*Current Biography,* June 1965

Continually is used especially when something continues to exist or happen, with or without interruptions, for an indefinite period of time:

The solar cells continually face the sun —Newlan MacDonnell Ulsch, *Boston Globe Mag.,* 21 June 1981

. . . the expression . . . of a beautiful secret continually tasted, was still on his face —John Updike, *Couples,* 1968

. . . tells of the loneliness that has been continually present in his life since he became blind and deaf —*Current Biography,* December 1966

The wines are the continually underrated local ones —John Vinocur, *N.Y. Times Mag.,* 9 Oct. 1983

Continually is also the adverb of choice when repetition is emphasized:

. . . and indeed I was deeply and continually honored wherever I went —Garrison Keillor, *Lake Wobegon Days,* 1985

My job is to edit copy continually —E. B. White, letter, September 1921

. . . there are two works I do reread continually —Muriel Spark, quoted in *N.Y. Times Book Rev.,* 12 June 1983

These examples show uses of *continually* and *continuously* in which a fastidious writer can make a rational choice. But these do not represent all usage. Many times the words are used as if they were interchangeable. The ma-

jority of the interchangeable uses are uses of *continuously* in contexts where *continually* would have worked as well and might have been expected; the use of *continually* in a context that is typical of *continuously* is relatively infrequent. The intrusion of *continuously* into the territory of *continually* is probably the result of the increase in the use of both *continuous* and *continuously* that has been going on for three centuries, rather than the result of confusion, indifference, or a failure of standards.

You can observe the distinctions described and illustrated above (or even the traditionally prescribed distinction), if you want to; quite a few writers, however, seem to make virtually no distinction at all.

continue on A half dozen or more commentators from Ayres 1881 to Garner 1998 have dismissed *continue on* as a redundancy, with the *on* considered (usually) superfluous. Ayres himself found the *on* to be "euphonious" in some expressions, but superfluous in others. Later commentators seem to have missed the euphony. Safire 1984, however, defends the expression when applied to travel.

Our evidence does not suggest that *continue on* is a favorite phrase in English; its use does not even make up a significant percentage of our evidence for *continue.* The citations we have are about evenly divided between use involving travel or movement and other use. Some of the travel examples:

They continued on for a quarter of a mile, squatting under the foliage and bellying over the ledges —Norman Mailer, *The Naked and the Dead,* 1948

The Iberian continued on to Palestine where he met St. Jerome as well —Bernard F. Reilly, *The Medieval Spains,* 1993

. . . bears due north through the coddled greenery of Wenham and Hamilton and at one time continued on past Ipswich —John Updike, *New England Monthly,* October 1989

And a few of the others:

. . . decides to make no investment at all and continues on with the old equipment —Ralph E. Cross, *Dun's,* January 1954

. . . an engineer who started with the Nike missile in 1946 and continued on to Deltas, Thors, and all the way up to the Hubble Space Telescope —Preston Lerner, *Air & Space,* February/March 1994

It continues on through Mr. Nixon's life after political death, documenting his relentless effort at self-exculpation —Sidney Blumenthal, *N.Y. Times Book Rev.,* 24 Nov. 1991

This is clearly a matter of no special importance. It hardly seems that anyone need worry about the space wasted by a two-letter word, especially one which may help the rhythm (or euphony) of a sentence or even serve usefully to underline continuation where cessation might have been expected. If you are one of the few who use *continue on,* you may keep right on using it. And if you do not use it, of course, there is no reason to begin.

See also REDUNDANCY.

continuous See CONTINUAL, CONTINUOUS.

continuously See CONTINUALLY, CONTINUOUSLY.

contractions Contractions became unfashionable in the 18th century and continued so until the early 20th century at least; in 1901 a correspondent of *The Ladies' Home Journal* was still wondering if *can't, couldn't,* and *won't* were permissible. Today many handbooks for writers recommend contractions to avoid sounding stilted. See AIN'T; AN'T; A'N'T; DON'T; WON'T. See also ABBREVIATIONS.

contrast 1. As a noun, *contrast* is used with the prepositions *between, with,* and *to:*

What a contrast . . . between this gray apathy and the way the Germans had gone to war in 1914 —William L. Shirer, *The Rise and Fall of the Third Reich,* 1960

The contrast between the wealthy citizenry of Potosí and the Indian miners —*Times Literary Supp.,* 23 Feb. 1967

. . . identified through comparison or contrast with the history of other societies —Peter J. Parish, *N.Y. Times Book Rev.,* 3 Feb. 1985

. . . a congenial contrast with his more bourgeois background —Gay Talese, *Harper's,* January 1969

The starting five was black, . . . and they made a startling contrast to Adolph Rupp's lily-white aggregation —Jack Olsen, *Sports Illustrated,* 15 July 1968

When preceded by *in, contrast* may be followed by either *to* or *with; to* seems somewhat more common in American English.

His gaily striped tie was in odd contrast to his haggard face —Van Siller, *Cosmopolitan,* March 1972

The enforced simplicity in this diary of half-living is in contrast to the intensity of his former life —*Times Literary Supp.,* 21 Mar. 1968

In contrast with Mr Chou, Mr Nguyen Huu Tho was strongly critical —David Bonavia, *The Times* (London), 19 Nov. 1973

Morrissey himself, in contrast with his present surroundings, is all New York —Melton S. Davis, *N.Y. Times,* 15 July 1973

2. The commentators are of several minds on the question of the verb *contrast* used with *with* or *to.* Alford 1866 allows both but prefers *to;* Bernstein 1965 and Safire 1984 allow both but think *to* implies a stronger contrast than *with;* Longman 1984, Simon 1980, and Garner 1998 think *with* the only choice in modern use. The OED finds *with* more common than *to,* and *with* predominates in our most recent evidence.

Some examples of *with:*

. . . contrasting her with other women and thinking how deliciously ingenuous she was —Vita Sackville-West, *The Edwardians,* 1930

It does not contrast the woman riveter with the chic mannequin —Arthur Miller, *Harper's,* September 1969

. . . a mountain whose majestic calm contrasts with the extraordinary scenes of human cruelty —Diane Johnson, *N.Y. Times Book Rev.,* 27 Mar. 1983

Some examples of *to:*

It is interesting to contrast the policies of the two German states to the use of German and English —Richard E. Wood, *English Around the World,* November 1976

. . . and what more comfortingly square profession could there be to contrast to the danger and self-righteousness of his parents' endeavors? —Mopsy Strange Kennedy, *N.Y. Times Book Rev.,* 25 Nov. 1984

We find little evidence of a difference of intensity between *with* and *to. With* is simply more often used.

convenient As a predicate adjective *convenient* can be followed by *to* and the infinitive:

. . . it is convenient to divide it into three parts —Norman Fisher, *London Calling,* 13 May 1954

. . . they find it more convenient to conform —John Foster Dulles, quoted in *New Republic,* 30 May 1955

It can also be followed by prepositional phrases introduced by *for* or *to. For* is used mostly for persons or their convenience:

. . . whichever is more convenient for you —Gwen Ford, *Young Miss,* November 1967

. . . convenient for carrying packages to the pantry shelf —*Phoenix Flame,* 1953

To is used for persons but also for places:

In a few constituencies it is convenient to the party managers if a good Jewish or

Catholic candidate wins —D. W. Brogan, *The English People,* 1943

. . . not located convenient to large cities —*Dictionary of American History,* 1940

. . . a point convenient to a group of plantations —*American Guide Series: Virginia,* 1941

conversant *Conversant* usually takes the preposition *with*:

. . . obviously conversant with all of Wodehouse's characters —*New Yorker,* 30 Oct. 1971

. . . woe to the liberal politician who was not quickly conversant with them —Norman Mailer, *Harper's,* March 1971

. . . two authors conversant with a large number of widely differing languages —Margaret Masterman, *Times Literary Supp.,* 19 Mar. 1970

It also takes *in,* but less frequently:

. . . may prefer to speak Spanish but are often conversant in English as well —John M. Crewdson, *N.Y. Times,* 8 Aug. 1979

convict When the verb *convict* is followed by a preposition, often the preposition is *of*:

. . . was convicted of perjury and sentenced to prison —Stanley E. Dimond & Elmer F. Pflieger, *Our American Government,* 1961

Big words are hopelessly out of place when they convict an author of insincerity —Eugene S. McCartney, *Recurrent Maladies in Scholarly Writing,* 1953

Less frequently, *convict* is used with *on*:

. . . was convicted . . . on the less serious charge —*Current Biography 1947*

Some language commentators deplore the use of *for* with *convict,* but it does not appear to be in widespread use. The Merriam-Webster files contain only one citation for it:

If we cannot convict some of them for their disloyal activities perhaps we can convict some of them for perjury —Joseph McCarthy, quoted in *New Republic,* 14 Feb. 1955

convince, persuade The use of *convince* in a construction in which it is followed by *to* and an infinitive phrase has been controversial since about 1958. Edwin Newman is often mentioned in discussions of this issue, but he came late (1974) upon the scene; Bernstein, Copperud, Follett, and Shaw all had preceded him. Most recent comment centers on criticism of the construction with *to* and the infinitive, but accepts as legitimate complement phrases beginning with *of* and clauses usually beginning with *that.* Some commentators try to distinguish *convince* and *persuade* on the basis of various subtle differences in meaning that they descry. A few—Bremner 1980, Barnard 1979—see no point in the controversy.

Barnard 1979 says that a half century ago, when he was a freshman in college, he was taught that *convince* meant "mental acceptance," and *persuade* mental acceptance followed by action. Barnard's summary connects that era with ours, because the ascribed meanings are currently put to use to make a point about syntax, whereas earlier they were used simply to distinguish the two words without explicit reference to syntax. The typical constructions—*convince* with *that* or *of* and *persuade* with *to* and the infinitive—were then used only in illustrating what was supposed to be a distinction in meaning.

In 1969 P. B. Gove, Merriam-Webster's editor in chief, answered a letter from a linguist about the construction in which *convince* is followed by the infinitive. He said that it was not in his idiolect and went on to explain why the construction was not illustrated in Webster's Third: the definer had only three examples of it as opposed to 61 of a clause following the verb. The definer no doubt thought it too infrequent a construction to be worth quoting. The definer has proved a poor prognosticator, however. Of the citations gathered between the editing of the Third and 1969, nearly 60 percent showed the infinitive construction. Flesch 1964 said that *convince to* was "a new idiom springing up under our noses," and he was right.

Our earliest evidence for the new idiom comes from 1952:

A new political party, the Constitutional Party, is formed to try to convince the Electoral College to vote for Gen. MacArthur and Sen. Byrd —*Current History,* November 1952

It had undoubtedly already existed in speech for some time, and it gradually increased in use in print:

. . . a method by which Congress in 1913 convinced Woodrow Wilson to modify his stand on currency reform —*New Republic,* 2 Aug. 1954

He convinced the Russians to let him exhibit anyway —*N.Y. Times,* 13 Sept. 1958

. . . something I could never convince him to read —John Lahr, *N.Y. Times Book Rev.,* 3 Dec. 1967

. . . to convince his compatriots to leave the country —Theodore Draper, *N.Y. Rev. of Books,* 12 Mar. 1970

The construction is fully established now:

> She said to hell with it, she would skip Italy. . . . You convinced her to go —Jay McInerney, *Bright Lights, Big City,* 1984

> . . . had helped convince them to drop a case or settle out of court —Edward Felsenthal, *Wall Street Jour.,* 19 Oct. 1994

> If sailors obsessed with saving weight on their racers can be convinced to recycle, then all sailors can —Sheila Heathcote, *Sailing,* November 1993

When Theodore Bernstein first noticed the construction in 1958, one of the corrections he suggested was the substitution of a *that*-clause for the infinitive phrase: "He convinced the Russians that they should let him. . . ." Such a use of the clause complement when action is involved is apparently rare, however. We do have a few examples:

> . . . was convinced by his teachers that he should take a senior high school biology course —C. Robert Haywood, *NEA Jour.,* January 1965

> When is a spoofy movie not quite convinced it should act like one? —Liz Smith, *Cosmopolitan,* December 1976

A review of the evidence in our files shows that almost always when *convince* is followed by a clause, mental acceptance only is connoted:

> . . . which is to convince itself that there are too many lines in a sonnet —James Thurber, letter, 23 June 1952

> . . . after he convinced himself that she was all right —"Centaur in Brass," in *The Collected Stories of William Faulkner,* 1950

> He had tried for weeks to forget her, he said, convinced that she was too young for him —Herman Wouk, *Marjorie Morningstar,* 1955

> The agency lawyers were convinced the decision was a fluke —Eileen Hughes, *Ladies' Home Jour.,* September 1971

But do not believe that *persuade* has disappeared from the use involving action:

> . . . Freud was persuaded to make an expedition to the great natural wonder of Niagara Falls —E. L. Doctorow, *Ragtime,* 1975

> Could language somehow be persuaded to come closer to experience? —Howard Nemerov, *Prose,* Fall 1971

> . . . denouncing those who tried to persuade him to come back in during one especially violent snowstorm —Simon Winchester, *The Professor and the Madman,* 1998

> And he confronted Cuban Marielitos . . . in the bowels of an Atlanta prison to persuade them to surrender hostages —Bill Lodge, *Dallas Morning News,* 17 Apr. 1999

To sum up: long ago *persuade* became established in a use connoting mental acceptance without following action. *Persuade* still has this use, often with the same *of* and *that* constructions regularly found with *convince.* Sometime around the middle of the 20th century, *convince* began to be used to connote mental acceptance followed by action, usually in a construction in which an infinitive phrase follows the verb. This construction is now a fully established idiom. Usage writers who have tried to block it (and some are still trying) have failed. But *convince that* is still more frequently used.

cop A few commentators worry about the status of *cop* for "police officer." Bremner 1980 says it is gaining respectability. It has gained respectability, and is used regularly in the general English of newspapers and magazines in the United States and in Great Britain and other countries using British English. It is, of course, used in novels and occasionally turns up in collections of essays and such, although it does not appear often in the most elevated kinds of writing.

cope *Cope* in the sense "to deal with and try to overcome problems and difficulties" has been used since Milton's time with the preposition *with*:

> . . . was beginning to feel a way towards a plan for coping with that old incubus —Stella Gibbons, *Cold Comfort Farm,* 1932

> . . . had simply not been able to cope with the revolutionary new tactics —William L. Shirer, *The Rise and Fall of the Third Reich,* 1960

Until the 1930s this appears to have been the only construction. *Cope* then came to be used absolutely, with no object added in a phrase introduced by *with.* This use is much like the absolute use of the verb *manage.* The Shorter OED dates it from 1932, the OED Supplement from 1934. It first appeared in British English and apparently became established there during World War II and its aftermath. In fiction it seems to have been primarily used in speech:

> "My cousin Pamela Lyson is coping. . . ." —Elizabeth Goudge, *Pilgrim's Inn,* 1948

> "She's not the sort to cope." —Joyce Cary, *A Fearful Joy,* 1949

> "We can cope," she said —H. E. Bates, *The Scarlet Sword,* 1951

But not all use was in fictional speech. Foster 1968 found it in a British soldier's account of his wartime experiences at Anzio in 1944. And it was used in general running text:

> . . . only 9 per cent were unable to cope at all —*Times Literary Supp.,* 10 Sept. 1954

> After all, since the flying boats stopped, the old aerodrome, opened in the 1920s, has been coping —Robert Finigan, *London Calling,* 3 Mar. 1955

In the 1950s the new construction began to appear in American English:

> . . . and on that occasion reliable old Schrafft will be on hand to help you cope —*New Yorker,* 8 Dec. 1951

> Four divisions of Russian occupation forces couldn't cope —*Newsweek,* 5 Nov. 1956

In the 1960s the usage came to the attention of American commentators. Copperud 1964 thought it correct but so unusual that people were likely to think it a mistake. The Heritage 1969 panel did not like it in formal writing (but the subject has been dropped in later editions), and Bremner 1980 does not like it at all, while the Harper 1975, 1985 panels accept it only in speech. E. B. White in his second and third editions of Strunk & White (1972, 1979) characterizes it as "jocular"; he seems to have been unfamiliar with the use of the construction in the *New Yorker.* None of these American commentators reveals knowledge that the construction is fully established in British use; no British commentator mentioned it until Burchfield 1996; he finds it standard. It has continued in British use:

> . . . the French authorities would either have to confess their inability to cope or would have to find new methods —*Times Literary Supp.,* 28 Apr. 1972

> . . . the struggles of a young middle-class married couple who could not really cope —Margaret Crosland, *British Book News,* May 1982

And it appears to be well established in general American use:

> . . . the astronauts would have been increasingly unable to cope —Henry S. F. Cooper, Jr., *New Yorker,* 18 Nov. 1972

> . . . candid interviews with families struggling to cope —Ellen Chesler, *N.Y. Times Book Rev.,* 28 Aug. 1983

The absolute use of *cope* is well established; it has had no effect whatsoever on the *cope with* construction.

cord See CHORD, CORD.

coronate Back in 1967 one Darcy Curwen wrote this:

> A short while ago I heard one of the better radio announcers say, "When Pope Pius was coronated. . . ." There is no such word; the fellow meant crowned —*Bulletin of Emma Willard School,* June 1967

Nickles 1974 doesn't like *coronate* either. William Safire in the *New York Times Magazine* for 16 March 1980 called it "wrong."

A look into Webster's Third or the OED will give you a different slant on the word. *Coronate* has been around since the 17th century. It is derived from Latin *coronatus,* past participle of *coronare* "to crown"; it is not a back-formation from *coronation.*

Coronate is a relatively rare verb. It last got fairly frequent play in American publications back at the accession of Queen Elizabeth II:

> Queen Elizabeth II will probably be coronated sometime between August and the spring of 1953 —*Wall Street Jour.,* 9 Feb. 1952

It has been used only occasionally since. Burchfield 1996 says it is not used in British English except as a term in biology. Most people use *crown.* But *coronate* is available if you need it, and it is a perfectly legitimate word.

correct *Correct* is on some lists of absolute adjectives (see ABSOLUTE ADJECTIVES). It has, of course, been frequently used in the comparative and superlative.

> . . has wrote a more correct account of Italy than any before him —Joseph Addison, preface to *Remarks on Italy,* 1705 (cited in OED under *any*)

> . . . recommends them to his readers as most correct —Baron 1982

> As far as we can judge, from rhymes and other clues, the American accent and stress of English is more 'correct', i.e. older, than the British accent —Howard 1984

correspond *Correspond,* in the senses meaning "to be in conformity or agreement" or "to compare closely, match," may be followed by either *to* or *with*; according to our evidence, *to* is used more often:

> . . . the man whose consciousness does not correspond to that of the majority is a madman —George Bernard Shaw, *Man and Superman,* 1903

> Their political position corresponds further to their military strength —*New Republic,* 3 May 1954

> . . . all quotations should *correspond* exactly with the originals in wording —*MLA Style Sheet,* 2d ed., 1970

When meaning "to write to someone," *correspond* is used with *with* exclusively:

In 1943 he began to correspond with a young Welsh poet, Lynette Roberts —Michael Glover, *British Book News,* July 1985

could care less, couldn't care less Everyone knows that *couldn't care less* is the older form of the expression. Eric Partridge in *A Dictionary of Catch Phrases* (2d ed., 1985) says that the phrase arose around 1940 and was probably prompted by an earlier catch phrase, "I couldn't agree with you more." If we assume Partridge's date of origin refers to speech, it is hard to quibble. We do have a 1945 citation from a BBC war correspondent covering a British commando operation:

You would have thought that they were embarking on a Union picnic; they just couldn't care less —Stewart Macpherson, 24 Mar. 1945, in *The Oxford Book of English Talk,* ed. James Sunderland, 1953

The OED Supplement and the editor of the second edition of Partridge's book cite the phrase as the title of a book published in 1946. It was established by the late 1950s and early 1960s in American use:

To me the elaborate framework, and symbolism, was too much for such petty characters. I couldn't have cared less what happened to any of them —Flannery O'Connor, letter, 17 Jan. 1958

". . . Some place with air conditioning. And without a TV set. I couldn't care less about baseball." —James Baldwin, *Another Country,* 1962

The origin of *could care less* is also obscure. All we know about it for sure is that it came later. Harper 1975, 1985 reports getting letters asking about the expression starting in 1960. That would suggest its existence in speech around that time. No printed examples have so far turned up that antedate the 1966 examples collected by James B. McMillan and cited in his article in *American Speech* (Fall 1978). Our earliest citation is from what appears to be a wire-service picture caption:

This roarless wonder at Chicago's Brookfield Zoo could care less about the old saying dealing with the advent of March —*Springfield* (Mass.) *Republican,* 2 Mar. 1968

The reason why the negative particle was lost without changing the meaning of the phrase has been the subject of much speculation, most of it not very convincing. No one seems to have advanced the simple idea that the rhythm of the phrase may be better for purposes of emphatic sarcasm with *could care less,* which would have its main stress on *care,* than with *couldn't care less,* where the stress

would be more nearly equal on *could* and *care.* You, however, may not find this argument very convincing either.

The attitude of the commentators toward *could care less* has in general been negative. Safire 1980 saw usage of *could care less* as having peaked in 1973; he dismissed it as defunct in 1980. But it has not disappeared:

The Americans, of course, could care less about British reaction —Joseph White, *Springfield* (Mass.) *Union-News,* 11 June 1993

. . . they could care less what anybody outside the team thinks of them —E. M. Swift, *Sports Illustrated,* 6 Apr. 1987

. . . instead of belonging to an old-line business lobby . . . she is a member of the more militant National Federation of Independent Business. . . . She could care less about the IMF. Her concerns are doing away with estate taxes . . . —Richard Dunham, *Business Week,* 14 Sept. 1998

Bernstein 1971 thought it not quite established then; if it becomes established, he says, it will be another example of "reverse English." Pairs of words or phrases that look like opposites but mean the same thing are not unknown in English: *ravel/unravel, can but/cannot but,* for instance. (For another case in which a negative construction and a positive construction mean the same thing, see BUT 4.)

This is what our present evidence suggests: while *could care less* may be superior in speech for purposes of sarcasm, it is hard to be obviously sarcastic in print. This may explain why most writers, faced with putting the words on paper, choose the clearer *couldn't care less.*

could of This is a transcription of *could've,* the contracted form of *could have.* Sometimes it is used intentionally—for instance, by Ring Lardner in his fiction. Most of you will want *could have* or *could've.* See OF 2.

council, counsel, consul A sizable number of handbooks and schoolbooks going back at least as far as Utter 1916 warn against the confusion of *council* and *counsel;* a few even add *consul* to the broth. According to the OED, *council* and *counsel* were hopelessly muddled in medieval times; and our present division of meanings, which apparently matches neither the Latin nor the French from which both are derived, began to establish itself in the 16th century. In current English, *council* generally stands for some sort of deliberative or administrative body, while *counsel* is used for advice or for a lawyer and as a verb meaning "to advise" or "to consult." *Consul* in modern use refers to a diplomatic official.

Our evidence shows that the chief confusion likely to be encountered is the substitution of *council*—the more common word—for one of the three main uses of *counsel*. In the following three examples, *counsel* should have been the spelling chosen:

> . . . who can council students —*Linguistic Reporter,* March 1979

> . . . his council is sought by leaders of city and nation —*Current Biography,* September 1966

> . . . they're still self-conscious about their council being a woman —*American Labor,* July–August 1969

Our advice to you is first, don't try to use *council, counsel,* and *consul* in a single sentence as some of the handbooks do—you'll only muddle people. And second, if you have some doubt about which form you want, a look in your dictionary will clear things up.

councillor, councilor, counselor, counsellor These derivative nouns follow the spellings of their root words. See COUNCIL, COUNSEL, CONSUL.

counterproductive, self-defeating Phythian 1979 and Harper 1975, 1985 are not pleased with the adjective *counterproductive,* a fairly recent (about 1959) addition to the English vocabulary. Phythian complains that it is too often used as "a loose alternative to *unprofitable, detrimental,* etc." Harper calls it a vogue word which "says nothing that *self-defeating* doesn't say quite as well."

Both these comments miss the point. *Counterproductive* seems to have found a little gap in the language in which to establish itself: no other word has quite the same meaning. Try, for instance, any of the three suggested substitutes in this example:

> . . . where everybody in the room is pretty sharp, competition in the counterproductive sense goes down, reciprocal respect goes up —John Barth, *N.Y. Times Book Rev.,* 16 June 1985

In the unprofitable sense? In the detrimental sense? In the self-defeating sense? None is a very likely replacement.

When applied to actions, *self-defeating* carries a strong suggestion of failure:

> . . . may have convinced millions of Americans . . . that violence is a self-defeating and futile way to relieve frustration —Frank K. Kelly, *Center Mag.,* May 1968

> . . . tried to rebut the reports, but his praise . . . was so fulsome as to be self-defeating —*Current Biography,* January 1968

Counterproductive stresses the producing of results contrary to those intended but tends to suggest a hindering rather than a failure of attainment:

> But some Protestant clergymen now tend to think that professional fund raising is counterproductive —*Time,* 4 Sept. 1964

> . . . retailers must be sure that its impact will not be advantageous in one season of the year only to be counterproductive in another —Michael LaBaire, *Publishers Weekly,* 28 Mar. 1980

> . . . diversity-training seminars are increasingly derided as window-dressing, and hiring and promotion quotas are under growing attacks as unfair or counterproductive —Claudia H. Deutsch, *N.Y. Times,* 20 Nov. 1996

Our evidence suggests that *counterproductive* has found a place in the language. You can use it if you need it.

couple, *noun* **1.** *Agreement. Couple* is a singular noun but it often takes a plural verb. Several commentators recommend the plural verb when the sentence also has a pronoun referring to *couple* since the pronoun will almost always be *they, their,* or *them.*

> The couple remain friends and share custody of their four children —*People,* 10 May 1982

The governing principle here is notional agreement; if the writer is thinking of two people, the verb is plural:

> The couple were married on April 21 —*Current Biography,* March 1966

> . . the couple have featured in sixteen plays —*Times Literary Supp.,* 8 Feb. 1974

> Before long the young couple have vanished —Patricia T. O'Conner, *N.Y. Times Book Rev.,* 16 Feb. 1986

When the writer thinks of the couple as a unit, the verb is singular:

> The couple has three children —*Current Biography,* February 1967

> The couple has an apartment in Dallas —*N.Y. Times,* 1 Dec. 1970

> The couple dislikes fussy food —Francesca Stanfill, *N.Y. Times Mag.,* 21 Dec. 1980

You will note that the verb seems naturally to be plural when the writing concerns a wedding, as two people are wed, and singular when it concerns children, as joint action is often involved. Consequently when children are mentioned and a pronoun reference follows, editors are likely to be upset:

> The couple has four children of their own —*N.Y. Times,* 24 Mar. 1966 (in *Winners & Sinners,* 31 Mar. 1966)

But *they, their,* and *them* are the standard pronouns of reference for *couple,* especially when people are referred to, regardless of the number of the verb. (See THEY, THEIR, THEM.) In the example just quoted, *his* or *her* are impossible and *its* would sound silly. The substitution of the plural verb might tend to suggest that the couple had children by previous marriages. Although *they, their,* and *them* have been used for centuries to refer to nouns and pronouns that take singular verbs, many newspaper editors seem not to realize it. If a sentence like the one above makes your editor see red, you'll have some complicated rewriting to do. In other instances you could simply use the plural verb:

A Dayton couple was slain in their home today —*N.Y. Times,* 30 July 1961 (in *Winners & Sinners,* 17 Aug. 1961)

In this example, the plural verb would work fine.

2. *A couple of.* The use of *couple* meaning "two" came under attack in the 19th century. Richard Grant White 1870 seems to have been in the vanguard (Hall 1917 gives 1867 as the first publication of the objection). The basis for the objection seems to be the etymological fallacy—*couple* is derived from Latin *copula* "bond." White's objection is repeated in several other American usage books—among them Bache 1869, Ayres 1881, and William Cullen Bryant's *Index Expurgatorius* (1877)—until sometime after the turn of the century.

But this usage had been around since the 14th century. Webster 1909, for instance, illustrated it with quotations from Sir Philip Sidney, the King James Bible, Addison, Dickens, and Carlyle. It is not surprising then, that White's objection rather fizzled out early in the 20th century. Here are some other old examples of the use:

A couple of senseless rascals —George Villiers, *The Rehearsal,* 1672

We finished a couple of bottles of port —James Boswell, *Life of Samuel Johnson,* 1791

The tribe lost a couple of their best hunters —Rudyard Kipling, *The Second Jungle Book,* 1895

. . . during a couple of years that I spent abroad —Henry James, *The Ivory Tower,* 1917

The objection shifted from White's etymological one to the more general charge of colloquialism or to an objection to the use of the phrase in the sense of "a small but indefinite number." Vizetelly 1906 seems to be the earliest to object to the indefinite use; many later commentators follow. Bierce 1909 takes the

opposite point of view, stating that *couple* should only be used when the idea of number is unimportant. The tendency of *couple* to be indefinite is shown in these examples:

For a couple of years the company succeeded in keeping clear of further disaster —E. K. Chambers, *The Elizabethan Stage,* 1923

. . . a cotton mill run by a hard-bitten North country working man who had borrowed a couple of hundred pounds to start the business —G. M. Trevelyan, *A Shortened History of England,* 1942

It apparently made relatively slow progress at the start, but after a couple of years it was in wide and indeed almost general use —H. L. Mencken, *The American Language, Supplement 1,* 1945

A couple of times I gave up —E. B. White, letter, 2 Jan. 1957

Some handbooks still stigmatize *a couple of* as colloquial or informal, but we think you need not worry too much about the propriety of a phrase that has been in use for 500 years. To those who might urge that it is to be questioned only when it means "a few," we point out that the works of E. K. Chambers, G. M. Trevelyan, and H. L. Mencken cited above are not noted for their breezy style.

For a more recent concern of the commentators, see COUPLE, *adjective.*

couple, *adjective* While the commentators were worrying whether the noun *couple* could be used to mean simply "two" and whether it could mean "a few" (see COUPLE, *noun*), the word itself was following the path of development that *dozen* had taken centuries earlier—dropping its following *of* and being used like an adjective. We are not sure when this process began in speech, but we begin to find written evidence in the 1920s. Sinclair Lewis heard it in the dictation of George W. Babbitt:

. . . all my experience indicates he is all right, means to do business, looked into his financial record which is fine—that sentence seems to be a little balled up, Miss McGoun; make a couple sentences out of it if you have to —Sinclair Lewis, *Babbitt,* 1922

Lewis was not the only one to use it:

. . . where the land rises to a couple or three or four feet —W. H. Hudson, *Far Away and Long Ago,* 1924

. . . in the phrases *a couple peaches, a couple of peaches,* only two should be meant —Krapp 1927

G. P. Krapp is the first commentator to mention the construction, but he evidently saw nothing wrong with it. A decade later, however, it was thought to be wrong:

> **couple.** Not an adj.; must be followed by "of" and preceded by article —Muriel B. Carr & John W. Clark, *An A B C of Idiom and Diction,* 1937

Of all the subsequent commentators who have disapproved the omission of *of,* Evans 1957 has the most interesting observation. While insisting that standard English requires *of* between *couple* and a following noun, he points out that the *of* is omitted before a degree word such as *more* or *less.* And indeed this construction is found in standard English:

> We can end this chapter by looking at a couple more examples of Middle English writing —Charles Barber, *The Flux of Language,* 1965

> . . . middle-aged men expecting a couple more promotions —Peter Preston, *Punch,* 28 Nov. 1973

These examples are British; the construction is explicitly recognized by a recent British dictionary, Longman 1984. The construction occurs in American English too:

> . . . till they had taken a couple more first-class lickings —Elmer Davis, *But We Were Born Free,* 1954

But American English usage seems to have been influenced by the number of commentators stressing the necessity of *of.* The result is the occasional "a couple of more":

> . . . a couple of more wins from Jim Palmer —Jim Kaplan, *Sports Illustrated,* 10 Apr. 1978

Nickles 1974 refers to this construction as a "garble" and opines that it results from confusion of *a couple of* with some such construction as *a few more*; he fails to recognize the standard *a couple more.* Theodore Bernstein seems to have encountered the construction, too; in a June 1967 *Winners & Sinners* he quotes Evans with a measure of approval, but questions whether all degree words fit the pattern. He comes a cropper by confusing Evans's "degree words" with ordinary adjectives. Bernstein was unable to find any specific comment in usage books on "a couple of more" and concludes therefore that it is not wrong, though "ungraceful." If you find it ungraceful also and do not care to omit the *of* before *more,* you can put the *more* after the noun instead; the example above would become "a couple of wins more from Jim Palmer." Bernstein also notes that when *more* is promoted to pronoun by omission of the following noun, *of* is not used, as in ". . . I think I'll have a couple more."

But we have strayed from the red-blooded, 100-percent-American adjective before a plural noun that Sinclair Lewis heard in the speech of the middle-class Middle West. The usage is not found in British English. Here are a few American ones:

> The first couple chapters are pretty good —E. B. White, letter, 26 Oct. 1959

> So let's start with a couple samples —Quinn 1980

> Afterward, I met Mark Mullaney upstairs for a couple beers —Ahmad Rashad, *Sports Illustrated,* 25 Oct. 1982

> . . . though Mr. Shaw himself still operated a couple wagons for hire —Garrison Keillor, *Lake Wobegon Days,* 1985

This construction seems well established in American English. Everyone who comments knows it to be common in speech. It is now quite common in general prose, but we have seldom found it in prose that aspires to formality and elegance. Its two most frequent uses are with periods of time and with number words like *dozen, hundred,* and *thousand*:

> . . . have surfaced dramatically in the last couple weeks —James P. Gannon, *Wall Street Jour.,* 16 Oct. 1970

> A couple thousand cases of liquor —*Wall Street Jour.,* 14 July 1969

> . . . contains a couple hundred poems —William Cole, *Saturday Rev.,* 18 Sept. 1976

To recapitulate: *a couple* without *of* seems to have begun being used like *a few* and *a dozen* in the 1920s. It is firmly established in American speech and in general writing (though not the more elevated varieties) when it is used directly before a plural noun or a number word. Before *more, a couple* is used without *of* in both British and American English and in this context is often preferred even by American commentators.

course 1. See COARSE, COURSE.
2. Copperud 1970, 1980 finds *course* as used in such phrases as *in the course of* or *during the course of* redundant for *during, at,* etc. Phrases like these are often used for rhythm or space in a sentence—to keep the content words spaced out so they don't interfere with one another; content words can be too tightly packed to be immediately understood. In addition, these phrases add emphasis to the notion of duration. Let us look at a few examples to see when these phrases are unnecessary and when they are useful:

> When in the Course of human events, it becomes necessary for one people to dissolve

the political bands which have connected them with another —*Declaration of Independence*, 1776

This example is perhaps unfamiliar to writers on usage. The phrase here helps build a stately and formal opening.

. . . the Italian star Silvana Mangano, whom De Laurentiis married in the course of making the picture —*Current Biography*, May 1965

If the phrase is reduced to *in* here, only puzzlement would result. "During the making of the picture" is no improvement either. *While* would be idiomatic here but might import a ludicrous hint that they were married on the set.

During the course of the Early Horizon, region after region seems to have broken free from the Chavín influence —Edward P. Lanning, *Peru Before the Incas*, 1967

Here "the course of" would seem omissible; it does no more than emphasize somewhat the length of the period and suggest a happening gradually. But if not at all essential, the phrase is at least harmless, and little is gained by its omission.

But it is not difficult to find instances where abridgment or omission would improve the sentence:

. . . both of which were merged into National Bank of North America in the course of the year —*Annual Report, CIT Financial Corp.*, 1971

During the course of this meeting, she told him about her overload —*AAUP Bulletin*, December 1967

We conclude that phrases like *in the course of* and *during the course of* can be useful as well as flatulent. You need not avoid them on principle, but you would do well to weigh their use.

craft 1. The editors of Harper 1985 asked their usage panel about *craft* used as a verb by President Reagan in "the wisdom to craft a system of government. . . ." Sixty-nine percent of the panel turned thumbs down on the use, but panelist James J. Kilpatrick saw nothing wrong with it. Bernstein 1965 seems to have been the first to notice the verb; he identifies the use of the past participle in advertising.

The OED has a single 15th-century example of *craft* used as a transitive verb, so the 20th-century use is a sort of revival. It does seem to have started in advertising, chiefly as a past participle, shortly after World War II:

Crafted with the great beauty and care that make every . . . shoe a masterpiece in footwear —advt., *Harper's Bazaar*, October 1947

Crafted in fine mahoganies and choice, hand-rubbed mahogany veneers —advt., *N.Y. Herald Tribune*, 15 July 1951

The intention is to suggest the workmanship and skill of master craftsmen. The revival was not long in reaching more general contexts:

Even the beautifully crafted mosaics on the walls were dingy —Lloyd C. Douglas, *The Big Fisherman*, 1948

There are ten stories in the collection, most of them superbly crafted —Ann F. Wolfe, *Saturday Rev.*, 3 Sept. 1955

Recent use has followed the same general lines. *Craft* and *crafted* are used literally:

. . . showing aborigines crafting boomerangs with Stone-Age techniques —*Smithsonian*, August 1970

. . . one of the most sophisticated and highly evolved machines that man has yet crafted —David F. Salisbury, *Christian Science Monitor*, 9 Oct. 1979

More frequently, though, they are found in figurative use, very often referring to writing:

. . . it's a carefully crafted poem —Robert Weaver, *Books in Canada*, January 1972

. . . fifty guidelines for crafting a sales pitch —Walter McQuade, *Fortune*, 21 Apr. 1980

The novel deal was crafted to avoid restrictions in federal law —*Business Week*, 2 Mar. 1981

. . . offering bribes to venal literary editors, crafting ecstatic reviews of each other's books —Martin Amis, *N.Y. Times Book Rev.*, 5 Apr. 1981

There are those in the current White House who spend all their time crafting the President's image —Alexander M. Haig, Jr., *TV Guide*, 15 Mar. 1985

The President, or his speech writer, was miles ahead of most of the Harper usage panel. *Craft*, both as verb and participial adjective, is well established in current American use. It has also been used in British English.

2. *Craft, kraft*. A few people unfamiliar with the word think that *kraft*, the kind of paper your brown supermarket bag is made of, is spelled *craft*. It is not; use *k* for this paper.

credence, credibility Phythian 1979 says that *credence* "is sometimes confused with *credibility*." A letter to the editor of *Nature* (6 Dec. 1984) makes the same point, calling the confusion "a new verbal abuse." It isn't very new; Fowler 1926 shows an example of the usage they are talking about in his discussion of the overlap in sense between *credence* and *credit*.

The crucial constructions here are *give credence to* and *lend credence to*. When the subject of the phrase is a person, the meaning of *credence* is the familiar one of "belief":

> . . . the directors of information in the Kremlin gave as little credence to their own agents as they did to Churchill —*Times Literary Supp.,* 4 July 1968

> . . . though I can't give much credence to that suggestion —Stanley Kubrick, quoted in *Playboy,* September 1968

The familiar sense is being used even when the construction is made passive:

> Should baseball statistics since World War II be given the same credence as those from the years . . . ? —William Claire, *Smithsonian,* April 1984

It is when the subject of these phrases is inanimate that we get a use closer in meaning to *credibility*:

> Two results stand out . . . ; neither of these gives any credence to the assertions of Lord Ridley —in Fowler 1926

> The nautical rope molding in the cornices and door trim gives credence to the theory that . . . —*American Guide Series: North Carolina,* 1939

> The evidence lends some credence to the view that American electoral politics is undergoing a long-term transition —Walter Dean Burnham, *Trans-Action,* December 1969

> His theory on the origin of human cancer has lent credence to the idea that cancer can be conquered by a massive infusion of funds —Lucy Eisenberg, *Harper's,* November 1971

The problem here is not really a question of confused usage. It is a problem created by the limits of lexicography. *Credence* in these typical constructions is a quality. When it inheres in humans, the lexicographer defines it by the name of a similar quality known to inhere in humans: *belief.* But when the quality of *credence* inheres in something inanimate—a theory, an action, evidence—the lexicographer has to resort to a different word—*believability*—to define the quality because *belief* is most readily understood as applying to humans. The difficulty for the lexicographer here is with *belief* and *believability,* not *credence,* for *credence* is applied to both persons and things in exactly the same constructions.

The criticized use seems to be of 20th-century origin. In its usual constructions it is certainly of the 20th century. Our evidence suggests that the application to things is increasing, especially in the construction *lend credence to.* There is nothing in the sources in which this construction is found to suggest that it is anything less than standard. It is used in both British and American English.

The OED notes that *credence* and *credit* have historically shared senses—*credence,* for instance, once had a financial sense that *credit* has taken over completely. One sense of *credit* that the OED marks obsolete means "credibility" or "believability." (The obsolete status is doubtful because Fowler's discussion of *credence* and *credit* includes two citations of what is apparently this sense.) Perhaps the dominance of the financial senses of *credit* has led to *credence*'s taking over this sense from *credit.* Compare these two examples:

> Many things which are false are transmitted from book to book, and gain credit in the world —Samuel Johnson, in James Boswell, *Life of Samuel Johnson,* 1791

> The legend gained new credence when dredging operations of recent years brought up several rotting wagon hubs —*American Guide Series: Tennessee,* 1939

And we note, finally, that *credence* is used with *lend* quite a bit more often than *credibility* is. Here, however, are two examples of *lend credibility to*:

> . . . cast him as a Parisian dress designer, a character to which he nevertheless managed to lend some credibility —*Current Biography,* January 1967

> . . . the blacks' report charged that blacks had been invited to the conference only to lend it credibility —Don Mitchell, *Harper's,* August 1971

In the first example, with its human subject, *credence* simply would not have been chosen. In the second we have an inanimate subject —an action. But the political overtones militate in favor of *credibility.* It may be that the recent politicization of *credibility* has also contributed to the increasing use of *credence* in other contexts.

credibility See CREDENCE, CREDIBILITY; CREDULITY, CREDIBILITY.

credible, creditable, credulous Commentators from at least as far back as Hodgson 1889 have been commenting upon or warning against confusion of these words. Hodgson gets off on the wrong foot, holding up the novelist Tobias Smollett for criticism for his use of *creditable* in this passage:

> Two creditable witnesses . . . affirmed the appearance of the same man —*The Expedition of Humphry Clinker,* 1771

Hodgson thought Smollett should have used *credible,* but Smollett was right: the first sense of *creditable* was "believable," and it was certainly current at the time Smollett was writing. This sense has mostly dropped out of use now; *credible* has taken over the field, and if this sense of *creditable* is not archaic, it is certainly rare. The sense meaning "credible" is entered in some law dictionaries. Most writers use *credible* for this meaning, however; *creditable* is most frequently used as a rather tepid word of praise:

> The restaurant's salads and vegetables are generally creditable, if not altogether imaginative —Jay Jacobs, *Gourmet*, September 1980

Credulous, which when applied to people contrasts with *skeptical,* does not appear to be misused very often. We do have one instance in which it is used to mean "credible":

> If it strikes you as credulous that the eminently successful producer of popular television games shows . . . doubled as a hit man for the CIA . . . , then you can credit this book —*Publishers Weekly,* 9 Mar. 1984

This leaves us with the substitution of *credible* for *creditable* or *credulous.* This has certainly happened, but our evidence for it indicates it is not common. We have one oldish example

> He has done credible work —*Anthology of Magazine Verse 1926*

in which *creditable* seems to have been intended. And we have a more recent one

> So long as our popular science writers depict science as an esoteric and inexact pursuit, the credible public will never dare judge the policy consequences or moral implications —*Trans-Action,* January/February 1967

in which *credulous* is apparently intended.

Apart from the question of whether the "credible" sense of *creditable* is still a live use, there appears to be very little to worry about here. Most writers know the differences of meaning that separate the three words, or they trust their dictionaries.

See also INCREDULOUS, INCREDIBLE.

credit   Simon 1980 seems to feel that *with* is the only preposition the verb *credit* is to be used with; he specifically objects to *for. With* is the most common preposition:

> . . . in his own era, Samuel Adams was often credited with or blamed for creating the Revolution all by himself —Carol Berkin, *N.Y. Times Book Rev.,* 12 Sept. 1976

> "Our company was credited with hundreds of kills," Reid told a reporter —Seymour M. Hersh, *Harper's,* May 1970

To and *as* are used:

> Historically, the quality of children's lives has been blamed on or credited to their par-

ents —Carll Tucker, *Saturday Rev.,* 15 Oct. 1977

> . . . overpopulation must be credited as a major factor in the vicious border war —F. Herbert Bormann, *Massachusetts Audubon,* June 1971

For is also in reputable use:

> These procedures proved successful . . . , and coupled with changes in agricultural practices, were credited for the success of control programs in a number of other tropical areas —Lloyd E. Rozeboom, *Johns Hopkins Mag.,* Spring 1971

> Credit Mobil, its final sponsor, for not being nervous about sex after 40 —Judith Crist, *New York,* 10 Feb. 1975

creditable   See CREDIBLE, CREDITABLE, CREDULOUS.

credulity, credibility   *Credulity* and *credibility* come close in meaning only when used with such verbs as *strain, tax,* or *stretch.* Even here use is quite straightforward in most instances. *Credulity* is used of the receiver:

> It is hard, without an inordinate strain upon the credulity, to believe any such thing —H. L. Mencken, *Prejudices: Second Series,* 1920

> He stretched credulity beyond the limits of all but the inner circle of the faithful — George E. Reedy, *N.Y. Times Book Rev.,* 18 Oct. 1981

Credibility is used of the sender:

> Howard's sudden transformation . . . puts a strain on the novel's credibility —Harry T. Moore, *Saturday Rev.,* 12 Feb. 1972

> . . . because the author places too much weight on these characters' shoulders, their credibility is strained —Susan Isaacs, *N.Y. Times Book Rev.,* 26 Sept. 1982

But *credulity* carries overtones of gullibility, an aspect often stressed in dictionary definitions. As a result, some writers have used *credibility* of the receiver in an apparent attempt to avoid the negative overtones of the alternative:

> . . . the contrast between the respectable exterior and the turbulent interior of this family strains her reader's credibility—*Times Literary Supp.,* 4 May 1951

> . . . wants us to believe that the narrator wrote this manuscript in a few hours on that Sunday afternoon, which somewhat taxes credibility —Ivan Gold, *N.Y. Times Book Rev.,* 12 Aug. 1979

Most writers, however, are content to use *credulity* of the receiver.

credulous   See CREDIBLE, CREDITABLE, CREDULOUS.

creep *Creep* is one of an interesting class of English verbs having a long vowel in the infinitive and a short one in the past and past participle. In Middle English *creep* was a strong verb—one that is inflected by internal vowel change—that came over into the weak class in the 15th century, developing the now-prevalent *crept* as past and past participle (the dental stop \t\ is the hallmark of past and past participle of weak verbs and also the clue to the regularity of this form). The dialectal *crep* and *crope* are survivors from Middle English.

Like other members of this class—*leap, kneel, dream*—*creep* has developed an even more regular past and past participle with the same vowel as the infinitive: *creeped.* The OED has examples of *creeped* from a 17th-century playwright, an 18th-century historian, and a 19th-century anthropologist. It is still used in the 21st century. Most of our recent evidence for *creeped* comes from speech; we have seen little of it in print yet, where *crept* is usual. Here are some recent examples:

> Bumbry may have creeped up —Tony Kubek, NBC baseball telecast, 5 Oct. 1983

> The interest rate has creeped up a little bit —Michael Ashe, Springfield (Mass.) news telecast, 11 July 1984

> That attitude made him one of the most hated men in the NBA, and it must have creeped into the way he did business off the court —Bryan Burwell, *USA Today,* 20 Apr. 1994

You might be interested in keeping your eyes and ears open for *creeped.* This verb has not yet settled down from the changes that began five centuries ago.

crescendo A few commentators, Bernstein 1958, 1965, Bremner 1980, Howard 1978, and Bryson 1984, object to the use of *crescendo* to mean "a peak of intensity." The proper use, they say, is to mean "a gradual increase in intensity." Since the increase has to reach some sort of climax, the extension of the word to the climax from the increase hardly seems surprising. The extended use may be American in origin:

> In July he was ordered abroad, and their tenderness and desire reached a crescendo —F. Scott Fitzgerald, "The Rich Boy," 1926

> The infrequent lamps mounted to crescendo beneath the arcade of a filling-station at the corner —William Faulkner, *Sanctuary,* 1931

> . . . the bombardment rose to a deafening crescendo —*N.Y. Times,* 12 July 1953

The sense is not limited to the United States, however:

> . . . it was built to order for the flies, and these rose to a crescendo of hungry activity —Farley Mowat, *People of the Deer,* 1952

> . . . gales were well-nigh continuous. One reached its crescendo at one o'clock in the morning with a gust that had everyone wondering what would go —*The Countryman,* Autumn 1950

And it is still with us:

> While no one yet imagines the protests reaching a Vietnam-like crescendo —Roger M. Williams, *Saturday Rev.,* 30 Sept. 1978

> . . . its episodes too neatly arranged to build to the quiet crescendo of the boy protagonist's weaning from his family —Tom Dowling, *San Francisco Examiner,* 19 Nov. 1985

The "peak, climax" sense of *crescendo* is still a minority use, and it shows no sign of driving the earlier senses from use, in spite of the opinion of Amis 1998. You can avoid it if you wish to, but it is clearly a fully established meaning.

cripple As a noun for a person with a physical disability *cripple* seems to have been largely replaced by such euphemisms as *handicapped, disadvantaged,* and *disabled*—a replacement noted by Malcolm Muggeridge (in *Esquire,* April 1974) and Robert A. Nisbet (in *Fair of Speech,* 1985). But it can still be found in fiction, in reference to the past, and occasionally in travel writing.

> Acts is studded with accounts of apostolic miracles, among them . . . Paul curing a cripple and doing other wonders —Dr. Ralph M. McInerny, *Miracles,* 1986

> . . . renowned for painting dwarves, cripples and children who obviously suffered from birth defects —Natalie Angier, *N.Y. Times,* 11 Sept. 1990

> Old Karachi teemed around me: tough-looking Pathan elders with turbans and orange-dyed beards; cripples and beggars, street hawkers —Mary Anne Weaver, *Smithsonian,* June 1990

> Whether it is . . . something as condemned as assaulting a cripple or as glorified as killing someone wearing the wrong uniform, if it is violent, we males excel at it —Robert Sapolsky, *Discover,* March 1997

When modified by some limiting adjective which takes it out of the realm where it is felt to be objectionable, *cripple* continues to flourish:

> . . . a sentimental, manipulating emotional cripple, who attempted to destroy her children —Anne Roiphe, *N.Y. Times Book Rev.,* 8 July 1984

... failure to have these talents would have set a man apart as a social cripple —Robert Pattison, *On Literacy,* 1982

criterion, criteria, criterions *Criterion* is a learned word taken from the Greek in the 17th century; in those more learned times, the OED informs us, it was not uncommon for writers to spell the word in Greek letters. Things are different in these less learned times, as we shall see.

Criterion has two plural forms, the classical *criteria* and the analogical English form *criterions.* The English *criterions* seems to have more approvers in usage books than actual users, if our citation file represents the matter fairly. It had a spate of popularity in the late 1940s and early 1950s, but is quite rare since then. It is still in occasional use, however:

... insisted in his lecture that language levels should be distinguished by social criterions —Harold B. Allen, *The Linguistic Institute in the Days of Bloomfield,* 1983

But the usual plural is *criteria,* by an overwhelming margin. *Criteria* is in fact so common that it is met more often than the singular *criterion.* And it is undoubtedly this frequency of *criteria* that has led to its perception by many as a singular. We cannot be sure when use of *criteria* as a singular first began. It probably occurred in speech before writing and in casual writing before print, but we have no direct evidence. Our first singular example appeared—perhaps fittingly, some would say—in a pamphlet on education published by an agency of the U.S. government:

In some cities the area to be covered, or number of schools rather than number of children, is the criteria considered in visiting teacher assignments —Katherine M. Cook, *The Place of Visiting Teacher Services in the School Program,* 1945

Our next example is from a publisher's advertising:

Dr. Harbage is writing about a criteria for great literature of all times —advt. flyer, Macmillan Co., October 1947

Then we found it in philosophy:

... Hsuntze proposes another criteria by which "we will not suffer from the misfortune of being misunderstood. . . ." —Jack Kaminsky, *Philosophy & Phenomenological Research,* September 1951

By 1964 the singular *criteria* had come to the attention of usage writers. We now know of twenty-some, one of which, through three editions, firmly believes *criteria* to be Latin.

The singular *criteria* seems pretty well established in speech. The following examples were all taken from radio or television broadcasts:

... to act independently and with complete liberty with only one criteria, the greatest good for the greatest number —Lyndon B. Johnson (in Harper 1985)

Let me now return to the third criteria —Richard M. Nixon, 20 Apr. 1970

The criteria was . . . —Caspar Weinberger, former U.S. Secretary of Defense, 14 Apr. 1986

If this sort of spoken testimony were all we had, it would be easy to dismiss the singular *criteria* as one of those inadvertences to which the spoken language is always liable. But there is this sort of evidence in cold print:

Professor Kira then examines the modern American bathroom from the standpoint of ergonomics or human engineering, whose criteria is that form follows function —*N.Y. Times,* 9 May 1966

No criteria, however, exists for gauging the longevity of a "new word" —Donald B. Sands, *College English,* March 1976

There is as yet no widely accepted test criteria for mopeds —*Consumer Reports,* June 1978

Into this he includes a criteria which assures proper and decent working conditions —advt. flyer, Oxford University Press, April 1981

... the induction committee waived its normal five-year retirement criteria for fear Kelley might never retire —Todd Balf, *Yankee,* 4 Apr. 1992

We have, incidentally, heard *criterias* used as the plural of *criteria,* but it is very rare in print:

... for establishing digestion process design criterias —flyer, CRC Press Inc., Fall 1984

Criteria is at this point: it definitely exists as a singular count noun, and it is definitely criticized. Only time will tell whether it will reach the unquestioned acceptability of *agenda.* In the meantime you should be aware that the singular *criteria* is still a minority use and that its legitimacy is disputed.

For other foreign plurals, see LATIN PLURALS.

criticize See CRITIQUE 2.

critique 1. *Noun.* It is hard to understand why there has been any controversy about this noun. Fowler 1926 disliked it (he gives us no reason for his dislike) and thought it might die out. It didn't. Flesch 1964 called it a "fad word" and Evans 1957 thought it "highfalutin." We don't understand this 20th-century antagonism to a word that had been in continuous use for more than two centuries. Copperud 1980 characterizes these criticisms as "dated and pedantic."

2. *Verb.* More recent criticism (Cook 1985, Harper 1985, Heritage 1982, 2000, Janis 1984, *Winners & Sinners,* 20 Jan. 1986) has been directed toward *critique* used as a verb. The assumption of most critics appears to be that *critique* is a neologism, but it has been in use since 1751, albeit not as regularly as the noun.

Our evidence suggests that the current use of the verb is more of a revival than a real continuation, starting apparently in the 1950s. *Critique* is at the first step of a line of historical development that began with *censure,* which originally meant "estimate, judge" but gradually came to be used only for fault-finding. *Criticize* has followed the same path, and even though its neutral sense is still in use, the usual negative overtones it carries for most people have probably prompted the choice of *critique.* The majority of our citations are quite clearly the result of a desire to avoid the negative implications of *criticize.*

In 1981 or 1982 the cover of a *New York Times Magazine* carried the headline "Betty Friedan Critiques the Women's Movement." You can see the reason for using *critique* here. *Criticize* would be interpreted as "censure," and *review* would have suggested more of a historical overview than a critical examination. Here are a couple of other examples:

... the insights of experts from many other countries invited to critique the plans —Hazel Henderson, *Saturday Rev.,* 18 Dec. 1973

... Theodore M. Bernstein, who critiqued *The New York Times* —Copperud 1980

You can use this verb or avoid it. It is sometimes particularly useful, and it does—so far—avoid the overtones of disparagement commonly carried by *criticize.*

culminate   1. When *culminate* is used with a preposition, the choice is usually *in:*

... must face the prospect of a steady physiological decline that culminates in senility and death —Albert Rosenfeld, *Saturday Rev.,* 2 Oct. 1976

If they were allowed their own way, every comedy would have a tragic ending, and every tragedy would culminate in a farce —Oscar Wilde, *The Picture of Dorian Gray,* 1891

Culminate is also used with *with* occasionally:

This rite ... culminates with the sacrifice of a llama —W. Stanley Rycroft, ed., *Indians of the High Andes,* 1946

Other prepositions—*as, at, into,* and *over*—have also appeared, but not so often:

... the forces ... culminate as a tendency to force the liquid toward the periphery and not to rotate it —Harry G. Armstrong, *Principles and Practice of Aviation Medicine,* 1939

... the mountain-building forces were active at irregular intervals culminating at the close of the Carboniferous —*American Guide Series: New Hampshire,* 1938

The pseudoplasmodium ... migrates for a considerable distance before it culminates into a sporocarp —Constantine John Alexopoulos, *Introductory Mycology,* 2nd ed., 1962

It culminates over the question of which of the two will complete the mission —Alan Brody, *Hartford Studies in Literature,* vol. 1, no. 1, 1969

2. Bernstein 1965 objects to *culminate* used transitively because it "is generally considered exceptional." The OED had labeled the sense *rare,* but the Supplement contains the note, "Delete *rare* and add later examples." The examples here are later than those in the Supplement:

The disagreement over Indo-China culminates a series of incidents —Denis Healey, *New Republic,* 17 May 1954

... the two Great Pyramids of Giza that culminated this period —Walter Sullivan, *N.Y. Times,* 29 Jan. 1975

cultivated, cultured The commentators who discuss these words seem to be going in several different directions, apart from agreeing that both adjectives mean "having or showing education and refinement." *Cultured* seems to have been condemned by some American commentators around the turn of the 20th century; it is defended by Hall 1917, who nevertheless uses *cultivated* himself. Gowers in Fowler 1965 would prefer *cultured* to *cultivated,* but fears it has been tainted by *kultur,* with its racist-imperialist associations. Copperud 1970, 1980 thinks *cultured* may also suffer from being linked with the institutionalized, ideological culture of the Communist world. While Copperud says that *cultured* has acquired an unfavorable connotation, Shaw 1975, 1987 thinks *cultured* is "the more elegant and refined word." And Daniel J. Kevles (*The Physicists,* 1971) thought that *cultivated* was going out of fashion "in part because it had acquired a connotation of preciousness."

Both words can be used with unpleasant connotations:

The cultivated lady in Bryn Mawr raises her sherry glass and stares speculatively at me over its rim —Laurence Lafore, *Harper's*, October 1971

Actually, the reason he is often asked to read a book is so that some day he can say that he read it, which will make him cultured —Jerry Richard, *Change*, October 1971

And both can be used without such overtones:

> . . . the indifference to modern drama which so many otherwise cultivated people feel —Thomas R. Edwards, *N.Y. Times Book Rev.*, 8 Sept. 1974

> That Smith himself was very widely read, immensely cultured, . . . these lectures leave no doubt —Patrick Cruttwell, *Washington Post Book World*, 26 Sept. 1971

When Copperud thinks more careful writers use *cultivated* because it is free from ideological and other taint, he may be right. Our evidence shows more use for *cultivated* recently than for *cultured*. The usage of those who write about language has clearly shifted to *cultivated*:

> And how much harder it has become, after forty-odd years, to pass judgment on usage, for if there has been a gain in what might be called educated speech and writing, there has been a loss in what might be called cultivated —Louis Kronenberger, *Atlantic*, September 1970

> . . . the informal conversation of cultivated speakers —William Card et al., *Jour. of English Linguistics*, 1984

> It is in cultivated homes that the babies without euphemism shit in their pants —Janet Whitcut, in Greenbaum 1985

cum   *Cum* is a Latin preposition that was taken over into English in the second half of the 19th century. Because it is Latin, it is considered snobbish by Flesch 1964 and pretentious and intellectually ostentatious by Copperud 1964, 1970, 1980. In his 1980 edition Copperud worries further about its puzzling those who do not know Latin. The examples below indicate that journalists and other writers need have no concern about the word's being widely understood. The matter of intellectual ostentation is for individual judgment, of course.

Cum is used in English usually as a conjunction linking preceding and following nouns or adjectives with or without hyphens. Even now it is fairly often italicized, a practice indicating that not all writers feel it is fully English.

> . . . whoops it up with them in the saloon-cum-cathouse —John Simon, *New York*, 31 May 1976

> . . . gives the role a tough-*cum*-innocent quality —Arnold Hano, *TV Guide*, 21 Apr. 1979

> . . . doing a 1929 gangster-movie-cum-musical spoof —Judith Crist, *Saturday Rev.*, 2 Oct. 1976

> It is true that the notion of Homer as a kind of Moses-cum-Jeeves is not dead —Colin MacLeod, *Times Literary Supp.*, 18 July 1980

> . . . the President threatened the economy with a new oil import fee cum gasoline tax —*Wall Street Jour.*, 15 May 1980

> . . . a fashionable restaurant cum boutique on the East Side —John Corry, *N.Y. Times*, 20 Apr. 1977

> . . . also visited the Maharajah, *cum* Governor, in his palace —John Kenneth Galbraith, *Ambassador's Journal*, 1969

It sometimes functions as an ordinary preposition:

> . . . would go there, cum wife and child, to say he had risen —Karl Shapiro, *American Scholar*, Winter 1985/86

cupful   The Oxford American Dictionary 1980 and Harper 1985 believe *cupfuls* is the only correct plural. They are wrong. It is, however, the more common plural. See -FUL.

cured   *Cured* is usually used with the preposition *of* in the sense and construction typified in the following quotations:

> A patient can be said to be cured of his infection —William A. Sodeman, ed., *Pathologic Physiology*, 1950

> . . . the students have been cured of their ignorance —William D. Schaefer, *Profession 78*, 1978

Evidence in our files seems to indicate that *cure* followed by *from* was once in use in the U.S. and still may be, as a regionalism:

> . . . thanks were thus rendered to the good carpenter for curing one of its [family] members from cancer —*Southern Folklore Quarterly*, September 1940

Some doubt is cast upon the matter, however, by the fact that this combination is not recorded in the Dictionary of American Regional English.

curriculum   *Curriculum* has two plurals: *curricula* and *curriculums*. *Curricula* is quite a bit more frequent, but both are standard. We have no very recent evidence of *curricula* being mistaken for a singular. For other foreign plurals, see LATIN PLURALS.

customer   See CLIENT.

D

dais This odd-looking word for a raised platform has suffered a lot of phonological knocking about in the course of its descent from Latin *discus* (it is also related to our word *dish*), and the pronunciation has reflected some uncertainty. For a time the recommended pronunciation was \'dās\, rhyming with *lace*, but this is largely restricted to British English. The most usual pronunciation now is \'dā-əs\, rhyming with *pay us*, and while this version was once denounced as "pedantic," it now is generally recommended. The second most common pronunciation is \'dī-əs\, as though the word were spelled (as it is, in fact, sometimes misspelled) *dias*.

See also PODIUM.

danglers See DANGLING MODIFIERS.

dangling adverb See SENTENCE ADVERB.

dangling constructions, dangling gerunds, dangling infinitives See DANGLING MODIFIERS.

dangling modifiers English has a common construction called the *participial phrase*:

> Happening to meet Sir Adam Ferguson, I presented him to Dr. Johnson —James Boswell, *Life of Samuel Johnson,* 1791

In Boswell's sentence, the subject of the main clause—I—is the same as that of the phrase, and it is accordingly omitted from the phrase, leaving the phrase to modify the subject of the main clause. But frequently the subject of the phrase is omitted when it would have been different from that of the main clause; the resultant participial phrase is often called a *dangling participle*—the most commonly mentioned kind of dangling modifier:

> 'Tis given out that, sleeping in mine orchard, a serpent stung me —Shakespeare, *Hamlet,* 1601 (in Burchfield 1996)

> Speaking as an old friend, there has been a disturbing tendency in statements emanating from Peking to question the good faith of President Reagan —Richard M. Nixon (cited by William Safire, *N.Y. Times Mag.,* 19 June 1983)

Now when the same construction can be found in a play of Shakespeare's in the 17th century and a speech of Richard Nixon in 1983, you might suspect that it is a very common one indeed. It is, and a venerable one: Hall 1917 cites studies that have found it as far back as Chaucer. Yet just about every rhetoric, grammar, and handbook written since the latter part of the 19th century warns against such constructions. Why the fuss?

Bryant 1962 states the reason succinctly: "in some sentences the reader is misled into attaching the modifier to a subject which it does not meaningfully modify." When such misleading actually occurs, the result can be a howler. Here are a few examples (the sources given are the books in which they are cited):

> Flying low, a herd of cattle could be seen —Paul Roberts, *Understanding Grammar,* 1954

> Walking over the hill on the left, the clubhouse can be clearly seen —Freeman 1983

> Quickly summoning an ambulance, the corpse was carried to the mortuary —Barzun 1985

The point that must be made here is that these funny examples have apparently been invented for the purpose of illustration. Actual dangling participles are seldom of such nature as to excite mirth; indeed, they may hardly be noticeable. We have already seen two genuine examples; here are a few more:

> Returning to a consideration of the extracurricular activities of the undergraduate, the continued significance of the intramural program of athletics should be stressed —James B. Conant, *President's Report, Harvard University,* 1950–1951

> . . . wanting to be alone with his family, the presence of a stranger superior to Mr. Yates must have been irksome —Jane Austen, *Mansfield Park,* 1814

When a genuinely funny dangler actually occurs, it is sure to be repeated in a collection of humorous mistakes, as this one was:

> After years of being lost under a pile of dust, Walter P. Stanley, III, left, found all the old records of the Bangor Lions Club —*Bangor Daily News,* 20 Jan. 1978 (reprinted in *SQUAD HELPS DOG BITE VICTIM and Other Flubs,* 1980)

Dangling participles are not the only dangling modifiers that students are warned against—clauses, prepositional phrases, infinitives, and appositives can all be misrelated in such a way as to be characterized as dangling:

> It is a fact often observed, that men have written good verses under the inspiration of passion, who cannot write well under any other circumstances —Ralph Waldo Emerson (in Hall 1917)

> The patience of all the founders of the Society was at last exhausted, except me and Roebuck —John Stuart Mill (in Barzun 1985)

> Distinguished public servant, exemplar for the United States Foreign Service, tireless seeker of peace, your work in arduous posts around the globe has repeatedly demonstrated —in Harper 1985

The usual reason given for avoiding such constructions is clarity, but in most cases the meaning can be readily discovered, even if the sentence is not expressed in the most elegant manner. The important thing to avoid is a juxtaposition that produces an unintended humorous effect. Unintentional humor seems most likely to be created when writing of an unusually compact nature is intended—a caption under a picture or a newspaper account. Here is an example from each; the perpetrators have not been named.

> After being crushed to predetermined particle size Babcock's fluidized bed combustor can be fired with any solid, liquid, or gas fuel —caption

> Jerry Remy then hit an RBI single off Haas' leg, which rolled into right field —newspaper account

Conclusion: dangling modifiers are common, old, and well established in English literature. When the meaning is not ambiguous, Bryant 1962 allows them to be "informal standard usage." The evidence in Hall 1917 and other sources shows they are not infrequent in literature of a more elevated sort. The one pitfall that must be avoided is unintended humor. The dangling modifier is a venial sin at most, but if you commit an unintentional howler, you are liable to be ridiculed.

See also SENTENCE ADVERB.

dangling participles See DANGLING MODIFIERS.

dare 1. Although almost everything you need to know about *dare* can be found in a dictionary, several usage books also comment on its peculiarities. These peculiarities arise from the fact that *dare* is both an ordinary verb and an auxiliary verb. As an auxiliary verb *dare* has in its present tense the uninflected third person singular *dare*, which

caught the eye of the first commentator to mention it, Robert Baker in 1770. He didn't like it. Neither did Campbell 1776. But they did not realize that they were dealing with what is now called a modal auxiliary, rather than with a misuse of the ordinary verb.

The modal auxiliary is regularly followed by an infinitive phrase without *to*:

> . . . they being so absolutely his masters that he dare not write a letter to a newspaper . . . without their approval —George Bernard Shaw, in *Harper's*, October 1971

> . . . the victory policy Nixon dare not too openly avow —*I. F. Stone's Bi-Weekly*, 17 May 1971

As a regular verb, *dare* has *dares* in the present third singular. It can be followed by an infinitive phrase with *to*:

> And yet Erica Mann Jong dares to call her book of poems "Fruits & Vegetables" —Erica Jong, *Barnard Alumnae*, Winter 1971

> . . . so one might dare to enter them —Norman Mailer, *Harper's*, March 1971

In other examples may be seen a blend of the modal and the ordinary uses; here *dare* is followed by the infinitive without *to*, yet is preceded by other auxiliaries (as *might, would,* and *do*):

> . . . not even there did I dare say the words —George P. Elliott, *Harper's*, September 1970

> . . . the hardiest germ would hardly dare approach her —Edith-Jane Bahr, *Ladies' Home Jour.*, October 1971

> Do we dare assume that . . . —Lloyd E. Rozeboom, *Johns Hopkins Mag.*, Spring 1971

The regular verb can also take a noun object:

> At the least one dares profound humiliation —Norman Mailer, *Harper's*, March 1971

2. The past tense *durst* has been superseded in modern use by *dared*. It is now archaic or dialectal.

daresay, dare say This compound verb is used in the first person singular of the present tense. It has hardly ever been used otherwise; the OED shows a single example of "he durst say" from Sterne in the 18th century, and Sylvia Townsend Warner ventured a "Philip . . . daresayed" in a story in the *New Yorker* in 1954. You can write it as one word or two. Our evidence shows the one-word styling slightly more common.

In its transitive use *daresay* is followed by a clause. Formerly the clause would never have been introduced by *that,* but in recent use *that* is used. Some examples without and with *that*:

> Well, I daresay my boiling point is lower than Baby Doll's —Harry Kurnitz, *Holiday,* February 1957

> If spousal privilege is taken for granted, how can there be no similar protection of communications between parent and child? It seems so obvious that I daresay many Americans believe it already exists —Anna Quindlen, *Newsweek,* 17 Jan. 2000

> . . . and I daresay that if it had been stuck into one of Mr. Buckley's novels . . . —Nora Ephron, *N.Y. Times Book Rev.,* 7 Aug. 1983

> . . . over the Connecticut River in Vermont, is one of the last remaining drive-ins. . . . I daresay that when the current owner retires it will go altogether —Bill Bryson, *I'm a Stranger Here Myself,* 1999

dassent, dassn't Safire 1984 quotes a correspondent who uses the spelling *dassent* and another who wonders if it shouldn't have been *dassn't.* This contraction—from *dares not,* apparently—was common in the 19th century and the early 20th (the Dictionary of American Regional English shows many spellings) and was used for *dares not, dare not* and *dared not.* The spelling variations are presumably intended to approximate speech. *Dassent* as a spelling is neither the most frequent nor the rarest:

> ". . . I whipped Ed Walker twice, Saturday. I don't like girls. You dassent catch toads unless with a string. . . ." —O. Henry, "The Ransom of Red Chief," 1907

Dassn't (now the commonest form) and its variations are basically dialectal but, as the use by a correspondent of Safire's suggests, are among those countrified terms trotted out for effect in otherwise straightforward writing.

> Like those beetles on the waterpond, you can bend the surface tension film but you dassn't break through —Christopher Morley, *The Man Who Made Friends With Himself,* 1949

> . . . chortling openly at the things a bigot thinks but dassn't utter —Jack O'Brien, *Springfield* (Mass.) *Union,* 1 Dec. 1973

dastard *Dastard* is a fairly rare word. It first meant a dullard, and then a coward. By the time Fowler 1926 was complaining about its being misused, the sense of "coward" was slipping into the past. The word, when used, generally means some sort of underhanded or treacherous villain:

> . . . a girl who took the wrong turning when some dastard, responsible for her condition,

had worked his own sweet will on her —James Joyce, *Ulysses,* 1922

> The most villainous villain in all of Shakespeare . . . is the evil Iago in "Othello," but the dastard gets off one great line —James J. Kilpatrick, *Springfield* (Mass.) *Union-News,* 11 July 1991

dastardly In 1926 H. W. Fowler, with his eye fixed firmly on the 19th century, pronounced the opinion that *dastardly* must mean "cowardly" and that to apply it to acts that involved or persons who took any risk was to misuse it. This opinion was repeated by Evans 1957 and carried unchanged by Gowers into Fowler 1965. Now, you can find such use if you look back far enough:

> Choosing the safe side, however, appeared to me to be playing a rather dastardly part —George Borrow, *The Romany Rye,* 1857

But it is hard to find this sense applied to persons. *Dastardly* seems to emphasize something done behind another's back, underhandedly, sneakily, or treacherously—or a person who would do such things—rather than mere cowardice. Even Fowler noted this aspect of meaning—"acts . . . so carried out as not to give the victim a sporting chance"—in deprecating the use.

But Flesch 1964 puts his finger on another characteristic that keeps *dastardly*—a fairly uncommon word in literary use—alive: "*dastardly* is a piece of old-fashioned rhetoric." It is quite regularly used in the public denunciation of some reprehensible deed:

> The horrible tragedy . . . has been summarily avenged, and the last of the perpetrators and participants have made atonement with their lives for the dastardly crime —*Tombstone Republican,* 28 Mar. 1884, in Douglas D. Martin, *Tombstone's Epitaph,* 1951

> I ask that the Congress declare that since the unprovoked and dastardly attack by Japan on Sunday, December 7th, a state of war has existed —Franklin D. Roosevelt, war message to Congress, 8 Dec. 1941, in *Nothing to Fear,* ed. B. D. Zevin, 1946

It would appear to be the faint odor of the black-caped villains of 19th-century popular melodrama, twirling their mustaches and gloating evilly over their misdeeds, that clings to *dastardly* and keeps it in contemporary use:

> Boris Karloff gives voice to that dastardly humbug Mr. Grinch —*TV Guide,* 30 Nov.–6 Dec. 1991

> . . . Peter Lorre and Sidney Greenstreet clones out to commit dastardly acts of espionage and other malevolent mischief —Pat Sellers, *US,* 28 Sept. 1982

The rhetorical use has even spawned another use of *dastardly* that simply expresses disapproval:

> What is this dastardly threat to pleasure at sundown . . . ? —Donald J. Gonzales, "Crisis at the Cocktail Hour," *Saturday Rev.,* 15 Nov. 1975

> Fat . . . has proven itself so dastardly a dietary villain that public-health authorities recommend trimming fat consumption to just 30 percent or less of a day's calories —*Consumer Reports,* September 1991

In effect, the "cowardly" sense of *dastardly* has been fading out of use for a century or more and seems destined to join the original sense of "dull, stupid" in the obscurity of the historical dictionaries. During a period from around 1850 to around 1950, *dastardly* often connoted underhandedness and treachery. Since about 1950 the word has been kept in use by its overtones of rhetorical denunciation and the stage villain of melodrama, and it is now even weakening into use as a generalized term of disapproval. There is no point in looking backward.

data, datum 1. The word *data* is a queer fish. It is an English word formed from a Latin plural; however, it leads a life of its own quite independent of its Latin ancestor and equally independent of the English word *datum,* of which it is supposed to be the plural. Ordinary plurals—that is, the plurals of count nouns, like *toes, women,* or *criteria*—can be modified by cardinal numbers; that is, we can say *five toes,* or *five women,* or *five criteria.* But *data* is not used with a cardinal number; no one, it seems, can tell you how many *data. Datum,* incidentally, is a count noun; in one of its senses it has a plural *datums,* which is used with a cardinal number:

> . . . in place of a single reference system today we have about 80 more or less independently derived reference systems or datums —Homer E. Newell & Leonard Jaffe, *Science,* 7 July 1967

In its current use, *data* occurs in two constructions: as a plural noun (like *earnings*) taking a plural verb and certain plural modifiers (such as *these, many, a few of*) but not cardinal numbers, and serving as a referent for plural pronouns (such as *they, them*); and as an abstract mass noun (like *information*), taking a singular verb and singular modifiers (such as *this, much, little*), and being referred to by a singular pronoun (*it*). Both of these constructions are standard. The plural construction is more common, since evidence suggests that the plural construction is mandated as house style by several publishers. Evans 1957 points out that usage differs in dif-

ferent sciences, although the passage of time has undoubtedly invalidated some of his specific observations.

The differentiation of *data* and *datum* was noticed at a fairly early date:

> . . . in ordinary use, "data" is not the mere plural of "datum." The two words possess quite different connotations. "Datum" appears to be almost exclusively used for a primary level in surveying while "data" connotes information or facts. Hence "data" as the plural of "datum" is a syntactical plural while "data" in the sense of facts is a collective which is preferably treated as a singular —*Science,* 1 July 1927

But insights such as those of the *Science* editor only slowly reached the citadels of usage pronouncement. And by about the middle of the 20th century, when usage writers began to recognize the mass singular use as established and standard (it was recognized without stigma in Webster's Second), more editors appear to have become convinced that only the plural construction was correct. So it happens that at present we have the anomaly of a majority of usage writers recognizing or approving the mass noun singular construction while a majority of the citations collected here are in the plural. That the preference for the plural is editorially inspired is indicated by such examples as these:

> . . . much of the data are still tentative —James Q. Wilson, *N.Y. Times,* 6 Oct. 1974 (the singular modifier *much* with plural verb shows that some copy editor routinely corrected the verb without thinking)

> There is no great amount of special data that begin to move upward many months before the economy as a whole —Leonard H. Lempert, *Christian Science Monitor,* 18 Sept. 1980 (the verb after *data* has been made plural even though the actual subject is *amount*)

Sometimes the singular construction is decorated with a supercilious [sic]:

> . . . "there is *[sic]* no scientific data which conclusively demonstrates *[sic]*" —Chief Justice Warren Burger, quoted by John Leonard, *N.Y. Times Book Rev.,* 8 July 1973

To summarize, *data* has never been the plural of a count noun in English. It is used in two constructions—plural, with plural apparatus, and singular, as a mass noun, with singular apparatus. Both constructions are fully standard at any level of formality. The plural construction is more common. If you are an editor for a publisher whose house style insists on the plural construction only, take care to be consistent (such care is advised by Evans 1957,

Bernstein 1971, 1977, Macmillan 1982, and Einstein 1985, among others).

2. *Datum.* There is a common misapprehension among usage writers that *datum* is rarely used. While it is not nearly so frequently used as *data,* it is far from being a rare word. It is well attested both as a surveying term (as mentioned above in the 1927 *Science* quotation) and as a term in other disciplines—philosophy, mathematics, and the social sciences, among others—and in criticism. All citations up until about the middle 1960s occur in decidedly learned media. There have been more occurrences of *datum* in popular sources since then. Perhaps the insistence of many editors that *data* is a plural has accelerated the tendency for *datum* to be used as a singular of *data:*

> Very soon I expect to be 52, a datum I do not expect will rouse the statisticians —William F. Buckley, Jr., *Pueblo Star-Jour.,* 5 Oct. 1977

In fact, it looks like *datum* is beginning to be simply a fancy substitute for *fact:*

> I'd estimate the median age of Manhattan Market's clientele to be well on the sunny side of thirty-five. Armed with this demographic datum, one may suspect . . . —Jay Jacobs, *Gourmet,* September 1981

> Let's be honest about the Glenn trip. The attempt to sell it as science . . . is entirely laughable. This enormous expense—and considerable risk—to pick up a datum or two about geriatrics? —Charles Krauthammer, *Time,* 9 Nov. 1998

For other foreign plurals, see LATIN PLURALS.

date When the verb *date* is used to point to a date of origin, it may be used with *from, back to,* or *to.*

> . . . a variety of ravishing screens dating from the late sixteenth to the mid-nineteenth centuries —John Gruen, *New York,* 8 Feb. 1971

> . . . the Cronkite film, though dating back to 1962, was the most popular —Martin Mayer, *Harper's,* December 1971

> Much of what would come about in 1968 . . . would date to this testimony in August of 1967 —David Halberstam, *Harper's,* February 1971

datum See DATA, DATUM.

daylight savings time See SAVING, SAVINGS.

days See ADVERBIAL GENITIVE.

dead Sometimes considered to be an absolute adjective. See ABSOLUTE ADJECTIVES.

deadwood *Deadwood* is what handbook writers call words that they feel should be pruned out to produce a desirably brief freshman English paper. While one may sympathize with the task of the freshman English instructor, many of the phrases and words so labeled have a useful function in the real world. The question will come up at various entries in this book. See also REDUNDANCY; WORDINESS.

deal 1. *Deal* belongs to a class of weak or regular verbs including *feel, creep, kneel,* and *mean* in which the past and past participle have a short vowel contrasting with the long vowel of the infinitive. Some of these (see KNEEL; CREEP) have variants. *Deal* seems always to have *dealt:*

> He dealt with them out of his constant sorrow —E. L. Doctorow, *Ragtime,* 1975

> It seemed everybody I knew either did drugs or dealt drugs —J. Poet, *Rolling Stone,* 17 July 1975

2. When the intransitive verb *deal* means "concern oneself" or "take action," its usual preposition is *with:*

> It deals with the illusions of youth —Paul D. Zimmerman, *Newsweek,* 4 Dec. 1972

> This was a state of mind, or point of view, which many of the anxious friends from another class of society found very hard to deal with —Katherine Anne Porter, *The Never-Ending Wrong,* 1977

When *deal* is used in relation to selling—literally or figuratively—the usual preposition is *in:*

> . . . never known to have actually dealt in the drug —Dan Rosen, *N.Y. Times Mag.,* 15 June 1975

> . . . the liberal arts deal in symbols and universal ideas —Scott Buchanan, "So Reason Can Rule," 1967

dear, dearly The adverbs *dear* and *dearly* are interchangeable only in contexts dealing with cost:

> The present version has cost Britain dear —*The Economist,* 1 Feb. 1985

> . . . negligence on the part of the British government (for which it later paid dear) —Samuel Eliot Morison, *Oxford History of the American People,* 1965

> Their high wages are dearly bought with monotonous labour —*Times Literary Supp.,* 5 Mar. 1970

. . . has cost the United States dearly in men and money —Richard H. Rovere, *New Yorker,* 5 June 1971

Dearly is used in other contexts:

The social word still matters dearly to her —Gail Cameron, *Ladies' Home Jour.,* August 1971

. . . in that he dearly loved a fight —*Times Literary Supp.,* 19 Feb. 1971

debacle This word was borrowed from French and is normally stressed in accordance with its pronunciation in that language: \dē-ˈbä-kəl\ or, less often, \dē-ˈba-kəl\, along with minor variants of these. Those who say \ˈde-bə-kəl\ have been the target of frowns, but one could argue that they have a point. The word as normally written has already lost both its original diacritics (the French form is *débâcle*); why should it not, after two centuries as part of English, fall in with the stress pattern of such other French-derived words as *miracle, manacle,* and *spectacle?*

debar When it is used with a preposition, *debar* most often appears with *from:*

. . . nothing can more surely debar the Germans from establishing and shaping the new Europe —Sir Winston Churchill, *The Unrelenting Struggle,* 1942

It seems to me axiomatic that a verse translator . . . shall not be debarred from a strictly literal translation —D. M. Thomas, *N.Y. Times Book Rev.,* 24 Oct. 1982

At one time, *debar* was also used with some frequency with the preposition *of;* however, nowadays it is infrequent:

. . . but the absence of some is not to debar the others of amusement —Jane Austen, *Mansfield Park,* 1814

. . . they would debar the citizen of his right to resort to the courts of justice —Justice Peter V. Daniel, quoted in *Harvard Law Rev.,* June 1953

debut The verb *debut* is disapproved of by many usage writers (as Bernstein 1977, Bremner 1980, Garner 1998, and the usage panels of both editions of Harper; Heritage 1982, 1992, 2000 objects to use outside of showbiz). Intransitive uses have been around since 1830 but transitive uses, which are even more strongly disliked and are less common, only since the 1950s. This verb comes in handy in newspaper and magazine articles, where it is most often found, since newsy writing often discusses first appearances of people, products, and the like. In general prose of this sort it is standard but it seems to have almost no

use in literature and other more elevated varieties of writing.

Since the gems debuted commercially a year ago, pawnbrokers and jewelry dealers across the country have gotten swindled —Tessie Borden, *Atlanta Jour.-Constitution,* 15 June 1999

Willie Nelson returns occasionally, after debuting on one of the first shows —Jorjanna Price, *Houston Post,* 30 Aug. 1984

When . . . Iverson debuted his signature cornrows as an NBA rookie two years ago, he rattled some sportswriters —*Newsweek,* 22 Mar. 1999

decide Intransitive *decide* is used with several prepositions, of which *on, upon, for,* and *against* are the most common:

. . . had also received an offer to play with a Canadian team for more money, but he decided on the Packers —*Current Biography,* January 1968

. . . led him to decide upon law as his career —*Current Biography,* December 1967

They decided against both the tea and the talk —Flannery O'Connor, letter, 5 May 1956

The trinity thought it over and gloomily decided for bacon and eggs —Honor Tracy, *Irish Digest,* January 1954

Sometimes a periphrastic preposition may replace *for:*

They decided in favor of a bridge —*The Americana Annual 1953*

Between and *about* are also used:

. . . helps you decide between . . . vegetable crops or flowers —radio commentator, 16 Apr. 1975

. . . I have already decided about the value of my work —William Faulkner, 13 Mar. 1958, in *Faulkner in the University,* 1959

decimate The Roman army took discipline seriously. They had a practice of keeping mutinous units in line by selecting one tenth of the men by lot and executing them. We are not certain how much the practice improved performance, but its memorable ferocity helped carry the word from Latin into English as *decimate.*

From Richard Grant White in 1870 down to the present day, numerous commentators have ridiculed or disapproved the way the word has been used in English. White ridiculed its use by war correspondents of the Civil War; another critic chastised war correspondents of the Crimean War. In 1941 the *Plain Dealer* (Cleveland, Ohio) criticized its use by war correspondents in World War II (and in 1944 took a slap at radio broadcasters too). War correspondents were not alone in taking their lumps; a poor farmer of 1859 was belabored in Hodgson 1889 for using the term to describe the destruction wrought on his turnip field by frost. And more recently, we read a troubled writer to the editor of the *Saturday Review* in 1971:

> I also grieve over what has happened to "decimate," though no less an authority than *The New York Times* has assured me I am wrong in thinking it can only mean "to destroy every tenth man."

All of these critics have learned the etymology of *decimate,* but none of them have bothered to examine its history and use in English. Such an examination would have relieved the grieving letter writer above; *decimate* has seldom meant "to destroy every tenth man" in English, and then only in historical references.

Aside from a few technical uses, *decimate* has had three main applications in English. The first, attested since 1600, refers to the Roman disciplinary procedure. The earliest citations note that the practice was revived by the Earl of Essex in Ireland; all later citations refer to the Romans.

The second application, attested from 1659, refers to a ten percent tax and specifically to a ten percent tax levied by Oliver Cromwell in 1655 on the defeated Royalists. This sense is of some literary interest—Dryden, for instance, refers to someone as being "poor as a decimated Cavalier"—but it has no current use.

The third, first attested in 1663, is the use that is criticized on etymological grounds. Labeled "*rhetorically* or *loosely*" in the OED, it is the only sense of the word that has continued to thrive in English. It is an emphatic word, and probably owes its continued use in English to the arbitrary ferocity of the Roman practice rather than to its arithmetic. It is most frequently used to denote great loss of life or serious or drastic reduction in number:

> . . . had survived an American ambush that decimated a group of stragglers he'd been travelling with —E. J. Kahn, Jr., *New Yorker,* 24 Mar. 1962

> Though the buffalo herds have been decimated, . . . this is still the frontier —John Updike, *New Yorker,* 30 Mar. 1987

> Smallpox, measles, influenza, typhus, bubonic plaque, and other infectious diseases endemic in Europe played a decisive role in European conquests, by decimating many peoples on other continents —Jared Diamond, *Guns, Germs, and Steel,* 1997

> California's Proposition 209, which has decimated the ranks of blacks and Hispanics at

the state's elite universities —William Raspberry, *Albany* (N.Y.) *Times-Union,* 29 May 1998

Often the word denotes great damage or destruction:

> . . . how parking lots decimated the downtowns they were intended to serve —Ada Louise Huxtable, *N.Y. Times,* 30 Aug. 1979

> . . . mercantile districts of cities are likely to be decimated by direct hits of explosive bombs or incendiary bombs —Horatio Bond, ed., *Fire Defense,* 1941

> . . . the ultimate underdog story: team decimated by scandal holding together and handling opponents they should have no chance against —John Feinstein, *A Season on the Brink,* 1989

> You'd think that the Asian crisis would have decimated this logic—but it didn't —Joseph Nocera, *Fortune,* 28 Sept. 1998

It is even used occasionally for humorous overstatement:

> One of them is murdered backstage. Then another. Somebody is out to decimate the country-and-western population —Newgate Callendar, *N.Y. Times Book Rev.,* 11 Oct. 1987

Sir James Murray inserted a definition in the OED, "To kill, destroy, or remove one in every ten of" before the extended sense just discussed. He presumably did this to provide a semantic bridge from the earlier senses (and especially the Roman sense) to the extended sense, but he produced no citations to indicate its actual use. Apparently *decimate* has never been so used in English.

Although a few commentators still cling to the Latin—"To reduce by one tenth, not to destroy entirely" (Macmillan 1982)—most recent usage books recognize that the Latin etymology does not rule the English word.

deduce, deduct *Deduce* and *deduct* formerly had a greater number of meanings than they do now. Some of the meanings, including the most common of today's senses, were shared by both words. *Deduce* once meant "subtract, deduct," and *deduct* meant "infer, deduce," but according to the OED both of these senses are now obsolete. It seems odd, then, that several modern usage books advise you not to get the two words confused.

We find that, in spite of what the OED says, *deduct* is still occasionally used to mean "infer, deduce." Such use shows that this sense is not obsolete after all, though it is very rare:

> ". . . leave the deducting to the cops. . . ." —Gypsy Rose Lee, *The G-String Murders,* 1941

. . . some anthropologists deduct that the ability to make tools . . . did not depend upon an enlargement of the brain —*Science News Letter,* 17 Apr. 1965

Why has the "infer" sense remained with *deduct* when it is now much more commonly associated with *deduce?* Probably because of the familiar noun *deduction,* which can refer to the action or result of either verb but is closer in spelling to *deduct.* Without the benefit of similar reinforcement, the "subtract" sense of *deduce* has not survived.

While the context will usually make your intention clear if you use *deduct* to refer to an operation of the mind, you might reasonably choose to avoid even the appearance of confusion and use *deduce* for that meaning.

deem A few commentators—Flesch 1964, Fowler 1926, 1965, Evans 1957—express variously some reservations about the old verb *deem.* At issue seems to be a use by politicians—including many U.S. presidents—that these people deem pretentious. The word is and has been in wide literary and journalistic use:

My parents deemed it necessary that I should adopt some profession —George Borrow, *Lavengro,* 1851

. . . to inspect all the sites that were deemed eligible —Emily Hahn, *New Yorker,* 24 Apr. 1971

The Congress, whenever two thirds of both houses shall deem it necessary —*Constitution of the United States,* 1787

. . . television was the last stop on the retail journey, a way to unload merchandise deemed unsalable by any other means —David Whitford, *INC,* June 1994

The book . . . was deemed a literary novel, meaning that it enjoyed glowing reviews and disappointing sales —Ann Patchett, *GQ,* November 1997

It can even be used in less elevated, even whimsical, contexts:

. . . supporting only those candidates deemed to be delectable —Wendy Kaminer, *Atlantic,* July 1992

It is hard to see that there can be any problem with this word.

defect Bernstein 1965 says that *defect* is followed by "*in* (an artifact); *of* (a person)" but the Merriam-Webster files do not support this distinction. Our evidence shows that the two prepositions are used interchangeably in both American and British English:

Language is alive only by a metaphor drawn from the life of its users. Hence every defect in the language is a defect in somebody —Jacques Barzun, *Atlantic,* December 1953

. . . defect in a work [of art] is always traceable ultimately to an excess on one side or the other —John Dewey, *Art as Experience,* 1934

All such fanaticisms have in a greater or less degree the defect which I found in the Moscow Marxists —Bertrand Russell, *London Calling,* 24 Mar. 1955

. . . a permanent aristocracy, possessing the merits and defects of the Spartans —*Selected Papers of Bertrand Russell,* 1927

. . . due to defects both of legislation and of administration —Lillian L. Shapiro, *Library Jour.,* 1 Jan. 1976

defective, deficient Some recent commentators (Phythian 1979, Bryson 1984, Chambers 1985, Burchfield 1996, Garner 1998) distinguish these words. Their consensus seems to be that *defective* emphasizes a flaw, while *deficient* emphasizes a lack—or, put another way, that *defective* is more qualitative and *deficient* more quantitative. Fair enough, if you remember that these are tendencies and not absolute distinctions. Contexts will occur in which either one might be used. Here are a few typical examples:

. . . some defective versions of the protein cause out-of-control proliferation of T cells and antibodies —*Science News,* 13 Jan. 2001

. . . her dedication as an artist was as total as her humanity was defective —Peter Davison, *Atlantic,* February 1972

. . . firewalls meant to defeat Hacker intrusions via the Internet are defective and password protections are poorly encrypted —David Hanson, *Chemical & Engineering News,* 21 Aug. 2000

Its answers were inadequate, . . . its vision deficient —Andrew M. Greeley, *Change,* April 1972

. . . which makes sprightly reading but is seriously deficient in American historical perspective —Walter Arnold, *N.Y. Times Book Rev.,* 11 Mar. 1973

See also DEFICIENT.

defend *Defend* may be followed by *against* or *from*:

. . . a part of Schleswig Holstein where strong dikes defend the land against the furor of winter storms —Samuel Van Valkenburg & Ellsworth Huntington, *Europe,* 1935

. . . watching him defend his high and rigid standards against the endless assault our times mount against them —Richard Schickel, *Harper's,* March 1971

. . . a floor of double boards to defend the old woman's bones from the dampness —Ellen Glasgow, *Vein of Iron,* 1935

The playwright defended *Come Back, Little Sheba* from the criticism that it was depressing —*Current Biography,* June 1953

defenestrate Defenestration has been a mode of political expression for centuries, and a member of the Harper 1975, 1985 usage panel wondered if there shouldn't be a verb *defenestrate* to go along with it. Almost two thirds of the panel thought there ought to be. Well, there is. It is a recent verb and has both literal and figurative use:

In a California college, I saw books thrown through a window. . . . Shouting and burning, defenestrating the memory of mankind, they feel at least they are doing *something,* not just sitting on their butts —Anthony Burgess, *American Scholar,* Autumn 1969

Perhaps the chief distinction of the picture is the number of things getting defenestrated in it: an overnight bag, a book, some manuscript pages, an attaché case —John Simon, *New York,* 8 Dec. 1975

He says that this used to make his colleagues rather cross, but that they have got used to it over the years. I am amazed that they have not defenestrated him —Howard 1980

To the lengthening list of Clinton stalwarts who have been defenestrated on the ground of political inconvenience was added the name of . . . the White House deputy chief of staff —Jane Mayer, *New Yorker,* 25 Nov. 1996

Our evidence indicates that usage of this back-formation is on the increase, but it is still not an especially common word. You can feel safe in using it if you need it.

deficient When *deficient* is used with a preposition, the preposition is almost always *in*:

The report that Diggory had brought of the wedding . . . was deficient in one significant particular —Thomas Hardy, *The Return of the Native,* 1878

But this view is held to be deficient in intelligence, liberalism, and democracy —Lionel Trilling, in *Forms of Modern Fiction,* ed. William Van O'Connor, 1948

See also DEFECTIVE, DEFICIENT.

defile When used with a prepositional phrase expressing means or agent, *defile* is fol-

lowed by *by* (more often) or *with* (a little less often):

. . . the academic institution . . . suddenly defiled by the crude political demands of people unfit to pass through its gates —Jerome Karabel, *Change,* May 1972

Now he saw why he had sanctified his body and refused to defile it with a woman —Sholem Asch, *The Apostle,* 1943

definite 1. Phythian 1979, Copperud 1980, and Garner 1998 warn against the misspelling *definate.* It, *definately,* and *defination* are all attested in our files. Watch out for that second *i.*

2. *Definite, definitely.* Copperud 1970, 1980, Phythian 1979, Bell & Cohn 1981, Janis 1984, Watt 1967, Prentice Hall 1978, and Perrin & Ebbitt 1972 all express objections to these words used as intensives. They call any use of the words in this way "meaningless," "imprecise," "vague," or "overworked." Such use is not faddish, however. The OED Supplement shows use of *definitely* as an emphatic *yes* from 1931. The evidence of our citations goes back to about the same time—1932 for the adjective and 1938 for the adverb. In 1938 the adverb was already being condemned as a fad use that would debase the word. But nearly seventy years is mighty long for a fad, and the use continues today. (Nor has it driven out older uses of the words.) The following examples evidence its establishment in general prose; it seems to have little use in literature and virtually none in any sort of elevated discourse, however:

Now "Ragtime" has brought an undisclosed amount of money and a definite, if indeterminate, quantity of hope to the block —Richard F. Shepard, *N.Y. Times,* 28 July 1980

He is a pupil of the late Edgar Wallace and has definitely made good in literature —*N.Y. Herald Tribune,* 24 July 1938

We had always hoped there would come a time when there would be dancing in the aisles of the U.N. But this was definitely not it —Goodman Ace, *Saturday Rev.,* 20 Nov. 1971

3. *Definite, definitive.* Warnings against the confusion of these words can be found in quite a large number of usage books and handbooks: Harper 1975, 1985, Sellers 1975, Copperud 1970, Bernstein 1965, Evans 1957, Fowler 1926, 1965, Phythian 1979, Chambers 1985, Shaw 1975, 1987, Prentice Hall 1978, Burchfield 1996, Garner 1998. Almost all of them tell you what the words mean—information readily available in dictionaries. Several say that the error consists in using *definitive* in

place of *definite*. We have little evidence of such substitution.

It is not always easy to tell in a given case whether *definitive* has been used in place of *definite* or has been used in one of its own well-established senses but in a context where error may be perceived by one so inclined:

> They all want definitive answers, not carefully hedged responses stated in terms of probabilities full of "ifs" and "buts" and other uncertainties —Seymour Martin Lipset, *N.Y. Times Mag.,* 30 Aug. 1964

Definite could fit smoothly into this sentence, but the author probably meant *definitive* in its sense "serving to supply a final answer." Nearly all our examples of the possible misuse of *definitive* are of this variety, as are several of Fowler's examples. Examples like the following are not numerous and not recent:

> No one denies that the cease-fire brings a definitive strengthening of the Communist position in Asia —Denis Healey, *New Republic,* 9 Aug. 1954

Most of the time, writers seem to have little trouble keeping these words distinct.

definitive See DEFINITE 3.

degree Various phrases based on *to a degree* receive some mention in a few usage books. Bernstein 1965 begins by observing that *to a degree* once had the meaning "to the last degree" or "to a remarkable extent" but that it now means "in moderate measure" or "in a small way." Fowler 1926 remarked on the first of these uses, calling it illogical but established and tracing it back to 18th-century literary sources. This older use seems fairly unlikely to appear in current American English, but its occurrences in older, more literary, and usually British English are not difficult to recognize, most of the time:

> She was indeed extraordinarily clever . . . ; but in some things she must have been stupid to a degree —Ira Victor Morris, *Covering Two Years,* 1933

The newer sense, the common one now in American English, was condemned by Follett 1966, but is recognized by Bernstein and dictionaries (as Merriam-Webster's Collegiate Dictionary, Tenth Edition). It emphasizes limitation. It can usually be told from the older use:

> To a degree this attitude is held by many in the Peace Now movement —David K. Shipler, *N.Y. Times Mag.,* 6 Apr. 1980

Sometimes, though, the context is such that you cannot be sure which meaning was intended. This example is probably of the newer meaning. but the older could be understood in its place:

> . . . the Princeton attitude toward passes thrown by other teams is still innocent to a degree —*New Yorker,* 6 Oct. 1951

In these quantified times, many American writers express the older sense with a different phrase, *to the nth degree*:

> . . . they were honest to the nth degree —John K. Fairbank, *Harvard Today,* Autumn 1968

Bernstein objects to phrases of the form *to an x degree,* in which *x* represents an adjective, as wasteful of space. But as Burchfield 1996 points out, the adjective generally serves to prevent ambiguity with the older sense. Here are a few typical examples:

> . . . they will be dealing to a large degree with government bodies —*Forbes,* 1 May 1967

> To a startling degree, the reverse seems to be true —Michael Lerner, *Change,* September 1971

> The staff, however, soon became bogged down in bureaucratic red tape and, to a certain degree, in its own idealism —Peter Linkow, *Change,* January–February 1971

déjà vu *Déjà vu* is a psychological term brought into English from French just after the turn of the century. It was used for an illusory feeling of having previously experienced something that was, in fact, happening for the first time. After about a half century, it began to appear on its own, unglossed, in nontechnical writing.

The point of divergence of popular use from technical use lies in the differing viewpoints of the technical writer and reader and the popular writer and reader. The psychologist and his reader are interested in the illusory experience. The popular author and his reader are interested in the fact that it all seems so familiar:

> For a while this bloated, exasperating, corny, interminable tear-jerker is apt to give the reader a maddening sensation of *déjà vu* —John Brooks, *N.Y. Times Book Rev.,* 16 Apr. 1950

The reviewer is pointing out that the author has done again what has been done before, but he is not suggesting that he has actually read the same material before. Here the book is new, but the situations, the characters, the sentiments, have been similarly treated before—the feeling that it is all familiar is no illusion.

Similar uses—stressing the familiar and especially the too familiar—abound:

. . . and to most liberals who had hoped for a fresh wind the appointment seems like a case of déjà vu —Edward B. Fiske, *N.Y. Times,* 10 Mar. 1968

To the American, on the other hand, who views them with a growing sense of *déjà vu,* they are likely to seem part of a syndrome he knows only too well —Hillel Halkin, *Commentary,* May 1972

Yet as one reads "Castles Burning," it is almost with a feeling of déjà vu, so closely does it follow the patterns established by the private eye writers of the 1930's —Newgate Callendar, *N.Y. Times Book Rev.,* 3 Feb. 1980

The popular use was established before it was discovered: it had been used in the *New York Times* for thirty years before the language guardians there took notice of it and raised objections. The popular use is established in standard sources written by professional writers. You can use it if you need it.

The word is usually written with both accents and no hyphen: *déjà vu.* The word is still italicized about half the time.

delusion, illusion   Although warnings not to confuse these two words have been issued since the late 1800s, *delusion* and *illusion* are often used in ways that apparently overlap in meaning. This is probably so because *delusion* refers to a misleading of the mind and *illusion* to a misleading of the mind as well as to a misleading of the senses. When *illusion* refers only to the senses, there is a neat differentiation. But real usage is (predictably) not so neat.

We will concern ourselves with popular use, where the two words appear to have overlapping areas of operation in referring to a misleading of the mind. H. W. Fowler was the first to recognize and come to grips with this situation. His treatment (in both the 1926 and 1965 editions) is the longest and most detailed that has been done. But in spite of its length, it is more suggestive than explicit. We will work with two points implicit in his discussion. First, *delusion* is the stronger word; it denotes a longer lasting, more tenacious, and sometimes more harmful or dangerous notion. Second, even when the two words are denotatively quite similar, they tend to be used in constructions where they are not actually interchangeable.

In the first of the examples below, the writer uses both words; *delusion* appears to be the stronger one. We think that you will seldom find the words interchangeable in the rest of the examples.

The illusion of continental self-sufficiency persists in an era when technology has utterly demolished it. That self-sufficiency

may have been an approximation of the truth fifty years ago. But today it is a delusion endangering our very existence —Marquis Childs, *Yale Rev.,* Spring 1947

Hess, always a muddled man . . . , flew on his own to Britain under the delusion that he could arrange a peace settlement —William L. Shirer, *The Rise and Fall of the Third Reich,* 1960

. . . I am under no illusion that such a school can always overcome the strong divisive community attitudes —James B. Conant, *Slums and Suburbs,* 1961

I indulged, on this last trip, the illusion of visiting again the Paris and London of my youth —Edmund Wilson, *A Piece of My Mind,* 1956

. . . the National Park Service, which in recent years has suffered the delusion that it is a federation of highway departments —Jon Margolis, *Esquire,* March 1970

. . . the shattering of an illusion about a boy with whom she had a long affair —Caroline Seebohm, *N.Y. Times Book Rev.,* 29 July 1979

But it is sham or delusion or both to label either "urban growth policy" —Donald Canty, *City,* March–April 1972

It is a snare and a delusion, says Herbert Hill —*Trans-Action,* October 1971

Delusion and *illusion* can sometimes be interchanged, but in most cases they cannot. The reasons for this are that *illusion* is the more common word, that *delusion* tends more often than *illusion* to be used technically, and that each tends typically to be used in its own surroundings. We believe that when you have a context in which either word fits comfortably, you will probably choose *illusion*—more writers do.

demand   The noun *demand* is idiomatically used with the prepositions *for, on* or *upon,* and *of:*

. . . the overwhelming demand for doctors during World War II —*Current Biography,* October 1967

. . . so many demands on our time —Jamienne Studley, *Barnard Alumnae,* Winter 1971

. . . the demands upon the infant must be limited —Ernest R. Hilgard & Richard C. Atkinson, *Introduction to Psychology,* 4th ed., 1967

. . . because of the increasing demands of her career she discontinued her studies —*Current Biography,* October 1967

demanding Bernstein 1965 notes that *demanding* is idiomatically followed by *of*.

> The short story . . . is one of the most demanding of all literary mediums —William Styron, *This Quiet Dust*, 1982

> Somewhat more demanding of sunlight is the Jamaican allspice tree —Linda Yang, *A New Look at Houseplants*, Winter 1993

demean *Demean* is two verbs. The first, related to *demeanor*, dates from the 14th century. The second, formed from the prefix *de-* and the adjective *mean*, apparently on the model of *debase*, dates from the 17th century. Some 18th-century pundits—Baker 1770 and Campbell 1776—disapproved of the second verb on the grounds that it was a misuse of the first.

The mistaken opinions of 18th-century commentators often have long lives. This one continued through the 19th century and into the 20th with Vizetelly 1906, Bierce 1909, MacCracken & Sandison 1917, and a great many other commentators of the 1920s. Fowler 1926 recognized that there were two verbs, but he disapproved of the second one. Still later we find Partridge 1942 and Follett 1966 registering disapproval.

In the meantime the second *demean* had appeared in dictionaries. Samuel Johnson seems to have been the first lexicographer to recognize it; he included it as a second sense under the first *demean*. Webster picked it up from Johnson and the OED notes it without censure, giving a 1601 citation as the earliest.

Partridge found the second *demean* to be growing obsolescent in the 1940's, but quite the opposite is the case today: the second *demean* is almost the only one in current use; the first *demean* has become rare. Here are some examples of the first *demean*:

> . . . it shall be my earnest endeavour to demean myself with grateful respect towards her Ladyship —Jane Austen, *Pride and Prejudice*, 1813

> Might not your paper demean itself with more attention to the niceties of diction? —letter to the editor, *Washington Post & Times Herald*, 21 Oct. 1954

And a few of the second:

> . . . expected the same services from me as he would from another, while I thought he demeaned me too much in some he required of me, who from a brother expected more indulgence —Benjamin Franklin, *Autobiography*, 1771

> . . . I don't think it demeans her elegant classical style in the least —Arlene Croce, *Harper's*, April 1971

The first *demean* is used reflexively, usually with a phrase specifying how one demeans oneself; the second *demean* may be used reflexively or not. The first *demean* is now a rather bookish word, and since the equally bookish *comport* is available as a replacement (not to mention the plainer *conduct* and *behave*), its continuing in vigorous use appears somewhat unlikely. The second *demean* has the field practically to itself. Both are standard.

demise Some commentators feel *demise* is pretentious for *death* in ordinary contexts, and Bryson 1984 considers the use "an unnecessary euphemism." Bryson's real objection, however, is to the use of *demise* in a sense close to *decline*. None of this criticism is borne out by recent evidence. In current nonlegal use *demise* means "death" or "a cessation of existence or activity" or "a loss of position or status." Here are some typical examples:

> . . . turns out to be a gratifyingly loutish, brutish fellow. It is quite clear that everyone who knows him would welcome his conveniently accidental demise —Richard Schickel, *Life*, 14 Aug. 1970

> The memoirs that spring forth after an Administration's demise —Walter Goodman, *N.Y. Times Book Rev.*, 29 May 1983

> Like books, board games appear headed for imminent demise at the hands of cathode-ray terminals —Will Manley, *Booklist*, 1 Mar. 1995

> This elegant little book is essential reading for anyone interested in the demise, the terminal silliness, of our culture —John Irving, *N.Y. Times Book Rev.*, 6 Apr. 1997

> . . . invited visitors to play a game in which points are awarded to those who predict the demise of yet another overhyped dot-com —Jeff Goodell, *Rolling Stone*, 14 Sept. 2000

These uses are standard.

Democrat, Democratic Harper 1975, 1985, Copperud 1970, 1980, Heritage 1982, and Garner 1998 all comment on the use of *Democrat* as an adjective by some Republican politicians. Heritage notes the usage does not have much acceptance off the campaign stump, and Copperud notes that it is not recognized in dictionaries. It is, however, unlikely to require notice in dictionaries because it is simply an attributive use of the noun.

The usage is primarily a spoken one. In print, *Democratic* with a capital *D* serves to distinguish the political designation from the broader lowercase use.

depart 1. Quite a number of prepositions are used with *depart*; the choice is determined by the meaning and purpose of the prepositional phrase. *On* or *in* for the time, *on* for the nature of the activity, *for* for the destination, and *from* for the point of departure, whether physical or nonphysical, are probably the most common, but others appear from time to time:

> Alvarado departed on the adventure late in 1523 —Chester Lloyd Jones, *Guatemala Past and Present,* 1940

> . . . and thus departed for Bucharest that December with his Queen —*Current Biography 1947*

> . . . persons who thus departed from the house —Herman Melville, *Pierre,* 1852

> . . . a measure of the amount by which a curve departs from a straight line —Bertrand Russell, *Foundations of Geometry,* 1897

> . . . monetary policy departed from acute restraint —John W. Schulz, *Forbes,* 1 Dec. 1970

> . . . he had a "formula" . . . and was not encouraged to depart from it —Seymour Krim, *Evergreen,* August 1967

2. From the evidence produced by a correspondent reprinted in Safire 1984, some wire service stylebooks (and perhaps some newspaper stylebooks too) insist on *from* after *depart,* disapproving the transitive use of the verb. Burchfield 1996 notes that except for *depart this life* the transitive is little used in current British English. But Copperud 1980 calls the use "unexceptionable," and it seems common enough in American English:

> The presidents of Columbia and Harvard have departed office —John Kenneth Galbraith, *New York,* 15 Nov. 1971

> . . . having seen the Greeks at last depart their shores after 10 years of siege —John Keegan, *N.Y. Times Book Rev.,* 11 Mar. 1984

> . . . comfortably ensconced in the first-class cabin of a Pakistani International Airlines flight that had departed John F. Kennedy International Airport for Karachi —Brian Duffy, *U.S. News & World Report,* 20 Feb. 1995

> Before departing the New England coastline, the developing gale appeared on a 96-hour "weatherfax" —Samantha Coit, *Bangor* (Maine) *Daily News,* 3 July 1999

depend In most senses *depend* is followed by *on* or *upon:*

> This is the way it goes with the writers: they resent you to the degree that they depend on you —Jay McInerney, *Bright Lights, Big City,* 1984

> If I whimpered about having to get up early in the morning, I could depend on her to say, "The early bird gets the worm." —Russell Baker, *Growing Up,* 1982

> . . . it was, rather, that no one could depend upon them —George F. Kennan, *New Yorker,* 1 May 1971

> . . . steam from 5 to 10 minutes, depending upon the type and age of the beans —James Beard, *American Cookery,* 1972

When *depend* means "hang down"—a live but not very common use—it often is followed by *from:*

> . . . a watch chain depended from his pocket —Paul Theroux, *N.Y. Times Book Rev.,* 22 July 1979

Depend is also used absolutely, though chiefly in conversation:

> In the time-honored phrase, it depends —Irving Kolodin, *Saturday Rev.,* 11 Dec. 1954

Many commentators point out that in speech this construction can be followed by a clause with *no on* or *upon* intervening, as in "It depends how many times you've seen it" or "It all depends whether it rains." We have no evidence of these conversational patterns in ordinary discursive prose.

dependant See DEPENDENT.

dependent **1.** *Adjective.* Like the verb *depend,* the adjective *dependent* is frequently used with *on* or *upon:*

> Parents have little escape and are dependent on each other for too many different roles —John Platt in *Information Please Almanac 1971,* ed. Dan Golenpaul

> . . . forsaken and dependent upon music for any interest whatsoever in their lives —Eve Babitz, *Rolling Stone,* 3 Feb. 1972

The spelling *dependant* is no longer current for the adjective.

2. *Noun.* The noun is usually spelled *dependant* in British English and *dependent* in American English.

depositary, depository The idea that a *depositary* is a person or an institution, while a *depository* is a place, is put forward in several usage guides. It is often tempered by a comment to the effect that such a distinction would be nice to make but isn't always made. The last observation is correct. In actual usage, *depositary* rarely appears as a noun, but when it does it usually refers to a person or institution. *Depository,* a much commoner word, often refers to a place, but the distinction is by no means strictly followed. Historically, both

deprecate

words have referred to persons and institutions since the 17th century and to places since the 18th century. And in many contexts either interpretation is possible. A bank, for example, is both an institution and a place. Here is a sampling of citations:

> ... the immense experience of which we are the depositaries and the inheritors —Max Ascoli, *The Reporter*, 1 Dec. 1955

> ... the stock had to be at Fluor's depositary that same day —Richard L. Hudson, *Wall Street Jour.*, 26 Nov. 1982

> ... family confidences; of which he is known to be the silent depository —Charles Dickens, *Bleak House*, 1853

> ... to cope with any large-scale attack on the bullion depository —Alan Hynd, *Saturday Evening Post*, 29 May 1954

> ... the ocean deeps ... cannot be considered a safe depository for radioactive wastes —*Current Biography*, December 1965

In current usage, *depositary* is almost always used as an adjective in phrases such as *depositary bank* and, most often, *American Depositary Receipts*.

deprecate, depreciate Contrary to the views of thirty or forty guardians of the language, *deprecate* and *depreciate* are seldom confused. Most of such confusion as exists has been introduced by those who have sought to illuminate, but have only befogged. Among the befoggers must be counted lexicographers, for our attempts to define and discriminate have not been notably successful.

Depreciate is the easier of the two words to deal with. Its oldest use is what for convenience we shall refer to as the disparaging sense. This sense manifests itself in two ways in modern English. First, it is used in its own right:

> True politeness in China demands that you should depreciate everything of your own and exalt everything belonging to your correspondent —Lord Frederic Hamilton, *Vanished Pomps of Yesterday*, 1934

> Knowledge is a great thing. Nobody should depreciate it —Robert M. Hutchins, *Center Mag.*, March 1968

This use appears to be receding, as *depreciate* comes more and more to be perceived as a technical term relating to monetary matters. But the figurative use of its monetary sense provides *depreciate* with a second way of denoting disparagement:

> The body-count by which the Vietnam war is officially and journalistically reported is as good an illustration as any of how we

have depreciated the value of human life —Ramsey Clark, *Center Mag.*, July/August 1970

> Such overuse depreciates the value of useful words —Howard 1977

We should note in passing that this latter use—with *value* as the direct object—is not replaced by *deprecate* in ordinary serious writing.

If *depreciate* is a relatively simple word to deal with, *deprecate* is not. Its early uses are strongly influenced by the religious associations of *deprecation*, its older relative, which was used as the name of a particular kind of prayer—a prayer for the removal or averting of something evil or disastrous. We can see this notion of praying or hoping to ward off or avert something in Samuel Johnson's use:

> ... to call upon the sun for peace and gaiety, to deprecate the clouds lest sorrow should overwhelm us, is the cowardice of idleness, and idolatry of folly —*The Idler*, 24 June 1758

The notion of seeking or hoping to turn aside or avert something undesirable, with or without the intercession of some higher power, can be seen in these examples:

> ... smilingly placed himself opposite him, with the look of one who deprecates an expected reproof —John Cowper Powys, *Ducdame*, 1925

> ... it would bring about the war we all dread and deprecate —Albert Guérard, *Education of a Humanist*, 1949

We might say that the thing deprecated in the foregoing examples is viewed with a certain amount of dread. One may also wish to ward off or avert something of which one does not approve. And in these next examples we can see the notion of disapproval mixed with that of seeking to avert or avoid:

> His eye, which was growing quick to read Naomi's face, saw at once ... that she deprecated even the slightest reference to her weakness —Sir Arthur Quiller-Couch, *The Delectable Duchy*, 1893

> As a Protector of the People Tiberius was held in great awe by the Rhodians. . . . But he insisted that he was merely a private citizen and deprecated any public honours paid to him. He usually dispensed with his official escort of yeomen —Robert Graves, *I, Claudius*, 1934

We may even find both dread and disapproval mixed with the seeking to ward off:

> Terrible as are the potentialities of the atomic bomb, we must not waste time in

deprecating its use. Instead, we must be more determined than ever to prevent the recurrence of war —Vera Micheles Dean, *The Four Cornerstones of Peace,* 1946

The notion of disapproval often takes over so thoroughly that the notion of seeking to ward off or avert is greatly diminished or even completely lost:

Master Cruncher . . . turning to his mother, strongly deprecated any praying away of his personal board —Charles Dickens, *A Tale of Two Cities,* 1859

Another group . . . deprecated all dogmas, and pled for a purely ethical religion —Will Durant, *The Age of Faith,* 1950

Novels, though not forbidden, were deprecated by their parents —K. M. Elisabeth Murray, *Caught in the Web of Words,* 1977

The use of dashes for commas is deprecated —Howard 1984

All needless repetition is to be deprecated —Barzun 1985

The editors of *Merriam-Webster's Dictionary of Synonyms* found a tinge of regret in *deprecate,* which would seem to move it in the direction of *deplore.* The notion of regret is stronger in some of the next group of examples than in others, but the interpretation is possible in all of them:

There is nothing I more deprecate than the use of the Fourteenth Amendment beyond the absolute compulsion of its words to prevent the making of social experiments —Oliver Wendell Holmes d. 1935, *Truax* v. *Corrigan,* 1921

I very much deprecate the House falling unduly into the debating of details and routine, and losing sight of its larger duty —Sir Winston Churchill, *The Unrelenting Struggle,* 1942

. . . is hardly his fault, and I will content myself with deprecating the conspicuous waste of a distinguished talent —Wolcott Gibbs, *New Yorker,* 16 Apr. 1955

I deprecate public debate about what the Cabinet should be doing, by members of the Cabinet —Harold Wilson, quoted in *The Listener,* 8 Aug. 1974

We should pause now to observe that we have entered the realm of controversy. The first use of *deprecate* to be criticized is its "disapprove" sense, by Ayres 1881, but this objection was lost in the growing controversy involving *depreciate.*

We do not really know how this most controversial use—or, really, two uses—of *deprecate* arose. Readers Digest 1983 has the most ingenious suggestion. They found it used by Thackeray in *Vanity Fair* (1848). He places the phrase "deprecate the value of" in the mouth of a fast-talking but ill-educated auctioneer, and in the view of Reader's Digest Thackeray has used a common malapropism of the day to mark his character. But since we have no genuine evidence of *deprecate* with *value* as object and no evidence of *deprecate* used for the monetary sense of *depreciate,* we are rather doubtful. And our earliest evidence for a changed sense is not for the "disparage" sense either; it is for what we could call the "modest" sense:

He said much of their kindness to him, and his wish that he could ever have the chance to do anything for them; while they politely deprecated anything that they had done —Margaret Deland, *Old Chester Tales,* 1898

This use might be defined as "to make little of, play down, belittle modestly." It is clearly related to similar uses of the adjectives *deprecating, deprecatory,* and their apparently later compounds with *self-.* It is a separate use of the verb that has continued:

I remember that he deprecated the very general belief in his success or his efficiency, and I think with sincerity —William Butler Yeats, *The Trembling of the Veil,* 1922

He speaks five languages . . . , but deprecates this facility —*Time,* 1 Dec. 1952

. . . was quite right to be confident, however much he might deprecate his own achievements —Goronwy Rees, *The Listener,* 30 Jan. 1975

He amusingly deprecates his melodic gifts by saying that canon is good for him as he only has to write one melody —*Record Roundup,* November–December 1984

You have noted that in this last use of *deprecate,* the making little of is always directed by the subject toward himself or what he has done. When it is directed toward a second person or toward a thing, *deprecate* comes closer in meaning to *disparage* or *belittle.*

"I am not deprecating your individual talent, Joseph," the Bishop continued, "but, when one thinks of it, a soup like this is not the work of one man. . . ." —Willa Cather, *Death Comes for the Archbishop,* 1927

Among Chicagoans of more than grade-school education, there is a disposition to deprecate the Colonel. . . . Some of the scoffers . . . —A. J. Liebling, *New Yorker,* 19 Jan. 1952

. . . perhaps the most reluctantly admired and least easily deprecated of twentieth-century American novelists —*New Yorker,* 17 Dec. 1955

And golfers by nature almost invariably deprecate any golf course they cannot break par on —Charles Price, *Esquire,* August 1965

. . . Western society places a premium on masculinity while often deprecating femininity —Marvin Reznikoff & Tannah Hirsch, *Psychology Today,* May 1970

It is instructive, we think, to try substituting *depreciate* for *deprecate* in these examples. In most of them *depreciate* simply does not sound quite right. We believe that it has become too strongly associated with the world of finance to sound totally suitable in literary or even psychological contexts. *Belittle* or *disparage* or even *denigrate* or *put down* will work better. It would appear that *depreciate* has been vacating this semantic area and that *deprecate* has been moving in.

If you have read all the examples here, you already know a good deal about how *deprecate* is used. To recapitulate, we see these historical trends: *depreciate* has for some time been retreating into specialization as a financial term; it is less and less used as a term of disparagement. *Deprecate* has taken over much of *depreciate*'s old territory, although its "modest" use is one *depreciate* was seldom used for. You can use *deprecate* in any of the ways here illustrated—the sources are impeccably standard. Or you can substitute some other word or phrase in order to avoid some of *deprecate*'s ambiguities.

See also DEPRECATING, DEPRECATORY, DEPRECIATORY; SELF-DEPRECATING, SELF-DEPRECATORY.

deprecating, deprecatory, depreciatory
These three adjectives have been introduced into the discussion of *deprecate* and *depreciate* by some commentators. Such introduction tends to be irrelevant to an understanding of the verbs, for only *deprecating* is derived from the verb and the adjectives have led their own separate existence.

The oldest of the set is *deprecatory.* The OED shows that it was originally used of prayer—this is the connection to *deprecation* that *deprecatory* shares with *deprecate.* Swift in 1704 took the adjective into the secular world, where it has been used in the sense "seeking to avert disapproval, apologetic" ever since.

. . . made a politely deprecatory little speech. "We may not be as good as you remember us," she said —*Time,* 18 Sept. 1950

Deprecatory later—probably under the influence of the verb—developed its second sense of "disapproving":

. . . quotation marks are not normally employed with words of common usage, *except* in a deprecatory or ironic sense —Rosemary Neiswender, *Library Jour.,* 15 Mar. 1966

In some examples of this sense, disparagement is clearly mixed with or is perhaps more important than disapproval:

. . . some deprecatory title such as "the moron course" —*Educational Research Bulletin,* 19 Jan. 1949

. . . the modernized disciplines have become academic again in the old, deprecatory sense of the term —Steven Marcus, *Times Literary Supp.,* 27 Aug. 1976

In such use the word is hard to distinguish from *depreciatory.*

Depreciatory is a 19th-century word that regularly means "disparaging":

. . . as *little* is not often used with depreciatory adjectives —Jespersen 1917

. . . nonart (the word is not to be taken as depreciatory) —Wayne Shumaker, *Elements of Critical Theory,* 1952

Deprecating, from the present participle of the verb, is another 19th-century word. It is used like *depreciatory:*

Mrs. Shane became falsely deprecating of Lily's charms. "She is a good girl," she said. "But hardly as charming as all that. . . ." —Louis Bromfield, *The Green Bay Tree,* 1924

They will turn off with a deprecating laugh any too portentous remark —Bertrand Russell, *The Scientific Outlook,* 1931

Allagash tells you, with a deprecating roll of his eyes, that Vicky is studying Philosophy at Princeton —Jay McInerney, *Bright Lights, Big City,* 1984

For me the word has a slightly humorous, slightly deprecating quality. I would use it only in joking —Peter S. Prescott, in Harper 1985

Do not be misled by the occasional failure of a critic to understand the older of the two modern senses of *deprecatory.* Our present evidence shows that the use of *deprecating* is increasing slightly while that of *deprecatory* and *depreciatory* is not.

See also DEPRECATE, DEPRECIATE; SELF-DEPRECATING, SELF-DEPRECATORY.

deprecative, depreciative These are relatively rare alternatives to *deprecatory* and *depreciatory.* See the article at DEPRECATING, DEPRECATORY, DEPRECIATORY.

deprecatory See DEPRECATING, DEPRECA-TORY, DEPRECIATORY.

depreciate See DEPRECATE, DEPRECIATE.

depreciative See DEPRECATIVE, DEPRECIA-TIVE.

depreciatory See DEPRECATING, DEPRECA-TORY, DEPRECIATORY.

deprive *Deprive* is usually used in the construction "deprive (someone or something) of (something)":

> It will not do merely to deprive the Court of its power to legislate —Rexford G. Tugwell, *Center Mag.,* January 1968

> . . . their acquiescence is a "singing" lyricism which deprived Yiddish poetry of intellectual bite —Irving Howe, *Commentary,* January 1972

Deprive is also used with *from* but apparently not very often:

> How can we improve a situation if we are deprived by terminology from knowing what the situation really is? —James B. Conant, *Slums and Suburbs,* 1961

de rigueur Bremner 1980, Bryson 1984, and Garner 1998 warn users of this adjective to be careful of its spelling. There is a *u* both before and after the *e*. Both *de rigeur* and *de riguer* have been spotted in print. This word requires some attention.

derisive, derisory *Derisive* and *derisory* both came into the language during the 17th century, the former in 1662 and the latter in 1618, as recorded in the OED. Both words then meant about the same thing, "causing or expressing derision." After a long period of time, in the late 19th and early 20th centuries, each word developed a second sense, "worthy of ridicule"; thus, the synonymy of the two words was extended. Despite the opinions of a few critics, *derisive* and *derisory* are to some extent still used synonymously in contemporary writing:

> . . . there was heard derisive laughter from the boorish revelers —Goodman Ace, *Saturday Rev.,* 25 Dec. 1971

> . . . pointing a derisory finger at me he roared, "Look at him! The Yellow Press lapdog!" —R. F. Delderfield, *For My Own Amusement,* 1968

> The put-on artist draws out that derisive moment —Jacob Brackman, *New Yorker,* 24 June 1967

> What a moment for "Pheeleep"—the derisory name by which that strange . . . baronet was known —*Times Literary Supp.,* 22 Oct. 1971

But there does seem to be a distinction growing between the two words. The evidence shows that over the last 50 years or so, writers have been more often choosing *derisive* for its original sense "causing or expressing derision,' while opting for *derisory* when they mean "worthy of ridicule":

> . . . he stopped just outside the door, waiting; and of course it came: the burst of derisive laughter —Morley Callaghan, *The Loved and the Lost,* 1951

> Instead, Mailer became his own most derisive critic . . . always finally being put down hardest by himself —John W. Aldridge, *Saturday Rev.,* 13 Nov. 1971

> From the audience, there was a growing volume of derisive laughter and catcalls —Nat Hentoff, *Village Voice,* 22 Feb. 1994

> . . . political instability and Asia's economic turmoil combined to reduce prices of Indonesian debt and equity to almost derisory levels —Walter Russell Mead, *N.Y. Times Mag.,* 28 June 1998

> He makes his rounds in a derisory excuse for an automobile, which is always in danger of breaking down —A. J. Liebling, *New Yorker,* 3 Nov. 1956

derive *Derive* is usually used with a prepositional-phrase complement, which nearly always begins with *from*:

> Mr. Vidal's Lincoln, however, derives from the mainstream of modern scholarship —Joyce Carol Oates, *N.Y. Times Book Rev.,* 3 June 1984

> . . . the social stratum from which he derived —Carl Van Doren, *The American Novel,* 1940

Derive is also found, though less frequently, with *therefrom* and *whence*:

> Her characters do not move in an ordered, stable world and derive therefrom a personal sense of order —William Van O'Connor, in *Forms of Modern Fiction,* and its ed., 1948

> . . . the sound-signs whence are derived the alphabets of the civilised world —Edward Clodd, *The Story of the Alphabet,* 1900

Now and then *derive* can be found with *in, of, out,* and *through*:

> . . . the two electoral triumphs by Woodrow Wilson derived essentially in the inability of the Republicans to compromise —Cortez A. M. Ewing, in *Aspects of American Government,* ed. Sydney D. Bailey, 1950

> . . . derived of the poorest African stock —Melville J. Herskovits, *Saturday Rev.,* 10 Jan. 1942

Modern international law, deriving out of the summary by Hugo Grotius —Frederic L. Paxson, *Pre-War Years 1913–1917,* 1936

. . . the cherub of our grave-stone cutters is derived through the Hebrews —Edward Clodd, *The Story of the Alphabet,* 1900

derogate In its intransitive senses, *derogate* is used with *from*:

. . . increase the authority of each Dominion and not derogate from it —Robert Gordon Menzies, *Foreign Affairs,* January 1949

. . . special agreements which do not derogate from the rights of prisoners —Dean Acheson, *Harper's,* January 1953

derogation *Derogation* when followed by a complement usually takes *of* or *from*, with *of* occurring more frequently:

. . . our . . . peevish derogation of the immense spectrum of cultures in what is referred to as the third world —Edward Hoagland, *N.Y. Times Book Rev.,* 22 Jan. 1984

While *derogation* may still be found with *from* sporadically in contemporary writing, it is more often found in writing from the 1950s and before:

It is no necessary derogation from his book that the humor is about the humor of alumni magazines —Howard Mumford Jones, *Saturday Rev.,* 12 Apr. 1941

descriptive genitive See GENITIVE 1.

desert, deserts, dessert This is really just a matter of paying attention to spelling. There are two nouns spelled *desert.* The first of these is the barren *desert,* and by reason of pronunciation if no other, it seems seldom to be mistaken for the others. The second *desert* is related to *deserve* and is pronounced like *dessert.* It is commonly used as a plural in the phrase *just deserts* (which one gets). Here we have the real spelling problem. We have found *desert* in place of *dessert* from 1833 to 1998 (and we suspect we have not seen the last of it). And the opposite error—*just desserts*—has been detected by Bernstein 1962 in the *New York Times,* by Simon 1980 in *Time,* and by one of our editors in *Newsweek* in 2000. Care is all that is needed here.

And don't you just know that somewhere there is an ice-cream emporium called Just Desserts?

desideratum The plural of this borrowing from Latin is *desiderata.* Evans 1957 says *desideratums* may also be used, but we have no record of its use in our files.

The use of *desiderata* as a singular is quite rare. Its development as a singular has probably been stunted by the flourishing condition of the singular *desideratum.* See the list at LATIN PLURALS for other borrowings whose plurals may or may not present problems.

The other desideratum is a pitcher with good control —Roger Angell, *New Yorker,* 12 Mar. 1984

Such knowledge and attitudes may not be just desiderata—they may be *imperatives* —Edwin O. Reischauer, *Saturday Rev.,* 29 May 1976

Whereas earlier philosophers had viewed "objectivity" as a methodological desideratum —Richard Wolin, *New Republic,* 15 May 2000

design, intend Einstein 1985 says that "common usage now freely substitutes *design* for *intend.*" He doesn't like it, however. Copperud 1970, 1980, opines that *design* is overused in journalism. Here are a couple of typical journalistic uses:

President Reagan, in an appearance at Jefferson Junior High School in Washington, D.C., that was designed to show his interest in educational issues —*Publishers Weekly,* 14 Sept. 1984

. . . a list of questions designed to find out just what our readers thought —*McCall's,* March 1971

The writer in each of these examples might have used *intend,* but it is hard to see how it would be an improvement. The use of *design* in senses close to *intend* dates back at least to the 17th century. Here is an example from a literary source:

The conference was neither so short nor so conclusive as the lady had designed —Jane Austen, *Mansfield Park,* 1814

This is not to suggest that *design* and *intend* are freely interchangeable. Einstein's advice to stop and think when you go to write *design* is sound; sometimes *intend* will indeed be the better choice. And sometimes not. In this last example, the use of *intend* would have muddled the intended meaning:

Then she went out in search of a new lifestyle, one better designed to elude threats to her well-being —Don Gold, *Cosmopolitan,* June 1976

desirous *Desirous* has been used with both *of* and *to* for a long time:

. . . desirous at once of having her time to herself —Jane Austen, *Mansfield Park,* 1814

I returned to London, very desirous to see Dr. Johnson —James Boswell, *Life of Samuel Johnson,* 1791

In contemporary writing, *desirous of* is more common than *desirous to*:

> They seem very desirous of getting back —Flannery O'Connor, letter, 1958

> . . . poetry designed to appeal to ears desirous of rhetoric —Eric Partridge, *British and American English Since 1900,* 1951

desist When *desist* takes a prepositional-phrase complement, the preposition is usually *from*; less frequently, *desist* is followed by *in*:

> . . . to desist from attempts at suppression —Elmer Rice, *New Republic,* 13 Apr. 1953

> . . . had desisted in his effort to press love upon her —Sherwood Anderson, *Poor White,* 1920

despair The verb *despair,* when used with a preposition, is usually used with *of*:

> Unless one despairs of mankind altogether —John Cogley, *Center Mag.,* July/August 1970

> Poetry has its roots in incantation . . . but it may well despair of competing with the incantation of Big Business, Bigger Navies, Brighter Churches —C. Day Lewis, *A Hope for Poetry,* 3d ed., 1936

Despair has also been used with *at,* but this use is much less frequent:

> . . . our parents sometimes despaired at our inability to understand —Paul Potter, *Johns Hopkins Mag.,* October 1965

despoil When *despoil* is used with a preposition, it is *of*:

> . . . individual monasteries were occasionally despoiled of their land and revenues —Owen & Eleanor Lattimore, *The Making of Modern China,* 1944

> . . . the Dons sought unsuccessfully in New Mexico the kind of wealth of which they had despoiled the Aztecs —*American Speech,* Spring/Summer 1975

despondent Simon 1980 makes the claim that *despondent* "can apply only to people." Wrong. It is usually applied to people but sometimes it is not:

> The house . . . needed paint badly, and looked gloomy and despondent among its smart Queen Anne neighbors —Willa Cather, *The Song of the Lark,* 1915

> . . . Mark Twain was filled with a despondent desire . . . to stop writing altogether —Van Wyck Brooks, *The Ordeal of Mark Twain,* 1920

> In the more despondent literatures of Europe —*Times Literary Supp.,* 14 Nov. 1968

dessert See DESERT, DESERTS, DESSERT.

destined *Destined* is almost always used with a preposition, either *to* or *for*. *Destined to* is most common when it is followed by an infinitive:

> . . . were destined to battle with each other for the control of the road —Harrison Smith, *Saturday Rev.,* 5 June 1954

> Frazer's *Golden Bough* suggested that the mere primitiveness of religious belief proves it is destined to be left behind on the march to civilization —Mary Douglas, *Commonweal,* 9 Oct. 1970

Destined to may also be followed by an object, although this is less frequent than the infinitive:

> . . . he was destined to a bright and leading role in the world —H. G. Wells, *Joan and Peter,* 1918

When *destined* is used with *for,* it is followed by a noun or noun phrase:

> . . . it seemed that her graph of accomplishment was destined for a downward dip —*Saturday Rev.,* 26 Mar. 1955

> . . . he's the kind of actor who seems destined for an Oscar —Stephen Schaefer, *US,* 11 Feb. 1985

destruct, self-destruct Ever since the 1950s people have been writing to ask if there is such a word as *destruct.* The *Chicago Tribune* in March 1962 reprinted a denunciation of the word that seems to have originated in the *Cedar Rapids Gazette.* Barzun 1985, prompted by an instance of *self-destruct* printed on the bottom of a grocery bag, claims there is no verb *destruct.*

The verb *destruct* has been entered in our unabridged dictionaries since 1909. It was originally formed in the 17th century from the past participle of the same Latin verb that gave us *destroy.* It was simply a rare alternative to *destroy* that had only the advantage of contrasting prettily with *construct.* When it was revived as part of aerospace jargon in the 1950s, its coiners and users probably had no idea that the verb already existed. They probably created it by back-formation from *destruction.*

The revived *destruct* is not used in quite the same way as *destroy.* For one thing, it is usually used with *self-,* and *destroy* is not. What is more, *destruct* carries the connotation of destroying for some positive purpose, such as safety.

> . . . a $50 million weather satellite which was deliberately destructed on launch —*Springfield* (Mass.) *Sunday Republican,* 19 May 1968

A noun *destruct* was formed at the same time as the revived verb. It is often used attributively:

> . . . an attaché case with instant destruct equipment —Walter Wager, *Telefon,* 1975

Both the noun and verb *destruct* are seldom found outside the areas of aerospace, the military, and cloak-and-dagger stories. Such is not the case, however, with *self-destruct. Self-destruct* was popularized by its use in the television series "Mission Impossible." The opening of each show included a tape of recorded instructions that burned itself up after the words, "This tape will self-destruct in five seconds."

We have evidence from technical sources for *self-destruct* used as an attributive (*self-destruct mechanism,* for instance), but not as a verb. The verb seems to have sprung full-grown from the heads of the "Mission Impossible" writers. The notion of self-destruction seemed to fill a need, for the verb rapidly became popular, established itself, and has continued to be widely used in general contexts. Here are some typical uses:

> . . . we've designed a leaf bag . . . which will self-destruct when it is left in the rain —Norman Seltzer, quoted in *Springfield* (Mass.) *Union,* 19 Aug. 1970

> A second homing device went into operation there this afternoon. Both devices will self destruct at 2:00 A.M. —Hugh C. McDonald, *The Hour of the Blue Fox,* 1975

> . . . an inventive time-travel story that unexpectedly self-destructs at the end —Gerald Jonas, *N.Y. Times Book Rev.,* 31 July 1983

destructive When it is used with a preposition, *destructive* is most often used with *of* or *to,* with *of* occurring more frequently:

> . . . whenever any form of government becomes destructive of these ends, the people have the right to alter it —Linus Pauling, *Center Mag.,* September 1968

> . . . a very violent . . . motion which is extremely destructive to the ligaments of the right shoulder —Ernest Hemingway, "African Journal," 1956

Much less often, *destructive* is used with *toward*:

> . . . persons . . . are apt to be *destructive* toward themselves or others —Kenneth Goodall, *Psychology Today,* May 1971

detract, distract Some language commentators warn against confusing the use of *detract* and *distract.* While it is true that *detract* is used most commonly to mean "to take away some-

thing," it is also used to mean "to divert." The OED records this sense as dating from the 16th century, and the citation it quotes from the early 19th century shows the verb with the word *attention* as its direct object. This sense of *detract* has been entered in Merriam-Webster dictionaries since Webster's Second (1934), and Merriam-Webster editors collected some half-dozen instances of its use during the 20th century:

> These exaggerated reports tend to detract attention from the real issue —John Scott, *Time,* 3 Mar. 1947

It is clear that *distract* is considerably more common with *attention* than *detract* is. Burchfield 1996 calls *detract* obsolete in British English in this use, but produces an over-the-air example from a BBC broadcast. We have no recent evidence for *detract* with *attention.*

When *detract* is used with a preposition, it is used with *from*:

> . . . the little room was furnished as a chapel, though very simply, so as not to detract from the glory of the frescoes —Elizabeth Goudge, *Pilgrim's Inn,* 1948

> An individual's image enhances or detracts from his power to persuade —Carll Tucker, *Saturday Rev.,* 25 Nov. 1978

deverbal nouns See NOUNS AS VERBS.

deviate When *deviate* is used with a preposition, it is now most often used with *from*:

> The building deviates considerably from the classic tradition —*American Guide Series: N.Y. City,* 1939

> . . . sticking as close as possible to . . . the printed score, deviating as little as possible from strict tempo —Winthrop Sargeant, *New Yorker,* 10 Mar. 1955

> . . . exercise censorship over any one of the Big Six Negro leaders who tried to deviate from the script —Malcolm X, *Evergreen,* December 1967

Deviate used with the preposition *into* is more commonly found in literature of the past:

> . . . Shadwell never deviates into sense —John Dryden, *Mac Flecknoe,* 1682 (OED)

> Our travellers deviated into a much less frequented track —Henry Fielding, *Tom Jones,* 1749 (OED)

But it continues to be found sporadically in modern writing, sometimes alluding to Dryden's use:

> For an additional 10¢ the driver will deviate into side streets —*American Guide Series: New Jersey,* 1939

. . . has been known to deviate into sense, but this is not one of those times —*New York,* 17 Nov. 1975

device, devise Several books call attention to the possibility of a spelling problem here. We have seen *devise* used for *device. Device* is a noun, *devise* primarily a verb and secondarily a noun used only in legal contexts. Checking your dictionary for the relevant meaning will keep you on the right path.

devolve When used with a preposition, *devolve* usually appears with *on* or *upon*:

. . . as they see the final power over curricular design slip from them and devolve on students —Lewis B. Mayhew, *Change,* January–February 1971

. . . the basic coverage of political conventions may devolve upon cable television —Neil Hickey, *TV Guide,* 1 Aug. 1980

Less frequently *devolve* is used with *to* or *into*:

. . . if the newspaper organization dissolves, no part of the assets should devolve to members —H. L. Ewbank, *AAUP Bulletin,* December 1969

The reason is that the economy had devolved into five separate economies that no longer act as one —*Business Week,* 1 June 1981

Curiously enough, while *devolve* followed by *from* had at one time faded from use, it now is appearing again, at least sporadically. *Evolve,* which commonly combines with *from,* may be an influence here:

His allegedly subversive campaigns . . . all devolve from his belief in basic American rights —Frank Deford, *Sports Illustrated,* 8 Aug. 1983

dialogue 1. The spelling *dialogue* is much more commonly used than *dialog.*
2. There is a variety of comment on the noun *dialogue.* Kilpatrick 1984 says, "At some point in recent semantic history, a curious notion took root that *dialogue* should be restricted to describe a conversation between two persons only." This is apparently a delicate allusion to, among others, Edwin Newman, whose discussion of Gerald Ford's use of *dialogue* (in *Esquire,* December 1975) is based on that notion, and Shaw 1975, 1987, where *dialogue* is said to be from the Greek for "two words." Not only is Shaw in thrall to the etymological fallacy, but the Greek etymon does not contain the notion "two" at all. Anyone who reads the etymology of the word in a good dictionary will see that Greek *dia* means "through, across, apart" and several other things, but never "two."
More commentators seem concerned about the sense of *dialogue* that means "an exchange

of ideas and opinions." This sense is called a "fad word" by Flesch 1964, and is mentioned or discussed also in Bremner 1980, Reader's Digest 1983, and Shaw 1975, 1987, and is the subject of Newman's remarks about President Ford's use. Here are some examples of the use:

Rhetoric and anger partially yielded to dialogue —Robert Liebert, *Change,* October 1971

Those staff meetings were a model of intellectual dialogue: tough, sharp, often acerbic —Wayne Booth, *PMLA,* October 1994

The answer to this may ultimately be the most important contribution that black intellectuals make to the dialogue about the appropriate role for American public intellectuals —Robert S. Boynton, *Atlantic,* March 1995

There is no doubt that this sense has enjoyed a considerable vogue which is still going on. It is standard in general prose.
3. Reader's Digest 1983 opines that the verb *dialogue* developed from the noun in the "exchange of ideas" sense discussed above, and the editors don't much care for it. That the verb is formed from the noun there is no question. And if the OED evidence is conclusive, Shakespeare was the first to use it—both transitively and intransitively. Among other users of the verb cited by the OED are Richardson, Coleridge, and Carlyle. What seems to have happened is that this verb has fallen out of serious literary use but has persisted or been revived in speech and speechlike writing. Here are some examples of typical recent use:

What I especially appreciate is your willingness to dialogue about issues —Louis Shores, *RQ,* Spring 1973

. . . to dialogue with Jesus Christ —radio talk show, 22 June 1975

This sort of use has been held up for our amusement by a contemporary satirical novelist:

Nor could he get her to dialogue with him beyond an inflectionless "Far out." —Cyra McFadden, *The Serial,* 1977

diamond, diaper See VEHICLE.

dice See DIE, *noun,* DICE.

dichotomy After reading and rereading our stack of citations for the use of *dichotomy,* we have come to the conclusion that many people who use this word have only a general idea of what it means. This haziness on the part of the word's users has resulted in a word whose meaning, aside from technical uses, is likewise hazy. For someone evaluating good and bad usage or even merely trying to describe usage accurately, *dichotomy* presents a ticklish problem.

Several usage commentators have responded to the uneasiness that *dichotomy* engenders by simply saying that it should not be used in general contexts to mean "division" or "split." Frankly, we welcome such uses because they, at least, can be pinned down to a single, clear definition.

. . . the sharp dichotomy between undergraduate education and graduate professional study —*Current Biography,* June 1964

. . . the dichotomy between mind and body —Rollo May, *Psychology Today,* August 1969

Howard 1978 disapproves of using *dichotomy* "to mean anything divided into two or resulting from such a division; and thence to mean something paradoxical or ambivalent." Howard has paraphrased these definitions from the OED Supplement. In one citation *dichotomy* means "paradox":

By a dichotomy familiar to us all, a woman requires her own baby to be perfectly normal, and at the same time superior to all other babies —John Wyndham, *The Midwich Cuckoos,* 1957 (OED Supplement)

We, too, have citations in which *dichotomy* means "paradox" or has some other vaguely similar meaning:

Herbert Hoover, a Quaker, fed milk to Belgian babies; Herbert Hoover as President of the United States had the war veterans of the Bonus Army bombed out of Washington by tear gas. What is this profound dichotomy? —Alfred North Whitehead, *Atlantic,* March 1939

It is a well-known paradox that the lover of the sea craves for dry land—the sailor's love-hate extension of our old dichotomy to want to be where we are not —William Sansom, *N.Y. Times Mag.,* 10 May 1964

. . . the dichotomy or contradictions within the American mind —Richard Beale Davis, *Key Reporter,* Spring 1968

. . . invoking a traditional . . . dichotomy, how can we understand an indefinable term except through acquaintance with what the term denotes? —Arthur Danto, *Columbia Forum,* Fall 1969

. . . spinning lovely dichotomies (all fairy stories have female heroines: all science comes from the ego, not the self) —*Times Literary Supp.,* 7 July 1978

The amusing spectacle of the recent presidential vote in Florida should remind us of the persistence of the federal-state dichotomy —Eugene Genovese, *Atlantic,* March 2001

The speed/stamina dichotomy should be obvious to anyone who has ever cooked a chicken —Michael Rogers, *National Wildlife,* October–November 1990

In many cases of such dichotomizing, the message that gets across to the reader is chiefly that the writer is using a fancy, academic-sounding word. If this is the impression you want to convey, *dichotomy* will surely serve you. If you are mainly interested in having your sentence understood, however, you might be better off finding another way to word it.

dictum While the plurals *dicta* and *dictums* are both in standard use, our evidence shows that *dicta* is quite a bit more commonly used.

Partridge 1942 contains an example of *dicta* used as a singular. Our files have no examples that are clearly singular; this does not appear to be a serious problem.

For other foreign plurals, some of which present usage problems, see LATIN PLURALS.

didn't ought See HAD OUGHT, HADN'T OUGHT; OUGHT 1, 3.

die, *verb* From as far back as Ayres 1881 there have been varying pronouncements as to which prepositions may be used with which objects after the verb *die.* Sometimes disapproval is expressed of one preposition or another; Vizetelly 1906 and Copperud 1964, 1970, 1980 do not like *from,* and Ayres 1881 and Jensen 1935 do not like *with.* Since as many specifically approve these two prepositions as object to them, there cannot be much of a question of propriety here. But there is still the question of idiom. Here we have some sample contexts in which prepositions are used with *die* in various senses. *Of* seems to be the most common:

. . . dying of kidney disease —Dr. C. L. Mengis, *National Observer,* 10 Mar. 1973

Diddloff is a dandy who would die of a rose in aromatic pain —W. M. Thackeray, *The Book of Snobs,* 1846

From:

. . . Alexander died from an infection —*Current Biography 1947*

. . . suspicions . . . which had withered and died since from too much doubt —Louis Bromfield, *The Green Bay Tree,* 1924

For:

It died for lack of support —James O. Goldsborough, *N.Y. Times Mag.,* 27 Apr. 1980

Men die from time to time, . . . but not for love —Lewis H. Lapham, *Harper's,* November 1971

. . . to do and die for the company —Clyde Haberman, *N.Y. Times,* 16 Jan. 1984

With:

. . . she, the children, and her father all died with the cholera —Raymond W. Thorp, *Bowie Knife,* 1948

And a few others appear less frequently:

. . . where the penal laws were dying through non-enforcement —*Dictionary of American Biography,* 1929

. . . at roll-top desks that were to die over —Cyra McFadden, *The Serial,* 1977

Many other prepositions are possible when the phrases are adverbial ones of location. Since these are not a matter of idiom with *die,* we have not included any here. In addition many varying older combinations can be found in the OED.

die, dice, *noun* The use of *dice* as a singular for one of the small cubes thrown in various games has been the object of some discussion. Krapp 1927 and Evans 1957 both mention its use, with Evans saying that *dice* is the usual singular. A letter to *Word Study* in 1947 made the claim that *dice* was the usual singular used by those who gambled with dice, and the Merriam-Webster editor who replied to the letter agreed, even though the use was not recognized in Webster's Second. Copperud 1970, 1980 and Garner 1998 disapprove the use.

The OED shows that the singular *dice* has been in use since the 14th century. It is apparently primarily a spoken use, for it is fairly rare in print. If dice players scorn *die* as a singular in speech, they (or their editors) seem to prefer it in print.

differ The basic advice of the usage books is this: when *differ* means "to be unlike," it is followed by the preposition *from;* when *differ* means "to disagree," it is followed by the preposition *with* or *from.* This advice is more or less a consensus of upwards of twenty commentators from Ayres 1881 to the present. Writers have apparently had no difficulty using these words, and the only controversy has been the disagreement of the usage writers among themselves about the propriety or desirability of *with* or *from* in the "disagree" sense.

Most of the commentary consists of a few observations and a made-up example or two. Here are some actual examples. They include some other prepositions usually not mentioned, as well as those that stir contention.

The sense "to be unlike" does, in fact, select *from:*

. . . the mind of the mature poet differs from that of the immature one —T. S. Eliot, "Tradition and the Individual Talent," 1917

Society folk in Philadelphia certainly differ from the Boston breed —Bennett Cerf, *Saturday Rev.,* 23 Apr. 1955

In its "disagree" sense, *differ* in current use takes *with* most frequently:

. . . said that only one player had differed with the majority —Murray Chass, *N.Y. Times,* 30 Mar. 1980

. . . he arrives at interpretations that often differ with those of other critics —Richard Ellmann, *N.Y. Times Book Rev.,* 4 Apr. 1976

. . . the secretary, who told me how he had differed with his friends in parliament —Jonathan Swift, *Journal to Stella,* 29 Apr. 1711

Differ from in the "disagree" sense is not so frequent:

I read the *Cicero,* not because I differ a whit from you as to the author, but because it offered me some information I wanted —Oliver Wendell Holmes d. 1935, letter, 8 Jan. 1917

I differed from him, because we are surer of the odiousness of one, than the errour of the other —James Boswell, *Life of Samuel Johnson,* 1791

Among is also found with this sense:

Primitive rules of moral action, greatly as they differ among themselves, are all more or less advantageous —Havelock Ellis, *The Dance of Life,* 1923

Sometimes *differ from* can be interpreted in either sense:

. . . the economic man has become dominant almost to the point of excluding values and interests that differ from his —Kenneth S. Davis, *N.Y. Times Mag.,* 27 June 1954

When *with* is used with *differ* in its "be unlike" sense, as happens occasionally, it does not quite parallel the use of *from* with this sense of the verb. Here *with* means something like "in the case of":

. . . details of the car-hire arrangement differ with each company —Richard Joseph, *Your Trip to Britain,* 1954

Several prepositions are used to indicate the subject of the difference. Here are a few typical examples:

. . . frequently differed on policy matters —*Current Biography 1949*

Opinions differ as to who were the first white visitors to Arizona —*Dictionary of American History,* 1940

. . . if they differ about the end itself —Brand Blanshard, *Saturday Rev.,* 29 Jan. 1955

. . . there was little persecution of those who differed in religious matters —*American Guide Series: New Hampshire,* 1938

different At least three different commentators—Cook 1985, Copperud 1970, 1980, and Bryson 1984—say that *different* as just used in this sentence is unnecessary. Unnecessary it may be, but including it is no great sin. The use of *different* after a number is simply an emphatic use. Let your ear be your guide. Note that the following writers found no need to excise the emphatic *different*:

I'll make it up to you twenty different ways —Samuel Johnson, in Boswell's *Life,* 1791

. . . published at least five different books on grammar —Simon 1980 (in Bryson 1984)

Concur has three different meanings —Harper 1985

different from, than, to We have about 80 commentators in our files who discourse on the propriety of *different than* or *different to.* The amount of comment—thousands and thousands of words—might lead you to believe that there is a very complicated or subtle problem here, but there is not. These three phrases can be very simply explained: *different from* is the most common and is standard in both British and American usage; *different than* is standard in American and British usage, especially when a clause follows *than,* but is more frequent in American; *different to* is standard in British usage but rare in American usage. Here are a few examples of each construction:

My wish has been to try at something different from my former efforts —Lord Byron, letter, 20 Feb. 1816

. . . English would be a very different tongue from what it is —Brander Matthews, *Essays on English,* 1921

Auden is gentleness itself . . . and the evening is smooth, quiet, affectionate. How different he is from his new public persona —Robert Craft, *Stravinsky,* 1972

She, too, had one day hoped for a different lot than to be wedded to a little gentleman who rapped his teeth —W. M. Thackeray, *Pendennis,* 1848

. . . and when Helen handed it to me, I said, "I thought these things were different than

they used to be." —James Thurber, letter, 31 July 1952

Life in cadet school for Major Major was no different than life had been for him all along —Joseph Heller, *Catch-22,* 1961 (in Guth 1985)

". . . Perhaps gentlemen are different to what they were when I was young. . . ." —E. M. Forster, *A Room with a View,* 1908

. . . it soon became apparent that I would find an architectural style there quite different to anything else —Neil Ray, *Geographical Mag.,* December 1983

. . . gives a sense different to the one intended —Howard 1984

The history of the controversy about *different than* and *different to* has two strands. The first is the history of the usage itself. The evidence shows *to* and *unto* as the first prepositions used, as early as the 1520s. The OED cites a 1603 comedy coauthored by Thomas Dekker for the use *different to* and a 1644 work by Sir Kenelm Digby for *different than.* From the 18th century the OED lists Addison with *different from,* Fielding with *different to,* and Goldsmith with *different than.*

The OED entry notes that *different from* was then (1897) usual, and that *different to* was well-attested and common in speech, but disapproved by some as incorrect. No mention is made of disapproval of *different than,* but a long list of standard British authors who had used it is appended.

The original objection to *different than* appears in Baker 1770. He found this sentence in William Melmoth's translation of Cicero's letters, published in 1753:

I found your Affairs had been managed in a different Manner than what I had advised.

Commented Baker: "*A different Manner than* is not English. We say *different to* and *different from;* to the last of which Expressions I have in another Place given the Preference, as seeming to make the best Sense." Leonard 1929 found the subject in no other 18th-century grammars, but Sundby et al. 1991 shows that Baker's opinion was carried down to the 19th century by a few less well known grammarians.

At any rate, Hodgson 1889 and Raub 1897 object to *different than,* and it has become a favorite topic of 20th-century comment. In the first half of the century *different than* was regularly condemned. In the second half some still condemned it, but a majority found it acceptable to introduce a clause, because insisting on *from* in such instances often produces clumsy or wordy formulations. But there is still quite a bit of residual hostility to *than,* especially when it is followed by a noun or pronoun. This may have more to do with the question of whether *than* can be a preposition (see THAN 1) than with *different* itself.

Different to has been the subject of more nearly continuous dispute. Disapproval began with Priestley in 1768. Baker 1770 preferred *from* to *to* and he raised the often repeated point that the verb *differ* takes *from* and not *to.* Fowler 1926 dismissed this point as mere pedantry; notwithstanding his scorn, the argument can be found in remarks from several late 20th-century commentators.

Fowler 1926 stoutly defends *different to,* and his defense has probably done much to lessen British objection to the expression, although objection still lingers in many letters to *The Times,* as Howard 1980 reports.

In summary we can say that there need have been no problem here at all, since all three expressions have been in standard use since the 16th and 17th centuries and all three continue to be in standard use.

differentiate When *differentiate* is used with a preposition, it is most often *from*:

At his best he could differentiate one poem from another —Randall Jarrell, *N.Y. Times Book Rev.,* 15 Aug. 1954

. . . it was the end of a continuous spectrum, differentiated from other states only by degree —J. Anthony Lukas, *N.Y. Times Mag.,* 14 Jan. 1973

Less frequently, *differentiate* is used with *between*:

. . . without ever being able to differentiate between their relative significances —Lois Armstrong, *People,* 5 July 1976

Differentiate is also used with *among,* but very infrequently, perhaps because it tends to lead to somewhat muddled sentences like this example:

Then he will try to differentiate among those who might assume larger responsibilities from those who cannot —Harry Levinson, *Think,* May–June 1967

dilemma Contrary to the beliefs expressed by members of what Kilpatrick 1984 calls the "Society for the Protection of *Dilemma,*" the word has several meanings.

The earliest use of *dilemma* in English was in the 16th century as a term in rhetoric for an argument presenting usually two alternatives to an opponent, both of which were conclusive against him. By the end of the 16th century, the word had spread from argument to situations involving action. The earliest citation for such use shown in the OED comes from the dramatist and poet Robert Greene:

Every motion was entangled with a dilemma: . . . the love of Francesco . . . the feare of her Fathers displeasure —*Never Too Late,* 1590

In Greene's play the heroine is faced with a hard choice between alternatives—Francesco's love and her father's good will—that appear to be unattainable at the same time, perhaps mutually exclusive.

Shakespeare extended the word to the state of mind of a person faced with such a choice:

Here, Master Doctor, in perplexity and doubtful dilemma —*The Merry Wives of Windsor,* 1601

By the middle of the 17th century, a third use had arisen: the application of the word to a situation in which a person is faced with alternatives each of which is likely or sure to be unsatisfactory. This use is closest to the original use in rhetoric.

. . . this doleful Dilemma; either voluntarily, by resigning, to depose himself; or violently . . . to be deposed by others —Thomas Fuller, *The Church-History of Britain,* 1655 (OED)

All three of these extended senses—Greene's, Shakespeare's, and Fuller's—have continued in use down to the present. Here, for instance, we find Greene's sense of a choice between alternatives that appear to be mutually exclusive, although perhaps they should not be:

. . . presents the dilemma of whether one wants to be correct or endure —Heywood Hale Broun, in Harper 1985

For the Greeks, the Roman Empire was a necessity of life and at the same time an intolerable affront to their pride. This was, for them, a formidable psychological dilemma —Arnold J. Toynbee, *Horizon,* August 1947

Here we have Shakespeare's extension to the decider's state of mind:

. . . lived in a constant dilemma between disapproval of Lucy's frivolity, and rapturous fascination —Vita Sackville-West, *The Edwardians,* 1930

Here are some examples of Fuller's use, with unsatisfactory or undesirable options:

. . . the unpleasant dilemma of being obliged either to kill the father or give up the daughter —Jedidiah Morse, *The American Universal Geography,* 1796 (OED)

. . . Goldschmidt was faced with a real dilemma: to grant the permit and further anger those upset by the first demonstration, or to refuse the permit and deny the constitutional right to demonstrate peaceably —Manson Kennedy, *City,* Summer 1972

The Greene sense and the Fuller sense are in essence the same; the difference between them is entirely a matter of how the author presents the dilemma. Fuller, for instance, might have presented his instance as a choice between resigning and staying alive or being deposed by force and perhaps not staying alive: the choice between life and possible death is not one between two equally undesirable options. Often what is most unsatisfactory, even positively painful, is the necessity of making the choice:

> . . . mothers tend to put themselves in a cruel dilemma. They know they want a life beyond their children, but they also want to be everything to their children —Bruno Bettelheim, *Ladies' Home Jour.,* September 1971

> . . . like most of the other professionals of the era, he could not escape the tragic dilemma of the Western liberal world, confronted by two brutal and regressive dictatorships neither one of which it could overcome without the help of the other —Walter Mills, *Center Mag.,* March 1968

The word has come gradually to be used in contexts in which just what the choice is or just what the alternatives are is not made explicit, leaving the reader to infer part of what is intended:

> . . . the dilemma between art and life in our own times —*Times Literary Supp.,* 28 Dec. 1951

> But they were in a real dilemma. It seems to be a law of the imagination that bad characters are more fun to write and read about than good ones —W. H. Auden, *New Yorker,* 1 Apr. 1972

And if no alternatives are mentioned at all, the word becomes very close in meaning to *problem, difficulty, predicament*:

> . . . man's relation to nature and man's dilemma in society —E. B. White, *Yale Rev.,* Autumn 1954

> . . . with Kennedy's withdrawal, the Democrats' dilemma becomes glaringly apparent —Kilpatrick 1984

> . . . to take man's dilemma, the old familiar things in which there's nothing new . . . and . . . to make something which was a little different —William Faulkner, 1 May 1958, in *Faulkner in the University,* 1959

This use of *dilemma* without specific alternatives is now by far the most common one. H. W. Fowler noted it, with disapproval,

around the turn of the last century. After a false start in *The King's English* of 1907, he laid down the law for the fraternity of usage prescribers in 1926:

> The use of *d*[ilemma] as a mere finer word for *difficulty* when the question of alternatives does not definitely arise is a SLIPSHOD EXTENSION; it should be used only when there is a pair, or at least a definite number, of lines that might be taken in argument or action, & each is unsatisfactory.

We can see that Fowler has two points here: first, he objects to the relatively new extension of *dilemma* to uses involving no question of alternatives, and second, he recommends confining the word within limits it had already outgrown in 1590. Fowler's followers have done little more than pursue their own reasoning into regions more and more remote from actual usage, such as deciding that a choice between two beautiful women is not a true dilemma (Copperud 1964). Freeman 1983 tells us that a choice between two desserts is not a dilemma; we have no evidence of the word's having been used of such a trivial matter.

Conclusion: *dilemma,* in the senses extended from the original application to argument, has never been as restricted in meaning as Fowler and his successors have wished it to become. Its further extension to instances in which no alternatives are expressed or implied has become the prevailing use, even though disapproved by Fowler and two leading usage panels. Your use of the word in the sense of *problem* or *predicament* should not be a concern—even E. B. White used it that way.

diminution For pronunciation problems with this word, see NUCLEAR.

diphtheria, diphthong See PHTH.

direct, directly These adverbs are sometimes interchangeable:

> . . . suggesting I write to her direct —John Willett, *Times Literary Supp.,* 26 Mar. 1970

> . . . letters . . . sent directly to me —John C. Messenger, *Psychology Today,* May 1971

> . . . flown direct to Hong Kong —Geri Trotta, *Town & Country,* March 1980

> . . . flew directly to Boston —Gail Cameron, *Ladies' Home Jour.,* August 1971

Directly is always used in preference to *direct* as a contrasting adverb paired with *indirectly*:

> . . . problems related directly or indirectly to the Vietnam War —Mary & Kenneth Gergen, *Change,* January–February 1971

Overall, *directly* is used quite a bit more often than *direct*. It has uses and meanings that it does not share with *direct*. An important exclusive use of *directly* is before the word or phrase it modifies:

> Directly in front of us, two men . . . began attacking the pavement with a crowbar —James Jones, *Harper's,* February 1971

> Nobody left, unless he was directly told to —Jane O'Reilly, *New York,* 15 Feb. 1971

> . . . hand-stitch them to the pocket pieces directly underneath —Mary Johnson, *Woman's Day,* October 1971

In addition, *direct* will not fit into the following uses:

> . . . landing directly against the microphone —Robert Thompson, *Harper's,* October 1971

> . . . the mountain that rose directly above our camp —Jane Goodall, *Ladies' Home Jour.,* October 1971

directly 1. A sense that *directly* does not share with the adverb *direct* is "immediately." Vizetelly 1906 notes the existence of some objectors to this use in America (we can count Bierce 1909 among these), but he says the use is popular in England. It has been in British use since Shakespeare's time.

> With undoubting decision she directly began her adieus —Jane Austen, *Mansfield Park,* 1814

> . . . reading it directly after Rowe's most tense contribution to the form —Bonamy Dobrée, *English Literature in the Early Eighteenth Century, 1700–1740,* 1959

It is also in American use:

> . . . in the 50 or 75 years directly before he began to write —Irving Howe, *New Republic,* 4 July 1955

> Directly after his graduation —*Current Biography,* January 1965

2. There is also a weakened sense that means "after awhile, shortly"; it is chiefly American.

> Pretty soon it darkened up, and . . . directly it begun to rain —Mark Twain, *Huckleberry Finn,* 1884 (*A Mark Twain Lexicon,* 1938)

The Dictionary of American Regional English shows this to be most common in the southern parts of the U.S.

3. The conjunction *directly* meaning "as soon as" has drawn fire from American critics in the past but is in standard British use.

> See how silly H. I. is directly I turn my back —Ellen Terry, letter, 26 Dec. 1896

> . . . and directly we enter it we breast some new wave of emotion —Virginia Woolf, in *A*

Century of the Essay, ed. David Daiches, 1951

> Directly you slip it on, this shoe feels like an old friend —advt., *Punch,* 24 Jan. 1951

> . . . I decided that directly I had £500 I would escape —Alan Moorehead, *A Late Education,* 1970

> . . . it gets very cold at sea directly the sun sets —Robin Brandon, *The Good Crewman,* 1972

See also IMMEDIATELY.

disagree Phythian 1979 says *disagree* takes *with,* not *from.* The OED shows that *from* is obsolete. *To* seems still to be found in legal contexts, especially in *disagreed to,* which may be paired with the more modern-sounding *agreed to.*

In ordinary use, *with* is common but other prepositions can be found, especially when the object refers to the general subject of discussion rather than the rejected viewpoint:

> One can disagree with his views, but one can't refute them —Henry Miller, *The Air-Conditioned Nightmare,* 1945

> It is possible to disagree with the U.S. proposal —Norman Cousins, *Saturday Rev.,* 30 Oct. 1971

> . . . the authorities disagree about the procedure to be followed —F. S. C. Northrop, *The Logic of the Sciences and the Humanities,* 1947

> Mr. Beard and Miss Compton disagreed on the distance of meat from heat —Jane Nickerson, *N.Y. Times Mag.,* 27 June 1954

disappointed When *disappointed* is used with a preposition in contemporary writing, it may take any one of several prepositions: *about, at, by, in, over,* or *with.* It may also be followed by *to* used with an infinitive. At one time, *disappointed of* was common, but over the past century, *disappointed in* has become the most prevalent usage:

> . . . to be contradicted by events, to be disappointed in his hopes —Sir Winston Churchill, quoted in William L. Shirer, *The Rise and Fall of the Third Reich,* 1960

> By 1843, when he came home disappointed in journalism but eager to write books —Henry Seidel Canby, *Thoreau,* 1939

During the 19th and early 20th centuries, some writers used *disappointed* with the word *agreeably.* The juxtaposition was deliberate, and, while some usage commentators cautioned against the use, others conceded that under the right circumstances it served a legitimate purpose: to convey a certain whimsical paradox. The use is not attested in contemporary writing:

> On approaching the house I was agreeably disappointed at having no pack of loudmouthed, ferocious dogs rushing forth —W. H. Hudson, *The Purple Land,* 1885

disapprove When used with a preposition, *disapprove* is generally used with *of*:

> ... the familiar agreement that a reporter need not sign an article of which he disapproves and may withhold permission to management for the use of his name —John Hohenberg, *Saturday Rev.,* 13 Nov. 1971

> ... was to have a "house-wedding," though Episcopalian society was beginning to disapprove of such ceremonies —Edith Wharton, *The Old Maid,* 1924

When the object of the preposition is the one disapproving, however, *by* appears:

> The Faribault alliance was disapproved by the annual Faribault school meeting in 1892 —*American Guide Series: Minnesota,* 1938

disassemble, dissemble *Dissemble* means "to hide under a false appearance" or "to put on a false appearance":

> ... had been trained to dissemble and conceal his real thoughts —M. S. Handler, introduction to *The Autobiography of Malcolm X,* 1966

Disassemble means "to take apart":

> Then we disassembled the mixers and examined them for signs of wear —*Consumer Reports,* July 1980

Several commentators caution their readers not to confuse these words. Our files contain no evidence of such confusion, but Gowers in Fowler 1965 and Garner 1998 cite instances in which *dissemble* is used when *disassemble* is meant.

disassociate See DISSOCIATE, DISASSOCIATE.

disburse The Oxford American Dictionary and Garner 1998 warn against confusion of *disburse,* which usually means "to pay out (money)" or "to distribute (property)," with *disperse.* Such confusion probably accounts for this:

> Cottontail rabbit management study indicates ... that stocked or marked rabbits disburse widely —*Biological Abstracts,* June 1954

James J. Kilpatrick in his newspaper column (29 Sept. 1985) has also mentioned having found an instance in which demonstrators were "asked to disburse." Garner has some examples in which a crowd is "disbursed."

discomfit Several usage commentators have, in the past, tried to convince their readers that *discomfit* means "to rout, completely defeat" and not "to discomfort, embarrass, disconcert, make uneasy." However, most of the recent commentary agrees with the evidence we have: the sense "to discomfort, disconcert" has become thoroughly established and is the most prevalent meaning:

> ... his habit of discomfiting an opponent with a sudden profession of ignorance —T. S. Eliot, "Francis Herbert Bradley," in *Selected Essays,* 1932

> Discomfited by Labor heckling ... , Eden lost his usual urbanity —*Time,* 19 Mar. 1956

> ... he saw that his boss was discomfited and at a loss —David A. Stockman, *Newsweek,* 28 Apr. 1986

The use of *discomfit* to refer to defeat in battle is now rare, and extended uses meaning "to frustrate the plans of, thwart" are uncommon. Although, as Harper 1985 says, "*discomfit* has now come to be practically synonymous with 'discomfort,'" there is a difference between the two words. *Discomfit* is used almost exclusively as a verb (*discomfiture* is the related noun), while *discomfort* is much more commonly used as a noun than a verb.

discontent The noun *discontent* may be followed by *with*:

> ... a widely voiced discontent with the Vietnam war —John J. Corson, *Saturday Rev.,* 10 Jan. 1970

> ... their growing discontent with British rule —Margaret Stimmann Branson, ed., *America's Heritage,* 1982

Less frequently, *discontent* is used with *over*:

> Some discontent over ROTC lingers —D. Park Teter, *Change,* September 1971

discourage When *discourage* is used with a preposition, it is usually *from,* which in turn is often followed by a gerund phrase as its object:

> ... some employers discourage them from taking that much time —David Butwin, *Saturday Rev.,* 23 Oct. 1971

Occasionally *discourage from* is followed by a noun phrase:

> ... directors who ... are being discouraged from the normal play of their talents —Gilbert Seldes, *Perspectives USA,* Summer 1953

Discourage has also been used occasionally with *into* and *with* as the following examples show:

> . . . a generally negative attitude toward the environment had almost discouraged me into discounting my own high estimation of that exceptional project —John Lear, *Saturday Rev.,* 6 Nov. 1971

> . . . certain books which . . . tend to discourage us rather with Renanian irony and pity —Edmund Wilson, *Axel's Castle,* 1931

discover, invent The original meaning of *invent* in English is "to come upon, find, discover," a meaning quite close to the meaning of the Latin word from which it was taken. Toward the end of the 18th century this original sense was decreasing in use, while two newer senses—still in use today—were flourishing. The OED has a citation from the Scots rhetorician Hugh Blair in 1783 that is probably the first discrimination between *invent* and *discover,* whose current sense was taking the place of *invent's* original sense:

> We invent things that are new; we discover what was before hidden. Galileo invented the telescope; Harvey discovered the circulation of the blood —*Lectures on Rhetoric and Belles Lettres,* 1783

What Blair was doing, in effect, was distinguishing a current sense of *invent* from a current sense of *discover* which was in competition with a dying sense of *invent* (it is now archaic).

Blair's book was widely used in schools. Perhaps Noah Webster was familiar with it from its use as a textbook. At any rate he included Blair's discrimination in his 1828 dictionary:

> *Discover* differs from *invent.* We *discover* what before existed, though to us unknown; we *invent* what did not before exist.

Noah changed Blair's "what was before hidden" to "what before existed, though to us unknown" in the explanation of *discover.* He may have thought this a sharper point of discrimination than Blair's wording. It has since become the only point of dispute.

Webster's discrimination has become a regular part of school textbooks and handbooks. Here is a modern example:

> *Discover* means "to find something existing that was not known before." *Invent* means "to create" or "to originate." —Battles et al. 1982

Now, if we look at typical examples given to show the distinction, we find:

> Marie Curie *discovered* radium.
> Edison *invented* the phonograph.

But does anyone write "Marie Curie invented radium" or "Edison discovered the phonograph'? The plain fact is that no one with a school child's command of the language confuses these two words used in such an obvious way. But look at this:

> Newton invented the differential and the integral calculus and discovered the laws of motion. I might perhaps have said that he discovered the calculus and invented the laws of motion, for the distinction between "discovery" and "invention," which used to be so carefully drilled into us at school, is not so sharp in the upper strata of mathematics and physics —K. K. Darrow, *Renaissance of Physics,* 1936

What Professor Darrow was questioning is the appropriateness of Noah Webster's "what before existed" to the conditions of abstract physics and mathematics. We don't need to dally in the upper strata of mathematics and physics to discover that even if Noah's comment was appropriate in 1828 it may no longer be today.

> We shall never know who first discovered how to pound up metal-bearing rock and heat it in the fire —Tom Wintringham, *The Story of Weapons and Tactics,* 1943

> Long before vaccination was discovered, attempts had been made to lessen the ravages of smallpox —Victor Heiser, *An American Doctor's Odyssey,* 1936

None of the processes above can really be said to have existed before. Yet *invent* cannot be used in place of *discover* in any of the sentences. The reason is syntactical: *discover* can take a noun, clause, or *how to* phrase as its object, but *invent* takes only a noun. Thus in many cases the distinction between the two words will be entirely grammatical.

And when a noun is the direct object? Here we find some disputed usages:

> The material was discovered in 1954 by Goodrich-Gulf scientists —*N.Y. Times,* 16 Oct. 1956

> A number of drug companies that hope to discover new medicines are synthesizing variants of the THC molecule —Solomon H. Snyder, *Psychology Today,* May 1971

The first of these examples refers to a synthetic rubber, and was criticized in *Winners & Sinners* on the basis of Noah Webster's then 128-year-old "what before existed." But it is a good idea to remember that even Noah did not make this criterion part of his definition—it was simply part of a word discrimination. His definition of this sense of *discover* reads:

To find out; to obtain the first knowledge of; to come to the knowledge of something sought or before unknown.

Nothing in the definition suggests *discover* is inapplicable to synthetic rubber—a substance undreamt of in 1828.

The second example contains an important clue. We have learned that inventions may have unexpected consequences. A man who hoped to invent an artificial substitute for quinine actually produced the first artificial dye. In other words, he invented a substance and discovered that it had an entirely different use. The same result can occur when scientists synthesize or invent new compounds in hopes of discovering new medicines. *Discover* can suggest serendipity or surprise:

After trying hundreds of hydrocarbons on several mosquito species, they discovered a hydrocarbon approximately thirty-five times more active —Lawrence Locke, *The Lamp,* Summer 1971

To summarize, Noah Webster's "what before existed" applies well enough to *discover* in uses that do not compete at all with *invent.* In some constructions *discover* can be used where *invent* cannot. And in sentences with noun objects where the two words can compete, *discover* is more likely than *invent* to suggest an accidental, unexpected, or merely hoped-for result.

discreet, discrete A number of usage books define *discreet* as "prudent," "judicious," "tactful," or "circumspect" and *discrete* as "separate" or "distinct," with the implication that these are two completely different words which should not be confused. However, the history and spelling of *discreet* and *discrete* are more closely intertwined than is commonly realized. Both words come from the same Latin source. In its early life *discrete* was infrequently spelled *discreet. Discreet,* on the other hand, used to have the spelling *discrete* as a common variant.

Since the first half of the 17th century, the two spellings have been perceived as separate words with separate meanings. In that time, confused spellings have undoubtedly occurred (hence the interest shown by usage book writers).

In spite of misspellings the separate identities of the two words have been firmly established. But are they irrevocably established? Although there is no way to tell whether a particular misspelling is merely a typographical error or whether it originated with the author, the "misspelled" forms of *discreet* and *discrete* seem to be appearing more frequently in reputable publications lately. We wonder if too many writers and editors are depending on computer spelling checkers in lieu of thinking.

He is conservatively dressed. . . . so discrete is he that there is almost nothing to mark him physically —*N.Y. Times Mag.,* 27 Apr. 1980

. . . discretely silent —*Christian Science Monitor,* 26 June 1980

He looks smooth and discrete, like a mortician —*Boston Globe Mag.,* 23 Nov. 1980

. . . tries to count the uncountable (i.e., cultures, which . . . are not discreet units) —*American Anthropologist,* September 1976

. . . breaking up the desired educational task into discreet parts —*College English,* September 1977

Examples like these, while surprisingly numerous, are by no means usual. The separate identities of the two words remain standard for now.

disinterest, disinterestedness, uninterest Robert F. Ilson, in an article in Greenbaum 1985, states that "the spread of *disinterested* at the expense of *uninterested* is bound to be helped by the existence of the noun *disinterest* and the non-existence of a noun *uninterest.*" Not only has *disinterest* strengthened the position of the adjective, it has also fueled the controversy surrounding the adjective. What of this word *disinterest?*

The OED editor, James A. H. Murray, had little evidence for the noun. He finds three senses. The first, "something . . . disadvantageous," is labeled "Now *rare*"; the second, "disinterestedness, impartiality," is labeled *"Obs.";* the third, "absence of interest," is labeled *"rare."* The Supplement of 1933 drops the second and third labels, adding citations from the early 20th century. The 1972 Supplement adds nothing to the second sense, but several citations to the third; the "absence of interest" sense appears to be flourishing.

Evidence in the Merriam-Webster files shows that both OED senses 2 and 3 continue in use. Its primary use is to mean "absence of interest":

. . . seemed always to display a disinterest in current affairs —Osbert Lancaster, *With an Eye to the Future,* 1967

She greeted Moses with marked disinterest —John Cheever, *The Wapshot Chronicle,* 1957

The officers heard this with disinterest —E. L. Doctorow, *Ragtime,* 1975

The OED's second sense also is in use:

. . . flourish best only as they achieve a degree of disinterest and detachment —Nathan M. Pusey, *President's Report, Harvard University,* 1966–1967

. . . reexamine these contentious issues . . . with admirable disinterest and dispassion —Bernard Wasserstein, *N.Y. Times Book Rev.,* 24 May 1987

This sense might be in more frequent use if it were not in competition with the synonymous *disinterestedness,* which is almost never used except in the sense of "freedom from selfish motive or interest":

I had a feeling of noble disinterestedness in my anger —Malcolm Cowley, *Exile's Return,* 1934

. . . his assumptions of scholarly disinterestedness and moral superiority —Angus Wilson, *Death Dance,* 1957

. . . no longer enlightened self-interest, but enlightened disinterestedness —Donald Milner, *The Listener,* 30 May 1974

The evidence indicates that *disinterestedness* is quite a bit more frequent than *disinterest* in the same sense. Thus there appears to be a tendency to use *disinterest* for "lack of interest" and *disinterestedness* for "freedom from selfish interest."

The last term of our trio, *uninterest,* does in fact exist. The OED lists a single 1890 example; our files contain some others. It means "lack of interest" but is not a commonly used word.

. . . his blank uninterest in poor and black citizens —Julian Symons, *Times Literary Supp.,* 9 Jan. 1981

. . . in angry reaction to the apparent uninterest of his strangely oblivious mother —Geoffrey C. Ward, *American Heritage,* December 1992

Most of our evidence for this word is fairly recent and comes from sources in which the controversy over *disinterested* is frequently mentioned; it is used, perhaps, to avoid *disinterest* and guilt by association.

disinterested, uninterested The controversy over these words is one in which it is stylish to lament what has been lost. For instance, Copperud 1970 says: "The umpire, ideally, would be *disinterested*; one who did not care about the game would be *uninterested.* A useful distinction is being blurred. Flesch concludes the battle is already lost, and Fowler wistfully wonders whether rescue is still possible. . . . Despite the critics, the battle does seem lost. . . ." Dozens of other commentators on the subject echo the same sentiments.

So far from being lost or blurred, however, the ethical sense of *disinterested* makes up some 70 percent of the citations for the word gathered by Merriam-Webster from about 1934 to the present. The ethical sense is alive and well, as it was throughout the 20th century; reports of its demise are greatly exaggerated.

The discovery that *disinterested* and *uninterested* were differentiated in meaning seems to have been an American one, and it was made at nearly the same time as the discovery that *disinterested* was being used to mean "uninterested." Our earliest evidence is from The Century Dictionary of 1889, where in a synonymy the editors note, "*Disinterested* and *uninterested* are sometimes confounded in speech, though rarely in writing." They then distinguish between the two. Many commentators, from the beginning of the 20th century through the 1940s, repeated the distinction; lament for the lost distinction does not appear to have begun until about 1950:

. . . the noble word "disinterested" is thus being lost, because so few writers (and virtually no journalists) will write the word "uninterested" any longer —Ruth Shepard Phelps Morand, letter to the editor, *American Scholar,* Winter 1949–50

The sense of loss continues unabated today:

. . . she must be—to use a good old word that is rapidly losing its usefulness—disinterested —Wayne C. Booth, in *Introduction to Scholarship in Modern Languages and Literatures,* ed. Joseph Gibaldi, 1981

The notion that the ethical sense is older, as expressed by numerous commentators, is erroneous. The OED shows that the earlier sense of *disinterested* is the simple negative of *interested*; it is dated before 1612; the earliest attestation of the ethical sense is 1659. Curiously, the earliest uses of *uninterested* are for ethical senses (both 17th century); the modern use is not attested until 1771. The OED editor, James A. H. Murray, was uncertain of the status in his time of the simple negative sense of *disinterested,* marking it "? *Obs*[olete]." The 1933 Supplement removed the label and presented, without comment, three modern citations, all British, all dated 1928. This evidence refutes the assertion of Anthony Burgess, quoted in Harper 1985, that this use of *disinterested* is "one of the worst of all American solecisms." On the contrary, it is the discovery of the usage problem that is American. The issue was unknown to Fowler 1926 (the Fowler mentioned by Copperud 1970 is, in fact, Sir Ernest Gowers in his 1965 revision of Fowler), and it is unremarked in the 1933 OED Supplement. The vehemence of opinion directed against the earliest sense of *disinterested* (Burchfield 1996 says it is a 20th-century revival; the Century Dictionary comment suggests the revival may have begun in the 1880s) appears to have increased over the years. Harper 1985, for example, shows 100 percent rejection of the use; in 1975 it had only been 91 percent.

What of actual usage, historical and modern? As with many issues of English usage, when much heat of opinion is generated, the subtleties of genuine use by purposeful writers are frequently overlooked (compare, for instance, ENORMITY, ENORMOUSNESS). The evidence shows a marked distinction between the way in which the ethical sense is used and that in which the simple negative sense is used. The ethical sense is applied more than half of the time to abstract nouns:

Disinterested intellectual curiosity is the life-blood of real civilization —G. M. Trevelyan, *English Social History,* 1942

. . . the old man was tripped up by a gaily-colored hoop sent rolling at him, with a kind of disinterested deliberation, by a grim little girl —James Thurber, *Fables for Our Time, and Famous Poems Illustrated,* 1940

Jane Austen uses the term with a suggestion of being free from selfish sexual motive:

He was now the Mr. Crawford who was addressing herself with ardent, disinterested love; whose feelings were apparently become all that was honourable and upright —*Mansfield Park,* 1814

This use finds an occasional modern echo:

Usually it was just the three of us, but we would often end the evening with a friend of his. These junkets were in all ways delightful and disinterested. Lewis had a serious interest in a classmate of Elaine; and at that time neither Elaine nor I had any serious interests whatever —Katherine Hoskins, "Notes on a Navy Childhood," *Prose,* 1974

You will perceive that these two uses are not far from the simple negative sense, except that the underlying *interested* is in these cases more heavily charged with meaning than it usually is at present. The word *interested,* indeed, was a more intense word in the past than now:

No day has passed . . . without my most interested wishes for your health —Samuel Pepys, letter, 4 Sept. 1665 (OED)

Here *interested* is close in meaning to modern uses of *concerned.* It is the greater intensity of *interested* that makes earlier simple negative uses of *disinterested* hard for us moderns to distinguish from uses of the ethical sense. Here is Jane Austen again; the interest must be chiefly monetary:

His choice is disinterested, at least, for he must know my father can give her nothing —*Pride and Prejudice,* 1813

The ethical sense is also applied to people:

. . . to insure that all work is well evaluated . . . by knowledgeable yet disinterested referees —Eugene Wall, *American Documentation,* April 1967

Don't you think that priests make more disinterested rulers than lay politicians? —Wilfrid Sheed, *People Will Always Be Kind,* 1973

It is when the ethical sense is applied to people that its meaning can be understood as the simple negative sense, especially if the construction and context are not unmistakable:

A clergyman cannot be disinterested about theology, nor a soldier about war —Bertrand Russell, *Education and The Good Life,* 1926

The construction in which *disinterested* is followed by a preposition can create some ambiguity and raise the possibility of misinterpretation, especially when the moral sense is the one intended. The modern simple negative sense is followed by a preposition just about half the time, but it is almost always *in*:

Unsocial, but not antisocial. . . . Contemptuous of other people. Disinterested in women —Dr. James A. Brussel, profile of a so-called "Mad Bomber," reprinted in *Rolling Stone,* 15 Nov. 1979

The simple negative sense, in its earlier uses, carries the stronger senses of *interested,* which are now largely out of use. Here is an example of it in a context where lack of financial interest is the underlying meaning:

But they are far from being disinterested, and if they are the most trustworthy . . . , they in general demand for the transport of articles, a sum at least double to what others of the trade would esteem a reasonable recompense —George Borrow, *The Bible in Spain,* 1843

By the early 20th century, our weakened sense of *interested* is detectable in the use of *disinterested*:

The only discordant note now is the services conducted perfunctorily by ignorant or disinterested priests —William Roscoe Thayer, letter, 26 Oct. 1906

. . . an editor who in a disinterested voice sat issuing assignments for the day —Ben Hecht, *Erik Dorn,* 1921

In most recent citations, the weakening is patent:

Although Sister Bear is anxious to learn baseball, Papa Bear forces lessons on her disinterested brother —*TV Guide,* 2 May 1985

Lamberts 1972 makes the point that in English many pairs beginning with *dis-* and *un-* are differentiated: *unarmed, disarmed; unengaged, disengaged; unproved, disproved; unable, disable; unaffected, disaffected; unconnected, disconnected.* He notes the *dis-* in each case means "was once but is no longer." "From here," he says, "it is only a short jump to *uninterested, disinterested.*" This meaning of *dis-* does, in fact, color many uses of *disinterested,* beginning early in the 20th century:

> When I grow tired or disinterested in anything, I experience a disgust —Jack London, letter, 24 Feb. 1914

> Those spotted are usually taught so slowly they grow disinterested and quit —*N.Y. Times,* 25 June 1967

The simple negative sense of *disinterested,* then, has lost, with the weakening of *interested,* the more highly charged meaning that it had in the 17th and 18th centuries, but it has gained a subsense with the meaning "having lost interest."

Uninterested is, of course, in use, although with not so great a frequency as *disinterested* in the same sense. Here are a few examples:

> . . . but the greater part of the young gentlemen having no particular parents to speak of, were wholly uninterested in the thing —Charles Dickens, *Nicholas Nickleby,* 1839

> My fear of deep water left the Navy simply uninterested —Russell Baker, *Growing Up,* 1982

Conclusion: The alleged confusion between *disinterested* and *uninterested* does not exist. Nor has the ethical sense of *disinterested* been lost—Merriam-Webster files show it used more than twice as often as the other senses. *Disinterested* carries the bulk of use for all meanings; *uninterested* is much less frequently used. In current use, *disinterested* has three meanings: an ethical one, "free from selfish motive or bias"; a simple negative one, "not interested"; and a slightly more emphatic one, "having lost interest." Of these the simple negative is the oldest, the ethical one next, and "having lost interest" the most recent.

The ethical sense of *disinterested* is applied both to human and abstract subjects, but more often to the latter; the simple negative sense is usually applied to human subjects. About half the time it is used in the construction *disinterested in*—this construction is not used for the ethical sense.

Uninterested originally had ethical senses (its earliest), which appear to be dead.

For another contributor to the *disinterested/uninterested* problem, see DISINTEREST, DISINTERESTEDNESS, UNINTEREST.

disinterestedness See DISINTEREST, DISINTERESTEDNESS, UNINTEREST.

disjuncts See IRONICALLY.

dislike 1. *Noun. Dislike* can take the prepositions *of, for,* and *to; to* is the least common. A few examples:

> . . . his dislike of Robbe-Grillet is bizarre —*Times Literary Supp.,* 19 June 1969

> Dislike of America ran much deeper —*Time,* 13 Jan. 1947

> . . . contempt and dislike for human beings —Angus Wilson, *The Middle Age of Mrs. Eliot,* 1958

> My dislike for the tidies of the world is particularly strong this week —*And More by Andy Rooney,* 1982

> I have always had a dislike to managers losing money over me —W. Somerset Maugham, *The Summing Up,* 1938

> . . . a man who takes an unreasonable dislike to another —*Time,* 26 May 1952

It would appear that *take a dislike* tends to be followed by *to.*
2. *Verb.* Besides a noun object, the verb *dislike* can take a participial phrase or an infinitive phrase, according to Evans 1959. Longman 1984 says that the infinitive complement is not possible in British English; our evidence is not extensive enough to confirm but certainly does not refute. It is possible in American English, though not common and especially rare in edited prose. The *-ing* construction is more common. An example of each:

> . . . reports that Miss West disliked working with Fields —*Current Biography,* November 1967

> I dislike to bother you with "trivia" —letter received at Merriam-Webster from Forest Park, Illinois, 26 Jan. 1983

dismayed Colter 1981 recommends *with* after *dismayed,* which is a little surprising, as *by* is the usual preposition. *With* and *at* may also be used:

> Dismayed by the plans —*Current Biography,* July 1965

> . . . dismayed by the fall of Premier Mendes-France —Mollie Panter-Downes, *New Yorker,* 19 Feb. 1955

> I am dismayed by the frequent assumption of our modern critics that only nervous degenerates can really write —Harold J. Laski, letter, 19 Feb. 1917

> . . . became dismayed with the timidity and nationalist bickering displayed there —*Current Biography,* September 1953

. . . was dismayed at the "yawning listlessness" of many —*Dictionary of American Biography,* 1928

disparate Reader's Digest 1983 notes *disparate* as a useful word meaning "strongly different, differing in real character." Safire 1984 disputes this use, feeling that *disparate* means "unequal" rather than "markedly dissimilar." It does seem to mean "unequal" in some legal contexts, notably in the phrase *disparate treatment,* which crops up in employment-discrimination cases. And inequality can easily be seen in these uses:

. . . election of local government officials from districts of disparate size —*American School Board Jour.,* June 1968

. . . economically disparate groups do not make congenial neighbors —Urban Land Institute finding, in *Center Mag.,* September 1968

Still, "markedly dissimilar" is the most frequent sense. It is hard to find the notion of inequality in these examples:

Pianists as disparate as Vladimir Horowitz and Fats Waller get equal consideration —Hans Fantel, *N.Y. Times Book Rev.,* 22 July 1979

. . . the disparate interests of heterogeneous faculties —Lewis B. Mayhew, *Change,* March 1972

The welding together of such disparate creeds into a coherent work of art is in itself no mean achievement —*Envoy,* May 1968

Disparate is also used of what is made up of diverse or incongruous elements:

This disparate and uneasy coalition —Maurice R. Berube, *Commonweal,* 11 Apr. 1969

. . . a disparate gathering of art that hasn't focused on any one period or style —David L. Shirey, *N.Y. Times,* 14 July 1971

dispense When *dispense* is used with a preposition, *with* is the usual choice, since *dispense with* is a fixed expression with its own meanings, "to suspend the operation of" and "to do without":

. . . why the government is so vigorously asserting its right to dispense with warrants in national-security cases —Alan M. Dershowitz, *Commentary,* January 1972

Miss de Momerie seemed ready to dispense with convention —Dorothy L. Sayers, *Murder Must Advertise,* 1933

When the verb is used in any of its senses involving portioning out or administering and the phrase denotes the receiver, *dispense* is naturally used with *to:*

We were in Yeats' debt because he dispensed some of his worthwhile sketches to his humble listeners —Fred R. Jones, *N.Y. Times Book Rev.,* 16 May 1954

When it is used in the less-frequent meaning "to exempt," *dispense* may be found with *from:*

. . . claiming to dispense the clergy from obeying the very laws which as bishops they are pledged to enforce —W. R. Inge, *The Church in the World,* 1928

disposal, disposition The comments about *disposal* and *disposition* made by Fowler 1926 and revived by a few latter-day usage writers are correct for the most part. The two words overlap in some areas of usage, but each tends to specialize in certain jobs.

Disposal refers to the getting rid of or destruction of something. It also gets used in the phrases *at one's disposal* and *at the disposal of.* Instances in which *disposition* replaces *disposal* in these uses are quite uncommon:

. . . the disposal of 300 tons of solid waste —*Annual Report, Eastman Kodak Co.,* 1970

. . . can use any means at their disposal —James F. Reed III, *Center Mag.,* May 1969

. . . to place the facilities of both institutions at the disposal of graduate students —*Current Biography,* December 1964

Disposition is the usual choice when talking about things that are administered, arranged, settled, or taken care of; *disposal* is only infrequently used in such cases. And *disposal* does not, of course, refer to temperament or inclination, as *disposition* does.

. . . the board's disposition of his case —*AAUP Bulletin,* December 1967

. . . the future disposition of the Panama Canal —Stanley Karnow, *Saturday Rev.,* 24 July 1976

. . . showed no disposition to be bored —Vita Sackville-West, *The Edwardians,* 1930

dispossess *Dispossess* is sometimes used with a preposition. When it is, *of* is the one generally used, although the use of *from* is also attested:

. . . dispossessing the nobles of their wealth —C. B. A. Behrens, *N.Y. Rev. of Books,* 3 June 1971

. . . dispossessing the French from the southern shores of the Mediterranean —Percy Winner, *New Republic,* 9 June 1952

disqualify When used with a preposition, *disqualify* is used with either *from* or *for:*

. . . Teachers of English or even of writing are not thereby disqualified from writing stories —William Saroyan, *N.Y. Times Book Rev.,* 8 June 1980

. . . failure to pass [examinations] would presumably disqualify them for parenthood —Vance Packard, *Saturday Rev.,* 20 Aug. 1977

disregard The noun *disregard* may be followed by *for* or *of.* At one time use of *of* predominated; now the two appear with about equal frequency:

. . . the slave-owners' total disregard for the humanity of their workers —*Times Literary Supp.,* 27 Aug. 1971

. . . his flip disregard for the consequences of his actions —Arthur Knight, *Saturday Rev.,* 26 June 1954

. . . a disregard of the judicial system —Julian Towster, *Saturday Rev.,* 19 Dec. 1953

. . . the Administration's disregard of the realities of power —Richard J. Whalen, *Harper's,* August 1971

The phrases *with disregard for* and *with disregard of* are both quite common; however, when *disregard* is preceded by *in,* it is followed by *of:*

. . . with complete disregard of danger —*Current Biography,* February 1953

. . . rears her orphaned nephew with a disregard for convention —*Current Biography,* September 1967

. . . he was like a flame burning on in miraculous disregard of the fact that there was no more fuel —Aldous Huxley, *The Olive Tree,* 1937

Disregard has been used with *to,* but infrequently:

. . . a total disregard to the ordinary decencies —Charles G. Norris, *Brass,* 1921

disremember On the whole, criticism of *disremember* has softened over time. Bache 1869 labels it both "obsolete" and "a low vulgarism." Ayres 1881 says it is "vulgarly used in the sense of *forget.*" Vizetelly 1906 commands: "Avoid this term as provincial and archaic, and use *forget* instead." Krapp 1927 says it is "dialectal and humorous." Reader's Digest 1983 calls *disremember* "a dialectal word" which "is sometimes used by standard speakers for folksy effect; this is an informal use." Burchfield 1996 and Garner 1998 call it dialectal.

Disremember can be found in dialect studies of the U.S. (especially the South) and Great Britain. It has been used in narrative and dialogue by fictional characters from various parts of the U.S., often for humorous effect or to suggest the rustic and uneducated. And it is very occasionally found in nonfiction.

. . . there didn't happen to be no candle burnin if I don't disremember —Frances Miriam Whitcher. "Hezekiah Bedott," 1855, in *The Mirth of a Nation,* ed. Walter Blair & Raven I. McDavid, Jr., 1983

". . . one of those Massachusetts fellers— I disremember his name. . . ." —Kenneth Roberts, *Oliver Wiswell,* 1940

"It was the British who did it," I said quickly. "I disremember the place and time" —E. L. Doctorow, *Loon Lake,* 1979

. . . when the composer, well on toward the patriarchal age of eighty-one . . . , disremembered so much —Irving Kolodin, *Saturday Rev.,* 29 May 1954

Trilling's fate was still worse: he was made out to be a convert. His lifelong commitment to greater social liberality was disremembered, as was his often repeated condemnation of social niggardliness —Benjamin DeMott, *Atlantic,* September 1988

We are not sure how common *disremember* is in standard spoken English, though it does not appear in the million-word corpus analyzed by Hartvig Dahl in *Word Frequencies of Spoken American English* (1979). Nonetheless, we suspect that it is basically a spoken word that only occasionally finds its way into print, and then usually for a particular effect.

dissatisfied, unsatisfied Though *dissatisfied* and *unsatisfied* appear to be synonyms, there are distinctions evident in the examples in the Merriam-Webster files. These show that *unsatisfied* is more frequently used to modify nonhuman terms (such as *ambition, debts, curiosity, demands, claims*) than human ones and that in all instances the meaning is generally of something or someone being "unfulfilled" or "unappeased":

. . . although every one was curious the curiosity was unsatisfied —Sherwood Anderson, *Poor White,* 1920

. . . a large unsatisfied demand for education at university level —*Times Literary Supp.,* 5 Feb. 1970

Dissatisfied, in contrast, is used primarily with respect to persons or groups in the sense of "not pleased or gratified":

Dissatisfied landowners stopped action —*American Guide Series: Minnesota,* 1938

. . . the young adult is dissatisfied more often with the job than the older worker

—Dale B. Harris, in *Automation, Education, and Human Values,* ed. W. W. Brickman & S. Lehrer, 1966

While both *dissatisfied* and *unsatisfied,* when used with a preposition, are usually followed by *with,* both words, according to our evidence, may be followed by *by*:

... became dissatisfied with most of what was then known . . . as psychological research —David Loye, *Psychology Today,* May 1971

They were unsatisfied with the composition of the appointed embassy —William Mitford, *History of Greece,* 1808 (OED)

... he was dissatisfied by the picture she represented —Eric Linklater, *Private Angelo,* 1946

... unsatisfied by what he characterized as "nothing but double talk" —*Library Jour.,* 1 Dec. 1966

dissemble   See DISASSEMBLE, DISSEMBLE.

dissent   The OED and our files show that *dissent from* is the usual combination of verb and preposition:

All who dissent from its orthodox doctrines are scoundrels —H. L. Mencken, *Prejudices: Second Series,* 1920

... he must dissent from the central doctrine of that encyclical —Neil H. Jacoby, "The Progress of Peoples," 1969

The use of *dissent to* has raised some hackles in the past. While it is not a very common usage, it may still be found, along with *dissent against*:

... dissenting to the most outrageous invasion of private right ever set forth as a decision of the court —Julian P. Boyd, *American Scholar,* Winter 1952–1953

It is summarized, dissented against and reviewed at ever-higher levels —David Binder, *N.Y. Times,* 26 Dec. 1976

The noun *dissent,* when used with a preposition, is also usually followed by *from*:

... was writing in dissent from a majority position —Willard Gaylin, *Harper's,* November 1971

Rarely it may also be found with *to*:

... Maryland had confirmed its 88-year-old dissent to the 14th Amendment —*Time,* 18 Apr. 1955

dissimilar   Some language commentators insist that *dissimilar* should be followed by *to* when it takes a complement or a prepositional phrase, but our evidence shows *dissimilar* is just as likely to be followed by *from*:

These pumps . . . were not dissimilar to those once familiar to everyone on a farm —James B. Conant, *On Understanding Science,* 1947

... but the military requirements are not dissimilar from those for defense —Fletcher Pratt, *New Republic,* 24 Feb. 1941

dissociate, disassociate   *Dissociate* and *disassociate* share the sense "to separate from association or union with another," and either word may be used in that sense. *Dissociate* is recommended by a number of commentators on the ground that it is shorter, which it is by a grand total of two letters—not the firmest ground for decision. Both words are in current good use, but *dissociate* is used more often. That may be grounds for your decision.

When used with a preposition, both *dissociate* and *disassociate* are usually used with *from*:

... some flight attendants dissociate themselves from the job —Gail Sheehy, *N.Y. Times Book Rev.,* 23 Oct. 1983

... she tries to disassociate herself from the film's apocalyptic ending —Stephen J. Sansweet, *Wall Street Jour.,* 10 Dec. 1981

Both words, however, are used with other prepositions from time to time:

... the restaurant, which he became disassociated with in June 1983 —Julie Gilbert, *Houston Post,* 3 Sept. 1984

... Albertine is . . . dissociated into so many different images —Edmund Wilson, *Axel's Castle,* 1931

distaff   Although disparaged by Copperud 1964, 1970, 1980 as "journalese" and by Flesch 1964 as pretentious, and viewed cautiously by Reader's Digest 1983 as liable to annoy women, the adjective use of *distaff* shows no sign of waning usage. Its primary use is as an alternative to *female.* We do note that almost all of our most recent citations come from magazines reporting on sports or the entertainment industry. Here are some examples:

... felt that most tournaments did not allot a big enough share of the prize money to the distaff side of the proceedings —Herbert Warren Wind, *New Yorker,* 2 Oct. 1971

... spun off a distaff line after women began snapping up her small size men's jackets —Martha K. Babcock, *People,* 2 Mar. 1981

... the first distaff jockey to win a race in Mexico —*Horse Illustrated,* July 1980

Imperiously glamorous with her suavely coiffed hair, tinted harlequin glasses, and uncut-emerald ring the size of a horse chestnut, Fleur ruled the distaff side of the Look empire —Amy Fine Collins, *Vanity Fair,* October 1996

Joe Smith, the director of Women's Basketball News Service, who has covered the distaff game since 1973 —John Walters, *Sports Illustrated,* 22 Jan. 2001

It is also applied to horses with some frequency:

Another with notable distaff relations is Mr. D. Simpson's Joshua colt from the Sandwich Stakes heroine Mayfell —Alan Yuill Walker, *British Racehorse,* October 1979

Two distaff champions, Landaluce and Princess Rooney, both completed their 2-year-old campaigns undefeated —Janet Carlson, *Town & Country,* July 1983

Our evidence at the present time shows little objection to the adjective *distaff* by women writers.

distaste When used with a preposition, *distaste* overwhelmingly takes *for:*

. . . made no effort to conceal his distaste for the drink —Terry Southern, *Flash and Filigree,* 1958

. . . had an obvious distaste for the corruption of modern politics —Irving Howe, *Harper's,* January 1969

Less often, *distaste* may also be used with *at, of, toward,* or *towards:*

. . . the girls in Women's Lib who talk about their distaste at being thought of as sex objects —John Corry, *Harper's,* November 1970

. . . well known for his distaste of books too forthrightly sexual —Norman Mailer, *Advertisements for Myself,* 1959

. . . the attitude of fear and distaste toward mathematics —Bruce Dearing, in *Automation, Education, and Human Values,* ed. W. W. Brickman & S. Lehrer, 1966

. . . the personal distaste Churchill and de-Gaulle nursed towards each other —*Atlantic,* October 1945

distill, distil *Distill* and *distil* are variant spellings, and although the spelling *distil* is used in contemporary writing, *distill* is found far more often. The word may be used with any one of various prepositions, but it occurs most frequently with either *from* or *into:*

The authors distil a mass of detailed information from the company's account books —Richard Dorment, *Times Literary Supp.,* 24 Apr. 1992

. . . has distilled into these two volumes a lifetime of research and thought —Allan

Nevins, "Book-of-the-Month-Club News," December 1945

Other prepositions used with *distill* are *out of, through,* and *to:*

. . . the preciousness of existence may be distilled out of its very precariousness —Frederic Morton, *Saturday Rev.,* 22 May 1954

Most filmmakers distill life through the conventions of fiction —Susan Rice, *Media & Methods,* March 1969

Distilled to its essence, the Marshall Plan is simply this —Clarence B. Randall, *Atlantic,* October 1950

Of is a much less common alternative to *from* and *out of:*

. . . the place had an overmastering silence, a quiet distilled of the blue heavens —John Buchan, *Castle Gay,* 1930

distinctive, distinct, distinguished Several British publications (as Sellers 1975, Chambers 1985) warn against confusing *distinctive* with *distinct* and a few, mostly American, (as Copperud 1970, 1980) warn against confusing *distinctive* with *distinguished.* We are frankly puzzled by all these warnings, for we have no recent evidence that suggests any confusion at all. The words are adequately defined in standard dictionaries and require no further clarification here. We offer a few typical examples of each:

. . . the platypus has a distinct reptilian walk —Janet L. Hopson, *Smithsonian,* January 1981

The functions of banking as distinct from the procedures —Martin Mayer, *The Bankers,* 1974

The reprinting of old guide books, then, is a distinct service to scholars —*Times Literary Supp.,* 19 Feb. 1971

. . . what its distinctive contribution is to society —Robert A. Nisbet, *Psychology Today,* March 1971

The distinctive feature of this compilation was its emphasis on science —*Times Literary Supp.,* 19 Feb. 1971

. . . acted in 1527 before Henry VIII and a distinguished audience —F. P. Wilson, *The English Drama 1485–1585,* 1968

. . . even the layman was able to make distinguished contributions —Nicolas H. Charney, *Saturday Rev.,* 19 Feb. 1972

distinguish When *distinguish* is used with a preposition, the preposition is most likely to be either *between* or *from.* They are used with about equal frequency:

. . . a child under four will hardly distinguish between yesterday and a week ago —Bertrand Russell, *Education and the Good Life,* 1926

. . . a transistorized instrument accurate enough to distinguish between sandy, hard, or rocky bottom —Jan Adkins, *Harper's,* October 1971

It had its stone wall . . . to protect it, distinguishing it from an open village —G. M. Trevelyan, *English Social History,* 1942

. . . permits us to distinguish the styles of the North American Indians . . . from those of the better-known African, Mesoamerican and South Pacific primitive cultures —Barbara Rose, *New York,* 10 Jan. 1972

Less often, *distinguish* is used with *among.* From the few examples which we have of *among,* it seems that the writers may have been influenced by the notion that *between* can be used only of two items and that *among* must be used for more than two:

. . . impossible to distinguish among the fat vases, fancy lampshades, and ladies' hats —David Denby, *Atlantic,* September 1971

See BETWEEN 1.

Very infrequently, *distinguish* may be used with *into*:

The following is a summary of the various suggestions . . . distinguished into the following categories —Felix M. Keesing, *Social Anthropology in Polynesia,* 1953

distinguished See DISTINCTIVE, DISTINCT, DISTINGUISHED.

distract See DETRACT, DISTRACT.

distrait Whatever controversy this word excited in the past seems to have faded away. Two of our most recent commentators, Burchfield 1996 and Garner 1998, find no problem; they merely give the word's meaning and show some examples. We agree there is no problem. *Distrait* is a fairly rare literary word, more used in British English than in American. Although it has been used in English since the 14th century, it is still treated like a French word, often italicized, and sometimes used in the French feminine spelling *distraite.* A few examples:

Scythrop grew every day more reserved, mysterious, and *distrait*; and gradually lengthened the duration of his diurnal seclusions in his tower —Thomas Love Peacock, *Nightmare Abbey,* 1818

. . . she habitually seated herself on any paper or papers she had collected; at the post, to be forced off her papers by any duty made her as *distraite* as a mother bird

—Elizabeth Bowen, *The Heat of the Day,* 1949

She was just a touch distraite throughout the evening, and her friends rallied her jocosely because she could not bear to spend even a few hours at the theater without her Ernest —Katherine Anne Porter, *Ladies' Home Jour.,* August 1971

. . . the signs of boredom under the perfection of the royal manner. Not that the King could be called distrait; no, but he had begun to fiddle with the silver bracelet round his wrist —Vita Sackville-West, *The Edwardians,* 1930

distrustful *Of* is the preposition used with *distrustful*:

. . . the Russians were at once distrustful of their new comrades —William L. Shirer, *The Rise and Fall of the Third Reich,* 1960

dive, dived See DOVE.

divest When followed by a prepositional phrase, *divest* appears with *of*:

It will divest itself of its local phone companies —Laura Landro, *Wall Street Jour.,* 18 Mar. 1982

. . . divesting themselves of all claim to moral and intellectual leadership —George F. Kennan, *New Republic,* 24 Aug. 1953

Until recently, *divest* in its business sense was usually a reflexive verb, as shown in the first example above. Although that usage is still predominant, another has recently cropped up alongside it in which *divest* takes as a direct object the thing that is given up:

GAF Corp. is in the process of divesting eight businesses—about half of its revenue base —*Business Week,* 1 June 1981

. . . a Texas Board of Education dominated by the Religious Right voted to divest $43 million in company stock —Richard Dunham, *Business Week,* 14 Sept. 1998

Barzun 1985 considers that, with this use, "an important verb has lost its bearings." This use might be seen as a contemporary revival of a sense "to lay aside, abandon" labeled "now rare" in the OED and "archaic" in Webster's Third, though earlier instances of this sense show no orientation to business. But whether the recent use is a new sense or a revival, we must wait to see how well it establishes itself.

divide 1. The verb *divide* is used with a large number of prepositions, some of which are used rarely, others of which are used frequently. In the Merriam-Webster citation files there are occasional instances of *divide* being used with *as to, to, against,* and *towards,* but there is extensive evidence for its use, depending upon the sense, with a variety of other prepositions. The one used most often is *into*:

> People who respond to international politics divide temperamentally into two schools —Arthur M. Schlesinger, Jr., *Harper's*, August 1971

> Those concerned with this matter divide into several groups —Lewis Mumford, *New Yorker*, 9 Feb. 1957

Divide is also used with *between* and *among*, with *between* occurring far more often. The choice seems often to be dictated by the old distinction that insists on *between* for two and *among* for more than two. However, some citations show that writers may ignore that distinction:

> . . . divide their time between Paris and Athens —*Current Biography*, July 1965

> . . . the initiative, instead of being concentrated, is divided between many laboratories —A. W. Haslett, *London Calling*, 18 Mar. 1954

> . . . the remainder is to be divided equally among his four sons —Mary P. Dolciani et al., *Modern Algebra and Trigonometry*, 1973

The use of *divide* with *from* is also common especially when both divisions are mentioned and one is the direct object:

> . . . the piece of knowledge that more than anything else divides women from girls —Herman Wouk, *Marjorie Morningstar*, 1955

In addition to the common mathematical use of *divide* with *by*, *divide by* is used in other contexts:

> . . . that town was roughly divided in half by the high and rugged Gardner Mountain Range —*American Guide Series: New Hampshire*, 1938

> . . . more alike . . . in feeling than any other two writers divided by three centuries —G. M. Trevelyan, *English Social History*, 1942

Divide may be used with *on, upon* or *over* when the matter that causes the division is the object of the preposition. *On* occurs most frequently, *upon* and *over* less often:

> The doubtful civil liberties cases are those on which the court divides —John P. Frank, *N.Y. Times*, 3 Oct. 1954

> Experts divide over whether Mr. Reagan represents the vanguard of a tidal swing in the 1980s —Richard J. Cattani, *Christian Science Monitor*, 15 July 1980

Agricultura workers are divided upon the question —F. D. Smith & Barbara Wilcox, *The Country Companion*, 1950

Divide with occurs, but not very often:

> . . . the *American Weekly Mercury* divided the honor with the *Boston Gazette* —*American Guide Series: Pennsylvania*, 1940

2. Many language commentators deplore what they consider the unnecessary use of the adverb *up* with various verbs, *divide* among them. *Divide up* has been around for quite some time and continues to be used by writers of standard English:

> . . . to enable women to divide up domestic tasks —Sir Winston Churchill, *The Unrelenting Struggle*, 1942

> . . . he might divide up a supply of jelly beans —John Holt, *Atlantic*, May 1971

divorce The verb *divorce* is almost always used with *from* when followed by a prepositional phrase:

> . . . some of them [artists] quite divorced from any earthly, temporal dimension at all —Joyce Carol Oates, *Saturday Rev.*, 6 Jan. 1973

> The isolationism of the 1920's had not divorced America from the world's perplexing problems —Oscar Handlin, *The American People in the Twentieth Century*, 1954

divulge A few commentators criticize *divulge* used as a casual variant for *say, tell,* or *announce*. Though the most recent of these books was published in 1998, we have no recent examples of such use in our files. We have a few older examples like this one:

> . . . it seemed to me an occasion to divulge my real ideas and hopes for the Commonwealth —Logan Pearsall Smith, *All Trivia*, 1934

More typical of the current use of *divulge* are these examples:

> As a special mark of favor to Elena, whom she had invited to tea, she confided a family recipe, which was not to be divulged even to me —Edmund Wilson, *New Yorker*, 5 June 1971

> Another folder . . . divulges Nixon's early fixation on discrediting his left-wing detractors —Paul Grabowicz, *Mother Jones*, May 1979

> . . . does not divulge prices to journalists —Janet Malcolm, *New Yorker*, 10 Apr. 1971

> One hesitates to ask another fisherman to divulge the location of a hot spot —William G. Tapply, *Yankee*, May 1996

do   Quirk et al. 1985 has a section on the use of *do* as a pro-form—that is, as a substitute for the predicate of an earlier part of the sentence. The uses discussed, in which *do* follows a modal auxiliary like *may* and *must* or perfective *have* (usually with a modal auxiliary), are idioms principally found in British English. These are not recent idioms; they have been under attack and examination at least since Cobbett 1823. Let's put down some examples here to relieve the abstractness of this grammatical talk. First, *do* after a modal (or after *used to,* here functioning somewhat like a modal):

    . . . Mrs. Stent gives us quite as much of her company as we wish for, & rather more than she used to do —Jane Austen, letter, 30 Nov. 1800

    . . . and she said, Does money grow on trees Bill?
    It might do, I said . . .
          —*The Stories of Frank Sargeson,* 1974

Here are some examples of *do* after perfective *have:*

    'She must have transferred her affections to some foul blister she met out there.'
    'No, no.'
    'Don't keep saying "No, no." She must have done.'
          —P. G. Wodehouse, *Right Ho, Jeeves,* 1934

    "We felt this man did not have the same service he would have done had he been white," said Mr. Hunte —*Evening Mail* (Birmingham, England), 13 June 1974

As you will have noted, most of these examples come from quoted or fictional conversation or from letters. It would thus appear that British writers tend to avoid the construction in more dignified prose. Our few recent American examples show no such limitation, probably because the idiom is not a common conversational one in American English.

    . . . the OCF didn't begin as well as it could have done —Stanley Kauffmann, *Before My Eyes,* 1980

dock   The distinction between *dock* and *pier* or *wharf* seems to have been first made by Richard Grant White in 1870. His dictum has been carried in newspaper lists of proscribed usages and in usage books written by journalists (as Bernstein 1962) ever since, but most current (and nonjournalistic) commentators accept the use as standard in American English.

It appears to be chiefly an American usage. The Dictionary of Americanisms gives citations from as early as 1817, but the OED does not recognize it in spite the first citation here:

    . . . staring about me, until we came alongside the dock —Charles Dickens, *American Notes,* 1842

    Jean was on the dock when the ship came in —Mark Twain, *Harper's Monthly Mag.,* January 1911

    . . . I thought of Gatsby's wonder when he first picked out the green light at the end of Daisy's dock —F. Scott Fitzgerald, *The Great Gatsby,* 1925

    Then she walked across the dock and up the steep sandy road —*Short Stories of Ernest Hemingway,* (1926) 1938

    . . . was on the dock waving a bill —Samuel Eliot Morison, *John Paul Jones: A Sailor's Biography,* 1959

doesn't   See DON'T.

donate   *Donate* is one of those pesky backformations that have frequently come under the gun of critics. Critics in the 19th and early 20th centuries found the word vulgar, but no recent critics carp at it.

Donate is an original Americanism, first attested in 1785. It has some British use, too. Fowler 1926 does not condemn it, but calls it "chiefly U.S." and notes it as a back-formation; Gowers in Fowler 1965 and Burchfield 1996 observe that it has become a formal word for *give* in British English. In American use it seems to be the word of choice when the giving, usually to a cause or charity, is public or is intended to be publicized. It is no longer controversial.

    Magazines donated space. Artists and writers donated their services. Peace was what people were groping for, and when Americans grope for something they turn naturally to display advertising —E. B. White, *The Wild Flag,* 1946

    . . . the receipts of the gala premier performance of the film would be donated to the League —Tom Buckley, *Harper's,* August 1971

done   1. *Done* in the sense of "finished" has been subject to a certain amount of criticism over the years for reasons that are not readily apparent. The use of *done* as an adjective in this sense dates back to the 14th and 15th centuries, but the construction usually objected to—*be done*—is of more recent origin, attested by examples in the OED from the second half of the 18th century. Otto Jespersen, in his seven-volume grammar (1909–1949), has examples of the construction from several well-known 19th-century writers beginning with Dickens. In earlier English the usual auxiliary with *done* had been *have.* From Jespersen's examples it would appear that during the 19th century the use of *have* with *done* became more and more limited to the fixed expression *have done with,* which is still in use; if his examples are indeed representative, this tendency may well have strengthened the position of *be done.*

The earliest objection to *be done* in our files is from MacCracken & Sandison 1917. They do not say what is wrong with it but prescribe *have finished* in its place. (The fact that the OED and Curme 1931 note it as chiefly Irish, Scots, and U.S. may show how the objection originated.) This must have been a regular part of many schools' grammar lessons, for 47 percent of the usage panel of Heritage 1969 remembered them well enough to disapprove the construction. The construction, however, is standard.

> A terrible sound arose when the reading of this document was done —Charles Dickens, *A Tale of Two Cities,* 1859

> I am done with official life for the present —Mark Twain, *Sketches, New and Old,* 1872 (Dictionary of American English)

> . . . as soon as she is done shooting this movie —Richard Boeth, *Cosmopolitan,* June 1976

2. The use of *done* as the past tense rather than past participle of *do* is not recorded in the OED. Evidence in the English Dialect Dictionary and the Dictionary of American English suggests that it may be more recent than one might expect, dating only from the 19th century. It may be of dialectal origin, and it is quite possible that there will never be a sufficient early record to date the use with any certainty. It is likely that the form was corrected by schoolteachers almost as soon as it was noticed; it is still in school grammars for correction (we note it in Warriner 1986, for instance). Our oldest comment on the use is from Richard Grant White 1870, who says it is common among completely illiterate people. Reader's Digest 1983 calls the usage nonstandard; Bryant 1962 says it is colloquial but is a receding usage. It is very seldom used in standard contexts, and only in such specialized ways as this:

> To outline the highly intricate plot . . . is impossible in a short review, and in any case would be comparable to revealing who done it in a review of a whodunnit —Peter Lewis, *Times Literary Supp.,* 21 May 1982

3. *Done* used as a completive or perfective auxiliary. Raven I. McDavid, in his 1963 abridgment of H. L. Mencken's *The American Language,* observes that the usage occurs chiefly but not exclusively in Southern and South Midland dialects; it is also mentioned in works on Black English and Appalachian English. The Dictionary of American Regional English labels it chiefly Southern and Southern Midland. The DARE editors raise a grammatical problem—they analyze some uses of *done* as an adverb denoting completion. Adverb or auxiliary, the usage is basically regional. It is probably subject to some social restrictions as well. Some examples:

> Old Eagle had done already took off —William Faulkner, *Saturday Evening Post,* 5 Mar. 1955

> . . . her voice, which had all the sad languor of the upper Pamunkey River. "The Japanese," she said, "they done bombed Pearl Harbor." —William Styron, *This Quiet Dust and Other Writings,* 1982

> . . . and you play the same thing, then it ain't great no more. It's done been played —Carlton Haney, quoted in *Bluegrass Unlimited,* September 1983

See DO.

don't In the 17th century several contracted negative verb forms came into use—among them *don't, won't, shan't, an't* (an ancestor of *ain't*), *han't, wa'n't*—that are noticeable because their pronunciation differs rather markedly from that of the positive elements from which they were formed. This somewhat obscured phonological relationship allowed several of these to be multipurpose forms: *an't* was used for *am not* and *are not; don't* for *do not* and *does not; han't* for *has not* and *have not.* The 17th century got by with fewer of these contractions than we use today.

No one is sure how *don't* came by its pronunciation; it matches neither *do* nor *does.* The most likely explanation, accepted by Strang 1970 and tentatively accepted by Jespersen 1909–49, is that the pronunciation comes by way of analogy with *won't.* The spelling obviously comes from *do* and *not,* but how this spelling came to be used for the third person singular is not so obvious, though (since *don't* was a spoken form long before it was written down) it seems likely that one or more phonological processes were involved. A contributing factor may well have been the unsettled condition of the third person singular of *do* in the 17th century. The northern form *does* had long been competing with the southern *doth* (both variously spelled) for several centuries. In addition to these two there was in the 16th and 17th century an uninflected form *do.* This form was regularly used by Samuel Pepys in his diary:

> . . . the Duke of York do give himself up to business, and is like to prove a noble prince; and so indeed I do from my heart think he will. . . . but I should be more glad that the

King himself would look after business, which it seems he do not —21 Jan. 1664

It is possible that this uninflected form had some influence on the written *don't*.

From the 17th century through the 19th century, *don't* seems to have had unimpeachable status:

> Putting as much contempt as I could into my look and tone, I said, "Dr. Johnson don't!—humph!" —Horace Walpole, letter, 26 May 1791

> . . . and if Wordsworth don't send me an order for one upon Longman, I will buy it —Charles Lamb, letter, 7 June 1809

> However, it don't matter if you've read the play —George Bernard Shaw, letter, 24 Dec. 1897

Indicative of the social status of third singular *don't* in the mid-19th century is this example:

> There is one other phrase which will soon come to be decisive of a man's social *status,* if it is not already: "That tells the whole story." It is an expression which vulgar and conceited people particularly affect, and which well-meaning ones, who know better, catch from them. It is intended to stop all debate, like the previous question in the General Court. Only it don't —Oliver Wendell Holmes d. 1894, *The Autocrat of the Breakfast-Table,* 1858

The attack on third singular *don't* seems to have begun in the second half of the 19th century and in the U.S. It must have rapidly gotten into school books and handbooks; almost all of our early 20th-century sources condemn the use. The usage survey reported in Crisp 1971 shows that third singular *don't* then had lower status than it had had in the survey of Leonard in 1932.

Earlier in this century it could still be found in both British and American poetry:

> To-night he's in the pink; but soon he'll die.
> And still the war goes on; he don't know why
> —Siegfried Sassoon, in *Georgian Poetry 1916–1917,* 1919

> "He don't consider it a case for God" —Robert Frost, *Mountain Interval,* 1921

And in American fiction of that period, third singular *don't* was being put into the mouths of ordinary middle-class and working-class characters, whose conversations tended to depart considerably from the norms taught in grammar school:

> "Old wind-bag," he sputtered. "Why does he want to be bragging? Why don't he shut up?" —Sherwood Anderson, *Winesburg, Ohio,* 1919

> ". . . It makes elegant reading, but it don't say nothing . . ." —Sinclair Lewis, *Babbitt,* 1922

> "I says 'Lay it down,' " says Cap. "If that don't mean 'bunt,' what does it mean?" —Ring Lardner, *How to Write Short Stories,* 1924

It still is used in speech, mostly but not exclusively by the less educated, and in casual writing:

> . . . the carpenter don't build a house just to drive nails —William Faulkner, 11 Mar. 1957, in *Faulkner in the University,* 1959

> . . . I judge Fr. C. belongs to the tribe that knows what's bad but don't know what's good —Flannery O'Connor, letter, 19 Apr. 1958

> And them bass fiddles that's electrified, they're so loud, and the average man that plays 'em don't know how to turn 'em down —Birch Monroe, quoted in *Bluegrass Unlimited,* September 1982

Doesn't, though dating back to 1639, seems not to have been much used until the 19th century. Byron seems not to have known it; at least he used only *don't* for all persons throughout *Don Juan,* although he uses both *does* and *doth* in positive constructions. Nor will *doesn't* be found in the fiction of Jane Austen. Although third person singular *don't* appears in her dialogue, *does not* is the preferred form. *Don't* is, of course, still standard in all uses except the third person singular, but in that use it has lost all the status it once enjoyed. As Flesch 1964 notes, *don't* is not an illiteracy. But neither is it standard any longer in edited prose.

See also AIN'T.

don't seem See CAN'T SEEM.

don't think The placement of the negative in such sentences as "I don't think it will rain tonight" and "I don't think they have a chance" is a characteristic English idiom that is sometimes objected to on the grounds of logic. Such sentences are briefly discussed at RAISING.

dote When *dote* is used with a preposition—and it almost always is—*on* is the overwhelming choice, although our files show instances of *dote upon* and *dote over:*

> . . . the spectators dote on his quips and his banter —Herbert Warren Wind, *New Yorker,* 17 July 1971

> How he doted on this terrible lodger of theirs —Glenway Wescott, *Apartment in Athens,* 1945

. . . it is precisely the sort upon which the dilettante etymologist dotes —Thomas Pyles, *Words and Ways of American English,* 1952

He has been assembling the stamps since boyhood and still dotes over them —*N.Y. Times,* 7 Oct. 1951

double comparative See DOUBLE COMPARISON.

double comparison Double comparison consists chiefly of the use of *more* or *most* with an adjective already inflected for the comparative or superlative degree. Lamberts 1972 observes that besides marking the comparative and superlative, *more* and *most* were used as intensives long before Shakespeare's time. This use is still with us: when we say to our host or hostess, "That was a most enjoyable meal," we are using *most* as an intensive, in much the same way as we might use *very*. Back in the 14th century *more* and *most* came to be used in intensive function with adjectives already inflected for comparative and superlative. OED evidence suggests that the practice continued from the 14th through the 17th centuries. It was fairly frequent in Shakespeare's plays and also occurred in the King James version of the Bible.

More fairer than fair, beautiful than beauteous —Shakespeare, *Love's Labour's Lost,* 1595

This was the most unkindest cut of all —Shakespeare, *Julius Caesar,* 1600

. . . that after the most straitest sect of our religion I lived a Pharisee —Acts 25:5 (AV), 1611

The OED evidence for this use of *more* and *most* suggests a marked decline after the 17th century. Part of the decline can be attributed to the attack mounted against the construction by several 18th-century grammarians, including Lowth in 1763. "Double comparatives and superlatives are improper," says he, and sets out Shakespeare and the translators of the book of Acts, cited above, for correction. The bishop, however, was willing to indulge poets in occasional improprieties, and he could not bring himself to condemn "most highest" applied to God in an old translation of the Psalms. Priestley, who was not a bishop, was not diffident about criticizing this construction in his revised edition of 1798, nor was Lindley Murray 1795. And by the middle of the 19th century, Goold Brown felt no compunction about telling Shakespeare and King James's translators what they should have written.

Lindley Murray's grammar was widely used as a school grammar, and widely imitated by other writers of school grammars. So the strictures on the double comparative and double superlative became part of every schoolchild's lessons—and they still are. The result has been that double comparison has pretty much vanished from standard writing. Double comparison does, however, linger in speech and in such familiar writing as letters—wherever it may serve some specified purpose.

See also LESSER, considered by some to be a double comparative.

double genitive Almost every native speaker of English has read or heard expressions like these:

. . . that place of Dorothy Thompson's is only sixty miles away —Alexander Woollcott, letter, 18 Mar. 1940

. . . two very nice girls who were friends of yours —Flannery O'Connor, letter, 9 Apr. 1960

The most noticeable thing about "place of Dorothy Thompson's" and "friends of yours" is that the possessive relationship is marked both by the preposition *of* and the genitive inflection. This construction is known as the *double genitive* or *double possessive*. It is an idiomatic construction of long standing in English—going back before Chaucer's time—and should be of little interest except to learners of the language, because, as far as we know, it gives native speakers no trouble whatsoever.

But the double genitive was discovered by the 18th-century grammarians and has consequently been the subject of considerable speculation, explanation, and sometimes disapproving comment.

The genitive in English has more functions than the simple indication of possession (see the article at GENITIVE). The double genitive construction is a characteristic that separates the possessive genitive from all other functions of the genitive. Here is how the matter is typically explained: "Jane's picture," out of context, can be considered ambiguous. If *Jane's* is an objective genitive, we can clear up the possible confusion by using the *of* construction: "a picture of Jane." If the picture belongs to Jane, and *Jane's* is a possessive genitive, using the *of* construction, we get "a picture of Jane's." In other words, when *of* is used with a possessive genitive, the noun or pronoun regularly retains its genitive inflection. No native speaker of English would write our first example as "that place of Dorothy Thompson."

The double genitive is a perfectly acceptable, perfectly normal form in modern English. But those 18th-century grammarians weren't so sure. Lowth 1762 may have been the first to notice it. He ran afoul of "a soldier of the king's." He seems to have mulled it over awhile; then he adds that "here are really two possessives; for it means 'one *of* the soldiers *of* the king.' " This is a partitive construction in which two *of*s are used to explain away the supposedly redundant *'s*. The partitive explanation has persisted down to 1990, even though the grammarian Otto Jespersen exploded it 1926 with an example from *Tristram Shandy*: "This exactness of his." The phrase cannot be turned into "one of the exactnesses of him." An even plainer example is another Shandean phrase, "that long nose of his."

The double genitive is standard English and should not be worried about.

double modal   *Double modal* is a term used by linguists to describe such expressions as *might can, might could,* and *might should.* Several of these have received comment in usage books. Those that survive in present-day American English tend to be used in speech rather than writing, and are generally old-fashioned or dialectal. *Might could* (which see) seems to be a still flourishing speech form in the Southern U.S. There are other combinations at OUGHT.

double negative   Otto Jespersen, in *Negation in English and Other Languages* (1917), has an interesting observation. He notes that negation in a sentence is very important logically but that it is often formally unimportant in the structure of the sentence—in many instances in English it is marked by no more than an unstressed particle like old *ne* or modern *-n't*. Hence, there has long been a tendency to strengthen the negative idea by adding more negative elements to the sentence. This tendency is perhaps properly called *multiple negation,* but it is usually referred to in modern handbooks and commentaries as the *double negative.*

The double negative functions in two ways in present-day English: as an emphatic negative, and as an unemphatic positive. We will examine each of these separately.

1. *Emphatic negative.* The multiple negative for emphasis or reinforcement of the negative idea of a sentence is very old, going back much farther than Chaucer. The construction was common at least through Shakespeare's time:

> . . . they could not find no more forage—Lord Berners, translation of Froissart's *Chronicles,* 1523

> And that no woman has; nor never none
> Shall mistress be of it
> —Shakespeare, *Twelfth Night,*
> 1602 (in Strang 1970)

> She cannot love,
> Nor take no shape nor project of affection
> —Shakespeare, *Much Ado About Nothing,*
> 1599 (in Lowth 1762)

The more effusive multiple negatives seem to have gone out of literary favor some time after Shakespeare, but the double negative—like Lord Berners'—kept in use:

> QUACK. . . . your process is so new that we do not know but it may succeed.
> HORNER. Not so new neither; *probatum est,* doctor.
> —William Wycherly, *The Country Wife,* 1675

I cannot by no means allow him, that this argument must prove. . . . —Richard Bentley, *Dissertation on Epistles of Phalaris,* 1699 (in Lowth 1775)

. . . lost no time, nor abated no Diligence —Daniel Defoe, *Robinson Crusoe,* 1719 (in McKnight 1928)

It was during the 18th century that the double negative began to attract the unfavorable notice of grammarians. Lowth 1763 gave the classic form to the statement:

> Two negatives in English destroy one another, or are equivalent to an affirmative. . . .

Lowth's statement was repeated word for word by Murray 1795 and in various forms by many other grammarians; it has become part of the warp and woof of pedagogy.

Lowth's statement is not original with him—it is simply a rule of Latin grammar. And it was a well-known rule; as early as 1591 Sir Philip Sidney in *Astrophel and Stella* had written a joking sonnet based on the principle that two negatives make an affirmative (quoted in Baron 1982). Lowth was aware of earlier use of multiple negation for emphasis, but he thought the old practice was obsolete.

It was later and lesser grammarians that made absolute the dictum about two negatives making a positive. From the absolute position seems to have arisen the often urged argument that the statement is based on logic. As Lamberts 1972 has pointed out, it all depends on what logic you choose. Two negatives may make a positive in the logic of Latin grammar, but not in the logic of algebra: $-a + -a = -2a$. Algebraic logic yields approximately the same result as the old multiple negative—simply a stronger negative.

The old multiple negative and the common or garden double negative were passing out of literature in Lowth's time. What was happening was that their sphere of use was contracting; they were still available but were restricted to familiar use—conversation and letters. And, since old forms persist the longest among the least educated, the double negative became generally associated with the speech of the unlettered. In modern use, the double negative is widely perceived as a rustic or uneducated form, and is indeed common in the speech of less educated people:

> ... I never had nary bit of desire to drink no strong drinks since I felt the Lord forgive me —Sam Johnson, quoted in *Our Appalachia,* ed. Laurel Shackelford & Bill Weinberg, 1977

> I went and saw the Allen Brothers in a free concert ... and I didn't know nothing about bluegrass —Rick Stacy, quoted in *Bluegrass Unlimited,* July 1982

And of course, the double negative is put into the speech of similar characters in fiction:

> ". . . and then there warn't no raft in sight. . . ." —Mark Twain, *Huckleberry Finn,* 1884

> I won't have nothing to do with those people, Houdini told his manager —E. L. Doctorow, *Ragtime,* 1975

It still occurs in the casual speech and writing of more sophisticated and better-educated people:

> There's one more volume which I hope will be the last but I haven't no assurance that it will be —William Faulkner, 5 June 1957, in *Faulkner in the University,* 1959

> You can't do nothing with nobody that doesn't want to win —Robert Frost, letter, 20 Sept. 1962

The double negative may even be trotted out in discursive prose for effect:

> The sailplane sure ain't no 747! —Susan Ochshorn, *Saturday Rev.,* 14 Apr. 1979

The range of use of the double negative has shrunk considerably in the past 400 years, but it has not disappeared. If it's part of your normal speech, you certainly don't need to eradicate it when talking to your family and friends. But it is not a prestige form; you are not likely to impress the boss, the teacher, or the job interviewer by using double negatives. But, as the examples above show, it does have its uses. You just have to pick your occasions.

2. Weak affirmative. Lowth, when he lays down the rule about two negatives making an affirmative, quotes Milton. The double negative as a weak positive was in use as early as 1537; it was a rhetorical device (the usual name for it is *litotes* or *meiosis;* see LITOTES) that would have been included in 16th-century books on rhetoric. The intention of this double negative is just the opposite of the traditional one: instead of emphasizing, it is meant as understatement. Here are a few examples:

> Fanny looked on and listened, not unamused to observe the selfishness which, more or less disguised, seemed to govern them all —Jane Austen, *Mansfield Park,* 1814

> ... had what *Opera News* not unfairly called "the kind of performance that gives the composer a bad reputation." —Andrew Porter, *New Yorker,* 29 July 1985

When this device is overused, reviewers and commentators on style can get annoyed:

> ... an annoying penchant for the double negative ("should not pass unnoticed" appears three times, "not dissimilar" twice) —Graham Forst, *Books in Canada,* February 1976

double passive The construction known as the *double passive* looks like this:

> The mystery was assiduously, though vainly, endeavoured to be discovered —in Fowler 1926, 1965

It involves a passive verb followed by a passive infinitive. It is awkward. The subject is examined in some detail in Bernstein 1965, Fowler 1926, 1965, Burchfield 1996, and Garner 1998; it gets shorter treatment in Copperud 1970, 1980 and Janis 1984. We cannot tell how much of a problem the double passive presents in current use; Burchfield says the fashion for writing them had virtually disappeared by 1900, but both he and Garner give recent examples. Some of these are plain enough, but many would be improved by revision.

We suspect these complex constructions will not be a problem in most of your writing.

See also PASSIVE VOICE.

double possessive See DOUBLE GENITIVE.

double subjects In 1672 John Dryden wrote an essay called "Defence of the Epilogue," in which he asserts that the English used by writers of his day is more proper, more correct, than the English used by writers in the age of Shakespeare, Fletcher, and Jonson. To illustrate his point, Dryden introduces several passages from Jonson's play *Catiline,* in which he finds various improprieties of diction. One of the lines criticized reads "Such Men they do not succour more the cause. . . ." Dryden observes: "*They* redundant."

Ben Jonson's *they* after *men* is what grammarians refer to as a *double subject.* The appositive pronoun after the subject of the sentence is an old technique for emphasizing the subject. It goes back to Old English and Middle English; it still survives to a certain extent in poetry (mostly older poetry, now) and in some dialects (it is sometimes mentioned, for example, as a characteristic of Black English), and, to judge from its stigmatized appearance in schoolbooks, it occurs in the speech of children and other unschooled persons.

Hall 1917 has an imposing list of poets who

have used the double subject. One familiar example will do here:

The eye—it cannot choose but see;
We cannot bid the ear be still
—William Wordsworth, "Expostulation and Reply," 1798

The old-fashioned mode of expression is obviously helpful in getting lines of poetry to scan.

The double subject is rare in modern prose. Older writers—including Dryden himself—occasionally fall into the old pattern, but it is seldom used today. It can, however, still be heard in casual speech:

But a first-rate scoundrel, like a first-rate artist, he's an individualist —William Faulkner, 7 Mar. 1957, in *Faulkner in the University*, 1959

Anyone who sees any illegal dumping on state land, they should get the plate number and we can take it from there —Carroll Holmes, quoted in *Springfield* (Mass.) *Sunday Republican*, 6 Dec. 1987

In both of these examples, the repeated subject comes after an intervening phrase or clause; in Black English, and in other ordinary speech, it can also follow the subject directly, but after a pause, which may or may not be indicated by punctuation when the spoken is written down.

In any case, the double subject is too informal to find much use in edited prose. Garner 1998 allows formal rhetorical use: "We the people of the United States . . ."

double superlative See DOUBLE COMPARISON.

doubt, *verb* The transitive verb *doubt* may take a clause as its object. The clause may be a sort of contact clause (which see) without a conjunction or a clause introduced by *that*, *whether*, or *if*:

Some cancer researchers doubt hyperthermia will ever emerge as a primary therapy —Walter L. Updegrave, *N.Y. Times Mag.*, 23 Mar. 1980

There is nothing for it but to doubt such diseases exist —H. G. Wells (in Fowler 1907)

. . . but I doubt that this represents a judgment of relative merit —Malcolm Cowley, *New Republic*, 22 Sept. 1941

. . . I doubt that this kind of disagreement produces many divorces —Elizabeth Janeway, *Atlantic*, March 1970

. . . I seriously doubt whether the stuff I give them makes anyone else feel good —*And More by Andy Rooney*, 1982

I doubt if he had read a play of Shakespeare's even at the end of his life —*The Autobiography of William Butler Yeats*, 1953

. . . I doubt if one writer ever has a satisfactory conversation with another writer —William Faulkner, 16 May 1957, in *Faulkner in the University*, 1959

The clause that follows *doubt* could also in the past be introduced by *but* or *but that*, especially when the main clause is negative or interrogative; these constructions now seem to be rare with the verb, although we do have examples of *but that* with the noun.

. . . I don't doubt but she may endure —Sir John Vanbrugh, *The Relapse*, 1696

. . . nor do we doubt but our reader . . . will concur with us —Henry Fielding, *Jonathan Wild*, 1743

So far, things are reasonably simple. Now enter the usage writers, who, in the first quarter or so of the 20th century, put forth several lists of differing rules. Over the course of time, American sets of rules and those given in Fowler 1926 became conflated. The ministrations of a couple of dozen commentators since Fowler have resulted in this contemporary consensus:

1. Use *that* for questions and negative sentences.
2. Use *whether* or *if* to express uncertainty.
3. Use *that*, even in positive statements, to express disbelief rather than uncertainty.

You can follow these rules to guide your own practice if you want to. But can you judge the practice of others by them? No. The reason is simple: to know whether uncertainty or disbelief is intended, you must have either a clearly indicative context or an almost clairvoyant knowledge of an author's intentions. And the point to remember is this: you need not pay any attention to the rules to understand these writers:

I doubt myself whether this would have made much difference —Quintin Hogg, *Times Literary Supp.*, 22 Jan. 1970

It was quite wonderful that she should . . . never have doubted that it would occur —Louis Auchincloss, *A Law for the Lion*, 1953

. . . Jordanian and Israeli army officers doubt that the systems they live within do provide means for peaceful change —*Commonweal*, 9 Oct. 1970

The house is furnished but they ask me to buy dishes and carpets, or bring these with me which I doubt if I can do —Robert Frost, letter, 16 July 1921

In his thirty-eight years as a critic I doubt if he ever wrote a single paragraph that was not carefully planned —Deems Taylor, *Music to My Ears,* 1949

We would conclude that *that* is used when the main clause is negative; *that* also seems to be picked for use with a third-person subject more often than *whether* and *if.* But most of our examples have a first-person subject, and in those sentences the writers seem to pick *if, that,* or *whether* according to personal preference.

See also IF 1.

doubt, *noun*   Doubt, whether as a singular or a plural, is followed idiomatically by a number of prepositions:

> . . . if there was any doubt about his condition —Daphne du Maurier, *Ladies' Home Jour.,* August 1971

> . . . had some doubts about sending this boy on a man's job —Ellen Lewis Buell, *N.Y. Times Book Rev.,* 16 May 1954

> . . . in Bolshevik theory the slightest doubt of the regime is interpreted as bitter enmity —*New Republic,* 17 Mar. 1952

> . . . so that all who could vote might be under no doubt of the road to reward —J. H. Plumb, *England in the Eighteenth Century,* 1950

> . . . Byron's . . . may have been intended for some other woman, but there is no doubt over Shelley's —*Times Literary Supp.,* 3 July 1969

> There is no doubt as to the accuracy of his portrayal —Klaus Lambrecht, *New Republic,* 2 June 1941

doubtful   Fowler 1926 included *doubtful* in his disquisition upon the verb *doubt,* and numerous later commentators have followed suit. In practice, *doubtful* is usually not followed by a clause, but when it is the clause can begin with *that, whether,* or *if.* We also find the conjunction omitted occasionally.

> . . . it seems doubtful that the university can expect a substantial reduction of conflict —Jerome H. Skolnick, *AAUP Bulletin,* September 1969

> . . . it is doubtful whether the Czechs resented it —*Times Literary Supp.,* 9 Apr. 1970

> . . . it is doubtful if any brief biography can recapture the essence of Benjamin Franklin —Carl Bridenbaugh, *N.Y. Herald Tribune Book Rev.,* 4 July 1954

> It is doubtful France would be willing to forswear testing —Gerard Smith, *Interplay,* February 1969

See also DUBIOUS, DOUBTFUL.

doubtless, no doubt, undoubtedly   The basic premise of the usage writers (Fowler 1926, Evans 1957, Follett 1966, Bremner 1980, and Bryson 1984) who discuss the relative strength of these words is correct: *doubtless* and *no doubt* are often used to mean "probably"; *undoubtedly* tends to carry more conviction, but it too is often used with less than literal force.

> In due time, "The Other" will doubtless become one of the classics of horror tales —Dorothy B. Hughes, *Los Angeles Times,* 23 May 1971

> To-day, in search, no doubt, of new subscribers, the exploiters of snobbery go forth —Aldous Huxley, *The Olive Tree,* 1937

> . . . she will undoubtedly be more careful next time —Lenore Hershey, *Ladies' Home Jour.,* January 1971

doubtlessly   Because *doubtless* functions as an adverb, *doubtlessly* has remained an uncommon word during its half-millennium sojourn in the English language. Commentators from Bierce 1909 to Garner 1998 would like to get rid of it altogether, but after such a long time it seems unlikely to disappear. Burchfield 1996 observes that it seems to have gotten a new lease on life in 20th-century American usage. Some examples:

> The actual person doubtlessly suffered enough —Robert McAlmon, *Being Geniuses Together,* 1938

> . . . they will doubtlessly be looting Mr. Westlake's book for story ideas —Molly Ivins, *N.Y. Times Book Rev.,* 10 July 1988

> The idea for the picture was doubtlessly based on Callot's direct study of nature —Jennifer Milam, *Antiques,* October 1995

The choice of *doubtless* or *doubtlessly* is the writer's. Many more of them chose the former than choose the latter.

See also DOUBTLESS, NO DOUBT, UNDOUBTEDLY.

dove   *Dive* is a weak verb with the past tense *dived.* In the 19th century it developed a past tense *dove*—probably by analogy with *drive, drove*—in some British dialects and in North America. As far as we know, Longfellow was the first person to put it into print:

> Dove as if he were a beaver —*The Song of Hiawatha,* 1855

Hall 1917 notes that Longfellow changed this to *dived* in later editions, probably at the suggestion of critics. The OED Supplement shows an 1857 comment on the prevalence of *dove* in Canada.

Most recent commentators accept both

dived and *dove* as correct. The usage of *dove* is really governed by geography rather than by social class or notions of correctness. The Dictionary of American Regional English finds both *dived* and *dove* widespread, with *dived* more prevalent in southern areas and *dove* in northern ones. *Dove* is also found in some parts of Canada.

Here are a few examples of both forms:

When I dived in, several others climbed out —John Kenneth Galbraith, *Ambassador's Journal,* 1969

One of the women dove in smartly and rose up past the tank window —E. L. Doctorow, *World's Fair,* 1985

The plane dived and smartly landed —John Updike, *Bech is Back,* 1982

Black dove the airplane, from a dizzy height that permitted him to see simultaneously London and Cherbourg —William F. Buckley, Jr., *Cosmopolitan,* October 1976

Although *dived* is somewhat more common in writing in the U.S. and is usual in British English, *dove* is an acceptable variant. We suggest that you use whichever is more natural to you.

downplay Copperud 1980 terms this verb "journalese," and William Safire publicly apologized in his *New York Times* column of 24 July 1983 for using it. New York journalists seem a bit diffident about using compound words of which adverbs form the first part (see, for instance, UPCOMING).

Downplay is a relatively new verb, evidently going back no farther than 1954. Its main use does seem to be in journalism: almost all of our evidence comes from newspapers and magazines. Fifty years in the business seems to have established it for general use.

Actor Stewart happily downplays his boyish charm —*Time,* 2 Aug. 1954

. . . he will downplay the need for economic and social reform —*Newsweek,* 30 Mar. 1964

White doggedly downplays this kind of talk —Wilfrid Sheed, *N.Y. Times Book Rev.,* 21 Nov. 1976

. . . downplays any territorial competitiveness —David McQuay, *Sunday Denver Post,* 23 Sept. 1984

I don't mean to downplay the significance of a firm resolution for the evolutionary relationship between birds and dinosaurs —Stephen Jay Gould, *National History,* November 2000

dozen *Dozen* has two plurals, a zero form *dozen* (just like the singular) and an inflected

dozens. When a number is put before the noun, the zero form plural is used:

He that kills me some six or seven dozen of Scots —Shakespeare, *I Henry IV,* 1598

. . . consuming . . . twelve dozen oysters, eight quarts of orange juice —Frank Sullivan, *The Night the Old Nostalgia Burned Down,* 1953

When the number is not specified, *dozens* is used:

. . . worked in dozens of minor roles in television plays —*Current Biography,* June 1965

Evans 1957 notes that *of* used to be common after *dozen*:

I bought you a dozen of shirts —Shakespeare, *I Henry IV,* 1598

This construction is now felt to be old-fashioned and is no longer used much. We do, of course, retain *of* after *dozens*:

Dozens of times since . . . I have been asked . . . —Joseph Wood Krutch, *American Scholar,* Spring 1955

draft, draught Longman 1984 and Chambers 1985 remind us that in current British English *draft* is used for a preliminary sketch and for the corresponding verb, and also for an order for payment (a bank draft). But *draught* is used for beer, horses, and a current of air, and *draughts* is used as the name for the game of checkers. American English uses *draft* in all cases, except, of course, that it calls checkers *checkers*.

drank See DRINK.

drapes, draperies A food and restaurant critic for the *New York Times* and the cartoonist of the strip "Garfield" are taken to task by Kilpatrick 1984 for using the noun *drapes.* "Drape isn't a noun," says Kilpatrick. "It's a verb." Simon 1980 also wrinkles his nose at the word, but his criticism has a social rather than a grammatical basis.

These are brave men, however, apparently the first males ever to venture into this subject, hitherto an exclusively female domain. The only earlier comment that we have found in a usage book is in Margaret Nicholson 1957. The subject seems to have originated with Emily Post, about 1927. Post's approach is straightforward: Never say *drapes*; say *"curtains,* or, if necessary, *draperies."*

The earliest citations for *drapes* are from the catalogs of Montgomery Ward and Sears and Roebuck. Mail-order words were not for Mrs. Post. No, that's for Miss Nobackground: "Say, Murree, the new drapes in my home are dandy" (1945 edition).

Post's substitutes, *curtains* and *draperies,* deserve brief comment. *Curtains* has long been in use on both sides of the Atlantic. Her qualifying words, "or, if necessary," may represent tacit recognition of the fact that in America *curtains* and *drapes* or *draperies* often designate somewhat different hangings. The earliest citation for *draperies,* interestingly enough, is from an 1895 Montgomery Ward catalog.

Nicholson appears to have originated the dictum, repeated by Kilpatrick, that *drape* is properly a verb and that the noun is *drapery.* This objection has no foundation in fact: the OED shows that *drape* as a noun referring to cloth is older than its use as a verb and than *drapery.* We must conclude that there is no linguistic reason for choosing between *drapes* and *draperies.* Both are of the same plebeian North American origin and the same age, and are equally well established. If you have always used one instead of the other, by all means you should continue to do so. If you have no fixed preference, *draperies* is the safer choice.

draught See DRAFT, DRAUGHT.

dream 1. The verb *dream* has the past and past participle forms *dreamt* and *dreamed.* Evidence in the OED suggests *dreamt* is somewhat older than *dreamed*; both forms are nearly 700 years old. Phythian 1979 says that *dreamt* is the more common form in England; our evidence confirms his observation. Watt 1967, Shaw 1987, and Lamberts find *dreamed* more common in the U.S.; the Brown Corpus (Kučera & Francis 1967) strongly backs their contention, while our evidence finds both forms flourishing in American use.
2. Shaw 1987 mentions *dream* taking *of* before a gerund; *of* can also be used with a noun object, and so can *about:*

. . . men who might never have dreamed of advocating massacres —*New Yorker,* 10 Apr. 1971

. . . she often dreamt of the assassination of Kennedy —Joyce Carol Oates, *McCall's,* July 1971

I dreamt about the boy who Rock and big Stoop had thrown off that roof —Claude Brown, *Manchild in the Promised Land,* 1965

drench *Drench* is often used with a complement introduced by *in* or *with*:

She was drenched in furs and diamonds —Richard Brautigan, *A Confederate General from Big Sur,* 1964

. . . desserts drenched in brandy or Cointreau —Dwight Macdonald, *New Yorker,* 18 July 1953

". . . after detonation the ground-zero circle is drenched with fallout" —Don DeLillo, *End Zone,* 1972

The sun went up in triumph and drenched the parkland with gold —Elizabeth Taylor, *New Yorker,* 14 Apr. 1956

When *drench* is used in the passive voice, *by* may begin the phrase:

She was drenched . . . by compassion for the immense disaster of her sister's life —Arnold Bennett, *The Old Wives' Tale,* 1908

The locution *drench to the skin,* or *drench one to the skin* is occasionally attested in our files:

. . . a thunderstorm which would have drenched them to the skin —Marcia Davenport, *My Brother's Keeper,* 1954

Particular contexts also allow *drench* to be used with *on* or *from*:

. . . snow and sleet, which drenched cruelly down on little townships —Mollie Panter-Downes, *New Yorker,* 21 Feb. 1953

Sometimes they . . . make awful confidences, or drench us from sentimental sloppails —Logan Pearsall Smith, *All Trivia,* 1934

drink The usual 20th-century past tense of this verb is *drank* and the past participle, *drunk.* Usage is not entirely uniform yet, although it is closer to uniform than it has been in the past. The OED notes that the past tense *drunk* was in good use from the 16th through the 19th centuries; Johnson's 1755 Dictionary gives it as a standard variant. Its status has receded since, and it now seems to be relegated to dialect and to what H. L. Mencken called the vulgate:

"He said he drunk very little," she reminded me —Ring Lardner, *The Big Town,* 1921

The past participle *drank* is a more complex problem. The OED says that it came in during the 17th century. It seems to have been used commonly at least until Jane Austen's time:

. . . having read somewhere that cold water drank plentifully was good for a fever —Benjamin Franklin, *Autobiography,* 1771

Monboddo dined with me lately, and having drank tea, we were a good while by ourselves —James Boswell, letter, 14 Feb. 1777

It is evening; we have drank tea —Jane Austen, letter, 2 Mar. 1814

Johnson's Dictionary did not give *drank* as a past participle—only *drunk* and *drunken*—but to illustrate one sense of *drink* Johnson quotes Dr. Arbuthnot using *had drank,* and the OED shows that Johnson himself used the form. Hall 1917 cites authors as recent as Robert Louis Stevenson for the form and further informs us that it had in his own time considerable vogue in polite spoken English.

Still, most early 20th-century comment ran against the form. Handbooks such as Utter 1916, Krapp 1927, and Lurie 1927 did not approve it; the editors of Webster's Second (1934) moved it from the main entry of *drink*, where it had been in Webster 1909, and stuck it in the pearl section at the bottom of the page, labeled erroneous.

Linguistic geographers around the middle of the century discovered, however, that the handbooks and Webster's Second were treating *drank* with less respect than it deserved. It was still in polite spoken use in some parts of the U.S. and Canada, and indeed was the majority use in a few areas. It is primarily a spoken form, but it does pop up from time to time in prose written by someone whose dialect still contains the form:

> Two inmates at the Berkshire County House of Correction were taken to Hillcrest Hospital Tuesday evening after they had reportedly drank Lysol —*Springfield* (Mass.) *Morning Union,* 21 Nov. 1984

In writing, you will want to use the past *drank* and the past participle *drunk*. The past *drunk* is essentially dialectal. The past participle *drank* is still in standard spoken use in some parts of the U.S. and Canada, but it is seldom used in print.

See also DRUNK, DRUNKEN.

drought, drouth These variant spellings for the dry spell receive more diverse comment than you would suspect: Shaw 1987, Harper 1985, and Watt 1967 say that both are correct but that *drought* is more common than *drouth*. Our evidence confirms this. Copperud 1980 finds *drouth* in greater favor, a comment that is not supported by our evidence. Longman 1984 says that *drouth* is poetic except in Irish, Scottish, and North American English; our evidence cannot dispute this. Evans 1957 calls *drouth* dialectal in England, but standard and interchangeable with *drought* in the U.S.; our evidence shows that *drouth* was more common in 1957 than it is now. The Oxford American Dictionary says that careful writers and speakers do not use *drouth*. This remark is simply not true; Burchfield 1996 has several examples from standard sources, and we have some others:

> 'Tis not enough on roots and in the mouth,
> But give me water heavy on the head
> In all the passion of a broken drouth
> —Robert Frost, *A Witness Tree,* 1942

> . . . the desolation, the aesthetic and spiritual drouth, of Anglo-Saxon middle-class society —Edmund Wilson, *Axel's Castle,* 1931

> A drouth or a plague of insects may cause crop failure along the river —Charles F. Hockett, *Man's Place in Nature,* 1973

At the present time, *drouth* is less frequent than *drought* in American English, but both forms are standard.

drown 1. *Drowned, drownded.* Sometime between the age of Chaucer and that of Shakespeare, several English verbs ending with a nasal vowel acquired an unetymological *-d* at the end. The added *-d* became permanent in some of these: *astound, lend, sound.*

Drown was one of the verbs that acquired an intrusive *d.* The variant *drownd,* says the *OED,* flourished in the 16th and 17th centuries. By the 18th century it seems to have been felt to be dialectal: Swift puts it into the mouth of Tom Neverout in *Polite Conversation* (1738):

> . . . don't throw Water on a drownded Rat.

But other characters in this piece say *drown'd*; for instance, Colonel Atwit:

> . . . he that is born to be hang'd, will never be drown'd.

Drownd was apparently first attacked by John Witherspoon in *The Druid,* 16 May 1781, who called it "a vulgarism in England and America" (cited in Mencken 1963, abridged). It has been used in rural humor:

> "Mebby I shall be drounded on dry land, Josiah Allen, but I don't believe it." —Marietta Holley, "A Pleasure Exertion," in *Mark Twain's Library of Humor,* 1888

It is still put into the mouths of fictional characters of rural background or of little education. It is no longer part of standard written or spoken English.

2. *Drowned, was drowned.* It is a convention of newspaper writers and editors that *drowned* should be used for an accidental drowning, and *was drowned* for an intentional drowning. Thus, "she drowned in the lake" should imply an accident, and "she was drowned in the lake" should bring *An American Tragedy* to mind.

The convention may be usefully observed in journalistic reports of drownings, but it is not much observed in other kinds of writing, especially when there is no implication of foul play:

> . . . Cessair, a fictitious granddaughter of Noah, comes to Ireland forty days early to escape the Flood . . . only to be drowned . . . with her brother and fifty maidens — George Brandon Saul, *The Shadow of the Three Queens,* 1953

Unless you are reporting an actual drowning, you probably need not worry about using the passive.

drunk, drunken The usual observation is that *drunk* is regularly used as a predicate adjective and that *drunken* is usual in the attributive position, before the modified noun. This observation is, in general, still true.

Drunk is used both literally and figuratively as a predicate adjective:

> By nine he was incoherently drunk —Gregory McDonald, *Fletch,* 1974

> . . . he was drunk with the shape and sound of words —Morris Dickstein, *N.Y. Times Book Rev.,* 3 July 1983

Overall it has only occasional attributive use in speech:

> It occurred to me then that no general can win a war with a drunk army —Jesse Jackson, quoted by Robert Friedman, *Esquire,* December 1979

But it is regularly used attributively before the words *driver* and *driving.* It has been so used for some time, judging from the frequency with which Theodore Bernstein censured its appearance in the *New York Times,* and, especially since the 1980s, it is preferred in that use:

> . . . the Europeans are particularly tough on drunk driving —Paul Hoffman, *Saturday Rev.,* 10 Feb. 1973

> . . . about three Americans are killed and 80 are injured by drunk drivers every hour of every day —*Newsweek,* 13 Sept. 1982

> Law enforcement is only one part of the nationwide campaign against drunk drivers —editorial, *Springfield* (Mass.) *Daily News,* 16 Dec. 1985

When *drunk* is a past participle modifying a noun, it may also precede the noun:

> . . . and a half drunk cup of black coffee . . . on the bedside table —Tim Cahill, *Rolling Stone,* 2 Mar. 1972

Drunken is the usual choice in attributive uses with words other than *driver* or *driving*:

> The drunken slaughter over the past decade is a staggering one-quarter of a million Americans —*Newsweek,* 13 Sept. 1982

Drunken, rather than *drunk,* is used to indicate habitual drinking as distinguished from a state of intoxication. In this use it may even be found as a predicate adjective:

> A brother drinks and the family is dubbed drunken —Carll Tucker, *Saturday Rev.,* 23 June 1979

dual A thousand years ago and more, Old English had a grammatical number system consisting of singular (for one), dual (for two),

and plural (for more than two). The plural long ago supplanted the dual, and all we have as reminders of its former existence are such words as *either, neither, between, both, other,* and *whether,* whose ancestors were connected with it. These words and the comparative inflection *-er* can still serve to remind us of things in twos. but the notion is greatly weakened now and in some instances nearly forgotten. It is, however, useful to remember how long the formal dual number has been defunct when a commentator invokes it to justify a supposed limitation on usage.

dual comparison See AS GOOD OR BETTER THAN.

dubious, doubtful Is it permissible to say that you are dubious about something? Follett 1966 states that "when the word is used with discrimination, the doubt is elsewhere than in the person or thing described as *dubious*. This person or thing is the object of doubt by another or others, not the author or abode of doubt." Macmillan 1982 is of the same opinion. Garner 1998 finds the use acceptable. *Dubious* certainly has been used—even by writers of discrimination—to mean "doubting, unsettled in opinion, suspicious."

> Mr. Cruncher was soothed, but shook his head in a dubious and moral way —Charles Dickens, *A Tale of Two Cities,* 1859

> When I was hired, old George was dubious, and with reason, because as a salesman I was tongue-tied —Bill Gerry, *Yale Rev.,* Winter 1948

> . . . one project about which their top management was very dubious —Peter F. Drucker, *Harper's,* January 1972

due to Concern over the propriety of *due to* is a long-lived controversy that began in the 18th century as a mere adjunct to a dispute about *owing to.* Johnson's Dictionary of 1755 noted under *owe* that a writer avoided *owing to* by using *due to.* Johnson thought *due* was used only of debt, and ignored *due to.* But he did enter it in a later edition with a quotation and the annotation. "proper, but not usual."

Handbooks of the 19th and early 20th centuries repeated Johnson's original comments on *due* (at *owe*), but with Utter 1916, MacCracken & Sandison 1917, Fowler 1926, and Krapp 1927, the sense "attributable" is acceptable as long as *due* is clearly an adjective; when *due to* is used as a preposition introducing a phrase that modifies anything but a particular noun, it is objectionable. A new issue has been born, and subsequent commentators have generally followed the newer line of attack.

Owing to and *due to* developed along precisely parallel lines, according to a detailed study by John S. Kenyon published in *American Speech,* October 1930. The difference is that *owing to* crept imperceptibly into use as a preposition while the focus of criticism was on the active-passive issue. *Due to* did not begin life as a preposition until nearly the 20th century (the OED Supplement has an 1897 citation). Once the critics noticed the new use, they laid aside all objections and belabored *due to* for its new function.

The basic argument is this: *due to* is all right when it clearly has a noun or pronoun to modify or when it follows a linking verb:

> . . . the failure to nail currant jelly to a wall is not due to the nail —Theodore Roosevelt, 1915, quoted by William Safire, *N.Y. Times,* 6 Apr. 1986

> It must be due to my lack of polish —Robert Frost, letter, 25 Apr. 1915

But when there is no linking verb, the construction is suspect:

> Although I myself, due doubtless to defective skill, have to work pretty hard — George Jean Nathan, *Testament of a Critic,* 1931

> . . . Ross is famous for his old conviction that women do not belong in offices. This has mellowed somewhat, partly due to his discovery during the war that several of them could be as competent as men —James Thurber, letter, 6 Sept. 1947

> . . . there is an outside chance at least that Ben Reid—due to those considerations of environment and mentality . . . —may have his sentence commuted —William Styron, *This Quiet Dust and Other Writings,* 1982

Perhaps it is time for the critics to find a new basis for disparaging *due to.* A sure sign of the knee-jerk quality of the present objections is beginning to appear in careless restatements of them. Two college handbooks of the 1980s call *due to* an adjective rather than a preposition, for example. A general handbook of the same time says that *due to* is a wordy way of saying *because. Because,* however, is a conjunction and *due to* is a preposition; *due to* competes with *because of.*

In our judgment, *due to* is as impeccable grammatically as *owing to,* which is frequently recommended as a substitute for it. There never has been a grammatical ground for objection. The preposition is used by reputable writers and is even officially part of the Queen's English—the OED Supplement gives a quotation from Queen Elizabeth II. There is no solid reason to avoid using *due to.*

due to the fact that Most of the commentators who mention this phrase condemn it as "wordy for *because.*" There are a couple of things you should keep in mind when presented with such advice. First, remember that, being human, we tend to see wordiness as a characteristic of someone else's writing; we ourselves always use just the right number of words.

> Most importantly, remember that *due to the fact that* is a wordy way of saying the short and simple word *since* —Shaw 1970

Second, it is a good idea to test the advice in a real context. Here are a few examples:

> The success of the Channel 13 report was due mainly to the fact that it let both sides . . . speak for themselves —Stephanie Harrington, *Village Voice,* 28 Feb. 1968

Would you improve this passage by changing it to "was mainly because it . . ." or "was mainly since it . . ."?

> This is due to the fact that the cost of prescription drugs borders on the exorbitant —Henry Gewirtz & Saxon Graham, *Trans-Action,* February 1970

"This is because" is usable here (*since* is not). You should be aware, though, that there is a considerable amount of opinion to the effect that *because* should not be used to introduce a clause functioning as a noun, though *because* is indeed often so used. So our handbook writers, in effect, recommend a usage here that they warn you against elsewhere in the book.

But enough. You can usually work your way around *due to the fact that,* if you want to. But you obviously cannot simply replace it with *because* or *since* in every context. Adding *the fact that* to *due to* allows the preposition to function as a conjunction; it may even come in handy sometime.

dumb Commentators as far apart as Utter 1916 and Harper 1985 have decried the use of *dumb* to mean stupid. In spite of the opposition of these commentators, the usage has become well established, even in writing:

> He assured me that musical people, though singularly dumb, were so sexually depraved that we could acquire platoons of budding sopranos for the price of a Coke and a hamburger —Russell Baker, *Growing Up,* 1982

The result of this sense's becoming established is that the "mute" sense of *dumb* has come to be considered offensive to those persons who cannot speak. The substitute usually recommended is *mute.*

dummy subject See THERE IS, THERE ARE.

dwell 1. Although there are two spellings, *dwelt* and *dwelled,* for the past tense of *dwell,* the original form *dwelled* has steadily lost ground over the centuries. *Dwelled* is still used, but *dwelt* is found far more often:

> . . . the great-hearted . . . sufferer who dwelt behind the hulking and lugubrious facade —William Styron, *This Quiet Dust and Other Writings,* 1982

> . . . it was on Roelf that her eyes dwelt and rested —Edna Ferber, *So Big,* 1924

> He dwelled on his own sensations and liked to talk about them —E. L. Doctorow, *Ragtime,* 1975

2. Some language commentators warn against using *dwell* when (to them) the more everyday word *live* is meant. The commentators were contending as far back as the early part of the 20th century that *dwell* had given way in use to *live.* While *live* may be the more common usage, *dwell* has by no means disappeared:

> . . . now dwells within a half-mile of a subway —*American Guide Series: N.Y. City,* 1939

> . . . less [people] than had dwelled in his own town —C. S. Forester, *The Sky and the Forest,* 1948

> . . . I learned that she dwelt at 16 Charlotte Street —Samuel Flagg Bemis, *New-England Galaxy,* Fall 1969

3. *Dwell* may take any of any number of prepositions. In addition to *behind, on, within,* and *at* (shown in the quotations above), *dwell* is used with *among, beneath, outside, over, under, upon,* and *with:*

> . . . God . . . taking flesh and coming down and dwelling among us as a man —Samuel Butler, *The Way of All Flesh,* 1903

> . . . "by my twin soul which dwells beneath the banana plant, will I do it!" —Charles Beadle, *Witch-Doctors,* 1922

> . . . elements of the society which support but dwell outside the campus —Anthony Lambeth, *Change,* Summer 1971

> It is useless to dwell over the sufferings of these heroic men —John Buchan, *The Last Secrets,* 1923

> One cannot turn over any old falsehood without a terrible squirming and scattering of the unpleasant little population that dwells under it —Van Wyck Brooks, *The Flowering of New England, 1815–1865,* rev. ed., 1946

> . . . divert attention from the sorrow and prevent the sufferer from dwelling upon it —Edith Sitwell, *I Live Under a Black Sun,* 1937

> Yet Goldsmith has a peculiar reticence which forbids us to dwell with him in complete intimacy —Virginia Woolf, *The Captain's Death Bed and Other Essays,* 1950 ed.

To judge by the evidence found in the Merriam-Webster citation files, *dwell* is used most often with *on,* followed by *in* and *upon.* The other prepositions are used less frequently.

dying, dyeing Several commentators warn, sensibly enough, against the careless use of *dying,* the present participle of *die,* when *dyeing,* the present participle of *dye,* is intended.

E

each There are a number of niggling problems about *each* and its agreement with either verb or pronoun. These problems mostly were discovered in the 18th century, when the conflict of grammatical agreement and notional agreement first began to trouble grammarians. We will take up a few of these separately. See also AGREEMENT: INDEFINITE PRONOUNS.
1. *Each,* pronoun, as simple subject. The rule of thumb from the 18th century on has been that *each* takes a singular verb. This is the usual case in modern practice:

> . . . for each who achieves it —*Times Literary Supp.,* 28 Mar. 1968

> Each derives its authority directly from the Constitution —*N.Y. Times Mag.,* 27 Feb. 1955

Notional agreement interferes with the singularity of *each* only when *each* has a plural antecedent. In this case, a plural verb may be used.

> . . . in Naples a number of families will join in a carriage, and each have their own emblazoned doors —*The Journals of Arnold Bennett,* ed. Frank Swinnerton, 1954

> . . . the quarrel scene between the two leaders was superbly conducted and each die in the grand manner —T. C. Worsley, *Britain To-Day,* June 1953

Sticklers for grammatical agreement will insist on a singular verb, and the singular is more usual.
2. *Each,* pronoun, followed by a phrase introduced by *of.* Since the *of* phrase always con-

tains a plural noun or pronoun, notional plurality is strong in these constructions. Those who always insist on grammatical agreement insist on the singular verb, but Copperud 1970, 1980 notes that the commentators he summarizes are evenly split on the propriety of the plural verb. Copperud also says that instances of *each (of)* with a plural verb are increasing in carefully edited prose. First a few examples with singular verbs:

Each of them is a decisive way —Ronald Reagan, *Abortion and the Conscience of the Nation,* 1984

But each of us harbors our own special interests —Tom Lewis, *Harper's Weekly,* 26 July 1976

And each of them was busy in arranging their particular concerns —Jane Austen, *Sense and Sensibility,* 1811 (in Hodgson 1889)

Now some plural examples:

Each of the novel's four strong, articulate, and high-energy women are in their mid-thirties —Donna Seaman, *Booklist,* 1 Apr. 1992

. . . it will be well and decorous that each of us appoint several consulting surgeons —Mark Twain, *A Tramp Abroad,* 1880

. . . how important each of the possible harms and benefits are —Robert Charles Clark, *Corporate Law,* 1986

It seems likely that notional agreement is the decisive force in most of these examples, singular and plural. If you are thinking of *each* as individualizing, you will use the singular verb; if you think of it as collecting, you will use the plural. Both singular and plural are standard, but singular is much more common.

3. *Each,* adjective, following a plural noun subject. The usage panel of Heritage 1969 rejected "they each have large followings" by a whopping 95 percent. They were marching alone, apparently; Copperud 1970, 1980 cites his commentators (except the panel) as accepting the plural verb, while Heritage 1982, Chambers 1985, Johnson 1982, Freeman 1983, Garner 1998, and Bernstein 1958 all allow it. Heritage 1982 also approves the plural pronoun in such instances. The examples of this construction in our files are plural:

. . . they each have too many possible meanings —Linda Costigan Lederman, *New Dimensions,* 1977

Our containerboard mills each conduct five-year programs —*Annual Report, Owens-Illinois,* 1970

Gates and Mifflin each publicly avowed

their entire confidence in Washington —Horace E. Scudder, *George Washington,* 1885

4. Pronoun reference. It is abundantly clear that *each* shares with many indefinite pronouns the tendency to take a plural pronoun in reference, and equally clear that notional agreement rules in most instances, singular or plural. Nonetheless, use of a plural pronoun in reference to *each* has often been censured, for example by Lurie 1927, Follett 1966, Phythian 1979, and Heritage 1982. Garner 1998 disapproves too, but does note the use of the plural pronouns to avoid the problems of sexism. Here are some examples in which the notion of *each* is singular:

Each house shall keep a journal of its proceedings —*Constitution of the United States,* 1787

The romanticist and the realist try to capture them, each in his own way —Leacock 1943

. . . to each according to his weakness and his heart's desire —Glenway Wescott, *Prose,* Fall 1971

Each claimed as of right the part which came nearest to his or her speciality; and each played all his or her parts in exactly the same way —George Bernard Shaw, preface, *The Shaw–Terry Letters,* 1931

More often, however, the notion is plural:

I found myself that same morning with three or four of the groundkeepers, each of us with a pick or shovel on our shoulders —E. L. Doctorow, *Loon Lake,* 1979

. . . but in lowliness of mind let each esteem other better than themselves —Philippians 2:3 (AV), 1611

Each in their own way, the Indians, Indo-Chinese and Indonesians, were asking —*Time,* 3 Dec. 1945

Each in their way broke fresh ground —*Times Literary Supp.,* 5 Nov. 1971

Note that *each,* like other indefinite pronouns, partakes of that idiomatic construction in which the pronoun takes a singular verb but a plural pronoun:

And each of them was busy in arranging their particular concerns, and endeavoring, by placing around them their books and other possessions —Jane Austen, *Sense and Sensibility,* 1811 (in Hodgson 1889)

Each woman enrolled in the WAAC has postponed the induction of a man since they are counted as a man in computing . . . manpower requirements —George C. Marshall, *The United States at War,* 8 Sept. 1943

Each, first of all, has to provide their home listeners with the best possible service —Robert McCall, *BBC Year Book 1952*

In pronoun reference to *each,* trust notional agreement.

5. *Each,* pronoun, referring to a plural subject, but following the verb. Copperud 1970 reports the agreement of Fowler 1965 and Bernstein 1965 that when *each* follows the verb, the reference to the subject should be singular; Copperud gives this example:

We are each responsible for his own family.

Not only does the example seem awkward, but the Merriam-Webster files have not a single example of the prescribed form with the singular. Actual usage seems to prefer the plural:

. . . strong unsubsidized lines can each carry their share of money-losing routes —*Time,* 17 May 1954

Bernstein and Fowler appear to be agreeing on theory only; the examples they present have plural pronouns. Our files have very few examples of this particular construction, which suggests this problem may be relatively uncommon.

each and every *Each and every* is an emphatic form, damned on all sides (Copperud 1970, 1980, Watt 1967, Shaw 1975, Bryson 1984, Janis 1984, Garner 1998, and more) as pompous, redundant, wordy, officialese, trite, and a cliché—a wide-ranging selection from the language critic's stock of disapproving descriptors. Strunk & White 1972, 1979 calls it "pitchman's jargon," to be avoided except in dialogue. It is, in fact, used in fictional speech. In this example, the author has purposely created a context that seems to justify the critics' adjectives:

"My friends, the time has come when each and every one of us must face the fact that pornography, no matter what disguise it wears, still remains outright obscenity and a threat to our families, to our future, and to the health of this great nation. . . ." —Irving Wallace, *The Seven Minutes,* 1969

But mostly *each and every* is simply used as an emphatic modifier:

When you pick an investment return—say 8 percent—the calculators assume that you get the return each and every year —Jane Bryant Quinn, *Newsweek,* 25 Oct. 1999

By now, every woman knows it's all right not to get an orgasm each and every time

she goes to bed with a man —Jane DeLynn, *Cosmopolitan,* December 1976

The evidence suggests that writers fail to take the strictures of the commentators very seriously and that they use *each and every* simply as an emphatic form of *each* or *every* or they use it, as Irving Wallace did in his fictional political speech, to help achieve a particular effect. It is available for you to use, if it seems useful, or to avoid, if it strikes you as it does the commentators.

each other **1.** *Each other, one another.* Bardeen 1883 indicates that the use of *each other* for *one another* is legitimate, though carped at by some critics; he lists Ayres 1881. Actually the prescriptive rule that *each other* is to be restricted to two and *one another* to more than two goes back even farther. Goold Brown 1851 cites the rule with approbation, and quotes it from an even earlier grammarian, one T. O. Churchill (*A New Grammar of the English Language,* London, 1823). But Churchill did not invent the rule. Sundby et al. 1991 have found it in a 1785 grammar by a George N. Ussher. Goold Brown also notes that "misapplications of the foregoing reciprocal terms are very frequent in books" and goes on to cite Samuel Johnson and Noah Webster in error. He further notes that "it is strange that phrases so very common should not be rightly understood." It is easier now to see why: evidence in the OED shows that the restriction has never existed in practice; the interchangeability of *each other* and *one another* had been established centuries before Ussher or somebody even earlier thought up the rule.

Fowler 1926 notes that some writers follow the rule but goes on to state that "the differentiation is neither of present utility nor based on historical usage. . . ." Even Fowler's high reputation among usage commentators has not convinced those to whom the rule is dear; many, at least as recently as Garner 1998, still prescribe it. A few examples may illustrate the rule's baselessness:

Sixteen ministers who meet weekly at each other's houses —Samuel Johnson, *Life of Swift* (in Brown 1851)

The spouse aspires to an union with Christ, their mutual love for one another —chapter gloss, *Canticle of Canticles* (Douay Version), 1609

Two negatives in English destroy one another —Lowth 1763

It is a bad thing that men should hate each other; but it is far worse that they should contract the habit of cutting one another's throats without hatred —T. B. Macaulay (in Webster 1909)

. . . Janet and Marcia would, by way of greeting, neigh at one another —John Updike, *Couples,* 1968

They had been marrying one another for so many centuries that they had bred into themselves just the qualities, ignorance and idiocy, they could least afford. At the funeral of Edward VII in London they had pushed and shoved and elbowed each other like children for places in the cortege —E. L. Doctorow, *Ragtime,* 1975

A few commentators believe the rule to be followed in "formal discourse." This belief will not bear examination: Samuel Johnson's discourse is perhaps the most consistently formal that exists in English literature, and he has been cited in violation of the rule.

We conclude that the rule restricting *each other* to two and *one another* to more than two is simply an invention. There is no sin in its violation. It is, however, easy and painless to observe if you so wish.

2. *Each other's, one another's.* Goold Brown 1851 cites some unidentified writer as using *each others',* which he finds wrong in that instance. In Johnson's use, cited above, however, he thinks *each others'* more logical. The evidence in Merriam-Webster files indicates that the possessive is regularly *each other's, one another's.* We have no evidence that Goold Brown's reasoning has been followed.

Johnson 1982 notes that the following noun can be either singular or plural; our evidence agrees:

. . . all entities or factors in the universe are essentially relevant to each other's existence —Alfred North Whitehead, *Essays in Science and Philosophy,* 1947

. . . its members still frequently exchange visits to each other's homes —*Current Biography,* January 1968

3. Henry Bradley, in the *E* volume of the OED, observes that the use of *each other* as the subject of a clause is "a vulgarism occasionally heard"; he does not, however, present evidence substantiation or quoted example. Fowler 1926 and Partridge 1942 agree; so does Heritage 2000. Evidence in the Merriam-Webster files indicates that such use is nearly nonexistent in edited prose. If *each other* is by now a fully established pronoun, there is no grammatical reason it could not be the subject of a clause, but it is simply not so used.

eager When *eager* is used with a preposition, the preposition is usually *to* and an infinitive:

He himself was eager to have the Cathedral begun —Willa Cather, *Death Comes for the Archbishop,* 1927

. . . wine connoisseurs eager to visit cellars and late-fall pilgrims seeking the increasingly rare white truffle —Corby Kummer, *Atlantic,* August 2000

Although in the past *eager* was used with a variety of prepositions besides *to,* the Merriam-Webster files attest to the continuing use of only *for* and *in* during the last 100 years. *Eager for* is much more frequent than *eager in* today.

. . . all were eager for more trips —Ruth Saberski Goldenheim, *Barnard Alumnae,* Winter 1971

. . . so many religions were steeped in an absolutist frame of mind—each convinced that it alone had a monoploy on the truth and therefore eager for the state to impose this truth on others —Carl Sagan, *The Demon-Haunted World,* 1996

. . . he was less learned than swift and eager in his reading —Horace Gregory, *The Shield of Achilles,* 1944

early on This adverb is sometimes objected to in American writing as an obtrusive Briticism. It is a relative newcomer to the language, having arisen in British English around 1928.

'It might have been *given* him earlier.' . . . 'Well—not too early on, Peter. Suppose he had died a lot too soon.' —Dorothy L. Sayers, *The Unpleasantness at the Bellona Club,* 1928 (OED Supplement)

Early on came into frequent use in American English in the late 1960s and is now well established as standard on both sides of the Atlantic.

Early on, I was a conservative, snobby, Buckley type —Gore Vidal, quoted in *Look,* 29 July 1969

But the biggest impact of the Napster effect is yet to come. From early on, Shawn Fanning saw his program as "a cool way to build community" —Steven Levy, *Newsweek,* 27 Mar. 2000

. . . very early on, Samuel Johnson learnt to fear the hours of stagnant idleness —John Wain, *Samuel Johnson,* 1974

earth The names of planets other than our own are invariably capitalized, but *earth* is more often than not lowercased. Capitalization is most likely when the earth is being referred to in astronomical terms:

. . . the effects which the cosmos has on the planet Earth —David W. Hughes, *Nature,* 14 June 1969

When the other planets are also referred to, there is some tendency both to capitalize

Earth and to omit the definite article *the* which normally precedes it:

> . . . for the moon, Mercury, Venus, Mars, and Earth —Brian T. O'Leary et al., *Science,* 15 Aug. 1969

Some writers, however, choose to lowercase *earth* and to include *the* even when referring to the other planets:

> The earth is uniquely favored among the planets. . . . The large planets (Jupiter, Saturn, Uranus and Neptune) have only a small solid core —Sir Edward Bullard, *Scientific American,* September 1969

Both treatments are perfectly acceptable.

easy, easily As an adverb, *easy* has a long history of reputable use. It dates back to the 14th century and can be found in the works of such authors as Spenser, Shakespeare, and Byron. In current English it has many uses, most of which have a somewhat informal quality:

> . . . Bauer knows when to go easy on players —*Current Biography,* February 1967

> In the daytime I'm working in the studios, $10 an hour. Making $300, $400 a week easy —Jimmy McPartland, quoted in Studs Terkel, *Hard Times,* 1970

> . . . lets no one off easy —Richard Howard, *N.Y. Times Book Rev.,* 24 Nov. 1974

> Go easy on the salad dressing —Martha Smilgis, *People,* 21 July 1980

> Take it easy when you first start a new exercise program —Martha Davis Dunn et al., *Living, Learning, and Caring,* 1981

These uses of *easy* are, in general, distinct from the uses of *easily. Easily* is a more common adverb than *easy,* and it has a wider range of applications. It often comes before the verb it modifies, in which position *easy* is not possible:

> . . . need not be so easily fooled —Stephen Steinberg, *Commentary,* January 1972

Easily usually cannot be replaced idiomatically by *easy,* even when it follows the verb:

> . . . seem to be able to suppress the drug's effects easily —Solomon H. Snyder, *Psychology Today,* May 1971

> . . . a gentleman who moves easily in exalted circles —John Thompson, *Harper's,* October 1971

In contexts where both adverbs are possible (such as "Laughs come easy" or "Laughs come easily"), you should choose whichever seems most natural and most appropriate to the tone of your writing.

Since *easy* is an adverb, its comparative *easier* is not an error, as Garner 1998 asserts.

> . . . says he wants to travel less, take things easier —Kim Masters, *Vanity Fair,* March 1996

> His health was bad . . . but his response was to arrest the Kremlin doctors who told him to take things easier —Norman Stone, *Times Literary Supp.,* Mar. 1991

echelon *Echelon* is originally a French word meaning literally "a rung on a ladder." It was borrowed into English in the late 18th century in a figurative sense denoting a step-like military formation, and it remained primarily a military word for about 150 years, developing additional senses during that time. One military sense it had developed by the end of World War II was "a level in a chain of command":

> It is a principle that a higher echelon maintain communications to the next lower echelon —*Coast Artillery Jour.,* November–December 1944

In this sense, *echelon* began to be applied to civilian as well as military organizations:

> . . . twelve men who formed the party's top echelon —*Newsweek,* 2 Aug. 1948

This is now the most common use of *echelon.*

Several commentators have objected to the popular extended sense of *echelon,* essentially because they regard it as overused. However, as Copperud 1980 notes, the new sense "is now so popular that uprooting it would be a fearsome task.' It would, in fact, be impossible.

ecology *Ecology* is a scientific word that in recent years has come into widespread use among nonscientists. In its oldest sense, it means "a branch of science concerned with the interrelationship of organisms and their environments." It can also refer in scientific use to the interrelationship itself, rather than to the study of it:

> . . . must be sought among the complex interactions of living organisms and their environments, in other words, in their ecologies —George L. Rotramel, *Systematic Zoology,* September 1973

This use of *ecology* is well established and above reproach. The difficulties that arise with *ecology* have to do with its use by general (nonscientific) writers to mean "the environment." Several recent commentators have noted and criticized this use of the word. Our files contain a few clear-cut examples of it:

> As to the furor over the ecology, it seems to me that its proponents are jousting wind-

mills —letter to the editor, *Johns Hopkins Mag.*, Spring 1971

And it not only saves money; it's good for the ecology, too —television commentator, 30 Aug. 1977

Most of our evidence for *ecology* in this sense is from the early 1970s, when the environmental movement was first coming into its own and its terminology was still relatively new and unfamiliar to many people. No doubt *ecology* is still sometimes used to mean "environment," but our evidence suggests that such usage, which was never very common, is becoming increasingly rare. A current writer or speaker is far more likely to use *environment* than *ecology* in such contexts.

economic, economical *Economic,* which usually refers to economics or an economy, has a wider range of application than *economical,* which usually refers to the quality of economy and means "thrifty" or "not wasteful." The discussion of these words in usage books generally consists of a description of their separate meanings and an injunction not to confuse the two.

However, many *-ic* and *-ical* adjectives (such as *geologic* and *geological* or *symmetrical* and *symmetric*) are variant forms of the same word and are partially or wholly synonymous with each other, so it is not surprising to find that occasionally there is some crossover of meaning between *economic* and *economical.*

. . . he plays remarkably pure, fundamental, indeed economic basketball —David Halberstam, *Inside Sports,* 30 Apr. 1980

. . . the political, economical and cultural history of Europe —Geoffrey Bruun, *N.Y. Herald Tribune Book Rev.,* 21 June 1953

You can easily avoid such crossover if you wish.

ecstacy Copperud 1980 says that *ecstacy* is "likely to be regarded as a misspelling; only Webster gives it as a variant." The Webster he's referring to is Webster's Third, which lists it as a relatively uncommon variant of *ecstasy.* These citations from our files show why *ecstacy* was included:

I get carried away in an ecstacy of mendacity —George Bernard Shaw, *Man and Superman,* 1903

. . . his meditations approached ecstacy —Thornton Wilder, *The Cabala,* 1926

. . . religious ecstacy —*Harper's,* June 1969

Although *ecstacy* is definitely an infrequent variant, it has been in use since the late 17th century. It persists because *-acy* words (as *celibacy, delicacy, democracy, diplomacy, fal-*

lacy, intestacy, privacy) are much more numerous in English than *-asy* words (as *apostasy, fantasy*).

ect. See ETC.

edifice This word has been cited as a pompous synonym for *building* by commentators dating back as far as Fowler 1926, but our evidence suggests that pomposity is not so much a characteristic of the word itself as of the buildings it describes. *Edifice* almost always refers to a large, massive, and imposing structure, in which use it is not pompous but descriptively appropriate:

The lastest Hilton edifice is scheduled to open for business in July in Beverly Hills. It is a $15,000,000 450-room hideaway on an eight-acre tract —Gladwin Hill, *N.Y. Times,* 10 Apr. 1955

. . . an immense, cupolaed edifice of red brick on the hill —Richard Wolkomir, *Vermont Life,* Winter 1969

editorial we See WE 1.

educationist, educationalist In British English, *educationist* is an ordinary word synonymous with *educator:*

The author is a well-known educationist who for twenty years has taught at St. Luke's College —*Times Literary Supp.,* 2 Apr. 1970

But in American English, *educationist* rarely describes an actual, specific person. It most often serves instead as a term of disparagement for a stereotypically muddleheaded educational theorist, whose dubious ideas have contributed greatly—in the writer's view—to the downfall of American education:

. . . the educationist is someone who can take an easy subject and make it difficult —Dr. Laurence T. Peter, *The Peter Prescription,* 1972

. . . English grammar has been denigrated by large numbers of influential educationists —Thomas H. Middleton, *Saturday Rev.,* 1 Mar. 1980

The variant *educationalist* is primarily British:

The title of this book is guaranteed to make even the hardened educationalist stifle a yawn —Noël Gilroy Annan, *Times Literary Supp.,* 11 Apr. 1986

It seems to be relatively little used.

educator A few commentators have called *educator* a pompous synonym for *teacher.* Evans 1957 notes that it is more often used of administrators in education than of actual teachers, and our evidence confirms this. *Educator* is also used to denote a scholar or theorist in the field of education. Its application to an actual teacher is relatively rare and usually carries implications of responsibility or achievement outside the classroom.

> Margaret Mead, sociologist, anthropologist, educator, philosopher —Donald Robinson, *Ladies' Home Jour.,* January 1971

-ee One of the two suffixes *-ee* in English—the one in *trainee,* not the one in *bootee*—comes via Middle English from Middle French. It has proved surprisingly productive in English and is used in many words where its use would have been prohibited in French. These extensions of the suffix, Jespersen 1905 tells us, first took place in legal language and later reached the general language. The most common use of the suffix is to form what Jespersen calls "passive nouns"—that is, nouns designating the receiver of the action of a verb, words like *appointee, draftee, grantee.*

A number of observers are not especially pleased with the productiveness of the suffix; they discourage the coining of such words. But *-ee* is often used for nonce coinages, often for humorous effect. There seems to be a long-standing tradition of easy witticism based on contrasting *-er* (or *-or*) and *-ee* forms. It can be found as far back as Laurence Sterne (who, interestingly enough, felt the suffix still to be French):

> The *Mortgager* and *Mortgagée* differ the one from the other, not more in length of purse, than the *Jester* and *Jestée* do, in that of memory —*Tristram Shandy,* 1760

And so it has gone, down to our own time. It is probably this sort of joking that lends the humorous or whimsical quality to many coinages:

> I have . . . a luncheon engagement for Friday which I am now trying to break. The lunchee is out of town —Archibald MacLeish, letter, 24 Nov. 1931

> In times past I was the giver; now things are reversed, and I'm the givee —Harry S. Truman, diary, 14 Feb. 1948

But not all coinages with *-ee* are whimsical or facetious; your dictionary will show you quite a few that have stuck around as useful.

Some of these same commentators may not like the receiver-of-an-action *-ee* but have been pushed into embracing it by the appearance of another sense of the suffix that can be viewed as nearly synonymous with *-er,* that designates more of a doer than a receiver. Gowers in Fowler 1965, for instance, abominates *escapee* (which see). Gowers is about a century too late to prevent the establishment of *escapee* (and so are Follett 1966 and Nick-

les 1974). Since *absentee* (1605) is about the earliest of the productions of this sense of *-ee,* you can see how untimely and futile are the complaints. Another commonly mentioned example is *standee,* which has been with us since around 1880. They may be illogical if the receiver sense is taken as the logical norm, but it's just too late for logicians to turn back the clock. All we can do is accept the fact that a number of these formations exist, as Safire 1982 advises. You do not have to use them yourself, of course.

effect, affect *Effect* and *affect* are probably the two most frequently looked up words in the dictionary, and for good reason. There are two verbs *affect.* The first means, among other things, "to make a show of liking; to put on a pretense of," and the second, "to produce an effect in or on, influence." *Effect* has been used for the second of these since at least 1494 and for the first since 1652. Clearly, we are talking about a long-term confusion here. It happens that *effect* is a verb, too, with a meaning roughly "to bring about." And, to complete the picture, both *affect* and *effect* are nouns. Even though *effect* is the only one in common use (*affect* is a technical term in psychology), *affect* is sometimes put in its place.

All of this history of befuddlement has left us with a fat collection of warning notices. Nearly every handbook published in the 20th century—from Vizetelly 1906 to Garner 1998—contains one. Does anybody pay attention? Our evidence suggests that most published writers do, although we have substantial evidence for mistaken usage too. Most likely it is often simply inattention to spelling. Many other of our examples of the mistake probably attest to poor proofreading; a few suggest ordinary inattention in writing.

Here is a handful of correct usages of the several verbs:

> . . . the luxury of contemporary London, which he affected to find nauseating —Paul Fussell, *Samuel Johnson and the Life of Writing,* 1971

> No one at AAI measured how day care affects the company —Andrea Fooner, *Inc. Mag.,* 5 May 1981

> . . . this President has a mandate to effect some serious changes —Andrew Hacker, *N.Y. Times Book Rev.,* 24 Oct. 1982

And of *effect,* noun (we will omit *affect,* noun):

> Economic effects of such high speed change are also unpredictable and somewhat chilling —Genevieve Stuttaford, *Publishers Weekly,* 29 July 1996

> In the Spanish conquest of the Incas, guns played only a minor role. . . . They did pro-

292

duce a big psychological effect on those occasions when they managed to fire —Jared
Diamond, *Guns, Germs, and Steel,* 1997

An unimaginative crescendo of stage effects
—Jon Pareles, *N.Y. Times,* 16 Jan. 1984

The verbs *affect* and *effect* and the nouns *affect* and *effect* are clearly enough differentiated in meaning that it is unlikely that you will
go wrong if you pay attention to your intended meaning. If you are a person who has trouble with this pair of words, you're not alone.
But a check of your dictionary should clear up
any doubts.

effectuate *Effectuate* is not a new verb (it
was first recorded in 1580), but it has something of the quality of an awkward neologism,
and its use has been subject to occasional criticism since the 19th century. It is not a word
that occurs naturally in casual conversation;
most often it occurs in prose having a formal
or legalistic quality, and it describes actions
taken on an official or governmental level:

> . . . the principle that the majority . . . ought
> to be able to effectuate its desires —Thur-
> good Marshall, *Center Mag.,* September
> 1969

> . . . emphasizing the importance of institu-
> tions in effectuating good works —Aaron
> Wildavsky, *N.Y. Times Book Rev.,* 9 Dec.
> 1984

effete *Effete* is derived from the Latin *effe-
tus,* meaning "no longer fruitful." It had some
early use in English in its literal sense, chiefly
describing domestic animals no longer capable of producing offspring, but its principal
English uses have always been figurative.
Until the 20th century, its usual figurative
sense was "exhausted, worn out":

> They find the old governments effete, worn
> out —Edmund Burke, *Reflections on the
> Revolution in France,* 1790 (OED)

But the uses in which the word is now familiar
to most people are not suggestive of exhaus-
tion so much as of overrefinement, weakness
of character, snobbery, and effeminacy. *Effete*
first showed signs of acquiring these shades of
meaning in the 1920s:

> "You're much too effete—that's your great
> shortcomin'. You don't feel—you are no
> child of nature. . . ." —S. S. Van Dine, *The
> Bishop Murder Case,* 1929

But it wasn't until the 1940s that the new *effete*
clearly established itself in reputable writing:

> . . . there are a few critics (principally effete
> members of English Departments) who at-
> tack me in order to belabor the entire tradi-

tion of realism —James T. Farrell, *New Republic,* 28 Oct. 1940

> . . . now and then some effete customer
> would order a stinger or an anisette —John
> Steinbeck, *Cannery Row,* 1945

> She cannot manage masculine men. Her
> males are either overtly effete . . . or pos-
> sessed by a feline power-mania —Edward
> Sackville West, *Horizon,* June 1946

These new uses of *effete* have made it a much
more common word than it ever was in its
"exhausted" sense, which is now almost never
seen.

The new *effete* has received occasional criticism from such commentators as Evans 1957,
Bernstein 1965, Bryson 1984, and Garner
1998, but resistance to it has not been widespread. Current dictionaries routinely recognize it as standard.

e.g. See I.E., E.G.

egregious We agree with some earlier usage
writers that this word's former positive sense
"distinguished, outstanding" has been replaced by a usually pejorative meaning, but
just what that meaning is is harder to pin
down than you might think. It is probably its
nebulous quality that prompted Flesch 1964
to say of *egregious,* "Many people don't know
its exact meaning, and so it's better to avoid
it." However, it can be useful to have available
a word that encompasses a range of meanings
not easily expressed in any other way.

> . . . the egregious Rorschach test, which
> turns students . . . into helpless victims of
> modern diviners —William F. Albright, *N.Y.
> Herald Tribune Book Rev.,* 20 June 1954

> . . . the most egregious idiot —John P.
> Roche, *New Republic,* 24 Jan. 1955

> . . . so many egregious errors —*Times Liter-
> ary Supp.,* 2 May 1968

> . . . a rather egregious box of imitation os-
> trich leather complete with two plastic
> tiger-teeth clasps —*N.Y. Times Book Rev.,* 5
> Dec. 1976

> . . . lines of such egregious insipidity
> —Arthur M. Schlesinger, Jr., *Saturday Rev.,*
> 13 May 1978

> The most egregious padding of the evi-
> dence, in this year's report, concerns Greece
> —Christopher Hitchens, *The Nation,* 10 July
> 2000

either 1. One of the older strictures on the
use of *either* is the objection to its use in the
sense of "each." The examples that seem to
have started the controversy are biblical:

And the king of Israel and Jehoshaphat king of Judah sat either of them on his throne —2 Chronicles 18:9 (AV), 1611

. . . and on either side of the river, was there the tree of life —Revelation 22:2 (AV), 1611

The discoverer of these "improper" uses was Bishop Lowth in 1763. From Lowth the subject was picked up by many other grammarians, including Lindley Murray 1795. Bache 1869 disapproves, as do many commentators in the 20th century.

But the sense had been recognized in Johnson's 1755 Dictionary, and it had a few defenders (Utter 1916) as well as a few who would tolerate it (Ayres 1881), though preferring each. The OED shows the use as an adjective to go back to King Alfred and as a pronoun to about the year 1000. It is the oldest sense of either. And the opposition of the grammarians appears to have had little effect on writers: Hall 1917 lists forty or so writers from the 19th and early 20th century using this sense of either.

Fowler 1926, who had obviously never seen or heard of Hall 1917, decided that the sense was archaic, but Fowler was wrong:

The two men walked one on either side of the cart —James Stephens, The Crock of Gold, 1912

. . . she had a spot of colour in either cheek —Henry James, The American, 1877

Gowers in Fowler 1965 revised the entry to express a preference for each, but he finds either idiomatic. Bernstein 1971 and Harper 1985 find the use acceptable. But what the commentators have not done is to distinguish the adjective use from the pronoun use. If you look back at the two biblical examples, you will see that either is a pronoun in the first and an adjective in the second. If the first sounds a little strange to you, don't be surprised. The pronoun in this sense has pretty much dropped out of use; Webster's Third marks it archaic. The adjective, however—and it was the adjective that Fowler 1926 called archaic—is still in common use, though it is probably not as common as each. Some examples:

An antique torchère and an ornate Ch'ing Dynasty lacquered screen anchor either end of the room —Anthony Haden-Guest, Architectural Digest, November 1985

. . . a majestic sweep of flesh on either side of a small blunt nose —William Faulkner, Sanctuary, 1931

. . . fragilely bound into the house by French windows at either end —F. Scott Fitzgerald, The Great Gatsby, 1925

2. Either of more than two. Now here we have an odd situation. This topic, into which neither is often introduced, is a fairly old one, but the older commentators in our collection—Richard Grant White 1870, Ayres 1881—treat it rather liberally. They find either in relation to more than two to be in use, and both White and Ayres find it a convenient usage that they think will prevail. It is commentators from the late 19th century on (and at least as recent as Trimmer & McCrimmon 1988) who insist on the limitation to two.

Bernstein 1971 in his discussion of the problem distinguishes between the use of either as a conjunction, and as a pronoun and adjective. (Many commentators, such as Garner 1998, do not make this distinction.) He observes that when either is a conjunction, use of more than two is not at all uncommon. Our files confirm his observation:

. . . the scantiest serious attention from either biographers, scholars, or critics —Edmund Wilson, The Wound and the Bow, 1941

. . . Bleak House is topped either by Pickwick, David Copperfield, or Great Expectations —Alexander Woollcott, letter, 21 Feb. 1941

The majority of his paintings feature either children, fishermen or old people —This England, Autumn 1983

Use of the pronoun for more than two, on the other hand, is fairly uncommon:

. . . beside him was a telephone through which he could communicate with anyone, on either of the three trains —Hector Bolitho, A Century of British Monarchy, 1951

We have no really recent examples of the pronoun used of three or more, and we have almost none at all of the adjective. You can therefore conclude that either is rarely used of more than two when a pronoun or adjective, but that the conjunction is commonly so used.

3. A minor question raised in a few recent handbooks has to do with parallelism in either . . . or constructions. Some commentators refer to it as misplacement of either. Here's a case in point:

. . . there is no record of his having taken a Doctor's degree either at Oxford, Cambridge, or Dublin —William Barclay Squire, in Grove's Dictionary of Music and Musicians, 3d ed., 1927

The commentators would prefer that either followed at, or that at be repeated before Cambridge and Dublin. There is no question that such a correction would be an improvement in elegance, but the sentence poses no problem of understanding as it is. We think you should try for the improved parallelism, but it is fair to say that this is not a life-and-death matter.

4. The question of the number of the verb governed by the pronoun *either* or by nouns or pronouns joined by *either . . . or* has been treated by various commentators from Baker 1770 to the present. The result has been an abundance of rules, conditions, and invented examples. But evidence of actual use of *either* as a subject seems almost to be less common than rules prescribing that usage. The paucity of evidence comes from the fact that *either* is less frequently used as a pronoun than as a conjunction, adverb, or adjective and that even as a pronoun it appears more often as an object than a subject.

Bremner 1980 has a compendious summary of the rules that are usually given:

When *either* is the subject of a clause, it takes a singular verb and singular referents. . . .

When *either* and *or* join singular subjects, the verb is singular. . . .When *either* and *or* join a singular subject and a plural subject, put the plural subject second and make the verb plural. . . .

When *either* and *or* join subjects of different person, make the verb agree with the nearer subject. . . .

These rules are commonsensical enough, and you will not go wrong if you follow them. But the little evidence we have suggests that there is some deviation from them—mostly on account of notional agreement. Several commentators, such as Longman 1984, Heritage 1982, Copperud 1964, 1970, 1980, Janis 1984, Perrin & Ebbitt 1972, and Evans 1957, recognize this.

When the pronoun *either* is the subject of the verb, we do find singular agreement:

. . . Welsh and Irish are closer to each other than either is to English —William W. Heist, *Speculum,* April 1968 (in Perrin & Ebbitt 1972)

And although almost everyone agrees that singular is usual, plural agreement is also attested. Plural agreement seems most likely when *either* is followed by *of* and a plural noun or pronoun:

. . . either of them are enough to drive any man to distraction —Henry Fielding, *Tom Jones,* 1749 (in Jespersen 1909–49)

. . . it was not a subject on which either of them were fond of dwelling —Jane Austen, *Sense and Sensibility,* 1811 (in Jespersen)

I personally do not find that either of these critics make my flesh creep —John Wain,

New Republic, 28 Jan. 1960 (in Perrin & Ebbitt)

It seems likely that plural agreement is more common in spoken than written English in such constructions.

See NOTIONAL AGREEMENT, NOTIONAL CONCORD and AGREEMENT: INDEFINITE PRONOUNS; see also NEITHER.

either . . . or   See EITHER 3, 4.

eke (out)   Evans 1957, Bernstein 1977, Bryson 1984, and Barzun 1985 all say that a supply can be eked out, or made to last, "either by adding to it or by consuming it frugally" (Bryson). Fowler 1926 and Phythian 1979 are more restrictive, saying that *eke out* means only "to make something, by adding to it, go further or last longer or do more than it would without such addition" (Fowler). The commentators' approval, such as it is, of the use of *eke out* is derived from the verb *eke*'s archaic meaning "to increase or lengthen."

These commentators are unanimous in objecting to the use of *eke out* in "they managed to eke out a living." This sense, "to get with great difficulty," which is sometimes expressed simply by *eke* without the *out,* has been the predominant sense since the 1950s. It is attested as far back as the first half of the 18th century, and it has continued in use since then with increasing frequency:

Some runaway slaves . . . contrived to eke out a subsistence —Charles Darwin, *The Voyage of the Beagle,* 1845 (OED)

. . . eked out a subsistence upon the modest sum his pen procured him —George Meredith, *Diana of the Crossways,* 1885

. . . using obsolete equipment and back-breaking labor to eke out small hauls from old veins [of coal] —*Time,* 20 Aug. 1956

. . . eking out a torpid but endurable existence —Richard Freedman, *Washington Post,* 26 Sept. 1971

As long as the *Times* continues to eke out profit and circulation gains and the rest of the company keeps going strong —Lucia Moses, *Editor & Publisher,* 6 Nov. 1999

So although someone may criticize you for saying that you're eking out a living, you should be well protected by the knowledge that it falls well within standard English usage.

elder, eldest   There is no real controversy concerning these words, but certain observations regarding them have been included in many books on usage, dating back as far as Vizetelly 1906.   The primary point stressed by the commentators is that *elder* and *eldest* are used only of persons ("her elder brother"), while *older* and *oldest* are used of both persons and things ("her older brother," "an older house"). This observation is generally true, but it should not be thought of as a hard and fast rule. While *eldest* is usually applied to a family member, *elder* is more versatile (think of *elder statesman*, for example). Its additional meanings can be found in a good dictionary.

elegant British travelers in America during the 19th century frequently commented unfavorably on the American use of *elegant* as a synonym of *fine* or *excellent,* as in "it's an elegant morning." H. L. Mencken, in *The American Language, Supplement I* (1945), notes that various commentators have recorded the use of *elegant* with such nouns as *potatoes, mill, lighthouse, hogs, bacon, corn,* and *whiskey,* to name a few. Such usage seems to have been confined almost entirely to speech. Here's an example of it from the dialogue of a novel set in Virginia around 1870:

"I'll take her right to the hospital and give her to the doctor in charge. . . . She has an elegant chance of pulling through, there. . . ." —Joseph Hergesheimer, *Mountain Blood,* 1915

Chances are you've never seen or heard *elegant* used in this way; the use seems to have died out.

A somewhat similar use of *elegant* is in such sentences as "we had an elegant time" and "we were served an elegant meal":

. . . until dinnertime, when an elegant roast was served —Andrew W. Turnbull, *New Yorker,* 7 Apr. 1956

Criticism of such usage was common in the early 20th century, and it can still be heard on occasion. But the criticized uses of *elegant* are less common than they once were, and the strong objections they once invited seem to have been largely forgotten.

elegant variation *Elegant variation* is a term invented by Fowler 1926 for the inelegant use of a synonym merely to avoid using the same word two or more times in a sentence, or in a short space of text. It also receives mention in Janis 1984, Johnson 1982, Copperud 1970, 1980, and Garner 1998. The sensible advice generally given is to avoid elegant variation. Fowler 1926, 1965 has the most extended treatment.

elegy, eulogy Strictly speaking, an elegy (from the Greek *elegos,* "song of mourning") is a sorrowful or melancholy song or poem, and a eulogy (from the Greek *eulogia,* "praise") is a formal statement or oration expressing praise. A funeral oration is called a eulogy because it typically praises the accomplishments and character of the person who has died. It also, of course, expresses sorrow, and many

people no doubt associate the word *eulogy* more strongly with sorrow than with praise. Such associations might be expected to cause some tendency to confuse *elegy* and *eulogy,* but we have little evidence of such confusion. *Eulogy* is never used to mean "a sorrowful song or poem." Nor is *elegy* used to mean "a speech of praise." *Elegy* is, however, sometimes used in figurative contexts to mean in essence "a funeral oration":

They write like undertakers: an elegy on every page —David Rains Wallace, *N.Y. Times Book Rev.,* 22 July 1984

If you use *elegy* in this way, you may find yourself being corrected.

elicit, illicit Warnings against confusion of the verb *elicit,* "to draw forth," and the adjective *illicit,* "unlawful," can be found in a few usage handbooks. While such confusion is unlikely in the real world because the words are different parts of speech, pronunciation tends to bring them together, and our files provide some evidence that confusion does exist:

The court majority said, and I quote: "We hold only that when the process . . . focuses on the accused and its purpose is to illicit a confession. . . ." —*Police,* September–October 1967

A good desk dictionary will sort the matter out for you, should you be confused for a moment.

eligible *Eligible* may be used with a complementary prepositional phrase, and *for* or *to* are the prepositions used most often. When the construction is *eligible for,* a noun phrase almost always follows it:

. . . were eligible for the university —William L. Shirer, *The Rise and Fall of the Third Reich,* 1960

. . . there's some standard [insurance] policy she's eligible for —James Gould Cozzens, *Guard of Honor,* 1948

When *eligible* is used with *to,* an infinitive usually follows, although occasionally a noun may follow instead:

He's eligible to start receiving benefits after the second week —Bill Moyers, *Harper's,* December 1970

. . . membership in State and county organizations made one eligible to membership in A.M.A. —*Current Biography 1950*

elope, elopement People who elope don't necessarily get married, as Bernstein 1965 points out. In its original sense, still sometimes seen, *elope* describes the actions of a married woman who runs away from her husband with her lover:

. . . his unfaithful wife had eloped with her latest lover —Harrison Smith, *Saturday Rev.,* 20 Mar. 1954

It can also be used to mean simply "run away." with no implications of love or marriage:

> . . . she finally eloped to London, to try her luck in the theatre —Peter Quennell, *The Marble Foot: An Autobiography,* 1976

In general use, however, *elope* calls to mind strong images of young lovers stealing away to be married in the dead of night. The associations that *elope* and *elopement* have with marriage are so strong that it is usually unnecessary to state specifically that two people who have eloped have, in fact, gotten married:

> Defying her family, they eloped, built a crude cabin here, and lived happily the rest of their lives —*American Guide Series: Connecticut,* 1938

When the marriage does not come off, on the other hand, it is a good idea to say so:

> Sixteen-year-old Christine . . . ended a two-week elopement without benefit of marriage with tears in her eyes —*Springfield* (Mass.) *Union* (UPI), 3 July 1957

else 1. In present-day English, compound pronouns with *else—anybody else, somebody else, who else,* for instance—take the *-'s* of the possessive on the *else.*

It seems strange, perhaps, to readers today that this subject needs to be mentioned at all. But a century ago it was a red-hot issue in usage. The reason for the dispute was a shift in general practice: before about 1840 the *-'s* went with the pronoun, and forms like *somebody's else* were considered standard. Gould 1870 and Ayres 1881 were still calling for these forms in the face of changing usage, but early in the 20th century the modern forms began to gain increasing acceptance by the commentators. But change comes hard for some people; there is evidence that some English instructors were still trying to inculcate *somebody's else* as late as the 1950s. The old forms may still be heard or seen, but the form with *else's* is now the overwhelming choice.

2. *else but, else than.* A curious controversy that arose around the 1880s and reached the 1990s concerns whether *else* must be followed by *than* or *but.* While most of our commentators prescribe *than,* at least one prescribes *but.* These contradictory prescriptions should tell you that both were, and are, in use:

> He had no idea of being anything else than an irreproachable husband —George Eliot, *Middlemarch,* 1872

> . . . the crime of trading with anybody else but himself —Joseph Conrad, *Lord Jim,* 1900

> Morbidity seems to me little else than sentimentality of a peculiar tint —Elizabeth Bowen, *The Mulberry Tree,* 1986

> . . . thought of little else but foreign markets —Arthur M. Schlesinger, Jr., *The Cycles of American History,* 1986

Our recent evidence shows *but* more frequently used than *than.*

Garner 1998 damns both constructions, saying delete *else* before *but* and replace *else than* with *other than.* This would seem to work all right; you can try it if you like.

elude See ALLUDE 2.

elusive, illusive Admonitions not to confuse *elusive* ("hard to perceive or comprehend") and *illusive* ("based on illusion; illusory") can be found in a few books on usage. The usual mistake is the use of the relatively uncommon *illusive* in place of *elusive*:

> . . . probably the appendix acting up. It was very illusive and not detected until the day of the operation —letter received at Merriam-Webster, 2 Sept. 1954

Garner 1998 has recent examples from the press. These may be evidence of reliance on computer spelling checkers rather than checking in a dictionary.

emanate *Emanate* is usually used with the preposition *from*:

> . . . these bursts emanate from galaxies billions of light years away —*Astronomy,* November 1998

Very rarely you might encounter *in*:

> All works will have emanated in either Spanish, Portuguese, or French . . . whether or not they have been translated —*Library Jour.,* 1 May 1967

embark *Embark* may be used with a number of different prepositions, but by a large margin the usual choice is *on* or *upon,* the former being more common:

> . . . the Federal Board was about to embark on a string of tightenings to cool down the economy —James J. Cramer, *Time,* 12 July 1999

> . . . the fact that we embark on each of these stories so willingly testifies to our trust in where they'll lead us —Anne Tyler, *N.Y. Times Book Rev.,* 18 Mar. 1990

Embark is used with *for* when the object denotes destination:

> Clark embarked most of the party . . . for the Three Forks —Bernard DeVoto, *The Course of Empire,* 1952

And we have a few citations for *embark from* to indicate the point of departure:

> . . . four companions, embarking from Floyd Bennett Field, circled the globe —*American Guide Series: N.Y. City,* 1939

At one time, *embark in* was a fairly common construction; however, it seems to have been dropping out of use during the last 40 years or so, as travel by ship has decreased.

embellish *Embellish* is most often used with *with* when it takes a complement:

> The book is embellished with some excellent photographs —*Times Literary Supp.,* 12 Feb. 1970

Embellish is also used with *by*:

> His text is embellished by a large number of extremely well-produced illustrations —*Times Literary Supp.,* 24 June 1955

emend See AMEND, EMEND.

emerge When *emerge* is used with a preposition, the choice is most often *from*:

> She began it officially by emerging from the back room clad in a dragon-embroidered kimono —Thomas Pynchon, *V.,* 1963

It is also very frequently used with *as*:

> . . . America, emerging as the greatest power after the Second World War . . . —Hannah Arendt, *N.Y. Rev. of Books,* 18 Nov. 1971

Sometimes it appears with both:

> . . . emerged from the war as a creditor nation —*The Encyclopedia Americana,* 1943

Emerge is also sometimes followed by *that* and a clause:

> It emerges that her husband is somehow involved with the dead girl —Anthony Quinton, *Encounter,* December 1954

Emerge can also be used with a number of other prepositions—*at, in, into, on, onto, out of, through, upon, with*—in sentences in which the choice of preposition is dictated by the sense of the sentence rather than by idiomatic co-occurrence.

emigrate, immigrate *Emigrate* and *immigrate* make a case in which English has two words where it could easily have made do with only one. The two words have the same essential meaning—"to leave one country to live in another"—and differ only in emphasis or point of view: *emigrate* stressing leaving, and *immigrate* stressing entering. A large number of handbooks, from MacCracken & Sandison 1917 to Garner 1998, warn us not to confuse the two. Our evidence shows that almost no one does, at least in edited prose. A handy clue

to identity is provided by the prepositions each takes. *Emigrate* tends to go with *from*:

> . . . Ezekiel Wapshot, who emigrated from England aboard the *Arbella* in 1630 —John Cheever, *The Wapshot Chronicle,* 1957

Bernstein 1965 recommends only *from*. However, when the writer is thinking in terms of the new country, *to* is also used:

> He was a Dane, a big, yellow-haired, outgoing man in his late forties, and a widower. He had emigrated to the United States after his wife's death —Russell Baker, *Growing Up,* 1982

Immigrate, with its stress on entering, usually is used with *to* and *into*:

> The family then immigrated in 1921 to London —Marilyn Berger, *N.Y. Times,* 7 Nov. 1997

> . . . the foreign scientists and engineers who immigrate into the United States —Robert M. Hutchins, *Center Mag.,* March 1968

Immigrate is sometimes used with *from*. Just as *emigrate to* can be understood as "to leave there and come to," *immigrate from* can be understood as "to come here from":

> Pettigrew comes from Richmond, Virginia, but his father immigrated from Scotland —Godfrey Hodgson, *Atlantic,* March 1973

Distinguishing these words may be less of a problem than is often suggested, as your meaning is essentially the same no matter which you use. To emphasize the notion of leaving, use *emigrate* with *from*; to emphasize the notion of arriving, use *immigrate* with *to* or *into*.

eminent, imminent Almost all books on usage include a warning about confusion of *eminent* and *imminent* (occasionally the much less used word *immanent* is included for good measure). The meanings are distinct: *eminent* means "prominent" (as in "an eminent author"); *imminent* means "soon to occur, impending" (as in "imminent danger"). Use of one word in place of the other is rare in edited prose, but it does occur from time to time in writing that has not been very closely scrutinized or has been left to the care of a spelling checker.

See also IMMINENT 1.

emote The verb *emote* is a back-formation that was formed from the noun *emotion* in the early 20th century. From the first, its use has tended to be something less than entirely serious:

> And you let me sit there and emote all over the place —Megrue & Hackett, *It Pays to Advertise,* 1917 (OED Supplement)

The basic meaning of *emote* is "to express emotion." Its most familiar use is undoubtedly in humorously describing the work of actors:

> A Method actor can sit on a stage, feeling deeply and emoting strangely, but it's no good if the audience hasn't the faintest idea of what is going on —Carol Tavris, *Harper's,* January 1983

It is also used in a similar way to describe theatrical behavior by nonactors:

> Remember, this is politics; it doesn't have to make sense so long as you emote instead of asking questions —Russell Baker, *N.Y. Times,* 8 May 1976

> Nor are men merely chary of expressing pain and neediness, particularly in an era where emoting is the coin of the commercial realm —Susan Faludi, *Newsweek,* 13 Sept. 1999

Uses of *emote* without humorous connotations are relatively uncommon, but we do encounter them from time to time:

> Crying, especially on-camera, is considerably more difficult for the actress, but Bob Fosse . . . helped her learn to emote —Peter Greenberg, *Cosmopolitan,* October 1976

Like many another back-formation, *emote* has met with some disapproval among usage commentators, but because its normal uses are facetious rather than serious, it does not invite strong criticism. Recent commentators (such as Bernstein 1965) have limited their censure to cases in which *emote* is used without humorous intent. Such usage cannot be called nonstandard, but it is inconsistent with the usual connotations of the word, and you may well want to avoid it for that reason.

emotional, emotive The use of these adjectives in British English has undergone an interesting development in recent decades. H. W. Fowler described *emotive* as a "superfluous word" in 1926, feeling that it served no purpose not better served by *emotional.* In his 1965 revision of Fowler's *Modern English Usage,* however, Sir Ernest Gowers noted that *emotive* had come to be used in a distinct way and had become the preferred choice in the sense "appealing to the emotions; evoking an emotional response," as in "an emotive speech" or "an emotive political issue." Gowers' observation is confirmed by our evidence from British sources:

> . . . an emotive and currently much discussed topic —Ann Oakley, *British Book News,* June 1979

> . . . it was reflected in the calm treatment of an emotive issue: euthanasia —*The Economist,* 30 Aug. 1985

Emotive is now so well established in this use among the British that one recent commentator, Phythian 1979, warns against confusion of *emotional* and *emotive,* by which he apparently means the use of *emotional* to mean "appealing to or evoking emotions." Such usage is in fact perfectly reputable, as H. W. Fowler could have told him. It is especially so in American English:

> . . . he is already . . . identified with a strong emotional issue —Joseph P. Albright, *N.Y. Times Mag.,* 1 Sept. 1974

> The nuclear-power controversy has become so emotional —Wadsworth Likely, *Saturday Rev.,* 22 Jan. 1977

employ *Employ* is occasionally cited as a pretentious substitute for *use.* The two verbs are in fact often interchangeable, but *employ* is most appropriately used when the conscious application of something for a particular end is being stressed:

> . . . his best poems employ ironically the conventions he rejects —Kenneth Fields, *Southern Rev.,* April 1970

> . . . will refrain from employing their military strength in new political power plays —Anatole Shub, *Harper's,* January 1972

employe, employee The French word *employé* (rhymes with *say*) was first used in English in the early 19th century. The feminine form is *employée,* "a female employee." The feminine form never had much success in English, but *employé* continued in occasional use well into the 20th century:

> The depositors were wage-earners; railroad employé's, mechanics, and day labourers —Willa Cather, *A Lost Lady,* 1923

Eventually, of course, both *employé* and *employée* were superseded by the English *employee,* formed by combination of *employ* and the familiar suffix *-ee.* The earliest known occurrence of *employee* is in Thoreau's *Walden,* published in 1854. The OED indicated in 1897 that *employee* was rare in the U.S., but by 1926 it was well enough established for H. W. Fowler to promote its use by describing it as "a good plain word with no questions of spelling & pronunciation & accents & italics & genders about it. . . ." Fowler had no use for the French *employé,* and he would be glad to know that *employee* appears now to be the invariable choice in British English.

In the U.S., however, the ghost of *employé* lives on. Although *employee* is undoubtedly the usual spelling in American English, there are some publications and writers that show a preference for the variant *employe,* apparently out of deference to *employé.* *Employe* aims to be a more logical and precise spelling than *em-*

ployee, but it fails on both counts. Its use is not incorrect, however. It occurs regularly in highly reputable publications, and it has clearly established itself as a respectable spelling variant in American English:

> . . . stemming from poor employe training —*Wall Street Jour.,* 3 June 1980

> . . . is studying "cafeteria-style" benefits for state employes —*USA Today,* 23 Apr. 1984

emporium The literal meaning of *emporium* in Latin is "a place of trade; marketplace." As used in English, it now typically denotes a store or restaurant that is notably large, notably busy, or notably pretentious. It has two plurals, *emporiums* and *emporia,* both of which are in good use:

> One of the most renowned hummus emporiums is Abu-Shukri on El-Wad Road —Calvin Trillin, *Travel & Leisure,* August 1994

> On the Upper West Side, the great style emporia dominate —Cynthia Ozick, *New Yorker,* 22 Feb. & 1 Mar. 1999

Emporiums is the more common of the two.

enamor In current English, *enamor* is used most often in the passive and when used with a preposition usually appears with *of*:

> . . . we are enamored of the notion that we are a country of people forever inventing ourselves —Wendy Kaminer, *N.Y. Times Book Rev.,* 11 Feb. 1990

Less frequently, *enamor* is used with *with*:

> . . . a peculiar mélange . . . that will, alas, disappoint those enamored with the Yugoslavian filmmaker —Judith Crist, *New York,* 1 Nov. 1971

Although some language commentators frown on the practice, *enamor* is used with *by,* but not very often:

> . . . she wouldn't have been quite so enamoured by the list of ingredients —June Bibb, *Christian Science Monitor,* 17 Feb. 1965

enclose, inclose These variant spellings are equally old (both date from around 1400) and equally respectable, but *enclose* has now become so much the more common of the two that *inclose* is rarely seen. The same distribution holds true for *enclosure* and *inclosure.* The *in-* forms seem now most likely to be found in legal writing:

> Rights of common may be . . . wholly extinguished by inclosure —E. H. Burn, *Cheshire's Modern Law of Real Property,* 11th ed., 1972

encounter Kilpatrick 1984 notes that he was once criticized by a correspondent for using *encounter* to mean "meet with" or "come across," as in "books I have encountered." He agrees with his critic that such usage is incorrect and that *encounter* properly means "to meet as an adversary or enemy; to engage in conflict with; to run into a complication." Certainly *encounter* has those meanings, but we wonder why Kilpatrick is so ready to abandon its 'meet with' sense, which the OED shows to have been in use since the 14th century. J. Leslie Hall investigated the pedigree of this sense in 1917 and found that it had been used by such writers as Samuel Johnson, Sir Walter Scott, Edgar Allan Poe, Nathaniel Hawthorne, George Eliot, and Robert Louis Stevenson. Our evidence shows that its occurrence in current English is common and perfectly idiomatic:

> . . . she stole on tiptoe downstairs . . . praying devoutly that she would encounter no one —Katherine Anne Porter, *Ladies' Home Jour.,* August 1971

> Within the publishing industry, it's rare to encounter such near unanimity of positive assessments —Robert Dahlin, *Publishers Weekly,* 21 Sept. 1998

encroach When used with a preposition, *encroach* is usually used with *on* or *upon*:

> Today, the enemy is vague, the work seems done, . . . the expert encroaches on the artist —Norman Mailer, *Advertisements for Myself,* 1959

> . . . groups of houses encroaching suddenly upon the desolation of the marshland —William Styron, *Lie Down in Darkness,* 1951

Occasionally *encroach* is used with *into, onto,* and *to*:

> . . . the highly flammable fir and lodgepole . . . are encroaching into new territory —Rick Bass, *Audubon Mag.,* September/October 1995

> . . . burnt-out cars had been dragged to the gutters, sometimes encroaching up onto the sidewalk —James Jones, *Harper's,* February 1971

> . . . fishermen encroached closer and closer to the Alaskan waters —Frank Abbott Magruder, *National Governments and International Relations,* 1950

end When *end* is used intransitively with a preposition, it may be used with *by*:

> Van Dusen ended by setting up the entire itinerary and going along —*Time,* 19 Apr. 1954

Somewhat less frequently (but still commonly), *end* is used with *as, at,* and *on:*

> . . . he ended as an Air Service supply officer —James Gould Cozzens, *Guard of Honor,* 1948

> The bridge ended at the island —*American Guide Series: Minnesota,* 1938

> The interview ends on a note of close harmony —Stuart Chase, *Power of Words,* 1953

> See also END UP.

endeavor   As a synonym for *attempt* or *try,* the verb *endeavor* has several distinguishing characteristics, the most obvious of which is its relative formality. It also carries connotations of a continuing and earnest effort, as in attempting to enact a long-range policy or to achieve a lasting result:

> And, I might add, I would endeavor to have these schools offer a far broader array of practical courses —James B. Conant, *Slums and Suburbs,* 1961

> . . . white-gloved policemen who endeavor to unsnarl traffic at the blind intersections —Michael Pollan, *Condé Nast Traveler,* November 1993

ended, ending   These words have caused some minor disagreements among usage commentators. The point at issue is whether *ending* can properly be used in describing a period that is in the past, as in "We were there for the week ending July 22." A few critics, dating back to Weseen 1928, have contended that *ended* is required in such a context (". . . for the week ended July 22"), and that *ending* is only appropriate when speaking of the future ("We'll be there for the week ending April 4"). Other commentators, such as Partridge 1942, have argued that the use of *ending* to speak of the past is common and respectable. The most telling point has been made by Sir Ernest Gowers, who has noted (in Fowler 1965) that we always use *beginning* rather than *begun* when referring to a past period in terms of its start ("We were there for the week beginning July 15"). This use of *beginning* has been criticized by no one. Gowers calls the criticism of *ending* "pedantic," and we agree. Both *ended* and *ending* are idiomatic when speaking of the past. Use the one that seems more natural to you.

endemic, epidemic   We have no evidence showing that these words have ever been confused, but the similarities of their spelling, pronunciation, and application are such that they look confusable, and books on usage have been explaining the distinction between them for many years. One more time can't hurt: medically speaking, *endemic* describes a disease that is constantly present to a greater or lesser extent in a particular place; *epidemic* describes a severe outbreak of a disease affecting many people within a community or region at one time. To the basic distinction we may also add that *endemic* can be followed by either *in* or *to:*

> . . . the gravely debilitating . . . parasitic disease that is endemic in lower Egypt —William Styron, *This Quiet Dust and Other Writings,* 1982

> . . . to study diseases endemic to the developing areas of the world —*Johns Hopkins Mag,* Summer 1967

Epidemic is more commonly used as a noun than as an adjective:

> . . . a typhus epidemic that killed more than 65,000 people in the British Isles in 1816 —Timothy Ferris, *N.Y. Times Book Rev.,* 31 July 1983

Its most familiar adjectival use is in the phrase *epidemic proportions:*

> . . . AIDS was proclaimed as reaching *epidemic* proportions —Edwin Diamond, *TV Guide,* 28 Oct. 1983

Both words, of course, are also commonly used in nonmedical contexts:

> The problems endemic to translating poetry —Genevieve Stuttaford, *Publishers Weekly,* 22 Oct. 1982

> Early in this century there was an epidemic of picture postcards —*People,* 14 Dec. 1981

Another point of some concern to usage commentators is the use of *epidemic* to describe outbreaks of disease affecting animals rather than people. Bernstein 1965 considers this a "loose usage," since *epidemic* is derived from the Greek *demos,* "people." He argues that the correct word for an outbreak among animals is *epizootic.* The distinction he promotes is in fact sometimes observed, particularly in scientific writing:

> An epidemic of plague in human beings is usually preceded by a rat epizootic —*Merck Manual,* 8th ed., 1950

But the etymological connection between *epidemic* and "people" is now entirely lost in general usage, and the use of *epidemic* to describe nonhuman outbreaks of disease is established as standard, as Gowers in Fowler 1965 and Copperud 1980 have observed.

> . . . epidemics of the disease during winter and spring months —H. E. Biester & L. H. Schwarte, ed., *Diseases of Poultry,* 2d ed., 1948

ending   See ENDED, ENDING.

endorse 1. *Endorse on the back. Endorse* is derived from the Old French verb *endosser,* "to put on the back." This etymology has led some critics, from Vizetelly 1906 to Garner 1998, to contend that the phrase *endorse on the back* is redundant. A good argument against that contention is made by Krapp 1927, who points out that the "on the back" connotations of *endorse* are "no longer strongly felt," and that the main idea in endorsing a check is to prepare it for cashing by signing it—that the signing is done on the back is almost incidental. The association with the idea of "back" is secondary to the principal idea of signing one's name. The redundancy of *endorse on the back* is more imaginary than real. 2. *Endorse* meaning "approve." The use of *endorse* to mean "approve, sanction" originated in the 19th century:

> This book . . . the world has endorsed, by translating it into all tongues —Ralph Waldo Emerson, *Representative Men,* 1847 (OED)

Criticism of it followed soon afterward from such commentators as Richard Grant White 1870 and Ayres 1881. Its foremost critic in the 20th century has been Fowler 1926, who described it as a "solecism." Fowler objected in particular to its use in advertisements. Some resistance to this use of *endorse* has persisted among British commentators, but its place in American English has long been established. Its most common occurrences continue to be in advertising and politics:

> . . . [players] of the Baltimore Colts football team also endorse UNIROYAL's All-Sports shoes —*Annual Report, UNIROYAL Incorporated,* 1970

> . . . he alienated Democratic leaders by endorsing Richard Nixon for President —*Current Biography,* January 1967

But it occurs commonly in other contexts as well:

> He fully endorses the modern appreciation of Erasmus as a deeply religious writer —*Times Literary Supp.,* 30 July 1971

3. *Endorse, indorse.* These spellings are equally reputable, but *endorse* is now far and away the more common of the two. Most of the recent evidence we have for the *in-* spelling is from legal contexts:

> . . . a specially indorsed writ —*Palmer's Company Law,* 22d ed., 1976

endow *Endow* is very often used with a preposition, and usually the preposition is *with*:

> Endow such men with religious zeal —Vernon Louis Parrington, *Main Currents in American Thought,* 1930

> I was endowed with rights to a White House car —John Kenneth Galbraith, *Ambassador's Journal,* 1969

There is also, of course, the common construction of *endow* used with *by* when the verb is used in the passive and the object names the agent:

> The library, which was endowed by Andrew Carnegie, has approximately 36,000 volumes —*American Guide Series: Louisiana,* 1941

Our files show *endow* with other prepositions, but these are fairly rare:

> . . . people who have been overgenerously endowed in the way of height —Hamilton Basso, *The View From Pompey's Head,* 1954

> . . . the mellow wisdom which once he had dreamed that the slow advance of years would endow upon him —James T. Farrell, *What Time Collects,* 1964

end result, end product Those people to whom redundancy is anathema do not take kindly to *end product* and *end result.* Of the two terms, *end result* is closer to a simple redundancy; it basically means "result" but may emphasize the finality of the result.

> . . . economic losses will continue to mount. . . . The end result will be a substantial reduction in the American standard of living —Lawrence A. Hunter, *Wall Street Jour.,* 19 Sept. 1999

End product, on the other hand, has two uses. Especially in science and manufacturing, an end product is the final product of a series of processes or activities and is often distinguished from a by-product. In most general contexts it simply means "result" or "product."

> . . . the digestible materials have been acted on by enzymes and their end-products —Edwin B. Steen & Ashley Montagu, *Anatomy and Physiology,* 1959

> . . . this is the end product of a lot of work —Jeremy Bernstein, *N.Y. Times Book Rev.,* 28 Feb. 1982

In *end result* and the looser, noncontrastive uses of *end product,* the question of whether *end* is superfluous or whether it serves as an intensifier depends occasionally on the context but usually on your opinion of redundancy (which see).

end up 1. *End up* is an "unacceptable colloquialism for *end* or *conclude,*" proclaims Macmillan 1982. Setting aside for now the matter of whether *end up* is a colloquialism, let's take a look at the difference between *end* and *end up.* The first point to notice is that *end up* is not substituted for all senses of the verb *end* but almost always is used to mean "to reach a specified ultimate rank or situation."

> . . . the dinner-glasses disappeared one by one . . . , the last one ending up, scarred and maimed, as a tooth-brush holder —F. Scott Fitzgerald, "The Cut-Glass Bowl," 1920, in *The Portable F. Scott Fitzgerald*, 1945

> Hollywood parties, those celebrated institutions which so frequently . . . end up in romance or in tragedy —Peter Ustinov, *London Calling*, 5 Aug. 1954

> They ended up fighting it out among themselves —Tom Wolfe, *New York*, 27 Sept. 1971

Although *end* also gets used in contexts like these, such use is far outnumbered both by the use of *end up* and by the use of *end* in other senses. We suspect, moreover, that *end* used with this meaning often reveals the hand of a copy editor who followed the advice of a handbook like Macmillan. *End* alone does not sound as natural as *end up* in many contexts:

> . . . he was warned his body would end in a ditch if he did not stop complaining —A. H. Raskin, *N.Y. Times Mag.*, 7 Nov. 1976

Because *end up* so commonly expresses the meaning "to wind up," its use emphasizes the notion of everything that led up to a certain result, while *end* emphasizes the notion of finality and more or less ignores what came before. As a result, *end* can be not only an awkward synonym for *end up*, but sometimes no synonym at all. This is especially true when *end up* is followed by a word or phrase modifying the subject. *End* cannot be substituted in the following sentences without changing the meaning.

> . . . like everyone else I don't want to end up a festering heap —John Lennon, quoted in *Current Biography*, December 1965

> . . . the October "election" in South Vietnam will end up an utterly meaningless exercise —Richard H. Rovere, *New Yorker*, 18 Sept. 1971

In the course of this discussion you have seen a sampling of the kinds of contexts in which *end up* normally appears. Clearly "colloquialism" is not an appropriate label for *end up*. There is really no difference between the formality of the contexts that *end up* appears in and those that *end* appears in. The only difference between the two verbs is one of meaning.

2. When *end up* is followed by a preposition, the preposition is usually (in rough order of frequency) *with*, *in*, *as*, *by*, or *at*. Some examples appear in section 1 above.

enervate A number of usage books warn their readers not to use *enervate* to mean "stimulate," "invigorate," or "energize." Don't be misled by the superficial resemblance of *enervate* to *energize*. It means "to lessen the vitality or strength of" or "to reduce the mental or moral vigor of."

> . . . compelled the sluggish arms of an enervated system to begin to flail —Donald Kirk, *Saturday Rev.*, 8 Jan. 1977

engage *Engage* may be used with many prepositions, but by far it is most often used with *in*, which in turn is most often followed by a gerund or a noun:

> . . . but was busily engaged, on the farther side of the piano, in examining a picture —Edith Wharton, *New Year's Day*, 1924

> The police are engaged in the rounding up of suspects —Anthony Burgess, *MF*, 1971

> . . . the reader (whom Miss Piercy does engage in argument, however feverish) —John Updike, *New Yorker*, 10 Apr. 1971

Less frequently *engage* is used with *with* or *on* (*upon* being less common); our files show *engage on* is chiefly a British usage:

> . . . he might engage on topics that his brother might like to regard as private —Ford Madox Ford, *The Last Post*, 1928

> The class under whose work he was engaged on this particular evening —Robertson Davies, *Tempest-tost*, 1951

> . . . he was no longer as actively engaged with his old publishing house —Bennett Cerf, *Saturday Rev.*, 19 Dec. 1953

Engage may be used with *to*, especially in the familiar "engaged to be married" and "the man she was engaged to" expressions. We also find other uses with the infinitive:

> I was engaged to lunch with him in New York —Edmund Fuller, *Wall Street Jour.*, 10 July 1980

> "Engage somebody to stay with him, or—or send him away?" —Ellen Glasgow, *Barren Ground*, 1925

Engage may be used with *for*:

> . . . she engaged for the London cast of David Belasco's production —*Current Biography 1949*

Engage is also used with *by*:

> . . . I was engaged by a newspaper to be its first dance critic —Walter Terry, *Saturday Rev.*, 27 Nov. 1976

and with *as*:

> . . . she had engaged herself as a servant —Kenneth Roberts, *Oliver Wiswell*, 1940

enhance The use of *enhance* with a personal object was called obsolete by Fowler 1926 and is cited as an error in one recent dictionary (Longman 1984). Evidence in the OED shows that *enhance* with a personal object was once common, but that it fell into disuse during the 17th century. Its occurrence in current English is rare but not obsolete:

> I think clothes should enhance the woman, not the designer —Margaret Gunster, quoted in *Women's Wear Daily,* 6 Dec. 1976

> A successful run enhances a runner in his own eyes —Dr. Brent Waters, *Runners World,* June 1981

Enhance now almost always has a thing—often an abstract quality—as its object:

> . . . the general effect, enhanced by a ceiling of pale-blue metal plates —*New Yorker,* 10 Apr. 1971

> The fresh flavour of the vegetables is . . . enhanced by the other ingredients —Marguerite Patten, *Health Food Cookery,* 1972

Enhance normally describes the improvement or heightening of something desirable, but its use with a negative object is not incorrect:

> . . . the very circumstance which at present enhances your loss, must gradually reconcile you to it better —Jane Austen, letter, 8 Apr. 1798

Bernstein 1965 finds that such usage occurs "not uncommonly." Our evidence shows, however, that it is now about as rare as the use of *enhance* with a personal object.

enjoin 1. Fowler 1926 dislikes the use of *enjoin* with a personal object followed by an infinitive, as in "They enjoined him to be careful." He finds some support for such a construction in the OED, but he argues that "ordinary modern use" requires an impersonal object followed by *upon,* as in "They enjoined caution upon him." Sir Ernest Gowers retains this argument in his 1965 revision of Fowler, but our evidence suggests that whatever validity it may have had in 1926 is now lost. As Evans 1957 notes, when *enjoin* is used to mean "to direct or admonish" it now usually takes the infinitive:

> . . . and enjoined him to bequeath them to his heirs —*Times Literary Supp.,* 28 May 1971

> . . . my temperament enjoins me to believe —Arthur M. Schlesinger, Jr., *Harper's,* August 1971

The construction favored by Fowler (with *upon* or *on*) is now relatively uncommon. Note that the sense of *enjoin* differs somewhat in this construction, being not so much "to direct" as "to impose" or "to urge as a duty or necessity':

> . . . displayed the charity enjoined on Christians —Naomi Bliven, *New Yorker,* 17 July 1971

2. A point of interest raised by several commentators is that *enjoin* has two main senses which are almost directly opposite to each other: "to direct or urge" and "to forbid or prohibit." Both senses are centuries old, and there is no question about the respectability of either. The "forbid or prohibit" sense is most familiar in—but not limited to—legal contexts:

> . . . girls enjoined from getting soiled; boys forbidden to play with dolls —Letty Cottin Pogrebin, *New York,* 27 Dec. 1971

> . . . a judge permanently enjoined him from shipping excess oranges —Guerney Breckenfeld, *Saturday Rev.,* 10 July 1976

enjoy Two uses of this verb have drawn occasional criticism since the 19th century. One of them, in the phrase *enjoy oneself,* can now safely be classed as a dead issue. Its supposed offense was that it illogically (and, perhaps, indecently) implied taking pleasure in oneself, inasmuch as the "correct" meaning of *enjoy* is "to take pleasure or satisfaction in." Even its principal critic (Hodgson 1889) admitted, however, that "this supposedly incorrect phrase was used 'by the best writers.'"

The other criticized use appears in such a sentence as "He enjoys poor health," in which *enjoy* is being used as if it were simply a neutral synonym of *experience.* This use is quite old, having been recorded as early as 1577. Such commentators as Richard Grant White 1870 and Ayres 1881 took unfavorable notice of it in the late 1800s, and objections to it can still be found in some usage handbooks. It is not now—and never has been—common in writing, but it does persist in making written appearances from time to time:

> . . . Mendes appears to have enjoyed poor health —Stephen Birmingham, *The Grandees* 1971

The problem is that *enjoy* so strongly suggests "take pleasure in" that its use with a negative object sounds peculiar. That is why such usage is criticized and why it continues to be uncommon.

enormity, enormousness The usage experts insist that *enormity* is improperly used to denote large size and is properly used only to denote wickedness, outrage, or crime. *Enormousness* is the word recommended for large size. This recommendation from Strunk & White 1979 for *enormity* is typical: "Use only in the sense 'monstrous wickedness.' " The recommendation is not just simple, it is an oversimplification, as the first definition of *enormity* in Webster's Second shows:

1. State or quality of exceeding a measure or rule, or of being immoderate, monstrous, or outrageous; as, the *enormity* of an offense.

This suggests a much wider range of application than just "monstrous wickedness." Let's have a look at some of these applications.

First, we find that *enormity* can carry overtones of moral transgression:

Sin, remember, is a twofold enormity —James Joyce, *A Portrait of the Artist as a Young Man,* 1916

Twenty years after the war we stand shocked and amazed at the enormity of the German crimes —*Times Literary Supp.,* 30 Dec. 1965

It may also denote an outrage against one's sense of decency or one's sense of what is right:

One should pause to absorb this in its full innovative enormity—a United States Senator tapped and trailed on his legislative rounds by *American* Army agents? —Andrew St. George, *Harper's,* November 1973

At other times it may stress the gravity of a situation, the seriousness of what may happen because of some act or event. The emphasis here is on the dire consequences, rather than the immorality:

I confess the crime, and own the enormity of its consequences, and the danger of its example —Samuel Johnson, letter written for Dr. Dodd, June 1777

She perceived as no one in the family could the enormity of the misfortune —E. L. Doctorow, *Ragtime,* 1975

The grave situation described may carry distinct overtones of being a considerable departure from what is normal:

They awakened; they sat up; and then the enormity of their situation burst upon them.
"How did the fire start?" asked Pablo plaintively, and no one knew —John Steinbeck, *Tortilla Flat,* 1935

But in spite of what the critics say, *enormity* is often used simply to denote great size or extent. It is applied to things that are literally or figuratively great in size:

. . . explains to a certain extent the enormity of its craters and the loftiness of its mountain peaks —*The Strand,* May 1905

. . . he knew . . . that he had conquered the language, and that the dictionary, which he had assembled out of the enormity of the English language, was to have no peer —John Willinsky, *Empire of Words,* 1994

Husband doubts friend appreciates enormity of his good fortune —John Barth, *The Floating Opera,* 1956

Quite often *enormity* will be used to suggest a size that is beyond normal bounds, a size that is unexpectedly great. Here the notion of monstrousness may creep in, but without the notion of wickedness. This use can be either literal or figurative. For instance, the first quotation below describes the dirigible *Hindenberg* as seen by a child on the streets of New York:

The enormity of her was out of scale with everything, out of scale with the houses and the cars on the street and the people now shouting and pointing and looking up; she was like a scoop of sky come down to earth, or a floating building —E. L. Doctorow, *World's Fair,* 1985

. . . it was as though one had flown near enough to the sun to realize its monstrous enormity, and had then returned to earth again appalled by its distance from us —Sacheverell Sitwell, *All Summer in a Day,* 1926

In many instances the notion of great size is colored by aspects of the first sense of *enormity* as defined in Webster's Second. One common figurative use blends together the notions of immoderateness, excess, and monstrousness to suggest a size that is daunting or overwhelming:

. . . the enormity of the task of teachers in slum schools —James B. Conant, *Slums and Suburbs,* 1961

In view of the enormity of population pressures in India, the condom machine is like a black joke —Michael T. Kaufman, *N.Y. Times,* 11 Nov. 1979

Interestingly, it is this use that most often catches the eye of the commentators:

"Impressed by the enormity of the job and the far-reaching scope of the military, Mr. Lovett knows . . ." "The enormity of the collection long ago discouraged the academy with its limited staff." Authorities on usage are virtually unanimous in reserving "enormity" for the idea of wickedness —Bernstein 1958

On the challenge of the Presidency, Mr. Reagan said: "I have always been well aware of the enormity of it, the difficulties. . . ." —William Safire, *N.Y. Times,* 8 Mar. 1981

Writers since the last half of the 19th century have used the interplay of the notions of enormous size and of wickedness or outrageousness to give their uses of the word a richness of meaning that they have directed in various ways. Here, for instance, we have a writer combining size with moral outrage:

The enormity of existing stockpiles of atomic weapons —*New Republic,* 21 Dec. 1953

Another writer uses it for humorous effect:

That is one of the lessons that buses remind you of . . . the enormity of the female behind —Beverly Nichols, *Punch,* 12 Dec. 1973

Sometimes even the "enormous wickedness" sense has been employed tongue-in-cheek:

. . . that solemn warning against the enormity of the split infinitive —Havelock Ellis, *The Dance of Life,* 1923

But what about *enormousness?* It has simply never been a very popular word. It developed in the 17th century, later than *enormity,* and its original sense, too, was associated with wickedness:

Such is the infinitenesse and enormousnesse of our rebellious Sin —John Donne, sermon, ca. 1631 (OED)

This sense appears to have dropped out of use. It developed the meaning of "enormous size" about the same time that *enormity* did; the earliest OED example for this sense is dated 1802 and the earliest two for the same sense of *enormity* are 1792 and 1802. It is, indeed, sometimes used in this sense, as the critics recommend that it be:

The plane, the hangar, the assembly equipment, the very workers themselves conveyed an impression of almost antiseptic cleanliness, and this, along with the enormousness of everything, gave the scene a feeling of unreality —John Brooks, *New Yorker,* 26 Apr. 1969

It is also used on occasion as what appears to be a mechanical replacement for *enormity*—in contexts where standard, well-attested uses of *enormity* (like those we have already examined) would have been at least as appropriate:

. . . Bengali civil servants . . . are dispirited, unhopeful, buried in mindless routine, and crushed by the enormousness of their daily challenges —C. Stephen Baldwin, *Saturday Rev.,* 6 Nov. 1971

But what really gives oxygen to O'Neill's fantasy and life to his dialogue . . . is the enormousness of need which Richardson and Neeson winkle out from behind the words —John Lahr, *New Yorker,* 1 Feb. 1993

But in spite of the adjurations of the critics, *enormousness* does not find a great many users. The reasons for stigmatizing the size sense of *enormity* are not known. It was simply characterized without explanation by Henry Bradley, editor of the *E* volume of the OED (1893), in these words: "this use is now regarded as incorrect." The sense was labeled obsolete or rare in Webster 1909, but the labels were removed in Webster's Second, leaving the sense unstigmatized. Both editions have synonymy notes that distinguish between *enormity* and *enormousness* by stressing the sense of wickedness for *enormity.* It seems possible that the critics derived their opinion from the synonymy notes, since they clearly have not heeded the definitions.

There is some recent evidence that a different view is beginning to find expression:

. . . I think the time has come to abandon the ramparts on "enormity's" connotation of wickedness —William Safire, *N.Y. Times,* 8 Mar. 1981

Conservatives hold that *enormity* means only 'extreme badness,' never 'enormous size.' We feel that this rule is obsolete and that it is acceptable to use the word in either sense, or in both at once —*Reader's Digest* 1983

We agree with these two commentators. We have seen that there is no clear basis for the "rule" at all. We suggest that you follow the writers rather than the critics: writers use *enormity* with a richness and subtlety that the critics have failed to take account of. The stigmatized sense is entirely standard and has been for more than a century and a half.

enquire See INQUIRE, ENQUIRE.

enquirer See INQUIRER, ENQUIRER.

enquiry See INQUIRY, ENQUIRY.

en route This French phrase was first used in English in the 19th century. Its assimilation into our language was completed long ago, and there is no longer any need to underline or italicize it as a foreign term. It is written both as one word and two. Copperud 1980 prefers the two-word form, and our evidence shows that it is the more common choice:

. . . essential that the civil en route services be provided —R. W. Faulks, *Principles of Transport,* 1973

The Apollo can be calibrated en route —Richard L. Collins, *Flying,* March 1984

Because the *en* of *en route* sounds just like *on* in one of its pronunciations, the potential for an embarrassing error exists:

. . . in spite of the fact that, on route to the show, the van brakes failed —*Chronicle of the Horse,* 3 Aug. 1984

Authors and proofreaders beware: your spelling checker won't help.

ensure, insure, assure Quite a few commentators insist on distinctions between these words, but Bernstein 1977 says there are none, flatly contradicting Einstein 1985, who says that each means something different. Usage agrees better with Bernstein. Here is what the synonymy paragraph in Merriam-Webster's Collegiate Dictionary, Tenth Edition, says:

> *Ensure, insure,* and *assure* are interchangeable in many contexts where they indicate the making certain or inevitable of an outcome, but *insure* sometimes stresses the taking of necessary measures beforehand, and *assure* distinctively implies the removal of doubt and suspense from a person's mind.

And here are three typical examples:

> . . . but the state has blocked the sale until Witco assures that any pollution on the property will be cleaned up —Barry Meier, *Wall Street Jour.,* 7 Aug. 1985

> . . . claims that his system will ensure uniformity in pronunciation —Baron 1982

> . . . held that school officials had the right to insure that a high-school assembly proceed in an orderly manner —William Safire, *N.Y. Times,* 24 Aug. 1986

A few commentators, such as Trimble 1975 and Sellers 1975, suggest *assure* for people, *ensure* for things, and *insure* for money and guarantees (insurance). These are nice distinctions, and you can follow them if you want to. *Assure* is almost always used of people, in fact:

> But I am writing to assure you no jury would convict if you wanted to join me in murdering Eddy Duchin —Alexander Woollcott, letter, 22 Feb. 1933

The rest of the recommendation rests on using *ensure* for general senses and reserving *insure* for financial senses. This distinction has been urged at least since Fowler 1926, especially by British commentators. It is in general true that *insure* is used for the financial uses. However, both *insure* and *ensure* are used in general senses:

> A solicitor is a man whose profession ensures that whenever you telephone him, he is in court —Alan Brien, *Punch,* 11 Sept. 1974

> . . . so simple a thing as ensure that all third-grade teachers will be expert in spelling —Mitchell 1979

> . . . would insure against any awkward second marriage —Mollie Hardwick, *Emma, Lady Hamilton,* 1969

> . . . his sudden fame probably insured a backlash —Calvin Tomkins, *New Yorker,* 6 Dec. 1982

Our most recent evidence shows that the distinction between *ensure* and *insure* is made more often in British written English than in American written English.

enter *Enter* is a verb which may be used with many prepositions, but most often it is used with *into* or with *upon* or *on*; of these, *into* occurs most frequently:

> Mr. Sloane didn't enter into the conversation —F. Scott Fitzgerald, *The Great Gatsby,* 1925

> Nor shall I enter into details concerning the ensuing half-dozen nights —Katherine Anne Porter, *Ladies' Home Jour.,* August 1971

> . . . wondered whether . . . this marriage had been entered upon late —Jean Stafford, *Children Are Bored on Sunday,* 1953

> . . . the house has now entered on a distinctly new phase —Edmund Wilson, *New Yorker,* 5 June 1971

Enter is also used with complements introduced by *for, as, at, by,* and *with*. Of this group *for* and *as* appear more often than the others:

> Six . . . were entered for the English Derby —George Whiting, *Irish Digest,* June 1954

> . . . the United States Army, which he entered as a captain —*Current Biography,* December 1964

> . . . he had come to America, probably entering at the port of Charleston, S.C. —*Dictionary of American Biography,* 1928

> . . . even though such language entered by way of the ruling classes —W. F. Bolton, *A Short History of Literary English,* 1967

> . . . a United States Naval Reserve chaplain, entering with the rank of lieutenant (j.g.) —*Current Biography,* January 1964

enthrall Usually, when *enthrall* is used with a preposition, it is used with *by*:

> . . . I am most enthralled by the past world that Borges offers up —John Riley, *Los Angeles Times Book Rev.,* 23 Jan. 1972

Enthrall may also be used with *with*:

> . . . Nelly, with whom he is enthralled —Tom Bishop, *Saturday Rev.,* 5 Feb. 1972

enthuse The road to respectability has been a long one for *enthuse,* and there are some who feel that it still has not arrived. It originated as a back-formation of the noun *enthusiasm* in the early 19th century.

Enthuse has been the object of critical attention at least since Richard Grant White 1870 called it "ridiculous." Ayres 1881 was somewhat more moderate in his judgment than White, saying only that *enthuse* had not yet won acceptance and that "for the present . . . it is studiously shunned by those who are at all careful in the selection of their language." Unlike White, Ayres recognized the possibility that *enthuse* might one day cease to be "shunned." Its written use during Ayres's time seems to have been chiefly confined to newspapers (as it is now), but journalists were not the only writers to employ it:

> . . . I have been very much interested in the memorial; and I have been enthused over what I conceive to be Lanier's theories of art —Robert Frost, letter, 10 June 1894

The attitude of usage commentators toward *enthuse* has been fairly consistent throughout the 20th century. In general, their criticism has been expressed more in the relatively moderate tones of Ayres than in the strident tones of Richard Grant White. The origins of *enthuse* as a back-formation are not now usually regarded as an unpardonable sin, but doubts persist about its suitability in formal writing. The typical advice now given is to avoid written use of *enthuse* because its reputation remains suspect.

Like opinion about it, actual usage of *enthuse* seems to have changed little through the years, except that it occurs much more commonly in writing than it once did. One of its most familiar uses is in the form of the past participle *enthused,* which functions as an adjective more or less equivalent to *enthusiastic*:

> I can think of few startups an intelligent executive would be less enthused about joining than yet another PC clonemaker —Joseph R. Garber, *Forbes,* 6 April 1998

> Researchers were especially enthused about the findings —Ron Winslow, *Wall Street Jour.,* 28 Sept. 1998

> The President was enthused —H. R. Haldeman, *Forbes,* 15 Mar. 1982

Its other common uses are as a transitive verb meaning "to say with enthusiasm":

> "Tremendously useful" he enthused —Hardcastle, *Punch,* 27 May 1975

> "I think it's great," a woman from Omaha enthused —Marquis Childs, *Smithsonian,* June 1985

or "to make enthusiastic":

> . . . the competitive spirit that has enthused blackberry-pickers down the years —Dennis Johnson, *Manchester Guardian Weekly,* 27 Sept. 1992

and as an intransitive verb meaning "to express enthusiasm":

> I must enthuse a little, too, over some old favourites —Harold J. Laski, letter, 1921

> . . . to hear the youngsters of today enthusing about the croissants —Frank Sullivan, *The Night the Old Nostalgia Burned Down,* 1953

> . . . and I was enthusing over it —Julian Huxley, *Memories,* 1970

> . . . enthuses over the joys and beauties of . . . homestead crafts —John D. Tierney, *Wall Street Jour.,* 18 Aug. 1981

Our evidence does not show that *enthuse* is a remarkably informal word, but it does confirm that it is not used in highly formal writing. The common applications of the word make it most useful—and most often used—in journalistic prose. The stigma attached to it is not a strong one, but it is persistent; we would not bet against its lingering for some years yet.

entitle *Entitle* has two common meanings: "to give a title to, title" and "to give a right to." Sources as diverse as Emily Post 1927 and Bremner 1980 have expressed disapproval of using *entitled* to mean "titled." However, this well-established usage has been common for over 500 years and is the older of the two senses.

> . . . a sermon entitled "Popular Government by Divine Right" —Stuart W. Chapman, *Yale Rev.,* Summer 1954

> I was impelled to entitle a recent political column about the Saudi oil minister, Sheik Ahmed Yamani, "Yamani or Ya Life" —Safire 1984

enure See INURE, ENURE.

envelope The two pronunciations of the noun, \'en-və-ˌlōp\ and \'än-və-ˌlōp\, are used with about equal frequency and are both fully acceptable, but the \'än-\ version is sometimes stridently decried. Evans 1962 calls it "a strange, ignorant mispronunciation," and approvingly cites Kenyon and Knott's dismissal of it as "pseudo-French" in A Pronouncing Dictionary of American English (1944).

It is really not pseudo-French, nor ignorant, and as used by most speakers today it appears naturally, with no affectation or striving for style. If you were to try to anglicize the French word *enveloppe,* \'än-və-ˌlōp\ is exactly what you would come up with—a pronunciation like that of *encore, ennui,* and many others. A fairly reasonable objection one might make to it is that *envelope* has been in our language since the early 18th century, so that it deserves to be spoken like such other old borrowings from French as *envy* and *environ* rather than to vary between two versions, as do *enclave* and *en route,* which were borrowed more recently.

Such a calmly philological consideration cannot well be the source of the peculiar venom directed against \'än-\, however. For this we must look to more revealing animadversions, such as one in the February 1926 issue of *American Speech,* which refers to someone who "is tempted to invest in a very high silk hat such as the doorkeeper uses at the British Museum, take to using *onvelopes,* write only *cheques* at the bank. . . ." Or this from Vladimir Nabokov's *Lolita* (1958):

> Oh, she was very genteel: she said "excuse me" whenever a slight burp interrupted her flowing speech, called an envelope an ahn-velope. . . .

Thus, \'än-və-ˌlōp\ is (or was) considered not so much wrong as non-U: a dreadful indication of the middle classes getting above themselves.

envious, enviable At one time, *envious* and *enviable* shared a sense, "highly desirable," but *envious* has lost the sense while *enviable* has retained it. Some language commentators warn not to mix up the two words, but our files show that such confusion is unlikely, because *envious* is not now used in the shared sense except in such contexts as poetry:

> Theirs was an envious gift, but lightly held —Thomas Cole, *Interim,* vol. 4, 1954

Envious, when used with a preposition, is usually used with *of*:

> . . . were envious of the easier way of life of their Kikuyu neighbours —L. S. B. Leakey, *Mau Mau and the Kikuyu,* 1952

envisage, envision *Envisage* got started in English in the early 19th century with the sense, now archaic, of "to meet squarely," "confront," "face."

> Must I recognize the bitter truth? . . . I have envisaged it —George Meredith, *The Egoist,* 1879 (OED)

By 1837 a second sense was developing which the OED defines as "To obtain a mental view of, set before the mind's eye; to contemplate; *chiefly,* to view or regard under a particular aspect." This use was attacked for no very obvious reason by Fowler 1926, and his objections were carried forward by two of his revisers, Nicholson 1957 and Gowers 1965.

Envision appeared on the scene by 1919—late enough, apparently, to escape Fowler's criticism and that of Nicholson and Gowers. Burchfield 1996 reports that *envisage* is favored in British English and *envision* in American but that the preferences are not exclusive. Garner 1998 concurs.

Here are some citations which show how *envisage* and *envision* are, in many respects, interchangeable:

> . . . I could envisage without difficulty a typical . . . day —P. G. Wodehouse, *Joy in the Morning,* 1946

> . . . all utopias . . . envisage a different kind of men and women from any that we know —*Times Literary Supp.,* 23 Apr. 1971

> . . . we envisage booming demand for political scientists —Alan Abelson, *Barron's,* 8 May 1972

> The dingy office, pathetic with an outmoded elegance of brass rail and threadbare carpet, was exactly what Mr. Campion had envisioned —Margery Allingham, *More Work for the Undertaker,* 1949

> . . . had envisioned only the possibility of humiliation —Stanley Marcus, *Minding the Store,* 1974

> . . . we may envision the appalled face of Emerson —Robert Penn Warren, *Democracy and Poetry,* 1975

epic Various popular uses of this literary word have been criticized from time to time. In its primary sense, *epic* denotes a long narrative poem such as the *Iliad* or the *Odyssey,* in which the deeds of historic or legendary figures are recounted. It also has several extended senses in which it applies to such modern phenomena as big-budget historical movies and double-overtime basketball games. These extended senses are sometimes criticized as hyperbolic, but they continue in widespread and largely uncontroversial use:

> The most spirited and satisfying new Western epic in several years —*New Yorker,* 31 Oct. 1983

> . . . an upset, lacrosse followers say, of nearly epic proportions —Bob Kravitz, *Sports Illustrated,* 4 Aug. 1986

epicene pronouns A problem of long standing in English is finding a gender-neutral singular pronoun to use in reference to indefinite pronouns like *anyone, everyone,* and *someone.* The spoken language has long used *they, their,* and *them,* but this folk solution has not sufficed for the academically trained and grammatically oriented, for whom number sometimes seems to be more important than common sense. The most usual grammarian's solution (buttressed at least once by the British parliament) has been to recommend the masculine *he, his, him.* Some grammarians and theorists, beginning in the 19th century, have chosen the road of neologism. This has led to such proposed forms as *ne, nis, nim, hiser, thon, en, unus, talis, ir, iro, im, ons, he'er, shis, heris, co, cos, tey, ter, tem, s/he,* and so on and on. The latest we have heard of are *che, chim, chis, chimself,* proposed by someone from Texas in December 1985. There may never be an end to these ingenious proposals. The best, most informative, and most entertaining summary of this whole matter is an article by Dennis E. Baron in *American Speech,* vol. 56, no. 2, Summer 1981. The same discussion is presented in a somewhat revised form as the tenth chapter of his book *Grammar and Gender* (1986).

Under this heading Nickles 1974 disapproves of *they, their,* and *them* used in reference to indefinite pronouns. We discuss the matter at THEY, THEIR, THEM 1.

epidemic See ENDEMIC, EPIDEMIC.

epithet An *epithet* can be either an adjective or a noun. Its use for a noun was disapproved during the 19th century, but such use is accepted now. Johnson's 1755 Dictionary noted that epithets may describe both good and bad qualities. Both uses are still current, but negative overtones are more common.

> . . . was what we now call a lowbrow; but that epithet had not then been invented —George Bernard Shaw, *American Mercury,* January 1946

> . . . forbade the union . . . from using epithets or offensive language against the company's employes —*Wall Street Jour.,* 5 Aug. 1948

> . . . his name has come to be almost as much of an epithet as that of the late Quisling —Bob Considine, *Springfield* (Mass.) *Union,* 26 Nov. 1954

This sense of *epithet* has not displaced the older, nonpejorative sense, which also continues in regular use:

> . . . earned him the affectionate epithet of "peanut ambassador" —*Current Biography,* April 1966

> . . . their search for the just adjective, the refined epithet —Kathleen Raine, *CEA Chap Book,* 1969

epitome The best-known sense of *epitome* is "a typical or ideal example," "embodiment." A few usage writers mention that *epitome* can be used of something bad as well as something good; this is true.

> He was the epitome of the ruthless business titan —S. N. Behrman, *New Yorker,* 27 Oct. 1951

> Even when apparently used with the intended meaning "embodiment," *epitome* can be interpreted as meaning "acme," "high point."

Such rides are my earliest recollection. They remain in memory as the epitome of happiness —Frank Swinnerton, *Tokefield Papers,* 1949

> . . . many Americans see the F.D.A. . . . as the epitome of foot-dragging bureaucracy —Herbert Burkholz, *N.Y. Times Mag.,* 30 June 1991

Harper 1985, Garner 1998, and others advise against using *epitome* to mean "acme." The "embodiment" sense is usually clear when *epitome* refers to a person; it is when it applies to something nonhuman that the meaning is uncertain. It may be that an "acme" sense is developing. Garner has an "epitome of boredom" example, and we have these:

> It's the epitome of game shows, the Olympics of game shows —Marvin Shinkman, quoted by Joanne Lipman, *Wall Street Jour.,* 7 Nov. 1986

> . . . the Blue Devils were being hailed as the epitome of college basketball —*Basketball Digest,* December 1993

This use does not appear to be established quite yet.

epoch Bernstein 1965 considers the proper meaning of *epoch* to be "the beginning of a new period, a turning point." That is, in fact, one of the oldest senses of the word, but it is now rarely seen:

> The adherence of the United States to such a convention would mark an epoch in the international copyright relations of this country —Arthur Fisher, *Annual Report of the Librarian of Congress,* 1952

Far more common is the use of *epoch* to mean "an extended and distinct period of time." Some commentators have attacked this sense, but it is entirely proper:

> . . . the leading international lawyer of his epoch —*Times Literary Supp.,* 25 Jan. 1974

> In the Cartesian epoch . . . man conceived of the universe as a watch —Robert Penn Warren, *Democracy and Poetry,* 1975

equal 1. When *equal* is used with a preposition, it is used most often with *to*:

> . . . whether the idea of maximum personal liberty is equal to the idea of maximum personal discipline —Adlai E. Stevenson, *Speeches,* ed. Richard Harrity, 1952

> He was equal to extended walks by this time —Thomas B. Costain, *The Black Rose,* 1945

Equal to may also be used with a gerund or an infinitive:

> . . . become equal to solving the problems of every conceivable environment —William

J. Reilly, *Life Planning for College Students,*
1954

She was very equal, therefore, to address
Mr. Bingley on the subject of the ball
—Jane Austen, *Pride and Prejudice,* 1813

Although the use of *equal* with *with* occurs
more often in older writings, it is still in occasional use:

. . . maintain social services in his country
on a level equal with those in the rest of the
United Kingdom —*Current Biography,* September 1968

2. *Equal* is one of those adjectives that commentators such as Partridge 1942, Bernstein
1965, and Shaw 1970, 1987 insist are absolute
and incapable of comparison. They therefore
disapprove of the combination *more equal.*
This opinion suffers from two weaknesses. It
ignores history—*equal* has been compared
since at least the 17th century—and it fails to
recognize the common use of *more* and *most*
to mean "more nearly," "most nearly." Here
are some ordinary uses of *more equal* in the
sense of "more nearly equal":

. . . but if we keep edging toward it, American society will become more just, more
equal, and more evenhanded in the distribution of power —John Fischer, *Harper's,*
March 1971

So even though income distribution among
unmarried individuals grew more equal
over the decade, among families it grew less
equal —David Osborne, *Harper's,* January
1983

More equal cannot be allowed to depart
without a notice of George Orwell's use of the
phrase in *Animal Farm.* There he used *equal* in
a way not normally compared and put *more*
with it to show the duplicitous ways in which
totalitarian regimes use the language for their
own advantage. All animals, say the ruling
pigs, are equal, but some are more equal than
others. Orwell's *more equal than* has frequently been echoed by later writers:

. . . those who are less equal than others
must find the power —Tom Hayden, *American Scholar,* Autumn 1967

. . . a rule of all great egalitarian bureaucracies, as George Orwell pointed out, is that
some people are more equal than others
—John Hersey, *New Yorker,* 31 May 1982

equally as This phrase has been denigrated
in books on English usage for more than a
hundred years. Nineteenth-century commentators such as Ayres 1881 concerned themselves in particular with the phrase *equally as
well,* which Ayres described as "a redundant
form of expression." Commentators through-

out the 20th century have expressed much the
same opinion. The definitive seal of disapproval was given by Fowler 1926, who called
equally as "an illiterate tautology."

The reason *equally as* is considered redundant is that either *equally* or *as* can stand
alone in most of the contexts in which the
phrase is used. However, as Bernstein 1965
notes, that *as* by itself is far less emphatic than
either *equally as* or *equally.*

Equally as is certainly not "illiterate," and its
redundancy is more apparent than real. We
would describe it as an idiomatic phrase that is
equivalent to *just as* and that is widely regarded as redundant. It no doubt occurs commonly in speech, but its reputation is bad enough
to make it relatively rare in edited prose:

There are others equally as dedicated
—*Forbes,* 15 Sept. 1970

. . . retaliated with two thorough slaughters
of the Redmen. . . . Their two get-back
whippings of Syracuse were equally as brutal —Curry Kirkpatrick, *Sports Illustrated,*
25 Mar. 1985

This innocuous phrase has drawn more vehement criticism than is warranted, but you may
well want to prefer *just as* in your writing or to
use *equally* by itself for emphasis where your
construction permits it.

equivalent **1.** When the adjective *equivalent*
is used with a preposition, the choice is usually *to:*

It is also misleading to talk as if a mere liking . . . for the ritual . . . of one of the Christian churches were equivalent to a religion
—Edmund Wilson, *A Piece of My Mind,*
1956

Much less often it is used with *with:*

A third additional trial would be equivalent
with the first one made originally —J. M.
Wolfe, *First Course in Cryptanalysis,* vol. II,
rev. ed., 1943

2. When the noun *equivalent* is used with a
preposition, it is usually used with *of:*

In economics, the equivalent of a beautifully composed work of art is the smoothly
running factory —Aldous Huxley, *Brave
New World Revisited,* 1958

Less frequently it may be used with *to,* and
still less frequently with *for:*

. . . the intellectual equivalent to a certain
surgical operation —*The Autobiography of
William Butler Yeats,* 1953

. . . France is almost without an equivalent
for the old "newspapers of information"
—*Manchester Guardian Weekly,* 10 Nov.
1944

erotica *Erotica* has the form of a Greek plural, but it is now usually understood as a mass noun meaning "erotic material," and, as Bernstein 1971 observes, it is now more often than not construed as singular:

> . . . the erotica is explicit —Thomas Lask, *N.Y. Times,* 15 Oct. 1966

> Is all erotica male fantasy then . . . ? —Shana Alexander, *Newsweek,* 5 Feb. 1973

Treatment of *erotica* as a plural still occurs, however, and is not incorrect:

> There is also a top row of erotica and I asked the man if he sold many of these —Bill Moyers, *Harper's,* December 1970

For other foreign plurals, see LATIN PLURALS.

err The dust of controversy swirls thickly about the pronunciation of this word. The traditional pronunciation can be illustrated from the works of Alexander Pope, who also gave us the phrase "to err is human" and is thus partly responsible for the continued familiarity of the word:

> In doubt his Mind or Body to prefer;
> Born but to die, and reas'ning but to err
> —"Essay on Man," 1734

But in our own century we find this witness, from a less celebrated pen, to the existence of an untraditional pronunciation:

> Those who err and call it *air*
> Can be met with everywhere.
> Educated men and women
> Fondly quote: "To air is human."
> —Katherine Buxbaum, in a publication of the Iowa State Teachers College, no date

Those who condemn \'er\ for *err* typically advance no reason other than the implicit one of tradition. Since *err* is both a semantic and etymological relative of *error,* \'er\ has what commentators usually call "logic" on its side; and the tradition has, in fact, partly dissolved in current usage, where \'er\ preponderates. Further, some speakers who are quite aware that they are "supposed" to say \'ər\ nevertheless eschew that version for its indistinct vowel. We may, then, endorse the further sentiments of Katherine Buxbaum:

> Blame the speakers? Let's be fairer:
> Blame the language for the error.
> *Error* is a proper word,
> "Ur-ur" would be quite absurd.
> Is it natural to infer
> That making errors is to err?
> Wherefore, purists, don't despair,
> Thoughts of punishment forbear,
> Just give the erring ones the air.

For a related but distinct question of pronunciation, see ERRANT, ARRANT 2.

errant, arrant 1. *Errant* and *arrant* were once synonymous words, but they long ago came to be distinguished from each other in their principal senses. The fundamental meaning of *errant* is "wandering" (as in "an errant knight"), while *arrant,* which also once meant "wandering," now has the sense "utterly bad" (as in "arrant nonsense"). The OED shows that *arrant* originated as a variant of *errant,* and that its current sense developed from its use in such phrases as "an arrant thief," which originally meant a wandering, vagrant thief but came eventually to be understood as an utterly bad thief. "Utterly bad" has been the principal sense of *arrant* since at least Shakespeare's time:

> We are arrant knaves all; believe none of us —Shakespeare, *Hamlet,* 1601

Errant has also been used in this sense:

> They are errant cowards —Daniel Defoe, *Robinson Crusoe,* 1719 (OED)

But this sense of *errant* seems never to have been very common and is now usually considered obsolete.

As a topic for discussion by usage commentators, the distinction between *errant* and *arrant* has a long but otherwise unimpressive history. The distinction in which *errant* means "wandering" and *arrant* "utterly bad" is generally observed in modern usage, but *errant* still turns up on rare occasions in place of *arrant:*

> . . . it is errant stupidity to look for simplicity in so-called simple cultures —Farley Mowat, *People of the Deer,* 1952

Such usage can be defended on historical grounds, but you would probably do better to choose *arrant* when you mean "utterly bad." 2. In accordance with the difference in spelling between *errant* and *arrant,* there has arisen a distinction in pronunciation, \'er-ənt\ versus \'ar-ənt\; but for a great many speakers who do not distinguish \e\ and \a\ before \r\ the distinction is impossible to maintain. Both pronunciations must therefore be considered acceptable for either word. See also ERR.

errata This little-used word leads a double life. Its primary existence is as the plural of *erratum,* a fancy synonym for "error" that is used principally to mean "an error in a printed work discovered after printing and shown with its correction on a separate sheet." But *errata* is also used in the publishing world in a distinct sense denoting either a list of such errors or the page on which such a list is printed. Usage commentators such as Shaw 1975, Harper 1975, 1985, and the panelists of Heritage 1969 and Heritage 1982 take a peculiar attitude toward this sense of *errata*. They accept the sense itself but advise that *errata* should always be construed as a plural, even when its meaning is "a list" or "a page." This advice seems impossible to follow:

> The Errata, if included, is a list of errors —C. A. Hurst & F. R. Lawrence, *Letterpress Composition and Machine-Work,* 1963

One could not say "The Errata are a list . . ." When *errata* is clearly being used in its singular sense, it cannot logically be used with a plural verb—such usage would be equivalent to saying, "The list are . . ." or "The page are . . ." In cases where a plural verb can be substituted without resulting in an ungrammatical sentence, the effect of the substitution is to change the meaning of *errata*. For example, if "The errata is in the appendix" is revised to "The errata are in the appendix," *errata* no longer means "list" in the revised sentence, but is serving instead as the plural of *erratum* and suggesting that there are errors in the appendix.

Confusing, isn't it? The point is that when the commentators say *errata* should always be treated as a plural, they are saying in effect that the use of *errata* to mean "a list" or "a page" is incorrect. What our evidence says is that the singular use of *errata* is limited to—and is correct in—the world of publishing:

> . . . this reissue . . . differs from the original only in the additions of an explanatory preface and an end errata —Glenn O. Carey, *CEA Critic,* January 1972

For other foreign plurals, see LATIN PLURALS.

erstwhile, quondam, whilom These three strange-looking words are all adjectives that mean "former."

The adjective *erstwhile* has a somewhat mysterious and confused history. It is not mentioned in the OED, and the earliest citation we know of appears in OED II and is dated 1903; yet, Webster 1909 and Webster's Second (1934) mistakenly label it archaic. Whatever its past, *erstwhile* now is widely used as an adjective:

> John Hennessey—erstwhile dean of the engineering school —Tom McNichol, *Wired,* October 2000

> . . . George Harrison of the erstwhile Beatles —Faubion Bowers, *Atlantic,* February 1972

> . . . started an erstwhile wide receiver . . . at quarterback —Paul Zimmerman, *Sports Illustrated,* 10 Jan. 1983

Though less common than *erstwhile, quondam* appears in a variety of contexts:

> Wheatleigh, originally a wedding present from a quondam robber baron to his daughter —Jack Beatty, *Atlantic,* May 1993

> A quondam grocery store now displays early prints and maps —Alan L. Otten, *Wall Street Jour.,* 10 June 1981

Whilom gets used occasionally:

> . . . the whilom seaport that once rivaled Philadelphia —William Least Heat Moon, *Blue Highways,* 1982

Harper 1985 says that "*erstwhile* is seldom used except in formal writing and even then it is often misunderstood." While we cannot agree that this is true of *erstwhile,* we do think it is true of *quondam* and *whilom.* If you decide to use one of these last two for reasons of style, you run the risk of confusing or mystifying your readers.

escalate *Escalate* is a back-formation from the noun *escalator.* It was first used in the early 20th century with the literal sense, "to ride up on an escalator":

> I dreamt I saw a Proctor 'escalating', Rushing up a quickly moving stair —*The Granta,* 10 Nov. 1922 (OED Supplement)

This sense seems to have disappeared. Figurative use of the verb seems to have developed from figurative senses of *escalation* and *escalator* that originated in the 1930s.

Escalate became a common word in the 1960s, when it was used constantly in speaking of the increasing U.S. involvement in the war in Vietnam. As its range of applications expanded, it was inevitably criticized as a vogue word, especially by British commentators.

Escalate typically implies a continuing and usually undesirable increase or expansion, often with the added implication that each stage of the increase provokes even further increases:

> . . . the violence escalated to include gunfire and gang warfare —*Newsweek,* 6 Mar. 1967

> The costs are already too high, and they escalate higher each year —Lewis Thomas, in *The Contemporary Essay,* ed. Donald Hall, 1984

Less often, *escalate* serves simply as a synonym of *increase* or *grow:*

> His interest escalated as his knowledge and skill deepened —Margaret Carter, *Living,* July 1974

escalator For pronunciation problems with this word, see NUCLEAR.

escape Does a prisoner escape jail or escape *from* jail? *Escape from* is the usual idiom, but *escape* is also occasionally used as a transitive verb in such a context, without *from:*

> . . . after escaping a Russian prison camp in his youth —Stanley Ellin, *N.Y. Times Book Rev.,* 20 July 1975

This sense of the verb is "to get free of." Its use, like that of the intransitive *escape (from),* is not limited to descriptions of jailbreaks:

> . . . machine-gunned those who tried to escape the burning ruins —William L. Shirer, *The Rise and Fall of the Third Reich,* 1960

A distinctive modern use of transitive *escape* is in contexts relating to space travel:

> . . . the second spacecraft to escape the Solar System —S. W. H. Cowley, *Nature,* 27 Mar. 1980

Evidence in the OED shows that this transitive *escape* is extremely old, being first attested in the 14th century. By the end of the 1600s, however, it had fallen into disuse, and until quite recently it was either omitted altogether from dictionaries or was labeled obsolete, as it is in the OED and in Webster's Third. Its recent revival—more accurately, its recent recoinage—dates only from the late 1950s, according to our evidence. A few usage commentators (Bernstein 1962, 1965; Harper 1975, 1985; and the usage panel of Heritage 1969) regard it as an error, arguing that as a transitive verb *escape* properly means "to avoid" (as in "escape possible punishment"). More recent commentators, such as Burchfield 1996 and Garner 1998, and most current dictionaries consider *escape* in the sense "get free of" as standard.

escapee *Escapee* has been criticized as a mistake for the older and seemingly more logical *escaper.* It is, however, a standard word and is recognized as such by all current dictionaries.

See also -EE.

especial, especially See SPECIAL, SPECIALLY, ESPECIAL, ESPECIALLY.

espresso, expresso The strong coffee made by forcing steam under pressure through finely ground coffee beans is known in Italian as *caffé espresso,* or just *espresso* for short. Contrary to a popular belief of English-speakers, the *espresso* means not "fast" but "pressed out"—it refers to the process by which the coffee is made, not the speed of the process. The idea that *caffé espresso* means "fast coffee" may have contributed somewhat to the occurrence in English of the variant *expresso,* or the variant may have originated simply because it more closely resembles a familiar English word than does *espresso.* In any case, *ex-* *presso* is in widespread use, both on menus and in edited prose:

> Jérôme sidled to the expresso bar —Jerome Charyn, *Antaeus,* Winter 1976

> . . . thick expresso with a shot of Calvados —Patricia Wells, *N.Y. Times,* 6 June 1982

Several current dictionaries, including Merriam-Webster's Collegiate Dictionary, Tenth Edition, and the OED Supplement, recognize *expresso* as an established variant, but others omit it altogether or treat it as a mistake. *Espresso* is the more common form.

Esquire *Esquire* is used in British English as a respectful title used in addressing correspondence to any man who could otherwise be referred to as "Mr."—in other words, just about any man at all. It is usually abbreviated to *Esq.* Its use in American English is far less common, persisting mainly among attorneys, who use it when referring to or addressing each other in writing.

There has recently been some controversy in American legal circles about using *Esq.* after the name of a woman lawyer. Garner 1998 reports that the usage is standard.

Note that when *Esq.* is used as a title following a name, no other title or term of address is used before the name.

-ess In 1855 Archbishop Richard Chevenix Trench, in *English Past and Present,* devoted a chapter to English words that were disappearing from use. One class of words he found greatly diminished in 19th-century English was feminine nouns—most of them designating occupations—ending in *-ess.* From the literature of the 14th, 15th, 16th, and 17th centuries he brought forth such interesting specimens as *teacheress, sinneress, neighbouress, herdess, constabless, ministress, flatteress, saintess, soldieress, impostress,* and *builderess.* According to H. L. Mencken (*The American Language, Supplement I,* 1945), a copy of Trench's book found its way into the hands of Mrs. Sarah Josepha Hale, editress (her term) of *Godey's Lady's Book,* in 1865. In the period around the Civil War, American women had begun their movement for civil rights, for the vote, and for a more active role in public life generally. Mrs. Hale made a stirring plea for the revival and establishment of many of these terms; it was her belief, apparently, that the regular use of these terms would add dignity to the women whose professions or occupations they described. She set forth one list of twenty-five occupational or professional titles and another of thirty-three more general titles which had, or for which she proposed, *-ess* equivalents (the lists are in Mencken).

Many of the words on these lists had been in

general use all along—*empress, duchess, princess, lioness, abbess, goddess, waitress, prioress,* and so forth—and had never been the subject of much discussion—indeed, most of these are impeccable today. But others of them, including such established words as *authoress* and *poetess,* ran afoul of the male establishment. They were derogated by the intellectually elite as ugly, pedantic, and unnecessary. At the other end of the spectrum, 19th-century American humorists like Artemus Ward and Petroleum V. Nasby used such terms as *beastess, championess,* and *prestidigitateuress* to satirize the serious use by women and of women of some of the terms Mrs. Hale had recommended. Mamie Meredith has an interesting survey of such use in *American Speech* (August 1930).

By the time we get to the 20th century, we find women turning against many of these terms too; the words are held to be demeaning in that they inject the consideration of sex where it is unnecessary. This argument had already been one of many put forth by 19th-century male critics of *poetess* and *authoress.* Most recent feminist opinion also opposes such forms. Wilson 1987 notes with wry amusement that it is almost always the masculine term (*actor, priest, shepherd*) that feminists want to have as the standard generic noun (but the same is not true for pronouns— see EPICENE PRONOUNS).

These feminine forms have not lacked defenders. One surprising one is Fowler 1926. Fowler thought that *-ess* words (and other feminine forms) were useful, and he thought there should be more of them. Interestingly, some of the less successful *-ess* words that Fowler champions can be found on the 1865 list in *Godey's Lady's Book.*

So far we have seen that *-ess* forms have been urged by women and condemned by women, and condemned by men and defended by men. A mixed bag of opinions, at least through the period of Fowler. Is modern opinion clearer? Yes and no. Though *-ess* forms would find few proponents among feminists today, the commentators—mostly men, of course—present less than a clear picture. For instance, Shaw 1975, 1987 says that *Negress* and *Jewess* were considered offensive long before the Women's Liberation movement; Simon 1980 says that these words are not pejorative. Kilpatrick 1984 advises a man married to a sculptor not to call her a sculptress; Simon thinks *sculptress* is not a pejorative term.

In this book the four *-ess* words most frequently mentioned by usage commentators—*authoress, poetess, Jewess, Negress*—are accorded individual treatment. But we cannot give you any easy advice about *-ess* words in

general. We can offer only a few indications. There seem to have been at least a few people in 19th century England who found some *-ess* forms polite:

> Mr. Lewis Carroll has much pleasure in giving to the editresses of the proposed magazine permission to use . . . —Lewis Carroll, letter, 6 Feb. 1888

And some found them rather humorous:

> How do you like the Mandarinesses? Are you on some little footing with any of them? —Charles Lamb, letter, 29 Mar. 1809

> Now enough of political economy, which I inflict on you only to educate you as a manageress —George Bernard Shaw, letter, 3 Oct. 1899

And at least a few modern writers have found the virtue noted by Fowler of packing two kinds of information in a single word useful:

> As Bech talked, and his translatress feverishly scribbled notes upon his complicated gist —John Updike, *Bech Is Back,* 1982

> . . . immediately my young love becomes a young giantess looking down at me —E. L. Doctorow, *Loon Lake,* 1979

One would probably do well to approach these words in a somewhat gingerly manner. Some are unmistakably out of favor now. Others, however, such as the traditional titles of female nobility, go their merry way. Even those of humbler station often continue in frequent use. *Waitress* shows no real sign, at this point, of being permanently displaced by the genderless neologisms *waitperson* and *waitron* (although *server* may be gaining); indeed, *waitress* has even become more common in print as an informal verb over the last 20 years or so. And the word *manageress,* which Shaw seems to have used humorously, continues in frequent and serious use in British English, our evidence suggests. Clearly this portion of our vocabulary is still evolving.

essay See ASSAY, ESSAY.

essential, *adjective* **1.** *Essential* is used most often with the preposition *to* when the construction requires a preposition:

> . . . you are essential to her perfect happiness —Charles Dickens, *A Tale of Two Cities,* 1859

Somewhat less frequently *essential* may be used with *for:*

> . . . a good liberal education during the undergraduate years is essential for every librarian —*Current Biography,* June 1964

Sometimes it is used with *in*:

> . . . he possesses the charismatic warmth, color, and conviction essential in a national leader —*Current Biography,* September 1964

Still less often *essential* is used with *as*:

> . . . socioeconomic status classifications are essential as a means of giving some meaning to the huge amounts of data —*Annual Report, Educational Testing Service,* 1966–1967

2. Some commentators claim *essential* is an absolute adjective and object to its use with adverbial qualifiers (see ABSOLUTE ADJECTIVES). Follett 1966 says it does not admit of *more* or *less* or even *so*. Partridge 1942 and Jacques Barzun, in *American Scholar,* Summer 1957, seem to be making the same objection. Harper 1975, 1985, while objecting to *more,* finds *most essential* acceptable because it is an idiom used for emphasis rather than comparison. But these commentators are merely expressing their opinion. Our evidence clearly shows *essential* to be a gradable adjective capable of taking adverbial qualifiers.

> The animal nature, indeed, is a most essential part of the Faun's composition —Nathaniel Hawthorne, *The Marble Faun,* 1860
>
> . . . it is now fairly clear that they are absolutely essential to him as a man and as a writer —Richard Poirier, *Saturday Rev.,* 22 Apr. 1972
>
> . . . critics will say that allowing kidney sales is the beginning of a slippery slope toward selling other, more essential organs —Bruce Gottlieb, *New Republic,* 22 May 2000
>
> The most essential characteristic of mind is memory —Bertrand Russell, in *Encore,* July 1946
>
> Once the ranks are filled with career soldiers, a "civilian-oriented leadership" will be more essential than ever —D. Park Teter, *Change,* September 1971

essential, *noun* When the noun *essential* is used with a preposition, it is used most often with *of*:

> . . . these mountain people, albeit unlettered, have acquired so many of the essentials of culture —F. R. Leavis, *The Common Pursuit,* 1952

Less frequently, *essential* appears with *in, for,* or *to*:

> . . . felt that religion was decent and right, an essential in an honest man's life —Pearl Buck, *The Long Love,* 1949

> . . . has plenty of at least one essential for success as an Albany lobbyist —Dwight Macdonald, *New Yorker,* 22 Aug. 1953
>
> . . . a change of underclothes and of socks are almost an essential to me —Graham Greene, *Travels with My Aunt,* 1969

estimate 1. When the verb *estimate* is used with a preposition, it is usually *at*:

> . . . German populations estimated at between 10 and 15 million —Vera Micheles Dean, *The Four Cornerstones of Peace,* 1946

See also ABOUT 2.
There is also evidence in our files for the use of *as, by,* and *from*:

> . . . half a dozen ears of dried corn which Chuck estimated as being over seven hundred years old —*Boy's Life,* February 1953
>
> The child is sexless, the adult estimates his virility by his sexual activities —Ruth Benedict, in *Personality in Nature, Society, and Culture,* ed. Clyde Kluckhohn & Henry A. Murray, 1948
>
> Their attainments in their studies will be estimated from their school records —*1952 Catalogue of Phillips Academy,* Autumn 1951

2. The noun *estimate* is often used with *of*:

> . . . it involved making an estimate of a man's character —C. S. Forester, *The African Queen,* 1935

estrange When used with a preposition *estrange* is used with *from*:

> . . . such critical approaches . . . can only estrange him from the audience he deserves —Irving Howe, *New Republic,* 28 Mar. 1955

Estrange is now found used most often in the passive:

> . . . she telephoned her husband, who was estranged from her and living in Boston —John Updike, *Playboy,* January 1982

et al. This Latin abbreviation means "and others" or "and the others." The most frequent use of *et al.* is in citing (as in a footnote or bibliography) a publication that has several or many authors. To save space, one or two of the authors' names are given, followed by *et al.*:

> Quirk, Randolf, et al. *A Comprehensive Grammar of the English Language.* London: Longman, 1985

Commentators generally discourage the use of *et al.* and similar abbreviations in expository writing, but our evidence shows that such use is common. There is considerable variation in the way *et al.* is styled. It sometimes is printed in italics, and the period following *al* is sometimes omitted; but the favored choice is to retain the period and to print *et al.* in regular roman type:

> Apparently John Updike, Saul Bellow et al. were going to welcome me —Susan Brownmiller, *N.Y. Times Book Rev.,* 12 Jan. 1986

etc. This abbreviation of the Latin *et cetera* means literally "and others of the same kind." Most commentators have one or two things to say about its proper use.

The most frequently repeated point is that *etc.* should not be preceded by *and,* since *et* means "and" in Latin. Our evidence suggests that this is not a serious problem in edited prose. A few commentators also warn that *etc.* should not be used at the end of a list introduced by *for example* or *such as* (as in ". . . such photographic materials as lenses, filters, etc."). The redundancy of *etc.* in such contexts is not strongly felt, however, and the usage does occur in standard writing:

> . . . had such Indian names applied to them as *coon, moose, possum, skunk,* etc. —Mathews 1931

> . . . by such function words as *can, must, should, have,* etc. —C. C. Fries, *The Structure of English,* 1952

There is disagreement about the contexts in which *etc.* can be appropriately used. Some critics favor restricting it to such special contexts as footnotes and technical writing, but others find its use in ordinary prose unobjectionable, recommending only that it be avoided in formal usage. Our evidence shows that *etc.* now occurs commonly in ordinary expository writing:

> . . . the full texts of pastoral letters, . . . private communications, speeches, etc. —Doris Grumbach, *N.Y. Times Book Rev.,* 8 July 1979

> . . . street language, dialects, admixtures of foreign tongues, etc. —Simon 1980

The use of *etc.* in reference to persons rather than to things is defended by Fowler 1926, but other commentators have been less tolerant of it (Partridge 1942 considers it "insulting"). Its occurrence is rare enough that the question of its acceptability is largely moot.

Et cetera is often mispronounced \ek-'set-ər-ə\. The analogous mispronunciation, substituting \ek-\ for \et-\, also occurs in French, and the reason is doubtless the same in both languages: assimilation of an unusual initial sound-sequence (no other familiar word in either language begins with \ets-\) to a common one. Words like *exceptional, ecstatic,* and *eccentric* abound in English. Whether influenced

by this pronunciation or by purely orthographical considerations (*ct* being a more common sequence of letters than *tc*), *etc.* itself is often misspelled *ect.* This was, for instance, the form regularly used by F. Scott Fitzgerald in his letters. Remembering that the phrase begins with Latin *et* "and" should prevent you from committing either the mispronunciation or the misspelling.

ethnic designations: pronunciation The word *Italian* is not infrequently pronounced with initial long *i,* \ī-'tal-yən\, in some regions of the United States, especially among older or less well-educated speakers. Less common is *Arab* with a long initial vowel and secondary stress on the last syllable: \'ā-ˌrab\. Both of these local and, in intent, socially neutral pronunciations are sometimes mimicked by others with humorous intent:

> . . . the seeming rebelliousness of a nice Jewish girl from Central Park West marrying an A-Rab —Erica Jong, *Fear of Flying,* 1973

But such variant pronunciations can give strong offense even if innocently meant. We suggest you use the short vowels, and pronounce these words as \'ar-əb\ and \ə-'tal-yən\ or \i-'tal-yən\.

etymological fallacy *Etymological fallacy* is a term used by philologists and linguists to describe the insistence that a word in present-day English derived from a foreign (and especially Greek or Latin) word must have the same meaning as the foreign word or must have its meaning limited in some way. Such insistence has long been popular with many usage writers, from Richard Grant White 1870 and earlier right down to the present. The appeal to etymology is a very seductive one, especially to those who know a little Latin or Greek. You will find the etymological fallacy mentioned in quite a few of the articles in this book.

One thing to remember when you read or hear someone insisting that an English word must have a certain meaning because of its Latin or Greek roots is that these insisters apply their etymologies very selectively. You will find few of them who object to *December* being used for the twelfth month, when its Latin root means "ten," or to *manure* being used as a noun meaning "dung" when it originally was a verb meaning "to work (land) by hand." So when you read, for example, that *caption* must refer to matter above a picture because it comes from Latin *caput* "head," keep *manure* in mind.

eulogy See ELEGY, EULOGY.

euphemisms 1. A euphemism is an inoffensive expression substituted for another that may offend or suggest something unpleasant.

Euphemisms have been around much longer than the word itself, which dates only from the 17th century. Euphemisms are culturally and socially mediated; they are perhaps less a subject for the student of grammar and usage than for the student of the social sciences more generally.

Euphemism is used as a pejorative label by quite a few writers on usage. It probably has little point as a label, most of the time, since one salient fact about euphemisms is that almost everyone knows what they are being used in place of; only the newest and most abstruse euphemisms are likely to puzzle the reader. But usage writers tend to fancy themselves blunt, forthright, and plainspoken people, and poking a little fun at the po-faced and the mealy-mouthed is one of their favorite sports. Of course, even the plainspoken can miss a euphemism now and then: witness Copperud 1980 who gets in a jab at *bathroom* and *restroom* being euphemisms for "the more exact toilet," but does not mention that this use of *toilet* was itself originally a euphemism (as, indeed, once was *privy*).

The use of euphemisms for political purposes—when *taxes* become *revenue enhancements,* *invasions* become *incursions,* and *murder* becomes *liquidation*—has been viewed with alarm by various writers, among them George Orwell. Bolinger 1980 also discusses the subject, especially in reference to the deceptive use of euphemisms.

You probably need not be very concerned about euphemisms in your writing. It is not practical to worry about any except those you recognize as euphemisms; those that you recognize, you will use or avoid according to what you are writing and the audience you are writing for.

2. *Euphemism, euphuism.* Fowler 1907, 1926, 1965 has a warning about confusing these words. It is doubtful that these words are often confused, as Fowler asserts. *Euphuism* is a literary word that seldom reaches the nonliterary public. Inadvertency would probably account for *euphuism* used as a gloss on the misspelling *uphemism* in Peter & Craig Norback, *The Misspeller's Dictionary,* 1974.

even   *Even* is an adverb whose placement can affect its meaning, according to the relatively few commentators who bother to mention it. In speech the location of *even* in the sentence is not especially important, since its intention is clearly signaled by stress. In this respect it is like *only,* which almost every commentator has discussed at length.

Burchfield 1996 notes that *even* can be placed before the verb instead of next to the word it qualifies: "it might even cost £100." The meaning of this example would be perfectly clear in speech and, in fact, is hard to

misunderstand even in print. But the example is very simple. Safire 1984 produces a more complex example from the headline of a book advertisement:

> Only NAL Could Publish a Book That Even Scared Stephen King

Here we find *even* placed in the familiar speech pattern, but the context is sufficiently complex to raise at least some doubt as to the meaning of the sentence. It pleased a correspondent of Mr. Safire's to ring several possible interpretive changes upon the sentence, which can be easily disambiguated in print by placing *even* directly in front of *Stephen King,* though at the cost of a possibly humorous *even Stephen.*

This, then, is our general advice: if your sentence is complex enough to cause possible confusion when it is read silently, without the assistance of the voice, put the *even* directly in front of the word or phrase it qualifies, as has been done in this example:

> Colloquialisms are necessarily used even in the formal writing of dialogue —Shaw 1980

See also ONLY 1.

event   The phrase *in the event that* serves as a somewhat formal substitute for *if:*

> . . . next in line for the Presidency in the event that there is no Vice-President —*Current Biography 1947*

The *that* is often omitted:

> In the event a vehicle is disabled by shelling —Carl Mann, *He's In The Signal Corps Now,* 1943

Both versions invite predictable criticism for wordiness and pomposity, and there are certainly plain contexts in which neither would be appropriate. But their distinctive tone and rhythm make them useful in writing that has an elevated quality:

> . . . which currency would, moreover, be available for immediate use in the event our negotiations with the Russians should utterly collapse —Jack Bennett, *Annals of the American Academy of Political and Social Science,* January 1950

eventuate   *Eventuate,* which means "to result, come to pass, come about," started life as an Americanism in the late 18th century and was stigmatized for that reason in the 19th century. Both British (Alford 1866) and American (Richard Grant White 1870 and Ayres 1881) commentators took whacks at it. In the 20th century Fowler 1926 and Krapp 1927 tried blaming journalists for using *eventuate.* Modern-day critics (as Garner 1998) are still at it.

In our time *eventuate* has been used on both

sides of the Atlantic primarily in scholarly and scientific writing and in the rather dry prose of textbooks and reference works. It has also had some use in popular magazines and newspapers, but it is not the best choice when you are aiming for simplicity or informality in your style.

> . . . this usually eventuated in some kind of legislation —Frederic A. Ogg & Harold Zink, *Modern Foreign Governments,* 1949

> . . . the Nazi-Fascist millenium [sic] which mercifully never eventuated —*Times Literary Supp.,* 15 Aug. 1980

> . . . a decline of the Visigothic Kingdom . . . which will eventuate in the conquest of the Iberian peninsula —Bernard F. Reilly, *The Medieval Spains,* 1993

> . . . most of the projects would eventuate in a pretty good gift for a relative you really like —John Kartman, *Booklist,* 15 Nov. 1992

every **1.** *Subject-verb agreement.* Since *every* regularly modifies a singular noun, it is not too surprising that a singular verb usually follows. The pronoun *every* is archaic, so *every* is not bedeviled by quite the same number of conflicts between grammatical agreement and notional agreement that *each* and the other indefinite pronouns are.

> . . . every snob thinks that the common people must be kept in their present place —George Bernard Shaw, *The Intelligent Woman's Guide to Socialism and Capitalism,* 1928

> By now, every woman knows it's all right —Jane DeLynn, *Cosmopolitan,* December 1976

When *every* modifies two or more nouns joined by *and,* there is mixed usage, at least in part because of the rule that compound subjects joined by *and* are both grammatically and notionally plural. *Every,* however, tends to emphasize each noun separately, and the singular verb is common. The possibility of nouns joined by *and* being considered individually and thus taking a singular verb was recognized as early as Lowth 1762; Fernald 1916 makes a specific exception to the rule of a plural verb for nouns modified by *each, every,* and *no.* Our evidence shows that the singular verb is more common:

> Every legislator, every doctor, and every citizen needs to recognize . . . —Ronald Reagan, *Abortion and the Conscience of the Nation,* 1984

> Every kitchen, office and shop in Sun Valley was on his beat —Peter J. Ognibene, *Smithsonian,* December 1984

But the plural verb is not rare:

> Every single word and meaning of great ancient writers like Geoffrey Chaucer were recorded in the OED —Robert Burchfield, *U.S. News & World Report,* 11 Aug. 1986

2. *Pronoun reference.* Longman 1984, in a usage note at *every,* opines that since *every* modifies a singular noun, it would seem logical that it would be followed by singular pronouns. But it often is not; the effect of notional agreement and considerations of sex often work to bring in plural pronouns. Evans 1957 has a rather succinct set of rules (we omit the examples) to sum up the situation:

> It *[every]* is also followed by a singular pronoun when there is no question whether it is males or females that are being talked about. . . . But when the reference is to both men and women, or the sex is unknown, a plural pronoun is generally preferred, . . . although some grammarians insist on the generic *his.* The plural pronoun is required in speaking of something owned in common . . .

The difference in Evans's approach and that of "some grammarians" is illustrated by this excerpt from Harper 1985:

> "I want *every* supervisor and employee to continually ask themselves these questions" is an example of a common error in choice of personal pronoun.

Evans would prefer *themselves,* since the sex is unknown, but Harper—in 1985 liberated enough not to require the generic *his*—calls for *himself or herself.* But notional agreement suggests the plural here too.

Actual usage may not be quite as tidy as Evans's rules are. Still, when there is no problem about males or females, the singular pronoun is usually used:

> . . . every woman knows it's all right not to get an orgasm each and every time she goes to bed with a man —Jane DeLynn, *Cosmopolitan,* December 1976

> Every bumptious idiot thinks himself a born ruler of men —George Bernard Shaw, *The Intelligent Woman's Guide to Socialism and Capitalism,* 1928

> . . . she lived in every moment entire as it came —Pearl Buck, *The Long Love,* 1949

Sometimes notional agreement will by itself attract a plural pronoun, even when there is no question of gender:

> I said, 'Now you wait and see. Every man in this United States that's got a daughter will be on my side,' and it turned out they were

—Harry S. Truman, in Merle Miller, *Plain Speaking*, 1973

The pull of notional agreement is especially strong when inanimate objects are involved:

Every kitchen, office and shop in Sun Valley was on his beat, and he visited them all —Peter J. Ognibene, *Smithsonian*, December 1984

When the reference is to men and women or when the sex is unknown, the plural pronoun is almost always used:

If we can succeed in persuading every man and woman, every nation to do their utmost —Herbert Hoover, quoted in *Time*, 27 May 1946

. . . the right of every nation, of every people, of every individual to develop in their own way —Dean Acheson, *New Republic*, 23 Jan. 1950

I saw every student before they went away —example from the Survey of English Usage (spoken), quoted in Longman 1984

Evans's observations are very close to the mark.

everybody, everyone Most of the discussions written about the indefinite pronouns *everybody* and *everyone* in usage books overlook important considerations. Here is a typical example:

Pronoun after "everyone." The pronoun to be used after the word "everyone" apparently troubles even our most careful writers, as witness: "Give everyone credit for having the courage of their convictions." This might get by in colloquial speech but it is not sanctioned in good writing —Bernstein 1958

The problem is, of course, the same one we find with almost all the indefinite pronouns (see AGREEMENT: INDEFINITE PRONOUNS)— *everyone* and *everybody* are grammatically singular but notionally plural. Their natural tendency is to take singular verbs and plural pronouns. Some four years later Bernstein is concerned about *everybody*:

"And so everybody took their guitars and songs, their poetry and perambulators, their high-bouncers and dogs, and went peacefully home." Here is an instance in which the proper pronouns—"his" or "his or her" won't work —Bernstein 1962

Indeed, the "proper pronouns" would make silly stuff out of the sentence. Bernstein's solution, of course, is to write the sentence over, to "face frankly this inadequacy of the language." But there is really nothing wrong with the pronouns in the sentence as it stands.

Bernstein is one of numerous modern descendants of the 18th-century grammarians Lowth and Lindley Murray, who first decided such pronouns should be singular. Bernstein has company: Bremner 1980, Shaw 1975, Nickles 1974, Colter 1981, Kilpatrick 1984, Simon 1980. On the other side, Copperud 1970 cites Evans 1957 and Flesch 1964. Longman 1984, Heritage 1982, and Reader's Digest 1983 find the plural pronouns acceptable. Jacques Barzun puts it more strongly:

. . . it seems to me clear that good sense requires us to say "Everybody took their hats and filed out." —*Atlantic*, January 1946

One of the points made about notional plurality in several sources is that a pronoun in a coordinate or in a following sentence referring back to *everyone* or *everybody* is always plural, and must be plural in normal English. To demonstrate this point we will call on dancer Sally Rand, as recorded by Studs Terkel:

Flashlights went off and the music played, and everybody was happy. They said: do it again —*Hard Times*, 1970

Try substituting *he* or *he or she* in that second sentence, and see how absurd it is.

In our first citation from Bernstein above, there is an assertion that reference to *everyone* (or *everybody*) by *they, their, them* is not sanctioned in good writing. The assertion is false. Such reference may be found in important literature and other reputable writing from the 16th century to the present. Here are several examples (some of these are taken from Jespersen 1909–49):

. . . but God send every one their heart's desire —Shakespeare, *Much Ado About Nothing*, 1599

. . . when every body else is upon their knees —*The Spectator*, No. 171 (in Jespersen)

. . . everybody had their due importance —Jane Austen, *Mansfield Park*, 1814

Let us give everybody their due —Charles Dickens, *Nicholas Nickleby*, 1839 (in Jespersen)

Experience is the name everyone gives to their mistakes —Oscar Wilde, *Lady Windermere's Fan*, 1893

Everybody ought to do what they can —Willa Cather, *O Pioneers!*, 1913

. . . can time any little irregularity of your own so that everybody else is so blind that they don't see or care —F. Scott Fitzgerald, *The Great Gatsby*, 1925

. . . I want everyone here in this country and in the world to feel their personal concern in the success of the United Nations —Clement Attlee, speech, 22 Nov. 1945

Everybody has a right to describe their own party machine as they choose —Sir Winston Churchill, in *Encounter,* April 1954

Everyone knew where they stood —E. L. Doctorow, *Loon Lake,* 1979

. . . everybody was too busy microwaving their dinners and cackling over The Brady Bunch —Christopher Hitchens, *Vanity Fair,* January 1996

They, their, them have been used in reference to *everybody* and *everyone* for more than 400 years in literature. You should not be dismayed by the fact that *everyone* and *everybody* regularly take a singular verb but a plural pronoun referent. That's just the way the indefinite pronouns behave in idiomatic English. Reader's Digest 1983 says "If you prefer *everyone . . . they* as being more natural, don't apologize." We agree. But do not feel that you have to use *they, their,* or *them,* if they do not seem natural to you. The choice is yours.

See also NOTIONAL AGREEMENT, NOTIONAL CONCORD; THEY, THEIR, THEM.

everyday, every day The single word *everyday* is an adjective ("an everyday occurrence," "part of everyday life"); the two-word phrase combining *every* and *day* functions either as a noun ("Every day is new") or as an adverb ("I see her every day"). The adverbial phrase is now frequently written as a single word:

Everyday it seems as though I am treated to matching scandals —Meg Greenfield, *Newsweek,* 16 Nov. 1987

. . . the junk we get on e-mail everyday —Bill Ott, *Booklist,* 15 Oct. 1997

This form may well get into the dictionaries someday, but for now the two-word styling for the adverbial phrase is still more common.

everyone See EVERYBODY, EVERYONE.

everyplace The history of *everyplace* parallels that of *anyplace.* It is a word of apparently American origin that has only recently begun to appear in print with any regularity. The objections that have been made to *anyplace* have also been made to *everyplace* (and also to *no place* and *someplace*). Its status in current English is as a somewhat informal synonym of *everywhere*:

. . . the answer I got everyplace I asked was no, he wasn't —B. J. Oliphant, *Dead in the Scrub,* 1990

Christian geography had become a cosmic enterprise, more interested in everyplace than in anyplace —Daniel J. Boorstin, *The Discoverers,* 1983

See also ANYPLACE; NOPLACE; SOMEPLACE.

everytime, every time *Every* and *time* form a common adverbial phrase that is normally written as two words ("They'll do it every time"; "Every time it rains . . ."). There is, however, a persistent tendency to treat this two-word phrase as a single-word adverb, especially when it occurs at the beginning of a clause and is essentially synonymous with *whenever*:

Everytime I read an Irish story —*Irish Statesman,* 13 Sept. 1924

For a week, everytime he ran into this man, Wallach would smile at him —Tracy Kidder, *The Soul of a New Machine,* 1981

Such usage seems to be growing slowly more common, but the two-word styling is still more widely preferred.

every which way This expressive Americanism, attested as early as 1824, has made a few commentators nervous: Vizetelly 1906 calls it "a pleonastic colloquialism"; MacCracken & Sandison 1917, Shaw 1962, 1970, and Prentice Hall 1978 all call it colloquial. Baker 1927 labels it incorrect and appends the following instruction:

Instead of saying, "He ran *every which way,*" one should say, "He ran in all directions."

It is a mystery why American commentators tend to be so timorous about Americanisms. Burchfield 1996 reports that it is fast gaining ground in British English. Here are a couple of American samples:

. . . dozens of cameras perched all over the city . . . always relentlessly prying and probing every which way —Philip Hamburger, *New Yorker,* 19 July 1952

. . . to send the company on a wild-goose chase shipping its damn machines every which way —E. L. Doctorow, *Loon Lake,* 1979

. . . fiberglass walls undulate from shower to bath . . . The surfaces flow every which way —Joseph Giovannini, *N.Y. Times,* 18 Sept. 1997

evidence *Evidence* has been used as a transitive verb for many centuries, but it has retained something of a formal quality that has invited occasional hostility from usage commentators. Fowler 1926 approved its use when its meaning was clearly "to serve as evidence of; prove the existence, occurrence, or truth of," but he considered it incorrect when used simply as a synonym of *show* or *exhibit.* Later commentators have not concerned themselves with any such distinction, but simply disapprove.

The distinction promoted by Fowler is not widely observed:

Exceptional, of course, is a common word of which the basic meaning is "forming an exception":

> . . . very much in keeping with the exceptional moral nature of America —Milton Viorst, *Interplay,* February 1969

It often describes someone or something that is significantly better than average:

> His talent was too exceptional to allow for casual predictions —Norman Mailer, *Advertisements for Myself,* 1959

See also UNEXCEPTIONABLE, UNEXCEPTIONAL.

excess See ACCESS 1; IN EXCESS OF.

excessively See EXCEEDINGLY, EXCESSIVELY.

exclude When *exclude* is used with a preposition, it is usually *from:*

> The humane judgement of the experienced literary man is excluded from consideration —Iris Murdoch, *The Fire and the Sun,* 1977

> He was shut up in a room from which all light was excluded —Thomas Hardy, *The Return of the Native,* 1878

exclusive When *exclusive* is used with a preposition and the object names what is excluded, the preposition is *of:*

> Few tourists come to Guadalcanal; the number last year was 1,809 . . . exclusive of one-day callers from occasional cruise ships —Robert Trumbull, *Saturday Rev.,* 23 Oct. 1971

When the object names what is actually included and excludes others, the preposition is *to:*

> The belief in "peaceful coexistence" is not exclusive to Socialists in Britain —*Time,* 20 Sept. 1954

excuse When the verb *excuse* is used with a preposition, it ordinarily is used with *from,* less often with *for.* Moreover, it is usually but not always passive:

> . . . the compulsory education law permitted children to be excused from public schools —*American Guide Series: Minnesota,* 1938

> . . . enabled an even greater number of officers to excuse themselves from any personal responsibility —William L. Shirer, *The Rise and Fall of the Third Reich,* 1960

> . . . one may be excused for supposing that he, too, would have been in the Canadian League long ago —Jack Olsen, *Sports Illustrated,* 29 July 1968

The Merriam-Webster files also show *excuse* with *of* instead of *from,* but not often:

> Has any other General been excused of the necessity of giving an accounting —*New Republic,* 29 Aug. 1949

exemplary *Exemplary* is etymologically related to *example,* and its fundamental meaning is "serving as an example or pattern." More often than not, it describes something praiseworthy:

> . . . with exemplary tact and discretion —George F. Kennan, *New Yorker,* 1 May 1971

> . . . every exemplary act of bravery —Marge Piercy, *N.Y. Times Book Rev.,* 23 May 1976

But it can also be used in neutral contexts:

> . . . presents exemplary details and sums up over large areas —John Hollander, *Harper's,* March 1971

And Garner 1998 notes its use in legal phrases like "exemplary damages," in which the idea is that the wrongdoer has been been made an example of.

Commentators have sometimes warned against using *exemplary* as if it were simply a synonym of *excellent,* but clear-cut instances of such usage are hard to come by. When *exemplary* describes something excellent, it seems always to carry the further suggestion that the thing described, because of its excellence, is worthy of imitation. The usage disliked by the commentators is presumably in such a context as the following:

> . . . they serve exemplary pastries —George V. Higgins, *N.Y. Times Mag.,* 9 Oct. 1983

Such usage is atypical, but it is not incorrect. *Exemplary* is a stronger word than *excellent,* even when it only describes a pastry.

exhilarate, exhilaration Spell these words with caution, noting well that they contain not just one *a,* but two. The first *a* can easily turn into an *i* or an *e:*

> . . . we feel so comfortable and so exhilerated —*Massachusetts Audubon News Letter,* December 1970

It may help to remember the etymological connection of these words with *hilarious.*

exhorbitant See EXORBITANT.

exhuberance, exhuberant See EXUBERANCE, EXUBERANT.

existence, existent The spelling *existance* for *existence* has been reported by Irmscher 1976 and Copperud 1980 and has caught our eye several times over the years. We also have some evidence for an *-ant* spelling of *existent.*

Both *existance* and *existant* are still considered misspellings and should be avoided.

exonerate *Exonerate,* when used with a preposition, is usually used with *from* or *of. From* is more common:

> . . . a society in which an understanding of human frailty means to exonerate ourselves from all moral judgment —Harold Clurman, *Harper's,* May 1971

> . . . exonerated him of complicity in the Iquitos uprising —*Current Biography,* April 1967

Two other prepositions are found in our files:

> . . . he cannot be exonerated for his negligence —O. S. Nock, *The Railways of Britain,* 1947

> . . . the contents of which tended very strongly to exonerate defendant as to the charge in the indictment —*State* v. *Pietranton,* 72 S.E. 2d 617, 13 Nov. 1952

exorbitant Note that there is no *h* following the *x* of *exorbitant.* This is a spelling error that's easily made, although its occurrence in published writing is relatively rare.

> . . . with tickets being sold at exhorbitant prices —*Variety,* 3 Oct. 1979

expatriate, expatriot The spelling *expatriot,* created by the influence of *patriot,* is occasionally used for the noun *expatriate.*

> . . . potentially dangerous expatriots such as Lee Harvey Oswald —*N.Y. Times,* 24 May 1965

> . . . the German expatriot poet Heine —*N.Y. University Bulletin,* Spring 1967

Expatriot is perceived as a misspelling and is not entered in current dictionaries. However, its use is frequent enough to allow the possibility of its becoming an acceptable variant spelling in the future. Until that happens, expect criticism if you use it.

expect **1.** We have collected over 40 comments and admonitions about *expect* from the past century or so, and all of them discuss the same issue: using *expect* to mean "suppose" or "think" in sentences such as "I expect you were sorry to hear that." Criticism of this usage has more often than not been based on such reasoning as that used by Richard Grant White in 1870: "*Expect* refers only to that which is to come, and which, therefore, is looked for. . . . We cannot expect backward." Many commentators echoed White's opinion during the late 19th and, in particular, early 20th centuries.

The OED shows that the "suppose" sense of *expect* is actually quite old, dating back to the 16th century. But the OED's editors, writing in 1894, were evidently no more fond of this sense than was Richard Grant White; they described it thus:

> Now *rare* in literary use. The misuse of the word as a synonym of *suppose,* without any notion of 'anticipating' or 'looking for', is often cited as an Americanism, but is very common in dialectal, vulgar or carelessly colloquial speech in England.

Questions about whether the Americans or the British were to blame for this sense persisted for some years, but that part of the controversy has now died out entirely. Our evidence shows that the "suppose" sense of *expect* is now common on both sides of the Atlantic.

Many recent handbooks have followed the OED's lead in calling the "suppose" sense colloquial (White's point about "expecting backward" is now rarely heard). Our evidence gives some support to that characterization, but only if *colloquial* is understood as meaning "characteristic of informal conversation" rather than as a term of disparagement. When *expect* means "suppose," it is almost invariably used in the first person, and it therefore appears most often in speech and in the kinds of writing which make use of the first person— correspondence, dialogue, and informal prose:

> I shall be able, I expect, to dispatch the waggon —Thomas Jefferson, letter, 27 Feb. 1809

> I expect that Shakespeare devised Iago with a gusto —W. Somerset Maugham, *The Moon and Sixpence,* 1919

> "George knows, I expect," said Virginia —Agatha Christie, *The Secret of Chimneys,* 1925

> To be fair, I expect that the same situation obtains in the editorial page —Lawrence Dietz, *Los Angeles Times Book Rev.,* 27 Feb. 1972

The "suppose" sense of *expect* is now far less controversial than it once was, although it still has its detractors. It has also had some staunch defenders in its time, including Fowler 1926, who declared, "This extension of meaning is, however, so natural that it seems needless PURISM to resist it. . . . there is no sound objection to it." We agree.
2. *Expect* is very often followed by *to* and the infinitive:

> For the system to work, the individual must not only expect to pay that price, he must consider it proper to do so —Ramsey Clark, *Center Mag.,* July/August 1970

. . . Bainbridge's men could expect to be starved and cold —C. S. Forester, *The Barbary Pirates,* 1953

Less often, but still very commonly, *expect* is used with *from* or *of:*

As was to be expected from such a large number of writers —Morris R. Cohen, *The Faith of a Liberal,* 1946

. . . he was not interested in poetry and there could be small hope of expecting poetry from him —John Ciardi, *Saturday Rev.,* 11 Mar. 1972

What he expected of me was to extricate him from a difficult situation —Joseph Conrad, *Chance,* 1913

A fine ear for the music of words is expected of a poet —Michael Williams, in *Little Reviews Anthology 1949,* ed. Denys Val Baker

expectorate Back in the days when chewing tobacco was a common habit, *expectorate* enjoyed some popularity among the genteel as a euphemism for *spit.* Like most euphemisms, it provoked a certain amount of criticism.

Expectorate is still sometimes used to mean "spit," but the user is now more likely to be trying for humor than politeness.

Q. Do you spit out the food or do you swallow it?
A. Everyone has the choice to swallow or, we like to call it, expectorate —Alexandra Bandon, *N.Y. Times Mag.,* 10 Mar. 1996

Such usage no longer provokes letters, pro or con. *Expectorate* now occurs chiefly in medical writing, in which it usually describes the expulsion of material from the lungs.

expel 1. When *expel* is used with a preposition, the choice is almost always *from:*

. . . had been expelled from his seat in the Senate for plotting with the British —Richard B. Morris, *N.Y. Times Book Rev.,* 25 July 1954

. . . if powerful blowers could be set up to expel the fumes away from the area —Bertrand de Jouvenel, *Center Mag.,* September 1969

An interesting twist on this use of *expel* may be seen in the following example, which is, however, not typical:

. . . the Chilean government expelled an American expatriate named Michael Townley into United States custody —Thomas Hauser, *N.Y. Times Book Rev.,* 27 July 1980

2. Although some language commentators warn their readers not to misspell *expel* as *ex-*

pell, apparently few people do. Our files show *expell* hardly ever occurs in print.

experience When the verb *experience* is used with a preposition, it is usually the past participle, and the preposition most frequently is *in:*

Also experienced in expressing his ideas in writing —*Current Biography 1953*

. . . highly experienced in industrial management and financial policy —*Times Literary Supp.,* 9 Mar. 1967

Less frequently, *experience* is used with *as:*

. . . with the help of a staff of twenty-three people experienced as parents —*Current Biography,* May 1965

expert 1. *Adjective.* When the adjective *expert* is used with a preposition, it is usually *in:*

. . . he is an artist expert in shaping his material into one comprehensive design —Samuel C. Chew, *N.Y. Herald Tribune Book Rev.,* 15 Apr. 1951

It may be used with *at:*

Lanny had become expert at learning scientific formulas —Upton Sinclair, *Presidential Mission,* 1947

2. *Noun.* The noun *expert,* when used with a preposition, is most often used with *on:*

. . . half a dozen specialists—experts on various regions of the world —Ernest O. Hauser, *Saturday Evening Post,* 29 May 1954

Somewhat less frequently, *expert* is used with *in,* and still less frequently, with *at:*

. . . a highly qualified lawyer, an expert in education —Jack Witkowsky, *Saturday Rev.,* 20 Nov. 1971

. . . the town's expert at repairing cane-seated chairs —Elizabeth Van Steenwyk, *Ford Times,* November 1967

expertise This French borrowing was first used in English more than a century ago, but its establishment as a full-fledged English word has occurred only in recent decades. Its older sense, "expert opinion or commentary," is now relatively rare:

But there is no evidence in the fairly numerous records of such expertises as have survived of any attempts at similarly precise analyses —Rowland Mainstone, *Developments in Structural Form,* 1975

But its newer sense, "expert knowledge or skill," is extremely common:

. . . with what sort of expertise does he judge a poet to be great? —Iris Murdoch, *The Fire and the Sun,* 1977

. . . showed his expertise at civil service —Joseph Wambaugh, *The Black Marble,* 1978

. . . the professionalism and increasing expertise of nurses today —Laurie Repchull, *Health Care,* 14 June 1982

Because it is both highly popular and fairly new, *expertise* is susceptible to criticism as a vogue word, and a number of commentators have called it one. Harper 1985 suggests that it "may well fall into disuse," but our growing collection of evidence for it suggests the process has not begun yet. It is equally possible that the voices of criticism will themselves eventually die out, as it becomes increasingly obvious that *expertise* is here to stay.

exposé *Exposé* can be written either with or without an acute accent:

. . . an exposé of female oppression —Daniel Seligman, *Fortune,* 29 Dec. 1980

. . . this particular expose is a bit of a revelation —Walter McVitty, *Nation Rev.* (Melbourne), 15 May 1975

Both forms are widely used. The accented form is the more common of the two, perhaps because it clearly indicates how the word is pronounced, \ˌek-spō-ˈzā\.

expressive When it takes a prepositional-phrase complement, *expressive* is used with *of:*

. . . her stiff back and neck eloquently expressive of outraged innocence —Thomas Wolfe, *You Can't Go Home Again,* 1940

expresso See ESPRESSO, EXPRESSO.

exquisite In a 1926 issue of *American Speech,* we read the following admonition:

Another word by which social reputations rise and fall is *exquisite.* Here the antepenultimate accent is the hall-mark of linguistic propriety; the penultimate accent gives the signal for the ejection to an outer social limbo. —John L. Haney, *American Speech,* April 1926

Similar advice is offered by later usage writers. Half a century later, educated speakers of English remain unimpressed: second-syllable stress in *exquisite* is as widespread as initial stress.

extended Used as an adjective, *extended* often has the sense, "notably long; prolonged, lengthy":

. . . went on an extended vacation —*Current Biography,* October 1965

. . . had been to Europe on an extended trip —Gail Cameron, *Ladies' Home Jour.,* August 1971

This sense is both old and respectable, but two fairly recent commentators (Flesch 1964 and Copperud 1970, 1980) have expressed disapproval of it, regarding it as, at best, a poor substitute for *long.* We see little basis for such an opinion, and the usage is, in any case, clearly standard.

extension The spelling *extention* was once a respectable variant of *extension,* but it fell into disuse several centuries ago. It occurs now only as an occasional error:

. . . the southern extention of the new road —*Country Quest* (Wrexham, Wales), July 1975

extract When the verb *extract* is used with a preposition, the choice is almost always *from:*

He seemed to extract a vicious enjoyment from her reaction —Harry Hervey, *Barracoon,* 1950

Extract has also been used with *out of* for several hundred years, but in our century this use has been sporadic:

May it be possible, that foreign hire Could out of thee extract one spark of evil? —Shakespeare, *Henry V,* 1599

. . . its captain resolved to extract the uttermost fare out of every refugee he took to London —H. G. Wells, *Mr. Britling Sees It Through,* 1916

exuberance, exuberant The same spelling error that occurs with *exorbitant* also occurs with *exuberance* and *exuberant*—an *h* slips in unobtrusively following the *x:*

He has an exhuberance, and abounding interest in good living —*The Californian,* Fall 1952

. . . the exhuberant clapping and backslapping —*Automation, Education and Human Values,* 1966

Watch out for that *h.*

exude *Exude,* when used with a preposition, is usually used with *from:*

. . . oil exudes from discrete openings that are typically 0.5 cm in diameter —Alan A. Allen et al., *Science,* 27 Nov. 1970

. . . Mr. Stryver, exuding patronage of the most offensive quality from every pore —Charles Dickens, *A Tale of Two Cities,* 1859

F

fabulous A number of commentators disparage the weakened sense of *fabulous*, in which it becomes a sort of generalized word of approval. Given the taste of English speakers and writers for hyperbole, such a development seems inevitable. With a little care you can still use the word in a heightened sense, but the word carries the germ of its own weakening, as you may notice in these examples:

> His manner was very much that of a man who has sailed strange seas and seen . . . the fabulous buried cache of forgotten pirates' plundering —Thomas Wolfe, *You Can't Go Home Again*, 1940

> . . . a man fabulous, rather than famous, in many of the diplomatic and social salons of the Europe of his day —George F. Kennan, *New Yorker*, 1 May 1971

> . . . the voice of a man divulging fabulous professional secrets —Roald Dahl, *Someone Like You*, 1953

> . . . her final fabulous success as a real estate magnate —James Purdy, *Cabot Wright Begins*, 1964

faced When *faced* is used adjectivally with a preposition, it is usually *with*:

> . . . a federal system faced with the challenges of a militant civil-rights movement —James Q. Wilson, *Commentary*, January 1972

When it means having covered the front or surface of something, *faced* is used equally with *with* or *in*:

> . . . an enormous foyer faced with marble —Eleanor Munro, *Saturday Rev.*, 24 July 1976

> . . . insisting that the house be faced entirely in the native Virginia beige fieldstone —Robert A. Caro, *Atlantic*, November 1982

face up to *Face up*, which is almost always followed by *to*, is considered to be an Americanism and has been soundly belabored by British critics going back to 1942. The apparent spur to comment was the growing use of the expression in British English:

> . . . he could face up to the fact that Ernest was not everybody's cup of tea —Nevil Shute, *Most Secret*, 1945

> . . . not facing up to life —Angus Macleod, *New Statesman & Nation*, 26 Dec. 1953

The general thrust of British criticism is that the *up to* is superfluous, since *face* says it all. This charge is rebutted by Bernstein 1965, Copperud 1970, 1980, and Harper 1975, 1985.

The claim that the phrase is an Americanism is made on doubtful grounds. Printed American evidence for *face up to* does not appear in our files until 1924 and the OED Supplement has British examples from 1925. The phrase seems to have been on both sides of the Atlantic at the same time.

Face up to is common in American English:

> It faces up frankly to Russia's known opposition —Adlai E. Stevenson, *Saturday Rev.*, 28 Feb. 1953

> I wanted to get her to face up to what would happen —Claude Brown, *Manchild in the Promised Land*, 1965

> Custine finally faced up to this situation —George F. Kennan, *New Yorker*, 1 May 1971

> It's time to face up to the fact that trust-fund accounting is a hoax —Peter G. Peterson, *Atlantic*, May 1996

British use seems to have continued unabated in spite of the critics. It is interesting to compare these examples two decades apart:

> . . . though it could be wished that the author had not been so "genuinely bilingual" as to adopt with enthusiasm the phrase "facing up to" —*Times Literary Supp.*, 16 Dec. 1949

> The British educational establishment did not on the whole face up to the Hegelian-Marxist challenge —*Times Literary Supp.*, 5 Mar. 1970

facilitate Fowler 1926 said that only things could be facilitated and that an example he had in which police officers were facilitated was "a slipshod extension." Fowler is wrong on style but right in substance. *Facilitate* with a personal direct object is attested in the OED from the 17th to the 19th centuries; Fowler found it in the 20th. It is, however, a rare use now.

Flesch 1964 and Zinsser 1976 disparage *facilitate* where *ease* would do; Garner 1998 finds it can be jargonistic. The shorter word, though, is not always the automatic choice. Neither *ease* nor *help* would convey the full intended meaning in these examples:

> . . . a practice facilitated, once the war broke out, by the blackout —William L. Shirer, *The Rise and Fall of the Third Reich*, 1960

> . . . the World Bank concentrated on facilitating loans and investment —*Current Biography*, July 1965

Simple solutions are not always good solutions, and monosyllabic words are not always the best words.

fact   **1.** Quite a few phrases built around *fact*—*the fact that, in point of fact, the fact is*—are attacked in various handbooks as wordy. What few commentators seem to notice, however, is that such phrases serve just as often to help the writer get a sentence organized or make an awkward transition. Try deleting or replacing the *fact* phrase in these examples and see if you have improved things:

> The fact is not that officials do uniquely badly but that they are uniquely vulnerable —Gowers 1948

> Although Al Capone was easily the best-known gangster of his own or any other time, he was in point of fact rather a parochial figure —Joseph Epstein, *Commentary*, January 1972

You should note that a preposition in English cannot take a *that*-clause as complement, but the insertion of *fact* before the clause solves the problem:

> Apart, however, from the fact that he was a younger son . . . —P. G. Wodehouse, *Something Fresh*, 1915

> . . . when you are alerted to the fact that the meaning of *because* is *for the reason that* it becomes obvious —Bernstein 1977

2. See TRUE FACTS.

fact that   See FACT 1.

factor   Most of the criticism that *factor* is imprecise or vague suffers from exactly the same fault—it is imprecise and vague. We are also told that the word is overworked, and maybe it is. A few commentators will allow *factor* to be used for "a cause contributing to a result"—one of about eight senses in Merriam-Webster's Collegiate Dictionary, Tenth Edition. Some of the "more precise" words that *factor* displaces are *consideration, circumstance, characteristic, constituent, component, ingredient*—all of them longer and windier. Let's test these criticisms on an example:

> But such factors as Reid's youth at the time of his crime, his slum background, his mar-

ginal mentality, had caused Wright . . . to feel that execution would be an injustice —William Styron, *This Quiet Dust and Other Writings*, 1982

Now, what are these factors? *Contributing causes* to the crime? *Mitigating circumstances?* Simply *considerations* that the judge is taking into account? Or perhaps all of these at once? If we substitute any of these more precise terms, do we then improve the sentence, or do we simply add syllables?

Contributing factor is criticized in a few books as a redundancy. As *factor* is a word of several senses, the addition of *contributing* probably serves to narrow the word's focus; the question of redundancy in such a context is irrelevant.

We think it is perfectly all right to use *factor* in favor of any of those longer, "more precise" substitutes. But remember that *factor* is a well-worked word; you should not beat it to death.

faculty   *Faculty* has several senses that relate to the world of academics. The British use it chiefly to denote a particular branch of learning in an educational institution, as in "the Faculty of Philosophy," which in the U.S. would be "the Department of Philosophy." *Faculty* in American English most often serves as a collective noun meaning "the teaching and administrative staff in an educational institution":

> Most of the faculty . . . does not favor or see as possible any such ambitious role for the university —Nathan Glazer, *American Scholar*, Spring 1967

But *faculty* is also used in the U.S. as a plural having the sense "faculty members." This use of *faculty* was first recorded in 1843:

> That was all I could ever get from him on the subject—'that the Faculty were funny fellows . . .' —*Yale Literary Mag.* (OED Supplement)

Evidence of its common occurrence in writing was a long time coming, however. We at Merriam-Webster came across it only in 1953, and we did not encounter it frequently until the 1960s:

> Faculty from many colleges and disciplines are participating —*AAUP Bulletin*, September 1965

> . . . not all faculty even yet concur in this resolve —Nathan M. Pusey, *President's Report, Harvard University*, 1968–1969

> Senior faculty say that the women are coming by these figures honestly —Gary Bass, *New Republic*, 8 & 15 Sept. 1997

This plural use of *faculty* has drawn the disapproval of several commentators. It continues to be common, however, and has clearly established a secure place for itself in the language of academics. If you dislike it, use "faculty members" or "teachers" instead.

fail 1. Some commentators say that the verb *fail* should be used only when an attempt of some sort is involved. Others are somewhat less restrictive, allowing *fail* to be used when an obligation or expectation is not met. But all disapprove the use of *fail* as a sort of general-purpose negative. They are fighting for a lost cause, nonetheless, for the use is established:

One might question the wisdom of a man who made two trips to Spain and failed to visit the Escorial —*Times Literary Supp.*, 19 Feb. 1971

. . . those who failed to see that pain is as necessary morally as it undoubtedly is biologically —Havelock Ellis, *The Dance of Life*, 1923

. . . he trailed around after his unit, buttoned into an uncomfortable uniform . . . but he obviously failed to enjoy it, and soon gave it up —George F. Kennan, *New Yorker*, 1 May 1971

2. When *fail* is used with a preposition, the construction often involves *to* and the infinitive:

Amy . . . had criminally failed to latch the streetdoor of the parlour —Arnold Bennett, *The Old Wives' Tale*, 1908

. . . that one-horse teachers' college whose recruiter failed to sway me thirty years ago —Tom Wicker, *Change*, September 1971

Fail is also used with *of*, but this use is not so common as it was before the 1950s:

. . . voters by the million could not fail of having some effect upon public affairs —Gerald W. Johnson, *Our English Heritage*, 1949

A lottery bill, for which King voted, failed of passage —*Current Biography*, May 1964

Fail is also used with numerous other prepositions:

Many men are almost as afraid of abandonment, of failing in marriage —Germaine Greer, *McCall's*, March 1971

He sold the farm to become an architect, at which he failed —Donald Hogan, *Harper's*, January 1972

The one piece in the collection which fails as a short story —Robert Kiely, *N.Y. Times Book Rev.*, 3 June 1973

. . . this enterprise failed from lack of capital —*Dictionary of American Biography*, 1928

. . . he falls for the Hollywood fleshpots, drinks too much, fails on his deadlines —Anthony Burgess, *Saturday Rev.*, July 1981

He turns then to Delphine, and with her he does not fail —E. K. Brown, *Rhythm in the Novel*, 1950

false comparison *False comparison* is a name used by a few commentators for a writer's careless omission of a word or two that would make a comparison perfectly clear and logical—"carrying ellipsis too far," Copperud 1970, 1980 calls it. Handbooks sometimes treat it as a variety of *illogical comparison* or *incomplete comparison*. This is a rather insignificant mistake in terms of its hindrance of communication, because readers tend to go right past such false comparisons without even noticing them. Here are a couple of examples of the fault from a well-known writer with the probable missing words supplied in brackets:

. . . in many counties Negroes outnumber whites in a ratio resembling [that in] parts of Alabama and Mississippi —William Styron, *This Quiet Dust and Other Writings*, 1982

. . . that fine and funny book, in which horror and laughter are commingled like [in] the beginning of a scream —William Styron, *This Quiet Dust and Other Writings*, 1982

From these and the examples in Johnson and Copperud it appears that *in* is often the word or one of the words omitted in false comparison. There are, however, others (see ANY 3; AS GOOD OR BETTER THAN). We think that you can see from the examples how easily the construction slips by. But even if readers are not likely to be often puzzled by false comparisons, we think it is a good idea for you to try to avoid them.

false titles This is a term for the journalistic practice of placing descriptive terms in front of a person's name in a news story: "globe-trotting diplomat Henry Kissinger" or "consumer advocate Ralph Nader." Some commentators associate the practice with *Time* magazine, which probably popularized the practice if it did not invent it. American commentators find the practice distasteful, and so do some British commentators who have found it in British journalism.

The practice seems to show no sign of waning and at any rate presents no problem of understanding to the reader. The practice probably derives its appeal from the compact way in which it identifies people for the reader.

If you're not a journalist, you need never worry about it in your writing. Examples such as this are highly unlikely outside of journalism:

. . . famed New Left philosopher Herbert Marcuse —Marcia Gillespie & Ronald Van Downing, *Essence*, November 1970

famed *Famed* has been aspersed by several commentators as journalese, but the OED tells a different story: the first journalist listed there is Shakespeare. The OED also has examples from Sir Richard Steele, George Washington, Lord Byron, and Nathaniel Hawthorne. Webster's Second has a quotation from Milton. With these important literary sources, it is no wonder that dictionaries recognize *famed* as standard.

In present-day use *famed* is both a predicate adjective, often with *for*, and an attributive adjective.

. . . leptin, a chemical already famed for its role in controlling body fat —Natalie Angier, *N.Y. Times*, 7 Jan. 1997

Stanley Kubrick, famed for his media allergy —Adam Hanft, *Civilization*, October/November 1999

One location was the famed Media Lab at the Massachusetts Institute of Technology —James Fallows, *Atlantic*, April 1996

. . . the desire to gain spiritual merit, to do penance for repented sin, . . . to find adventure, escape home drudgery, partake of the famed luxuries of the East —Jacques Barzun, *From Dawn to Decadence*, 2000

familiar The usual prepositions used with *familiar* when it is a predicate adjective are *with* and *to*; someone is *familiar with* something, and someone or something is *familiar to* someone.

Most people are familiar with the parachutes worn by aviators —Jim Wilson, *Popular Mechanics*, October 1999

Some authors, such as Richard Rodriguez and Ruben Martinez, will be familiar to media mavens outside the region —Ray Olson, *Booklist*, 15 Oct. 1996

From may identify a source of familiarity:

Biopharming raises many questions familiar from the debate about genetically engineered foods —Aaron Zitner, *Los Angeles Times*, 4 June 2001

farther, further About every usage commentator in the 20th century has had something to say about *farther* and *further* (and sometimes *farthest* and *furthest*) and how they should be used or how they seem to be used. Only a few go beyond the notion that *farther* should designate distance, and *further* quantity or degree. These observations are not highly accurate, as we shall see.

Farther and *further* are historically the same word, so it is not surprising that the two have long been used more or less interchangeably. Neither word was originally connected with *far*, but gradually they have both become so.

Fowler 1926 noticed that *farther* and *further* were becoming differentiated, and that *farther*'s range of application was shrinking. He thought that this development would lead to the demise of *farther*. But so far, *farther* is still with us.

Fowler's differentiation is most noticeable when *farther* and *further* are used as adjectives. Both words could at one time be used in the sense "additional":

. . . I have now no farther thought of danger —Thomas Gray, letter, 12 Sept. 1756

You will e'er long I suppose receive further intelligence of him —Jane Austen, letter, 11 Feb. 1801

But in present-day English *further* has taken over this function entirely:

"Well," he began, without any further greeting —Katherine Anne Porter, *Ladies' Home Jour.*, August 1971

. . . no further deliveries of military equipment —Chester Bowles, *Saturday Rev.*, 6 Nov. 1971

. . . hums like a tuning fork between all these fainter and further thoughts—William H. Gass, *Harper's*, February 1984

Farther as an adjective is now limited to instances where literal or figurative distance is involved:

The farther floe was pulling away in the grip of the tide —Berton Roueché, *New Yorker*, 22 Oct. 1966

. . . at the farthest remove imaginable from regional writing —Ivan Gold, *N.Y. Times Book Rev.*, 24 Apr. 1983

And *further* competes even in this function:

The Viking settlements had cut greater Northumbria in two, and the further part had fallen under the influence of the Celtic Highland powers —Frank Barlow, *The Feudal Kingdom of England 1042–1216*, 3d ed., 1972

. . . it was the furthest thing from everyone's mind —E. L. Doctorow, *Loon Lake*, 1979

So for the adjective we can see that *further* has squeezed *farther* out of the "additional" sense and is giving it pressure in the "more distant" sense.

As adverbs, *farther* and *further* are less well differentiated. Differentiation is most nearly complete in the "degree" sense, where there is no notion of distance. We can find *farther* in this sense, but our examples are showing their age:

> . . . without consulting farther with any soul living —Laurence Sterne, *Tristram Shandy*, 1759

> Please see to it that I do not have to act any farther in the matter —Bernard DeVoto, letter, 7 June 1943

Further is now the usual choice:

> DeGaulle's violent remarks . . . further strained relations —Stephen E. Ambrose, *Johns Hopkins Mag.*, April 1966

> . . . I recommend that you have nothing further to do with this person nor with these arms transfers —Robert C. McFarlane, quoted in *The Tower Commission Report*, 1987

> . . . her example gave me courage to develop my own voice further —Rita Dove, *Essence*, May 1995

Further is used as a sentence adverb; *farther* is not.

> Further, I am monolingual and have no way of knowing whether a translation is faithful to the original —E. B. White, letter, 13 May 1957

But when spatial, temporal, or metaphorical distance is involved, *farther* is still thriving:

> . . . too tired, too unhappy to go farther —Bernard Malamud, *The Magic Barrel*, 1958

> I asked how much farther it was to Dublin —Renata Adler, *Pitch Dark*, 1983

> Nothing could be farther from the truth —Godfrey Hodgson, *N.Y. Times Book Rev.*, 30 Jan. 1983

> . . . Mr. Donald is too scrupulous ever to push the evidence farther than it should go —Geoffrey C. Ward, *N.Y. Times Book Rev.*, 22 Oct. 1995

> . . . huge, reckless washoffs that gully the soil, robbing it of nutrients and disrupting ecologies farther downstream —Bill Bryson, *A Walk in the Woods*, 1999

But *further* is giving *farther* plenty of competition for the same uses:

> He could not only walk further but he walked faster —Mordecai Richler, *The Apprenticeship of Duddy Kravitz*, 1959

> . . . 300 miles further down the river —Noel Perrin, *N.Y. Times Book Rev.*, 6 Sept. 1981

> I park my car in a better spot, further from the curve —Renata Adler, *Pitch Dark*, 1983

> The Russian artillery fire and bombs are reaching further into the southern sections

of the city —Alessandra Stanley, *N.Y. Times*, 17 Jan. 1995

So in adverbial use *further* dominates when there is no sense of distance and as a sentence adverb, but both *farther* and *further* are in use when spatial, temporal, or metaphorical distance is involved.

Further is more commonly attested than *farther* in our recent files and in the Brown University corpus (Kučera & Francis, 1967). Fowler's prediction of the demise of *farther* has come true only in certain uses, however. *Further* has all but eclipsed *farther* in adjective use, with *farther* competing only for a portion of the "more distant" use. *Further* has pretty well eliminated the adverbial *farther* from non-distance uses, and it has the sentence adverb function all to itself. But both forms are in vigorous competition in the adverbial distance uses.

farthest See FARTHER, FURTHER.

fascinated Some language commentators have noted that when *fascinated* is used with a preposition, *by* is used for a human fascinator, and *with* for a nonhuman fascinator. Our evidence shows that the situation is not so simple. First, *fascinated* is more often used with *by* than with any other preposition, and *by* can take as its object either a human or nonhuman fascinator:

> . . . I continued to be fascinated by the Senator and especially his two assistants —Ernest Hemingway, "African Journal," 1956

> She was at once fascinated and repelled by the disclosures —Herman Wouk, *Marjorie Morningstar*, 1955

Fascinated with does seem to be used only of something nonhuman:

> The male, of course, has long been fascinated with combat —Vance Packard, *The Sexual Wilderness*, 1968

Nonhuman objects are also usual in the scattered examples we have of the use of *fascinated* with other prepositions or *to* and the infinitive:

> He was fascinated at the thought of what the day meant to Grant —Sherwood Anderson, *Poor White*, 1920

> . . . he became fascinated in the detailed lineaments of what he claimed to find oppressive —Richard Poirier, *A World Elsewhere*, 1966

> I was fascinated to hear Mr. Harrington equate power with the status quo —Henry Steele Commager, *Center Mag.*, July/August 1971

fascination *Fascination* is most often used with the prepositions *for, of,* or *with*:

> . . . there is a pride and fascination for them in a new love adventure —H. G. Wells, *Joan and Peter*, 1918

> He felt the strange fascination of shadowy religious places —D. H. Lawrence, *Sons and Lovers*, 1913

> . . . Hunt's fascination with the mechanics and engineering of public opinion —Theodore H. White, *The Reporter*, 8 June 1954

Sometimes it appears with *about, by,* or *in*:

> There is, however, a terrible human fascination about the miniature —Loren C. Eiseley, *Harper's*, March 1953

> . . . an intensely strong attraction toward beauty and an equally intense fascination by the ugliness which is contrasted with it —T. S. Eliot, "Tradition and the Individual Talent," 1917

> There is today, among some labor bosses, the same childlike fascination in finance, in deals, in handling big chunks of money —Eric Sevareid, *The Reporter*, 18 Sept. 1958

fatal, fateful Quite a few writers on usage are at pains to distinguish between *fatal* and *fateful*. It all began when H. W. Fowler found a passage in a newspaper using *fateful* where he felt *fatal* would have been better. Fowler's OED would have told him that the sense used in the newspaper was first attested in 1764 and the sense he thought *fateful* was created for was not attested until 1800.

Fowler also made the pronouncement that *fateful* could indicate a good outcome as well as an unpleasant one. Almost all subsequent commentators repeat this part of Fowler's treatment. To it, many recent ones add a limitation on *fatal*. Perhaps the most compendious summary is that of Copperud 1980:

> *Fatal* means death-dealing, *fateful* productive of great consequences, for either good or evil.

As a description of actual usage, this is something of an oversimplification, and it especially oversimplifies the range of use of *fatal*.

Fatal is the original adjective for *fate*. It carries the usual simple relational sense: the Fates are "the fatal sisters." It also has (and has had since Chaucer's time) the sense of "involving momentous consequences, portentous" that the critics prefer to assign to *fateful*. The usual direction of this portent is toward evil, as Fowler observed:

> . . . if I had been superstitiously inclined to observe days as fatal or fortunate —Daniel Defoe, *Robinson Crusoe*, 1719

> Then came the fatal letter, the desolating letter — Arnold Bennett, *The Old Wives' Tale*, 1908

> . . . ever since she had got back to the Vassar club that fatal morning —Mary McCarthy, *The Group*, 1963

Fateful is used in about the same way:

> . . . the Gulf of Tonkin resolution, the fateful declaration adopted by Congress —*The Progressive*, January 1970

> The fateful decision to cover up what we knew to be the true budget numbers —David A. Stockman, *Newsweek*, 28 Apr. 1986

Fateful does sometimes have at least a neutral, if not quite positive, connotation:

> . . . the day when the fateful letter from the college admission office is due —James B. Conant, *Slums and Suburbs*, 1961

> It is sixty years since Mann undertook that fateful holiday in Venice . . . which gave him the basic material for the novella —*Times Literary Supp.*, 30 July 1971

Fatal developed its sense "causing death, destruction, or ruin" in the 16th century. When the meaning is strictly "causing death," it is a sense not shared by *fateful*:

> . . . demonstration had been set off by the fatal shooting of . . . a prisoner —Paul Jacobs, *Center Mag.*, May 1969

> The infection of the fallopian tubes could be fatal —*Human Reproduction* (9th grade textbook), 1981

Fatal also indicates destruction or ruin, often with the notion of death commingled:

> Queen's favours might be fatal gifts, but they were much more fatal to reject than to accept —Henry Adams, *Mont-Saint-Michel and Chartres*, 1904

> He discerns a fatal flaw in the theory —Ronald Gross, *N.Y. Times Book Rev.*, 25 Mar. 1973

Fateful has been used sporadically in this sense. It is never constructed with *to*, however, as *fatal* can be.

> He hath loosed the fateful lightning of His terrible, swift sword —Julia Ward Howe, "Battle Hymn of the Republic," 1862

And *fatal* has a weakened sense that has developed from the "causing death or destruction" sense. The OED suggests that this sense may have come from the human tendency to hyperbole:

Being that is a fatal way to begin any sentence —Barzun 1985

Tediousness is the most fatal of all faults —Samuel Johnson, *Life of Prior*, ca. 1781

Fateful is not used in this sense. Nor is it used in the sense of *fatal* that applies to a powerful and dangerous attraction:

... I look forward to becoming a middle-aged sex object of fatal charms —Joan Rivers, *McCall's*, October 1971

... has a fatal attraction for the stalest figures of speech in the language —Joseph Lelyveld, *Saturday Rev.*, July 1980

Fatal has the wider range of application, and is the more common of the two adjectives.

fault There have been complaints by Follett 1966, Copperud 1964, and the usage panel of Harper 1975, 1985 about the transitive use of the verb *fault* in the sense "to find fault with." Some commentators (as Bernstein 1971) wonder what the fuss is about—the use has been around since the middle of the 16th century. It appears to have become common only in the middle of the 20th century, however, which is probably why its critics have thought it a fad. It is no fad; it is standard.

No one can fault the performers in this comedy —*New Yorker*, 19 Oct. 1963

It is difficult to fault this book —*Times Literary Supp.*, 29 Dec. 1972

faulty parallelism *Faulty parallelism* is a term used by composition teachers for the placement of different structures in coordination with each other. Very often such faulty parallelism occurs with the conjunctions *and* and *or* with such other coordinators as *either* and *neither*. Here are a couple of made-up examples for illustrative purposes:

The old car was a relic and rusty.

To drink heavily and taking too many drugs are bad for your health.

These examples show the vice in a plain and simple form. In the first a noun and an adjective are coordinated; in the second, an infinitive phrase and a participial phrase. Those who teach composition naturally are very fierce on such constructions.

But when we get away from the writing of the tyro and into the world of the professional and presumably polished writer, we have a different problem. Faulty parallelisms still occur, but they tend to be almost invisible. This new invisibility would suggest that in edited prose faulty parallelism may generally be accounted a venial sin—if the writer doesn't notice it and the editor doesn't notice it and the reader doesn't notice it, how serious can it be?

Moreover, what if the usage writer doesn't notice it? In Strunk & White 1959 we find this rule:

15. Express co-ordinate ideas in similar form.

We assume that E. B. White believed in the rule. E. B. White the grammarian, at least. What about E. B. White the essayist? Joseph M. Williams, in "The Phenomenology of Error" (*College Composition and Communications*, May 1981), quotes this passage:

I have written this account in penitence and in grief, as a man who failed to raise his pig, and to explain my deviation from the classic course of so many raised pigs. The grave in the woods is unmarked, but Fred can direct the mourner to it unerringly and with immense good will ... —"Death of a Pig," *Essays of E. B. White*, 1977

Did you notice any faulty parallelisms there? (Williams says there are two.) But White presumably didn't notice any, and neither have most of his readers. You could probably find many similar examples in edited prose if you were to sharpen your eye so as to be able to detect them readily. These are only venial sins, but we think you should try to avoid them in your writing. But if you slip, no one may notice.

favorable *Favorable* is followed by the prepositions *to* and *for* when it means "advantageous." *To* is more common:

Existing credit law, sometimes archaic and traditionally favorable to the lender —Lucia Mouat, *The Consumer Fights Back*, 1970

... the proposed deal has some aspects favorable to the rank-and-file —Phil Taylor, *Sports Illustrated*, 4 Sept. 1995

... the supply/demand balance will start to turn favorable for fed cattle —Bob Utterback, *Farm Journal*, April 1997

For is the usual preposition when *favorable* means "suitable":

... to select those most favorable for hybridization —*Current Biography*, January 1964

... conditions on the early Earth may not have been favorable for the natural synthesis of these molecules —*Sky & Telescope*, September 1994

To is used when *favorable* means "feeling or expressing support or approval":

... strengthened the hand of those favorable to the council —Paul Sigmund, *Change*, March 1973

... a similar national effort is the most effective to date in promoting candidates favorable to environmental issues —John Walsh, *Science*, 19 Nov. 1982

Toward is sometimes used instead of *to*:

... reviewers were not too favorable toward the production —*Current Biography 1953*

faze, phase, feaze, feeze 1. *Faze* is a 19th-century American variant of a much older verb *feeze* (spelled in about a dozen different ways) with a meaning not attested for the older word: "disconcert, daunt." It has existed in American use in four chief spellings, *faze, phase, feaze,* and *feeze.* Of the four variants, *faze* is by far the most usual. *Phase* (considered a misspelling by some commentators) is next most frequent:

A woman arriving alone in sunglasses and Nike jogging shoes did not phase the solitary waiter —*Town & Country*, May 1983

Rainstorms do not phase them —*Christian Science Monitor*, 11 Nov. 1977

... not even the sight of the evening's star in purple-pink underwear ... seemed to phase anyone —*Rolling Stone*, 16 Mar. 1972

Feaze and *feeze* are becoming quite rare.

The unrelated *phase* is usually a noun, but it is also a verb and it seems to be getting more play as a verb in recent years, especially in such combinations as *phase out, phase in,* and *phase into.*
2. *Faze*, being an Americanism, was naturally suspect by the usage and dictionary community. Vizetelly 1906 seems to be the earliest commentator to recommend avoiding it as slang. Its entry in older dictionaries was variously labeled colloquial, dialectal, slang, or informal, and a few usage commentators still carry similar warnings. But Merriam-Webster dictionaries, Reader's Digest 1983, and Bernstein 1971 know that it is standard.

Quite a few commentators note that *faze* is most commonly found in negative contexts: While this is true, it is incidental to the meaning of *faze*—not being fazed is more worthy of remark than being fazed. Here are a couple of examples:

He had ice water in his veins. Nothing fazed him, not insult or anger or violence —Robert Penn Warren, *All the King's Men*, 1946

... the wines, which do not faze him, fuddle me —Robert Craft, *Stravinsky*, 1972

feasible *Feasible* has three senses. As defined briefly in Merriam-Webster's Collegiate Dictionary, Tenth Edition, they are, in historical order, "capable of being done or carried out," "capable of being used or dealt with successfully," and "reasonable, likely." In 1926 H. W. Fowler announced that he did not like the third sense, which he had noticed coming into

common use. It was his opinion that the third sense of *feasible* was simply a fancy substitution for *possible* or *probable*, and he insisted that *feasible* be limited to its first sense (he ignores the second). He believed the third sense was not justified etymologically. He omitted to note that the sense goes back to Thomas Hobbes in the 17th century and had already been in use for about 250 years.

To clinch his point about the proper uses of *possible* and *feasible*, Fowler tells us that a thunderstorm is possible but not feasible (an example repeated, with minor changes, by several later commentators). The example, however, is beside the point: writers do not use *feasible* of storms.

There are three definitions of *feasible* because sometimes lexicographers have to sort out the senses of an adjective according to the kinds of nouns it modifies. The second and third senses account for the application of *feasible* to things that are not doable, even though the underlying notion of *feasible* is not much changed.

The most feasible interpretation is that dust and breccia probably were formed at an early stage in the history of the moon —Mitsunobu Tatsumoto & John N. Rosholt, *Science*, 30 Jan. 1970

They read between the lines. ... they fire off ten or twenty interpretations of a line, a phrase, among them one or two feasible readings, the rest ludicrous —D. J. Enright, *Interplay*, 1995

Egyptian hieroglyphics ... are also usually assumed to be the product of independent invention, but the alternative interpretation of idea diffusion is more feasible —Jared Diamond, *Guns, Germs, and Steel*, 1997

None of the things described as *feasible* in these examples can be done; in each case the word suggests that whatever is in question is within the realm of practical possibility or reasonable likelihood. *Possible* cannot be substituted for *feasible* in some of these contexts and still make sense; in those where it can be substituted it often changes the meaning.

Whatever is feasible is more reasonable or more likely than what is merely possible. To point a finger at a use of *feasible* and say that *possible* was meant is to try to read the writer's mind. These are cases where we would do better to give the writer credit for having chosen the right word.

feature 1. Back in the 1920s there was much negative comment in usage circles and in various handbooks on the propriety of *feature* as a verb in advertising and journalism. Fowler 1926 saw it as a repulsive Americanism that he feared would make its way into popular

British use. (It did.) Because it was mentioned in handbooks then, it is still in handbooks, though now chiefly to explain that it is in standard use (as it had been since about 1888). Here are a couple of examples:

> The exhibition will feature first editions and related manuscripts —Erica Jong, *Barnard Alumnae*, Winter 1971

> The film . . . evolved into a series, featuring Mickey Rooney as Andy Hardy —*Current Biography*, September 1965

> There are two popular, in the sense of common, mistakes made in speech and in informal prose. Both feature that innocent-looking word *because* —Kingsley Amis, *The King's English*, 1998

2. Strunk & White 1959 (and subsequent editions) also considers *feature* hackneyed, but it differs from most in disliking the older noun use as well as the verb. The example of disapproved use (which goes back to the original Strunk circa 1920) is interesting:

> A feature of the entertainment especially worthy of mention was the singing of Miss A.

The advice given is this: "Better use the same number of words to tell what Miss A. sang and how she sang it." This advice seems a bit naive; it is distinctly possible that the example is a minor masterpiece of tact. If Miss A. happens to have more friends than talent, it may be more politic not to tell what she sang and how she sang it.

feaze See FAZE, PHASE, FEAZE, FEEZE.

February A succession of \r\'s in different syllables of the same word presents an articulatory hurdle to many speakers, not only in English but in other languages. One solution is for one of the \r\'s to dissimilate, either becoming a different sound, or dropping out altogether. Several words that come to us from Romance languages show the first process, with \l\ substituted for \r\: compare *pilgrim* with the etymologically related *peregrine*. Within English, in a number of words with unstressed \ər\ before a consonant, the \r\ drops from this position in favor of another \r\ more prominently placed. Thus *caterpillar* is often pronounced \'ka-tə-ˌpi-lər\, and the first \r\ of *elderberry, governor, offertory, surprise, thermometer*, and *vernacular* and the second \r\ of *paraphernalia* are often dropped without exciting any notice or comment. *February*, by contrast, is a shibboleth. The most widespread pronunciation of this word among educated speakers is \'fe-byə-ˌwer-ē\, and while the consensus of usage writers is tolerant of this version, most of us can recall having been admonished to say \'fe-brə-ˌwer-ē\ at some point in our school days.

The status of other words in which \r\ sometimes dropped from the end of a consonant cluster (as in *February*) varies. *Library* is perhaps pronounced \'lī-ber-ē\ more often by children than by adults, and that pronunciation draws general disapproval. But *synchrotron* and *temperature* often come out \'siŋ-kə-ˌträn\ and \'tem-pə-chər\ without causing eyebrows to be raised.

feed *Feed*, when used with a preposition, is most often used with *on*:

> When writing turns to mush, thought, which feeds on writing, suffers from malnutrition —Thomas H. Middleton, *Saturday Rev.*, 24 Nov. 1979

> . . . a common mosquito, *Culex pipiens*, that feeds on birds and mammals primarily at dusk —M. A. J. McKenna, *Atlanta Jour.-Constitution*, 13 May 2001

Feed is also used less frequently with *upon* or *off*, but use of these prepositions is becoming more common:

> . . . to think again; to feed upon memory —Walter De la Mare, *Encounter*, December 1954

> The virus needs healthy cells to feed upon —Katie Leishman, *Atlantic*, October 1985

> The dread of the new place mounts up in her and feeds off the complaints in his letters —Oscar Handlin, *The Uprooted*, 1951

> . . . the embryos feed off nutrients in the egg-food —Natalie Angier, *N.Y. Times*, 28 Oct. 1997

feel Copperud 1964 quotes one Alice Hamilton, M.D., from an article in the *Atlantic* (September 1954), as being amused by "the increasing rejection of *believe* and *think* in favor of *feel*." This is our earliest attested objection to the use, although Copperud seems to know of earlier objections based on the assertion that nothing can be felt that is not apprehended by the sense of touch. The evidence in the OED shows this presumed restriction has never existed.

Various commentators and college handbooks object to the use. Copperud defends it, noting that it has been around for a long time (it goes back to Shakespeare) and that a number of respected authors—Trollope, Hardy, Lincoln—have used it. He also mentions that Webster's Third quotes an Alice Hamilton for the "think, believe" sense. Could it be the same Alice Hamilton? Yes, indeed, and from the same article:

> I am a reader, so I feel I have a right to criticize authors —Alice Hamilton, M.D., *Atlantic*, September 1954

In the examples below you will see that this sense of *feel* tends to be colored by the notion of emotion or intuition; it doesn't seem to mean "think" in the sense of using powers of reasoning.

> But I feel that I have not yet made my peace with God —Emily Dickinson, letter, 8 Sept. 1846

> ... there still remained my relation with the reader, which was another affair altogether and as to which I felt no one to be trusted but myself —Henry James, *The Art of the Novel*, 1934

> ... some of us felt that this wasn't an appropriate time to celebrate —Tip O'Neill with William Novak, *Man of the House*, 1987

This use is entirely standard.

feel bad, feel badly It is a standard joke of usage writers to remark that someone who says "I feel badly" must be complaining about a defective sense of touch. This hoary witticism goes back as least as far as Vizetelly 1906 and has been frequently repeated from Bierce 1909 to Kilpatrick 1984. Of course, they know and we know that people who say "I feel badly" simply mean they feel bad.

The continuing use of *feel badly* in competition with *feel bad* in spite of the long opposition of 20th-century schoolbooks is not easily explained. There are at least two important contributing factors.

First, the *feel bad, feel badly* choice is related to the *feel good, feel well* choice, where many people choose one or the other depending on whether they are talking about a physical or mental state (see GOOD 1). Those who differentiate use *feel well* for health and *feel good* for emotion; many make the same distinction with *bad* and *badly*, choosing *feel bad* for health and *feel badly* for emotion. Here, for instance, is Harper 1985 panelist David Schoenbrun:

> "I use 'I feel bad' to express a physical condition, but 'I feel badly' to express an emotional response."

Many others use *badly* for emotion:

> We feel very badly about your only having one turkey —James Thurber, letter, Fall 1938

> ... I was laughing, but trying not to for some reason, feeling badly that I laughed, feeling ashamed —E. L. Doctorow, *Loon Lake*, 1979

But Bryant 1962 and others point out that the evidence of surveys shows that many people do not differentiate, and use *badly* for health as well as *bad* for the emotional state:

> I do not feel so badly this forenoon—but I have bad nights —Walt Whitman, letter, 17 June 1864

> Still, I feel bad about not having written you —E. B. White, letter, 23 June 1946

In fact Bryant sums up several surveys by saying they show usage to be almost evenly divided between *feel bad* and *feel badly*, regardless of whether health or emotional state is the topic. Our printed evidence, however, shows *feel badly* is used most often for the emotional state.

Second, Evans 1962 notes that some people may choose *badly* because they think "*bad* could only mean wicked." This is not an idle supposition. Bache 1869 explicitly prescribes the usage now decried as erroneous:

> "He feels very *bad* " is sometimes said as descriptive of one's feeling very sick. *To feel bad* is to feel conscious of depravity; to feel *badly* is to feel sick.

It is possible that the association of *bad* with moral turpitude has survived in many American families and has strengthened the use of *badly*.

Conclusion: the controversy over *feel bad* and *feel badly* is founded in two opposing prescriptive standards—that of the 1869 handbook prescribing *feel badly* and that of the 20th-century schoolbooks prescribing *feel bad*—it is unlikely to die out very soon. People will go on about as they do now—some differentiating *bad* and *badly*, some not, some avoiding *badly*, some not. You can see that the question is not as simple as it is often claimed to be, and, with those considerations in mind, make your own choice.

feet See FOOT.

feeze See FAZE, PHASE, FEAZE, FEEZE.

fell swoop The phrase *at one fell swoop* is uttered by Macduff in Shakespeare's *Macbeth* when he learns that Macbeth has murdered his wife and children, as several commentators remind us. The metaphor is that of a hawk swooping down on defenseless prey, and *fell* here means "cruel, savage, ruthless." Bremner 1980 calls the phrase a cliché in modern use, and Evans 1957 says "the phrase is now worn smooth of meaning and feeling."

Fell has become a rarely used literary, rhetorical, poetic term, rather removed from common experience. It is not obsolete and you can still find it, but not often, and not in ordinary places. So the present-day reader of the Shakespearean phrase tends to understand Macduff's sense of the suddenness of the attack and to skip over the meaning of *fell*.

And the phrase has become an idiom, really; it has lost its literal meaning and has come to mean "all at once." It is neutral in application, not necessarily introducing a disastrous event. And Shakespeare's *at* often becomes *in* or *with*.

> These controls should be ended at one fell swoop —Milton Friedman, reprinted column, 1969

> What cosmic process created the stars and planets? Are new ones still being formed? Or were all that now exist made in one fell swoop? —Fred L. Whipple, *Scientific American Reader*, 1953

> With one fell swoop, I seized the door and pulled it wide open —Cleveland Amory, *Saturday Rev.*, 6 Sept. 1975

> Universal Studios had made "Back to the Future" II and III at once; why not film three "Lord of the Rings" movies in one fell swoop —Laura Landro, *Wall Street Jour.*, 1 Dec. 1999

The phrase does get quite a lot of work, and you are not unreasonable to consider it a bit of a cliché; but it has a fine pedigree.

female The status of *female* as a noun equivalent in meaning to *woman* has gone through some remarkable changes over the centuries.

Lounsbury 1908 traces its slow progress in literature from occasional use in Chaucer and Shakespeare to fully established literary use in the 18th century. Its use in literary works continued unabated into the first half of the 19th century; it is found in such writers as Fanny Burney, Jane Austen, Sir Walter Scott, James Fenimore Cooper, Poe, Dickens, Thackeray, and Hawthorne. Hall 1917 lists a great many others.

In the middle of the 19th century, however, numerous commentators began to condemn the use. Commentators such as Alford 1866 and Richard Grant White 1870 condemned the use as equating women with the lower animals. Similar sentiments are expressed by a number of other critics of the mid-to-late 19th century.

There are a few interesting observations to be made about all this late Victorian furor. First, the most vociferous objectors are men, so we really do not know if most women found the usage offensive or not. Clearly they had not earlier; Fanny Burney had used *female* of the Princess Royal, and Jane Austen not only of the characters in her novels but of herself:

> I think I may boast myself with all possible vanity to be the most unlearned and uninformed female who ever dared to be an authoress —letter, 1 Dec. 1815 (in Lounsbury)

Second, the objection is ostensibly based on the word's leveling of women with lower animals, but the gallantry of this argument may well be largely factitious. The real basis for objection to this use of *female* is much more likely to have been its regular appearance in the newspapers of the day. The transparency of the stated basis for objection is clear from our earliest evidence, a letter written to a Manchester newspaper in 1858. The passage to which the writer objects reads "a female had been found dead at a road-side." He purports to be anxious to discover whether it had been "a cow, or a mare, or a she ass." Had it been a cow, mare, or she ass, of course, it wouldn't have made the newspapers, even in 1858.

The critics and even the defenders of *female* have not been over-generous in their supplying of 19th-century examples. Still, we can trace a few distinct uses. *Female* as a term correlative to *male* seems not to have been much objected to. A typical example of this use Hall quotes from Macaulay:

> Though in families the number of males and females differs widely, yet in great collections of human beings the disparity almost disappears.

This sort of use is specifically approved by some commentators as scientific or statistical.

The use as a simple synonym of *woman* we have seen from Jane Austen earlier. Another example:

> The alarmed female shrieked as she recovered her feet —James Fenimore Cooper, *The Pilot*, 1823

Mark Twain, writing after the mid-Victorian assault, made fun of Cooper's penchant for using it.

The "woman" use seems to have led in two directions. First, and perhaps most handily, *female* was used in the singular when the age of the person referred to was unknown or uncertain, and in the plural to indicate a group of mixed or undetermined ages:

> ... the females of the family —Jane Austen, *Pride and Prejudice*, 1813

> In short, there was not a female within ten miles of them that was in possession of a gold watch, a pearl necklace, or a piece of Mechlin lace, but they examined her title to it —Joseph Addison, *The Guardian* (cited by Hall)

Second, a humorous or facetious use:

> ... I sometimes add my vocal powers to her execution of
> "Thou, thou reign'st in this bosom,"—
> not, however, unless her mother or some other discreet female is present, to prevent misinterpretation —Oliver Wendell Holmes d. 1894, *The Autocrat of the Breakfast-Table*, 1858

The frequent statements made in the 19th century on the opprobrium attached to the use of *female* were overstated. The most opprobrious citation produced to back up the assertion is from an 1889 daily newspaper by an anonymous author who says it is a term of opprobrium. There is, however, a faintly or mildly pejorative flavor in some use. Hodgson says the "contemptuous sense is justified by ample precedents" and produces this example:

> He did not bid him go and sell himself to the first female he could find possessed of wealth —Anthony Trollope, *Doctor Thorne*, 1858

Trollope's contempt here does not seem especially strong.

At the end of the 20th century and the beginning of the 21st, how is *female* faring? The neutral journalistic use has staged a comeback. It usually contrasts implicitly or explicitly with *male*:

> . . . is believed to be the only female among more than 1,000 head coaches of men's Division 1 sports teams —Craig Neff, *Sports Illustrated*, 21 Mar. 1988

> . . . to become the first female to win a national title ahead of men —Alan Dunn, *Manchester Guardian Weekly*, 5 Jan. 1992

> For centuries, men of the region have engaged in "honor killing," the intrafamily slaughter of allegedly errant females —Lisa Beyer, *Time*, 18 Jan. 1999

The application to lower animals continues to flourish:

> When researchers attached satellite tags . . . to relocated animals, they found that lone females seemed to make a beeline for home —Sharon Begley et al., *Newsweek*, 31 Jan. 2000

Scientific and statistical use is still common:

> . . . an X chromosome spends two-thirds of its time in females —Matt Ridley, *Genome*, 1999

> . . . during the preceding year, 37.9 million females age 10 and over in the U.S. had read at least one romance novel —Paul Gray, *Time*, 20 Mar. 2000

The more-or-less mildly pejorative use is still around:

> I shudder to think what Father would say to me here, skulking among a tribe of papist females —Barbara Kingsolver, *The Poisonwood Bible*, 1998

Bolinger 1980 maintains that *female* in ordinary conversation is always derogatory. We can neither prove nor disprove the assertion.

feminine forms, female-gender word forms, feminine designations Long, learned, and speculative discussions of nouns whose terminations in English mark them as intended for women can be found under these and related headings in Fowler 1926, 1965, Reader's Digest 1983, Copperud 1970, 1980, and other sources. The largest group of these words, those ending in *-ess*, we have treated separately under that heading in this book.

Writers who express opinions about feminine forms in general can be divided into three groups: those (mostly men) who believe them falling into disuse; those (some 19th-century women and Fowler 1926) who find them desirable; and those (chiefly women) who find them offensive.

See - ESS; see also PERSON 2.

fewer See LESS, FEWER.

field It is a bit of a convention in the field of college handbooks to disparage the phrase *in the field of* as deadwood, which it certainly is in such examples as "He is majoring in the field of physics." The complaint is probably more of a warning to freshman English students and other college writers than a generalization on usage at large.

In our files we have a handful of citations from which the phrase could have been harmlessly omitted. But our citations seldom have it attached to well-known areas of intellectual endeavor such as psychology, history, or medicine. More often it is used to flag some other noun as standing for a field of study or endeavor when that meaning might not otherwise be the first to come to mind:

> Until Lévi-Strauss entered the field of mythology —John Bamberger, *N.Y. Times Book Rev.*, 3 June 1973

> . . . a writer of the utmost distinction in the crime field —Julian Symons, *N.Y. Times Book Rev.*, 30 Sept. 1979

The phrase *the field of* is probably generally omissible before the name of a well-known field such as chemistry or mathematics or philosophy, but it may be useful in preventing misunderstanding if the field is something like mystery novels.

fillers *Filler* is a term used for words, phrases, and sounds (often spelled *er, uh, um*) that are used to fill gaps or pauses in discourse by speakers, as Burchfield 1981 diplomatically puts it, "who temporarily lose their fluency." A number of these—*actually, like, you know*, for instance—have been denigrated by usage writers, many of whom seem unaware of their function.

One astute observer of the language describes the function of fillers this way:

For the speaker, they give time for formulating the coming material, and for both speaker and hearer, they signal that the speaker will continue; the hearer's turn to reply has not come —Archibald A. Hill, in *Studies in English Linguistics*, ed. Sidney Greenbaum et al., 1979

Some fillers—*well, oh*—introduce an utterance, and others—*actually, you know, isn't it?*—are used as tags at the end of an utterance. Robert F. Ilson, in *The English Language Today* (1985), notes that British English has a wider variety of these than American English. It also appears that some of the British fillers are considered indicative of social class.

Fillers have been studied to some extent by linguists, but there is undoubtedly a great deal that we do not know about their functions and the constraints under which they are used. Just remember that fillers are characteristic of speech, not of written prose.

final   Phythian 1979, Partridge 1942, Einstein 1985, Ayres 1881, and Copperud 1970, 1980 all carry brief warnings that *final* used with such words as *completion, ending, upshot,* and *culmination* is redundant. That our files—which are fairly wide-ranging—contain no examples of these combinations suggests that the problem does not arise often. When *final* is used with such words, or with *end, consumer, destination, outcome,* it is merely intended to reinforce the notion of finality.

See REDUNDANCY.

finalize   It has been fashionable to scorn *finalize* for more than four decades now. Denigration began in 1942 both in the U.S. and in England. British critics were the more vigorous early on; most American criticism seems to have waited until after President Eisenhower used the word in a speech in 1958.

There was early confusion about the origin of *finalize*. Some commentators were sure it was an Americanism, while others thought President Eisenhower had introduced it. But all the while it had been sitting quietly at the foot of page 948 in Webster's Second 1934—in the pearl section that holds the lower-frequency words.

Although the earliest use we now know of is Canadian, *finalize* got into Webster's Second from Australia, chiefly. In 1923 our agent in Melbourne wrote to report losing the sale of a dictionary because *finalize* was not in it. The word was apparently quite common in Australia and New Zealand in the 1920s, especially in business circles. By 1927 the word had reached the U.S., apparently through the medium of the U.S. Navy; it turns up in the U.S. Naval Institute *Proceedings* in May of that year. The OED Supplement has British examples from 1930. It seems never

to have been considered anything but standard in Australia and New Zealand. It is probably the widespread adoption of the word by various bureaucracies around the time of World War II that brought it to unfavorable notice.

Evidence in our files and in the OED Supplement shows that *finalize* is used in all of the major English-speaking areas of the world. It is still a favorite in business and official English. It is most often used in contexts like these:

> No advertising budget has been finalised —*Evening Press* (Dublin, Ireland), 5 June 1974

> Final regulations were proposed last April, and an I.R.S. official testified today that they may be finalized in about 2 1/2 weeks —Frances Cerra, *N.Y. Times*, 22 Sept. 1976

> In the last few weeks, the Justice Department has been working to finalize plans —Michael Isikoff, *Newsweek*, 3 July 2000

You do not have to use *finalize* at all, of course, but it is now standard. Garner 1998 and Burchfield 1996 note that there is nowadays little objection to the word. Garner also notes the single word is preferred by many to longer equivalents.

fine   1. A number of handbooks call *fine*, when used to denote superior quality, an overused counterword. But it is obvious that the writers represented in our files don't seem to feel it the least bit empty of content. It is used especially, though not at all exclusively, by reviewers, for whom it apparently suggests a measured or discriminating appreciation of something good. It seems to be able to denote superior quality without the suggestion of overstatement. It is frequently used in the superlative. Here are some samples of use:

> . . . where a translator, however fine a scholar, is not a writer . . . —Leo Rosten, *Harper's*, July 1972

> A fine detective story, admirably bolstered with trade expertise —*Times Literary Supp.*, 22 Oct. 1971

> Yet his writing over the past two decades has included some of his finest poems —*Times Literary Supp.*, 16 Apr. 1970

As a predicate adjective it tends to be a more generalized (and less emphatic) term of approval:

> The job was fine—for a while —Vivian Cadden, *McCall's*, October 1971

> This is no "value-free" book, which is fine with me —Peter Steinfels, *Commonweal*, 9 Oct. 1970

2. The adverb *fine* used as a term of approval is called colloquial by a number of commentators, but they probably intend *colloquial* as a disparaging label rather than as a descriptor of standard spoken English. Here are some examples of the use:

> I liked your Maine poems fine —Archibald MacLeish, letter, 25 Jan. 1929

> The dress . . . is beautiful and fits fine —Flannery O'Connor, letter, 1 Jan. 1959

It can be found in discursive prose as well as in speech and friendly correspondence:

> This bloodless September stuff suits me fine —Edward Hoagland, *Harper's*, February 1971

> They could walk fine in real life, but in front of the fashion photographers' cameras they were forced to become physical incompetents —*New Yorker*, 5 Oct. 1981

In this use the adverbial *fine* is not idiomatically interchangeable with *finely*.

finished In 1985 an American woman living in Germany wrote to us to complain that the sentences "I'm not finished yet" and "You aren't finished yet" had been marked wrong by a German instructor on an English examination taken by her son (who had attended elementary school in the United States). The instructor was looking for *haven't* in each case, which was prescribed by the British textbook. The explanation was that *am not* and *are not* with *finished* were not standard British usage, although they were "popular" in the U.S. and might occur in "informal" British speech.

That the textbook is based on an artificial standard is fairly obvious from Strang 1970, who says that the construction *be finished with* arose in the 19th century, and from Otto Jespersen 1909–49 (volume 4), who found the construction in English literature as far back as Oliver Goldsmith's *Vicar of Wakefield* (1766). Jespersen also found examples in numerous other writers of British English. To his list we can add James Joyce:

> Are you not finished with him yet . . . ? —*Ulysses*, 1922

Since a good many of the examples appear to have been spoken by characters in these books, it seems reasonable to suppose that the construction is commonly found in ordinary speech.

It seems apparent that *finished* began to become common in this construction during the 19th century, at the same time that the participial adjective was becoming established. It also seems clear that the dispute over the propriety of the construction centers upon its use with a personal subject. With an inanimate subject, the construction can be understood as passive rather than as intensive. Here's an example of this usage, which has not been a matter of dispute:

> At three o'clock his business was finished —Sherwood Anderson, *Poor White*, 1920

See also DONE 1; THROUGH.

firm **1.** *Noun.* Bernstein 1965 and Copperud 1970, 1980 object to the nontechnical use of *firm* as a synonym for any sort of business: Bernstein objects in particular to its use for a corporation, a different sort of legal entity; Copperud claims no dictionary recognizes the "corporation" use except Merriam-Webster dictionaries. The technical sense is "a partnership of two or more persons not recognized as a legal person distinct from the members composing it."

There are two matters to set straight here. First, no Merriam-Webster dictionary equates *firm* with *corporation*; our dictionaries do recognize a current extended sense, however, "a business unit or enterprise." This sense is well attested:

> . . . the engineering firm that built the Chesapeake Bay bridge —*Dun's*, October 1971

> The new firm started operations in early 1971 as a major supplier of die cast parts —*Annual Report, National Lead Co.*, 1970

The second point is that the reader of these and similar examples has no need to know and probably does not care to know what legal basis the firm is established on. The consideration is irrelevant to the reader, and so is the objection.

Firm is a collective noun that is treated as singular in American English. In British English, however, it may take a plural verb:

> One sympathetic firm have sent Mr. Lawrence a pair of "indestructible" socks —*The People*, 25 Feb. 1968

2. *Adverb.* The adverb *firm* is usually found in just a few fixed phrases, such as *hold firm* and *stand firm*:

> On legalization of the Communist Party the Government is also standing firm —David Holden, *N.Y. Times Mag.*, 3 Oct. 1976

Firmly serves for other adverbial uses.
    See also FIRSTLY.

first and foremost This alliterative phrase is disparaged as redundant, trite, and meaningless by several commentators. No doubt there is some justice in such comments, and you may want to keep them in mind the next time you are called upon to make a campaign speech. *First and foremost* has other uses than as an introduction to windy oratory, however. Its alliteration and rhythm give it an emphatic quality which may make it attractive as an occasional alternative to *primarily* or *primary*:

> Its first and foremost component is the conscious cultivation of man's intellectual and expressive powers —Thomas F. O'Dea, *Center Mag.*, May 1969

> . . . what they needed first and foremost was a giant statistical brain —David Halberstam, *Harper's*, February 1971

> First and foremost, Bunnies work in a traditionally dead-end female occupation: they're waitresses —Gloria Steinem, *TV Guide*, 23 Feb.–1 Mar. 1985

> As a practical matter, though, the poison pill is a legal device: Takeover battles now revolve first and foremost around whether a poison-pill defense should be allowed —Joseph Nocera, *Esquire*, February 1990

firstly Two objections have been lodged against this word. The first is a 19th-century prejudice against *firstly* on the grounds of propriety. Thomas De Quincey, for instance, said in 1847 that he detested the pedantic neologism *firstly*. Ayres 1881 seems to agree, although he does mention the approbation of Moon 1864; both Ayres and Gould 1870 note that Webster 1864 called it improper. Later commentators who are lined up against *firstly* include Vizetelly 1906 and Bierce 1909.

All this criticism involved a certain amount of misunderstanding, however. De Quincey thought *firstly* a neologism, but it had been in use for more than 300 years when he wrote. Moon seems to have approved *firstly* because he thought *first* wasn't an adverb; but it is. Fowler 1926 pooh-poohed the whole fuss as "one of the harmless pedantries."

Fowler's dismissal of the objections to *firstly* rather took the wind out of the sails of the controversy, though, and it gradually drifted to a stop, although occasional objections continued to be voiced until at least 1981. Evans, in support of Fowler, lists such well-known 19th-century writers as Dickens, Scott, Gladstone, Byron, Thackeray, and Kingsley as users of *firstly*.

Since Fowler took the original objection away from the commentators, they have come up with another one. Almost universally they admit that *firstly* is all right, but they still prefer that you not use it. They want you to use *first* instead because it is shorter. Whether or not the commentators' advice has had any effect, *first* is a much more common and much more generally useful word than *firstly*, which is almost never used except to begin an enumeration. Our evidence also suggests that *first-*

ly is more frequent in British English than in American English.

All of this brings us to a final point. A good many recent handbooks feel you should be consistent in your enumerations. They prefer *first, second, third*, etc., but will allow you *firstly, secondly, thirdly*, etc. if you really favor those. Now there is nothing wrong with consistency, but it is only fair to note that consistency in the employment of these enumerators does not appear to have been a high priority with many good writers, who have often played fast and loose with them.

first two, two first When *first* and a cardinal number are used together, there are two ways of ordering them: either "the three first Gospels" (an example from Alford 1866) or "the first three Gospels." The OED shows that the first of these constructions is the older, dating back to at least the 14th century. The latter construction is attested from the late 16th century. The OED editor suggests that the latter construction is the result of the common people's perception of *first* as an ordinal.

The OED explanation works very well for *first*, but Jespersen 1909–49 (volume 2) notes that the same competition in word order occurs with *last* and *next* as well as *first*. The development of the two competing constructions, then, is not likely to be explained by simple logic; let us just accept it as historical fact.

The older construction—"the two first"—became the subject of commentary and controversy in the second half of the 19th century. The first of the usage writers in our collection to mention the issue is Alford 1866, who defends his use of "the three first Gospels" against critics. Since that time, the subject has been reviewed in a large number of usage books, most of them coming between Alford and the 1930s, although it does appear in some more-recent books.

There is no shortage of literary evidence for the older construction:

> I cast my eyes but by chance on *Catiline*; and in the three or four first pages, found enough to conclude that *Johnson* writ not correctly —John Dryden, "Defence of the Epilogue," 1672

> . . . and procure a transcript of the ten or twenty first lines of each —Samuel Johnson, letter, 7 Aug. 1755

> Why, the two last volumes are worse than the four first —Thomas Gray, letter, 8 Mar. 1758

> . . . the three next pictures —*The Spectator*, No. 167 (in Jespersen)

> The two last days were very pleasant —Jane Austen, letter, 8 Sept. 1816

The basis for the objection to the older construction is logic, supposedly; the argument urged is that there can be one first and one last. Jespersen comments on this argument:

Pedants have objected to combinations like *the three first lines* on the absurd plea that there is only one first line (as if it were not possible to speak of the first years of one's life!)

Alford attacks the logic of the usage from a somewhat different angle. He objects to "the first three Gospels"—the correction urged upon him by his critics—on the grounds that "the first three" to him implied the existence of a second three—and there are only four Gospels. Lounsbury 1908 also makes use of this argument.

Neither appeal to logic against the older construction nor the argument of Alford and Lounsbury defending it is very compelling. A few more simple-minded commentators have merely called the older construction wrong, but, of course, it is not. What is happening is that the older construction is falling out of use. Longman 1984 describes it as old-fashioned. The usage panel in Harper 1975, 1985 shows that 81 percent use the newer construction. Our files have very few recent examples of the older construction. The newer construction is the one you will usually find:

Between his last two comedies he went on some diplomatic mission to Constantinople —Bonamy Dobrée, *Restoration Comedy*, 1924

The first couple chapters are pretty good —E. B. White, letter, 26 Oct. 1959

The first six volumes set a high standard —*Times Literary Supp.*, 31 Oct. 1968

We think that the newer construction is now the more common one idiomatically, and if you have been born since the 1920s, it is the one you will use automatically. But remember that anyone who happens to still use the older order is not wrong.

fit, fitted   There seems to be a bit of confusion about the alternative past and past participle forms of the verb *fit*. Both *fitted* and *fit* are used in the United States; only *fitted* appears to be used in British English. Theodore Bernstein 1962, 1965, 1971, 1977 insists on *fitted* (in 1971 he allowed *fit* fit for speech, but not for print), and so does his successor, as recently as 20 Mar. 1987. The Dictionary of American Regional English shows that *fit* predominates in most parts of the U.S. except New England (and the *New York Times* offices).

Evans 1957, Bryant 1962, Lamberts 1972, and Heritage 1982 present opinion or evidence

showing some preference for *fitted* when the verb is used in a causative sense:

During the off-season he was fitted with glasses —Rick Telander, *Sports Illustrated*, 2 Aug. 1982

Our evidence for this sense does not confirm the dominance of *fitted*, even though it may seem right intuitively. For instance, we have this example:

A fine shirtmaker will tell you that . . . you are perfectly capable of being fit —G. Bruce Boyer, *Town & Country*, February 1983

For now you need only remember that in American English both *fitted* and *fit* are correct; your preference in a particular instance will probably be conditioned by where you were born. British English uses *fitted*. The Dictionary of American Regional English shows *fit* more common than *fitted* in the U.S. Our files show *fitted* somewhat more common than *fit* in print.

fix   **1.** Back in 1839 Captain Frederick Marryat, the nautical novelist, paid a visit to America. Among the things he noticed was the American use of the verb *fix*. "The verb 'to fix' is universal. It means to do anything," he wrote in his diary. The editors of the Dictionary of American English used Marryat's comment to preface their treatment of the verb, for which they were able to descry some thirty senses and subsenses of American provenience. While a good many of these originated later than 1839, some go back to the 17th and 18th centuries.

Schele de Vere 1872 expanded quite a bit on Marryat's comment, and it was perhaps from this source that the subject was picked up by turn-of-the-century commentators, such as Vizetelly 1906, Bierce 1909, and MacCracken & Sandison 1917.

From these older sources *fix* has found its way into quite a large number of handbooks. Many of these complain that the word is overused or has too many meanings and recommend that some more exact word be substituted for it. On examination you can see that the reasons given for these recommendations are inexact. Is "repair my watch" more specific than "fix my watch"? Or is "prepare some supper" more precise than "fix some supper"? Clearly not. Shaw 1987 says that it doesn't make much sense to use the same word for such widely diverse meanings. But *fix* is no more semantically diffuse than many common verbs in English. For instance, you can "take a swim," "take a drink," "take your time," "take it on the chin," or "take a size six." Who is confused by such everyday phrases?

This seems to be another case of the inexplicable nervousness of American usage commentators when faced with Americanisms. There is no reason for Americans to be diffident about their own language. Here are a few examples of senses that are mentioned in the usage books:

> . . . the Windham Garage, where cars and farm machines get fixed —Vance Bourjaily, *Atlantic*, February 1973

> "Do you want me to fix you a piece of jelly bread?" she asked —Russell Baker, *Growing Up*, 1982

> Her hair looked as if it had just been professionally done, although she fixes it herself —Lally Weymouth, *N.Y. Times Mag.*, 26 Oct. 1980

> . . . fixing traffic tickets for wayward drivers —William Nack, *Sports Illustrated*, 22 Sept. 1980

> . . . don't bother either to have their cats fixed or to feed them —Anthony Bailey, *New Yorker*, 20 Nov. 1971

These uses are all standard in American English though not, perhaps, characteristic of the most elevated prose.

2. The noun *fix* has less frequently been aspersed, but it receives occasional mention. Bernstein 1971 says most senses of the noun are useful and acceptable, but he questions the sense "a shot of a narcotic." The examples here will show you how that sense has developed since 1971:

> . . . the urgent frisking for notes and small change of boys desperate for a fix —Anthony Burgess, *MF*, 1971

> . . . Dopey Americans will pay anything for their coffee fix —William Safire, *N.Y. Times*, 13 Jan. 1977

> Beauty contest addicts can get another giant fix tomorrow —John J. O'Connor, *N.Y. Times*, 9 Sept. 1977

flack See FLAK, FLACK.

flagrant See BLATANT, FLAGRANT.

flair, flare A number of handbooks warn against confusing these homophones. Part of the trouble is that *flair* is an occasional variant of *flare* in the sense of "a spreading outward." When pants with flared legs were fashionable, they were sometimes spelled *flairs* and sometimes *flares*. Aside from this, we have little recent evidence for *flair* in this sense.

flak, flack *Flak* was originally antiaircraft fire, and more recently hostile or at least unfriendly criticism. *Flack* was originally a press agent. Copperud 1980 is worried that the difference between the two is threatened. As far as spelling is concerned, the difference has already eroded to a certain extent: *flack* is established as a variant spelling of *flak*, and *flak* is used occasionally for *flack*. However, neither variant is as common as the original spelling, so spelling will clue you to meaning most of the time. In other cases, you will have to pay attention to the context. The words are never confused, even if their spellings are sometimes interchanged. We recommend that you use the original and still-dominant spellings for each word.

flammable, inflammable These two words are synonymous. *Flammable* is a much newer word, apparently coined in 1813 to serve in a translation from Latin. In the 1920s it was adopted by the National Fire Protection Association in place of *inflammable*. Underwriters and others interested in fire safety followed suit. The reason given for its adoption was the possibility that the *in-* of *inflammable* might be misunderstood as a negative prefix. We do not know whether such a misunderstanding has ever actually occurred. We do have occasional citations that show some uncertainty about the meaning of the words, so there seems to be some basis for the concern about misunderstanding.

The publicity campaign undertaken to urge wider adoption of *flammable* put the word in the public eye on numerous occasions over the years. Eventually the ivory tower—where nothing burns, apparently—began to be heard bemoaning the loss of a fine literary word (*inflammable*) which was being shunted aside by a "corrupt" form. The combination of publicity and occasional outbreaks of lamentation have helped land the subject in many usage books.

Our files show that both forms continue to be used. *Flammable* is less common in British English than it is in American English. *Flammable* is used literally; figurative use belongs to *inflammable*:

> The vision of a single young woman is said to have overcome the inflammable Monk —George Meredith, *The Ordeal of Richard Feverel*, 1859

> But the inflammable and inflammatory materials were there to be ignited by critics of the scientific-military Establishment —Donald Fleming, *Atlantic*, September 1970

Nonflammable is the usual negative compound of *flammable*.

flare See FLAIR, FLARE.

flat adverbs A flat adverb is an adverb that has the same form as its related adjective: *fast* in "drive fast," *slow* in "go slow," *sure* in "you sure fooled me," *bright* in "the moon is shining bright," *flat* in "she turned me down flat," *hard* and *right* in "he hit the ball hard but right at the shortstop." Flat adverbs have been a problem for grammarians and schoolmasters for a couple of centuries now, and more recently usage writers have continued to wrestle with them.

Flat adverbs were more abundant and used in greater variety formerly than they are now. They were used then as ordinary adverbs and as intensifiers:

> . . . commanding him incontinent to avoid out of his realm and to make no war —Lord Berners, translation of Froissart's *Chronicles*, 1523

> . . . I was horrid angry, and would not go —Samuel Pepys, diary, 29 May 1667

> . . . the weather was so violent hot —Daniel Defoe, *Robinson Crusoe*, 1719

> . . . the five ladies were monstrous fine —Jonathan Swift, *Journal to Stella*, 6 Feb. 1712

> . . . I will not be extreme bitter —William Wycherly, *The Country Wife*, 1675

You would be hard pressed to find modern examples of these particular uses.

Originally such adverbs had not been identical with adjectives; they had been marked by case endings, but over the course of Middle English the endings disappeared. The 18th-century grammarians, such as Lowth 1762, Priestley 1798, and Murray 1795, could not explain how these words were adverbs. They saw them as adjectives, and they considered it a grammatical mistake to use an adjective for an adverb. They preferred adverbs ending in *-ly*.

Two centuries of chipping away by schoolmasters and grammarians has reduced the number of flat adverbs in common use and has lowered the status of quite a few others. Many continue in standard use, but most of them compete with an *-ly* form. Bernstein 1971, for instance, lists such pairs as *bad, badly; bright, brightly; close, closely; fair, fairly; hard, hardly; loud, loudly; right, rightly; sharp, sharply; tight, tightly.* Many of these pairs have become differentiated, and now the flat adverb fits in some expressions while the *-ly* adverb goes in others. And a few flat adverbs—*fast* and *soon*, for instance—have managed to survive as the only choice.

Several articles in this book deal with the question of flat adverbs; see BAD, BADLY; CHEAP 2; CONSIDERABLE 2; NEAR, NEARLY; QUICK, QUICKLY; SCARCELY 1; SLOW, SLOWLY; TIGHT, TIGHTLY.

flaunt, flout A letter to the editor of the *San Francisco Chronicle* in 1932 noted "the curious new error" of confusing *flaunt* with *flout*. This is the first record we have of anyone objecting to this use. Our earliest evidence of the error itself is from 1918:

> They flaunt his every title to affection or respect —*Yale Rev.*, October 1918

Further evidence turned up sporadically in the 1920s and 1930s, but we began to see this use of *flaunt* frequently only in the late 1940s.

This is one issue about which there is no dissent among usage commentators. All of them regard the use of *flaunt* to mean "flout" as nothing less than an ignorant mistake. Many of them also note with dismay or astonishment that this ignorant mistake is extremely common, and that it occurs even among the well-educated (Partridge 1942 even candidly admits to having made it himself). Nowhere is there the least suggestion, however, that its common occurrence among the highly educated makes it at all defensible.

Flaunt in its approved senses can mean "to display oneself to public notice," "to wave showily," and especially "to display ostentatiously":

> . . . some books that flaunt a brand name are doing little more than beckoning to a market —Hugh Kenner, *Harper's*, March 1984

> . . . to allow a minority to openly flaunt its differences with the rest of society —*Houston Post*, 16 Sept. 1984

Flout means "to treat with contemptuous disregard":

> . . . is crushed by the conventions she flouts —Robert Pattison, *On Literacy*, 1982

> . . . many of them flout the rules on amateurism —Bob Ottum, *Sports Illustrated*, 6 Feb. 1984

Both words are used to describe open, unashamed behavior, and both typically suggest disapproval of such behavior. They are, in fact, used in such similar ways that they go together easily in a single sentence:

> . . . a young woman notoriously wild, flaunting her sexual power, flouting the decorum deemed fitting a maiden queen —Maureen Quilligan, *N.Y. Times Book Rev.*, 3 Apr. 1983

Add to this similarity of use the obvious similarity of the words themselves, and you have a situation ripe for confusion.

It is an oversimplification, however, to say that the use of *flaunt* to mean "to treat with contemptuous disregard" is merely the result of confusion. Certainly this sense originated from confusion, but those who now use it do so not because they are confused—they use it because they have heard and seen it so often that it seems natural and idiomatic.

They observed with horror the flaunting of their authority —Marchette Chute, *Shakespeare of London*, 1949

. . . she flaunted the rules, was continually reprimanded —Louis Untermeyer, *Saturday Rev.*, 7 June 1969

. . . whose code of respectability he flaunts or violates —Philip Roth, *Reading Myself and Others*, 1975

So in 1997, a number of Burgundians ignored the law. . . . What's new in 1997 is that they flaunted the law openly —Per-Henrick Mansson, *Wine Spectator*, 31 Jan. 1998

And a nation that flaunts God's moral dictates cannot survive, he warns in *Character & Destiny* —Michelle Cottle, *New Republic*, 10 May 1999

No one can deny that this sense of *flaunt* is now alive and well.

Nevertheless, the notoriety of *flaunt* used for *flout* is so great that we think you well-advised to avoid it, at least when writing for publication. We also suggest that you avoid using *flout* to mean "to display ostentatiously; flaunt." Such usage does turn up in print on occasion:

"The proper pronunciation," the blonde said, flouting her refined upbringing, "is pree feeks" —Mike Royko, *Springfield* (Mass.) *Union-News*, 30 June 1988

. . . she flouted a kind of Oriental black-widow sexuality —William Prochnau, *Once Upon a Distant War*, 1995

See also MITIGATE.

fleshly, fleshy A few critics, starting with Fowler 1926, distinguish between *fleshly* and *fleshy* and warn against confusing them. The two words, the OED shows, have been occasionally synonymous for many years—at least since Chaucer used them both in the sense of "plump." To show the main directions of development while not getting bogged down in unnecessarily specific details, we can say that each word has two main divisions of meaning. The first relates to the flesh as substance, the second to flesh as opposed to the spirit or to what is immaterial.

The senses relating to flesh as a substance and its physical attributes have come to predominate with *fleshy*:

A charming, fleshy, latter-day Jay Gatsby —Aljean Harmetz, *N.Y. Times Mag.*, 5 Oct. 1980

The senses contrasting with *spiritual* are those that have come to predominate with *fleshly*:

Paul has to bring these fleshly pagans over to a more ascetic faith —Anthony Burgess, *TV Guide*, 5 Apr. 1985

There are quite a few instances in which both words can be used similarly, or even synonymously. These uses are well justified historically and are not wrong, but they tend to be counter to what the reader would normally expect.

floating adverb See SENTENCE ADVERB.

flounder, founder A person flounders by struggling to move or obtain footing, while a ship founders by filling with water and sinking. Usage writers say that these two words are often confused, and we have found that *flounder* and *founder*, whether used literally or figuratively, do sometimes borrow each other's meaning.

. . . Cabeza de Vaca's boat had floundered in 1528 —Bernard DeVoto, *The Course of Empire*, 1952

. . . our political parties must never flounder on the rocks of moral equivocation —Adlai E. Stevenson, *Speeches*, ed. Richard Harrity, 1952

. . . bloodhounds . . . raced confidently through the campus right to the highway . . . and there they foundered —Edward Corsetti, *True Police Cases*, October 1959

Flounder for *founder* is a substitution much likelier to be encountered than the reverse. And the uses of *founder* for *flounder* tend to read as though some third verb might be what the writer really wanted. Crossover uses of *flounder* are more straightforwardly cases of confusion with *founder*. We do not have enough evidence to say that a new sense has become established in either case, so it is better to keep the meanings of these two words distinct.

Critics such as Bernstein 1958 and Freeman 1983 also disapprove of *founder* paired with *sink* as redundant:

The ship carrying Manoel's rhinoceros foundered off the coast of Genoa and sank with all hands —Calvin Tomkins, *New Yorker*, 20 Nov. 1971

The redundancy is undeniable, but the offense seems minor.

flout See FLAUNT, FLOUT.

flunk A number of college handbooks and at least one high-school handbook stigmatize *flunk* as "colloquial"—whatever that may mean to their respective editors. Flesch 1983, in contrast, approves the term, which he finds more forceful than *fail*. It is probably this forcefulness that is moving *flunk* from the schoolroom and the campus into wider general use. Here are a couple of examples:

. . . why Professor Schlesinger flunks Nixon as a President —Garry Wills, *N.Y. Times Book Rev.*, 18 Nov. 1973

. . . I had, I recall, flunked trigonometry four times in a row —William Styron, *This Quiet Dust and Other Writings*, 1982

Both know their positions have gaping logical holes, but they are trapped by their parties in old thinking that flunks logic —Jonathan Alter, *Newsweek*, 10 Apr. 2000

foist 1. And *fob off*. Fowler 1926 discovered a sentence in a British newspaper beginning, "The general public is much too easily foisted off with the old cry. . . ." This construction, said Fowler, was wrong; *fob off* could be used in "the public can be fobbed off with something" or in "something can be fobbed off on the public," but *foist* could only be used in the second construction. Fowler was right, but the example he found may have been unique; we have no examples of the construction in our files. Garner 1998 notes that Fowler's first *fob off* construction is found mostly in British English.
2. *Foist* has gathered a lot of comment for a word that is not awfully common, but once Fowler had set the ball rolling, others were sure to join in. The dispute involves which prepositions are or should be used with *foist*. We will cut through the conflicting opinions and tell you that it is used with *on, upon, off*, and *off on*. *On* and *upon* are the most common:

The welfare reform Clinton now basks in was foisted on him by the Republican Congress —Andrew Sullivan, *New Republic*, 28 Aug. & 4 Sept. 2000

. . . patients who couldn't look at a piece of broccoli because they had so much of it foisted on them when they were children —Ellyn Satter, *Reader's Digest*, August 1990

The cause of their sorrow was a unique coffin foisted upon them by their chief supplier of funeral goods —Russell Baker, *Growing Up*, 1982

. . . a harrowing trip to a West Village salon where fake nails were foisted upon her —Helmut Newton, *Vogue*, June 1997

Foist off on is next most common:

. . . prefers her wine uncut . . . not the watered-down version some parents might foist off on their offspring —James Laube, *Wine Spectator*, 15 Sept. 1997

. . . seductively foisted off on the inhabitants as not only "normal" but utterly desirable —Thomas Byrne Edsall, *Atlantic*, May 1992

There is also plain *foist off*:

. . . authors who try to foist off the ancient Greek philosopher as some sort of modern biologist —Jeremy Bernstein, *N.Y. Times Book Rev.*, 2 Oct. 1983

Had Bender been posing as his partner while foisting off his phony boxes of Per-Fo and bilking widows out of their pensions? —T. Coraghessan Boyle, *The Road to Wellville*, 1993

These are all standard. Garner corrects an instance of *foist with*; it appears to be a rare combination.

follow, follows See AS FOLLOWS.

following An editor of Webster's Second 1934 used *following* as a preposition in the fourth definition of the preposition *after*: "following the expiration of." However, it passed unnoticed by other editors working on the dictionary, and *following* was not entered as a preposition in Webster's Second until the Addenda Section of 1955. The omission caused a couple of American commentators to deny its existence. British commentators have recognized it but don't like it. It has been in use since at least 1926, when it was first complained about. A few British commentators will accept the preposition when it means "after and because of," as it does here:

Japan's financial system is a wreck following the collapse of the "bubble economy" —Bill Powell, *Newsweek*, 13 Dec. 1993

. . . suffering an infection following a face lift —*TV Guide*, 5 Sept. 1998

But more often it is just an alternative to *after*:

Following a preliminary tasting, we poured the residue of the bottle down the lavatory —Anthony Powell, *Casanova's Chinese Restaurant*, 1960

In June 1955, following his college graduation, David Halberstam tossed a suitcase into his banged-up Chevy and headed south —David M. Oshinsky, *N.Y. Times Book Rev.*, 15 Mar. 1998

It can suggest itself to a writer as a counterpart to another participial preposition, *during*:

During World War II, we helped train and equip twenty Nationalist divisions to oppose the Japanese and following the war helped train and equip forty more to oppose Mao Tse-tung —Chester Bowles, *Saturday Rev.*, 6 Nov. 1971

The use of *following* as a preposition is established as standard.

fond *Fond*, when it is used with a preposition and has a sense involving affection, is most often used with *of* followed by a noun phrase or a gerund:

. . . a round, amiable, commanding man of whom he was very fond —Donald Barthelme, *New Yorker*, 3 May 1982

He is also fond of swimming, reading, and going to the theater —*Current Biography*, October 1966

In the past, *fond* in this sense was used with *on*, most notably by Shakespeare:

That he may prove More fond on her than she upon her love —Shakespeare, *Midsummer Night's Dream*, 1596

fondness *Fondness* is usually used with the preposition *for*, followed by a noun or a gerund:

They have no particular fondness for organizations —Norman Cousins, *Saturday Rev.*, 20 Nov. 1971

. . . a strange fondness for keeping a brief diary on beech trees —John Mason Brown, *Daniel Boone*, 1952

foot *Foot* has three plurals. The regular one is *feet*. The second is *foots*, which is used in only a couple of specialized senses (for instance, when *foots* means "footlights"). The third is the zero form *foot*. This plural also has a limited use. It is used in the chiefly British sense of "foot soldiers, infantry":

. . . the majority of the foot, as of old, were pikemen and billmen —James A. Williamson, *The Tudor Age*, 1964

The more common use of the plural *foot* is in the sense of the nonmetric unit of measure, and even here it is restricted. It regularly occurs (and *feet* does not) between a number and a noun. In this position it is usually joined to the number with a hyphen.

. . . cleared a seven-foot fence to get away —*Sports Illustrated*, 24 Apr. 1967

. . . a 340-by-120-foot auditorium —Norris Willatt, *Barron's*, 9 Feb. 1970

. . . the twenty-eight foot thirteen-ton cutter *Gipsy Moth III* —*Current Biography*, December 1967

The plurals *feet* and *foot* both occur between a number and an adjective:

. . . is five feet six inches tall —*Current Biography*, October 1965

. . . neither the Russians nor the Chinese were ten foot tall —Michael Howard, *Times Literary Supp.*, 21 Dec. 1979

In present-day American printed use, *feet* is more common than *foot*, and is prescribed by many handbooks. *Foot* seems to be more frequent in print in British English. In speech, *foot* is common in both varieties:

He was a short man, only about five foot six —Harry S. Truman, quoted in Merle Miller, *Plain Speaking*, 1973

. . . ten to eleven thousand foot deep —Margaret Thatcher, speech to National Press Club, 19 Sept. 1975

Evans 1957 points out that formerly *foot* could always be used as a plural after a number, even when not immediately followed by a noun or adjective. This practice is less common now. We see it sometimes in British English:

. . . at heights up to 5,000 foot —V. B. Wigglesworth, *Nature*, 16 Nov. 1973

In American English we find it chiefly in speech:

. . . which is 15 foot in diameter —Leon Lederman, speech at meeting of American Association for the Advancement of Science, 1977

Many of the handbooks take the erroneous position that *foot* is only a singular and that *feet* is the only correct plural. The plural *foot* is limited to the uses shown here, but in them it is not an error. Belief that *foot* is wrong leads to this sort of unthinking hypercorrection:

. . . which grows to a height of one feet —*N.Y. Times*, 6 July 1980

forbid *Forbid* is commonly followed by *to* and the infinitive following a direct object:

. . . wine books forbid people to have wine with salad —Jerry Anne DiVecchio, *Sunset*, August 1995

The airlines forbid account holders to sell the tickets —Betsy Wade, *N.Y. Times*, 8 Mar. 1998

Occasionally *to* is followed by an object:

. . . had died in some awful combination of exile and expatriation, since their health forbade England to them —Mary McCarthy, *N.Y. Rev. of Books*, 9 Mar. 1972

Forbid is also used with *from*. Critics deny that this usage is idiomatic, but it has been around for a long time—since 1526. Our evidence shows that *from* follows the direct object and is followed by a gerund:

The Vatican issued an order forbidding all Catholic clergy from participating in Illich's Center —"Radical Cleric," *A Center Occasional Paper*, February 1971

The new rules would . . . forbid them from giving the Soviet Union technology and expertise —Richard Burt, *N.Y. Times*, 19 Mar. 1980

Forbid is also used with a gerund phrase as object:

Foxy wasn't sure if the rules forbad using associations others had used —John Updike, *Couples*, 1968

... a promise to her family forbids her writing another book for a year —*Publishers Weekly*, 24 Jan. 1966

forceful, forcible, forced There probably never would have been a problem about these words had not H. W. Fowler taken offense at a vogue for *forceful* in the British press in the 1920s. Fowler 1926 sprang to the defense of *forcible*, calling it "the ordinary word" and saying that *forceful* was reserved for poetic and other special contexts. Burchfield 1996 says that Fowler was off the mark, and numerous other commentators from 1957 on have tried to clarify the issue. Here is our summary of actual usage.

Forceful is generally used figuratively in present-day American English:

... has been a forceful advocate of the Army's viewpoint —*Current Biography*, November 1965

It is less often used literally; when it is it means "characterized by force":

... an explosion perhaps 500 times as forceful as the atomic bomb —Richard L. Williams, *Smithsonian*, January 1981

Forcible is most commonly—almost always in America—used literally. It suggests something done by force:

In those 10 decades China suffered forcible entry from Western imperial powers —Horace Sutton, *Saturday Rev.*, 17 Mar. 1979

Forcible also has an older figurative use, practically identical with modern *forceful*:

A copious and forcible language —T. B. Macaulay, *The History of England*, vol. I, 1849

This was probably the use Fowler wished to defend. It is still found in British English, but not in American:

To his contemporaries he seemed clear-cut and forcible —*Times Literary Supp.*, 19 Mar. 1964

Forced is added to the group by a couple of commentators. It shares with *forcible* the notion of being produced or done by force. But it tends to be legal force or force of circumstances rather than physical force:

... a discussion of forced busing —Judith Crist, *Saturday Rev.*, 16 Oct. 1976

Protection against forced labor —Carol L. Thompson, *Current History*, November 1952

Forcible is not normally used in this way. *Forced* is also used of something produced by willpower or effort:

... in this vein of forced lightness —Katherine Anne Porter, *Ladies' Home Jour.*, August 1971

foreign plurals For a list of those that are most frequently the subject of usage writers, see LATIN PLURALS.

for free *For free*, as far as we know, was first aspersed in the *Saturday Evening Post*, 20 Feb. 1943; the citation is in the American Dialect Dictionary. What is interesting is that the earliest citation shown in the ADD is an anonymous quotation printed in an article in the same magazine, 12 Dec. 1942—just about two months earlier. The phrase must have had quite a bit of popular use at the time. Since 1943 it has become rather fashionable for writers of usage books (such as Bernstein 1965, Shaw 1975, 1987, Harper 1985) to disparage the phrase.

A couple of commentators dissent. James J. Kilpatrick in a newspaper column (11 Aug. 1985) wonders if the phrase is becoming respectable. He says it is "shorter than the stiff and formal" phrase *without charge*. Flesch 1983 defends *for free* as an idiom.

When an idiom that seems to be as recently formed as *for free* begins to compete with *free*, *gratis*, and *without charge*, speakers and writers probably feel some real need for it. Kilpatrick has given us one hint as to why. You can discover another hint by trying *free* where these writers wrote *for free*:

The drivers will pay their transportation ..., but will have the run of the inn for free —*N.Y. Times*, 25 Dec. 1963

... it seemed best to find a way to live for free then —Jane Harriman, *Atlantic*, March 1970

You can see here that the *for* obviates the ambiguous combinations *inn free* and *live free*. In the next example, the removal of *for* would require its replacement with *away* in order to preserve normally idiomatic English:

... to avoid accusations it was giving billable services for free —*Datamation*, 15 Aug. 1970

And many writers clearly think it lends the right informal note:

... sunset, the only thing they get for free —Christopher Morley, *The Man Who Made Friends With Himself*, 1949

Then offer it—for free—to the British Museum —Bennett Cerf, *Saturday Rev.*, 31 Jan. 1948

More recently, reports about the software industry seemed to have relied heavily on this phrase:

That means Microsoft pays for Apple goods when it uses them, but Apple apparently gets to use Microsoft technology for free

—Rebecca Eisenberg, *San Francisco Examiner*, 10 Aug. 1997

He made Linux available for free on the Internet —Janice Maloney, *Time*, 26 Oct. 1998

By including a database application in its Office suite and a browser in Windows, Microsoft essentially offered these products for free —J. Bradford Delong & A. Michael Froomkin, *Harvard Business Rev.*, January 2000

This idiom is well established in general prose.

forget The past tense of *forget* is *forgot*; the past participle is *forgot* or *forgotten*. Both past participles are used in American English (*forgotten* is more common):

> . . . I've forgot, don't remember, the name of the other —Harry S. Truman, quoted in Merle Miller, *Plain Speaking*, 1973

> . . . one of the shabbier pretensions gets almost forgotten —Robert Penn Warren, *Democracy and Poetry*, 1975

Longman 1984 and Evans 1957 remind us that *forgotten* is standard in present-day British use; *forgot* is considered archaic.

> . . . an acknowledgment that he had quite forgot her —Jane Austen, *Mansfield Park*, 1814

formal *Formal* is a term used in a great many usage books to distinguish that kind of writing and speech that is most mannered and remote from ordinary conversational English. In spite of its wide use, it presents problems as a label, because there is a good deal of uncertainty about just what *formal* is meant to cover. Two responsible commentators can use the term differently. Bryant 1962, for instance, includes among formal sources many of the same sources Perrin & Ebbitt 1972 considers general.

When *formal* is used in this book, it is used only as a vague indicator of general tendency and not as the marker of a class of writings with uniform characteristics. We would suggest that you take prescriptions of "not used in formal English" or "unacceptable in formal English" with a considerable grain of salt. Perhaps Bishop Lowth's "elevated style" would have been a more generally useful label.

See also INFORMAL.

formal agreement See NOTIONAL AGREEMENT, NOTIONAL CONCORD.

former *Former, latter.* Just about any usage book will tell you that *former* is used to refer to the first of two and *latter* to the second of two and that *former* and *latter* should not be used when three or more persons or things are being discussed.

Let's take a look at the evidence: *former* and *latter* are certainly used when two persons or things are being discussed:

> This book is addressed . . . both to "new" and to "experienced" collectors. The former will be misled and the latter irritated by the text —*Times Literary Supp.*, 5 Feb. 1970

> . . . a fundamental trade-off between capitalist prosperity and economic security. As a nation we have chosen to have less of the former in order to have more of the latter —David A. Stockman, *Newsweek*, 28 Apr. 1986

But more often only one word or the other is used:

> . . . the decision to base the civil rights bill on both the commerce clause and the 14th Amendment, with the heavier emphasis on the former —*Current Biography*, February 1965

> . . . the home of Dr. and Mrs. Perley Marsh, the latter a descendant of Colonel Hinsdale —*American Guide Series: New Hampshire*, 1938

And *former* and *latter* are not restricted to just two possible referents; they are often used with three or more—often enough that such use really can be considered acceptable, at least in most varieties of general prose.

> . . . there were three sorts of recruits: . . . The former of these probably joined with a view to an eventual captaincy —*Times Literary Supp.*, 30 Dec. 1949

> . . . though her bibliography includes Hecht, Snyder, and Daiches, she omits the latter's first name —DeLancey Ferguson, *Modern Language Notes*, February 1957

Even less restricted uses of *latter* occur. Sometimes it refers to a group of things:

> Among these latter were the great German poet, Friedrich Schiller, and New England's Henry Wadsworth Longfellow —*American Guide Series: Minnesota*, 1938

> He is a fellow of the three latter societies —*Current Biography*, November 1966

And sometimes *latter* simply refers to the last person or thing named previously, especially at the end of a clause or phrase:

> The skipper, or if the latter is the navigator, the bos'n, will be having a final look around —Peter Heaton, *Cruising*, 1952

When discussing more than three items, you can, of course, use the alternatives (such as *last* or *last-named* instead of *latter*) that many usage books recommend.

formula Both plural forms, *formulas* and *formulae*, are common and correct. Our evidence reveals no general patterns that show that one form or the other is preferred in a particular field.

forte This word in the sense of "one's strong point" is derived from the French. In this sense, usage writers recommend that the word be pronounced like *fort*. It is also very often pronounced like the musical term *forte*, which represents the same Latin root meaning "strong" but which in this case is derived immediately from the Italian. The musical term is pronounced, with usage experts concurring, \\'fȯr-ˌtā\\ or \\'fȯr-tē\\ (like *forty*). All three versions may be heard from well-educated speakers in reference to a strong point, but the last two have incurred vociferous disapproval.

Those who object to the pronunciations in question point out that the word comes from the French, and \\'fȯr-ˌtā\\ is not at all the way the French pronounce it. Against this objection several points may be made:

First, it is now an English word, which we may pronounce as we see fit. A comparable case is that of *apostrophe* in the sense of a punctuation mark. This comes probably from the French and would be pronounced by them without the long *e*, roughly \\ˌä-pȯs-'trȯf\\, yet we pronounce it \\ə-'päs-trə-fē\\, just like the rhetorical term (meaning "addressing of an absent person") that comes to us via Latin from the ancient Greek. With both *forte* and *apostrophe* we have to do with a very old word that has reached us twice by different routes.

Second, the spelling isn't French either—in French the word is *le fort*—so any quest for Gallic purism is doomed from the start.

Third, the recommended pronunciation, rhyming with *fort*, also is not the French one, which rhymes rather with *for*.

A more ticklish objection is that the pronunciation \\'fȯr-ˌtā\\ isn't exactly English either, but pseudo-foreign: we are here pronouncing the word as if it were Italian, or French with an acute-accented *e*, when in fact it is French with an unaccented *e*. In this view, the pronunciation represents a failed attempt at foreignness (see HYPERFOREIGNISMS).

Since there is, in fact, no etymologically respectable pronunciation available for this word, you might as well select one that feels natural and that aids communication. All three discussed here are standard.

forthcoming Janis 1984 and Copperud 1980 are worried about a sense of *forthcoming* that they believe is displacing *forthright*. The use, which dates back to 1835 and seems to be originally British, is almost always a predicate

adjective and only rarely an attributive adjective. It is often used in negative constructions. It is applied to people and, less often, to what they say or write. In its earliest attestations it describes a social characteristic that suggests openness and willingness to talk. In these applications it is perhaps closer in meaning to *outgoing* than to *forthright*.

> But though she was friendly she was not very forthcoming. She replied courteously and sweetly when spoken to, but she never told anybody anything —Elizabeth Goudge, *Pilgrim's Inn*, 1948

> From Bertram Shaw, who was candid and forthcoming, he obtained what he required without appreciable trouble —Edgar Lustgarten, *Defender's Triumph*, 1951

When people are in a position where they are, for reasons of policy, expected to be closemouthed or evasive, *forthcoming* comes fairly close to *frank* or *candid* or *forthright*:

> The doctor was forthcoming and impregnable in the best tradition of American technicians. His understanding of events was too coherent to permit him to be tricked into inconsistency —Suzanne Garment, *Wall Street Jour.*, 3 Apr. 1981

> . . . the publisher, a pale, languid man of 30, was even more forthcoming. "I'm in it for the money", he said —*The Times* (London), 1 Nov. 1973

> Asked if he thinks Motown is promoting the album aggressively enough, an otherwise totally forthcoming Smokey replies, "I won't comment on that right now." —Tom Sinclair, *Entertainment Weekly*, 26 May 2000

It may suggest generosity or readiness to give out information:

> . . . the dust-jacket gives no information about him, except that he lived in West Cornwall for several years. The publishers should be a little more forthcoming —D. M. Thomas, *Times Literary Supp.*, 1 Aug. 1980

> The woman on the other end is clearly new, else she would not be so forthcoming with the information —Jay McInerney, *Bright Lights, Big City*, 1984

> Foremost of the century, old-money families were proud and forthcoming about their cultural booty —Alan Deutschman, *GQ*, May 1998

These are the chief ways in which the disputed sense is used. *Forthright* is in no danger of being usurped.

fortuitous Our evidence at the present time is not conclusive, but it appears that sometime after World War I—certainly by the 1920s—

fortuitous began to be used in a sense meaning "fortunate, lucky." Fowler 1926 seems to have been the first to notice the use. He laid the development to the sound of *fortunate* and the meaning of *lucky*. *Felicitous* may also have had some influence. After all, *fortuitous* sounds like a blend of *fortunate* and *felicitous*, and its new meaning resembles a blend of its original meaning and the meaning of *felicitous*.

Fowler was apparently alone in noticing the new sense (he considered it an error) until well after World War II. The next commentator in our collection who mentions the use is Bernstein 1958. After Bernstein there are many commentators (we have about twenty) who disapprove the use. A couple (Harper 1975, 1985 and Copperud 1970, 1980) notice that the sense is already recorded in American dictionaries.

The oldest meaning of *fortuitous*—which has been the predominant sense all along—is "occurring by chance":

> . . . a certain Fortuitous Concourse of all Mens Opinions —Jonathan Swift, *A Tale of a Tub*, 1710

> His presence in Berlin was quite fortuitous. He had come to deliver a memorial address —William L. Shirer, *The Rise and Fall of the Third Reich*, 1960

There is, as Reader's Digest 1983 observes, a use intermediate between "by chance" and "fortunate." It is applied to something that is a chance occurrence, but has a favorable result.

> I think I reported not long ago in *The New Yorker* . . . how I was saved in college one night by the fortuitous appearance in the night skies of the most brilliant aurora borealis seen in Ohio since the Civil War —James Thurber, letter, 21 May 1954

> She panted into the underground, snatched a ticket from the machine, belted down the stairs, and there was a fortuitous train —Doris Lessing, *The Good Terrorist*, 1985

The earliest evidence we have for the "fortunate" sense dates from 1920, but we did not collect any more examples until after World War II.

> . . . a fortuitous escape from the seemingly inevitable death sentence —Franklin L. Ford, *Saturday Rev.*, 10 May 1947

> This circumstance was a fortuitous one for Abraham Lockwood —John O'Hara, *The Lockwood Concern*, 1965

> But from a cost standpoint, the company's timing is fortuitous —*Business Week*, 13 Dec. 1982

> Her $170,000 bid on what is now Matanzas Creek's vineyard was accepted. The south-

facing slope was a fortuitous find . . . its worth more than 10 times as much today —Jeff Morgan, *Wine Spectator*, 15 May 1996

In present-day English we have three senses of *fortuitous* forming a gradation: "happening by chance," "happening by a lucky chance," and "lucky, fortunate." The third of these has been in use for almost seventy years and is recognized in several dictionaries. There is no question that it is established, especially in newspaper and magazine use, and even though it has lately received a great deal of unfavorable notice, it is showing no signs of going away. You can use the sense, but you should be prepared to catch a little flak if you do.

It is harder to advise you about the intermediate use. It seems likely to continue in use, and because the element of chance is present in its meaning, it is unlikely to cause much stir. Only one commentator has noticed it so far, and it has not yet been recognized in most dictionaries. Our guess is that if you use *fortuitous* to mean "happening by a lucky chance," you have nothing to worry about.

fortuitously The adverb *fortuitously* has been subject to the same strictures as *fortuitous*, but not as often, possibly because the adverb is a good deal less frequent than the adjective. It got quite a bit of attention in Safire 1984. Safire in a newspaper column (22 Nov. 1981) found fault with a sentence in a *Time* article about airplanes that had been ordered by the Shah of Iran shortly before his fall. The offending sentence ended ". . . planes that fortuitously were never delivered." Safire interpreted the adverb to mean "fortunately" because it seemed obvious to him that it was fortunate that the Ayatollah didn't get his hands on the planes. The *Time* writer defended his choice of the word. He said he had picked it deliberately because the planes had been not delivered by happenstance, or, as he put it, "sheer dumb luck."

We have here perhaps the first recorded dispute that can be ascribed to the failure of dictionaries to recognize the intermediate sense of *fortuitous* (see FORTUITOUS and its citations from James Thurber and Doris Lessing for this sense). The *Time* use of the adverb falls midway between "by chance" and "luckily." The blending of the notions of chance and luck seems to be present in these examples, too:

> The needs of the gross anatomy laboratory have been fortuitously met by the big refrigerators of the former dining hall —John Walsh, *Science*, 6 Oct. 1972

> We followed him out the door, into the elevator, and into a taxi that had fortuitously stopped in front of the hotel —*New Yorker*, 1 Dec. 1951

The other two meanings of *fortuitous* also exist in the adverb.

founded *Founded,* when used with a preposition in general applications, is used most often with *on*:

> . . . tales of real life, high and low, and founded on fact! —Henry David Thoreau, *Walden*, 1854

> . . . his instinctive dislike of the middle class was founded on its intellectual sterility —Vernon Louis Parrington, *Main Currents in American Thought*, 1927

Founded is used in the same way with *upon*, but our evidence suggests that this use has diminished somewhat over the last 40 years:

> . . . early poems founded upon old French models —*The Autobiography of William Butler Yeats*, 1953

Founded is also used with *in*:

> . . . this criticism is founded in misconception of the true significance of literature —*Selected Writings of Benjamin N. Cardozo*, ed. Margaret E. Hall, 1947

founder See FLOUNDER, FOUNDER.

Frankenstein Since 1905, when the first lecture was delivered, commentators have been informing us that *Frankenstein* stands for the creator of the monster and not the monster, so we should use *Frankenstein monster* or *Frankenstein's monster* instead. Barzun 1985, however, termed such insistence pedantry, and several other commentators from Evans 1957 to Garner 1998 recognize that the "monster" sense of *Frankenstein* is established. It has been recorded in Merriam-Webster dictionaries since 1934. The phrase *Frankenstein monster*, interestingly enough, has a fair number of users. The phrase actually antedates the prescription of its use: it turns up as early as Oliver Wendell Holmes' *The Autocrat of the Breakfast Table* in 1857. You are free to use either *Frankenstein* or *Frankenstein monster*.

free The adjective *free* is most commonly followed by *of*:

> . . . a pleasure and admiration not entirely free of dutifulness —John Updike, *Hugging the Shore*, 1983

Less commonly it is followed by *from, with,* or *to* plus the infinitive:

> I am free from your besetting fault — George Bernard Shaw, letter, ca. 4 Nov. 1934

> As scrupulous with historical detail as she is free with plot —Timothy Pfaff, *N.Y. Times Book Rev.*, 15 June 1980

> . . . information he didn't feel free to print —Russell Baker, *The Good Times*, 1989

The verb *free* takes *from* somewhat more often than *of*:

> They had time to free some debtors from jail —James MacGregor Burns, *The Vineyard of Liberty*, 1981

> . . . to free themselves of other obligations —Harrison E. Salisbury, *N.Y. Times Book Rev.*, 20 Jan. 1985

freedom *Freedom* is used with *of* far more often than with any other preposition:

> There is a great deal of fuss nowadays about freedom of speech —T. S. Eliot, "Charles Whibley," in *Selected Essays*, 1932

Of other prepositions, those occurring most often are *for, from, in,* and *to* followed by an infinitive:

> . . . the concept of freedom for the individual —*Current Biography*, February 1966

> . . . a reasonably stable government . . . and at least a modicum of efficiency and freedom from graft —Elspeth Huxley, *N.Y. Times Mag.*, 18 July 1954

> . . . freedom in thought, the liberty to try and err —H. L. Mencken, *Prejudices: Second Series*, 1920

> . . . limited freedom to preach and teach —Tom Whitney, *Wall Street Jour.*, 25 Mar. 1954

free gift *Free gift* is cited as a redundancy by many commentators. It appears most commonly nowadays in advertising copy. Since most of us don't have to write advertising copy, the criticism seems rather trivial. The phrase has been in use since at least the 18th century, and older use serves to distinguish what is given voluntarily from what is cajoled or required. (Gibbon, in his *Decline and Fall*, tells us that Roman emperors exacted gifts from the people on certain state occasions.) The notion of "freely given" can still be found:

> . . . grace is the free gift of God —Flannery O'Connor, letter, 21 June 1959

The commentators uniformly assume *free* means "without charge" in *free gift*. The assumption may not always be warranted.

friend The preposition used with *friend* is most often *of*:

> . . . known in Boston, . . . as the inexhaustible friend of all good causes —Van Wyck Brooks, *The Flowering of New England, 1815–1865*, rev. ed., 1946

Less often, *friend* is used with *to*:

> . . . the oversensitive ones, and the displaced ones, do not need it, and it is no friend to

them —Edna O'Brien, *Cosmopolitan*, February 1973

Friend is also used with *with*, especially in the idiomatic phrases *be friends with* or *make friends with*:

Whitman could be friends with anyone who was genuine, not a snob, not a prig —Henry Seidel Canby, *Walt Whitman*, 1943

friendly, *adjective* When *friendly* is used with a preposition, it is most often *to*:

. . . she had always been extremely friendly to me and to my work —Eric F. Goldman, *Harper's*, January 1969

Less frequently, *friendly* is followed by *with*:

"His Grace is never very friendly with anyone. . . ." —Sir Arthur Conan Doyle, *The Return of Sherlock Holmes*, 1904

You might expect to find *friendly toward* or *towards* paralleling the use of *friendly to*; however, we have very little evidence in our files for either preposition.

friendly, friendlily, *adverb* Both *friendly* and *friendlily* have been in use as adverbs for quite some time. According to the OED, the first written example of *friendly* dates from around the 12th century, and the adverb has had continuous use through the ensuing centuries. According to our evidence, it is still in use but very rare:

He was . . . friendly disposed towards the British —W. Gordon Harmon, *Royal Central Asian Jour.*, January 1951

The use of *friendlily*, according to the OED, dates from 1680. The Merriam-Webster files show that *friendlily* is currently preferred to *friendly*, at least in edited prose, although it too is rare. Krapp 1927 called it "too awkward for general use."

The invitation was made friendlily and genuinely enough —Alec Waugh, *My Place in the Bazaar*, 1961

Came out into the reception area to greet them friendlily —Lawrence Sanders, *The Second Deadly Sin*, 1977

. . . it begins by friendlily prompting you for those good and evil combinations —Daniel Seligman, *Fortune*, 3 Mar. 1986

It seems likely that most writers avoid the choice by means of paraphrase.

frightened The prepositions used after *frightened* are *of*, *by*, *at*, and *about*. *Frightened of* has a history of being criticized which apparently started in the middle of the last century. The OED quotes an 1858 issue of *Saturday Review* as saying, "It is not usual for

educated people to perpetrate such sentences as . . . 'I was frightened *of* her.' " The OED's own comment is that "in recent colloquial use *frightened of* (cf. 'afraid of') is common."

More than a century after the *Saturday Review*'s criticism, the stigma attached to *frightened of* lingers in the minds of some usage writers. Some critics suggest *by* and *at* as replacements for *of*, and others recommend *afraid of* instead of *frightened of*. Our evidence indicates that when a preposition follows *frightened, of* is probably more common than *by* and certainly more common than *at*. All three can be considered standard.

What is the use of free expression to people so frightened of the future that they prefer the comforts of the authoritative lie? —Lewis H. Lapham, *Harper's*, November 1990

. . . frightened out of their wits by the fierce impact —Thomas B. Costain, *The Black Rose*, 1945

. . . people who like classical music but are frightened by its scope —Ann M. Lingg, *Think*, September 1954

They were all frightened at the collapse of their lives —D. H. Lawrence, "The Horse Dealer's Daughter," in *England, My England*, 1922

Frightened about also sounds idiomatic:

. . . the owning and managerial classes were then frightened, not only of Labour, but also about their own economic survival —G. D. H. Cole, *New Statesman & Nation*, 21 Nov. 1953

from whence, from thence, from hence Present-day usage writers take the position that *from* is redundant with *whence, thence,* and *hence.* The basis for this assertion is that the notion of *from* is already present in the words.

The questioning of these phrases is not recent. Samuel Johnson in his Dictionary of 1755 termed *from whence* "A vitious mode of speech." (*Vicious* was not so strong a word in 1755 as it is now.) And after the comment, Johnson quotes Spenser and Shakespeare. He used it himself:

There is nothing served about there; neither tea, nor coffee, nor lemonade, nor anything whatever; and depend upon it, Sir, a man does not love to go to a place from whence he comes exactly as he went in —Samuel Johnson, in James Boswell, *The Life of Samuel Johnson*, 1791

Among the 18th-century grammarians who discussed the subject, Priestley 1798 reached the heart of the problem: he noted that writers used the preposition when it sounded right and left it out when leaving it out sounded right.

Priestley was aware of literary usage and so was Hodgson 1889. American usage writers of the late 19th century (Bache 1869 and Ayres 1881) are more severe towards the phrases and less interested in literary practice. More recent usage commentators are for the most part dogmatic, for two reasons: the phrases are much less common than they were two centuries earlier, and many commentators appear to be unacquainted with the older literary sources.

Here are a few instances from the past:

I shall be able, I expect, to dispatch the waggon with the servants from hence, about the 9th. of March —Thomas Jefferson, letter, 27 Feb. 1809

I from thence considered industry, as a means of obtaining wealth and distinction —Benjamin Franklin, *Autobiography*, 2d part, 1784

Let them be whipp'd through every market town till they come to Berwick, from whence they came —Shakespeare, *2 Henry VI*, 1592

Even though Benjamin Franklin knew and used all these phrases, there is little likelihood that you will. *From hence* has hardly penetrated the 21st century. One reason may be that *hence* is little used today in reference to a physical location. It is more often used of time and in other senses. *From hence* is to all intents and purposes an archaism.

From thence has had 20th-century use, but it could hardly be called frequent.

. . . he timed the run from Watford to Mark Lane, and the farther walk from thence to the entrance to the docks —Freeman Wills Crofts, *The Loss of the 'Jane Vosper'*, 1936

Thence, however, is used of place, and therefore *from thence* is a possibility. Most of our 20th-century examples come from British publications; it seems to be less common in American English.

From whence is still alive in both British and American English. Its frequency has made it the chief focus of critical comment. We have plenty of current evidence of its use, although it is not nearly as common as *whence* alone. *From whence* may have been kept fresh in the public consciousness by its occurrence in the King James Bible, especially in the 121st Psalm: "I will lift up mine eyes unto the hills, from whence cometh my help." This passage may also help account for the frequent occurrence of *from whence* with the verb *come*.

Mr. Praeger, as orderly and meticulous as Vienna, (from whence he came) —*N.Y. Times*, 11 Aug. 1957

The fourth lesson was to remember, always, from whence I came —Tip O'Neill with William Novak, *Man of the House*, 1987

. . . gathering data that appear destined to mock, ridicule and otherwise lampoon the raw material (a.k.a. people) from whence the data came —Steve Friedman, *GQ*, November 1997

From whence is the only one of the three phrases that shows signs of continuing vitality, even though it is undoubtedly less common than it was a century or two ago. We see no great fault in using it where it sounds right—and great writers have used it where it sounded right all along.

frown Of all the prepositions used with *frown*, *upon* and *on* are the most frequent:

. . . the fact that he is frowned upon by some people —Roy Blount Jr., *Sports Illustrated*, 23 Aug. 1982

Music was not desired by Quakers, it was frowned on —Catherine Drinker Bowen, *Atlantic*, March 1970

Less often, *frown* is used with *at*:

. . . turning his head to frown grotesquely at the man in the back —Terry Southern, *Flash and Filigree*, 1958

fruitful When *fruitful* is used with a preposition, it is most often followed by *of*, less often by *in*, and occasionally by *for* or *to*:

. . . its mathematical aspect . . . is less complicated and less fruitful of controversy —Bertrand Russell, *Foundations of Geometry*, 1897

History is fruitful of recurrences and therefore of analogies —Reinhold Niebuhr, *Atlantic*, July 1954

The year 1892 was fruitful for Chekhov —*Times Literary Supp.*, 22 Oct. 1971

. . . the fund of available analogies that prove fruitful to diverse minds —Morris R. Cohen, *The Faith of a Liberal*, 1946

fruition The original sense of *fruition* is "enjoyment." The sense is found in the King James Bible and the Book of Common Prayer, and it is common in older literature:

. . . I must observe it once more, that the hours we pass with happy prospects in view are more pleasing than those crowned with fruition —Oliver Goldsmith, *The Vicar of Wakefield*, 1766

Sometime in the 19th century the word began to be used in the sense of "a bearing of fruit" or, in its more usual figurative application, "realization, accomplishment." The OED was one of the first dictionaries to record this use; the editor of *F*, Henry Bradley, thought it must be a blunder based on an erroneous association with the word *fruit*.

The new sense seems not to have excited much comment at first. There was a little flurry of interest in the 1920s, mostly because Webster 1909 had omitted the sense. But Webster's Second entered it in 1934, and after that the interest waned until the middle 1960s, when several commentators discovered the original sense practically all at once. Flesch 1964, Bernstein 1965, and Gowers in Fowler 1965 all disparaged the new sense. Copperud 1970, 1980 observes that the old sense was practically unknown by then and dismisses their objections as pedantry. Howard 1977 and Bryson 1984 also accept the figurative use.

The original sense, because of its liturgical use, is not yet archaic, though it is pretty unusual in everyday contexts. The original extension to the ripening of fruit or crops is also seldom met. The ordinary use is the entirely figurative one:

> . . . we then think of him as still mindful of the old ideals and sure to bring them elsewhere to fruition —William James, *Pragmatism*, 1907

> . . . harbors large ambitions that require a helpmate rather than a playfellow to bring them to fruition —Joseph P. Lash, *McCall's*, October 1971

> These were dreams of long standing that had finally come to fruition —Nicholas Fraser, *Harper's*, September 1996

fugitive When the noun *fugitive* is followed by a preposition, the preposition is usually *from*:

> . . . the character seems like a fugitive from a Molière comedy —*Time*, 20 Aug. 1951

In its specialized sense "likely to evaporate, deteriorate, or change," the adjective *fugitive* may be followed by *to*:

> . . . good money value pigments are generally very fugitive to light —William von Fischer, ed., *Paint and Varnish Technology*, 1948

In other senses, the adjective is occasionally used with *from*:

> . . . poor Indians . . . whose clothes were sometimes fugitive from better wardrobes —John Steinbeck, *Tortilla Flat*, 1935

-ful Nouns ending in *-ful*, such as *cupful*, *spoonful*, *bagful*, and so forth, regularly form the plural by adding *-s* at the end: *cupfuls*, *spoonfuls*, *bagfuls*.

The plural of these words has long been a puzzle to the public. The earliest commentary we have encountered is Dean Alford's 1866 response to a query about the plural of *spoonful*. The Dean prescribed *spoonfuls*, if it was to be written as one word; *spoons full* if it was to be written as two words. This advice has been repeated often.

There seem to be two factors contributing to the public's continuing perplexity. One is that many of these words began as two-word compounds of noun and adjective, and the noun took the plural. The other is that somewhere, sometime, there seem to have been teachers who were convinced that internal pluralization was more proper or more elegant. We have had many letters from people who remember their teachers telling them that the proper plural is *cupsful* or *handsful*. We have not discovered what schoolbooks prompted these teachers; all of our usage books disagree. But the notion is surely alive.

The result of the continuing uncertainty is the existence of less frequent variants such as *cupsful* or *teaspoonsful*. These variants are called wrong by some recent handbooks. They are not wrong, but most people use *cupfuls* and *teaspoonfuls*.

full *Full* is very often followed by *of*:

> All his motions were full of tender concern —Morley Callaghan, *The Loved and the Lost*, 1951

> Then one night, Ring came round, fuller of bounce than ever —Frank O'Connor, *Harper's*, April 1971

The phrase *to have one's hands full*, however, is followed by *with* when it takes a preposition:

> . . . a man who already had his hands full with two such posts —Harold Taylor, *Saturday Rev.*, 14 Apr. 1973

fulsome The considerable comment about the frequent use or misuse of *fulsome* is an American phenomenon of fairly recent occurrence, starting in the late 1940s or early 1950s in response to the word's beginning to appear with some frequency in newspapers and magazines. The following filler from the June 30, 1951, issue of the *New Yorker* is typical:

> Nick Schenk, head of Loew's Inc., is at work now drafting the letter of acceptance of L. B. Mayer's resignation—to make it so fulsome that even Mr. Mayer will like it. —*Leonard Lyons in the Post.*
>
> You mean so coarse, gross, foul, satiating, nauseating, sickening? Or you mean so repulsive, disgusting, and offensive to moral sensibility?

All of the synonymous terms supplied by the *New Yorker* editor are taken from Webster's Second, published in 1934. They illustrate the contribution of this dictionary and its predecessor to the problem. The editor of *fulsome* for Webster 1909 had available in the OED the full history of the word, but little evidence of current use. He used the OED information in revising the definition of the 1890 unabridged. But he did two things that would have future repercussions: he included in the definition hints from two definitions the OED editor considered obsolete, or probably obsolete; and he added at the end, apparently out of his own head, the words "insincerity or baseness of motive." Both of these characteristics of the 1909 definition were carried over into the 1934 book.

The addition of "insincerity or baseness of motive" was especially unfortunate. It appears to have been the 1909 editor's notion of why fulsome praise might be offered, but it has never been a meaning of the adjective itself.

So one major contributor to the controversy has been the dictionary definition written sometime before 1909, reprinted in the 1934 unabridged (and, with variations, in numerous smaller dictionaries and handbooks on usage) and then repeated, with varying degrees of accuracy of recall, by members of usage panels. A measure of misreading has sometimes added to the problem: the first string of adjectives listed by the *New Yorker* editor are from a definition labeled obsolete in both the 1909 and 1934 Webster.

Then what does *fulsome* actually mean in current usage? A number of the earlier senses listed in the OED still persist, if attested only occasionally. The etymologically purest sense (OED 1)—"characterized by abundance; copious, full"—is still in use. This sense draws the most frequent criticism:

> . . . illustrating with fulsome quotations both the underlying philosophy and the nature of its expression in poetry —*Times Literary Supp.*, 16 June 1966

> The Ecclesiological Society, which the author describes in fulsome detail —George N. Shuster, *Key Reporter*, Spring 1963

The sense applied to the roundness or fullness of the figure (OED 2) turns up now and then:

> Crisp sheer shantung dresses over crinolines give fulsome billowy figure flattery —*Women's Wear Daily*, 2 Apr. 1952

The sense applied to the flavor or taste of food (OED 3b) was alive as late as 1927, although much weakened in force:

> . . . an exquisite wine, Sainte Croix du Mont, which called itself a Sauternes. I could not make out why it lacked the rather fulsome sweetness of ordinary Sauternes . . . —Stephen Gwynn, *In Praise of France*, 1927

The sense of "offensive to normal tastes or sensibilities" (OED 6) also finds occasional use:

> Color photography . . . has already reflected, in its uses, the true fresh beauties (as well as the fulsome inanities) of the age —Walker Evans, *Fortune*, July 1954

There is one relatively new use. It pertains to music and is related to the earliest sense of the word:

> . . . and she was in generally fulsome, limpid voice, a few rough moments aside —Thor Eckert, Jr., *Christian Science Monitor*, 13 Feb. 1980

But most of our citations deal with complimentary language or those who produce such language. In most cases the use is pejorative and causes the critics no concern. It emphasizes the notion of excess or effusiveness:

> ". . . A cast of your skull, sir, . . . would be an ornament to any anthropological museum. It is not my intention to be fulsome, but I confess that I covet your skull." —Sir Arthur Conan Doyle, *The Hound of the Baskervilles*, 1902

> I gazed at her with an admiration whose extent I did not express, lest I be thought fulsome —A. J. Liebling, *New Yorker*, 15 Oct. 1955

> Her books had long, fancy-pants titles with semicolons, and fulsome tributes on their acknowledgements pages to the noble institutes that had subsidized them —Zoë Heller, *New Republic*, 3 July 2000

But there is a real problem with the use of *fulsome* when it is applied to praise, to an introduction, or to similar ceremonial devices. *Fulsome* does not immediately connote disparagement to the mind of the hearer, reader, or user encountering it for the first time. There is plenty of evidence that *fulsome* is taken to be either neutral, meaning approximately "full and detailed," or even complimentary, meaning approximately "generous" or "lavish." President Reagan used it as a neutral term:

> I got a very fulsome apology from the President of Iraq —quoted on NBC News, 19 May 1987

When the writer's or speaker's intent is not clear, the sense can be ambiguous:

> In both the House of Commons and the House of Lords, the adoption of the traditional "humble address" of congratulation provided the setting for fulsome tributes to the royal family —*Washington Post*, 17 Nov. 1948

Back came some of the most fulsome praise for a vegetable that Thomas ever received —*Christian Science Monitor*, cited by James J. Kilpatrick, syndicated column, 3 July 1985

Comity was the rule of the day; Senate Republicans were almost as fulsome in their tributes and backslaps as were their democratic colleagues —Robert C. Schmults, *Insight*, 15 Feb. 1993

The watchword obviously must be care. If you are tempted to use *fulsome*, remember that it is quite likely to be misunderstood by both the innocent reader and the gimlet-eyed purist unless your context makes your intended meaning abundantly clear. It is not a word familiar enough to carry an ambiguous context to a clear conclusion.

Let's try to sum this up. *Fulsome* is probably more commonly used today than it has been at any time since the end of the 17th century. Its most common use is in mildly depreciatory contexts, but keep in mind that several nonpejorative meanings, one limited to music, are still current.

Most usage commentators and handbooks are still measuring current usage by looking back to the definition of 1909. Modern lexicography will eventually catch up with present-day use, and the commentators, one hopes, will soften their remarks. One commentator in fact changed his position. Rudolf Flesch in his 1964 book censured the usual modern examples of the word. But in his 1983 book, he said:

If you want to use *fulsome* in the sense of copious and abundant, go right ahead.

We would urge a bit more caution. If you do use the nonpejorative senses, make sure your context is unambiguous.

fun   A few commentators and handbooks notice the use of *fun* as an adjective, mostly to deplore it. Quite a few of them believe the usage is new—Flesch 1983, for instance, thinks it only about twenty years old; Copperud 1980 concurs; Harper 1985 finds it a vogue usage of the early 1970s; Macmillan 1982 thinks it transitory.

The OED Supplement, however, shows that it is a bit older. The Supplement calls it an attributive use of the noun passing into an adjective and cites examples from the middle of the 19th century on.

The flurry of use that has caught the attention of the commentators seems to have started after World War II:

This language problem has its fun side, too —*Time*, 2 Sept. 1946

New fun ideas are the poncho and the all-in-one shirt and shorts "walking suit" —Virginia Pope, *N.Y. Times Mag.*, 13 June 1954

The usage had really caught on by the middle 1960s, helped, probably, by advertising for fun cars and fun furs. It is used nowadays just the way it was used in 1946:

Vocabulary is, indeed, the fun part of dialectology —Robert Claiborne, *Our Marvelous Native Tongue*, 1983

The examples shown so far are for attributive uses. No commentator has attempted to tackle the question of whether *fun* is a predicate adjective as well, and probably with good reason, for there is no sure way to prove that *fun* in "That was fun" is either an adjective or a noun. But it is often linked with another adjective:

They think it is fun and good for young people —Rosemary Brown, *Ladies' Home Jour.*, September 1971

These are disappointing books. *Starvation or Plenty?* is more fun; *Famine in Retreat?* is safer —*Times Literary Supp.*, 4 Mar. 1970

These uses suggest that some writers may well feel it to be a predicate as well as an attributive adjective. We have evidence from speech for *so fun*, *funner*, and *funnest*, which attest to adjective status in speech.

As an attributive adjective, *fun* is not often found in elevated contexts; as a quasi-predicate adjective, it is found in all contexts.

funny   It is a bit funny that the sense of *funny* that means "strange, odd, peculiar" is still being treated as something less than standard. Here is a recent comment:

Often used in conversation as a utility word that has no precise meaning but may be clear enough in its context. It is generally too vague for college writing —Trimmer & McCrimmon 1988

This is little more than an elaboration of Mac-Cracken & Sandison 1917:

. . . inaccurate colloquialism for *strange, odd*.

The OED traces this sense back to 1806. It labels the sense colloquial, and its examples seem to be from letters or transcribed conversation. It does appear to be a spoken use in origin.

She supposes my silence may have proceeded from resentment of her not having written. . . . &c. She is a funny one —Jane Austen, letter, 7 Jan. 1807

It was moving into more general use even before the turn of the century, and it is still common in standard, although perhaps not stodgily formal, sources.

> "I am in Lady Agatha's black books at present," answered Dorian, with a funny look of penitence —Oscar Wilde, *The Picture of Dorian Gray*, 1891

> For some funny reason we have never been accepted as Vermonters —Robert Frost, letter, May 1931

> She was funny that way—that was the only explanation —Mary McCarthy, *New Yorker*, 23 Mar. 1957

> Considering how hard a man works to get himself into the White House, it's funny that once he gets there he can't wait to leave —*And More by Andy Rooney*, 1982

Unless your prose is of a truly elevated sort, there seems to be no real reason to avoid this use of *funny*.

further, furthest See FARTHER, FURTHER.

fused participle See POSSESSIVE WITH GERUND.

G

gage See GAUGE.

gainsay This synonym for *deny* has a vaguely Shakespearean quality. Fowler 1926 classes it as a literary word, and he (as well as Burchfield 1996) notes that it now usually occurs in negative contexts. Our evidence shows negative contexts are more common:

> Afro-Americans . . . have been a central feature of America's history, and no amount of gainsaying can eradicate their importance —John Hope Franklin, *Race and History*, 1989

> In the context supplied, there is no gainsaying such evidence as Cistercian bookmarks designed to aid memorizing —Alastair Fowler, *Times Literary Supp.*, 28 Dec. 1990/3 Jan. 1991

> There is no gainsaying such certainty of misinformation —John Algeo, in Greenbaum 1985

But positive contexts are not unusual:

> Biological impossibility . . . was more frequently invoked to gainsay the possiblity of hybrid strains —Harriet Ritvo, *The Platypus and the Mermaid*, 1997

> . . . a look of dejection of which, perhaps, she was conscious, because she gave him an occasional, hesitant smile as though to gainsay it —Paula Fox, *A Servant's Tale*, 1984

galore *Galore* is derived from the Irish Gaelic *go leor*, "enough." Some usage commentators have written about it as if it still had a strongly Irish quality, but in fact it has been used in English since the 17th century and has long since been thoroughly assimilated into the mainstream of our language. Its most strident critics have been Fowler 1926, who considered it "no part of the Englishman's natural vocabulary," and Bernstein 1965, who found it appropriate only for "jocular or breezy or slangy effect." Our evidence shows that it is a common, standard word most likely to occur in writing that has an informal tone (Burchfield 1996 calls it "a refreshingly informal" word). It occasionally appears in more formal contexts, but it would be out of place—and therefore is not used—when a somber or highly serious tone is called for. Here are some examples of typical use from our files:

> . . . tables (several of them, covered with Oriental carpeting), chairs galore, plush settees —Truman Capote, *New Yorker*, 27 Oct. 1956

> . . . with loyalty galore to invest if only he could earn it back with interest —John le Carré, *N.Y. Times Book Rev.*, 14 Oct. 1979

> So reasons galore are adduced for not giving up —Russell Baker, *N.Y. Times*, 9 Nov. 1993

gambit A *gambit* is a chess opening in which a player risks one or more minor pieces to gain an advantage in position. Some usage writers would like to rein extended uses in as close as possible to the original meaning. Bernstein 1958, Follett 1966, and Bryson 1984 all think that a gambit should involve some sort of concession or sacrifice. When this happens in actual practice, the writer is usually deliberately employing the metaphor of a chess game, and such uses are rare.

> . . . it is clear that the U.S.S.R. was playing a gambit: among the captured Russian material exhibited in Helsinki at the close of the

campaign was none of the first-class equipment that the Germans subsequently came up against on the Russian front —Eric Dancy, *Foreign Affairs,* April 1946

In the evidence we have accumulated, *gambit* is freely used to mean merely "a calculated move" or "stratagem." Other common meanings are "a remark intended to start a conversation or make a telling point" and "a topic."

Yes, this sounded like the usual Richard gambit, stirring the pot for attention —S. L. Price, *Sports Illustrated,* 3 Apr. 2000

Agritainment, also known as agritourism, is the latest gambit in small-farm survival tactics —Julie V. Iovine, *N.Y. Times,* 2 Nov. 1997

. . . uses a foxier gambit to achieve his ends. He employs the infantile, or blubber-mouth approach —S. J. Perelman, *New Yorker,* 9 July 1949

In desperation one seeks an artificial gambit. I remember one from an English girl: "Oh, I say, are you frightfully keen on cats and dogs?" —George C. McGhee, *Saturday Rev.,* 28 June 1975

. . . the bulk of the exchange between the Americans and the Japanese was carried on through interpreters, in that uniquely disjunctive idiom. One strained gambit followed another —Connie Bruck, *New Yorker,* 9 Sept. 1991

Bryson objects to the phrase *opening gambit* as a redundancy, but with extended meanings so far removed from the original, the question of redundancy loses whatever importance it might have in more literal contexts:

Rose's very title, *The Haunting of Sylvia Plath,* and the book's opening gambit, "Sylvia Plath haunts our culture," strike the ear as excessive —Joyce Carol Oates, *Times Literary Supp.,* 21 June 1991

The move to Cambridge was the opening gambit in the Danish attempt to defeat and dismember Wessex —Michael Wood, *In Search of the Dark Ages,* 1987

If you happen to be criticized for using *gambit* in a general way, we do not think you should take the criticism too seriously.

gamut *Gamut* in its literal sense, which is now almost never used, means "the whole series of recognized musical notes." Most people are familiar with *gamut* as a figurative word meaning "an entire range or series." It occurs especially in the phrase *run the gamut,* which usually has the sense "to range all the way; vary":

. . . ran the gamut from mildly piquant and creamy to firmer, well-ripened specimens —Mimi Sheraton, *N.Y. Times,* 2 May 1979

. . . the outdoor furniture runs the gamut from prim poolside pieces to the frankly zany —*N.Y. Times,* 10 Apr. 1980

Possible confusion of *run the gamut* with *run the gauntlet* is noted by several commentators. Reader's Digest 1983 and Harper 1985 cite a few examples of such confusion, but it does not appear to be a widespread problem. See, however, GAUNTLET 2. Garner 1998 has three examples of *run the gambit* for *run the gamut,* all from newspapers. These may indicate overreliance on computer spelling checkers.

gantlet See GAUNTLET 1.

gap The use of *gap* in such phrases as *generation gap* and *credibility gap* is discouraged as hackneyed by several commentators. Its popularity continues unabated, however, and there seems to be no end to the variety of its applications:

Vanishing Livestock Breeds Leave Diversity Gap —headline, *N.Y. Times,* 14 Nov. 2000

Bush advisers serve up some happy x factors to fill in the promise gap —James Carney et al., *Time,* 24 Apr. 2000

. . . the gender gap in primary and secondary education is slowly closing —Katha Pollitt, *The Nation,* 26 June 2000

. . . strong evidence of an energy gap between different spin-carrying excitations —Eduardo Fradkin, *Nature,* 1 May 1997

gauge Note well the spelling of *gauge.* A common error puts the *u* before the *a:*

. . . when you guage present progress with past aspirations —*Rolling Stone,* 13 May 1971

The old and respectable variant spelling *gage* avoids the problem altogether, but it is now rarely used for the verb. Its most common use is in reference to scientific instruments used to make measurements:

. . . gages for measuring extremely high pressures —Benjamin Petkof, *Mineral Facts and Problems,* 1965

gauntlet 1. *Gauntlet, gantlet.* Some confusion exists about the status of these spelling variants. The argument is sometimes heard that they represent etymologically distinct words, and that *gantlet* is the only correct choice—or at least is the preferable one—in the common phrase *run the ga(u)ntlet.* This argument is mistaken. There is, in fact, more than one *gauntlet* in the English language, but *gauntlet* and *gantlet* are not themselves etymologically distinct—they are spelling variants, pure and simple.

The older *gauntlet* was borrowed from French in the 15th century. Its literal meaning in French is "little glove," and it originally described a protective glove worn with medieval armor. The phrases *throw down the gauntlet* and *pick up the gauntlet* arose from the medieval custom of throwing down a glove to issue a challenge. These phrases (with many variations) persist in figurative use, and *gauntlet* also now describes several varieties of glove, both protective and fashionable:

> In the first paragraph he throws down the gauntlet —*Time,* 12 Dec. 1983

> . . . wears his engineer's cap, coveralls and work gauntlets —*Saturday Evening Post,* 16 Nov. 1956

> Wool-knit gauntlets in navy, cobalt, or black —*New Yorker,* 21 Nov. 1983

The *gauntlet* of *run the gauntlet* has a more complex history. The reference in *run the gauntlet* is to a form of military punishment in which a prisoner was made to pass between two rows of men armed with clubs or other weapons. The original name for such a punishment in English was *gantlope. Gauntlet* came to be used in place of *gantlope* through the process of folk etymology—that is, the substitution of a familiar word for an unfamiliar one. The earliest citations for *gauntlet* meaning "gantlope" are from the 17th century:

> To print, is to run the gantlet —Joseph Glanvill, *The Vanity of Dogmatizing,* 1661 (OED)

Gantlet was simply one of several spelling variants. It has also been used for the "glove" sense of *gauntlet*:

> The gantlet was down, and the embattled city prepared for war —John A. Crow, *Spain: The Root and the Flower,* 1985

We do not know exactly how *gantlet* came to be regarded as the "preferred" spelling in *run the ga(u)ntlet*. The distinction *gantlet* (punishment)/*gauntlet* (glove) seems to have arisen in the U.S. during the 19th century. Our own dictionaries recognized it—for reasons which are not at all clear—up until the publication of *Webster's Third* in 1961. British dictionaries have never recognized the distinction, and *gantlet* is no longer used as a spelling variant in British English. In American English, mistaken notions about its correctness have assured its continued use as a variant of *gauntlet* in its "gantlope" sense, especially in a few well-known publications:

> . . . it must pass through a gantlet of people —Roger Rosenblatt, *N.Y. Times Mag.,* 5 June 1994

> But multiracial teens who run the gantlet often emerge with a stronger sense of self —Lynette Clemetson, *Newsweek,* 8 May 2000

> . . . ideas must survive a brutal peer-review gantlet —Hal Lancaster, *Wall Street Jour.,* 8 Nov. 1994

Gauntlet is the more widely used spelling:

> . . . if you choose to run the gauntlet and win a seat at an actual table, there's food at the end —Jeff Weinstein, *The Village Voice,* 12 July 1994

> Every development that requires a zoning change must be submitted to the local community board. That's a difficult gauntlet to run —Tamar Jacoby et al., *New Republic,* 23 Aug. 1999

> . . . found himself running a gauntlet of 1,200 women —Linda Marx, *People,* 4 Oct. 1982

> . . . running a gauntlet of hostile bulls —Fred Bruemmer, *National Wildlife,* June/July 1985

2. Many commentators warn against confusion of *run the gauntlet* for *run the gamut.* Such confusion does not appear to be widespread, but we do have some evidence of it:

> Customers run the gauntlet from state and local governments to public libraries and big corporations —*Datamation,* May 1977

When the sense of the phrase is "range," the correct choice is *gamut.*

See also GAMUT.

gay By now everyone knows that homosexuals have made *gay* the word of choice for "homosexual." Copperud 1980 notes that *gay* shares with *black* and *Chicano* the distinction of being both self-applied by the segment of society it describes and adopted generally. The general acceptance of the term in its new sense has brought it to the attention of usage writers, many of whom are sure that the homosexual use of *gay* has destroyed the word for its older uses. Our evidence shows, however, that the older senses of *gay* are still with us.

It would take a certain willful perverseness to read "homosexual" into the use of *gay* applied to inanimate nouns in contexts like these:

> . . . crossed the street under the clear starry sky toward the gay lights of the municipal tree —Garrison Keillor, *Lake Wobegon Days,* 1985

> . . . stepping nimbly between the piles of garbage to the gay marimba rhythms in your head —Jay McInerney, *Bright Lights, Big City,* 1984

. . . the Little Diner's [sandwich pockets] are notable for their refined texture and gay orange hue —Jane & Michael Stern, *Gourmet,* September 1995

Applied to humans, it can be more easily ambiguous:

> We walked along Beauchamp Place encountering a gay fellow dressed as King Charles —Robert Morley, *Punch,* 10 Feb. 1976

But note how the placement of *gay* in the next two examples makes the meaning clear:

> Where would a gay student feel most comfortable? —*People,* 17 Sept. 1984

> . . . the leader of a gay band of Sorbonne students —Mary McCarthy, *Occasional Prose,* 1985

The bemoaning of the loss of the traditional senses of *gay* is premature, to put it mildly. The traditional senses are still in regular use. Attention to the context will almost always ensure that your intended meaning comes through clearly. Nonetheless, the new sense creates enough potential for unintended humor or serious miscommunication to exact some thoughtful care from you in your use of the word.

gender The use of *gender* to mean "sex" has been cited with disapproval in books on usage for many years. Fowler 1926 seems to have been the first to raise the issue, and his remarks are typical:

> **gender** . . . is a grammatical term only. To talk of *persons* or *creatures of the masculine* or *feminine g.,* meaning *of the male* or *female sex,* is either a jocularity (permissible or not according to context) or a blunder.

The grammatical *gender* denotes a subclass of words that is usually partly based on sex and that determines agreement with other words or grammatical forms. For example, a French noun of the feminine gender, such as *femme,* "woman," takes the definite article *la,* while a noun of the masculine gender, such as *fils,* "son," takes *le.* As many commentators point out, sex does not always enter into it: the French word for "pen," *plume,* belongs to the feminine gender and takes *la;* the word for "pencil," *crayon,* is masculine and takes *le.*

So much for grammar. The "sex" sense of *gender* is actually centuries old. The OED records it as early as the 1300s, and it was included as a standard sense in the dictionaries of both Samuel Johnson (1755) and Noah Webster (1828). Its use during much of the 19th century seems to have been, if not common, at least unremarkable:

> . . . black divinities of the feminine gender —Charles Dickens, *A Tale of Two Cities,* 1859

But by the turn of the century dictionaries had begun to give it restrictive labels. The OED described it as "now only *jocular*" in 1898, and Merriam-Webster dictionaries at the same time were calling it "obsolete or colloquial."

Whether obsolete, colloquial, or jocular, the "sex" sense of gender continued in occasional use. By the publication of Webster's Third in 1961, we had accumulated enough evidence of its straightforward use in written contexts to see that the restrictive labels of the past no longer applied. But the real boom in its popularity was still to come. Since the 1970s, the "sex" sense of *gender* has become increasingly common in standard writing:

> . . . have nothing to do with the author's gender —Erica Jong, *N.Y. Times Book Rev.,* 12 Sept. 1976

> . . . excluded persons of their gender —Daniel Seligman, *Fortune,* 5 Apr. 1982

> . . . our ratiocinations and observations bear the imprints of ethnicity, gender, and class —Roger G. Newton, *The Truth of Science,* 1997

> When Vermont law specifies that the town clerk may issue a license to either the "bride" or "groom" it is clear that the legislature had gender in mind —Dennis O'Brien, *Commonweal,* 14 Jan. 2000

Its use as an attributive adjective where *sexual* would otherwise appear is especially widespread:

> . . . shifts in gender identity —Robert T. Rubin et al., *Science,* 20 Mar. 1981

> . . . what we call gender harassment —*People,* 15 Oct. 1984

> Racial segregation and gender discrimination still exist —*Teen Voices,* Winter 1996

> . . . academic works on history, literature, political science, gender studies —Calvin Reid, *Publishers Weekly,* 10 Jan. 2000

And it has given rise to the derivative term, *genderless:*

> In these genderless times —James J. Kilpatrick, quoted in Harper 1985

The revival of *gender* in its "sex" sense may be partly attributable to the increased public attention now being given to issues involving men and women, as well as to the increased use of the word *sex* in senses relating to physical intercourse. In any case, there is no denying that the "sex" sense of *gender* is now more common than it has ever been. Most current dictionaries recognize it as standard, but there are still some books on usage that discourage its use.

genealogy *Genealogy* is formed ultimately from the Greek roots *genea* "race, family" and *-logia,* a combining form derived from *logos* "word, reason" and denoting expression or study. The exact English correspondent of *-logia* is *-logy,* as in *eulogy.* However, *-logy* frequently follows combining forms ending in a thematic vowel *-o-,* which in these combinations (rather perversely from a semantic standpoint) receives the stress (as in *psychology*). As a result, many speakers think of *-ology* as being the suffix. Yielding to the tug of this neologistic suffix, most speakers pronounce *genealogy* \jē-nē-'äl-ə-jē\, as though it were spelled *geneology.* Sometimes the inattentive even spell it that way. Those who understand the formation of the word or whose pronunciation is simply more influenced by spelling will tend to say \jē-nē-'al-ə-jē\ (rhyming with *analogy*) or, even more meticulously, \jen-ē-'al-ə-jē\ (with the first *e* short—no doubt in reminiscence of the epsilon of the Greek).

general consensus See CONSENSUS 2.

genitive 1. Back in the 18th century some grammarians began to refer to the genitive case as the possessive case. Between then and now many of them convinced themselves that denoting possession is the only function of the genitive (it is not) and therefore began to find fault with instances where the genitive marker *'s* is added to nouns denoting something inanimate. Why? Because it is not supposed to be possible to ascribe possession to something inanimate. But this is merely fooling oneself by one's own terminology; a change in name does not mean a change in function. Look at these examples: *the nation's capital, a week's pay, a dollar's worth, a stone's throw, the Hundred Year's War, land's end, on a winter's night.* Not one of these shows possession, but all of them are standard. A few commentators are still befuddling themselves, but you can pay them no heed.
2. There is mixed usage with regard to indicating the genitive case of a singular noun ending in an \s\ or \z\ sound with an apostrophe plus *s* or an apostrophe alone. Our evidence shows that for common nouns more writers use *'s* than the apostrophe alone: *the boss's desk, the princess's wedding* are more common than *the boss' desk, the princess' wedding.* But when a polysyllabic *s* or *z* noun is followed by a word beginning with an *s* or *z* sound, the apostrophe alone is more frequent: *for convenience' sake.*

This same basic observation can be made of proper nouns: *Jones's house, Dickens's novels* are more common than *Jones' house, Dickens' novels.* There are more exceptions with proper names, however: *Jesus' time, Moses' law.* Multisyllabic names and particularly those of biblical and classical origin usually take only the apostrophe: *Odysseus' journey, Aristophanes'*

plays. Single-syllable names, however, even the classical ones, more often have *'s: Zeus's anger.*
3. See also APOSTROPHE 2, 4; DOUBLE GENITIVE; POSSESSIVE WITH GERUND.

genuine The usual pronunciation of this word among educated speakers has a short final vowel, \'jen-yə-wən\ or \'jen-yə-win\. A variant with long final vowel, \'jen-yə-ˌwīn\, is found in most regions of the United States, and in some places is even the predominant form in less-educated speech. This variant has a friendly, folksy ring to it and is often used in jest by educated speakers. But these observations are generalizations; our pronunciation files show occasional use of \'jen-yə-ˌwīn\ in a nonfacetious context by educated speakers.

gerund See POSSESSIVE WITH GERUND.

gesticulation, gesture Fowler 1926 notes that the principal meaning of *gesticulation* is abstract, "the use of gestures," and the principal meaning of *gesture* is particular, "an act of gesticulation; an expressive bodily movement." But he also observes that either word can serve in place of the other when its connotations (or lack of connotations) make it an appropriate choice—that is, *gesticulation* can be used to denote a particularly theatrical or emotional gesture, and *gesture* can be used to mean "the use of gestures" when the writer wants to avoid the overtly theatrical connotations of *gesticulation.* Fowler's observations still obtain:

. . . show the same interest in dramatic gesticulation and facial expression —E. H. Gombrich, *N.Y. Rev. of Books,* 12 Mar. 1970

. . . the meeting regresses to its more natural state—passionate shouting, wild gesticulation —Bob Shacochis, *Harper's,* February 1995

. . . dismiss legislation with the impatient gesture of an old man's hand —Lewis H. Lapham, *Harper's,* January 1972

. . . the resources of . . . gesture from which a characterization is composed —Irving Kolodin, *Saturday Rev.,* 3 Apr. 1971

get 1. One of the more important verbs in English, *get* is handled with considerable diffidence in the handbooks. Part of the problem, as the handbooks see it, is the large number of vigorously expressive idioms *get* enters into; the "Choice English"—to use the term of Roberts 1954—that college freshmen are expected to cultivate much prefers colorlessness to vigor. Vigorous expressions are often suspected by usage critics of being "colloquial"—that is, slightly improper in some way or other not easily specified. If you are writing with the idea of getting your point across, however, you will not avoid the rich fund of idiomatic phrases with *get*.

One very important use of *get* is to form a sort of passive with the past participle. Bryant 1962 says that this construction emphasizes the idea of process. A couple of other commentators call it emphatic and unambiguous. Roberts 1954 says it is felt to be somewhat colloquial and thus avoided in Choice English. Evans 1957 says that the construction was condemned by grammarians in the 19th century, who prescribed *become* or *be* as substitutes. Both Evans and Flesch 1964 think that such substitution results in a weaker, less emphatic statement. Here are examples of the passive with *get*:

> There are times when the French get aggravated and displeased by us —Jimmy Carter, quoted in *N.Y. Times,* 14 Feb. 1980

> . . . propaganda in the form of news items which I doubt ever got printed —Katherine Anne Porter, *The Never-Ending Wrong,* 1977

> He enquired who she was, and got introduced —Jane Austen, *Pride and Prejudice,* 1813

> . . . got pillaged by the young brigands —Charles Dickens, *A Christmas Carol,* 1843

2. There has been some mild controversy over *get* in the sense of *obtain.* Bernstein 1965 prefers *obtain,* which he thinks stronger than *get,* but Copperud 1970, 1980 considers the substitution of *obtain* for *get* an affectation. Garner 1998 considers *obtain* and *procure* formal, and observes that confident, relaxed writers use *get.* You can use whichever sounds better to you without concern. Here are some samples of *get*:

> . . . sign the inventory. Get a copy —Anna Fisher Rush, *McCall's,* March 1971

> . . . has missed out on the help that can be gotten from the academic community —Barry Commoner, quoted in *N.Y. Times,* 17 Mar. 1980

> . . . administrators can easily get agreement from almost every unit —Ivar Berg, *Change,* September 1971

3. The past tense of *get* is *got*; the past participle is *got* or *gotten.* See GOT, GOTTEN; HAVE GOT.

4. The pronunciation \('git\ has been noted as a feature of some British and American dialects since the 16th century. In the phonetic spelling of his own speech Benjamin Franklin records *git.* However, since at least the 17th century some grammarians and teachers have deprecated this pronunciation. It nonetheless remains in widespead and unpredictable use in many dialects, often, but not exclusively, in

weakly stressed positions followed by a strong stress, as in "get up!"

get ahold of See AHOLD.

gibe See JIBE, GIBE.

gift The use of *gift* as a verb has drawn scorn and even expressions of despair from some commentators on language. Their criticism is directed specifically at its use in contexts where it serves essentially as a synonym of *present,* as in "He gifted her with a new coat," although a number of the critics acknowledge that such usage dates back to the 17th century. The OED has several citations:

> The Regent Murray gifted all the church Property to Lord Sempill —J. C. Lees, *Abbey of Paisley,* 1878 (OED)

Gift did not become a controversial verb until it began to appear with some regularity in American newspapers and magazines. Its adoption by Hollywood gossip columnists probably did nothing to help its reputation:

> Glen Ford gifted Eleanor Powell with a brand new kitchen —*Movieland,* March 1951

> He gifted her with a large heart-shaped diamond —Louella O. Parsons, syndicated column in *Springfield* (Mass.) *Daily News,* 28 July 1958

Most of the criticism of this verb has been from American sources. Usage panelists in particular cannot abide it—the major panels have consistently rejected it by better than a nine to one margin. The British seem to regard it with somewhat greater tolerance, perhaps because of its long history of reputable use in Scotland. Burchfield 1996 says that in spite of the history of Scottish use, it is not now much used in British English. Dictionaries, both British and American, treat it as standard. There is nothing fundamentally wrong with the verb *gift.* It is, however, an uncommon word, and an unpopular one as well. Unless you happen to be either Scottish or a gossip columnist, you probably won't have much occasion to use it.

See also FREE GIFT.

gild the lily This idiomatic phrase is cited as a misquotation by many commentators, who point out that the passage in Shakespeare's *King John* (1597) from which it is derived actually reads:

> To gild refined gold, to paint the lily. . . .

Of course, those who use *gild the lily* are not actually quoting Shakespeare—they are simply using an established idiom (Garner 1998 calls it a cliché) in a familiar way:

> . . . blini, the buckwheat pancakes that are a classic for caviar. . . . Also topping them

with smoked salmon is a delightful way to gild the lily —Lane Crowther, *Bon Appétit,* January 1998

An appeals court, gilding the lily of nonsense, agreed —George F. Will, *Newsweek,* 21 July 1986

Garner 1998 has examples in which *gild* is misspelled *guild.* This looks like too much reliance on computer spelling checkers.

Gipsy See GYPSY, GIPSY.

gladiolus One gladiolus may make for a sparse bouquet, but at least it spares you from having to figure out what to call more than one of them.

Gladioli is the commonest plural of *gladiolus* and is found in both specialized and general sources.

. . . sweet corn, gladioli, butter and potatoes —John Cheever, *The Wapshot Chronicle,* 1957

. . . she recognized tulips . . . gladioli, and violets —Cynthia Ozick, *Atlantic,* May 1997

My friend selected two dozen gladioli —Robin Wright, *New Yorker,* 5 Sept. 1988

Gladioli, with their rich, varied colors —catalog, Springhill Nurseries, Spring 1987

The plural *gladiolus,* though not quite as common, also appears in a wide range of sources.

Other gladiolus are giants growing more than 6 ft. tall —Paul Franklin, *Fine Gardening,* May/June 1990

He looked at gladiolus, clay pots of daisies, Easter lilies —William Cobb, *New Yorker,* 11 Dec. 1989

Hardy Gladiolus have long been a favorite —catalog, Park Seed Co., Spring 1987

Gladioluses is less common and appears in general periodicals and books but not in technical sources.

. . . his gold lamé shirt draped in gladioluses in homage to Oscar Wilde —Paul Evans, *Rolling Stone,* 6 Apr. 1995

. . . lilies, gladioluses, dahlias —*N.Y. Times,* 31 Jan. 1982

The spelling *gladiola* originated by backformation when people heard the word *gladiolus* and thought it was a plural. *Gladiola* and *gladiolas* are relatively uncommon in print but are frequent enough not to be considered simple misspellings. *Gladiola* now sometimes appears as a plural form as well. Both *gladiola* and *gladiolas* appear in general publications only.

. . . lit by candelabra and flanked on both sides by large baskets of pink and white

gladiola —Neil Sheehan, *A Bright Shining Lie,* 1988

. . . gardens of peonies, roses, gladiola, irises —Ron Hansen, *Harper's,* December 1986

. . . lush gladiolas, display dahlias —John Updike, *Couples,* 1968

. . . gladiolas, scarlet salvia, wax begonias . . . are all non-U —Eleanor Perenyi, *Green Thoughts,* 1983

Some commentators, such as Garner 1998, despise *gladiola* and *gladiolas.* You could dodge the whole problem by shortening the plural to *glads.*

glamour The spelling variant *glamor* originated in the U.S. on analogy with such other American spellings as *honor* and *odor.* Some commentators have been reluctant to accept it as a respectable variant, but our evidence shows that it occurs fairly often in American periodicals:

. . . the glamor of the stage —*Wall Street Jour.,* 19 Nov. 1980

. . . the woman whose screen image bespoke glamor so dazzling —*People,* 1 June 1992

. . . glitz and glamor packages —*Wine Spectator,* 30 June 1993

Glamour is, however, much more common than *glamor* in the U.S. and is the only spelling used in Great Britain.

glance See GLIMPSE, GLANCE.

glimpse, glance Discussion of this pair of words goes back to Fowler 1926, who points out that "you *take* or *give* a glance at something, but *get* a glimpse of it." On the basis of the citations he gives as examples of what not to do, it would seem that his specific complaint was about the use of "a glimpse at" instead of "a glance at." In the same vein, Garner 1998 corrects "a first glimpse . . . at" to "a first glimpse . . . of." Our evidence shows that while *of* is considerably more common, *at* is neither nonstandard nor rare after *glimpse:*

I had only a glimpse at the child —Jane Austen, *Letter,* 25 Nov. 1798

A glimpse at sexual advice manuals scotches the myth —Roy Porter, *London Rev. of Books,* 7 July 1988

. . . for a moment, one has a glimpse at the seriousness of his calling —Michael Coffey, *Publishers Weekly,* 14 Nov. 1994

. . . provides a rare glimpse at how a big law firm handled reports of alleged bigotry —Amy Stevens & Benjamin A. Holden, *Wall Street Jour.,* 19 Aug. 1994

glow When the verb *glow* is used with a preposition, use of *with* occurs most frequently:

. . . the fire that burned within him, that glowed with so strange and marvellous a radiance —Aldous Huxley, *The Olive Tree,* 1937

. . . she was a positive creature, self-assured, beautiful and glowing with an interior smile —Jean Stafford, *The Mountain Lion,* 1947

. . . the whole tiered and layered place glowed with new paint —Bernard Malamud, *The Assistant,* 1957

Glow is less frequently used with *about, at, from, in, into, of, over,* and *to* in various relations and senses:

. . . regard it as perfectly proper to study and glow about the marvels of Roman aqueducts —Sidney Hook, *Education for Modern Man,* 1946

. . . sitting alertly in the drawing-room, glowing at friends —Elizabeth Bowen, *The Hotel,* 1927

. . . her gentle, eager personality glowing from her fine features —Rex Ingamells, *Of Us Now Living,* 1952

. . . the leaves of the maple trees glowed red and yellow in the sunlight —John P. Marquand, *So Little Time,* 1943

Opposing opinions glow into acrimony —Morris Longstreth, *Book-of-the-Month Club News,* March 1951

. . . the Gilbert apartment, never brightly lit, glowed of itself —Lloyd Alexander, *Discovery,* March 1954

. . . he glowed over the marvels of modern gadgetry that could reduce hard work —James Aldredge, *Irish Digest,* February 1955

They kindled him and made him glow to his work —D. H. Lawrence, *Sons and Lovers,* 1913

go 1. The past tense of *go* is *went*; the past participle is *gone*. Those of you who are interested in etymology might try looking up the history of *went,* which was borrowed by *go* from another Middle English verb. In the speech of the less educated—H. L. Mencken's vulgate—the two forms are often interchanged.

The people on our place always say, "we gone to see it," or "we gone and done it," when the action is past—never "went" when "went" would be correct —Flannery O'Connor, letter, 4 May 1955

Miss O'Connor herself used *went* as a past participle facetiously:

. . . I can forget about going to Europe, having went —letter, 17 May 1958

Others use it unconsciously:

. . . would have went home —radio sports announcer, 1 June 1984

These uses are not standard.

2. The newest sense of *go* as a transitive verb means "say." This sense has been noticed in Safire 1984 and by various correspondents to this company and to newspapers. The use, which seems to have first attracted attention in the mid 1970s, has been noted as common in the speech of children and young adults. It is a speech form, seldom seen in print. Here is one of our few examples:

I'm the last person to admit I've achieved anything. . . . But now my friends say it to me, and I go, "You're right, I can't deny it any more. We've made it." —Steve Martin, quoted in *Newsweek,* 3 Apr. 1978

One of Safire's correspondents points out that in speech *go* can differentiate between direct and indirect quotation. In speech there is little or no difference between "She says you're cute" and "She says, 'You're cute.' " But "She goes, 'You're cute' " is always direct quotation. This is a clever explanation, but there are ways to disambiguate "She says you're cute" through intonation, stress, and juncture without using *go* for *say.*

The usage appears to exist in British English too. Our pronunciation editor noted this pun on it in a British radio comedy called "I'm Sorry, I'll Read That Again" in June 1976:

ANNOUNCER. . . . the Lone Stranger's horse went lame.
HORSE. Neigh. Lame, lame, lame.

Just remember that this sense of *go* is a spoken use.

3. See GO AND.

go and *Go and* is often used to emphasize a following verb:

. . . but now she has gone and . . . married that monsieur de Wolmar —Thomas Gray, letter, December 1760

. . . a subject too well painted by others for me to go and daub —Charles Reade, quoted in *PMLA,* March 1945

It went a long way toward making him touchy about what Uncle Daniel had gone and done —Eudora Welty, *The Ponder Heart,* 1954

"What's he want to go and do that for?" —Helen Eustis, *The Fool Killer,* 1954

This emphatic use does not imply any actual motion. It can be used without *and*—"Go jump in the lake"—as well. It has the punch and directness of speech and is seldom used in ordinary discursive prose.

See also TAKE AND; TRY AND; UP, *verb* 2.

gobbledygook This word for turgid and generally unintelligible prose has been in use only since the 1940s, but the phenomenon it describes is much older. Many usage books from Cobbett 1823 to Bailey 1984 have entertaining and horrifying examples. Entries under *gobbledygook* can be found in Janis 1984, Watt 1967, Copperud 1970, 1980, Perrin & Ebbitt 1972, Evans 1957, Shaw 1970, and Burchfield 1996. If you want to look at some samples for amusement or instruction, we recommend these books to you. Garner 1998 under this heading comments that the spelling *gobbledygook* is more common than the variant *gobbledegook*. Burchfield, however, prefers *gobledegook*.

See also JARGON.

goes without saying It is surprising to learn that this common idiomatic phrase is hardly more than a hundred years old. A translation of the French *cela va sans dire*, it was first recorded in 1878, and it was still enough of a novelty for Lewis Carroll to feel a bit self-conscious about using it:

> To say I am well "goes without saying" with me —Lewis Carroll, letter, 21 Aug. 1894

By 1926, however, it was well enough established for H. W. Fowler to regard it with a somewhat grudging acceptance, despite its Gallic origins.

Fowler's approval of *goes without saying* might have marked the beginning and end of its career as a usage topic, except that a few recent critics such as O'Connor 1996 have seen fit to fault it on logical grounds, pointing out that if something truly goes without saying there is no need to say it. Such literal-minded criticism of an idiomatic phrase is itself illogical, however, and it has not caught on widely. *Goes without saying* continues in common and reputable use:

> It goes without saying that the two timbres should complement each other —William F. Buckley, Jr., *N.Y. Times Mag.*, 2 Jan. 1983

> It goes without saying that seafood is the dominant source of animal protein on the Caribbean coast of Colombia —Raymond Sokolov, *Why We Eat What We Eat*, 1991

> The unspoken subtext of this high-minded appeal, it goes without saying, was that I could do more —John Hersey, *N.Y. Times Book Rev.*, 10 Sept. 1989

See also NEEDLESS TO SAY.

good 1. *Good* as an adverb. Although the adverbial use of *good* dates back to the 13th century, the patterns it appears in in present-day English seem to have established themselves in the 19th century. And in the 19th century also we find the beginning of the tradition of reprehending those uses—our earliest commentator is Bache 1869. We can fairly confidently assume a spoken origin here; Bache antedates the earliest 19th-century example in the OED by about twenty years.

All of the schoolbooks and many of the college handbooks and other usage books that we have consulted insist that *good* is an adjective only. The more enlightened commentators recognize the adverb's existence. They correctly associate it primarily with speech. The schoolmasterly insistence on *well* for the adverb may have contributed to the thriving condition of adverbial *good*:

> Insistence on *well* rather than *good* . . . has created a semantic split related to the adjective-adverb distinction but extending beyond it: *good* has become emotionally charged, *well* is colorless. *He treats me good* expresses more appreciation than *He treats me well*, and *She scolded him, but good* can hardly be expressed with *well* at all —Bolinger 1980

The justice of Bolinger's observation is nowhere better illustrated than in the world of American professional sports, where *good* is the emotionally charged adverb of choice:

> Guidry hung a slider. I just exploded all over it. I mean, it was *kissed*. I hadn't hit the ball good in a month —Reggie Jackson with Mike Lupica, *Playboy*, June 1984

> "The boys did good," Manager Bamberger said, smiling —Roger Angell, *New Yorker*, 10 May 1982

The adverbial *good* is not, however, limited to sports:

> . . . the press which implies only a kind of competitive point-scoring with the Communists. They goose us; we goose them back good —John Kenneth Galbraith, *Ambassador's Journal*, 1969

> This works pretty good. Roxanne pats his hand and tells him not to get upset —Garrison Keillor, *Lake Wobegon Days*, 1985

> . . . Doc Moore's car had a tree fall on it and smash it up real good —Bill Paul, *Wall Street Jour.*, 27 May 1975

Our evidence shows that adverbial *good* is common in the speech of the less educated, but is also known and used by the better educated. It is almost de rigueur in professional sports. Bernstein 1977 reports that the adverb as used in sports grates on Edwin Newman (1974). But it does not grate on Reggie Jackson, who knows the lingo. And one should not assume that *well* is avoided out of ignorance—a professional basketball coach interviewed on television after a game began by saying that the team played good but in mentioning the contributing factors said that they shot well and they rebounded well. The nuances here are plain to sports fans but are overlooked by usage writers.

As the quotations above suggest, adverbial *good* is still primarily a speech form. It is not likely to be needed in a book review or a doctoral dissertation.

See also BAD, BADLY.

2. Most commentators fail to mention the intensive use of adverbial *good*. It often modifies *many* or a number and is preceded by *a*:

> . . . something Hilaire Belloc noted a good 50 years ago —John Simon, *N.Y. Times Book Rev.,* 14 Oct. 1979

> But a good many other Americans at that time could take a college education or leave it alone —Tom Wicker, *Change,* September 1971

This is an entirely standard use. It was listed as an "incorrect phrase" in Joseph Hervey Hull's *Grammar* of 1829, however.

good and *Good and* functions as an intensive adverb. A few other adjectives—*nice* is the most familiar one—can also be joined by *and* to another adjective to function as an intensive. *Nice and* is generally restricted to approving phrases (like *nice and warm*), but *good and* is a straight intensive:

> Why you *have* been good and busy! —Ellen Terry, letter, 1 Dec. 1896

> His Irish was good and up —Wilfrid Sheed, *People Will Always Be Kind,* 1973

> . . . she'll be good and ready to come home by then —Flannery O'Connor, letter, 16 May 1963

> I'll be good and damned if I give Hussey a bottle of vermouth to change the padré into a Presbyterian —George Jean Nathan, letter, in *The Intimate Notebooks of George Jean Nathan,* 1932

As these examples suggest, *good and* is not often found in very lofty surroundings. Evans 1961 thinks it is used chiefly in spoken American English; several handbooks also suggest it is informal or colloquial. In spite of Ellen Terry, the usage seems to be primarily American.

goodwill, good will *Goodwill* can be spelled either as one word or as two. Our evidence shows that *goodwill* is the prevalent form, but

good will is also very common, especially when the sense is "benevolent interest or concern":

> . . . he left with nothing but good will —Eugene DiMaria, *Metropolitan Home,* November 1982

> Warmth and good will were in the air —Heywood Hale Broun, *N.Y. Times,* 2 Apr. 1995

When the sense relates to the value of a business, the single word *goodwill* is almost invariably used:

> In most leveraged buyouts, goodwill is a substantial part of the price —Matthew Schifrin, *Forbes,* 9 Mar. 1998

And when the term is being used adjectively ("a goodwill tour") it is written either as a single word or, less often, as a hyphenated compound:

> . . . the first lady's ostensible role as the administration's goodwill ambassador — Seth Gitell, *New Republic,* 9 Aug. 1999

> . . . most hotels run their lost-and-found departments as a good-will operation —Robert J. Dunphy, *N.Y. Times,* 13 Nov. 1977

got, gotten The past participle of *get* is either *got* or *gotten.* In British English *got* has come to predominate, while in North America *gotten* predominates in some constructions and *got* in others. Marckwardt 1958 points out that in North American English *have gotten* means that something has been obtained, while *have got* denotes simple possession:

> . . . the IMF has already gotten pledges for more than $55 billion —E. J. Dionne, Jr., *Commonweal,* 16 Jan. 1998

> *Wise Blood* finally came out in England and has gotten good reviews —Flannery O'Connor, letter, 21 Oct. 1955

> I haven't got a son —Mordecai Richler, *The Apprenticeship of Duddy Kravitz,* 1959

> . . . as long as I have got a chance to win —Dwight D. Eisenhower, quoted in *U.S. News & World Report,* 16 July 1954

This practice is not absolutely uniform, however:

> If you haven't got your license yet —James Thurber, letter, 1937

Gotten has been under attack in American handbooks as somehow improper. Lindley Murray 1795 apparently started the controversy by calling *gotten* nearly obsolete. It was passing out of use in British English at that time, though it was still being used in the 1820s:

As the Greeks have gotten their loan, they may as well repay mine —Lord Byron, letter, 9 Apr. 1824

Murray's books were widely used in American schools, and his opinion was adopted by American usage books like Bache 1869 and Ayres 1881; MacCracken & Sandison 1917 called *gotten* "less acceptable in general" and Jensen 1935 repeated Murray's judgment that it was obsolete. One version of this notion, even though it is wrong, persists as recently as Einstein 1985, who insists on *got* only. The schoolmastering has perhaps kept *got* more current than it might have been had natural selection been allowed free play. Thus we find both *got* and *gotten* in use as past participle. Freeman 1983 says that *gotten* is preferred to *got* when there is a notion of progression involved. This is frequently true:

> Squirrels had gotten into the mattress —John Cheever, *The Wapshot Chronicle*, 1957

> . . . it was recommended that the President not inform Congress until we had gotten the hostages back —Edwin Meese 3d, quoted in *The Tower Commission Report*, 1987

> Have investors gotten any smarter . . .? —Jane Bryant Quinn, *Newsweek*, 31 Jan. 2000

But it is also used where there is no idea of progression:

> I had gotten up to go to the men's room —William Styron, *This Quiet Dust and Other Writings*, 1982

> . . . explains why your having gotten flu two years ago didn't protect you against the different strain that arrived this year —Jared Diamond, *Guns, Germs, and Steel*, 1997

And *got* is used both when the notion of progression is present and when it is not:

> . . . in composing my list of guests I haven't got beyond him and Anne Parrish —Alexander Woollcott, letter, 19 Nov. 1936

> Since he has got grown, it's the races, of course, he likes —Peter Taylor, *The Old Forest and Other Stories*, 1985

> They had then got to the approaches of French Canada —John Cheever, *The Wapshot Chronicle*, 1957

> . . . until a small group of friends could be got to sit still for a few minutes —Russell Lynes, *Harper's*, April 1970

> . . . had got word that Tom Bird wanted to meet with him again —Calvin Trillin, *New Yorker*, 6 Jan. 1986

English speakers in North America seem to use both *got* and *gotten* in a way that is almost

freely variable. The observation of Marckwardt is largely true; that of Freeman less so. The learner of English might find it useful to follow their distinctions, but the native speaker will pick whichever form seems more natural at the time.

For other questions involving this verb, see GET; HAVE GOT.

gourmand, gourmet These similar words have dissimilar histories. *Gourmand* was a synonym for *glutton* when it was borrowed from French in the 15th century. *Gourmet,* which once meant "a wine merchant's assistant" and, later, "a connoisseur of wine" in French, did not appear in English until the 19th century, by which time it had developed the sense "a connoisseur of food and drink." *Gourmand* had by that time developed a similar "connoisseur" sense of its own, but it still retained suggestions of a hearty appetite. The distinction between the two words became a topic for discussion as soon as *gourmet* entered the language:

> The *gourmand* unites theory with practice. . . . The *gourmet* is merely theoretical —A. D. MacQuin, footnote, *Tabella Cibaria,* 1820 (OED)

More recently, the distinction has been expressed somewhat differently; Garner 1998, for instance, describes a gourmet as a connoisseur of food and drink, and a gourmand as a glutton. *Gourmand* is often described as having contemptuous overtones that *gourmet* lacks.

What our evidence shows is that *gourmet* is a more common word, but the contemptuous overtones of *gourmand* are no longer strong:

> Unless you've a gourmand instead of gourmet, dinner for two . . . will not cost more than $70 plus wine or beer —John Dornberg, *N.Y. Times,* 20 Mar. 1994

> . . . old-style New York testimonial steak dinners, in which utensil-disdaining, greasy-to-their-ears, gourmands merrily put away many, many animals' worth of steak —Roy Blount, Jr., *Atlantic,* August 1992

> The okapi is an eclectic feeder but never a gourmand —Terese B. Hart et al., *Natural History,* November 1992

But more often it serves as little more than a synonym of *gourmet:*

> . . . the black truffle, the feted fungus for which gourmands will pay up to $90 per ounce —Jeffrey Brune, *Discover,* January 1991

> In Healdsburg, gourmands enjoy the creative menus and fresh ingredients at Tre

Scalini —Cynthia V. Campbell, *Sunday Advocate* (Baton Rouge, La.), 18 Feb. 1990

Today Port is no longer a drink of the common man; it is the drink of sophisticates and gourmands —Anthony Dias Blue, *Bon Appétit,* May 1998

. . . a pasta to please the most exacting gourmand—as well as the most despotic macrobiotnik —*Elle,* June 1990

So some people make a distinction, but others do not. *Gourmand,* however, is not used as an attributive adjective, while *gourmet* is common in such use: a *gourmet meal, gourmet cooking.*

government　Both *government* and *environment* are often pronounced with varying degrees of compression, reaching as far as \'gəm-int\ and \in-'vīr-mint\. But even educated speakers speaking slowly are likely to omit the *n* before the *m,* and this pronunciation must be considered standard. Our files bristle with professors and senators saying \'gəv-ər-mənt\ and \en-'vī-rə-mənt\. One accordingly runs across the misspellings *goverment* and *enviroment* from time to time; *goverment* is even listed in the OED as an "obsolete form" of *government.* Recalling the connection with *govern* and *environs* will immunize you against such spelling errors.

graduate　The verb *graduate* first became controversial in the 19th century, when its use as an intransitive in a construction such as "He graduated from college" was censured by several American commentators, including Gould 1880 and Ayres 1881. The critics argued that since the college conferred the degree on the student, *graduate* should only be used transitively with the student as its object or in the passive construction "He was graduated from college." How such an idea originated is not clear. The OED shows that the intransitive *graduate* occurred in writing as early as 1807 (the transitive *graduate* is older, dating from the 15th century):

> Four years are then to be passed at college before the student can graduate —Robert Southey, *Letters from England,* 1807 (OED)

By 1828 it was well enough established for Noah Webster to include it in his dictionary. In spite of the objections of the critics some 50 years later, its widespread use by the well-educated seems not to have been seriously affected:

> I graduated from the Lawrence High School as many as five years ago —Robert Frost, letter, 11 Sept. 1897

The continued common use of the intransitive *graduate* has long since persuaded most

commentators to admit its acceptability, but the older use has not entirely disappeared.

But the usage of *graduate* has again shifted; a new transitive sense meaning "to graduate from" is now the object of critics' scorn:

> . . . won't graduate high school in New York —advt., *N.Y. Times,* 19 June 1979

This use of *graduate* without *from* has been cited as an error since Evans 1957. While the new use is probably established by now, it appears to be more frequent in speech than in writing, and is not nearly as frequent as the longer established intransitive.

> "I graduated college in 1974," says Schwartz —Robert Lipsyte, *N.Y. Post,* 2 May 1977

> . . . graduated high school at age 14 —Carl Zimmer, *Discover,* November 1997

graffiti, graffito　Before the 1960s, *graffiti* and its singular *graffito* most often referred to writings or drawings on ancient walls or artifacts. Art historians, language historians, archaeologists, and the like were the main users of this term (which came into English from Italian), and they discriminated between the singular and plural forms.

> . . . a graffito in hieroglyphic Hittite —Maurice Vieyra, *Hittite Art 2300–750 B.C.,* 1955

> Among the many *graffiti* left on the pedestal —M. R. Dobie, translation of Alexandre Moret, *The Nile and Egyptian Civilization,* 1927

In the 1960s the creation of graffiti evolved from an incidental to an obtrusive cultural phenomenon, and as the phenomenon overspread public places, the word *graffiti* invaded the household. Many people came to know the word only as *graffiti,* not realizing that *graffito* was available when a singular was needed. As a result, *graffiti* is sometimes used as a mass noun with a singular verb:

> Graffiti comes in various styles —S. K. Oberbeck, *Newsweek,* 1 Oct. 1973

> Graffiti mars buildings across the street —Kelly Barron, *Forbes,* 30 Nov. 1998

> There doesn't seem to be a lot of graffiti in Lisbon —Robert Murray Davis, *Commonweal,* 10 Mar. 2000

This use is not yet as well established as the mass-noun use of *data,* but it does fill a gap left by *graffito,* which is virtually always a count noun, not a mass noun.

> . . . a crudely drawn graffito —Herbert Mitgang, *N.Y. Times,* 13 Mar. 1983

> . . . a lovely graffito I saw recently —David Halberstam, *Playboy,* July 1973

Use of *graffiti* as a singular count noun is rare in print, but together with the rare use of *graffito* as a plural, it reveals how confusing some people find this word—even (or maybe especially) when they are trying their hardest to get it right:

. . . a graffiti on the wall —*Times Literary Supp.*, 30 Apr. 1971

. . . one of the most sophisticated graffito I have ever encountered —Clive Barnes, *Punch*, 23 Mar. 1976

Graffiti . . . is evidently growing by leaps and occasionally out of bounds. . . .
. . . told us he has collected more than 2,000 individual graffito—yes, that's the singular —Cleveland Amory, *Saturday Rev.*, 7 Jan. 1967

Mass-noun use of *graffiti* continues to grow and is pretty well established by now. You, however, may want to choose the count noun use as the safer alternative. For other foreign plurals, see LATIN PLURALS.

grammatical agreement See NOTIONAL AGREEMENT, NOTIONAL CONCORD.

grammatical error It must have been a humorist who in the 19th century attacked the phrase *grammatical error* in exactly the same way the guardians of the language had attacked many an idiom: "How can an error be grammatical?" This slyboots elicited a lengthy defense of the phrase from Bache 1869, which was reprinted in Ayres 1881. It must have been a later wit who drew a similar defense from Follett 1966.
It should be pointed out, however, that the phrase is used as a generalized term of abuse in usage commentary. Phythian 1979, for instance, calls the use of *uninterested* that he disapproves a grammatical error, even though no grammar is involved in the problem.

grapple *Grapple* is usually used as an intransitive verb, and as such it is almost always used with *with*:

. . . the Administration will soon realize that it is grappling with fact, not theory —John Kenneth Galbraith, *The Reporter*, 14 Apr. 1953

. . . the crisis of the American spirit grappling with its destiny —Robert Penn Warren, *Democracy and Poetry*, 1975

Very occasionally it is used with *for, on,* or *over*:

. . . in her incessant grappling for affection —Frederic Morton, *N.Y. Herald Tribune Book Rev.*, 31 Aug. 1952

I'll not be overanxious to venture my life
In meddling with Death. What Death grapples on
Is better abandoned
    —Donagh MacDonagh, "Gravedigger,"
    in *New World Writing*, 1954

. . . men sweating and grappling over state problems —Emily Taft Douglas, *New Republic*, 4 Oct. 1954

Modern transitive uses of *grapple* with *to* are echoes of one of Shakespeare's famous lines:

Those friends thou hast, and their adoption tried,
Grapple them unto thy soul with hoops of steel
    —*Hamlet*, 1601

The once detested Mr. Carlyle was grappled to our souls with hoops of steel —Samuel Hopkins Adams, *Grandfather Stories*, 1955

grateful *Grateful* in its sense meaning "appreciative" may be used with the prepositions *for* or *to*. In general, *grateful for* is used with benefits received, *grateful to* with people:

Separated from his dream, he was sickened at its ugliness and grateful for the lights and sounds of day —John Cheever, *The Wapshot Chronicle*, 1957

The world was grateful for this moment of fresh air —Thomas Merton, *Center Mag.*, September 1969

I am uncommonly grateful to you for drawing my attention to it —Dorothy L. Sayers, *The Nine Tailors*, 1934

She was touched by the offer of the rings, and grateful to George —Herman Wouk, *Marjorie Morningstar*, 1955

When *grateful* means "pleasing" and is used with a preposition, the preposition is usually *to*:

. . . gave me ample room to develop my theme, but forced upon me a concision that my practice as a dramatist had made grateful to me —W. Somerset Maugham, *The Summing Up*, 1938

gray, grey Both spellings are correct and common. In American English, the preference is for *gray,* but *grey* is also widely used. The British have a very definite preference for *grey.*

Grecian, Greek The distinction between these adjectives has been variously described by commentators dating back to Fowler 1926. What our evidence shows is that the distinction is not observed as consistently as some of the commentators would like. Both adjectives are used in referring to both ancient and modern Greece, although *Greek* is certainly the more common and more widely applied of the two. Some commentators have wanted to restrict *Grecian* to the architecture and art of ancient Greece and to human features suggestive of that art ("a Grecian nose"), but the evidence simply does not support such a narrow restriction:

> A Grecian pruning saw . . . is perfect for this —Millicent Taylor, *Christian Science Monitor*, 26 Dec. 1975

> . . . German tourists are beginning to people Grecian beaches —Frank Riley, *Saturday Rev.*, 30 Oct. 1976

Such usage may now deserve to be called atypical, but it is not actually incorrect. *Grecian* and *Greek* are basically synonymous words. We recommend that you rely on your own sense of idiom to choose between them in a given context.

grey See GRAY, GREY.

grieve When *grieve* is used with a preposition, it is used most often with *for*:

> They entirely despaired of my recovery . . . and began to grieve for me as one whose days were numbered —Mark Twain, "Early Rising, As Regards Excursions to the Cliff House," 3 July 1864

> How can you grieve for a person who's not dead —Terry McMillan, *Waiting to Exhale*, 1992

Somewhat less frequently *grieve* is used with *at* or *over*:

> . . . somewhat grieved at the smallness of this customer's appetite —Osbert Sitwell, *Noble Essences*, 1950

> . . . the President . . . grieved over the people's disappointment which he was helpless to prevent —Samuel Hopkins Adams, *Incredible Era*, 1939

Grieve is also used with *to* and the infinitive:

> . . . he grieved, like an honest lad, to see his comrade left to face calamity alone — George Meredith, *The Ordeal of Richard Feverel*, 1859

grievous In contravention of its spelling, *grievous* is sometimes pronounced \'grē-vē-əs\, so that it rhymes with *previous*. We have evidence for this pronunciation from some educated speakers of the language, including several prominent politicians, but it is not common by any means and is widely regarded with scorn. The standard pronunciation of *grievous* is \'grē-vəs\.

Usage commentators warn against the \'grē-vē-əs\ pronunciation, and some of them also warn against the spelling *grievous*. We have little evidence of this misspelling. A couple in our files are probably typographic errors, but *Grevious Bodily Harm*, the name of a street drug, is undoubtedly a real misspelling.

See also MISCHIEVOUS.

grisly, grizzly The adjective that means "inspiring horror or disgust" is usually spelled *grisly*:

> . . . that grisly and still mysterious disease —Nan Robertson, *N.Y. Times Mag.*, 19 Sept. 1982

> . . . one of the grisliest bloodbaths in all history —*Wall Street Jour.*, 26 Jan. 1982

The adjective that means "somewhat gray" is spelled *grizzly*:

> . . . the grizzly old Field Marshal —William L. Shirer, *The Rise and Fall of the Third Reich*, 1960

> . . . the man, a grizzly old country preacher —Richard M. Levine, *Harper's*, April 1971

The grizzly bear is so named because its fur has a grayish appearance. When most people think of grizzly bears, however, the images that come to mind (rightly or wrongly) are of a fierce and terrifying animal, the color of whose fur is of no special importance. The association of grizzly bears with fierceness may be part of the reason why the "inspiring horror or disgust" adjective is often spelled *grizzly*. Another part of the reason is that this spelling reflects the word's pronunciation, \'griz-lē\, more accurately than *grisly* does.

> Why otherwise torture their victims . . . ? . . . It is not for themselves or for us these grizzly dramas are played out —Archibald MacLeish, *Atlantic*, June 1950

> . . . three dozen or so grizzly murders —*People*, 20 Sept. 1982

We have substantial evidence for this spelling, and like the OED we treat it as a legitimate variant in our dictionaries. It is far less common than the *grisly* spelling, however, and there are many people who regard it simply as an error.

grope *Grope* is used most often with *for*:

> . . . his eyes groping painfully for a sight of whoever stood on the landing —Kay Boyle, *A Frenchman Must Die*, 1946

> We must all grope for richer roles, however we can —Francine Du Plessix Gray, *N.Y. Times Book Rev.*, 10 Oct. 1976

Much less frequently, *grope* in this sense is used with *after*:

> Even the costumes . . . seemed to grope ineptly after some notion of eroticism —Mimi Kramer, *New Yorker,* 26 Oct. 1987

In other relations, *grope* may be used with any number of prepositions, among them *into, through, to, toward,* and *towards*:

> Let me grope into a series of formulations, not intended to be sequential-cumulative —William Stafford, *Writing the Australian Crawl,* 1978

> But tens of thousands of people groped through it [fog] and crowded the city —Robert D. McFadden, *N.Y. Times,* 24 Nov. 1979

> Government mediators . . . groped closer to a solution to the dispute —*Newsweek,* 18 Apr. 1955

> Like other state governments, California's is . . . often thwarted as it gropes toward a future of awesome complexity —Trevor Armbrister, *Saturday Evening Post,* 12 Feb. 1966

> . . . they grope towards an understanding of their loss —*Times Literary Supp.,* 19 Feb. 1971

grow About the only current usage problem with *grow* concerns the recent extension of the transitive from the ordinary "grow tomatoes" and "grow flowers" to such uses as "grow the economy" and "grow your investment." Garner 1998 doesn't like it. Our modest evidence suggests it is primarily political or business jargon:

> . . . management-speak on how to "grow" your business —Max Boot, *Wall Street Jour.,* 24 Aug. 1994

> . . . the only way to grow the business —John Kerr, *Inc.,* March 1995

> It's hard for any league to grow its business in that environment —E. M. Swift, *Sports Illustrated,* 15 May 2000

Only time will tell if this use is going to become more widely used.

guarantee, guaranty As a look in any good dictionary will show, these two words are interchangeable in almost all of their uses. The principal distinction to be made between them is the one made by Copperud 1970, 1980: ". . . *guarantee* is by far the more commonly used." Some writers formerly preferred *guaranty* for the noun and *guarantee* for the verb, but *guarantee* is now the usual choice for both. The advice given by Fowler 1926 is still sound: "Those who wish to avoid mistakes have in fact only to use *-ee* always."

guerrilla, guerilla The literal meaning of *guerrilla* in Spanish is "little war." It was once used in English, as in Spanish, to denote irregular warfare carried on by independent bands of fighters, but the word in that sense was replaced more than a hundred years ago by such phrases as *guerrilla war* and *guerrilla warfare.* The principal use of *guerrilla* in English has long been to denote a fighter engaged in such warfare:

> . . . would train our new guerrillas for all kinds of conditions —Garry Wills, *Atlantic,* February 1982

The spellings *guerrilla* and *guerilla* are established as reputable variants in English (the Spanish spelling is *guerrilla*). Most of the evidence in the OED is for the *guerilla* spelling, but our modern evidence shows clearly that *guerrilla* is now the more common form. Usage commentators accept both.

guess Look at the use of *guess* in these examples.

> I guess I'll be on hand this time —Mark Twain, letter, 8/9 Feb. 1862

> I guess I missed the boat with that one —Groucho Marx, letter, Summer 1941

> Something about the Gold Room awakened my greed, I guess —Charles N. Barnard, *National Geographic Traveler,* July/August 1997

> "I guess I'll use lemon instead of vinegar," she said —*And More by Andy Rooney,* 1982

Such uses of *I guess* were long accounted Americanisms and have long been looked down on by some of our British cousins (Phythian 1979 still thinks the expression "worth resisting"). American defenders from James Russell Lowell (*Introduction to the Bigelow Papers,* 2d series, 1867) to H. L. Mencken (*The American Language,* 3d edition, 1923) to Harper 1975, 1985 have shown that the expression is an old one in English that came over to this country straight from the language of Shakespeare's time. Howard 1977 agrees: "*I guess,* in the sense I am pretty sure, was good English before it became good American." Howard finds it coming back into British use from American.

Some American commentators—Guth 1985, Macmillan 1982, for instance—have been diffident about it. American uncertainty goes back at least to 1829, but American English is nothing to be ashamed of.

We are not advising you to use *I guess* in your starchiest formal discourse, and we doubt that you would be inclined to. In contexts like those shown above, however, it is perfectly acceptable.

guts The sense of *guts* meaning "courage" has been around for quite some time now: the OED Supplement gives the first use as occurring in 1893.

Its use makes the commentators a little nervous even today. Evans 1957 found it "coarse but effective"; Copperud 1970, 1980 thinks the word is always used with the deliberate intent to shock or to sound rough-hewn; Flesch 1983 quotes a use by William Safire and seems a little surprised that his editors let him get away with it; both Flesch and Shaw 1975, 1987 feel that it is slang. As you read through the following examples, you will see that critical opinion has not caught up to actual use yet. However, the word is indeed plain and forthright, and if you are not prepared to be plain and forthright (or feel your audience is not prepared to have you so), you might want to choose an alternative such as *courage, mettle, pluck, spirit, resolution*—or even that old periphrastic warhorse, *intestinal fortitude*.

> ... what had taken place ... apparently involved just guts, the revolt of a man against the pure footlessness which had held him in bondage —William Styron, *Lie Down In Darkness*, 1951

> These facts speak eloquently of the guts and stamina of these two men —Sir John Hunt & Sir Edmund Hillary, *Geographical Jour.*, December 1953

> There was no one in the house who had guts enough to say that *Some Came Running* was a washerwoman at 1,200 pages, and could be fair at 400 —Norman Mailer, *Advertisements for Myself*, 1959

> ... Charlotte shows some guts in telling the Matron how to run her hospital —*Times Literary Supp.*, 19 May 1966

> ... those who might have challenged him didn't have the guts to do it —Merle Miller, *N.Y. Times Book Rev.*, 23 Nov. 1975

> ... but people so much want a poet with guts that they cling to him like a port in a storm —Virginia Woolf, letter, 1930 (in *Times Literary Supp.*, 28 May 1982)

> ... *The Washington Post* was the only news organization. ..unpeeling what happened at the Watergate break-in. No other editor or news executive had the guts —Nicholas von Hoffman, *The Nation*, 23 Oct. 1995

guttural Bryson 1984 and Garner 1998 warn that this word is frequently misspelled *gutteral*. This observation is borne out by evidence in our files. Remember that there are two *u*'s.

guy Stephen Leacock put it this way:

> The fact is we are always hard up for neutral words to mean "just a person"; each new one gets spoiled and has to be replaced. . . . Hence the need for "guy," which will gradually rise from ridicule to respectability —Leacock 1943

Flesch 1983 announces that *guy* has reached respectability. A few commentators, however, demur. Shaw 1975, 1987, Bell & Cohn 1981, and Macmillan 1982 are not sure it belongs in standard English. Harper 1985 is more neutral. But *guy* has filled the need described by Leacock and is in common use in standard journalism. This use of *guy* was once thought to be an Americanism (the only citation in the original OED is from a late 19th-century American source), but evidence in the OED Supplement shows that it had a British origin around the middle of the 19th century.

Here are some current examples. You will note that it can also be used of women and corporations; it truly has become a term for "just any person."

> Fans cheer the good guys and hiss the bad guys —Jody Berger, *ESPN*, 9 Aug. 1999

> Cunning is the refuge of the little guy —Stephen Jay Gould, "Were Dinosaurs Dumb?," 1980, in *The Contemporary Essay*, ed. Donald Hall, 1984

> In short, small banks can go down in flames. The big guys? Never. —Milton Moskowitz, *Houston Post*, 3 Sept. 1984

> Amy Irving likes it that Santa Fe isn't a swinging place. "The people are down-home—I'm just a normal guy here," she says —Andrea Chambers, *People*, 16 Aug. 1982

> ... the inability of people to put themselves in the other guy's shoes —Ishmael Reed, *N.Y. Times Book Rev.*, 4 Nov. 1984

> But he was a tenacious old guy who wrote some interesting poems —William Stafford, *Writing the Australian Crawl*, 1978

gynecology The most widespread pronunciation of *gynecology* among both physicians and laypeople is \ˌgī-nə-ˈkäl-ə-jē\. A respectable runner-up among physicians is \ˌjin-ə-ˈkäl-ə-jē\; this version is less well known to the general public. Some medical sources even sanction \ˌjī-nə-ˈkäl-ə-jē\, though one physician has expressed the opinion that he had never heard the \ˌjī\ version from anyone that he felt "ought to be using the word."

gyp For some time now there has been a tendency to call attention to oneself or one's group by taking public umbrage at some term or other as an ethnic slur. The verb *gyp*, reports Safire 1986, is one of those words. *Gyp*, which means "to cheat or swindle," is probably derived from a noun that is probably short for *Gypsy*. This is a fairly remote derivation to take offense at, and we have no evidence that *gyp* is ever used in an ethnically derogatory way. But since a few have taken offense, it is likely that others will follow. You should at least be aware that the issue has been raised and that sensitivities are now keener in this area than perhaps they were formerly. The

verb, incidentally, is an Americanism of late 19th-century origin.

Gypsy, Gipsy These spelling variants have established themselves on opposite sides of the Atlantic: *Gypsy* is the almost invariable choice in American English; *Gipsy* was predominant in British English. But Burchfield 1996 reports that *Gypsy*, which Fowler 1926 preferred, is now gaining ground.

h

> Hear them down in Soho Square,
> dropping aitches ev'rywhere,
> Speaking English any way they like.
> —Alan Jay Lerner, "Why Can't the
> English?" in *My Fair Lady*, 1956

The pattern that elicited this plaint from Professor Higgins was the familiar Cockney one, a pattern not found in the United States. The emotion with which the question was fraught sprang from the fact that, in England, *h*-dropping is the verbal class distinction par excellence. In America, on the other hand, although there is one pattern in which \h\ is normally dropped by some people and not by others, the variation does not correlate so starkly with social class.

The pattern in question is that of \h\ before the semivowels \w\ and \y\, as in *when* or *human*. Some educated people say \hwen\ and \'hyü-mən\; others—probably the majority—say \wen\ and \'yü-mən\. The \wen\ style has long prevailed in southern England, home territory of standard British English, and cannot be regarded as incorrect, though it is under persistent pressure from the spelling. In America, \hw-\ gets an additional boost from the admixture of the northern strand of English speech, where \hw-\ did not die out. Accordingly, in this country, when language is put under a lens, the \wen\ style sometimes appears in an invidious light, as when Ring Lardner suggests the semi-educated vernacular of one of his characters by making him say

> She was playing bridge w'ist with another gal and two dudes —*The Big Town*, 1921

All the same, it is entirely standard.

Another subclass of *h*-words may be defined not phonologically but etymologically: those borrowed from French, the *h* not being pronounced in the lender language. In many of

these, \h\ has been added at the suggestion of the spelling: the \h\ we now pronounce in *hotel, habit, heritage*, etc., is an innovation. In others, the \h\-less pronunciation persists—*hour, honor, honest, heir*, etc.—though here too there have been struggles, as Charles Lamb attests:

> Martin Burney is as odd as ever. We had a dispute about the word 'heir' which I contended was pronounced like 'air'—he said that it might be in common parlance, or that we might so use it, speaking of the 'Heir at Law' a comedy, but that in the Law Courts it was necessary to give it a full aspiration, & to say *Hayer*—he thought it might even vitiate a cause, if a Counsel pronounced it otherwise. In conclusion he 'would consult Sergeant Wilde'—who gave it against him. Sometimes he falleth into the water, sometimes into the fire —letter, 24 May 1830

In the case of *herb* (from French *herbe* \erb\), the battle fell out differently in different ages and areas:

> "When my Father was a boy every well-brought-up Canadian child learned that 'herb' was pronounced without the 'h'; you still hear it now and again, and modern Englishmen think it's ignorance. . . ." —Robertson Davies, *The Rebel Angels*, 1981

The situation today is: Americans normally do not pronounce the \h\, Englishmen normally do, and Canadians are divided. Canadian phonology in general matches the American much more nearly than it does the British, but anglophone Canadians tend to follow Britain's lead on individual lexical shibboleths like *herb* and *schedule*.

See also A, AN.

had better, had best These are standard English idioms.

. . . a word which had better be eschewed by all those who do not wish to talk high-flying nonsense —Richard Grant White 1870

. . . somewhat mysteriously hinted that I had better be at his house . . . at seven o'clock in the evening —*The Intimate Notebooks of George Jean Nathan,* 1932

. . . he had better think again —Barzun 1985

It had best be a good letter —Penelope Gilliatt, *New Yorker,* 1 May 1971

A great many handbooks find it necessary to assure you that *had better* and *had best* are standard, because these expressions were attacked as illogical in the 19th century. But the point to remember is that these phrases have been standard all along.

A few of the critics who approve *had better* are less certain about it when the *had* is omitted. See BETTER 1.

had have, had of   See PLUPLUPERFECT.

had ought, hadn't ought   Bache 1869 said that he had it on good authority that the New Englandisms *had ought* and *hadn't ought* were "making progress among us"—Bache's anonymous book was published in Philadelphia—and he therefore gave the expressions some room for disapproval. Since 1869 many schoolbooks and handbooks have taken up the cudgels against them, but apparently to little or no avail, for they are still the speech forms that they seem to have been all along. You will not find them in polished personal essays or in art criticism or even in ordinary reporting.

There has been a notion from the beginning that *had ought* and *hadn't ought* are regionalisms. Linguistic surveys show that Bache was not too much off base in 1869 in calling them New Englandisms. They seem to be predominantly Northern forms, although we have seen a few anomalous examples. E. Bagby Atwood's *A Survey of Verb Forms in the Eastern United States* (1953) shows *hadn't ought* in New England, New York, northern Pennsylvania, and New Jersey, as well as in small areas of Ohio and northeastern North Carolina. The Dictionary of American English reports them as widespread but more frequent in Northern areas.

The fullest account seems to be in Visser 1969. He suggests that the expressions are more common in normal conversation than the printed record would indicate, and he has a generous half page of printed citations dating from 1836 to 1964.

Regardless of what the schoolbooks and handbooks might say, neither *had ought* nor *hadn't ought* is wrong; they are simply regionalisms. But they are still confined to speech and fictional speech.

See also OUGHT 1, 3.

had rather   *Had rather* is a standard English idiom. It seems to have come into use during the 15th century. It eventually replaced the older *had liefer.* From the middle of the 18th century until early in the 20th, it was the subject of considerable controversy. It appears in present-day handbooks chiefly in the form of notices that both *had rather* and *would rather,* the alternative prescribed during the controversy, are standard.

hail, hale   Confusion about which of these spellings should be used in a particular context one would expect to be common, but we have relatively little evidence of it in our files. Perhaps proofreaders and copy editors have especially sharp eyes when it comes to *hail* and *hale.* Even so, it seems worthwhile to point out possible areas of confusion.

The spelling *hale* is the established choice for the verb meaning "to compel to go":

. . . he was haled before a summary court —Hugh Trevor-Roper, *American Scholar,* Winter 1981/82

Usage commentators find that this verb is often mistakenly spelled *hail.*

. . . Albania was challenging Great Britain's competence to hail it before the International Court of Justice —*Collier's Year Book,* 1949

Hale is also the spelling used for the adjective meaning "healthy":

. . . a tall, hale blond of thirty —Sara Davidson, *Harper's,* June 1972

The spelling *hail* occurs here too:

. . . most young Israelis . . . are tough, confident, hail-and-hearty —*The Economist,* 26 July 1985

The spelling *hail* is correctly used for the noun and verb relating to icy lumps of precipitation and for the verb meaning "greet" or "acclaim." It also occurs in the idiom "hail from":

They hail from any number of Western states —Gary Schmitz, *Denver Post,* 31 Aug. 1984

And in the term *hail-fellow-well-met*:

. . . a fun guy, a genuine hail-fellow-well-met —William Taaffe, *Sports Illustrated,* 10 Mar. 1986

hairbrained   Most often this word is spelled *harebrained,* and that is how usage writers tell you to spell it. Heritage 2000, for instance, says that *hairbrained* has a long history, but should be avoided. One might wonder just what the long history of *hairbrained* may be. Going to the OED, we see that a third of the citations quoted at *harebrained* and related terms are for the *hair-* spelling and that both spellings are attested from the 16th century onward. *Hairbrained* has continued to the present day as an infrequent but regular variant.

> . . . on such a hairbrained being as myself —Lord Byron, letter, 16 Feb. 1808

> . . . he'll pull some hair brained deal —James Jones, *From Here to Eternity*, 1951

> . . . their hairbrained folly —Christopher Lasch, *N.Y. Times Book Rev.*, 25 Jan. 1976

> . . . a hairbrained scam puts them in dutch with the Mafia —*Selec TV Mag.*, May/June 1986

Its history shows that *hairbrained* is established, but it remains an infrequent variant. Most people use *harebrained*.

hale See HAIL, HALE.

hale and hearty This is one of those alliterative duplications, says Evans 1957, which become clichés. The phrase denotes robust good health and is almost always used of older persons. It is so familiar that it can be misspelled by those who, as the saying goes, "spell by ear."

> . . . who at 91 years of age looked hale and hardy —*Johns Hopkins Mag.*, Spring 1983

If you use the phrase, mind the spelling. See also HAIL, HALE; HARDY, HEARTY.

half 1. A few commentators—among them Sellers 1975, Longman 1984, Chambers 1985, and Corder 1981—discuss *half* with respect to verb agreement. They all tell us that when *half* is followed by a singular noun it takes a singular verb; when followed by a plural noun, a plural verb. This makes good sense, because it follows notional agreement and also allows for the principle of proximity.

Burchfield 1996 adds that when a noncount noun follows *half*, a plural verb may also be properly used.

> . . . half of whose population votes —Gustave Mersu, *American Mercury*, October 1952

> . . . a half of the children drop out —James B. Conant, *Slums and Suburbs*, 1961

> . . . half the citizens don't know or care —Robert Penn Warren, *Jefferson Davis Gets His Citizenship Back*, 1980

2. Handbooks from MacCracken & Sandison 1917 to Garner 1998 say that both *half a* (or *an*) and *a half* are all right, but *a half a* is redundant. A few, like Scott, Foresman 1981, notice that the *a half a* construction seems to be mostly a spoken usage. This is our opinion, too, for we have very little evidence of its use in print.

In edited prose *a half* and *half a* and *half an* are usual:

> . . . eating a half grapefruit —E. L. Doctorow, *Loon Lake*, 1979

> Given half a chance —Aristides, *American Scholar*, Autumn 1981

> . . . to make you listen with half an ear —Donal Henahan, *N.Y. Times*, 28 Nov. 1967

hamstring H. W. Fowler made the verb *hamstring* a minor usage issue in 1926 by arguing that its past tense and past participle should be *hamstringed* and not *hamstrung*, inasmuch as it is derived from the noun *hamstring* and has no relation to the verb *string*. Later commentators have had to balance their respect for Fowler's opinions against the evidence of actual usage, which shows clearly that *hamstrung* is the form now established in standard use. Some commentators compromise by saying that both *hamstringed* and *hamstrung* are acceptable, but our own evidence indicates that *hamstringed* has now fallen entirely out of use—we have no 20th-century example of it in our files, except in the context of usage commentary.

handful *Handful* has two plurals, *handfuls* and *handsful*. The first is the more common, and the one recommended in several handbooks. See -FUL.

hands-on This now-common adjective is a recent coinage. Our earliest evidence of its use is from 1969:

> The high point of the classes is the great amount of hands-on time available to the students —Philip H. Braverman, *Datamation*, November 1969

It first became widespread in the phrase *hands-on experience*, denoting practical experience in the actual operation of something, such as a computer, or in the performance of a job. Much of our early evidence for it relates to education.

> . . . unusual teaching methods that emphasize active, hands-on experience —Larry A. Van Dyne, *Change*, February 1973

But by the early 1980s, *hands-on* was being more widely applied, describing everything from a museum featuring articles meant to be touched to a corporate executive taking an active role in running a business:

> ". . . didn't think Valente was hands-on enough." Mr. Valente, he [unidentified speaker] said, "didn't dig into the business enough. . . ." —Jeffrey A. Tannenbaum, *Wall Street Jour.*, 19 June 1980

Its adoption in the world of business has given *hands-on* a measure of notoriety that it never had in the world of education, and such commentators as Safire 1986 and the usage panel of Harper 1985 have considered it jargon. Whatever validity that description may have, the use of *hands-on* in the business world is established, and it will probably gain in respectability in the non-business world as its occurrence becomes less of a novelty. Our only recommendation is that you avoid it in contexts where it may be more suggestive of physical groping than of practical involvement:

> ". . . we're all looking for ways to get a hands-on feel for the consumer" —Alexander MacGregor, quoted in *N.Y. Times Book Rev.*, 3 Apr. 1983

hang, hanged, hung One of the more widely known and frequently repeated observations on usage is that *hanged* is preferred as the past and past participle of *hang* when the verb has the sense "to hang by the neck until dead" and that *hung* is the correct choice for all other senses of the word. This distinction arose out of the complex history of *hang*. The OED shows that *hang* developed from two Old English verbs, one of which was a weak (or, in effect, regular) verb giving rise to the inflected form *hanged*, and the other of which was a strong (or, in effect, irregular) verb giving rise to *hung*. (These verbs, Lamberts 1972 tells us, were originally a transitive–intransitive pair, like *set–sit, lay–lie*, that eventually fell together as a single verb.) The two forms were more or less interchangeable for many centuries, but the weak form was eventually superseded by the strong form except in the "execute by hanging" sense, in which *hanged* probably persisted because it was the form favored by judges in pronouncing sentence. Even in the "execute" sense, however, the strong form made inroads:

> . . . for these rogues that burned this house to be hung in some conspicuous place in town —Samuel Pepys, diary, 4 July 1667

> . . . to-day I am laid by the heels, and to-morrow shall be hung by the neck —George Farquhar, *The Constant Couple*, 1699

> . . . should not escape unpunished. I hope he hung himself —Jane Austen, letter, 6 Dec. 1815

> These men were . . . at last brought to the scaffold and hung —Percy Bysshe Shelley, *Address*, 1817 (OED)

> I have not the least objection to a rogue being hung —W. M. Thackeray, *The Newcomes*, 1853 (cited by Otto Jespersen, *S.P.E. Tract 25*, 1926)

In 1898, the OED noted that writers and speakers in southern England often used *hung* in this sense.

The distinction between *hanged* and *hung* has been a topic for commentary since Joseph Priestley first broached the subject in 1769. The issue was raised by only a few writers in the 19th century, but 20th-century commentators took up the cause wholeheartedly, and almost all books on usage now include some mention of *hanged* and *hung*. The primary concern of the critics is that *hung* should not be used in the "execute" sense, or that such use should at least be avoided in formal writing. Many commentators recognize that *hung* for *hanged* is now common in standard English, but more than a few persist in describing it as an error, pure and simple.

Our evidence shows that *hung* for *hanged* is certainly not an error. Educated speakers and writers use it commonly and have for many years:

> The negro murderer was to be hung on a Saturday without pomp —William Faulkner, *Sanctuary*, 1931

> . . . soldiers convicted of appalling crimes are being hung and shot —*Times Literary Supp.*, 29 Nov. 1941

> . . . insists that IRA terrorists can be hung by the law now —Noyes Thomas, *News of the World* (London), 24 Nov. 1974

> . . . a 13-year-old evangelist, who hung himself because his mother spanked him for sassing her —Flannery O'Connor, letter, 23 Apr. 1960

> . . . the 334 men and women who have hacked, stabbed, shot, hung, poisoned, or flung themselves to death —Ron Rosenbaum, *Explaining Hitler*, 1998

Hanged is, however, more common than *hung* in writing. It is especially prevalent when an official execution is being described, but it is used in referring to other types of hanging as well:

> Nobody is hanged for stealing bread any more —William Faulkner, 15 Feb. 1957, in *Faulkner in the University*, 1959

> . . . were promptly hanged outside the Portcullis Gate —John Updike, *Bech Is Back*, 1982

> . . . he had fled Europe . . . to avoid being hanged —Russell Baker, *N.Y. Times Mag.*, 15 Feb. 1976

> . . . he would rather be hanged at home than starved abroad —Lawrence Millman, *Smithsonian*, October 1999

Hanged also occurs in several old-fashioned idiomatic expressions in which *hung* is not possible:

But equally I'm hanged if I want to be bullied by it —Sinclair Lewis, *Main Street*, 1920

I'll be hanged if I'll be mournful —Peter B. Kyne, *The Pride of Palomar*, 1921

But *hung* is more likely than *hanged* when the hanging described is in effigy:

. . . by morning I'll be hung in effigy —Ronald Reagan, quoted by William Safire, *N.Y. Times Mag.*, 8 Mar. 1981

. . . the Tar Heels returned to campus . . . to find that students had hung their coach in effigy —Alexander Wolff, *Sports Illustrated*, 22 Dec. 1997

And E. Bagby Atwood's *A Survey of Verb Forms in the Eastern United States* (1953) found that in speech "*hung* . . . predominates in all areas and among all types [of informants considered with respect to age and level of education]."

The distinction between *hanged* and *hung* is not an especially useful one (although a few commentators claim otherwise). It is, however, a simple one and certainly easy to remember. Therein lies its popularity. If you make a point of observing the distinction in your writing, you will not thereby become a better writer, but you will spare yourself the annoyance of being corrected for having done something that is not wrong.

hangar The name for a building in which aircraft are housed is *hangar*, not *hanger*. The spelling mistake is easily made:

. . . a variety of military buildings including jet hangers —*Johns Hopkins Mag.*, Summer 1971

hanker *Hanker*, when used with a preposition, is most frequently combined with *after*:

. . . betrays himself when he hankers too yearningly after common human fulfilments —Aldous Huxley, *The Olive Tree*, 1937

. . . a moment when he hankered after other, strange delights —Robertson Davies, *Tempest-tost*, 1951

Nearly as often, *hanker* is used with *for* or with *to* and the infinitive:

. . . the most invaluable library of pictorial reference books that any gardener could hanker for —Linda Yang, *N.Y. Times Book Rev.*, 22 Aug. 1993

. . . we hanker to accumulate all the information in the universe and distribute it around among ourselves —Lewis Thomas, *The Lives of a Cell*, 1974

The evidence also includes an occasional use of *hanker* with *toward*:

. . . those who were soon to call themselves 'sophisticated' were hankering toward Dorian Gray's aesthetic life —James D. Hart, *The Popular Book: A History of America's Literary Taste*, 1950

harass 1. Several commentators point out that *harass* is sometimes misspelled with two r's. Our evidence confirms this.
2. *Harass* may be pronounced with the stress on the first syllable \'har-əs\ or on the second \hə-'ras\. Some authorities favor first-syllable stress, but second-syllable stress prevails in the U.S. Burchfield 1996 reports that second-syllable stress is gaining ground in Britain, where formerly first-syllable stress was the only pronunciation heard.

hard, hardly Of these two adverbs, *hard* is the older by a couple of centuries. *Hardly* was formed in the 13th century as an ordinary adverbial derivative of the adjective *hard*. Its oldest senses have passed out of use, but the senses "with force," "harshly," and "with difficulty" are still alive, although they are more common in British use than in American.

. . . where the means of existence was wrung so hardly from the soil —Sir Winston Churchill, *The Unrelenting Struggle*, 1942

Professor Bowers has been hardly treated by those he is anxious to help —*Times Literary Supp.*, 24 Mar. 1966

The problem that hangs over these senses is the likelihood of confusion with the "scarcely" sense of *hardly*, which is the dominant use in present-day English. This sense can even modify the same verbs as the early senses, and the reader must concentrate on the context in order not to be misled:

Marquis' vocabulary and literary and historical references are pleasures to play with. Because they are different and hardly used, students delight . . . —Winfield Carlough, *Media & Methods*, November 1968

The recommendation of all the commentators is that you use *hard* in all uses where it fits. Our evidence suggests that most American writers seem to find other words—like the glosses given above—to use in place of *hardly* when it doesn't mean "scarcely."

hardly The hastier usage commentators and schoolbook compilers assure us that *hardly* is a negative. More cautious observers say that *hardly* has the force of a negative or that it has a negative meaning. *Hardly* is not a negative. There is an important difference between

I hardly studied at all —Harvey Wheeler, in *A Center Occasional Paper*, April 1971

and the same sentence expressed negatively:

I didn't study at all.

Try making a negative out of *hardly* in the following examples and you will see what we mean:

They had hardly known each other then —Robert Canzoneri, *McCall's*, March 1971

. . . mothers are often tired but hardly ever lazy —Bruno Bettelheim, *Ladies' Home Jour.*, January 1971

Trembling in every limb, hardly able to set one foot before the other, she opened the door —Katherine Anne Porter, *Ladies' Home Jour.*, August 1971

. . . provide the translators with the problem—which they hardly solve—of finding reasonable English equivalents for his florid indignation —*Times Literary Supp.*, 2 Oct. 1970

You can see that *hardly* approaches a negative but doesn't quite get there. Otto Jespersen (*Negation in English and Other Languages,* 1917) calls it an *approximate negative.*

Approximate negative or not, the school-books and handbooks are nearly universal in calling *hardly* with a negative (*can't* is the one most frequently named) a *double negative.* This is a misnomer in two ways. First, a word not a negative plus a negative cannot logically be called two negatives; second, and more important, the effect of two genuine negatives is usually reinforcement of the negation (see DOUBLE NEGATIVE 1), while a negative with *hardly* is actually weakened (*softened* is Jespersen's word). To see the difference, let's compare the constructions.

I got up and tried to untie her, but I was so excited my hands shook so I couldn't hardly do anything with them —Mark Twain, *Huckleberry Finn,* 1884

Huck is saying in this passage that his hands were shaking so much that he had considerable trouble in untying her, but he did untie her. Now let's make a true double negative out of it:

My hands shook so much I couldn't do nothing with them.

If Mark Twain had had Huck say that, the female in question would still be tied up.

So analysis of *can't hardly* as a double negative is wrong, and if it is to be stigmatized, that must be done on some other basis than association with *don't never* and the like.

Now let's see where these constructions with *hardly* and a negative occur. They are found in speech:

. . . and you couldn't hardly get a job —Edward Santander, quoted in Studs Terkel, *Hard Times,* 1970

There's not hardly an hour goes by that his face, or just the thought of him, doesn't flash through my mind —Terry Bradshaw, quoted in *Playboy,* March 1980

Prenuptial agreements, [Mick] Jagger recently said, "don't stand up in court hardly." —*Time,* 12 Mar. 1984

. . . and nobody hardly took notice of him —Jonathan Swift, *Journal to Stella,* ca. 1712 (in Jespersen)

It occurs in fictional speech and in fictional first-person narration:

. . . it gave us not time hardly to say, O God! —Daniel Defoe, *Robinson Crusoe,* 1719 (in Jespersen)

"I don't know," she says. "He acts kind of shy. He hasn't hardly said a word to me all evening." —Ring Lardner, *The Big Town,* 1921

Now here's a funny thing about me: the first night on a sleeper, I can't hardly sleep at all —Sinclair Lewis, *The Man Who Knew Coolidge,* 1928

The combination *without hardly* seems to turn up in newspaper reporting from time to time:

The rest are left to wander the flat lowlands of West Bengal without hardly a trace of food or shelter —*N.Y. Times,* 13 June 1971

. . . a nice spacing of seven hits by Nelson to win without hardly breaking a sweat —Gerry Finn, *Springfield* (Mass.) *Morning Union,* 2 Aug. 1985

Summary: *hardly* with a negative produces a weaker, not a stronger, negative; it is not, therefore, a double negative. But it is a speech form not used in discursive prose. The difference between *hardly* with a negative and *hardly* without a negative is neatly illustrated in the examples from Katherine Anne Porter and Mark Twain. Katherine Anne Porter is writing as the omniscient narrator, and she uses *hardly* without a negative. Mark Twain uses Huck Finn as first-person narrator; Huck uses *hardly* with a negative—the construction that would have been natural to his speech. Keep this distinction in mind if you use *can't hardly* or other negative constructions with *hardly* in writing: use them only where they are natural to the narrator or speaker.

See also HARD, HARDLY; SCARCELY 2.

hardly . . . than   The sequence *hardly . . . when* is considered correct and standard by all commentators.

His studies had hardly begun when he was drafted into a cavalry unit of the *Wehrmacht* in 1943 —*Current Biography,* February 1967

This sequence means the same thing as *no sooner... than.* The perhaps more familiar *no sooner... than* sticks in the minds of some writers using *hardly,* and *hardly... than* results:

... hardly had the applause died down than some of them were found to have been invented ... by one of the painters who had worked on the restoration —John Russell, *N.Y. Times,* 12 Feb. 1984

Hardly... than is a syntactic blend (which see). It seems to be of rather recent origin; the OED has, at the third sense of *than,* a single instance from 1903 (and a *scarcely... than* from 1864).

Fowler 1926 was the first to make an issue of this construction. He called it "surprisingly common" and gave three instances, all probably taken from British newspapers. Jespersen 1909–49 (volume 7) has examples from two little-known authors (one of whom used the construction several times in the same book). Bryant 1962 has a 1958 example but cites a study which found the construction rare. Our file of citations has little evidence of it.

Most of the commentators in our collection who mention the construction consider it an error; several of them point out that both *barely* and *scarcely* can occur with *than* in the same syntactic blend. Our evidence suggests that neither the approved *hardly... when* or the disapproved *hardly... than* is a commonly met construction. Use of the syntactic blend is only a minor error.

See also SCARCELY... THAN.

hardy, hearty These two words do not look alike, but they sound much alike in American English. They are vaguely similar in meaning in some of their senses, but they are not interchangeable. The substitution of one for the other, then, must be accounted a mistake. We have a "hearty crop" from *Newsweek* in 1976, and "a particularly hearty flower" from *Parade Magazine* in 1977, both of which should have been *hardy.* And from the *New York Times Magazine* we have a 1982 "hardy soups," which should have been *hearty.*

English is a very difficult language to spell by ear. We suggest you consult a dictionary whenever you are in any doubt—even if you are using a word processor.

harebrained See HAIRBRAINED.

hark back, harken back, hearken back To understand the problem here, we have to spend a moment on *hark, harken,* and *hearken.* These words are related, and all have the basic sense "to listen, listen carefully;" *Harken* is just a spelling variant of *hearken*; the OED shows *harken* to have been used earlier, but *hearken* came to predominate. *Harken* was probably given some impetus in American use by its having been put forward as a reformed spelling—the *Chicago Tribune* adopted it in 1934—and most of our 20th-century evidence for it is American. Both *harken* and *hearken* are still used in their basic meaning.

Hark, however, is now rare in its sense of "listen." From its use as a cry in hunting, it had developed various uses for actions in hunting; in these it was usually accompanied by an adverb such as *away, on, forward,* or *back. Hark back* was a 19th-century formation which quickly acquired a figurative meaning "to turn back to an earlier topic or circumstance." This has become an established use and is the most frequent employment of *hark,* although it can still be found with *forward, after,* and *to.*

In the early 20th century *hark back* began to influence *hearken*:

... it was not sleep at first, but a mental hearkening back to scenes and incidents from his Chicago life —Theodore Dreiser, *Sister Carrie,* 1900

Hearken back developed a variant *harken back*:

This ancestral harkening back to Mark Twain —John Henry Raleigh, *New Republic,* 8 Feb. 1954

It appears from our most recent evidence that the spelling *harken* is beginning to prevail in this use in American English. In the 1980s both *harken* and *hearken* began to develop a sense meaning "hark back" without *back*:

One very dusty bottle in the cellars ... harkens to the days of Napoleon —Anne Marshall Zwack, *Gourmet,* September 1985

... the many ancient hedgerows hearken to an ancient blood-sports tradition —Joseph Wambaugh, *The Blooding,* 1989

Some seventy years after Dreiser used it, critics noticed the *h(e)arken back* construction. They decided it must be a mistake. But they came too late. It is already fairly well established in general writing and is continuing to gain ground. If the present trend continues, *harken* and *hearken,* with or without *back,* may come to be regularly used to mean "hark back" in American English. We have no evidence that *hearken back* is establishing itself in British use, though it has occasional use in the U.S. At the present time, however, neither *hearken back* nor *harken back* appears to be replacing *hark back,* which continues to be more frequently used, both in British and American English.

has got See HAVE GOT.

hassel See HASSLE.

hassle The spelling *hassel* is a variant of *hassle* but is not much used anymore. Its heyday was in the early 1950s, when the word usually referred to a heated argument or a fight, but even then *hassle* was more common.

have got 1. Marckwardt 1958 points out that to many—perhaps most—Americans *have got* denotes mere possession, while *have gotten* denotes obtaining:

> I haven't got a dime myself —E. L. Doctorow, *Loon Lake,* 1979

> However much money you have gotten from Thaw it is only as much as he wanted to give you —E. L. Doctorow, *Ragtime,* 1975

Have got is believed by several British commentators (including Longman 1984 and Strang 1970) to be more common in British English than in American English.

Have got came under fire in American English from Richard Grant White 1870. White considered the *get* superfluous in the construction. White's objection went into later handbooks and grammar books. Hall 1917 mentions three such from about the turn of the century. Bierce 1909 objects, and so do many others. But by the time of Evans 1962 and Bernstein 1971 a greater tolerance had developed. Bernstein quotes Gowers in Fowler 1965 on the side of acceptance. Curiously, later British commentators—Phythian 1979, Longman 1984, Chambers 1985—pick up criticizing where the Americans left off. This resumption of an old theme is even more curious with the conjoined names of Fowler and Gowers on the side of acceptance. Here are some examples of the use:

> . . . ask George if he has got a new song for me —Jane Austen, letter, 27 Oct. 1798

> . . . has not Hobhouse got a journal? —Lord Byron, letter, 3 May 1810

> Haven't you got your little camera with you? —Lewis Carroll, letter, 10 Aug. 1897

> The Chinese haven't got anybody who'll protect them —Gough Whitlam, quoted in *The Listener,* 3 Jan. 1974

> . . . how we have achieved the spelling that we have got today —Howard 1984

> "But have you got the grit, the character, the never-say-quit spirit it takes . . . ?" —Russell Baker, *Growing Up,* 1982

> What do you call xenophobia when it's actually the opposite . . . ? Whatever it is, Theroux has got it, and he uses it to good effect —Adam Goodheart, *N.Y. Times Book Rev.,* 18 June 2000

Have will do perfectly well in writing that avoids the natural rhythms of speech. But in speech, or prose that resembles speech, you will probably want *have got.*

2. *Have got to.* Here we have another curiosity. *I have got to go* is listed as an incorrect expression in Joseph Hervey Hull's *Grammar* of 1829. But our earliest printed examples come from the middle of the 19th century. The early examples are British and literary—Disraeli, Dickens, George Eliot, Trollope, Ruskin, Oscar Wilde, H. G. Wells, George Bernard Shaw—while Hull's grammar book was written for school use and published in Boston. Later negative comment on this construction comes from Vizetelly 1920, Jensen 1935, Shaw 1970, 1975, 1987, and Harper 1975, 1985. In addition to the literary names mentioned (they are from Jespersen 1909–49, volume 4), we have these examples:

> South Carolina has got to eat dirt —Henry Adams, letter, 2 Jan. 1861

> But I've got to face the situation —Harry S. Truman, letter, 14 Nov. 1947

> We have got to come into court—the high court of public opinion—with clean hands —Dwight D. Eisenhower, quoted in *Newsweek,* 30 June 1952

> But I, as President, have got to maintain the accurate image that we do have a crisis —Jimmy Carter, quoted in *N.Y. Times,* 14 Feb. 1980

> "You've got to be kidding," I said —Tip O'Neill with William Novak, *Man of the House,* 1987

> Every man has got to stand on his own feet —William Faulkner, 8 May 1957, in *Faulkner in the University,* 1959

Have got to, have to, and the frequently recommended *must* can all be used in the present tense, but only *had to* can be used in the past. *Got to,* with the *have* omitted, is also used in the present tense, but primarily in speech. It is not, as Harper says, illiterate.

> "You just got to grow up a little, honey," she said —John Irving, *The Hotel New Hampshire,* 1981

> You got to get away where you can see yourself and everybody else. I really believe you got to do that —James Thurber, letter, 20 Jan. 1938

havoc See WREAK, WRECK.

he, he or she Many handbooks, among them Scott, Foresman 1981, Little, Brown 1980, 1986, Corder 1981, Irmscher 1976, Ebbitt & Ebbitt 1982, Trimmer & McCrimmon 1988, and other usage books such as Reader's Digest 1983 and Copperud 1970, 1980 have articles of varying length dealing with the problem of what third person singular pronoun to use in referring to a singular noun antecedent that can apply to either sex.

Everybody says that the traditional solution has been to use *he, his, him, himself,* the masculine third person singular. This prescription goes back no farther than 1788, when a Charles Coote, who considered himself a historian, mentioned it in a footnote in his grammar. The actual practice, however, is much older, but it was not the only solution available.

The use of generic *he* as a common-gender and common-number pronoun has lately been attacked as offensive by feminists and others. Bolinger 1980 points out that the problem was not discovered by feminists, but is an old one in the language. The lack of a common-gender and common-number pronoun has been felt since at least as far back as Middle English. The common solution has been to substitute the plural *they* (or *them* or *their*); even Chaucer used this dodge. We have many examples of how writers have dealt with the difficulty at THEY, THEIR, THEM 1, at the articles dealing with pronouns at AGREEMENT, and at the separate entries for the indefinite pronouns.

The use of the double pronoun *he or she, him or her, his or her,* is not recent either. Bolinger notes that it dates back at least to the 18th century and cites a quotation found by Otto Jespersen in a work by Henry Fielding: "the reader's heart (if he or she have any)." The double pronoun works well at times, but its frequent use leaves the writer open to two kinds of error. The first is the failure to follow through. Reader's Digest 1983 has an example: "The true measure of a human being is how he or she treats his fellow man." The other likely fault is the use of the double pronoun when the antecedent is plural. Allan Metcalf, in *American Speech,* Fall 1984, has this example: ". . . would add little or nothing to the citizens' understanding of the situation and advance his or her accomplishments." Besides susceptibility to these inconsistencies, the double pronoun has the disadvantage of awkwardness, as numerous commentators point out, especially when a context calls for it repeatedly.

Many of the books mentioned above suggest and exemplify other ways of avoiding generic *he*. Among them are casting the sentence in the plural, addressing the reader directly in the second person, and revising to avoid the pronoun altogether.

We suggest that you solve the difficulty in the way that you think will work best in a given situation—it is not likely you will want to use the same strategy every time for every audience. Those who are committed to the generic *he* will undoubtedly keep on using it.

Those who are not will search for other solutions. See SEXISM 2.

The lack of a common-gender third person singular pronoun has stimulated many ingenious folk over the years to invent such a form. See EPICENE PRONOUNS.

head up Like many other verbs, *head* is often used with *up*; a person can either *head* a committee or *head up* a committee. Because the *up* appears to add nothing to the meaning of *head,* language watchers regard it as superfluous and therefore, as Harper 1985 puts it, "unacceptable to careful speakers and writers." Evidence of actual usage shows, however, that *head up* is extremely common both in speech and in writing. We have found it to be in widespread use since the 1950s:

. . . who unselfishly headed up the fund —Harvey Breit, *N.Y. Times Book Rev.,* 18 Apr. 1954

. . . a dynamic young businessman who was heading up a forty-million-dollar a year enterprise —Tom McCarthy, *The Writer,* November 1968

. . . Saxophonist Cannonball Adderley . . . heads up his quintet —*New Yorker,* 20 Aug. 1973

. . . who now heads up his own firm —Diane Sustendal, *N.Y. Times Mag.,* 25 Mar. 1984

. . . was retained as special counsel to head up an outside investigation —Peter Elkind, *Fortune,* 9 Nov. 1998

We see nothing wrong with such usage, but you should be aware that it stands some chance of being criticized.

healthy, healthful In the *Saturday Review* of 17 Mar. 1979 Thomas H. Middleton wrote, "The sad truth is that *healthy* has so often been used to mean 'healthful' that any dictionary worth its flyleaf just has to list 'healthful' as one of *healthy*'s meanings." This and a notice in a column by James J. Kilpatrick (28 June 1985) attest to the flourishing condition of the old issue of the distinction between *healthful* and *healthy*. Here is the gist of the prescription: *healthful* means "conducive to health" (it does) and *healthy* means "enjoying or evincing health" (it does), and never the twain shall change places. The trouble is that *healthy* is used for the sense of *healthful* just given. How long has this sloppy confusion of distinct words been going on? Since the middle of the 16th century—in other words, for more than four hundred years.

The distinction itself was invented by Alfred Ayres only in 1881. It has certainly been repeated many times since, right up into the 1990s. But it should surprise no one that the distinction has often not been observed: there never was a distinction in the first place.

Burchfield 1996 notes that *healthful* has little use in British English.

Healthy, since its introduction in the middle of the 16th century, has been used much more frequently than *healthful* in both senses. So if you observe the distinction between *healthful* and *healthy* you are absolutely correct, and in the minority. If you ignore the distinction you are absolutely correct, and in the majority.

Here are some examples of each word in its main acceptations:

> . . . they demand more food and beer than the natives consider either decent or healthful —Anthony Burgess, *Saturday Rev.,* 22 July 1978

> He felt incapable of looking into the girl's pretty, healthful face —Saul Bellow, *Herzog,* 1964

> . . . would almost certainly result in a healthy marine back to normal duty within a week —Thomas C. Butler, *Johns Hopkins Mag.,* Summer 1971

> . . . to achieve more genteel or healthier living habits —J. M. Richards, *Times Literary Supp.,* 27 Nov. 1981

> . . . even when they are poorer and eat a less healthy diet —Jim Holt, *N.Y. Times Book Rev.,* 16 Apr. 2000

Bernstein 1965, 1971 disapproves *healthy* meaning "considerable," thinking it slangy. You can see from these examples that it is not:

> Count Frontenac, who had a healthy respect for the Iroquois —Samuel Eliot Morison, *Oxford History of the American People,* 1965

> Signed manuscripts by living novelists generally drew the healthiest prices —Richard R. Lingeman, *N.Y. Times Book Rev.,* 21 May 1978

hearken back See HARK BACK, HARKEN BACK, HEARKEN BACK.

heartrending A few commentators (Shaw 1987, Copperud 1980, and Garner 1998) recommend *heartrending*—to be found in almost every dictionary—over *heart-rendering*—not to be found in any dictionary that we know of. *Heartrendering* does exist, but it is of such low frequency that we do not think you will ever be much tempted to use it.

hearty See HARDY, HEARTY.

heave In standard English *heave* has two past tense and past participle forms, *heaved* and *hove.* In nautical contexts *hove* is used.

> . . . cable can be hove in or veered under power —Great Britain Admiralty, *Manual of Seamanship,* 1951

> . . . the vessel is hove ahead by the capstan or windlass —Carl D. Lane, *The Boatman's Manual,* 1951

> We . . . hove up the anchor —Roland Barker, *Ships & the Sea,* July 1953

> Aspinwall backed the foresail a bit and hove to on the starboard . . . tack —Anthony Burgess, *MF,* 1971

> . . . a small skiff that had just hove in sight —Nelson Bryant, *N.Y. Times,* 2 Jan. 1983

Hove is also used when the nautical uses are borrowed for general contexts, especially in fixed phrases.

> I hove to at the stripling's side —P. G. Wodehouse, *Joy in the Morning,* 1946

> She first hove into view on a *Family* episode last season —*Time,* 25 Sept. 1972

> . . . long before Mr. Agee hove on the horizon with a 46-page critique —Frederick Taylor, *Wall Street Jour.,* 21 Aug. 1981

Other uses of *hove* have for the most part dropped out of current use.

> . . . whoever hove those things in here —Mark Twain, *Tom Sawyer,* 1876

When a past tense or past participle is needed for *heave* in a context not involving nautical lingo, *heaved* is usually used.

> The Sheriff heaved massively in the chair —Robert Penn Warren, *All the King's Men,* 1946

> His stomach heaved —Marcia Davenport, *My Brother's Keeper,* 1954

> . . . heaved a sigh of relief —Daphne du Maurier, *Don't Look Now,* 1966

> . . . the Earth's crust was heaved up —Paul F. Brandwein et al., *Concepts in Science,* 1975

hectic This word is mentioned in several books of usage, including Bremner 1980, Copperud 1970, 1980, Bernstein 1965, and Evans 1957, and has been submitted to the usage panels of Heritage 1969 and Harper 1975, 1985—all because of its treatment in Fowler 1926. Fowler was upset with what is now the prevalent sense of the adjective: "filled with excitement or confusion." He based his objection on etymology, thus, as Copperud observes, failing to take note of his own observation that etymology does not always determine meaning, an observation which he had tucked under the heading *True & False Etymology.* (See ETYMOLOGICAL FALLACY.)

Hectic is derived from a Greek word meaning "habitual." In English it was applied to a persistent fever present in some diseases, and then it came to mean "having such a fever" and then "red, flushed" and eventually acquired (around 1904) its present usual sense, which is similar to the figurative use of *feverish*. Here are a couple of examples of the fever senses, in case you are unfamiliar with them:

> Hectic spots of red burned on his cheeks —Oscar Wilde, *The Picture of Dorian Gray,* 1891

> . . . identify it with the hectic flush of a consumptive —Robert M. Adams, *N.Y. Rev. of Books,* 20 May 1971

These will probably seem more familiar:

> I had a pretty hectic time for a while —John Buchan, *Greenmantle,* 1916

> No single reporter could do justice to the hectic weekend at the Waldorf —Joseph P. Lash, *New Republic,* 18 Apr. 1949

> . . . which had survived the hectic activity —Norman Mailer, *Harper's,* March 1971

No one after Fowler finds fault with the extended sense.

height There are two problems here. The first is spelling. This word was originally formed in Old English from the Old English version of *high* and the suffix *-th*; the formation is exactly analogous to *breadth, width,* and *length*. The spellings *heighth* and *highth* are, therefore, the purest from the standpoint of etymology. However, they have been replaced in prevalent standard use by *height*.

Height comes into use by way of northern English dialects. The OED tells us that the *th* after the sound our *gh* used to stand for was pronounced \t\ in the north and \th\ in the south. As a result, northern spelling had no final *h* while southern spelling did. Milton spelled the word *highth*. But the northern version has come to prevail in modern use. *Highth* seems to have dropped out of use altogether, but *heighth* persisted into the first half of the 20th century at least, and is still occasionally used to stand for the pronunciation \ˈhītth\. Even though *heighth* and *highth* are etymologically pure and are not errors, we recommend that you stick to the mainstream spelling *height*.

Pronunciation is a different matter. The modern \ˈhītth\ is a bit of a phonological curiosity in itself, being a sort of combination of the more usual \ˈhīt\ and an older and apparently mostly disused \ˈhīth\, which would have been used for *highth*. It may have been influenced by the usual pronunciation of *eighth*. It is, however, a pronunciation too widespread among the highly educated and the highly placed to be considered anything but a standard variant. If it is your natural pronunciation, stick with it, but be aware that some commentators believe it an error.

heist Copperud 1980 pronounces *heist* only fit for casual use and says well-edited publications avoid it. Flesch 1983 flatly contradicts him, saying that it is frequent in well-edited publications. Flesch produces evidence that he is right. He notes that all dictionaries label it *slang,* and suggests that it is in widespread use because it lends color to writing.

> The whole affair was neatly reckoned as *"le fric-frac du siècle,"* the heist of the century —Peter Andrews, *N.Y. Times,* 29 July 1979

> Missing the big jewel heist . . . was the low point for me —William Safire, *N.Y. Times,* 23 Sept. 1974

> Enter Supercrook, determined to heist the heroin —Newgate Callendar, *N.Y. Times Book Rev.,* 3 June 1979

help See CANNOT BUT, CANNOT HELP, CANNOT HELP BUT.

helpmate, helpmeet Both these words are standard. *Helpmeet* is the older and is formed by a misunderstanding from a verse in the King James Bible:

> And the Lord God said, It is not good that man should be alone; I will make him an help meet for him —Genesis 2:18

In the passage, *meet* is an adjective meaning "suitable." However, the reference was to the impending creation of Eve, and gradually *help meet* came to be understood as one word meaning "wife." *Helpmate* was formed by folk etymology from *helpmeet*. *Helpmeet* is not archaic, as Garner 1998 says:

> . . . a suffering artist cured of influenza and lovesickness by a beautiful helpmeet and a bottle of cognac —Julian Barnes, *New Yorker,* 19 Sept. 1994

> The owner of the flat socked her in the jaw . . . whereupon her helpmeet cold-cocked him —George F. Will, *Newsweek,* 1 May 1995

But *helpmate* is the more common word.

hence See FROM WHENCE, FROM THENCE, FROM HENCE.

he or she See HE, HE OR SHE.

her See IT'S ME.

herb See H.

here is, here are See THERE IS, THERE ARE.

hers *Hers* is another one of those pronouns from the northern dialects of Britain that became ultimately successful, driving the southern form—*hern*—out of standard use. *Hern* still exists in nonstandard varieties of English.

Hers was frequently spelled with an apostrophe two or three hundred years ago:

. . . I sent for a dozen bottles of her's —Samuel Pepys, diary, 17 June 1663

Bishop Lowth used the form with the apostrophe in his grammar book of 1762. But in present-day use, *her's* is accounted a mistake in spelling.

See also YOURS.

herself See MYSELF.

hesitant *Hesitant* may often be followed by *about* or by *to* and the infinitive:

. . . was not at all hesitant about presenting his strong objections to the Bay of Pigs plan —Irving Janis, *Psychology Today*, November 1971

. . . is hesitant to offend any of the fraternity by impertinence —Paul Potter, *Johns Hopkins Mag.*, October 1965

Less often, *hesitant* is used with *in*:

. . . we would be even less hesitant in embarking on foreign adventures of the Vietnamese sort —Joseph Shoben, *Change*, November–December 1969

hiccup, hiccough *Hiccup* is the older spelling, and the one preferred by usage commentators, but *hiccough* has also been in use for several centuries (from 1628). *Hiccough* undoubtedly originated through a misunderstanding of *hiccup*, and the OED suggested in 1898 that it "ought to be abandoned as a mere error." It hasn't been, however. *Hiccup* is the more common spelling, but *hiccough* continues in occasional reputable use:

. . . from laboratory to field trial to commercial sale with relatively few hiccoughs —Matt Ridley, *Genome*, 1999

. . . with hardly a hiccough —*The Economist*, 12 July 1985

The word is pronounced so that it rhymes with *stickup*, regardless of its spelling.

him See IT'S ME.

him or her See HE, HE OR SHE.

himself See MYSELF.

hinder When *hinder* is used with a preposition, the choice is usually *from*:

He could not hinder himself from dwelling upon it —Stephen Crane, *The Red Badge of Courage*, 1895

. . . did not hinder her from giving spirited interpretations in comedy —*Current Biography*, March 1953

Occasionally, *hinder* may be found with *in*:

My various societies . . . boost or hinder me in my scholarly endeavors —Wayne C. Booth, in *Introduction to Scholarship in Modern Languages and Literatures*, ed. Joseph Gibaldi, 1981

In the passive voice, *hinder* is often used with *by* to express agency or means:

. . . whose scientific work is hindered by extreme eccentricity —*Times Literary Supp.*, 22 Oct. 1971

hindrance 1. *Hindrance* is the common spelling for this word, but the variant *hinderance* is still occasionally found in 20th-century writing:

The subsequent omission of this facility is not a great hinderance as it is located in an urban enclave —James L. Mulvihill, *Professional Geographer*, August 1979

2. When used with a preposition, *hindrance* is usually used with *to*:

. . . his very superiorities and advantages would be the surest hindrance to success —Edith Wharton, *The Age of Innocence*, 1920

. . . all these are great hindrances to the development of the world on a liberal scale —Arnold J. Toynbee, quoted in Arnold J. Toynbee et al., "Will Businessmen Unite the World?" April 1971

Less frequently but still commonly, *hindrance* is used with *of*, as in the following:

. . . he still felt his rebellion against odious fate, everyone's fate, death, war; his tremor of knee and hindrance of speech —Glenway Wescott, *Apartment in Athens*, 1945

hint When used with a preposition, *hint* is usually used with *at*:

. . . a slender selection of essays, which hint quietly at what may be expected —Edmund Wilson, *Axel's Castle*, 1931

. . . a submerged feeling or memory, that the two of them can only hint at but cannot express —Joyce Carol Oates, *Harper's*, August 1971

Less frequently, *hint* is used with *of*:

The face of the old retainer hinted of things still untold —Thomas B. Costain, *The Black Rose*, 1945

The evidence shows that once in a while *hint* is also used with *about*, *against*, or *for*:

"Why do you even hint about shame to me? . . ." —E. Temple Thurston, *The Green Bough*, 1921

Her husband's tutor was found to hint very strongly against such a step —Thomas Hardy, *A Group of Noble Dames*, 1891 (OED Supplement)

. . . not answering letters hinting broadly for invitations to visit —Grace Metalious, *Peyton Place,* 1956

his It was at one time believed—and the story still crops up from time to time—that the origin of the possessive *-'s* was as an elision of *his.* Although the supposition is wrong, *his* was actually sometimes used to mark the possessive.

. . . my cozen Edward Pepys his lady —Samuel Pepys, diary, 17 June 1663

See APOSTROPHE 2, 4; GENITIVE.

his or her See HE, HE OR SHE.

hisself Anyone who stops to think about it will notice that our standard reflexive pronouns are not very consistently formed. Some are formed on the genitive case of the pronoun: *myself, ourselves, yourself, yourselves. Herself* might be considered as a genitive as might *itself* if we allowed for merging of the two *s's.* But then we have *himself* and *themselves,* patently formed on the objective case, and we have to admit that the third person reflexives are just different. Bishop Lowth back in 1762 was aware of the anomaly and opposed *himself* and *themselves* as corruptions. He plumped for *his self* and *their selves* instead, citing the first from Sir Philip Sidney and the second from some statutes of Henry VI.

But usage paid no attention to the Bishop's plea for a more rational and consistent set of pronouns. *Hisself* and *theirselves* still exist, but they are considered nonstandard. You will find them, and *theirself,* in dialectal speech, in fiction as part of the speech of rustic characters, and occasionally used for humorous effect.

They run off as though Satan hisself was a'ter them with a red-hot ten-pronged pitchfork —Artemus Ward, "Interview with President Lincoln," 1861, in *The Mirth of a Nation,* ed. Walter Blair & Raven I. McDavid, Jr., 1983

I wouldn't want nobody to have to strain hisself —Flannery O'Connor, letter, 28 Feb. 1960

See also THEIRSELVES.

historic, historical *Historic* and *historical* are simply variants. Over the course of two or three hundred years of use, they have tended to diverge somewhat. *Historical* is the usual choice for the broad and general uses relating to history:

. . . a historical survey of popular music —John J. O'Connor, *N.Y. Times,* 10 May 1981

. . . an historical interpretation of Bonhoeffer's theology —*Times Literary Supp.,* 30 July 1971

. . . a possible way out of a political and historical tangle —Norman Cousins, *Saturday Rev.,* 30 Oct. 1971

Historic is most commonly used for something famous or important in history:

What I think marks both those times is that people who were in either of them knew they were in a historic moment —Arlo Guthrie, quoted in *Yankee,* August 1986

On May 10, 1973, in a historic decision, the House voted 219 to 188 to stop the Defense Department from spending any more money on the war in Vietnam —Tip O'Neill with William Novak, *Man of the House,* 1987

But this is not a complete differentiation. *Historic* still crops up in the general sense:

. . . the literal satirist, who might be only of limited historic significance —Robert B. Heilman, *Southern Rev.,* April 1970

Historical also means "important in history," but this sense does not appear to be very widely used any more:

. . . the Dean, speaking from that most historical pulpit —Hamlin Garland, *Back-Trailers from the Middle Border,* 1928

Most of the usage writers pretend that the differentiation is more absolute than it actually is. But we would suggest that you go along with the general trend; bucking it may be historically justified but is more likely to interfere with the smooth transfer of your ideas from paper to reader.

You will have noticed that both *a* and *an* are used before *historic* and *historical.* A number of commentators prescribe *a* here, but you should feel free to use *an* if it sounds more natural to you. We find that more writers use *a* than *an* but that both are common. For more on the use of *a* and *an,* see A, AN.

hither 1. *Hither, thither, whither.* These three analogous adverbs, which basically mean "to here," "to there," and "to where," have been described by various commentators as old-fashioned, archaic, obsolescent, formal, pompous, and literary. The adequacy of any of those descriptions may be questioned ("old-fashioned" is probably best), but it is clear, in any case, that these are not ordinary words in common, everyday use.

Of the three, *hither* is least likely to be used alone.

Hither Beecher removed his household in 1810 —*Dictionary of American Biography,* 1929

It occurs most often in the company of *thither* or *yon:*

... cursing at the loss of the phone, running hither and thither with messages —Penelope Lively, *City of the Mind,* 1991

... have continued to do, hither and thither in the world —Glenway Wescott, *Prose,* Fall 1971

... elegant wood carvings jutting out hither and yon —Russell Baker, *Growing Up,* 1982

When hauling the dead hither and yon became less a chore and more an honor, men took it over with enthusiasm —Thomas Lynch, *The Undertaking,* 1997

It also continues to be used in the adjective *come-hither*:

... a come-hither photograph of the sultry young cosmetics marketer —*New Republic,* 15 Mar. 1999

Thither occurs considerably more often as a solitary adverb than *hither*. When used straightforwardly, it usually relates to movement to a geographical location:

... the merchants had flocked thither from the South and West with their households to taste of all the luscious feasts —F. Scott Fitzgerald, "May Day," in *The Portable F. Scott Fitzgerald,* 1945

... to support any British army that marched thither —Samuel Eliot Morison, *Oxford History of the American People,* 1965

... the international press corps, sped thither by the taxi fleet that hovers at the hotel's door —John Keegan, *Atlantic,* April 1984

Thither is also sometimes used to deliberately evoke the language of the past:

... has assembled accessories from all over the store, and thither we advise you to hie —*New Yorker,* 10 Dec. 1949

It is also used with *hither*, of course, and less commonly, with *yon*:

... random couples necking thither and yon —Bennett M. Berger, *Trans-Action,* May 1971

The most common—or least uncommon—of these adverbs in current English is *whither*. It occurs in the same kinds of contexts as *thither*:

... had left Chicago, whither he had emigrated, for the Soviet Union —Horace Sutton, *Saturday Rev.,* 5 June 1971

... and I have often wondered whither they were removed —Robert Stone, *Harper's,* November 1988

Whither would they go? —Simon Schama, *The Embarrassment of Riches,* 1988

Whither is also used figuratively:

The ... self-serving leader must try to imagine whither this restlessness may lead in the next five years —Michael Novak, *Center Mag.,* March–April 1971

... describe the general musical situation in America and whither we are heading —Thomas Lask, *N.Y. Times,* 12 Mar. 1971

A related figurative use is in rhetorical questions, which typically consist simply of *whither* followed by a noun, with no accompanying verb:

So now, with 500 years of Canadian brewing history gone like so much ullage, whither Canadian beer? —Jamie MacKinnon, *Globe and Mail* (Toronto), 26 June 1995

Others weigh in with the 'whither America?' doomspeak —Ian Hamilton, *London Rev. of Books,* April 1998

For forty years ... "Whither NATO?" was a cud that could be placidly chewed not only by editorialists but also by think-tankers —*New Yorker,* 17 Jan. 1994

The rhetorical question is frequently found in titles of articles.

Hither, thither, and *whither* show no sign of passing into obsolescence in the near future. Their place in current English is not large, but it appears to be firmly established.

2. In addition to its adverbial uses, *hither* has been used as an adjective meaning "near" since the 14th century:

... this was just the hither edge of the oil slick —Archibald MacLeish, *N.Y. Times,* 17 June 1973

... in the steppes of eastern Europe or hither Asia —W. P. Lehmann, *Language,* January–March 1954

Although not in the vocabulary of most people, this adjective has staying power.

hitherto   There are two complaints about *hitherto*. Flesch 1964 and Janis 1984 suggest avoiding *hitherto* because it is old-fashioned. For Janis if it is not old-fashioned, it is overformal. But neither label is borne out by the evidence. *Hitherto* is in frequent current use. And Bremner 1980 produces an example from the sports pages, not noted for their overformality, to complain about.

Bremner 1980 says the word means "up to now" and not "up to then." This is the gist of the second complaint, which can also be found in Bernstein 1965, Copperud 1970, 1980, and Bryson 1984.   We find the argument back in a 1956 *Winners & Sinners*; there Bernstein says that now is the time implied by *hitherto.* It is, but we must be careful not to restrict our notion of time so severely that *now* refers only to today and everything else is *then*. For look at this example, which is typical of a certain approach to writing about the past:

> Bogus naturalization of immigrants and repeating at elections were now carried to hitherto unknown lengths —*Dictionary of American Biography*, 1936

The *now* in that passage refers to 1869 or 1870 (the article is about Boss Tweed) and means "at the time we are talking about," and *hitherto* there means "up until the time we are talking about." This use of *hitherto* is not rare in the 20th century:

> Hitherto when in London I had stayed with my family in Bedford Park —William Butler Yeats, *The Trembling of the Veil*, 1922

> No, Owen was a poet—a War Poet only because the brief span of his maturity coincided with a war of hitherto unparalleled sweep, viciousness and stupidity —Osbert Sitwell, *Noble Essences*, 1950

> In refined London literary circles . . . Kipling was hailed for . . . the opening up of the hitherto unknown worlds of military and civilian life in British India —Richard Eder, *N.Y. Times Book Rev.*, 30 Apr. 2000

> . . . not only upset his Liberal colleagues and negated the delicacy with which he had hitherto been endeavouring to bring them along —Roy Jenkins, *Gladstone*, 1995

> Andrea had seemed to Glenn rather opaque and standardized hitherto —John Updike, *New Yorker*, 27 July 1992

Underlying the critics' objection, though not always mentioned, is the existence of a contrasting word for *hitherto* that decidedly means "up until then"—*thitherto*. It is a nice word but very rare. Here are two examples:

> . . . the ruts in the lane—thitherto as deep as the Union trenches before Vicksburg—had mysteriously filled up by themselves —S. J. Perelman, *New Yorker*, 6 June 1953

> The surprise hit of this past Christmas season was a talking bear . . . manufactured by a thitherto unknown company —David Owen, *Atlantic*, October 1986

Now if you want to devote yourself to the preservation of *thitherto*, we commend it to your use—it is a fine word. If not, you can go right ahead and use *hitherto* in the sense of "up until the time we are talking about" like William Butler Yeats or John Updike.

hoard, horde These words are homophones, and Chambers 1985, Bryson 1984, Shaw 1987, and Copperud 1980 all warn against confusing them. But as your dictionary will show you,

there is no reason to confuse them from the standpoint of meaning. This is a spelling problem. Our evidence suggests that *hoard*—maybe the spelling just seems more familiar—is used in place of *horde*: "hoards of local golfers," "hoards of warriors." One creative misspeller, in a journal designed for educational consumption, managed to combine the two words: "hoardes of seagulls." If you think you are apt to misspell either of these words, check your dictionary.

hoi polloi 1. *Use with "the."* Hoi polloi is a Greek term that literally means "the many." Its use in English stretches back to a time when a good education consisted largely of mastering Greek and Latin. *Hoi polloi* was adopted by the well-educated as a term for the unprivileged masses. Early on it was written in Greek letters:

> . . . one or two others, with myself, put on masks, and went on the stage with the οἱ πολλοι —Lord Byron, *Detached Thoughts*, 1821

As its use became more widespread in the 19th century, the transliterated form *hoi polloi* (rarely *oi polloi*) came to be preferred:

> After which the *oi polloi* are enrolled as they can find interest —James Fenimore Cooper, *Gleanings from Europe*, 1837 (OED Supplement)

> The *hoi polloi*, as we say at Oxford, are mindless—all blank —*Read & Reflect*, 1855 (OED Supplement)

Proper usage of *hoi polloi* did not become a subject of controversy until the early 20th century, when the argument that this term should not be preceded by *the*—because *hoi* literally means "the"—was advanced. This was a silly argument to begin with, since *hoi* has no meaning in English, and its earliest users, who actually knew Greek, always prefixed the phrase with *the*. Nevertheless the argument is still heard, and some writers do omit *the*:

> . . . status-seeking moviegoers can now order from waiters, use private bathrooms and generally avoid mixing with hoi polloi —Lisa Gubernick, *Wall Street Jour.*, 11 Dec. 1998

> . . . Lord Wilson . . . who looked visibly strained when dealing with *hoi polloi* —Stephen Vines, *Manchester Guardian Weekly*, 13 Sept. 1992

> . . . where Old New York mixes with hoi polloi —*New Yorker*, 28 Nov. 1988

More writers retain *the*:

> . . . wearing the badge sets one apart from the hoi polloi —Franklin Leonard, *George*, November 1997

When most of us apply for a passport, we have to stand in line for hours in a windowless government office, pressed against the hoi polloi —Eric Konigsberg, *New Republic,* 1 Mar. 1993

. . . designed so that dignitaries could reach their trains without having to brush shoulders with the hoi polloi —Alice Rubinstein Gochman, *Gourmet,* November 1990

. . . with a sigh, we resign ourselves to being part of the hoi polloi —Shirley Slater, *Bon Appétit,* April 1993

In summary, more writers keep *the* than omit it. A few italicize *hoi polloi.* All these methods are standard.

2. An issue about which there has been much less comment is the use of *hoi polloi* to mean "the snobby elite," a sense which is almost directly opposed to the term's original meaning. A few commentators (as Bernstein 1977, Bryson 1984, Garner 1998, and Heritage 2000) mention and censure this sense. It rarely occurs in print. Our earliest example is this one:

I could fly over to Europe and join the rich hoi polloi at Monte Carlo —Westbrook Pegler, *Times News-Tribune* (Tacoma, Wash.), 25 Sept. 1955

Since Pegler's time we have found only three or four more examples (Garner has a 1997 example). It appears, however, that this sense of *hoi polloi* is extremely common in speech. It has been reported to be well established in spoken use in such diverse locales as central New Jersey, southern California, Cleveland, Ohio, and Las Vegas, Nevada. Several members of our editoral staff have also testified to its common occurrence. We do not know for certain how this new sense originated. Bernstein 1977 speculates that it may have come about because of association of *hoi* with *high.* Another possibility is that the new sense developed out of the inherent snobbery of *hoi polloi.* In its original sense, *hoi polloi* is a term used by snobs or—more often—in mocking imitation of snobs. Even its sound has a quality of haughtiness and condescension (much like that of *hoity-toity,* a term that underwent a similar extension of meaning in the 20th century, from its former sense, "frivolous," to its current sense, "marked by an air of superiority"). It may be that people unfamiliar with the meaning of *hoi polloi,* but conscious of its strong associations with snobbery, have misunderstood it as an arrogant term for the haves rather than a contemptuous term for the have-nots.

hold See AHOLD.

holocaust Usage writers who claim that *holocaust* is not a synonym for *disaster* and

who, because of the older sense of a completely burnt sacrificial offering, say that *holocaust* has the more specific meaning "fiery destruction entailing loss of life" (Bernstein 1965) or "wholesale destruction by fire" (Bremner 1980) are taking advantage of the critic's license to discuss only a small incident in the whole story. *Holocaust* has had a more complicated semantic development than this restriction suggests.

The "burnt sacrifice" sense appeared in English by the middle of the 13th century, and related figurative uses are attested in the OED from 1497 on, although they are rarely found today. Uses in which the notions of death and destruction are preeminent did not develop until a couple of centuries later, but once started, they flourished more vigorously than the uses related to sacrifice. As a result, *holocaust* commonly refers to large-scale destruction, loss of life, fire, or all three at once:

The scientists say that the chances of pandemic holocaust are extremely remote, because they have seen no evidence of it in their animal experiments —*The Economist,* 25 Feb. 1989

. . . predicting the downfall of Rome and of all priests and friars in a holocaust that would leave no unworthy clergy alive —Barbara W. Tuchman, *The March of Folly,* 1984

The possibility of nuclear holocaust —Barry Gewen, *N.Y. Times Book Rev.,* 19 Oct. 1997

. . . the building burns . . . in a luridly awful holocaust —Valentine Cunningham, *Times Literary Supp.,* 23 Sept. 1983

Both shared Pol Pot's complicity in the Cambodian holocaust —Sydney H. Schanberg, *Vanity Fair,* October 1997

One specific application of the word is, of course, to the genocidal slaughter of European Jews by the Nazis during World War II. When used this way, *holocaust* is usually capitalized and preceded by *the* unless it is used as an attributive:

. . . a survivor of the holocaust —Barbara A. Bannon, *Publishers Weekly,* 3 Jan. 1977

. . . a country so obsessed by the Holocaust —*Atlantic,* April 1983

. . . concentration camps where Holocaust victims were exterminated —William R. Doerner, *Time,* 13 May 1985

Figurative meanings branch out in various directions from the basic meanings discussed above. While the commentators tend to disapprove many of these, our evidence shows them infrequent when compared to the most common uses, which refer to the Nazi Holocaust or to nuclear war. Here is a sample of broader use:

The Edsel holocaust threw us into The Dark Age of Applied Science —Jim Siegelman, *Harper's Weekly*, 12 July 1976

. . . awakens to the ethical holocaust around him —Judith Crist, *Saturday Rev.*, 2 Oct. 1976

. . . turn an ordinary matrimonial war into an explosive do-or-die end-of-the-world holocaust —J. Alan Ornstein, *The Lion's Share: A Combat Manual for the Divorcing Male*, 1978

. . . Jackson's policy of Indian removal—a particularly shocking episode in America's home-grown holocaust —Eric Foner, *N.Y. Times Book Rev.*, 2 Mar. 1980

. . . after the tornado . . . in a township garage that had survived the holocaust —Civia Tamarkin, *People*, 9 July 1984

home, house, *noun*   The folks who disparage the use of *home* in the sense of "house" divide roughly into two groups. One group is often associated by usage writers with Edgar A. Guest and his famous line, "It takes a heap o' livin' in a house t' make a home." They write like this:

We build a *home* with love and time, and build a *house* with a hammer and saw —A. M. Stires, Jr., letter to editor, *Fine Homebuilding*, February/March 1981

How can you in English buy a home any more than love or Killarney? You can buy a house and hope to make your home there —Ian Robinson, *Encounter*, January 1975

The other group distinguishes the words on the basis of class: Simon 1980 identifies *home* as non-U, while Paul Fussell, in *Class* (1983), identifies it with the middle class. Both of these gentlemen were anticipated by Emily Post 1927, who based her opinion on exactly the same grounds.

Both groups like to place the blame for *home* meaning "house" on the advertising of real-estate agents. Bernstein 1965, 1971, 1977 at least partially exculpates them from the charge. And well he should. The usage is much older than modern real-estate agents. In Merriam-Webster's Collegiate Dictionary, Tenth Edition, you will find the first sense of *home* divided into two parts, "domicile" and "house." The distinction represents modern use. The OED does not separate these senses, probably because the distinction is hard to make in the oldest examples. The earliest citation comes from the Lindisfarne Gospels, which are dated around 950, and is a translation of a passage from the New Testament that in the King James Version is the familiar "In my father's house are many mansions" (John 14:2). In the *Lindisfarne Gospels* the word rendered as *mansions* by the King James translators is *hamas*—the Old English for *homes*. Modern use seems to have begun with Felicia D. Hemans around 1835, in a reference to "the stately homes of England." Mrs. Hemans is nearly a century earlier than Babbitt and his real-estate promoters.

If we forget the practice of real-estate agents and advertising writers and turn to ordinary prose writers, we find that Bernstein is right in his observation that *home* and *house* are often interchangeable. Writers sometimes contrast them and at other times do not.

Their house, I assume, gives them a large measure of happiness. Yet why does my calling their home vulgar also give me such a measure of happiness? —Aristides, *American Scholar*, Winter 1981/82

. . . had come down to New York from her home in Bridgeport, a clapboard house —E. L. Doctorow, *Ragtime*, 1975

Our house is our home. We live there —*And More by Andy Rooney*, 1982

. . . 107 acres of land with a home on it —Stephen Singular, *New York*, 8 Dec. 1975

. . . half of Foxy's home rested on a few cedar posts and Lally columns footed on cinder block —John Updike, *Couples*, 1968

A number of commentators have remarked on the tendency to buy a home and sell a house:

They talked about buying a new, smaller home. . . . They figured they could get $75,000 for their old house —*And More by Andy Rooney*, 1982

There is nothing wrong with distinguishing *home* and *house* if you want to. But be aware that many writers other than those involved in real estate will sometimes use them interchangeably.

home in   See HONE IN ON.

homograph, homophone, homonym   Our correspondence shows that people are occasionally muddled by these words. *Homograph* is used for words that are spelled alike but are different in meaning or derivation or pronunciation: the *bow* of a ship, a *bow* and arrow. *Homophone* is used for words that sound alike but are different in meaning or derivation or spelling: *to, too, two; magnate, magnet; rack, wrack*. *Homonym* is used for homographs or homophones; sometimes it is used more specifically to designate words that are both homographs and homophones, like the verb *quail* and the noun *quail.*

John Algeo, in *The English Language Today* (1985), reports that confusion of homophones is a major subject of usage in the popular press. Homophones certainly present spelling problems, and you will find plenty of them in this book. Homophones are also a primary source of puns.

Hon. See HONORABLE.

hone in on The few usage commentators who have noticed *hone in*—Garner 1998, for instance—consider it to be a mistake for *home in.* It may have arisen from *home in* by the weakening of the \m\ sound to \n\ or may perhaps simply be due to the influence of *hone.* Our earliest citation is from 1965:

> ... looking back for the ball honing in to intercept his line of flight —George Plimpton, *Paper Lion,* 1965

Recent evidence suggests that *hone in on* is becoming increasingly common.

> ... a barrage of phone calls, direct mail and paid canvassers honing in on Republican-leaning people —Robert Dreyfus, *The Nation,* 26 Oct. 1998

> If sideline cameras honed in on golfers the way they do football players, the pros would say, "Hi, Dad" —Tom Callahan, *Golf Digest,* April 1996

> He's using a scope to hone in on their hindquarters —Stanley Bing, *Esquire,* August 1990

> ... investigators had honed in on not the sperm protein but a common protein —*N.Y. Times,* 30 Apr. 1996

Since a number of our citations are from reported speech, *hone in* seems to be common in speech. The phrase seems to have become established in American English, and is apparently beginning to be used in British English (Garner has a British example). If you use it, you should be aware that some people will think you have made a mistake. *Home in* and *zero in* are safe alternatives.

honor When used with a preposition, the verb *honor* may select *by* or *with,* the former occurring a little more frequently than the latter:

> ... would honor its obligation to provide equal treatment to the would-be Negro attorney by establishing a law school —Harry S. Ashmore, *Center Mag.,* May 1968

> ... the only American of Norwegian birth honored by a statue in Oslo —*American Guide Series: Minnesota,* 1938

> In 1945 the Museum of Modern Art honored Strand with a widely praised one-man show —*Current Biography,* July 1965

> ... the only Englishman in all history that the world honors with the surname of Great —Kemp Malone, *Emory University Quarterly,* October 1949

Honor is used less frequently with *for, at,* or *in:*

> ... was honored for excellence in teaching —*Emory & Henry Alumnus,* Summer–Fall 1970

> ... has been honored at half a dozen public luncheons —Joe Alex Morris, *Saturday Evening Post,* 10 July 1954

> ... this principle has been honored in the original allocation of powers —Scott Buchanan, *Center Mag.,* September 1969

Very occasionally, *honor* may be found with *through:*

> The creators were honored through association of their names with their achievements —Lawson M. McKenzie, *Science,* 25 Dec. 1953

Honorable *Honorable* is a title of respect in American use but one with no official standing, and—perhaps not surprisingly—it is the subject of a number of conflicting commentaries. We set aside the vexed question of who is entitled to an *Honorable* and who is not as essentially a matter for books on etiquette, and concentrate here on the more linguistic aspects of the issue.

We can tell you this: the word is capitalized when used as an honorific. It is generally preceded by *the.* It is generally followed by the given name, initials, or some other title (as *Mr.*). It is abbreviated to *Hon.* when appropriate.

Copperud 1980 points out that H. L. Mencken was using the term derisively fifty years ago, and there is evidence that others do not always use the term with solemnity either:

> My former Secretary of Agriculture, the Hon. Charlie Brannan —Harry S. Truman, diary, 24 June 1955

It looks like this in more straightforward surroundings:

> ... the court of the Honorable Harmon T. Langley —Frank De Felitta, *Cosmopolitan,* August 1976

Copperud opines that the term seems "to be going out of use in our blunter age," but that sort of prediction does not always come true.

See also REVEREND.

hoof Both the plurals *hoofs* and *hooves* are in standard use. Phythian 1979 and Copperud

1970, 1980—citing older commentators—say that *hoofs* is more common. But in contemporary print, *hooves* is more common, and especially so in the trade journals of those concerned with horses, cattle, goats, and mules:

> . . . trampled the grass with their hooves —Daniel B. Weems, *Raising Goats,* 1983

> A farrier visits every four to five weeks to trim hooves and reset shoes —Marcia Werts, *Morgan Horse,* July 1984

And it is also more common in general sources:

> The hooves furnished glue —William Least Heat Moon, *Blue Highways,* 1982

> . . . a horse with golden trappings and gilded hooves —E. J. Kahn, Jr., *New Yorker,* 9 July 1984

> . . . the broken swath of weeds its slashing hooves left bowed —Dick Allen, *New Republic,* 10 Apr. 2000

> . . . shoes . . . that look like the hooves of an Icelandic reindeer —André Leon Talley, *Vogue,* April 1998

But *hoofs* is not rare:

> . . . its tiny hoofs —Charles C. Mann, *Natural History,* June 1986

> . . . the muted sound of horses hoofs —Bill Turque, *Newsweek,* 14 Feb. 2000

> . . . sand dunes, where the animals' cloven hoofs would flounder —Ian Frazier, *New Yorker,* 20 Feb. 1989

hope 1. *Hope,* when used with a preposition, is usually followed by *of* or, a little less frequently, by *for:*

> . . . the next year low water defeated hopes of grand-scale river navigation —*American Guide Series: Minnesota,* 1938

> . . . the ability of the present Soviet leaders to fulfil their hopes of efficiency —*Times Literary Supp.,* 9 Apr. 1970

> . . . it was sufficiently promising to arouse hopes for his future —*Times Literary Supp.,* 15 Sept. 1966

> . . . he took his manuscript back from a large New York firm that had low hopes for it —Judith Appelbaum, *N.Y. Times Book Rev.,* 11 May 1983

Very occasionally *hope* is used with *in, on, over* or *to* plus the infinitive:

> He had previously put his hopes in Gambetta —*Times Literary Supp.,* 12 June 1969

> . . . she does not place her hopes on books . . . smuggled out of Russia —*Times Literary Supp.,* 18 May 1967

> . . . a faint stirring of hope over the possibilities of a Korean truce —*Current History,* July 1952

> . . . was their only hope to keep North Carolina from voting so heavily for Wallace —Robert Sherrill, *Saturday Rev.,* 17 June 1972

Hope may also be followed by a clause introduced by *that:*

> . . . expressed his hopes that such programs could reverse "the worst tendency in . . . education . . ." —*Current Biography,* January 1966

2. *Hope* is used idiomatically in all the following phrases: *in the hope(s) of, in hope(s) of, in the hope(s) that,* and *in hope(s) that.*

> In the hope of bringing about a peaceful settlement —Senator Mike Mansfield, in *A Center Occasional Paper,* June 1968

> They put to sea . . . in the hopes of drifting across the Pacific —Geoffrey Murray, *Christian Science Monitor,* 4 June 1980

> . . . do not invert the normal order of words in hopes of sounding more genteel —Barzun 1985

> . . . doping out basketball scores in hope of one day winning a pool —Evan Hunter, *N.Y. Times Book Rev.,* 13 Nov. 1983

> . . . in the hope that the issue could be resolved —Bernard Gwertzman, *N.Y. Times Mag.,* 4 May 1980

> We're lumping them all together here in the hopes that somewhere in the pile you will come across just what you need —*New Yorker,* 17 Dec. 1950

> In hopes that something good might be brought out of the ruins, he began to pick up —John Fischer, *Harper's,* December 1969

At one time an infinitive may have followed *in hopes,* but this construction seems not to occur in contemporary writing:

> . . . to see the End of it, and in Hopes to make something of it at last —Daniel Defoe, *Moll Flanders,* 1722

Also occurring in idiomatic use are the phrases *with the hope(s) of* and *with the hope that.* The former occurs with either the singular or plural of *hope,* although the singular occurs more often. The latter is attested in our evidence only in the singular:

> . . . with the hope of establishing a government that was both anti-Communist and anti-Fascist —*Current Biography,* June 1964

> . . . and with the hopes of having it repaid them with interest, whenever they have oc-

casion to return the visit —Thomas Gray, letter, 9 Oct. 1740

. . . to ascertain student views with the hope that they might understand —Donald Mc-Donald, *Center Mag.*, July–August 1970

With the hope of has some slight variations, such as *with little hope of, with any hope of,* and *with its hope of.*

hopefully No one knows why a word or phrase or construction suddenly becomes popular—it just happens. And when it does, it is sure to attract the displeased attention of some guardian of the language. The split infinitive, for instance, seems to have become suddenly popular during the 19th century, and there are still people who worry about it. The sentence-modifying use of the adverb *hopefully* is a like case, and it is recent enough that its history can be traced reasonably clearly.

One problem in tracing the history of *hopefully* as a sentence adverb has been the paucity of pre-1960s evidence. The OED has a single 1932 example, and Merriam-Webster only a couple from the 1950s. This shortage has happily been remedied by Fred R. Shapiro (*American Speech,* Fall 1998 and Winter 1999). Using recently available electronic databases, he found that sentence-adverbial *hopefully* was both older (he found 1702 and 1851 examples) and more common than had been supposed. His evidence shows the construction well established in the 1930s:

. . . a settlement final until now, which drew boundaries in a viable and hopefully permanent form —Albert Howe Lybyer, *American Historical Rev.,* 1933 (in Shapiro, *American Speech,* Fall 1998)

. . . we will have a perfectly swell script and, hopefully, one that is near the proper length —David O. Selznick, memo, 25 Feb. 1938 (in Shapiro, *American Speech,* Fall 1998)

The use seems to have continued in a fairly frequent fashion through the 1940s and 1950s, below the radar of the usage commentators. (Much of Shapiro's evidence comes from professional journals, where commentators never look.) And his evidence corroborates the observation of Copperud 1970, 1980, that the rapid expansion of use of *hopefully* as a sentence modifier began "about 1960." The evidence in our files shows a considerable increase beginning in 1964.

The onslaught against *hopefully* in the popular press began in 1965 and reached a peak around 1975, which is the year the issue seems to have crossed the Atlantic. Viewers with alarm there would repeat all the things American viewers with alarm had said, and add the charge of "Americanism" to them.

The *locus classicus* of most of the charges

leveled against sentence-modifying *hopefully* is Follett 1966. Follett died in January 1963, and it is likely that his analysis was one of the earliest to be written down. He seems to have been the originator of the theory that this use of *hopefully* was un-English and that it came from "hack translators" of German who used it to translate the German *hoffentlich.* But he does not produce any hack translations to back up his assertion; all his examples seem to be from American newspapers. Besides the irrelevant German objection he also complains that this *hopefully* lacks point of view and adds a social objection demeaning people who use vogue words. His discussion lacks only a complaint about the loss of the original sense of the word, but others were around to supply it. (This complaint appears as recently as Garner 1998.)

Hopefully in its vilified use is a sentence adverb, or, to use a term from Quirk et al. 1985, a disjunct. Disjuncts serve as a means by which an author or speaker can comment directly to the reader or hearer, usually on content of the sentence to which they are attached. Many other adverbs (such as *interestingly, clearly, frankly*) are used in this way, and most of them are so common as to pass entirely unnoticed.

We should point out that opinion has not been unanimously opposed to this usage. Besides a defender or two, there were handbooks that noted both acceptance and objection. After a few years some commentators changed their minds and others gave up the fight. On 10 November 1985 the Prince of Wales used the word during a televised press conference at the Smithsonian Institution in Washington. What more prestigious cachet can be put on it?

The sentence-modifying *hopefully* has by no means driven the older senses from use:

. . . tempers the gloom, adding hopefully, "and there may be a lesson in that." —Baron 1982

. . . many who have set out hopefully upon it have turned back, frustrated and disheartened —Barnard 1979

To sum up: *hopefully* had been in sporadic American use as a sentence modifier for some thirty years before it suddenly caught fire in the early 1960s. What is newly popular will often be disparaged, and criticism followed rapidly, starting in 1962 and reaching a high point around 1975. There has been a considerable abatement in the fuss since and many commentators now accept the usage, but it seems safe to predict that there will be some who continue to revile it well into the new century. You can use it if you need to, or avoid it if you do not like it. There never was anything wrong with it.

See also SENTENCE ADVERB.

horde See HOARD, HORDE.

host This 15th-century transitive verb dropped out of sight during the 17th century and reappeared in the late 19th. Around 1960 it was discovered by American usage writers, who forthwith condemned it as the creation of either society columnists or ordinary journalists. Usage panels have rejected it. The basis of all this disapprobation seems to be the mistaken notion that the verb is a modern coinage. Although its origin has been well documented, *host* is still being disparaged by a few commentators. One of our most recent would replace *host* with an intransitive phrase, ignoring grammar, and another believes it can routinely be replaced by *entertain*. Try that solution in these examples:

> Moscow had backed out of its promise to host the World's Fair —Frank Deford, *Sports Illustrated*, 28 Sept. 1970

> . . . on television in Pittsburgh, where he briefly hosted an afternoon variety show —*Current Biography*, February 1967

> . . . a reception hosted by the governor of Styria —Nina FitzPatrick, *Fables of the Irish Intelligentsia*, 1991

> Great Britain has not hosted the Games since the London Olympics of 1948 —*British Heritage*, October/November 1993

> We can also make a case for sexually dimorphic species hosting fewer parasites —Deborah A. McLennan & Daniel R. Brooks, *Quarterly Rev. of Biology*, September 1991.

Perhaps an acquaintance with actual usage would help our commentators. *Host* is fully established and standard.

house See HOME *noun*, HOUSE.

hove See HEAVE.

how *How* as a conjunction in the sense of *that* is aspersed by Ayres 1881, Vizetelly 1906, Bernstein 1965, and Phythian 1979—which makes nearly a century of aspersing. The usage itself is a bit older, however; the OED tracks it back to Aelfric, the Anglo-Saxon grammarian and writer of religious prose, around 1000. It is a little unfair to equate the usage flatly with *that*, although the OED does so and our dictionaries do too. It is, in fact, a usage in which the underlying notion of "the way or manner in which" is weakened to varying extents, and in many cases appears—at least to the modern reader—to be entirely absent. Here are a few older examples of the use:

> And anon the tidings came to king Philip of France how the King of England was at Boulogne —Lord Berners, translation of Froissart's *Chronicles*, 1523

> When therefore the Lord knew how the Pharisees had heard that Jesus made and baptized more disciples than John —John 1:4 (AV), 1611

> And it is pretty to hear how the King had some notice of this challenge a week or two ago, and did give it to my Lord General to confine the Duke —Samuel Pepys, diary, 17 Jan. 1668

> I have heard how some critics have been pacified with claret and a supper, and others laid asleep with soft notes of flattery —Samuel Johnson (in Ayres 1881)

> Bob Cratchit told them how he had a situation in his eye for Master Peter —Charles Dickens, *A Christmas Carol*, 1844 (in OED)

If there is a problem with this use of *how*—and Evans 1957 declares it standard—it may be that it is falling out of literary and written use and being more and more confined to speech. We do have 20th-century evidence, but not a great deal since mid-century, except in speech:

> It was odd how writers never seemed to have anything to do except write or live —Martha Gellhorn, *Atlantic*, March 1953

> I won't waste your time this afternoon in telling you, in the political tradition, all about how I am myself a farmer —Adlai E. Stevenson, *Speeches*, ed. Richard Harrity, 1952

The OED notes that this sense of *how* has appeared as part of the compounds *how that* (found in Chaucer and the King James Bible) and *as how* (attested as early as Smollett's *Roderick Random* in 1748); *how that* is apparently no longer used, but *as how* continues in modern use. See AS HOW.

how come *How come* is a familiar phrase of obscure origin that first came to attention as an Americanism in the middle of the 19th century. We say "of obscure origin" because for a time there was considerable speculation about its origin. Interest in its origin seems to have waned in the last half century.

Krapp 1927 labels it colloquial and slang; Evans 1957, Bernstein 1965, and Harper 1975, 1985 find *how come* unsuitable in writing. Reader's Digest 1983 dismisses it as "informal only." Garner 1998 calls it "very informal." Flesch 1964 finds it an acceptable and useful idiom, however, and Safire 1982 defends it spiritedly against Bernstein, Evans, and Harper, as well as a couple of correspondents.

How come is a little bit like the verb *bust*: its use in writing is on a higher level than its use in speech seems to be—it is a social climber in print. Its rise in respectability probably started after World War II. We have many journalistic examples:

> And yet for all this self-indulgence, he has managed somehow to achieve what Max Beerbohm called in his own case "a very pleasant little reputation." How come? —Joseph Wood Krutch, *Saturday Rev.*, 30 Jan. 1954

> . . . and how come he's our moral tutor in this fear-and-loathing tour of the Clinton sex scandals? —Christopher Hitchens, *N.Y. Times Book Rev.*, 30 July 2000

> If you use a laptop, you will recall gratefully that it does not matter whether the electrical source is 220 volts or 110, you just plug it in. How come? —William F. Buckley, Jr., *National Rev.*, 29 Sept. 1997

> And, for that matter, how come they never have donuts in Peking . . . ? —*And More by Andy Rooney*, 1982

> Construction was obviously not stone, but iron. How come? —Edwards Park, *Smithsonian*, February 1985

> . . . how come British rock and rollers . . . have such admirable longevity compared to American counterparts . . .? —Jay McInerney, *Times Literary Supp.*, 27 July–2 Aug. 1990

Writers simply seem to find *how come* a sassier—Safire says "nastier"—and more emphatic *why*. We have not yet found it in surroundings more elevated than those we have quoted.

however   The main problem raised by the commentators about *however* is its placement in the sentence. When used to mean "on the other hand, nevertheless, but" some commentators—Strunk & White 1959, 1972, 1979 and Zinsser 1976 among them—hold that *however* should not begin a sentence. This opinion is older than Strunk & White, but we are not certain where it began. Harper 1975, 1985, Bremner 1980, Bernstein 1971, and Heritage 1982 disagree with the prohibition; Bremner calls it a myth. Copperud 1970, 1980, Bremner, Bernstein, and Janis 1984 make the point that the *however* should be placed where it most effectively emphasizes the words the writer wants to emphasize. Here are a few examples of how other writers have chosen to place *however*:

> Critics were in general agreement in praising his sensitivity and fluent technique. . . . Some, however, found fault —*Current Biography*, July 1967

> Clearly the Guevara diaries were documents of the greatest political and historical inter-

est and importance. However, neither the Bolivians nor the Americans . . . were at first prepared to authorize their publication —*Times Literary Supp.*, 14 Nov. 1968

> Black revolutionaries also face ethical dilemmas, however —Denis Goulet, *Center Mag.*, May 1969

> It would have to come when I was in no state to answer your letter with words of cheer. However, better late than never —James Thurber, letter, 19 Mar. 1940

The only point that needs to be made is that there is no absolute rule for the placement of *however*; each writer must decide each instance on its own merits, and place the word where it best accomplishes its purpose.

The treatment of the subject in Strunk & White suggests that placing *however* first in the sentence makes it mean "to whatever extent" or "in whatever way." In fact, the context determines this sense of *however* no matter where it occurs in the sentence:

> Such are the harsh facts, and no new formulas, however ingenious, . . . can make them disappear —Walter Laqueur, *Commentary*, January 1972

human   At the noun entry for *human* in the OED, Murray, the editor, observes that it was formerly much used, but, he continues, it is "now chiefly *humorous* or *affected*." It is hard to find much that seems either humorous or affected in the 19th-century examples he offers, however. Murray was very conscious of competing with the American *Century Dictionary*, and he may have picked up his *humorous* from their "Now colloq. or humorous." The *Century* label perhaps came by a circuitous route from the examples from American humorists in Bartlett's *Dictionary of Americanisms*.

From such slender beginnings arose a minor industry of disparaging the noun use—an industry almost entirely based on not looking at the OED examples, dating back to Lord Berners in the 16th century.

The curious thing about this issue is its persistence in what may be called the folklore of usage—that is, persistence in believing something is wrong with this noun in spite of its having been declared standard by such commentators as Bernstein 1965, 1971, Evans 1957, and Flesch 1964. The persistence of both views is reflected in contemporary handbooks: Guth 1985 says it is not generally accepted while Irmscher 1978 says it is acceptable. Copperud 1970, 1980 says there is still substantial objection to it. And the evidence seems to show that writers tend to avoid it even now; our recent citations include a great many more examples of *human being* than of *human.*

> . . . he can give scientific reasons for thinking that humans (or some humans) might have been expected to have tails —Howard 1983

> . . . that microbes . . . caused diseases and that insects carried them to humans —*Johns Hopkins Mag.,* Summer 1967

> While lower animals can deceive and mislead through camouflage and similar devices, as far as we know only humans can consciously and deliberately lie —Carol Z. Malatesta, *N.Y. Times Book Rev.,* 31 Mar. 1985

Our conclusion is that even though this noun has been standard for some 450 years, many people still believe that it is somehow tainted and avoid it.

hung   See HANG, HANGED, HUNG.

hypallage   See RAISING.

hypercorrection   Sir Isaac Newton set down three laws of motion, the third of which is often stated thus: "For every action there is an equal and opposite reaction." If we were to translate this—albeit roughly—to apply to usage and grammar, we might get something like "For every correction there is an equal and opposite hypercorrection." *Hypercorrection* is a term used by linguists and grammarians for "equal and opposite" errors made in the course of avoiding other errors which are frequently subjected to correction.

The most frequently discussed hypercorrections involve pronouns, especially the use of a nominative pronoun in a slot calling for an objective pronoun. Examples:

> . . . the most irritating thing to we military people —four-star general on television, 6 Nov. 1983

> . . . designed for you and I —radio commercial, 3 Mar. 1980

Such pronoun mistakes are particularly frequent in compound objects such as *you and I, my wife and I.* How many of these are really the result of hypercorrection is a matter that can be disputed, since such usages can be found dating back farther than the inception of traditional grammar. *Between you and I* is frequently mentioned as a hypercorrection; yet it can be found as long ago as the diary of Samuel Pepys, who wrote "between my wife and I" on 5 July 1663. And we hear it put in the mouths of characters in Restoration comedies:

> . . . Impertinent people, which, between you and I *Jack,* are so numerous —Thomas Shadwell, *The Sullen Lovers,* 1668

You will find more on this subject at BETWEEN YOU AND I and at PRONOUNS.

Another hypercorrect pronoun usage is the substitution of *whom* for *who* in sentences like "Whom shall I say is calling?" You will find more on this at WHO, WHOM 1.

Another common hypercorrection involves the use of an *-ly* adverb where an adjective or flat adverb is called for:

> . . . there's an awfully lot of methane and ammonia in the universe —exobiologist, quoted in *Science News,* 16 Aug. 1969

> . . . the seldomly used player —network television baseball announcer, Fall 1986

> . . . because he tested positively for steroids —network television sports announcer, 25 Dec. 1986

> . . . unless my eyes have gone badly —cable television sports announcer, 3 Nov. 1985

> . . . go home and think deeply, longly, and . . . —Boston city councilman, 4 Aug. 1983

> I once had a dentist who never failed to say "open widely" —John Ciardi, in Harper 1985

Lamberts 1972 lists the disputed adverbs *muchly, thusly,* and *soonly* as forms created by hypercorrection.

Similarly we will sometimes find *well* for *good*:

> . . . make your dog look as well as possible —dog handler at Westminster dog show, 11 Feb. 1985

> A correct use, cited just to show how well it sounds —Copperud 1964

Some instances of what look like hypercorrect adverbs after linking verbs may be lingering traces of an older style of using adverbs instead of adjectives after such verbs. You will find one common example of this practice discussed at LOOK 1.

Another substitution occasionally mentioned as a hypercorrection is the use of *as* in place of *like*:

> All three lamps are pure brass, and not brass plated, as some similar looking products —advt., *New Yorker,* 1 Feb. 1988

This is another practice with long-standing antecedents. See LIKE, AS, AS IF 2.

Perrin & Ebbitt 1972 also mentions as hypercorrections the substitution of some verb forms for others, such as using *lie* for *lay,* and certain pronunciations. Robert F. Ilson, in *The English Language Today* (1985), mentions the involuted sentences typically produced in trying to avoid a terminal preposition. And Allan Metcalf, in *American Speech,* Fall 1984, mentions a new one: the insistence by some on using *his or her* as a nonsexist substitute for generic *his* or disapproved *their* is leading to the use of the singular form even when the antecedent is plural. See HE, HE OR SHE.

Hypercorrections are also called *hyperurbanisms*.

See also SUBJUNCTIVE.

hyperforeignisms By analogy with the terms *hypercorrection* (which see) and *hyperurbanism* ("aiming for a prestige form and overshooting the mark"), we suggest the term *hyperforeignism* to denote an unsuccessful attempt to give an authentic foreign pronunciation to a foreign-derived word being used in English context. Such flubs open the speaker up to ridicule much more than garden-variety, down-home mispronunciations such as \'rev-ə-lent\ for *relevant*, since the spectacle of people seemingly trying to get above themselves and then coming a cropper attracts the hoots of both democrats and aristocrats. A veteran columnist writes:

> One of our most famous TV anchorpersons . . . pronounces coup de grâce "coo dee grah." How refeened —Herb Caen, *San Francisco Chronicle*, 16 Oct. 1987

The hapless anchorperson may have misguidedly dropped the final \s\ with *Mardi Gras* (pronounced \'märd-ē-ˌgrä\) in mind. More than one ambitious diner has likewise overgeneralized and committed the faux pas (\fō-'pä\) of ordering vichyssoise as \ˌvē-shē-'swä\. (As a rule of thumb, French leaves *s* silent only when it is the last letter of a word.)

Another Gallic trap lies in the pronunciation of *e*, especially at the end of a word, where most of the problems arise. When surmounted by an acute accent (as in *café* or *attaché*) or followed by silent *r* or *t* (as in *beret* or *pourparler*), the pronunciation is \ā\; but when not so accompanied (as in *cache* \'kash\ or *vichyssoise* or *à la carte*) the final *e* is silent. Yet we have occasionally recorded educated speakers rendering *cache* as \ka-'shä\, perhaps misled by *cachet*, which is indeed pronounced that way. A different problem arises in the cases of words like *chancre*, where a truly French pronunciation would violate phonological constraints of English. The usual solution, especially with older loanwords of this type (*massacre, mediocre, reconnoitre/reconnoiter, theatre/theater*), is to end the word with a fully anglicized \-ər\. *Raison d'être*, a more recent loan and still quite foreign-looking, gets either an authentic French pronunciation with voiceless final \r\ or the nearest more-or-less-English equivalent, with \-rə\. *Cadre* is a special case, the most common pronunciations being \'kad-rē\ and \'käd-rā\—the latter rhyming with, and possibly modeled on, the

Spanish loan *padre*. For more on final *e*, see FORTE.

Our passing reference above to "silent *r*" skirts another area of difficulty. Again a rule of thumb: French *r* is silent only at the end of a word after *e*, and not always then. The rather widespread pronunciation of *reservoir* as \'rez-ə(r)-ˌvwä\ is pseudo-French.

In a curious position are a couple of words long naturalized in English which sometimes get partly French pronunciations even from people who have no idea that the words were borrowed from French. The case of *envelope*, of which the \'än-\ version has attracted some withering comment, is discussed at ENVELOPE. The pronunciation \'sänt-ə-ˌmēt-er\ for *centimeter* may have conceivably been influenced by *centime*, though it is specially prevalent not among money people but among nurses and doctors. These pronunciations are not incorrect—they are French as far as they go—but by now one would expect to hear consistently the fully anglicized \en\ in these words.

Queen of the hyperforeignisms is *lingerie*. Of the multitudinous pronunciation variants for this word, the most common seems to be \ˌlän-jə-'rā\, the product of some extremely tenuous analogies with words like *entrée*. An approximation to the French would be \ˌlaⁿ-zhə-(ˌ)rē\, but, while that pronunciation is certainly established, so many others are also established that it is unlikely to sweep the field.

In another category of hyperforeignism, a form is created not by the overly enthusiastic application of sound-spelling correspondence rules from the lender language, but by the application of more familiar rules from a *different* language. Thus, Americans are aware, from examples like *chancre* and *cachet* and a dozen others, that the French pronounce *ch* as \sh\. Having mastered this much, they proceed to rechristen Chile's president Augusto Pinochet (\ˌpē-nō-'chet\) Gallically as \ˌpē-nō-'shä\, though Spanish *ch* is pronounced \ch\ as in English. Among generic words, Italian-derived *adagio* \ä-'dä-jō\ gets Frenchified as \ä-'däzh-ō\, but gets its revenge when we pronounce the Latin-derived *viva voce* (\ˌvī-və-'vō-sē\) as if it were from Italian, \ˌvē-və-'vō-chä\. Both of these pronunciations are well established.

hyphen, hyphenate Phythian 1979 objects to *hyphenate* as unnecessarily long since *hyphen* is already a verb. *Hyphenate*, however, is the more common of the two:

> . . . although long-lived is hyphenated —Simon 1980

> Photocomposition is particularly stupid at breaking words and hyphenating them in the wrong places —Howard 1984

Hyphenate is probably reinforced in its preferred position by the noun *hyphenation,* the noun *hyphenate,* and the adjective *hyphenated.* There is also a verb *hyphenize,* which is very seldom used.

hypothecate, hypothesize Einstein 1985 admits that in his head *hypothecate* and *hypothesize* mean essentially the same thing and that his ear prefers *hypothecate.* He then bemoans the fact that they mean different things—as you will be told they do if you listen to Shaw 1987 or Bernstein 1962 or Garner 1998 or Fowler 1926, or if you look in an old dictionary. But if you look in Webster's Third you will find two verbs spelled *hypothecate* with different derivations. The newer one (dating from 1906) does mean "hypothesize." The newer one can also be found in the OED Supplement, which, however, does not accord it a separate entry.

Neither verb *hypothecate* is often used, and the two appear not only in different contexts but in different sources. The older *hypothecate,* which has to do with pledging something for security, appears in business and legal contexts. The newer *hypothecate,* meaning "hypothesize," seems to be found most often in scientific writing and in linguistics, and only occasionally elsewhere—the OED Supplement has a letter of Ezra Pound's and we have an example from a high-school text on art history.

So, Mr. Einstein and others can feel free to use the word their ear prefers. Many more writers use *hypothesize*; in our files it is more than twice as common as both verbs *hypothecate* put together.

I

I The entries at *I* in many usage books—Cook 1985, Nickles 1974, Copperud 1970, 1980, Venolia 1982, and Bryson 1984, among others—deal primarily with issues discussed to some extent elsewhere in the same book or in someone else's book. The leading topic of commentary is the use of *I* in some object position where *me* would be expected, and especially as the second part of a compound of the "someone and I" type.

> I have been planning a piece on personal pronouns and the death of the accusative. Nobody says "I gave it to they," but "me" is almost dead, and I have heard its dying screams from Bermuda to Columbus: "He gave it to Janey and I." . . . Love to you and she from Helen and I —James Thurber, letter, 25 June 1956

You will find more on this and related subjects in the articles at BETWEEN YOU AND I; HYPERCORRECTION; IT'S ME; MYSELF; PRONOUNS.

Other aspects of the first person singular pronoun and its use or avoidance can be found at WE 1 and PRESENT WRITER.

-ic, -ical English contains a considerable number of adjective pairs ending in *-ic* and *-ical*: for instance, *biologic, biological; electric, electrical; ironic, ironical; mythic, mythical.* Some of these pairs are essentially interchangeable while others are differentiated in use. A number of these pairs have been treated in usage books, and you'll find some of them here: see CLASSIC, CLASSICAL; ECONOMIC, ECONOMICAL; HISTORIC, HISTORICAL.

If you are uncertain which of a given pair of these adjectives to use, you had better rely on a good dictionary, such as Merriam-Webster's Collegiate Dictionary. A good dictionary will show you which senses belong to which variants if they are indeed differentiated in use. Sometimes there is less differentiation than usage writers would like there to be.

ideal *Ideal* is sometimes considered to be an absolute adjective. See ABSOLUTE ADJECTIVES.

identical *Identical,* says Bernstein 1965, takes the preposition *with* or *to.* But in *Winners & Sinners,* 15 Oct. 1964, he had taken a different view. Criticizing this sentence,

> He said that Presidents Dwight D. Eisenhower and John F. Kennedy, faced with similar legislation, had taken positions identical to his —*N.Y. Times,* 9 Oct. 1964

Bernstein said "the favored preposition is 'with', not 'to.' " Where he derived this idea is uncertain, unless he saw Follett 1966 in manuscript (Follett prescribes *with* but shows only examples with *to*) or Treble & Vallins 1937 (who prescribe *with,* not mentioning *to*).

Opinion on the matter is divided between Treble & Vallins 1937, Sellers 1975, Phythian 1979 (all British), Colter 1981 (Canadian), Himstreet & Baty 1977 (U.S.), and Follett 1966 (U.S.), who prescribe *identical with* and Bernstein 1965, Copperud 1970, 1980, Harper

1975, 1985, Heritage 2000, Longman 1984, and Garner 1998, who accept both *with* and *to*.

Evidence shows *identical with* to be the older form, attested in the OED as far back as the 17th century. Follett claims that *identical to* is an Americanism, but the evidence is too sketchy to be certain of that. Its use is not exclusively American; Longman 1984 recognizes British use, and we have a few examples:

> Apart from their size the young are almost identical to the adults —Mark Carwardine, *Encyclopedia of World Wildlife*, 1986.

> . . . almost identical to 'true' pitcher plants found elsewhere —John Vandenbeld, *Nature of Australia*, 1988

> This situation is identical to the survival in North America of earlier English terms that have long since passed out of use in the mother country —John Geipel, *The Viking Legacy*, 1971

Our evidence shows *identical with* to be almost twice as frequent as *identical to*. Neither preposition appears to be eclipsing the other, and both are fully acceptable. We note only one trace of preference in our evidence: all of our mathematical citations use *with*. Here are a handful of examples of both constructions:

> The boat was small, identical to the one in which they landed —Norman Mailer, *The Naked and the Dead*, 1948

> . . . so the theater we visit today is architecturally identical to the one Jefferson knew —Diana Ketcham, *American Heritage*, April 1995

> . . . when 0 is added to any given number, the sum is identical with the given number —Mary P. Dolciani et al., *Modern Algebra and Trigonometry*, 1973

> . . . my own early convictions—which were identical with his —E. B. White, letter, 30 Jan. 1976

> . . . Those adverbs that take comparative inflections are generally identical with adjectives —Sidney Greenbaum, *The Oxford English Grammar*, 1996

identify   When *identify* is used with a preposition, it is usually *with*:

> He identified vigorously with J. Edgar Hoover, the great sleuth —A. J. Liebling, *New Yorker*, 9 Oct. 1954

> . . . my father in some way identified himself with the Great Commoner, and this seemed to me purely a pose —Edmund Wilson, *A Piece of My Mind*, 1956

> . . . the reader watches an imagined consciousness unfold and identifies with it —Howard Mumford Jones, *Saturday Rev.*, 23 Apr. 1955

> . . . Whitman found himself as man and artist by identifying with New York —Alfred Kazin, *Harper's*, December 1968

This sense of *identify* apparently was borrowed from the field of psychology in which it began to be used in the early 20th century. There is no disagreement among language commentators with the fact that the use is firmly established and is acceptable. Rather, disagreement arises about the use or nonuse of the reflexive pronoun. Follett 1966, Macmillan 1982, Harper 1985, and Simon 1980 all maintain that omission of the pronoun is an error arising from the jargon of psychology. Up until the 1940s, our evidence shows that the pronoun was used more often than not; more recently, however, use of the pronoun has become optional, as you can see from the examples above. The usage panel of Heritage 2000 finds either use or nonuse of the pronoun acceptable.

idiom   *Idiom* is a word you will find with some frequency in this book, as in most usage books. It is not an especially precise word, and it is generally used by usage writers for some construction or expression that they approve of but cannot analyze.

The word is frequently applied to those expressions or constructions that either are not transparent from the usual current meanings of the individual words that make them up or that appear to violate some grammatical precept.

The tension between idiomatic usage and logical analysis is one of the chief sources of usage comment, and has been since at least the middle of the 18th century. For a typical 18th-century treatment of an idiom, see HAD RATHER.

idiosyncrasy, idiosyncracy   A number of critics since Fowler 1926 (Watt 1967, Copperud 1964, 1970, 1980, Bryson 1984, Burchfield 1996, Garner 1998) warn against the *-cy* spelling, calling it a misspelling.

The evidence in the OED shows that the *-cy* spelling goes back as far as Sir Thomas Browne's *Pseudodoxia Epidemica* in 1650; there are also some 19th-century examples. It has been in occasional use since. It was recognized as a secondary variant in Webster's Third because of its appearance in reputable publications. Some examples:

> . . . indulged for his "genius" of which he took his idiosyncracy to be one indicator —Garry Wills, *N.Y. Times Book Rev.*, 10 Sept. 1989

> . . . showing us merely the idiosyncracy of people —V. S. Pritchett, *A Man of Letters*, 1985

. . . brings his own talents and idiosyncracies to conservation —Ken Slocum, *Wall Street Jour.*, 21 June 1983

Since *idiosyncracy* has been in use for nearly 350 years, it is probably time to stop thinking of it as a misspelling; it is a misspelling only from the standpoint of etymology, not of educated usage. But we remind you that it is a secondary variant—*idiosyncrasy* is much more common—and you will probably be better off sticking to the more common spelling.

i.e., e.g. Usage books note that these two abbreviations tend to be confused with each other. Our evidence shows that the usual error is the use of *i.e.* in place of *e.g.* The error is relatively rare in edited material, but it does seem to occur widely in speech and casual writing. To avoid it, remember that *i.e.* is an abbreviation for the Latin *id est* and means "that is"; *e.g.* is an abbreviation of *exempli gratia* and means "for example." *I.e.*, like *that is*, typically introduces a rewording or clarification of a statement that has just been made or of a word that has just been used:

Most of the new books are sold through 3,500 Christian (i.e., Protestant) bookstores —*N.Y. Times Book Rev.*, 31 Oct. 1976

It is money that wasn't absorbed by government, i.e. the administration tax cuts, that is spurring current growth —Joe Sneed & John Tatlock, *Houston Post*, 31 Aug. 1984

E.g. introduces one or more examples that illustrate something stated directly or shortly before it:

Poets whose lack of these isn't made up by an inescapable intensity of personal presence (e.g. Sylvia Plath) simply aren't represented —Hugh Kenner, *N.Y. Times Book Rev.*, 17 Oct. 1976

. . . rent them to responsible tenants, e.g., retired naval officers —David Schoenbaum, *N.Y. Times*, 3 July 1977

If you feel uncertain about which abbreviation is called for in a particular context, try substituting *that is* or *for example*, or else revise the sentence so that neither is required.

if 1. *If, whether.* The notion that *if* may not introduce a noun clause, as *whether* may, goes back to an obscure 18th-century dictionary editor, J. Johnson. This Johnson—not to be confused with Samuel Johnson—prefixed a 20-page grammar to his New Royal and Universal English Dictionary of 1762 and in it he attacked a number of Scotticisms, among which was *question if* for *question whether.*

We know of no other comments on *if* "whether" after J. Johnson until the issue turns up a century later in Alford 1866. Alford clearly had the question raised by a correspondent who thought that *if* should not be so used. Alford says, "I cannot see that there is anything to complain of in it" and duly notes its use in the Book of Genesis and in Dryden and Prior. But Ayres 1881 condemns it, and so do a great many commentators of the 1920s and 1930s.

More recent American commentators, however, tend to take Alford's attitude. Evans 1957, Copperud 1964, 1970, 1980, Bernstein 1965, 1971, Perrin & Ebbitt 1972, Watt 1967, Irmscher 1976, Bryant 1962, and others find the usage standard. A number of these, as well as Janis 1984 and Shaw 1987, also add that *whether* is the word more often used in formal contexts. Holdouts for Ayres's position include Harper 1975, 1985 and a few British sources—Sellers 1975, Phythian 1979, and Chambers 1985 (Burchfield 1996 prefers *whether* without condemning *if*).

The OED and Jespersen 1909–49 (vol. 3) trace the construction back to Old English. Jespersen finds it in Shakespeare:

How shall I know if I do choose the right? —*The Merchant of Venice*, 1597

As Evans points out, this use of *if* has never actually been restricted; the whole question of its propriety is the invention of J. Johnson and his successors. Yet the notion that *whether* and not *if* should be used to introduce such a clause is still at large; Mary Vaiana Taylor in *College English*, April 1974, found 20 percent of the teaching assistants she polled marking *if* wrong in such sentences. It may be the persistence of this notion that makes *whether* predominate in formal contexts. Here are a few examples of this use of *if*:

. . . I asked her if she was engaged to Sam Fiske —Emily Dickinson, letter, 19 Mar. 1854

Dr. Crowther fingered his tie to feel if it were straight —Aldous Huxley, *Point Counter Point*, 1928

We've been having days I doubt if you could beat in Colorado —Robert Frost, letter, 1 Nov. 1927

. . . I doubt if one writer ever has a satisfactory conversation with another writer —William Faulkner, 16 May 1957, in *Faulkner in the University*, 1959

And keep an eye on the temperature gauge to see if the engine runs too hot —*Consumer Reports*, April 1980

If there's a swindler in the bookkeeping department at the bank, I doubt if he's going to pick my account to steal from —*And More by Andy Rooney*, 1982

We can use the example by Andy Rooney to illustrate a point made by Otto Jespersen: the "whether" sense of *if* is not used at the beginning of a sentence. Initial *if* (the first word in the example) is understood as the ordinary conditional use. The "whether" sense is rarely found except after a verb, although it is sometimes used after adjectives:

> It is extremely doubtful if it could be used with any success —Raymond W. Bliss, *Atlantic,* November 1952

2. Copperud 1970, 1980 cites Flesch 1964 and Fowler 1965 as being opposed to *if* in the sense of "though"; Harper 1985 and Garner 1998 also dislike it. These seem to be examples of the construction questioned:

> . . . sets out to make a fairly routine, if exhaustive, search of the caves —John S. Bowman, *Saturday Rev.,* 23 Oct. 1971

> . . . a man possessed of such satanic, if controlled, fury on a football field —George Plimpton, *Harper's,* May 1971

> . . . the excellence of its traditional, if routine, services —Nicholas Pileggi, *New York,* 24 July 1972

The construction is standard—and it is quite common.

if and when This rather innocuous-looking phrase has been the subject of attack from Fowler 1907 to Garner 1998. The gist of the problem is that you can get by with either *if* or *when* and that you shouldn't use both. One commentator puts it succinctly: "Use whichever one you mean, but not both." This advice will work in quite a few instances:

> . . . can sell out at full fair market value if and when it chooses to do so —Laura Saunders, *Forbes,* 1 Mar. 1993

> But we will have to do our part if and when the time comes —*New Republic,* 19 Apr. 1999

> . . . such a mortgage becomes established if and when the property is acquired by the mortgagor —*Louisiana Civil Code,* 1980

It might be noted that either *if* or *when* could be used alone without substantially altering the meaning. Burchfield 1996 thinks the phrase could be useful when both notions are wanted:

> When a player "blew out" his knee team officials were more concerned with if and when he might return to action than with which ligament he had shredded —Richard Demak, *Sports Illustrated,* 29 Apr. 1991

The amount of critical fire seems disproportionate to the problem. The addition of two probably unnecessary syllables is likely to cause no crisis of space in print nor loss of breath in speech.

We suspect you will seldom have a real need for *if and when,* but if it slips out, it is a trivial offense.

if worst comes to worst See WORST COMES TO WORST.

ignoramus Fowler 1926, Burchfield 1996, Evans 1957, and Garner 1998 insist that the only plural for *ignoramus* is *ignoramuses,* not *ignorami.* This assertion is based on the grounds that *ignoramus* is derived from a Latin verb and not from a noun. Well, in legal language it is. But the common use comes from a character in a play (*Ignoramus,* 1615, by George Ruggle) whose name came from the legal term. The objected-to plural does have some actual use—perhaps facetious, in some cases—but not a great deal. It began to turn up in our files in the 1920s.

> . . . the gawks and ignorami who circulated around the schoolhouse back in Hickory Creek —*Literary Digest,* 5 May 1923

We have about half a dozen examples from the 1920s, but nothing after that until the mid-1960s:

> And you can't think how it annoys me to see the New Ignorami of criticism refer to him merely as *Twain,* as if that were his real name —Katherine Anne Porter, *N.Y. Herald Tribune Book Week,* 26 Dec. 1965

> Such missteps, while often howlingly funny to ignorami like us, are deadly serious concerns to psychologists and linguists —Roger Rosenblatt, in *The Bedford Reader,* ed. X. J. Kennedy & Dorothy M. Kennedy, 1985

> These ignorami should never have been invited to the party —Michael I. Miller, *American Speech,* Summer 1984

The revival is continuing, and *ignorami* is beginning to be recorded in dictionaries as a secondary variant. *Ignoramuses* is still the usual plural, however.

I guess See GUESS.

ilk The story of *ilk* is a familiar one to readers of usage books. The word in Old English was a pronoun synonymous with *same.* It persisted in that sense only among the Scots, who used it in the phrase *of that ilk,* meaning, as the OED explains, "of the same place, territorial designation, or name: chiefly in names of landed families, as *Guthrie of that Ilk, Wemyss of that ilk* = Guthrie of Guthrie, Wemyss of Wemyss." This pronoun was converted to a noun by a Scot in the late 18th century and was recorded disapprovingly in the OED by James Murray, its editor and a Scot. Somehow this usage migrated to the U.S., perhaps carried here by linguistically improper Scots immigrants. By the last third of the 19th century expressions of the "Boss Tweed and men of that ilk" type were turning up in American newspapers. This use was first recorded as an Americanism in 1872 by one Maximillian Schele de Vere, a Swede who had lived in Prussia before emigrating to the U.S. Schele de Vere did not merely record the use; he found out how the Scots used the word and instructed all Americans who might read his book in the correct Scottish usage.

From this improbable start the subject has been picked up by a long list of 20th-century commentators from Fowler 1926 to Burchfield 1996 and Garner 1998. Most of our recent commentators recognize that the "kind, sort" sense of *ilk*—it is the only sense used outside of Scotland—is standard.

Our evidence shows that the "kind or sort" sense of *ilk* commonly carries a suggestion of contempt, which was apparent in the two examples cited by Schele de Vere in 1872, and which is still apparent in much current use:

> The titillating mush of Cartland and her ilk —Germaine Greer, *The Female Eunuch,* 1970

> . . . pilgrims of that Beautiful People ilk park their limos on West 10th Street —Gael Greene, *New York,* 3 Mar. 1975

But *ilk* is also commonly used with no disparaging connotations:

> . . . Twain, Conrad and others of the lofty ilk —Leonard Michaels, *N.Y. Times Book Rev.,* 16 May 1976

> . . . the success of Michael Arlen, P. G. Wodehouse and their ilk —Margaret Crosland, *British Book News,* May 1982

It is clear that the defense of the old and little-used Scottish sense of *ilk* is more passionate than reasonable. No commentator has asked what practical use there is in explaining the proper Scottish use of *ilk* to Americans or even Englishmen. There is very little certainly. The "kind, sort" sense of *ilk* is perfectly standard.

ill Raub 1897 advocated using *ill of* when a preposition was called for. Some years later, *Literary Digest* was saying that the preferred modern use was *ill with* (1929). More than 50 years later, it does appear that *ill with* is the more commonly found construction; however, the evidence in our files shows that *ill of* is still in use:

> Actually I only once went ill with thirst —T. E. Lawrence, *Seven Pillars of Wisdom,* 1935

> . . . incurably ill with cancer —*Time,* 14 Mar. 1949

> . . . he was ill with tuberculosis —*Current Biography,* July 1966

> . . . she was ill of a fever —Harrison Smith, *Saturday Rev.,* 28 Feb. 1953

> He was put in bed ill of the fever —Joseph Whitehill, *American Scholar,* Winter 1967–68

illegible, unreadable The distinction to be made between these words is that *illegible* means "impossible to read; indecipherable" and *unreadable* chiefly means "lacking interest or attraction as reading; extremely dull or badly written"; the distinction rests on leaving literal use to *illegible* and confining *unreadable* to figurative use.

> . . . the handwriting, though expressive, is almost illegible —*Times Literary Supp.,* 12 Feb. 1970

> Protect prescription labels with transparent tape, so they won't become smudged and illegible —Dodi Schultz, *Ladies' Home Jour.,* August 1971

> The novel is almost unreadable now, cloying in its account of its young hero's sexual longings —Christopher Benfey, *New Republic,* 8 & 15 Sept. 1997

> . . . issued their second highly technical, distinctly unreadable text —Marcia Seligson, *McCall's,* March 1971

Some commentators, from Fowler 1926 to Garner 1998, would limit *unreadable* to figurative contexts but others, as Evans 1957 and Shaw 1975, recognize that literal use also exists (it has been around since 1830). Literal *unreadable* is not rare; it is often found in technical contexts:

> Encryption . . . is the science of designing code techniques so people can make information unreadable to all but the intended recipients —Peter Wayner, *N.Y. Times,* 28 May 1998

> Unlike bar codes . . . the tag cannot be stripped away, torn off, or made unreadable —Jim Rosenberg, *Editor & Publisher,* 19 Dec. 1998

It is also found in general contexts:

> Braille, finding the embossed Roman alphabet unreadable, determined to devise a system that would enable the blind to write as well as read —Daniel J. Boorstin, *The Discoverers,* 1983

> God's unreadable mind could not act in separate stages —Garry Wills, *Under God,* 1990

illicit See ELICIT, ILLICIT.

illogical comparison See ANY 3; FALSE COMPARISON.

illusion See DELUSION, ILLUSION.

illusive See ELUSIVE, ILLUSIVE.

illustrate When *illustrate* is used with a preposition, it may be used with *by, in,* or *with*:

> . . . a large number of new behaviors to meet new situations are abundantly illustrated by the plight of the current group of European refugees —Ralph Linton, *The Cultural Background of Personality,* 1945

> How is this illustrated by the books in hand? —Thomas Caldecotte Chubb, *Saturday Rev.,* 13 June 1953

> The rich diversity of his life is abundantly illustrated in the correspondence which flowed across the Channel —Dumas Malone, *N.Y. Times Book Rev.,* 1 Aug. 1954

> The same competitive spirit was illustrated in Smith's coverage of President Kennedy's assassination —*Current Biography,* December 1964

> His portly hard middle hung over with a shirt illustrated with pineapples —Saul Bellow, *The Adventures of Augie March,* 1953

> Mr. Tracey illustrates, with recordings, how drums are used for different purposes —*London Calling,* 18 Feb. 1954

Illustrate may occasionally be used with *from* to suggest a different relation:

> . . . then proceeded to discuss and illustrate these apophthegms from his own knowledge of books —Gilbert Highet, *The Classical Tradition,* 1949

The use of *illustrate* with these prepositions will most often call for the verb to be a past participle; however, as the Highet and *London Calling* examples above show, there are instances using other verb forms.

illy This little-used adverb was once the object of impassioned criticism:

> The Illy Haters Union is not so strong in numbers as the Anti-Infinitive Splitters Guild, but its members are of more desperate and determined character —*N.Y. Sun,* 10 Nov. 1931

Illy is actually quite an old word, recorded in writing as early as 1549. Its written use has never been truly common, however. Samuel Johnson did not include it in his dictionary of 1755, and British travelers, hearing it spoken in the U.S., mistook it for an Americanism in the early 1800s (as is noted in Mencken 1936). *Illy* did not originate in America, but it does

seem to have had far more use in the U.S. than in Great Britain. Its career as a usage issue has also been chiefly American. It has been routinely vilified by American commentators from the late 19th century to Garner 1998.

The argument against *illy* runs as follows: since *ill* is established as both an adverb and adjective, *illy* is superfluous. and its use is equivalent to using *welly* in place of *well*. What this argument ignores is that there are many similar adverbial pairs in English—for example, *full* and *fully, right* and *rightly*. There is, in fact, nothing intrinsically wrong with *illy*. The reason for its existence may be that adverbs ending in *-ly* are normally preferred when the adverb precedes the verb or participle it modifies ("It was rightly done" or "It was done right" but not "It was right done"). Most of the evidence for *illy* shows it occuring before a verb or participle:

> Beauty is jealous, and illy bears the presence of a rival —Thomas Jefferson, *Writings,* 1785 (OED)

> Never were two beings more illy assorted —Washington Irving, *Oliver Goldsmith,* 1849 (OED)

> I fear it has been illy and inadequately done —*The Private Papers of Senator Vandenberg,* ed. Arthur H. Vandenberg, Jr., 1952

> . . . no graceful memoir of a life well or illy spent —*Saturday Rev.,* 5 June 1965 (OED Supplement)

Of course, *ill* is also used before verbs and participles, and is far more common than *illy*. (More common than either are such synonymous adverbs as *poorly* and *badly*.)

You will probably never need the rarely used *illy,* but it is not an illiteracy.

image *Image* in its relatively recent sense of "popular or perceived conception, public impression" is called a fad word by Flesch 1964, Bernstein 1965, Fowler 1965, and Watt 1967, although Flesch thinks it seems to fill a need. The usage panel of Harper 1975, 1985 disapproves it. Phythian 1979 and Ebbitt & Ebbitt 1982 say it is established, and by implication so does Janis 1984, who merely explains it. Bernstein thought the fad would probably fade out, but that has not happened. It is well established, as Burchfield 1996 points out.

> . . . how his media consultants formed, marketed and sold an image —Ronald Steel, *N.Y. Times Book Rev.,* 5 Aug. 1984

> He's devoted a large part of his creative life to demolishing the image of the ballerina as nun —Arlene Croce, *Harper's,* April 1971

> . . . has been quite frank in discussing the image he hopes Germany will present to the

world at Munich —William L. Shirer, *Saturday Rev.*, 25 Mar. 1972

It can be used attributively, too:

I recall a session that a roomful of image makers held with a Presidential candidate before a televised news conference —William Safire, *N.Y. Times Mag.*, 16 June 1991

. . . the decisive battle for the Reagan Revolution got reduced to an image contest between the Speaker and the President —David A. Stockman, *Newsweek*, 28 Apr. 1986

imaginary, imaginative Shaw 1975, 1987, Phythian 1979, Copperud 1970, 1980, and Burchfield 1996 all differentiate between *imaginary* and *imaginative*, agreeing roughly that the first means "existing in the imagination, not real" and the second "characterized by or showing use of the imagination." No problem really; it is hard to imagine the words interchanged in examples like these:

Many of the ailments were imaginary —Joyce Carol Oates, *Harper's*, August 1971

. . . threatening her with some very imaginative mutilations —Katherine Anne Porter, *The Never-Ending Wrong*, 1977

He had liked each tree—one for climbing, another to play beneath with tiny, imaginary people —Robert Canzoneri, *McCall's*, March 1971

. . . an imaginative and unassuming . . . architectural genius —P. W. Stone, *Catholic Digest*, December 1968

But the words can be closer in meaning:

His canvases, chiefly imaginary, somber landscapes —*Current Biography*, June 1965

. . . works that create through language an essentially imaginative environment for the hero —Richard Poirier, *A World Elsewhere*, 1966

In such use, relating to art and literature, *imaginative* is more common, and it stresses what is produced by the imagination as distinct from what merely exists in the imagination, for which *imaginary* is the usual word.

imbecile, imbecilic Simon 1980 says in passing that *imbecilic* is "a substandard adjective derived by faulty analogy." We do not know on what basis this assertion is made, but the formation from the noun *imbecile* and the adjective ending *-ic,* as shown in the OED Supplement, is entirely regular.

The word *imbecilic* appears to be a 20th-century coinage. The earliest citation in the OED Supplement is dated 1918.

It was written down as early as 1917:

. . . two statements by Professor Harry Elmer Barnes, of Smith College. The first was written in June, 1917: ". . . the extreme Pan-Germanic junker party—allied itself to the semi-imbecilic Crown Prince." —*American Mercury*, August 1927

It cannot be considered substandard English:

. . . a remark more imbecilic than the first —Jean Stafford, *Children Are Bored on Sunday*, 1953

. . . the imbecilic but eternally triumphant Inspector Clouseau —Arthur M. Schlesinger, Jr., *Saturday Rev.*, 28 Oct. 1978

. . . Arnheiter's imbecilic game of hide-and-seek with the Chinese submarine —William Styron, *This Quiet Dust and Other Writings*, 1982

immanent See EMINENT, IMMINENT; IMMINENT 2.

immediately *Immediately* has been used as a conjunction equivalent to *as soon as* for well over a hundred years, but it has never really succeeded in establishing itself in American English. Some American commentators have cited it as an error, and our evidence shows that its use by American writers has been rare. In British English, however, it is common and standard:

Immediately he had finished tea he rose —D. H. Lawrence, *Sons and Lovers*, 1913

I started writing *Jill* immediately I left Oxford —Philip Larkin, *Required Writing*, 1983

See also DIRECTLY 3.

immigrate See EMIGRATE, IMMIGRATE.

imminent 1. *Imminent* in the past has been spelled *eminent* (see EMINENT, IMMINENT), but the spelling is now avoided as an error. It was denounced as long ago as Baker 1770. The opposite mistake may have been made in the following example, but it is possible that a pun involving *imminent arrival* and *eminent* was intended:

Miami Beach's tensely anxious Sans Souci Hotel readied the full treatment for its imminent guests, the touring Shah of Iran and his luscious Queen —*Time*, 24 Jan. 1955

2. *Imminent, immanent.* Sellers 1975 and others warn against confusing these words, which would appear hard to do from the disparity in their meanings; *immanent* is more likely to be found in philosophy than in ordinary discourse. But the spellings are close, and sure enough *imminent* has been used in the sense of "immanent" since 1605. The OED has

three 17th-century examples, and one from the 19th. Here are a couple of ours from the 20th:

> . . . suddenly the young woman she is to be is imminent in her manners and her looks —Irwin Edman, *American Scholar*, Winter 1950–1951

> It is possible to act to change the world because we are not totally imminent in it —Richard Lichtman, *Center Mag.*, September 1969

Now it is likely that these are simply typographical errors and not deliberate revivals of the 17th-century spelling. We firmly recommend that you keep the two words distinct in spelling so that you do not confuse your readers.

immune In general, when *immune* is used with a preposition, *from* and *to* appear about equally:

> . . . had some source of strength that made him immune from being imposed on by a woman of character like herself —Frank O'Connor, *New Yorker*, 2 Aug. 1952

> . . . it could hardly have been immune from scrutiny by curious and critical official eyes —George F. Kennan, *New Yorker*, 1 May 1971

> And what pilot is immune to errors? —Charles A. Lindbergh, *The Spirit of St. Louis*, 1953

> . . . these were not problems wholly immune to those immutable laws of change that eventually affect all societies —George F. Kennan, *Saturday Rev.*, 6 Mar. 1976

Much less frequently, *immune* is used with *against*:

> His name is now immune against partisan rancor —Richard M. Weaver, *The Ethics of Rhetoric*, 1953

In its biological/medical sense, although *immune* has been used with *against, from,* and *to*, current evidence shows a preference for use of *to*:

> . . . furnish satisfactory evidence . . . to the effect that he was immune against smallpox —Victor Heiser, *An American Doctor's Odyssey*, 1936

> . . . immune from nervous and organic disorders —Alexis Carrel, *Man, the Unknown*, 1935

> An individual is immune to a virus as long as the corresponding antibodies are present in his circulatory system —J. D. Watson, *Molecular Biology of the Gene*, 1965

Some language commentators have said that *immune* may be used with *of*; if it has been or is now so used, the occurrence is not common. Our files have no evidence for this usage.

immunity When *immunity* is used with a preposition in its general sense, it is most commonly found with *from* when the object names the threat:

> Testifying under immunity from prosecution —Laura A. Kiernan, *Boston Globe*, 9 Oct. 1992

Of is common to mark other relations:

> . . . prohibiting the abridgement of the privileges or immunities of citizens —Kenneth S. Tollett, *Center Mag.*, November/December 1971

Less frequently, *immunity* is used in its general sense with *against* or *to* when the object names the threat, and with *for* in other relations:

> . . . give the youngsters some kind of immunity against the slums and social injustices —Gertrude Samuels, *N.Y. Times Mag.*, 13 June 1954

> . . . a feeling of security . . . of absolute immunity to onslaught from above —H. L. Mencken, *Prejudices: Second Series*, 1920

> . . . offering him immunity for past offenses —*American Guide Series: Louisiana*, 1941

In its biological/medical sense, *immunity* is used most often with *to*, and less frequently with *against* or *from*:

> No instance of natural immunity to cowpox has been conclusively demonstrated —Kenneth F. Maxcy, *Preventive Medicine and Hygiene*, 7th ed., 1951

> . . . episodes of mild malaria may generate immunity against more severe malaria —Louis H. Miller, *Nature*, 10 Oct. 1996

> Since there was complete immunity from symptoms due to bubbles —Harry G. Armstrong, *Principles and Practice of Aviation Medicine*, 1939

Occasionally, this sense is found with *in* or *of* marking other relations:

> . . . may produce fairly satisfactory immunity in man which lasts for several months —Henry Pinkerton, in *Pathology*, ed. W. A. D. Anderson, 1948

> . . . the passive immunity of the newborn provided by nature is a highly efficient mechanism —T. F. McNair Scott, in a seminar given by the Medical Division of Sharp and Dohme, Summer 1953

immure When used with a preposition, *immure* is most often found with *in*. *Immure* is most commonly found in the form of the past participle, although occasionally other forms are found:

> . . . one cannot immure himself in an ivory tower —Gerald W. Johnson, *New Republic,* 14 Mar. 1955

> . . . immured in the deep, dark, stony bowels of a pyramid —Walter de la Mare, *Encounter,* December 1954

> . . . a professor of English . . . whom I had presumed safely immured in the research for his long-promised book —Lewis H. Lapham, *Harper's,* September 1996

In the same relation *immure* is used less frequently with *behind* or *within*:

> . . . accretion of objects . . . behind which he seems to immure himself in order to feel at ease —Janet Flanner, *New Yorker,* 9 Mar. 1957

> He immured himself so closely within the walls of the old theocratic temple —Vernon Louis Parrington, *Main Currents in American Thought,* 1927

In other relations, *immure* has been used occasionally with *at, against,* and *with*:

> . . . she was taken off and immured at La Roche —Sir Basil Thomson, *The Mystery of the French Milliner,* 1937

> She is as wary of good fortune as she is immured against the bad —Walker Percy, *The Moviegoer,* 1961

> . . . in the dingy office on lower Sixth Avenue where I daily immured myself with an intractable typewriter —S. J. Perelman, *New Yorker,* 1 Jan. 1972

impact This word comes in for adverse criticism as a verb in figurative use. Since part of the criticism seems to be based on the erroneous notion that the verb is derived from the noun by functional shift, we must first pursue a little etymology. *Impact* was a verb in English before it was a noun; it is first attested in 1601 and was brought in straight from the past participle of the Latin verb that also gave us *impinge.* The relatively recent figurative uses of the verb are parallel to, though no doubt influenced by, figurative use of the noun; this is not a case of a verb derived from an earlier noun.

Our earliest evidence for figurative use of the verb is primarily literary:

> The world did not impact upon me until I got to the Post Office and picked up my mail —Christopher Morley, *The Man Who Made Friends with Himself,* 1949

> . . . the images impacting the human retina —Thomas Hart Benton, *University of Kansas City Rev.,* Autumn 1950

> How will total war impact on such a poet? —*Times Literary Supp.,* 4 May 1951

> It hardly impacted even on the guests' subconscious —Enid Bagnold, *Atlantic,* October 1952

The verb had only a trickle of use in the 1950s and 1960s; not until about 1970 is there a noticeable increase in use, and even through the 1970s the increase is modest. The biggest jump in use in our files occurs around 1980, and it is this advance that attracted criticism in Heritage 1982, Harper 1985, Kilpatrick 1984, Cook 1985, and Garner 1998.

There is now a difference in where the word is found, too. The newer citations come from quotations from politicians, from business and financial sources, and from other reportage. Some examples:

> More governmentese—Environmental Protection Administrator Ruckelshaus talks of ways to "advantageously impact" the auto pollution problem —*Wall Street Jour.,* 2 Mar. 1973

> . . . a variety of efforts to impact energy —Senator Edward M. Kennedy, quoted in *N.Y. Times Mag.,* 24 June 1979

> . . . lets us spend more on R&D without impacting the bottom line —Jessie I. Aweida, quoted in *Business Week,* 26 Jan. 1981

> Minority student-athletes and low-income student-athletes are impacted to a greater degree —Graham B. Spanier, *N.Y. Times,* 29 Aug. 1999

> . . . said the proposal . . . could impact all women seeking abortions —*Denver Post,* 5 Sept. 1984

> Economizing has impacted the entire realm of shipboard life, from first class to cabin class —Myra Yellin Outwater, *Nautical World,* February 1998

The verb seems to be no longer prominent in the literary sources from which it sprang. The critics recommend the use of *influence* or *affect* instead of *impact.* But clearly *impact,* with its overtones of impacting bombs and asteroids, sounds more forceful. In addition, many people seem to have trouble with *affect* and *effect; impact* presents no spelling problem. It is too late now for complaint to prevent the establishment of this use.

impatient When used with a preposition, *impatient* is most often followed by *of*:

His sisters . . . were quite as impatient of his advice, quite as unyielding to his representation —Jane Austen, *Mansfield Park,* 1814

He was always impatient of delay —Edmund Wilson, *A Piece of My Mind,* 1956

Less frequently, *impatient* is used with *for, to,* or *with,* and occasionally with *at:*

. . . a Cadillac cowboy impatient for his father's death —*Current Biography,* September 1964

Winterbourne was impatient to see her again —Henry James, *Daisy Miller,* 1879

. . . had always been impatient with doctrines and systems —William H. Whyte, Jr., *The Organization Man,* 1956

. . . impatient at Benson's presence —George Meredith, *The Ordeal of Richard Feverel,* 1859

impeach 1. When used with a preposition, *impeach* is usually used with *for:*

. . . (who, by the way, was later impeached for corruption!) —Julian Huxley, *Memories,* 1970

. . . why should he be impeaching the Reverend George Barnard for exceptional futility? —Compton Mackenzie, *The Parson's Progress,* 1923

Once in a while, *impeach* is used with *on:*

. . . attempted to impeach Culligan on a variety of counts of misfeasance —Richard R. Lingeman, *N.Y. Times,* 14 Feb. 1970

At one time *impeach* was used with *of,* but in modern prose that combination seldom occurs:

. . . in the name of all the commons of England, impeached Thomas earl of Strafford . . . of high treason —Earl of Clarendon, *The History of the Rebellion and Civil Wars in England,* 1647 (OED)

2. Look again at the citation from Julian Huxley in section 1 above saying that somebody "was later impeached for corruption." Was this person removed from office or simply charged with misconduct? This question is related to the central usage problem involving *impeach.*

Theodore Bernstein in 1970 conducted a small poll in connection with a number of news reports about the threat of impeachment proceedings against Justice William O. Douglas of the Supreme Court. He polled thirteen people, all of whom worked for the *New York Times,* and found that ten of them thought *impeach* meant "to remove from office." This is not a new understanding of the word. We have evidence of it going back to before World War

I. But it is rarely found in print (our earliest printed evidence is from an editorial in the *New York Sun* in 1913). You could call the meaning "remove from office" a folk usage—it exists in people's minds, in their conversation (two of our earliest citations involve arguments about whether President Andrew Johnson was impeached or not), and on signs ("Impeach Earl Warren" signs used to be fairly common). Once in a while it pops up in print:

When the supreme court found several of Peron's early decrees illegal, he had his rubber-stamp congress impeach it, then filled the vacancies with his followers —Michael Scully, *Reader's Digest,* January 1956

If a great many people believe *impeach* means "to remove from office," then it does mean that. The interpretation is scarcely devoid of reason since removal from office is the whole point of impeachment. The meaning can be found in Webster's Third, but it is too rarely used in print to be entered in desk dictionaries. Still, a writer must reckon with its existence. If you need to use *impeach* in your writing and wish not to be misunderstood, you had better phrase your context carefully.

impecunious Evans 1957 calls *impecunious* "formal" and Flesch 1964 tags it as "an unnecessarily long word for *poor.*" Although the word is not encountered all that often, when *impecunious* is used our evidence shows that it can carry connotations of its own. As Merriam-Webster's Dictionary of Synonyms says, *impecunious* "may imply the deprivation of money but it more often suggests a habitual being without money. . . ."

. . . the impecunious artists and writers of New York gathered for cheap meals and free talk —Jerome Mellquist, *Perspectives USA,* Summer 1953

. . . a society of Oxford dons, dedicated to the charitable work of giving an occasional square meal to impecunious scions of the Anglo-Irish aristocracy —Felipe Fernández-Armesto & Derek Wilson, *Reformations,* 1996

The ideal secular post for an impecunious scholar in those days was as librarian to some dilettante nobleman —Daniel J. Boorstin, *The Discoverers,* 1983

Time was when the impecunious reviewer could join the queue at Gaston's in Chancey Lane and receive 50 per cent of the cover price—in cash—for as many books as he had strength to lug to the counter —*Times Literary Supp.,* 3 Nov. 1995

Impecunious can upon occasion be a useful word.

impenetrable *Impenetrable* is now usually used with *to* when a complementary prepositional phrase is needed:

Five volleys plunged the files in banked smoke impenetrable to the eye —Rudyard Kipling, *Wee Willie Winkie and Other Child Stories*, 1888

This gentleman was impenetrable to ideas —Padraic Colum, Introduction to James Joyce, *Dubliners* (Modern Library Edition), 1926

. . . why should black novels, paintings, or symphonies be impenetrable to whites? —Robert F. Moss, *Saturday Rev.*, 15 Nov. 1975

At one time, *impenetrable* also occurred with *by*, but this use is now extremely infrequent:

Aristocracies are, as such, naturally impenetrable by ideas —Matthew Arnold, *Essays in Criticism*, 1865 (OED)

impervious When *impervious* is used with a preposition, the choice is almost always *to*:

. . . so hard a bark, as to be almost impervious to a bullet —Herman Melville, *Omoo*, 1847

But he had long since grown impervious to these alarms —Arnold Bennett, *The Old Wives' Tale*, 1908

He looked at her, impervious to her tears —Jean Stafford, *Children Are Bored on Sunday*, 1953

. . . Berlin struck me, above all, as impervious to any political reactions whatever —Stephen Spender, *N.Y. Times Mag.*, 30 Oct. 1977

implement The OED shows that the verb *implement*, meaning "to carry into effect," originated in the language of Scottish law at the beginning of the 19th century. Its more widespread use began to occur about a hundred years later:

. . . council has been prepared to implement that agreement —*Westminster Gazette*, 30 Aug. 1909 (OED Supplement)

Implement proved to be such a useful verb that before long it became common, thereby attracting the attention of usage commentators. Its early popularity was among the British, and its early critics were also British. They seem to have regarded it as too fancy and obscure a word for general use. Burchfield 1996 notes that the word passed from early objection to being considered jargonish to acceptance. Some American commentators still object to it, charging overuse.

Overuse tends to be in the eye of the beholder, but we do concede that *implement* is a very common word. It typically describes the taking of concrete measures to carry out an official policy or program:

States remain years behind in implementing child support regulations —*N.Y. Times*, 30 Dec. 1997

. . . since 1994, when the "Don't Ask, Don't Tell" policy was implemented —*National Rev.*, 4 May 1998

. . . drew scattered snickers when he implemented a dress code for Senate staffers —Michelle Cottle, *New Republic*, 12 July 1999

In such contexts, *implement* is an entirely appropriate word. You should feel no uneasiness about using it.

implicit *Implicit* is often used with a preposition, and that preposition is usually *in*:

The movies borrowed from other arts on the way to finding methods implicit in their medium —Bernard DeVoto, *The World of Fiction*, 1950

This assumption, implicit in innumerable statements by President Reagan —Henry Steele Commager, *Atlantic*, March 1982

In other relations and other senses *implicit* may also be found, less frequently, with *from*, *with*, or *within*:

. . . in the best stories the end is implicit from the beginning —Joan Aiken, *The Writer*, May 1968

The black dead ocean looked like a mirror of the night; it was cold, implicit with dread and death —Norman Mailer, *The Naked and the Dead*, 1948

The goodness and strength implicit within Pen unfold but slowly —John DeBruyn, *LIT*, Spring 1966

implicit comparative We are indebted to Quirk et al. 1985 for the name of this topic. Implicit comparatives make up a small group of words which were comparative adjectives in Latin and have come to be used in English in some of the ways that true English comparatives are. According to Quirk, "they are not true comparatives in English, since they cannot be used in comparative constructions with *than* as explicit basis of comparison."

The implicit comparatives are comparative not so much through syntax as through meaning. In some cases, though, the comparative meaning affects the syntax. *Minor, major, inferior,* and *superior,* for example, are apparently perceived as having more absolutely comparative connotations than *junior* and *senior*: of these six adjectives, only *junior* and *senior* are regularly used with *more* and *most*:

> When a more junior man leaves, does it make any difference? —Elizabeth Drew, *Atlantic,* August 1970

> The more senior the officer, the more time he has —George S. Patton, Jr., *War as I Knew It,* 1947

> . . . power and prestige for even the most junior Congressmen —Gerald R. Rosen, *Dun's,* October 1971

> Tribute should be paid here to certain of our most senior colleagues —*Professional Geographer,* March 1949

Usage commentators generally cover this difference not by discussing implicit comparison but by proclaiming that *more* should not be used with *major, inferior,* or *superior* while ignoring *junior* and *senior.*

See also INFERIOR, SUPERIOR; MAJOR.

imply See INFER, IMPLY.

important 1. *Important, importantly, more* (or *most*) *important, more* (or *most*) *importantly.* Copperud 1970 reports that the usage panel of Heritage 1969 was evenly divided on the question of the acceptability of *more importantly* but notes that the subject is (at that time) mentioned in no dictionary of usage. The phrase *more importantly* had come to our attention only a short time before:

> "More importantly, Shafer will be trying to take the first of the uncommitted power blocs into the Rockefeller camp . . ." (June 13). The adverbial phrase "more importantly" modifies nothing in the sentence. What is wanted in constructions of this kind is "more important," an ellipsis of the phrase "what is more important." —*Winners & Sinners,* 11 July 1968

The subject gained momentum only slowly, reading its peak in the 1980s. But Bernstein changed his mind in 1977, concluding that neither *important* nor *importantly* was wrong. Safire 1984 agreed.

American commentators have tended to object to the adverb and to recommend the adjective. Objections are made primarily on grammatical grounds. Many repeat Bernstein's original statement that *more importantly* modifies nothing in the sentence. But from the same point of view, neither does *more important.* So a longer phrase, *what is more important,* is postulated and ellipsis adduced to explain the inconvenient absence of *what is.* Quirk et al. 1985 describes the grammar of the adjective as a "supplementive adjective clause"; no longer expression needs to be postulated to explain it. Quirk adds that a corresponding adverb can replace the adjective with little or no change in meaning. The OED Supplement simplifies the grammar by calling *more important* "a kind of sentence adjective" and *more importantly* "a kind of sentence adverb." Both forms can be explained grammatically, so there is no real ground for objection in grammar. Only one grammatical limitation needs to be kept in mind: the adjective is used in this way only with *more* or *most;* the adverb can stand alone, but usually has *more* or *most.*

Proponents of the adjective also assert— as Newman 1974 does—that the adjective construction is much older. This assertion cannot be proved with the information now available. The OED Supplement shows *more important* from 1964 and *more importantly* from 1938. Our evidence tells us that both are older than that, but we know this only by chance. Our oldest examples of each phrase are found on citations marked originally for some other term. There are undoubtedly earlier examples to be found, if someone interested were to look for them. So far, the adverb is still older:

> No one could overestimate the cost of that struggle to the English, not only in men and money, but also and more importantly in the things of the spirit —H. L. Mencken, *Prejudices: First Series,* 1919

> In this country a frontier is no more than something which affects the hours during which licensed premises may be open . . . or, more importantly, where the system of government of the Established Church changes —*Times Literary Supp.,* 3 Apr. 1937

> More important, the passion of Giovanni and Annabella is not shown as an affinity of temperament —T. S. Eliot, "John Ford," in *Selected Essays,* 1932

> But at the end, on every point, unanimous agreement was reached. And more important even than the agreement of words, I may say we achieved a unity of thought and a way of getting along together —Franklin D. Roosevelt, address, 1 Mar. 1945, in *Nothing to Fear,* ed. B. D. Zevin, 1946

You can, then, use either the adjective or the adverb: both are defensible grammatically and both are in respectable use. Usage writers use both:

> More important, there is no verb *destruct* —Barzun 1985

> More important, do not confuse *masterful* with *masterly* —Safire 1984

> . . . but, more importantly, I thought it would help users and readers of English —Bernstein 1977

Importantly, the editor of Webster's New World Dictionary, David Guralnik, agrees —Safire 1980

Most importantly, remember that *due to the fact that* is a wordy way of saying the short and simple word *since* —Shaw 1970

2. *Important* may be complemented by prepositional phrases beginning with *for, in,* or *to*:

Impressions and experiences which are important for the man —T. S. Eliot, "Tradition and the Individual Talent," 1917, in *American Harvest,* ed. Allen Tate & John Peale Bishop, 1942

What kinds of involvement with language are most important for students? —Dwight L. Burton, in *The Range of English,* 1968

. . . tea is very important in British life —Michael Davie, *London Calling,* 19 May 1955

. . . was important in the development of the cotton oil business —*Current Biography 1950*

. . . the matter imitated is important at least to the sale of the goods —Oliver Wendell Holmes d. 1935, in *The Dissenting Opinions of Mr. Justice Holmes,* ed. Alfred Lief, 1929

. . . an end she thinks more important than extra health to her family —Herbert Spencer, reprinted in *Encore,* November 1944

To is sometimes followed by an infinitive phrase:

It is no doubt important to resist pain, but it is also important that it should be there to resist —Havelock Ellis, *The Dance of Life,* 1923

After the superlative, *most important,* one may often find a prepositional phrase beginning with *of*:

The most important of these opportunities came in May 1965 —*Current Biography,* December 1965

impose When used with a preposition, transitive *impose* is used most often with *on*; while *impose* is also used with *upon, on* occurs almost twice as often:

He had greatly disliked the outlandish style imposed on him —Arthur Mizener, *The Saddest Story,* 1971

To impose the baler on those big, hay-grown fields, mastering all their produce —Edmund Wilson, *New Yorker,* 5 June 1971

By making forms he understands the world, grasps the world, imposes himself upon the world —Robert Penn Warren, *Democracy and Poetry,* 1975

Much less frequently, *impose* occurs with *as* or *from*:

A great writer—yes; that account still imposes itself as fitting —F. R. Leavis, *The Common Pursuit,* 1952

Order is something evolved from within, not something imposed from without —E. M. Forster, in *Encore,* November 1944

Occasionally, *impose* is used with *against, around, between, in, into,* or *over*:

If there were any risk that I might be simply imposing one interpretation against another —Frederick J. Hoffman, *Southern Rev.,* April 1965

. . . the United Kingdom's Defense Ministry imposed a new 200-mile war zone around the Falklands —*Wall Street Jour.,* 29 Apr. 1982

He imposed the huge, native stone building between his rambling lodge and his old stable —*Ford Times,* February 1968

They imposed respect if not affection in Europe —D. W. Brogan, *The English People,* 1943

. . . the imposing of reason and moderation into the bosoms of some fifteen gentlemen of birth —Stella Gibbons, *Cold Comfort Farm,* 1932

. . . the Romans imposed a uniform organisation over the whole of Lowland Britain —L. Dudley Stamp, *The Face of Britain,* rev. ed., 1944

impossible This word is sometimes considered to be an absolute adjective. See ABSOLUTE ADJECTIVES.

impractical, impracticable *Impracticable* applies to what is not feasible:

". . . a delicious idea, but so impracticable it doesn't really bear thinking about at all." —Roald Dahl, *Someone Like You,* 1953

Because lion hunting is impracticable without dogs —David Quammen, *Outside,* May 1994

Impractical is a 19th-century word that was quite rare when the OED was originally edited. It has since outstripped the older (17th-century) *impracticable* in use. It is sometimes just an antonym of *practical*:

For Clyde's parents had proved impractical in the matter of the future of their children —Theodore Dreiser, *An American Tragedy,* 1925 (OED Supplement)

It may be applied to what has no practical value:

> . . . in fact, "book learning" beyond the Three R's was historically considered somewhat impractical —Tom Wicker, *Change,* September 1971

It is also used for what is not feasible:

> Visits . . . were impractical for a considerable number of students living in isolated areas —Peter J. Smith, *Saturday Rev.,* 29 Apr. 1972

Impractical is easier to pronounce and spell than *impracticable*; that fact may in the future make it even more dominant than it already is.

impresario Copperud 1970, 1980 notes this is often misspelled *impressario*; we can confirm his observation. It has nothing to do, etymologically or semantically, with *impress,* and you should not let this more common word influence your spelling of a less common one. Only one *s,* please.

impress *Impress* is used with any one of numerous prepositions; among them *by* or *with* occur most frequently:

> . . . her first novel . . . impresses by its assurance and finish —*British Book News,* August 1967

> . . . he sure had been impressed by the fellow with the Stacomb in his hair —David Halberstam, *Harper's,* July 1969

> He had impressed the village with his urbanity and his sharp clothes —John Cheever, *The Wapshot Chronicle,* 1957

> . . . I am impressed with the way it [a book] hangs together thematically —Erica Jong, *Barnard Alumnae,* Winter 1971

Impress is also found quite often with *on* or *upon:*

> . . . it was the general custom for boys to be whipped on certain days to impress things on their memories —Thomas B. Costain, *The Black Rose,* 1945

> His view of art . . . impressed itself upon a number of writers —T. S. Eliot, "Arnold and Pater," in *Selected Essays,* 1932

Somewhat less frequently, *impress* is used with *as* or *into:*

> Her full lower lip was impressed into a suggestion of voluptuousness —E. L. Doctorow, *Loon Lake,* 1979

> . . . [Khrushchev] impressed us as a very rugged, forceful individual —Don Dallas, *London Calling,* 21 Apr. 1955

Very occasionally, *impress* is used with *at, for,* or *in:*

> . . . neither awed nor visibly impressed at being the center of attention —Joseph N. Bell, *Saturday Evening Post,* 25 Dec. 1954

> All able-bodied survivors were impressed for the task —*American Guide Series: Texas,* 1940

> The poem does not contain a series of . . . fine phrases. It only impresses in its totality —A. T. Tolley, *Southern Rev.,* April 1970

improve When *improve* is used with a preposition, it is usually *on* or *upon:*

> . . . remembered all the backwoods stories his customers told him—and doubtlessly improved on them a little —George Sessions Perry, *Saturday Evening Post,* 3 July 1954

> The book is hard to improve on —Daniel Melcher, *Children's House,* Holiday issue, 1969

> It is a common fallacy that a writer . . . can achieve this poignant quality by improving upon his subject-matter —Willa Cather, *Not Under Forty,* 1936

> . . . a mass of people as a whole seems to improve upon the better nature of the parts —Edward Hoagland, *Harper's,* October 1970

Very occasionally, *improve* is used with *over:*

> . . . although he improves over Johnson by entering more respellings —*Language,* January–March 1946

improvement The chief prepositions used with *improvement* are *on, in, of,* and *to.*

> . . . some of whom offered improvements on Patterson's original proposal —*Current Biography 1947*

> . . . where life would be such an improvement on dull dingy Paris —Vladimir Nabokov, *Lolita,* 1958

> . . . studies for possible improvements in State and Federal social security legislation —*Current Biography 1947*

> . . . spent every dollar he earned on the comfort of his family and the improvement of their station in life —Herman Wouk, *Marjorie Morningstar,* 1955

> . . . the patents taken out by Watt for improvements to the steam engine —*Times Literary Supp.,* 5 Mar. 1970

in, into You will not find many subjects in this book over which more ink has been spilled to as little purpose as this one—the distinguishing of the prepositions *in* and *into*. The real distinction is simply stated: *into* is used with verbs of motion; *in* is used with verbs that show location and also with some verbs of motion. The OED gives the history: in Old English *in* originally had all the work; with verbs of location it took a noun in the dative case, and with verbs of motion a noun in the accusative case. Eventually the two cases became indistinguishable, and *to* was dragged in to help with the accusative instances. By modern times, *into* had carved out a pretty sizable piece of the original territory of *in*.

The grammarians, though, want usage to be even simpler. There must be one function for *in*, one function for *into*, and no sharing. They have been insisting on this simplification of English since at least Joseph Hervey Hull's *Grammar* of 1829 (and he very likely was not the first), and they are still beating the same drum.

But *in* has remained in use with verbs of motion all along. There seem to be various reasons for its survival. The OED lists several verbs with which *in* is regularly and idiomatically associated. There are other idiomatic expressions that require *in* rather than *into* (the poker game, for instance, is *spit in the ocean*). And there is the constant influential presence of the adverb *in*, which combines idiomatically with many verbs.

Here are a few examples of *in* with verbs expressing motion, spread over about 300 years:

FLORIO. My Rosaura! *They embrace.*
Enter Podesta *and* Bricklayer.
ROSAURA. My husband! Faint, faint in my arms!
—John Crowne, City Politiques, 1683

Your plants were taken in one very cold blustering day & placed in the Dining room —Jane Austen, letter, 1 Oct. 1808

. . . will turn round halfway in his chair and spit in the fire! —Mary Chesnut, diary, 1 Jan. 1864

You never know when something you may say might make them go jump in the lake —Flannery O'Connor, letter, 20 May 1960

You can't get a waiter to wait ten seconds. You go in a restaurant, he hands you a menu . . . , and in three seconds he starts tapping his pencil —*And More by Andy Rooney*, 1982

The last example above makes another point: *into* would have given more prominence to the fact of entering the restaurant than the writer wanted.

The points to remember are these. Sometimes you need *into* to distinguish motion from location, as in this example:

. . . their sturdy little ship, the Roosevelt, backed out of her berth into the East River —E. L. Doctorow, *Ragtime*, 1975

Some verbs and some expressions idiomatically call for *in*—we've seen "go jump in the lake," for instance. And when you have a choice, remember that *into* gives more prominence to the idea of entrance; if you want to deemphasize that, as Andy Rooney did, you use *in*. Both *in* and *into* are standard with verbs of motion no matter how some commentators might wish things to be. But you must, as always, use your ear.

inaccessible *Inaccessible*, when used with a preposition, is almost always used with *to*:

Mary was not . . . so inaccessible to all influence of hers —Jane Austen, *Persuasion*, 1818

. . . there were things in us fundamentally inaccessible to one another —George Santayana, *Persons and Places*, 1944

. . . our classical authors remained uncollected, with much of their work inaccessible to the reading public —Malcolm Cowley, *N.Y. Times Book Rev.*, 25 Apr. 1982

Very occasionally, *inaccessible* may be used with *for*:

. . . its deliberately national and middle-class image make it inaccessible or unattractive for most of the children —Wallace Roberts, *Change*, November–December 1969

In its physical sense *inaccessible* may be used with *by*:

Places inaccessible by any road may be quickly reached by plane —George Gaylord Simpson, *Attending Marvels*, 1934

. . . areas near the capital were inaccessible by rivers —Chester Lloyd Jones, *Guatemala Past and Present*, 1940

in advance of Copperud 1980 disparages *in advance of* as wordy for *before*; Janis 1984, with greater insight, notes that *before* is simpler but does not always carry the same force. The phrase is more specific than *before* in that it has fewer meanings, and it may be occasionally preferred to *before* for that reason.

However, Washington never really ceased to give substantial military assistance to Chiang Kai-shek in advance of democratic performances —Lawrence K. Rosinger, *New Republic*, 5 Aug. 1946

And other senses of *advance* may occur in the phrase:

. . . the laws were in advance of English common law —*Dictionary of American Biography*, 1936

in any case   See CASE.

inasmuch as   This phrase is disparaged by several commentators (such as Follett 1966, Evans 1957, Copperud 1960, 1964, 1970, 1980, Flesch 1964) in terms only slightly varied from those of Fowler 1926. Fowler calls it "pompous," and later critics apply such labels as "formal" and "stilted." As Janis 1984 and Evans 1957 point out, *since, as,* and *because* are simpler. But if you want a longer expression, there is nothing wrong with *inasmuch as*; the objections are trifling.

> . . . inasmuch as he was a Kennedy, his name entitled him to enter another, even more powerful fraternity —Neal Gabler, *New Republic,* 9 Aug. 1999

> . . . which is just as well, inasmuch as it is by no means clear that he'd have understood it —William F. Buckley, Jr., *National Rev.,* 25 Aug. 1970

inaugurate   Copperud 1960, 1964, 1970, 1980 is following a long journalistic tradition when he disparages *inaugurate* for *open, begin,* or *start* as journalese; it goes back to Bierce 1909 and before him to William Cullen Bryant's *Index Expurgatorius,* compiled when he was editor of the *New York Evening Post* and published in 1877. *Inaugurate* was also disparaged by Richard Grant White 1870 and Ayres 1881, and (according to Vizetelly 1906), by Yale professor William Lyons Phelps, inaugurating (if we may) an extra-journalistic tradition. Vizetelly notes that lexicographers ignore these strictures, and indeed they have—the sense "to begin" was recognized in Samuel Johnson's Dictionary (1755).

To be frank, were it not for the strength of the tradition, this would have been a dead issue long ago. Here are a few examples of what is clearly a standard, and not especially journalistic, usage:

> . . . Raleigh ordered them to take the tradewind route inaugurated by Columbus —Samuel Eliot Morison, *The European Discovery of America,* 1971

> . . . thereby inaugurating a terror which would become dreadfully familiar to hundreds of millions —William L. Shirer, *The Rise and Fall of the Third Reich,* 1960

> On this legal basis Frederick inaugurated his great feudal trial against his Guelph enemy —Norman F. Cantor, *The Civilization of the Middle Ages,* 1993

> Yet it would be unreasonable to demand that a writer both inaugurate a new era of scholarship and solve all the problems he has raised —Richard Sennett, *N.Y. Times Book Rev.,* 19 Oct. 1980

in back of   See BACK OF, IN BACK OF.

in behalf of   See BEHALF 1.

in case   See CASE.

in case of   See CASE.

incentive   When *incentive* is used with a preposition, it is usually *to*:

> . . . add that terrible but effective incentive to greater effort: fear of losing a job —*New Republic,* 19 Sept. 1949

> This of course provides an incentive to make the next release particularly interesting —Chris Albertson, *Saturday Rev.,* 27 Nov. 1971

Less often but still quite commonly, *incentive* is used with *for*:

> . . . reducing the incentives for South Africans, Israelis and Pakistanis to use nuclear weapons —James Fallows, *N.Y. Times Book Rev.,* 26 June 1983

Incentive also occasionally is used with *toward*:

> . . . rivermen provided the first incentive toward establishing a settlement here —*American Guide Series: Pennsylvania,* 1940

When the prepositional phrase specifies the incentive, the preposition is, naturally enough, *of*:

> . . . the old incentive of competition —S. P. B. Mais, *The English Scene To-day,* 2d ed., 1949

incentivize, incent   These two recent coinages (*incentivize* dates from 1970 in our files; *incent* from the 1990s) have little or no use outside of business contexts. More than half of our evidence comes from quoted speech, which suggests that neither is much used in writing. Predictably they have been condemned by commentators including Harper 1985 (against *incentivize*) and Garner 1998 (against both). A couple of examples of the words in action:

> Stock options are a winning invention by management to incentivize people who are most deserving of being incentivized— namely management —Alan Abelson, *Barron's,* 26 May 1997

> We like people who are vested through their ownership in the business, and are incented accordingly —O. Mason Hawkins, quoted by Sandra Ward, *Barron's,* 3 Feb. 1997

Our evidence so far does not show these verbs working their way into mainstream English.

inchoate   A number of British commentators, beginning with Ivor Brown 1945 and including Gowers in Fowler 1965 and Howard

1977, complain about the extension of meaning of *inchoate* from "incipient, immature, or just beginning" (Howard's definitions) to "amorphous, incoherent, or disorganized" (Howard again). A couple of American commentators agree. But the extended use is natural and probably inevitable: what is just begun is also unfinished, incomplete, and often also disorganized or incoherent. And unfortunately for the complainers, the extension of meaning was already three decades old or more when Brown noticed it.

> . . . all the world of men outside seemed inchoate, purposeless, like the swarming, slimy, minute life in stagnant water —Mary Webb, *The Golden Arrow,* 1916

> . . . had to seek the help of their conquered subjects, or of more vigorous foreigners, to administer their ill-knit and inchoate empires —T. E. Lawrence, *Seven Pillars of Wisdom,* 1935

> Sometimes her sweltering and inchoate fury was so great that she threw him on the floor and stamped on him —Thomas Wolfe, *Look Homeward, Angel,* 1929

It is now one of the words regularly used by reviewers:

> . . . it threatens to dominate their narratives, as something inchoate, unchannelled, mysterious —John Updike, *New Yorker,* 10 Apr. 1971

> . . . about 132 pages of inchoate material in this new collection —Joyce Carol Oates, *N.Y. Times Book Rev.,* 1 Apr. 1979

It is also used in other kinds of writing:

> . . . his unique set of blocks, inhibitions, and inchoate anxieties —Norman Mailer, *Harper's,* March 1971

> . . . articulating the inchoate feelings of the beyond-the-beltway, traditional-values voters —Michael Barone, *U.S. News & World Report,* 20 Feb. 1995

American dictionaries and at least one British one have already acknowledged this spread of meaning.

incident Harper 1975, 1985 and Copperud 1970, 1980 are disturbed by the use of *incident* as an all-purpose word for some unpleasant or potentially dangerous occurrence—Copperud, Gowers in Fowler 1965, and Garner 1998 call it a euphemism. The basis of their concern is found in the assertion that *incident* means only "a minor or unimportant occurrence." But the assertion is without foundation and suggests that dictionaries have not been "perused with attention" (to use a line from Dr. Johnson). Here are three examples of actual use:

> There were frequent border incidents leading to armed clashes —*Current Biography,* November 1967

> The students were earlier declared ineligible following a weekend incident involving alcoholic beverages —*Ouray County* (Colo.) *Plaindealer,* 8 Mar. 1973

> Whenever an incident occurred in the neighborhood, he was one of the first to be suspected —C. Knight Aldrich, *Psychology Today,* March 1971

The sense displayed in these examples has been established since before World War I in reference to occurrences of serious diplomatic import, and in the period since World War I has spread to other areas. The OED Supplement has numerous examples from 1913 on. When Gowers says that it is often used as a euphemism for *affray,* its value becomes apparent—it suggests an unfortunate occurrence while avoiding the need to specify its character, which may not always be immediately certain. The sense is impeccably standard. Its potential for being used euphemistically should not be overlooked, however. Here, for instance, is Thomas H. Middleton reporting on the jargon of the nuclear power people:

> A nuclear accident isn't called an accident; it's an "abnormal occurrence" or an "incident." —*Saturday Rev.,* 1 May 1976

incidental When used with a preposition, *incidental* is usually combined with *to*:

> . . . labor problems incidental to rapidly expanding factories —*American Guide Series: Massachusetts,* 1937

> These projects were always incidental to our games, which dominated our days —Jim Strain, *Sports Illustrated,* 22 June 1981

Very occasionally, *incidental* occurs with *on*:

> One oligarchic critic emphasises the casual profits incidental on Athens' position as an imperial city —A. H. M. Jones, *Past and Present,* February 1952

incidentally 1. The spelling *incidently* is a rare variant of *incidentally* that is noted in a number of large dictionaries, including the OED and Webster's Third; it goes back to Sir Thomas More. It has never been entirely out of use:

> Incidently, May . . . had previous theatrical experience —George Mann, *Theatre Lethbridge,* 1993

> Here, you got yer sheriff by the name of Wayne . . . who incidently, might I add ominously, owns the Reo Rock Bar —Julie Lang, *Village Voice,* 12 Apr. 1994

Some commentators consider it an error, but it is not. It is not a spelling that we recommend your using, however.

Incidently would also be the spelling of an adverb derived from the adjective *incident,* should one be needed.

2. Fowler 1926 and Gowers at greater length in Fowler 1965 disparage the use of *incidentally* as a sentence adverb. When used this way—as it commonly is in speech, letters, and lighter prose—*incidentally* introduces an aside or digression; there is nothing wrong with such use.

> Incidentally, I had lunch with T. S. Eliot the other day —James Thurber, letter, 12 Dec. 1950

> . . . Cervantes's masterpiece . . . —incidentally, now available in a new and accomplished translation —Malcolm Muggeridge, *Punch,* 8 Apr. 1953

> Incidentally, I am only coming to Princeton to research, not to teach —Albert Einstein, letter, quoted in *Change,* January–February 1971

incidently See INCIDENTALLY 1.

inclose, inclosure See ENCLOSE, INCLOSE.

include There are quite a few commentators—Bryson 1984, Barzun 1985, Flesch 1964, Copperud 1960, 1964, 1970. 1980, Bernstein 1965, and Garner 1998 among them—who maintain that *include* should not be used when a complete list of items follows the verb.

> The prison includes 22 enclosed acres and a farm of 1,000 acres west and south of the walls —*American Guide Series: Minnesota,* 1938

> His clubs include the Athenaeum, the Carlton, the Farmers', the Beefsteak, and Grillion's —*Current Biography,* September 1964

There is nothing wrong with either of these examples. They fit the requirements of Fowler 1926, 1965 perfectly:

> With *include,* there is no presumption (though it is often the fact) that all or even most of the components are mentioned. . . .

The critics above, however, have somehow reasoned themselves into the notion that with *include* all of the components must not be mentioned, which has never been the case. Fowler's comments accurately describe how *include* is used.

incomparable A number of derivatives ending in *-ble* are accented on a syllable other than the one corresponding to the stressed syllable of the underlying verb. Thus *incomparable, irrevocable, irrefutable,* and *irreparable* are normally stressed on the second syllable. The

disparity of stress often corresponds to a certain disparity of meaning. *Incomparable,* for example, typically does not mean literally "not subject to comparison" but "matchless, beyond compare."

A few words of this type have not definitely settled on a single pronunciation style: *lamentable* varies widely between the specially stressed \'lam-ən-tə-bəl\ and \lə-'ment-ə-bəl\, stressed by analogy with the verb *lament.* And a minority of educated speakers use verb-like pronunciations even for words like *irrevocable,* although such pronunciations are scorned by some. But we are not dealing here with mere error. Every so often we receive a letter from a correspondent consciously defending \kəm-'par-ə-bəl\ for *comparable* when the sense is not "roughly equal" but "suitable for comparison," a meaning more closely tied to the underlying verb. Thus, five cents and a billion dollars would be (in this view) \kəm-'par-ə-bəl\, whereas one hour and one acre would not be.

There are similar cases of different pronunciations for different senses of a word. *Ablative* gets stress on its first syllable when it is used in the grammatical sense but is pronounced \a-'blāt-iv\ when it means "tending to ablate." *Protractor* may be pronounced \'prō-₁trak-tər\ when it designates the geometrical instrument and no longer, in the speaker's mind, has connection with any verb, but \prō-'trak-tər\ when it refers to "something that protracts."

incomparables See ABSOLUTE ADJECTIVES.

incomplete comparison AS GOOD OR BETTER THAN; FALSE COMPARISON.

incongruous *Incongruous* may be used with the preposition *to* or *with*:

> . . . it would be . . . incongruous to meet her at the end of a chapter —Herman Wouk, *Aurora Dawn,* 1947

> He ate enormously, with a zest which seemed incongruous with his spare frame —Willa Cather, *The Song of the Lark,* 1915

Less frequently, *incongruous* occurs with *about, in,* or *on*:

> There is something incongruous about Oslo —Hugh C. McDonald, *The Hour of the Blue Fox,* 1975

> . . . settlements incongruous in material and often startling in their ugliness —S. P. B. Mais, *The English Scene To-day,* 2d ed., 1949

> He was smoking a cigar which looked incongruous on his thin face —Norman Mailer, *The Naked and the Dead,* 1948

in connection with *In connection with* and one or two other phrases containing *connection* are disparaged as wordy in such books at

Phythian 1979, Janis 1984, Copperud 1960, 1964, 1970, 1980, and Shaw 1975, 1987. The usual argument is that some simple preposition—*about* is the one most often mentioned—is preferable. The guess here is that the commentators have paid little attention to the way their corrections would read in a range of actual contexts.

> Our financial practices put the Company in a very favorable position in connection with the currency disturbances in Europe —Paul E. Wallendorf, quoted in *General Electric Investor*, Summer 1971

"A favorable position about the currency disturbances"? Not likely.

> The World Bank . . . was founded in connection with the United Nations at the end of World War II —*Current Biography*, July 1965

About? By? From? At? Of? Concerning? Several of these substitutes are clearly impossible; others will produce a meaningful sentence but not a sentence with the same meaning as this sentence. Our files contain many examples where it is not easy to replace the phrase with one of the suggested single-word prepositions.

True, the phrase does also occur in simpler contexts where a shorter preposition is a viable option:

> . . . offered the following in connection with this aspect of the situation —*AAUP Bulletin*, December 1967

> One thing I want to point out . . . in connection with these prices —Richard Joseph, *Your Trip to Britain*, 1954

In connection with, then, can sometimes be replaced by a shorter preposition and sometimes not. You as a writer are going to have to make that decision. The automatic substitution of *about* or *concerning* can result in gibberish.

incorporate When *incorporate* is used with a preposition, it is used usually, with about equal frequency, with *in* or *into*:

> . . . the Germans had just simply dropped on Mr. Schatzweiler in their pleasant way, incorporated him in their forces and had sent him to the front —Ford Madox Ford, *The Last Post*, 1928

> . . . so our allies can incorporate the bomb in their military plans —Omar N. Bradley, *Saturday Evening Post*, 10 Apr. 1951

> . . . to incorporate into the community of scholars a community of students —James B. Conant, *Atlantic*, May 1946

> . . . to accept new findings of fact . . . and incorporate them into our teaching —W. Nelson Francis, *College English*, March 1953

Incorporate is sometimes used with *with*:

> . . . where music has been for a hundred and fifty years integrated and incorporated with the whole intellectual tradition —Virgil Thomson, *The Musical Scene*, 1947

Incorporate is used only infrequently with *on*:

> . . . innovations in engine and body design which may be incorporated on coming car models —*The Americana Annual 1953*

incredulous, incredible Many books on usage explain the distinction between these words, which is that *incredible* means "impossible to believe" or "hard to believe" ("an incredible story") and *incredulous* means "unwilling to believe; disbelieving" ("an incredulous audience"). The commentators are chiefly concerned about the use of *incredulous* where *incredible* is usual:

> . . . so began the incredulous success story we all know —*Disco 45 Annual 1976*

Such usage was once in good repute. The OED gives "not to be believed" as an obsolete sense of *incredulous* and shows it occurring in the works of such writers as Sir Thomas Browne and William Shakespeare:

> No obstacle, no incredulous or unsafe circumstance —Shakespeare, *Twelfth Night*, 1602

But this sense of *incredulous* had fallen into disuse by the end of the 18th century. Its reappearance in recent years has been sporadic, although there are signs that the usage may be growing more widespread:

> . . . for the FBI to be called in . . . seems incredulous —Peter Gammons, *ESPN.com*, 17 Sept. 2000

> . . . their tales of woe seemed almost incredulous —William L. Shirer, *The Nightmare Years*, 1984

> . . . her incredulous performance. . . . It does strain credibility —*People*, 3 June 1985

Even so, *incredible* is still the usual and standard word in such contexts. Most writers continue to restrict *incredulous* to its "disbelieving" sense, and we recommend that you do so as well:

> He was greeted with incredulous laughter —Robert M. Hutchins, *Center Mag.*, September 1968

> The author was incredulous and investigated. "It was true," he discovered. —Mel Gussow, *N.Y. Times Mag.*, 1 Jan. 1984

See also CREDIBLE, CREDITABLE, CREDULOUS.

inculcate When *inculcate* is used with a preposition, and the direct object denotes what is inculcated, the preposition is usually *in* or *into*:

> His task, rather, is to inculcate in the government and the people basic ecological attitudes —William Murdoch & Joseph Connell, *Center Mag.,* January–February 1970

> By the time I was four years old "Take a Pair of Sparkling Eyes" . . . had been fairly inculcated into my bloodstream —Noel Coward, *Punch,* 8 July 1953

Infrequently, *inculcate* is also used with *on* or *upon*:

> . . . thorough instruction in all phases of weather . . . designed to inculcate judgment on what to do in emergency —Phil Gustafson, *Saturday Evening Post,* 12 June 1954

> . . . the figure primarily responsible for inculcating upon vast numbers of young and needy minds . . . the primer-simple notion that LSD has "something" to do with religion —Theodore Roszak, *The Making of a Counter Culture,* 1969

More controversial is the use of *inculcate* with *with* and a personal direct object. This practice is disapproved by some language commentators (Evans 1957, Phythian 1979, Bryson 1984, Garner 1998, for example) but the sense of the verb is little different from that when *inculcate* is used with the other prepositions mentioned above: "to cause to be impressed" rather than "to impress."

> The children . . . were early inculcated with their parents' moral code —*Current Biography,* July 1965

Indoctrinate, the word suggested by Garner, would seem too strong in the examples above. This construction is standard but is much less common than the uncontroversial one discussed first.

incumbent When the adjective *incumbent* is used with a preposition, it is usually used with *upon* or *on*: *upon* occurs a little more frequently. Use of *on* or *upon* usually means that the object of the preposition is followed by *to* with an infinitive:

> After taking off his coat, he felt it incumbent upon him to make some little report of his day —Theodore Dreiser, *Sister Carrie,* 1900

> It is incumbent upon the press to act not in its own best interests, but in society's best interests —Carll Tucker, *Saturday Rev.,* 23 June 1979

> . . . Mr. Lorry felt it incumbent on him to speak a word or two of reassurance —Charles Dickens, *A Tale of Two Cities,* 1859

> It is not the Russian people as a whole on whom it is incumbent to respond to the challenge —George F. Kennan, *New Yorker,* 1 May 1971

Occasionally, the preposition is simply followed by a noun:

> . . . the various types of obligation incumbent on the members of the profession —R. M. MacIver, *Annals of the American Academy of Political and Social Science,* January 1955

Far less frequently, *incumbent* is used with *for*:

> . . . is it therefore incumbent for us to abandon our search . . . ? —Ernest Nagel, *New Republic,* 28 June 1954

indefinite pronouns Many indefinite pronouns, such as *anyone, somebody, none, each, either,* and *one,* are involved in usage questions of one kind or another. You will find most of these treated separately. They are also part of the discussions in the articles at AGREEMENT: INDEFINITE PRONOUNS; NOTIONAL AGREEMENT, NOTIONAL CONCORD; THEY, THEIR, THEM.

independence When used with a preposition, *independence* is used with either *from* or *of*:

> . . . and he would say, with enough diffidence to mark his respect for his elders, yet a complete independence of their views —Edith Wharton, *The Spark,* 1924

> Countries that have been sluggish in their social and economic adaptations have not attained independence of foreign aid —Neil H. Jacoby, "The Progress of Peoples," 1969

> . . . to work toward Korea's independence from Peking —David J. Dallin, *The Rise of Russia in Asia,* 1949

> . . . the logical independence of the axiom of parallels from the rest, is the guiding motive of the work —Bertrand Russell, *Foundations of Geometry,* 1897

independent *Independent,* when used with a preposition, is usually used with *of*:

> . . . our anxiety to make judges independent of the popular will —Morris R. Cohen, *The Faith of a Liberal,* 1946

> . . . they would . . . unanimously bring up to me, independent of any questions I'd ask them, the claim that the morale in the field was . . . high —William Ruckelshaus, quoted in *N.Y. Times Mag.,* 19 Aug. 1973

Perhaps by analogy with *independence, independent* is occasionally used with *from*:

. . . all . . . apparently on a par and independent from each other —*Newsweek*, 1 May 1972

Indian See NATIVE AMERICAN.

indifferent The preposition used with *indifferent* is almost always *to*:

. . . aspects of language that the earlier grammarians were indifferent to —Geoffrey Nunberg, *Atlantic*, December 1983

. . . singularly indifferent to landscape —*Times Literary Supp.*, 21 May 1971

Rarely we find a compound preposition—*as to* or *with respect to*—instead:

For it is commonly said and commonly believed that science is completely neutral and indifferent as to the ends and values which move men to act —John Dewey, *Freedom and Culture*, 1939

individual The contention of most commentators in the controversy over *individual* as a noun meaning "a human being" is this: it is acceptable when the individual is contrasted with a larger unit, such as society or the family, and it is acceptable when it stresses some special quality. These two examples illustrate:

The individual rebelled against restraint; society wanted to do what it pleased; all disliked the laws which Church and State were trying to fasten on them —Henry Adams, *Mont-Saint-Michel and Chartres*, 1904

But Donne would have been an individual at any time and place —T. S. Eliot, "Andrew Marvell," in *Selected Essays*, 1932

But there is something wrong with it when it points to no obvious contrast or no obvious special trait and simply means "person":

There were many individuals of dashing appearance, whom I easily understood as belonging to the race of swell pick-pockets —Edgar Allan Poe, "The Man of the Crowd," reprinted in *Encore*, September 1945

The above distinction is essentially that given in Fowler 1926. But the controversy is older than Fowler, dating back at least to Alford 1866, who discovered it occurring with some frequency in English newspapers. American commentators picked up his comments by 1869 and heightened his objections into vulgarism; later they added a charge of pomposity. In the 1880s an etymological objection was raised, but it died out after Bierce 1909. This etymological objection did give rise to the assertion that *individual* should only be used to contrast the individual with a group—an assertion forwarded by Fowler to

recent times. Dictionaries like the OED and the *Century Dictionary*, apparently lacking much evidence, repeated the epithets of the commentators.

It's not clear why this sense of *individual* has been picked out for objection. We know from Alford that it was common in English newspapers of his time, and H. L. Mencken remarked that the same could be said of American papers. We know that 19th-century American humorists like Artemus Ward used it—perhaps this use, a half century earlier, brought on the change of jocosity added to other objections around 1917. But Hall 1917, who actually looked for examples in literary sources, was puzzled by the controversy, for he had found the word in the works of some 38 authors. And we suspect that what might be termed high-toned use of the disputed sense of *individual* was never questioned:

Every decent and well-spoken individual affects and sways me more than is right —Ralph Waldo Emerson, "Self-Reliance," 1841

Alas and alas! you may take it how you will, but the services of no single individual are indispensable —Robert Louis Stevenson, *Virginibus Puerisque and Other Papers*, 1881

Faith, in the agonized hands of the individual, becomes an imaginative experiment —R. P. Blackmur, "Emily Dickinson," in *American Harvest*, ed. Allen Tate & John Peale Bishop, 1942

If we are correct in our guess that late Victorian journalistic practice was the probable cause of the outcry, the whole issue should have died with the cause. But it has not. We find it mentioned (after Fowler) in a large number of commentators. What do these people say about a subject that has been empty of content for, say, half a century? Mostly they repeat Fowler 1926 in one way or another. It is interesting that not one of these mentions the literary background—going back to Sir Francis Bacon in the 17th century—of the use. Evidence of the pointlessness of the continuing criticism comes from Shaw 1987, who calls *individual* "loosely overused" and notes it "often has a humorous or contemptuous meaning" but at the same time sprinkles his book with passages like "a taciturn individual is usually considered surly, dour, sullen and severe."

Our evidence from the last fifty years or so shows that *individual* as a noun is most often used in contrast to some larger group—just as Fowler said it should be. When the contrast is not evident, the word almost always seems to carry the notion of one person considered separately. We have no recent evidence of facetious or disparaging use. The following examples are typical:

> There would be stiff penalties for any individual caught mailing out Christmas cards before the tenth of December —*And More by Andy Rooney,* 1982

> . . . just to be myself, just to be a simple individual with no particular axe to grind —William Faulkner, 1 May 1957, in *Faulkner in the University,* 1959

> . . . I am here concerned . . . with what a more or less aware individual may experience as his own selfhood —Robert Penn Warren, *Democracy and Poetry,* 1975

> . . . a hedge fund—a little-regulated private investment partnership, geared to wealthy individuals —Connie Bruck, *New Yorker,* 23 Jan. 1995

We see no need for continuing concern over *individual.* This sense has always been standard, the practices of Victorian journalists notwithstanding, and still is standard.

For some other controversies that have been at least partly fueled by 19th-century journalistic fashion, see FEMALE; PARTY; TRANSPIRE.

indorse, indorsement   See ENDORSE 3.

indulge   When *indulge* is used intransitively and with a preposition, the preposition is usually *in:*

> People who know the facts can never be quite so free to indulge in fantasy as those who don't —Aldous Huxley, *The Olive Tree,* 1937

> . . . the ordinary man's occasional fear of indulging involuntarily in overstrong language —Osbert Sitwell, *Noble Essences,* 1950

When *indulge* is used transitively and with a preposition, the preposition is usually *in* cr *with; in* occurs a little more frequently:

> I thank the House for having indulged me in this manner —Sir Winston Churchill, *The Unrelenting Struggle,* 1942

> . . . indulged themselves in factitious pity —William Styron, *Lie Down in Darkness,* 1951

> . . . and it was only on occasion of a present like this, that Silas indulged himself with roast-meat —George Eliot, *Silas Marner,* 1861

> . . . continues to indulge his whimsy with brocade and doeskin neckties —*Current Biography,* March 1965

Transitive *indulge* is occasionally used with *by;* when it is, the object of *by* is generally a gerund:

> . . . a post-war Italy that brims with talent yet indulges its recent shame by condescending toward its greatest novelist —*New Republic,* 4 Aug. 1952

indulgent   When *indulgent* is used with a preposition, it may be *in, of, to* or *with:*

> . . . is so indulgent in its enumerations of irrelevant detail —*N.Y. Times Book Rev.,* 24 Dec. 1978

> . . . less indulgent of the conflicting impulses of Malcolm X —Henry Louis Gates, Jr., *New Yorker,* 8 Apr. 1996

> . . . would perhaps be more indulgent to my vivacity —Matthew Arnold, preface to *Essays in Criticism,* First Series, 1865

> The fans could afford to be indulgent with the antics of Moose —*Boy's Life,* February 1953

inedible, uneatable   A few commentators disagree over the distinctions between these words. Our evidence indicates that the words are used more or less interchangeably except in strictly scientific contexts, where *inedible* is preferred. *Inedible* is a considerably more common word overall than *uneatable:*

> . . . the accounts of inedible food, nasty bug bites —Karen Karbo, *N.Y. Times Book Rev.,* 4 June 2000

> The bacon was perfect; the burger was almost charred, too, but not inedible —Ruth Heimbuecker, *Pittsburgh Press,* 13 Sept. 1989

> . . . the edible members of the genus *Cucurbita* are commonly referred to as squash and pumpkins; the inedible or ornamental members are called gourds —Judith Leet, *JAMA,* 4 Oct. 1995

> The sour orange used as a base for the Mars orange is virtually uneatable, while the fruit of the Mars is very sweet —Whitney Otto Villard, *How to Make an American Quilt,* 1991

> . . . we were served with almost uneatable pieces of pork and quite uneatable yucca —Graham Greene, *Getting to Know the General,* 1984

in excess of   This phrase has drawn some criticism as a pompous or verbose substitute for *more than* or *over.* It seems to be most at home in writing that has to do with large quantities of material or large sums of money:

> . . . a fifteen-year project costing in excess of $6,000,000 —*Current Biography,* February 1967

> . . . a capacity in excess of 450,000 tons a year —*Annual Report, The Mead Corp.,* 1970

> Total expenditure will be in excess of $5.5 million —*Area Development,* July 1970

infatuated *Infatuated* takes *with* when it uses a preposition:

> Stock investors are infatuated with growth —Heinz G. Biel, *Forbes*, 15 Aug. 1972

> . . . he is infatuated—via newspaper pictures—with Evelyn Nesbit Thaw —Stanley Kauffmann, *Saturday Rev.*, 26 July 1975

infectious See CONTAGIOUS, INFECTIOUS.

infer, imply We have in our collection more than fifty writers on usage, from 1917 to 1988, who insist that a certain distinction between *infer* and *imply* be observed and preserved. Rather than explain, let us illustrate:

> Given some utterance, a person may infer from it all sorts of things which neither the utterance nor the utterer implied —I. A. Richards, *Confluence*, March 1954

Richards' usages are exactly those approved and recommended by our more than fifty commentators. They are not, however, the only usages of these words. And there's the rub. Real life is not as simple as commentators would like it to be. A glance at any good dictionary would suggest the same to you: Merriam-Webster's Collegiate Dictionary, for instance, lists four transitive senses of *imply* (one is obsolete) and five of *infer*. We will not confuse you by discussing all of these, but there are three distinct uses of *infer* we must deal with, and a couple of *imply*. We will start with *imply*, which is simpler and less controversial.

For simplicity we lump together the two chief uses of *imply*, noting only that the first involves no human agent and that the second may or may not. Examples of each, in order:

> Amnesty, like pardon, implied crime, and he admitted none —Robert Penn Warren, *Jefferson Davis Gets His Citizenship Back*, 1980

> And further, an utterer may imply things which his hearers cannot reasonably infer from what he says —I. A. Richards, *Confluence*, March 1954

There once was minor controversy about a sense of *imply* meaning "hint" used with a personal subject.

> *Imply* carries with it a tinge of offensiveness when we say, "What do you mean to *imply*?" —*Literary Digest*, 4 Apr. 1931

This use is not especially common in edited prose but turns up in letters to the editor and in fictional speech:

> "Don't imply you inherit your flibbertigibbet ways from me. . . ." —*American Girl*, December 1951

But keep this *imply* in mind. It is used in exactly the same way as a disputed sense of *infer*, though not so often.

Now, for *infer*, which is the real bone of contention. We are going to identify only three main uses of *infer*, and for the sake of convenience we label them historically. The first is the use of *infer* that everybody approves. We will call it "More 1528," because Sir Thomas More introduced it to English in that year:

> Wherupon is inferred . . . that the messenger wold have fled fro by force —*A Dyaloge . . . of the Veneration and Worshyp of Ymagys*, 1528 (OED, sense 3)

The second use we will call "More 1533," for Sir Thomas gave it to English in that year (in fact he had introduced the usual use of *imply*, too, in 1528). It means the same as *imply*:

> The fyrste parte is not the proofe of the second, but rather contrary wyse, the seconde inferreth well ye fyrst —*Answer to Frith*, 1533 (OED, sense 4)

A distinguishing characteristic of More 1533 is that it does not occur with a human subject.

Now More 1528 and More 1533 coexisted in literary writing for 400 years or so, and no one was confused, so far as the record shows. Here are some examples of More 1528:

> I found that he inferred from thence . . . that I either had the more money, or the more judgment —Daniel Defoe, *Moll Flanders*, 1722

> . . . nor can any thing be more fairly inferred from the Preface, than that Johnson . . . was pleased —James Boswell, *Life of Samuel Johnson*, 1791

> She seldom saw him—never alone; he probably avoided being alone with her. What was to be inferred? —Jane Austen, *Mansfield Park*, 1814

> Mr. Anderson did not say this, but I infer it —Henry Adams, letter, 17 Jan. 1861

> . . . I infer that Swinburne found an adequate outlet for the creative impulse in his poetry —T. S. Eliot, *The Sacred Wood*, 1920

More 1533, the OED shows, was used continuously up to the time the book was edited; Milton and James Mill are among those quoted. Here are some examples not in the OED:

> He used Metcalf as an agent in all proceedings which did concern that foundation; which will infer him to be both a wise and an honest man —Thomas Fuller, *The Holy State and the Profane State*, 1642

> However, as I have often heard Dr. Johnson observe as to the Universities, bad practice

does not infer that the *constitution* is bad —James Boswell, *Life of Samuel Johnson,* 1791

Lucy . . . reseated herself with an alacrity and cheerfulness which seemed to infer that she could taste no greater delight —Jane Austen, *Sense and Sensibility,* 1811

. . . to be a literary man infers a certain amount of—well, even formal education —William Faulkner, 25 Feb. 1957, in *Faulkner in the University,* 1959

More 1533 is not itself really the subject of much controversy, but it is recognized in dictionaries, and that recognition leads the commentators not to trust the dictionaries.

We may call the real disputed sense "personal *infer*" because—in distinct contrast with More 1533—it usually has a personal subject. And contrary to all those fifty or more commentators, it does not really equal *imply* in the latter's full range of meanings—it means "hint, suggest," in other words, *imply* only in the sense considered a bit less than acceptable in the 1930s. The personal *infer* is relatively recent. We have found no examples earlier than this one:

I should think you *did* miss my letters. I know it! but . . . you missed them in another way than you infer, you little minx! —Ellen Terry, letter, 3 Oct. 1896

Our earliest American example comes from a list of Kansas words submitted to *Dialect Notes* in 1914 by Judge J. C. Ruppenthal of Russell, Kansas. His example of the use reads this way:

He *infers* by his remarks that things are not going right.

This sense is clearly an oral use at the beginning—we have no examples of it in print, except in usage books, until the middle of this century. But it is obscure in origin—was it a theater usage? Or possibly an Americanism Ellen Terry picked up on one of her American tours?

The development of *infer–imply* as a usage issue is curious, too. The earliest mention of the subject is in MacCracken & Sandison 1917, an English handbook apparently originally intended for use at Vassar College. Here is what it says:

A speaker or his statement *implies* (suggests, expresses, though not explicitly) something which a hearer *infers* (draws or deduces) from the statement. *Infer* is constantly used where *imply* is intended. CORRECT: Do you mean to *imply* [not *infer*] that I am deceiving you?

You will note that the example shown has a personal subject and that the authors say "*infer*

is constantly used." Since we know of no printed evidence existing in 1917, we infer the usage to be spoken.

The OED defined More 1533 without comment, as did Webster 1909 and undoubtedly other dictionaries. But in 1932 a member of the philosophy department at Boston University wrote to the Merriam-Webster editorial department questioning the definition of More 1533 in Webster 1909. In his opinion the sense was no longer in current good use. After some preliminaries about logic, he got to the point:

. . . no cultured person has in my hearing ever confused the two words. It is, however, the constant practice of the uneducated and the half-educated, to use *infer* for *imply.*

The logician is, of course, talking not about More 1533 but personal *infer.*

The editors gave serious consideration to the complaint—and by that time they also had collected some early commentators and a couple of clippings from the *Literary Digest* that rather preferred *infer* in this use to *imply,* because *imply* seemed a bit offensive. One editor suggested adding a note to the definition of More 1533, but he was overruled by another who observed that the sense in question was not quite the same as More 1533. Instead they added a new definition, "5. Loosely and erroneously, to imply," which appeared in Webster's Second (1934). Thus the dispute was established, although most of the usage-book comment came after World War II.

What can we conclude from all this? The first obvious point is that all the commentators from the very beginning missed the fact that it was an oral use they were objecting to—no one distinguished book use from spoken use. And the dictionaries did not support the distinction the commentators were trying to make because the dictionaries recorded only book use. The second point is that the words are not and never have been confused. We have seen that the same writer could use both More 1528 and More 1533 without mental distress. And personal *infer* has never been muddled with anything else, although it may have replaced the similar use of *imply* that was mildly disparaged in the 1930s. Third, logic is irrelevant to the dispute. *Infer* and *imply* are not interchanged by logicians. The personal *infer* is never used in logic. The objection is social—the personal *infer* has been associated with uncultured persons. Fourth, no distinctions are being lost. The distinctions between the main uses of *infer*—More 1528, More 1533, personal *infer*—and *imply* have remained the same all along. They are not the same distinction the commentators are talking about, but the commentators' distinction—roughly, that *imply* always means transmission and *infer* reception—is wishful and has not existed in usage since 1533. Fifth, it seems likely that the repeated injunction not to use *infer* for *imply* has diminished the literary use of More 1533, and if anything is in real danger of being lost, it is that long-standard use.

We have no evidence of personal *infer* in print before the 1950s—setting aside Ellen Terry's letter quoted above, which was published in 1932. Here is a sampling of what we have collected:

I have heard Italians complain of the American accent, inferring that American culture is unworthy of notice —W. Cabell Greet, *Word Study,* October 1952

The actor . . . may, by using a certain inflection or adopting a certain attitude, give a quite contrary impression, infer a meaning or eliminate one —Cyril Cusack, *Irish Digest,* January 1953

. . . "fit to be President," the New York *Post* was digging up evidence to infer that he is not —*New Republic,* 9 Mar. 1953

Jake liked to think of himself as a high-rolling bronc-buster, and if somebody inferred that he couldn't ride a particular horse, that was the horse Jake was bound to try —Fred Gipson, *Cowhand: The Story of a Working Cowboy,* 1953

May I remark here that although I seem to infer that private communication is an unholy mess of grammatical barbarism, . . . such is not my intent —V. Louise Higgins, "Approaching Usage in the Classroom," *English Jour.,* March 1960

One probable effect of the controversy should be noted here. Although our collection of usage books is by no means exhaustive, the ones we have show that the *imply–infer* issue did not become intensely treated until the very end of the 1950s. The writers just quoted—excepting Gipson, who was consciously using a colloquial expression (probably a direct descendant of our 1914 Kansas use)—probably did not even know there was a usage question here. Later, it became virtually impossible not to know, and our evidence shows a marked decline of occurrence of personal *infer* in edited prose. It pops up here and there, as in letters to the editor, but it is scarce in edited material. As far as we know, spoken use has not been affected.

When you are weighing the importance of the controversy in your mind, consider this example:

Leavis infers that Eliot's whole achievement is compromised by the inadequacies which his criticism reveals —*Times Literary Supp.,* 30 Nov. 1967

If a writer says that a third person infers something, it is not possible without the preceding context (missing from our clipping) to know for certain whether the third person is hinting or suggesting or is deducing or concluding. But even though you cannot be sure about the meaning of *infer* in the sentence, do you have any trouble understanding what is being said about Eliot?

If you have had the fortitude to stick with us this far, you know that the commentators' intense concern over preserving the all-important distinction between *infer* and *imply* goes back to a spoken use prevalent among certain less-cultured undergraduates at Vassar before 1917. It has been the chiefly oral use of *infer* with a personal subject that has been under attack all along, and that seems not to pose much of a problem for writers. The dwindling use of the More 1533 sense of *infer,* however, may well suggest that writers are increasingly following the commentators' preferred distinction between *infer* and *imply.* That distinction is easy enough to observe, certainly.

inferior, superior   *Inferior* and *superior,* as a result of the somewhat tricky role they have as implicit comparatives in English, are favorite subjects of usage commentators. The most commonly raised issue is that idiomatically they should be followed by *to* rather than *than* (a telling point that shows they are not true comparatives, according to Quirk et al. 1985). All the commentators are agreed on this. And, unlike Partridge 1942 and Shaw 1975, we find that writers do follow *inferior* and *superior* with *to:*

. . . regarded as inferior to the earlier work —*Current Biography,* June 1966

No longer do workers and peasants feel inferior to the university-trained —Rhea Menzel Whitehead, *Saturday Rev.,* 4 Mar. 1972

. . . nor is the tuition greatly superior to that of the tax-supported schools —B. K. Sandwell, *The Canadian Peoples,* 1941

On the whole, they were infinitely superior to the situation —Andrew Sarris, *Village Voice,* 28 Feb. 1968

The only evidence we have for *than* is second-hand from usage books.

See also IMPLICIT COMPARATIVE.

infest   When *infest* is used with a preposition, the choice is most often *with:*

. . . a brisk, gorsy, suburban place infested with fox terriers and healthy children —Anthony West, *New Yorker,* 10 Nov. 1951

. . . a division's command post . . . in an apple orchard infested with snipers —A. J. Liebling, *New Yorker,* 10 Dec. 1955

Less frequently, *infest* is used with *by*:

> . . . her tenement was infested by rats and overpriced —*New Yorker*, 10 Dec. 1966

As may be seen in the examples given above, when *infest* is used with a preposition, the verb form is usually the past participle; exceptions, however, do occur:

> . . . I curse computers for infesting the language with terms like *input, readout,* and *interface* —Thomas H. Middleton, *Saturday Rev.*, 1 Apr. 1978

infiltrate When *infiltrate* is used with a preposition, *into* is by far the one used most often:

> . . . a super-saver passenger will try to infiltrate his garment bag into a first-class section —Erma Bombeck, *Pittsburgh Press*, 6 Oct. 1987

> . . . how much of a force they had in reserve as opposed to the force they had infiltrated into the South —David Halberstam, *Harper's,* February 1971

Occasionally, *infiltrate* may be found with *to*:

> Another complete failure followed—this time in a step-ladder factory to which his father had infiltrated him —*English Digest,* May 1953

When the object names the one doing the infiltrating, *infiltrate* is also used with *with* or *by*:

> . . . there will be efforts to infiltrate the bandits with police operatives —*Christian Science Monitor*, 23 Apr. 1952

> . . . a language that has become infiltrated by patterns and loan words from English —R. Somerville Graham, *Word*, December 1956

Less frequently and in various relations, *infiltrate* is used with *through, among,* or *from*:

> . . . it will be next to impossible to keep the Reds from infiltrating through any dividing line —*Newsweek,* 17 May 1954

> They learn how to keep out of the street itself (it's a deathtrap) and how to infiltrate instead from house to house —*Newsweek,* 22 Mar. 1943

> . . . the salt water trickles down on the rocks; steam rises. The salt steam infiltrates among the clams —Hugh Cave, *New England Journeys,* 1953

In technical use the choice of prepositions used with *infiltrate* is even wider: the military does not restrict itself to *into, to,* or *through*; use of *toward, within,* and *around* also occurs:

> . . . a momentary glimpse of Guillermo's section to our left, infiltrating rapidly toward the rise —Alvah Bessie, *Men in Battle,* 1939

> . . . one or two lone infantrymen . . . could infiltrate within rifle range and quickly kill the gun crew —*Coast Artillery Jour.,* September–October 1942

> Their storm troops could infiltrate around points offering real resistance —Norman Friedman, *Desert Victory,* 1991

infiltration When *infiltration* is used with a preposition, *of* is often chosen:

> The charges of heavy communist infiltration of the book trade —*Publishers Weekly,* 3 Mar. 1951

> . . . articles expounding at length on the Soviet infiltration of the international disarmament movement —Elizabeth Grossman, *N.Y. Times Book Rev.,* 30 Jan. 1983

Somewhat less frequently, *infiltration* is used with *into*:

> . . . the danger of infiltration of professional gamblers into college athletics —*Current Biography 1951*

> . . . the progressive infiltration into their staffs of persons bringing with them the professional . . . standards —*AAUP Bulletin,* May 1965

Infiltration has also been used with *among,* although infrequently:

> . . . to keep an eye on Guatemalan infiltration among its neighbors —*Time,* 21 June 1954

Occasionally, *in* is used:

> . . . investigations into charges of Communist infiltration in the State Department —*Current Biography 1953*

infinitive The infinitive is the simple form of a verb. It can be used as a noun or as a modifier and it can control a word group used as a noun or modifier. The preposition *to* frequently but not always occurs with the infinitive. Since the 18th century there has been an assumption that the *to* is part of the infinitive, though that is not so. This belief has given us two usage controversies, which you will find at SPLIT INFINTIVE and TRY AND.

inflammable See FLAMMABLE, INFLAMMABLE.

inflict, afflict Are *inflict* and *afflict* in conflict? Quite a few commentators think so, and they warn us not to confuse the two. As is often true in these cases, the confusion is imaginary. What is perceived as confusion is in fact persistence of the oldest sense of *inflict*, which means the same as *afflict*.

Inflict typically occurs in constructions in which something is inflicted on, or upon, somebody:

> . . . once in a great while I inflict it upon people —Thomas H. Middleton, *Saturday Rev.*, August 1981

> . . . I am resolved not to inflict boredom on even the most deserving —Oliver St. John Gogarty, *It Isn't This Time of Year At All!*, 1954

Afflict typically occurs in constructions in which someone is afflicted with or by something:

> I found myself afflicted with a sense of the staleness and glibness of my verse —Donald Hall, *Goatfoot Milktongue Twinbird*, 1978

> . . . how a composer's work is both aided and afflicted by the power of record companies —Langdon Winner, *N.Y. Times Book Rev.*, 17 April 1983

These are not the only constructions in use, but they are typical. And they match the guidelines set up by the commentators. The thing to note is that the typical direct object of *inflict* is some unpleasant circumstance and the typical direct object of *afflict* is a person. The older sense of *inflict* works just like *afflict*:

> The miners are still out, and industry, as a result, is inflicted with a kind of creeping paralysis —Harold J. Laski, letter, 30 May 1926

> . . . a sick man inflicted with an incurable ailment —*Manchester Guardian Weekly*, 20 Nov. 1936

> An estimated 17.6 million people in Africa are infected with the parasites, experts say, with about half being inflicted with the "savanna" strain of the disease —Warren E. Leary, *N.Y. Times*, 28 Mar. 1995

Garner 1998 thinks this use is increasing, but we do not find much of it in our files. It never has been very common, and we do not recommend that you try to resurrect it.

influence 1. When the noun *influence* is used with a preposition, *of* predominates and usually introduces the influence itself:

> The influence of Seneca is much more apparent in the Elizabethan drama —T. S. Eliot, "Shakespeare and the Stoicism of Seneca," in *Selected Essays*, 1932

> All confessions are carefully scrutinized for the influence of fear and coercion —William O. Douglas, in *Omnibook*, October 1953

In the opposite relation, introducing the one influenced, it is often used with *on* or *in*; use of *on* occurs a little more frequently:

> I had read *The Sound and the Fury* a month or two earlier and it had a long influence on me —Norman Mailer, *Advertisements for Myself*, 1959

> . . . the need to conform has a powerful influence on the thinking and behavior of Americans —Ralph White, *Psychology Today*, November 1971

> . . . his enormous influence in the party organization —*New Republic*, 8 Mar. 1954

> . . . her dresses have become an important influence in the fashion industry —*Current Biography*, May 1953

In the same relation but less often, *influence* is used with *over* or *upon*:

> For this reason, he gained unbounded influence over Alexis's mother, the Tsarina —*Times Literary Supp.*, 1 Feb. 1968

> . . . heredity . . . exercised a greater influence upon him than did living people —Osbert Sitwell, *Noble Essences*, 1950

Influence has occasionally also been used with *among, for, from*, or *with*:

> It thus became a major goal of American foreign policy to weaken Communist influences among unions —*Collier's Year Book*, 1949

> She didn't approve of Mack in the least. Thought he was a bad influence for Duveaux —Olive Higgins Prouty, *Now, Voyager*, 1941

> . . . the younger man was subjected to a deep and lasting influence from the older writer —Emile DeLaveny, *Times Literary Supp.*, 17 Apr. 1969

> . . . the Russians took steps to gain influence with the governments of Eastern Europe —C. E. Black & E. C. Helmreich, *Twentieth Century Europe*, 1950

2. Simon 1980 is not gentle with people who stress this word on the second syllable:

> What makes *influence* so ghastly is not necessarily its sound (though I think it is ugly) but its demonstration of the existence of people so uneducated, so deaf to what others are saying, so unable to learn the obvious that they are bound to be a major source of verbal pollution, linguistic corruption, cultural erosion.

We cite this passage to illustrate what passions a fairly minor linguistic variation can arouse. The pronunciation \in-ˈflü-əns\ is chiefly Southern—we have recorded it spoken by former President Jimmy Carter, journalist Tom Wicker, and various Southern senators and governors. The point to notice is that, in some communities, \in-'flü-əns\ *is* what others are saying. It is thus largely a mark, not of the nescient, but of those who happen to have been born and raised in the South.

The same variation is found in *congruence*, some stressing the first syllable and some the second. In this case, however, so far as we know, the variation correlates neither with schooling nor with region.

informal Informal is often used—even overused—by usage writers, handbook writers, and dictionaries as a replacement label for the much misunderstood label *colloquial*. It is of vague application; beyond the fact that it represents a different part of the usage spectrum from *formal*, its meaning is rather elusive. Here are two attempts to pin it down:

> Informal style is marked by relatively short loose sentences, the use of simile rather than metaphor, casual rhythms and stresses —Barnard 1979

> Informal English is the spoken language of cultured people and the language used in writing when casual or familiar expression is desired —Janis 1984

When we have used it in this book, we have used it much as others have—simply in contrast to *formal* (which see).

informant, informer An *informer* may simply be someone who informs but is usually someone who informs against someone else underhandedly, as a spy or a police informer who gets paid for information. An *informant* may be the same thing as an *informer*, but most often *informant* denotes someone who informs in a general way or provides cultural or linguistic information to a researcher.

> . . . a rich storehouse of information . . . the informers are (among others) Herodotus, Frank Stockton, Marco Polo —Jean Stafford, *New Yorker*, 3 Dec. 1973

> Still another cause for disciplinary action is the charge of being an informer —J. Edgar Hoover, *Masters of Deceit*, 1958

> The intrigue in Mrs. Gutierrez's life has been created by her career. She is a professional informant. . . . Between 1968 and the present, Mrs. Gutierrez has been a paid informer —Nicholas M. Horrock, *N.Y. Times*, 2 Apr. 1975

> . . . choosing informants for the preparation of a dialect atlas —G. L. Brook, *English Dialects*, 1963

> . . . some of Mayer's other findings were more surprising. One informant after another revealed that American films stirred a deep discontent —David Robinson, *Saturday Rev.*, 13 Dec. 1975

infringe Although Fowler 1926 disliked *infringe* used as an intransitive verb, few other commentators have followed his lead, and his most recent reviser, Burchfield 1996, says that intransitive use is fully established, as, indeed, it was when Fowler was writing. It is usually followed by *on* or *upon*:

> . . . did not . . . infringe upon the interests of other groups —Frances Fox Piven, *Columbia Forum*, Summer 1970

> . . . tried to infringe on their power —Pete Axthelm, *New York*, 1 Nov. 1971

> . . . might infringe on that talismanic privacy —Francine Du Plessix Gray, *N.Y. Times Book Rev.*, 15 July 1979

The transitive *infringe* is also alive and well. It occurs most often in writing relating to the law:

> . . . many modern statutes have infringed it —David M. Walker, *The Scottish Legal System*, 3d ed., 1969

> . . . is not free to infringe the patent —John D. Upham, *Chemical & Engineering News*, 9 Feb. 1987

infuse When *infuse* is used with a preposition, it is usually *with*:

> . . . we know that broad social feelings should be infused with warmth —Lionel Trilling, in *Forms of Modern Fiction*, ed. William Van O'Connor, 1948

> His facile, free use of pen and brush infuses the massive subjects with a joyful vitality —Ada Louise Huxtable, *N.Y. Times*, 27 Apr. 1980

Less frequently, *infuse* is used with *by*:

> Subsequent chapters . . . are infused by a remarkable grasp of the facts —Hal Lehrman, *N.Y. Times Book Rev.*, 7 Aug. 1955

In another often encountered sense—"introduce, insinuate"—*infuse* is used with *into*:

> . . . infusing life into an inanimate body —Mary Shelley, *Frankenstein*, 1818

> . . . a tendency to infuse more and more of myself into the apprehension of the world —George Santayana, *Saturday Rev.*, 15 May 1954

Infuse also has been used with *in* or *to*:

> These words, these looks, infuse new life in me —Shakespeare, *Titus Andronicus*, 1594

. . . with the arrival of Sir Gerald Templer early in 1952 a new spirit was infused both to civilians and security forces —*The Americana Annual 1953*

Shakespeare, in addition to using *infuse* with *in, into,* and *with,* also used it with *on;* this last use is not found in contemporary prose:

> With those clear rays which she infused on me That beauty am I bless'd with which you see —*Henry VI,* 1592

A few critics object to "infusing a person with something." But it is a long-established use dating back to the 16th century. It may be that the OED, in labeling the use obsolete, influenced the commentators against it. The OED, it turns out, was premature in calling the sense obsolete. In the first OED Supplement (1933) this sense of *infuse* receives further treatment, including a directive to remove the obsolete label, and the sense is illustrated with two modern quotations. Our own files indicate continuing use:

> The spirit infused Deacon Jackson and Sister Wilson . . . at the same time —Maya Angelou, *I Know Why the Caged Bird Sings,* 1969

> And though the Red Sox fell 4–2 to the Indians on Sunday, they were infused with new confidence —Peter Gammons, *Sports Illustrated,* 19 Sept. 1988

> . . . the episode . . . infused him with a new sense of passion and purpose —John Lancaster, *Washington Post,* 9–15 Sept. 1991

ingenious, ingenuous, ingenuity Confusion of *ingenious* and *ingenuous* is not now much of a problem, but the distinction between these words was not so widely observed several centuries ago. *Ingenious* is the older word, having been borrowed from French in the 1400s. It is derived from the Latin *ingeniosus,* which means "talented, clever." *Ingenuous* was first used in English in the late 1500s. The Latin source from which it arose is *ingenuus,* "native, free born." Both words have developed several senses since their first use in English, but the fundamental meaning of *ingenious* has always been "clever":

> . . . the plot is ingenious and the going is good-humored —*New Yorker,* 1 May 1971

> . . . an ingenious method of checking errors —W. David Gardner, *Datamation,* June 1982

Ingenuous had some early use in the sense "noble or honorable," but its primary use in English has been to describe a person or personality characterized by frankness and openness, owing either to good character or—now more often—innocence:

. . . proposing serious budget cuts, and doing so with an ingenuous, at times charming, optimism —Robert Wright, *New Republic,* 6 Mar. 1995

. . . his frankness of expression, his ingenuous American informality —William F. Buckley, Jr., *Cosmopolitan,* October 1976

The OED shows that, in addition to their customary and distinct uses, *ingenious* and *ingenuous* were used fairly regularly as synonyms for many years:

> Our Lord having heard this ingenious confession —William Beveridge, *Sermons,* ca. 1680 (OED)

> If their Sonnes be ingenuous, they shall want no instruction —Shakespeare, *Love's Labour's Lost,* 1595 (OED)

But they appear to have ceased being used as synonyms by about 1800. Many 20th-century usage commentators warn that these words are often confused, but we have little evidence of it in our files.

A related subject is the history of the noun *ingenuity. Ingenuity* is derived from *ingenuous,* but its meaning is "the quality or state of being ingenious":

> . . . substituting technical ingenuity for a lack of good musical material —Peter Hellman, *Cosmopolitan,* January 1973

> . . . the tenacity and ingenuity of Vermont hill farmers —*N.Y. Times,* 21 Aug. 1983

Ingenuity acquired this sense in the 17th century, when *ingenuous* and *ingenious* were being used as synonyms. It was sufficiently well established in the 18th century for Johnson to include it in his 1755 Dictionary, and for Baker 1770 to disapprove of it: "It is a considerable Blemish in our Language, that the Word *Ingenuity* has two Senses; for hereby it often becomes unintelligible." Baker wanted *ingenuity* to be used only in its older "ingenuous" sense. He was fighting a battle already lost, however. The older sense of *ingenuity* had already been largely superseded by *ingenuousness* in Baker's time. It is now obsolete.

in hope(s) of See HOPE 2.

in hope(s) that See HOPE 2.

inhuman See UNHUMAN, INHUMAN.

inimical, inimicable When *inimical* or its less often encountered synonym, *inimicable,* is used with a preposition, the preposition is *to:*

> Pleasure is by nature immoderate and indefinite and inimical to right proportion —Iris Murdoch, *The Fire and the Sun,* 1977

> . . . those deficits seem to me directly inimicable to the progress we want to see on in-

flation —Paul Volcker, quoted in *Wall Street Jour.*, 10 Mar. 1982

initialisms See ACRONYMS.

ink Bremner 1980 and Copperud 1980 both look down on the verb *ink* as sportswriterese or sports headlinese, but this transitive verb has long since leaked from the sports pages into wider use:

The contract safely inked, I was interviewed —Jessica Mitford, *Atlantic*, October 1974

. . . she has been inked to do the part of a judge in an HBO special —Marge Crumbaker, *Houston Post*, 12 Sept. 1984

CBS has inked a talent holding deal with former "ER" star Gloria Reuben —Josef Adalian et al., *Variety*, 6–12 Dec. 1999

Pepsi-Cola Co. this month inked a strategic marketing and vending alliance —*Advertising Age*, 26 Jan. 1998

You should not expect to find it or use it in the more solemn kinds of discourse, however.

in line See ON LINE.

innate When *innate* is used with a preposition, it is usually *in*:

The faculty for myth is innate in the human race —W. Somerset Maugham, *The Moon and Sixpence*, 1919

. . . the delays innate in both serial and book publication —Walter Rundell, *AAUP Bulletin*, September 1971

Very occasionally, *innate* is used with *to*:

. . . the materials for conflict are innate to social life —Richard Sennett, *Psychology Today*, November 1970

innocent Back in 1926, H. W. Fowler decided that *innocent of* in the sense "lacking in" was worn-out humor. Gowers continued the notice in Fowler 1965. Burchfield 1996 finds it acceptable. If it was humorous at one time, it no longer seems to be especially so:

. . . finds the story is "meaningless," apparently because it is innocent of satire or moral —James Thurber, letter, 13 Dec. 1950

Her oval face is innocent of any wrinkle, though the pursed lips and focused brow indicate where wrinkles will come —John Updike, *Hugging the Shore*, 1983

Oddly for the work of an anthropologist "China Misperceived" is quite innocent of ethnographic insight —Marilyn B. Young, *N.Y. Times Book Rev.*, 11 Nov. 1990

See also PLEAD 2.

inoculate Bremner 1980 and Copperud 1970, 1980 note that this word is misspelled

with two *n*'s. The mistake does turn up in print from time to time, and so *inoculate* appears to be a bit of a problem word for copy editors and proofreaders as well as writers. Distinguish *inoculate* from *innocuous*, which does have two *n*'s.

in order that There is a chiefly British issue concerning this phrasal conjunction that began with Fowler 1926. Fowler likes *may* or *might* after the phrase and will tolerate *should* and sometimes *shall*, but he calls use of *can*, *could*, *will*, and *would* "unidiomatic." Burchfield 1996 finds that the restriction to the first four modals has gone out of date and that clauses introduced by *in order that* are currently more like those introduced by *so, that,* and *so that*.

in order to Commentators concerned with saving words (including Bremner 1980, Flesch 1964, Bernstein 1965, Copperud 1960, 1964, 1970, 1980, and Garner 1998) would have you regularly delete *in order* from this useful phrase. Follett 1966, on the other hand, says that objections to the phrase are pedantic.

One thing the phrase accomplishes is to eliminate the possibility of ambiguity. It is often used in contexts where reduction to *to* would be ambiguous.

I had to borrow $2,500 from Elliott Nugent, and damn near left *The New Yorker* for Paramount Pictures in order to live —James Thurber, letter, 2 June 1958

It may therefore, perhaps, be necessary, in order to preserve both men and angels in a state of rectitude —Samuel Johnson, in James Boswell, *Life of Samuel Johnson*, 1791

Of course, there are many contexts where ambiguity is not a problem. It may prove useful to look over these examples to see how many would be improved by deleting *in order*:

. . . even went the length of reading the play of "King John" in order to ascertain what it was all about —George Bernard Shaw, *Cashel Byron's Profession*, 1886

I dreamed last night that I had to pass a written examination in order to pass the inspection there —Robert Frost, letter, 22 Mar. 1915

With which understanding one may with all propriety open a discourse on poetry in order to show that poetry is older than prose —Leacock 1943

. . . it is always strange to what involved and complex methods a man will resort in order to steal something —William Faulkner, "Centaur in Brass," in *The Collected Stories of William Faulkner*, 1950

The critic betrays an unconscious admiration . . . in the sublime images he is driven to in order to express the depths of his exasperation —John Butt, *English Literature in the Mid-Eighteenth Century*, edited & completed by Geoffrey Carnall, 1979

First let me say that it is with great reluctance that I am raising my own allowance. In order to do that, I am increasing the self-imposed debt limit —*And More by Andy Rooney*, 1982

We suspect you will not find many improvements made simply by dropping *in order*. In some cases (perhaps especially those of Frost and Butt/Carnall) *in order* avoids real awkwardness. In others considerations of rhythm and emphasis (considerations allowed by Burchfield 1996) may be judged to apply. The thoughtful writer strives not for mere conciseness, but also for ease of communication. Many of the little phrases that brevity buffs think unnecessary are the lubrication that helps to smooth the way for your message to get across.

input This fashionable word, which has spread into general use from the world of computers, is disparaged as jargon and bureaucratese by Heritage 1982, Shaw 1987, Bremner 1980, Bryson 1984, Janis 1984, Mitchell 1979, Zinsser 1976, and Garner 1998. Most of the objections are directed at the noun. And the sense which seems to provoke the most irritation is a broad one: "advice, opinion, comment."

Let us concede *input* to be jargonish and faddish; yet, it must be in some way useful if it continues to be chosen so frequently by such a variety of writers as the ones quoted below. We'll let you decide how useful it can be in this sampling of the citations in our files.

Some lakes can withstand inputs of acids for many years because they sit in or near beds of limestone —Robert Alvo, *Natural History*, September 1986

. . . getting the process started would require an input equivalent to that spent on the Apollo program —Isaac Asimov, *Saturday Rev.*, 28 June 1975

. . . the best way for farmers to protect their profits is to cut input costs —*Wall Street Jour.*, 18 Dec. 1985

. . . a reporter . . . called for input on an article he was writing —Michelle Cottle, *New Republic*, 10 & 17 July 2000

. . . the raw sensory material, actually, the input right into his own ear from the streets —Allen Ginsberg, *American Poetry Rev.*, Vol. 3, No. 3, 1974

Where, as in Vietnam and Laos, the frustration has been nearly total, the bureaucratic input has been all but infinite —John Kenneth Galbraith, *ADA World Mag.*, March 1971

. . . the musical design was rounded rather than rugged, the level of expressivity restrained by Kim's much too restricted scale of personal input —Irving Kolodin, *Saturday Rev.*, 3 Apr. 1976

. . . had learned to just listen to these monologues. He knew that Knight wasn't looking for input as much as he was looking for a sounding board —John Feinstein, *A Season on the Brink*, 1989

With so little public input and few outspoken opponents —Jonathan Watts, *Lancet*, 6 Mar. 1999

These examples may give you some idea of the semantic spread of *input* as used outside bureaucracy and the worlds of science and technology. Whether you use it is obviously your choice.

inquire, enquire 1. Both *inquire* and *enquire* are used in American and British English. *Enquire* appears more frequently in British English than in American English. When *enquire* does appear in American English, it is usually in bookish or formal contexts. Overall, in American English *inquire* occurs more often than *enquire*; in British English *inquire* occurs about as often as does *enquire*.
2. When *inquire* and *enquire* are used with a preposition, it is most often *about* or *into*:

. . . their host inquired about the horses —*American Guide Series: Louisiana*, 1941

. . . but he did inquire about it. . . . —*Times Literary Supp.*, 17 July 1969

. . . before we enquire into the affirmative aspects of this hope —McGeorge Bundy, ed., *The Pattern of Responsibility*, 1951

. . . he enquired into dynamical problems involving the measures of time and velocity —S. F. Mason, *Main Currents of Scientific Thought*, 1953

Inquire and *enquire* are used less frequently with *after* or *for*:

The parents of the boys he played with always inquired after his father and mother —F. Scott Fitzgerald, "The Rich Boy," 1926

. . . as if she enquired after a favorite child —Katherine Anne Porter, "The Source," in *Mid Country*, ed. Lowry C. Wimberly, 1945

It was soon evident that this was the reddleman who had inquired for her —Thomas Hardy, *The Return of the Native*, 1878

. . . enquiring for news of the war —*Yale Rev.,* October 1919

There is also some evidence of use with *as to* and *concerning*:

. . . when he told a man who enquired as to the progress of his comedy that he had finished it —Matthew Arnold, reprinted in *Encore,* November 1944

. . . a man who was carrying a load of pottery to market stopped his horse against my field and inquired concerning Wyman the younger —Henry David Thoreau, *Walden,* 1854

Inquire and *enquire* are usually used with *of* when the object is the person asked; less frequently *from* is used in this relation:

Let spendthrifts' heirs enquire of yours—who's wiser —Lord Byron, *Don Juan,* Canto XII, 1823

. . . he had long inquired of himself what great principle or idea it was that had created the Union —Archibald MacLeish, *Saturday Rev.,* 13 Nov. 1971

. . . when he inquired from his friend, David Garnett, whether the rest of the party really liked him —*Times Literary Supp.,* 19 May 1971

inquirer, enquirer   Of the variants *inquirer* and *enquirer,* the former appears more frequently. When *enquirer* is used, it is likely to be found in British prose; however, it has not gone entirely out of use in the U.S.—witness the newspaper title the *National Enquirer.*

inquiry, enquiry   1. The evidence for *inquiry* and *enquiry* points to a pattern of usage much like that of *inquire* and *enquire,* but with one difference: *enquiry* appears in current American usage more often than does the spelling *enquire.* Still, both *inquiry* and *enquiry* are used in American and British English, with the *i* spelling occurring more often.
2. When *inquiry* and *enquiry* are used with a preposition, *into* is found most often:

. . . distinguish between legitimate legislative inquiry into the acts of a man . . . and illegitimate inquiry into opinions —Norman Thomas, in *New Republic,* 28 Feb. 1955

This book is an enquiry into the causes of the English blindness to Racine —John Loftis, *Modern Language Notes,* November 1958

Less frequently, the two words are used with *about, as to, in, of, on,* or *with* in various relations and senses:

The next day I made such exhaustive enquiries about women with golden hair, that

some people thought me mad —John Berry, *Antioch Rev.,* December 1956

. . . his head was tilted at the precise angle of inquiry as to where he should put Muhlenberg's drink —Theodore Sturgeon, *E Pluribus Unicorn,* 1953

. . . Research Council fosters scientific inquiry in the social fields —*Current Biography 1950*

. . . made inquiries of other libraries when a particular book was needed —*Current Biography,* June 1967

During the Parliamentary enquiry on the Liverpool and Manchester Railway Bill —O. S. Nock, *The Railways of Britain,* 1947

. . . his casual inquiry with other publishers who thought they had not had the same experience —Curtis G. Benjamin, letter to the editor, *Times Literary Supp.,* 19 June 1969

in regard to, in regards to   See REGARD 1.

in respect of, in respect to, with respect to   These phrases have been the subject of considerable dispute in the past. None of the varied opinions about the phrases has a solid, practical connection to actual usage. Our evidence tells us that all three of these phrases are in current good use. You will notice that our examples tend to come from academic writing rather than the popular press. *In respect of* has much more British than American use.

Hull remains completely obdurate about not using the word "recognition" in respect of the French Committee —Sir Winston Churchill, *Closing the Ring,* 1951

This is particularly so in respect of his concept of lateral thinking —*Times Literary Supp.,* 12 Feb. 1970

In respect to is the least common of the three. It is much more frequent in American English than British English:

The most intriguing in the group of paintings is the one which, in respect to its replicas, has figured simply as the *Weavers* in the modern literature —W. R. Rearick, *Johns Hopkins Mag.,* Spring 1967

. . . perhaps prejudices my judgment in respect to the perfection of her model —George Santayana, *Persons and Places,* 1944

With respect to is currently the most common of the three in American English, and it has British use as well:

. . . creates its share of problems with respect to language —Albert H. Marckwardt, *Linguistics and the Teaching of English,* 1966

. . . a more advantageous position with respect to the larger more comprehensive problem —Nehemiah Jordan, *Themes in Speculative Psychology,* 1968

. . . our conception of the physical world can be exhibited as a theory with respect to our experiences —A. J. Ayer, quoted in *Times Literary Supp.,* 19 Feb. 1970

inroad *Inroad,* according to our evidence, is often used in the plural. When *inroad* is used with a preposition, it is used with several. Occurring frequently are *into* and *on:*

. . . he had drunk three times as much brandy as was his custom and had made a great inroad into the package of Egyptian Prettiests which he never smoked after supper —Jean Stafford, *Children Are Bored on Sunday,* 1953

. . . the appearance, if not the reality, of Republican inroads into a Democratic stronghold —Iver Peterson, *N.Y. Times,* 7 Nov. 1979

. . . another sharp inroad on the principle of free speech —*Civil Liberties,* February 1954

. . . the continuing inroads on moviegoing . . . via the Public Broadcasting Service, cable, and Home Box Office —Judith Crist, *Saturday Rev.,* 8 Jan. 1977

Inroad is also used, somewhat less frequently, with *in* or *upon:*

. . . the idea of making inroads in the Democratic camp to split off the Southerners —C. Vann Woodward, *Reunion and Reaction,* 2d ed. rev., 1956

Sometimes the inroads upon justice are subtle and insidious —*Selected Writings of Benjamin N. Cardozo,* ed. Margaret E. Hall, 1947

Very occasionally, *inroad* is used with *against, among,* or *with:*

. . . their power to make dramatic inroads against an injustice of long standing —Milton S. Eisenhower, *Johns Hopkins Mag.,* February 1966

. . . trade unionism made some inroads among the skilled construction crafts —Murray Ross, *Annals of the American Academy of Political and Social Science,* November 1947

A rapidly growing Mexican sulphur industry . . . is now making inroads with domestic customers —*Newsweek,* 2 July 1956

insanitary See UNSANITARY, INSANITARY.

insensible When *insensible* is used with a preposition, it is usually *to:*

. . . Archer had never been insensible to such advantages —Edith Wharton, *The Age of Innocence,* 1920

. . . the strange thing is that a boy so sentient of his surroundings should have been so insensible to the real world about him —*The Autobiography of William Allen White,* 1946

I never knew a member of the Vietnam press corps who was insensible to what happened when the words "war" and "correspondent" got joined —Michael Herr, *Esquire,* April 1970

At one time, *insensible* was also used with *of,* but we find almost no recent evidence.

If there was one man in the world she hated because he was insensible of her attraction it was Mark —Ford Madox Ford, *The Last Post,* 1928

. . . the primitive . . . mind . . . is untrammelled by logic, and insensible of the law of contradiction —Sir James G. Frazer, *Aftermath,* 1937

insensitive When *insensitive* is used with a preposition, it is used with *to:*

He was insensitive to all kinds of discourtesy —James Joyce, *Dubliners,* 1914

. . . we will only impede progress if we rely on threats or are insensitive to many difficulties and basic fears —Adlai E. Stevenson, *New Republic,* 28 Sept. 1953

One would have to be astonishingly insensitive to these pleas —Fred M. Hechinger, *Saturday Rev.,* 29 May 1976

inseparable When used with a preposition, *inseparable* is followed by *from:*

. . . the strengthening of discipline, the summoning of moral resources are by no means inseparable from the formulas of religion —Edmund Wilson, *A Piece of My Mind,* 1956

. . . employment policy is inseparable from demographic policy —Anthony Wolff, *RF Illustrated,* August 1975

inside of Bierce 1909 seems to have been the first to insist on the omission of *of* from the compound preposition *inside of.* He has had a considerable number of followers over the past fifty years. There are two types of dissent that counter the tradition established by Bierce.

Bryant 1962 cites two studies that show *inside of* occurs in standard contexts as a variant of *inside*; she thus concludes that *inside of* is standard, as it is.

The second form of dissent finds *inside of*

less reprehensible when used with expressions of time.

It seems likely that *inside of* originated as a speech form in which *of* served to create a bit of space between *inside* and the next content word. It would, therefore, be fair to characterize it as colloquial in the nonpejorative sense of the word. You use it or omit it according to the rhythmic requirements of your sentence. Here are a few examples:

> ... had such a roaring time of it that she killed herself inside of two years —George Bernard Shaw, letter, 31 Dec. 1897

> "... inside of a week I got a package from Croirier's with a new evening gown in it." —F. Scott Fitzgerald, *The Great Gatsby*, 1925

> Isn't it disheartening to see a magnificent sunburn ... disappear entirely inside of a fortnight? —Bennett Cerf, *Saturday Rev.*, 11 Apr. 1953

> He went inside of the office that he was directed to enter —Ishmael Reed, *Japanese by Spring*, 1993

> The yokel had simply stepped inside of his opponent's sense of time —Ralph Ellison, *Invisible Man*, 1952

As these suggest, the use with expressions of time is the more frequent. *Inside of* is standard, but *inside* is much more frequently used. See also OUTSIDE OF.

insight When *insight* is used with a preposition, the choice is usually *into*:

> ... the sudden insight into the nature of things —Edmund Wilson, *A Piece of My Mind*, 1956

> ... realizing this gave me no insight into how to correct it —Bartley McSwine, *Change*, May–June 1971

Occasionally, *insight* is also used with *about, as to, on, regarding,* or *to*; of this group *on* occurs a little more frequently than the others:

> ... I had a big insight and a little insight about the book —Rust Hills, *Esquire*, April 1973

> ... might well offer fresh insights as to the character and extent of the social adaptation involved —George C. Barker, *ETC*, Summer 1945

> There is no doubt that certain unusually able ex-Communists ... can offer brilliant insights on our present difficulties —*New Republic*, 22 Oct. 1951

> ... shows a keen insight regarding the genetic relationships of American Indian lan-

guages —*Dictionary of American Biography*, 1929

> ... gave us new insights to their concerns and objectives —Chester Bowles, *Promises to Keep*, 1971

insightful This relatively new adjective (first recorded in 1907) has lately become something of a minor irritant to a few usage commentators, who have described it variously as "journalese" (Zinsser 1976), "a suspicious overstatement for 'perceptive'" (Strunk & White 1979), and "jargon" (Janis 1984). Dictionaries, on the other hand, routinely treat it as an ordinary, inoffensive word. It is in common use, especially in reviews.

> ... as readable as it is insightful —William Manchester, *N.Y. Times Book Rev.*, 12 Sept. 1976

> ... is also very insightful about Burton's acting —*Wall Street Jour.*, 18 Dec. 1981

> Judiciously feminist in her sensibility and continually insightful —E. L. Doctorow, *N.Y. Times Book Rev.*, 13 Feb. 1994

> ... offers insightful commentary on everything from development and environmental issues to local lingo —Genevieve Stuttaford et al., *Publishers Weekly*, 18 May 1998

insignia *Insignia* has the form of a Latin plural, the singular of which is *insigne*. But as an English word, *insignia* is used both as a plural and as a singular:

> ... the magazine's insignia has been a rabbit dressed in evening clothes —*Current Biography*, September 1968

> ... all the insignia and stigmata of Old World nationalism —Henry Steele Commager, *Saturday Rev.*, 13 Dec. 1975

When *insignia* is understood as a singular, it often has *insignias* as its plural:

> Precise or elegant usage is seen as one of the insignias of class —Anatole Broyard, *N.Y. Times Book Rev.*, 22 Mar. 1981

The singular *insignia* is recorded in the OED as early as 1774, but its use seems not to have become common until the 20th century. Usage commentators have in general regarded it with tolerance, although it has had its critics (such as Follett 1966). The alternative singular *insigne* is preferred by some writers:

> ... a red beret with the Amtrak arrow insigne —David Butwin, *Saturday Rev.*, 22 Jan. 1972

However, *insignia* is a far more common choice in such contexts, and *insigne* is itself sometimes criticized as pretentious. *Insignia* appears still to be used primarily as a plural in

British English, but in American English, the singular *insignia* and the plural *insignias* (as well as the plural *insignia*) are now unquestionably standard. You need not hesitate to use them.

insist When *insist* is used with a preposition, it is used with *on* or (less often) *upon*:

... he liked to insist more strongly than ever on the altruistic, the self-sacrificingly patriotic character of his whole career —Aldous Huxley, *The Olive Tree*, 1937

... she insisted on reading them pleasant stories about nice boys and girls —Louis Auchincloss, *A Law for the Lion*, 1953

... but he himself, though capable of firm opinions, never insisted upon them —Robert Penn Warren, *Commonweal*, 15 Aug. 1947

In its transitive use, *insist* is used with a clause as object:

... in some suburban schools where parents insist their children take certain academic subjects —James B. Conant, *Slums and Suburbs*, 1961

inspire When *inspire* is used with a preposition, it generally is used with *by* and the verb form is usually the past participle:

... inspired by the most genuine passion for the rights and liberties of mankind —Virginia Woolf, *The Second Common Reader*, 1932

... inspired by a subconscious desire to compensate for these humiliations —George F. Kennan, *New Yorker*, 1 May 1971

Inspire is also used quite frequently with *in, to,* or *with; to* and *with* occur more often than *in*. The verb may take any of its forms.

The bribe had inspired nothing but fright in the old man —Irving Wallace, *The Plot*, 1967

... inspiring Americans to visit Europe —Horace Sutton, *Saturday Rev.*, 1 Jan. 1972

The old rooms in the candlelight inspired him with a tenderness —Vita Sackville-West, *The Edwardians*, 1930

in spite of the fact that See FACT 1.

instance Two commentators, Phythian 1979 and Copperud 1970, 1980, say that *instance* is frequently used in wordy phrases. They both single out *in the instance of*:

... a place to bemoan the fact that, once again, this time in the instance of oneself, the world in its ignorance is failing to recognize another genius —Aristides, *American Scholar*, Winter 1985/86

Their number, in the instance of Freud, is immense —Steven Marcus, *N.Y. Times Book Rev.*, 16 Feb. 1997

Our evidence does not show the phrase to be overused. Both commentators object to *instance* on the same grounds as they object to *case*. See the article at CASE for a discussion of phrases that have been criticized as wordy.

instil, instill 1. Both *instil* and *instill* are used, but the double *l* spelling occurs more frequently. The single *l* spelling seems to be favored by the British, but it occurs also in American English use.
2. When *instil* or *instill* is used with a preposition, it is most often *in*:

His desire to share this understanding with his countrymen and to instil in them a persistent impulse toward inquiry —Roger Burlingame, *Backgrounds of Power*, 1949

School teachers, anxious to instil a love of the outdoors in young folk —*Scots Mag.*, July 1958

... inevitability of violence could be instilled in the minds of his contemporaries —Richard Hofstadter, *Harper's*, April 1970

Less frequently, but still quite often, the preposition *into* is used:

My plan is one for instilling high knowledge into empty minds —Thomas Hardy, *The Return of the Native*, 1878

... the conventional English education instils into us a prejudice against that kind of disquisition —Max Beerbohm, *Atlantic*, December 1950

Some language critics object to the use of *instil, instill* with the preposition *with*. This use has been around for a long time; the OED shows Milton used it in 1664. *Instill with* is still in use. It is not unidiomatic, especially in a passive construction:

... does not believe that the young should be instilled with old "moral dogmas" —Mark Crispin Miller, *Atlantic*, November 1984

... Taiwanese students returning from America instilled with new values and ideas —Andrew Tanzer, *Forbes*, 8 Apr. 1996

It is also idiomatic in active constructions:

... it was the Chinese who instilled them with principles of national communism —*Times Literary Supp.*, 13 May 1965

Instil and *instill* have also been used, although infrequently, with *among, through,* or *within*:

The police also back the Church in her endeavors to instil modesty of dress among women —*Living Church*, 27 Mar. 1926

He planned to instil lofty ideals through his painting —*Times Literary Supp.*, 30 Oct. 1981

The aim was to instill within bright children a desire to continue their education —James B. Conant, *Slums and Suburbs*, 1961

instruct When *instruct* is used with a preposition, the one that occurs most frequently is *to* followed by an infinitive:

. . . they told them so because they had been instructed to tell them so —H. R. Trevor-Roper, *New Statesman & Nation*, 5 Dec. 1953

. . . an urgent call from the White House instructing him to draw up a legal brief —*Current Biography*, July 1965

Almost as frequently *instruct* is used with *in*:

. . . present need should instruct America in drawing the plans of a new system of government —Vernon Louis Parrington, *Main Currents in American Thought*, 1930

. . . a teacher was secured in Philadelphia to instruct in English grammar —*American Guide Series: Delaware*, 1938

Occasionally, *instruct* is used with *as to* or *for*:

. . . instruct them as to which candidate to vote for —Dayton D. McKean, *Party and Pressure Politics*, 1949

Of the 382 delegates thus chosen, 278 were instructed for Roosevelt, 68 for Taft —David Saville Muzzey, *Our Country's History*, new ed., 1961

insure See ENSURE, INSURE, ASSURE.

integral See METATHESIS.

intend Here are the chief constructions (besides the simple direct object) that are used with *intend*:

It may be followed by an infinitive:

They never intended to strike Jacksontown —E. L. Doctorow, *Loon Lake*, 1979

It may be followed by a direct object and an infinitive phrase:

. . . seems to have intended the happy ending to show the purification of our corrupt society —John Butt, *English Literature in the Mid-Eighteenth Century*, edited & completed by Geoffrey Carnall, 1979

It may be followed by a gerund:

. . . I saw that the child had reached the fence and intended climbing it —Peter Taylor, *The Old Forest and Other Stories*, 1985

It may be followed by a clause, with or without *that*. The verb in the clause will be a sub-

junctive or the equivalent of a subjunctive. This construction seems less common than the foregoing:

. . . in everything Richelieu undertook things happened as Richelieu had intended they should happen —Hilaire Belloc, *Richelieu*, 1930

Intend may take a prepositional phrase introduced by *for*:

At first intended for the church, he was educated at . . . —*Australian Dictionary of Biography*, 1967

In speech and speechlike writing, it is sometimes followed by *on* and a gerund:

. . . I intend on protecting myself and my loved ones —letter to the editor, *Saturday Evening Post*, October 1981

Longman 1984 warns against *intend* followed by *for*, a noun or pronoun object, and an infinitive with *to*, as in "I didn't intend for her to hear." We have no examples of this construction in edited prose, and assume that it is a verbal use like *intend on*.

See also DESIGN, INTEND.

intense See INTENSIVE, INTENSE.

intensifiers A recent correspondent of ours was curious to know what an intensifier is—a new part of speech? she asked. Not really a new part of speech. An intensifier—or intensive, as it is also called—is a linguistic element used to give emphasis or additional strength to another word or a statement. Intensifiers come from several parts of speech and other grammatical categories. Our correspondent sent us a couple of nouns:

Where *the dickens* have you been?
What *the hell* are you doing?

Adverbs are the largest class:

a *very* hot day
it was *so* sweet of you
a *mighty* fine time
You know that *full* well.
a *really* big show
awfully bad weather
wet *clear* through

Adjectives are used too:

you *bloody* idiot
It's a *complete* lie.
utter nonsense

And participles:

stark raving mad
a *blooming* fool

And pronouns:

She *herself* did it.
Borrowing is *itself* a bad habit.

Prepositional phrases can serve as intensifiers:

> Where *in heaven's name* have you been?
> What *in the world* does he think he's doing?

Good and and *nice and* are also used:

> when I'm *good and* ready
> It's *nice and* warm here.

Intensifiers are a frequent bone of contention in usage books. Since they very often indicate a conversational style, many handbooks discourage their use. And there are long-standing disputes about the propriety of adjectives and flat adverbs in intensive function.

Historical observers like Lamberts 1972 and Strang 1970 note that the words used as intensifiers have tended to change over the years. Such intensifiers as *sore, wondrous, plaguey, powerful, devilish, prodigious,* which were formerly quite common, are little used nowadays. Those that survive from older use are often objects of dispute.

intensive, intense The controversy over these two words was started by Fowler 1926. His complaint was that *intensive* was replacing *intense* in a sense meaning approximately "highly concentrated." He laid the blame for this change on two phrases that apparently began to appear frequently around the time of World War I—*intensive farming* (this sense of *intensive* now has become more specialized and has a separate definition) and *intensive bombardment.* He thus charged other use of this *intensive* with being a popularized technicality and plumped for *intense* instead.

What Fowler seems to have noticed was a change in usage in progress. The OED shows that the two earliest senses of *intensive* are synonymous with two senses of *intense*: "very strong or acute" and "highly concentrated." The OED marked both these senses of *intensive* obsolete because their evidence ended with the 17th century. The first of these is indeed obsolete: Robert Burton wrote *intensive pleasure* but nowadays only *intense* is used in such a context. The second sense, if indeed it was obsolete, was revived in the 20th century, and in the second half of the 20th century it all but replaced *intense* in the "highly concentrated" sense.

In the 20th century the words tended to differentiate along different lines from those Fowler was defending. *Intense* has tended to become limited to describing some inherent characteristic:

> . . . in the intense sunlight —Nancy Milford, *Harper's,* January 1969

> . . . requiring intense concentration —Stanley Marcus, *Minding the Store,* 1974

> . . . the intense dislike she arouses —Alfred Kazin, *Harper's,* August 1971

Intensive would never be used in those contexts. *Intensive* tends to connote something that is applied from outside:

> . . . gave them six years of intensive training for leadership —William L. Shirer, *The Rise and Fall of the Third Reich,* 1960

> . . . Grissom and Glenn underwent intensive preparation for the next space flight —*Current Biography,* June 1965

> . . . nine days of intensive screenings, panel sessions, and lectures —Arthur Knight, *Saturday Rev.,* 12 Feb. 1972

> The foreign children in Cologne are taught intensive German for two years —Deborah Churchman, *Christian Science Monitor,* 7 July 1980

It would appear that the "highly concentrated" sense is generally viewed as externally applied rather than an inherent characteristic and is thus displacing *intense* in this use. *Intense* is not dead in this use, but it is dwindling:

> . . . an intense barrage of anti-personnel gunfire —*Current Biography,* April 1966

> But some of them, in spite of care and intense treatment, can never fly well enough to defend themselves or hunt —Margery Facklam, "Kay McKeever and a Parliament of Owls," in *Chains of Light* (8th-grade textbook), ed. Theodore Clymer, 1982

intensives See INTENSIFIERS.

intent When the adjective *intent* is used with a preposition, it is usually *on*:

> . . . he would walk right past purple cows, so intent was he on his quest —James Thurber, *Fables for Our Time, and Famous Poems Illustrated,* 1940

> . . . the author is so intent on being clever that he usually forgets to be anything more —Babette Deutsch, *Yale Rev.,* December 1953

Less frequently, *intent* is used with *upon*:

> . . . comes Fred MacMurray, so intent upon making his way in the corporation —Lee Rogow, *Saturday Rev.,* 23 Oct. 1954

Intent has also been used, but not very often, with *in* or *to* plus the infinitive:

> . . . several lanes of traffic . . . intent in tracing the most direct route between two given points —Emily Hahn et al., *Meet the British,* 1953

> The Federalists were intent to create a strong government —Claude G. Bowers, *Atlantic,* January 1953

intention When *intention* is used with a preposition, it is used most often with *of,* which is followed by a gerund or a noun:

". . . may we very humbly entreat you to sign this gentleman's manifesto with some intention of putting your promise into practice?" —Virginia Woolf, *Three Guineas,* 1939

The great novelists knew that manners indicate the largest intentions of men's souls —Lionel Trilling, in *Forms of Modern Fiction,* ed. William Van O'Connor, 1948

The main intention of the poem has been to make dramatically visible the conflict —Allen Tate, *On the Limits of Poetry,* 1948

Almost as frequently, *intention* is used with *to,* which is followed by an infinitive:

. . . a young child's statements are often objectively untrue, but without the slightest intention to deceive —Bertrand Russell, *Education and the Good Life,* 1926

. . . the government's intention to implement the Industrial Training Act —*Current Biography,* July 1967

Intention has also been used with *against, behind, toward,* or *towards:*

"He said the U.S. harbors no military intentions against Saudi Arabian oil fields" —NBC radio newscast, 19 Mar. 1975

. . . in her wise innocence she had divined the intention behind her mother's tolerance —James Joyce, *Dubliners,* 1914

. . . their keen perception of Soviet actions and intentions toward Yugoslavia —Alex Dragnich, *Current History,* July 1952

Recently, Young informed the ICC of his intentions towards the Central —*Time,* 1 Feb. 1954

intercede *Intercede* is used with a variety of prepositions; those found most often are *for, in, on,* or *with:*

. . . to intercede for her afore she commits the sin that cannot be forgiven —Sir Arthur Quiller-Couch, *The Delectable Duchy,* 1893

. . . and she it was now . . . who interceded for the old woman with her uncle —Hilaire Belloc, *Richelieu,* 1930

It was not the task of the government to intercede in this process —Herbert I. London, *Arts and Sciences,* Spring 1967

. . . beseeching him to intercede in my behalf with *Post* pooh-bah Ben Bradlee —John Leonard, *The Nation,* 26 June 2000

. . . will intercede with the deity on their behalf —*National Geographic,* October 1947

. . . the frantic prefect of Canton asked Warren to intercede with the British —Geoffrey C. Ward, *American Heritage,* August/September 1986

Once in a while, *intercede* is used with *against* or *between:*

Only the law, it seems, can effectively intercede against the threat of irreversible depredations —Hilton Kramer, *N.Y. Times,* 22 Apr. 1979

"Resists making judgments that intercede between teenagers and the codes and beliefs of their parents" —publisher's catalog, August 1981

interesting, interestingly *Interesting* has drawn occasional criticism from usage commentators dating back to Partridge 1942, primarily on the grounds that it is an overused and imprecise adjective. It is, of course, an extremely common word.

What was most interesting about Daniel's speech . . . —Gay Talese, *Harper's,* January 1969

. . . for more interesting part-time jobs —Jane Schwartz Gould, *Barnard Alumnae,* Winter 1971

. . . these letters are interesting but not fascinating —Robert F. Byrnes, *Saturday Rev.,* 5 Apr. 1975

Its imprecision is part of what makes it useful, and we see no need to make a policy of avoiding it.

The adverb *interestingly* is often now used as a sentence modifier. Such usage has been common since the 1960s:

. . . and, interestingly, no public funds at any level could have been used —James B. Conant, *Slums and Suburbs,* 1961

Interestingly, Young thinks the Atlanta experience is essentially national —Richard Reeves, *New York,* 12 July 1976

Interestingly, Weinberger once served as a young captain —Hedrick Smith, *N.Y. Times Mag.,* 1 Nov. 1981

It occurs commonly with *enough:*

Interestingly enough . . . , the students who have the most trouble . . . —John Coyne, *Change,* March 1973

Interestingly enough, these handbooks . . . are bound in the manner of real books —Erik Sandberg-Diment, *N.Y. Times,* 20 Mar. 1984

The sentence-modifying *interestingly* is somewhat similar to the sentence-modifying *hope-*

fully (which see), but no usage commentator that we know of has so far criticized it.

interface *Interface*, like *input*, is a word given wide currency by the computer revolution, and as both noun and verb it is viewed with alarm and distaste by many commentators from the 1970s on. Our evidence, however, suggests there is not much reason for alarm. We have a great many citations from the 1990s but they are almost entirely from technical contexts, especially those involving computers, computer games, and the Internet. It appears to have occasional facetious use, but is otherwise rare in general edited prose. Burchfield 1996 makes a similar observation from a British standpoint.

in terms of *In terms of* is a compound preposition that seems to have taken hold only after World War II. It apparently struck a responsive chord, for we have many examples of its use from the early 1950s. It did not take long to draw unfriendly attention: the editor of the *Journal of Communication* disapproved it in 1954, and usage books soon followed suit. The usual advice is to omit it or to substitute a simple preposition for it. Sometimes it may be possible to find a simple substitute:

> Windows 98 and Mac OS are more alike in terms of function them they have ever been —Peter Haynes, *N.Y. Times,* 5 Nov. 1998
>
> . . . holding U.S. physicians to an increasing degree of accountability, particularly in terms of cost-effectiveness and the quality care they provide —Jonathan P. Weiner et al., *JAMA,* 17 May 1995

Perhaps simple *in* would have served in the first example, and *for* in the second. But we find that in most cases *in terms of* cannot easily be revised out. Its very imprecision seems to be its greatest virtue. Here are some examples in which we think you will find no easy replacement for *in terms of*:

> . . . the method is delightfully remote from academicism, and the theme comes to life in terms of people and wagons, horses and dogs —*Times Literary Supp.,* 28 Dec. 1951
>
> And so McCarthy in the hearings saw all issues and conditions in terms of himself —Michael Straight, *New Republic,* 28 June 1954
>
> . . . a scheme for an orderly arrangement of the elementary particles. The particles were described in terms of eight quantum numbers —*Current Biography,* February 1966
>
> . . . he has no thought of overdoing the simple life; he is thinking in terms of £500 a year, with a few good servants and horses

> —James Sutherland, *English Literature of the Late Seventeenth Century,* 1969
>
> . . . the contrast between male and female behaviour in terms of what might be called conversational etiquette —Michael Rundell, *English Today,* July 1995
>
> It is not a tempera painting merely updated and translated into oil. It may be, instead, the first Florentine painting planned fundamentally in terms of the capacities of oil —Andrew Butterfield, *New Republic,* 5 July 1999
>
> . . . on a quixotic mission to simplify perhaps the most inelegant aspect of the Web: its addresses. Inelegant in terms of the spoken word, that is —J. C. Herz, *N.Y. Times,* 28 May 1998

internecine *Internecine* is a useful word today because of a mistake that wasn't caught. The word began its history in English in Samuel Butler's satirical poem *Hudibras* (1663). According to the OED, Butler apparently used the phrase *internecine war* as a translation of Latin *internecīnum bellum,* which was a term for a war of extermination. Samuel Johnson's Dictionary (1755) was the first dictionary to enter the adjective, and Johnson, apparently misled by Latin *inter-* (which does not have in this word its usual "mutual" or "reciprocal" sense), defined it as "endeavouring mutual destruction." Johnson's definition was of course carried into later dictionaries—lexicographers are frequently respectful enough of their predecessors to copy them. Before too long, Johnson's sense was the dominant meaning of the word. And a good thing, said Fowler 1926, for without Johnson's misunderstanding, the word would have had no particular use in the language, since its Latin sense has plenty of substitutes in English, including *destructive, slaughterous, murderous, bloody,* and *sanguinary*.

So Johnson's mistake has given English a useful, if somewhat learned, word. It is really more of an interesting story than a usage issue; even the major usage panels find the mistaken use acceptable. The last complaint we know of is in Bernstein 1958; he objected to its use for internal conflict without the notion of slaughter. It is true that other words are available for this use, but *intramural* sounds too much like fun and games and *intertribal* too anthropological. The bloodless sense is well established:

> The rivalry between the various cities of Texas is an interesting phenomenon. . . . The Easterner, or tenderfoot, will not comprehend this keen, internecine rivalry —Frank Sullivan, *The Night the Old Nostalgia Burned Down,* 1953

Did you then remember that, for all their internecine squabbling, trade unionists always call one another "brother"? —Grundy, *Punch,* 20 July 1976

Meanwhile, internecine warfare broke out among the team's big egos —Michael Riley, *Time,* 21 Nov. 1988

He doesn't say, though the internecine bureaucratic struggle for honours is one amusing side of his story —Paul Barker, *Times Literary Supp.,* 21 Mar. 1997

interpose When used with a preposition, *interpose* most commonly appears with *between* in modern writing:

She actually interposed her body between him and the street door —Edna Ferber, *Cimarron,* 1929

. . . interpose himself between the police and the body of one demonstrator —Norman Mailer, *Harper's,* November 1968

Much less often, *interpose* is used with *in:*

. . . the Senate has shown restraint in interposing vetoes in the case of major appointments —Lindsay Rogers, in *Aspects of American Government,* ed. Sydney D. Bailey, 1950

And, once in a while, *interpose* is followed by *against, on, upon,* or *with* in various senses and relations:

. . . 1966, when Robert Kennedy interposed his formidable presence against what appeared to be the certain election of Arthur Klein —Richard Cohen, *New York,* 13 Sept. 1971

For a while I listened . . . and at length interposed once more on the old man's side —W. H. Hudson, *Green Mansions,* 1904

Mountain systems are significant . . . because of the barriers that they interpose upon the movements of people —Vernor C. Finch & Glenn T. Trewartha, *Elements of Geography,* 2d ed., 1942

. . . the McCarthy fight against Harvard and Dr. James Conant was interposed with the statement that Conant had so little understanding of Communism —*The Reporter,* 16 Feb. 1954

interpretative, interpretive These words are synonyms. *Interpretative* is older by a century or so. The OED labeled *interpretive* "rare," having only one 17th-century and one 19th-century citation, but the OED Supplement contains plenty of 20th-century evidence, as do our files. Fowler 1926 and Gowers in Fowler 1965 prescribe *interpretative* on the basis of the underlying Latin form and call *interpretive* wrong. Evans 1957 and Bernstein

1965 give the nod to the older and longer form: Bernstein notes that some writers appear to use *interpretive* on the analogy of *preventive.* Copperud 1960, 1964 prefers *interpretive*; in his consensus books (1970, 1980) he notes ruefully that the consensus seems to run against him and concedes that dictionaries favor *interpretative.*

The definitions in Webster's Third are at *interpretative,* and *interpretive* is defined only by a cross-reference to *interpretative.* This arrangement probably reflects nothing more than alphabetical chance—*interpretative* comes first. The editors of the Third had about equal evidence for both words.

Recent evidence, however, runs heavily in favor of the shorter *interpretive.* Both forms are well established.

intervene *Intervene* is used with a variety of prepositions, but it occurs most often with *in:*

. . . the new board was shorn by Congress of any power to intervene in industrial disputes —Mary K. Hammond, *Current History,* November 1952

There were, at that time, only two places where the Allies could intervene in Russia —George F. Kennan, *Soviet Foreign Policy, 1917–1941,* 1960

Less frequently, *intervene* is used with *between* or *with; between* occurs a little more often:

. . . the trained self-consciousness . . . intervenes between the poet's moods and his poetry —C. Day Lewis, *A Hope for Poetry,* 3d ed., 1936

. . . had called for the government to intervene with Federal troops —Malcolm X, *Evergreen,* December 1967

Intervene has also been used with *against* and *into:*

. . . appealed to Pope Paul VI to intervene against possible obstructive tactics —*Current Biography,* December 1964

. . . Mr. Dubos says that man must continue to intervene into nature, but we must do it with a sense of responsibility —William Kucewicz, *Wall Street Jour.,* 13 June 1980

in that case, in the case of See CASE.

in the circumstances See CIRCUMSTANCES.

in the course of See COURSE 2.

in the event that See EVENT.

in the hope(s) of, in the hope(s) that See HOPE 2.

in the worst way See WORST WAY.

into 1. See IN, INTO.

2. *Into, in to.* Quite a few handbooks, beginning at least as far back as Fowler 1926, point out that the adverb *in* followed by the preposition *to* is not to be confused with the preposition *into.* The matter is probably not one of real mental confusion but of inadvertence or carelessness; it seems most likely to occur where *in* idiomatically belongs to the preceding verb and *to* goes with a human object. *Turn* is a verb often chosen for illustration, because *turn something in* carries the notion of handing over and contrasts strikingly with the "transform, change" sense of *turn* which is idiomatically used with *into.* Thus, we find in the handbooks more than one illustrative instance of "suspects turned themselves into police." Our own bad example is not quite as striking, but you may still say "abracadabra" at the end of it:

> . . . turn this form into your department head —internal memo, Merriam-Webster Inc., 1986

It should be *in to.*

intrigue The most common sense of the verb *intrigue* is "to arouse the interest and curiosity of," as in "the story intrigued them." This sense is now so well established and widely used that anyone unfamiliar with its history will probably be surprised to learn that it did not exist until about a hundred years ago. The earliest evidence of its use (in the OED Supplement) is from 1894. Once it had been introduced, however, it caught on quickly, and within a few decades it had become both extremely common and, among certain people, extremely unpopular.

The new and common sense of *intrigue* was widely disliked in the early 20th century. Its frequent appearance in newspapers sent some readers to their dictionaries, where they found only such definitions for the verb *intrigue* as "to cheat or trick," and "to plot or scheme." Where had the new sense come from? It appears to have been borrowed directly from French, where it had developed from a sense essentially synonymous with *puzzle* (which had itself developed from the "cheat or trick" sense). Its French origin enabled Fowler 1926 to attack it as a "Gallicism." Fowler condemned *intrigue* as a worthless and pretentious substitute for such verbs as *puzzle, fascinate,* and *interest.*

The new sense of *intrigue* was already firmly established in English by the time Fowler censured it. It has been included as a standard sense in Merriam-Webster dictionaries since 1919, when it was added to the New Words section of Webster 1909. Its widespread use has continued unabated throughout the 20th century. Critical attacks against it have also

continued, but almost all commentators now acknowledge that the disputed sense of *intrigue* is standard. A couple of recent exceptions are Simon 1980 and Garner 1998.

We include all this information solely as a matter of interest—not to suggest that you should feel the least hesitation about using *intrigue.* This useful verb may have been a gallicism in the 1890s, but it is certainly not a gallicism now. As several commentators have pointed out, it has connotations that distinguish it from *fascinate, interest,* and other such verbs; something that intrigues us not only fascinates us, it fascinates us by making us curious, by making us want to find out more. Sir Ernest Gowers rightly suggests in Fowler 1965 that the popularity of *intrigue* is largely explained by the fact that no other verb has quite the same meaning.

> "I must confess," he said, "the New Woman and the New Girl intrigue me profoundly. . . ." —H. G. Wells, *Ann Veronica,* 1909

> I wish in your Upper-class Usage you had touched on a point that has long intrigued me —Evelyn Waugh, letter, 1 Sept. 1955

> . . . a problem that intrigued the seventeenth-century mind as fully as it does our own —Noam Chomsky, *Columbia Forum,* Spring 1968

> . . . friends would be intrigued by the difference in Bundy —David Halberstam, *Harper's,* July 1969

> . . . tried to solve a problem that had intrigued me: whether the first player in a game of ticktacktoe can always win, given the right strategy —Martin Gardner, *Scientific American,* August 1998

> . . . intriguing stories that everyone swears happened to a friend of a friend . . . and that circulate for years in nearly identical form in city after city, but that can never be documented as real events —Steven Pinker, *The Language Instinct,* 1994

introduce When *introduce* is used with a preposition, it is usually used with *to* or *into*; use of *to* occurs just a little more frequently:

> ". . . I dressed, had some dinner at that little Italian restaurant in Rupert Street you introduced me to. . . ." —Oscar Wilde, *The Picture of Dorian Gray,* 1891

> Craft introduced her to the noted composer Igor Stravinsky —*Current Biography,* July 1967

> . . . the first Merino sheep ever imported into this country . . . and introduced into Claremont by his kinsman —*American Guide Series: New Hampshire,* 1938

The artist evenings at the Museum . . . seem to have introduced a new spirit into Virginia art —*Southern Literary Messenger,* September 1940

. . . the suspense of someone who introduces one part of life into another, feeling insecurely that they may clash —John Cheever, *The Wapshot Chronicle,* 1957

Once in a while *in* occurs:

General David Humphreys, . . . and the first man to introduce merino sheep in America —*American Guide Series: Connecticut,* 1938

Introduce has also occurred with *among, at, between, for, round,* and *within:*

. . . a Russian campaign to divide Germany from the Atlantic Community and to introduce friction among the European powers —*Current History,* May 1952

In 1819, the use of the power loom was introduced at the Amoskeag Mills —*American Guide Series: New Hampshire,* 1938

. . . the inhabitants saw Penn's claim to revenue from soil and trade as a wedge introduced between them and the Crown —*American Guide Series: Delaware,* 1938

During the second year of his ministry he introduced a gradual change for this evening service —Virginia Douglas Dawson & Betty Douglas Wilson, *The Shape of Sunday,* 1952

. . . small figures in relief, called 'weepers', were introduced round the base of the tomb —O. Elfrida Saunders, *A History of English Art in the Middle Ages,* 1932

When directed change is, however, introduced within segments of a culture, latent dissatisfactions are brought to the surface —Lewis S. Feuer, *Jour. of Philosophy,* 11 Nov. 1954

intrude When *intrude* is used with a preposition, the choice most often is *into:*

. . . the old-established aristocratic society into which they intruded with their outlandish ways —G. M. Trevelyan, *English Social History,* 1942

Thereafter Nazi influences intruded ever more forcefully into the organized life of German-Americans —Oscar Handlin, *The American People in the Twentieth Century,* 1954

Just a little less frequently, *intrude* is used with *on* or *upon:*

. . . he was someone intruding too quickly on that moment of understanding shared

with Peggy in the hall —Morley Callaghan, *The Loved and the Lost,* 1951

. . . he was not sure that he should intrude upon his uncle's sorrow —Jean Stafford, *The Mountain Lion,* 1947

Intrude is occasionally also used with *between* or *in:*

. . . we are kept at a distance because Mailer's personality intrudes between us and the experience —Tom Seligson, *N.Y. Times Book Rev.,* 15 July 1973

We will not allow any other people to intrude in our way of life —*Current Biography 1947*

inundate When *inundate* is used with a preposition, *with* is usual:

Her face was inundated with an angry colour —James Joyce, *Dubliners,* 1914

We were soon inundated with letters —William H. Whyte, Jr., *The Organization Man,* 1956

Less often *inundate* is used with *by:*

CBS was inundated by calls, telegrams, and letters —Marya Mannes, *The Reporter,* 27 Apr. 1954

Infrequently *inundate* has been used with *in:*

. . . this gluts the market and inundates the viewer in a morass of mediocrity or worse —Amos Vogel, *Evergreen,* June 1967

inure, enure The spelling *inure* is found much more often than is the variant *enure.*

Inure, when used with a preposition, almost always takes *to,* whatever its meaning:

Inured to television and radio, that audience is accustomed to being distracted —Aldous Huxley, *Brave New World Revisited,* 1958

Americans have become inured to red meat, well tabascoed —Anthony Burgess, *Saturday Rev.,* 3 Feb. 1979

Inure, however, has also at times been followed by *against* or *with:*

. . . we have learned, too, that museums can inure us against the reality of function —Leonard Kriegel, *Change,* March–April 1969

. . . those people still inured with gentler passions —George W. Bonham, *Change,* October 1971

Enure when used with a preposition in its meaning "habituate" is usually used with *to,* in much the same way as *inure* is used. The variant *enure* in this sense is found more often in British than in American use:

... the jungle odour renders it difficult for anyone, not enured to it, to complete the tour —Osbert Sitwell, *Escape with Me!*, 1939

... a people that is by now enured to crises —*The Economist*, 9 Aug. 1947

Enure, in its sense "accrue," has a more complicated pattern of usage than does *inure.* As shown above, *inure* in both senses is used with *to. Enure,* when meaning "accrue," is used with *to* or *for* in British English and usually with *to* in American English:

... like all fair bargains, it should enure to the benefit of both sides —*The Economist*, 28 June 1947

... even though they enure not for the company's benefit but for that of the secretary himself —*Palmer's Company Law*, 22d ed., 1976

invent See DISCOVER, INVENT.

invest There are two different verbs *invest,* the first preceding the second by some 80 years (1533; 1613). The earlier *invest,* which comes directly from the Latin *investire,* is usually used with *with*:

During a few years the book was invested with a significance . . . which its . . . merits could not justify —Aldous Huxley, *The Olive Tree*, 1937

... which permitted the Victorians to invest medieval art and architecture with Victorian values —Janet Malcolm, *New Yorker*, 18 Sept. 1971

When this *invest* is used with *by,* the verb is usually in the form of the past participle:

Dukes were originally invested by girding them with a sword, as earls had long been invested —*Chambers's Encyclopaedia*, new ed., 1950

The western base of Big Round Top was invested by the Confederates —*American Guide Series: Pennsylvania*, 1940

When the second verb *invest,* which comes through the Italian *investire,* is used with a preposition, it is usually *in*:

Pension plans are less heavily invested in stocks than generally believed —George Anders, *Wall Street Jour.*, 18 Dec. 1981

... the superficial adoption of this tradition by one who was unwilling to invest in its authentic vitality —George Steiner, *Times Literary Supp.*, 27 June 1980

in view of the fact that See FACT 1.

invite The noun *invite* was formed by the same process—functional shift—that gave us the nouns *command* and *request.* It has been in use for more than 300 years—since 1659— and its users include Fanny Burney (in her diary) and Thackeray (in a letter), among others. It has been disparaged by commentators from Gould 1867 to Garner 1998. It has been labeled ignorant, vulgar, humorous, informal, slang, dialectal, barbarous, colloquial, unrespectable, incorrect, and ill-bred. Such a variety of opinion is uninformative about the nature of the problem, but it does suggest that the critics consider *invite* just a bit below the salt. It is used chiefly in speech and light informal prose.

"What are you dressing up for, Nobby?" asked someone. "Didn't your invite say evening dress optional?" —C. S. Forester, *Saturday Evening Post*, 15 Nov. 1958

He said, "I wish I'd known you wanted to come. I'd have got an invite for you" —*New Yorker*, 30 May 1988

Charlie MacArthur said an invite of Woollcott's was like a call to the jury panel —Ruth Gordon, *Myself Among Others*, 1971

Listen up, all you 16–12 teams waving your RPI rating and crowing about your invite to the Big Dance —Jack McCallum, *Sports Illustrated*, 8 Mar. 1999

... one Nobel Peace Prize nominator wants to call him with an invite to Oslo —Jonathan Cooper, *People*, 5 Aug. 1985

invoke See EVOKE, INVOKE.

involve 1. Some language critics, among them Phythian 1979, Follet 1966, and Evans 1957, deplore the use of this word as imprecise when there is no suggestion of complication or entanglement, as in sentences like "Representatives of several groups were involved in the discussions." However, the choice of *involve* in these cases may have been deliberate on the part of a writer who was looking for a less specific but no less meaningful word than *entail, necessitate,* or *affect* (all of which Phythian suggests as substitutes). At any rate, *involve* has over the centuries acquired various shades of meaning. It is standardly used in any number of senses without apparently generating misunderstandings on the part of the reading public, and also without any serious loss of use of those other putatively more precise words, which continue to be called upon when writers need them.
2. When *involve* is used with a preposition, it occurs with many, but the one chosen most often is *in*:

Involved in these imaginings she knew nothing of time —Thomas Hardy, *The Return of the Native*, 1878

. . . approve the costs that were involved in building new roads —Edwin O. Reischauer, *N.Y. Times Book Rev.*, 23 May 1954

It seems inconceivable that such a man could be involved in questionable deals —Trevor Armbrister, *Saturday Evening Post*, 12 Feb. 1966

Involve is also used often with *with*:

The less parochial among British radical students . . . are rightly involved with the problem of world hunger —*Times Literary Supp.*, 9 Apr. 1970

When Jo is away, he finds himself simultaneously involved with Anna, a Brooklyn waitress . . . and Imogen, the romantically beautiful wife —Alfred Kazin, *Partisan Rev.*, Summer 1946

The second floor of a three-story frame building is fully involved with fire —Dennis Smith, *Report from Engine Co. 82*, 1972

Infrequently, *involve* has been used with *against, around,* or *into*:

At present about 400,000 soldiers, some 95,000 of them European, are involved against Ho's forces —Frank Gorrell, *New Republic*, 3 Aug. 1953

. . . the true business of the literary artist is to plait or weave his meaning, involving it around itself —Samuel C. Brownstein & Mitchel Weiner, *How to Prepare for College Entrance Examinations,* ed. Stanley H. Kaplan, 1954

"That'll be quite enough." He involved a thousand-volt charge into his primness and succeeded in looking like the Angel of the Lord —Margery Allingham, *More Work for the Undertaker*, 1949

invulnerable This word is sometimes considered to be an absolute adjective. See ABSOLUTE ADJECTIVES.

iridescent Reader's Digest 1983 and Gowers in Fowler 1965 remind us that this is sometimes misspelled *irridescent*. It should have only one *r*.

ironically Bremner 1980 advises us to let the reader decide whether something we write is ironic or not, and not to preface the remark with *ironically*—and especially not with *ironically enough*. Bremner is objecting to *ironically* as a sentence adverb, but he has missed the point. *Ironically* as a sentence adverb is what some grammarians call a disjunct; disjuncts tell you what the writer or speaker thinks about a statement, not what the reader or hearer is supposed to think.

Bremner is about the only American usage writer we have found who mentions this primarily British issue. The British commentators—Howard 1978, Burchfield 1981, Longman 1984, and Robert F. Ilson in *The English Language Today* (1985)—base their objections on semantic grounds. Howard may speak for the group:

Ironically is a powerful and explicit word. It is being weakened by use as an all-purpose introductory word to draw attention to every trivial oddity, and often to no oddity at all.

Howard's summary fits the objections of the other British commentators reasonably well. Part of the fun of this line of criticism is trying to think up plausible substitutes for *ironically. Oddly, embarrassingly, incongruously, paradoxically, strangely,* even *sadly* and *tragically* have been suggested.

The usage is about as old as sentence-adverbial *hopefully* (half a century or so), but is only now being discovered. Here are some examples from over the years:

Ironically enough, it was Boston and Cambridge that grew to seem provincial —Van Wyck Brooks, *The Flowering of New England, 1815–1865,* rev. ed., 1946

Ironically, the President found himself agreeing with the same companies his administration had just indicted . . . as a wicked oil cartel —*Time*, 8 Sept. 1952

Ironically the bombing of London was a blessing to the youthful generations that followed —Iona & Peter Opie, *Children's Games in Street and Playground*, 1969

. . . Ironically enough, philanthropy works best . . . in the area where it is least needed —Wendy Lasser, *The State of the Language*, 1990

. . . aggressive technology . . . may, ironically enough, deprive us, in the end, of bread itself —Robert Penn Warren, *Democracy and Poetry*, 1975

The show, which . . . was scripted and orchestrated to within an inch of its life, gave Groucho a whole new audience and, ironically, consolidated his reputation as an improvisational genius —Adam Gopnik, *New Yorker,* 17 Apr. 2000

These should be enough to give you a good idea of the standardness of the usage. Burchfield 1996, who had disparaged the use earlier, thinks it is settling down into standard use. The older use of *ironically,* incidentally, seems to be moving right along unaffected by the newer use.

irrefutable See INCOMPARABLE.

irregardless This adverb, apparently a blend of *irrespective* and *regardless,* originated in dialectal American speech in the early 20th century (according to the American Dialect Dictionary, it was first recorded in western Indiana in 1912). Its use in nonstandard speech had become widespread enough by the 1920s to make it a natural in a story by Ring Lardner:

> I told them that irregardless of what you read in books, they's some members of the theatrical profession that occasionally visits the place where they sleep —Ring Lardner, *The Big Town,* 1921

Its widespread use also made it a natural in books by usage commentators, and it has appeared in such books regularly at least since Krapp 1927. The most frequently repeated comment about it is that "there is no such word."

Word or not, *irregardless* has continued in fairly common spoken use, although its bad reputation has not improved with the years. It does occur in the casual speech and writing of educated people, and it even sometimes finds its way into edited prose.

> . . . allow the supplier to deliver his product, irregardless of whether or not his problem is solved —John Cosgrove, *Datamation,* 1 Dec. 1971

> . . . irrespective of whether the source is identified and irregardless of whether all that news is disseminated to the general public —Robert Hanley, *N.Y. Times,* 25 Oct. 1977

> The spherical agglomerates occur in these powders, irregardless of starting composition —*Predicasts Technology Update,* 25 Aug. 1984

But *irregardless* is still a long way from winning general acceptance as a standard English word. Use *regardless* instead.

irrelevant Fowler 1926 notes that the OED contains a warning against the misspelling *irrevelant*; the same problem is mentioned by Copperud 1970, 1980, Bremner 1980, and Janis 1984. We have examples of the misspelling in our files, so care is warranted.

Fowler also says that *irrevelant* is probably spoken a hundred times for every time it appears in print. The process that produces *irrevelant* from *irrelevant* in speech is called metathesis (which see). Metathesis has had a hand in producing some of our common words, like *burn.* Transposing the *l* and the *v* in speech could lead to the same transposition in writing. A similar metathesis is discussed at CALVARY, CAVALRY.

irreparable See INCOMPARABLE.

irrevocable See INCOMPARABLE.

is because See BECAUSE 1; REASON IS BECAUSE.

isolate When *isolate* is used with a preposition, the choice is usually *from*:

> Daphne looked at him brightly, her eyes isolated from them all —Hugh MacLennan, *Two Solitudes,* 1945

> . . . peoples were so isolated from one another, so impeded by their different languages —Edmund Wilson, *A Piece of My Mind,* 1956

Occasionally, *isolate* is used with *in*:

> . . . isolated in the conventional productivity statistics —Robert M. Solow, *Think,* May–June 1967

And, once in a while, *isolate* is found with *by* or *with*:

> The unit was isolated by standard isolation pads located between it and the steel beams —*Trane Weather Magic,* April 1955

> The tooth was isolated with cotton rolls, the caries removed and the cavity dried —*1952 Year Book of Dentistry*

issue In British English, the transitive verb *issue* is often followed by *with*:

> . . . schoolchildren are not issued with school-books, but with vouchers for buying them —Margaret Lane, *Times Literary Supp.,* 9 Mar. 1967

> . . . at lunch yesterday I was issued with a roll whose "crust" must literally have been painted on —Kingsley Amis, *Times Literary Supp.,* 15 July 1983

Such usage first occurred in the early 20th century. Its common occurrence has led to its acceptance by British commentators (such as Partridge 1942 and Gowers in Fowler 1965). Speakers of American English would say "provided with" or "supplied with" instead.

is when, is where See WHEN, WHERE.

it For *it* in reference to preceding ideas, topics, sentences, or paragraphs, see THIS 1.

Italian See ETHNIC DESIGNATIONS: PRONUNCIATION.

iterate See REITERATE.

its, it's It is easy to state the standard rule: *it's* is the contraction of *it is* and *it has; its* is the third person neuter possessive pronoun. But these two forms have been frequently interchanged and entangled throughout their history, and you can be sure that they still are.

Both forms seem to have come into use

around the beginning of the 17th century. The pronoun is first attested in 1598 as *its* in an Italian-English dictionary written by John Florio. Before this the usual possessive (in writing, at least) was *his*. Richard Mulcaster, for instance, in his *Elementarie* of 1582 has this:

> . . . euerie word almost either wanting letters, for his necessarie sound, or having . . .

Another popular solution to the neuter possessive problem was to use the uninflected *it*, as Shakespeare did:

> . . . it had it head bit off by it young —*King Lear*, 1606 (in Strang, OED)

Shakespeare seems not to have used *its*, although the OED says he might have written the *it's* used as an absolute adjective in *Henry VIII* (acted in 1613). Editors began putting *its* in Shakespeare's plays later (McKnight 1928 gives an example of *it* changed to *its* in the Third Folio, 1664). Wyld 1920 notes that *its* is not used in the 1611 Bible. And it does not appear as one of the possessive pronouns in Ben Jonson's grammar (published posthumously in 1640). Nevertheless it established itself during the 17th century, and Strang 1970 says that after midcentury the alternative *his* signifies an element of personification.

The troublesome fact for us moderns is that the predominant form in printing was *it's*. The apostrophized form was used by the above-mentioned Florio as early as 1603. It may have been given this form because it was felt not to be a separate possessive pronoun like *his, her,* or *their* but simply *it* with the *'s* of the genitive attached to it. This possibility is borne out to a certain extent by Priestley 1761; he lists *it's* as the genitive of *it* and does not include it in the list of possessive pronouns at all. *It's* was apparently the more common form of the pronoun throughout the 17th and 18th centuries. In the 18th century we find such uses as these:

> . . . our language has made it's way singly by it's own weight and merit —Lord Chesterfield, letter to *The World*, 28 Nov. 1754

> . . . of it's real import —Adam Smith (in Leonard 1929)

> . . . when it is omitted and it's Place supplied with an Apostrophe —Baker 1770

Late 18th-century users carried it into the early 19th century:

> . . . estimate it's merit —Thomas Jefferson, letter, 21 May 1787

> . . . will work it's effect —Thomas Jefferson, letter, 21 Aug. 1818

> . . . the assurance of it's being . . . —Jane Austen, letter, 8 Nov. 1800

The unapostrophized *its* was in competition with *it's* from the beginning and began its rise to dominance in the mid 18th century. Lowth 1762 gave *its* as the possessive form of *it* (even though he seems to have favored *her's*, etc.). Baker gave *it's* in 1770, as we saw above, but switched to *its* in his 1779 edition.

The modern assumption that *its* came to predominate for the pronoun in order to distinguish it from *it's* "it is" is supported by Campbell 1776, who complained of *it's* being misused for *'tis*, the usual contraction of *it is*. But even if *'tis* predominated, *it's* was in at least occasional use:

> . . . and it's come to pass . . .
> This tractable obedience is a slave
> To each incensed will
> —Shakespeare, Henry VIII, 1613

> Why, sir, it's your own fault —Sir John Vanbrugh, *The Relapse*, 1696

Since we all know that *it's* predominates over *'tis* today, we may reasonably suppose that *its* came to be preferred as a contrasting pronoun form.

Another more recent assumption is that this distinction, which presumably developed during the 19th and early 20th centuries, is being lost. The reappearance of prenominal *it's* (which may never have completely disappeared) is certainly well documented. It is frequently noticed in signs and posters, as by Simon 1980, for instance. We have also found it in letters, advertisements, flyers, mail-order catalogs, and animal-husbandry journals. But—and if you are an alarmist, you may view this with alarm—we have also found it in edited, more widely circulated publications: *Vogue* (1985), *New York Times Magazine* (1984), *Southern Living* (1983), *Springfield* (Mass.) *Morning Union* (1983), *This England* (1983), *People* (1982), and *Gourmet* (1981). These cannot all be typos, can they?

And the distinction is under milder pressure from the other side—from the George Bernard Shaws who eschew the apostrophe in general and use only *its* for all purposes.

We tend to agree with Reader's Digest 1983 that the insistence on *its* for the pronoun as necessary to distinguish the pronoun from the contraction does not make much sense, since the *'s* does everything for the noun. *Jean's* can be possessive in "Jean's coat" and it can be a contraction in "Jean's here" and "Jean's already read it." Use of one form in three functions with the noun does not seem to trouble anyone.

Still, we do not recommend that you rush to espouse the apostrophized pronoun. The possessive pronouns were a complete muddle in the 18th century. Over time the confusion has sorted itself out, and we now have a modestly consistent set of unapostrophized pronouns. So even though the apostrophe is on the rise (see the article at APOSTROPHE), we see no particular reason to go back to 18th-century usage. We recommend that you stick with *its* for the pronoun and *it's* for the contraction.

it's me The venerable argument over the nominative versus the objective case after the verb *to be* is a memorable part of our linguistic heritage. Nearly everyone has heard it in one form or another. You should be aware that, while the discussion is still going on, its grounds have been shifted:

> The choice between "It is I" and "It's me" is a choice not between standard and nonstandard usage but between formal and colloquial styles —Trimmer & McCrimmon 1988

So instead of the old choice between right and wrong we are now choosing a style; it is a choice that is much closer to the reality of usage than the old one was.

Copperud 1970, 1980 cites Follett 1966 as prescribing the nominative in constructions where a personal pronoun follows *to be*, and we do find instances when the nominative is used, but probably for the reason alluded to above by Trimmer & McCrimmon: these constructions tend to be rather formal.

> Let me urge you not to forget that it was I . . . whom you burdened with the job —*The Intimate Notebooks of George Jean Nathan*, 1932

> It was she who . . . paid no longer any attention to religion —William Styron, *This Quiet Dust and Other Writings*, 1982

In older English we find the nominative even in speech written for the stage:

> Is't he that speaks nothing but Greek or Latine, or English Fustian? —Thomas Shadwell, *The Humorists*, 1671

> Alas, this is not he whom I expected —Aphra Behn, *The Dutch Lover*, 1673

But the more relaxed colloquial style could also be found in earlier writing:

> It is not me you are in love with —Sir Richard Steele, *The Spectator*, No. 290, 1 Feb. 1712

From the beginning in the 18th century, there were two camps. The earlier, apparently, is represented by Priestley 1761, who favors accepting *it is me* on grounds of custom. Priestley mentions that grammarians opposed his position, but he doesn't say who they were. Lowth 1762 heads the partisans of *it is I*, who clearly had Priestley outnumbered: Baker 1770, Campbell 1776, and Lindley Murray

1795 were on the side of the nominative. And these were the commentators whose preachments were accepted as gospel by the schoolmasters. Priestley's opinion had to wait until Alford 1864 to find a sympathizer.

If the great tide of expressed opinion favored *it is I*, how is it that *it is me* survived to reach its at least semi-respectable status today? The strongest force operating in favor of *it is me* is probably that of word position: the pronoun after *is* is in the usual position for a direct object, and the objective case feels right in that position. It is probably just as simple as that—we find the strength of word order at work on initial *whom* also, turning it frequently into *who*, even when it is an object in its clause—but early grammarians knew nothing of the power of word order in English, and they had to find other explanations.

One of the more interesting explanations was the "French analogy." This was apparently first set forth by Priestley. In his discussion of the uses of the oblique (Priestley preferred Johnson's *oblique* to Lowth's *objective*) cases of the pronoun in place of the nominative, he notices that French has similar constructions, notably *c'est moi*.

Priestley also asserts that the reason the grammarians won't accept *it is me* is that it does not match the pattern of Latin (which is why he brought up French). It is probably true that Latin is the theoretical reason for the insistence on the nominative. But besides theory, there was actual usage. Unless all the Restoration playwrights had tin ears or were for some unfathomable reason following an artificial convention, the people of quality they portrayed on the stage did use the nominative:

> MARCEL. By Heavens, 'tis she: Vile Strumpet! —Aphra Behn, *The Dutch Lover*, 1673

> MRS. LOVEIT. Oh, that's he, that's he! —George Etherege, *The Man of Mode*, 1676

> LADY TOUCHWOOD. . . . but when you found out 'twas I, you turned away —William Congreve, *The Double Dealer*, 1694

> LYRIC. . . . If ever the muses had a horse, I am he —George Farquhar, *Love and a Bottle*, 1698

A number of recent commentators maintain that *me* is more common than *us, them, him*, or *her* after *be*. This at least sounds likely, but we do not know how it can be proved. We do know that all of the objective pronouns can be found in the construction:

> "It's me," I said.
> "How are you?" she replied
> —Russell Baker, *Growing Up*, 1982

From the way the president moved his head, I realized that his real audience wasn't us at all —Tip O'Neill with William Novak, *Man of the House*, 1987

. . . if I were them, I would —George Schultz, Secretary of State, television interview, 6 Dec. 1985

. . . can sometimes act like it's him against the world —Penelope Wang, *Newsweek*, 29 Dec. 1986

. . . but it's her, the same girl, returned to my life —E. L. Doctorow, *Loon Lake*, 1979

Clearly, both the *it is I* and *it's me* patterns are in reputable use and have been for a considerable time. *It is I* tends to be used in more formal or more stuffy situations; *it's me* predominates in real and fictional speech and in a more relaxed writing style. *Him, her, us,* and *them* may be less common after the verb *to be* than *me* is, but they are far from rare and are equally good.

For more on the vagaries of pronouns, see BETWEEN YOU AND I; PRONOUNS; THAN 1; THEY, THEIR, THEM; WHO, WHOM 1.

-ize 1. *-ize, -ise.* The American form of this suffix is *-ize*; the British typically use *-ise*, although some of the more etymology-conscious publishing houses may insist on the *-ize* termination for some words, following OED practice. Longman 1984 has a list of verbs (such as *advertise, chastise, circumcise, despise,* and *surmise*) that must be spelled *-ise* in both language varieties, but these words are not formed from the suffix *-ize*.
2. According to the OED, the suffix *-ize* itself was first mentioned by Thomas Nashe in 1591. He was none too politely tweaking the noses of his "reprehenders," whom he was apparently pleased to have nettled with his verb coinages ending in *-ize*. Ever since, it has been possible to raise hackles with newly coined verbs that end in this suffix.

Such verbs aroused much comment in the 19th century. Critics were upset by Noah Webster's inclusion of *demoralize, Americanize,* and *deputize* in his 1828 dictionary. Bache 1869 hated *jeopardize* (which was almost as big an object of scorn in the 19th century as *finalize* was in the 20th) and *signalize*. Richard Grant White 1870 denounced *resurrectionize*; his denunciation led Fitzedward Hall 1873 to rain

down dozens of other similarly formed *-ize* verbs on him. Not content with pelting White, Hall produced a few dozen additional examples in another part of the book. Compton 1898 wanted to ban *deputize* and *jeopardize*.

With this admirable head of steam built up, the issue roared into the 20th century, where *finalize* replaced *jeopardize* as the object of the most heat and least rationality. But plenty of other *-ize* words have come under the gun: *accessorize, burglarize,* and *prioritize* are some you will find discussed in this book. The anathematizing (we couldn't resist) of *-ize* verbs shows no sign of letting up: a recent handbook, Trimmer & McCrimmon 1988, counsels students to "avoid such pretentious and unnecessary jargon as *finalize, prioritize,* and *theorize.*" The pretentious and unnecessary *theorize* has been with us since 1638 and has been used by Coleridge, Howells, Joyce, Dreiser, and Forster, among others.

If you are one of those persons of tender sensibilities whose nerves are grated by *-ize* verbs, you would be better off learning to live with the problem, as everybody knows that the jargoneers of the government, the military, and the various hard and soft sciences have a sweet tooth for these words. And they are not the only ones. Truman Capote used *artificialize*, Mary McCarthy *sloganized* and *scanorized*, Coleridge *melancholize*, Charlotte Brontë *colloquize*, and Robert Southey *physiognomize*.

But you can take some comfort in the thought that many of these coinages do not last. A check through Hall's 1873 list turns up such confections as *excursionize, pulpitize, scrorize, sultanize, sensize, dissocialize, soberize*—have you ever encountered them? One suspects that more recent coinages such as *laymanize, impossibilize, disasterize, explitize, incentize,* and *prominentized* will be similarly forgotten.

So *-ize* is a very productive suffix in English; for 400 years or more it has been freely attached to nouns, adjectives, proper names, and sometimes other roots to produce verbs for immediate use. These are often nonce words (we have a *Colorado-ize* used by someone getting ready to go backpacking in the mountains), but many others have stuck. Who today blinks at *popularize, formalize, economize, legalize, politicize, terrorize,* or *capitalize?*

J

Jap, Japanese The word *Jap* is a clipped form of *Japanese* that has been around since the end of the 19th century. Clipped terms are often felt to be somewhat less than respectful—even such inoffensive terms as *prof* and *doc* have been criticized—and clipped ethnic terms are doubly suspect. In the United States, this term has a considerable history of pejorative use from the first decade of the 20th century. Such use did not take long to appear in fiction:

> I've got that boundary line to patrol—to keep out Chinks and Japs —Zane Grey, *Desert Gold*, 1913

World War II gave a great boost to the usage. Not only did *Jap* have brevity to recommend it, but it probably served a psychological purpose:

> The epithets "Kraut," "Jap," "Gook"—all are shorthand ways of excluding the enemy from the ranks of human beings —Anne Roiphe, *Cosmopolitan*, April 1975

But World War II is more than fifty years behind us. *Jap* is generally either used disparagingly or taken to be offensive, even in innocent use. Unless your intent is to recreate the atmosphere of World War II for some purpose, use *Japanese*.

jargon Chaucer used *jargon* to mean the twittering of birds; the word has declined in status since then. The OED shows that it embarked upon its career as a pejorative term in the 17th century. According to Perrin & Ebbitt 1972, Sir Arthur Quiller-Couch, in his *On the Art of Writing* (1916), popularized the word as an all-purpose bludgeon for various kinds of verbal fuzziness. Sir Arthur's treatment would hardly pass muster nowadays for an investigation of jargon; he wanders too easily from the subject. Much more to the point is the chapter in Bolinger 1980.

In modern use *jargon* is a pejorative term meaning more or less "obscure and often pretentious language." This meaning is very closely related to another: "the technical terminology or characteristic idiom of a special activity or group." The pejorative meaning represents the outsider's opinion of the specialist's or insider's technical terminology. Let the outsider beware, then. If you are going to pry into material written for the specialist,

you are going to have to learn the specialist's language. Of course many outsiders resent having to learn the language—and not without some reason. The defenders of jargon may point out that it eliminates ambiguities and is the quickest way for one professional to talk to another, but there is good reason to suspect that part of the function of jargon is to keep outsiders in the dark.

The jargon that is most likely to distress the ordinary person is that used by governments; few citizens these days can avoid directly confronting bureaucratic jargon in such places as tax returns and other official forms that must be dealt with. Consequently, bureaucratic jargon has probably drawn more hostile criticism than any other jargon. Bureaucratic jargon is the official language bureaucrats write for bureaucrats to read. If you need the official approval of a bureaucrat, you will probably have to learn how to cope with the idiom. It is not going away.

We do not intend to apologize for jargon, but to be fair you have to recognize that many of its critics simply refuse to understand it. For one small example, Barzun 1980 disparages the word *containerize* as unnecessary jargon. Not needed, he says, since we already have the verb *to box*. He then goes on to explain that *box* wouldn't do because, as he mockingly suggests, "it wouldn't have sounded like the heroic, scientific conquest of mind over matter." He omits to notice that *box* (or for that matter *crate* or *package* or *wrap* or *carton*) was not used because it does not mean the same thing to people in the business as *containerize* does. Willful misunderstanding is no corrective to jargon.

jealous 1. Some language commentators warn against confusing the words *jealous* and *zealous*. At one time, as the OED indicates, the two words were considered synonyms and were used as such, most particularly in the Bible and in related religious writings:

> And he said, I have been very jealous for the Lord God of hosts —1 Kings 19:10 (AV), 1611

> To spoyle the zelous God of his honour —*Homilies* II, 1563 (OED)

According to our evidence, *jealous* and *zealous* are not otherwise used interchangeably. Their closest approach in meaning now occurs when *jealous* is used to mean "vigilant in guarding a possession":

> . . . toward a more passionate assertion of the demands of individual freedom, or a more jealous insistence upon the precedence of the community —Archibald MacLeish, *American Scholar*, Autumn 1953

2. When *jealous* is used with a preposition, it is usually used with *of*:

> I know that religion, science, and art are all jealous of each other —W. R. Inge, *The Church in the World*, 1928

> . . . the 1944 campaign cost the French many lives and untold property, of which the Normands are so traditionally jealous —David Butwin, *Saturday Rev.*, 21 June 1969

Once in a while, *jealous* is used with *for*:

> They were like sons to him, he was jealous for their welfare, and was always available for advice and help —*Dictionary of American Biography*, 1929

Infrequently, *jealous* has been used with *to* and an infinitive or with *over*:

> The old legal constitution of the country gave him the whole judicial power, and William was jealous to retain and heighten this —John Richard Green, *The History of the English People*, 1880

> Ape-women, mannish Russian scientists, stewardesses wearing impossible caps, . . . they are all there, and who would get jealous over *them?* —Robert Plank, *Hartford Studies in Literature*, vol. 1, no. 1, 1969

jeer When *jeer* is used with a preposition, it is usually followed by *at*:

> Isabelle knew she would be jeered at as yet another American heiress who had forced her way —Rebecca West, *The Thinking Reed*, 1936

> . . . the exiles of an earlier period, who . . . had jeered at the United States —Edmund Wilson, *Memoirs of Hecate County*, 1946

Jeer has also been infrequently used with *to*:

> . . . The women jeered to one another, "What can be done with a new world like this?" —Josephine Young Case, *Atlantic*, May 1946

jejune Todd & Hancock 1986 call attention to a curious fact about *jejune*; derived from a Latin word originally meaning "fasting, hungry," it is usually used figuratively for what is devoid of substance or nutriment for the mind—uninteresting, insipid, or trite stuff. But it has also become associated with an un-

originality that bespeaks immaturity, and so it is used in senses approximating "puerile, juvenile, naive." Todd & Hancock suggest that this semantic "slide," as they put it, may be due to contamination from French *jeune* "young." Others have made the same suggestion. Burchfield 1996, however, thinks it unlikely. The mainstream of current use runs in this channel:

> It was a gasbag of a speech, soft, loose, jejune, thin gruel for a man who has been at the center of events for more than two decades. . . . Is this all he has to say? —Ward Just, *New England Monthly*, October 1984

But uses that suggest or hint at youthfulness are not hard to find:

> We pass in the world for sects and schools, for erudition and piety, and we are all the time jejune babes —Ralph Waldo Emerson, "Spiritual Laws," 1841

> If I were Harvard University, or the General Motors Corporation, I would buy and remove The Anchor . . . to somewhere in the States; to show the young and jejune what a pub should look like —Christopher Morley, in *A Century of the Essay*, ed. David Daiches, 1951

> In fact they thought more of my jejune prentice work than I did myself —George Bernard Shaw, letter, 11 Sept. 1943

> The hero's jejune temperament also leaches into the language, which seems flat at times —William C. Taylor, *N.Y. Times Book Rev.*, 27 July 1997

> So downplay your romantic and adolescent past. This means no jejune wall art —Allison Glock, *GQ*, May 1997

Edmund Wilson, in *The Bit Between My Teeth* (1965), comments without etymologizing on the use of *jejune* in the sense "callow." Wilson was familiar with this use, for in 1922 he received this in a letter:

> I changed the meaning of *jejune* eight or ten years ago. That is to say, I added a new special meaning, to wit, that of youthful feebleness —H. L. Mencken, letter, 17 May 1922

If you look back at the Emerson quotation, you may feel that Mencken was perhaps taking a bit more credit for invention than he deserved. *Jejune*, like *effete*, seems a sort of intellectual-sounding pejorative of uncertain meaning. If you use it, it would seem wise to be certain what you intend it to mean.

jeopardize Richard Grant White called *jeopardize* "a foolish and intolerable word" in 1870, and he was not the only one who thought so. A popular view among American critics in the 19th century was that the proper verb was *jeopard,* an older word which, according to the OED, had fallen into disuse by the end of the 1600s. The first record of *jeopardize* is from 1646, but there is no further evidence of its use until it turns up in Noah Webster's American Dictionary in 1828 with the note, "This is a modern word used by respectable writers in America, but synonymous with *jeopard,* and therefore useless." Useless or not, *jeopardize* became increasingly common, both in America and in Great Britain, as attempts to resurrect *jeopard* met with predictable failure. The voices of protest against *jeopardize,* all of which had been American, began to die down by about 1900. Now the shoe is on the other foot, and we have Garner 1998 finding *jeopard* the useless word. It is rarely used.

See -IZE 2.

Jew, jew down   *Jew* used as an adjective and the phrasal verb *jew down* are usually considered offensive. The former should be replaced by *Jewish,* and the latter avoided altogether.

jewelry   This word is sometimes pronounced \'jü-lə-rē\, a switched-around form of \'jü-əl-rē\ that is an example of *metathesis* (which see). A similar case is *Realtor,* often pronounced \'rē-lət-ər\. Neither pronunciation is very well established as standard.

Jewess   *Jewess* is a word of relatively low frequency and of uncertain status. Copperud 1964, 1970, 1980 and Evans 1957 say it is often considered derogatory. *Jewess* is often bracketed with *Negress,* with commentators finding them both derogatory (Evans) or not (Simon 1980).

An important factor in the status of such words is who uses them. We have evidence, for instance, that Jewish women may use *Jewess* of themselves:

> I sat and thought to myself, here is the head of the church, sitting face to face with the Jewess from Israel, and he's listening to what I'm saying —Golda Meir, quoted in *N.Y. Times,* 20 Jan. 1973

Most of our literary evidence seems to be neutral, although it is not always easy to detect covert social commentary that may underlie a usage. Here are a few American examples:

> His wife had been a German Jewess, above him socially, so she thought —Saul Bellow, *Mr. Sammler's Planet,* 1969

> The sexual yearning is for the Other. The dream of the shiksa —counterpart to the Gentile dream of the *Jewess,* often adjectively described as "melon-breasted." —Philip Roth, *Reading Myself and Others,* 1975

> . . . they had been refugees in Portugal during World War II, and when it was over, only Australia would let them in. An Australian Jewess, Bech thought —John Updike, *Bech Is Back,* 1982

Jewess seems to be a word that can be used by those who are deft enough to illuminate social attitudes in a subtle way; perhaps most of us are not clever enough to use it. It seems neutral in a historical context. Our British evidence is enigmatic; the little we have suggests from the way it is used that it could give offense, but British sensibilities may be different on this point.

See also -ESS; NEGRESS.

jibe, gibe   The distinction between *jibe* and *gibe* is not as clear-cut as some commentators would like it to be. *Jibe* is the more common spelling. It is used both for the verb meaning "to be in accord; agree" ("jibe with") and for the verb and noun of nautical parlance ("jibe the mainsail," "a risky jibe in heavy seas"). It is also used as a variant of *gibe* for the verb meaning "to utter taunting words; to deride or tease" and for the noun meaning "a taunting remark; jeer." *Gibe* is more common in these uses and is preferred by the critics, but *jibe* is also in widespread use, and the evidence shows clearly that it is a respectable spelling variant:

> . . . my jibe at the Socialists of the eighteen-eighties —George Bernard Shaw, *The Intelligent Woman's Guide to Socialism and Capitalism,* 1928

> . . . with some new jibe at Mr. Dillon or Mr. Redmond —*The Autobiography of William Butler Yeats,* 1953

> . . . a blasphemous boy jibes at them —Robert Craft, *Stravinsky,* 1972

> . . . applause for any jibe at the expense of the decade known as the Sixties —Christopher Hitchens, *Harper's,* July 1990

Jibe has been recognized as a standard variant of *gibe* since the publication of the fourth volume of the OED in 1900. The critics worry that its use may cause confusion, but the context in which it occurs always makes its meaning clear.

There is some evidence for *gibe* used as a variant of *jibe* in both the "agree" sense and the nautical uses, and it is recognized as such in both Webster's Second and Webster's Third. However, this use is very rare and in most contexts would probably be considered an error by readers.

join   1. *Join* is used with any of several prepositions; those occurring most often are *in, to,* or *with.* When *in* is used, it is followed by a noun or by a gerund:

... Snowy felt ashamed to have joined in the laugh —Richard Llewellyn, *A Few Flowers for Shiner,* 1950

... urged the United States to join in the acceptance of Communist China by the United Nations —*Current Biography,* January 1966

Scientific management thus joined trade-union pressure . . . in shortening the work week —Stuart Chase, *N.Y. Times Mag.,* 30 May 1954

Join is also used with *to* and *with*:

All my life I have looked for . . . a writer with spiritual health and goodness joined to literary genius —Francis Hackett, *Saturday Rev.,* 16 Feb. 1946

... it describes its author's struggle to assert her sexuality, to join it to creativity —Leonard Kriegel, *N.Y. Times Book Rev.,* 11 May 1980

... I joined with a group of persons to go in a taxi to the prison —Katherine Anne Porter, *The Never-Ending Wrong,* 1977

... Pennsylvanians under Wayne . . . joined their units with men from New Hampshire —F. Van Wyck Mason, *The Winter at Valley Forge,* 1953

... detailed research joined with a splendid narrative style —*American Scholar,* Spring 1953

When *join* is being used of persons, *with* is the more likely preposition. However, *join to* may also be found:

He was then joined to Gen. Scott's command and was actively engaged at the seige —*Dictionary of American Biography,* 1929

Occasionally, *join* is used with *into*:

... when the thirteen colonies joined into a Federal Union —Vera Micheles Dean, *The Four Cornerstones of Peace,* 1946

2. There are many language commentators who disapprove using *together* with *join*; they call it redundant. *Join together* is primarily a spoken idiom in which the purpose of *together* is to add emphasis. Probably the best known example of these words is in the Bible:

What therefore God hath joined together, let not man put asunder —Matthew 19:6 (AV), 1611

Contemporary examples can also be found:

... the art which joins all men together at their deepest and simplest level of response —Leslie A. Fiedler, *Los Angeles Times Book Rev.,* 23 May 1971

... communities on Cape Cod and Martha's Vineyard have joined together to win lower prices —*The Nation,* 28 June 1999

So secular and fundamentalist Palestinians have joined together in a loud cry for war —Joel Brinkley, *N.Y. Times Mag.,* 16 Dec. 1990.

There is no need to avoid familiar idioms like *join together* simply because the second word iterates and emphasizes part of the meaning of the first.

See REDUNDANCY; WORDINESS.

judgment, judgement Both ways to spell this word have been in use for centuries. *Judgment* was once the only spelling shown in dictionaries, but that changed with the publication of the OED, in which *judgment* and *judgement* are treated as equal variants. Most dictionaries now show both spellings. Usage commentators generally allow that both are acceptable, but the Americans among them tend to prefer *judgment* while the British preference is for *judgement.* Our own most recent evidence shows both spellings are in reputable use on both sides of the Atlantic and that the preference of the critics is reflected in the general practice on both sides.

judicial, judicious These two adjectives are close etymological relatives whose meanings have shown a tendency to overlap ever since *judicious* entered the language in the late 16th century (*judicial* is an older word, first recorded in a work written before 1382). The distinction between their principal senses remains clear, however: *judicial* has to do primarily with judges and the law (as in "the judicial branch of the government"), while *judicious* relates to sound judgment of a general kind (as in "a fair and judicious critic"). *Judicious* was also once used in a sense synonymous with *judicial,* but that use was last attested in 1632 and is now obsolete. Use of *judicial* as a synonym of *judicious,* which first occurred in 1581, has also been labeled obsolete, but our evidence shows that label to be mistaken:

... made an evident effort to be judicial and fair minded —John C. McCloskey, *Philological Quarterly,* January 1946

One likes one's academicians objective, critical and judicial —*Times Literary Supp.,* 14 Nov. 1968

... requires the judicial appraisal of other people's management —Franklin D. Roosevelt, 12 Mar. 1935, in Donald Day, *Franklin D. Roosevelt's Own Story,* 1951

This sense of *judicial* is considered erroneous by usage commentators. As the above quotations show, it occurs in standard, even academic, contexts, but it is not common. Most writers will choose *judicious* in its place.

juncture *Juncture* has several meanings, the most common of which is "a point in time." It is used especially to denote an important or critical point brought about by a concurrence of circumstances or events:

> At this critical juncture in history only the fullest resources . . . can do the job —*City*, March–April 1972

> . . . stave off the danger of a schism that has seemed looming at some junctures in the last few years —Paul Hofmann, *N.Y. Times*, 14 Jan. 1980

Use without implications of particular importance or crisis is not uncommon, however:

> At this juncture, the future looks bright in the extreme for Barbra Streisand —Burt Korall, *Saturday Rev.*, 11 Jan. 1969

> . . . All-Star point guard Gary Payton, who at one juncture last season had expressed unhappiness about being in Seattle —Mike Wise, *N.Y. Times*, 10 Oct. 1999

Dictionaries treat these uses of *juncture* as standard, as they are, but critics like Evans 1957, Gower in Fowler 1965, and Garner 1998 dislike *juncture* when *point* or *time* would serve as well—that is, when there is no underlying sense of events converging or coming to a head.

junior See IMPLICIT COMPARATIVE.

junta Though this Spanish-derived word has been in English since the early 17th century, the pronunciations we most frequently record are the still Spanish-sounding \'hün-tə\ and \'hùn-tə\. (English retains the Spanish \h\ pronunciation of *j* in *jai alai, jalapeño*, and *jicama* as well.) Also well attested is the frankly anglicized \'jən-tə\. Less frequent but still standard are the hybrids \'jün-tə\ and \'hən-tə\, the latter heard from Presidents Kennedy and Reagan. Very occasionally we hear someone overshooting Spanish and landing in pseudo-French: \'zhən-tə\ (see HYPERFOREIGNISMS).

jurist The use of *jurist* as a synonym for *judge* is deprecated by several commentators, who point out that *jurist* has the general sense "one who is versed in the law" and is therefore not strictly limited in application to judges. It should be noted, however, that *jurist* is now little used in American English except in referring to a judge (although Garner 1998 found an example referring to jurors). The British use it differently, to denote a legal scholar or writer. It does not, as a rule, stand alone in place of *judge* as a pure synonym; it typically serves as a respectful term for a person whose status as a judge is already known:

> Mr. Murphy went to Judge Kaufman in chambers and threw the problem in the jurist's lap —A. J. Liebling, *New Yorker*, 23 July 1949

just As an adverb, *just* has many uses, almost all of which have a somewhat informal quality. It can mean "exactly" ("just right"), "very recently" ("someone just called"), "barely" ("just in time"), "immediately" ("just west of here"), "only" ("just a reminder"), "very" ("just wonderful"), and "possibly" ("it just might work"). Handbooks on writing occasionally cite one or more of these senses as a colloquialism, but all of them occur commonly in writing that is not unusually lofty in subject matter or tone.

The phrase *just exactly* has been frequently criticized as a redundancy since Fowler 1926. It is not remarkably frequent in edited prose, and where it does appear it is usually in informal surroundings.

> What was said sounded as if it should be understood, but just exactly what was said remained uncertain —Jacob Stein, *American Scholar*, Summer 1996

> And there was T. S. Eliot. . . . Looking, I mean, just exactly what you expected he'd look like —Stanley Elkin, *Harper's*, April 1989

> . . . glanced around nervously to see just exactly where it was that Packer wished to conduct the frisk —John Grisham, *The Chamber*, 1995

justify When *justify* is used with a preposition, it often occurs with *by* or *in*. When *by* is used, it is followed more often by a noun, less often by a gerund; when *in* is used, it is followed more often by a gerund, less often by a noun:

> . . . their immediate jubilant reaction has been abundantly justified by the sales —Peter Forster, *London Calling*, 20 May 1954

> . . . he did not so much apologize as justify both by argument and instance the life he had led —Irwin Edman, *Atlantic*, February 1953

> . . . he tried to justify his enthusiasm by pretending that it was in truth an intellectual interest —Douglas Hubble, *Horizon*, August 1946

> When is a physician justified in not being completely candid with the patient? —Norman Cousins, *Saturday Rev.*, 1 Oct. 1977

> . . . their own lives are to be justified . . . only in the accomplishment of their children —Romeyn Berry, *N.Y. Times Mag.*, 16 May 1954

Less frequently, *justify* is used with *as* or *to*:

> ... the playhouse was forced to justify itself as a serious cultural endeavor —*American Guide Series: Pennsylvania*, 1940

> ... Ruark himself justifies it as a journalistic device —Bruce Bliven, Jr., *Saturday Rev.*, 23 Apr. 1955

> She loved him so much that she justified to herself his every fault —Ruth Park, *The Harp in the South*, 1948

> ... the physician is duty bound and morally justified to relieve suffering —Louis Lasagna, *Johns Hopkins Mag.*, Spring 1968

Justify has occurred infrequently with *for* or *of*:

> The decision to keep the original arrangement of the poems ... is entirely justifed for

its critical value —*Times Literary Supp.*, 19 Feb. 1971

> It is not necessarily and uniquely poetic, though it justifies itself of his poetic experience —Cyril Connolly, *Horizon*, April 1946

Justify, with some frequency, is also followed by the idiom(s) *on* (or *upon*) *the ground(s)*:

> ... Batista justified his seizure of power on the grounds of an alleged conspiracy —*The Americana Annual 1953*

> Locke justified the right of revolution not upon the ground of hostile acts of the people —*Dictionary of American History*, 1940

> The plan is justified on the ground that the farm cannot be divided —Walter Prescott Webb, *The Great Frontier*, 1952

karat   See CARAT, KARAT, CARET.

ketchup   See CATSUP, KETCHUP, CATCHUP.

kid   Admonitions not to use *kid* to mean "child" seem to have come more from English teachers than from usage commentators, although they do appear in many books written in the early 20th century. As is now generally recognized, the "child" sense of *kid* is actually quite old, having been recorded as early as 1599. The OED indicates that it was originally "low slang," but it became established in more general use during the 19th century.

The "child" sense of *kid* first became common among the British, but its career as a usage issue has been strictly American. No British commentator that we know of has criticized it. The early resistance to it by Americans has also now largely subsided in the face of many years of widespread use, although it does still have some detractors (Harper 1975, 1985 finds that it is "viewed with distaste by many"). Copperud 1970, 1980 sums up its status: "The consensus is that it is informal, which means well suited to most contexts."

> When I was a kid, there were no such things as holidays for me —Frank O'Connor, *New Yorker*, 28 July 1956

> ... looking like a somber little man among the American kids —Mary McCarthy, *Occasional Prose*, 1985

> This can drive some kids to even greater rebellion, which often lands them in jail —*The Economist*, 11 Apr. 1986

kilometer   In North America, *kilometer* is most often pronounced with the principal stress on the second syllable: \kə-ˈläm-ət-ər\. This pronunciation has drawn heated objections from some quarters. Since *centimeter, millimeter*, etc., are pronounced with principal stress on the first syllable, it stands to reason that *kilometer* should be too. For just one word of the series to receive second-syllable stress seems to violate the very spirit of uniformity which the metric system represents.

The proposal to use only first-syllable stress in these words is not a lost cause. First, \ˈkil-ə-ˌmēt-ər\ is a fairly close runner-up already, especially among scientists. Second, those who have been saying \kə-ˈläm-ət-ər\ and are made aware of the issues are sometimes contrite.

Interestingly enough, second-syllable stress was, in fact, the only option shown for *millimeter* and *centimeter* in Noah Webster's original 1828 dictionary: in that book, *kilometer* rhymed with *barometer*, and *centimeter* rhymed with *perimeter*. The analogy between these sets of words is false in the sense that the semantic relations between prefix and suffix are different in the two cases, but in both cases the same Greek word meaning "measure" is at the root of -*meter*. Nor will European example help us much. The \kə-ˈläm-ət-ər\ variant is quite widespread in the British Isles as well, as Burchfield 1996 attests. The stress pattern in non-English-speaking European countries is not especially relevant to questions of English pronunciation, but for what it may be worth, the local equivalent of *kilometer* is pronounced with second-syllable stress in Spanish and Italian, and with third-syllable stress in German, French, and Russian.

It might seem desirable to many to have a standard pronunciation for *kilometer,* but in the present case there is an inherent dilemma which cannot be dismissed out of hand. Normally a pronunciation wins out over its rivals not by reason of etymology or logical niceties but because of the bandwagon effect. In the case of *kilometer,* however, there is at present no bandwagon. The currently most widespread American pronunciation, \kə-ˈläm-ət-ər\, faces a plausible challenge from \ˈkil-ə-ˌmēt-ər\, and it is anyone's bet what the outcome will be. It is entirely conceivable that there will be no outcome, in the sense that one variant will drive out the other.

We may be wise to remember that it is really not all that unusual for words that might well be pronounced analogously to differ, even in the vocabulary of science. For instance, two closely related areas of mathematics are *homology* theory and *homotopy* theory, often pronounced in the same breath. But the former is pronounced \hō-ˈmäl-ə-jē\, the latter \ˈhō-mə-ˌtäp-ē\. And there is another odd-man-out among the *-meter* words of the metric system: *centimeter* is often given a quasi-French pronunciation \ˈsänt-ə-ˌmēt-ər\, especially by doctors and nurses (see also HYPER-FOREIGNISMS).

kilt In Scotland, the traditional knee-length skirt worn by men is called a kilt. Outside of Scotland, the established singular form is also *kilt,* but analogy with such familiar words as *pants* and *trousers* occasionally leads to the addition of an *-s:*

> The Indian wearing kilts was supposed to represent the "Mohawks" who had staged the Tea Party —Leslie Thomas, *Long May It Wave,* 1941

This use of *kilts,* which our evidence shows to be rare, has been cited as an error by several commentators. You can be sure that the Scots dislike it as well.

kin The usual sense of *kin* is collective— "relatives":

> . . . the pressures close kin . . . can exert on the would-be childbearer —Shirley Lindenbaum, *N.Y. Times Book Rev.,* 29 Apr. 1984

But it also has occasional use as a countable singular—"kinsman":

> . . . below it, Old Heidelberg, a close kin to Liederkranz —*Esquire,* February 1974

The singular *kin* is not new; the earliest record of its use is from the 13th century. It is, how-

ever, uncommon enough to call attention to itself. Bernstein 1965 and Harper 1985 call it as an error. What our evidence shows is simply that it is rare.

See also KITH AND KIN.

kind 1. *These* (or *those*) *kind* (or *sort*) *of.* Most of the handbooks and usage books tell us to use *this* or *that* with singular *kind* or *sort* and follow *of* with a singular noun, and use *these* or *those* with plural *kinds* or *sorts* and follow *of* with a plural noun. But this advice applies only to American English, and it presents an unrealistically narrow set of options. Real usage—even in American English—is much more varied and much more complex.

The history of these expressions as a usage issue goes back to the 18th century. Leonard 1929 reports that Robert Baker in his 1779 book disapproved *these* or *those* before singular *sort* and Lowth 1762 (in one of his later editions) and Lindley Murray 1795 touched on the construction; Murray cited "these kind of sufferings" for correction.

Leonard says the issue was considered a more serious problem in the 19th century. In this country Noah Webster (*Grammatical Institute,* 1804), Goold Brown (*Grammar of English Grammars,* 1851 and later), Richard Grant White 1870, and Ayres 1881 disapprove; presumably there were many others. And if White and Ayres are typical, most American commentators were entirely ignorant of any literary precedent for the expressions (Goold Brown does mention Shakespeare but still calls his use an impropriety).

> These kind of knaves I know —Shakespeare, *King Lear,* 1606

> . . . these kind of Testimonies —John Milton, *Of Prelatical Episcopacy,* 1641

> . . . these kind of thoughts —John Dryden, *Of Dramatick Poesie, An Essay,* 1668 (in McKnight)

> . . . these kind of structures —Jonathan Swift, *A Tale of a Tub,* 1710

> . . . these sort of authors are poor —Alexander Pope (in Alford 1866)

> These Sort of people ask Opinions —Sir Richard Steele, *The Tatler,* No. 25, 7 June 1709

> You don't know those Sort of People Child —Daniel Defoe, *Moll Flanders,* 1722

> . . . engaged in these sort of hopes —Jane Austen, *Mansfield Park,* 1814

> These sort of people —Charles Dickens, *Nicholas Nickleby,* 1839 (in Jespersen 1909–49)

> . . . these sort of impertinences —Sydney Smith, letter, 6 Jan. 1843 (in Hodgson 1889)

These constructions do not stop in the middle of the 19th century, but the examples should give you a general idea of what could have been found by 19th-century commentators had they chosen to look.

The reaction to the expressions has been more mixed in Great Britain. You might expect more tolerance from British commentators, since the examples above are all from British literature. Alford 1866 is a defender of the construction, but Hodgson 1889 is a critic. Fowler 1926 is somewhat tolerant, while Gowers in Fowler 1965 promotes it to the status of "sturdy indefensible." Chambers 1985 finds it acceptable in informal language. But Phythian 1979, Howard 1980, and Bryson 1984 take the American point of view (or perhaps they have come full circle to Baker and Lindley Murray again).

The phrases did not develop uniformly. *Manner*, which most commentators simply ignore, seems to have been the first so used (as in Shakespeare's "all manner of men"), followed shortly by *kind*. It is important to note that the constructions with *kind* have many premodifiers other than *these* and *those*—in fact *these* apparently occurs only twice in Shakespeare. He uses *such* ("such kind of men"—*Much Ado About Nothing*), *some* ("some kind of men"—*Twelfth Night*), *all* ("all kind of natures"—*Timon of Athens*), and other modifiers ("the newest kind of ways"—*2 Henry IV*) as well as a singular before with a plural after ("a kind of men"—*Othello*). Milton, writing about forty years later, also uses this last pattern. He has in his English prose works "what kind of Bishops," "such kind of deceavers," "which kind of Monsters," "such kind of incursions," and "a kind of Chariots" in addition to his uses with *these*.

Sort, which comes along later, probably gives us a clue to how the idioms developed. Shakespeare regularly uses it with *a* before and the plural after ("a sort of men"—*Merchant of Venice*, "a sort of vagabonds"—*Richard III*). When Shakespeare uses a plural premodifier, he uses *sorts* ("all sorts of deer"—*Merry Wives of Windsor*, "several sorts of reasons"—*Hamlet*). A concordance of Milton's English prose works shows that Milton follows the same pattern. We might conjecture then, from this little information about *sort*, that the idioms first form with the singular felt to be a mass noun, frequently with a plural complement, and gradually the *kind of*, *sort of* comes to be felt to be more or less of an adjective (this is the supposition of the OED and Jespersen) —with no particular effect on the preceding modifier or the following noun. *Sort* falls into the same patterns as *kind*—with plural modifiers and plural nouns—in the 18th century.

To complete the picture, we find both Shakespeare and Milton using plural *kinds* followed by a singular, too—the singular being a mass noun. Shakespeare gives us "Some kinds of baseness"; Milton, "various kinds of style," "other kinds of licensing." Shakespeare (but not Milton, apparently) also has *kinds* with a plural: "All kinds of sores and shames."

To sum up: we can find both *kind* and *sort* in the singular preceded by a singular and followed by a singular; in the singular preceded by a singular and followed by a plural; and in the singular preceded by a plural and followed by a plural. And *kinds* and *sorts* are followed both by singulars and plurals. All these permutations have been in use since the 18th century or earlier, and they are still in use:

"What kind of angel is this?" —Bernard Malamud, *The Magic Barrel*, 1958

I hate to write this kind of thing —Flannery O'Connor, letter, 26 Oct. 1958

. . . started as a kind of narrative —John Houseman, quoted in *Publishers Weekly*, 19 Aug. 1983

. . . a sort of Modern Authors —Jonathan Swift, *The Mechanical Operation of the Spirit*, 1710

I love this sort of poems —Charles Lamb, letter, 20 Mar. 1799

. . . stockbrokers, sugar-bakers—that sort of people —W. M. Thackeray, *Punch*, 27 Sept. 1845

. . . the kind of questions that must be asked —Herbert J. Muller, *The Uses of English*, 1967

. . . this kind of records —Dan Gibson, quoted in *New Yorker*, 16 July 1984

. . . to see what sort of books occupied the lowest . . . bookshelves —Lewis Carroll, letter, 11 May 1859

If there are any other kind of farmers —Leacock 1943

. . . what kind of adjustments he must make —Gideon Ariel, quoted in *Popular Computing*, November 1982

. . . those kind of guys —Ring Lardner, *The Big Town*, 1921

. . . these kind of sensational statements —Sir Winston Churchill, *The Unrelenting Struggle*, 1942

These are the kind of worries I can handle —*And More by Andy Rooney*, 1982

Those kind of letters —Art Buchwald, *Springfield* (Mass.) *Republican*, 2 Oct. 1983

Those are the kind of thoughtful comments —Jeff Greenfield, *Springfield* (Mass.) *Morning Union*, 2 May 1986

. . . a trend toward different kinds of living —Margaret Mead, *Barnard Alumnae*, Winter 1971

. . . a writer of several kinds of distinction —R. W. B. Lewis, *N.Y. Times Book Rev.*, 2 Jan. 1983

. . . those kinds of excess —Jeff Greenfield, *Springfield* (Mass.) *Morning Union*, 2 May 1986

These are the kinds of books a grandmother should give —*People*, 14 Feb. 1983

And although it is seldom mentioned by the handbooks, *type* has fallen into the same sort of pattern:

And in America we don't do those type of things —Carl Ekern, quoted in *Newsweek*, 21 July 1986

Conclusion: *kind* and *sort*, in the singular, preceded by *these* or *those* and followed by a plural noun is an idiom well established in British usage—from the 16th century to the present. It is a bugbear of American handbooks, and such use as it has had in American English has until quite recently been confined chiefly to speech. It seems now to be establishing itself in written American English. The grammar books and handbooks may nonetheless continue to repeat themselves. Many of them will be so concerned with *these* and *those* that they will entirely miss the fact that "that kind of sailboats" (from a recent 7th-grade English text) is just as anomalous from the point of view of narrow grammatical logic as "those kind of sailboats." But you are aware by now that a much greater variety of constructions is in respectable use than the handbooks realize.
2. See KIND OF, SORT OF; KIND OF A, SORT OF A.

kindly *Kindly* is used both as an adjective ("a kindly smile") and as an adverb ("he smiled kindly"). In one of its many adverbial uses it serves as a synonym of *please*:

The old woman did not know it but she spoke in a hoity-toity voice. . . . "Kindly order me a conveyance" —Rumer Godden, *Ladies' Home Jour.*, December 1970

"And now you'll kindly do me the favor to pack a suitcase full of clothes and send it on to me. I'll give you just one week for it, too." —Katherine Anne Porter, *Ladies' Home Jour.*, August 1971

These passages illustrate two ways in which *kindly* differs from *please*: it tends to have a highly formal sound, and it often has an impe-

rious quality, so that the request being made comes across as a command. If someone you disliked were to clap a hand on your shoulder in a hearty gesture of insincere friendship, you might find yourself saying, "Kindly take your grubby paw off me." *Please* just wouldn't be appropriate at such a moment.

The "please" sense of *kindly* is standard.

kind of, sort of These phrases slid imperceptibly into adverbial function around the end of the 18th century. They began to be viewed askance in the early 20th century. The earliest disparager, Vizetelly 1906, called *kind of* an American provincialism, but it is not, having early Scots, Irish, and English sources as well as American. No subsequent commentator (and there are many of them) has done more than repeat early condemnations; none has put forward a cogent reason for avoiding the phrases. This is simply so much self-perpetuating malarkey. Our evidence shows both phrases in widespread general and informal use. No one seems to use them in formal discourse. A few examples:

And I kind of want to make *her* Moyra —Henry James, "Notes for *The Ivory Tower*," 1917

". . . You see, they're tennis shoes, and I'm sort of helpless without them. . . ." —F. Scott Fitzgerald, *The Great Gatsby*, 1925

We've been having practice raids here, and I dash around the roads at night blowing a horn and feeling kind of silly —E. B. White, letter, 21 May 1942

He wasn't even a politician, and it's kind of hard to explain why he stayed in politics —James Thurber, *New Yorker*, 9 June 1951

. . . they all sort of work together —Lord Snowden, quoted in *Australian Women's Weekly*, 30 Apr. 1975

. . . I kind of liked him too —*And More by Andy Rooney*, 1982

Jim believed that God sort of generally watched over the world —Garrison Keillor, *Lake Wobegon Days*, 1985

. . . they were to be transferred in amounts sort of as drawn —Caspar Weinberger, Secretary of Defense, quoted in *The Tower Commission Report*, 1987

kind of a, sort of a Here we have another English idiom that has come under the disapproving scrutiny of the critics. From 1779 when omitting the *a* was held to be more elegant to 1998 when including it was held to be illiterate, numerous critics advise us to omit the *a* (or *an*).

Writers have been using the construction with *a* from Shakespeare's time to the present:

. . . and yet I have the wit to think my master is a kind of a knave —Shakespeare, *The Two Gentlemen of Verona*, 1595

. . . he left off the study of projectiles in a kind of a huff —Laurence Sterne, *Tristram Shandy*, 1759

You know what sort of a man King is —Henry Adams, letter, 17 Jan. 1861

. . . saints casting down their crowns (in what kind of a tantrum?) —Elizabeth Bishop, *The Collected Prose*, 1984

Witnesses today cannot even agree as to . . . what sort of a coffin was used —Hugh Brogan, *Times Literary Supp.*, 27 June 1986

. . . she felt so inadequate as a wife for what kind of a Mrs is it that cannot cheer up her man —Salman Rushdie, *The Satanic Verses*, 1989

. . . what sort of a man would give up sex for a low-prestige job with pauper's wages like the Catholic priesthood? —*Commonweal*, 23 Apr. 1999

Type, incidentally, can also be found in this construction:

. . . that type of a threat —Joseph McCarthy, 1954, quoted in Pyles 1979

Our files show that *kind of a* and *sort of a* are primarily spoken idioms—we find them in both reported and fictional speech. But they do appear in edited serious prose—even in articles on law and philosophy—when they are the writer's idiom. But the *a* (or *an*) is much more often omitted. You are more likely to use the form without the article in most writing. Still, there never has been a sound reason for aspersing the less common idiom. If it is your idiom, there's no need to avoid it, especially in speech or in familiar writing.

kith and kin   This alliterative phrase has been cited as an overworked cliché by several commentators. As overworked clichés go, it is not an especially popular one; we have collected only a handful of examples of its use during the past several decades. The commentators like to point out that *kith* means—or formerly meant—"fellow countrymen," so that *kith and kin* should not, in their view, be taken as referring only to kinsfolk. What our evidence shows is that *kith and kin* is variously used and variously understood in current English. More often than not, it does seem to imply nothing more than "kinsfolk," but its exact meaning is often hard to pin down. Clearly some writers do apply it to friends as well as to relatives:

. . . began to interview Sedgwick kith and kin. She talked with friends from Edie's

years in Cambridge —Geoffrey Wolff, *N.Y. Times Book Rev.*, 4 July 1982

For 2,000 years, Sri Lankans have lived in the same towns, worshiped at the same shrine and walked the same roads. To them, the people buried at Sigiriya are kith and kin —Barbara Crossette, *N.Y. Times*, 25 June 1991

kneel   *Kneel* belongs to a group of verbs which offer a choice of variants for the past and past participle. Either *kneeled* or *knelt* is considered standard. *Knelt* occurs more frequently than does *kneeled* in contemporary usage:

The boy knelt and held out his arms —E. L. Doctorow, *Ragtime*, 1975

Warren walked in bowed, kneeled on the straw mat —E. L. Doctorow, *Loon Lake*, 1979

The OED tells us that *kneeled* was the regular spelling until the latter part of the 19th century, when *knelt* began appearing. Shakespeare, for instance, never used *knelt*.

knit, knitted   As many commentators observe, the past tense and past participle of *knit* can be either *knit* or *knitted*. A few critics in the early 20th century regarded *knitted* as an error, but that issue was apparently laid to rest when Fowler 1926 accepted both forms, while noting some distinctions in their use. Our evidence shows that the two forms are interchangeable in most contexts ("a knit/knitted shirt"; "he knit/knitted his brows in concentration"). *Knit* is definitely preferred, however, with such adverbs as *closely* and *tightly* in figurative use:

They rejected the closely knit but stifling family interaction —A. I. Rabin, *Psychology Today*, September 1969

. . . a loosely knit state which allows for great variety —John W. Holmes, *The Lamp*, Fall 1971

Always alone among strangers, the family grew tightly knit —Ross Milloy, *N.Y. Times Mag.*, 6 Apr. 1980

knot   Nautically speaking and strictly speaking, a knot is a unit of speed equal to one nautical mile per hour, and a vessel is described as traveling at (or "making") a certain number of knots. Also occasionally heard is such usage as "The ship was under way at 20 knots an hour," in which *knot* has the meaning "nautical mile." This sense of *knot* is widely derided by those in the know as a landlubber's mistake, and you would probably be prudent not to indulge in its use, at least within earshot of sailors or usage commentators. If you do happen to use it, however, and if some seafaring or word-watching type accuses you of gross ignorance, you might just point out that it was first entered in a dictionary in 1864 and was first recorded a century before that in the written works of two famous English sailors:

> The ship went ten knots an hour —Admiral George Anson, *Anson's Voyage Round the World*, 1748 (OED)

> The strong tide, though even here it ran five knots an hour —Captain James Cook, *Voyages*, published in 1790 (OED)

know *Know* belongs to a class of verbs most of which (like *blow, fly, show*) have at least some irregular forms in the past and past participle but a few of which (like *flow*) have only regular ones. In standard English *know* has only *knew* and *known*. *Knowed*, although old—the OED dates it back to the 14th century—is now found only in dialectal and uneducated speech. *Knowed* has been frequently used by fiction writers for their special purposes:

> "I knowed it!" sighed Mrs. Davids —Francis Lee Pratt, "Captain Ben's Choice," in *Mark Twain's Library of Humor*, 1888

> Old Eagle had done already took off because he knowed where that old son of a gun would be laying as good as we did —William Faulkner, *Saturday Evening Post*, 5 Mar. 1955

kraft See CRAFT 2.

kudos, kudo *Kudos* is a Greek word that was dragged into English as British university slang in the 19th century. The OED so notices, calling it in addition (and curiously) a colloquialism. Early users, conscious of its origin, sometimes printed it in Greek letters, but no one does anymore.

In its earliest use, the word referred to the prestige or renown one gained by having accomplished something noteworthy. The word became more popular than one might have expected for a bit of university slang. By the 1920s it had developed a second sense, "praise given for some accomplishment"—a reasonable extension of the original use. *Time* magazine is frequently credited with the popularizing of this second sense, but it probably did not originate with *Time* editors.

In construction *kudos* is originally a noncount noun, a mass noun, like *glory, acclaim, renown,* or *prestige*:

> . . . they had acquired much kudos among the pilgrims —John Buchan, *The Last Secrets*, 1923

> . . . Oliphant, who gained a little kudos —Leonard Merrick, *The Actor-Manager*, 4th ed., 1919

> . . . she was proud of sharing in Bresnahan's kudos —Sinclair Lewis, *Main Street*, 1920

During the 1920s the "praise" sense of *kudos* came to be understood as a plural count noun. *Time* magazine does seem to have been influential in this process. It was a policy of the editors to announce honorary degrees and like awards under an opening like this (from 28 June 1926):

> Another week of Commencements . . . and distinguished citizens from all walks of life were called to many rostra to be honored. . . . Kudos conferred during the week:

And a list would follow. The notion of plurality also became associated with the word when it was linked with a plural noun:

> They were the recipients of honorary degrees—kudos conferred because of their wealth, position or service to humanity —*Time*, 27 June 1927

Our earliest unmistakably plural citation is a bit earlier and from a different source:

> Colonial mechanics have very few kudos thrown in their path —letter to the editor, *Rand Daily Mail* (Johannesburg), 23 Dec. 1925

Demonstrably plural citations have not been as frequent as you might expect from the amount of attention *kudos* has received. Here are a couple more of our earlier ones:

> There is no other weekly newspaper which in one short year has achieved so many kudos —*Time*, 9 June 1941

> Its kudos for brilliance are few —Saul Carson, *New Republic*, 26 Jan. 1948

Far more of our citations are of uses in which *kudos* could be taken to be either a mass noun or a plural.

Once *kudos* was perceived as plural, though, it was inevitable that someone would prune the *s* from the end and create a singular. The earliest pruner in our files is Fred Allen. He did it in an all lowercase letter (he often ignored the shift key on his typewriter) written to some of his writers who were in the service in World War II:

> Mrs. a wishes to send a kudo, she rented from variety, to tempy —29 Feb. 1942

What Fred Allen could do in a letter, someone else was bound to do in print:

> To all three should go some kind of special kudo for refusing to succumb —Al Hine, *Holiday*, June 1953

A surprising number of commentators are in denial and tell us that there is no such thing as a kudo. But they are wrong. If there is no such thing as a kudo, there is no such thing as a cherry, a pea, an asset, a caterpillar, or a one-hoss shay. All of these terms were formed by back-formation from a supposed plural. Jespersen 1909–49, in his second volume, has many other examples. Mencken (1963 edition) also lists a number of similarly formed singulars that exist in the American vernacular.

Like it or not, *kudo* is here as a singular count noun and *kudos* as a plural count noun. A few more examples:

He then goes on to quote various kudos that the secretary-general received —David Rieff, *New Republic,* 1 May 2000

This last in Mariani's pick as his Restaurant of the Year, another kudo for the chef —Herb Caen, *San Francisco Chronicle,* 21 Oct. 1987

... two châteaus have been added to the list of premiers grands crus classés, the top kudo under the ranking —James Suckling, *Wine Spectator,* 30 Nov. 1996

We think that *kudo* and *kudos* as count nouns are by now well established, although you will note that they have not yet penetrated the highest range of scholarly writing or literature. If you do choose to use the word, keep in mind that there are three separate uses: *kudo* as a singular count noun, *kudos* as a plural count noun, and *kudos* as a singular noncount noun.

Kudos is usually pronounced \'k(y)ü-₁däs\ or \'k(y)ü-₁dōs\ by those who treat it as singular, \'k(y)ü-₁dōz\ by those who make it plural.

L

labor   See BELABOR, LABOR.

lack   *In* and *for* are the prepositions used with the verb *lack.* The usage panel of Heritage 1969, 1982 prefers *lack* to *lack for* when no difference of meaning would result. But *lack for,* found in negative contexts, is standard. Burchfield 1996 notes that it is also used in British English.

She never lacked for self-knowledge in the matter of vanity —Wright Morris, *Plains Song,* 1980

Steve Lasker hasn't lacked for news experience since his teens —Frederick C. Klein, *Wall Street Jour.,* 22 June 1983

Leon didn't lack for visitors the last few years —Garrison Keillor, *Lake Wobegon Days,* 1985

Lack is occasionally used in negative constructions without *for:*

... certainly the river did not lack a few travelers —William Styron, *This Quiet Dust and Other Writings,* 1982

laden   When *laden* is used with a preposition, the choice is almost always *with:*

... he ceased to speak to her as though she were a child and he a person laden with wisdom —Sinclair Lewis, *Arrowsmith,* 1925

... enigmatic space and Edward Hopper American houses that seem laden with disquiet —Irving Howe, *N.Y. Times Book Rev.,* 11 Sept. 1983

lady   *Lady* is one of the fine old words of English. After perhaps 1100 years of use it began

to be the subject of considerable discussion in usage books during the 19th century. While the commentators disagreed on specific points, there was generally more agreement on the broader issues. Almost everyone agreed that *woman* was a better general designation for the sex than *lady,* but almost all of them allowed *lady* to be an acceptable word for a woman of superior breeding or social refinement. The occasion of all this discussion seems to have been an American journalistic convention of the time that mandated referring to women in news reports as *ladies.*

The commentators of the early 20th century contented themselves with reviewing the same 19th-century topics in pretty much the 19th-century way. After World War II, however, commentators began to be a little more sophisticated in their approach because American women had become more emancipated in their attitudes. Reader's Digest 1983 seems to grasp particularly well not only the diversity of attitudes towards *lady* but also the complexity of actual usage when they call *lady* "a word so full of social overtones and built-in gender assumptions that no one can prescribe rules of its usage for others." The subject matter, however, has not changed; it is almost entirely the same question of which is better, *lady* or *woman,* to use as a general indicator of sex (*woman* is now the all but universal choice), and which is better to use in light of what is known about a person's social position or refinement. A good dictionary can tell you nearly all of this. All the uses commented upon are listed as separate senses of the noun *lady.*

If the subject matter of the commentators has remained essentially constant for more than a century now, what about usage? Is it any different? We can reply with some assurance that the 19th-century journalistic habit of referring to all women as *ladies* has nearly passed from the scene. Then too, *lady* has picked up at least one use since the old days: it is now used, especially in the gossip sheets and personality magazines, as a word for the young woman who is the usual but unmarried companion of a man who happens to be a television actor, a rock star, or some similar focus of fascinated attention.

> With lady Josephine and daughter Leah, 4, along for the ride . . . —*People,* 9 May 1983

The examples that follow will tell you more about how *lady* is used in print; some simply use the word while others offer comment. One of the things you will probably notice is that no simple rule about when to use or not use *lady* will stand up against actual usage. People will choose between *lady* and *woman* in ways that seem most natural to them, although—as you will see—they sometimes do so to the displeasure of those to whom or about whom they are speaking.

> . . . the trunk had been lost but was now found that contained what some lady was going to wear —Robert Frost, letter, 10 Nov. 1920

> A lady is—or in Ellen Terry's generation was—a person trained to the utmost attainable degree in the art and habit of concealing her feelings and maintaining an imperturbable composure under the most trying circumstances —George Bernard Shaw, preface, *The Shaw–Terry Letters,* 1931

> It was years ago, I remember, one Christmas Eve when I was dining with friends: a lady beside me made in the course of talk one of those allusions —Henry James, *The Art of the Novel,* 1934

> . . . it . . . no more enhances the quality of a lady's output than does the assumption of . . . cute and booksy *noms de plume* —James Thurber, *Thurber Country,* 1953

> . . . [my mother]'s usually the only lady present at these things and gets treated in highstyle by the auctioneer —Flannery O'Connor, letter, 6 Oct. 1956

> Whatever the fops and bullies may have thought of it, tragedy had a special appeal to the ladies —James Sutherland, *English Literature of the Late Seventeenth Century,* 1969

> At the end of the lecture Miss Stein rose; we all got up; and amid the babble of good-nights the ladies came forward from their compound —Allen Tate, *Prose,* Fall 1971

> She never has more than eight and serves sumptuous Haitian delicacies cooked by her Haitian lady —André Leon Talley, *Women's Wear Daily,* 17 Apr. 1978

> . . . another female stereotype—the elderly lady who seems to be everybody's white-haired grandmother but actually is a sharp, observant old dame who knows much more than she pretends to —Newgate Callendar, *N.Y. Times Book Rev.,* 28 Aug. 1983

> Despite the efforts of feminists, working-class women across America, young and old, still resolutely refer to themselves as ladies —Michael Brody, *Fortune,* 11 Nov. 1985

> His mother had been a scrubwoman, and he wasn't going to let these ladies suffer the way she had —Tip O'Neill with William Novak, *Man of the House,* 1987

> At an information office on the pier, a smiling lady provides me with a town map —Charles N. Barnard, *National Geographic Traveler,* July/August 1997

> The ultimate lady entrepreneur, Chan . . . has an enviable collection of Prada bags, a pricey pad on the Upper East Side and a little black book full of Wall Street power brokers —Leah Platt, *The Nation,* 9 July 2001

> One of my few unpublished stories . . . was written on the advice of the lady agent just mentioned —Donald Hamilton, in *Colloquium on Crime,* ed. Robin W. Winks, 1986

lady . . . avoid using this in place of "woman" unless you intend shadings of meaning that describe someone who is elegant, "refined," and conscious of propriety and correct behavior. In most contexts this word is perceived as (and often is) condescending —Rosalie Maggio, *The Nonsexist Word Finder,* 1987

lag When *lag* is used with a preposition, it is usually *behind*:

> Behind him lagged the girl —Harriet La Barre, *Discovery,* March 1954

> . . . the organized workers thus saw their pay lag behind the corporate returns —Michael Harrington, *Center Mag.,* September 1969

lament The verb *lament,* when used with a preposition, is used with *about, for,* or *over*:

> . . . we need not gloat or lament about the limitations of finite minds —Antony Flew, *A New Approach to Psychical Research,* 1953

And Jeremiah lamented for Josiah —2 Chronicles, 35:25 (AV), 1611

. . . instigating some journalist friends of his at the same time to lament over the decay of the grand school of acting —George Bernard Shaw, *Cashel Byron's Profession,* 1886

lamentable See INCOMPARABLE.

large, largely The adverb *largely* is described as unidiomatic following the verbs *bulk* and *loom* by several commentators, dating back to Fowler 1926. Our evidence confirms that *large* is the usual choice:

These inner planets . . . do not bulk very large in the solar system as a whole —Carl Sagan, *Scientific American,* September 1975

. . . and America loomed large in their imagination —Garrison Keillor, *Lake Wobegon Days,* 1985

We have no evidence for *bulk largely* in our files more recent than 1949. Our only example of *loom largely* is from speech.

last Some usage writers make the distinction that *last* means "final" and *latest* means "most recent." Other writers admit that both words can mean "most recent" but insist that only *latest* conveys this meaning unambiguously.

Topics such as a last/latest issue of a magazine or a writer's last/latest book are the typical illustrations chosen by commentators, presumably because such contexts might be ambiguous if the wrong word is chosen. However, we agree with Bryson 1984 that "the chances of ambiguity . . . are probably not as great as some authorities would have us believe." Our citations bear this out:

. . . which was reproduced in facsimile in the last issue of this news letter —Ruth Wedgwood Kennedy, *Renaissance News,* Autumn 1951

. . . some hostile review in the *New Republic* of my last book —Harold J. Laski, letter, 28 Nov. 1920

This is another scrappy note written as a stop-gap between my last long letter to you and the next —Alexander Woollcott, letter, 26 Jan. 1918

. . . indicates that respondents tend to remember best the last words they hear —Stanley L. Payne, *The Art of Asking Questions,* 1951

We believe that the general context or the subject under discussion, if not the immediate context, will usually provide enough information to make such uses of *last* unambiguous.

When nouns denoting time (such as *night, week, May, Tuesday*) are being modified,

idiom calls for *last* or *past,* but not *latest,* even though the meaning is clearly "most recent" and not "final."

. . . the last three or four years —William R. Eshelman, *Wilson Library Bulletin,* November 1968

For eight of the past nine years —*Bowdoin Alumnus,* January 1971

See also FIRST TWO, TWO FIRST.

last analysis See ANALYSIS.

late Much thought has been given to the use of *the late* before the name of a dead person. The most frequently considered aspect of such use is just how long a person referred to as "the late" can have been dead. Here are a few opinions:

. . . the statute of limitations might run for half a century —Bernstein 1971

As a general rule, late is used in reference to persons whose death has occurred within the twenty or thirty years just past —Harper 1975

. . . "the late" is used for about ten to fifteen years after death —Safire 1984

What everyone does agree on is that there is no hard and fast rule to be followed. Our evidence shows that *the late* can be applied to people whose lives were recent enough to exist at any point within the living memory of the writer or speaker. You should use your own judgment to decide whether it is appropriate in a particular instance.

Still another consideration is the use of *the late* in referring to a famous person whose death is common knowledge. Bernstein 1971 and Safire 1984 discourage such use, regarding *the late* as superfluous. Safire acknowledges, however, that "some people use the phrase . . . to pay respects to the subject." Most people, in fact, use the phrase that way. *The late* is primarily a term of respect for a person who has recently died, and its use in referring to a famous person is both common and appropriate:

The late Henry Ford —*N.Y. Times,* 27 Sept. 1950

The late President John F. Kennedy —*Current Biography,* June 1967

. . . the late H. L. Mencken —Paul Fussell, *Los Angeles Times Book Rev.,* 25 Apr. 1971

Another aspect of the use of *the late* has also drawn comment. Kilpatrick 1984 warns against such a sentence as "The bill was signed by the late President Johnson" which, he says, "creates a startling and indeed a macabre image," implying that President Johnson was already "late" when he signed the bill. That seems to be an excellent point until you realize that *the late* can almost always be read in a macabre way by anyone determined to do so:

> In a talk to Harvard's Nieman Fellows twenty years ago, the late A. J. Liebling declared that . . . —Joseph P. Lyford, *Center Mag.,* September 1969

> The late Prof. Louise Pound collected them in a study of 1936 —Allen Walker Read, "The Geolinguistics of Verbal Taboo," 10 Jan. 1970

> On Lowenstein's first day in the House, the late L. Mendel Rivers accosted him —John Corry, *Harper's,* April 1971

The late can legitimately be used in this way because it does not simply mean "the dead," it means "the now dead." It is actually no more macabre to say "the bill was signed by the late President Johnson" than to say "the bill was signed by the now dead President Johnson."

later on The *on* of *later on* was much criticized as superfluous in the first half of the 20th century, but it no longer provokes controversy. It occurs commonly in both speech and writing:

> . . . if you don't report him, he'll probably get into worse trouble later on —J. Edgar Hoover, *NEA Jour.,* January 1965

> Later on their diagnoses got more specific —Conrad Rooks, quoted in *Evergreen,* December 1967

> . . . his ability to resist, later on, the temptation to steal a television set —C. Knight Aldrich, *Psychology Today,* March 1971

For a parallel, but more recent, case see EARLY ON.

Latin plurals One of the favorite subjects of usage writers over the years is the misuse of the plurals of foreign words—mostly but not all Latin—as singulars. For discussions of individual foreign plurals that are used as singulars, see AGENDA; BACTERIA; BONA FIDES; CANDELABRA; CRITERION, CRITERIA, CRITERIONS; CURRICULUM; DATA, DATUM; DESIDERATUM; DICTUM; EROTICA; ERRATA; GRAFFITI, GRAFFITO; MAGI; MEDIA; MEMORANDUM; MINUTIA; PAPARAZZO, PAPARAZZI; PARAPHERNALIA; PHENOMENON; PROLEGOMENON, PROLEGOMENA; STADIUM; STRATA, STRATUM; TRIVIA.

latter See FORMER.

laudable, laudatory Usage commentators are concerned about maintaining the distinction between these words, which is that *laudable* means "deserving praise; praiseworthy" ("laudable attempts to help the poor") and

laudatory means "giving praise; praiseful" ("a laudatory book review"). This distinction is a real one, observed by almost everyone. *Laudatory* is sometimes used in place of *laudable*:

> Librarians are alert to . . . the need to re-allocate certain routine chores to others less qualified; this is laudatory —Mary Lee Bundy & Paul Wasserman, *College & Research Libraries,* January 1968

> . . . both take pay cuts in order to do what really makes them happy. This laudatory stance fails to save either man from banality —Philippe Van Rjndt, *N.Y. Times Book Rev.,* 3 July 1983

But this use is still quite rare, and it cannot be regarded as standard.

laugh The verb *laugh,* when used intransitively with a preposition whose object is what caused the laughter, is usually used with *at*:

> . . . the ridiculous, *le rire,* the comic is what we laugh at —John Dewey, *Art as Experience,* 1934

> . . . a butt, a clod, laughed at by looking-glasses —Virginia Woolf, *Between the Acts,* 1941

> . . . a professor on this side of the Atlantic would be laughed at in the English weeklies —E. K. Brown, *Rhythm in the Novel,* 1950

Laugh is also used with *over*:

> . . . a misjudgment he still laughed over when I first met him —Anthony Loyd, *My War Gone By,* 1999

> . . . watched this newcomer squeeze Betty's cheeks while they laughed over some little private joke —Edna O'Brien, *New Yorker,* 1 Jan. 1990

lay, lie These verbs are one of the most popular subjects in the canons of usage. They first attracted attention in the second half of the 18th century, when educated usage seems to have been rather indifferent to the distinctions between them.

The earliest commentator in our collection to mention *lay* and *lie* is Baker 1770. Early in his book he sets down the principal parts of the two verbs and gives examples of how they should be used. Later on he observes that *lie* is very seldom used for *lay* (this is still a true observation) but that he has found *lain* (the past participle of *lie*) used for *laid.* He cites a writer named Bluet who wrote, "after they have lain aside all Pretences to it." Emily Dickinson made the same substitution:

> Thank you for "the Sonnet"—I have lain it at her loved feet —letter, Spring 1886

The opposite change is much more common. Campbell 1776 criticized this passage:

> . . . my studies having laid very much in churchyards —*The Spectator,* 24 Oct. 1712

Once the grammarians had picked up *lay* and *lie* as a subject, it was soon entrenched both in the schools and in the handbooks and usage books. Our collection includes about sixty commentators upon the subject. To them you could add the standard dictionaries, all of which mark the intransitive *lay* for *lie* as nonstandard in one way or another (Flesch 1983 cocks a snook at the dictionaries for being so prissy). Almost all of these commentators tell you what the principal parts of each verb are and note that even though many people have confused them, you should not; the details are in your dictionary.

Let's look first at the history of the usage. The OED shows that *lay* has been used intransitively in the sense of "lie" since around the year 1300. From then until the latter part of the 18th century, the usage was unmarked: Sir Francis Bacon, for instance, used it in the final and most polished edition of his essays in 1625. Lounsbury 1908 notes its occurrence in such 17th- and 18th-century writers as Pepys, Fielding, Horace Walpole, and Mrs. Montagu.

But from the 19th century on, there are fewer and fewer literary examples. Byron has a rather famous, or infamous, "there let him lay" in *Childe Harold's Pilgrimage,* 1818; it is cited in the OED and many other places, but it does not really count. Byron was driven to it: he needed a rhyme for *spray* and *bay*.

If the grammarians and the schoolmasters and the schoolmarms and the usage writers have succeeded in largely establishing the transitive-intransitive distinction between *lay* and *lie* in standard discursive prose, they have not done so well in speech. The persistence of *lay* "lie" in speech in spite of the marshalled opposition of the schoolteachers is reinforced by several factors. First, there is the failure of what Bolinger 1980 calls contrast. The two verbs overlap in some ways: they share an identical form, *lay*; in the past tense the common use with *down* sounds about the same whether spelled *lay down* or *laid down*. Evans 1957 and the OED note in addition that *lay* once had a use with a reflexive pronoun that meant the same as *lie down*: "Now I lay me down to sleep."

> . . . I laid me down flat on my belly —Daniel Defoe, *Robinson Crusoe,* 1719

Evans says that the pronoun dropped out but was understood, giving intransitive *lay*. Then we have some idioms in which *lay* functions intransitively:

> . . . I see that you, too, plan to lay off for Holy Week —Alexander Woollcott, letter, 21 Feb. 1941

> He begins by saying he can't get hold of enough books to find out whether we have any literature or not and then he proceeds to say we have none. I am sure he will lay for me somewhere —Robert Frost, letter, 22 Feb. 1914

And, finally, there is the simple longevity of intransitive *lay*, almost 700 years of continuous use.

The conflict between oral use and school instruction has resulted in the distinction between *lay* and *lie* becoming a social shibboleth—a marker of class and education. Thus, writers can use it to identify characters, or to build up a dialectal integrity.

> Old Eagle had done already took off because he knowed where that old son of a gun would be laying —William Faulkner, *Saturday Evening Post,* 5 Mar. 1955

> "I mean, I don't change sheets in the morning, after I wait on the breakfast eaters . . . without having no place to lay down. . . ." —John Irving, *The Hotel New Hampshire,* 1981

A linguistic shibboleth is only a reliable social marker when an individual either uses or avoids it on all occasions. Persons whose education or status would lead them to avoid such use in formal situations may use the stigmatized word in informal, friendly circumstances:

> She thinks every story must be built according to the pattern of the Roman arch . . . , but I'm letting it lay —Flannery O'Connor, letter, 25 July 1964

> . . . I didn't want anybody, the workers or the contractors or anybody, to lay down on the job —Harry S. Truman, quoted in Merle Miller, *Plain Speaking,* 1973

And there is another curious influence on the use of transitive *lay* in speech: a folk distinction between *lay* and *lie* seems to be in operation that cuts across the distinction of the school books. Evans 1957 says, "There is a tendency in present-day English to prefer the verb *lay* in speaking of inanimate objects, and the verb *lie* in speaking of living creatures." A baseball announcer on television has put it in the pithier folk form: "*Lay* is for things, *lie* is for people." We even have some printed evidence of this "*lay* is for things" use:

> . . . the book really lays flat when opened —Mabel C. Simmons, *New Orleans Times-Picayune,* 23 May 1976

> The System Unit Board, laying flat at the bottom of the box, includes a 5 Mhz 8088

microprocessor —Sergio Mello-Grand, *InfoWorld*, 19 Dec. 1983

Notwithstanding the belief of some that social judgments can be solidly based on language use, the *lay–lie* shibboleth may be changing its status. For instance, several commentators, such as Evans 1957, Follett 1966, and Flesch 1983, are perfectly willing to give the distinction up; Bolinger 1980 thinks it is already a lost cause not worth defending; Copperud 1970, 1980 judges the consensus of his experts to be that at least some uses of *lay* for *lie* are verging on standard. Flesch even goes so far as to recommend using *lay* for *lie* if it comes naturally to you.

If *lay* "lie" is on the rise socially, however, it is likely to be a slow rise, as indignant letters to the editor attest. Bolinger observes sensibly that if you have invested some effort in learning the distinction, you will not want to admit that you have wasted your time. And by far the largest part of our printed evidence follows the schoolbook rules. On the other hand, evidence also shows no retreat of intransitive *lay* in oral use. So what should you do? The best advice seems to be Bolinger's:

Many people use *lay* for *lie*, but certain others will judge you uncultured if you do. Decide for yourself what is best for you.

lead, led The past tense and past participle of the verb *lead* is spelled *led*:

... he led negotiations in a strike —*Current Biography*, February 1967

The strong tendency to spell it *lead* is presumably attributable in large part to analogy with the verb *read*, as well as to the influence of the noun *lead*.

... has lead a life of action —*American Poetry Rev.*, vol. 3, no. 5, 1974

... has lead the field —*Southwest Art*, May 1984

This is a common mistake in casual writing. Watch out for it.

See also MISLEAD, MISLED.

lean 1. While both *leant* and *leaned* can be found in the past tense and past participle in British English, *leant* is preferred. In American English, *leaned* is used almost exclusively.

The train started. Snopes leaned into the aisle, looking back —William Faulkner, *Sanctuary*, 1931

Jake leaned against the counter. 'Say what kind of a place is this town?' —Carson McCullers, *The Heart Is a Lonely Hunter*, 1940

She leant out of the porthole —Ngaio Marsh, *Death of a Peer*, 1940

Mr. Pondoroso leant his scooter against the Wayne Mews wall —Colin MacInnes, *Absolute Beginners*, 1959

... entered her child's room and leant over his sleeping form —Ray Smuts, *Sunday Times* (South Africa), 10 Nov. 1974

His anger vanished. His whole soul leaned out eagerly towards Gallagher, craving support —Liam O'Flaherty, *The Informer*, 1925

2. *Lean* is used with a great number of prepositions, but by far the one most frequently found is *on*:

They leant on the counter, laughing and talking —John Fountain, *The Bulletin* (Sydney, Australia), 24 Feb. 1954

Both items lean heavily on nostalgia —Bennett Cerf, *Saturday Rev.*, 22 May 1954

This is a straight deal or the senora wouldn't be in it. You have no reason to lean on me —Pierre Salinger, *On Instructions of My Government*, 1971

... a factor ... never pointedly leant on by the playwright to underpin his case —John Bayley, *Times Literary Supp.*, 20 June 1980

Lean with *to, toward,* or *towards* is also quite common:

... Mr. Horgan leans too heavily to the side of the friars and paints them whiter than the evidence justifies —Oliver La Farge, *American Scholar*, Spring 1955

... nearly everybody leans toward a timid conservatism with regard to unfamiliar music —Virgil Thomson, *The Musical Scene*, 1947

... his aesthetic appreciation ... leaned towards the old rather than to the modern —A. L. Rowse, *West-Country Stories*, 1947

Lean is also found with other prepositions. Following are examples of *upon, in,* and *against*:

Shakespeare leaned, as it were, even as craftsman, upon the general fate of men and nations —*The Autobiography of William Butler Yeats*, 1953

I wasn't being lonely and sitting home and crying. I was leaning over in the opposite direction —Ethel Merman, quoted in *Saturday Evening Post*, 5 Mar. 1955

The old man leaned the mast with its wrapped sail against the wall —Ernest Hemingway, *Life*, 1 Sept. 1952

Earlier in this article are examples of *lean* with *into, out of,* and *over*.

leap *Leaped* and *leapt* are interchangeable both as the past tense ("He leaped/leapt over the ditch") and past participle ("The song has leaped/leapt to the top of the charts") of *leap*. *Leapt* is the more common choice in British English. In American English, *leaped* and *leapt* seem to be used with about equal frequency:

> . . . remarks leaped to his tongue —Norman Mailer, *Harper's*, March 1971

> . . . fairly leapt at life in a hundred directions —James Dickey, *N.Y. Times Book Rev.*, 3 Oct. 1976

learn 1. The use of *learn* to mean "teach" was once perfectly respectable:

> Sweet prince, you learn me noble thankfulness —Shakespeare, *Much Ado About Nothing*, 1599

> . . . having learned him English so well that he could answer me —Daniel Defoe, *Robinson Crusoe*, 1719

> I have too much pride to stand indebted to Great Britain for books to learn our children the letters of the alphabet —Noah Webster, letter, *Weekly Monitor*, 15 Feb. 1785

The OED includes many citations for the "teach" sense of *learn*, dating back to the beginning of the 13th century. Samuel Johnson treated it as a standard sense in the first edition of his dictionary, published in 1755. But the 1785 edition included the note "This sense is now obsolete." By the last decades of the 18th century it had lost prestige. Noah Webster noted in his American Dictionary (1828) that "this use of learn is found in respectable writers, but is now deemed inelegant as well as improper." The OED labeled it "vulgar" in 1902.

The "teach" sense of *learn* has persisted in dialectal and uneducated speech, but its only use in writing is now in the representation or deliberate imitation of such speech:

> . . . if he'd only learned himself to speak good grammar he would probly be a Major today —James Jones, *From Here to Eternity*, 1951

> I'll learn him to touch my gun! —Agnes Sligh Turnbull, *The Gown of Glory*, 1951

2. Even though Lindley Murray disapproved *learnt* in 1795, the British use both *learnt* and *learned* as the past tense and past participle of *learn*:

> . . . learned to live off man's left-overs —Gordon Hard & Frank Manolson, *Observer Mag.*, 25 Nov. 1973

> When I went to my prep school, I learned the piano —Charles, Prince of Wales, quoted in *Observer Rev.*, 9 June 1974

> . . . Magistrate Riley's colleagues have learnt their lesson —*Private Eye*, 5 Apr. 1974

> . . . he first learnt, really learnt, the pleasure of reading —*British Book News*, July 1983

Learnt is no longer very common in American English. It turns up occasionally:

> . . . according to the system learnt in their course —Ring Lardner, *How to Write Short Stories*, 1924

But the usual form in American English is *learned*:

> . . . a slightly reticent girl who had learned to carry her beauty well —Frank Conroy, *Harper's*, November 1970

> . . . was horrified when she learned what had happened —Jay McInerney, *Bright Lights, Big City*, 1984

learned See ALLEGED 2.

leary See LEERY, LEARY.

leave, let 1. Ayres 1881 condemns such expressions as "leave me be" and "leave it alone" as vulgarisms. Compton 1898 and Vizetelly 1906 agree and so does Bierce 1909. Bierce is apparently the first to distinguish the "solitary" sense of *leave alone* from its "untouched" sense.

Since World War II, opinion has been divided between the insisters on the Biercian distinction (Copperud 1960, 1964, 1970, 1980 and Bernstein 1958, 1965, 1977) and just about everyone else (including Evans 1957, Bryant 1962, Watt 1967, Shaw 1975, 1987, Harper 1975, 1985, Trimmer & McCrimmon 1988, and Garner 1998) who find *let alone* and *leave alone* acceptably interchangeable. Some examples of *leave alone*:

> But a good many other Americans at that time could take a college education or leave it alone —Tom Wicker, *Change*, September 1971

> My mother hated whisky and admired men who could leave it alone —Russell Baker, *Growing Up*, 1982

You should note that the "solitary" sense can still be used unmistakably when it is wanted:

> . . . she was afraid that she would be left alone. Once you have lived with another, it is a great torture to have to live alone —Carson McCullers, *The Ballad of the Sad Café*, 1951

Leave alone is standard in both uses.
2. Many of the American commentators on *leave* and *let*—particularly those who write schoolbooks and college handbooks—make no mention of *leave* (or *let*) *alone* but concentrate on other uses of *leave* meaning "let." The

construction usually condemned is *leave* followed by a pronoun and an infinitive without *to*. *Leave* in this use is often a mild imperative:

> Leave us only add that . . . —Jonathan Evan Maslow, *Saturday Rev.,* 12 Apr. 1980

This construction is primarily oral. It has been so long and so often reprehended in the schools that one of its chief uses in print is to be facetious:

> Leave us not enquire how I happened to be running —Alan Coren, *Punch,* 7 Oct. 1975

When it is used seriously in print, the use has been taken from speech:

> If you put them in drums, and this is the easiest way to handle them, and you leave them stand, some free-liquid will surface over time —John Hernandez, quoted in *Civil Engineering,* December 1982

> As for the gap left by Sweet, "We will probably leave it be," says NBC casting chief Joel Thurm —*TV Guide,* 31 May 1985

One curious thing about these constructions is that they are held to be more reprehensible in American English than in British English. Perhaps British tolerance accounts for occasional serious (but not literary) use in British publications:

> Leave it steep for at least 4 hours —Elizabeth David, *Italian Food,* 1969

This example points out how minor the problem really is. In American English, "Let it steep" or "Leave it to steep" would both be acceptable. But no matter how you choose to define *let* and *leave* here, the same message has been given.

3. See also LET; LET ALONE.

lectern   See PODIUM.

led   See LEAD, LED.

leery, leary   When *leery* or its less common variant *leary* is used with a preposition, it is most likely to be followed by *of*:

> . . . the presidency of the world would be an office of comparatively little power—nothing to be leery of —E. B. White, *Harper's,* July 1942

> . . . is leery of wise New York politicians and reporters —Richard Reeves, *New York,* 27 Dec. 1971

> . . . with nervous Republicans still leery of the supply-side theology —William Greider, *Atlantic,* December 1981

Leery or *leary* is also used less frequently with *about* and very occasionally with *as to*:

> ". . . I'm kind of leery about churches, and I'm kind of leery about preachers too."

> —Claude Brown, *Manchild in the Promised Land,* 1965

> ". . . This was something new and, frankly, some of us were a wee bit leery as to the outcome." —Edward N. Saveth & Ralph Bass, *Think,* July 1953

legitimate, legitimatize, legitimize   Fowler noted in 1926 with some asperity that *legitimatize* and *legitimize* were edging out the usage of the older verb *legitimate*. *Legitimate* dates from 1586, *legitimatize* from 1791, and *legitimize* from 1848. Phythian in 1979 echoed Fowler's complaint but had perhaps neglected to check current usage. While growth in the usage of *legitimatize* and especially of *legitimize* did occur in the first half of the 20th century, that growth has not had the effect of producing "the virtual exclusion of *legitimate*" that Phythian claims. In fact, according to Garner 1998, *legitimate* is used more frequently than *legitimize* (they are about equally frequent in our files):

> . . . the ways in which schools and colleges legitimate and maintain inequality —Christopher Jencks, *N.Y. Times Book Rev.,* 15 Feb. 1976

> Poland has ceased being a nation with even a pretense of Communist rule, a rule that is legitimated by Marxist ideology —Irving Kristol, *Wall Street Jour.,* 11 Jan. 1982

> Ethnicity began to be legitimized as part of the fabric of American life —Arthur M. Schlesinger, Jr., *Saturday Rev.,* 12 Nov. 1977

> . . . that format went from English first into Fortran . . . and then back into English, which sort of legitimizes its descent —Howard 1983

Legitimatize is used less often than are the other two words:

> The only reasons for placing this story in 1916 were to legitimatize the fact that every idea in it is shopworn, and to build sets —Pauline Kael, *New Yorker,* 21 Nov. 1970

> . . . perception and more broadly subjective experience had become legitimatized in mainstream American psychology —Howard E. Gruber, *N.Y. Times Book Rev.,* 8 Jan. 1984

lend   1. See LOAN, LEND.

2. Some of the commentators who want to discourage the use of *loan* as a verb go on to comment that only *loan* is a noun, not *lend*. Well, almost right but not quite. *Lend* is a noun, though not in ordinary American English. It has been in the language since the end of the 16th century, but was at first spelled *len* or *lenne,* acquiring its terminal *d* only in the 18th century (the *d* on the verb *lend* is

also unetymological). It seems to have been used chiefly on the outskirts of mainstream British English, in northern dialects, in Scotland, in Australia and New Zealand; one of our American citations is from an Irish-American milieu, so it may have been used in Irish English too.

> "Run out to Mrs. Mullins in the Front Room and ask her for the lend of her brass fender," she cried —Mary Lavin, *Atlantic*, June 1956

> ". . . Why don't you get the lend of a truck one night. . . ." —Ross Franklyn, in *Coast to Coast: Australian Stories 1946*

lengthy   *Lengthy* started its career as a usage issue in the late 1700s, when British critics began to attack it as an Americanism. The first record of its use is from about a hundred years earlier. Among the 18th-century American writers who used it were Thomas Jefferson, John Adams, Alexander Hamilton, George Washington, and Benjamin Franklin:

> An unwillingness to read any thing about them if it appears a little lengthy —Benjamin Franklin, letter, 1773 (OED)

The British first regarded *lengthy* as an unneeded synonym for *long*, but they soon began to use it themselves:

> This address . . . was unusually lengthy for him —Charles Dickens, *Pickwick Papers*, 1837 (OED)

Noah Webster included it in his *Compendious Dictionary* of 1806, and it began to appear in English dictionaries by 1835. But it was included in William Cullen Bryant's *Index Expurgatorius* of 1871 and has been subject to unfavorable comment by occasional American commentators for more than a century. Most recent commentators have been more tolerant. A typical opinion can be found in Evans 1957: "*Lengthy* is largely restricted to speeches and writings and carries the reproachful suggestion that they are longer than they need be." Evans' opinion has been more or less repeated by commentators as recently as Garner 1998, although some of them disagree about whether *lengthy* need connote tedium or not.

Our evidence shows that *lengthy* frequently retains its "overlong, tedious" connotations:

> They were given lengthy lectures on the importance of neatness and lettering —David Wellman, *Trans-Action*, April 1968

> Completion of a lengthy form . . . is often followed by equally lengthy delays —Robin Prestage, *Saturday Rev.*, 1 Jan. 1972

But typically it describes something that is long in a noteworthy way, whether because of tediousness or, very often, because of comprehensiveness:

> . . . embarked upon lengthy studies of all aspects of therapeutic application of X-rays —*Current Biography 1949*

> Commission members launched a lengthy probe —Trevor Armbrister, *Saturday Evening Post*, 12 Feb. 1966

> . . . to undergo lengthy training in programming —Herbert A. Simon, *Think*, May-June 1967

Our evidence also shows that its use in describing things other than speech and writing is common:

> . . . would certainly involve lengthy delays —Richard Eells, "Pacem in Maribus," *A Center Occasional Paper*, June 1970

> . . . its lengthy Christmas holidays —Donna Martin, *Change*, Winter 1972-73

Its use in describing physical objects, however, is relatively rare:

> He twirled his lengthy key chain —Don Davis, in *The Best from Yank*, 1945

Lengthy is a venerable synonym of *long* which has been used by excellent writers for about three centuries. You need not hesitate to use it yourself.

less, fewer   Here is the rule as it is usually encountered: *fewer* refers to number among things that are counted, and *less* refers to quantity or amount among things that are measured. This rule is simple enough and easy enough to follow. It has only one fault—it is not accurate for all usage. If we were to write the rule from the observation of actual usage, it would be the same for *fewer*: *fewer* does refer to number among things that are counted. However, it would be different for *less*: *less* refers to quantity or amount among things that are measured and to number among things that are counted. Our amended rule describes the actual usage of the past thousand years or so.

As far as we have been able to discover, the received rule originated in 1770 as a comment on *less*:

> This Word is most commonly used in speaking of a Number; where I should think *Fewer* would do better. *No Fewer than a Hundred* appears to me not only more elegant than *No less than a Hundred*, but more strictly proper —Baker 1770

Baker's remarks about *fewer* express clearly and modestly—"I should think," "appears to me"—his own taste and preference. It is instructive to compare Baker with one of the most recent college handbooks in our collection:

> *Fewer* refers to quantities that can be counted individually. . . . *Less* is used for collective quantities that are not counted individually . . . and for abstract characteristics —Trimmer & McCrimmon 1988

Notice how Baker's preference has here been generalized and elevated to an absolute status, and his notice of contrary usage has been omitted. This approach is quite common in handbooks and schoolbooks; many pedagogues seem reluctant to share the often complicated facts about English with their students.

How Baker's opinion came to be an inviolable rule, we do not know. But we do know that many people believe it is such. Simon 1980, for instance, calls the "less than 50,000 words" he found in a book about Joseph Conrad a "whopping" error.

The OED shows that *less* has been used of countables since the time of King Alfred the Great—he used it that way in one of his own translations from Latin—more than a thousand years ago (in about 888). So essentially *less* has been used of countables in English for just about as long as there has been a written English language. After about 900 years Robert Baker opined that *fewer* might be more elegant and proper. Almost every usage writer since Baker has followed Baker's lead, and generations of English teachers have swelled the chorus. The result seems to be a fairly large number of people who now believe *less* used of countables to be wrong, though its standardness is easily demonstrated.

In present-day written usage, *less* is as likely as or more likely than *fewer* to appear in a few common constructions. One of the most frequent is the *less than* construction where *less* is a pronoun. The countables in this construction are often distances, sums of money, units of time, and statistical enumerations, which are often thought of as amounts rather than numbers. Some examples:

> The odometer showed less than ten thousand miles —E. L. Doctorow, *Loon Lake,* 1979

> . . . he had somewhat less than a million to his name when he went to Washington —David Halberstam, *Harper's,* February 1971

> I was never in Europe for less than fourteen months at a time —James Thurber, letter, 18 July 1952

> Her agency, less than 5 years old, is a smashing success —Donald Robinson, *Ladies' Home Jour.,* January 1971

> . . . an allied people, today less than 50,000 in number —W. B. Lockwood, *A Panorama of Indo-European Languages,* 1972

> ". . . I've known you less than twenty-four hours. . . ." —Agatha Christie, *Why Didn't They Ask Evans?,* 1934

Fewer can be used in the same constructions, but it appears less often than *less.* It is sometimes used in such a way as to make one suspect that an editor rather than a writer is responsible for the *fewer.*

> . . . has never gained fewer than 1,222 yards in a season —Rick Telander, *Sports Illustrated,* 5 Sept. 1984

Some contemporary usage writers concede that this use of *less* is acceptable.

The *no less than* construction noticed by Baker tends still to have *less* more often than *fewer:*

> The class of 1974 . . . included no less than 71 new Democrats —Tip O'Neill with William Novak, *Man of the House,* 1987

> It is spoken by no less than 100 millions in Bengal and bordering areas —W. B. Lockwood, *A Panorama of Indo-European Languages,* 1972

Less is the usual choice in the "twenty-five words or less" construction:

> . . . readers are encouraged to keep their comments to 500 words or less —*Change,* January–February 1971

> . . . of all the millions of families in the country, two out of three consist of only three persons or less —Mark Abrams, *London Calling,* 9 Oct. 1952

> . . . and now know enough to create little fictions that in 30 seconds or less get right to the heart of desire itself —Mark Crispin Miller, *Johns Hopkins Mag.,* Winter 1984

Kilpatrick 1984 defends this *less* and the one just above. *Less* is also frequent when it follows a number:

> . . . almost $10 million less than for 1969 —*Annual Report, Borg-Warner Corp.,* 1970

> Many bulls fought in Madrid weigh 100 kilos less —Tex Maule, *Sports Illustrated,* 29 July 1968

> . . . at thirty-three on my part, and few years less on yours —Lord Byron, letter, 17 Nov. 1821

And of course it follows *one:*

> . . . one less scholarship —Les A. Schneider, letter to the editor, *Change,* September 1971

One less reporter —Don Cook, *Saturday Rev.,* 24 June 1978

Less is also frequently used to modify ordinary plural count nouns. In present-day English this usage appears to be more common in speech (and reported speech) than it is in discursive writing. It is likely that some of the plural nouns in the examples were thought of as uncountable amounts rather than numbers.

. . . Goldsmith took less pains than Pope . . . to create images of luxury in the reader's mind —John Butt, *English Literature in the Mid-Eighteenth Century,* edited & completed by Geoffrey Carnall, 1979

. . . Americans pay less taxes than most of the inhabitants of developed countries —Robert Lekachman, quoted in *Center Mag.,* January–February 1970

The less sodium you consume, the less drugs you're likely to need —Jane E. Brody, *N.Y. Times,* 11 July 1979

You have to make less mistakes —Victor Temkin, quoted in *N.Y. Times,* 4 May 1980

. . . lower rates . . . lazy days, and less crowds —L. Dana Gatilin, *Christian Science Monitor,* 23 Oct. 1979

Less people exercise their right to vote —William Scranton, quoted in *Celebrity,* October 1976

Uses such as the above, even those where *fewer* might have been more elegant, have been standard for more than a millennium. If you are a native speaker, your use of *less* and *fewer* can reliably be guided by your ear. If you are not a native speaker, you will find that the simple rule with which we started is a safe guide, except for the constructions for which we have shown *less* to be preferred.

lesser   1. Samuel Johnson in his 1755 dictionary aspersed the formation of *lesser* as a "barbarous corruption" because he considered it a double comparative (see DOUBLE COMPARISON). *Less* does serve as a comparative of *little,* and it did so in Middle English when *lesser* was formed. Whoever coined *lesser* seems to have considered *less* not a comparative of *little,* but an independent adjective meaning "unimportant." At any rate Johnson recognized that the irregularity of its formation had had no effect on its literary use; he presents citations from Spenser, Shakespeare, Bishop Burnet, John Locke, and Pope. But many 19th-century grammarians pruned Johnson's remarks down to the "barbarous corruption" part, omitting his mitigating comments, and then lumped *lesser* with *badder, gooder,* and *worser.* This treatment created a usage problem that sputtered through the 19th century and died out.

Though its propriety was a 19th-century issue, *lesser* still appears in handbooks, usually paired with *less.* The handbooks tend to hold that *lesser* is used to indicate a difference in value or importance. The observation is broadly correct:

. . . would have turned any lesser man to madness or suicide —Robert Graves, *New Republic,* 21 Mar. 1955

The discussion has been confined so far to the lesser ode, but most poets attempted the greater ode as well —John Butt, *English Literature in the Mid-Eighteenth Century,* edited & completed by Geoffrey Carnall, 1979

It is also used of numerical quantities in contexts where *smaller* or *lower* is more usual:

So $1 million a day would be taken out for each day they bargain. They would be bargaining for a lesser amount each day —Peter Ueberroth, quoted in *Springfield* (Mass.) *Morning Union,* 2 Aug. 1985

It is also used of size. Such use was more common in the past than it is now; most present-day use for size is confined to names of plants and animals like *lesser celandine* or *lesser yellowlegs.*

. . . offered to share the booty, and having divided the money into two unequal heaps, and added a golden snuff-box to the lesser heap, he desired Mr. Wild to take his choice —Henry Fielding, *Jonathan Wild,* 1743

2. The adverb *lesser* raises an occasional question too. Shakespeare used it several times in his plays. In present-day use it is limited to modifying past participles—especially *known* —to which it may or may not be joined by a hyphen.

The lesser known is the epitaph on Ben Franklin's tombstone —Harper 1985

. . . the lesser-known places within America's National Park System —Horace Sutton, *Saturday Rev.,* 14 Apr. 1979

lest   This conjunction is almost always followed by a verb in the subjunctive mood:

It is an idea that cannot safely be compromised with, lest it be utterly destroyed —E. B. White, letter, 29 Nov. 1947

Lest there be any doubt —Alan M. Dershowitz, *N.Y. Times Book Rev.,* 26 June 1983

. . . to be very wary lest one become an accomplice —Robert Stone, quoted in *Publishers Weekly,* 21 Mar. 1986

It can also be followed by a *should* clause, a construction that seems to have been more common in the past than it is now:

... lest it should betray her into any observations seemingly unhandsome —Jane Austen, *Mansfield Park*, 1814

... the anxiety of the socialists lest they should lose —*Times Literary Supp.*, 19 Mar. 1970

The use of a verb in the indicative mood following *lest* has been cited as an error as recently as 1998. Our evidence shows that such usage occurs in standard writing, but is atypical:

... lest its drift is lost on us —Roger Owen, *Times Literary Supp.*, 14 May 1982

let 1. See LEAVE, LET.
2. *Let's*. This contraction of *let us* is found only in the imperative. It dates back at least to Shakespeare's time:

If you deny to dance, let's hold more chat —*Love's Labour's Lost*, 1595

By the 20th century *let's* is frequently treated as a unit, rather than as a contraction, and then it takes a following pronoun. When the pronoun is *us,* the construction is criticized as redundant, especially by the earlier commentators. Quirk et al. 1985 characterizes *let's us* as "familiar American English."
Let's is also followed by a pair of pronouns in either the nominative or the objective case; the constructions occur in both American and British English.

Let's you and I take 'em on for a set —William Faulkner, *Sartoris,* 1929 (in OED Supplement)

... let's you and I go together —Arthur Wing Pinero, *The Benefit of the Doubt,* 1895 (in Jespersen)

Let's you and me duck out of here —John D. MacDonald, *The Brass Cupcake,* 1950 (in OED Supplement)

... the resulting photograph was really amusing. The caption under it read, or so Liz quipped: "Lady Bird, after this is over, let's you and me go out and have a drink." —Lady Bird Johnson, *A White House Diary,* 1970

These are idiomatic constructions—no matter what the case of the pronoun—found almost exclusively in spoken English. You can use whichever of them sounds right to you wherever you would use speech forms in writing. You will probably not need any of them in anything you write that is at all removed from speech.
3. The negative of *let's* is formed in three ways: *let's not,* which is widely used; *don't let's,* which is chiefly found in British English; and *let's don't,* which is an Americanism. This form is typical of speech and casual writing:

In all events, let's don't celebrate it until it has done something —Alexander Woollcott, letter, 26 Jan. 1918

let alone The phrase *let alone* is used as a conjunction to introduce a contrasting example for purposes of emphasis. In sentences with a negative construction or negative overtones, its sense is close to "much less":

". . . Great to read but bloody to speak, let alone sing. . . ." —Robertson Davies, *The Lyre of Orpheus,* 1988

... it does so much worse for a million others that I don't feel justified in worrying let alone complaining —Robert Frost, letter, November 1914

This is no mean feat for any author, let alone one who is also a Harvard professor —Rosemary Herbert, *Publishers Weekly,* 23 Jan. 1987

Vizetelly 1922 and Lincoln Library 1924 disapproved of this usage. No subsequent commentator—Krapp 1927, Opdyke 1939, Evans 1957, Bryant 1962, Bremner 1980, Einstein 1985—has agreed, so the issue can be called dead.
Evans, Bryant, and Bremner do agree, however, that *leave alone* is not standard in the same use. This opinion seems to be related to American sensitivity to *leave–let* substitutions that British commentators seem to ignore. Our evidence for *leave alone* in this function is quite sparse, and British:

... Mr. McKenzie deplored the fact that, when his shop had been recently broken into, the thieves would not even burgle, leave alone buy, his books —Michael Barratt, *The Bookseller,* 1 June 1974

They knew nothing of microbes and viruses, leave alone the role of fleas and lice as vectors of disease —Keith Thomas, *Manchester Guardian Weekly,* 5 Apr. 1992

We suspect that Americans simply do not use *leave alone* in this way. It seems to be only a rather rare variant in British English, but it does not appear to be substandard there.

let's See LET 2.

level 1. *Noun.* Flesch 1964, Gowers in Fowler 1965, Follett 1966, Prentice Hall 1978, Bremner 1980, Howard 1980, and Bryson 1984 are all censorious of the use of *level* in the sense "position in a scale or rank." Several object at considerable length to this relatively innocuous term that writers and especially journalists find very handy. If you are inclined to be influenced by such epithets as *automatic, vague, clutter,* and *avoidable,* you may want to avoid this use of *level*; however, consider the following examples, and ask yourself if they would be substantially improved by revising to eliminate the word *level*:

> Mr. Gardner writes at a fine level of sophistication, neither oversimplifying nor talking down —*New Yorker*, 3 Feb. 1973

> Their story of a young Baltimore lawyer harried to distraction by the demented unfairness of courts and judges is out of control. The decibel level is too high —Arthur M. Schlesinger, Jr., *Saturday Rev.*, December 1979

> At the White House level the Office of Budget Management has been working for two years on a new government publication —John Lear, *Saturday Rev.*, 15 Apr. 1972

> *Like to have*, in the sense of almost or nearly, is common on the level of folk or Dialect speech —Harper 1975

The complete avoidance of *level* in this sense seems hardly worth aiming for.

2. *Verb*. The transitive verb takes *at* when it suggests aiming:

> The conduct of Harris so infuriated the men that some of them leveled their muskets at him —George V. Rogers, *New-England Galaxy*, Fall 1970

> ... echo the charges ... leveled at Surrealism —Annette Michelson, *Evergreen*, August 1967

The intransitive sense "to deal frankly or openly" takes *with*:

> ... the girls in the office who leveled with him about what it means to work for a company riddled with brilliant men —*Women's Wear Daily*, 8 June 1972

liable 1. When *liable* means "responsible" and is followed by a prepositional phrase, the preposition is *for*:

> ... each alleged conspirator can be held liable for the statements and actions of the other conspirators —Herbert L. Packer, *N.Y. Rev. of Books*, 6 Nov. 1969

> ... a general partner liable for any excess of liabilities over the paid-in capital —*Dun's*, October 1971

When it means "in a position to incur," *to* is used:

> Outside of eating with a sharp knife, there is no rule in the Book that lays you liable to as much criticism —Will Rogers, *The Illiterate Digest*, 1924

> ... will render a man liable to certain diseases of the personality —John Butt, *English Literature in the Mid-Eighteenth Centu-*

ry, edited & completed by Geoffrey Carnall, 1979

2. *Liable, apt, likely*. These three words are often used in the same construction—with *to* and an infinitive following—and in meanings that are very nearly synonymous. Usage commentators have been discriminating between them since Richard Grant White 1870.

Most commentators expend their critical efforts on *liable*. The emphasis is on the undesirable aspect of whatever it is that follows *liable*, although this aspect tends to be somewhat exaggerated by examples in which boilers are liable to explode. The disastrous is not required.

Let's begin with a few examples of *likely* which no one criticizes and everybody recommends. They can perhaps serve us as a sort of benchmark by which to judge examples of *apt* and *liable*. We think they present contexts in which different writers might have used *apt* or *liable*.

> ... strange subjective experiences, and because they are strange they are also likely to be upsetting —*Trans-Action*, March 1968

> She is a down-to-earth woman who is likely to shake her head at being celebrated as "a living legend" —*Current Biography*, February 1968

> ... my interests being what they are I am not likely to make even a good start —Charlton Laird, in *The Range of English*, 1968

Now we come to *apt*:

> I wish, however, that the instrument might be less apt to decay, and that signs might be permanent —Samuel Johnson, preface to the Dictionary, 1755

> Solitary reading is apt to give the headache —Charles Lamb, letter, 26 Feb. 1808

> ... discovering the Church is apt to be a slow procedure —Flannery O'Connor, letter, 16 July 1957

If we remember that what is undesirable or unwanted is not necessarily a disaster of large proportions, we will find that *liable* is rather more often used of the undesirable than not:

> ... it seems to me that their cause is, I do not say, desperate, but liable to be overturned at what would seem to be a small thing —Henry Adams, letter, 23 Apr. 1863

> ... I am so liable to say what I do not mean —Lewis Carroll, letter, 9 June 1879

> ... the pastor must set an example, he must illustrate his morality in public; and this is liable to result in hypocrisy —Edmund Wilson, *A Piece of My Mind*, 1956

She is not as prone to fight with other dogs, and is less liable to stray —*The Complete Dog Book,* 1980

We do have good evidence of *liable* as simply synonymous with *likely*:

It's all kudu country," Pop said. "You're liable to jump one anywhere." —Ernest Hemingway, *Green Hills of Africa,* 1935

. . . the parrot does not act as if it is liable to say anything important in the next hour —Damon Runyon, *Runyon à la Carte,* 1944

Even while observing Arab etiquette . . . he is liable to drape an arm across royal shoulders and boom, "Well, your Excellency, how's the doubles game? . . ." —J. D. Reed, *Sports Illustrated,* 17 Nov. 1980

Our conclusion is that, except in the handbooks, which seem simply to repeat their predecessors, this is essentially a dead issue. Both *apt* and *liable* are still synonyms of *likely,* as they have been for some 400 years now. *Liable* is still more frequently used of things that are undesirable.

liaise This back-formation from *liaison* dates from 1928. It was originally a military word, but by the 1940s it became fairly well established in more general use among the British. Its occurrence in British English is now common and unremarkable:

. . . while liaising between management and men —Jeremy Kingston, *Punch,* 20 Mar. 1974

He also liasied with the aged primate, Cardinal Frantisek Tomasek, when the latter became politically embroiled with the State —Michael Simmons, *Manchester Guardian Weekly,* 15 Nov. 1992

It is relatively uncommon but not unknown in American English.

Why should an administration need so many people to liaise with itself? —Michael Kinsley, *New Republic,* 4 & 11 Jan. 1993

liaison With its French origin and unusual sequence of vowels, *liaison* is inevitably going to present a puzzle to some people when it comes time to pronounce it. And, in fact, a bewildering array of pronunciations of this word can be found in our files. The two most common pronunciations in American English are \'lē-ə-ˌzän\ and \lē-'ā-ˌzän\, both of which are established in standard speech. The variant \'lā-ə-ˌzän\ is well entrenched in the military, but in other circles it is widely regarded as an error. Its use by Ronald Reagan, for example, is criticized by Safire 1984.

The spelling of *liaison* also gives many people trouble. The tendency is to drop the second *i*:

. . . permanent liason officer to the International Control Commission —*Village Voice,* 28 Feb. 1968

This error is rare in edited prose, but it is easily made in casual writing.

library See FEBRUARY.

lie See LAY, LIE.

lighted, lit A puzzled editor once wrote to ask about the acceptability of *lighted* versus *lit* as past and past participle of *light.* His letter was prompted by one of his authors—a university professor—who claimed that only *lighted* was proper; *lit* should be reserved for drunks.

The professor is right about drunks, but wrong otherwise. Both *lit* and *lighted* are acceptable and standard, and have been all along. The evidence in the Merriam-Webster files shows both forms to be used about equally. A few of the handbooks opine that *lighted* may be more frequent in adjectival use ("a clean, well-lighted place"), but even here our evidence shows about equal use of both forms. We have reputable citations for "a lit cigar" and "a lighted cigar" and "a lit window" and "a lighted window." The matter, then, is simply one of the author's preference—choose whichever sounds better in a given context.

Lit seems to have been originally called into question by an obscure grammarian who in 1765 opined that it was "rather low." His opinion must somehow have been passed down to the professor. The opinion is without basis.

light-year In scientific usage, a light-year is a unit of distance equal to the enormous distance light travels in one year in the vacuum of space. But nonscientists sometimes have trouble thinking of a "year" as anything other than a unit of time:

It seems light years ago that Scott Fitzgerald rhapsodized the lissome girls in grown-up gowns —*People,* 11 Oct. 1982

A thousand light-years ago, I thought —Dick Francis, *Straight,* 1989

Three light-years later, those college sophomores have graduated —Amely Greeven, *Vogue,* April 1998

Such usage is not especially common in standard writing (*from* is much more common with *light-years* than *ago* or *since*). It attracts disapproval from the astronomically educated. It should not be confused with the widespread and established figurative use of *light-year* to mean "a very great distance":

. . . [this team] is light-years away from where we need to be —Bill Parcells, quoted by Gerald Eskenazi, *N.Y. Times,* 22 Aug. 1999

In 1939, light-years away from her cloistened beginnings, she met Freud —Daphne Merkin, *N.Y. Times Book Rev.,* 8 June 1997

In terms of nuclear power safety, the United States and other advanced nations are light-years ahead of the countries that used to make up the Soviet Union —Russell Watson, *Newsweek,* 11 Oct. 1999

like, as, as if **1.** *Conjunction.* Those who are old enough may still remember an American cigarette commercial back in the 1950s and early 1960s that contained the line "Winston tastes good, like a cigarette should." This line provoked a considerable controversy in the popular press, which is probably what the advertising agency hoped to achieve. The controversy lasted quite a long while, passing from the newspapers to magazines to usage books. Even the editors of the *New Yorker* took note of it:

> We hope Sir Winston Churchill, impeccable, old-school grammarian that he is, hasn't chanced to hear American radio or television commercials recently. It would pain him dreadfully, we're sure, to listen to the obnoxious and ubiquitous couplet "Winston tastes good, like a cigarette should." That pesky "like" is a problem for us Americans to solve, we guess, and anyway Sir Winston has his own problems —*New Yorker,* 26 May 1956

That pesky *like* seems not to have bothered the impeccable, old-school grammarian as he dealt with his other problems:

> We are overrun by them, like the Australians were by rabbits —Sir Winston Churchill (in Longman 1984)

So what is the problem with this pesky *like*? Is it a solecism typical of the uneducated? Some commentators think so:

> *Like* has long been widely misused by the illiterate; lately it has been taken up by the knowing and the well-informed, who find it catchy, or liberating, and who use it as though they were slumming —Strunk & White 1959, 1972, 1979

Let's take a look at the history of conjunctive *like* and see if Strunk & White's opinion is right.

Like was used as a conjunction as long ago as the late 14th century, along with a compound form *like as.* It first turned up around 1380 to mean approximately "as if," and Chaucer used it in about 1385 to introduce a full clause in *The Complaint of Mars.* Both "as" and "as if" uses are attested in the 15th

and 16th centuries. In 1608 or 1609 Shakespeare (or his collaborator) used it to introduce a full clause near the end of the first scene of *Pericles*:

> ANTIOCHUS.   As thou
> Wilt live, fly after; and, like an arrow shot
> From a well-experienc'd archer hits the
>   mark
> His eye doth level at, so thou ne'er return
> Unless thou say Prince Pericles is dead.

Shakespeare also used conjunctive *like* followed by a nominative pronoun:

> And yet no man like he doth grieve my heart —*Romeo and Juliet,* 1595

So we can say this much about conjunctive *like*: in the 14th, 15th, and 16th centuries it was used in serious literature, but not often.

Evidence from the 17th and 18th centuries is not plentiful either. In these centuries it comes mostly from nonliterary works, including less formal sources such as letters and journals. This suggests that conjunctive *like* may be primarily a speech form only occasionally used in print. It might also suggest that the evidence has simply not been dug out yet.

In the 19th and 20th centuries conjunctive *like* becomes much more common; Jespersen 1909–49 (vol. 5) tells us that "examples abound" and lists them from Keats, Emily Brontë, Thackeray, George Eliot, Dickens, Kipling, Bennett, Gissing, Wells, Shaw, Maugham, and others. So we must conclude that Strunk & White's relegation of conjunctive *like* to misuse by the illiterate is wrong.

Where did the idea that *like* as a conjunction is an illiteracy come from? We are not sure. We do know that *like* became a subject of dispute in England during the 19th century. Jespersen cites an account by the English philologist Frederick Furnivall in his memoirs of an argument Furnivall had with Tennyson on the subject. Tennyson had corrected Prince Albert for using conjunctive *like*; he thought the use was recent, and incorrect. Furnivall pointed out that it was to be found in Shakespeare. Alford 1866 also found conjunctive *like* "quite indefensible."

In America the earliest mention of the subject comes from Noah Webster's *Rudiments of English Grammar,* 1790. Webster included the sentence "He thinks like you do" in an 8-page list of "improper and vulgar expressions." A Philadelphia schoolmaster, Joseph Hutchins, followed in 1791. Joseph Hervey Hull, in an 1828 grammar, included the sentence "It feels like it has been burned" in a list like Webster's. Hull added a new construction to the controversy, but we don't know if he realized it. And we are not even sure that Webster originated the dispute. Apparently few other 19th-century grammarians noticed this use, but some 19th-century American commentators did, including Bache 1869 and Richard Grant White 1870.

Although 19th-century commentators were in substantial agreement on this matter, the dictionaries were not quick to take it up. The conjunctive use of *like* was not controversial in the 18th century, and Samuel Johnson's Dictionary of 1755 had *like as* under the adverb entry; there was no preposition or conjunction. Webster 1828 and Worcester's Dictionary simply followed Johnson. The conjunction was unrecognized until the Century Dictionary entered it in 1889, with quotations from Shakespeare and Darwin and commentary from James Russell Lowell, who ascribed its use to Henry VIII and Charles I of England. Webster 1890 had no entry for a conjunction. Funk & Wagnalls 1890 entered the conjunctive use as sense 2 of the adverb, labeled it *Colloq.*, and added a quotation from Colonel John S. Mosby of Civil War fame. Webster 1909 recognized the conjunctive use in a synonymy note, calling it a provincialism and contrary to good usage.

The objection to conjunctive *like,* then, appears to be a 19th-century reaction to increased conjunctive use at that time, and the objectors were chiefly commentators on usage rather than grammarians or lexicographers. After World War I all three of these groups got in step to present a united front on the issue: it was incorrect to use *like* for *as* or *as if; like* was a preposition, not a conjunction.

It might be useful here to give some of our many examples of conjunctive *like.* Most of these are 20th-century examples, with a few earlier ones thrown in as a reminder of the historical dimension of this usage. They typify the chief constructions in which we find conjunctive *like.*

Since the "as if" sense seems to be the earliest attested, we will start with it. It is mostly used to introduce a full clause:

Seemed like I'd die if I couldn't scratch —Mark Twain, *Huckleberry Finn,* 1884

When they worked she looked like she had moles burrowing under her hide —Jessamyn West, *Atlantic,* July 1944

. . . and it looked like we were a pretty good combination —Harry S. Truman, quoted in Merle Miller, *Plain Speaking,* 1973

. . . looking like it aimed to run right through the shed —William Faulkner, *The Town,* 1957

. . . the accounts of all the women in Mr. Reagan's life look like they were edited by Nancy Reagan —Maureen Dowd, *N.Y. Time Book Rev.,* 18 Nov. 1990

. . . middle-aged men who looked like they might be out for their one night of the year —Norman Mailer, *Harper's,* November 1968

She felt like I was talking to her —William L. Shirer, *The Nightmare Years,* 1984

. . . the back wheels spinning, stones flying like they were shot from guns —Garrison Keillor, *Lake Wobegon Days,* 1985

. . . you wake like someone hit you on the head —T. S. Eliot, "Sweeney Agonistes," 1932 (in OED Supplement)

The worst thing we could do is act like we know we have him beat —Douglas Foster, *New Republic,* 6 Dec. 1999

I remember that scene like it was yesterday —Tip O'Neill with William Novak, *Man of the House,* 1987

This sense of *like* seems especially common after verbs like *feel, look,* and *sound. Like* "as if" is also used in a few common short idiomatic phrases where it is followed by an adjective, especially *mad* or *crazy,* and the phrase is used adverbially:

Thence by coach; with a mad coachman, that drove like mad —Samuel Pepys, diary, 13 June 1663

And other writers were in the library studying like mad —William Stafford, *Writing the Australian Crawl,* 1978

. . . Brooks and friends are horsing around like crazy —Stanley Kauffmann, *Before My Eyes,* 1980

. . . we had to jump out with our equipment just as the helicopter touched down and run like crazy —Pamela Grim, *Discover,* November 1998

At the same time as he had been spending like mad —Michelle Cottle, *New Republic,* 5 June 2000

Like in the sense "as" occurs in more than one construction. The first—this is the single most heavily criticized use of *like*—is to introduce a full clause:

I expect we shall shortly carry our knives and forks, like the Chinese do their chop sticks, in our pockets —Washington Irving, *Morning Chronicle* (New York), 22 Jan. 1803

Nobody will miss her like I shall —Charles Dickens, letter, 7 Jan. 1841 (in Jespersen)

We go into litigation instinctively, like a young duck goes into the water —Mark Twain, *Morning Call* (San Francisco), 15 Sept. 1864

Do you still recite, like you used to?
—Arnold Bennett, *Hilda Lessways,* 1911

Just like you used to be —Willa Cather,
O Pioneers!, 1913

. . . I can go hungry again like I have gone
hungry before —Carl Sandburg, *Smoke and
Steel,* 1920

. . . instead of being embarrassed by the
waiter, like he used to be —Sinclair Lewis,
Babbitt, 1922

People in the South are like they are anywhere —Sherwood Anderson, letter, 18 Oct.
1925

Sir Oswald played bridge, like he did
everything else, extremely well —Agatha
Christie, *The Seven Dials Mystery,* 1929

This morning he was taken ill. . . . Some
diagnosed pleurisy, like you had (as H.
Yorke would write) —Evelyn Waugh, letter,
15 Jan. 1940

I expected him to look a little haunted, like
Humphrey sometimes used to —Angus Wilson, *Death Dance,* 1957

. . . just scratches him off like the old
dog does fleas —William Faulkner, 15 Feb.
1957, in *Faulkner in the University,* 1959

. . . she might not be an early riser, like he is
—Jay McInerney, *Bright Lights, Big City,*
1984

As parents you may be wondering, like I do
on frequent occasions —Charles, Prince of
Wales, quoted in *N.Y. Times Mag.,* 28 Sept.
1986

In the Ukraine they string them up, just like
they do in the Conservative party —Michael
White, *Manchester Guardian Weekly,* 22
Dec. 1991

. . . made people think we can live on the air
like they do in Hollywood —J. William Fulbright, quoted in *Arkansas Times,* 13 May
1993

Another construction is the one in which
like introduces a clause from which the verb
—and sometimes even more—has been omitted. The verb is usually to be understood from
the preceding clause. The classic example of
this construction is "He takes to it like a duck
to water." Here are some more:

. . . as if it followed like the night the
day, that "language is a living thing. . . ."
—Simon 1980

It is intended to stop all debate, like the previous question in the General Court —Oliver Wendell Holmes d. 1894, *The Autocrat of
the Breakfast-Table,* 1857

Here I am, Madam, gazing whole hours at
the Maison quarrée, like a lover at his mistress —Thomas Jefferson, letter, 20 Mar.
1787

I've had my share of criticism, but for the
most part it has rolled off me like water off
a duck —Tip O'Neill with William Novak,
Man of the House, 1987

. . . so I stared at it, like Kant at his church
steeple, for half an hour —F. Scott Fitzgerald, *The Great Gatsby,* 1925

. . . are related to those of Africa, like those
of the Galapagos to America —Charles Darwin, *On the Origin of Species by Means of
Natural Selection,* 1859

. . . until it sat like a walnut in icing —E. L.
Doctorow, *Ragtime,* 1975

. . . the fog began to rise and seemed to be
lifted up from the water like the curtain at a
playhouse —Benjamin Franklin, *Autobiography,* 1788

When the subject of the clause is a pronoun,
the nominative case may tip off the use of the
conjunction:

. . . she, like they, was one of the last of
that Anglo-American cultural aristocracy
—John Henry Raleigh, *New Republic,* 5 Apr.
1954

. . . [the Russians] like we, have a common
interest in avoiding war —Prime Minister
Harold Macmillan, quoted in *Springfield*
(Mass.) *Union* (UPI), 20 Mar. 1959

. . . even if they, like we, have a few problems with electronic processing equipment
—*Los Angeles Times,* 28 Sept. 1983

These examples should suffice to show that
conjunctive *like* is widely used in standard English prose, and that it is used in some constructions where it goes unnoticed—as it is in
the citation from Simon 1980; Simon in the
same book takes another writer to task for
using conjunctive *like.* They also show that although it occurs in many literary sources, it is
almost always used where a construction that
is primarily a speech form may be used appropriately. If you keep that in mind, you are not
likely to go wrong.

The belief that *like* is a preposition but not a
conjunction has entered the folklore of usage.
Handbooks, schoolbooks, newspaper pundits,
and well-meaning friends for generations to
come will tell you all about it. Be prepared.
2. Preposition. The frequent adjuration against
conjunctional *like* is believed to have frightened some people into using *as* for all purposes, even for a preposition. This sort of overre-
action is called hypercorrection, and it has
given the commentators an additional usage

to condemn when they have finished with conjunctive *like.* Here are a couple of samples drawn from handbooks:

> He was built as a swordfish —Ernest Hemingway (in Fennell 1980)

> . . . the Basenji is the size of a fox-terrier and cleans itself as a cat —Natalie Winslow, *Providence Sunday Journal,* 17 Jan. 1971 (in Perrin & Ebbitt 1972)

Like is what the handbooks prescribe for these. Here are a few examples of *as* from our files:

> Delicate problems as this are pivotal factors in establishing enduring leadership —Joseph A. Jones, *Exporters' Digest and International Trade Rev.,* October 1951

> New York, as most major cities, has found that the general public is very apathetic —*N.Y. Times,* 12 Oct. 1970

> . . . beaches do not naturally smell as rotten eggs —*Massachusetts Audubon News Letter,* April 1971

You could argue plausibly that each of these is a hypercorrection, but what could you say about the following?

> Golden lads and girls all must,
> As chimney sweepers, come to dust . . .
> —Shakespeare, *Cymbeline,* 1610

> O God, I thanke thee, that I am not as other men —Luke 18:11 (Geneva Bible), 1560

Prepositional *as,* then, is not a modern phenomenon, born in holy terror of using *like. As* has been used prepositionally, in one way or another, since the 13th century. But it probably is used hypercorrectly some of the time. In all of the examples from our files, we would recommend *like.*

like, such as The few commentators who mention *like* and *such as* express rather diverse opinions. Little, Brown 1980, 1986 and Sellers 1975 make a distinction between the two, reserving *such as* for examples and *like* for resemblances. Kilpatrick 1984 does not care for *like* used in place of *such as. Winners & Sinners,* 27 Apr. 1987, on the other hand, does not want *such as* used before a single example; *like* is to be used there. Bernstein 1971 and Follett 1966 think that the example-resemblance distinction is too fine to worry about; Bernstein describes those who do worry about it as nit-pickers. Kilpatrick says Follett and Bernstein are wrong.

The fact that opinions vary so greatly on this matter is enough to suggest that standard usage itself varies a good deal. We think that Bernstein and Follett are right here and that the issue of ambiguity, which evidently underlies the thinking of those who urge the distinction, is probably much overblown. In the examples that follow, the quotation from Emily Post is clearly an example of *like* used for resemblance; that from Guth is an example of *like* used for examples. In the passages from Copperud and Flannery O'Connor, you cannot be sure whether examples or resemblances are intended, but the meaning of each sentence works out to be the same under either interpretation. And in none of the examples is there any ambiguity of meaning:

> "Attended" instead of "went to" is taboo with people like Mrs. Worldly —Emily Post, *Etiquette,* 1927

> . . . and you get more benefit reading someone like Hemingway, where there is apparently a hunger for a Catholic completeness in life —Flannery O'Connor, letter, 16 Jan. 1956

> Phrases like *three military personnel* are irreproachable and convenient —Copperud 1964

> It has been used in advertising copy like the following —Harper 1975, 1985

> Avoid clipped forms like *bike, prof, doc* —Guth 1985

> . . . a mere box-office success like *Kiss and Tell* —George Jean Nathan, *The Theatre Book of the Year, 1949–1950*

> A writer like Auden for instance, or like Rex Warner, might do a fruitful parody —G. S. Fraser, in *Little Reviews Anthology 1949,* ed. Denys Val Baker

> . . . some very outré works, things like Swift's poem "A Beautiful Young Nymph Going to Bed." —Paul Fussell, *Samuel Johnson and the Life of Writing,* 1971

liked to See LIKE TO, LIKED TO.

like for *Like for* is a particular instance of the case where a verb takes an infinitive clause as its object and the clause is introduced by *for.* Jespersen 1909–49 (vol. 5) presents examples of many verbs so complementized, but only a single example of *like for,* from a novel by George Eliot. George Eliot put it in the mouth of a Warwickshire character, and we presume the *like for* was intended to be dialectal. Here is an example typical of American use:

> I'd like for you to go ahead —Jesse Stuart, *Beyond Dark Hills,* 1938 (in American Dialect Dictionary)

American commentators seem to have picked out the combination *like for* because it is fairly common in spoken American English. The Dictionary of American Regional English says it is mostly a Southern and southern Midland expression. Evidence from California (a letter in our files and a citation from Richard Nixon in Reader's Digest 1983) suggests that the locution has also moved where its speakers moved. Bryant 1962 says it is used by cultivated speakers throughout the country.

Those who object to the locution apparently favor the Northern dialects in which *like for* does not occur naturally. The fact remains, however, that *like for* is hard to find in edited prose and seemingly always has been, even though Bryant traces it back to 1474. Our evidence suggests that the request, as in the quotation from Jesse Stuart above, is its most frequent use, though it does occur in other constructions. Here is one:

> . . . women are unanimous on one point: They don't like for their breasts to be handled roughly —"M," *The Sensuous Man,* 1971

likely Although this adverb has been in use since the 14th century, 20th-century commentators have been sniping at it since Bierce 1909; there has been a campaign against its use the *N.Y. Times* (where it appears pretty often) going on for more than thirty years. The problem is the use of the adverb without premodifying intensifiers such as *very* or *most,* which very frequently accompany it. Fowler 1926, for instance, insists that the intensifier is required, but he is referring to British usage; he allows that American usage may be different.

What about the evidence? The OED shows the unmodified *likely* from 1380 to 1895, but the two late 19th-century citations are from Scotland and the north of England. Editor Henry Bradley marks the unqualified adverb as rare except in Scotland and in dialect. Gowers in Fowler 1965 notes spoken use in Scotland and Ireland. We have examples from Scotland, Ireland, and New Zealand in our files. The OED Supplement says the unqualified adverb is frequent in North America.

If the OED citations are representative, it would appear that the unqualified adverb began to drop out of use in mainstream British English in the 19th century while it continued to be used in areas remote from the influence of London—Scotland, Ireland, North America (both the U.S. and Canada), and later New Zealand.

Our evidence shows the unmodified *likely* used chiefly in what some handbooks call "general English"—the everyday language of the press and of most periodicals. We have only a little literary evidence of its use in discursive prose. Here are some typical examples:

> A six-room apartment is not a house, and if you cook onions in one end of it, you'll like-

ly smell them in the other —*New Yorker,* 29 Mar. 1952

> Canada likely will emphasize in the next few days that . . . —*The Gazette* (Montreal), 15 Apr. 1953

> Currants for Christmas puddings will likely be dearer this year —*Sunday Post* (Glasgow), 15 Aug. 1954

> Mr. Lowenstein, whose district likely never will win recognition for its wheat farms —*N.Y. Times,* 31 Jan. 1969

> . . . and that money in turn will likely buy less —*Carnegie Quarterly,* Winter 1975

> It will likely occur to some readers that there is something self-justifying and even defensive in these essays —Robert Penn Warren, *Democracy and Poetry,* 1975

> The painting was likely finished in the winter of 1795 —Michael Olmert, *Smithsonian,* February 1982

> Otherwise he or she will likely make their mistakes again —Kilpatrick 1984

> . . . has been the most contentious issue between the U.S. and China for 35 years, and will likely remain so —Kurt Andersen, *Time,* 7 May 1984

> But Ruthton women likely hadn't gone to college —Andrew H. Malcolm, *N.Y. Times Mag.,* 23 Mar. 1986

> Some entries would likely have been stamped TOP SECRET if they had gone through the classification process —*Newsweek,* 14 Feb. 2000

To sum up, the use of *likely* as an adverb without a qualifier such as *more, most, very,* or *quite* is well established in standard general use in North America. Burchfield 1996 notes it is almost always accompanied by an intensifier in English usage.

See also LIABLE 2.

liken The verb *liken* regularly takes the preposition *to*:

> . . . one colonist likened it to sending a cow in pursuit of a hare —John Mason Brown, *Daniel Boone,* 1952

> . . . economist Gary Becker would liken the institution of marriage to Adam Smith's pin factory —Peter Passell, *N.Y. Times Book Rev.,* 1 May 1983

like to, liked to The *like* and *liked* in these expressions has been variously identified as adjective, verb, and auxiliary verb (the last is our present dictionary rubric). If the grammar is a bit perplexing, the meaning is not: "came near (to), almost." As idioms go, it is modestly old, dating back to the 15th century. Around 1600 Shakespeare used both forms:

> We had lik'd to have had our two noses snapp'd off —*Much Ado About Nothing*, 1599

> . . . I have had four quarrels, and like to have fought one —*As You Like It*, 1600

The idiom—if we call both variants one idiom—was quite common in literary sources during the 17th and 18th centuries:

> Stumbling from thought to thought, falls headlong down
> Into doubt's boundless sea, where, like to drown
> Books bear him up awhile. . . .
> —John Wilmot, Earl of Rochester, *Satire Against Mankind*, 1675

> . . . I had like to have lost my Comparison for want of Breath —William Congreve, *The Way of the World*, 1700

> Mr Prior was like to be insulted in the street for being supposed the author of it —Jonathan Swift, *Journal to Stella*, 9 Feb. 1711

> And such bellows too! Lord Mansfield with his cheeks like to burst —James Boswell, *Life of Samuel Johnson*, 1791

The evidence in the OED and OED Supplement shows that at least in the form *like to* the idiom continued in English literary use through the 19th century. But its translation to American English seems not to have been so literary. Consequently, Americans are likely to equate the terms with countrified or uneducated or old-fashioned speech. With the idiom's dropping out of literary use generally in the 20th century, most of our city-bred commentators think it uncouth. Nowadays it is found mostly in the Southern and southern Midland areas, with some occurrence in more northern regions. It is a speech form that you will not need in discursive prose.

> . . . Grover went to chewing on it and it liked to burn him up —Henry P. Scalf, quoted in *Our Appalachia*, ed. Laurel Shackelford & Bill Weinberg, 1977

> . . . and he like to have never got away —Flannery O'Connor, letter, 11 Jan. 1958

limited This innocuous word first became controversial when Hodgson 1889 asserted that it was "often faultily employed" for such adjectives as *small, slight,* and *scant.* He quoted examples of what he considered to be misuse—"limited price" for "low or reduced price" and "limited acquaintance" for "slight acquaintance." Vizetelly 1906 repeated Hodgson's opinions almost exactly and cited the same examples in slightly reworded versions.

His remarks were in turn repeated by other commentators, right up into the 1990s. Despite their protests, however, such usage has continued to be common in standard speech and writing:

> . . . a narrow mind, capable at most of the limited range of Marston —T. S. Eliot, "Cyril Tourneur," in *Selected Essays*, 1932

> . . . by young women of limited means —Morris R. Cohen, *The Faith of a Liberal*, 1946

> . . . my experience is probably a limited experience —William Faulkner, 25 Feb. 1957, in *Faulkner in the University*, 1959

> . . . despite the use of a diverse and ostensibly large archival base, the footnotes reveal a very limited acquaintance with any secondary material —John Turner, *Times Literary Supp.*, 17 Dec 1993

While one recent commentator (Freeman 1990) is still grousing about *limited acquaintance* (in an obviously contrived sentence), the example above is the only one we've seen in many years. *Limited price* is equally scarce. This issue is pointless.

lingerie See HYPERFOREIGNISMS.

linking verbs See LOOK 1.

lion's share A clutch of commentators, including Kilpatrick 1984, Bernstein 1965, and William Safire (*N.Y. Times Mag.*, 16 Mar. 1986), complain that *lion's share* is frequently misused. Bernstein's criticism is typical:

> The *lion's share,* as conceived by Aesop, is all or almost all, not merely a majority or the larger part.

The dependency of these commentators on the fable of Aesop may well be the fault—as much as we hate to admit it—of Merriam-Webster dictionaries.

Lion's share was entered in Webster 1864 with the definition "the larger part" and an explanatory note identifying Aesop's fable as the source of the phrase. The 1890 editor had apparently read Aesop too, and he interpreted Aesop as Bernstein would later. He put a new definition "all, or nearly all" in front of the 1864 definition, now elaborated into "the best or largest part." Editors of Webster 1909 and Webster's Second left the 1890 version untouched.

The trouble with the 1890 treatment was that the second part described English usage all right, but the first part, the part that Bernstein and the rest fixed on, represented only Aesop. And Aesop spoke no English, of course. The OED was not fooled by Aesop; the definition there reads "the largest or principal portion." The examples given, starting with

Edmund Burke in 1790, illustrate the stated definition, not "all, or nearly all." Nor, in fact, do any of the citations that were in our files before 1934 unmistakably illustrate "all, or nearly all" as a separate sense. Our citations show that it is often practically impossible to tell whether "most" or "nearly all" is intended but that when it is possible, the meaning is always the one criticized by the commentators, but recorded by modern dictionaries. Here are a few examples, beginning with some of our earliest:

> . . . partly from my own fault in assigning perhaps rather a lion's share to myself —Oliver Wendell Holmes d. 1935, letter, 1 Dec. 1899

> The central Government collects and spends the lion's share of the citizens' tax dollar —Cabell Phillips, *N.Y. Times,* 1 Dec. 1957

> It was his life, rather than his art, that commanded the lion's share of attention —Hilton Kramer, *N.Y. Times Book Rev.,* 10 Aug. 1975

> . . . it worked wonders for the rich . . . by giving them the lion's share of new tax breaks —Sean Wilentz, *New Yorker,* 25 Oct. 1995

> . . . the cello's solo literature is so small (the piano and the violin got the lion's share of concerti) —Laura Jacobs, *Vanity Fair,* September 1998

The moral of this tale is that usage commentators and lexicographers have to look at English usage to understand how English speakers use a term, no matter what source it comes from.

lit See LIGHTED, LIT.

litany 1. *Litany* refers literally to a type of prayer in which a series of invocations and supplications are recited by the leader of a congregation, with alternate responses being made by the congregation as a whole. Recent decades have seen the development of two figurative senses, the first of which, "a repetitive recital," relates to the chantlike quality of a litany:

> . . . a litany of cheering phrases. "One of us is going to make it. . . . There's always room at the top. . . ." —Herman Wouk, *Marjorie Morningstar,* 1955

> . . . recited with her . . . a good-night prayer, a little litany of blessings into which Piet never knew whether or not to insert the names of his parents —John Updike, *Couples,* 1968

The second figurative sense is "a lengthy recitation or enumeration."

> . . . she launched into a litany of complaints about . . . the producers of her hit show —Tracy Young, *Vogue,* March 1991

These figurative uses of *litany* have so far met with little criticism. Among the best-known commentators, only Bernstein 1965 recommends restricting *litany* to its literal sense.

2. *Litany, liturgy.* Many commentators are at pains to distinguish between *litany* and *liturgy,* which means "a rite or body of rites prescribed for public worship." The literal senses of these words do not appear to be subject to confusion, but we have a few citations in which *liturgy* is used figuratively where *litany* seems to be called for:

> . . . the final words of the liturgy rang through the blockhouse public address system: "Ignition . . . Mainstage . . . Lift-off!" —Carmault B. Jackson, Jr., M.D., *National Geographic,* September 1961

> . . . such slogans as "Not An Inch," "No Surrender," and "No Pope Here" are part of their political liturgy —Arthur Roth, *Harper's,* April 1972

literally The *L* volume of the OED, published in 1903, contained a citation for *literally* that had occasioned the editor of the volume, Henry Bradley, to append the note "Now often improperly used to indicate that some conventional metaphorical or hyperbolical phrase is to be taken in the strongest admissible sense." The citation in question was written by the English actress Fanny Kemble and published in 1863: "For the last four years . . . I literally coined money." Fanny Kemble did not originate the use; Charles Dickens had employed it years earlier in *Nicholas Nickleby* (1839):

> 'Lift him out,' said Squeers, after he had literally feasted his eyes in silence upon the culprit.

The use must have gained popularity by the time Bradley was doing his editing, and it continued to be popular enough to warrant notice in Webster 1909, where it was accorded the laconic usage note "often used hyperbolically." By 1922 H. W. Fowler sounded the call, and there has followed a steady stream of protesters and viewers-with-alarm ever since. Copperud 1980 writes, "Seldom is the word employed in its exact sense, which is *to the letter, precisely as stated.* Some examples: 'The actor was literally floating on applause.' The word wanted was *figuratively,* unless levitation occurred. . . ."

How did things come to such a pass? The course of development is clear from the entry in the OED. There are four living uses of *literally*. The first (OED sense 2) means "in a literal manner; word for word"; *the passage was translated literally.* The second (OED sense 3) means "in a literal way"; *some people interpret the Bible literally.* The third (OED sense 3b) could be defined "actually" or "really" and is used to add emphasis. It seems to be of literary origin. Dryden in 1687 complained that his "daily bread is litt'rally implor'd"; Pope in 1708 commented "Euery day with me is literally another yesterday for it is exactly the same." In 1769 the political writer Junius asked rhetorically, "What punishment has he suffered? Literally none."

The purpose of the adverb in the foregoing instances is to add emphasis to the following word or phrase, which is intended in a literal sense. The hyperbolic use comes from placing the same intensifier in front of some figurative word or phrase which cannot be taken literally. Pope, with his "literally another yesterday," had already in 1708 prepared the way.

Has the hyperbolic use all but eclipsed the earlier uses of *literally*, as Copperud asserts? No. Merriam-Webster files show the three living earlier senses to be still in regular use; furthermore, these uses as monitored by our readers outnumber the hyperbolic use by a substantial margin.

Now a word about the critics. The chief assertions they make are that the hyperbolic use of *literally* is a misuse of the word or a mistake for *figuratively*. As we have seen, it is neither; it is an extension of intensive use from words and phrases of literal meaning to metaphorical ones.

If the hyperbolic use of *literally* is neither a misuse nor a mistake for some other word, should you use it? The point to be made here is that it is hyperbolic, and hyperbole requires care in handling. Is it necessary, or even useful, to add an intensifier like *literally* to a well-established metaphorical use of a word or phrase? Will the use add the desired emphasis without calling undue attention to itself, or will the older senses of *literally* intrude upon the reader's awareness and render the figure ludicrous? Here are a few examples to judge for yourself.

. . . make the whole scene literally glow with the fires of his imagination —Alfred Kazin, *Harper's,* December 1968

They will literally turn the world upside down to combat cruelty or injustice —Norman Cousins, *Saturday Rev.,* 20 Nov. 1971

Even Muff did not miss our periods of companionship, because about that time she grew up and started having literally millions of kittens —Jean Stafford, "Bad Characters," 1954

He literally glowed; without a word or a gesture of exultation a new well-being radiated from him and filled the little room —F. Scott Fitzgerald, *The Great Gatsby,* 1925 (Reader's Digest 1983)

And with his eyes he literally scoured the corners of the cell —Vladimir Nabokov, *Invitation to a Beheading,* 1960 (OED Supplement)

Lily, the caretaker's daughter, was literally run off her feet. Hardly had she brought one gentleman into the little pantry . . . than the wheezy hall-door bell clanged again and she had to scamper along the bare hallway to let in another guest —James Joyce, *Dubliners,* 1914

. . . yet the wretch, absorbed in his victuals, and naturally of an unutterable dullness, did not make a single remark during dinner, whereas I literally blazed with wit —W. M. Thackeray, *Punch,* 30 Oct. 1847

litotes *Litotes* is a classical rhetorical device with a classical name—it is a form of understatement in which you assert a positive by using the negative of the contrary. The common expression "not bad" is an example. Litotes often takes the form *not un-* (as in "not unlikely") and in this form constitutes an acceptable kind of double negative; however, litotes does not require two negatives.

Not a few commentators have entries at *litotes.* Most of them are content to explain the term; a few have reservations about it. Safire 1980 does not care much for it; his objection is primarily to the *not un-* version. Howard 1978 quotes George Orwell in disapproval; again the *not un-* form is the one criticized. Kilpatrick 1984, however, notes that litotes can be used to convey subtleties not easily expressed otherwise. Everybody is against overusing the device.

The idea of litotes, the textbooks say, is to get emphasis by means of understatement. Bernstein 1958 suggests that humor and sarcasm are possible, too:

I spoke to goody this a.m., and dropped several hints that you would not be averse to getting a few laughs on the tallulah show come sunday —Fred Allen, letter, 30 Apr. 1951

He was not unaware that in his dress and as the owner of a car he was a provocation to many white people —E. L. Doctorow, *Ragtime,* 1975

Litotes can also be found in a number of fixed expressions:

. . . enclosing a check . . . , and telling me in No Uncertain Terms, what I could do with it —Frank Sullivan, letter, 25 Oct. 1965

You will find *litotes* mentioned at DOUBLE NEGATIVE 2.

liturgy See LITANY 2.

livid *Livid* is ultimately derived from the Latin verb *livere*, which means "to be blue." Its original use in English was as a synonym, more or less, of *black and blue*, describing flesh that was discolored by or as if by a bruise:

> There followed no carbuncle, no purple or livide spots —Francis Bacon, *The Historie of the Raigne of King Henry the Seventh*, 1622 (OED)

Its first extension of meaning gave it the sense "ashen or pallid," with the idea of blueness now secondary, if not entirely lost:

> The light glared on the livid face of the corpse —Ann Radcliffe, *The Italian*, 1797 (OED)

> ... the shuddering native, whose brown face was now livid with cold —W. M. Thackeray, *Vanity Fair*, 1848

> Mugridge's face was livid with fear at what he had done —Jack London, *The Sea-Wolf*, 1904

In this sense *livid* came to be used especially to characterize the appearance of a person pale with rage:

> He was livid with fury —Compton Mackenzie, *The Early Life and Adventures of Sylvia Scarlett*, 1918 (OED Supplement)

This use gave rise in turn to a pair of new senses. Because the faces of angry people are reddened at least as often as they are ashen, and because *livid* is easily associated with such words as *lurid* and *vivid*, the images called to mind by such a phrase as *livid with fury* were for many people colorful rather than pallid, and the color they were full of—or at least tinged with—was red:

> ... she saw the girl's head, livid against the bed-linen, the brick-rose circles again visible under darkly shadowed lids —Edith Wharton, *The Old Maid*, 1924

> ... the plate window where a fan of gladiolas blushed livid —Truman Capote, *Other Voices, Other Rooms*, 1948

Livid also began to be understood as describing the angry state itself rather than the appearance produced by it:

> The owners of large estates were ... livid at the prospect of his breaking up the bankrupt estates in the East —William L. Shirer, *The Rise and Fall of the Third Reich*, 1960

> "Oh, Vernon, isn't it scrumptious?" some woman was exulting. "Those faculty wives will be livid! . . ." —S. J. Perelman, *New Yorker*, 26 Nov. 1966

Such is the mottled history of *livid*. The history of critical comment about it is briefer and somewhat less varied. Most of the criticism has been directed at the "reddish" sense. Bernstein 1958, 1965, 1977 sets the tone for more recent criticism by accepting both the "black and blue" and "ashen" senses while regarding the "reddish or red-faced" sense as an error. He does not mention the "furious" sense. The opinion of Freeman 1983 is like that of Bernstein. Bremner 1980 and Bryson 1984 also reject the "reddish" sense, but they both take note of—and accept—the "furious" sense. Kilpatrick 1984 is alone in regarding the "reddish" sense as established.

Our own evidence shows that the usual meaning of *livid* in current English is "furious." This sense is so well established that a phrase like *livid with anger* now sounds almost redundant. The other senses are now somewhat rare.

It is often hard to tell whether "black and blue," "ashen," or "reddish" is meant:

> Suddenly Jerry seemed to petrify, features livid. . . . For a second, Barrett wondered whether Jerry might strike her or attempt to strangle her —Irving Wallace, *The Seven Minutes*, 1969

The truth is that *livid* seems no longer to have strong associations with any color. Whether red-faced or pale, a person who is filled with rage is now aptly described as *livid*.

loan, lend Copperud 1970, 1980 states flatly that the idea that *loan* is not good form as a verb is a superstition, but a surprisingly large number of commentators nonetheless express reservations about it. Among them are these, all Americans: Einstein 1985, Kilpatrick 1984, Bell & Cohn 1981, Bernstein 1965, 1971, 1977, Strunk & White 1959, 1972, 1979, Nickles 1974. In addition other commentators such as Perrin & Ebbitt 1972 and Garner 1998 note a preference for *lend* in formal discourse. Here is a recent comment:

> We do not accept, for example, that the noun *loan* can be used as a verb when *lend* is already there for that purpose, even though the banking community not only accepts it but is its most frequent user (or abuser) —Einstein 1985

Mr. Einstein is essentially repeating a century-old opinion that can be traced back at least as far as Richard Grant White 1870.

But before we go into the history of the usage dispute, we should examine the history of the word. The verb *loan* was among the words brought to America by early English-speaking settlers who, in the words of James Russell Lowell, "unhappily could bring over no English better than Shakespeare's." The

OED shows that verbal *loan* fell into disuse in England after the 17th century but continued in use in America, which was essentially cut off from the literary and intellectual life of England. In 1796 an English traveler in America named Thomas Twining noticed *to loan* used by "the least cultivated ranks of society" (quotation in Dictionary of American English).

By the middle of the 19th century British letters were not as unfamiliar in the United States as they had been in earlier centuries, and American men of letters show some awareness of a certain provincial tone in the use of *loan* as a verb. James Russell Lowell put it in a fictitious press notice he wrote to fill up a blank page in the first series of *The Biglow Papers* (1848):

. . . a pastoral by him, the manuscript of which was loaned us by a friend.

Lowell probably thought the word just right for a small-town editor. He commented on it in the introduction to the second series of *The Biglow Papers* (1867):

Loan for *lend,* with which we have hitherto been blackened, I must retort upon the mother island, for it appears so long ago as in 'Albion's England.' (in Dictionary of American English)

Oliver Wendell Holmes's *Elsie Venner* (1861) also contains a comment:

Loaned, as the inland folks say, when they mean 'lent.' (quoted in Lounsbury 1908)

Boston literary lights such as Holmes and Lowell may have felt the verb *loan* to be provincial, but what about the rest of the country? From the middle part of the 19th century the OED cites James C. Calhoun of South Carolina. To the west we find

. . . officers of the Bank have loaned money at usurious rates —Abraham Lincoln, speech in the Illinois legislature, 11 Jan. 1837

Former president Martin Van Buren, a New Yorker, in his autobiography, begun in 1854, wrote

. . . he pressed me to enter one of the prominent law offices in the city of New York, and offered to loan me the necessary funds. . . .

Benjamin Lundy, a New Jersey-born abolitionist editor and lecturer, noted in his journal in December 1834

He also loaned me files of the Vermont Chronicle. . . .

Perhaps only the Brahmins felt diffident about verbal *loan.*

Still Richard Grant White 1870 went beyond a charge of provincialism and declared it wrong: "Loan is not a verb, but a noun." White based his objection on his derivation of the noun from the past participle of the Anglo-Saxon verb *laenan*; Lounsbury 1908 demonstrated that White was unable to tell a verb from a noun in Old English. Nevertheless, the pronouncement stuck; from White it spread to William Cullen Bryant's *Index Expurgatorius* for the *New York Evening Post* (first published in 1877), and so on down to 1985.

British commentators appear satisfied in the main to label *loan* an Americanism and to assert the correctness of *lend* in British English. Fowler 1926 notes *loan*'s survival in the U.S. and "locally in U.K." Burchfield 1996 finds it used chiefly outside of England, but does have some English evidence.

How is the verb *loan* actually used? The most striking thing is that it is used literally: you can loan money, books, art works, clothing, equipment, people or their services. *Lend* is also used for these purposes, but only *lend* is used for figurative purposes, such as lending a hand, lending an ear, or lending enchantment. Here are some samples of how *loan* has been used:

I wonder if Frederic Melcher of The Publishers Weekly wouldnt loan you his copy —Robert Frost, letter, 26 Mar. 1936

Colonel Sartoris invented an involved tale to the effect that Miss Emily's father had loaned money to the town —William Faulkner, "A Rose for Emily," in *The Collected Stories of William Faulkner,* 1950

. . . to the National Gallery he loans a picture —Eric Partridge, in *British and American English Since 1900,* 1951

. . . an island cottage that Mittler owned and loaned them —John Cheever, *The Wapshot Chronicle,* 1957

. . . telling him he wasn't going to loan him the eighty dollars —*And More by Andy Rooney,* 1982

. . . the Magna Carta, which was being loaned to the United States for the Bicentennial —Tip O'Neill with William Novak, *Man of the House,* 1987

Loan as a verb is entirely standard; its use is predominantly American and includes literature but not the more elevated kinds of discourse. If you use *loan* remember that its regular use is literal; for figurative expressions, you must use *lend.*

loath, loathe, loth Copperud 1970, 1980 points out that *loath* is an adjective, *loathe* a verb; so do several others. Bernstein 1977 begins, "A reputable newspaper contained this sentence: 'But, curiously, in an institution *loathe* to make decisions, they are ready to judge a President.' That is a gaffe that is not uncommon." Reader's Digest 1983 and Garner 1998 call the spelling *loathe* for the adjective an error. Few dictionaries record the spelling: the OED notes *loathe* as a 17th-century variant; Webster's Third allows it as a secondary (*also*) variant, as do its derivative dictionaries (Merriam-Webster's Collegiate Dictionary, Tenth Edition, for instance) and Longman 1984, which advises sticking to *loath* for the adjective, *loathe* for the verb.

If people would follow this advice, the language would no doubt be tidier; unfortunately they do not. The reason seems to be pronunciation: many people rhyme the adjective with the verb, voicing the *th*, and some of them use the spelling *loathe* which represents their pronunciation. There appears to be no confusion; all of our citations using the *loathe* spelling for the adjective are unambiguous (as is Bernstein's example)—no one is likely to be misled. A recent example:

> . . . eager specialists who impressed me not only because they seemed to know what they were about but because they were articulate and not loathe . . . to let me learn —Laurence Urdang, *Datamation,* March 1984

The spelling *loth* is more common in British usage than American; American usage of *loth* was more common in the past than it is at present.

Things will be neater if you use *loath* (or *loth*) for the adjective, *loathe* for the verb. But if *loathe* represents your pronunciation of the adjective, you need not be afraid to use it. It is a legitimate variant.

locate   *Locate* seems to have come into use as an Americanism, and as an Americanism it has been subject to disparagement since the 1870s.
1. *Located* "situated." William Cullen Bryant put *located* on his *Index Expurgatorius* (published in 1877) without a gloss, so we do not really know what it was about the word that offended him. We do know that Bernstein 1962 found it objectionable in the sense of "situated." Maybe he was the inheritor of the Bryant tradition. He considerably moderated his views in his 1965 book; apparently no one else agreed. The use is entirely standard.

> Located in a bad slum area now undergoing redevelopment, this school . . . —James B. Conant, *Slums and Suburbs,* 1961

> She lived in Brooklyn . . . and was an avid fan of the Dodgers baseball team when it was located in that borough —*Current Biography,* April 1968

> Settlements were typically located on or near the shore —Edward P. Lanning, *Peru Before the Incas,* 1967

Located is also disparaged as unnecessary or as deadwood in several books, such as Bernstein 1965, Flesch 1964, Perrin & Ebbitt 1972. If we take the Lanning quotation for an example, we can see that the sentence can still be understood when *located* is omitted. But its omission does not make a better sentence, just a shorter one. You should not hesitate to use *located,* even though it may be omissible for sense, when it gives a sentence better rhythmic structure.
2. *Locate* "find." This curious objection, which began in 1917, has been repeated by more recent commentators. Evans 1957 would restrict *locate* for finding something by hunting for it. Flesch 1964 objects to *locate* as being a "stilted synonym" of *find.* Gowers in Fowler 1965 sets up a distinction: you *locate* the place where something or someone is, but you *find* the something or someone there. This is rather a subtle distinction, and it is not observed by the writers represented in our files.

> The young policeman was . . . trying to locate with his eyes the place in the garden where . . . —Doris Lessing, *The Good Terrorist,* 1985

> . . . one or more dogs that will locate the lion —J. Stevenson-Hamilton, *Wild Life in South Africa,* 1947

> . . . sent out to reconnoitre and to locate the kraal of the Kaffirs —Stuart Cloete, *The Turning Wheels,* 1937

> . . . he soon located about two dozen other concerned students —*Johns Hopkins Mag.,* October 1965

> . . . instructed to locate two others with whom you would like to be in a group —Clyde Reid, *Christian Herald,* June 1969

> . . . this excerpt is very difficult to locate —George Jellinek, *Saturday Rev.,* 12 June 1954

> CIA officials sought to locate the source of the funding —*The Tower Commission Report,* 1987

You will note that not one of these violates Evans's distinction, but all except the first violate Gowers's distinction. All of these examples are standard.

While we cannot say with Janis 1984 that "the quibbling about this word has ceased," none of these usages need worry you.

look   **1.** Perrin & Ebbitt 1972 and Longman 1984 note that when *look* is used as an intransitive verb in the sense of "use one's eyes" it may be qualified by an adverb of manner: "look carefully," "look longingly." But when it functions as a linking verb, it takes an adjective: "You look beautiful," "You look tired."

This is the modern analysis, and it dates from about the time of Alford 1866. But the OED shows that *look* in the latter meaning was formerly felt to be an intransitive and not a linking verb, and was usually qualified by an adverb of manner. An 1829 grammar lists *look beautiful* as a "blunder." Old examples with the adverb are not especially hard to find:

> . . . my Lord Sandwich, who is in his gold-buttoned suit, as the mode is, and looks nobly —Samuel Pepys, diary, 17 June 1663

> The beauty remarks how frightfully she looks —Samuel Johnson, *The Rambler,* No. 193 (in Hall 1873)

> . . . holds a great deal commodiously without looking awkwardly —Jane Austen, letter, 8 Nov. 1800

> She has got her new teeth in, and I think they look very nicely —Emily Dickinson, letter, 20 June 1852

Here we have an instance where the general perception of how the verb functions has changed over the years. The OED notes that because the grammarians have insisted on the use of the adjective and condemned the adverb, the adverb of manner is rarely seen, unless it is *well, ill,* or *badly.* The first two are acceptable, of course, because they are adjectives as well as adverbs.

> "My house looks well, doesn't it?" he demanded —F. Scott Fitzgerald, *The Great Gatsby,* 1925

But you had better stick to adjectives. The occasional adverb of manner is beginning to look like some sort of hypercorrection, as indeed the passage just quoted from Fitzgerald does.

2. We have had a couple of inquiries over the years about the propriety of *looking to* followed by an infinitive, and James J. Kilpatrick in a 1985 syndicated column recorded a correspondent's complaint about the same construction. Here is a typical example:

> I'm not looking to set a longevity record in this job —Dean Rusk, quoted in *Christian Science Monitor,* 17 Jan. 1968

There are actually three different uses in which *look* is followed by *to* and an infinitive. Let's take a look at them.

The first is a sense of *look* expressing anticipation or expectation. The OED shows that it began to be followed by an infinitive construction in the 17th century:

> Bruce, good morrow. What great author art thou chewing the cud upon? I look'd to have found you with your headache and morning qualms —Thomas Shadwell, *The Virtuoso,* 1676

This construction can still be found in the 20th century but is now less common than the others:

> In any reasonable world, the noted writer in question, and the young lady interviewers, could look to have their mouths washed out with soap —Emile Capouya, *Saturday Rev.,* 25 July 1964

In the 19th century this construction begins to turn up with *look* in the form of the present participle. The OED has Robert Southey in a letter written in 1830:

> I too had been looking to hear from you.

And a citation from A. E. Housman's *A Shropshire Lad* (1896):

> Two lovers looking to be wed.

Examples with *looking* are very common in recent use.

From our current point it is easy to look back at Southey and find hope as well as expectation and at Housman and find intention as well as anticipation. It is the notions of hope and intention that predominate in our most popular current use of *look* followed by *to* and the infinitive. It is most commonly found with *looking* but other forms of the verb are used as well.

> Long as I'm playin', I'm not lookin' to be on no high pedestal —Louis Armstrong, quoted in *N.Y. Times,* 20 Jan. 1960

> . . . Kierkegaard, whose work . . . looked to demonstrate that we cannot know the moral role we enact —Norman Mailer, *N.Y. Times Mag.,* 26 Sept. 1976

> . . . two men have been around looking to kill him —Lewis H. Lapham, *Harper's,* November 1971

> . . . Gremlins will arrive, looking to scare you silly —Richard Corliss, *Time,* 4 June 1984

> . . . everyone is tired and looking to go home —Larry Cole, *TV Guide,* 12 Nov. 1982

The newer use is differentiated from the older chiefly by the notions of trying or hoping or intending to do something, the greater frequency of the present-participle construction, and the greater ease of using it in the negative.

There is a third use in which *look* is followed by *to* and the infinitive. This is the linking verb use of *look* in which it comes close in meaning to *seem* or *appear.* It has been used with an infinitive complement—almost always *to be*—since the later 18th century. It is almost always used with some form of *look* other than the present participle and is still common in current use:

It looked to be hard, mean work —John G. Mitchell, *Smithsonian,* May 1981

. . . looks to be a slow and laborious and rather uninteresting business —Howard Nemerov, *American Scholar,* Summer 1967

And this is the only film that Spielberg has ever made where the editing looks to be from desperation —Pauline Kael, *New Yorker,* 30 Dec. 1985

loose, lose Many handbooks include warnings about confusion of these two common words. The real problem, of course, is simply spelling. The verb *lose* rhymes with *choose,* and the urge to spell it with an extra *o* sometimes proves irresistible:

. . . they loose her to a worthless motorcycle punk named Falbuck —*Media & Methods,* March 1969

This error is rare in edited material but fairly common in casual writing. A quick look in any dictionary is all that is needed to avoid it.

lost Sometimes considered to be an absolute adjective.
See ABSOLUTE ADJECTIVES.

loth See LOATH, LOATHE, LOTH.

lots, a lot Sir Ernest Gowers in Fowler 1965 notes that the Concise Oxford Dictionary labels *a lot* colloquial but that modern writers do not hesitate to use it in serious prose. He cites Sir Winston Churchill as one of his examples. *Colloquial* is the favorite handbook label for *a lot* and *lots:* about three-quarters of those in our collection use it. And many of them think *colloquial* means something bad:

Lots of, a lot of, a whole lot. These terms are colloquial for "many," "much," "a great deal." The chief objection is that each is a vague, general expression —Shaw 1970

Other people have noticed what Gowers noticed. Crisp's 1971 survey of attitudes toward usage problems listed all the surveyed groups as finding *lots, a lot* established. Perrin & Ebbitt 1972 says they are established in general, though not formal, usage. Our evidence confirms Perrin & Ebbitt's observation and Gowers's too. These expressions have been used in serious but not overformal writing for a long time, and they still are.

There were lots of people in Oxford like that —John Galsworthy, *The Dark Flower,* 1913

There is a lot of good in it —John Galsworthy, *Another Sheaf,* 1919

As to favorable comments I can stand a good lot —Oliver Wendell Holmes d. 1935, letter, 1 Nov. 1916

. . . there are lots of young men with their girls —Virgil Thomson, *The Musical Scene,* 1947

It was used a lot by the dons —Oliver St. John Gogarty, *It Isn't This Time of Year At All!,* 1954

. . . will have to sacrifice a lot of academic sacred cows —John Fischer, *Harper's,* February 1971

Lots of Swiss are worried —Mollie Panter-Downes, *New Yorker,* 26 Nov. 1950

. . . we must have lots of consumers' representatives —Christopher Hollis, *Punch,* 9 Dec. 1953

I had spent a lot of time —James Jones, *Harper's,* February 1971

See also ALOT, A LOT.

loud, loudly *Loud* is most familiar as an adjective, but it is also an established adverb. Its adverbial uses are more limited than those of *loudly;* it always follows the verb that it modifies, and it occurs chiefly with only a few simple and familiar verbs:

. . . if he talks loud and is rude to the waiters —Frank Swinnerton, *Tokefield Papers,* 1949

. . . and who screams loudest —A. C. Spectorsky, *The Exurbanites,* 1955

. . . those who shout loudest against the draft —Malcolm S. Forbes, *Forbes,* 1 Dec. 1970

. . . cheering as loud as their lungs would allow —R. W. Apple, Jr., *N.Y. Times,* 30 July 1981

Loudly could be substituted in any of the above passages and is the adverb of choice with most other verbs and in most other contexts:

A clock on the wall ticked loudly —Daphne du Maurier, *Ladies' Home Jour.,* August 1971

. . . his loudly amplified guitar —Pete Welding, *Rolling Stone,* 11 May 1972

. . . a raucous company of sightseers comes loudly down the quay —Jan Morris, *N.Y. Times Mag.,* 20 July 1975

. . . are loudly proud of their gift for understatement —Herb Caen, *Architectural Digest,* June 1986

luxuriant, luxurious Readers of other usage books are warned not to confuse these words, but uses of *luxuriant* to mean "of, relating to, or marked by luxury" or "of the finest or richest kind" have appeared periodically since 1671 and uses of *luxurious* to mean "fertile," "lush," or "prolific" have been around since 1644.

   ... in luxuriant restaurants —Theodore Dreiser, *Sister Carrie,* 1900

   ... a dozen records with luxuriant gold and red seals —Walter Van Tilburg Clark, "The Portable Phonograph," 1941

   ... luxuriant suede, slate floors, crystal chandeliers —Margaret E. Morse, *Southern Accents,* September–October 1984

   ... some luxurious misty timber jutted into the prairie —Henry David Thoreau, *A Week on the Concord and Merrimack Rivers,* 1849

   ... his luxurious whiskers —George Meredith, *The Ordeal of Richard Feverel,* 1859

   ... a luxurious growth of wet moss and lichen —Nathaniel Nitkin, *New-England Galaxy,* Fall 1967

These uses are standard but are much less frequent than those recommended by the usage writers who wish that differentiation between the two words was more complete than it is. Garner 1998 has examples showing that the disputed uses still can be found. We suggest, however, that you stick to the mainstream uses.

mad   1. The use of *mad* to mean "angry" was criticized in 1781 by the Reverend John Witherspoon (reprinted in Mathews 1931), who said "In this instance mad is only a metaphor for angry. . . . It is not found in any accurate writer, nor used by any good speaker" except for rhetorical effect. He was uncertain of its geographical province, discussing it under the heading of Americanisms but saying it was "perhaps an English vulgarism." The issue resurfaced a century later when an Englishman named Richard A. Proctor blamed the usage on Americans, who had "manifestly impaired the language." In rebuttal, Ayres 1881 quoted from Shakespeare and the Bible to show that the "angry" meaning had a proper English pedigree; however, the notion that it is an Americanism recurs from time to time in later commentators. Several of Ayres's contemporaries also found the usage unexceptionable.

But attitudes changed early in the 20th centuty—no one knows why—and numerous commentators raised their pens in unanimous protest. A common complaint labeled the usage a "careless colloquialism"; the proper, formal meaning was held to be "insane" or "crazy."

More recent commentators hold a wider variety of opinions; many find the use to be perfectly acceptable, though somewhat informal. As Garner 1998 points out, there never was a reason for stigmatizing the use.

As Ayres pointed out, the "angry" sense can be found in earlier British usage. Evidence shows the "angry" sense of *mad* used on several levels. There is evidence of some—though not much—literary use. More common use is found in general nonfiction, in fictional narra-

tive and dialogue, in informal writing such as correspondence, and of course in speech:

Being mad that he did not answer, and more at his laughing so —William Butler Yeats, *The Green Helmet,* 1910

You may be mad at your boss, but rather than risk getting fired you could displace your aggression by yelling at the people you live with —Ronald B Adler & Neil Towne, *Looking Out/Looking In,* 1987

This book will make ordinary readers mad —Jay Nordlinger, *National Rev.,* 22 May 2000

They do not much mind if Papandreou makes those important people mad —Jane Kramer, *New Yorker,* 24 May 1982

I was so mad the way father was talking that I thought I could shoot the man —Liam O'Flaherty, *The Informer,* 1925

"I was mad," he said. "I have a pretty bad temper. . . ." —John Steinbeck, *The Moon Is Down,* 1942

When you're mad at somebody, you pick out the most obvious thing about him and abuse him with it —Ken Dryden, quoted by Michael Farber, *Sports Illustrated,* 4 Oct. 1999

   ... they get mad and stay that way about six hours and then everything is dandy again —Flannery O'Connor, letter, 5 Oct. 1957

He used to call me "boy." That made me mad —Senator Burton K. Wheeler, quoted in Studs Terkel, *Hard Times,* 1970

2. *Mad* can be followed by the prepositions *about, at, for, on, with,* and occasionally *over.* People who are angry are *mad at* or less often *mad with* people or things; they are also sometimes *mad about* things. People who are carried away by enthusiasm are *mad about, mad for,* or, if they are British, *mad on* something or someone. People who are frantic or wild are *mad with* something.

> . . . the farmers' union, mad at the administration because of low agricultural prices —Tad Szulc, *Saturday Rev.,* 29 Apr. 1978

> This boy is not calling me up to find out if I am mad with him —Flannery O'Connor, letter, 1 Aug. 1957

> Mad about the prices, mad about the sloppy workmanship and mad at myself for being so dumb about cars —Vivian Gerber, quoted in *Progressive Woman,* October 1972

> My family are nearly all gone, and I'm not mad about the few that are left —Sir John Gielgud, quoted in *People,* 19 Oct. 1981

> Jim, mad for the sea after his first taste of salt water, acquired a small schooner yacht —John Dos Passos, *Chosen Country,* 1951

> . . . middle-class Robbie and working-class Kevin, who are both mad on cars —*Times Literary Supp.,* 3 Dec. 1971

> . . . a stupid *cocotte* who has begun by driving him mad with jealousy —Edmund Wilson, *Axel's Castle,* 1931

> . . . he made his first appearance in Paris, which promptly went mad over him —Deems Taylor, *Music to My Ears,* 1949

madding crowd Evans 1957, Reader's Digest 1983, and Harper 1985 claim that the phrase *madding crowd,* which comes down to us from Thomas Gray's "Elegy in a Country Churchyard" (1750) via the title of Thomas Hardy's novel, *Far from the Madding Crowd* (1874), is commonly miscorrected to *maddening crowd.*

Our evidence shows that the phrase is in fact rarely changed to *maddening crowd* in print.

magi Those who know this word only in the context of the Three Wise Men may possibly be caught in the same mistake that others have made before them:

> She is a kind of Magi —work of literary criticism, 1966

> . . . a power-seeker, a Magi if you will —*Publishers Weekly,* 16 Feb. 1976

Magi is the plural of *magus* and is likely to remain so. Plural spellings used as singulars are often strongly—but not always suc-

cessfully—resisted. For examples, see the list at LATIN PLURALS.

magic, magical According to Fowler 1926 the distinguishing features of *magic* and *magical* are that (1) *magic* is almost always used attributively and (2) *magic* is used literally and in fixed phrases while *magical* is used with extended meaning. But Burchfield 1996, the latest reviser of Fowler, finds that except for a few fixed phrases such as *magic carpet* and *magic square,* there is no tidy distinction between the two words. Here is what we have found in the evidence we have collected.

The adjective *magic* is almost exclusively an attributive adjective. *Magical* can be either an attributive or a predicate adjective, but attributive uses are about three times as common as the others. So nonattributive uses of either word are relatively uncommon.

Both words are used with literal force to refer to the supernatural.

> . . . bulls and stags represented a greater magic potency —Katharine Kuh, *Saturday Rev.,* 20 Nov. 1971

> The practice of using human fat as a powerful magical ingredient —A. W. Howitt, in *A Reader in General Anthropology,* ed. Carleton S. Coon, 1948

And both are commonly used with extended meanings, though their connotations may differ. *Magic* often implies some kind of instant effect, while *magical* often involves a feeling such as enchantment. These are only tendencies, however, because the figurative uses of the two words overlap quite a bit.

> . . . the magic solution to the defense problem in Europe —J. F. Golay, *New Republic,* 19 Apr. 1954

> . . . a man who really had the magic touch —Leonard Bernstein, *Atlantic,* April 1955

> . . . the magic plainness of La Fontaine's language —Richard Wilbur, *N.Y. Times Book Rev.,* 14 Oct. 1979

> . . . looked more and more magical and silvery as it danced away —G. K. Chesterton, *The Innocence of Father Brown,* 1911

> . . . its magical mornings and its incomparable sunsets —Paul Bowles, *Holiday,* March 1957

> . . . the magical ease with which they are summoned forth —Daniel Menaker, *Harper's,* October 1972

Magna Carta, Magna Charta There is some debate over whether or not this term should be spelled with *h.* You may want to use the *Carta* spelling because (1) it agrees with the pronunciation \ˌmag-nə-ˈkärt-ə\ that is used for either spelling, (2) it agrees with the vote by the House of Lords discussed by Gowers in Fowler 1965 (and therefore may be construed as the officially sanctioned spelling), and (3) it agrees with the larger portion of the citational evidence for this term in the Merriam-Webster files.

> Later generations undoubtedly read into the Magna Carta a great many guarantees —Henry W. Littlefield, *History of Europe 1500–1848*, 1959

> The first great step on the constitutional road was Magna Carta —G. M. Trevelyan, *A Shortened History of England*, 1942

On the other hand, if you already use and prefer the *Charta* spelling, you can defend your usage on the grounds that it has been around for over three and a half centuries and has been used by numerous reputable writers on both sides of the Atlantic. (By the way, the claim of Partridge 1942, echoed by Copperud, that *Charta* isn't Latin, is not true.)

> Considered to represent the penn'orth appointed by Magna Charta —Charles Dickens, *Our Mutual Friend*, 1865 (OED)

> The county law . . . has been called the *Magna Charta* of Prussian local government —Woodrow Wilson, *The State*, rev. ed., 1898

One further point is worth mentioning: when the original document and not a latter-day counterpart is being referred to, *Magna C(h)arta* is usually not preceded by *the* (see the Trevelyan and Dickens citations above). Although literal American use with the definite article is occasionally found in print (see the Littlefield citation above), in British usage the article is omitted. We suspect, however, that many Americans who are familiar with the term only from their school days use the definite article.

magnate, magnet These two words are occasionally confused.

> His manager was William Butler, textile magnet and baron of Massachusetts politics —*Boston Sunday Globe*, 24 Feb. 1985

Better check your dictionary if you are in doubt about them.

See also HOMOGRAPH, HOMOPHONE, HOMONYM.

magus See MAGI.

major The two main points made about the adjective *major* by usage writers are that it is overused and that when it is used, it should be as a comparative and not a positive adjective.

It is true that *major* does tend to get a lot of use and that in contexts where it invariably appears its meaning gets diluted. The announcement of a "major motion picture," for example, means nothing more than that a movie is being released. But you should not be dissuaded from using a word simply because other people use it too much. Just don't overuse it yourself. And while *major* may not be a particularly precise or dazzling adjective, many of the words suggested as possible replacements are not exactly eye-openers either. Gowers in Fowler 1965 recommends "*chief, main, principal,* etc."; Phythian 1979 lists "*large, important, big, momentous, main, prominent, chief, principal,* etc."; and Bremner 1980 suggests "*big, great, important, serious, chief, main, principal.*" It is hard to see what advantage these hold over *major*.

The argument that *major* is a comparative like *greater* is based on the word's origin as the comparative of Latin *magnus*, which conveniently ignores the fact that Latin and English are different languages. Although *major* can be used as a synonym of *greater* (as in "the major part of her writings"), Burchfield 1996 points out that it is not a true English comparative because it cannot be construed with *than*. In other words *greater than* is standard English but *major than* is simply not used. There seems to be little substance to the argument except to note that *major* is very rarely compared with *more*.

See also IMPLICIT COMPARATIVE.

majority 1. *Majority* is a singular noun in frequent use as one of those collectives that take either a singular or plural verb depending, in this case, on the writer's notion of the majority as a unit or as a collection of individuals. Our evidence of recent use shows a couple of trends. When *majority* stands alone as the subject, it tends to be used with a singular verb:

> . . . the majority has decided to go with front-wheel drive —*Blair & Ketchum's Country Jour.*, May 1980

> The silent majority . . . has dwindled —I. F. Stone's *Bi-Weekly*, 17 May 1971

> The majority was persuaded that . . . —Paul Lerman, *Trans-Action*, July/August 1971

Less often it takes the plural verb:

> . . . hope that the silent majority are more or less happy with the Daily Service —Rev. Hubert Hoskins, *Home & Family*, September 1974

When *majority* is followed by *of* and a plural noun, a plural verb is usual:

> The majority of its members were girls —Oliver St. John Gogarty, *Mourning Became Mrs. Spendlove*, 1948

The majority of the residents of Crown Heights are black —Lis Harris, *New Yorker,* 16 Sept. 1985

... the majority of the letters are to Russell —*Times Literary Supp.,* 23 Mar. 1967

Occasionally we find a singular verb:

The immense majority of the students is apathetic —Thomas Molnar, *Yale Literary Mag.,* December 1981

2. The use of *majority* is rather discouraged by most of the commentators, both British and American, when it is applied to something regarded as not countable. Our evidence shows that while plural nouns are considerably more common after *majority of* than singular nouns, the use with a singular is neither rare nor nonstandard:

The vast majority of matter is thought to be ... dark matter —Roy Cowen, *Science News,* 4 July 1998

... Dr. McCormick, who narrates the majority of the book —Robin Marantz Henig, *N.Y. Times Book Rev.,* 18 Aug. 1996

... more educational, dramatic and positive than the vast majority of programming —Joel Stein, *Time,* 17 Jan. 2000

... cable networks began to periodically capture a slight majority of the audience tuned in to television —Johnnie L. Roberts, *Newsweek,* 28 Dec. 1998

We note that most of these singular nouns are or are felt to be mass nouns.

3. Bremner 1980 and Bryson 1984 think that *vast* as a modifier of *majority* is a bit of a cliché. Our files show *vast* to be the most common modifier, but it is unlikely to run *great, overwhelming, large,* and several others out of business. Bryson notes that *vast majority* has been used by Partridge, Fowler, and Bernstein, so you will not find a united front on the subject. We see no reason for you to worry about it.

4. *Majority, plurality.* More of our handbooks undertake to rehearse the familiar distinction between these words in their electoral use than to comment on any other aspect of *majority*'s usage. Any decent dictionary will tell you that this use of *majority* refers to more than half the total votes while *plurality* refers to a number of votes that is less than half the total yet is greater than the number for any other candidate.

malapropism No writer likes to waste good material. Usage writers are no different, and we suspect that the heading *malapropism* in several books attests to this natural frugality. Entries can be found in Todd & Hancock 1986, Harper 1975, 1985, Reader's Digest 1983,

Bremner 1980, Phythian 1979, Perrin & Ebbitt 1972, and Watt 1967, among others. We are joining the group.

Malapropism is much older as a phenomenon than it is as a word. The word, coined from Mrs. Malaprop, a character in Richard Brinsley Sheridan's *The Rivals* (1775), only came into use in the 19th century. But the botching of big words goes back at least to the 16th century, when writers of scholarly intent introduced many words from Latin into the language. McKnight 1928 notes that considerable fun was derived by writers from the difficulty uneducated or partially educated people had with hard words. Sir Thomas Wilson, in his *Arte of Rhetorique* of 1553—not a place you would ordinarily look for laughs—has several such passages purporting to be from genuine speech. McKnight observes that Shakespeare used the same sort of speech for some of his comic characters, notably the police officers Elbow and Dogberry, as well as Mrs. Quickly and various clowns and country folk. Jespersen, in *Growth and Structure of the English Language* (1905), makes the point that English literature is richer in this sort of humor than that of any other language.

Jespersen and Bolinger 1980 discuss the causes of malapropism. Bolinger identifies it as a failure of contrast—the words are close enough in sound or appearance to be used one for the other. Jespersen notes that hard words are usually cut off from ordinary words; they share neither etymological roots nor associations of ideas with the common stock of the vocabulary. They must therefore be learned in isolation, and this isolation makes it easier for them to be exchanged for a similarly isolated hard word. Bolinger says that malapropism is a regular adornment of jargon, jargon being language that is full of specialized terms unconnected to ordinary discourse. He gives as an example from jargon a linguist's substitution of *tenant* for *tenet*; we have a like example in our own files:

... posits counter-arguments for some of Chomsky's basic tenants —*Linguistic Reporter,* September 1974

So we have two kinds of malapropism—the deliberate confusion of hard words for humorous effect that has been used by writers from Shakespeare's time and before, and inadvertent malapropisms committed by people not trying to be funny. Unconscious malapropisms are undoubtedly more common in speech than in writing. They can be found in reported speech:

... the ability to zero in on the essence of a problem and synthesize it for the Governor —in *N.Y. Times Mag.,* 29 June 1980

. . . what it's gonna affect is our truth and velocity with the citizens — in *Playboy*, November 1983

And they turn up in writing too:

The vision of Safirius Arbiter is an awesome one, since Safire is neither an entomologist nor an expert on usage —reviewer, *Saturday Rev.*, November 1980

. . . the most famous diet-conscious Red Sox because of his chicken regiment —reporter, *Springfield* (Mass.) *Morning Union*, 4 Sept. 1985

. . . you'll use these porcelains to dramatize a table or as limelights on an important armoire shelf —advt., *N.Y. Times*, 26 Apr. 1981

. . . recommended the merger as a money-saving mechanism that would eliminate the duplicity of services —reporter, *Springfield* (Mass.) *Morning Union*, 2 Nov. 1983

Malapropisms are venial sins. They are sometimes funny, and many writers on usage collect them. Humor writers will probably never stop using them. But they represent only a failure of the memory to retain the distinctive features of two different words. If you are trying to expand your vocabulary, you will probably drop a clanger now and then. We all do. An occasional linguistic pratfall seems not to be too high a price to pay for a richer vocabulary.

A related phenomenon is the mixed metaphor, likewise prominently displayed for fun in many usage books. And, yes, see also MIXED METAPHOR in this book.

man *Man* in its generic sense "a human being" has come under considerable attack in recent years by people who feel that because it is so widely understood in its somewhat more recent sense of "a male person," its generic sense slights women. This is not an unreasonable objection; however, the replacement of this generic *man* has been slowed by some mild resistance to replacing it with the four-syllable *human being* and greater, if less comprehensible, resistance to the two-syllable *human*. (For more on the *human–human being* controversy, see HUMAN.) *Human* and *human being* are making some progress as replacements on the schoolbook level; however, when we see them being used in place of *Man* by the intellectual elite of religion, science, and philosophy—those who deal with problems of cosmic dimension and treat everything in the large—we will know we have seen a successful revolution.

You, in the meantime, can use *human* or *human being* or even *person* if you dislike the generic *man*. Or you can keep on using *man*.

One way or the other, you will probably please someone and displease another. You will find longer discussions in McMahan & Day 1980, 1984, Reader's Digest 1983, Irmscher 1976, and other handbooks, as well as in books that deal extensively with the questions of gender and sexism in English, such as Dennis Baron's *Grammar and Gender* (1986), Rosalie Maggio's *The Nonsexist Word Finder* (1987), and Casey Miller and Kate Swift's *Words and Women* (1976). Some of these also take up the matter of compounds with *-man* (*policeman, fireman*, etc.), which in this book are covered at SEXISM 1.

manifold, manyfold The adjective having such senses as "various" and "many" is almost always spelled *manifold*:

. . . all are part of Roderick's manifold adventures —John Butt, *English Literature in the Mid-Eighteenth Century*, edited & completed by Geoffrey Carnall, 1979

The adverb meaning "by many times" is now almost always spelled *manyfold*:

This investment, too, will be returned to us manyfold —Abraham Ribicoff, *Saturday Rev.*, 22 Apr. 1972

Manifold does have some adverbial use:

. . . the total extent of scientific knowledge gathered throughout history will be exceeded manifold within a few decades —John G. Meitner, ed., in preface to *Astronautics for Science Teachers*, 1965

But such usage, although dating back to before the 12th century, is rare in modern English, and may be thought to be an error.

mankind *Mankind* has been open to some of the same objections as the generic use of *man* (which see). If our usage books are right, this is a subject less fervently pursued than *man*, probably because *mankind* in modern use is used almost exclusively to mean "the human race." It does, however, have a sense "men":

PERT. Your knowing of Mr. Dorimant, in my mind, should rather make you hate all mankind.
MRS. LOVEIT. So it does, besides himself. —George Etherege, *The Man of Mode*, 1676

This sense seems to be quite rare in the 20th century. Most modern use is of this type:

It was to be more than a compilation of national histories; it was to tell the story of mankind —*Times Literary Supp.*, 19 Feb. 1971

If *mankind* is offensive to you, you have available *humankind, human beings, humans*, and *people*, at the very least, for replacements. *Humankind*, like *mankind*, is a mass noun that will force you to make up your mind about agreement; some people make such nouns plural, some singular. The other alternatives are all comfortably plural.

manner In *Hamlet* there is the phrase *to the manner born* which is used to mean "accustomed to a practice from birth." It seems to have caught the fancy of the literary set and has subsequently been stretched in one way or another to fit various somewhat similar contexts. This one is not too far from Shakespeare's meaning:

> She looks very pretty, breakfasting in bed as to the manner born —Vita Sackville-West, *The Edwardians,* 1930

For at least sixty years various commentators have warned against the spelling *manor* in place of *manner.* Some of them recognize that the spelling *manor* gives the phrase a different twist, but still disapprove. Reader's Digest 1983, however, simply treats *to the manor born* as a phrase meaning "of upper-class birth and education"—a sort of equivalent to *born with a silver spoon in one's mouth.* Some examples:

> They were dedicated to shoring up the prerogatives of the self-made entrepreneurial male; she was a cradle feminist and to a manor born —Nelson W. Aldritch, Jr., *N.Y. Times Book Rev.,* 28 July 1996

> At 42, New Yorker Jim Erwin has the Gatsbyesque dash of a man to the manor born —Ann Butler, *Pittsburgh Press,* 16 July 1990

> These are certainly the grandest accommodations in the area, if not the entire state; if you weren't to the manor born, here you can pretend you were adopted —Jeffrey Bauman, *Travel & Leisure,* June 2000

We think Reader's Digest has taken a reasonable approach. If someone intends a meaning that is not Shakespeare's, why use Shakespeare's spelling? But you should note that both of these phrases are conspicuously literary, and you should not throw them around carelessly.

mantel, mantle These two words are now usually regarded as distinct from each other, with *mantel* used for a shelf above a fireplace, and *mantle* used for a cloak or a cover. However, they were originally nothing more than spelling variants (both derived from the Old French *mantel,* "cloak"), and *mantle* still occurs on occasion as a variant of *mantel:*

> An autographed picture of John Dewey dominates the mantle —William D. Lewis, *AAUP Bulletin,* December 1967

> Hand hewn beams, original mantle, plank floors throughout —advt., *N.Y. Times Mag.,* 25 May 1980

This use of *mantle* seems now to be largely confined to American English (American dictionaries treat it as standard, but British dictionaries do not recognize it). The few commentators who take note of it are all American, and all of them prefer *mantel* in such contexts. Our evidence shows that most writers prefer *mantel* as well:

> . . . a bottle of J & B on the mantel —Donald Barthelme, *New Yorker,* 17 July 1971

> . . . in a fishbowl on his mantel —Joseph Wambaugh, *The Black Marble,* 1978

> . . . he pauses by the fireplace mantel —John Updike, *Playboy,* September 1981

many a The phrase *many a* is followed by a singular noun, and when that noun is the subject of a verb, a singular verb:

> . . . many a student graduates without forming a firm conviction —Carl R. Woodward, *Phi Gamma Delta,* December 1968

> . . . many a man before him has become confused —Ashley Montagu, *Psychology Today,* April 1968

But pronoun reference, when it occurs, is governed by notional agreement and may thus be plural or singular:

> . . . and misled many a good body that put their trust in me —Thomas Gray, letter, 6 Sept. 1758

> Many a prophet who had predicted that business would slip . . . changed his mind —*Time,* 30 Mar. 1953

manyfold See MANIFOLD, MANYFOLD.

mar When the verb *mar* is modified by a prepositional phrase, the preposition is usually *by:*

> . . . all these gifts and qualities, . . . were marred by prodigious faults —Virginia Woolf, *The Second Common Reader,* 1932

> . . . his intellect, which was amazingly spotty, marred by great gaps —Norman Mailer, *The Naked and the Dead,* 1948

Less frequently, *mar* is followed by *with:*

> . . . a painstaking compilation, but . . . marred with unscholarly remarks —*Dictionary of American History,* 1940

marital, martial The issue here is not usage but typography. A slip on the keyboard easily transposes the *i* and the *t,* changing *marital* to *martial* or vice versa. We do not know how often this typo makes it into print, but it is common enough to have caught a few critical eyes.

marshal, marshall The usual spelling of both the noun and verb is *marshal,* but a look in the OED shows that *marshall* has seen occasional use as a variant for centuries. We have some recent evidence of its occurrence in edited prose:

> . . . a sort of medieval Marshall Dillon who rides into town to root out corruption —Michael A. Lipton, *People,* 30 Mar. 1992

> . . . plants can marshall a complex array of chemical countermeasures —J. A. Miller, *Science News,* 25 May 1985

Nevertheless, *marshall* is regarded as a spelling error by several commentators. It seems to be a bit more likely in British English, where *marshalled* and *marshalling* are common for the inflected forms of the verb. In American English, especially, *marshal* is the better choice.

martial   See MARITAL, MARTIAL.

martyr   1. *Noun.* When *martyr* is used with a preposition, it is usually followed by *to*:

> He'd been a martyr to asthma all his life —A. J. Cronin, *The Citadel,* 1937

> . . . Chaucer, as an amorous poet, made Aeneas fickle instead of a martyr to duty —Gilbert Highet, *The Classical Tradition,* 1949

Occasionally *martyr* is followed by *for* or *of*:

> . . . she died as martyr for the new morality against the old —John Ardagh, *Washington Post Book World,* 26 Sept. 1971

> . . . the common picture of her (Cleopatra) as a martyr of love, a mortal Aphrodite —John Buchan, *Augustus,* 1937

Raub 1897 suggests using "martyr *for* or *to* a cause, *to* a disease." According to our evidence, the distinction still exists. Of those citations in the Merriam-Webster files that show *martyr* used in connection with a physical condition, all follow it with *to,* as in the Cronin example above.

2. *Verb.* When the verb *martyr* is used with a preposition whose object is the reason, it is usually *for*:

> . . . he is determined to martyr himself, if need be, for the anti-Nazi cause —*Time,* 14 Apr. 1941

> . . . martyred by Diocletian for refusing to abjure the Christian faith —E. R. Leach, *London Calling,* 24 June 1954

massive   More than 35 years ago a couple of commentators decided that the figurative use of *massive,* which dates from the 16th century, was being overused. These critics were repeated by other critics, right down to the present. But what constitutes overuse? The commentators offer no explanation. *Massive*

is not a rare word, but the little word *back* appears in our files 13 or 14 times as often as all the senses of *massive.* The judgment of overuse is strictly subjective and you can feel free to ignore it.

masterful, masterly   The Fraternal Order of Usage Commentators, right down to the end of the 20th century (and doubtless beyond), just about uniformly insist that *masterful* must mean "domineering" and *masterly* "skillful, expert" and that it is a misuse of *masterful* to use it in the sense given for *masterly.* The two adjectives are thus distinct, and each—especially *masterful*—is to be kept in its proper place.

This distinction, however neat and convenient, is an invention, created by H. W. Fowler in 1926. Fowler knew, as anyone who looks at the OED can, and said that the two words were for a long time interchangeable. Each of them had a "domineering" sense and a "skillful, expert" sense. The "domineering" sense of *masterly* dropped into disuse around the end of the 18th century. Fowler seems to have thought the world of English usage would be a tidier place if *masterful* too were limited to one sense. He therefore declared the differentiation between the two words to be complete, and followed with a number of examples that showed it was not, but that he declared ex post facto to be misuses. From then until now, usage writers have followed Fowler, condemning as misuse all the evidence that proved Fowler's opinion was only wishful thinking in the first place.

It hardly needs to be said that the decried sense of *masterful* is in standard and respectable use—the usage that likes nothing better than repining for some lost cause.

> Lafe is a masterful letter writer, a practised hand, as it were —Henry Miller, *The Air-Conditioned Nightmare,* 1945

> . . . Murray's hand . . . can be seen in the masterful design of the dictionary's page —John Willinsky, *Empire of Words,* 1994

> . . . sole ballottine blessed with a frame of masterful brioche —Gael Greene, *New York,* 3 Mar. 1975

> Coraghessan Boyle writes a rich and masterful prose —Andrew Rosenheim, *Times Literary Supp.,* 22 Mar. 1991

> A masterful place hitter and bunter, Keeler . . . bridged the gap between ancient and modern baseball —David Nemec, in *The Ultimate Baseball Book,* ed. Daniel Okrent & Harris Lewine, 1984

> . . . the Constitution is in many respects a document of calculated omission and mas-

terful ambiguity —Arthur M. Schlesinger, Jr., *The Cycles of American History*, 1986

Gibbon created ironic distance by masterful deployment of footnotes —Robert Darnton, *The Kiss of Lamourette*, 1990

But neither the use of *masterly* nor the use of the "domineering" sense of *masterful* has been eclipsed:

> . . . artists in their own right—several of them masterly ones —William Styron, *This Quiet Dust and Other Writings*, 1982

> This is a masterly poem —Flannery O'Connor, letter, 30 Nov. 1957

> They were masterly statesmen, not masterful supermen —David Thomson, *Europe Since Napoleon*, 2d ed., rev., 1962

> "But then you don't seem powerless to me, either. Quite masterful, the way you run your TV crew." —John Updike, *Bech Is Back*, 1982

The only doubts among the Fowler followers have been occasioned by adverbial use. *Masterful* has the perfectly ordinary *masterfully*, but *masterly* has a problem. The standardly formed *masterlily* has been talked about, but evidently never used. *Masterly* is itself used as an adverb, but using the same form for both adjective and adverb makes some commentators a bit uncomfortable. Most of them don't dare recommend *masterfully* (although a couple do) and thus imply that *masterful* might be acceptable. Mostly they have recourse to circumlocution: *in a masterly way*. This must be painful to inveterate savers of words, but it is a matter of little concern to most of us.

There is some degree of differentiation between *masterful* and *masterly* used in the "skillful" sense. Our backing suggests that *masterly* is stronger in literary use; *masterful* in general use—in reviews, in sportswriting, in speech, and in other areas where high formality is not the order of the day. Both words are entirely standard and in quite respectable use. The recommended distinction is easy to observe, and you may prefer to do so, but you are in good company if you choose to ignore it.

mastery   Both Lincoln Library 1924 and Bernstein 1965 note a distinction in preposition usage with the word *mastery*: it is *mastery of* a subject but *over* a person. Actual usage shows that things are not so clearcut. Generally, *mastery of* is found when something impersonal is involved:

> . . . had still far to go before he obtained absolute mastery of the government —J. H. Plumb, *England in the Eighteenth Century*, 1950

> Mastery of one's own discipline can be a lifework —Irving Kolodin, *Saturday Rev.*, 29 Jan. 1972

> . . . mastery of managerial techniques —William H. Whyte, Jr., *The Organization Man*, 1956

However, use of *mastery of* may occasionally involve persons:

> . . . leading on towards mastery of ourselves and our environment —Bertrand Russell, *Education and the Good Life*, 1926

Mastery over is found less often, but it too involves something impersonal more frequently than it involves persons:

> . . . the mastery of the Alexandrians over the difficult art of the textbook —Benjamin Farrington, *Greek Science*, 1953

> The sun resumed its blessed mastery over the land —Oscar Handlin, *The Uprooted*, 1951

> It's amazing . . . the complete mastery he's held over them —Ned Martin, radio baseball broadcast, 30 Apr. 1975

materialize   Several common uses of this verb have been the object of critical commentary throughout much of the 20th century. In its oldest sense, *materialize* is a transitive verb meaning "to give material form to," a sense that dates back to 1710. The 19th century saw the development of several additional senses, including "to make materialistic," "to cause (a spirit) to appear in bodily form," and "to assume bodily form," as in "The ghost materialized." None of these senses have been disputed. But two other senses from the 19th century have been—"to make an appearance; appear suddenly":

> Some fifteen or twenty hounds that suddenly materialized among the bee-hives —Miss Murfree, *The Prophet of the Great Smoky Mountain*, 1885 (OED)

and "to come into existence; develop into something tangible":

> Year after year passed and these promises failed to materialise —*Blackwell's Mag.*, May 1891 (OED)

These uses have been treated as standard in dictionaries since 1905, when the OED entry for *materialize* was first published. They have been treated as standard in Merriam-Webster dictionaries since the publication of Webster 1909. They have been criticized at least since 1917.

No commentator that we've read has set forth a cogent argument against these senses; they simply refuse to accept them. Yet, *materialize* is a common verb in its disputed senses, and its use is by no means limited to careless or pretentious writers. In its "appear" sense, it is especially useful in describing an appearance that is made suddenly, as if by magic:

> An instant later, a silk hat materialized in the air beside me —J. D. Salinger, *New Yorker,* 19 Nov. 1955

> . . . an LBJ staffer materialized to get Sam into his formal attire —Larry L. King, *Harper's,* April 1970

> The drinks . . . materialized on glass tables —John Updike, *Bech Is Back,* 1982

The sense "come into existence" also has distinct qualities. It usually occurs in negative constructions ("failed to materialize"), describing something that was hoped for or anticipated but did not happen or appear:

> The rain didn't materialize—instead we had a beautiful day —E. B. White, letter, 27 Aug. 1940

> The expected rally in Emerson failed to materialize —Malcolm Cowley, *The Literary Situation,* 1954

> . . . a research fellowship would have been possible. . . . The fact that none ever materialised was a source of lasting disappointment —K. M. Elisabeth Murray, *Caught in the Web of Words,* 1977

> . . . a large sum of money that had been promised by an Eastern benefactor did not materialize —Garrison Keillor, *Lake Wobegon Days,* 1985

The old prejudice against these uses of *materialize* lingers on, but their place in standard English is nonetheless established, and has been for many decades.

may 1. See CAN, MAY.
2. *May, might.* Since the late 1960s commentators have noticed and been puzzled by uses of *may* where they had expected *might.* There seem to be two places where such substitution occurs: in describing hypothetical conditions, and in a context normally calling for the past tense. Perhaps some examples would make things clearer. The first describes a hypothetical situation; it is taken from speech, as the *'d have* for *had* also indicates. It was spoken by a color analyst on a professional football telecast:

> If he'd have released the ball a second earlier—when [the pass receiver] made his cut—he may have had a touchdown —Dan Dierdorf, CBS television, 20 Dec. 1986

Here "might have had a touchdown" would have been expected.

In the second example we have a context where the past is called for:

> Born in Buffalo, N.Y., he may have gone to Princeton . . . but he made his reputation as a railroader —*Forbes,* 15 Sept. 1970

This one is confusing since *may* in such surroundings suggests that the writer does not know whether he went to Princeton; *might* (which is the verb we would have expected) would suggest that he could have gone if he had wanted to.

No one has a satisfying explanation for why these substitutions occur, and we are as stumped as everyone else. Here is about all we can tell you: we have more British evidence for the substitution (and more notice is taken of it by British commentators) than we have American evidence. But we do have both. The substitution is more frequent in speech than in writing. British evidence and British comment suggest that in print it is most likely to be found in the newspapers. It can be a puzzler when it occurs; notice in this example how you are at first led to believe that the boy survived:

> At first it was believed that the boy may have survived in a pocket of air, but when divers reached him yesterday it became obvious that he drowned soon after the trawler went over —*The Guardian,* 30 Oct. 1973

It will probably be some years before we know much more about this use of *may* for *might.* It has received no large-scale investigation, as far as we know. We don't know how long it has been going on or whether it started in the U.K. or the U.S. It may not be too recent:

> The fields are so small and the trees so numerous along the hedges that . . . you may think from a little distance that the country was solid woods —Robert Frost, letter, 18 May 1914

We may be seeing here a slow shift in the boundaries between *may* and *might.* But we also find a commentator or two worrying about examples where *might* has replaced *may.* Our advice to you is to use *may* and *might* as they naturally occur to you and not to worry about it.

may of See OF 2.

me Everyone expects *me* to turn up as the object of a preposition or a verb:

> ". . . He's not a damned show-off like me." —Ernest Hemingway, *Green Hills of Africa,* 1935

> Now he was going to show me something —Ernest Hemingway, *Green Hills of Africa,* 1935

But *me* also turns up in a number of places where traditional grammarians and commentators prescribe *I*. Many of these disputed uses of *me* result from the historical pressure of word position; language historians tell us that since sometime around the 16th century *me* has been appearing in places where *I* had before been regular—such as after *as* and *than* and the verb *be*—because those places are much like similar positions—such as after prepositions and transitive verbs—where *me*, or any other objective form, is usual.

Thus we find *me* used after *as* and *than*:

> I had met a young man, barely older than *me* —Marya Mannes, *Out of My Time*, 1971

> LoPresti, who was a few years older than me —Tip O'Neill with William Novak, *Man of the House*, 1987

It is also common after *be* (there is more on this aspect of the subject at IT'S ME):

> . . . and I will say, whether anyone calls it pride or not, that if he *does* get up and around again it's me that saved his life —Walt Whitman, letter, 30 June 1863

> In gratitude, Churchill rolled off a recorded message to the workers: "This is me, Winston Churchill, speaking himself to you, and I am so glad to be able to thank you in this remarkable way." —*Time*, 1 Apr. 1946

> I meant it was me that couldn't encompass but one bill of goods metaphysically —Flannery O'Connor, letter, 31 Oct. 1959

Me is also used absolutely and in emphatic positions in the sentence:

> "Who, me?" said the lion —James Thurber, *Fables for Our Time, and Famous Poems Illustrated*, 1940

> "Why me?" I was going to ask —Simon 1980

> Me, I'll take the old sentimental shows —George Jean Nathan, *The Theatre Book of the Year, 1946–1947*

> Me, I am in transition from one college to another —Robert Frost, letter, 15 July 1943

All of the constructions so far mentioned are generally accepted by commentators as historically justified. You will note, however, that they are most likely to be found in speech and in writing of a relaxed personal or conversational style. In more formal contexts you may want to use *I* after *be* and after *as* and *than* when the first term of a comparison is the subject of a verb.

More problematical is what one of our correspondents dubbed "The *Someone and I* Syndrome" (this subject appears in another guise at BETWEEN YOU AND I and PRONOUNS). While traditional opinion prescribes *someone*

and I for subject use—*I and someone* seems a bit impolite—in actual practice we also find *me and someone* and *someone and me*:

> Me and Enoch are living in the woods in Connecticut —Flannery O'Connor, letter, 1950

> . . . you and me can shake the eye-teeth of both the Democratic and Republican national parties —George C. Wallace, quoted in *Springfield* (Mass.) *Sunday Republican*, 30 June 1968

Of these two constructions, *me and someone* does have the minor virtue of putting the *me* in the emphatic position, where it is slightly less noticeable. Both are speech forms often associated with the speech of children, and are likely to be unfavorably noticed in the speech and writing of adults except when used facetiously (as in Flannery O'Connor's letter).

Another *me* is the one used occasionally, especially in this country, as an indirect object where *myself* is more common:

> But one day I bought me a canary bird —Oliver Wendell Holmes d. 1894, *The Autocrat of the Breakfast-Table*, 1857

> . . . I must get me a place just like it —Alexander Woollcott, letter, March 1938

> . . . I have bought me some peafowl —Flannery O'Connor, letter, 17 March 1953

The OED Supplement says this is common in American speech; it does not appear to be much used in serious formal prose.

Our final use is of *me* for *my*. Our evidence suggests that this use is chiefly associated with Irish dialect; it is used humorously by others as well:

> ". . . wasn't me whole world lost?" —Paul Vincent Carroll, in *44 Irish Stories*, ed. Devin A. Garrity, 1955

> . . . I'll surely sleep through the day and I'll lose me job —Robert Gibbings, *Lovely Is the Lee*, 1945

> They are paying me well and unfortunately I have to earn me bread —Flannery O'Connor, letter, 2 Feb. 1959

meaningful The history of *meaningful* shows how extreme popularity can, perversely, have a bad effect on a word's reputation. For about a hundred years after its first recorded use in 1852, *meaningful* existed quietly as an uncommon, unremarkable adjective. Even after it had become a fairly common word in the 1950s, it continued to pass unnoticed by the critics. But in the 1960s *meaningful* ceased to be ordinary. Its common use in such phrases as *meaningful dialogue* and *meaningful relationship* made it suddenly notorious, and it began to be criticized. E. B. White called it "a bankrupt adjective" in Strunk & White 1972, 1979, and the usage panel of Harper 1975 rejected it both in speech and in writing by a large majority. It was found to have various faults, but its chief failing was a simple one: it was overused. In the 1960s and 1970s, many people got sick of *meaningful*, and some have not yet recovered.

In the meantime, *meaningful* has continued in common use. It serves essentially as an antonym of *meaningless*, for which purpose it is well suited:

> Even his Christmas Eve assault on Trenton was more a coup de théâtre than a strategically meaningful step —Garry Wills, *Atlantic*, April 1994

> They said that what is important to our children and our grandchildren will be remembered; what is forgotten is no longer meaningful —Leslie Marmon Silko, *Yellow Woman and a Beauty of the Spirit*, 1996

> The incident produced a certain panicky, just discernible exchange of meaningful glances —Adam Gopnik, *New Yorker*, 4 Aug. 1997

> . . . men could at least feel they belonged to a meaningful brotherhood and provided a utility beyond mere earning power —Susan Faludi, *Newsweek*, 16 Aug. 1999

Its notoriety is no longer great and will most likely continue to diminish as the years go by. Its use with *relationship* or *dialogue*, however, can still be counted on to draw a few groans.

means 1. In the sense "material resources affording a secure life," *means* takes a plural verb:

> . . . he came under the care of his maternal grandparents, whose means were sufficiently ample to enable them to afford him unusual educational advantages —*Dictionary of American Biography*, 1928

> . . . while their means were always modest there was no trace of dire poverty —J. T. Ellis, *Irish Digest*, January 1954

At one time, this sense was also used in the singular construction; the OED labels it obsolete, and its latest use dates from the 17th century.

2. When used with a preposition, *means* is most often followed by *of*:

> . . . agreement about the best means of organizing the state —Aldous Huxley, *Ends and Means*, 1937

> . . . having developed the means of survival in the Harlem ghetto —*Current Biography*, November 1967

> . . . essential to find a means of conveying the lessons —*Times Literary Supp.*, 19 Feb. 1971

Less frequently, *means* is used with *to, toward*, or *for*:

> Many of our wants are means to a higher set of goals —Charles L. Schultze, *Saturday Rev.*, 22 Jan. 1972

> High wages and slum clearance were the means toward abolition of group hatred —Oscar Handlin, *The American People in the Twentieth Century*, 1954

> . . . technology has not as yet developed a means for dependable underground transmission of high voltage power —*Annual Report, Union Electric Co.*, 1970

3. See also BY MEANS OF.

meantime, meanwhile Many American commentators have noted differences in the use of these two words. The usual observation is that *meantime* normally functions as a noun and *meanwhile* as an adverb. The use of *meantime* as an adverb and *meanwhile* as a noun is generally discouraged, although most commentators allow that such usage is not incorrect; Bernstein 1971 defends the adverb *meantime* at some length, noting its frequent use by Shakespeare.

The evidence shows that *meantime* and *meanwhile* have been used interchangeably as nouns since the 14th century and as adverbs since the 16th century. The general observation that *meantime* is now the more common noun and *meanwhile* the more common adverb is undoubtedly true, but the adverb *meantime* and the noun *meanwhile* have been in continuous use for hundreds of years, and their use in current English is not rare:

> Meantime there was a core of older contributors —*Times Literary Supp.*, 19 Feb. 1971

> Meantime, he is headed in the right direction —E. B. White, letter, 4 Feb. 1974

> Meantime, the Shakers . . . lived extremely sober lives —Jacques Barzun, *From Dawn to Decadence*, 2000

> And in the meanwhile, mum's the word —Alexander Woollcott, letter, 19 Nov. 1934

> But in the meanwhile a lot of people learned to read —Bergen Evans, "The Language We Speak," speech, June 1968

> In the meanwhile, the whole area of Gettysburg . . . was one makeshift burial ground —Garry Wills, *Lincoln at Gettysburg*, 1992

There is no need to make a point of avoiding such usage.

meddle   When *meddle* is used with a preposition, it often is followed by *with*:

> . . . it is inexpedient to meddle with questions of State in a land where men are highly paid to work them out for you —Rudyard Kipling, *Plain Tales from the Hills,* 1888

> . . . she did not like other people to meddle with her property —Edmund Wilson, *New Yorker,* 5 June 1971

Meddle is also used with *in* and *into*:

> . . . not in a condition to meddle nationally in any war —Claude G. Bowers, *The Young Jefferson, 1743–1789,* 1945

> Congress . . . has meddled in affairs that are properly within the jurisdiction of the courts —*New Yorker,* 10 Apr. 1971

> . . . to abstain from the temptation to meddle into the inner affairs of other departments —*ACLS Newsletter,* vol. 5, no. 2, 1954

We also note that *meddle in* and *meddle into* often have *affairs* as their object; it appears that *meddle with* does not.

media   *Media,* the plural of *medium,* has developed into a singular noun in English. It seems at present to be developing in two somewhat contrary directions. The older, which is the use of *media* as a singular count noun, is not very recent; it dates back to at least the 1920s. Louise Pound in *American Speech,* October 1927, has two unattributed citations for *media* as a singular; one, in the form of a plural *medias,* is clearly from advertising. The OED Supplement has a 1923 citation from a book on advertising using *mass media* as a singular. It thus appears that *media* as a singular count noun originated in advertising jargon, and our evidence shows that it has stayed in use in that field ever since.

> The Japanese, who have invested $12 billion in American entertainment companies over the past three years, have a name for this so-called new media —John Huey, *Fortune,* 31 Dec. 1990

It should be noted that singular *media* and plural *media* are both used by advertising people.

Media has turned up as early as 1939 as a singular noun in a medical text for the stuff on which cultures are grown. It is a use that has persisted, although it is obviously nowhere near as common as the "mass media" use. Here are a couple of fairly early examples:

> . . . producing a suitable media for organic life —*Britannica Book of the Year 1946*

> . . . various salts of penicillin in an aqueous media can not be administered orally —*Science,* 16 Feb. 1945

A third independent singular *media* turned up in the field of art in a local museum bulletin in 1937. We have relatively little subsequent evidence of this use, but it too appears from time to time:

> . . . "Experiments in Design" with Mrs. Varty which will include tissue paper, ink, string, a different media every day —Gladys E. Guilbert, *Spokesman-Review* (Spokane, Wash.), 30 Jan. 1966

And we have other miscellaneous uses of singular *media,* some of which we show you here. Note that the two most recent are technical:

> . . . partly as a cultural media —K. L. Little, *American Jour. of Sociology,* July 1948

> . . . necessary to rely on the mails as the contact media —Henry M. Ellis, *Stamps for Fun and Profit,* 1953

> Films . . . will inevitably become more a media of personal expression —*Saturday Rev.,* 28 Dec. 1963

> These expatriate stars have become too large for one company or even one media to handle —Iris M. Fanger, *Christian Science Monitor,* 14 Sept. 1979

> . . . a new ultra-high-density recording media —*Annual Report, Eastman Kodak Co.,* 1983

> . . . an optical disc media —*Predicasts Technology Update,* 5 Jan. 1987

The singular count noun *media,* then, is fairly well established in a number of different specialized areas as the equivalent of *medium.* The plural *medias* is much less common than the singular *media,* and both are much less common than the plural *media* at the present time.

The other direction in which singular *media* is moving is toward use as a collective noun. A collective noun can take either a plural or a singular verb, and when *media* takes a plural verb no one notices it because the agreement does not differ from that of the traditional plural. When it takes a singular verb, it is distinguishable from the singular count noun in that it takes *the* rather than *a* or *one* or *this* and does not have a plural *medias.* The range of application of this *media* is narrow: it almost always refers to the mass media—television, radio, and the press especially. (It is also now being used as a plural collective to refer to representatives or members of these organizations.) It is a use well established in speech:

> Adds Fordham's Father Culkin: "Now the media goes directly to the public. . . ." —Paul D. Zimmerman, *Newsweek,* 13 Nov. 1967

You know, the news media gets on to something, and there's a certain herd instinct among writers —Edwin Meese 3d, quoted in *N.Y. Times,* 25 Sept. 1981

I understand the media . . . and it apparently understands me —Jesse Jackson, quoted in *Esquire,* December 1979

There have been many changes in the media since you first came into it, since I first came into it —Marquis Childs, address to National Press Club, 17 Oct. 1975

The media consumes you when you approach a milestone —Reggie Jackson, quoted in *Sports Illustrated,* 12 Aug. 1985

And it occurs in writing too, especially of a journalistic kind:

. . . the media is boomer-dominated and boomer-obsessed —David Martin, *Newsweek,* 1 Nov. 1993

. . . the media gives insufficient coverage to what they do and say —William Davis, *Punch,* 12 Oct. 1976

His accessibility allows the media, and through it the voters, to glean a deeper insight into his person —*New Republic,* 6 Mar. 2000

The media pokes its nose into every nook and cranny of your life —*Ms.,* June/July 2000

The commentators by and large reject both of these developments, and many of them are unaware that there are two different uses of singular *media*. However, the illustrated uses of *media* are not on the wane. The evidence suggests that use of *media* is going to remain unsettled for some time because of these somewhat opposing pulls. But you should remember that *media* and *medium* are English words, even if naturalized, and are no longer subject to the rules of Latin. The evidence is that the singular count noun has been with us for more than fifty years, and shows no sign of retreat in spite of the hostility of the pundits. The collective use is more recent and seems to be following the direction of development of *data*. It too is likely to survive (Garner 1998 considers it standard). And this is also worth remembering: our evidence shows that *media* is still being construed as a plural more often than it is either as a singular count noun or as a collective noun with a singular verb.

For more of these interesting foreign plurals, see the list at LATIN PLURALS.

mediate *Mediate* is most often used with *between* when it takes a preposition:

I want to mediate between the two of you now, because if this breach continues it

will be the ruin of us all —Robert Graves, *I, Claudius,* 1934

. . . he mediates between the pole of nature and that of civilization —Robert Penn Warren, *Democracy and Poetry,* 1975

Occasionally, *mediate* is used with *for:*

The learned professions have evolved to mediate for the individual —Ralph Crawshaw, *Center Mag.,* May 1969

Although Bernstein 1965 notes the use of *mediate* with *among,* our evidence shows that this use is infrequent:

. . . the process of mediating among conflicting purposes and the anticipated needs of more than one reader —C. H. Knoblauch, *College Composition and Communication,* May 1980

Mediate is also found quite frequently in its transitive uses with *to* or *through:*

. . . the individuals who, in the various cultural settings, mediate the culture to the child —Margaret Mead in *Personality in Nature, Society and Culture,* ed. Clyde Kluckhohn & Henry A. Murray, 1950

. . . whose ideas are never likely to reach the common reader, except as mediated through the prose of shallower . . . disciples —*Times Literary Supp.,* 3 Sept. 1954

mediocre This word is sometimes considered to be an absolute adjective. See ABSOLUTE ADJECTIVES.

meditate When *meditate* is used with a preposition, the choice is usually *on:*

. . . our only condition is that he turn them into poetry, and not merely meditate on them poetically —T. S. Eliot, "The Metaphysical Poets," in *Selected Essays,* 1932

. . . meditated with concentrated attention on the problem of flight —Havelock Ellis, *The Dance of Life,* 1923

. . . meditate on the fact that they were commanded by a man who meant business —C. S. Forester, *The Barbary Pirates,* 1953

Less frequently it is used with *upon:*

While they went out of doors together, she meditated upon the fact of his usefulness —Ellen Glasgow, *Barren Ground,* 1925

. . . the young priest blotted himself out of his own consciousness and meditated upon the anguish of his Lord —Willa Cather, *Death Comes for the Archbishop,* 1927

medium See MEDIA.

meld As a verb meaning "to blend or merge," *meld* is a fairly new word. although not nearly as new as some people believe. We first encountered it in 1936:

... apple, currant, and raisin all melded into one sweetly tart aroma —Della Lutes, *The Country Kitchen*, 1936

By 1939, the editors of Webster's Second had seen enough evidence of this blend of *melt* and *weld* to be satisfied that it was established in standard use, and they added it to the "New Words Section." It has been included in our dictionaries ever since.

Because the new *meld* is now a common word, it has attracted some unfavorable attention. Complicating the picture is the existence of an older *meld,* used to mean "to declare or announce (a card or cards) for a score in a card game (as pinochle or gin rummy)." Those who regard the new *meld* as an unwelcome development tend to perceive it as a misuse of the cardplayers' word. But the new *meld* is not a misuse of the older word. It is, instead, an entirely new coinage. It suggests a smooth and thorough blending of two or more things into a single, homogeneous whole. Connotations of smoothness are its most distinctive characteristic, and its sound reinforces those connotations.

We do not think you should feel nervous about using *meld.* Dictionaries have long recognized it as a standard word, and its use in reputable writing has been common for years.

He melded the operation of five U.S. affiliates into a smoothly functioning division —*Time*, 18 Feb. 1974

... in which he melds the musical traditions of these countries —Hans Fantel, *N.Y. Times Book Rev.,* 22 July 1979

... where Indian philosophy and custom met and melded with their Chinese counterparts —Geri Trotta, *Gourmet,* May 1981

The verb has also given rise, by functional shift, to a related noun:

... the choreographer's meld of classic and folk idiom —Anna Kisselgoff, *N.Y. Times,* 25 Feb. 1971

... this meld of the mundane and the poetic —Robert Kirsch, *Los Angeles Times Book Rev.,* 6 June 1976

memento see MOMENTO.

memorandum Quite a bit has been written about the plural forms of *memorandum,* starting back in the 1870s when Richard Grant White put forward a plea for the English plural *memorandums.* Hall 1917 noted that *memorandums* was well established, citing Boswell and Defoe, among others.

Modern concern is over *memoranda* used as a singular and dates back to 1906. Since then quite a few commentators take on the subject, right up to Garner 1998. Almost everybody

discourages *memoranda* as a singular and abominates *memorandas.*

Ordinarily when there is so much discussion of a Latin plural, we have a lot of evidence for the alleged misuse, but not in this case: *memoranda,* singular, and *memorandas* almost never appear in print. We do have a little evidence from speech, particularly from congressional hearings.

So apparently there is not much of a problem here, and no real writing problem at all. *Memoranda* and *memorandums* are about equally common and both have good literary precedent; you can take your pick.

For more foreign plurals that vex English speakers, see LATIN PLURALS.

mentality This was an uncommon word until the early 20th century, when it first came to be widely used in the sense "way of thinking; outlook." Its newly common use was noted with disapproval by Fowler 1926, who considered it a "superfluous word" and hoped that it would be allowed to "lapse into its former obscurity." That hope has not been realized. The "outlook" sense of *mentality* has continued to be common, and it has attracted relatively little critical attention since Fowler's time. As Burchfield 1996 notes, it often carries overtones of disparagement:

... top officers tended to have banana-boat mentalities in a jet age —Albert H. Johnston, *Publishers Weekly,* 2 Aug. 1976

... a study of greed, of the small-town mentality, of alienated youth —Newgate Callendar, *N.Y. Times Book Rev.,* 21 Aug. 1983

Bestowing a million-dollar payday on a single survivor ... reflects the day-trader mentality of the dot-com era —James Wolcott, *Vanity Fair,* September 2000

metathesis The process whereby a sound hops out of its proper place, so to speak, and pops up elsewhere in the word, or switches places with another sound in the word, is called *metathesis* (\mə-'tath-ə-səs\). A good example of metathesis is one pronunciation of *integral,* in which the \r\ has moved from after the \g\ to after the \t\, thus yielding \'in-trə-gəl\, as though the word were spelled "intregal." We have recorded this pronunciation from numerous educated speakers over the years, including former President Gerald Ford, Governor Nelson Rockefeller, broadcaster Edward R. Murrow, and professors Lionel Trilling and Marvin Harris. The reason for this alteration in the sequence of sounds is probably attraction to the pattern exemplified by such words as *intricate, introvert,* and (in one pronunciation variant) *interesting,* and also, at one remove, by words like *gentrified* and *centrally.* It is not a matter of \intr-\ being simply "easier to say" than \int . . . r-\, since under different accentual conditions that cluster is sometimes broken up in relaxed pronunciation: thus *introduced* commonly becomes \ˌint-ər-'düst\, in which form the first \t\, no longer protected by an immediately following \r\, drops out, and the word is pronounced as though spelled "innerduced." Again, such variations come from the lips of quite well-educated speakers; we have recorded \ˌkänt-ər-'byü-shən\ from no less a figure than Mitford M. Mathews, author of A Dictionary of Americanisms.

In the above examples, a single consonant has hopped out of place. But consonants can also exchange places, as in the mispronunciation of *relevant* as \'rev-ə-lənt\. Once again we apparently have a case of attraction to pattern: compare *reveille, revel(ing)*, and more distantly, *envelope, invalid* (noun), and *revelation*.

When we hear such shifts occurring sporadically around us, they may sound to some like gross and hopeless slipups that could never become standard in the language. But the products of metathesis have indeed been taken up over the course of history. One notorious variant of *ask,* \'aks\, in effect goes all the way back to Old English, where *axian* and *ascian* existed side by side, and it is only by comparison with cognate forms in other languages that we can deduce that *-sk-* is the historically earlier order. In the case of *wasp,* it is rather the metathesized form that has become standard, since while Old English has both *wæsp* and *wæps* and Latin has *vespa,* overall comparative evidence points to a prehistoric *-ps-* as original. Similar vicissitudes mark the history of *bird, hasp,* and *tamarisk.* In the latter case the metathesis took place within the development of Latin, *tamariscus* out of earlier *tamarix* (where *sc* = \sk\ and *x* = \ks\), and English simply took over the result. Both metathesized and unmetathesized forms are visible in English *scintilla,* taken direct from the classical Latin *scintilla* "spark," and *stencil,* borrowed (via French) from a Vulgar Latin form we reconstruct as *stincilla. Palaver* and *parabola* are likewise metathetic doublets, though further sound change has obscured the relationship between them.

See also CALVARY, CAVALRY; IRRELEVANT.

meticulous This adjective, which is derived ultimately from the Latin *metus,* "fear," was a rare word until about the turn of the 20th century, after which it became both common and, for a time, controversial. The OED shows that it had some use in the 16th and 17th centuries as a fancy synonym of *fearful* and *timid,* but by 1700 it had fallen into disuse. In the 19th century it acquired (perhaps by way of the French *méticuleux*) a second sense, "overly careful about small details":

The decadence of Italian prose composition into laboured mannerism and meticulous propriety —John Addington Symonds, *Renaissance in Italy,* 1877 (OED)

This sense in turn gave rise to what is now its almost invariable sense, "painstakingly careful." *Meticulous* has been widely used in this sense for many decades:

. . . gave to the fashioning of the written word all the fastidious, meticulous austerity of devotion that she knew —Rose Macaulay, *Told by an Idiot,* 1923

His meticulous integrity in business and his accuracy in money matters —Henry Seidel Canby, *Thoreau,* 1939

. . . she had observed a meticulous neutrality. . . . nothing could have been more correct than the behavior of her Government —Sir Winston Churchill, *The Unrelenting Struggle,* 1942

The meticulous care with which the operation in Sicily was planned has paid dividends —Franklin D. Roosevelt, fireside chat, 28 July 1943, in *Nothing to Fear,* ed. B. D. Zevin, 1946

. . . a meticulous eye for detail —Howard E. Gruber, *N.Y. Times Book Rev.,* 22 July 1979

. . . some kind of fine and meticulous craftsman —Doris Lessing, *The Good Terrorist,* 1985

In dense, meticulous arguments . . . Brooten mounts an assault on that view —Cullen Murphy, *Atlantic,* August 1993

She was very much the craftswoman, all her work meticulous, slow, perfect —Simon Winchester, *The Professor and the Madman,* 1998

The newly common *meticulous* attracted predictably unfavorable attention in the first half of the 20th century. Its early critics (such as Fowler 1906) had no use for it in any sense, regarding it as a foreign affectation. But by about the 1930s the standard critical view had come to be that it was correctly used in its older and less common sense, "overly careful," and incorrectly used in its newer and popular sense, "painstakingly careful." The older sense was considered correct because it retains, however slightly, connotations of timidity and fearfulness, while the newer sense has lost such connotations altogether. Dictionaries, including our own, were also slow to recognize the newer sense, and its failure to appear in standard references no doubt encouraged many people to regard it as an error. Theodore Bernstein, whose dictionary of choice was Webster's Second 1934 (in which the newer sense does not appear), was still insisting in 1965 that *meticulous* should only mean "timorously careful and overcareful." A newer dictionary would have told him differently, as would most of his fellow commentators (such as Evans 1957. Follett 1966, and Copperud 1970, 1980). The use of *meticulous* to mean "overly careful" is now rare. Its use to mean "painstakingly careful," on the other hand, is extremely common, and there is absolutely no question about its propriety.

might   See MAY 2.

might could   *Might could* is a double modal found in regional American speech, chiefly in Southern and southern Midland areas, according to the Dictionary of American Regional English. *Might could* is the most conspicuous of a number of double modals with *might*; others include *might can, might should,* and *might would.*

These constructions are not found in print except as part of reported or fictional speech. Dialect surveys and fictional use associate them with less educated or uneducated speakers. Dialect surveys report that cultured informants tend to avoid the construction; we cannot tell whether this is a result of schooling or is a mark of social status or is simply a typical pattern for a familiar form not used in the presence of strangers. Here are a few examples:

". . . My boy Sammy might could pay it for me. . . ." —Erskine Caldwell, *A House in the Uplands,* 1946

He might could help 'em —John Faulkner, *Men Working,* 1941 (in ADD)

I might can do it. I don't know now —Aunt Arie, quoted in *The Foxfire Book,* ed. Eliot Wigginton, 1972

He might should've called a timeout the play before —John Hannah, professional football telecast, 16 Nov. 1986

might of   See OF 2.

might should   See MIGHT COULD.

might would   see MIGHT COULD.

mighty   The use of *mighty* as an adverbial intensifier has been looked at askance since at least 1829, when the sentence "That is a mighty big dog" was given in Joseph Hervey Hull's *Grammar* as an "incorrect phrase" to be corrected. The issue is largely an American one; it does not appear much in British usage sources. And its origin appears to be in the assertion of Bostonian cultural superiority: not only was Hull's *Grammar* published in Boston, but the Boston *Pearl* of 20 Feb. 1836 is recorded in Thornton 1912 as labeling *mighty* a southern corruption.

Similar labels have, of course, been repeat-

ed right down to the present day by writers of usage books and college handbooks. The labels applied are most often *colloquial* and *informal*; others include *old-fashioned* and *quaint,* and several handbooks discourage its use in "most writing."

Hall 1917 seems to have been the first to investigate the use of *mighty*. The intensive use is not recent—the OED records it from before 1300; Hall adds many instances of his own finding from literature right down to his own time. He is unable to discover when the word dropped out of the literary language.

Since the stigmatizing of *mighty* appears to have started in Boston, one would assume that it was not current in everyday English in New England. But such is not the case. *Mighty* turns up in the writing of such proper Bostonians as Oliver Wendell Holmes, the elder:

But he said a mighty good thing about mathematics —*The Autocrat of the Breakfast-Table,* 1858

And Henry Adams:

. . . man knows mighty little, and may some day learn enough of his own ignorance to fall down and pray —quoted in John Buchan, *Pilgrim's Way,* 1940

It is common in the letters of the younger Oliver Wendell Holmes:

. . . I am mighty sceptical of hours of labor and minimum wages regulation —letter, 8 Jan. 1917

His Corsican chauffeur was mighty careful not to run down a hen —letter, 29 July 1923

It is probably safe to assume, then, that the commentators who started questioning the propriety of *mighty* were not even thoroughly acquainted with the vocabulary of Bostonians.

Hall 1917 opines that *mighty* was brought to the U.S. at a time when it was current in London English—a conclusion safe enough, since the word seems to have been in current use in London English from the 17th through (at least) the 19th centuries. Boswell records it frequently in his *Life of Samuel Johnson* (1791) as appearing in the speech of the great man:

An ancient estate should always go to males. It is mighty foolish to let a stranger have it because he marries your daughter. . . .

Although our evidence of the currency of *mighty* in British English is equivocal because scarce, there is no doubt it is firmly established in American English—especially in the Southern and southern Midland areas, but by no means limited to them.

In current American English it usually conveys a folksy, down-home feeling or a rural atmosphere:

"It's plain and simple fare," said Aunt Tennie Cloer, "but mighty filling and mighty satisfying. . . ." —quoted by John Parris, *Asheville* (N.C.) *Citizen-Times,* 18 Jan. 1976

A man must be mighty serious about his squirrel hunting —Stuart Williams, *Field & Stream,* February 1972

It is also a feature of a relaxed and chatty style:

. . . fried chicken, country ham, baked cheese grits, candied apples, turnip greens, corn bread and biscuits. That sounds mighty good to me, and I am all for trotting out American regional cooking —Julia Child, *N.Y. Times Mag.,* 16 Jan. 1977

It sounded mighty formidable, like someone not to be trifled with —Garrison Keillor, quoted in *Update* (Univ. of Minn.), Fall 1981

. . . a Tennessee whisky and a mighty tasty one —Terry Sullivan, *GQ,* January 1998

It is common in the letters of literary people:

. . . and a mighty fine fellow you'll say he is —Robert Frost, letter, 1 July 1914

. . . a curious voyage that has really been mighty enjoyable —Alexander Woollcott, letter, 11 Sept. 1917

All in all we have had a mighty good winter —E. B. White, letter, 18 Jan. 1940

It was mighty thoughtful of you to send me that quote from dear old Sam Adams's letter —James Thurber, letter, 3 Dec. 1958

It is even used from time to time in more formal or more sophisticated contexts, where it can be counted on to add emphasis by being unexpected:

. . . the chairman made sure that there were mighty few of them —Mollie Panter-Downes, *New Yorker,* 30 Oct. 1971

Has E-phoria ended? Highflying Internet stocks look mighty weak —Gretchen Morgenson, *N.Y. Times,* 30 May 1999

Hall 1917 thought perhaps you would not want to use *mighty* in a sermon, but judged it useful in other contexts where you might find it handy. Reader's Digest 1983 says this: "If not quite suitable for the most ceremonial of formal contexts, the adverb *mighty* is Standard American English in all others." We agree with both; *mighty* does have a force and flavor all its own, and if it is natural to you, you should not be afraid to use it where you think it will serve a purpose.

militate 1. According to our evidence, *militate* is almost always used with a preposition, and that preposition almost always is *against*:

. . . what he hated about America . . . was everything that militated against such a free life —Mark Schorer, *New Republic,* 6 Apr. 1953

. . . this has happened rarely so far, and a factor militating against the possibility is the variety of outlets of the reprint houses —James T. Farrell, *Literature and Morality,* 1947

Occasionally *militate* is used with *in favor (of):*

This fact alone militates in favor of Tunisia's French connection —Ray Alan, *New Republic,* 20 Sept. 1954

. . . considerations which at the time militated in their favor —Walter Millis, *N.Y. Herald Tribune Book Rev.,* 9 Feb. 1947

Although Richard Grant White writing in 1870 cautioned against using *militate against* and Ambrose Bierce in 1909 declared "there is no such word," *militate* has been around since 1642 and continues in widespread use in contemporary English. Modern commentators do not object to it.

2. See MITIGATE.

millennium With the coming of the year 2000, the word *millennium* received a great deal of use, but frequency of reference did not eliminate the single *-n* spelling *millenium.* This spelling has long been well attested in our files and still claims nearly 10% of the occurrences of the word. But no dictionary or spelling book that we are aware of recognizes *millenium.* You had better spell it with as many *n*'s as *l*'s.

mineralogy See GENEALOGY.

minimal Why is there a problem about *minimal?* There seem to be two reasons: increase in use of the word in recent years, and dictionary definitions that fail to explain that use any too clearly. As a result the commentators have been concerned, because they did not know how to gauge the usage that they saw. The overcrammed definitions in some earlier dictionaries have been improved in Merriam-Webster's Collegiate Dictionary, Tenth Edition. It shows that the nonspecialized uses of *minimal* fall into three broad groups. The first of these is the "least possible" sense; it is identified most readily by the application of *minimal* to a noun denoting something undesirable:

Their object was to deal China a crushing blow with a minimal expenditure of men and materials —Nathaniel Peffer, *Harper's,* September 1938

. . . it is contoured to slice through the air with minimal fuel-wasting drag —advt., *Wall Street Jour.,* 28 May 1980

The formula could work this year if injuries are minimal —Paul Zimmerman, *Sports Illustrated,* 1 Sept. 1982

A more frequently met sense is one meaning "barely adequate":

... for the maintenance of minimal German living standards —William Harlan Hale, *Harper's,* December 1945

... held back in agreeing to even the minimal inspection —Norman Cousins, *Saturday Rev.,* 30 Oct. 1971

... too poorly trained and motivated to hold even minimal jobs —Sylvia Nasar, *Fortune,* 17 Mar. 1986

The third is "very small or slight":

... brought together everything, with minimal exceptions —Irving Kolodin, *Saturday Rev.,* 28 June 1975

... had a minimal interest in the world outside —Joyce Carol Oates, *N.Y. Times Book Rev.,* 15 Apr. 1973

... public opinion soon wrote off the Atlantic Charter as of minimal importance —*Times Literary Supp.,* 9 Apr. 1970

minimize The commentary on *minimize* in the usage books primarily consists of objecting to the sense meaning "to estimate in the least possible terms" (a sense recorded in most dictionaries).

The complaint seems to hinge either on a wrongheaded insistence on the word's having only one meaning or on excessive concern with the word *estimate,* which is used in the definition in several dictionaries, including ours and the OED, as if *minimize* were therefore some technical term and hence could not mean "play down." However, *play down* is simply an idiomatic equivalent of what the dictionary definitions are really saying. Here are some examples of the sense:

... sources which have steadily rigged statistics to minimize adverse trends —*American Mercury,* February 1953

... did not try to hide or minimize the uglier aspects of the Resistance —*Times Literary Supp.,* 18 Dec. 1969

... urged the public not to minimise the bomb problem —Andrew Boyle, *The Listener,* 30 Aug. 1973

... dresses for the maid of honor—all selected to minimize her sister Margaret's stockiness —Shirley Ann Grau, *Cosmopolitan,* January 1972

This sense is a century old and entirely standard.

miniscule, minuscule This word is derived from the Latin adjective *minusculus* and is etymologically related to *minus.* If you aim to be consistent with its etymology, therefore, you should spell it *minuscule.* Most people do:

... the chances of ... being caught cheating are minuscule —Andrew Zimbalist, *Brill's Content,* April 2000

... genetic variation among ... populations was minuscule —Jim Holt, *N.Y. Times Book Rev.,* 16 Apr. 2000

... home run records of monumental and minuscule proportions fell —David Sabino, *Sports Illustrated,* 17 July 2000

... the minuscule demonstrations against the Korean War —Harold Meyerson, *Atlantic,* August 2000

The spelling *miniscule* is also common, however. This spelling was first recorded at the end of the 19th century (*minuscule* dates back to 1705), but it did not begin to appear frequently in edited prose until the 1940s. The spelling presumably owes something to association with the combining form *mini-* and with such familiar words as *minimal* and *minimum.* Our evidence indicates that it occurs in standard contexts:

... miniscule socialist parties —Franklin Foer, *New Republic,* 1 May 2000

Scalpers. Traders who try to eke out profits from miniscule movements of 1/8th or 1/16th of a point —Tia O'Brien, *Upside,* January 2000

And those that do wait successfully are miniscule in number —Ernest Holsendolph, *Emerge,* November 1999

Nevertheless, *miniscule* continues to be widely regarded as a spelling error. No usage commentator will tolerate it. Our own view is that any spelling which occurs so commonly in perfectly reputable and carefully edited books and periodicals must be regarded as a standard variant. You should be aware, however, that you stand some chance of being corrected if you use it.

minister The verb *minister* is most often used with *to:*

He pictured her then with a glow on her face ... that ministered to him alone —Winston Churchill, *The Crisis,* 1901

... something still eludes us in the career of Jonathan Edwards and in the community to which he ministered —Edmund S. Morgan, *N.Y. Times Book Rev.,* 13 July 1980

It has also occurred infrequently with *among*:

> While ministering diligently among his rural parishioners —*Dictionary of American Biography,* 1936

minor See IMPLICIT COMPARATIVE.

minus The use of *minus* as a preposition more or less equivalent to *without* has attracted occasional disapproval for many decades. Such usage dates back to the 19th century:

> We [arrived] . . . about six in the evening, *minus* one horse —J. B. Fraser, *Travels in Koordistan,* 1840 (OED)

This use of *minus* was discouraged in several handbooks on writing in the early 20th century. More recently, a few critics have stressed what they regard as its facetious quality; Bernstein 1965, for example, describes it as "a jocular casualism." Our evidence shows that it does sometimes occur in writing that has a playful tone:

> . . . a reissue of the bearded representative who refused to sponsor an antiwar resolution. . . . We find him about the same but minus the chin spinach —Julian Moynahan, *N.Y. Times Book Rev.,* 17 Oct. 1982

But *minus* is also commonly used in serious, if not highly solemn, writing:

> . . . a condition for dealing with the Saigon regime minus Thieu —I. F. Stone, *N.Y. Rev. of Books,* 9 Mar. 1972

> The property is now a state farm, the castle, minus most of its looted furnishings, a museum —Eleanor Perenyi, *Green Thoughts,* 1983

> . . . much of the National Democrats' vicious and intolerant nationalism—minus, of course, their Catholicism—was integrated into the official ideology of the Polish People's Republic —Norman Davies, *N.Y. Times Book Rev.,* 2 Sept. 1984

The full sense of *minus* in such contexts is usually "deprived of" or "having lost" rather than simply "without." The word still retains something of an informal quality, but that does not make it inappropriate in most current writing.

minuscule See MINISCULE, MINUSCULE.

minutia The meaning of *minutia* is "a minute or minor detail." The word is almost always now used in its plural form:

> . . . seldom are minutiae piled on —Bradley Miller, *American Scholar,* Winter 1981/82

> . . . only after . . . all minutiae of a complex protocol have been observed —Fred Bruemmer, *Natural History,* December 1984

Evans 1957 says that the plural can be either *minutias* or *minutiae,* but our evidence shows that the only form now used is *minutiae.* Bernstein 1965 cites as an error a sentence in which *minutiae* is used as a singular. This does not appear to be a widespread problem; we have no further evidence of the error in our files. Janis 1984, on the other hand, warns against using *minutia* as a plural, and for this we do have some evidence:

> She has described her early years in their minutia —Herbert Lottman, *Columbia Forum,* Fall 1970

> . . . acquiring encyclopedic knowledge about minutia —Frederick Goldman & Linda R. Burnett, *Need Johnny Read?,* 1971

This use of *minutia* is not established as standard.

For other foreign plurals, see LATIN PLURALS.

mischievous A pronunciation \mis-'chē-vē-əs\, and consequent spelling *mischievious,* is of long standing: evidence for this spelling goes back to the 16th century. Our pronunciation files contain modern attestations ranging from dialect speakers of the islands of the Chesapeake Bay to Herbert Hoover. The pronunciation and spelling must be considered nonstandard but are in a somewhat special category, as they may be used deliberately and humorously, not to make fun of someone else's speech, but because the folksy sound and the echo from *devious* often add an appropriate flavor to the semantics of the word. See also GRIEVOUS.

mishap Bernstein 1958, 1965, Harper 1975, 1985, Shaw 1975, Bryson 1984, and Garner 1998 all maintain that *mishap* should be reserved for minor unwanted accidents. There are, however, several factors working against the success of such a restriction.

First, there is history. The association of triviality with *mishap* is recent; older literary citations carry no such connotation. In Shakespeare's *The Comedy of Errors,* for instance, the old Syracusan merchant Ægeon tells "sad stories of [his] own mishaps," which include a shipwreck in which his wife and one of his twin sons were lost. Although Ægeon knows they were rescued and not drowned, the accident was not trivial.

Second, the word is of a convenient length for newspaper headline writers, who often use it in place of the longer *accident* no matter how serious the occurrence. Thus we see headlines like these:

> Practice Mishap Kills Driver —*Springfield* (Mass.) *Morning Union,* 8 Feb. 1984

30 die in mishap —*The Times* (London), cited in Bryson 1984

J. J. ASTOR DROWNED IN LINER MISHAP —headline over the report of the sinking of the *Titanic,* cited in Howard 1984

This use can carry over into ordinary prose:

> . . . no mention of his having been killed in an auto mishap —Gregory Corso, *Evergreen,* August 1967

> . . . a woman whose fiancé was mortally injured in a traffic mishap —James Podgers, *ABA Jour.,* January 1995

> . . . dangerous levels of radiation from hushed-up nuclear mishaps —John J. Stephan, *Current History,* October 1993

But undeniably *mishap* is also used for trivial occurrences:

> After an additional series of humorous mishaps, ugly duckling Bernice becomes a beautiful swam —Sue-Ellen Beauregard, *Booklist,* 1 May 1991

> All sorts of little mishaps can blight a Broadway production —Bowen Northrup, *Wall Street Jour.,* 24 July 1972

> . . . provoked by some mishap in the kitchen —Russell Baker, *Growing Up,* 1982

And sometimes no one can know how serious or trivial the mishap may be:

> They spent many hours in a simulated capsule . . . preparing themselves for the possibility of mishap during flight —*Current Biography,* November 1965

In actual use, then, *mishap* may be applied to either serious or inconsequential occurrences, always unfortunate for the person involved. It can be used to deliberately downplay the seriousness of what happened:

> A spokesman for Metropolitan Edison, owners of the plant, insisted for several hours that a "mechanical mishap" had occurred, not a nuclear accident —H. L. Stevenson, *UPI Reporter,* 5 Apr. 1979

While *mishap* most often connotes an occurrence that is not disastrous, it is often felt to be neutral, as its occasional modification by *minor, humorous,* or *major* attests.

mislead, misled The spelling error that occurs with the verb *lead* also occurs, not surprisingly, with *mislead.* The past tense and past participle, *misled,* is sometimes spelled *mislead:*

> . . . if a checklist format is used to project the findings, the user can be mislead —*Language Arts,* October 1976

Remember, when the verb is being used in the past tense or past participle, get the *-lead* out. See also LEAD, LED.

misplaced modifiers, misrelated modifiers See DANGLING MODIFIERS.

missile Bremner 1980 and Copperud 1970, 1980 note that *missile* is often misspelled *missle. Missile* is tough for us Americans; the same pronunciation also suggests such alternatives as *missal* and *mistle(toe).* If you think of the British pronunciation with \-ıīl\ at the end, you will have no trouble.

misspell Copperud 1970, 1980 notes that "with ultimate perversity" this word is often misspelled *mispell.* The error is rare in edited writing, but we do have some evidence of it:

> Catch boss's typos, mispellings, etc. —*The Affirmative Action Handbook,* 1978

This ranks high on the list of Most Embarrassing Spelling Errors.

mistrustful *Mistrustful* is usually used with *of* when it takes a preposition:

> . . . the Russians are so mistrustful of everybody that they never know what to believe —Upton Sinclair, *A World to Win,* 1946

> . . . be mistrustful of the ways of Western journalists —Norman Stone, *N.Y. Times Book Rev.,* 28 Oct. 1984

Sometimes *toward* is used:

> . . . has described three such motherless children as . . . mistrustful toward older people —Matthew Josephson, *Southern Rev.,* Winter 1973

mitigate This verb has several senses, but it functions primarily in current English as a synonym of *alleviate,* with suggestions of *moderate:*

> . . . to mitigate injustices in both communist and capitalist societies —John Wilkinson, *Center Mag.,* March 1969

> . . . did little to mitigate their unhappiness —*The Tower Commission Report,* 1987

It is not a rare word, but neither is it an extremely common one, and many people no doubt feel less than sure about its meaning. This uncertainty has in recent decades led to its being used with *against* in place of the similar but unrelated verb *militate,* meaning "to have weight or effect":

> . . . some intangible and invisible social force that mitigates against him —"Centaur in Brass," in *The Collected Stories of William Faulkner,* 1950

. . . his looks tend to mitigate against him intellectually —David Halberstam, *McCall's*, November 1971

. . . such things tend to mitigate against strong "character" —Jonathan Chait, *New Republic*, 20 Dec. 1999

Such usage is comparable in several ways to the use of *flaunt* to mean "flout": it has its origins in the confusion of two similar words, it occurs primarily among educated people, and it is universally regarded as an error by usage commentators.

Flesch 1983 and Garner 1998 think the confusion is very widespread, but our files show it is not as common as *flaunt-flout*. Flesch also says that we should give up and accept it as an American idiom. *Mitigate against* may reach that status someday—it shows no sign of going away—but it has not done so yet, and your use of it will probably attract some critical attention. We suggest you limit your use of *mitigate* to its moderating sense and use *militate against*.

See also FLAUNT, FLOUT.

mix When *mix* takes a preposition, it is most often *with*:

It must be remembered that he had never mixed on easy terms with boys and girls of his own age —Robertson Davies, *Tempest-tost*, 1951

. . . a peculiar ability to merge and mix with other social groups —Walter Lippmann, *Atlantic*, March 1955

. . . Mr. Strauss mixed a college deferment with some later luck on the draft lottery —J. Anthony Lukas, *N.Y. Times Book Rev.*, 11 June 1978

Mix is less often used with *in* or *into*:

He informs all office seekers that it is not in keeping with his position as judge to mix in politics —*American Guide Series: Nevada*, 1940

Unfortunately prestige gets mixed into education at every turn —James B. Conant, *Slums and Suburbs*, 1961

Once in a while *mix* takes *within*:

Political shifts and clashes which . . . were cast to mix within the vast crucible of the interior —Russell Lord, *Behold Our Land*, 1938

mixed metaphor This is an entry in several usage books and handbooks for the same reason *malapropism* is: it seems a shame to waste good comic material. Mixed metaphors are essentially a matter of beginning with one figurative expression and ending with another. These are doubtless more frequent in speech than in writing, for writers at least have the opportunity to go back and revise. Of course, they sometimes fail to do so. Here are a few samples without their authors' names:

This field of research is so virginal that no human eye has ever set foot in it —Ph.D. dissertation cited in *Linguistic Reporter*, April 1981

. . . seems rather tame during the first taste or two, but gradually builds up a head of steam that leaves one breathing fire —*Gourmet*, January 1979

. . . American scientists stole a trump on the Soviet Union —*Springfield* (Mass.) *Morning Union*, 12 Sept. 1985

. . . an almost universal crescendo of hysteria and violence is the path through the horns of the dilemma —*A Center Occasional Paper*, 1971

It should be noted that sometimes a mixed metaphor may result when the writer is so accustomed to the figurative sense of a word that he or she forgets its metaphorical origin. Thus some mixed metaphors can be useful evidence for the lexicographer that an extended sense is established. These last two examples are perhaps such evidence:

The ecologists are hammering away at the population growth bottleneck in an effort to shave it to reasonable proportions —cited in Bernstein 1971

Bond's knees, the Achilles' heel of all skiers, were beginning to ache —Ian Fleming, cited in Barzun 1985

All we can suggest is that you look back over what you have written for any figurative language that may draw an unintended laugh.

See also MALAPROPISM; SYNTACTIC BLEND.

mock As a verb, *mock* is usually transitive; however, when it is intransitive and is used with a preposition, it is most often used with *at*:

She was a handsome, insolent hussy, who mocked at the youth —D. H. Lawrence, *Sons and Lovers*, 1913

. . . voices screaming and mocking at me —Frank Reynolds, *Evergreen*, June 1967

modal See DOUBLE MODAL.

molten Several commentators point out that the adjective *molten* in its "liquefied by heat" sense is now limited in application to substances such as metals and rocks that require great heat to be melted. Our evidence, in general, supports that observation:

. . . a stream of molten metal —*Times Literary Supp.*, 30 July 1971

. . . effects that molten glass can produce —Helen Harris, *Town & Country,* August 1979

. . . a fresh batch of molten rock —Richard A. Kerr, *Science,* 1 May 1981

Molten does, however, have some persistent use in describing melted cheese:

. . . molten Parmesan cheese —C. S. Forester, *Holiday,* October 1957

. . . sautéed onions, molten cheese —Jane & Michael Stern, *Cook's,* September/October 1986

Such usage is not wrong, but it is atypical.

momentarily A relatively new sense of this word has drawn a fair number of attacks in recent years from a small but determined group of critics. The disputed sense is "at any moment; in a moment," as in "We'll be leaving momentarily." Its detractors insist that *momentarily* is correct only in its original sense, "for a moment," which was first recorded in 1654. This sense, however, appears to have been little used until the 20th century (the first of our dictionaries to enter it was Webster 1909), but it is now extremely common:

. . . the Pacific breezes momentarily gave way to a brisker wind —*Times Literary Supp.,* 16 Apr. 1970

. . . Tilden had such a striking manner on the tennis court that you could hardly take your eyes off him. even momentarily —Herbert Warren Wind, *New Yorker,* 15 Feb. 1988

Fowler 1926 brought the adverb *momently* into his discussion of *momentarily,* but we will ignore *momently* here, as we have no current evidence of its use in the U.S. and Burchfield 1996 finds it largely restricted to (British) literary use.

Burchfield also notes that the "in a moment" sense, which dates from the late 1920s, is American. It is not inherently inferior to the older and more frequently used "for a moment" sense. Although some critics claim that the newer sense makes the word ambiguous, it does not. The meaning of each is almost always made clear by the context in which it occurs:

. . . more than ever convinced that the small unfamiliar stateroom . . . had momentarily been filled and then emptied of black sea water —John Hawkes, *Fiction,* vol. 1, no. 4, 1973

The menu said that momentarily we should be sipping consomme from shallow silver cups —John Hawkes, *Fiction,* vol. 1, no. 4, 1973

Most people realize that it is possible for a word to have more than one meaning and still not muddle its users. There is no need to restrict yourself to the more common sense of *momentarily* if you have a use for the other.

momento *Momento* is a rather rare spelling variant of *memento.* It is unetymological, since it obscures the word's relation to *memory* and *remember,* and probably shows the influence of *moment.* Some call it a misspelling, but it appears often enough in edited prose to have been considered acceptable for entry in at least two dictionaries: Webster's Third and the OED Supplement.

. . . a nostalgic momento of an earlier century —Joseph Wechsberg, *New Yorker,* 28 Mar. 1953

. . . a satisfyingly real momento of my enjoyment —Margaret Forster, *The Writer,* October 1968

. . . lexical momentos of the pop culture —John Algeo, *American Speech,* Winter 1980

The spelling is attested as early as 1853 in a letter written by Chauncey A. Goodrich, professor at Yale, son-in-law of Noah Webster, and first editor in chief of Merriam-Webster dictionaries. The OED Supplement instances George Eliot from 1871 and Dylan Thomas from 1951.

moneys, monies In most of its uses, *money* has no plural, but when the reference is to discrete sums of money, usually obtained from various sources or distributed to various individuals or groups, the plural *moneys* or *monies* is often used:

. . . union pension-fund moneys are being used to destroy union jobs —Jeremy Rifkin & Randy Barber, *Saturday Rev.,* 2 Sept. 1978

. . . ad hoc collections of public and private monies —Fred Ferretti, *N.Y. Times,* 13 July 1980

The plural *monies* has occasionally been criticized because it suggests a singular *mony* rather than *money.* It is, however, an old and perfectly respectable variant that is used about as commonly as *moneys,* and it is recognized as standard in all current dictionaries.

monopoly *Monopoly* is used with several prepositions. Shaw 1972 and Bernstein 1965 prescribe the use of *of,* while Evans 1957 says that the use of *of* is British and the use of *on* is American. According to our evidence, *of* has been the preposition most commonly used with *monopoly* on both sides of the Atlantic:

... our illusions ... that we have a monopoly of energy, know-how, culture and morality —Adlai E. Stevenson, *Look,* 22 Sept. 1953

... a monopoly of atomic weapons —Barry Goldwater, *The Conscience of a Conservative,* 1960

... the clergy had enjoyed a fairly close monopoly of trained intelligence —G. M. Trevelyan, *English Social History,* 1942

The richer countries' monopoly of science and technology —*Times Literary Supp.,* 27 Aug. 1971

However, Evans may well have noticed a trend, as our evidence for the past 30 years or more indicates that the use of *monopoly on* is probably more common now in American English than *monopoly of*:

No one has a monopoly on virtue or truth —Bill Moyers, quoted in *N.Y. Herald Tribune,* 4 Jan. 1964

In the cities, however, cadre members can still be easily singled out by ... their monopoly on conversation —Jonathan Mirsky, *Saturday Rev.,* 1 July 1972

... the Soviet Union has a monopoly on the best sable —Angela Taylor, *N.Y. Times,* 29 May 1976

There still appears to be no use of *monopoly on* in British English.

Monopoly is also used, although less frequently, with *in* and *over*:

... exercising a complete and official monopoly in that field since January 1950 —*Current Biography 1953*

... we believe that monopoly in anything, including monopoly in religion, is a source of corruption —Reinhold Niebuhr, quoted in *Time,* 29 Sept. 1947

... entrenched institutional interests that had previously obtained a monopoly over beliefs in, say, astronomy —John Dewey, *Freedom and Culture,* 1939

... give English merchants an almost complete monopoly over the colonial import trade —Leon H. Canfield & Howard B. Wilder, *The Making of Modern America,* 1962

Although Shaw mentions use of *monopoly for,* our files show scant evidence for it:

... a few among them possessed a virtual monopoly for the underwriting of government loans —Rondo E. Cameron, *Jour. of Political Economy,* December 1953

moot The adjective *moot* has a sense that means "open to question; debatable" (and a related sense "disputed") which causes no real concern amongst prescribers of usage. The sense that means "deprived of practical significance; purely academic," however, makes a few of them uneasy. They know it originated in legal use, and they are reluctant to see the shift into general use as acceptable.

Webster's Third illustrates this sense of *moot* with two citations about legal matters. In the late 1950s, when Webster's Third was being edited, legal citations for this sense in our files outnumbered nonlegal ones by about four to one. Since then, this sense has become as firmly fixed in general English—at least in American English—as it is in legal English.

Whether this type of proliferation is good or bad is a moot question. The facts of life are that it exists —Representative Frank Thompson, quoted in *American School Board Jour.,* September 1968

Even inflation cannot justify charging $20 for a moderately-sized book. In Nash's case this complaint is moot, for his book would be expensive at any price —Philip Rosenberg, *N.Y. Times Book Rev.,* 20 June 1976

... a genuine Atlantic political culture might be the result—rendering the fears expressed in this article largely moot —John O'Sullivan, *National Rev.,* 6 Dec. 1999

moral, morale We have on hand a good number of handbooks and schoolbooks that try to distinguish these two words on the most simplistic of lines. However, if you look up these two nouns in a good dictionary, you will see that they are intimately intertwined. The chief problem seems to be the sense "esprit de corps." In present-day English *morale* is the usual spelling for this sense; *moral* is likely to be considered a misspelling. But it is not; the OED shows that *moral* was the original spelling for this sense. It was the spelling in French, and the sense was taken over from the French. And current dictionaries, such as Merriam-Webster's Collegiate Dictionary, Tenth Edition, still recognize this sense as one of the meanings of *moral.*

We recommend, however, that you use *morale* for the "esprit de corps" sense—most people do. Few, if any, use *morale* instead of *moral* for the lesson in a story.

more important, more importantly See IMPORTANT 1.

mortician This word is an Americanism that was coined as a synonym for *undertaker* in the 1890s. Mencken 1936 notes that it first occurred in a publication titled *Embalmers' Monthly* in 1895. Its euphemistic qualities have naturally attracted some derision over the years, but few people now are conscious of it as a euphemism, and its use in American English is common and unremarkable:

. . . asked by the hospital which mortician you wish to have called —*Harper's Weekly,* 9 Feb. 1976

. . . increased cancers among such occupationally exposed groups as beauticians and morticians —Ben A. Franklin, *N.Y. Times,* 20 Mar. 1984

Undertakers themselves, interestingly enough, apparently prefer the term *funeral director,* which is actually an even older euphemism, first recorded in 1886.

Moslem, Muslim *Moslem* is the older spelling, but *Muslim* is more used today perhaps because it is preferred by those of whom it is used and because it is a closer representation of the Arabic. Either is likely to be preferred to *Mohammedan* or *Muhammadan,* which some people find offensive.

most, almost The adverb *most* that is a shortening of *almost* has been attested in the written language since the early 17th century. It is in current use in speech and in standard writing of a not overly formal character.

Most "almost" is quite limited in application. It modifies the adjectives *all, every,* and *any*; the pronouns *all, anybody, anyone, anything, everybody, everyone,* and *everything;* the adverbs *always, anywhere,* and *everywhere.* There are other uses of *most* "almost" but they are dialectal or, perhaps, old-fashioned. Here are some examples of standard written use:

. . . with a technical equipment equal to most any demands —Irving Kolodin, *Saturday Rev.,* 30 Jan. 1954

. . . and most every conceivable type of four-wheeled vehicle —Malcolm S. Forbes, *Forbes,* 1 Dec. 1970

So most everybody in the bar was merely leaning on the bar —John McNulty, *New Yorker,* 31 Oct. 1953

. . . like most everyone else on the beach —David Arnold, *Boston Globe Mag.,* 2 Dec. 1979

These symbols . . . are most always used in pairs —Joseph Lasky, *Proofreading and Copy-Preparation,* 1949

. . . accompanies him most everywhere —Frank Deford, *Sports Illustrated,* 8 Aug. 1983

Most all of the poultry you purchase is ready-to-cook —Eva Medved, *The World of Food,* 3d ed., 1981

All of these uses are standard. Here are a few samples of dialectal or old-fashioned use:

It was most eleven when Josiah and me got to bed agin —Marietta Holley, "A Pleasure

Exertion," in *Mark Twain's Library of Humor,* 1888

It most froze me to hear such talk —Mark Twain, *Huckleberry Finn,* 1884, in *The Practical Cogitator,* ed. Charles P. Curtis, Jr., & Ferris Greenslet, 1945

"There's your moon, Midge," he said. . . . "I was watching it. It's most at the full."
                —Hamilton Basso, *The View from Pompey's Head,* 1954

A lot has been written about this *most.* From Bache 1869 to Trimmer & McCrimmon 1988 commentators and pedagogues disparage the word, calling it "inexcusable," "colloquial," "schoolgirlish," "dialectal," "incorrect," "folksy," "illiterate." Yet no native speaker of American English has any trouble with it, and it does not interfere with superlative *most.* As Evans 1957 observes, there is no theoretical or grammatical reason to object to the use. Indeed, the 120 years of opposition to *most* defy rational analysis. It is not even a covert marker of social status. It is simply an established American idiom. As you have noticed, its range of application is limited; it cannot be used everywhere that *almost* can. But within its sphere it is entirely respectable.

motive *Motive* is often followed by the preposition *for,* which is, in turn, often followed by a gerund:

Copernicus had no motive for misleading his fellowmen —George Bernard Shaw, *Man and Superman,* 1903

. . . had every motive for continued loyalty to Rome —*Times Literary Supp.,* 30 July 1971

. . . motives for doing something are often *not* good reasons for doing it —Wayne C. Booth, *Modern Dogma and the Rhetoric of Assent,* 1974

Motive is also sometimes followed by *of* or *behind*:

The Czechs at first suspected the purity of the mission's professed motive of helping them —*Current Biography,* May 1965

One of these pits contained twenty-seven skulls. . . . The motive behind this peculiar burial is not clear —Raymond W. Murray, *Man's Unknown Ancestors,* 1943

And sometimes *motive* is followed by *to* and an infinitive:

This was sufficient motive to endanger the peace of the frontier —Ray Allen Billington, *Westward Expansion,* 1949

Ms. *Ms.* is a blend of *Miss* and *Mrs.* and seems to have been originally devised as a convenience for business use in addressing letters when the sender did not know if the woman addressed was married or not. The utility of such a designation seems to have been recognized as long ago as the 18th century; the OED Supplement (under *certain*) has a 1754 citation in which the writer wishes such a term existed. It took a couple of centuries for one to be invented.

Once *Ms.* began to be used with some frequency, the feminist movement adopted it as a desirable honorific because, like *Mr.,* it was unmarked for marital status. The result of this adoption was a certain amount of controversy, most of it of the unenlightening variety, now mostly forgotten. Our evidence shows that it is now the standard form to use, especially in business correspondence, when a woman's marital status is unknown or irrelevant to matters at hand.

There are substantial treatments of the history and development of *Ms.* in Reader's Digest 1983 under *Miss* and in Copperud 1980 under *Ms.*

muchly Rather surprisingly, *muchly* has existed in our language for a long time. The first citation for it in the OED is dated 1621 and illustrates a straightforward use in a serious poetic context. The second OED citation, though, shows that in its early days *muchly* was also seen as something of an oddity:

> Commonly 'tis larded with fine new words, as Savingable, Muchly, Christ-Jesusness —J. Birkenhead, *Assembly-Man,* 1647 (OED)

Unlike *thusly* (which see), *muchly* has never really gained a foothold in mainstream English. It is rarely found in print and is most commonly used these days in speech, especially in the phrase "thank you muchly." People tend to use it instead of *much* when they want to inject a little interest or humor into a conventional or formulaic speech pattern; even after three and a half centuries, *muchly* retains the character of a novelty word.

mucous, mucus As has been pointed out by several commentators, the noun is spelled *mucus,* and the adjective is spelled *mucous.* This is not a troublesome matter for most writers, since neither word is likely to appear with great frequency except in strictly medical contexts; still, the occasional mistake may occur in general writing:

> The mucus membrane . . . could then proceed —*Harper's,* March 1971

> . . . a sticky mucous that acts like flypaper to trap ants and termites —*International Wildlife,* January/February 1983

multiple negation See DOUBLE NEGATIVE. Geneva Smitherman, in *Talkin and Testifyin*

(1977), has a discussion of the subtleties and nuances achievable in Black English with multiple negatives.

muse *Muse* is used about equally with *on, upon,* or *over:*

> . . . he took a moment or two to muse on it —Gertrude Samuels, *N.Y. Times,* 3 Oct. 1954

> . . . her silent mother mused on other things than topography —Thomas Hardy, *The Mayor of Casterbridge,* 1886

> They settled back into reposeful attitudes with airs of having accepted the matter. And they mused upon it —Stephen Crane, *The Red Badge of Courage,* 1895

> . . . muse upon the continuity and the tragic finality of life —Irving Howe, *New Republic,* 28 Mar. 1955

> . . . muse with kindly condescension over this token of bygone fashion —Virginia Woolf, *The Second Common Reader,* 1932

> . . . Cabot mused over the fact that the old bastard considered himself . . . one of the eminences of the great metropolis —James Purdy, *Cabot Wright Begins,* 1964

Muse also occurs, much less frequently, with *about:*

> Ever since man first mused about his own nature —Eric H. Lenneberg, *Biological Foundations of Language,* 1967

Muslim See MOSLEM, MUSLIM.

must of See OF 2.

mutual, common It has long been the practice of usage writers to condemn the use of *mutual* in the senses "shared in common" and "joint" because, they maintain, *mutual* must include the notion of reciprocity. The basis for this long-lived criticism goes back to two sources in the 18th century. The first of these is Samuel Johnson's 1755 Dictionary, which gave only one definition, "reciprocal." Fitzedward Hall 1873 points out that this is an error on Johnson's part; the first quotation under *mutual* is from Shakespeare's *Merchant of Venice* (1597) and is for the "common" sense. Johnson simply missed the meaning, and his omission is what we may call the passive 18th-century source.

The active 18th-century source is Baker 1770. Baker claimed never to have seen Johnson's Dictionary before writing his book, so he must have developed his opinion independently or gotten it from some unidentified source. Baker insists on the "reciprocal" sense and objects to expressions like "our mutual benefactor" and "our mutual friend"; although he gives no actual citations of such use, he says that many writers use such expressions. He prescribes *common* as correct in such expressions and quotes with approbation a letter of John Locke's using "our common friend."

Subsequent criticism of the "common" sense of *mutual* seems to derive directly from Baker. The subject got a considerable boost in popularity when Charles Dickens published *Our Mutual Friend* in 1864. After Alford 1866 (who does not mention Dickens, though) almost every 19th-century commentator known to us has something to say on the subject, and so do a great many 20th-century commentators. Among the most recent holdouts for Baker's position are Phythian 1979, Simon 1980, and Garner 1998.

The OED's first example of *mutual friend* is dated 1658. The other examples of its use are from Lady Mary Wortley Montagu, Edmund Burke, Sir Walter Scott, and George Eliot. Here are a few from our files:

> . . . by the hands of our mutual friend, Mr. Boswell —Sir Alexander Dick, letter (to Samuel Johnson), 17 Feb. 1777

> I had it from a dear mutual friend —W. M. Thackeray, *The Book of Snobs,* 1846

> . . . after I had paid ten dollars in court for having punched a mutual friend —Robert Frost, letter, January 1923

> . . . after the burial of a mutual friend —James Joyce, *Ulysses,* 1922

> . . . our mutual friend, T. R. Smith —*The Intimate Notebooks of George Jean Nathan,* 1932

> Our mutual friend Libba Thayer has given me your address —James Thurber, letter, 2 May 1960

> That same day, a mutual friend invited Mullins and myself to join him for a round of golf at his club —Tip O'Neill with William Novak, *Man of the House,* 1987

We even have an example or two of the stigmatized sense used with other nouns. Dean Alford managed to convince himself that the *mutual* in the following example denoted reciprocity, but it clearly does not: it refers to the faith of both Paul and the Christians in Rome in Jesus Christ:

> That is, that I may be comforted together with you by the mutual faith both of you and me —Romans 1:12 (AV), 1611

Here are a couple of other examples:

> . . . La femme de quarante ans has a husband and *three* lovers; all of whom find out their mutual connection one starry night —W. M. Thackeray, *The Paris Sketch Book,* 1840

> So they all nudged each other toward a mutual fate —Garry Wills, *Saturday Rev.,* 11 Dec. 1976

Objection to *mutual* "common" has no basis other than Baker's *ipse dixit* of 1770. The usages themselves go back to Shakespeare; they have been in continuous use for almost 400 years, they are eminently standard, and it is about time the matter was laid to rest.

myriad   Some of you may wonder how usage controversies originate. The case of *myriad* may provide some insight. The earliest mention of the word seems to be in Fowler 1926. He limits his commentary to the two meanings of the word. The two subsequent editions of Fowler similarly limit themselves, as do most of the books having an entry for *myriad*. In 1929, however, someone wrote to the language column of the *Writer's Digest,* apparently asking about the propriety of the plural *myriads*. The inquirer was informed that the use dated to the 17th century (it actually goes back to the 16th) and was standard. Milton was quoted using the plural. (Milton was quoted using the plural in Samuel Johnson's 1755 dictionary.) Opdyke 1939 noted both adjective and noun use (as does Heritage 2000). Margaret Nicholson, in her 1957 Americanization of Fowler, noted both singular and plural use, and provided examples of the plural and of the construction *a myriad of.* Harper 1985 mentioned noun and adjective use and gave an example of the construction *a myriad of.* The only comment even approaching controversy was in Shaw 1970, holding "myriad lights" (rather feebly attested in our files) to be a cliché. Then O'Connor 1996 recommends that both *myriads* and *a myriad of* be avoided. No reason given, no authority cited.

What possible basis can there be for this opinion? The author certainly has not looked up *myriad* in any standard reference. Perhaps she believes the word is an adjective only. But we have seen that the plural noun dates from the 16th century. The *a myriad of* construction is more recent. The earliest citation in the OED is from Walter Savage Landor in 1824, although there is an 18th-century citation for "one single myriad of." The earliest American use we have found is from Thoreau's *Walden* in 1854. Both constructions continue to be used in reputable standard English.

Have we witnessed the birth of a new usage dispute? All the usual makings are there: opinion asserted in contradiction to evidence of use—much of it rather literary—and in contradiction to previous comment. Only time will tell.

myself   In the *New York Times Magazine* for 1 Feb. 1981, William Safire quotes outgoing President Jimmy Carter:

I will work hard to make sure that the transition from myself to the next President is a good one.

Safire opines that the use of *myself* is "an unstylish, though not incorrect, use." He then goes on to recommend *myself* be used as an intensive, "not as a cutesy turning away from the harsh 'me'." Not mentioned in this article is the substitution of *myself* for *I*, in which Reader's Digest 1983 detected Safire indulging himself:

No longer were Price, Buchanan, and myself part of the innermost circle —*Before the Fall,* 1974

"One cannot escape the impression that over the last couple of decades or so there has been a marked increase in the use of 'myself' for 'me'," says Foster 1968. He gives a few examples, including this one:

The *Daily Express* immediately asked myself, Hastings and Osborne to contribute to a series of articles called "Angry Young Men" —Colin Wilson, *Encounter,* November 1959

If we look at the three examples so far given, we can see that in the first *myself* replaced *me* as the object of a preposition, in the second it replaced *I* as the subject of a verb, and in the third it replaced *me* as the object of a verb. These three functions are the chief ones in which *myself* replaces *I* or *me*. We will subdivide them somewhat, and pick out a few particular items for notice.

The substitution of *myself* for *I* or *me* had not escaped the notice of commentators earlier than Foster and Safire. Indeed it has been the subject of considerable comment for at least a century, from as early as Ayres 1881 to Garner 1998. Two general statements can be made about what these critics say concerning *myself*: first, they do not like it, and second, they do not know why. An index to their uncertainty can be found in this list of descriptors that they have variously attached to the practice: snobbish, unstylish, self-indulgent, self-conscious, old-fashioned, timorous, colloquial, informal, formal, nonstandard, incorrect, mistaken, literary, and unacceptable in formal written English. Goold Brown's remark seems apropos here: "Grammarians would perhaps differ less, if they read more."

The handful of commentators who have done real research have found the usage surprisingly widespread in literary sources. Hall 1917, for instance, found it in 37 authors from Malory to Robert Louis Stevenson. But Hall is longer on lists of names than on actual quotations. We will try to be long on examples. We have grouped the examples according to the three main types of usage we mentioned

above. Please note, by the way, that other reflexive pronouns—*ourselves, thyself, himself, herself*—are used in the same way as *myself*; a few examples of these are included among the greater number for *myself*.

First, *myself* as the subject of a sentence. As sole subject, *myself* is not common except in poetry:

Myself hath often overheard them say —Shakespeare, *Titus Andronicus,* 1594

Myself when young did eagerly frequent —Edward FitzGerald, *The Rubáiyát of Omar Khayyám,* 1859

Somehow myself survived the night —Emily Dickinson, poem, 1871

But when the reflexive pronoun is part of a compound subject, prose examples abound:

. . . Williams, and Desmoulins, and myself are very sickly —Samuel Johnson, letter, 2 Mar. 1782

From the moment Mrs. Washington and myself adopted the two youngest children —George Washington, letter (in Pooley 1974)

. . . both myself & my Wife must —William Blake, letter, 6 July 1803

. . . the Post & not yourself must have been unpunctual —Jane Austen, letter, 1 Nov. 1800

I will presume that Mr. Murry and myself can agree that for our purpose these counters are adequate —T. S. Eliot, "The Function of Criticism," in *Selected Essays,* 1932

The King, myself, Lord Halifax, a British Admiral, Adm. Leahy, Lascelles, the Secretary of State in that order around the table —Harry S. Truman, diary, 5 Aug. 1945

The Dewas party and myself got out at a desolate station —E. M. Forster, *The Hill of Devi,* 1953

When writing an aria or an ensemble Chester Kallman and myself always find it helpful —W. H. Auden, *Times Literary Supp.,* 2 Nov. 1967

Although Rosenman, others and myself continued to press for this postwar domestic legislation —Chester Bowles, *Promises to Keep,* 1971

We also find it tacked on to the subject in an appositive:

. . . the four of us, John, Wally, Tom, and myself, moved into the astronaut quarters —Virgil "Gus" Grissom, *Gemini: A Personal Account of Man's Venture into Space,* 1968

... in the course of which several other film critics, myself included, have to take their lumps —Simon 1980

The four of us—Baker, Darman, Regan and myself—were an odd lot —David A. Stockman, *Newsweek,* 28 Apr. 1986

Next, *myself* as the object of a verb and as a predicate noun. Most of these examples involve groups of names.

... appointed Mr. Francis, then attorney-general and myself to draw up constitutions for the government of the academy —Benjamin Franklin, *Autobiography,* 1788

... it will find him here, as it will myself —Thomas Jefferson, letter, 27 Feb. 1809

... T. R. Smith, then managing editor of the *Century Magazine,* telephoned Mencken and myself at our office —*The Intimate Notebooks of George Jean Nathan,* 1932

... which will reconcile Max Lerner with Felix Frankfurter and myself with God —E. B. White, letter, 4 Feb. 1942

... Brinsley said that he was prepared to give myself and Donaghy a pint of stout apiece —Flann O'Brien, *At Swim-Two-Birds,* 1939

During the lunch hour the male clerks usually went out, leaving myself and the three girls behind —Frank O'Connor, *New Yorker,* 11 Jan. 1958

He said with a smile, "You Unitarians"—meaning Ted Sorensen and myself—"keep writing Catholic speeches." —Arthur M. Schlesinger, Jr., in *Life,* 16 July 1965

Before we move on to use of *myself* as the object of a preposition, we will give you some examples where the reflexive pronoun seems particularly popular—after those words whose status as preposition or conjunction is a matter of some dispute, words like *as, than,* and *like*:

... when mortals no bigger—no, not so big as—ourselves are looked up to —Henry Adams, letter, 13 Feb. 1861

Some very odd people turn up hereabouts, usually hoping to find me as unconventional as themselves —Flannery O'Connor, letter, 6 Nov. 1960

We are not unwilling to believe that Man wiser than ourselves —Samuel Johnson, *The Rambler* No. 87, 15 Jan. 1751

... no one would feel more gratified by the chance of obtaining his observations on a work than myself —Lord Byron, letter, 23 Aug. 1811

... Mr. Rushworth could hardly be more impatient for the marriage than herself —Jane Austen, *Mansfield Park,* 1814

I think few persons have a greater disgust for plagiarism than myself —Oliver Wendell Holmes d. 1894, *The Autocrat of the Breakfast-Table,* 1857

... he judged her to be a year or so younger than himself —James Joyce, *Dubliners,* 1914

... her first husband, who was much older than herself —George Bernard Shaw, preface, *The Shaw–Terry Letters,* 1937

Her view is that he is a rare soul, a finer being either than herself or her husband —E. L. Doctorow, *Loon Lake,* 1979

To-morrow I bury her, and then I shall be quite alone, with nothing but a cat to remind me that the house has been full of living things like myself —Charles Lamb, letter, 12 May 1800

Like myself, she was vexed at his getting married —Samuel Butler, *The Way of All Flesh,* 1903

... to see a man, who ... in the dusk looked for all the world like myself —Robert Frost, letter, 10 Feb. 1912

You know by now what a word from you means to any of the rest of us—& particularly to one like myself —Archibald MacLeish, letter, 9 Sept. 1926

Only among older chaps like myself —Kingsley Amis, quoted in *The Writer's Place,* ed. Peter Firchow, 1974

... as to which I felt no one to be trusted but myself —Henry James, *The Art of the Novel,* 1934

Finally, *myself* as the object of some ordinary prepositions:

Ye have seen what I did unto the Egyptians, and *how* I bare you on eagles' wings, and brought you unto myself —Exodus 19:4 (AV), 1611

The pheasant I gave to Mr. Richardson, the bustard to Dr. Lawrence, and the pot I placed with Miss Williams, to be eaten by myself —Samuel Johnson, letter, 9 Jan. 1758

So much for my patient—now for myself —Jane Austen, letter, 17 Nov. 1798

... the Russians were playing a double game, between ourselves —W. M. Thackeray, *The Book of Snobs,* 1846

... it will require the combined efforts of Maggie, Providence, and myself —Emily Dickinson, letter, April 1873

. . . with Dorothy Thompson and myself among the speakers —Alexander Woollcott, letter, 11 Nov. 1940

There are also two captions for Hokinson, one by myself and one by my secretary —James Thurber, letter, 20 Aug. 1948

Indeed I hope that you will have time, amongst your numerous engagements, to have a meal with my wife and myself —T. S. Eliot, letter, 7 May 1957

. . . a monitoring exercise of BBC radio in mid-1979 undertaken by Professor Denis Donoghue, Mr Andrew Timothy and myself —Burchfield 1981 (Introduction)

. . . and the Druid cannot imagine the magazine without himself —Jay McInerney, *Bright Lights, Big City,* 1984

If you have read this whole article, you have seen examples spoken or written by forty or so people—poets, politicians, playwrights, novelists, essayists, diarists, statesmen, even lexicographers. The evidence should make it plain that the practice of substituting *myself* or other reflexive pronouns for ordinary personal pronouns is not new—these examples range over four centuries—and is not rare. It is true that many of the examples are from speech and personal letters, suggesting familiarity and informality. But the practice is by no means limited to informal contexts. Only the use of *myself* as sole subject of a sentence seems to be restricted; all our examples are from older poetry.

Two observations may be made here, both gleaned from Frank Parker et al., "Untriggered Reflexive Pronouns in English," *American Speech,* Spring 1990. First, Noam Chomsky suggests that compounds like *Harry and myself* block the assignment of case by a governing verb or preposition to the individual constituents of the phrase, so that if they are pronouns they may be nominative or objective or may even be reflexives. The second involves a linguistic study called discourse analysis. You will observe that almost all the instances of first and second person reflexive pronouns here occur in contexts where the speaker or writer is referring to himself or herself or the listener or reader as a subject of the discourse, rather than as a participant in it. According to discourse analysis this is the way that English ordinarily works. Discourse analysis doesn't explain third person reflexives very well, but, in spite of what the critics may think, this use of the first and second person reflexives is a common and standard, though not mandatory, feature of the language.

Some writers no doubt use the reflexive pronouns for some of the many invidious reasons suggested by the commentators' labels. As an example of what you will want to avoid, we present this bit from a letter of inquiry received here in 1985; in trying to elevate his style beyond his capacity, the writer has violated the tenets of discourse analysis:

Quite recently, while using your lexicon, a rather interesting enigma manifested itself; one which I hope you can elucidate for myself.

If you can resist this sort of temptation, reasonable use of *myself* ought not to give you much trouble.

See also YOURSELF, YOURSELVES.

N

naïf, naïve, naïveté, naivety Many commentators discuss the relative status of these words in current English. What our evidence shows is that *naïf* and *naïve,* which in French are the masculine and feminine forms of one word, are in English now usually differentiated according to part of speech rather than gender: *naïve* is a common adjective used for both men and women; *naïf* is rarely used except as a noun meaning "a naïve person." The diaeresis is now omitted at least as often as it is retained:

. . . the naïve statement of a sheltered man —Ken Auletta, *N.Y. Times Book Rev.,* 22 Dec. 1985

This thinking proved naive and fatal —Kenya Napper Bello, *Essence,* October 1995

I am . . . just a naïf at heart —Philip Roth, *Reading Myself and Others,* 1975

. . . amiable naifs marching into a war they don't quite get —Anne Marie Cruz, *ESPN,* 7 Feb. 2000

The noun *naïveté* is greatly preferred in American English to the Anglicized *naivety.* It is still usually written with a diaeresis and an acute accent, but two other stylings, *naiveté* and *naivete,* are not at all uncommon:

. . . an example of Mr. Wilson's naiveté —George F. Kennan, *Atlantic,* November 1982

. . . Whitman's campaign has been distinguished by its naiveté —Eleanor Clift, *Newsweek,* 25 Oct. 1993

. . . never confounds innocence and naïveté —Molly Winans, *Commonweal,* 7 Nov. 1997

The British use *naïveté* as well, but they now seem to prefer *naivety:*

. . . amusing because of their naivety —William Davis, *Punch,* 26 Mar. 1975

. . . balancing the charges of elitism on one side against those of naivety on the other —Andrew Ballantyne, *Times Literary Supp.,* 5 Apr. 1996

naphtha See PHTH.

nary *Nary* started out as a dialect word and, when not followed by *a* or *an,* it still is.

. . . nary whiskey under any circumstances —Walt Whitman, letter, 15 Apr. 1863

. . . they don't have nary constables now —Albert Potter (a deputy sheriff in Kentucky), quoted in *N.Y. Times,* 5 Dec. 1976

Nary a/an, on the other hand, is now also used in mainstream English.

One would think from "Don't Know Much About History" that nary an honest buck was earned between 1870 and 1914 —James M. Cornelius, *N.Y. Times Book Rev.,* 30 Sept. 1990

. . . parallel universes, neither capable of interacting with the other, and nary a wormhole in sight —Daniel Taylor, *Christianity Today,* 11 Jan. 1999

. . . sheds light on some very trendy issues with nary a word of jargonese —Alison Demos, *Civilization,* April/May 1999

. . . nary an officer could be seen —David Freed, *Los Angeles Times,* 8 Sept. 1984

Bremner 1980 says it "sounds phony and studiedly quaint except on provincial lips." Freeman 1990 finds it "provincial" and "affected." You can judge those views against the examples above. It is a standard use but one that is usually employed deliberately for effect.

native British sources, Longman 1984, Sellers 1975, and Burchfield 1996, note that *native* for a nonwhite, non-European person indigenous to some place is no longer considered polite. The offensiveness of the word, or the diffidence about it, seems to be a reaction to colonialism and its attitudes:

Plomer's voyagings put him in touch with people—"natives" as they were then called —Stephen Spender, *N.Y. Times Book Rev.,* 27 June 1976

The evil of colonialism is not oppression but contempt. Eminent Victorians despised their own lower classes and certainly the Irish . . . as much as they did any other people they called natives —Eugene Weber, *N.Y. Times Book Rev.,* 16 June 1985

In North America we find *native* used nonpejoratively, especially in Alaska and western Canada, in the sense "Native American." In this use it is frequently capitalized.

. . . education seminars on Native cultures —*Discover Alaska,* Winter 1986

Native American *Native American* is a relatively new term that is now being used frequently in competition with *American Indian* and *Indian.* It has not yet replaced the other terms. The *Native* is sometimes spelled with a lowercase *n.*

Native American means American Indian, Indian, Native Hawaiian, and Alaskan Native —*Federal Register Part IV,* 15 Dec. 1983

He tells of a daydreaming child who sees a native American pass by his classroom window, but when he relates this to his teacher, she insists there are no Indians in Connecticut —Linda Hirsh, *Hartford* (Conn.) *Courant,* 3 June 1986

. . . the most complex Native American society of North America —Jared Diamond, *Guns, Germs, and Steel,* 1997

nature *Nature* is one of those words, like *case, character,* and *fact,* that you find in handbooks accompanied by the label "wordy" or "superfluous" or "redundant" along with the assertion that such a quality is one of the chief characteristics of its use in English. Anyone who had to wade through the citational evidence for *nature* in our files in search of these wordy phrases would soon develop a contrary opinion; most uses of the word do not embed it in phrases like *in the nature of* or *of such a nature as to.*

The assumption the critics make when they call an example wordy or roundabout is that the sentence in which the construction occurs could be readily improved by omitting or shortening the expression. You might challenge this assumption by seeing what you would do with each of our examples below. How many can you shorten easily? And how many are noticeably improved by your revision? Does revision alter the meaning? Does it alter the tone?

Something in the nature of an ovation was their reward —Virgil Thomson, *The Musical Scene,* 1947

. . . the chapter dealing with the philosophical developments was in the nature of an afterthought —*Times Literary Supp.,* 19 Oct. 1951

. . . use a thin bookmarker. . . . Don't use scissors or old letters or anything of that nature —Lionel McColvin, in *The Wonderful World of Books,* ed. Alfred Stefferud, 1952

We are in a time of stress of a nature such as this country has never before experienced —Vannevar Bush, *N.Y. Times Mag.,* 13 June 1954

Yet the losses we inflicted upon them in the month of May were, I think, in the nature of three-quarters of the losses they inflicted upon us —Sir Winston Churchill, *The Unrelenting Struggle,* 1942

He also began to suffer from the intense nature of tennis —Adrian McGregor, *National Times* (Sydney), 5 Apr. 1975

Many stocks close for the month with prices a little lower than at the opening, but there has been nothing of a startling nature in the mild decline —*The Bulletin* (Sydney, Australia), 31 Mar. 1954

naught 1. *Naught, nought.* Two British commentators, Gowers in Fowler 1965 and Chambers 1985, prefer the spelling *nought* for "zero" and *naught* for "nothing." This, indeed, seems to be prevailing British practice:

It is when a certain number of noughts begins to appear at the end of the figures . . . that our eyes begin to glaze over —Hardcastle, *Punch,* 10 Apr. 1974

This precaution becomes as naught when the squad is turned about —John Peel, *Punch,* 13 May 1975

In American English, the word is not commonly used in either spelling to mean "zero"; *naught* is somewhat more common than *nought* when the meaning is "nothing."
2. Flesch 1964 and Copperud 1964, 1970, 1980 asperse *naught* "nothing" as quaint and bookish. Sometimes it is so for deliberate effect:

Say not the struggle naught availeth —Simon 1980

In most cases, however, the use of this word is limited not by quaintness but by the rather narrow range of constructions it idiomatically fits into. It is used primarily with *avail* or in such phrases as *come* (or *go* or *bring) to naught*:

It availed him naught —*The Economist,* 22 Sept. 1984

It occurred to me that the great care I was using in completing my diary might come to naught —Eric Randall, *Newsweek,* 15 Sept. 1986

. . . a tidal wave of red ink brought this plan to nought —Matthew Miller, *New Republic,* 6 Dec. 1999

. . . he saw his opening-round 65 go for nought last year —Steve Popper, *N.Y. Times,* 17 June 2001

nauseous, nauseating, nauseated Behind the intense, though relatively recent, controversy over these words is a persistent belief, dear to the hearts of many American commentators, that *nauseous* has but a single sense: "causing nausea." Of course, this belief is erroneous. Although the OED lists three senses, the focus of the controversy is a sense of *nauseous* meaning "affected by nausea, feeling sick to one's stomach" that seems to have arisen shortly after World War II, undoubtedly in speech first. It first came to our attention in 1949 in a letter to the editor of a periodical:

> SIR: One of the minor crosses which any physician has to bear is the experience of hearing patient after patient say, "Doctor, I am nauseous." . . . If the distinction I am making is not clear to you, may I point out that "nauseous" implies the quality of inducing nausea and that the person or animal in whom this sensation is induced is nauseated —Deborah C. Leary, M.D., *Saturday Rev.,* 4 June 1949

Dr. Leary was objecting to a similar use in an earlier *Saturday Review* article; before her objection we have no record of anyone's having made such a distinction. But by 1954 Theodore Bernstein had noticed it (*Winners & Sinners,* 28 Apr. 1954), and he reprinted the notice in Bernstein 1958. From this modest beginning, *nauseous* has become a standard entry in American usage books. We have found the subject discussed in more than 20 of them.

Dr. Leary's prescription is to use *nauseated* for "experiencing nausea" and *nauseous* for "causing nausea," and her prescription is repeated by almost all the subsequent usage books. A further concern is added by Perrin & Ebbitt 1972 and Ebbitt & Ebbitt 1982—the possibility that the use of *nauseous* to mean "sick" might be ambiguous to someone who had grown up with the distinction. But ambiguity is not a real problem. When *nauseous* means "sick," it is used in a restricted set of sentence patterns; it is regularly used as a predicate adjective following a linking verb such as *be, feel, become,* or *grow.* The subject of the verb is of necessity always personal. Use of this sense is generally literal but may occasionally be figurative.

But the heavy bread, the tepid meat, made him begin to feel nauseous —James Baldwin, *Another Country,* 1962

New, shorter-lived anesthetics make it possible for patients to come out of surgery without feeling groggy or nauseous for days, Dr. Jones explains —George Anders, *Wall Street Jour.,* 11 Aug. 1994

When a cat is nauseous, it will often drool —Robert K. Lynch, B.S., V.M.D., *Cats Mag.,* February 1973

When the medication makes her tired and nauseous, she works at home —Jane E. Brody, *N.Y. Times,* 16 May 1984

. . . I think that writing must be a bit like pregnancy. . . . often, when I get up in the morning and look at what I wrote the night before, sure enough—I become nauseous —Mike Nichols, *Life and Other Ways,* 1988

When *nauseous* means "causing nausea, nauseating" in a literal sense it is seldom used with a personal subject. It is also much more often used as an attributive adjective—in front of the noun it modifies—than as a predicate adjective:

. . . sucked in the sides of his mouth so he would not taste the nauseous alcohol —Donald Windham, *The Dog Star,* 1950

. . . dangling over the nauseous water on which bobbed craft —Elizabeth Bowen, *The Little Girls,* 1964

. . . the sickly sweet smell which makes the neighbourhood of the leper nauseous —W. Somerset Maugham, *The Moon and Sixpence,* 1919

But even more important to remember than the differing syntactic patterns is that when *nauseous* means "nauseating" it is most likely to be used figuratively and not literally. This figurative use began in the second half of the 17th century. It was used as a generalized term of disapproval:

I hate that nauseous fool, you know I do —George Etherege, *The Man of Mode,* 1676

You would be as nauseous to the ladies as one of the old patriarchs, if you used that obsolete expression —George Farquhar, *Love and a Bottle,* 1698

This use of the figurative *nauseous*—applied to persons—seems to have pretty much died out with the 17th century. But figurative use applied to other things was equally common then and has continued right up to the present.

I confess I have not been sneering fulsome Lies and nauseous Flattery —William Congreve, *The Old Bachelor,* 1693

Pray, Mr. Wild, none of this nauseous behaviour —Henry Fielding, *Jonathan Wild,* 1743

. . . when it was requisite to administer a corrective dose to the nation, Robespierre was found; a most foul and nauseous dose indeed —W. M. Thackeray, *The Book of Snobs,* 1846

. . . most evident and nauseous in the worst play which Ford himself ever wrote —T. S. Eliot, "John Ford," in *Selected Essays,* 1932

. . . a world ludicrously contrived, socially misleading, professionally nauseous —Anthony Powell, *Casanova's Chinese Restaurant,* 1960

. . . he is self-consciously on guard against the nauseous eulogies he reads in some of his colleagues' columns —Michael Holroyd, *Bernard Shaw,* 1988

. . . an addict friend, who exposes the nauseous act of shooting up —Annie Gottlieb, *N.Y. Times Book Rev.,* 16 June 1974

In present-day use, however, the "nauseating" sense of *nauseous* is less common than it once was. *Nauseating* seems to be taking over much of its use.

I especially hated the cod liver oil, a nauseating goo tasting of raw liquefied fish —Russell Baker, *Growing Up,* 1982

Anything more nauseating she could not conceive. Prayer at this hour with that woman —Virginia Woolf, *Mrs. Dalloway,* 1925

Chamberlain's obsequiousness, his exaggerated flattery, in these letters can be nauseating —William L. Shirer, *The Rise and Fall of the Third Reich,* 1960

The pomposity and self-satisfied moral rectitude of those bent on prosecution is, however, quite nauseating —J. H. Plumb, *N.Y. Times Book Rev.,* 5 Sept. 1976

. . . two nauseating children with fixed, dangerous grins on their faces —Gahan Wilson, *N.Y. Times Book Rev.,* 5 Dec. 1993

Nauseated, prescribed by many usage books in place of *nauseous,* is less frequently used than *nauseous.* It has some figurative use:

. . . the propaganda lies about the Czech treatment of the Sudeten Germans . . . made me even more nauseated —William L. Shirer, *The Nightmare Years,* 1984

But most of its use is literal:

Nauseated with pain, Armitage roused himself —Jean Stafford, *The Mountain Lion,* 1947

. . . was dizzy and nauseated when he penciled in the river that bears his name —Garrison Keillor, *Lake Wobegon Days,* 1985

There is a little evidence that *nauseous* and *nauseated* may be heading toward differentiation in their literal uses. Many of the citations we have for *nauseous* connote a queasy feeling, not actual sickness.

. . . he munched some treated corn. After some observation, the bereft farmer relaxed; Harriman felt slightly nauseous for two days —Jake Page, *Science 81,* April 1981

Suddenly, one of the contestants stepped back and shouted, Holy ———, I broke his ——— arm! I got nauseous —Melvin Durslag, *TV Guide,* 20 Mar. 1981

But a number of citations for *nauseated* suggest actual sickness:

He spent the next 10 days in a hospital, nauseated, literally wanting to die —Rick Telander, *Sports Illustrated,* 28 Feb. 1983

Chemotherapy and radiation help her toward remission, but they bald her skull and blast her mind, leaving her nauseated and irritable —Brina Caplan, *N.Y. Times Book Rev.,* 28 Nov. 1982

The evidence so far is only suggestive.

Conclusion: At present, *nauseous* is most often used as a predicate adjective meaning "nauseated" literally; it has some figurative use as well. Usage writers decry these developments of the last 40 or 50 years, but they are now standard in general prose. The older sense of *nauseous* meaning "nauseating," both literal and figurative, seems to be in decline, being replaced by *nauseating. Nauseated* is usually literal, but is less common than *nauseous.* Any handbook that tells you that *nauseous* cannot mean "nauseated" is out of touch with the contemporary language. In current use it seldom means anything else.

near, nearly The use of *near* in the sense "almost, nearly" has been around for more than 700 years. It has been used in literature:

. . . for he would as near as possible remove all whatsoever encumbrances —Thomas Nashe, *The Life of Gabriel Harvey,* 1596

My uncle *Toby's* wound was near well —Laurence Sterne, *Tristram Shandy,* 1759

. . . wicker-covered flask . . . containing near a pint of a remarkably sound Cognac brandy —W. M. Thackeray, *Vanity Fair,* 1848

. . . but a bloody sweep came along and he near drove his gear into my eye —James Joyce, *Ulysses,* 1922

By the second quarter of the 20th century this use had largely been taken over by *nearly* in general use. H. W. Fowler made note of this, and a number of later commentators began advising avoiding *near,* as if it were somehow tainted. But it is not tainted; rather its range has shrunk. It is still used to modify adjectives, used to modify expressions of time, distance, and number, used in negative contexts, and used when preceded by another adverb.

The piece is pretty near done —E. B. White, letter, 21 Feb. 1942

. . . in my case it's not anything near as neat as a filing case, it's more like a junk box —William Faulkner, 6 May 1957, in *Faulkner in the University,* 1959

It took guts . . . to publish this near 900-page volume —Susan Toepfer, *People,* 4 Feb. 1991

. . . making near perfect decisions —William C. Rhoden, *N.Y. Times,* 9 Oct. 1994

The youngest, Mark, nine months, . . . can darn near walk and talk —James Thurber, letter, 27 Aug. 1960

These uses are standard.
See also FLAT ADVERBS.

necessary When used with a preposition, *necessary* is most often used with *to:*

Tennyson is as much a part of the nineteenth century as steam and as necessary to its understanding as Ricardo —Thomas F. O'Dea, *Center Mag.,* May 1969

. . . use all the police presence necessary to stanch the crime rise —Fred P. Graham, *Harper's,* September 1970

Less often, necessary is used with *for:*

. . . re-inventing the institutions that are necessary for human happiness —John Cogley, *Center Mag.,* July/August 1970

Necessary occasionally is used with *in:*

. . . a recognition that non-economic considerations were necessary in the distribution of economic goods —Thomas F. O'Dea, *Center Mag.,* May 1969

necessity When *necessity* is used with a preposition, the preposition is usually either *of* or, less often, *for.*

. . . the necessity of civil, academic and scientific liberty —George Soule, *New Republic,* 20 Jan. 1941

. . . the necessity of adopting a program of action —Mary E. Murphy, *Annals of the American Academy of Political and Social Science,* May 1948

. . . the necessity for greater precision —T. S. Eliot, " 'Rhetoric' and Poetic Drama," in *Selected Essays,* 1932

Harper 1985 claims that "an infinitive is never used after *necessity,*" but we have occasionally found it in quite reputable sources:

. . . the necessity to seek commercial markets —Roger Benedict, *Wall Street Jour.,* 17 Dec. 1957

. . . the necessity to formulate plans —Noël Gilroy Annan, *Times Literary Supp.,* 30 Apr. 1970

née The literal meaning of this word in French is "born." Its usual function in English is to introduce a married woman's maiden name, as in "Mrs. John Jones, née Smith." Usage commentators dating back as far as Bierce 1909 have warned against following it with a woman's given name, "Mrs. John Jones, née Mary Smith," because, they argue, a person is born only with a last name—the given name comes later. What that argument ignores is that *née* is not normally understood as meaning "born" when used in English. Its sense in English is closer to "formerly or originally known as" than to "born" and its use before a woman's maiden name is clearly meant to indicate what the woman was known as before her marriage, not at the moment of her birth. *Née* is more often than not used as the critics say it should be, but its use with a given name is not uncommon. Such use is especially likely when the woman is referred to by her husband's full name ("Mrs. John Jones" rather than "Mrs. Mary Jones"), but it also occurs on occasion when the given name has already been indicated:

Mrs. Fanny Harwood, nee Fanny Pain —*The Times* (London). 3 Nov. 1973 (OED Supplement)

This citation also illustrates that *née* is sometimes written without an acute accent. Both versions are common.

Née has other uses which the critics do not generally consider, but which they surely would not like if they did:

Voltaire (nee François Arouet) —Aram Bakshian, Jr., *National Rev.,* 30 June 1970

. . . the Brewers nee Pilots who are also in their third year —Fred Ciampa, *Boston Sunday Advertiser,* 13 June 1971

John Davis, nee Helmut Otto Kase —*Private Eye,* 14 Dec. 1973

. . . in the Palace, née the Chalfonte-Haddon Hall —Joan Kron, *N.Y. Times,* 14 Apr. 1977

Such usage demonstrates the extent to which *née* has lost its literal, French meaning in English.

need, *noun* Chambers 1985 says that *need* takes *for* except in the phrases *have need of* and *in need of.* Bernstein 1962 thinks that choosing *for* rather than *of* avoids the possibility that the reader could misinterpret *of* as being the genitive *of* (which connects *need* with the person or thing whose need it is) instead of the idiomatic *of* (which, like *for,* connects *need* with the description of what is needed).

Looking at the evidence we have accumulated over just the past few decades, we find that, overall, *for* and *of* are used with about equal frequency after *need.* Of the uses with *of,* half are for the genitive *of* and half for the idiomatic *of.* Uses of the phrase *in need of* make up about a quarter of the uses of idiomatic *of.* Both *have need of* and *have need for* are used but are less common. So in actual usage, the preposition that follows *need* is usually *for,* but *of* is also a common choice:

. . . the need for devising ways —Harvey Wheeler, quoted in *Center Mag.,* November 1969

. . . the need for regular checkups —Glenn V. Carmichael, *Ford Times,* September 1966

. . . the need of efficiency —Scott Buchanan, "So Reason Can Rule," 1967

. . . a condition in need of amendment —Norman Mailer, *Harper's,* March 1971

Bernstein's point about the confusion of idiomatic *of* with genitive *of* is undercut somewhat by the fact that genitive *of* usually follows the plural *needs* rather than the singular *need:*

. . . adapting it to the needs of the welfare state —*Current Biography,* July 1965

Although the fact is not mentioned by the commentators, *need* is also commonly followed by *to* and an infinitive:

. . . the need to look into the ecology —*Times Literary Supp.,* 9 Apr. 1970

. . . had the need to confess —Joseph Wambaugh, *Lines and Shadows,* 1984

need, *verb* **1.** *Need* is both a finite verb and an auxiliary. In its function as an auxiliary it does not inflect and is followed by the bare infinitive without *to:*

No pressure group need apply —Harry S. Truman, diary, 20 Sept. 1945

. . . so that Louis need never know —Mavis Gallant, *New Yorker*, 8 July 1985

. . . all that Johnson or Nguyen need do is enroll —Michael Holzman, *College English*, March 1984

The finite verb does inflect; when followed by an infinitive, it requires *to*:

The church bells needed to ring three times —Virginia Black, *This England*, Summer 1983

It can also be followed by a gerund:

The facts are too well known to need repeating here —Tip O'Neill with William Novak, *Man of the House*, 1987

2. A curious construction in which *need* is followed directly by a past participle—"my car needs washed"—is called "widely disliked" by Longman 1984. The editors of *The Dictionary of American Regional English* know this as an American idiom found chiefly in the Midland area. The usual phrasing would be "needs to be washed," "needs washing," or "needs a wash."

needless to say Those who are determined to take their idioms literally are apt to have the same trouble with *needless to say* that they have with *goes without saying* (which see). If something truly need not be said, they wonder, then why say it? And if it does need to be said, why claim that it doesn't? The simple and obvious answer to these questions is that *needless to say* is not a logical, literal expression but an idiomatic phrase. It is used parenthetically for two main purposes—to emphasize that the writer or speaker regards the statement being made as in some way self-evident, and to provide a graceful transition between sentences or paragraphs:

. . . could then be discussions with the National Liberation Front. Needless to say, such discussions can hardly take place if the Saigon government regards even words of compromise as treasonable —Senator Mike Mansfield, in *A Center Occasional Paper*, June 1968

. . . steps which finally resulted in the atomic bomb. . . . Needless to say, . . . all these decisions were made with the utmost secrecy —*Times Literary Supp.*, 5 Feb. 1970

We agree with Copperud 1964: "Criticism of the expression, except for overwork, is quibbling."

negation See DOUBLE NEGATIVE; RAISING.

negative See AFFIRMATIVE, NEGATIVE; DOUBLE NEGATIVE.

negative-raising See RAISING.

neglectful *Neglectful* is used with *of*:

. . . are utterly neglectful of what we consider the first requirements of decency —Edward Westermarck, *The History of Human Marriage*, 5th ed., 1921

. . . improper and neglectful of the low-income and non-politically oriented student —Fred Hill, *Change*, June 1972

negligent When *negligent* is used with a preposition, the choice is usually *in* or *of*:

. . . was perhaps somewhat negligent in his relations with his mother —Arnold Bennett, *The Old Wives' Tale*, 1908

The insurer is negligent in failing to settle —R. E. Keeton, *Harvard Law Rev.*, May 1954

. . . almost deliberately negligent of the possibility of a war with Germany —H. G. Wells, *Mr. Britling Sees It Through*, 1916

. . . he was a careless workman, negligent of detail —Edith Hamilton, *The Greek Way to Western Civilization*, 1930

Negligent has also been occasionally used with *about*:

. . . is equally negligent about fiction —Charles Thomas Samuels, *Berkshire Rev.*, Winter 1970

Negress *Negress* is a word of fairly low frequency of use and of uncertain status. Our evidence shows that it is sometimes considered an offensive racial epithet, and some commentators also say that women consider it to be a patronizing term, like many other words ending in *-ess*. Most of our evidence is now more than a quarter century old; it is largely neutral and descriptive in tone, but one cannot be sure how such writings may have been viewed by black women who might have read them. It seems to have receded in use along with *Negro* as preferences in racial terminology changed. In American use the word is regularly capitalized; in British use it is often lowercased.

Negro See BLACK; COLORED.

neither *Neither* is a word about which many theoretical rules have been excogitated, beginning back in the 18th century, without regard to actual practice. Practice that deviates from the rules is regularly censured as error, regardless of the stature of the offending writer. But irregular (not to say, unruly) practice has continued in blithe disregard of the censorious grammarians, as materials collected in the OED, volume 2 of Jespersen 1909–49, and an article by William M. Ryan (*American Speech,* Fall–Winter 1976) abundantly attest. The worm in the apple of theory here is usually notional agreement, which was unknown to the grammarians who devised the rules and is unknown to or ignored by the handbook compilers who repeat them. We will take a look at four instances where precept and practice diverge.

1. *Pronoun. Neither,* the rules assure us, is singular. However, actual practice requires us to temper the absolute form of the rule and say that *neither* is usually singular. The reason it is sometimes plural is easy to see when you think about it. *Neither* serves as the negative counterpart of *either,* which is usually singular. But it also serves in the same way for *both,* which is usually plural. Suppose, for instance, you have written "when both are dead." If you wanted to use *alive* instead of *dead,* you might come up with Shakespeare's solution:

> Thersites' body is as good as Ajax'
> When neither are alive
>   —*Cymbeline,* 1610

Other writers have done the same:

> Both writ with wonderful facility and clearness; neither were great inventors —John Dryden, preface to *Fables, Ancient and Modern,* 1700 (in OED)

> Neither belong to this Saxon's company —Sir Walter Scott, *Ivanhoe,* 1819 (in Jespersen)

> Neither were as good or as popular as his First —*Time,* 20 July 1942

> The major characters dissolve into a stream of anxieties and musings, the minor ones are ferociously eccentric; and neither matter —Irving Howe, *New Republic,* 16 Nov. 1953

> He had two job offers, but neither were ones he felt he could accept —Diana Diamond, *N.Y. Times,* 20 Oct. 1974 (in Ryan)

It is worth noting that *neither* by itself is more frequently singular:

> Neither has a theatre of its own —Ronald Hayman, *The Set-Up,* 1973

> . . . neither was able to go —K. M. Elisabeth Murray, *Caught in the Web of Words,* 1977

The singular number of *neither* is most likely to be ignored when it is followed by *of* and a plural noun or pronoun, for then both notional agreement and the principle of proximity pull in the direction of a plural verb. A few commentators recognize this construction. The pull of these two forces is obvious in the first example below, where *neither* without the *of* phrase is singular:

Neither cares about decent homes for the citizens. Neither of these dragons care about skyrocketing prices —*Congressional Record,* 18 July 1951

> . . . neither of them are a bit better than they should be —Henry Fielding, *Tom Jones,* 1749 (in Jespersen)

> . . . but neither of these are the causes of it —John Ruskin, *The Crown of Wild Olive,* 1866 (in Jespersen)

> Do you mean to say neither of you know your own numbers? —H. G. Wells, *A Modern Utopia,* 1905 (in Jespersen)

> Neither of these two last examples were so intended —William Empson, *The Structure of Complex Words,* 1951

> . . . Marx and Trotsky, neither of whom were notably gentle or vegetarian —Dwight Macdonald, *Esquire,* October 1966 (in Perrin & Ebbitt)

> . . . the two hot spots, neither of which have ever been especially praised for their food —Judy Klemesrud, quoted in Simon 1980

> Neither of these indicators are particularly accurate —Pat Ingram, *Chronicle of the Horse,* 13 Jan. 1984

Even in this construction a singular verb is very common:

> . . . with whiskey and a deck of cards, but most of the time neither of these was available —J. L. Dillard, *American Talk,* 1976

> Neither of you speaks a word until you're in the cab —Jay McInerney, *Bright Lights, Big City,* 1984

> . . . neither of us was rational enough to be convinced of the other's position —John Barth, *The Floating Opera,* 1956

The pronoun *neither,* then, is not invariably singular, though it is more often so. When formal agreement obtains, it takes a singular verb. When notional agreement obtains, it takes either a singular or plural verb. These constructions are neither nonstandard or erroneous. If you are writing something in a highly formal style, you will probably want to use formal agreement throughout. Otherwise, follow your own inclination in choosing singular or plural constructions after *neither.*

2. *Neither . . . nor, neither . . . or.* Commentators from 1776 to 2000 insist that *nor* should follow *neither,* and not *or.* But although *nor* is usual after *neither, or* has also been used quite often from the 16th century to the present.

> . . . he would neither go with me, or let me go without him —Daniel Defoe, *Moll Flanders,* 1722

... for I neither ride or shoot or move over my Garden walls —Lord Byron, letter, 9 Sept. 1811

But justice is neither old or new —Mark Van Doren, *American Scholar,* Autumn 1951

... an author who is neither an infant, a fool, or a swindler —Eric Bentley, *New Republic,* 16 Feb. 1953

Neither Cadwallader, Oliffe or Mitcham would claim ... —Tom Mangold, *The Listener,* 7 Nov. 1974

... the satellites are in thermal balance, neither heating up or cooling off —Robert C. Cowen, *Christian Science Monitor,* 23 Dec. 1982

Now, we can see no particular reason why anyone would prefer *or* to *nor* in these examples. But obviously *or* seemed idiomatic to these writers, and their sentences are perfectly comprehensible. We suspect that you, like most people, will pick *nor* after *neither.* But if you do happen to use *or* instead, you will have committed no dreadful solecism.

3. Must *neither* refer to two only? The answer, as you might suspect from having read a few of the examples in the preceding section, is no. A few commentators (Follett 1966 and Fowler 1926, 1965, for instance) hold out for two, but more consider what Fowler called the loose use to be neither solecistic nor nonstandard. It dates back to the 17th century, according to the OED. The adjective, the pronoun, and the conjunction are all sometimes used of more than two; such use is quite common with the conjunction.

I could do neither one of those three things —Henry Adams, letter, March or April, 1894

... neither of these last three materials is found in Japan —G. B. Sansom, *Japan: A Short Cultural History,* rev. ed., 1943

... neither tea, nor coffee, nor lemonade, nor anything whatever —Samuel Johnson, in James Boswell, *Life of Samuel Johnson,* 1791

Neither *Hamlet,* nor *Macbeth,* nor *Othello,* nor *Douglas,* nor *The Gamester* presented anything that could satisfy even the tragedians —Jane Austen, *Mansfield Park,* 1814

Neither you nor I nor anyone we know —Archibald MacLeish, letter, 27 Mar. 1920

... people who were neither beautiful, exciting, nor amusing —William Butler Yeats, *Dramatis Personae,* 1936

... the rigid enforcement of antique decorum will help neither language, literature, nor literati —James Sledd, *English Jour.,* May 1973

We could cite dozens more. You may have noticed that the adjectival and pronominal uses are a bit jarring, but the conjunctional uses seem humdrum. This suggests that you will probably want to avoid the first two— *none* is a good substitute—but you can use the conjunction freely. Note that *nor* is sometimes repeated and sometimes omitted for the intermediate words.

4. *"Neither . . . nor" and verb agreement.* Fowler 1926 is a bit irritated that Samuel Johnson and John Ruskin, as cited in the OED, transgressed his rule, which requires that if both subjects are singular the verb be singular. Fowler, of course, did not understand notional agreement, which is what Johnson and Ruskin were following. Here is Johnson:

Neither search nor labour are necessary —*The Idler,* No. 44, 1759 (OED)

Dr. Johnson used singular agreement too:

... neither reason nor revelation denies —letter, 25 Sept. 1750 (in Fitzedward Hall 1873)

Conjunctional *neither . . . nor,* like the pronoun *neither,* acts as a negative for *either . . . or* (construed as singular) and for *both . . . and* (construed as plural); agreement therefore may be either singular or plural—notional agreement, pure and simple. Here are several examples with two singular subjects and with either a singular or a plural verb:

Neither wood nor plastic conducts heat the way metal does —*And More by Andy Rooney,* 1982

Neither moon nor Mars are habitable—Ashley Montagu, *Vista,* January–February 1970

Neither Cox nor Kepshire has shown any ill effects —Craig Neff, *Sports Illustrated,* 22 July 1985

... neither my father nor I were by nature inclined to faith in the unintelligible — George Santayana, *Persons and Places,* 1944

... neither George—nor the audience— knows what dragons await him —David Ansen, *Newsweek,* 16 June 1986

... has lasted almost a century because neither light, heat, nor humidity affect it —Ellen Ruppel Shell, *Science 84,* September 1984

Neither . . . nor with two (or more) singular subjects, then, is governed by notional agreement and may take either a singular or a plural verb, as if the writer were imagining it as the negative of "either this or that" or the negative of "both this and that." When the subjects are plural, or the last subject is plural, a plural verb is expected:

Neither *montaña* nor Mexican origins are at all likely —Edward P. Lanning, *Peru Before the Incas,* 1967

If you are a native speaker of English, you will probably follow notional agreement without thinking, just as Samuel Johnson did. If you need a rule to follow consistently, use formal agreement—singular verb with singular subject and the verb to agree with the nearest subject otherwise. Formal agreement is always the safe choice in cases where you are uncertain.

5. See also AGREEMENT, INDEFINITE PRONOUNS; EITHER.

never A couple of handbooks, Scott, Foresman 1981 and Colter 1981, would restrict *never* to the meaning "not ever, at no time" and disapprove its other chief meaning, "not in any degree," which is used like an emphatic *not.* The objection can be found as far back as Gould 1867. But just what is wrong with the typically spoken usages they give as examples is not made explicit. The use in question is quite old:

Thou canst not say I did it. Never shake
Thy gory locks at me.
—Shakespeare, *Macbeth,* 1606

Many uses of *never* seem to hover between a simple negative meaning and "at no time":

. . . the fly ash . . . is trapped and never enters the atmosphere —*Annual Report, Virginia Electric & Power Co.*, 1970

You never go through that kind of experience . . . and come out the same —Mary Vespa, *People,* 16 May 1983

. . . holding onto a bag—probably popcorn that Naomi never finished —Johanna Kaplan, *Harper's,* March 1971

Such uses are standard.

next See FIRST TWO, TWO FIRST.

nice The use of *nice* as a general-purpose term of approval seems first to have been censured by one Archdeacon Hare, who was a friend of Walter Savage Landor. He called it a vulgarism. His remarks were repeated by later 19th-century American commentators like Ayres 1881, and from there the subject was taken up vigorously by a great many commentators, some of whom are diffident about the use even now. The usual objection is—now that the class-conscious label "vulgarism" has fallen into disuse—that *nice* is overused.

The usage apparently antedates the criticism by about a century. Curiously, the earliest evidence seems to come from Dr. Johnson's circle. Hodgson 1889 quotes a 19th-century philologist named Kington Oliphant, who says the earliest instance he had seen was

in Mrs. Thrale's conversation as recorded in Fanny Burney's diary. The earliest citation in the OED is from a 1769 letter of Mrs. Elizabeth Carter, who was also an acquaintance of Dr. Johnson. The usage seems to have come down to the present chiefly as conversational English.

It is certainly familiar to American writers, who take no trouble to avoid it in their casual moments:

I have written you this nice long letter —Robert Frost, letter, 9 Oct. 1915

It was uncommonly nice of you to write —Archibald MacLeish, letter, 9 Sept. 1926

It was nice to see a great writer in our time —Ernest Hemingway, *Green Hills of Africa,* 1935

It's terribly nice, my boy, with the rosemary in bloom and the fragrance of the mimosa trees —James Thurber, letter, 20 Jan. 1938

Of course when they began to bring in a little money, that was nice —William Faulkner, 13 Mar. 1958, in *Faulkner in the University,* 1959

It was certainly damn nice of you to write me that telegram —F. Scott Fitzgerald, letter, 29 Jan. 1934

It was damned nice of you to write in your book for me —Robert Benchley, letter, 29 Apr. 1934

. . . the club cleared a nice profit at the bar —Groucho Marx, letter, summer 1940

There is certainly nothing wrong with an effort to get college freshmen to use a wider variety of adjectives in their writing, but there is also nothing inherently wrong with *nice* in its generalized use.

nickel, nickle *Nickel* is the original spelling, the usual spelling, and, in the opinion of many people, the only correct spelling. *Nickle* is undoubtedly common in casual writing, but we think you would be well-advised to join the majority and spell it *nickel.*

nite *Nite* is a bit of a curiosity. Some people have thought it was associated with the spelling reform movement of the late 19th and early 20th centuries, but it seems not to have been. It seems to have been poorly thought of even by the reformers, possibly because it had gained a bad reputation from its employment by the willfully misspelling 19th-century American humorists:

But the fack can't be no longer disgised that a Krysis is onto us, & I feel it's my dooty to accept your invite for one consecutive nite only —*Artemus Ward: His Book,* 1862

Although snubbed by the reformers, *nite* has made considerable headway in the 20th century. Mencken 1963 (abridged) associates *nite* with advertising writers. It is clear from the evidence that much of the advertising using *nite* was for entertainment and show business: combinations such as *nite club, nite life,* and *nite spot* are common. A slightly later development finds *nite* as part of the name of an event:

> The Tilbury Rotary Club will present a Holiday Festival Nite on Tuesday —*Chatham* (Ontario) *Daily News,* 26 June 1980

> Have this wish on Auction nite —*Prime Time,* April 1981

So *nite* is apparently an arbitrary respelling used by American humorists in the 19th century and by American advertisers from around 1930. The OED Supplement shows it appearing in British English in the 1960s. It does not seem to have made any inroads into standard written usage. *Nite* will continue to be used in advertising and in the names of events like "Las Vegas Nite," but it is not a spelling you will want to use in ordinary prose.

no 1. *No* is often used in conjunction with other negatives, especially in speech. See DOUBLE NEGATIVE.
2. Ayres 1881 insists that when *no* introduces some sort of compound expression, it should correlate with *nor:* "no this nor that." Heritage 1982 insists that *or,* not *nor,* is required in the same situation. From this divergence of opinion we can infer that *or* was sometimes used in Ayres's time and that it has become prevalent since:

> Mr Edwards is no scholar or man of letters —*Times Literary Supp.,* 22 Oct. 1971

> Rose sent no congratulations or messages —Gail Cameron, *Ladies' Home Jour.,* August 1971

> There would be no backing down or hiding behind a convenient wall —Billie Whitelaw, quoted in *Annabel,* April 1974

But *nor* is still found on occasion:

> . . . no experienced editors, no office staff nor a distributor for the books —Kenneth C. Davis, *Publishers Weekly,* 2 Aug. 1985

Nor could be considered more emphatic than *or,* but in present-day use, emphasis is usually achieved by repeating the *no:*

> There was no chair, no table, no sofa, no pictures —Graham Greene, *Travels with My Aunt,* 1969

> No pollution, no crime, no politics —John Fischer, *Harper's,* July 1972

3. *"No" in the sense of "not."* A few commentators around the end of the 19th century objected to *no* qualifying a verb and meaning "not"—a matter chiefly of objecting to the phrase *whether or no.* Vizetelly 1906 said the practice had literary sanction. We have usually found *or no* (with or without *whether*) used in place of *or not* in literary contexts or by literary figures:

> . . . depends on whether or no his personal ambition is combined with intellectual ability —W. H. Auden, *Antaeus,* Spring/Summer 1976

> Laryngitis or no, the play has started off with a bang —Alexander Woollcott, letter, 19 Feb. 1940

> But personality or no, I have been aware of how much a part of you she was —E. B. White, letter, 20 Apr. 1957

> . . . Sister Mary Teresa emerges as a real human, nun or no —Newgate Callender, *N.Y. Times Book Rev.,* 1 Apr. 1984

See also WHETHER OR NOT.

nobody, no one These indefinite pronouns for the most part follow the same pattern of notional agreement as the other indefinite pronouns: they regularly take a singular verb but may be referred to by either a singular or plural pronoun. The handbooks that take a traditional position—mostly older ones— insist on the singular pronoun; newer ones recognize plural reference, although some of them avoid actual approval by limiting *they, their,* and *them* to informal use. Formal agreement looks like this:

> Nobody attains reality for my mother until he eats —Flannery O'Connor, letter, 28 June 1956

You can see right away one of the problems that formal singular agreement brings up —the question of sexism, conscious or otherwise. So there is an added advantage to favoring the plural pronoun: you avoid having to decide whether to use *he* or *she, his* or *her,* or *him* or *her.* Sometimes the notion of the many is so strong that the context simply calls for a plural:

> . . . but nobody really wanted to hear him speak. They wanted to see him grin —Harry S. Truman, quoted in Merle Miller, *Plain Speaking,* 1973

And the plural pronoun is often used even when the singular would present no problem:

> Nobody here seems to look into an Author, ancient or modern, if they can avoid it —Lord Byron, letter, 12 Nov. 1805

Byron was writing from Cambridge, and his reference could only have been to males.

The use of the plural pronoun in reference to *nobody* and *no one* is not only very common, it is well established—the OED dates it back as far as 1548. It is as old-fashioned as Jane Austen and as modern as Doris Lessing:

Nobody was in their right place —Jane Austen, *Mansfield Park*, 1814

"But nobody uses it, do they?" —Doris Lessing, *The Good Terrorist*, 1985

Our advice to you is to not be afraid of using *they, their,* or *them* to refer to *nobody* or *no one* when the idea is clearly plural or when you simply want to avoid a choice between masculine and feminine singular pronouns. When the sense is not necessarily plural, you can use singular pronouns in accordance with formal agreement. But meaning should come first.

For more on agreement with indefinite pronouns, see AGREEMENT: INDEFINITE PRONOUNS; NOTIONAL AGREEMENT, NOTIONAL CONCORD; THEY, THEIR, THEM.

no doubt   See DOUBTLESS, NO DOUBT, UNDOUBTEDLY.

noisome   While almost all English usage books find a need to caution against confusing *noisome* with *noisy,* our citation files show that *noisome* is almost always used to mean "noxious" or "disgusting":

. . . is zoned against livestock, partly owing to the fact that noisome pig farms once existed there —Christopher Rand, *New Yorker,* 11 Apr. 1964

This morning's coffee shop is this afternoon's noisome, grease-spewing alfresco sandwich stand —Alexander Cohen, *N.Y. Times,* 13 Aug. 1972

We also find it with extended meaning:

Miss Karmel's debut is not of the noisome type with which so many "promising" writers enter upon—and usually depart from—the literary scene —Martin Rice, *Saturday Rev.,* 9 May 1953

The reception of Charles Osborne's life of W. H. Auden and Ted Morgan's Somerset Maugham was predictably noisome —Richard Holmes, *N.Y. Times Book Rev.,* 29 June 1980

And we have some evidence for *noisesome* meaning "noisy," but not enough to warrant its entry in the dictionary.

. . . the suggestion that modern mothers . . . quieten their noisesome offspring by filling them up with chlorodyne —*Times Literary Supp.,* 5 Jan. 1967

. . . our own necessarily noisesome and laborious progress through the thick bamboo forest —A. B. Anderson, *African Wild Life,* December 1950

no less than   See LESS, FEWER.

none   No one knows who set abroad the notion that *none* could only be singular, but abroad it is. Howard 1980 says, "A considerable number of readers of *The Times* are convinced beyond reason that the pronoun *none* is singular only"; Burchfield 1981 notes that listeners to the BBC are similarly convinced. The notion is not restricted to Britain: Mary Vaiana Taylor, in an article titled "The Folklore of Usage" in *American Speech* (April 1974), says that 60 percent of the graduate teaching assistants she surveyed marked *none* with a plural verb wrong in students' papers. William Safire, in the *New York Times Magazine* (1 Apr. 1984), mentions several correspondents who have written in protest of his "Obviously, none of these previous noun usages offer a clue. . . ."

The origin of the notion is based on the etymology of the word. The etymology explanation goes back at least to Lindley Murray 1795. Murray, after recording that "*None* is used in both numbers" goes on to observe, "It seems originally to have signified, according to its derivation, *not one,* and therefore to have had no plural. . . ." Murray is, in fact, only half right there. The Old English *nan* "none" was in fact formed from *ne* "not" and *an* "one," but Old English *nan* was inflected for both singular and plural. Hence it never has existed in the singular only; King Alfred the Great used it as a plural as long ago as A.D. 888. And even Murray concludes his observation by saying, "but there is good authority for the use of it in the plural number."

We will probably never know who transformed Lindley Murray's etymological explanation into a law of usage and spread it about widely. But no matter how difficult it may be to say how this notion got started, we can find a number of adherents to it, from Bierce 1909 down to Simon 1980. Most recent commentators, however, admit both singular and plural use.

Our evidence shows that writers generally make it singular or plural according to whatever their idea is when they write. This matching of verb (or referring pronoun) to a pronoun by sense, rather than formal grammatical number, is known as notional agreement (see NOTIONAL AGREEMENT, NOTIONAL CONCORD and the various articles at AGREEMENT).

For instance, when *none* is followed by an *of* phrase containing a plural noun or pronoun, you might expect the plural verb to be more natural. Our evidence, however, shows both the singular and plural verbs:

> None of these are love letters in the conventional sense —W. H. Auden, *New Yorker*, 19 Mar. 1955
>
> None of its inhabitants expects to become a millionaire —Bernard DeVoto, *Holiday*, July 1955
>
> None of the lines are strikingly brilliant —Wolcott Gibbs, *New Yorker*, 5 Mar. 1955
>
> None of them is happily married today —Judith Krantz, *Cosmopolitan*, October 1976

Or perhaps you might think that *none* is more likely to take a singular verb when it butts right up against its verb. But here, too, both singular and plural are used:

> While some were poor, none was rich —John Kenneth Galbraith, *The Scotch*, 1964
>
> None were deeper in that labyrinthine ambition —G. K. Chesterton, reprinted in *The Pocket Book of Father Brown*, 1946
>
> And if, among this wealth of possibilities, none seems exactly right —Barnard 1979
>
> . . . and none say they read poetry for fun —James Sledd, in Greenbaum 1985

Clearly, then, *none* takes a singular verb when the writer thinks of it as singular, and plural when the writer thinks of it as plural. The notion that it is singular only is a myth of unknown origin that appears to have arisen late in the 19th century. If in context it seems like a singular to you, use a singular verb; if it seems like a plural, use a plural verb. Both are acceptable beyond serious criticism.

nonrestrictive appositives See APPOSITIVES.

nonstandard *Nonstandard* is a label frequently used in dictionaries and handbooks. It generally designates forms and constructions that are not characteristic of educated native speakers; these are very often regionalisms. Some books, such as Webster's Third, differentiate between *nonstandard* and *substandard*, using *substandard* as an indicator of social status. But many other books simply use *nonstandard* as a blanket replacement for *substandard*, *illiterate*, and various other now dated pejoratives.

See also STANDARD, STANDARD ENGLISH; SUBSTANDARD.

no one See NOBODY, NO ONE.

noplace *Noplace*, meaning "nowhere," is condemned along with *anyplace*, *everyplace*, and *someplace* by a number of commentators

on the grounds that *place*, a noun, should not be used as an adverb to mean "where." The objection does not hold water, as Bernstein 1971 points out at *anyplace*, because *place* is often used in combinations where it has adverbial force.

The evidence in our files and in the OED Supplement shows that *noplace* is found in American English rather than British English and that it is used in print less frequently than *anyplace* or *someplace* and about as frequently as *everyplace*. It is apparently more a spoken than a written form. In print it looks like this:

> . . . hibernating toads go noplace until the temperature rises toward five degrees Celsius —*New Yorker*, 17 Aug. 1987

The adverbial *noplace*, which is sometimes spelled as two words, should be distinguished from the simple combination of *no* and *place*:

> Daring . . . had no place in the old role —Elizabeth Janeway, *Ms.*, April 1973

See also ANYPLACE; EVERYPLACE; SOMEPLACE.

nor 1. For *nor* after *no*, see NO 2; for *nor* after *neither*, see NEITHER 2, 4.
2. *Nor* frequently replaces *or* in negative statements:

> You cannot describe a house brick by brick, nor a wood leaf by leaf —Leacock 1943
>
> . . . I wasn't interested in literature nor literary people —William Faulkner, 13 Mar. 1958, in *Faulkner in the University*, 1959
>
> . . . not seeking to discount the study of grammar nor the analysis and practice of good written expression —Finegan 1980

It is clearly felt to be more emphatically negative than *or* in some instances:

> . . . I recommend that you have nothing further to do with this person nor with these arms transfers —Robert C. McFarlane, quoted in *The Tower Commission Report*, 1987

normalcy *Normalcy* became a notorious word during the 1920 Presidential election, when Warren G. Harding proclaimed that what the country needed was a return to the "normalcy" of the days before World War I. Those who opposed Harding often criticized him for his less than exemplary use of the language, and they loudly derided *normalcy* as a characteristically laughable malapropism. (Actually the word had been put into Harding's mouth by a speechwriter.)

Harding's supporters quickly came to his defense, however, even going so far as to look in the OED, where it was discovered that *normalcy* had been recorded as early as 1857. It had also appeared in Webster 1864. It was an unusual and uncommon word, certainly, but Warren G. Harding had not invented it, although the myth that he had was still being repeated in the 1990s:

> . . . "normalcy" (a word coined by Warren Gamaliel Harding) —John Lukacs, *American Heritage,* November 1993

What Harding *had* done, of course, was to popularize the word. Despite those who regarded it as a "spurious hybrid" (Fowler 1926, for one), *normalcy* established itself in widespread use during the 1920s. Its notoriety was such that many of those who used it did so self-consciously, often in direct—and usually critical—reference to Harding and his term of office, and there was a persistent tendency to enclose the word in quotation marks:

> . . . to fear that we may be slipping back to a state of "normalcy" in politics —*World's Work,* September 1926

Although it still is used in reference to Harding, in current use it is simply a straightforward synonym of *normality*:

> . . . from relative normalcy through marked eccentricity —John Barth, *The Floating Opera,* 1956

> . . . taking special pains to give an impression of completest normalcy —Saul Bellow, *Herzog,* 1964

> . . . the insight that the German Chancellor is driven by a need for national normalcy —William Safire, *N.Y. Times Mag.,* 27 June 1993

> . . . another sign that their city was gradually returning to prewar normalcy —Edward Sorel, *GQ,* December 1997

> . . . changing abnormal cell growth back to some level of normalcy —Paula Begoun, *Houston Chronicle,* 4 June 1998

Normalcy is now a perfectly reputable word, recognized as standard by all major dictionaries.

no sooner   Quite a number of commentators—Janis 1984, Phythian 1979, Longman 1984, Johnson 1982, Bernstein 1965, Copperud 1964, 1970, 1980—insist that *no sooner* must be followed by *than* and not *when.* It usually is followed by *than; when* is rare in print but we did find this example:

> The moderator had no sooner asked for comments from the audience when a little man arose —*National Observer,* 26 Sept. 1966

If *when* is common after *no sooner,* it must be so only in speech. In print, *than* is the regular choice:

> . . . he had no sooner completed training than he was called to Ottawa —*Current Biography,* June 1966

> No sooner does John Riggins reluctantly drop out of sight . . . than Joe T. limps up to the booth —E. M. Swift, *Sports Illustrated,* 1 Sept. 1986

not about to   The idiom *not about to* has all the earmarks of being a relatively recent Americanism. It is not, however. There is nothing about the words *not about to* that excites attention, and it is not unlikely that the phrase, expressing intention, has been in at least occasional use since this:

> By the by, I expect Hanson to remit regularly; for I am not about to stay in this province for ever —Lord Byron, letter, 12 Nov. 1809

In current use *not about to* usually connotes determination as well as intention, and Byron was perhaps not expressing determination. So modern use may not be a direct descendant of Byron's use, but no one knows for sure—there simply is no evidence.

The phrase did not come to the attention of critics until 1968, when Theodore Bernstein noticed it in the *New York Times* and decided it must be "substandard" (*Winners & Sinners,* 8 Aug. 1968). He later upgraded the phrase to "colloquial" (*Winners & Sinners,* 15 May 1969). Subsequent writers for the *Times* have not been deterred by Bernstein's objections; our files have numerous examples from *Times* writers right up to the present.

Reader's Digest 1983 says that it was "at first regarded as informal, suitable only for spoken use" but that it is "now acceptable in formal writing also." It has gained wide currency in American English, and we have also found it in Canadian, British, and Australian sources. It is used in edited prose, especially in newspapers and magazines.

> . . . although she considers herself passionate, she is not about to act in a headlong way —Mary Gordon, *N.Y. Times Book Rev.,* 8 May 1994

> Because I am a traditionalist, I am not about to recommend the abolition of turkey on Thanksgiving —Jasper White, *Yankee,* November 1991

> . . . Hearst was not about to deny the public what it wanted —Neal Gabler, *Life: the Movie,* 1998

> . . . I'd chimneyed 20 metres down a narrow chasm . . . and was not about to turn back —Amanda Burdon, *Australian Geographic,* January–March 1995

not all

. . . I'm not about to become a full-time
househusband like Lennon did —Mick Jagger, quoted by Michael Cable, *US,* 2 Jan.
1984

not all, all . . . not See ALL 3.

not all that See ALL THAT.

not as, not so See AS . . . AS 1.

not . . . but Under this heading a number of
commentators take up the issue of *but* following a negative. It is aspersed as a double negative by some, but it is not a double negative
(see the explanation at BUT 4). The construction is most frequently followed by a number
(which may be either cardinal or ordinal), but
other words (such as *few*) are used too.

The *not . . . but* construction is the older of
a pair of expressions (the other lacks the negative) that mean the same thing. It is most
common in speech, but not entirely limited to
it. Here are a few examples from speech and
letters:

The last duel I fought didn't take but five
minutes —Emily Dickinson, letter, 11 Jan.
1850

You haven't done it but once —Flannery
O'Connor, letter, 20 Sept. 1958

. . . we never lost but very few logs —Elbert
Herald, quoted in *Our Appalachia,* ed. Laurel Shackelford & Bill Weinberg, 1977

"You . . . can't wear but one suit of clothes
at a time," Mantzel says philosophically
—Nancy Schommer, *People,* 18 Mar. 1985

Here is one from fiction:

. . . and Miss Betty didn't have to be told but
once —Peter Taylor, *The Old Forest and
Other Stories,* 1985

Bryant 1962 calls this construction standard in
speech. But it seems to be a bit old-fashioned,
and like many old-fashioned expressions may
be more common in rural speech than in
urban speech, and hence suspect to the city-
dweller. It has been in the process of being replaced by the positive construction—especially in print—for quite some time now:

It makes but one mistake —Emily Dickinson, letter, early 1878

. . . had won 25 away games and lost but 15
—Anthony Cotton, *Sports Illustrated,* 30
Mar. 1981

. . . he had but 12 days to go —C. D. B.
Bryan, *N.Y. Times Book Rev.,* 16 Oct. 1983

Note that the meaning of *not . . . but* is
"only." When *but* means "except," it is also
common with negatives:

No respect was paid but to merit —John
Butt, *English Literature in the Mid-Eigh-
teenth Century,* edited & completed by
Geoffrey Carnall, 1979

. . . there's no place for the kids to play but
in the street —*And More by Andy Rooney,*
1982

For a negative followed by *but* and *that* or
what, see BUT 5.

not hardly See HARDLY.

notional agreement, notional concord As
Quirk et al. 1985 explains it, *notional agreement* (called *notional concord* by Quirk and
others) is agreement of a verb with its subject
or of a pronoun with its antecedent in accordance with the notion of number rather than
with the presence of an overt grammatical
marker for that notion. Another way to look
at the matter is that notional agreement is
agreement based on meaning rather than
form. This meaning is the meaning the expression has to the writer or speaker.

Notional agreement contrasts with formal,
or grammatical, agreement, in which overt
markers—form—determine singular or plural
agreement. Formal agreement could also be
called school-grammar agreement, for it is
what is taught in school. We do not know who
first realized that notional agreement exists as
a powerful force in English grammar, but it
must be a fairly recent discovery. The 18th-
century grammarians never tumbled to it,
even though their examples for correction
showed it being widely followed. Most school
grammars are based on their 18th-century
forebears and do not mention notional agreement. And many (perhaps most) usage commentators seem likewise unaware of it.

But notional agreement has often been
granted silent assent by normative grammarians in specific instances: formally plural
nouns like *news, means,* and *mathematics* have
long been accorded the privilege of taking singular verbs. So here is notional agreement at
work, but no one objects:

I don't think the barricades is an answer
—James Thurber, letter, 20 Jan. 1938

The Philippines likewise wasn't interested
—Chris Pritchard, *Christian Science Monitor,* 23 June 1986

Likewise, when a singular noun takes a plural
verb or pronoun—as in the case of many collective and institutional nouns in British English—we have notional agreement at work:

And so every Southern household when
they bought books they bought Scott
—William Faulkner, 13 May 1957, in *Faulkner in the University,* 1959

The Brandt Commission have estimated that . . . —Christopher Terrill, *Geographical Mag.,* May 1984

When in the Course of human events, it becomes necessary for one people to dissolve the political bands which have connected them with another —*Declaration of Independence,* 1776

More troubling to the traditional grammarian are instances in which a singular noun is used as if it were a generic collective and is referred to by a plural pronoun or is matched with a plural verb:

. . . and no small blame to our vaunted society that the man in the street . . . was debarred from seeing more of the world they lived in —James Joyce, *Ulysses,* 1922

. . . a game of donkey baseball sounds pretty dull, but people who have seen them tell me different —John O'Hara, letter, 11 Sept. 1934

I can usually spot a liberal Democrat or a conservative Republican at one hundred feet, and I have no trouble at all when they come close enough so I can hear them talk —*And More by Andy Rooney,* 1982

In this sort of notional agreement the plural pronoun is much more common than the plural verb.

Indefinite pronouns are heavily influenced by notional agreement, and in a peculiar way: they tend to take singular verbs but plural pronouns:

"But nobody uses it, do they?" —Doris Lessing, *The Good Terrorist,* 1985

. . . none has distinguished themselves —Carol Leggett, quoted in *Publishers Weekly,* 26 June 1987

And suddenly she is there. and everybody knows, and they crane their heads backward to see her —Alice Adams, *Listening to Billie,* 1977

Notional agreement will also at times produce a singular verb after compound subjects joined by *and* and a plural verb after compound singular subjects joined by *or.* This is just the opposite of what formal agreement says should be the case:

. . . time and chance happeneth to them all —Ecclesiastes 9:11 (AV), 1611

My admiration and affection for you both is bounded only by the Seven Seas —Groucho Marx, undated letter, in *The Groucho Letters,* 1967

. . . in periods when vellum, parchment, or even paper were prohibitively expensive

—Lee T. Lemon, *A Glossary for the Study of English,* 1971

". . . a feather or a fiddle are their pursuits and their pleasures. . . ." —Henry Fielding, *Jonathan Wild,* 1743

Notional agreement is mentioned at many entries in this book, because the conflict between notional and formal agreement is behind many disputed usages. (See, in particular, ONE OF THOSE WHO; THEY, THEIR, THEM; and the various articles at AGREEMENT.) Sometimes the conflict will drive a writer to produce a sentence even more startling than those produced by purely formal or purely notional agreement:

Granted only a small fraction of lawyers actually besmirches their profession —*San Francisco Chronicle,* 13 Aug. 1986

not only . . . but also   The *also* in this set of correlative conjunctions is optional and is frequently omitted. Freeman 1983 says that when *also* is omitted, the words following *but* receive greater stress. This may be so, at least sometimes, but it is hard to demonstrate.

. . . it is necessary not only that his designs be formed in a masterly manner, but that they should be attended with success —Samuel Johnson, in James Boswell, *Life of Samuel Johnson,* 1791

Also is often omitted in shorter constructions, where the omission is often desirable as it makes for tighter and smoother expression:

Human society is not only multifaceted but often contradictory —Finegan 1980

. . . an oafish brute who not only beat her but insisted on being addressed as father —Alexander Woollcott, letter, 24 Apr. 1942

I not only feel, but know as a fact, that . . . —James Thurber, letter, 20 Jan. 1938

It would not matter whether Johnson had used *also,* but the other three examples would have been more awkward with the *also.*

The chief concern of the many commentators who discuss the *not only . . . but (also)* construction is parallelism: they insist that for clarity identical constructions be placed after both the *not only* and the *but (also).* Despite the opinions of the commentators, the nonparallel construction is common enough to pass almost unnoticed. The fact that it often does pass unnoticed is evidence that it creates no confusion or misunderstanding. Hall 1917 collected about 125 nonparallel constructions from more than 50 authors, almost all literary. It is clear that constructions which are not precisely parallel are as much a part of standard English as those which are precisely parallel.

Here we have a few examples in which parallelism is not observed:

> Most of the luxuries, and many of the so called comforts of life, are not only not indispensable, but positive hindrances to the elevation of mankind —Henry David Thoreau, *Walden,* 1854

> North Haverhill is not only the seat of the country estate of Frances Parkinson Keyes but provides the locale for a number of her novels —*American Guide Series: New Hampshire,* 1938

> I was really impressed by your analysis of the show not only because of its complimentary tone, but because it so accurately described so many of the evils of radio —Groucho Marx, letter, 28 Dec. 1949

> A journal, both of them insisted, would give the Institute not only professional standing, but could provide a wide appeal for membership —Julia Child, *Jour. of Gastronomy,* Summer 1984

And here are a few examples in which it is observed:

> . . . for not only are their own Eleven all at home, but the three little Bridges are also with them —Jane Austen, letter, 30 June 1808

> . . . I am sure he would not only get over that trouble, but be as well and strong as he ever was —Walt Whitman, letter, 15 Apr. 1863

> . . . it was not only a Greek but a contemporary tragedy —Gilbert Highet, *The Classical Tradition,* 1949

> Miss Didion is wonderful not only at hearing her characters but at naming them —Mary McCarthy, *Occasional Prose,* 1985

We doubt that you had any trouble understanding any of the examples, though you may have preferred some over others. As long as you take care that the groups of words joined by the conjunctions are not so dissimilar as to call attention to themselves, you need not worry all the time about achieving precise parallelism. It is more important for your sentence to sound natural and to make sense.

For the related issue of the placement of *only* in a sentence, see ONLY 1.

notorious Usage writers from Ayres 1881 to Harper 1985 have warned all and sundry not to confuse *notorious* with *famous, notable,* or *noted.* They point out that *notorious* has a pejorative connotation: "widely and unfavorably known." Other usage writers, from Vizetelly 1906 to Copperud 1970, 1980, reply that the word is not always used pejoratively.

Notorious is quite frequently used. Part of its popularity is the tang that clings to all uses of the word from its frequent use to mean "widely and unfavorably known." Even in its neutral uses, as we shall see, its association with the unfavorable, disreputable, and unsavory gives it a piquancy, an emphatic quality, that a mere *noted, notable, famous,* or even *celebrated* lacks. Thus, it is often the word chosen by writers who are aware of its particular flavor; writers who are not aware of that flavor can get themselves into trouble, as did the advertising copywriter who wrote a radio commercial for a local boutique calling attention to the availability of a painter in residence who was "notorious for his portraits."

Our evidence shows that most writers who use *notorious* are well aware of its overtones. Here are the ways in which it is used.

It is always pejorative when linked with a noun for an undesirable person:

> . . . a notorious gunman for the Profaci family —Tom Buckley, *Harper's,* August 1971

> . . . a notorious muddle-head, as Lenin unkindly described him —*Times Literary Supp.,* 31 Dec. 1971

> . . . the most notorious serial killers of our time —Genevieve Stuttaford et al., *Publishers Weekly,* 26 May 1997

> . . . promoted in part by the notorious machine politican "Bath-House" John Coughlin —Howard P. Chudacoff, *The Age of the Bachelor,* 1999

When *notorious* is applied as an attributive or predicate adjective to a person, you can assume that it is being used pejoratively:

> . . . biography of someone as notorious as Adolf Hitler —John Kenneth Galbraith, *N.Y. Times Book Rev.,* 22 Apr. 1973

> . . . links to the notorious Osama bin Laden, the terrorist paymaster —Bill Powell, *Newsweek,* 27 Sept. 1999

> . . . when the notorious Captain Bligh sailed into port in 1793 —Caleb Pirtle III, *Southern Living,* November 1971

Often there will be clues that indicate a milder or even humorous use:

> . . . Alben and I had our pictures taken, as is usual when notorious persons leave or arrive in cities —Harry S. Truman, diary, 20 Sept. 1945

> . . . is a notorious soft touch for friends and strangers alike —*Current Biography,* April 1966

> Neither union officials nor executive vice presidents are notorious students of ab-

stract truth —Richard E. Danielson, *Atlantic*, February 1947

Notorious is frequently applied as an attributive or predicate adjective to nouns that the linguist would describe as "not human." The word verges on the neutral in many such applications. Still, in the absence of clues to the contrary, you will find the intent to be pejorative:

> Some weeds have become notorious in tropical forestry —Charles J. Taylor, *Tropical Forestry*, 1962

> . . . the President's veto of the notorious McCarran thought-control bill —Harold L. Ickes, *New Republic*, 29 Nov. 1950

> . . . a garish strip long notorious for fenderbenders and holiday mega-traffic-jams —Bruce Ingersoll, *Wall Street Jour.*, 26 July 1999

> . . . at Andersonville, the notorious Confederate prison —Gary Cartwright, *GQ*, November 1998

But very often there are no moral overtones; *notorious* is simply used as a more emphatic *celebrated, famous,* or *well-known*:

> . . . was a notorious hypochondriac and recluse —*Publishers Weekly*, 7 Apr. 1997

> . . . the notorious thoroughness with which Clay conducts inspections —E. J. Kahn, Jr., *New Yorker*, 13 Jan. 1951

> . . . they fill a notorious gap in the literature on ancient Rome —M. I. Finley, *N.Y. Rev. of Books*, 3 June 1971

The notorious "second novel" bugaboo of literature —Stanley Kauffmann, *New Republic*, 6 Mar. 2000

He was involved in a notorious controversy with the poet Swinburne —K. M. Elisabeth Murray, *Caught in the Web of Words*, 1977

In the construction *notorious for*, the strength of *notorious* is usually dependent on the matter following *for*:

> . . . Serb forces who became notorious in Bosnia for the atrocities of "ethnic cleansing" —Carlotta Gall, *N.Y. Times*, 26 Mar. 1999

> . . . I am notorious for my habit of looking on the bright side —John O'Hara, letter, 3 Aug. 1962

> Presidents are, in the eyes of bureaucrats, notorious for putting off decisions —Leslie H. Gelb & Morton H. Halperin, *Harper's*, June 1972

> Gell-Mann became notorious for his bad temper —George Johnson, *Atlantic*, July 2000

> . . . Galicia, a region notorious for the shrewdness of its sons —*New Republic*, 22 Nov. 1948

In the construction *it is notorious that, notorious* is nearly always neutral; any pejorative intent has to be supplied by the matter following *that,* which seldom happens:

> . . . and concerning taste it is notorious that there can be no dispute —Ashley Montagu, *Man's Most Dangerous Myth: The Fallacy of Race*, 2d ed., 1945

> We have commentators, but it is notorious that they are not allowed to comment —Jacques Barzun, *Atlantic*, February 1947

> That he was not always pleased is notorious —D. J. R. Bruckner, *N.Y. Times Book Rev.*, 16 Oct. 1983

You can see from the examples that most writers have no problem handling *notorious*. All you have to remember is that it always seems to have a certain piquancy, a certain bite, from its frequent association with persons and things of undesirable character. Even when it is neutral in denotation, it has that characteristic flavor.

not to worry   Sixty-two percent of the Harper 1985 usage panel disapproved the harmless British import *not to worry* in speech and 87 percent disapproved it in writing. Panelist Willard R. Espy dissented, finding *not to worry* diverting. In this he agrees with Flesch 1983.

The peculiarity of the expression lies in the imperative force of *not to*—equivalent to *don't*. The construction appears to be quite recent. The OED Supplement has a precursor of *not to worry* in "please not to mention that again" from George Eliot's *Middlemarch* (1872), but the earliest citation they show for *not to worry* is from 1958. Language historian Barbara M. H. Strang in a 1965 book review refers to it as a new construction.

The phrase began to appear in American English in the 1970s and is still to be found now and then:

> "I don't suppose you remembered that bagel," Megan says. "Not to worry, I'm not really hungry anyway. . . ." —Jay McInerney, *Bright Lights, Big City*, 1984

> Not to worry; there are still tons of them —Chris Taylor, *Time*, 10 Apr. 2000

The construction turns up once in a while with other verbs:

> "We're gonna go outside for a while, okay?" she said. "Not to panic or anything. But I have this freaky feeling." —Cyra McFadden, *The Serial*, 1977

not un-   See DOUBLE NEGATIVE 2.

nought   See NAUGHT 1.

nouns as adjectives   See ATTRIBUTIVE.

nouns as verbs   It occasionally comes as a surprise to the linguistically unsophisticated that nouns can be put to work as verbs. This, like the use of nouns as adjectives, is a practice with a long history. Dean Alford 1866 commented on the subject; among the verbified nouns he mentions are *progress, head,* and *experience.* The Dean was not upset by the practice, but several recent commentators—Freeman 1983, Harper 1975, 1985, and Strunk & White 1972, 1979 among them— have criticized specific instances of the practice. The verbified nouns (or denominal verbs, to use a term many linguists use) that are objected to include *chair, host, gift,* and *debut,* all of which are treated separately in this book.

The opposite practice, that of turning verbs into nouns, also occurs. There is commentary on the subject in Safire 1980 and 1984.

nouns joined by *and, or*   See AGREEMENT, PRONOUN: NOUNS JOINED BY AND, OR.

now   Use of *now* as an adjective dates back to the 14th century. Its oldest sense, "present, existing," has impressive historical backing and has excited no animosity:

> ... the now Bishop Asbury had become well acquainted with the role —Dr. Asbury Smith, *Maryland Mag.,* Autumn 1971

But in the 1960s the adjective *now* suddenly became popular—and somewhat notorious— in two new uses: describing the mores and manners of the younger generation, and characterizing the generation itself:

> One agency music director in search of the "now sound" —*Newsweek,* 27 Nov. 1967

> ... fairly typical of the Now Generation —Henry S. Resnik, *Saturday Rev.,* 26 Oct. 1968

These uses of *now* enjoyed a vogue of several years, but by the mid-1970s they had aged somewhat, as had the generation they applied to. In current English they have a distinctly dated quality and are most likely to occur when the era of their popularity is being deliberately evoked.

See also THEN 1.

no way   From the evidence at hand it appears that *no way* as an emphatic negative is an Americanism that cropped up in the late 1960s. Our earliest printed evidence is from 1968:

> ... I can't forget those first seventeen years, no way! —Arthur Ashe, quoted in *N.Y. Amsterdam News,* 7 Sept. 1968

Howard 1978 and Harper 1975, 1985 are sure the expression is on the way out; Reader's

Digest 1983 and Flesch 1983 are sure it is here to stay. Shaw 1975, 1987 merely thinks it is hackneyed. Our current evidence does not suggest that the phrase is losing popularity.

As Reader's Digest notes, *no way* occurs in several constructions. The first of these, the interjectional use, is the earliest and the most common:

> So I ask myself . . . do I want to go out on location in some godforsaken corner of McKeesport, Pennsylvania, and live in a motel for two months? No way —Robert Mitchum, quoted in *N.Y. Times,* 19 Sept. 1971

> The answer is—no way —Ada Louise Huxtable, *N.Y. Times,* 23 June 1974

> You remember the Bolivian Marching Powder and realize you're not down yet. No way, José —Jay McInerney, *Bright Lights, Big City,* 1984

No way also frequently occurs after *there is* (or *was*). This construction is very close to being a simple combination of *no* and *way.* When followed by *for,* the phrase seems entirely transparent:

> . . . said there was no way for Truman to win —Victor Emanuel, Sr., *Houston Post,* 15 Sept. 1984

But the *there is* construction without the *for* is more common:

> There's no way I could skate constantly for 20 minutes —Scott Hamilton, quoted in *Houston Post,* 4 Sept. 1984

> He was a turncoat, and there was no way we would support him —Tip O'Neill with William Novak, *Man of the House,* 1987

The *there is* can simply be omitted too:

> No way you can put a ball over that scoreboard —John Candelaria, quoted in *Sports Illustrated,* 16 July 1979

> No way the hottest name in Hollywood is supposed to act this uncool —Charles Leerhsen with Carl Robinson, *Newsweek,* 8 Dec. 1986

So far, *no way* seems to be limited to speech and prose of a personal or casual nature.

nowhere near   Usage handbooks typically describe *nowhere near* as a colloquial or informal substitute for *not nearly* and say it should be avoided. The OED shows that it is an extremely old phrase, attested in writing (in the form *nowhere nigh*) as far back as 1413. Its common use in writing, however, seems not to have occurred until fairly recently.

What that evidence shows is that *nowhere near* occurs widely in standard edited prose, and is not especially informal. It seems a bit more emphatic than *not nearly*:

> Yet this comes nowhere near to describing a certain ineffable style the Murphys were said to have had —Donna Rifkind, *Times Literary Supp.*, 6 Dec. 1991

> While this is hot, [it] is nowhere near the million kelvins of the corona —Leon Golub, *Astronomy*, May 1993

> . . . is one reason that "downsizing" sometimes produces nowhere near the results that companies expect —Joann S. Lublin, *Wall Street Jour.*, 6 Dec. 1993

> Any regret for what I may have made Hattie feel is nowhere near enough to have appeased her anger —William Maxwell, *New Yorker*, 23 Sept. 1991

> Defense study acknowledged that a ballistic-missile defense system is nowhere near technologically practical — *New Republic*, 6 Dec. 1999

A distinct use of *nowhere near* is in the sense "not at all close to":

> Teddy bears, thank goodness, are nowhere near extinction —Carolyn Meyer, *McCall's*, March 1971

> . . . our present health insurance policy comes nowhere near providing that —Sylvia Porter, *Ladies' Home Jour.*, August 1971

This sense has the same emphatic quality as the "not nearly" sense.

nowheres As several commentators point out, the adverb *nowheres* is not in standard use as a variant of *nowhere*. It occurs primarily in dialectal and nonstandard speech and in written representations of such speech:

> I hain't been nowheres —Mark Twain, *Huckleberry Finn*, 1884 (OED Supplement)

> I don't want to go nowheres and I'll take a job if it's the right kind —Ring Lardner, *The Big Town*, 1921

Nowheres, like *anywheres* and *somewheres* (which see), is an Americanism.

nth Fowler 1926 argues that since *n* means "an unspecified number" rather than "an infinite number" in mathematics, the derivative use of *nth* by nonmathematicians is more "utmost," as in "to the nth degree," is wrong. His opinion has not been heeded. No other commentator objects to the "utmost" sense of *nth* (Evans 1957 and Copperud 1970, 1980 consider it established in reputable use, and dictionaries have recognized it as standard throughout the 20th century. Here are a few examples of its use from our files:

> . . . in the characters . . . developed to the nth degree —Judith Crist, *New York*, 27 Dec. 1971

> . . . raised to the *n*th power of elegance —Audax Minor, *New Yorker*, 17 July 1971

> . . . has raised to the *n*th degree our national failings of lethargy and wishful thinking —David Wheeler, *The Listener*, 15 May 1975

nuclear In many recent usage books the reader is admonished to say \'nü-klē-ər\, not \'nü-kyə-lər\, and never mind what President Eisenhower used to say.

We wish first to confront a more interesting question. Why, when the pronunciation problems of *nuclear* are so well known that they are a continuing source of national wrath and mirth, do so many educated people—and especially members of Congress—persist in the condemned pronunciation? Why did \'nü-kyə-lər\ arise in the first place?

Since \'nü-kyə-lər\ is not a spelling pronunciation, it must have originated phonologically as a deviation from the target of \'nü-klē-ər\. The transformation is reminiscent of but cannot strictly be described as *metathesis* (which see); in any event *metathesis* is a label for a phenomenon, not an explanation. That the target pronunciation presents some articulatory difficulties is suggested by two other variants that may more clearly be seen as simplifications: the occasional \'nü-kyir\ and the fairly common \'nü-klir\ (which we have attested respectively from former President Jimmy Carter and from his mother, among others).

But besides any inherent difficulty involved in saying \'nü-klē-ər\, the pronunciation \'nü-kyə-ler\ was probably engendered by a process that functions in folk etymology as well: the replacement of a relatively less familiar sequence of sounds with one relatively more familiar. Now, there is *no* other common word in English that ends in \-klē-ər\, and just one uncommon one (*cochlear*). But there are several that end in \-kyə-lər\ or \-kyü-lər\: *particular*, *spectacular*, *molecular*, *secular*, *oracular*, *vernacular*. So we believe that *nuclear* became \'nü-kyə-lər\ for the same reason that *et cetera* became \ek-'set-ə-rə\ (see ETC.): speakers have succumbed to the gravitational tug of a far more prevalent pattern.

This explanation is further bolstered by the case of *similar*, *percolator*, and *escalator*, which the less educated often pronounce respectively \'sim-yə-lər\, \'pər-kyə-ˌlāt-ər\, and \'es-kyə-ˌlāt-ər\. Here the vague explanation that the folk version is "simpler" will not hold water, because the folk version arises by *adding* a sound, \y\. What actually happens is that when saying *similar*, *percolator*, and *escalator*, some speakers conform to the more familiar pattern (stop consonant plus \yəl\ plus vowel) that shows up in such words as *fabulous, cellular, ridiculous, angular, populated,* and *masculine.*

A number of other pronunciation variants that go against the spelling of a word—the common \'nəp-shə-wel\ for *nuptial* (compare words like *conceptual* and *voluptuous*) and the less common \,dim-yə-'nish-ən\ for *diminution,* for example—can be explained along similar lines.

Returning to the status of \'nü-kyə-lər\, we must make several points. First, it is a minority pronunciation; \'nü-klē-ər\ is still much more common among educated speakers. Second, it is nonetheless a common pronunciation among the educated. Most of our evidence for it is from prominent political figures and journalists, but we have also recorded it from the mouths of college professors in a variety of academic disciplines. Third, if it is your natural pronunciation and you choose to continue with it, you will have a lot of distinguished company, but you are also likely to draw some unfriendly attention from those who consider it an error.

number 1. All commentators agree that the plural verb in the first example that follows is correct, and so is the singular verb in the second:

> Current statistics already show that, of the unemployed, a large number are illiterate —Adolf A. Berle, in *The Great Ideas Today,* ed. Robert M. Hutchins & Mortimer J. Adler, 1965

> The number of foreign-language and second-language users together adds up to 300 to 400 million —Braj B. Kachru, in Greenbaum 1985

The rule of thumb for this construction is stated succinctly by Bernstein 1977:

> In general, *a number* takes a plural verb and *the number* a singular.

Evidence in the Merriam-Webster files shows that the rule of thumb is generally observed. Even when the sentence begins with *there, a number of* commands the plural verb:

> There are a number of things to be said about the V.I.P. list —Arnold Gingrich, *Esquire,* April 1970

An adjective like *increasing* or *growing* tends to emphasize the word *number* in its singularity, and results in rather more mixed usage:

> . . . an increasing number of these students are earning —William Hamilton Jones, *Johns Hopkins Mag.,* October 1965

> An ever growing number of films is available —Arni T. Dunathan, *Vocatio,* April 1968

But even in these constructions, the plural verb is the more common.

2. See AMOUNT 1.

3. See the articles at AGREEMENT.

numerous Normally an adjective ("Numerous species were sighted"), *numerous* gives occasional indications of taking on the function of a pronoun:

> . . . blunted the awareness of numerous of its inhabitants to the historical significance of many of its buildings —Norman Harrington, *N.Y. Times,* 7 Apr. 1968

> . . . the ill repute in which they fear they are held by the undergraduates and numerous of their neighbors —John Kenneth Galbraith, *A Tenured Professor,* 1990

Numerous is equivalent to *a number* or to the pronoun *many* in such a construction. Its use is similar to the use of *various* as a pronoun (as in "various of them"), except that it occurs far more rarely.

See also VARIOUS.

nuptial See NUCLEAR.

O

O, oh Usage writers from Ayres 1881 to Shaw 1987 have been explaining the fine distinctions between these two variants of the same interjection. To us the matter looks much simpler. If you meet a capital *O* all by itself in current American prose, the odds are that you are looking at an abbreviation or a symbol or some other arbitrary designation. If you see it used interjectionally, you may be sure that you are reading a highly rhetorical writer fond of apostrophe:

> O for the times when one tended to go by the second edition of Webster's —Simon 1980

> O, the gallant self-effacement of the mountaineering fraternity —John G. Mitchell, *Wilderness,* Summer 1985

Most plain people use *oh* nowadays. It is customary to separate *oh* from following matter with a comma or exclamation point. *Oh* is generally capitalized only when beginning a sentence. *O* is a rare spelling in ordinary interjectional use. When you see it, you are permitted to suspect that someone is after a particular effect, such as mockery:

> O, lackaday, the organization had betrayed me —Wayne C. Booth, *Now Don't Try to Reason with Me,* 1970

obedient When *obedient* is used with a preposition, it is *to:*

> Van Helsing stepped out, and, obedient to his gesture, we all advanced too —Bram Stoker, *Dracula,* 1897

> They [stories] are obedient not only to a genre . . . but also to the ideas they wish to see prevail —Thomas Sutcliffe, *Times Literary Supp.,* 2 Sept. 1983

object When *object* is used with a preposition, it usually takes *to.* What follows *to* may be a noun, pronoun, gerund, or infinitive:

> She had the desire to do something which she objected to doing —Arnold Bennett, *The Old Wives' Tale,* 1908

> Mademoiselle Lucy corrected her uncle's French, but objected to do more —George Meredith, *The Ordeal of Richard Feverel,* 1859

> ". . . But our silly husbands have a way of objecting to that sort of thing." —Roald Dahl, *Someone Like You,* 1953

> . . . he at least strenuously objected to many of the German demands —William L. Shirer, *The Rise and Fall of the Third Reich,* 1960

The gerund is found more often than the infinitive. *Object to* followed by a noun phrase is the most common construction.

Bernstein 1965 notes that *object* can also be followed by *against.* Examples in the OED show that *object against* was at one time in common use; in the 20th century, however, it is rare, and we have little evidence for it:

> It would be objected against these men that they would still be themselves and wreck illusion —*New Republic,* 15 Feb. 1939

objective Copperud 1970, 1980 cites a few commentators who object to *objective* as a noun where *object* or *aim* could be used; Shaw 1975, 1987 states roughly the same view. The usage disapproved dates back, according to the OED, to the 1880s. It apparently arose as a shortening of the military phrase *objective point.* Our evidence shows that *objective* tends to be found in serious discursive prose more frequently than in lighter writing.

If you choose to reduce your *objective* to *object,* you will pick up one syllable or three let-

ters—not much of a gain, whether you are speaking or writing. We think it is your choice entirely. Here are three genuine examples for you to evaluate:

> In October, 1945 the Atomic Energy Commission laid down six objectives for the development of nuclear research —*Times Literary Supp.,* 27 Aug. 1971

> . . . their primary objective is not the enrollment of new voters but changing the party affiliation of old voters —Lawrence King, *Commonweal,* 9 Oct. 1970

> First objective is to collect old newspapers —James Egan, *McCall's,* March 1971

objet d'art Copperud 1970, 1980 notes that this term is often mistakenly spelled *object d'art.* We have a few examples of this misspelling in our files:

> . . . fine paintings, sculptures and objects d'art both antique and contemporary —advt., *Town & Country,* July 1980

> . . . supplies sculptural objects d'art for store display —*Metropolitan Home,* June 1982

A moment's reflection or a quick look in the dictionary is all that is needed to prevent this mistake. Or you can use instead the completely English equivalent, *art object.*

obligated, obliged Usage comment about the verbs *obligate* and *oblige* seems to concern itself mostly with uses of the past participles. The first of these uses involves a sense of *obligated* meaning "indebted for a service or favor." The OED has 17th-, 18th-, and 19th-century evidence for the sense, but marks it "not now in good use." The OED Supplement shows that the sense went out of use except in northern England, Scotland, and the United States. MacCracken & Sandison 1917 and Copperud 1970, 1980 warn against the use of this sense; Janis 1984 suggests it has been replaced by *obliged.* Our evidence supports Janis. *Obliged* does indeed seem to have replaced it:

> I would be much obliged if you would send me six copies —Flannery O'Connor, letter, 19 July 1952

Part of the diffidence toward *obligated* that is to be found in usage books may come from its having dropped out of use in British English while remaining in Scottish and American use. British commentators and commentators born in areas of British speech are hostile to *obligated.* Bremner 1980 quotes with obvious satisfaction the fun George Bernard Shaw made of Woodrow Wilson's use of the word. Wilson was not, however, the first American president to use it:

They were obligated, according to Promise, to give the Present —George Washington, *Writings,* 1753 (in DAE)

In the sense of being bound or constrained legally or morally, *obligated* and *obliged* are essentially interchangeable:

... Helen MacInnes feels obligated to make the background of her books as factual and authentic as possible —*Current Biography,* November 1967

... O'Connor from time to time felt obliged to answer those critics —Terry Pettit, *Averett Jour.,* Autumn 1970

... the false jauntiness that most of the high-circulation magazines still felt obligated to assume —Bruce Bliven, *New Republic,* 22 Nov. 1954

... to secure permissions which in many cases they have not been legally obliged to seek —*Times Literary Supp.,* 12 Feb. 1970

When the constraint is applied by physical force or by circumstances, however, *obliged* and not *obligated* is used:

Subway riders are frequently obliged to step around a limousine idling softly while madam shops —Elizabeth Dailley Heaman, *Ford Times,* February 1968

... he speculated unprofitably, and in 1815 was obliged to resume his practice —*Australian Dictionary of Biography,* 1967

... not one of those children has been obliged to suffer the experience of a home-cooked meal —Gordon Lish, *Saturday Rev.,* 22 July 1978

oblivious Usage writers and other concerned language watchers in the early 20th century insisted that the correct meaning of *oblivious* was "forgetful; no longer mindful" and that it should only be followed by the preposition *of.* The sense of *oblivious* to which the critics objected was "not conscious or aware," which was first recorded in the middle 1800s. The OED labeled this sense erroneous in 1902, and it was censured by many critics. Much criticism was directed specifically at the phrase *oblivious to,* meaning "unaware of."

The "unaware" sense of *oblivious* has continued in extremely common use, however, and criticism of it is now largely a thing of the past. Our evidence shows that in current English it is far and away the most common meaning of the word, and in this sense the word is usually followed by the preposition *to:*

... their campaign for a tax cut without appearing oblivious to the need to protect Social Security —Charles Lane, *New Republic,* 22 Mar. 1999

They were pushing and shouting and oblivious to anyone not in their group —P. J. O'Rourke, *Rolling Stone,* 14 Nov. 1996

Father was oblivious to the man's speculative notice of his wife —E. L. Doctorow, *Ragtime,* 1975

... go-go girls oblivious to the rout outside —William Styron, *This Quiet Dust and Other Writings,* 1982

The "forgetful" sense of *oblivious* is still sometimes used. It always takes the preposition *of:*

Oblivious of any previous decisions not to stand together ..., the three stood in a tight group —Doris Lessing, *The Good Terrorist,* 1985

Some writers and editors prefer *of* to follow *oblivious* in its "unaware" sense as well. Such usage is not uncommon in current writing:

He seemed entirely wrapped up in himself, totally oblivious of those about him —John Greenwood, *What, Me, Mr. Mosley?,* 1988

... looked up from his food, which he had been steadily shovelling in, completely oblivious of everyone —Antonya Nelson, *New Yorker,* 9 Nov. 1992

obnoxious *Obnoxious* in its oldest sense means "exposed to something unpleasant or harmful":

"... may render you only obnoxious to danger and disgrace. ..." —Henry Fielding, *Jonathan Wild,* 1743

This sense is etmologically accurate: *obnoxious* is derived ultimately from the Latin *ob-,* "exposed to" and *noxa,* "harm." This sense has, however, been entirely superseded by a sense "extremely offensive," which apparently (as the OED suggests) owes something to association with *noxious.* This sense is by no means new, having been first recorded more than 300 years ago:

A very obnoxious person; an ill neighbour —Anthony Wood, *Life,* 1675 (OED)

Mr. Arthur Lee could not but be very obnoxious to Johnson, for he was not only a *patriot* but an *American* —James Boswell, *Life of Samuel Johnson,* 1791

Some commentators in the late 19th and early 20th centuries were unhappy about the "offensive" sense of *obnoxious,* but most seem not to have realized that it was far too well established to be seriously opposed. No one now questions the correctness of this sense.

observance, observation The distinction between these words has been explained and recommended in books on usage for more than a century. It is a simple one: *observance* is to be used in the sense "an act or instance of following a custom, rule, or law," as in "observance of the Sabbath" and "observance of the speed limit"; *observation* is to be used in the sense "an act or instance of watching," as in "observation of a lunar eclipse." This distinction is usually followed:

> Her only hope lay in strict observance of court procedure —*American Girl,* March 1953

> His observation of the readiness of churchgoers to accept Hitler —*Current Biography,* September 1984

But *observance* and *observation* are also sometimes used as synonyms. Many commentators acknowledge that such usage was once respectable, but most of them now want it to be regarded as an error. A more reasonable view is to regard it simply as rare. The use of *observation* to mean "an act of following a custom or law" is especially uncommon:

> The South has never been solemn in the observation of this sacred day —*American Guide Series: North Carolina,* 1939

The use of *observance* to mean "an act of watching" occurs somewhat more often, although it is certainly far less common than the use of *observation* in this sense:

> ... evidence of Inge's faithful observance of life —*Current Biography,* June 1953

> ... made paranoiac by his observance of my rage —Sally Kempton, *Esquire,* July 1970

Dictionaries treat such usage as standard.

You will probably keep *observance* and *observation* distinct in your own writing, but there is certainly no rule that says you have to.

observant *Observant,* when used with a preposition, takes *of:*

> ... be meekly observant of religious custom on Sunday —*Selected Writings of Edward Sapir,* ed. David G. Mandelbaum, 1949

> ... acutely observant of traffic laws —*Current Biography,* June 1965

observation See OBSERVANCE, OBSERVATION.

obsess When *obsess* is used with a preposition, it appears as a past participle, often as part of a passive construction. It is used with *with* about twice as often as with *by:*

> ... they had grown so obsessed with the idea that they could not willingly contemplate any action —C. S. Forester, *The African Queen,* 1935

> ... become obsessed with the suspicion that most of the talk they cannot hear consists in

plottings —James Gould Cozzens, *Guard of Honor,* 1948

> ... were obsessed at this moment with the urgency of heading southeast —William L. Shirer, *The Rise and Fall of the Third Reich,* 1960

> ... as soon as he suspects her of infidelity, he becomes morbidly obsessed by jealousy —Edmund Wilson, *Axel's Castle,* 1931

> ... gamblers, obsessed by their own fictions of speculation —Thomas Wolfe, *You Can't Go Home Again,* 1940

It has also been used infrequently with *of* or *on:*

> ... too obsessed for our own good of the idea that our supposedly superior intelligence was all the insurance we needed —Norman Cousins, *Saturday Rev.,* 17 Jan. 1942

> The crop of Negro fiction written during the last decade is obsessed on the subject of race —Charles I. Glicksberg, *Western Rev.,* Winter 1949

obsolete The use of this word as a verb is called into question by a few recent commentators—a usage panelist in Harper 1985, Janis 1984, Copperud 1980. The functional shift of *obsolete* from adjective to verb was first recorded in 1640. Modern use appears to be an American revival dating, our files indicate, from the late 1930s:

> For radio itself deliberately obsoletes today what it built yesterday —David Sarnoff, *Television,* 1936

It is not common in current use, and almost always appears in technical contexts:

> ... older cpu's whose speed and efficiency never were fully tapped before they were effectively obsoleted by their manufacturers —Edith Myers, *Datamation,* November 1977

> While many ... do describe various small, quick-loading 35mm film cartridges, modern technology has obsoleted these —Herbert Keppler, *Popular Photography,* November 1993

obtain 1. The transitive *obtain* is denigrated as pretentious for *get* by some of the same commentators who tell you that *get* is overused. But if you look in your dictionary, you will see that *obtain* does not mean simply "get"; it means "to gain or attain usually by planned action or effort." We think you will not be tempted very often to slip it in for plain *get.*
2. The intransitive *obtain* is described as literary by Safire 1984 (he cites Krapp 1927 and

Nicholson 1957 in support) and viewed with distrust by Freeman 1983, who thinks *prevail* or *is/are still with us* might be better. This use of *obtain* looks like this in context:

> . . . in rural areas where a degree of casual familiarity has always obtained —William Styron, *This Quiet Dust and Other Writings,* 1982

There's nothing wrong with being a little literary now and then.

obtrude *Obtrude* is used with a great many prepositions; those which occur most frequently are *in, into, on,* or *upon*:

> . . . contemptuous of anyone who allows the past to obtrude in the present —Robert Craft, *Stravinsky,* 1972

> It is interesting to note how progressive divergencies in pattern obtrude themselves in some species —J. Stevenson-Hamilton, *Wild Life in South Africa,* 1947

> We have to wait until the seventeenth century for a real democratic movement, obtruding itself into the Civil War —A. J. P. Taylor, *New Statesman & Nation,* 29 Aug. 1953

> . . . by otherwise obtruding his ego into the picture —Winthrop Sargeant, *New Yorker,* 5 Dec. 1953

> . . . last summer he was again most painfully obtruded on my notice —Jane Austen, *Pride and Prejudice,* 1813

> I'm not sure whether Miss Murdoch's novel needs that extra dimension of allusion, but it never obtrudes on the excitement —Derwent May, *Saturday Rev.,* January 1981

> Phil stared at the sign with reproach, as though she thought it had . . . no business obtruding itself upon her attention —Donald Barr Chidsey, *Panama Passage,* 1946

> . . . a clergyman, committed to the religious point of view, but he obtrudes no dogma upon the reader —Gerald W. Johnson, *New Republic,* 8 Feb. 1954

Obtrude is also used with *before* and *between,* but these appear less often:

> . . . obstacles and impediments will obtrude themselves before your gaze —*Selected Writings of Benjamin N. Cardozo,* ed. Margaret E. Hall, 1947

> Whenever the mechanics of language obtrude between a poet and his experience —*Times Literary Supp.,* 22 Oct. 1971

obviate Bernstein 1958, 1965 and Follett 1966 seem to have invented the notion that *obviate* can mean only "make unnecessary," not

"anticipate and prevent." The editors of the OED, Webster's Second, Webster's Third, and recent editions of Merriam-Webster's Collegiate Dictionary were unaware of any such limitation, and so were the writers on whose work they based their definitions.

> He looked at a person once . . . and after that he remembered how they looked well enough to obviate another inspection —Tennessee Williams, *The Roman Spring of Mrs. Stone,* 1950

> . . . robs a dealer of gems to obviate his being slaughtered by yeggs —S. J. Perelman, *New Yorker,* 3 Mar. 1951

> . . . its most sizable service is simply in obviating further, future demonstrations of how dull sex can be as a subject for a full evening —Robert Craft, *N.Y. Rev. of Books,* 6 Nov. 1969

> . . . different in such a way as to obviate the second Russian Revolution of 1917 —George F. Kennan, *New Yorker,* 1 May 1971

> The object of engineering design is to obviate failure —Henry Petroski, *To Engineer Is Human,* 1992

occasion 1. *Occasion* is about equally followed by *for* or *of*:

> . . . a formula that has been the occasion for a considerable amount of misunderstanding —I. A. Richards, *Basic English and Its Uses,* 1943

> His death in 1945 was not an occasion for revising a harsh general opinion —Christopher Sykes, *Encounter,* December 1954

> The birthday, apparently, was merely the occasion, not the cause, of the guests' effusions —Lillian Ross, *New Yorker,* 24 May 1952

> . . . one of life's minor absurdities and small occasions of anguish —Robert Kiely, *N.Y. Times Book Rev.,* 1 July 1979

Occasion also is followed quite frequently with *to* and the infinitive. In this construction *occasion* is typically preceded by the verb *have* or, once in a while, another verb such as *find* or *take*:

> . . . I had occasion to see an unusual number of movies —Lewis H. Lapham, *Harper's,* November 1971

> . . . the Honourable Peter . . . found occasion to get some conversation with Adrian alone —George Meredith, *The Ordeal of Richard Feverel,* 1859

> . . . Lowell took occasion to describe the direction of his interest in American English

usage —Jayne Crane Harder, *American Speech,* October 1954

2. Andy Rooney writes (*And More by Andy Rooney,* 1982) that he has to check his spelling of *occasion* to make sure he hasn't stuck two *s*'s in the word. Copperud 1980 also reports the double *s* misspelling, and our files have plenty of examples of it. So check your spelling; if Andy Rooney can, so can you.

occupy When *occupy* is used with a preposition, *with* appears most frequently:

> I hadn't really thought about it, so occupied had I been with all the arrangements —Graham Greene, *Travels with My Aunt,* 1969

> He was occupied with turning human actions into poetry —T. S. Eliot, "Shakespeare and the Stoicism of Seneca," in *Selected Essays,* 1932

Occupy by is found almost as often:

> He occupied himself by taking long walks —Green Peyton, *San Antonio: City in the Sun,* 1946

> The center of the house was occupied by a magnificent mahogany staircase —Robert Morss Lovett, *All Our Years,* 1948

Occupy also occurs with *in*:

> . . . she occupied herself in social-service work —John Cheever, *The Wapshot Chronicle,* 1957

> They occupy themselves in showing that America started in the gutter —Percy Holmes Boynton, quoted in Charles I. Glicksberg, *American Literary Criticism 1900–1950,* 1951

octopus Do you know what the plural of *octopus* is? Three receive mention: *octopuses, octopodes, octopi.* But only *octopuses* and *octopi* are in use. The OED gives *octopodes* as the first plural (*octopuses* as the alternative), but the OED also enters *octopus* with double bars as a foreign word.

Octopi is attacked from time to time as improper, chiefly by those who know (or have been told) that a plural formed on the Greek would be *octopodes. Octopus,* however, is not directly imported from the Greek; it comes from New Latin, which took it from the Greek *oktopous. Octopi* is, however, irregularly formed—on analogy, we suppose, with the plurals of other Latin nouns of the second declension (like *alumnus*).

The history of these plurals in English shows *octopuses* the oldest, starting with the OED's 1884 example. *Octopi* first turned up in our files in 1922. The editors of Webster's Second had exactly the same number of citations for *octopi* and *octopuses,* and from about the same kinds of sources, so they included both, along with the OED's *octopodes.* The citations gathered for the books published after Webster's Second show *octopuses* slightly more popular than *octopi.* Evidence gathered in recent years shows *octopuses* leading *octopi* by a substantial margin. *Octopodes* is a nonstarter: we have no evidence of its use in context.

-odd When used to indicate a quantity somewhat greater than a given round number, *odd* is usually preceded by a hyphen.

> . . . the two-hundred-odd commercial stations —Stanley Gortikov, quoted in *Center Mag.,* September 1968

> . . . the 600-odd Scouts returned home —Dick Pryce, *Scouting,* January–February 1972

Unhyphenated examples do occur, but they entail a greater risk of being misunderstood, and often with unintended humorous results.

> . . . disciplinary regulations which . . . must apply to the five hundred odd officers —James Gould Cozzens, *Guard of Honor,* 1948

> . . . they sold four million odd records, more than the Beatles ever did in a year —Michael Thomas, *Rolling Stone,* 16 Mar. 1972

Our advice is to include the hyphen and so avoid possible ambiguity.

of 1. *Of* is involved as a part of various subjects in this book. See, for instance, the compound prepositions ALONGSIDE OF, ALONGSIDE; INSIDE OF; OFF OF; OUTSIDE OF. It is also part of the construction discussed at DOUBLE GENITIVE.

2. *Of* for 've or *have. Have* in a sentence like "I could have gone" rarely receives full stress and is consequently seldom pronounced \'hav\. In ordinary circumstances the *could have* would be pronounced \'kud-əv\, with the accent on *could* and no accent on *have.* Thus in ordinary conversation *have,* unstressed, is pronounced the same as *of,* unstressed. When the unstressed *have* is spelled, it is usually spelled 've, but children and others who are partly educated may equate the \əv\ with the spelling *of,* producing *could of* (and *should of, would of, ought to of, might of, may of, must of*). We call this naive use, and it is much warned against in schoolbooks.

In spite of the warnings, naive *of* can be found in print:

> This movie would of sunk (as would many others) if the male 'protagonist' was out bayoneting babies —letter to the editor, *Valley Advocate,* 5 Mar. 1980

It is also used deliberately by writers, usually to represent the speech of an uneducated character.

I could of beat them easy with any kind of support —Ring Lardner, *You Know Me Al,* 1916

"Everybody kept saying to me: 'Lucille, that man's 'way below you!' But if I hadn't met Chester, he'd of got me sure." —F. Scott Fitzgerald, *The Great Gatsby,* 1925

For *had of,* see PLUPLUPERFECT.

3. *Of* is used in a periphrastic version of the adverbial genitive (which see). The noun after *of* may be either singular or plural. The construction has a distinctly literary feel:

I walk out here of an afternoon, and hear the notes of the thrush —William Hazlitt, letter, February 1822

. . . settle down of an afternoon to compare audition notes —Kim Waller, *Town & Country,* September 1983

. . . will be like . . . sitting down of an evening with you —Robert Frost, letter, 10 Oct. 1920

I don't sleep well of nights, either —William Humphrey, *Sports Illustrated,* 14 Oct. 1985

of a On 2 April 1984 former shortstop Pee Wee Reese was asked (in front of a television camera) about the speech he would make when he was inducted into the Baseball Hall of Fame. "It won't be that long of a speech," said Pee Wee. Another former shortstop, Tony Kubek, on a nationally televised baseball broadcast (15 August 1987), remarked that some idea or other was "too radical of a theory." What have we here? Shortstop idiom? Not exactly. Golfers use it too:

. . . wouldn't be that difficult of a shot —Lee Trevino, golf telecast, 16 Nov. 1985

And newscasters use it:

How big of a carrier task force? —Jim Lehrer, television newscast, 24 Mar. 1986

And hosts of television cooking shows:

You can't get in here and make that big of a mess, can you? —Jeff Smith, "The Frugal Gourmet" (telecast), 14 Mar. 1987

And mayors:

I don't want to be considered too good of a loser —Edward Koch, quoted in *N.Y. Times,* 4 Oct. 1982

Even newspaper columnists will use it:

I don't care how good of a shape the economists say we're in —Erma Bombeck, *Springfield* (Mass.) *Union,* 16 Sept. 1976

What we have here is a fairly recent American idiom that has nearly a fixed form: *that* or *how* or *too,* or sometimes *as,* followed by an ad-

jective, then *of a* and a noun. (In the rare instances where a plural noun is used, *a* is omitted.) Our evidence shows the idiom to be almost entirely oral; it is rare in print except in reported speech. The earliest examples we have seen so far are in the American Dialect Dictionary and date back to 1942 and 1943. It is undoubtedly at least somewhat older.

This current idiom is just one of a group of idioms that are characterized by the presence of *of a* as the link between a noun and some sort of preceding qualifier. Perhaps the oldest of these is the *kind of a* or *sort of a* construction, which is used by Shakespeare and is even older than that. It has been aspersed by usage commentators since 1779 (see KIND OF A, SORT OF A).

The newspaperman has the same kind of a job as the housewife, eat it and forget it, read it and forget it —Flannery O'Connor, letter, 16 Feb. 1963

A possible forerunner of the current idiom is an older one in which the head is *considerable.* The Dictionary of American Regional English has examples going back as far as 1766 and shows two forms of the construction: *considerable of a* and *a considerable of a.*

A brick came through the window with a splintering crash, and gave me a considerable of a jolt in the back —Mark Twain, *Sketches Old and New,* 1875 (in DARE)

. . . who at that time was considerable of a Socialist —*The Autobiography of William Allen White,* 1946

. . . and it was quite evident that he fancied himself considerable of a sheik —Octavus Roy Cohen, in *Great Railroad Stories of the World,* ed. Samuel Moskowitz, 1954

The only sure thing is that when normative usage writers encounter these idioms their reaction is to condemn. Thus, we have had 200 years of condemnation of *kind of a* in spite of its literary use. And so it goes, right down to the current idiom:

. . . Is "honesty" too strong of a word? —advt., *N.Y. Times Mag.,* 10 Feb. 1980

Reader's Digest 1983, Copperud 1980, and Safire 2001 call this nonstandard. But the only stricture on it suggested by our evidence is that it is essentially a spoken idiom: you will not want to use it much in writing.

of any See ANY 3.

of course *Of course* is commonly used in writing to qualify some statement of fact that the writer is sure most of the readers already know, but some may not, and others may need reminding of. It is added as a sort of courtesy, as if the unvarnished statement might insult the intelligence of the majority who can be expected to know.

> On the Continent and in England, soccer is, of course, the most popular mass sport —Joseph Wechsberg, *New Yorker,* 22 Jan. 1955

> . . . but being Jewish she could not, of course, be accepted by a sorority —John Corry, *Harper's,* February 1971

> . . . on the commercial networks, and of course these same programs can also be viewed on cable —Thomas Whiteside, *New Yorker,* 3 June 1985

A few commentators mention that some people dislike the use of *of course* for the purpose of one-upmanship when it is attached to some little-known fact. Its invidious use is well illustrated by this example:

> Your reviewer quotes me: "A certain Spanish bishop called Simancas . . ." Thereupon he loftily observes: "Simancas, of course, was not a bishop, but a place." His *of course* is inimitable. He has *always* known all about Simancas, of course! —Wyndham Lewis, *Times Literary Supp.,* 16 Oct. 1948

It can be used less nastily:

> . . . mentioned quite casually that, of course, quasars had been a pet interest of his because he and a colleague had discovered the first one —Tom Buckley, *N.Y. Times Mag.,* 12 Sept. 1976

A couple of other commentators object to its use to buttress unsubstantiated assertions; the example given is of this sort: "The administration, of course, is corrupt." Our files have no good examples of this use, which may be more common in oral discussions and in partisan publications than in ordinary edited prose.

off *Off* in the sense of "from" is disparaged in a few books: Opdyke 1939, Longman 1984, Trimmer & McCrimmon 1988. The OED dates such use of the preposition from the middle of the 16th century, and adds "esp. with *take, buy, borrow, hire,* and the like." Burchfield 1996 says the use is now considered less than standard, which, judging from his examples, seems to mean no longer in general use. But we have some modern examples:

> . . . so I took the bike off Joe and we worked this stunt —Ian Cross, *The God Boy,* 1957

> . . . taking a long draw off a bottle of light brew —Glenn Lewis, *Houston Post,* 26 Aug. 1984

> . . . were hunted on foot as well as off a pony —Rex Hudson, *Shooting Times & Country Mag.,* 31 Mar. 1976

> . . . eventually the government banned them off the radio stations —Michael Manley, quoted in *Jamaica Jour.,* March/June 1973

> . . . videocassette recorders, with which they can record shows off their cable systems or off the networks —Thomas Whiteside, *New Yorker,* 3 June 1985

Some of the uses here were undoubtedly not even thought of by the critics. There is nothing wrong with *off* in the sense of "from," although it is perhaps more often a speech form than a written one and to many people it will suggest uneducated speech.

For discussion of *off of* used in the same way and drawing the same criticism, see OFF OF.

offensive When *offensive* is used with a prepositional-phrase complement, the preposition is almost always *to:*

> . . . it's offensive to a gentleman's feelings when his word isn't believed —Dorothy L. Sayers, *The Nine Tailors,* 1934

> This mannerism which has become so offensive to the friends of the Sperbers —Norman Mailer, *Advertisements for Myself,* 1959

off from The OED notes that the adverb *off* is frequently used with *from.* The OED treats this combination as if it were entirely standard but does not show many examples. A few commentators object to the *from* in *off from* as redundant in contexts where *off* can stand alone as a preposition. Watt 1967 calls it rare. He may be right.

The combination *off from* is very common, but usually the *off* is necessary to the preceding verb (*cut off from* and *take off from* occur frequently). Possibly redundant use is pretty infrequent:

> "You wanna beer?" Gabe asks me, plucking a can off from the vine of three he'd carried to the porch —Dagoberto Gilb, *The Magic of Blood,* 1993

> Paper must be slabbed off from rolls that have paper gouged out of them —Nelson R. Eldred, *The Lithographers Manual,* 1988

There is nothing to worry about here. The OED notes a peculiarity of this idiom—it can be reversed:

> Surreptitiously Miss Thriplow slipped the opal ring from off the little finger of her right hand —Aldous Huxley, *Those Barren Leaves,* 1925

offhand, offhanded, offhandedly *Offhand* has been in use as both an adjective and adverb for about 300 years. It is an older word and a shorter word than *offhanded* and *offhandedly,* and has therefore been preferred to one or both of them by a few usage commentators from the time of Utter 1916. About *offhanded* there is little to be said except that it is a standard word which was first recorded in 1835 and is used in much the same way as *offhand*, but is less common:

> . . . with offhanded humor and the intimate ironies of Yiddish inflections —Lincoln Caplan, *Saturday Rev.*, 15 Oct. 1977

> . . . an offhanded way with plot and structure —Richard Locke, *N.Y. Times Book Rev.*, 21 May 1978

The adverb *offhandedly*, however, is quite distinct from the adverb *offhand*. The most common adverbial use of *offhand* is as a sentence modifier which basically means "without premeditation or preparation":

> Offhand, I'd say that there will be at least nine starters —Audax Minor, *New Yorker*, 5 June 1971

> . . . but, offhand, this particular pair wouldn't have been my first choice —Max Lerner, *Saturday Rev.*, 29 May 1976

Offhandedly is never used in this way. It also differs from *offhand* in that it can modify adjectives (*offhand* cannot), it is sometimes modified by other adverbs (*offhand* never is), and it almost always means "casually" (*offhand* rarely does):

> As Kagan somewhat offhandedly sums up a portion of the findings —Anne Bernays, *Atlantic*, March 1970

> . . . the off-handedly monotonous renderings of Auden —*Times Literary Supp.*, 16 July 1971

> . . . imperturbably snobbish and offhandedly puncturing —John Simon, *New York*, 1 Nov. 1971

> . . . said it so offhandedly that one would think there was nothing particularly spooky —Robert F. Jones, *Sports Illustrated*, 1 June 1981

Summary: The adjective *offhanded* is a relatively uncommon synonym of *offhand*. It is standard and respectable, but can easily be replaced by the shorter word if you want it to. The adverb *offhandedly*, however, is common, useful, and distinct from the adverb *offhand*. If anyone tells you to replace *offhandedly* with *offhand*, pay no attention.

office The verb *office*, formed by functional shift from the noun, is condemned by Copperud 1980. Garner 1998 doesn't like it, but calls it common among businesspeople. Our files do not contain a great many examples. Here are some:

> When I took my first teaching job at the University of Manitoba in 1949 I taught and

officed in what was known as the old Broadway Buildings —James Reaney, preface, *Masks of Childhood*, 1972

> . . . in some cases they office right in their homes —Arlene Rossen Cardozo, *Woman at Home*, 1976

> . . . I came downtown, and I officed with Earl B. Dickerson —William S. White, *The Golden Thirteen*, 1993

Copperud criticized the passive transitive use. It is still around:

> . . . telecommuters who work at home but are officed elsewhere —Kathi S. Allen, et al., *American Demographics*, October 1997

There is also a gerund:

> . . . "alternative officing," the latest movement in the $20 billion office furniture business —Leigh Gallagher, *Forbes*, 7 Sept. 1998

This use is still mainly confined to business contexts.

officiate Harper 1975, 1985 assures us that *officiate* is only an intransitive verb, but *officiate* has been used transitively since the 17th century. Some transitive uses are still alive:

> Spencer, a master of ceremonies in Britain who has officiated some 700 royal occasions —Julie Gilbert, *Houston Post*, 27 Aug. 1984

And sports fans know that games, matches, and contests are officiated—often poorly. Let us assure you that *officiate* can be used transitively to mean "to carry out (an official duty or function)," "to serve as a leader or celibrant of (a ceremony)," or "to administer the rules of (a game or sport) esp. as a referee or umpire."

officious, official A handful of commentators (almost all British) and the Oxford American Dictionary warn against confusion of *officious* and *official*. This does not seem to be a problem in current American English.

Officious in current English is essentially synonymous with *meddlesome*. Here are a few typical examples of current use:

> . . . usually barges into things, officious and overconfident —Lloyd N. Jeffrey, *CEA Critic*, January 1971

> . . . experienced educators and teachers—rather than officious bureaucrats —Harold Howe II, *Saturday Rev.*, 20 Nov. 1971

> . . . the silence was shattered by the bustle and officious chatter —*Runner's World*, October 1980

off of *Off of* is a compound preposition made of the adverb *off* and the preposition *of* and has been in use at least since Shakespeare's "a fall off of a tree" (*2 Henry VI*).

In the last quarter of the 19th century some American commentators began to find fault with it, finding the *of* superfluous. Dozens of commentators have followed suit. What most of these commentators have in common is an unfamiliarity with the actual use of the phase. While British literary usage has receded into the past, American writers have found *off of* idiomatic:

". . . Who the hell do you eat off of . . . ?" —Ernest Hemingway, *To Have and Have Not,* 1937

. . . haven't enough ingenuity to master the art of getting cellophane off of bread —Fred Allen, letter, 20 Nov. 1941

. . . there were moments when, with several cars coming toward me, and two or three honking behind me, and a curved road ahead, I would take my foot off of everything and wail, "Where the hell am I?" —James Thurber, letter, August 1935

. . . I'd borrow two or three dollars off of the judge —Mark Twain, *Huckleberry Finn,* 1884 (*A Mark Twain Lexicon,* 1938)

. . . I'll occasionally take a roundabout route off of the parkway —Philip Roth, *N.Y. Times Book Rev.,* 18 Oct. 1987

. . . where you can make a nice dollar off of misery in crooked nursing homes —Roy Blount, Jr., *Playboy,* February 1983

'Did you take it off of his finger?' I asked —Robert Penn Warren, *Partisan Rev.,* Fall 1944

When he turned off of Stockton onto Webster —Andrew M. Greeley, *Patience of a Saint,* 1987

. . . Faust . . . is rejuvenated only after he has quaffed at a Witches' Sabbat a "filthy brew" that takes twenty years off of his life —Leslie A. Fiedler, *Memory and Desire,* 1986

. . . would be much obliged if you would send them a copy that I get the 40% off of —Flannery O'Connor, letter, 24 May 1952

. . . maybe you do need to be involved, to get the edges beaten off of you a little every day —William Faulkner, 25 Feb. 1957, in *Faulkner in the University,* 1959

. . . a moment when the nervousness would lift off of him as he spoke —Jay McInerney, *N.Y. Times Book Rev.,* 6 Aug. 1989

And it is common in standard edited prose, especially in journalism:

Traffic was routed off of the highway —*N.Y. Times,* 20 Jan. 1983

. . . searing decades off of weathered skin —*Vogue,* July 2000

. . . bouncing ideas off of a revved Robin Williams —David Ansen, *Newsweek,* 27 Sept. 1999

Danny Tartabull had a bases-empty shot off of Dave Stewart —Jack Curry, *N.Y. Times,* 12 June 1994

. . . retirees living off of Social Security —Peter B. Nelson, *Professional Geographer,* November 1997

Off of Cabo San Lucas, the mainsail blew out —Eric Sandstrom, *Multihulls,* July/August 1990

Mr. Clay's act works off of the basest instincts of society —John J. O'Connor, *N.Y. Times,* 29 July 1990

Were the twins, born off of the reservation, domiciled on it or in the state of Mississippi? —Marcia Coyle, *National Law Jour.,* 25 Feb. 1991

You can see that in American English *off of* is used in contexts ranging from uneducated (Huck Finn) to general. Recent commentators who still say *off of* should be avoided are out of touch with reality. If it is part of your personal idiom and you are not writing on an especially elevated plane, you have no reason to avoid *off of.*

offspring   *Offspring* functions both as a singular and as a plural:

Given a cooperative offspring of course mother is the best placed person of all to stimulate her child's intellect —*Times Literary Supp.,* 14 Nov. 1968

. . . others young enough to have been her own offspring —Peter Quennell, *N.Y. Times Book Rev.,* 10 Oct. 1976

Offsprings also has a long history of occasional use as an alternative plural:

. . . half a dozen male offsprings and a girl or two —Saki (H. H. Munro), *The Unbearable Bassington,* 1912

But our evidence indicates that the *-s* plural is now rarely used.

of which   See WHOSE 1.

oh   See O, OH.

O.K., OK, okay   1. *Spelling.* The spellings *O.K., OK,* and *okay* are the predominant ones today. We find a few publishers that use *ok* and *o.k.,* but they are in the minority. We have a Canadian instance of *okeh,* the form preferred by Woodrow Wilson because he believed it to be a Choctaw word meaning "it is so."

There is little to choose in frequency between the first three forms at the present time. Garner 1998 says *OK* is the most common. Some commentators—Reader's Digest 1983, for example—prefer *okay* because when used as a verb it has the advantage of taking regular inflections without apostrophes.

2. *O.K.* is used as an adjective, adverb, noun, and verb. It has been a bugbear of the college handbook from MacCracken & Sandison 1917 to Trimmer & McCrimmon 1988. You may safely infer from this that it is not okay to use *O.K.* in a freshman English paper. Flesch 1983 and Reader's Digest 1983 both point out that *O.K.* is widely used on a much higher level than the college handbooks and usage panels are willing to recognize. Flesch says that it has long been in standard use, not only in this country, but throughout the English-speaking world. The OED Supplement supports this view by showing examples of use in British English since the 1860s.

Here are a few examples from our files:

No OK comparison is too OK for the Hitchcock exegetes —Stanley Kauffmann, *Before My Eyes,* 1980

. . . and feel O.K. about ourselves in transit —Jay McInerney, *N.Y. Times Book Rev.,* 24 Mar. 1985

On April 4, the Fed OK'd an acquisition of a Columbus, Ohio thrift —*Wall Street Jour.,* 12 Apr. 1982

. . . he starts out with a couple of Ole and Lena jokes, which they like okay —Garrison Keillor, *Lake Wobegon Days,* 1985

With the old school, it's OK, too —Mary McGrory, *Boston Globe,* 22 July 1984

The sommelier looked particularly taken aback. But La Vanderbilt merely smiled sweetly, reasoning that it must be the OK thing to do —Callan, *Punch,* 6 Mar. 1974

Every project has received Brooke Astor's personal okay —Arthur M. Schlesinger, Jr., *Architectural Digest,* May 1986

The inescapable conclusion is that the handbooks are looking backward and not at contemporary usage. *O.K.* (or *OK* or *okay*) is widely used on every level of speech and on all levels of writing except the stodgiest. Unless you are taking freshman English, you can use it freely.

old adage The expression *old adage* has been called a tautology by commentators from Vizetelly 1922 to Kilpatrick 1984. All of these commentators base their opinions on the fact that *adage* is defined in dictionaries as "an old saying."

Whence this definition? Johnson 1755 defines *adage* as "a maxim handed down from antiquity." Noah Webster's 1828 definition, "an old saying, which has obtained credit by long use," continued in Merriam-Webster dictionaries until 1934. Editors of Webster's Second noted a change in the way the word was being used, however, a change exemplified by this citation from the *Yale Review* (October 1917):

It is an adage that the tired business man abets his wife in all. . . .

So the editors of Webster's Second snicked *old* out of the definition. At the time Webster's Third was edited, the definition was completely revised. It had become evident that an adage, while embodying some common observation, need not come down from antiquity:

Some people forget the lovely adage that people who live in glass houses should undress in the dark —*Publishers Weekly,* 12 Aug. 1950

. . . what is meant by the adage, "an imperfect democracy is better than a perfect autocracy" —Lucius Garvin, *A Modern Introduction to Ethics,* 1953

The adage that the rise of civilization is the result of a series of intellectual minorities pitting themselves against the barbaric masses is open to question —Richard L. Russell, *N.Y. Times Mag.,* 23 Jan. 1955

It is also worth our notice that *old* has gone with *adage* since the word first came into English:

'Much company, much knavery'—as true as that old adage 'Much courtesy, much subtlety.' —Thomas Nashe, *The Unfortunate Traveller,* 1594

So it is not surprising that *old* has continued to accompany *adage* both from force of habit and, in more recent use, to impute age to the adage, which may not be very old at all:

. . . racegoers remembered the old adage, "Second in the Trial, first in the Derby." After all, they'd seen it come true five times in sixteen years, which is quite enough to establish an adage —Audax Minor, *New Yorker,* 8 May 1954

Or the *old* may merely be factual:

Contrary to the old adage, practice won't make you perfect —Willie Mosconi, *Winning Pocket Billiards,* 1965

. . . the old adage "misery loves company" —Natalie Babbitt, *N.Y. Times Book Rev.,* 24 June 1979

. . . an old adage about robbing Peter to pay Paul —Peter G. Peterson, *Atlantic,* May 1996

That old adage applies, the one that says you should write about what you know best —Robert Cormier, *English Jour.*, January 2001

Old adage is as old as *adage* itself in English. Usage writers who object to it on grounds of redundancy have not taken note of a change of meaning. Go ahead and use it where it seems apt to you.

omitted relative For omission of the relative pronoun of a restrictive clause, see CONTACT CLAUSES.

on 1. *On, upon.* A sizable number of commentators recommend that you choose *on* when you have a choice between *on* and *upon*. *On* is certainly the more common word, but *upon* is very far from rare. Writers seem to ignore the handbooks' advice and choose whichever word sounds better at the moment. Some examples of *upon*:

Birds appear . . . as ornament on ceramics and upon copper breastplates —Roger G. Kennedy, *Hidden Cities,* 1994

. . . of course that depends upon who is looking at each one —William Faulkner, 13 May 1957, in *Faulkner in the University,* 1959

Lord Peter Death Bredon Wimsey burst upon the British mystery novel scene in 1923 —Joyce Carol Oates, *N.Y. Times Book Rev.,* 15 Mar. 1998

. . . until a rainstorm descends upon the neighborhood —*New Yorker,* 2 Oct. 2000

Garner 1998 notes that *upon* is the better choice for introducing something:

Upon Seaver's arrival, several of his teammates acted like star-struck teenyboppers —Ron Fimrite, *Sports Illustrated,* 14 July 1986

2. See ONTO, ON TO.

on account of 1. *On account of* is commonly used as a compound preposition equivalent to *because of*:

. . . partly on account of the violent attacks on their work —*Times Literary Supp.,* 18 Dec. 1969

It is especially likely in writing that has a conversational tone:

At first I figure I am going to like Otash on account of the lingo he uses —Dan Greenburg, *N.Y. Times Book Rev.,* 10 Oct. 1976

. . . lived in my house only on account of a pretty casual decision about real estate —Garrison Keillor, *Lake Wobegon Days,* 1985

On account of was first recorded in this use in 1792, and has long been established as standard in both British and American English. Usage commentators have no special fondness for it, but most of them give it at least grudging acceptance. Harper 1975, 1985, for example, describes it as "acceptable in speech." Our evidence shows that it is also common in writing, although certainly far less common than *because of.*

2. *On account of* is also sometimes used as a compound conjunction equivalent to *because.* This use of the phrase is limited almost entirely to dialectal and nonstandard speech. Its occasional occurrence in writing is strictly for the purpose of imitating or evoking the quality of such speech:

Scotsmen, we're told, are virile on account of they don't wear knickers under their kilts —Marje Proops, *Sunday Mirror* (London), 10 Nov. 1974

. . . his feet are on the ground on account of no money remained for a pedestal —Garrison Keillor, *Lake Wobegon Days,* 1985

Several usage commentators take the conjunctive *on account of* seriously enough to condemn its use, but we suspect that such condemnation serves little purpose. The nonstandard nature of the phrase will be obvious to anyone who encounters it in reading.

on behalf of See BEHALF.

one 1. The pronoun *one,* when it stands for a person, is usually the mark of a formal style. In such a context it may refer to a particular kind of individual or it may mean "anyone at all" or it may be used as a substitute for *I* or *me.* In the first two examples that follow, a particular kind of individual is referred to; in the third, the meaning seems to be "anyone at all":

One might wish that the book consisted entirely of such fresh and surprising matter —John Updike, *New Yorker,* 24 May 1982

In the next few years, one marched in Harlem and elsewhere . . . , went on sympathy marches for civil-rights workers who were killed . . . —Nora Sayre, *Esquire,* March 1970

. . . he now seemed to have a new girl friend, the wife of a gangster who was lying in hospital after a shooting affray, a rather dangerous relationship one would have thought —Graham Greene, *Getting to Know the General,* 1984

The use of *one* in place of *I* or *me* (or *one's* in place of *my*) is chiefly British, and it has been objected to by some commentators—mostly American.

I would reject a natural lawn even if it made sense in a garden like mine and wouldn't look . . . as though one were too slatternly to keep a garden decent —Eleanor Perenyi, *Green Thoughts,* 1983

In some cases like this, the use of *one* can broaden beyond *I.* In the first of the examples that follow, *one* can easily be taken to mean "you and I"; in the second, "I and others" may be intended:

. . . I do not think him so very ill-looking as I did—at least one sees many worse —Jane Austen, *Mansfield Park,* 1814

I'm watching this pretty carefully and I hope this issue will come up in the Lords and one may be able to speak about it —Donald Coggan, Archbishop of Canterbury, quoted in *The Economist,* 29 Mar. 1975

In some cases, the reader or the person being addressed is clearly one of the particular kind of individual being referred to, and in these cases, *one* comes close to meaning simply *you,* but even here, some broadening of view can be discerned.

At least one book on writing (Trimble 1975) recommends avoiding *one* and using *you* when addressing the reader on the grounds that the printed page itself puts enough distance between reader and writer, and that it need not be increased by using more formality. E. B. White agrees, but sees a problem:

As for me, I try to avoid the impersonal "one" but have discovered that it is like a face you keep encountering in the streets and can't always avoid bowing to —letter, 26 Sept. 1963

2. A question that comes up frequently in connection with *one* is what pronoun to use later in the sentence to refer to it. *He, they,* and *one* are all likely candidates, but which one do you choose? This choice has been a matter of contention since the 18th century.

It appears that the earliest solution was to use *he, him,* and *his* to refer back to a beginning *one.* Shakespeare did so; the OED has an example from the 15th century and says that use of *he* and *his* was usual. The practice was attacked by Baker 1770 and by Alford 1866; they both recommended the consistent employment of *one, one's,* and *oneself* after *one.* There has been a great deal of subsequent comment, and a divergence of usage. Since the second half of the 19th century, British usage has tended to follow the consistent use of *one.* American usage is divided. Americans do it both ways:

Besides, life is too short for one to waste his time reading any but our best writers

—Thomas Meehan, *N.Y. Times Book Rev.,* 14 Aug. 1983

If one were to take literally all the tales of market coups that one hears over lunch tables, one would be astonished at how often one is asked to split the check —*New Yorker,* 10 May 1982

. . . one is always paid for one's sins —Flannery O'Connor, letter, 5 May 1956

And one must be careful not to shoot himself —Stuart Chase, *The Tyranny of Words,* 1938

Sometimes you can even find *one* . . . *you:*

When one is very old, as I am . . . your legs give in before your head does —George Bernard Shaw, quoted in *Time,* 21 Oct. 1946

The consideration of gender apparently enters into the use of the sequence *one* . . . *they, their, them,* which, if overlooked by most handbooks, is not missed by the OED. The OED says that the plural pronouns "were formerly in general use on account of their indefiniteness of gender" but that the practice "is now considered ungrammatical." The ungrammaticality here is a violation of formal or grammatical number agreement (for a discussion of this subject, see THEY, THEIR, THEM).

Use of *they, their, them* in singular reference to *one* dates back to the 17th century. Some more recent examples are these:

. . . shut up in a nasty Scotch jail, where one cannot even get the dirt brushed off their clothes —Sir Walter Scott (in Bolinger 1980)

. . . one may escape the duty by demonstrating themselves to be a hopeless administrator —*Harvard–Radcliffe Parents Newsletter* (in *New Yorker,* 2 Dec. 1985)

What does one do to get to the stage where they can mentally orchestrate like this? —Ted Greene, *Guitar Player,* August 1981

You can see that for the American writer there is no simple solution: you just have to handle each case in the way that sounds best to you.

See also ONE OF THOSE WHO and the various articles at AGREEMENT.

one another, one another's See EACH OTHER 1, 2.

one in (out of) See AGREEMENT, SUBJECT-VERB: ONE OR MORE, ONE IN (OUT OF)____ 2.

one of the See ONE OF THOSE WHO.

one of the . . . if not the Phythian 1979 discusses this example:

545

The new National Theatre is one of the most imaginative, if not the most imaginative, buildings of our time.

The problem here, says Phythian (and his view of this construction is shared by several other commentators), is that the part of the sentence outside the commas calls for the plural *buildings,* and the part inside the commas calls for the singular *building.* The sentence is therefore ungrammatical.

This construction is somewhat similar to *as good or better than* (which see) in that it contains a grammatical anomaly or discontinuity that is more likely to be troubling to usage commentators than to ordinary readers. It does not hinder understanding and is at worst a stylistic blemish. You can revise the problem away easily enough by moving the noun forward to follow the first adjective; most of your readers are not likely to be aware of the difference.

We do not have much evidence for the construction. It is older, naturally, than the comment on it:

> . . . a busy America is one of the great, if not the greatest, influences —James Forrestal, quoted in *Time,* 20 Jan. 1947

one of those things See ONE OF THOSE WHO.

one of those who Under this heading we have gathered several similar constructions, all of which display the same disputed point of grammar. We begin with Kilpatrick 1984, who reproaches himself for having written this sentence:

> In Washington we encounter *to prioritize* all the time; it is one of those things that makes Washington unbearable.

For Kilpatrick the error is in *makes*; the theory that makes the verb culpable—a theory going all the way back to Baker 1770—says that the antecedent of *that,* which is the subject of *makes,* is *things* and therefore the verb should be plural: *make.*

The trouble with the firm rule of Follett 1966 and Baker 1770 (as well as Garner 1998, Bernstein 1962, and Shaw 1987) is that it has no firm foundation of usage to support it: it is largely airy theory. The practice these writers would correct can be found in Old English as early as the 10th century. The usages of the past cannot be undone, and if the same mental processes that led to past usages are still in effect, the reformers are going to have a hard time. In this case the mental process involves the pull of notional agreement (see NOTIONAL AGREEMENT, NOTIONAL CONCORD). Kilpatrick, in paraphrasing Follett, puts it this way:

By a mental shortcut, the *one* in whom we are interested jumps over the class . . . and links itself to the defining words. . . .

So it is simply a matter of which is to be master—*one* or *those.* In Kilpatrick's sentences and in those of a great many other writers, it has been *one*:

> My worthy Friend Sir ROGER is one of those who is not only at Peace within himself, but beloved and esteemed by all about him —Joseph Addison, *The Spectator,* No. 122, 20 July 1711

> Waugh is not one of those who finds the modern world attractive —Randolph S. Churchill, *Book-of-the-Month-Club News,* December 1945

> . . . he is one of the few serious young novelists who has tried to go directly toward the center of post-war experience —Irving Howe, *New Republic,* 10 Nov. 1958

> . . . one of those rare books which justifies the jacket blurb —Cleveland Amory, *N.Y. Times Book Rev.,* 28 Feb. 1954

> They would sail to the Caribbean on one of those ships that was your hotel while you were in port, and it had better be an English ship —John P. Marquand, *Point of No Return,* 1949

> . . . one of those film buffs who has seen everything and understood nothing —John Gregory Dunne, quoted in Simon 1980

The primacy of *one* in the writer's mind may be signaled by pronoun reference, too:

> . . . he is one of those that must lose his employment whenever the great shake comes —Jonathan Swift, *Journal to Stella* (in Jespersen 1909–49, vol. 2)

> About the Lourdes business. . . . I will not be taking any bath. I am one of those people who could die for his religion easier than take a bath for it —Flannery O'Connor, letter, 17 Dec. 1957

But do not think that *one* is always the master. An article in *The English Journal* in October 1951 reported a citation count (from 1531–1951) showing five plural verbs to one singular. The actual preponderance in favor of the plural verb may not be so great—certainly it is not in our files. But it is plain that *those* is often the master:

> I am one of those People who by the general Opinion of the World are counted both Infamous and Unhappy —Joseph Addison, *The Spectator,* No. 203, 1711 (in Kenyon, *American Speech,* October 1951)

> Tom Sawyer's Aunt Polly was one of those people who are infatuated with patent med-

icines —Mark Twain, "A Dose of Pain Killer," in *Mark Twain's Library of Humor*, 1888

I don't want you to think I'm one of those people who are always talking about their bodily ailments —Frank Sullivan, *A Rock in Every Snowball*, 1946

It is one of those bright ideas that do not come off —Newgate Callendar, *N.Y. Times Book Rev.*, 8 Feb. 1981

. . . for he is one of those authors who seem to write almost in collusion with their audience —Anatole Broyard, *N.Y. Times Book Rev.*, 9 Mar. 1986

The plural notion may also be signaled by pronoun reference alone:

. . . one of the Englishmen who came to Ireland for a visit, married, and made Ireland their home —John O'Hara, letter, 18 Oct. 1959

So the choice of a singular or plural verb, and of the matching singular or plural pronoun (which the commentators pass over), is a matter of notional agreement: is *one* or *those* to be the master? We cannot trace the practice of Old English down to our time in an unbroken line of descent, but there is abundant evidence that *one* has controlled number in modern English sentences from Shakespeare to James J. Kilpatrick, and there is likewise abundant evidence that *those* has controlled number in other sentences. Addison was not troubled by using both constructions. You need not be more diffident than Addison.

one or more See AGREEMENT, SUBJECT-VERB: ONE OR MORE, ONE IN (OUT OF)____ 1.

on line Do you stand *in* line or *on* line? Forty years ago *on line* would have marked a writer or speaker as a New Yorker. Bryant 1962 describes it as a regionalism peculiar to New York City and the Hudson Valley. A number of later commentators have repeated her. More recent commentators such as Geoffrey Nunberg in Shopen & Williams 1980 and Safire 1982 attest to the continued use of *on line* in New York. Copperud 1980 complains that New Yorkers are foisting their provincialisms on the rest of us.

Certainly *on line* has not replaced *in line*, but *on line* is certainly better known nationally than it used to be.

. . . hates waiting in lines —Robert R. Harris, *N.Y. Times Book Rev.*, 19 Dec. 1982

They go to movies and they don't have to stand on line —Nora Ephron, *Esquire*, June 1989

Hamden, Conn. (AP)—Many people get frustrated waiting on long lines at the De-partment of Motor Vehicles office —*Springfield* (Mass.) *Morning Union*, 3 Oct. 1985

. . . while waiting on line at our local movie theater —Joseph A. King, *Newsweek*, 14 Apr. 1986

Just before leaving the stable or while waiting on line for inspection . . . —P. Wynn Norman, *Chronicle of the Horse*, 11 May 1984

only **1.** Garner 1998 calls *only* "perhaps the most frequently misplaced word in English." This issue had its beginning with Bishop Lowth:

Thus it is commonly said, 'I *only* spake three words': when the intention of the speaker manifestly requires, 'I spake *only* three words.' —Lowth 1763

The problem has been lengthily discussed by many commentators for over two centuries. We note that writers are held to misplace it with some frequency. And we will see from the following examples that the chief mistake is the placing of *only* between the subject and the verb or between the auxiliary verb and the main verb—common locations for many common adverbs.

Who are the writers who misplace *only*? Hall 1917 calls them "the standard authors," and cites 104 of them from the 17th through the 19th centuries. Here is a sampler:

. . . I will only add this in the defence of our present Writers —John Dryden, "Defence of the Epilogue," 1672

. . . follies that are only to be killed by a constant and assiduous culture —Joseph Addison, *The Spectator* (in Hall)

Every other author may aspire to praise; the lexicographer can only hope to escape reproach —Samuel Johnson, *Preface to the Dictionary*, 1755

I set out immediately, with my son, for London, and we only stopped a little by the way to view Stonehenge on Salisbury Plain —Benjamin Franklin, *Autobiography*, 1788

. . . but which through a stupid blunder . . . only did cost one American dollar and a half —Henry Adams, letter, 15–17 May 1859

We see cherubs by Raphael, whose baby-innocence could only have been nursed in Paradise —Nathaniel Hawthorne, *The Marble Faun*, 1860 (in Hall)

I think that Stephen Spender was only attempting to enumerate oil and water colour pictures and not photographs —T. S. Eliot, letter, 16 Oct. 1963

We feel very badly about your only having one turkey —James Thurber, letter, Fall 1938

... the critics and scholars (most of them) gave him high marks in Speech when he had only earned them in Observation —John O'Hara, letter, 17 Feb. 1959

I only got wine by roaring for it —Evelyn Waugh (in Burchfield 1981)

He only planned to keep on going as far as each streetcar would take him —E. L. Doctorow, *Ragtime*, 1975

If writers from Dryden to Doctorow have ignored the rule that *only* must immediately precede the word it modifies, why the fuss? The answer is that the rule for correct placement is based on the application of logical thinking to written English. The "misplacing" of *only* is caused by the operation of idiom in spoken English. Lowth's original objection to "I only spake three words" depends on his interpreting *only* to apply ambiguously to either *I* or to *spake*, an interpretation that would not be possible if the words were spoken. Prose was not written laboriously in the 18th century; careful and painstaking revision was, in the main, reserved for poetry. Thus, 18th-century prose was undoubtedly closer to spoken English than it appears from this distance. We know that Dr. Johnson, who habitually put such things off until the last minute, dashed off many of his prose works and never revised them. We should not be surprised, therefore, that many instances of "misplaced" *only* can be found in his prose works.

A rule based on logic that is applied to written English and does not take into account the natural idiom of speech will create thousands of "violations" as soon as it is formulated. This plainly has been the case with the rule for placing *only*.

If the grammarians and rhetoricians who preached strict adherence to the placement rule viewed noncompliance only as so much more incorrect English, the disparity between rule and practice was seen by others in a different light. One of the earliest to comment was Alford 1866:

The adverb *only* in many sentences where strictly speaking it ought to follow the verb and to limit the objects of the verb, is in good English placed before the verb.

Goold Brown 1851 calls Lowth's criticism of "I only spake three words"—which he found with *spake* altered to *spoke* in a later grammar—hypercritical. Hall 1917 devotes six pages to the subject and lists 104 authors in over 400 passages in violation of the rule. But the most trenchant notice of the disparity is taken by Fowler 1926 (he is called "surprisingly permissive" by Garner). He begins with a quotation and appends his opinion:

I read the other day of a man who 'only died a week ago,' as if he could have done anything else more striking or final; what was meant by the writer was that he 'died only a week ago'. There speaks one of those friends from whom the English language may well pray to be saved, one of those modern precisians who have more zeal than discretion, & wish to restrain liberty as such, regardless of whether it is harmfully or harmlessly exercised.

He continues:

For *He only died a week ago* no better defence is perhaps possible than that it is the order that most people have always used & still use, & that, the risk of misunderstanding being chimerical, it is not worth while to depart from the natural. Remember that in speech there is not even the possibility of misunderstanding, because the intonation of *died* is entirely different if it, & not *a week ago*, is qualified by *only*; & it is fair that a reader should be supposed capable of supplying the decisive intonation where there is no temptation to go wrong about it.

Fowler has his contemporary followers:

To quibble about the position of *only* when meaning is not at stake is to waste time —Perrin & Ebbitt 1972

The placement of *only* in a sentence is a matter of great concern to a few self-styled purists, but happily not for most speakers and writers. . . . The simple fact is that the "rule" about placing *only* next to the element modified is honored now more in the breach than in the observance. Especially in speech, the normal placement of *only* is before the verb and this must be considered to be a perfectly acceptable part of the American idiom —Harper 1985

The placement in speech is well attested:

. . . I once tried to buy such a pair, for myself: but only got the crushing reply that "slippers of *that* kind are *only* worn by *ladies*"! —Lewis Carroll, letter, 11 Nov. 1896

There was a young man, who had only worked there six weeks —William Benton, in Studs Terkel, *Hard Times*, 1970

He only got in three innings' work all spring —Dick Howser, quoted in *New Yorker*, 9 Dec. 1985

All these examples that run counter to the rule for what Fowler terms "orthodox" placement might lead you to suspect, as Harper 1985 does, that few people use the orthodox placement. Such is not the case, however. What has happened is that both parties to this dispute have been at pains to find examples that disagree with the rule; the prescribers present them for correction, and the rule's critics present them as evidence that the rule and usage do not match. No one—at least until comparatively recent times—has bothered to collect examples that adhere to the orthodox placement. Such examples do exist, abundantly:

The Endymion is now waiting only for orders, but may wait for them perhaps a month —Jane Austen, letter, 1 Nov. 1800

She looked at the body only enough to make sure that it was all over —Glenway Wescott, *Apartment in Athens,* 1945

... I can only try to explain what was in my mind —Christopher Fry, *Atlantic,* March 1953

... I'd taken it only just in time —Christopher Isherwood, in *New World Writing,* 1952

... maybe we'd have only one more chance —William Faulkner, 25 Feb. 1957, in *Faulkner in the University,* 1959

He needed only to suffer —E. L. Doctorow, *Ragtime,* 1975

Indeed, we spent so little time in bed most of us had only one child —James Thurber, letter, 24 June 1959

But we can ultimately only guess about Davis —Robert Penn Warren, *Jefferson Davis Gets His Citizenship Back,* 1980

Bryant 1962 notes that the position of *only* with respect to the word or phrase it modifies is not fixed in standard English—especially not in speech—but in edited written English it is usually placed immediately before the word or words it modifies. An examination of the citations in the Merriam-Webster files made in 1982 reached a similar conclusion: in edited prose *only* tends to be placed immediately before the word or words it modifies.

To conclude, we offer these few summary observations. The position of *only* in standard spoken English is not fixed; ambiguity is prevented by clarifying stress and intonation. In literary English from the 17th century to the present, the placement of *only* according to the idiom of speech has been freely used; it is still used, especially in prose that keeps close to the rhythms of speech. In current edited prose—especially that for which ample time has been provided for revision—*only* tends to be used in the orthodox position—immediately before (or sometimes after) the word or words it modifies.

See also EVEN.

2. The conjunction *only,* for reasons not stated, is rejected by commentators from 1869 to 1984. The OED dates use of *only* as a conjunction back to the 14th century. Here are a few examples:

It is intended to stop all debate, like the previous question in the General Court. Only it don't —Oliver Wendell Holmes d. 1894, *The Autocrat of the Breakfast-Table,* 1858

... they were getting plenty of notice of German intentions and preparations. Only, they failed to heed them —William L. Shirer, *The Nightmare Years,* 1984

For, brethren, ye have been called unto liberty; only use not liberty for occasion to the flesh —Galatians 5:13 (AV), 1611

... they would have had an answer, only the old lady began rattling on —W. M. Thackeray, *History of Sam Titmarsh and the Great Hoggarty Diamond,* 1841 (in Jespersen 1917)

Rhododendron time in Seattle is fairly spectacular, only I can't think when rhododendrons are in bloom —E. B. White, letter, 23 June 1946

You can ask Shakespeare to speak for himself, only he won't do it —Eric Bentley, *New Republic,* 5 May 1952

These uses are standard. It may be that because the conjunction is sometimes found in dialectal contexts, some may feel it is not standard. Particular contexts may be dialectal; the senses in which *only* is used are not:

"Only I'm an old man now I'd change his tune for him. I'd take the stick to his back. ..." —James Joyce, *Dubliners,* 1914

... he kept telling how he could catch them thieves easy, only the rheumatiz was so bad he couldn't walk —Vance Randolph, *Western Folklore,* January 1951

on the part of This common idiomatic phrase can often be replaced by a single preposition, such as *by* or *among,* and several commentators think—not surprisingly—that it should be. Its use is easily avoided by anyone who finds it awkward or needlessly wordy. Many writers apparently do not find it so:

After a proper resistance on the part of Mrs. Ferrars —Jane Austen, *Sense and Sensibility,* 1811

... evinces, on the part of the author, an utter and radical want of the adapting or constructive power —Edgar Allen Poe, "The Literati of New York City," 1846

It determined on the part of poor Giovanelli a further pious, a further candid, confidence —Henry James, *Daisy Miller,* 1879

... ignorance on the part of many English teachers ... of the most elementary facts about the nature of language —Barnard 1979

onto, on to The preposition *onto*, which was originally spelled *on to*, was aspersed as a vulgarism or an unnecessary formation in the 19th century. Alford 1866 disapproved it, and so did Ayres 1881; other disapprovers are mentioned by Vizetelly 1906 and Bernstein 1971. As a two-word preposition, *on to* has been in use since the 16th century; perhaps it was not much used in the best-known literature, but several of its users who are quoted in the OED had at least minor literary reputations. Alford was probably unaware of its early use. Apparently he had many correspondents who defended the term, which suggests that it was then popular.

In current American usage *onto* is usually interchangeable with *on* in the sense "to a position on":

... with the McCarthy news pushed over onto page 4 —James Thurber, letter, 1 June 1954

... the crowd was so excited that they ran out onto the field —Tip O'Neill with William Novak, *Man of the House*, 1987

... some tramp who had wandered onto the grounds —E. L. Doctorow, *Loon Lake*, 1979

Some commentators contrast *onto* with *on* in uses like these, especially with verbs like *run*, *wander*, *walk*, and *step*, as *walk on* the roof suggests something different from *walk onto* the roof.

Onto is also used for attachment:

... my father's Model T with the isinglass windows in side curtains that had to be buttoned onto the frame in bad weather —Russell Baker, *Growing Up*, 1982

Nearly every commentator from Alford to the present warns about not confusing the preposition *onto* with the adverb *on*—associated with a preceding verb—followed by the preposition *to*:

Pass this on to MR. PAYNE and apprize Martin thereof —Charles Lamb, letter, undated (perhaps 1823)

... the decision to hold on to the price line —*Fortune*, December 1960 (in Bryant 1962)

A correspondent complains to us that this distinction is frequently not observed with *hold*, especially when the preposition follows its object:

I'd given this company, a bank, all my money to hold onto for me until I needed it —*And More by Andy Rooney*, 1982

The distinction between the adverb followed by the preposition and the compound preposition is not as readily discernible with *hold* as it would be with some of the other verbs, such as *travel* or *go*, and it may be that the preposition *onto* will become established with *hold*.

In American English the preposition is regularly spelled *onto*; the open compound *on to* is still preferred by some British writers and publishers.

Onto also is used in a sense close to "aware of." This use is originally American, but the OED Supplement says it is now also used in British English:

Alvarez is onto some kind of truth —Wilfrid Sheed, *The Good Word and Other Words*, 1978

onward, onwards As is noted by several commentators, *onward* serves both as an adjective ("an onward rush") and as an adverb ("rushing onward"); *onwards* is an adverb only ("from 1600 onwards"). Evans 1957 notes that *onward* is the preferred adverb in American English, and our evidence supports that observation. In British English, however, *onwards* is in common use, especially following a prepositional phrase beginning with *from*:

... dating from about 900 onwards —W. F. Bolton, *A Short History of Literary English*, 1967

... eighteenth-century art from the Goncourts onwards —*Times Literary Supp.*, 14 May 1970

ophthalmia, ophthalmologist See PHTH.

opine This verb has been used in English since the 15th century, and it certainly is not a rare word today, but not everyone is inclined to take it seriously. Several recent commentators have described it as a stilted word, appropriate only in facetious use, and it does turn up in humorous writing:

"Even *good* moon cheese ain't worth the trouble," Joe opines. "Bottom's plumb out of the moon-cheese market." —Larry L. King, *Cosmopolitan*, November 1976

It also commonly serves to imply some disagreement with the opinion being reported:

Many opine that a writer, and particularly a poet, for some reason, must love language —William Stafford, *Writing the Australian Crawl*, 1978

More generally, it serves to emphasize that the opinion being reported is just that—an opinion:

... has recently opined that melting the ice cap "would not mean the end of human so-

ciety." —Robert Claiborne, *Saturday Rev.*,
13 Nov. 1976

". . . They wanted to make a killing with a
stock scheme to go public," opines Cousins
—Lisa See, *Publishers Weekly*, 23 Sept. 1983

Garner 1998 reports that it is also found in reports of court cases where it connotes no arbi-
trariness of opinion.

opportunity In American usage, *opportunity*
is regularly used with *to* followed by an infinitive:

. . . it was a fine day and a good opportunity
to enjoy the salt air —John Cheever, *The
Wapshot Chronicle*, 1957

He gave them every opportunity to escape
—Saul Bellow, *Herzog*, 1964

Opportunity to seems to occur only infrequently in British English:

. . . offered new opportunities to these communities to enter an honourable and prof-
itable profession —D. W. Brogan, *The English People*, 1943

American usage favors *opportunity for* followed by a noun phrase somewhat less frequently than it does *opportunity to* followed by
an infinitive:

. . . offered unlimited opportunities for
water transport —*American Guide Series:
Rhode Island*, 1937

. . . opportunities for broad university reforms are endless —George W. Bonham,
Change, March–April 1969

British usage of *opportunity for* with a noun
phrase occurs only a little more often than
with *to*:

. . . a present that can offer little except an
opportunity for limited reparation —*Times
Literary Supp.*, June 1969

Opportunity for followed by a gerund is found
less frequently in both American and British
usage than the constructions already mentioned:

. . . gave him an opportunity for thinking
and writing —*Current Biography*, July 1965

. . . the street boy has not the same opportunities for working off his adventurous animal spirits —George Sampson, *English for
the English*, 1921

Opportunity of occurs in both American and
British usage. In fact, *opportunity of* followed
by a gerund appears from our evidence to be
the most common of these constructions in
British usage. Although it still occurs in American English now and then, it was more frequent thirty years ago and before:

He seldom loses an opportunity of disprais-
ing the present, of showing his profound
pessimism —*The Journals of Arnold Bennett*,
ed. Frank Swinnerton, 1954

. . . have an opportunity of becoming acquainted only with his work as a teacher
—*Times Literary Supp.*, 12 Jan. 1967

. . . affords the lay reader the opportunity of
entering into intellectual intimacy with
Judge Learned Hand —Felix Frankfurter,
N.Y. Herald Tribune Book Rev., 18 May 1952

Opportunity of followed by a noun phrase is
also found in both American and British English, but less often than the construction with
the gerund:

. . . would give the priest moderator an opportunity of more frequent personal contact —Thomas F. Cribbin, *Bulletin of the
National Catholic Education Association*,
August 1949

"This," I said, "would give us an opportunity of long-needed talks. . . ." —Sir Winston
Churchill, *Closing the Ring*, 1951

opposite Many commentators observe that
opposite as an adjective is followed by either *to*
or *from* and that *opposite* as a noun is followed
by *of*. Our evidence for the adjective supports
the observation:

. . . in a direction opposite to that hypothe-
sized —Robert F. Forston & Charles Urban
Larson, *Jour. of Communication*, June 1968

. . . almost exactly opposite from me —John
Hawkes, *Fiction*, vol. 1, no. 4, 1973

But our evidence for the noun is more equivocal. The usual preposition following the
noun is *of*:

The overall tone . . . is the opposite of scholarly —Norman Horrocks, *Library Jour.*,
July 1966

. . . for legislation precisely the opposite of
the Pastore bill —John Fischer, *Harper's*,
December 1969

But *to* has some reputable use with the noun:

. . . he perversely accomplishes the opposite
to what he presumably intended —*College
English*, January 1945

. . . the opposite to the goal actually sought
—Brian Crozier, *Interplay*, June/July 1969

There is no particular reason why this choice
of preposition should be considered incorrect;
it certainly does not violate idiom in any way.
It is atypical, however.

opposition *Opposition*, when used with a
preposition, is usually followed by *to*:

The early theater suffered the brunt of moral opposition to the arts —*American Guide Series: New York,* 1940

. . . was also in the vanguard of the opposition to a renewal of the demand for subsidies —C. Vann Woodward, *Reunion and Reaction,* 2d ed. rev., 1956

. . . he was in opposition to the Democratic majority —*Current Biography,* January 1968

Opposition also has been used—in a different relation and with paired objects—with *between* or *of*; they occur less frequently:

. . . Rousseau . . . accepts the natural opposition between imagination and reason —Irving Babbitt, *The New Laokoon,* 1910

. . . the opposition between the complete classical form and the open . . . blurred form of romantic poetry —René Wellek, in *Twentieth Century English,* ed. William S. Knickerbocker, 1946

. . . I propose . . . to consider how the concrete educated thought of men has viewed this opposition of mechanism and organism —Alfred North Whitehead, *Science and the Modern World,* 1925

. . . he is seldom content to allow his opposition of separateness and union to work on a reader's feelings —E. K. Brown, *Rhythm in the Novel,* 1950

Opposition has also been used, but considerably less often, with *against*:

. . . maintains a steady opposition against the general proposal of the Committee —*Manchester Guardian Weekly,* 18 Dec. 1936

opt When used with a preposition, *opt* is usually followed by *for, to,* or *out of*:

Some simply tire of the corporate same-old same-old. So they opt for the moon-shot into cyberspace —Patricia Sellers, *Fortune,* 7 Feb. 2000

Instead, more workers opted for preferred provider networks —Tim Bonfield, *Cincinnati Enquirer,* 27 Jan. 1999

If you have oily skin, opt for a water-based or oil-free formula —*Cosmopolitan,* May 2000

Why did he opt to select a wife from among a group of woman who agreed to a public competition . . .? —Nora Roberts, *Time,* 28 Feb. 2000

Since attendance at classes isn't mandatory, many students opt to cut —Rachel Donadio, *Lingua Franca,* March 2000

While most people spend their lives climbing the corporate ladder, these "down-shifters," as they're called, are opting to get off the ladder —Shari Caudron, *Industry Week,* 20 May 1996

. . . would require companies to give customers the chance to opt out of joint marketing programs —Daniel Eisenberg, *Time,* 6 Sept. 1999

. . . Nadar opted out of actually fighting in the popular uprising —Peter Plagens, *Newsweek,* 1 May 1995

optimum, optimal Contrary to the preference of a commentator or two, *optimum* is both noun and adjective, and has been since the late 19th century. It began its career in English as a scientific term and it still tends to be found mainly in technical surroundings:

Initially, early universes will be far from optimum and will die in roughly a Planck time —Robert H. March, *Physics Today,* March 1998

It is occasionally found in general sources:

. . . each person must discover the meaning . . . at an optimum moment in life —Barrett J. Mandel, *AAUP Bulletin,* September 1971

. . . it would be churlish, albeit accurate, to suggest that seeing these 25 plays and eight series on a big screen with an audience isn't the optimum viewing situation —Graham Fuller, *Village Voice,* 11 Feb. 1982

. . . the island's declared optimum quota of 820 tourists at a time —Jan Morris, *Locations,* 1992

Several critics contend that *optimum* is often inappropriately used to mean simply "best," but they give no examples of such usage. Our own evidence shows that *optimum* usually means "best possible" or "most favorable," not simply "best." *Optimal,* also common in technical contexts, has more general use than *optimum.* It can be close to "best" in meaning:

Today, investors are looking for the optimal broker, period —Dan Burke, *Fortune,* 20 Dec. 1999

But even here, and in most general contexts, it means "best possible":

. . . despite his determination to retain optimal health, smokes a pack of cigarettes a day —Ralph T. King, Jr., *Wall Street Jour.,* 10 Jan. 1996

or See AGREEMENT, SUBJECT-VERB: COMPOUND SUBJECTS 2; EITHER 3, 4; NEITHER 2; NO 2.

-or, -our In words like *color* and *honor* the ending *-our* is standard in British English. The elimination of the *u* is largely the doing of

oral   **552**

Noah Webster's spellers and dictionaries. It has become one of the regular features that distinguishes British from American spelling.

oral See VERBAL, ORAL.

orate Many commentators have noted, and our evidence confirms, that this back-formation from the noun *oration* is frequently used in a humorous or disparaging way to describe impassioned or pompous speech:

> An old man beside me was orating as to how anyone who lives to be 60 in New York deserves a medal —Alan Rich, *New York,* 26 Feb. 1973

It is also used straightforwardly, often with reference to the past:

> . . . Populists had orated from a wagon near the Odd Fellows Hall —Anthony Lukas, *Vanity Fair,* October 1997

> It was ironical . . . that the greatest platform campaigner of his age should . . . have been rejected in the constituency in which he had orated mightily —Roy Jenkins, *Gladstone,* 1995

> We must accustom ourselves to talking without orating —William Stafford, *Writing the Australian Crawl,* 1978

orchestrate Figurative use of the word *orchestrate* has drawn criticism from language commentators on the grounds that it is faddish or a cliché. However, if use of the figurative sense, "to arrange or combine so as to achieve maximum effect," is a fad, it is a long-lived one, as this use is attested as early as 1883.

Figurative use began with descriptions of paintings, but over the years its application has broadened considerably. It usually connotes a careful handling of details to reach a desired result:

> Kanin knows how to orchestrate a gag by timing it shrewdly —Brooks Atkinson, quoted in *Current Biography 1953*

> Disney World may be the world's first working socialist state. Everything is timed, planned, orchestrated —Caryl Rivers & Diana Zykovsky Anhalt, *Grand Tour,* Spring 1996

> . . . the thoughtful handselling and the carefully orchestrated store ambience —*Publishers Weekly,* 3 Jan. 2000

> On that note . . . the production cuts to a series of deftly orchestrated satiric vignettes —John Lahr, *New Yorker,* 19 Oct. 1998

If often connotes a behind-the-scenes or covert management:

> A few days later, in orchestrated pursuance of a policy to suppress criticism of seven

weeks of appeasement —William Safire, *N.Y. Times,* 27 Dec. 1979

> . . . the possibility that others could have orchestrated the crime —William Murray, *New Yorker,* 31 July 1989

> Before anything came of this, however, he was unceremoniously booked out of Honduras, an event he believes Lt. Col. Oliver North orchestrated —Genevieve Stuttaford, *Publishers Weekly,* 12 Oct. 1992

> . . . the sabbatical is the presentable public face that has been put on a very private ousting orchestrated by Microsoft's president —Janice Maloney, *Time,* 7 June 1999

It is clear that many professional writers find the figurative use of *orchestrate* perfectly acceptable.

order See IN ORDER THAT; IN ORDER TO.

ordinance, ordnance A number of usage commentators trouble themselves to distinguish between these words, along the following lines. *Ordinance* has several meanings, the most common of which is "a law set forth by a governmental authority":

> . . . the nation's first planning and zoning ordinance to set up controls for a historic district —David Butwin. *Saturday Rev.,* 15 Apr. 1972

Ordnance is a military word which is etymologically related to *ordinance* but is otherwise distinct from it. *Ordnance* can mean "artillery," "a service of the army in charge of combat supplies," or "military supplies for combat":

> . . . the danger from unexploded ordnance —Paul R. Ehrlich & John P. Holdren, *Saturday Rev.,* 4 Dec. 1971

Confusion of these similar words is rare, but not unheard of. The most likely mistake to be made is the substitution of the more common word, *ordinance,* for the less common *ordnance*:

> Early in 1944, Joe was drafted into the Army and trained in ordinance —*Guitar Player,* August 1981

organizations considered as collective nouns See AGREEMENT: ORGANIZATIONS CONSIDERED AS COLLECTIVE NOUNS.

Oriental See ASIAN, ASIATIC, ORIENTAL.

orientate *Orientate,* first attested in 1849 in the same issue of the same journal that first used *orientation,* has been under critical fire since 1945. The criticism boils down to this: *orientate* is three letters and one syllable longer than *orient.* That would seem like a rather trivial concern, but the word seems to draw criticism for no better reason than that. *Orientate* is quite common in British English:

> When they come to London, colonials orientate themselves by Piccadilly Circus —Ngaio Marsh, *Death of a Peer,* 1940

> . . . the propaganda of the period has to orientate itself in relation to these landmarks —Aldous Huxley, *The Olive Tree,* 1937

> . . . France and Italy, where the conservatives tend to be clerically orientated —*Times Literary Supp.,* 26 Apr. 1974

> . . . the struggle in Greece to promote the classically-orientated Katharevousa —Randolph Quirk, *Style and Communication in the English Language,* 1982

The shorter *orient* seems to be the usual choice in American English.

originate *Originate,* when used with a preposition, is most often used with *in:*

> The reports as presented in these meetings all originate in widely separated company departments —James K. Blake, *Dun's,* January 1954

> . . . television programs originating in Richmond —*NEA Jour.,* January 1965

> *Virginia Woolf: The Inward Voyage* shows signs of having originated in a doctoral dissertation —*Times Literary Supp.,* 30 July 1971

A little less often, *originate* is used with *from:*

> Originating from a commingling of Indians with runaway slaves, these people had fled . . . —*American Guide Series: Texas,* 1940

> . . . arranged for ten organ recitals originating from the Germanic Museum to be broadcast over CBS —*Current Biography 1950*

Originate is also used with *as, at, on, out of, outside of,* and *with:*

> The classical view is that the earth originated as a hot body —A. E. Benfield, *Scientific American Reader,* 1953

> The system originated at the end of World War I —*Current Biography 1950*

> . . . the concept of the separable soul has been originated on primitive "scientific" grounds —Weston La Barre, *The Human Animal,* 1954

> A poem does not originate out of an impulse to communicate —John Hall Wheelock, *N.Y. Times Book Rev.,* 23 May 1954

> . . . in the case of families that originated outside of North America —Ernst Mayr, *Wilson Bulletin,* March 1946

> Mr. Lowell . . . issued the invitation, but the idea had originated with Lawrence Henderson —Lucien Price, *Dialogues of Alfred North Whitehead,* 1954

or less See LESS, FEWER.

or no See NO 3.

or not See WHETHER OR NOT.

or otherwise See OTHERWISE.

other For uses of *other* in *of any other*—in what is called false comparison—see ANY 3.

other than *Other* has a propensity for being used with *than.* The trouble is, as the OED shows, that *other* can be an adjective, a pronoun, or an adverb, and still be used with *than.* This flexibility has created a variety of *other than* constructions and the consequent bewilderment of usage commentators, beginning with Fowler 1926. The critics who follow Fowler more or less repeat, with varying degrees of expansiveness, his dictum that *"other than* should be registered as a phrase to be avoided." Writers have paid scant attention to this advice; *other than* is not avoided.

The grammatical problem that Fowler brought on himself was a result of not paying attention to the OED. Fowler approved *other* as an adjective; he disapproved it as an adverb, even though the OED recognized it. And he overlooked the fact that the OED also covers it as a pronoun. This oversight left him stumped when, damning uses he had decided were adverbial, he ran up against an example to which his adverbial analysis did not apply:

> Up to the very end no German field company would look with other than apprehension to meeting the 25th on even terms.

This *other* is the seventh sense of the OED's pronoun. It has been around for quite a while and is still current:

> I can not in honesty or self-respect do other than protest —Dewitt Clinton Poole, quoted in *Current Biography 1950*

> . . . civil law, which regulates relationships between individuals, families, and corporations involving other than criminal activities —Norman F. Cantor, *Imagining the Law,* 1997

Fowler was similarly perplexed when *other than* was followed by an adjective:

> But it is doubtful if any of the leaders . . . would have been other than dismayed and frightened at the idea —Gerald Carson, *New-England Galaxy,* Winter 1965

> . . . he always wondered how she could be other than happy —Robert Canzoneri, *McCall's,* March 1971

When *other* is rather obviously an adjective or an adverb, the compound *other than* works much like a compound preposition meaning "besides" or "except":

> . . . a high-level dialogue, covering issues other than hostages —Oliver North, in *The Tower Commission Report*, 1987

> . . . discovering he has a lover other than her —Martin Tucker, *Commonweal*, 11 Apr. 1969

> The gene, he says, is too small to be anything other than a large molecule —Matt Ridley, *Genome*, 1999

> . . . prohibited the offering of advice on venereal disease by anyone other than medical practitioners —Richard Davenport-Hines, *Times Literary Supp.*, 13 Nov. 1998

This quasi-prepositional use is sometimes close in meaning to "apart from":

> Other than twisting and untwisting her hands, she sits perfectly still —Jim Jerome, *N.Y. Times Mag.*, 14 Jan. 1979

> Other than the bullet holes, the Parnasse was in decent shape —Neal Stephenson, *The Diamond Age*, 1995

In addition, you will sometimes find *other than that* used like *except that*:

> I do not recall in what territory it was, other than that it was west of Albuquerque —Agnes Morley Cleaveland, *No Life for a Lady*, 1941

All of these uses are standard English. It seems quite clear that the last word on the grammar of these phrases has not yet been written, but inability to analyze constructions in a satisfying way has never deterred writers from using them. There seems little point in changing *other than* to *except* or *besides* or *otherwise than* or *apart from* unless you think the change makes your sentence sound better. You surely need not avoid *other than* simply because usage writers are perplexed by its grammar.

otherwise   The problem here is that old devil grammar. The commentator with the problem is Fowler 1926, who, as Bernstein 1971 puts it, "worked himself into a thousand-word lather over what he deemed misuses of *otherwise*." This time Fowler had not missed something in the OED, as he had with *other than*; the construction upon which he intended mayhem was not really covered in the OED, having become established only at the end of the 19th century (the OED Supplement dates it from 1886). The problem, as Fowler saw it, was *or otherwise* tacked on after an adverb, adjective, or noun (or verb, the OED Supplement adds)

to indicate its contrary. (In actual use *otherwise* may also indicate an indefinite alternative, not necessarily a contrary.)

Fowler decided that *otherwise* had to be an adverb and so rejected *or otherwise* when attached to an adjective or noun. Bernstein and Copperud 1970, 1980 point out that *otherwise* is an adjective in most dictionaries, and they dismiss Fowler's objections (repeated by Phythian 1979) as pedantry. They tend to accept his objections to *or otherwise* attached to a noun, however.

The difficulty with all this ratiocination is that *otherwise*, one of our oldest everyday words, is far too flexible to be confined in the rigid part-of-speech categories of Latin. Here are some examples in which *or otherwise* (or *and otherwise*) suggests a contrary:

> . . . certain people whose deeds, admirable or otherwise, entitle them to more public attention —John Fischer, *Harper's,* December 1971

> . . . the stability or otherwise of this resolved and obstinate war Government —Sir Winston Churchill, *The Unrelenting Struggle,* 1942

> . . . we are shown portraits, prints, and drawings, contemporary and otherwise —*Times Literary Supp.*, 27 Aug. 1971

> . . . essays by 16 Hardy enthusiasts, scholarly and otherwise —Peter Gardner, *Saturday Rev.*, 21 Feb. 1976

> . . . endurance tests to prove their fitness or otherwise for the status of manhood —Francis Birtles, *Battle Fronts of Outback,* in *Wanderers in Australia,* ed. Colin Roderick, 1949

The phrases are not uncommonly linked with a noun used as an adjective:

> . . . personalities, show biz and otherwise —Daisy Maryles, *Publishers Weekly,* 5 July 1976

> . . . could be discussing their hits, baseball and otherwise —*People,* 22 Nov. 1976

Otherwise may also imply an unspecified alternative, rather than a simple contrary:

> . . . if vacancies happen by resignation or otherwise during the recess of the legislature of any State —*Constitution of the United States,* 1787

> . . . for most travelers, European or otherwise —Robin Prestage, *Saturday Rev.*, 1 Jan. 1972

> They also were too apathetic or inexperienced to set rules for themselves, either academically or otherwise —Edith Hollerman, *Change,* Summer 1971

These constructions are standard, every one.

ought **1.** *Ought* is a little awkward to put into the negative. In writing, *ought not* is the usual form, and it may be followed by the bare infinitive or the infinitive with *to:*

> A fellow, however, ought not to be satisfied with a recipe that is merely simple and delicious —Robert Draper, *GQ,* May 1998

> . . . ought they not ask for membership in the new U.N. Trusteeship Council? —*Time,* 17 Mar. 1947

> Such language ought not be allowed to go to waste —Laurence Urdang, *Verbatim,* Autumn 1994

> But thousands of others ought not to be in prison at all —Karl Menninger, quoted in *Psychology Today,* February 1969

Although *ought not* is used in speech, it does seem a bit stuffy for everyday use. *Oughtn't* is one spoken substitute. In the U.S. it is regionally limited, being found most commonly in Midland and Southern areas of the Atlantic Seaboard and in parts of the Northern Midland area. It has somewhat limited use in writing:

> You oughtn't to have to trot up there every time somebody gets it into his head he wants to ask you something —William Ruckleshaus, quoted in *N.Y. Times Mag.,* 19 Aug. 1973

> But if you think melodrama is innately vulgar, then you oughtn't watch TV at all —Frank McConnell, *Commonweal,* 10 Oct. 1997

> Those of us who are depressed at the political decline of Ronald Reagan oughtn't scold those who are delighted —Morton Kondracke, *Los Angeles Times,* 15 Jan. 1987

Bryant 1962 explains *hadn't ought* as a survival of an old use of *ought* as a past participle. It is found only in speechlike prose, speech, and fictional speech:

> . . . he hadn't ought to have shown my letter to you. (I use American, that lovely tongue.) —H. L. Mencken, letter, 4 Sep. 1911

> . . . and she kind of whispers to me, "Say, you hadn't ought to kid the servants like that." —Sinclair Lewis, *The Man Who Knew Coolidge,* 1928

> "But he hadn't ought to be telling lies about Cleve Pikestaff." —Hodding Carter, *Southwest Rev.,* Winter 1948

The British equivalent of the American *hadn't ought* is *didn't ought.* It is aspersed in various British usage books. It seems to be a spoken form only, and a footnote in Quirk et al. 1985 suggests that it may be a dwindling form, since it was the least popular negative form in a test of British teenage informants. Here are a couple of examples:

> Dixon was promoted in 1948 to be ambassador in Prague. [British Foreign Secretary Ernest] Bevin later commented, "I didn't ought to have sent you to that awful place" —*Times Literary Supp.,* 29 Feb. 1968

> Behind the salty paganism of country life stands the daily haggle of what people 'ought' or 'didn't ought' to do —V. S. Pritchett, *A Man of Letters,* 1985

2. Many commentators (Follett 1966 and Garner 1998, for example) insist on retaining *to* before the infinitive after *ought* in every instance; others (Evans 1957 and Freeman 1990, for instance) say *to* is optional in negative statements. Bernstein 1971 criticizes both sides, saying the *to* is optional in either negative or positive statements when something intervenes between *ought* and the infinitive, and he provides two examples of positive statements. Quirk et al. 1985 reports that tests of young people in both Great Britain and the U.S. showed the omission of *to* widely acceptable in what he calls "nonassertive contexts." Our files have only a couple of examples of omitted *to* in positive contexts from written sources; they would seem to fit the description of "nonassertive." Here is one:

> . . . find stronger rationalizations for why people ought better communicate —Allan G. Mottus, *Women's Wear Daily,* 27 Aug. 1973

Here is an example with the intervening matter mentioned by Bernstein:

> They ought logically go first to the standing committee —*N.Y. Times,* 28 Dec. 1966

But in edited prose, retention of the *to* is usual:

> . . . the standard against which men ought to be measured —Ward Just, *Atlantic,* October 1970

Things are different in negative contexts. If you look back at the examples in section 1, you will note that *to* was often omitted after *ought not* and *oughtn't,* but retained after the double modal forms. Quirk et al. 1985 says that *to* tends to be retained in assertive contexts.

3. *Hadn't ought* and *didn't ought* we have looked at above. In the U.S. *hadn't ought* is a geographical variant rather than a social variant. The positive forms *had ought* and *should ought,* however, are characteristic of uneducated speech. Bryant says that *had ought* is, like *hadn't ought,* a Northern form, but an uncultivated one:

. . . and so they had ought to be quiet, for they have nothin' to fight about —Thomas Chandler Halliburton, *The Clockmaker,* 1837

Should ought is a favorite of Ring Lardner's characters:

"They should only ought to of had one. . . ." —*You Know Me Al,* 1916

4. See HAD OUGHT, HADN'T OUGHT.

ought to of The *of* here stands for *'ve* or *have.* See OF 2.

-our See -OR, -OUR.

ours The possessive pronoun *ours,* like the possessive pronouns *its, theirs,* and *yours,* is properly spelled without an apostrophe.

ourselves See MYSELF.

out See OUT OF, OUT.

out loud *Out loud* was once widely decried as an error for *aloud,* and it is still sometimes described as a colloquialism to be avoided in formal writing. Its first recorded use was in the early 19th century:

Lord Andover in the presence of Lord and Lady Suffolk and speaking *out loud* —Maria Edgeworth, letter, 1821 (OED Supplement)

Its heyday as an object of criticism came about a hundred years later, when American commentators such as MacCracken & Sandison 1917, Ball 1923, Woolley & Scott 1926, and Krapp 1927 routinely prescribed against it in their books. While its notoriety has diminished, it still survives as a usage topic in composition textbooks for high school and college students and in Garner 1998.

Our abundant written evidence for *out loud* shows clearly that it is not a colloquialism. We would agree that *aloud* is more likely in solemn writing (Garner says it is much more frequent), but in general use the two terms are essentially interchangeable:

She read it aloud to my classmates —Russell Baker, *Growing Up,* 1982

He was reading my words out loud to the entire class —Russell Baker, *Growing Up,* 1982

. . . being permitted to think aloud with friends and colleagues —Bruce Dearing, *CEA Forum,* April 1971

. . . afraid to let themselves or others think out loud —Nehemiah Jordan, *Themes in Speculative Psychology,* 1968

A distinctive and exclusive use of *out loud* is in the idiom "for crying out loud!" It is also preferred to *aloud* following the verb *laugh:*

. . . *Mazeppa* makes him laugh out loud —Robert Craft, *N.Y. Rev. of Books,* 25 Feb. 1971

He laughed out loud —E. L. Doctorow, *Loon Lake,* 1979

out of, out A few commentators observe that the *of* is superfluous most of the time, or sometimes—depending on whose opinion you are reading—when *out* is used with verbs of motion. The observation, however, is not especially useful, for *out* and *out of* are interchangeable only in a very few restricted contexts; *out* simply cannot be substituted for *out of* in most cases.

Out is used much more often as an adverb than as a preposition. When used as a preposition, it seems most often to go with *door* or *window:*

We went out the door and got into the car —Paul Ernst, *Redbook,* March 1964

. . . old budgetary guidelines have gone out the window —Jerry Edgerton, *Money,* March 1980

. . . permits prevailing west breezes to carry warm greenhouse air out the door —Glenn Munson, *Blair & Ketchum's Country Jour.,* January 1980

He stares out the window —John Corry, *Harper's,* February 1969

With *window, out of* is about equally common:

. . . who stared blankly out of a window —Emmanuel Bernstein, *Psychology Today,* October 1968

. . . upstairs his fat wife leaned out of the window —Bernard Malamud, *The Magic Barrel,* 1958

With nouns that designate places or things that can be thought of as containing or surrounding, *out of* is usual:

You never need get out of your car —Eileene Coffield, *Ford Times,* November 1967

I would have done anything to get out of that kitchen —William M. Clark, *New-England Galaxy,* Fall 1969

A bathtub is, at best, a makeshift place to take a shower. It's hard to get into and out of gracefully —*And More by Andy Rooney,* 1982

Out has been used this way, but it sounds not quite part of the mainstream:

"Father! father!" exclaimed a piercing cry from out the mist —James Fenimore Cooper, *The Deerslayer,* 1841

Dock Knowital he Snuck Out the room an' Disappeared —Frank W. Sage, D.D.S., *Dental Digest,* November 1902

The woman came out the bath house —Flannery O'Connor, *Partisan Rev.,* February 1949

We conclude that prepositional *out* has a narrow range of application. It can seldom be idiomatically substituted for *out of.*

outside of 1. Bernstein 1965 sees nothing wrong with *outside of* as a synonym for *outside,* but a whole string of commentators from Bierce 1909 to Shaw 1987 do see something wrong. The culprit is *of,* all two letters and one syllable of it. Our evidence suggests that writers and speakers retain the *of* when it sounds right to them, and drop it when it does not. You have the same choice. *Outside of* was in common use by standard 19th-century authors such as Emerson, Thackeray, Hawthorne, and Henry James. Here are some 20th-century examples:

Well, as an old veteran sixth-grader, that question is I think outside of my province —William Faulkner, 11 Mar. 1957, in *Faulkner in the University,* 1959

If you order it outside of Boston, however, the waiter is not likely to know what you're talking about —Safire 1982

"Yes. He's a fine one," Pop said.
"Where did you get him?
"Just outside of camp."
                    —Ernest Hemingway, *Green Hills of Africa,* 1935

Most of the papers chosen had been written outside of class to meet regular assignments —James Sledd, in Greenbaum 1985

. . . but I was relatively unknown outside of Capitol Hill —Tip O'Neill with William Novak, *Man of the House,* 1987

2. Bernstein 1965 disparages *outside of* in the sense of "except for" or "aside from," and so do several others from 1927 to 1998. The usage is, however, quite respectable in ordinary writing:

Really outside of Hume no one in English philosophy has quite the same magic —Harold J. Laski, letter, 11 Apr. 1920

. . . Britain and France can buy all the supplies they want from us, outside of munitions —*New Republic,* 8 Mar. 1939

. . . all fish and shellfish—outside of a few specimens such as abalone and octopus—are tender in their raw state —Thomas Mario, *Playboy,* September 1968

Outside of Geraldine . . . the other characters tend to be stereotypes —Jane Green, *Publishers Weekly,* 10 April 2000

This hasn't been a particularly good year for political consultants—outside of all the money they made —Art Levine, *U.S. News & World Report,* 10 Mar. 1997

3. See INSIDE OF.

over Disapproval of *over* meaning "more than" is a hoary American newspaper tradition. It began with William Cullen Bryant's *Index Expurgatorius* of 1877. Bryant simply forbade *over* (and *above*) in this sense; he gave no reason. From Bryant the dictum passed to Bierce 1909. From Bierce *over* passed into almost all of the newspaper handbooks: we find it in Hyde 1926; George C. Bastien et al., *Editing the Day's News* (4th ed., 1956); and Bremner 1980. *Time* for 11 Oct. 1948 twitted the Detroit *Free Press* for disapproving the usage while the newspaper's motto is "On Guard for Over a Century"; New World 1988 mentions the stylebooks of the *Washington Post, Los Angeles Times* and the Associated Press. Garner 1998 is still disapproving: he calls it a "casualism."

Over in the sense of "more than" has been used in English since the 14th century. Here are some examples; you will note they were not written by American newspaper reporters:

. . . over 32,000 acres are under vineyards —*Encyclopædia Britannica,* 11th ed., 1910

Johnson's biographical writings cover a period of over forty years —John Butt, *English Literature in the Mid-Eighteenth Century,* edited & completed by Geoffrey Carnall, 1979

I have now a library of nearly 900 volumes, over 700 of which I wrote myself —Henry David Thoreau, journal, 30 Oct. 1853, quoted in *N.Y. Times Book Rev.,* 7 Nov. 1982

. . . Mr. Kallman and I have been close friends for over thirty years —W. H. Auden, *Harper's,* March 1972

. . . the phrase in question appeared over six hundred years earlier —W. F. Bolton, *A Short History of Literary English,* 1967

I have been in show business man and boy for over forty years —Groucho Marx, letter, 5 Sept. 1951

It has been almost twenty-two years since you were at "Shorelee" and it doesn't seem a day over seventeen —James Thurber, letter, 1 June 1954

Over two hundred friends from my district came —Tip O'Neill with William Novak, *Man of the House,* 1987

There is no reason why you need to avoid this usage.

overall This word became common only in the 20th century, and its newfound popularity has led to criticism from several commentators (such as Evans 1957, Gowers 1965, and Garner 1998). Their basic objection is not to the word itself but to its overuse, especially as an adjective in place of such familiar words as *general, total, complete,* and *comprehensive,* and as a sentence adverb. It is a common word, and although all of its common uses are standard, you may well want to give some thought to its value or appropriateness in a particular context before you use it in your writing. It is not, however, a word to be shunned. Here are a few examples of its use, both as an adjective and as an adverb:

> Despite an overall cultural similarity, the various parts of West Pakistan are dominated by different communal groups —Rosanne Klass, *Saturday Rev.,* 5 Feb. 1972

> . . . the overall effect of the book is numbing —Michael Kammen, *N.Y. Times Book Rev.,* 4 July 1976

> . . . the overall temper, the general disposition of the writer —I. A. Richards, *Times Literary Supp.,* 7 July 1978

> The sale, overall, appeared to have been successful —*Antiques and the Arts Weekly,* 29 Oct. 1982

> Overall, we need to promote public awareness —Russ Peterson, *Audubon Mag.,* November 1982

overlook, oversee A glance in any dictionary will show that the verb *overlook* has many senses, including one in which it is synonymous with *supervise.* This sense dates back to 1532, but in current English it has become extremely rare—for obvious reasons:

> The operators "overlook" the machines —Anglo-American Council on Productivity, *Packaging,* 1950

Take away the quotation marks and most readers will get an impression of distracted operators neglecting or perhaps tripping over their machines, since "to fail to notice; ignore" has long been established as the principal sense of *overlook.* The "supervise" sense now survives almost solely in the noun *overlooker,* a chiefly British synonym of *foreman:*

> . . . require an overlooker to take charge of our Fancy Yarn Department —advt., *Telegraph & Argus* (Bradford, Eng.), 4 June 1974

The history of *oversee* closely resembles that of *overlook,* except that the "supervise" sense is the one that has prevailed:

> . . . a few aides who were to oversee the major departments —*New Yorker,* 12 May 1972

Oversee also once meant "to fail to notice; disregard":

> . . . to oversee and wilfully neglect the gross advances made him by my wife —William Congreve, *The Way of the World,* 1700 (OED)

But that sense of the word is now obsolete.

overly Bache 1869 and Ayres 1881 succinctly insulted contemporaries who used this word, calling them vulgar and unschooled. Times have changed: modern critics merely insult the word itself. Follett 1966, for example, claims that *overly* is useless, superfluous, and unharmonious and should be replaced by the prefix *over-.* Bryson 1984 adds that "when this becomes overinelegant . . . , the alternative is to find another adverb: 'excessively' or 'unnecessarily' or even the admirably concise 'too.'" You may not want to go to such lengths to avoid *overly,* and some modern commentators (Evans 1957, for example) would agree that there is no need to. We concur. In fact, in some cases none of the alternatives sounds as good as *overly.*

> . . . a not overly clean tunic —Thomas B. Costain, *The Black Rose,* 1945

> . . . the author of various not overly inspired books —Robert A. Hall, Jr., *A Short History of Italian Literature,* 1951

> . . . make his otherwise overly comfortable life more interesting —Pauline Kael, *Harper's,* February 1969

Even when *over-, too, excessively,* or *unnecessarily* would be a successful substitute, the fact that a synonym is available does not mean that you have to use it. These writers used *overly:*

> . . . so much playing is overly concerned with notes —Howard Klein, *N.Y. Times,* 7 Apr. 1966

> . . . Russian leaders seemed overly suspicious —Norman Cousins, *Saturday Rev.,* 30 Oct. 1971

> . . . an overly educated European newspaperman —Norman Mailer, *N.Y. Times Mag.,* 26 Sept. 1976

> . . . an overly eager land developer —William Styron, *N.Y. Times Mag.,* 15 June 1980

Overly is not as commonly used in England as in the U.S., but according to the OED Supplement it is gaining ground there.

oversee See OVERLOOK, OVERSEE.

overwhelm When *overwhelm* is used in the passive voice or as an adjectival past participle, it is most often followed with *by; with* is also found sometimes:

> . . . we have not been overwhelmed by the air attack —Sir Winston Churchill, *The Unrelenting Struggle,* 1942

> . . . an irrational, heroic, mystic world, beset by treachery, overwhelmed by violence —William L. Shirer, *The Rise and Fall of the Third Reich,* 1960

> . . . Oxford's dreaming spires overwhelmed by factories —John Fischer, *Harper's,* July 1972

> . . . a village whose final fate was to be overwhelmed with drifting sand —Jacquetta & Christopher Hawkes, *Prehistoric Britain,* 1949

When some other form of *overwhelm* is used, *by* and *with* are also used. Occasionally, *in* is also found:

> Your letter overwhelms me a little by its affectionate generosity —Harold J. Laski, letter, 2 Apr. 1920

> The danger of historical parallels is their power to overwhelm the judgment with the pat and triumphant testimony of coincidence —Archibald MacLeish, *Saturday Rev.,* 9 Feb. 1946

> . . . a blast furnace burst, overwhelming some twenty men in a stream of molten metal —*Times Literary Supp.,* 30 July 1971

over with *Over with* has been cited as an error or as a colloquialism in usage handbooks for most of the past century. The critics typically regard the *with* as superfluous. Some advise using *over* by itself; others express a preference for *finished* or *ended.* Our evidence indicates that *over with* occurs primarily in speech and in writing that has the informal quality of speech. It serves especially to express a desire or determination to have something unpleasant done or finished as soon as possible:

> I will be real glad when this television thing is over with —Flannery O'Connor, letter, 18 May 1955

Its most characteristic use is with the verb *get:*

> We may both live to be sorry we didn't go through school . . . and get it over with —Robert Frost, letter, 26 May 1926

> We want to tackle a problem and get it over with —Henry Huglin, *Center Mag.,* January/February 1970

> The Carter administration, no doubt, will now try to ignore the flap and get the renominations over with —*Wall Street Jour.,* 3 June 1980

Such usage is perfectly idiomatic and need not be avoided in an appropriate context.

owing to For some comments about the history of this preposition, which has frequently been prescribed by the commentators in place of *due to,* see the article on DUE TO.

pace This 19th-century borrowing from Latin is one that English could well have done without, according to Fowler 1926, 1965. He warned that it was used to mean "according to"—a misapprehension not found in our files nor in those of Burchfield 1996. In English it is used primarily as a courteous apology for introducing a contradictory opinion. It tends to be used in writing of the learned sort, and is almost always italicized.

> *Pace* Anita Loos, six out of ten prefer brunettes —*Time,* 1 Sept. 1947

> Life, *pace* Jeremy Bentham, is not exclusively utilitarian —*Times Literary Supp.,* 11 Nov. 1965

> . . . the health-care fiasco had made liberalism look more than ever like a plot spun by

elitists and bureaucrats to straighten out (pace Kant) the crooked timber of humanity —Jack Beatty, *Atlantic,* August 1996

> Easiness is a virtue in grammar, *pace* old-fashioned grammarians of the Holofernes school, who confused difficulty with depth —Howard 1984

pachyderm, pachydermatous A handful of critics complain about these words. Copperud 1964, 1970, 1980 and Flesch 1964 object to newspaper use of *pachyderm* as a synonym for *elephant.* Fowler 1926, 1965 objects to *pachydermatous* as a favorite of what he calls "polysyllabic humorists," who use it to mean "thick-skinned."

There is really no problem with these words that a little restraint in using them will not eliminate. The chances are that you will be careful enough to avoid overkill. So go ahead and use *pachyderm* or *pachydermatous* if it suits your purpose. As you can see from the following examples, the purpose need not be dead serious.

> A mighty creature is the germ,
> Though smaller than the pachyderm.
> —Ogden Nash, "The Germ," reprinted in *Chains of Light* (8th-grade textbook), 1982

> . . . making one another laugh by sticking pins into venerable pachyderms like the royal family, the army, the Archbishop of Canterbury —Patrick Campbell, *Saturday Rev.*, 11 June 1977

> . . . the archetypal Seuss hero . . . was Horton, a conscientious pachyderm —Eric Paceolm, *N.Y. Times*, 26 Sept. 1991

> . . . when P. G. Wodehouse wrote, on the subject of one of his sabre-toothed and pachydermatous aunts, 'A massive silence prevailed in the corner where the aunt sat' —Howard 1977

> . . . even in dealing with the most pachydermatous political systems, patient pressure is neither counterproductive nor futile —*The Economist*, 19 July 1985

paid See PAY.

pair 1. *Plural: "pair," "pairs."* The usual plural is *pairs,* when there is no preceding number or indicator of number (as *several*):

> . . . maturity is the ability to live with conflicting pairs of truths —Faubion Bowers, *Saturday Rev.*, 12 Feb. 1972

When a number or indicator of number precedes *pair,* either *pair* or *pairs* may be used:

> . . . hung the pin-stripe suit with the two pair of pants —Wright Morris, *Real Losses, Imaginary Gains*, 1976

> . . . six pair of blue jeans —Marcia Cohen, *N.Y. Times Mag.*, 2 Mar. 1975

> It had oarlocks for three pairs of oars —Frances H. Eliot, *New England Journeys*, 1953

> In a saucepan soak 2 pairs of sweetbreads —Evan Jones, *Gourmet*, February 1973

A few commentators—Garner 1998, Harper 1985, Bremner 1980, Shaw 1987—disparage the plural form *pair* after a number. Our evidence shows that both *pair* and *pairs* are in reputable use in the U.S.

2. *Agreement. Pair* is one of those collective nouns that take a singular or plural verb according to notional agreement. If you are thinking of the individuals in the pair, you use a plural verb:

> A pair of elephants were grazing near the camp —Alan Moorehead, *No Room in the Ark,* 1959, in Henry I. Christ, *Modern English in Action,* 1982

If you are thinking of the pair as a unit, you will use the singular:

> Genuine crocodile loafers. . . . The handsome pair has a hand-sewn moccasin construction —catalog, *Trifles,* Fall 1987

pajamas, pyjamas Until the early 20th century, in the United States the spelling *pajamas* vied with the spelling *pyjamas.* However, *pajamas* is now the usual American spelling and *pyjamas* is the British:

> . . . old women in black pajamas, hair pulled back —Peggy Seeger & Diane Alexander, *N.Y. Times,* 13 Apr. 1975

> . . . perhaps it was the colour of his pyjamas —Graham Greene, *Travels with My Aunt,* 1969

Exceptions, of course, can occur:

> The Professor in pyjamas was not an unpleasant sight —Willa Cather, *The Professor's House,* 1925

> . . . a pair of puce pajamas newly laundered —Anthony Burgess, *MF,* 1971

Perhaps the biggest categorical exception occurs in contemporary American advertising, where the spelling *pyjamas* is found with some regularity, perhaps for snob appeal.

> Evening pyjamas made for us alone —advt., *Vogue,* June 1982

> . . . silky black jersey hostess pyjamas —catalog, *Horchow,* July–August 1982

palpable Fowler 1926 considers *palpable* a dead metaphor that can be brought to "angry life" by extended use. Krapp 1927 cautions that the word must be handled carefully, a sentiment echoed by Copperud 1970, 1980; Flesch 1964 thinks the word is bookish; Evans 1957 thinks *palpable lie* is no longer fresh. All of this cautionary exhortation is belied by the fact that published writers who use the word—and there are plenty of them—have no particular difficulty with it.

The primary meaning is "capable of being touched or felt," a sense that is common in medical use:

> The liver span was 18 cm, and the edge was palpable 8 cm below the right costal margin —Howard Wilson, M.D., et al., *JAMA,* 23 Feb. 1979

By the 15th century, *palpable* was being used figuratively, applied to what could be perceived by senses other than touch:

As palpable and constant as the smell in the house —Jean Stafford, *New Yorker,* 7 Apr. 1951

... the sharp drafts of autumn are palpable in the cool air flowing down the mountain —Stephen Goodwin, *Prose,* Fall 1972

Further extension, from the physical senses to mental perception, took place in the 16th century:

This vulgar notion is, indeed, a palpable error —Matthew Arnold, *Essays in Criticism,* First Series, 1865

That, I tell him, is palpable nonsense —David Brudnoy, *National Rev.,* 17 Dec. 1971

... has sued directors for a "palpable break of fiduciary duty" in a class action suit —Maria Shao, *Wall Street Jour.,* 8 June 1981

... I had dashed off my own offering on "the jury system." It was a palpable plagiarism from Mark Twain —*The Autobiography of William Allen White,* 1946

Figurative use is the predominant use in present-day English.

panacea A panacea literally is a magical medicine that cures all ailments and figuratively is a magical solution that solves all problems. Since no such medicine and no such solution actually exist, the word *panacea* almost always occurs in negative constructions or in contexts in which the writer is criticizing a single proposed or attempted solution to a broad array of problems as inadequate or simplistic:

Biotech is not a panacea, but it does promise to transform agriculture in many developing countries —Bill Gates, *Time,* 19 June 2000

Panacea is also sometimes used to speak—usually in a deprecating way—of a simple, easy solution to a single problem. Such use may seem inconsistent with the word's "cure-all" denotation, but the underlying logic of it is usually evident: it implies that the problem (or, in literal applications, the ailment) is a complex and difficult one having many aspects which no single solution can, by itself, put right:

She called it Steamed Crackers, and considered it a panacea for an upset digestive system —M. F. K. Fisher, *With Bold Knife and Fork,* 1969

... boot camps ... are the latest panacea in the fight against urban crime —Kevin Heldman, *Vibe,* September 1994

The movie musical ... has always posited dance as a panacea for social inequality —Mimi Kramer, *New Yorker,* 15 May 1989

Cases in which *panacea* has been used more broadly to mean "an easy and complete cure or solution," without the implication that the ailment or problem in question is especially complex, are rare, according to our evidence. Bernstein 1962, 1965 disapprovingly cites a passage from the *New York Times* in which the writer refers to a possible "panacea for mosquito bites." Other commentators who have criticized such usage include Evans 1957, Harper 1985, and Bryson 1984.

pander 1. *Pander, panderer.* Copperud 1980 says *panderer* is more common in the newspapers, but *pander* is the original noun. *Pander* is a 16th-century noun; *panderer* is a 19th-century word derived from the verb. Both are seen decidedly less often than the verb. Both nouns are also used in the figurative sense:

... at 50 he decided ... that he was nothing more than a pander to people who had nothing better to do with their time than read —E. L. Doctorow, *N.Y. Times Book Rev.,* 25 Aug. 1985

Basically he was a panderer, out to seduce, or amuse, or thrill his public —Harold C. Schonberg, *N.Y. Times,* 2 Apr. 1972

2. The intransitive verb *pander* is regularly used with *to:*

... the public interest could be served without pandering to idle curiosity —E. Pendleton James, *Business Week,* 19 Apr. 1982

... which panders to the frustrated, inarticulate ambitions of the illiterate lower middle classes —Robert Pattison, *On Literacy,* 1982

... a mercenary who has used his brilliant gifts to pander to popular taste —Hubert Saal, *N.Y. Times Book Rev.,* 13 Mar. 1983

pants Ambrose Bierce was no man to mince words, and his opinion of *pants* was characteristically unequivocal: "vulgar exceedingly" he called it in 1909. He was not the first to think so:

The thing named 'pants' in certain documents,
A word not meant for gentlemen, but 'gents'
—Oliver Wendell Holmes d. 1894,
Rhymed Lesson, 1846 (OED)

Pants, originally short for *pantaloons,* is an Americanism that was first recorded in 1840. Its bad reputation as a vulgar synonym for *trousers* lasted nearly a century, but its increasingly common use eventually quieted the critics, and no one now disputes that *pants* is standard and respectable. Such criticism as is now heard is directed at the singular form *pant,* which has seen occasional use since at least the 1890s:

> . . . the perfect complement for a handsome blazer and trim belted pant —advt., *N.Y. Times Mag.,* 29 Feb. 1976

> . . . exciting re-thinking on the new cropped pant —advt., *N.Y. Times,* 22 Sept. 1981

This use of *pant* is now common in clothing advertisements and catalogs but is otherwise rare.

The British have adopted *pants* from American English, but they use it primarily in a distinct sense, as a synonym for *underpants* or *drawers.* This is a distinction that Americans traveling in Great Britain may consider worth remembering.

paparazzo, paparazzi *Paparazzo,* usually seen in the form of its plural *paparazzi,* is a quite recent import from Italian. It usually refers to one of those free-lance photographers who are noted for their aggressive pursuit of celebrities:

> . . . only a remote chance that gossip columnists or paparazzi will crash the parties in the hotel's private suites —*Newsweek,* 10 Jan. 1966

> The duo has been hounded by the tabs since 1996, when paparazzi caught them kissing in the park —Elizabeth Gleik, *Entertainment Weekly,* 13 Feb. 1998

It should come as no surprise that a recent import from Italian suffers a certain amount of misspelling and has its plural taken as a singular. One wire service managed to do both at once:

> . . . a self-styled "papparrazi" who claimed he had taken and sold thousands of photos —*Transcript-Telegram* (Holyoke, Mass.), (UPI), 6 July 1972

Remember that the ending in *i* is the plural and that only the *z* is doubled. If you spell the word with two or three sets of double letters, you're in trouble.

See LATIN PLURALS for other plurals used as singulars.

paradigm *Paradigm* is a learned word that has been in use since the 15th century. Its original meaning was "example, pattern." At the end of the 16th century grammarians appropriated the word and applied it to a pattern of inflected forms in a language, which were usually displayed in tabular form. Flesch 1964, Reader's Digest 1983, Janis 1984, and Barzun 1985 all note that *paradigm* has become a popular jargon word.

The old sense has continued to flourish. Here we find it as "a typical example":

> The descriptions of Frankfurt as a paradigm of modern city life —Joseph P. Bauke, *Saturday Rev.,* 27 Nov. 1971

Here as "an outstanding or perfect example":

> Louis XIV, the paradigm of absolute monarchs —John Wilkinson, *Center Mag.,* March 1968

And as "a pattern of behavior":

> His logic is the familiar paradigm: If radicals take two steps forward, society will eventually take one —Robert Sklar, *The Progressive,* February 1967

> . . . by the standards of the 1960s, the paradigm of revolution; the cadre was thoroughly committed, socially heterogeneous, and tragically ineffectual —Bernard F. Dick, *Saturday Rev.,* 18 Mar. 1972

It can even appear in place of *paragon:*

> It is the finest cigar in all the world. . . . The photographic use we, at enormous self-sacrifice, have made of this paradigm of stogies is not to torment you with visions of the unobtainable —*Esquire,* September 1973

Such uses as these are clear when compared to the most active area of current popular jargonistic use—that of science. The father of the new use seems to be Thomas S. Kuhn, who, in the second edition of his influential *The Structure of Scientific Revolutions* (1973) admitted that in his first edition (1962) he had used *paradigm* at least 22 different ways. With such a diverse foundation, it is not surprising that the ways in which the scientific and theoretical writers throw the word around may sometimes puzzle us innocent bystanders. Here are a few examples. They share the broad central notion of "a theoretical framework":

> Western scientific medicine is undergoing a fundamental shift in basic beliefs and assumptions. . . . This paradigm shift from reductionism to holism is altering the practice of medicine in America today —*Interface,* Fall 1979

> For example, the beginnings of some paradigms might be Aristotle's analysis of motion or Maxwell's mathematization of the electromagnetic field —Mary A. Meyer, *Physics Today,* June 1983

> The adaptationist view bids fair to become the dominant paradigm within evolutionary biology and ecology —Stephen Rose, *N.Y. Times Book Rev.,* 8 May 1983

But we should not point at scientists alone. The literary critics have been known to throw the word about too:

Genet, then, as the very paradigm of existentialist schizophrenia, embodied not only the mystic heart of Sartrean philosophy but the entire preoccupation with the dialectics of negation and illusion —John Killinger, *Jour. of Modern Literature*, 1st issue, 1970

parallel 1. It is not hard to misspell *parallel*, what with all those *l*'s congregating in strange ways. If it gives you trouble, you can try thinking of the two *l*'s in the middle as parallel lines cutting through the word. Better yet, keep a dictionary handy.
2. Prepositions that occur idiomatically after the adjective *parallel* are *to* and *with*:

. . . an undertaking which ran parallel to the more orthodox . . . theorizing —*Times Literary Supp.*, 5 June 1969

. . . a form of expression that for many years ran parallel with his painting —*Current Biography*, April 1968

To seems to be preferred in mathematical writing:

. . . a plane parallel to the base of a cone —School Mathematics Study Group, *Geometry, Part II*, 1965

. . . with the line y = f(a) parallel to the x-axis —School Mathematics Study Group, *Calculus, Part I*, 1965

The noun *parallel* is idiomatically followed by *to*, *with*, and *between*:

. . . look for a parallel to the all-Brahms recital —Irving Kolodin, *Saturday Rev.*, 13 Nov. 1971

To cite another parallel with Vietnam —Ronald P. Kriss, *Saturday Rev.*, 26 Feb. 1972

The parallel between the treatment of blacks and women by our society —Ruth R. Hawkins, *Change*, November–December 1969

parallelism See FAULTY PARALLELISM; NOT ONLY . . . BUT ALSO.

parameter *Parameter* has drawn the disparaging fire of critics since the late 1950s, when its movement from mathematics into other technical and quasi-technical fields was first noticed.
A couple of critics put forward the notion that *parameter* is frequently used where *perimeter* is meant. Such confusion may occur in speech, but it is an odd observation to make of edited prose, for *perimeter* (before 1973) was quite rare in extended use, and whereas *parameter* in the criticized use is usually plural, *perimeter* in figurative use (before 1973) was usually singular. (The possible effect of

parameter-avoidance on the figurative use of *perimeter* is discussed at PERIMETER.)
The use of *parameter* most likely to attract comment about misuse for *perimeter* is that in which it is used in the plural in the sense of "limits." Note that in the first two examples below *parameters* clearly means "limits," but *perimeter* or *perimeters* could not be used; in the second two you could force *perimeters* in, but other words such as *bounds* or *range* or *confines* would work as well or better.

In the event that temperature levels exceed parameters, the system will warn the operator —*Datamation*, February 1976

. . . [it] is clearly within the parameters of Yariv's simple formula that Mr. Kissinger would seek to concoct his own equation for bringing Israel and the P.L.O. together —Edward R. F. Sheehan, *N.Y. Times Mag.*, 8 Dec. 1974

The Teachings of Don Juan and *Fire on the Moon* both fall within the parameters of science fiction as an attitude —Michael Baron, *Real Paper*, 3 Dec. 1975

Eno's eccentric music doesn't stray beyond rock's accustomed borders so much as it innovates within those parameters —Charley Walters, *Rolling Stone*, 6 May 1976

You may also notice that things tend to be *within* parameters. This was not the idiom with *perimeter(s)* before the middle 1970s.
By the time that most of the usage commentators were coming down hard on *parameter*, the computer became established in our lives, and with it came *parameter*, stronger than ever. It is unlikely to be dislodged until a swankier term comes along. It is found in general publications:

But a true novel is an extended piece of fiction: Length is clearly one of its parameters —Anthony Burgess, *N.Y. Times Book Rev.*, 5 Feb. 1984

They will need to remain within the budgetary parameters established by the EMU —Jorge Pedraza, *Commonweal*, 5 June 1998

. . . the infinite fantasies of the imagination, the divine and the wretched parameters of the human condition —Leo Rosten, *Harper's*, July 1972

. . . the . . . cliché expert, Dr. Arbuthnot, revealed the parameters of the new Presidentialese to the official translators —William Safire, *N.Y. Times*, 18 Nov. 1976

. . . the usual three parameters of wine—appearance, smell and taste —Steve Heimoff, *Wine Spectator*, 15 May 1992

. . . moving the discussion aggressively to the right and greatly expanding the parameters of the politically discussable —Michael Kelly, *New Yorker,* 24 Apr. 1995

. . . the airlines compete vigorously in every other parameter of service including schedule frequency —Anthony Lewis, *N.Y. Times,* 8 Nov. 1976

In spite of examples like these, our evidence shows that *parameter* is mostly a word used in technical and quasi-technical (such as investment and consumer electronics) writing. If you are uncertain about using it, you can probably substitute another word—*bounds, scope, limits,* for instance.

paramount *Paramount* is used as a sort of emphatic or superlative version of *first* or *important*; it designates what or who is preeminent or most important. Some commentators, Flesch 1964, Evans 1957, and Garner 1998, worry about *paramount*'s being used as a mere synonym of *first* or *important*. There seems to be little need for worry, as there is no pattern of disputable use in our files. Flesch also thinks that *paramount* is pompous. All the same, *paramount* is available to you, if you need to use it, and should cause no concern. Here are a few typical uses:

. . . refused to kowtow to the new paramount Viking chief —John Geipel, *The Viking Legacy,* 1971

When price is paramount, bargain hunters start here and let this site wheel 'n' deal for them —*Newsweek,* 26 July 1999

. . . it ought not to be forgotten that in biographical narrative the writer rather than the subject is paramount —Peter Ackroyd, *N.Y. Times Book Rev.,* 10 Jan. 1999

. . . dinner can range from 30 to as many as 250 guests. Under these circumstances, flexibility is paramount —Kristin K. Hubbard, *Harper's Bazaar,* July 1980

Harper 1985 believes *paramount* to be an uncomparable adjective— this bugaboo we discuss at ABSOLUTE ADJECTIVES.

paraphernalia *Paraphernalia* is a plural noun from medieval Latin for which there is no operative singular in English. The grammarian H. Poutsma in 1904 found its use with a singular verb (attested since 1788 in the OED) objectionable; three quarters of a century later the grammarian Randolph Quirk (*Style and Communication in the English Language,* 1982) expressed doubts that a native speaker of English, in spite of the insistence of dictionaries, would use it as a plural count noun. The evidence at this dictionary office falls somewhere between the two opinions.

We know from evidence that *paraphernalia* is used with both singular and plural verbs:

. . . the paraphernalia of Christianity is prophylactic against the taint —George Stade, *N.Y. Times Book Rev.,* 14 Jan. 1973

The paraphernalia of line fishing are found —Edward P. Lanning, *Peru Before the Incas,* 1967

Use with a plural verb does not in itself prove that a noun is a plural count noun, because many collective nouns, even though singular in form, can be used with plural verbs. But the next example seems to show a bona fide plural count noun:

. . . all those paraphernalia of women's lives —Judith Chernaik, *Saturday Rev.,* 6 Jan. 1973

Somewhat more often, however, the word seems to be perceived as a mass noun:

. . . every bit of transistorized paraphernalia gleams —Arlene Croce, in *The Film,* 1968

It's stuffed with every kind of oldfangled paraphernalia —*Playboy,* February 1981

Here we have notional agreement at work. Some feel *paraphernalia* is a plural count noun; some feel it is a singular mass noun. We cannot fault either use.

See LATIN PLURALS for other plurals used as singulars.

parenting Heritage 1982 contains a usage note informing us that the usage panel finds the verb *parent* unacceptable. This disapproval is misdirected. The transitive verb *parent* has existed since the 17th century, but it is not commonly used. You can occasionally see such examples as these:

The twins were parented, it is often held, by the Renaissance —*Times Literary Supp.,* 8 May 1948

. . . the ease with which I parented my own child —Brenda Maddox, *N.Y. Times Mag.,* 8 Aug. 1976

What the panelists were really objecting to is the noun *parenting,* a recent formation (1958) that has received decidedly mixed reviews in usage circles. While reviews may be mixed, the word is being used with some frequency, perhaps because it says in one word what formerly had to be said in several. Here are some examples:

The strategy for expanding the crane's population involves an ingenious system of surrogate parenting —*National Wildlife,* December 1982/January 1983

You will learn about marriage, parenting and caring for children —Frances Baynor Parnell et al., *Homemaking: Skills for Everyday Living,* 1981

One of the many important—but difficult—tasks of parenting is knowing when to step into a situation and take action and when to hold back —Lindsey Stokes, *Newsweek*, 13 Sept. 1999

parlous That this old adjective, both a synonym and a derivative of *perilous*, experienced a resurrection in the 20th century is a development noted with varying degrees of disapproval by Fowler 1926, Krapp 1927, and Evans 1957. By and large, the critics regard the word as an archaic affectation. It continues in fairly common use, however, occurring most frequently as a modifier of *state* and *times*. James J. Kilpatrick in a newspaper column (23 Feb. 1995) says that in *parlous times, parlous* contains a note of mockery. This may be true when modifying *times,* but it does not seem to hold when *state* or other nouns are modified:

Yes, these are parlous times on Publishers Row —Ray Walters, *N.Y. Times Book Rev.,* 18 July 1982

These are parlous times for radio personalities trying to make the transition to late-night TV hosts —David Hiltbrand, *People,* 12 Aug. 1991

Given its parlous financial state, Daewoo's relaxed approach has been mystifying —*Financial Times* (London), 20 July 1999

. . . the parlous state of the pound, which was at that time hovering just above its lowest permitted level —James Lewis, *Manchester Guardian Weekly,* 13 Sept. 1992

And we are reminded how parlous public service in China is even now —Orville Schell, *N.Y. Times Book Rev.,* 3 Apr. 1988

The flats have baths in the kitchens and are occupied mainly by one-parent families in parlous financial circumstances —Julian Nundy, *Independent on Sunday* (London), 25 Nov. 1990

Naturally China is eager to reassure potential foreign investors at this parlous moment —Terry McCarthy, *Time,* 21 Sept. 1998

part 1. Bernstein 1965 notes that the intransitive verb *part* is followed by *from* or *with* and indeed this is true, so far as it goes. In contemporary usage, *part* is found more often with *with* than with *from,* and in almost all instances, means "give up":

. . . used to pay for an elector's right, whose owner was willing to part with his right to vote —E. H. Collis, *Lost Years,* 1948

". . . It's simply that he can't bear to part with a dime." —Hamilton Basso, *The View From Pompey's Head,* 1954

. . . in carrying on this war, the British may have to part with that control —Franklin D.

Roosevelt, 12 Jan. 1940, business conference, in *Franklin D. Roosevelt's Own Story,* ed. Donald Day, 1951

. . . unwilling to part with favorite possessions —Gary E. McCalla, *Southern Living,* November 1971

Part from occurs less frequently. At one time, it was used for "relinquish" but in current usage it generally means "leave" or "separate":

His precious bag, which he would by no means part from —George Eliot, *Life,* 1885

The gold had to be left where it was. He parted from it philosophically —Geoffrey Household, *The Third Hour,* 1938

I parted from McNeil at Victoria —Nevil Shute, *Most Secret,* 1945

He parted from the British Army in 1946 —Barbara Campbell, *N.Y. Times,* 21 Jan. 1978

2. See ON THE PART OF.

partake As an intransitive verb, *partake* may be followed by *in* or *of.* The use of *in* implies active participation in something:

. . . have imagined myself partaking in some incredible romance —*The Autobiography of William Butler Yeats,* 1953

Monday's jump-rope session is bad enough; I will not be invited to partake in anyone's schoolyard double Dutch anytime soon —Josh Liberson, *GQ,* April 1997

Of is also used in such contexts:

Judges also partake of the more amusing type of malapropism —Bryan A. Garner, *The State of the Language,* 1990

Often, however, a less active role is implied by *of.* The underlying sense may be one of passive experience or simple sharing:

. . . he came while we were at dinner, and partook of our elegant entertainment —Jane Austen, letter, 1 Dec. 1798

Or the emphasis may be less on "sharing" than it is on "taking a portion or serving of," especially in contexts having to do with food and drink:

Johnson then called for a bottle of port, of which Goldsmith and I partook, while our friend, now a water-drinker, sat by us —James Boswell, *Life of Samuel Johnson,* 1791

At a Wisconsin celebration they partake of a traditional breakfast consisting of moose milk, coffee, and sweet rolls —Ralph Whitlock, *Manchester Guardian Weekly,* 2 Feb. 1992

Alceste can't partake of life's banquet. He is a kind of moral anorexic —John Lahr, *New Yorker,* 8 May 1995

All of the uses of *partake* in the above illustrations are old, well-established, and standard. A few critics simply consider *partake* inherently "overformal," "stilted," "bookish," or the like. Certainly a phrase like "partake of liquid refreshment" for "have a drink" would seem to merit those epithets, but the uses above do not strike us in the same way.

part and parcel Although a number of critics have denigrated this phrase, they seem not to understand its meaning very well. Some of them consider it verbose and easily reducible to *part* in all occurrences. But, as Burchfield 1996 points out, the phrase does not mean "part" but "an essential part."

Here are some examples:

As an element of the trivium, grammar was part and parcel of a liberal education —Dennis Baron, *English Today,* October 1988

. . . mannerisms that now seem old-fashioned but that were part and parcel of the virtuoso violin playing of the time —Winthrop Sargeant, *Saturday Rev.,* 4 Oct. 1975

Now the idea of higher dimensions did not arise from the brow of UFOlogy or the New Age. Instead, it is part and parcel of the physics of the twentieth century —Carl Sagan, *The Demon-Haunted World,* 1996

. . . a will to succeed that is part and parcel of their religion —Robert Lindsey, *N.Y. Times Mag.,* 12 Jan. 1986

partial *Partial* is used with the preposition *to* when it means "markedly fond of someone or something":

"But if a woman is partial to a man, and does not endeavor to conceal it, he must find it out." —Jane Austen, *Pride and Prejudice,* 1813

We have become very partial to bean sprouts —Jean Stafford, *The Mountain Lion,* 1947

. . . a Countess who is admired by both the Composer and the Poet, but cannot decide to which she is partial —Irving Kolodin, *Saturday Rev.,* 24 Apr. 1954

The OED traces this sense of *partial* to 1696; it labels the sense colloquial (in the standard descriptive way of dictionaries). In the early part of the 20th century, some American commentators also used the label *colloquial,* but in the pejorative sense. Recent commentators accept the use without quibble.

partiality *Partiality* is most often followed by the preposition *for*:

". . . I have a partiality for a man who isolates an issue and pleads to it. . . ." —James Gould Cozzens, *Guard of Honor,* 1948

". . . I think that it was done by him unawares, his partiality for her was so great." —Robert Penn Warren, *All the King's Men,* 1946

He has a partiality for suburban life —*Times Literary Supp.,* 29 May 1953

Occasionally, *partiality* has been used with *to* or *toward*:

Our aversion to raw meat is understood, our partiality to fish . . . appreciated —A. V. Davis, *Punch,* 6 July 1953

Sometimes newcomers to the fleet were a bit annoyed over the skipper's partiality toward this absent-minded youth —Lloyd C. Douglas, *The Big Fisherman,* 1948

partially, partly The long-lived controversy over the use of *partially* has ground on for more than a century. It began in 1870 when the American commentator Richard Grant White encountered the phrase "wholly or partially correct" in a book by Swinburne. White evidently believed that *partially* must mean "with bias" and could not be used like *partly,* even though educated people so used it. White's opinion was attacked by Fitzedward Hall in 1872 and 1873; he showed that *partially* had been used like *partly* for a long time (it has been in use since the 15th century). Ayres 1881 backed White's view with the comment "This use of the adverb *partially* is sanctioned by high authority, but that does not make it correct." In the meantime William Cullen Bryant put *partially* on his *Index Expurgatorius* for the *N.Y. Evening Post,* and the objection to *partially* for *partly* became an enduring part of newspaper tradition. In the early 1900s another commentator turned White's objection into a warning about possible ambiguity; this is repeated as recently as Garner 1998 in spite of the fact that the "with bias" sense of *partially* is unattested since 1819. Our critics seem to prefer their opinions to the facts.

Fowler 1926 introduced a distinction in usage between the two. Since Fowler's distinction is frequently repeated (by Bremner 1980, Nickles 1974, Janis 1984, Strunk & White 1972, 1979, Sellers 1975, Bryson 1984, Heritage 1969, Longman 1984, and Chambers 1985), it is worth examining. Fowler says that *partly* (which he opposes to *wholly*) is better used to mean "as regards a part and not the whole," while *partially* (opposed to *completely*) is better used to mean "to a limited degree." Bryson 1984 puts this point most succinctly, equating *partially* with "incompletely" and *partly* with "in part."

Fowler's distinction is a clear and simple one. It is, however, invented, the words both having been in use in more complex patterns for 300 years or more when Fowler devised it. Although most usage writers make up their examples to illustrate it, it is not hard to find examples that follow its general outlines. Here, for instance, we find *partially* used to mean "to a limited degree":

. . . their ramble did not appear to have been more than partially agreeable —Jane Austen, *Mansfield Park*, 1814

. . . steps were taken to furnish these partially trained forces with whatever equipment could be made available —George C. Marshall, *The United States at War*, 1943

. . . but he has only partially succeeded in it —*Times Literary Supp.*, 16 Apr. 1970

A sharp-featured face with a partially bald head —Norman Mailer, *The Naked and the Dead*, 1948

And here we find *partly* meaning "in part" with no hint of incompleteness or limited degree:

. . . a Reprimand, which partly occasioned that Discourse of the Battle of the Books —Jonathan Swift, *A Tale of a Tub*, 1710

. . . may at least partly explain their common genius —William Styron, *This Quiet Dust and Other Writings*, 1982

. . . I knew, partly from experience and partly from instinct —Charlotte Brontë, *Jane Eyre*, 1848

The last example shows a construction, *partly x, partly y*, in which *partly* is very common and *partially* quite rare.

You can follow Fowler's distinction if you want to. But more often writers seem to use the adverbs interchangeably:

. . . her figure was partly enveloped in a shawl —Charlotte Brontë, *Jane Eyre*, 1848

. . . her hat-brim partially shaded her face —Charlotte Brontë, *Jane Eyre*, 1848

. . . female religious (partly clothed . . .) —James Joyce, *Ulysses*, 1922

. . . a partially nude señorita, frail and lovely —James Joyce, *Ulysses*, 1922

. . . it only partly explains his lack of interest —Richard Poirier, *A World Elsewhere*, 1966

. . . scarcity of suitable screen material partially explains the trend —*Publishers Weekly*, 9 June 1951

From Fowler to the present time, little has changed; most commentators have been willing to repeat Fowler or some other earlier comment.

Our evidence shows that there is some tendency toward differentiation, but it is far from completely established. *Partially* is used more often than *partly* to modify an adjective or past participle that names or suggests a process:

The snow was partially melted —George Meredith, *The Ordeal of Richard Feverel*, 1859

. . . killed and partially eaten —J. Stevenson-Hamilton, *Wild Life in South Africa*, 1947

. . . a partially cleared grassy circle —John McNulty, *New Yorker*, 13 June 1953

. . . partially concealed by a reddish beard —Gay Talese, *Harper's*, February 1969

. . . a partially paid-for-car —Philip G. Schrag, *Columbia Forum*, Summer 1970

Partly, on the other hand, is used more often than *partially* before clauses and phrases offered by way of explanation:

. . . it is also partly because Chaucer's English lies almost directly behind our own —W. F. Bolton, *A Short History of Literary English*, 1967

Partly to reassure him, North invited Ghorbanifar to the United States —*The Tower Commission Report*, 1987

Partly for this reason, the search . . . was not undertaken —Noam Chomsky, *Columbia Forum*, Spring 1968

These observations may indicate a trend, but only time will tell whether more differentiation or less will be the result.

Most native speakers of English will have no difficulty with these words. If you are a learner, we suggest that you follow either Fowler's distinction, insofar as possible, or the current general trends as illustrated here.

participate For the most part, *participate* is used with the preposition *in*:

They participated, with a curious, restrained passion, in the speech made by the red-haired man —Christopher Isherwood, *The Berlin Stories*, 1946

. . . Stalin himself was personally participating in the negotiations —William L. Shirer, *The Rise and Fall of the Third Reich*, 1960

. . . the information they need to participate knowledgeably in public debates —Norman Cousins, *Saturday Rev.*, 25 June 1977

Occasionally, *participate* is followed by *with*:

. . . we also participate with banks which in turn use their funds for part of the loans —*Nation's Business*, April 1954

And, in what appears to be a British usage, *participate* is followed by *on*:

> . . . an illegitimate child . . . had no right to participate on the intestacy of either of his parents —S. M. Cretney, *Principles of Family Law,* 1974

> . . . while participating on the Programme —*Weight Watchers,* 1975

participle 1. See DANGLING MODIFIERS; POSSESSIVE WITH GERUND. 2. See VERY 1.

particular *Particular* is considered an overused adjective by Copperud 1964, Fowler 1965, Phythian 1979, and Janis 1984. They are especially leery of its use following the demonstrative adjectives *this* and *that*:

> Students get into this particular category too —Margaret Mead, *Barnard Alumnae,* Winter 1971

> . . . had brought me to this particular point in space and time —Norman Cousins, *Saturday Rev.,* 30 Oct. 1971

> . . . to change the rules to fit that particular reality —William Johnson, *Sports Illustrated,* 15 July 1968

Particular adds a certain emphasis in these passages which the critics regard either as unnecessary or nonexistent. Its omission in such cases, if you are of a mind to follow the critics' advice, is easy and painless. Note, however, that in some other cases, especially in negative constructions, *particular* after *this* or *that* has implications which go beyond simple emphasis:

> . . . discovered that Benítez was not guilty of that particular theft —*Current Biography,* January 1966

> . . . but I did not find this particular manual dull —Willoughby Newton, *Saturday Rev.,* 20 Nov. 1971

The implications are that Benítez was or may have been guilty of *other* thefts and that Newton did or might very well find *other* manuals dull. *Particular* can not be deleted from either passage without some loss of meaning.

partitive genitive See DOUBLE GENITIVE.

partly See PARTIALLY, PARTLY.

parts of speech The eight parts of speech are simply holdovers from Latin (and Latin took them from Greek) that are used for convenience—few grammarians want to be faced with the task of devising an adequate set of descriptors for English. And for English, the parts of speech are not categories of words, but of functions. Many of our English words— *out, fan, hit, back, like,* for instance—can func-

tion as more than one part of speech. In Latin a word functions as only one part of speech (at least when you lump prepositions and conjunctions together as particles). If you remember that, in English, words function as parts of speech but are not themselves parts of speech, you will not be misled by people who insist that *like* is not a conjunction or that nouns cannot be used as verbs.

party Copperud 1980 informs us that the use of *party* in the sense of "person" "comes from the jargon of the telephone service." In fact, the earliest complaint about this usage we are aware of comes from Dean Alford in 1866, ten years before Alexander Graham Bell patented the telephone. And the OED shows that the usage itself has been around since the 15th century. (The legal use of *party* goes back almost 200 more years.) Einstein 1985 similarly assures us that *party* was alive in the 17th century but fell into disuse and was reborn in the U.S. in the 1930s when many telephone subscribers had party lines. But if it was in disuse until the 1930s, why do we have commentators writing about the usage in 1866, 1869, 1870, 1873, 1878, 1881, 1906, and 1909?

What, then, is all the fuss about? In a word: class. The most penetrating analysis seems to have been made by Fitzedward Hall back in the 1870s. *Party* for *person* was apparently in common and serious use in the 15th, 16th, and 17th centuries. Hall seems to imply that its use went into decline—perhaps in the 18th and early 19th centuries, although he has evidence from both periods—and when it revived it became common in the speech of the uneducated, the vulgar, the unwashed. In the United States it was associated with the speech of shopkeepers and tradesmen. The usage was one of those held to distinguish the socially superior from the socially inferior.

From our vantage point it is hard to tell if there really was a decline in ordinary use that made its appearance in the mouths of the vulgar more striking. The OED has enough 18th- and 19th-century examples to suggest that there was no decline in use; perhaps it was simply an increase in use by the less cultured that led editor Murray to add (as of 1905) "now shoppy, vulgar, or jocular." Such evidence as we have suggests that ordinary use continued until at least the middle of the 19th century:

> "I know he must have exerted himself very much, for I know the parties he had to move. . . . " —Jane Austen, *Mansfield Park,* 1814

> Now I would give a trifle to know, historically and authentically, who was the greatest fool that ever lived. . . . Marry, of the present breed, I think I could without much

difficulty name you the party —Charles Lamb, "All Fools' Day," *Essays of Elia,* 1823

. . . my travelling companions were very disagreeable individuals; these parties being a pair of squalid females and two equally unwelcome personages of the male sex —William Cullen Bryant, *Letters of a Traveller,* 1850

We are doubtful that ordinary use ever disappeared:

. . . evidently recognizing in me a representative of the ancient parties he once so cunningly ruined —John Burroughs, *Wake-Robin,* 1871

. . . he is a shameless and determined old party —Winston Churchill, *The Crisis,* 1901

"Oh!" said the other party, while Densher said nothing —Henry James, *The Wings of the Dove,* 1902

The vulgar use that was objected to is probably exemplified by DeMorgan's apparently provincial Englishman and Flann O'Brien's garrulous Irishmen:

. . . he thought he could ackomerdate him at that too. Anyhow, he knew a party as could! —William DeMorgan, *Joseph Vance,* 1906

Now be damned but hadn't they a man in the tent there from the county Cork, a bloody dandy at the long jump, a man that had a name, a man that was known in the whole country. A party by the name of Bagenal, the champion of all Ireland —Flann O'Brien, *At Swim-Two-Birds,* 1939

The brother gave a promise to a certain party not to leave town during the emergency —Myles na gCopaleen (Flann O'Brien), *The Best of Myles,* 1968

Alford 1866 was the first to censure this use in England (the good dean was a bit embarrassed by earlier use of the word in the Apocrypha and in Shakespeare) and Richard Grant White 1870 was the first in the U.S. It received frequent mention in subsequent 19th-century sources and in early 20th-century sources. It got into newspaper tradition through William Cullen Bryant's *Index Expurgatorius* compiled before 1877 for the *New York Evening Post* (he was unmindful of his own earlier use) and the contemporaneous "Don't List" of the *New York Herald.* It was warned against in reference books, books on business correspondence, and college handbooks. It still is.

The phone company did not come in for mention until after World War II. Telephone company use seems to have served only to buttress the ruminations of those commentators disinclined to look at the OED. Nor has legal use—whence this use seems to have sprung some 500 years ago—ever been questioned.

What about current use? The "jocular" use mentioned by the OED has clearly flourished; it is quite common in light, breezy writing and is applied especially to persons who have reached a certain age:

The matriarch is Ma Jukes, a friendly old party —Frank Sullivan, *A Rock in Every Snowball,* 1946

. . . a six-foot, erect, florid party in his early eighties —Audax Minor, *New Yorker,* 17 July 1971

I, a respectable middle-aged party with long, tidy hair in a bun and a black dinner dress —Nika Hazelton, *N.Y. Times Book Rev.,* 11 Mar. 1973

Author Singer, a bossy old party of 79 —Brad Darrach, *People,* 12 Dec. 1983

It is used in more serious contexts when it clearly means "one of the persons involved":

. . . suggested that all three parties involved undergo psychological examinations —Eileen Hughes, *Ladies' Home Jour.,* September 1971

. . . argues that their authors are merely reminding themselves of what they know already, rather than recreating it for a third party —Philip Larkin, *Required Writing,* 1983

In summary, the strictures on *party* in the sense of "person" are a 19th-century social commentary that has carried into the latter part of the 20th century purely by inertia. The use by the uneducated that occasioned the issue no longer seems to be a matter of comment among those who play the game of identifying social status by lexical item. Perhaps there never was very much to the issue. At any rate, the phone company is not to blame. Current use is as we have shown it and is completely standard.

passed, past The thrust of the advice in all the handbooks and schoolbooks is that the unwary and unsophisticated student should not confuse the homophones *passed* (past tense and past participle of *pass*) and *past* (variously a noun, adjective, adverb, and preposition).

Passed and *past* are originally the same word; the adjective and preposition are derived from the past participle of the verb, and the noun and adverb are derived by functional shift from the adjective. The spelling *past* was at one time used for both the past tense and past participle:

I did not tell you how I past my time yesterday —Jonathan Swift, *Journal to Stella,* 25 Jan. 1711

... he was so much offended ... that he past the latter part of his life in a state of hostility —Samuel Johnson, preface to Johnson's edition of Shakespeare, 1765

He past; a soul of nobler tone —Alfred Lord Tennyson, *In Memoriam,* 1850 (OED)

Our latest citations show no instances of the spelling *past* used for the past tense or past participle of the verb; *passed* is the only spelling in current use for these functions. *Past* is becoming archaic as a spelling for the verb's inflected forms. It is, of course, still used for the adjective, preposition, noun, and adverb.

passive voice   A large number of commentators agree that sentences in which the verb is in the active voice are preferable to those in which the verb is in the passive voice. The passive has long been discouraged as the weaker form of expression. In spite of generations of textbooks, use of the passive has increased and, interestingly, studies show the passive to be much more frequently used by the educated than by the uneducated.

The passive has its uses. Even grammarians and usage commentators find it useful, or perhaps subtly enticing. Joseph M. Williams caught these two specimens for exhibit in *College Composition and Communications,* May 1981:

> Emphasis is often achieved by the use of verbs rather than nouns formed from them, and by the use of verbs in the passive rather than in the passive voice —S. J. Reisman, ed., *A Style Manual for Technical Writers and Editors,* 1972

> ... the passive voice is wherever possible used in preference to the active —George Orwell, "Politics and the English Language," 1946

Orwell's dictum in the same essay is "Never use the passive where you can use the active."

Orwell's essay is interesting in another regard. Bryant 1962 reports three statistical studies of passive versus active sentences in various periodicals; the highest incidence of passive constructions was 13 percent. Orwell runs to a little over 20 percent in "Politics and the English Language." Clearly he found the construction useful in spite of his advice to avoid it as much as possible.

There is general agreement that the passive is useful when the receiver of the action is more important than the doer; Bryant's example is "The child was struck by the car." Orwell also uses the passive for this purpose in "Politics and the English Language":

> ... noun constructions are used instead of gerunds. ...

> The range of verbs is further cut down. ...

> ... banal statements are given an appearance of profundity. ...

The passive is also useful when the doer is unknown, unimportant, or perhaps too obvious to be worth mentioning. Bryant exemplifies each of these with

> The store was robbed last night.

> Plows should not be kept in the garage.

> Kennedy was elected president.

Orwell makes use of the passive in this way too:

> People are imprisoned for years without trial, or shot in the back of the neck or sent to die of scurvy in Arctic lumber camps: this is called *elimination of unreliable elements.*

The passive with the unknown or unimportant doer is disapproved in some instances by quite a few commentators who consider it evasive. Copperud 1970 gives as an example of evasive use, "It is felt that your request must be denied." Whether this evasion is useful or not depends on your point of view: if it is your request that is denied, it is irritating not to know who denied you; if you are some poor functionary whose duty it is to inform people that their request has been denied, it may seem most helpful. Orwell in the passage just cited is generalizing rather than evading. The force of his statement would not be much strengthened by using the active with a general subject:

> Totalitarian regimes imprison people for years without trial ... ; they call this *elimination of unreliable elements.*

Indeed, the absence of a named agent might be seen as part of the writer's point.

A few commentators find the passive useful in scientific writing (one even believes it to be necessary) because of the tone of detachment and impersonality that it helps establish.

The point, finally, is that sentences cast in the passive voice have their uses and are an important tool for the writer. Everyone agrees you should not lean too heavily on passive sentences and that you should especially avoid awkwardly constructed passives. The few statistical studies we have seen or heard of indicate that you are likely to use the active voice most of the time anyway.

past   See PASSED, PAST.

past history   *Past history* is censured as a redundancy by several commentators, who point out that all history is in the past. The phrase probably occurs more often in speech than in writing, but its use in expository prose is not uncommon:

A child born into a family subject to decades of accumulated poverty is clearly affected by a past history of discrimination —Andrew Sullivan, *New Republic*, 10 May 1993

Its orbit is unstable over tens of thousands of years so that we have no idea of its past history —Fred L. Whipple, *Orbiting the Sun*, 1981

Such usage is idiomatic. Your use of *past history* is unlikely to be noticed or criticized by most readers, but if you share the commentators' enthusiasm for expunging redundancies, you will want to avoid it. See also RE-DUNDANCY.

past perfect   See PLUPLUPERFECT.

patient   In the senses "able or willing to bear" and "subject to," *patient* seems to be found most often with *of*:

> . . . the United States be patient of misrepresentations of its motives —*Current Biography 1948*

> . . . most scientific modern excavations are patient of chronological reassessment —*Times Literary Supp.*, 18 Dec. 1969

In the more common senses involving calmness and forbearance, *patient* is found with *with*:

> . . . I don't imagine that he would be very patient with dreams —Walter de la Mare, *Encounter*, December 1954

> He had been all too patient with her, too long —Herman Wouk, *Marjorie Morningstar*, 1955

In older literature we also find these senses of *patient* used with *toward, in, at,* and *under,* but we have no recent evidence for them. They still sound idiomatic, however.

pavilion   Bremner 1980 points out there is properly only one *l* in this word. It is not infrequently given two, but that spelling must still be considered an error.

pay   A few commentators (such as Watt 1967 and Bremner 1980) note that *paid* is the spelling for the past and past participle of *pay* except in the nautical *pay out,* where it is usually *payed.* The nautical spelling is sometimes used for the regular past tense, where it should not be:

> . . . she payed—or actually bought breakfast—for Scott —*Springfield* (Mass.) *Morning Union*, 23 Apr. 1984

peace   See PIECE, PEACE.

peaceable, peaceful   Several commentators note a distinction between these words, the upshot of which is that *peaceable* means "disposed toward peace; preferring peace" and *peaceful* means "characterized by peace." Those are in fact the usual meanings of *peaceable* and *peaceful* in current English:

> But if labor's leaders were feeling peaceable toward the administration, it was the best-kept secret in town —Meg Greenfield, *The Reporter*, 2 June 1966

> . . . would always have been as peaceful as a church social —John Kenneth Galbraith, *Saturday Rev.*, 6 Nov. 1971

However, *peaceable* and *peaceful* can also be properly used as synonyms, and they have been since the 14th century. The "characterized by peace" sense of *peaceable* and the "disposed toward peace" sense of *peaceful* are now relatively uncommon, but they are still standard, as a look in any good dictionary will show. Here are a few examples:

> . . . that through orderly, peaceable processes . . . change would come —*Center Mag.*, November/December 1971

> . . . assigned to a ladder company in remote and peaceable Staten Island —Tom Buckley, *N.Y. Times Book Rev.*, 3 Oct. 1976

> Congo natives are peaceful, and the drums often mean an invitation to a dance —Wallace W. Atwood & Helen Goss Thomas, *Visits in Other Lands* (textbook), 1950

> . . . the modest man becomes bold, the shy confident, the lazy active, or the impetuous prudent and peaceful —W. M. Thackeray, *Vanity Fair*, 1848

peak, peek, pique   These homophones have a way of being muddled by nodding writers. Most of the examples we have seen involve the substitution of *peak* for one of the other two. James J. Kilpatrick both in his 1984 book and later newspaper columns has caught a number of these, including "a peak at the machines" where *peek* was wanted, and "peaked our curiosity" where *piqued* was wanted. We have a few too:

> . . . she could peak into the bedroom —*N.Y. Times*, 2 Sept. 1983 (*peek*)

> . . . peaking students' desire to learn —an elementary-school principal, 16 May 1983 (*piquing*)

A writer needs to keep the meaning in mind and match it to the correct spelling.

peculiar   When *peculiar* is used to mean "characteristic of one only," it is usually followed by the preposition *to*:

> . . . a drowsy fervour of manner and tone which was quite peculiar to her —Thomas Hardy, *The Return of the Native*, 1878

. . . the French woman, from very early times, has shown qualities peculiar to herself —Henry Adams, *Mont-Saint-Michel and Chartres,* 1904

. . . they must be characters peculiar to *this* story and no other —Shirley Jackson, *The Writer,* January 1969

pedagogue The spelling *pedagog,* which seems to have been born in the spelling reform movement of the late 19th century, is still sometimes used:

. . . abdication of parent, priest, and pedagog —F. R. Buckley, *N.Y. Times,* 20 Nov. 1972

pedal, peddle Copperud 1980 and Bernstein 1962 both have found instances of the verb *peddle* used where *pedal* was meant. The OED has a late 19th-century *peddler* for *pedaler.* This is mere carelessness.

peek See PEAK, PEEK, PIQUE.

penultimate Safire 1984 records the efforts of a correspondent who sent a couple of newspaper clippings in which *penultimate* was used in the sense of "ultimate, final, last." It may be tempting to some people to use *penultimate,* which means "next-to-last," in this way. It has a more impressive look and sound than a mere *ultimate* or *final.* But it is not always easy to tell if *penultimate* is being used as an emphatic *ultimate.* It often requires extra-linguistic knowledge: you have to know if the penultimate whatever-it-is was in fact the last one or not. Or you have to persevere through enough context to find out whether or not the writer knows what is penultimate. Sometimes a writer provides a giveaway, though:

Just as the first of these three novels begins with a missionary teacher . . . so the third and penultimate volume . . . —Nancy Wilson Ross, *Saturday Rev.,* 24 June 1972

You may be a bit suspicious of what a writer had in mind when you find *penultimate* modifying a plural:

The penultimate days of the event —Benjamin DeMott, *American Scholar,* Winter 1962–1963

. . . the penultimate decades of the century —Gerald Taylor, *Silver,* 2d ed., 1963

But most of the time, unless you have knowledge to the contrary, you have to assume writers know the meaning of the word:

. . . regulations have cleared the penultimate hurdle and appear ready to become law —John Alcysius Farrell, *Sunday Denver Post,* 2 Sept. 1984

. . . rises to a rare moment of lyric power in the novel's penultimate paragraph —Joyce Carol Oates, *N.Y. Times Book Rev.,* 3 Oct. 1982

If you remember the meaning of *penultimate,* it should give you no trouble.

people, persons The questioning of the use of *people* to mean *persons* began in the middle of the 19th century. Around the turn of the century things heated up. *People* for *persons* went on the "Don't List" of the *New York Herald* and thereafter became a staple of the journalistic usage writers.

Like many controversial usages examined in this book, *people* managed to hold its place while the grounds of dispute shifted. At first *people* was objected to when the context gave any indication that the word was thought of as a plural—*several* and *many* were the disputed modifiers. Then followed the dispute about numerical designators—*1,500,000, a thousand,* etc. More recently the use of round numbers with *people* has been declared acceptable, but some still object to use with specific numbers, like *five* or *two.* Safire 1982 reports that an Associated Press style manual revised around 1980 prescribes *people* for all plural uses. Safire says this decision was greeted with joy by some people working in the *New York Times* newsroom, where the style manual still prescribed *persons* with specific numbers. Kilpatrick 1984 disagrees with the AP decision.

The use of *people* with a preceding number seems to have been missed by the OED, Webster 1909, the Century, and Funk & Wagnalls. If the dictionaries missed the use, the grammarians did not. Poutsma 1904–26 cited Dickens ("A Christmas Carol") and *Punch.* Jespersen 1909–49 found the usage to be as old as Chaucer's "a thousand peple"; he cited as later examples Defoe, Dickens, Disraeli, and others. He also found the construction *one or two people* in Dickens and H. G. Wells.

It is reassuring, at least, to know that recent handbooks and style books will now allow you to use *people* as Chaucer did nearly 600 years ago or as Dickens did more than a century ago. Here are modern examples of most of the originally disputed usages:

. . . many people who feel that the federal funds have not always been wisely spent —Lucy Eisenberg, *Harper's,* November 1971

More than 1,500 people . . . attended —Ron Fimrite, *Sports Illustrated,* 20 Mar. 1978

. . . equipped to seat six people comfortably —*Esquire,* April 1973

I told him I could give him a couple of people who would look after him —Ernest Hemingway, "Miss Mary's Lion," 1956

But what about *persons?* It has not vanished from these contexts. We find it chosen as an alternative where *people* has just been used:

> Some 400,000 people, most of them young persons —*Current Biography*, June 1968

> . . . has peopled his story with real persons —Liz Smith, *New York*, 9 Feb. 1976

We find it used naturally where the older style books would require it:

> . . . almost one million persons are today confined —Alan M. Dershowitz, *Psychology Today*, February 1969

> . . . only three persons lost their lives —*Current Biography*, May 1966

And occasionally it is put in place of *people* by inattentive writers and editors, as in this example from *Winners & Sinners*:

> Mike Curtis, who likes to hit persons hard, slammed his 232 pounds into . . . the Ram running back —*N.Y. Times*, 9 Nov. 1971

You can safely follow your ear in your choice of *people* or *persons* after a number—or simply use *people*, in accordance with the latest advisories.

per Bernstein 1971 traces opposition to the preposition *per* all the way back to William Cobbett in the early 19th century. Cobbett's objection was that *per* was not English and to most people was "a mystical sort of word." Later 19th-century and early 20th-century commentators disapproved *per* before English words. The same injunction can be found as recently as Freeman 1983.

Bernstein's point is that *per* is no longer a mystical word, yet newspaper reporters and editors are still told to replace it with *a* or *an*, even in statistical and economic contexts where *per* is appropriate. Here are a few of these contexts using *per*.

> About 8–9 parts per million of nitrate in an infant's drinking water may interfere with hemoglobin function —Barry Commoner, *Columbia Forum*, Spring 1968

> . . . contributions . . . will be made by sponsors who will pay per mile for distances covered —*Massachusetts Audubon News*, May–June 1971

> . . . the average use per residential customer —*Annual Report, Union Electric Co.*, 1970

> Dividends per share of Common Stock —*Annual Report, R. J. Reynolds Industries, Inc.*, 1970

> He referred to the $29.75 bite (including city taxes) per concert ticket —J. Sebastian Sinisi, *Denver Post*, 1 Sept. 1984

Sports writing is frequently statistical also:

> . . . twenty-nine and one-half points and fifteen rebounds per game —*Current Biography*, July 1967

> Both men gave career best performances in taking five wickets per piece as Notts. were dismissed in two hours 55 minutes for 94 —Terry Bowles, *Evening Post* (Nottingham, England), 13 July 1974

Probably no one needs to be reminded of *miles per hour, miles per gallon*, and such.

The demystification of *per* has gone so far that it can be found in rather more literary contexts than you might expect:

> . . . and on up to four more English writers per publishing season —Bernard DeVoto, *Harper's*, November 1952

> Complicating matters are two beautiful women, one per agent, and an assortment of double agents —Arthur Krystal, *N.Y. Times Book Rev.*, 18 Nov. 1984

> . . . gives us as much serious fun per word as anyone around —George Stade, *N.Y. Times Book Rev.*, 6 Mar. 1983

Janis 1984 notes a use of *per* meaning "according to," often found in business correspondence in such expressions as "per your instructions" and sometimes preceded by *as* (see AS PER). This use he calls stilted. It is not limited to business correspondence. Here are some examples, none of which sound particularly stilted:

> Kesselring still believes that even after the failure to destroy the Russian ground forces (per his advice) . . . Hitler could have changed the course of the war —A. J. Liebling, *New Yorker*, 26 Mar. 1955

> Many of them were rowdy and wasted, per tradition —John Rockwell, *N.Y. Times*, 16 June 1976

> The Soviets, per custom, besieged the U.S. women with questions —Demmie Stathoplos, *Sports Illustrated*, 2 Aug. 1982

No commentator seems to question the use of *per* to mean "by the means or agency of":

> . . . a narrator, opening the play, announces the plot; the voice is the voice of George Moore (per David Warrilow) —Edith Oliver, *New Yorker*, 28 June 1982

> . . . a cavernous saloon, where, per his invitation, a rambunctious dairyman who insulted him, the brother of a man he killed . . . , and a faro dealer . . . await him with guns —Judith Crist, *Saturday Rev.*, 21 Aug. 1976

Harper 1975, 1985 notes that when *per* is used, *each* is not necessary. We do not find this redundancy very often in print.

The examples shown above represent most of the common standard uses of *per*. You will notice that automatic substitution of *a* or *an* for *per*, recommended by some commentators, simply does not produce acceptable English in many instances. Bernstein is right: *per* is no longer a mystical word, and you need not worry about using it in contexts such as those we have illustrated.

peradventure As an adverb meaning "perhaps" *peradventure* is archaic (although Burchfield 1996 has found a 1984 use from a South African writer that may be facetious). As a noun it persists in occasional use, usually following the preposition *beyond*:

> It went without saying that you have specified a class beyond peradventure when you have clearly stated what is required for membership in it —W. V. Quine, *Quiddities*, 1987

> . . . American ophthalmic surgeons who know beyond all possible peradventure that eye-strain . . . is of exactly that transcendent importance denied by the oversea prejudice —*JAMA*, 20 Mar. 1996

percent, per cent You can use either the one-word or the two-word form. Both are correct; the one-word form is more common in American use. *Per cent* used to be perceived as an abbreviation of *per centum* and was commonly styled as *per cent.*, with a period. The form with the period is old-fashioned and rarely seen anymore.

Percent can be followed by either a plural or singular verb. This is rather like notional agreement but it is usually more explicit: the noun related to *percent* frequently follows but sometimes precedes, and its number tends to determine that of the verb:

> . . . 80 percent of family physicians do make them —Dodi Schultz, *Ladies' Home Jour.*, August 1971

> Of the . . . inhabitants, 75 percent are of African descent —Esther Silver, *Essence*, November 1970

> . . . 25 percent of the population was overweight —*Current Biography*, December 1967

One commentator complains that "a large percent" is vague; doubtless it is frequently intended to be so:

> . . . might be able to pick up a large percent of the delegates with a modest percent of the votes —Ken Auletta, *New York*, 29 Mar. 1976

A number of handbooks dislike the appearance of the percent sign % in discursive prose.

percolator For pronunciation problems with this word, see NUCLEAR.

perfect "The phrases, *more perfect*, and *most perfect*, are improper," declared Lindley Murray in his *Grammar* of 1795, starting a subject that has lasted at least into the 1990s.

> *Perfect* is viewed by many careful writers as one of the uncomparable adjectives —Harper 1985

Copperud 1970 reports that the consensus of his usage authorities is that *perfect* may be freely compared, and dictionaries agree. But some commentators do not: Bernstein 1965, 1971 favors keeping *perfect* free from comparison, and Simon 1980 believes that *perfect* can have no superlative. Here is the background of this disagreement.

Evidence in the OED shows *perfect*, in one sense or another, has been used in the comparative and superlative since the 14th century. Examples from the 18th century are numerous and include such authors as Addison, Swift, and Bolingbroke and such grammarians and rhetoricians as Hugh Blair, Campbell 1776, and Lowth 1762; Lindley Murray himself copied Blair's and Campbell's uses in his own grammar of 1795. For Americans, the best-known 18th-century example is the Preamble to the U.S. Constitution: "in order to form a more perfect union."

How did Murray and the grammarians who followed him come to believe *perfect* should not be compared in spite of usage? They applied rigorous logic, or so they thought. Lowth and Priestley 1798 had already seen certain adjectives as having, to use Lowth's words, "in themselves a superlative signification" to which they thought it improper or illogical to add a superlative ending, although they recognized that such in fact was done (for a complete discussion, see ABSOLUTE ADJECTIVES). Lowth noticed *chiefest* and *extremest*; it was Murray who added *perfect* to the list. And, of course, once other grammarians had copied Murray, *perfect* became solidly ensconced in ever-growing lists of adjectives not to be compared. The opinions of the grammarians were repeated in handbooks and thence passed on to our modern commentators.

And how is it that American grammarians and usage commentators have ignored the authority of the Constitution's example? Harper 1985 says that one rebuttal to the urging of the constitutional example is the argument that the usage of 1787 is not the same as today's. The argument, though a valid enough generalization in many respects, will not hold water in this case. The OED shows 19th-century examples and Merriam-Webster files have these in addition:

> . . . man and the more perfect animals —John Stuart Mill, *A System of Logic*, 1843–1872

> . . . made my reverie one of the perfectest things in the world —William Dean Howells, *Venetian Life*, enlarged ed., 1872

> . . . the stronger and more perfect parts of his music —John Burroughs, *Wake-Robin*, 1871

Twentieth-century examples are numerous. Here are a few:

> I believe this passage contains the most perfect poetry yet written by any of the younger poets —C. Day Lewis, *A Hope for Poetry*, 3d ed., 1936

> . . . utilizing the machine to make the world more perfect —Lewis Mumford, *Technics and Civilization*, 1934

> . . . some of the most perfect examples of early Colonial and Federalist architecture —John P. Marquand, *New England Journeys*, No. 2, 1954

> . . . a more perfect rake has seldom existed —Nancy Mitford, *Atlantic*, May 1954

> . . . the most perfect writer of my generation —Norman Mailer, *Advertisements for Myself*, 1959

> To produce a more perfect wool, some Australian farmers are keeping their sheep indoors —*Time*, 25 Mar. 1985

> It seemed to me that I had never seen a more perfect, a cleaner animal —Ptolmey Tompkins, *Harper's*, January 1997

> The more perfect the translation the more absolute its ephemerality —Roy Harris, *Times Literary Supp.*, 28 Aug. 1987

The comparison of *perfect* has been in respectable use from the 14th century to the present; it has never been wrong, except in the imagination of Lindley Murray and those who repeat after him.

If we say, "This is *more perfect* than that," we do not mean that either is perfect without limitation, but that "this" has "more" of the qualities that go to make up perfection than "that"; it is *more nearly* perfect. Such usage has high literary authority —Fernald 1946

perfectly Both Harper 1985 and Heritage 1982 record that *perfectly* used as an intensive, as in

> . . . knew perfectly well that *The Songs of Bilitis* were made 'out of the whole cloth' —Gilbert Highet, *The Classical Tradition*, 1949

is sometimes objected to but is very common. Such objection as we have found (Watt 1967, Partridge 1942) is not very strong. We think you can use it without fear of criticism.

perimeter One of the most persistent criticisms of the word *parameter* has been that it is misused in place of *perimeter*. A typical example of the criticized sense of *parameter* is this:

> . . . readers with earthier appetites will find *Chiaroscuro* well within the parameters of their crime fiction menus —Peter Plagens, *Art in America*, July 1986

The frequent assumption of those who criticize *parameter* is that *perimeter* is regularly used in this way, in a figurative sense meaning "limits" or "outer limits," and, in fact, such a sense was in use before 1973, when *parameter* critics began making their assumption. Let's consider a few examples of that use:

> The most useful division is between criticism which attempts to bring to literature insights found outside its perimeter, and criticism which dives directly to the center of the literature and works outward to the perimeter —Wayne Shumaker, *Elements of Critical Theory*, 1952

> . . . it had become a flexible philosophy . . . and its supernatural perimeter attracted many a young searcher for truth —William Manchester, *Disturber of the Peace*, 1951

> . . . being aware, on the perimeter of his mind, of the rest of the court —John Creasy, *Alibi*, 1971

It was also, somewhat illogically, used in the plural:

> The limits of the world have already been reached by exploration; . . . the "perimeters of the future" are already in sight —*Times Literary Supp.*, 27 July 1951

> The perimeters of his poetic estate are clearly defined by the seas on all sides and his refusal to cross them —Raymond Gardner, *The Guardian*, 13 Oct. 1971

As these figurative evidence are a goodly portion of all our figurative evidence earlier than 1973, we conclude that such was not at all a common use of *perimeter* then. We may note also that figurative use then was as often singular as plural; this contrasts with *parameter*, almost always plural in the criticized construction. And we find *within* commonly used with *parameters* (see also the examples at PARAMETER), but not with *perimeter*. On the basis of these features, then, we think it unlikely that the criticized use of *parameter* developed out of its substitution for the figurative sense of *perimeter*.

The mainstream figurative use of *perimeter*

—now apparently somewhat more frequent in the plural than in the singular—has continued beyond 1973:

> . . . a rich boy eager for experience beyond the perimeters of his sedate world —Frederic Morton, *N.Y. Times Book Rev.,* 7 Sept. 1980

> . . . because its fulfillment was possible within the perimeter of Soviet ideology —Stanley Kauffmann, *Before My Eyes,* 1980

But now we are finding *within perimeters* as well:

> Let us do good things within their own proper perimeters —James A. Michener, *N.Y. Times Book Rev.,* 27 Feb. 1977

> . . . within the perimeters of what is considered correct business attire —Diane Sustendal, *N.Y. Times Mag.,* 16 Sept. 1984

The use of *within* with *perimeters* is quite new. It may come simply as a carryover from the very frequent use of *within* with *parameters* or, conversely, it may result from people's consciously replacing *parameter* with what they are told is the "correct" word, yet unconsciously using the familiar preposition. In either case, we have an increase in the figurative use of *perimeter,* now sometimes the object of *within,* that has co-occurred with the increase of hostile criticism of *parameter.* This development may be entirely fortuitous, but it is hard to dismiss the possibility that the use of *perimeter* has been stimulated by either the use or the criticism of *parameter.*

period of time This phrase has been censured as a redundancy by Shaw 1987, Janis 1984, Copperud 1980, and Phythian 1979. The basis for objection is put this way by Shaw: "The word *period* conveys the idea of time. . . ." But consider these examples:

> The account of the loss of the ship makes a fitting period to a brave and hopeful voyage into a new world —Farley Mowat, *Westviking: The Ancient Norse in Greenland and North America,* 1965

> Most of the characters speak in rounded periods, often with a touch of malicious wit —Newgate Callendar, *N.Y. Times Book Rev.,* 19 Jan. 1986

The point is simple: *period* does not necessarily convey the idea of time. *Period* is a word of several senses—Merriam-Webster's Collegiate Dictionary, Tenth Edition, defines over a dozen of them—and people who write *period of time* (or *period of years,* or other similar formulations) are merely taking care that you do not miss their meaning.

> Over a period of thirty years the late Wilder Hobson and I played a name game —John O'Hara, *Holiday,* May 1967

When using such a phrase improves the clarity of your sentence, we think you can sensibly afford to ignore the criticism.

peripheral When the adjective *peripheral* is used with a preposition, the preposition is *to*:

> . . . the political issue has been seen as peripheral to the psychological and the stylistic —Helen Muchnic, *N.Y. Times Book Rev.,* 4 Mar. 1979

> The accumulation of art objects is peripheral to the activity of art —William Stafford, *Writing the Australian Crawl,* 1978

permeate *Permeate* is used with *by* or *with* about equally. When it is used with *by,* the verb is almost always in the passive; when *permeate* is followed by *with,* the verb may appear in either the active or the passive voice:

> The German philosophers were of the view that the universe was permeated by a similar spiritual activity —S. F. Mason, *Main Currents of Scientific Thought,* 1953

> . . . a language that was still permeated by the assumption that politics could *not* be an objective science —Irving Kristol, *Encounter,* December 1954

> . . . a general joylessness that permeates their lives with frustration —Stanley Kubrick, *Playboy,* September 1968

> . . . his stories are permeated with a sense of vague regret not far removed from fright —William Peden, *Saturday Rev.,* 11 Apr. 1953

Sometimes *permeate* is used intransitively and may then be followed by *beyond*:

> . . . the influence of the Court permeates even beyond its technical jurisdiction —Felix Frankfurter, in *Aspects of American Government,* ed. Sydney D. Bailey, 1950

permissive, permissivism These are two of the words used by those who think they are defending English to belittle those who offer information on which opinions about language matters might be based more soundly. The use of either by a commentator is almost certainly a sign that a lexicographer, a linguist, or another writer on usage has trodden upon one of the commentator's cherished beliefs. The periphrastic equivalent of *permissive* is *anything goes.*

permit of Copperud 1964, 1980 regards the *of* in *permit of* as superfluous, but he concedes that its use is standard. Like *admit of* and *allow of, permit of* is almost always used with an impersonal subject. Its sense is "to make possible." It is not an especially common construction.

> . . . there are very few matters . . . that do not permit of a difference of opinion —O. S. Nock, *The Railways of Britain,* 1947

> Enough ratings are to hand to permit of some definitive judgment —Jack Gould, *N.Y. Times,* 1 Dec. 1957

> . . . a circular piece of stout leather with a hole in its centre to permit of its being passed up and over the grip —F. J. Norman, *Dragon Times,* 8 July 1998

See also ADMIT 3.

pernickety, persnickety When a correspondent in 1986 wants to know whether *pernickety* or *persnickety* is the preferred form of the word, you know you are hearing from someone with a long memory. From the mid-1940s to about 1961 a dispute about the propriety of *persnickety* was waged fitfully in the pages of newspapers and weekly newsmagazines.

The controversy seems to have had its origin in Webster's Second 1934. That book was the first Merriam-Webster to recognize the version with *-s-,* but it tucked the spelling away in the pearl section (the small type at the foot of the page in older dictionaries)—several pages away from *pernickety.* Apparently some of the objectors to *persnickety* failed to notice the pearl section and assumed that the *-s-* spelling was not in the dictionary.

Pernickety was introduced into English by Scottish writers in the early 19th century. *Persnickety* is an Americanism, first attested in the early 20th century.

> This detachment caused him to be looked upon as slightly finicky, not to say persnickety —*American Mercury,* August 1926

> . . . The Atchison Globe . . . thumbed a persnickety snoot at Emporia —*Emporia* (Kans.) *Gazette,* 10 May 1927

Today *persnickety* is much more common than *pernickety* in the United States; *pernickety* is the only form used in British and Commonwealth English.

> If the *tamago* is not up to snuff, a really persnickety eater will ask for the check and leave —Harvey Steiman, *Wine Spectator,* 15 May 1990

> A tweed-encased fogey, he's allergic to technology, persnickety about language —John Powers, *Vogue,* March 1998

> . . . such a presentable assortment it seems persnickety not to be pleased by any of them —George F. Will, *Newsweek,* 17 Aug. 1987

> He was pernickety about decent English —J. M. Cameron, *N.Y. Rev. of Books,* 8 May 1986

> The insurance company, pernickety about such matters, threatened suit for fraud —Robertson Davies, *The Lyre of Orpheus,* 1988

You can use whichever spelling you prefer.

perpetrate, perpetuate Many handbooks on usage either state or imply that these two familiar words are frequently or occasionally confused, but we have few examples of the mistaken use. The error warned against is the use of *perpetrate,* "to commit (as a crime)," in place of *perpetuate,* "to cause to continue or to last." Copperud 1964 quotes a clear-cut instance of *perpetrator* used for *perpetuator,* and Kingsley Amis, in Michaels and Ricks 1980, quotes a news report in which *perpetuate* is obviously the word wanted, but *perpetrate* is the word used. Garner 1998 has four examples from 1990s newspapers and says the number could be easily multiplied. Check your dictionary if you are uncertain.

perquisite, prerequisite Shaw 1987 says these two words get their prefixes confused; the Oxford American Dictionary warns against confusion; Copperud 1980 distinguishes them. If you do not know the meaning of these words, you will find them plainly defined in any good dictionary. We have almost no evidence of the words' being interchanged in our files, but Garner 1998 has several instances.

If you tend to mix up the spelling of the two words, here are a few clues to go by. First, if you want an adjective, it must be *prerequisite; perquisite* is a noun only. And the prepositions typically used with each word are different. *Perquisite* regularly takes *of:*

> It is one of the perquisites of membership —*PMLA,* March 1982

> . . . the perquisites of his position—a chauffeured limousine, a chef —Tony Schwartz, *N.Y. Times Book Rev.,* 9 Dec. 1979

Prerequisite, on the other hand, usually takes *for* or *to:*

> . . . has come to be nearly a prerequisite for leadership —Robert Pattison, *On Literacy,* 1982

> . . . a prerequisite for graduation —James Cass, *Saturday Rev.,* 29 May 1976

> . . . making unfair demands as a prerequisite to improved relations —Lynda Schuster, *Wall Street Jour.,* 3 Feb. 1982

> . . . registration before an election is a prerequisite to casting a vote —*American Girl,* November 1952

Of is used, but somewhat less frequently:

> . . . oratorical abilities—the first prerequisite, as he had always maintained, of a successful politician —William L. Shirer, *The Rise and Fall of the Third Reich,* 1960

persevere   *Persevere* is most often followed by *in*:

> Up to this time he had persevered in his resolve not to invite her back —Thomas Hardy, *The Return of the Native,* 1878

> . . . he may feel that to persevere in that suggestion would alienate Washington's already fluctuating affections —*New Statesman & Nation,* 19 Dec. 1953

> In the retail motor-gasoline business, affiliates persevered in their efforts at greater selectivity —*Annual Report, Standard Oil Co.* (New Jersey), 1970

Persevere may sometimes be used with *with*; although it is found in American English, it seems more often to occur in British and Commonwealth English:

> . . . many people would persevere with the Victorian conception of a schizophrenic culture —Robin Boyd, *Meanjin* (Australia), Autumn 1952

> . . . his suggestion that they persevere with their medicine —A. J. Cronin, *The Citadel,* 1937

> . . . the great Oxford English Dictionary, for instance, which no commercial publisher could have persevered with —John Russell, *N.Y. Times Book Rev.,* 16 Apr. 1978

persnickety   See PERNICKETY, PERSNICKETY.

person   1. See PEOPLE, PERSONS.
2. One of the more noticeable outgrowths of the concern about sexism in language during the 1970s and beyond has been the coinage of compound terms in which the terminal element *-man* (as in *draftsman*) and sometimes *-woman* (as in *chairwoman*) is replaced by *-person*. A few of those compounds were enthusiastically adopted by those endeavoring to be nonsexist: *chairperson, anchorperson, spokesperson,* for instance, are now well established. Critical opinion of such compounds in the press and in usage books has been chiefly negative and chiefly written by men. Perhaps the hostile attitude of commentators has helped winnow out the weakest of such proposed compounds, but the most useful have persevered in use widely enough to gain admission to dictionaries.

Bolinger 1980 observes that there is a tendency in actual use for the new compound, such as *chairperson* or *spokesperson,* to be ap-

plied chiefly to women, so that where once we had *spokesman–spokeswoman* we now begin to find *spokesman–spokesperson.* This tendency—and our files suggest it is only a tendency, not an accomplished fact—has also turned some women against some of the *-person* compounds. The disaffection of women with *chairperson* and *anchorperson* has probably furthered the use of *chair* and *anchor* as replacements for the compound forms, but we have not spotted a *spokes* yet.

Janis 1984 notes the effect of the employment ads on such usages.

Unless you are constrained by particular circumstances, you are free to use or avoid compounds such as *spokesperson* as you wish. If you do choose to use them, we suggest that you check with a recent dictionary or two to be sure that the compound you have picked is in current use.

See also SEXISM.

persona   *Persona* seems to have been brought into English from Latin by Joseph Addison in 1704; he used it in its original Latin sense "an actor's mask," and he was writing about Roman actors. This etymologically primary meaning has subsequently been used in English context, but its users have often tended to treat *persona* as a Latin word, though Addison did not. Here is another writer who has used this sense as English:

> . . . and, to employ a metaphor that has become fashionable in erudite circles, he appears to his readers in a persona and thus shows not a face but a mask, as though he were an actor in a drama presented to an audience in ancient Athens —Eric Partridge, *British and American English Since 1900,* 1951

No dictionary of which we are aware includes this sense as English; it is certainly of low frequency.

It was the sense of "mask" that appealed to Ezra Pound, who is one of the people responsible for enlarging the word's domain. Pound used the word as a title as early as 1909. It is from Pound's use and from criticism of Pound's work that *persona* acquired its use as a term in literary criticism.

According to a citation in the OED Supplement, some of the works of C. G. Jung had been translated into English by 1917. *Persona* was a term Jung used:

> I term the outer attitude, or outer character, the *persona,* the inner attitude I term the *anima,* or *soul* —*Psychological Types,* translated by H. G. Baynes, 1924

Jung's theories had many explicators in English, and each one seemed to give a little individual twist to Jung's notion:

The persona is the agent responsible for the adaptation of the individual's inner constitution to the environmental world —*Times Literary Supp.*, 9 May 1942

Persona is Jung's celebrated word for the mask that the ego wears before society —*Times Literary Supp.*, 12 May 1950

A related concept is the "persona," which refers to the role played by the individual in society. . . . The persona is not a part of the true character but is firmly attached to it and acts as a sort of protection of the inner man —Gerald S. Blum, *Psychoanalytic Theories of Personality*, 1953

It is hard to tell just how close each of these explanations is to Jung's original notion, but it is worth noting that the concept appears to have become externalized: if Jung considered the *persona* an aspect of the individual's personality, it has become in the last two explanations a kind of separate entity acting as a protection or buffer. This view of the persona from the outside as a kind of independent entity—perhaps influenced by the original "mask" sense of the word—proved to be suggestive to writers.

It invaded the world of literary criticism, providing new life and new dimension to the Ezra Pound–centered use:

You might call it a mask, or as Jung would say, a *persona* that soon had a life of its own —Malcolm Cowley, *New Republic*, 18 Mar. 1946

And it also started on an independent life of its own as a word for a person's public personality:

A likeable personality, he seemed to me, quite without the arrogance I had been led to expect. But he may have been giving his *persona* a night off —J. B. Priestley, *Irish Digest*, April 1955

. . . his major work . . . is an appendage to his public persona rather than a great book —Anthony West, *New Yorker*, 10 Dec. 1955

Few Englishmen have such an officially English persona —V. S. Pritchett, *N.Y. Times Mag.*, 21 Sept. 1958

. . . the differences between the modern author's *persona* as conveyed to the public and his character as seen by his intimates —Frank Swinnerton, *Saturday Rev.*, 2 Mar. 1957

You may have noticed that each of the examples given so far has a certain amount of age; they are not brand-new. The literary use is flourishing, as is the "public personality" use. Some more recent examples of each:

. . . one might argue the "I" of the poem is more often than not a *persona* created by the poet especially for the occasion —*Times Literary Supp.*, 25 Jan. 1974

But even a lyric poem posits some self that is moved to utterance. The posited self of a lyric may be taken as purely fictional or as a shadowy persona of a literal self, the author —Robert Penn Warren, *Democracy and Poetry*, 1975

Wayne and Cooper developed personae which they controlled and exhibited skillfully —Stanley Kauffmann, *Before My Eyes*, 1980

. . . masked her frightful bouts of pain and debility with the glamorous, heavily made-up, in the end sybilline persona who sought to be entertaining —John Updike, *N.Y. Times Book Rev.*, 23 Feb. 1986

personal 1. *Personal* is a word of frequent occurrence and critics tend to disparage its use as redundant, especially in the expressions *personal friend, personal opinion,* and *personal physician.* While these objections have been repeated into the 1990s, they are essentially trivial. *Personal opinion* can be found in speech:

. . . a criticism is after all a personal opinion, and any personal opinion on any work is valid because the work itself is only the writer's personal opinion on a situation —William Faulkner, 1 May 1958, in *Faulkner in the University*, 1959

But it is also used in edited prose when the writer finds it useful to emphasize the individual:

After some months he had his own column called "Hors du M. Le Coq," a heading signifying a personal opinion —Patricia Highsmith, *Times Literary Supp.*, 17 Apr. 1992

. . . his frank personal opinion of any of his most celebrated analysands might have been . . . "The man's bonkers. . . ." —Calvin Trillin, *New Yorker*, 15 Aug. 1994

. . . placed the government in the odd posture of relegating the president's assessment to the inconsequential level of personal opinion —Doug Ireland, *Village Voice*, 28 Jan. 1992

But he adds this personal opinion about the secondary meaning: "Realistically, I suppose it is here." —Bernstein 1977

The critics who sniff at *personal physician* miss the point: the phrase is usually used of the rich or powerful:

One of his ancestors . . . was the personal physician of Napoleon Bonaparte's brother —*Current Biography*, July 1965

. . . Dr. Burton Lee, the President's personal physician, rushed to his aid —*People,* 20 Jan. 1992

. . . the personal physician to England's Charles II —John Berendt, *Esquire,* December 1990

Personal physician may also be used to contrast with consulting specialists:

Fortunately, Emily's personal physician disagreed, and surgery was done —Laurie Garrett, *Elle,* December 1992

Personal friend is found in speech and letters:

. . . I wish you as a personal friend of mine, would tell him you have reason to believe he is mistaken —Abraham Lincoln, letter, 14 Feb. 1843

In edited prose, it most often contrasts with a professional or business relationship:

In one persona, he was a millionaire boat designer, a personal friend of then Vice President George Bush —John Katzenbach, *N.Y. Times Book Rev.,* 25 Nov. 1990

. . . Rabbi Stephen Wise . . . a personal friend and close advisor of President Roosevelt —William J. Vanden Heuvel, *American Heritage,* July/August 1999

In short, the censured uses of *personal* do not seem to be simple redundancies, and when they do appear, authors generally have a good reason for them. We think you need not be too concerned about the critics' censures as long as you have a good reason for using *personal.*

2. *Personal, personnel.* A surprisingly large number of books warn against confusing these two words. Such confusion would appear unlikely because they are pronounced differently and function as different parts of speech. It is possible that they both may be misspelled sometimes as *personel.*

personality The use of *personality* to designate a person prominent in the public eye has been disparaged as overused and at least mildly objectionable by a number of critics. Some believe the use to be recent, but it is not, dating back to 1889. Our files don't show the word to be overused, so the basis of objection may lie in the word's association with showbiz, flacks, and hype. It does occur in such contexts:

In Filmland's army of public personalities, the front rank is made up of actors —Stanley Kauffmann, *New Republic,* 1 July 1996

At 60 Minutes, the on-air personalities were involved in six or seven stories at the same time —Marie Brenner, *Vanity Fair,* May 1996

When rap became a big business, the industry wanted personalities to market —Frank Owen, *Vibe,* December 1994/January 1995

It is also used for persons of striking presence in other contexts:

Excessive personalities from history . . . Caligula, Attila, Gilles de Rais, Vlad the Impaler —Stephen O'Shea, *Elle,* December 1990

It was associated with the prohibition underworld and with two of its most flamboyant personalities, Larry Fay and Texas Guinan —Dalton Gross et al., *Notes and Queries,* September 1994

These uses are standard.

personally The objections raised to the use of *personally* are about the same as those made to *personal*; they call it redundant, unnecessary, or verbose, especially when used with *I.* The use of *personally* with *I* in print is the mark of an informal conversational style; it is commonly found in letters, interviews, and fictional speech.

To date I personally haven't seen a flake of snow —Robert Frost, letter, 25 Dec. 1912

Personally I have found it a good scheme to not even sign my name to the story —Ring Lardner, preface, *How to Write Short Stories,* 1924

Personally, I am never happy when I am away from my beloved books —Myles na gCopaleen (Flann O'Brien), *The Best of Myles,* 1968

Personally, I am most grateful to Mr. Hibben for his salvation of the gazelles —John Fischer, *Harper's,* October 1971

Admittedly, these usages are not precisely parallel . . . and I personally couldn't care less —Robert Claiborne, *Our Marvelous Native Tongue,* 1983

We suggest that you limit your use of this construction to such deliberately informal contexts; to use it in a passage of serious discussion may leave you open to criticism.

Personally is, however, used in serious contexts where it emphasizes personal contact, or the doing of something in person that might have been delegated, or the exclusion of considerations other than personal ones. Here are some examples of such uses:

Palmer was at pains to get the oldest and most doddery doctors . . . with whom he was personally on friendly terms, to sign the death-certificates of the victims —*Times Literary Supp.,* 27 Aug. 1971

. . . excellent on the problems of which he was personally in command —John Kenneth Galbraith, *Saturday Rev.,* 6 Nov. 1971

. . . which President Carter planned to tour personally to determine the extent of the devastation —Wayne King, *N.Y. Times,* 22 May 1980

It is also used to mean "as a person":

. . . with a look of being personally unusual —Ivy Compton-Burnett, *The Last and the First,* 1971

Sympathetic to New Deal purposes, he disliked the New Dealers personally —Edwin M. Yoder, Jr., *Harper's,* February 1971

personal pronouns Usage problems with personal pronouns are covered under the names of the individual pronouns. For discussions of the use of the nominative versus the objective case, see AS . . . AS 3; BETWEEN YOU AND I; HYPERCORRECTION; IT'S ME; THAN 1.

personnel See PERSONAL 2.

persons See PEOPLE, PERSONS.

perspicacious, perspicacity, perspicuous, perspicuity Fowler 1926 was perhaps wise in his approach to this subject: he lumped all of these hard words under the heading *perspic-* and avoided a lot of tedious spelling. In case you are uncertain, the pair with *a* go together and the pair with *u* go together. The purpose of Fowler's discussion, and that of commentators since, is to point out confusion—the substitution of one or another of each pair for one or another of the other pair.

One easy way to keep out of trouble with these words is not to use them, of course. Any good thesaurus will give you several alternatives for each. A bolder approach is to check your desk dictionary before you use them. We say desk dictionary, not unabridged, because your desk dictionary has the present-day mainstream meanings. An unabridged dictionary has all the meanings, and that is the problem.

According to the commentators, the chief mistake is substitution of *perspicuity* for *perspicacity* (it has been going on since 1662) and of *perspicuous* for *perspicacious.* The latter is a real problem for the commentators: *perspicuous* was used in the sense of *perspicacious* in 1584, two years before it was used in its current mainstream meaning (1586) and 56 years before *perspicacious* (1640) is attested in English at all.

The meanings we are concerned with are "of acute discernment; keen" (you might even say "shrewd")—the chief modern meaning of *perspicacious*—and "acuteness of discernment or insight"—the chief modern meaning of *perspicacity.*

The trend of development since the 16th and 17th centuries has been toward differentiation, with *perspicacious* and *perspicacity* used

chiefly in the senses just given, and *perspicuous* and *perspicuity* used in the senses of "clear to the understanding; plain, lucid" and "clarity, lucidity." Here are some examples of mainstream use:

. . . she took some comfort in her perspicacity at having guessed his passion —Vita Sackville-West, *The Edwardians,* 1930

. . . triumph is itself fortuitous, and is therefore no great credit to his perspicacity —George F. Kennan, *New Yorker,* 1 May 1971

The dictum of Ben Jonson . . . that "the chief virtue of style is perspicuity. . . ." —*Times Literary Supp.,* 18 Mar. 1944

. . . the problems that still confound us were formulated with remarkable clarity and perspicuity —Noam Chomsky, *Columbia Forum,* Spring 1968

. . . St. Augustine has some very perspicacious remarks on Plato —I. F. Stone, *N.Y. Times Mag.,* 22 Jan. 1978

Being not only sane but perspicacious, General Grigorenko kept mum —Robert C. Tucker, *N.Y. Times Book Rev.,* 2 Jan. 1983

One must be extremely exact, clear, and perspicuous in everything one says —Lord Chesterfield, *Letters to his Son,* 1774

. . . offering a perspicuous picture of the movement of empires —*Times Literary Supp.,* 12 Feb. 1970

If you follow the example of these, you will not go wrong. Garner 1998 has examples of *perspicacity* used in place of *pertinacity* too. It is a good idea to keep your desk dictionary handy.

persuade *Persuade* is most often used with *to* and an infinitive:

. . . persuading young people to make one of the sciences . . . their life's work —Russell H. Johnsen, *Scientific Monthly,* January 1954

. . . his test is not so much what happened as what he believes he can persuade other people to believe —John Kenneth Galbraith, *Saturday Rev.,* 6 Nov. 1971

Occasionally *to* is followed by a noun:

Persuaded to the hospital for examination and medications, he insisted on returning home —Larry L. King, *Harper's,* April 1971

Persuade occurs quite frequently with a clause:

The reading of the card persuaded me that he was dead —James Joyce, *Dubliners,* 1914

Slowly his anger grew. . . . He even persuaded himself that he felt jealousy —Edith Sitwell, *Fanfare for Elizabeth,* 1946

. . . the palpable effort of that book to persuade that Concord was a Brook Farm where no Hawthorne ever worked on a dung-hill —Alfred Kazin, *Partisan Rev.,* September–October 1940

It is somewhat less often used with *of, by,* or *into:*

. . . his anxiety to refute polemical over-simplifications and persuade the reader of his objectivity —Dennis H. Wrong, *Change,* April 1972

. . . I might be persuaded by your eloquence —Lewis H. Lapham, *Harper's,* January 1972

The speech . . . persuades us into accepting her surrender —T. S. Eliot, "Thomas Heywood," in *Selected Essays,* 1932

And, to give you an idea of the wide assortment of prepositions used with *persuade,* here are examples of *as to, from, out of, with,* and *upon,* with which it is found occasionally:

She could not persuade herself as to the advisability of her promise —Theodore Dreiser, *Sister Carrie,* 1900

Pickets are then sent to the plant gates to persuade others from taking the places of the strikers —*New Republic,* 20 Jan. 1937

". . . This brother of yours would persuade me out of my senses, Miss Morland. . . ." —Jane Austen, *Northanger Abbey,* 1818

. . . to persuade the intelligence with reason rather than to overwhelm it with a profusion of detail —Walter Prescott Webb, *The Great Frontier,* 1952

. . . his ministers will clearly have difficulty in persuading it upon ordinary people —David Wood, *The Times* (London), 19 Nov. 1973

See also CONVINCE, PERSUADE.

persuasion Back in the 19th century writers like Dickens or Trollope commonly used *persuasion* to mean "religion"—either as a system of beliefs or as a group of people adhering to those beliefs. (The use actually goes back to the 16th and 17th centuries.) Thus a Roman Catholic might be referred to as "a person of the Catholic persuasion" or a Jew as "a person of the Hebrew persuasion." This use must have been so common as to invite parody; in 1866 Dean Alford was complaining that he had seen and heard "Jewish persuasion" and "Hebrew persuasion" so often he expected soon to encounter "an individual of the negro persuasion." So, from a word used to indicate a set of religious beliefs or believers, *persuasion* came to be used for any group or kind.

Fowler 1926 objected to such use as "worn-out humour." Recent critics following Fowler's lead call it facetious and tiresome. Their reservations have been ignored by writers. We find it used sometimes facetiously and sometimes matter-of-factly:

I have cooked hundreds of batches of chili and have eaten chilies of all makes and persuasions —Craig Claiborne, *N.Y. Times,* 5 Nov. 1980

Western writers, says Slade, particularly those of the liberal persuasion, are anti-clericalist —Bernard Lewis, *Islam in History,* 1993

. . . listen to fiddlers of every musical persuasion —Robert E. Tomasson, *N.Y. Times,* 25 May 1979

The introductions went on and on. Celebrities of every stripe and persuasion got up to take a bow —Bill Barich, *New Yorker,* 29 Aug. 1988

. . . where no man had ever been beaten in one-on-one basketball by an opponent of the female persuasion —Joseph Honig, *N.Y. Times,* 6 Jan. 1980

This use does not appear to be as popular now as it was in the 19th century.

pertinent *Pertinent* is usually used with *to* and a noun object:

This is a play that she would like to see revived as she feels it is very pertinent to the present —*Current Biography,* June 1964

. . . the "digging up" of all facts and figures pertinent to the project —Axel Bruzelius, *Area Development,* July 1970

Sometimes *pertinent* is followed by *to* and an infinitive:

. . . it is pertinent to take stock of the position and consider what it implies for the future —*The Economist,* 21 May 1953

Occasionally, *pertinent* has been followed by *as regards, for,* or *in:*

This is especially pertinent as regards corporations that operated at less than optimum —C. E. Ferguson, *Southern Economic Jour.,* October 1952

. . . although pertinent for some points of view, is irrelevant to our purpose here —George B. Hurff, *Social Aspects of Enterprise In the Large Corporation,* 1950

. . . find a new instrument for the 1970s and '80s which will be more pertinent in achieving those still valid goals —Calvin H. Plimpton, *Amherst College Bulletin,* November 1968

peruse *Peruse* is a literary word. Marlowe and Shakespeare used it; so did Pope and Swift and Johnson, Wordsworth and Tennyson. In poetry it was a useful alternative to the monosyllabic *read*. But taste in literature has changed, and *peruse* is no longer used as frequently as it was in times past.

Early in the 20th century, when regular literary use of *peruse* began to wane, there arose the notion among American critics that the word should only be used in a narrow sense. Vizetelly 1906 seems to have been the earliest to propound this view:

> **peruse** should not be used when the simple *read* is meant. The former implies to read with care and attention and is almost synonymous with *scan*, which is to examine with critical care and in detail. A person is more apt to *read* than to *scan* or *peruse* the Bible.

Vizetelly has been followed by numerous critics right up to Garner 1998.

While we cannot be sure, it appears that this notion of the correct use of *peruse* was Vizetelly's own invention. It was certainly born in disregard of dictionary definitions of the word and in apparent ignorance of the literary traditions on which those dictionary definitions were based.

The sense that is criticized was defined by Samuel Johnson in his 1755 Dictionary simply as "To read." We know from the evidence that *peruse* was in Johnson's working vocabulary and that he was familiar with its use. It meant "to read" to him. Later lexicographers elaborated on Johnson's treatment. Webster, for instance, defined it in 1828 as "To read, or to read with attention." At least part of the reason for elaborating on Johnson's definition was probably the sense development of *read*. Johnson recognized three senses of *read*; his reviser, Archdeacon Todd, a half century later, doubled that number. No doubt Webster's addition at *peruse* was made partly to narrow the focus of *read* as a defining term.

James A. H. Murray, editing the word for the OED from an undoubtedly greater range of citational evidence than was available to either Johnson or Webster, framed a definition in three parts: "To read through or over; to read thoroughly or carefully; hence (loosely) to read." Most American dictionaries of the 20th century have taken the same approach. Murray's three components can be considered as broad (to read), medium (to read through or over), and narrow (to read thoroughly or carefully). All three of these have coexisted at least since the time of Marlowe and Shakespeare; the broadness or narrowness is usually shown by the context. For instance here we find the narrow use being signaled:

> In meantime take this book; peruse it thoroughly
> And thou shalt turn thyself into what shape thou wilt
> —Christopher Marlowe, *Dr. Faustus,* 1604

> Have you with heed perused
> What I have written to you?
> —Shakespeare, *Coriolanus,* 1608

> Having carefully perused the Journals of both Houses —Edward Hyde, Earl of Clarendon, *A History of the Great Rebellion,* 1647 (OED)

> . . . especially let his Method of Phisick be diligently perused —George Herbert, *A Priest to the Temple,* 1652

> Let the Preface be attentively perused —James Boswell, *Life of Samuel Johnson,* 1791

> . . . many books
> Were skimmed, devoured, or studiously perused,
> But with no settled plan
> —William Wordsworth, *The Prelude,* 1805

By the same means the broad sense could be signaled:

> Whatever is common is despised. Advertisements are now so numerous that they are very negligently perused —Samuel Johnson, *The Idler,* 20 Jan. 1759

> I've even found myself idly perusing the Yellow Pages —Lesley Conger, *The Writer,* October 1968

> Those of us who have been idly perusing the latest flock of holiday brochures —*The Guardian* (in Bryson)

The bulk of the evidence is not marked by the use of adverbial modifiers to point the reader in the narrow or the broad direction. Most of it, we would assume, falls into the middle range (read through or over):

> I have perused the note —Shakespeare, *The Taming of the Shrew,* 1594

> Oh! Mr. Pamphlet, your servant. Have you perused my poems? —George Farquhar, *Love and a Bottle,* 1698

> He only is the master who keeps the mind in pleasing captivity; whose pages are perused with eagerness, and in hope of new pleasure are perused again —Samuel Johnson, *Lives of the Poets,* 1783

> . . . nor do we doubt but our reader, when he hath perused his story, will concur with us in allowing him that title —Henry Fielding, *Jonathan Wild,* 1743

> . . . resolved instantly to peruse every line before she attempted to rest —Jane Austen, *Northanger Abbey,* 1818

I have a letter from William which you may peruse —Henry Adams, letter, 18 Aug. 1863

I perused a number of public notices attached to the wall —Flann O'Brien, *At Swim-Two-Birds*, 1939

How depressing political allegory can be may be discovered by perusing Addison's *Trial of Count Tariff* —Bonamy Dobrée, *English Literature in the Early Eighteenth Century, 1700–1740*, 1959

You may have noticed by now that the plain word *read* can readily be substituted in any of these examples, even where the idea of "read through or over" is pretty obvious. Sometimes the suggestion of the broader sense is equally plain:

Or else, to shew their learned Labour, you May backward be perus'd, like Hebrew —Jonathan Swift, "George Nim-Dan-Dean Esq.," 1721

. . . but when I returned to Boston in 1733, I found this change had obtained favour, and was then become common, for I met with it often in perusing the newspapers —Benjamin Franklin, letter, 26 Dec. 1789

O the old books we shall peruse here! —Charles Lamb, letter, 18 Sept. 1827

I have also perused *But Gentlemen Marry Brunettes*—that nothing be lost —Oliver Wendell Holmes d. 1935, letter, 17 June 1928

Mr. Warburton then and therefrth seemed to lose his appetite for information. He ceased perusing the *Wall Street Journal* —James Purdy, *Cabot Wright Begins*, 1964

Sometimes the narrower sense is implied, too:

. . . I beg the favour that you will peruse the inclosed, and . . . correct the mistaken passages —Edmund Cave, letter, 15 July 1737

. . . having written scandalous speeches without license or approbation of those that ought to peruse and authorise the same —Vita Sackville-West, *Aphra Behn*, 1928

With Dickinson and his cohorts perusing it in the meantime with critical eyes —Claude G. Bowers, *The Young Jefferson, 1743–1789*, 1945

In conclusion we recommend that you reread the examples and see for yourself in how many Samuel Johnson's simple "read" definition would work perfectly well. There are likely to be only a few in which adding the adverbs used by later dictionary definers will enhance anyone's understanding of the passage. Vizetelly's strictures do not stand the test of being tried against actual usage by people

familiar with the word. *Peruse* has not changed much since Shakespeare's time, but it is not a word we use very often any more. Therefore if you choose to use it, you are best advised to use it in a literary context.

pervert *Pervert* is used with *into, to,* or *by:*

. . . those who pervert honest criticism into falsification of fact —Franklin D. Roosevelt, fireside chat, 28 Apr. 1942, in *Nothing to Fear*, ed. B. D. Zevin, 1946

According to Sadat, Ali Sabri perverted it into an instrument that gave him personal control over large parts of the country —Joseph Kraft, *New Yorker*, 18 Sept. 1971

. . . those who pervert good words to careless misuse —Jacques Barzun, *Atlantic*, December 1953

There is no possible way to prevent peaceful atoms from being perverted to warlike purposes —Morehead Patterson, quoted in *The Reporter*, 12 Jan. 1956

The habit of perverting values by subordinating the eternal to the temporal —*Times Literary Supp.*, 23 May 1942

They have perverted the concept of academic freedom by broadening its scope to include social action —Ronald Reagan, *Change*, July–August 1969

Somewhat less frequently, *pervert* is followed by *for, from,* or *with:*

. . . perverting justice for reactionary political ends —William L. Shirer, *The Rise and Fall of the Third Reich*, 1960

. . . were not only impeded but spoiled and perverted from their true nature —Robert A. Hall, Jr., *A Short History of Italian Literature*, 1951

Luther protested against a Catholic Church that had . . . perverted it [Scripture] with casuistry —Irving Babbitt, *The New Laokoon*, 1910

phase See FAZE, PHASE, FEAZE, FEEZE.

phenomenon 1. The plural is *phenomena* or *phenomenons. Phenomena* is much more frequent at the present time, but *phenomenons* prevails in the sense "an exceptional or unusual person, thing, or occurrence."

2. Perhaps we in the dictionary trade should get around to recognizing that *phenomena* is used as a singular. The OED dates the use as far back as 1576; the plural form *phenomenas* goes back to 1635, and among its 17th century users the OED numbers Robert Boyle, the famous chemist and physicist. It cannot be simply an illiteracy used by those ignorant of Latin and Greek; Robert Boyle undoubtedly

knew more Latin and Greek than most of the subsequent commentators who have disparaged the form. Philip Howard, who seems to have some classical background, has this comment:

> It is a notable recent *phenomena* that one *criteria* of education in an influential *strata* of the community is to be good at criticizing what the *media* is saying about all this *data* on the decay of English. Instead of crying barbarism, it is more constructive to investigate why this should be happening. Fewer people know Latin and Greek these days, and accordingly there are fewer around to be pained by outrages upon their methods of word-formation. And, in any case, English grammar evolves with majestic disregard for the susceptibilities of classical scholars —*Weasel Words,* 1978

Evidence in our files for the singular *phenomena* goes back to the mid-1920s. The OED has a note that the form was found in the 18th and 19th centuries. We have some modern examples from print; they mostly come from sources more concerned with explication than with the niceties of language:

> The scientific name for this phenomena is meteorotropism —*Farm Jour.,* January 1998

> . . . the Borgia were, in modern terms, a media phenomena —*The Economist,* 23 Nov. 1974

> . . . a fine analysis of this phenomena —*Publishers Weekly,* 31 May 1976

But the majority of our evidence comes from speech. It has been reported or recorded in the speech of university professors, U.S. Senators, poets, and literary critics as well as from the speech of well-known figures from the world of professional sports. In current American English, then, the singular *phenomena* is primarily a speech form that is occasionally found in print other than reported speech. Its occurrence in print is not nearly as common as that of the plural *phenomena,* which we also have attested from speech.

A case can be made that the singular *phenomena,* now more than 400 years old, ought to be a recognized form. It is no more etymologically irregular than *stamina, agenda,* and *candelabra,* all of which are accepted as standard. As a form found mostly in speech, it has nowhere near the use in print that, say, *stamina* has. Until it gets more regular use in print, however, it must be considered a borderline form at best. You can be a pioneer, if you wish, but we do not recommend it.

For other foreign plurals, see LATIN PLURALS.

phone Prentice Hall 1978 and Bell & Cohn 1981 tell us in all seriousness that *phone* is colloquial and not to be used in formal writing. The ban on *phone* was announced by Emily Post back in 1927. It was one of a number of clipped forms—*auto* and *photo* were two others—that were viewed askance by linguistic etiquette books (such as MacCracken & Sandison 1917) in the early years of this century. In the same list with *phone,* Emily Post included *mints.* No usage writer has commented on that one.

If Emily Post's ideal Mrs. Worldly would never have said *phone* in 1927, she probably would say it today. You need not give its use in writing at any level a second thought, though the unclipped *telephone* is equally available if you prefer it.

phony, phoney Copperud 1980, who is primarily concerned with American use, says that while Fowler 1965 and the dictionaries recognize the spelling *phoney,* it is not used. This statement is not accurate.

Here is how the spellings stack up today. *Phoney* is the usual spelling in British English; *phony* is seldom found there (though we do have Australian evidence for it). Both *phony* and *phoney* are found in American English, but *phony* is the predominant form by quite a wide margin.

phth When this cluster of consonants occurs in words such as in *diphtheria, diphthong,* or *naphtha,* the recommended pronunciation is with \fth\, but the most usual version is \pth\. The popular version may even be heard in the speech of specialists: our pronunciation files attest \'dip-ˌthäŋ\ from linguists and \'thir-ē-ə\ from distinguished doctors. *Ophthalmia* and *ophthalmologist,* being rarer words, are more likely to get \f\, but again we have heard \p\ versions even from physicians. (This last-named word presents another trap: we have instances of ophthalmologists and professors of medicine saying \ˌäf-thə-ˈmäl-ə-jəst\, skipping over the *l* before the *m.*)

pianist One sometimes reads that musicians themselves say \'pē-ə-nəst\; one sometimes hears, on the other hand, that this pronunciation, while posh, is prissy and obnoxious. In our own file of pronunciations, \pē-ˈan-əst\ seems to prevail among classical musicians and radio announcers, while some very unassuming people have been recorded as saying \'pē-ə-nəst\. In any event, if our pianist accompanies a violinist, he or she is an \ə-ˈkəmp-ə-nəst\, not an \ə-ˈkämp-ə-nē-əst\. Although we note that Dickens once wrote *accompanyist,* the accepted pronunciation matches the accepted spelling, *accompanist.*

piece, peace A few schoolbooks and handbooks warn against confusing *piece* with *peace.* This would seem a schoolchild's error, but in fact adults in their less attentive moments do sometimes botch the two.

Piece is also one of those *-ie-* words that get misspelled with *-ei-*. The old reminder for vowel order used to be "piece of pie." Our examples of the misspelling are old, but they are genuine. We suggest you take care with these homophones.

pique When the verb *pique* is used in passive constructions and is followed by a preposition, the preposition is usually *at* or *by*. Either preposition is possible when the meaning of *pique* is "to irritate":

> . . . she had been piqued at my discovery of her in one of her most secret hiding-places —W. H. Hudson, *Green Mansions,* 1904

> The Swiss will be piqued at the U.S. because of the higher tariff —*Wall Street Jour.,* 30 July 1954

> . . . he seemed piqued, too, by what he considered to be a premature disclosure of the plan —Trevor Armbrister, *Saturday Evening Post,* 12 Feb. 1966

> . . . I think she was piqued . . . by my victory —George P. Elliott, *Esquire,* March 1970

When *pique* means "to excite or arouse," the preposition of choice is *by*:

> One's interest is piqued but not captured by the chronicle of this weak-willed man —*N.Y. Times,* 25 May 1952

In an old sense, now much less often used, *pique* means "to pride" and is followed, like *pride,* by either *on* or *upon:*

> . . . Mary, who piqued herself upon the solidity of her reflections —Jane Austen, *Pride and Prejudice,* 1813

> Horace Winterton piqued himself on this —Sylvia Townsend Warner, *New Yorker,* 8 Mar. 1952

See also PEAK, PEEK, PIQUE.

piteous, pitiable, pitiful What *piteous, pitiable,* and *pitiful* have in common is that each of them is used to mean "arousing pity or compassion." The OED notes that in this sense, *piteous* first occurred around 1290, *pitiable* in 1456, and *pitiful* around 1450. While all three words are still used in this way, *piteous* seems to occur less often than *pitiable* or *pitiful:*

> . . . no piteous cry or agonised entreaty, would make them even look at me —Bram Stoker, *Dracula,* 1897

> Such piteous reports arrived of poor persons camped on the Philadelphia common and orphans taking refuge in almshouses —James MacGregor Burns, *The Vineyard of Liberty,* 1981

> . . . Gatsby, a man who happened to have a lot of money but was not a rich man, was made so pitiable that there were those who loved him —John O'Hara, Introduction to an edition of *The Great Gatsby,* 1945

> He felt a tender pity for her, mixed with shame for having made her pitiable —Bernard Malamud, *The Assistant,* 1957

> As a woman, she had to feel sorry for any girl, no matter what a pitiful, poor, pathetic creature she was —James T. Farrell, *What Time Collects,* 1964

> . . . has arrived at the knowledge that man is the pitiful victim of a pointless joke —Archibald MacLeish, *Saturday Rev.,* 13 Nov. 1971

Pitiable and *pitiful* also share a second sense, "evoking mingled pity and contempt especially because of inadequacy.' *Pitiful* is somewhat more frequent:

> The resorting to epithets . . . is a pitiable display of intellectual impotence —Morris R. Cohen, *The Faith of a Liberal,* 1946

> . . . revolutionary rhetoric nourishes resentments and self-deceptions that are worse than ludicrous or pitiable —Benjamin DeMott, *Atlantic,* March 1970

> The most important impediment to obtaining efficient administrative officials . . . has been the pitiful wage scale —Harry S. Truman, *Message to Congress,* 6 Sept. 1945

> The man who after Eugene O'Neill was our best playwright—I say *was* because his later plays have been pitiful travesties of his beautiful early ones —Simon 1980

Although *piteous* is not often used in this sense, it does occur:

> In the club "library," a piteous collection of a couple of hundred dated, dog-eared Victorian popular editions —Benny Green, *Punch,* 27 Apr. 1976

place See ANYPLACE; EVERYPLACE; NOPLACE; SOMEPLACE.

plan 1. A few commentators—Harper 1985, Janis 1984, Copperud 1970, 1980, Bryson 1984—take note of various combinations of words with *plan* that they consider redundant. These combinations tend to serve the purpose of narrowing the focus of the verb—the verb having more than one sense (although the commentators take no account of this very relevant consideration). Among such combinations are *plan ahead, plan in advance,* and, presumably, *plan out,* which is an old idiom:

> It grieved Piet to see her beg, to see her plan ahead —John Updike, *Couples,* 1968

. . . I would take up my seven-page single-spaced typed outline, and see what I had planned ahead for the next day —Irving Wallace, *The Writer,* November 1968

You can use the automatic toll gates only if you have the exact change. That means to go through all of them without waiting in line at the manned gates, you have to plan in advance to have six quarters, two dimes and a nickel —*And More by Andy Rooney,* 1982

As he was ready to entertain himself with future pleasures, he had planned out a scheme of life in the country —Samuel Johnson, *Life of Savage,* 1744

. . . she was not yet incapable of planning out a day for herself —Elizabeth Bowen, *The Hotel,* 1927

. . . lesser towns like Silchester, which the Romans planned out in their rectangular fashion —G. M. Trevelyan, *A Shortened History of England,* 1942

The noun combinations of *future plans* and *advance plans* are also mentioned by the critics—they seem to be primarily spoken usages. **2.** *Plan on, plan to. Plan on,* followed by the gerund, is a standard American idiom, according to Evans 1957 and Watt 1967. A few handbooks insist that in formal use it be replaced by *plan to* followed by the infinitive:

Always signal well in advance if you plan to slow down for a turn —Julie Candler, *Ford Truck Times,* Summer 1970

Give them away, or plan to take them with you —Anna Fisher Rush, *McCall's,* March 1971

Our evidence suggests that *plan on* is more often found in spoken than in written use; we have few printed examples.

I will be discharged from the service in early 1979 and plan on returning to the States —Russ Sherlock, *Cats Mag.,* December 1977

Plan on is also used with a noun object:

If you're having a luncheon, plan on cheese sandwiches with . . . —radio broadcast, 4 Mar. 1975

playwright, playwrite The *-wright* in *playwright* is from an obsolete sense of *wright* that meant "maker" (in the formation of words such as *wheelwright, shipwright,* and *wainwright* it means "maker" or "worker in wood"). The potential for confusion with *write* is always lurking in *playwright,* though it finds its way into print less frequently than you might think—so infrequently that *playwrite* remains a misspelling.

A simplistic work about an idealistic black playwrite —*New York,* 3 Feb. 1975

When we move to verb and verbal use, though, the dormant tension between the two spellings and between the equally appropriate meanings of their second elements rises to the surface. Usage writers disagree: Shaw 1987, Bremner 1980, and Bernstein 1977 prefer *playwriting*; Garner 1998 prefers *playwrighting.* Our current evidence shows *playwriting* more common than *playwrighting*:

. . . Racine gave up playwriting as soon as he won a pension and a place in court —Robert Darnton, *The Kiss of Lamourette,* 1990

. . . most of my playwriting life —S. N. Behrman, *New Yorker,* 20 May 1972

. . . took a break from playwriting one summer to knock out a best seller —David Quammen, *N.Y. Times Book Rev.,* 30 Oct. 1988

"Polished, urbane, and adult playwrighting in the musical field," Porter ruefully observed at the time, "is strictly a creative luxury" —Ethan Mordden, *New Yorker,* 28 Oct. 1991

. . . an Obie Award for playwrighting —Glenna Sloan, *Language Arts,* November–December 1981

plead **1.** *Plead* belongs to the same class of verbs as *bleed, lead, speed, read,* and *feed,* and like them it has a past and past participle with a short vowel spelled *pled* or sometimes *plead.* Competing with the short-vowel form from the beginning was a regular form *pleaded.* Eventually *pleaded* came to predominate in mainstream British English, while *pled* retreated into Scottish and other dialectal use. Through Scottish immigration or some other means, *pled* reached America and became established here.

In the late 19th and early 20th centuries, *pled* was attacked by many American commentators. In spite of occasional backward-looking by a commentator or two, it is fully respectable today. Both *pled* (or *plead*) and *pleaded* are in good use in the U.S. *Pled* seems still to be current in Scottish use. A few examples of the disputed form:

Both pled not guilty —Ernest McIntyre, *Glasgow Herald,* 12 June 1974

. . . a scene, for whose life I pled, vainly —Sinclair Lewis, "The Art of Dramatization," 1933

My mother pled with the girl's mother to allow her to let the dress down —Nancy Hale, *New Yorker,* 20 Nov. 1965

please

2. A few commentators are fond of pointing out that in the courtroom one must plead "guilty" or "not guilty" and that one may not plead "innocent." In life outside the courtroom, however, *plead innocent* is very common and perfectly respectable. *Plead innocent* is the usual phrase used on radio and television, undoubtedly because it cannot be misheard for *plead guilty*. Both forms can be found in newspaper accounts:

> . . . pleaded innocent before Criminal Court Judge Jerome Kay —*Springfield* (Mass.) *Morning Union,* 13 May 1986

> . . . pled not guilty and was found not guilty —*Monte Vista* (Colo.) *Jour.,* 18 Jan. 1973

please When *please* is used in the passive voice or when it takes a direct object, it is often followed by *to* and an infinitive:

> "I'm always pleased to meet a new member of the Company." —James Jones, *From Here to Eternity,* 1951

> . . . have ceased to lie to themselves, ceased the pretense we are pleased to label sanity —Richard Schickel, *Harper's,* April 1971

Also found quite frequently with the passive *pleased* are prepositional phrases beginning with *with, about,* or *by,* and clauses:

> He gets more pleased with himself with each new film —Arthur M. Schlesinger, Jr., *Saturday Rev.,* 1 Apr. 1978

> I am very much pleased about what you have done with the manuscript —Flannery O'Connor, letter, 3 Feb. 1949

> . . . were more irked than pleased by these signs of progress —Virginia Douglas Dawson & Betty Douglas Wilson, *The Shape of Sunday,* 1952

> People in Britain are pleased that Sir Winston Churchill and Anthony Eden are meeting the President —Hugh Gaitskell, *N.Y. Times Mag.,* 27 June 1954

pleasing The adjective *pleasing,* when used with a preposition, is usually followed by *to* and a noun or by *to* and an infinitive:

> . . . its streamlined shape is pleasing to the eye and appeals to the esthetic sense —Harry G. Armstrong, *Principles and Practice of Aviation Medicine,* 1939

> Clapp's Unitarian doctrines were pleasing to some of his old congregation —*American Guide Series: Louisiana,* 1941

> That is why the form (the short story) is so infinitely pleasing to work on —Margaret Shedd, *The Writer,* May 1968

pled See PLEAD 1.

plentitude A couple of critics say that *plentitude* is not the word; it is *plenitude*; Garner 1998 finds *plentitude* a common misspelling. But it is only a less frequent variant of *plenitude* formed under the influence of *plenty*. It has been around since 1615 (*plenitude* is a couple of centuries older). It is used in the same sorts of contexts that *plenitude* is, but not nearly as often. Here are a couple of samples:

> It was an attrition strategy that relied on a plentitude of American-supplied resources —Neil Sheehan, *A Bright Shining Lie,* 1988

> . . . uses punny free-associative wordplay to decode the obvious and vacuum up the teeming plentitude of apparent nothing —James Wolcott, *New Republic,* 12 June 1995

plenty *Plenty* is a short word with all the vigor of speech. As such it has long been a source of worry for those who concern themselves with purity and propriety of speech. The critics started on *plenty* back in the 18th century and have not stopped yet. Like some other long-lived controversies, this one has developed new grounds for objection as the old grounds have lost interest. We will take up four separate issues here.

1. *Predicate adjective.* The original objection to *plenty* was to its use as a predicate adjective. Samuel Johnson in his Dictionary of 1755 may have been the first to take a stand; he deemed *plenty* a noun substantive and he thought it used "barbarously" as an adjective meaning "plentiful." He gave two citations, however, one from the 16th-century writer Thomas Tusser and the other from Shakespeare. Shakespeare's line has subsequently been quoted often:

> If reasons were as plenty as blackberries, I would give no man a reason upon compulsion —*I Henry IV,* 1598

Joseph Priestley in his 1768 edition also deemed *plenty* a noun and noted its use where *plentiful* would have served; he did not especially disparage the use, but he did seem to consider it aberrant. Campbell 1776, however, is forthright: he calls it "so gross a vulgarism" that he would not have included it at all had he not "sometimes found it in works of considerable merit."

The OED shows that the adjectival *plenty* had been in use since the 14th century. At the time Campbell was being outraged, the following writers were using *plenty* (both quotations are from the Century Dictionary):

> They seem formed for those countries where shrubs are plenty and water scarce —Oliver Goldsmith

When labourers are plenty, their wages will be low —Benjamin Franklin

Nineteenth-century and early 20th-century commentators kept *plenty* under fire. An exasperated editor working on Webster's Second wrote on a slip noting some of their opinions, "This is cheap pedantic Bosh." And bosh it was. The evidence shows that the predicate adjective *plenty* was in respectable literary use at least through the 19th century, although it is not very common in the 20th. Here are three older American examples:

Their peculiar oaths were getting as plenty as pronouns —Richard Henry Dana, *Two Years Before the Mast,* 1840

. . . churches are plenty, graveyards are plenty, but morals and whisky are scarce —Mark Twain, *Innocents Abroad,* 1869 (OED Supplement)

Bread is never too plenty in Indian households —Willa Cather, *Death Comes for the Archbishop,* 1927

2. *Attributive adjective.* Fowler 1926, finds the attributive use similar to others in which a noun has come to be used as an attributive adjective with *of* omitted: "a little brandy," "a dozen apples." The construction was used by Robert Browning:

One block, pure green as a pistachio-nut, There's plenty jasper somewhere in the world. . .
—"The Bishop Orders His Tomb at Saint Praxed's Church," 1855

Fowler opined that this construction was "still considered a solecism"; those few American commentators who bother to mention the construction all find something wrong with it.

The evidence for this use of *plenty* is hard to characterize. Browning is certainly literary, and we do have some later literary use. Most use, however, would appear to be spoken. OED and OED Supplement evidence seems to show that the main use lies outside of standard British English; besides the OED Scots examples, the Supplement provides American, Irish, Australian, and Caribbean examples and a hint of African use via Graham Greene. Here are some examples from our files:

He is not only a Humorist but has got plenty money to show that he is —Will Rogers, *The Illiterate Digest,* 1924

The answer to that was that if they did, he would immediately do something else, and find plenty reasons to support him —Maurice Hewlett, *Halfway House,* 1908

. . . Greek ships had plenty freight —U.S. Naval Institute, *Proceedings,* June 1938

. . . she would close up at 5 P.M. and leave plenty memos —Christopher Morley, *The Man Who Made Friends With Himself,* 1949

There were plenty days when they didn't even eat —John Dos Passos, *Number One,* 1943

After the arms program tapers off, there is plenty work to be done —*Time,* 5 Jan. 1953

But we have found little evidence in print recently, which leads us to suspect that the attributive adjective *plenty* is at present chiefly in spoken use.

3. *Adverb.* The OED dates adverbial use—more or less as an intensifier—to the 1840s. The OED notes that the adverb is in widespread British and American colloquial use. Fowler 1926 calls it "colloquial, but not literary, English." Some more recent commentators—Harper 1985, for instance—term the adverbial use "informal," while others—such as Readers' Digest 1983—consider it nonstandard. A few handbooks prescribe *very, quite,* or *fully* in place of *plenty,* but the prescription is not a remedy in every case—*plenty* can carry a notion of "more than enough" that the suggested replacements lack. The adverbial *plenty* has its own place and may not always be easily substituted for.

We know the adverbial *plenty* to be common in speech. It is also frequent in writing, although not in writing of the starchier sort. Here are numerous examples of use:

It's already plenty hot for us in the kitchen without some dolt opening the oven doors —Colton H. Bridges, *Massachusetts Wildlife,* November–December 1975

I've played under four managers in the big leagues, and each one was plenty smart —Ted Williams, *Saturday Evening Post,* 17 Apr. 1954

A couple of minutes later she came down looking plenty excited —Erle Stanley Gardner, *The Case of the Stuttering Bishop,* 1936

. . . I am a lot better and plenty good enough for my purposes —E. B. White, letter, January 1945

The boat still averaged 71.9 mph—plenty fast enough —Bob Ottum, *Sports Illustrated,* 19 Nov. 1984

. . . a calm, thoughtful man of forty-five, who has got around plenty . . . in belles-lettres —Bernard Kalb, *Saturday Rev.,* 9 May 1953

The drinks may have been soft, but . . . the advertising claims were plenty hard —David M. Schwartz, *Smithsonian,* July 1986

That memory made me feel freshly linked up with my father. . . . I fought plenty with him —Benjamin DeMott, *N.Y. Times Mag.*, 17 Feb. 1985

While Gutman goes easy—too easy—on Parcells, Parcells is plenty hard on himself —Allen St. John, *N.Y. Times Book Rev.*, 22 Oct. 2000

4. *Used with "more."* Evans 1957 says that *plenty* may be followed by *more*, with or without a noun following *more*, wisely avoiding the trap of trying to categorize such use of *plenty* as belonging to one or another of the traditional parts of speech. Here is one of those annoyingly hard-to-classify constructions where something that may or may not follow the word in question presumably has a hand in determining its part of speech. Here are a couple of examples, for which we will let you pick your own part of speech:

. . . we have plenty more to say on the subject —*New Yorker*, 22 Nov. 1952

The accidental century surely has plenty more accidents in store —*Times Literary Supp.*, 31 Mar. 1966

I do not regret these two sentences. . . . There were plenty more where they came from —Anthony Loyd, *My War Gone By*, 1999

Conclusion: The use of *plenty* will always have its detractors among the usage commentators. It is too vigorous, too much like plain talk for the sort of writing they seem to prefer. Almost every use that *plenty* has has been questioned at one time or another; all the same, the uses that are still current are also standard, at least in relaxed surroundings. We think you should feel free to use *plenty* where it sounds right to you.

plethora   **1.** Sometimes the remarks of a usage commentator will alert the lexicographer to the development of a new sense of a word, and sometimes they can remind the lexicographer that dictionary treatment has not been quite as clear as it should have been. The complaint of Bryson 1984 that a plethora "is not merely a lot, it is an excessive amount" seems to indicate the latter problem. Lexicographers have tended to lump together the common uses of the word, and "excessive amount" is the primary organizing notion. Reader's Digest 1983, however, descries two closely related but slightly different senses— "abundant supply" and "overabundant supply"—which more accurately describe 20th-century usage.

We can shed a bit more light on this matter by showing some examples of how the word has been used in the past hundred years. First,

here are some examples of the undesirable or overabundant *plethora*:

Organization chokes now and then on the plethora of detail —Wallace Stegner, *N.Y. Times Book Rev.*, 24 Feb. 1985

. . . a plethora of regulatory bills is pending before Congress —Ted Lewis, *Scientific American*, November 1997

. . . one needs the patience of Job and the leisure of Sardanapalus to plough through the plethora of references —Dwight Macdonald, *New Yorker*, 29 Nov. 1952

These all connote excess. In the next two examples we see the undesirable *plethora* without any clear connotation of excess:

. . . the term began with a plethora of irritating duties —Harold J. Laski, letter, 29 Sept. 1917

Early meetings experienced, as most early ones do, a dearth of good horses and a plethora of complaints —Red Smith, *Saturday Evening Post*, 29 June 1957

And we can sometimes find the notion of excess without a strong suggestion of undesirability:

Callow, inexperienced, and unripe despite his plethora of wives —Irving Howe, *Harper's*, October 1970

. . . a plethora of therapeutic choices make the acceptance of treatments an arduous process —Charles Marwick, *JAMA*, 3 Dec. 1997

Then we have the plain "abundance, profusion" sense of *plethora* in which there are connotations neither of excess nor of undesirability:

. . . Leonardo, with his plethora of talents —*Atlantic*, February 1939

The ads for the six gadgets promise a plethora of benefits —*Consumer Reports*, November 1978

. . . he also dangles the names of a plethora of other suspected traitors —Edward Jay Epstein, *N.Y. Times Book Rev.*, 18 May 1980

Daily the world enters our homes through the newspapers, magazines, television, and a plethora of new books, to feed the natural curiosity of the young —Milton S. Eisenhower, *Johns Hopkins Mag.*, February 1966

The lagoon of the marsh already attracts a plethora of wildlife —Jane Kay, *San Francisco Chronicle*, 30 Apr. 2001

Plethora, then, may connote an undesirable excess, an undesirably large supply but not an excess, an excess that is not necessarily or not greatly undesirable, and simply an abundant supply. All of these uses are well attested and standard.

2. *Plethora* is a singular noun with a plural *plethoras* that is seen only once in a while. It often occurs in the phrase *a plethora of* followed by a plural noun. When this unit governs the verb of a sentence, notional agreement holds sway. Writers who view the plethora as a lump use a singular verb; those who view it as a collection of discrete items use a plural verb:

> . . . the plethora of retellings which descends on the market —*Times Literary Supp.*, 22 Oct. 1971

> . . . a plethora of spurious Rodin drawings were glutting the market —Katharine Kuh, *Saturday Rev.*, 25 Dec. 1971

plunge   When *plunge* is used with a preposition, it is used most often with *into*:

> . . . Mr. Hawkins, snatching the receiver, plunged into a long conversation with some unknown person —Dorothy L. Sayers, *Murder Must Advertise*, 1933

> He plunged at once into the two reviews that I had recently written —Allen Tate, *Prose*, Fall 1971

Plunge is also frequently used with *in*:

> . . . bending over the dish-pan with her arms plunged in soapsuds —Ellen Glasgow, *Barren Ground*, 1925

> . . . a puritan of a different type, who regards most of us as pretty irrevocably plunged in illusion —Iris Murdoch, *The Fire and the Sun*, 1977

Less frequently, *plunge* is used with *through* or *to*:

> . . . rock-walled coulees through which a mighty river once plunged —*American Guide Series: Washington*, 1941

> The bears fare best who take a risk, such as . . . plunging through a populated area —Edward Hoagland, *Harper's*, February 1971

> . . . saboteurs stuck limpet mines on two gun-running yachts, plunging them to the harbor's bottom —*Newsweek*, 30 Dec. 1957

> We drove into the smoke, and visibility plunged to near zero —Fred Ward, *National Geographic*, January 1972

Plunge is also used with *beneath, down, for, on, over, toward,* or *towards*:

> . . . the road plunged beneath over-arching trees —Dorothy L. Sayers, *Murder Must Advertise*, 1933

> . . . the whole herd . . . plunged down the steep bank of Sugar River —Edmund Wilson, *New Yorker*, 5 June 1971

> Those who plunge for any uncomplicated view of society are bound to have trouble in understanding . . . natural law —Robert M. Hutchins, *Center Mag.*, November/December 1971

> . . . embezzling about $400,000 to plunge on the stock market —*Times-Picayune* (New Orleans), 6 May 1952

> . . . plunged headlong over the side of the boat —Elizabeth George Speare, *The Witch of Blackbird Pond*, 1958

> . . . showed the world was plunging toward destruction —Oscar Handlin, *The American People in the Twentieth Century*, 1954

> . . . as the Age of Reason plunged towards revolution —*Times Literary Supp.*, 12 Nov. 1954

plupluperfect   English abounds in surprising constructions. Various observers have commented on the fact that in speech the ordinary past tense (*ate*) often replaces the present perfect tense (*have eaten*) or the pluperfect or past perfect tense (*had eaten*). And we find other observers commenting on the fact that the pluperfect is—in speech again—often supplied with an extra auxiliary (*had have eaten*). A correspondent of the magazine *English Today* named Ian Watson wrote in April 1986 commenting on this use, which he dubbed *plupluperfect*. He quoted a British politician named Jim Prior who used the plupluperfect in a radio interview:

> If I had've been there. . . .

Subsequent correspondence in the same magazine showed that the construction was by no means new, having been traced by historical grammarians to the 15th century. The OED under *have*, definition 26, notes that in the 15th and 16th centuries there are many instances of a superfluous *had* or *have* in compound tenses. The editors give several examples, of which the most recent is dated 1768.

The present-day version of the construction seems usually to show *have* as the extra auxiliary. In speech this *have* tends to be unstressed and reduced, and in written representations of speech it comes out spelled *'ve, a,* or *of*. We have already seen an example of *'ve*. Paul Christophersen in *English Today*, October 1986, gives these examples of *a*:

> . . . if we'd a left the blame tools at the dead tree we'd a got the money —Mark Twain, *Tom Sawyer*, 1876

> If we'd a-known that before, we'd not a-started out with you so early —John Galsworthy, *Strife*, 1909

We have these examples spelled *of*:

"It was four o'clock in the morning then, and if we'd of raised the blinds we'd of seen daylight." —F. Scott Fitzgerald, *The Great Gatsby,* 1925

"The army ain't got none like mine," says Daley. "I guess they wished they had of had. . . ." —Ring Lardner, *The Big Town,* 1921

(The contraction *-'d* in the examples from Twain, Galsworthy, and Fitzgerald makes it impossible to be sure that these are not, rather, examples of *would have* and so not the true plupluperfect.)

Partridge 1942 points out that the construction is by no means confined to the illiterate, although the fictional examples presented so far are surely intended for characters of little education. Partridge cites an unnamed novel in which an educated character has these musings:

"But then . . . should I have been any more understanding if I hadn't have happened to have been there that afternoon. . . ."

And Christophersen gives an example from a 1976 English examination paper:

If the two had have been married, Criseyde would not have had to be exchanged for Antenor.

The construction would have to be judged nonstandard in ordinary written discourse, but we have no evidence that it ever occurs there, at least in the edited varieties.

Christophersen's article in *English Today* gives a historical account of the construction and two explanations of its origin that have been put forward. No one is really certain how the construction arose, and no one seems to have advanced a theory to account for its use. In its modern manifestation the plupluperfect seems to occur in the conditional clause of a hypothetical or counterfactual statement, so it may be related to the limitations of the modern subjunctive which, except for the verb *be,* is unmarked for tenses of past time. This construction, a similar one with *would,* may simply represent an attempt by the speaker to impose a subjunctive marker on the standard past perfect.

So we have, on the one hand, a tendency to replace the pluperfect with the simple past and, on the other, a tendency to emphasize the pluperfect with an extra auxiliary or even to create a sort of pluperfect subjunctive. Who said English was plain and simple?

plurality See MAJORITY 4.

plurals Rules for the formation of plurals can be found in many dictionaries, handbooks, and style manuals, and we do not intend to summarize them all here. Several special aspects of plural formation, however, have received attention in a number of usage books, and we will note them briefly.

1. *Proper names.* Personal names, especially those ending in *-s,* seem to be the proper nouns most often mentioned in usage books. The standard way of pluralizing most problematic proper names is shown in this example:

. . . to think of these characters of fiction—from the Charlie McCarthys and the Mr. Chipses and Mrs. Minivers of the present hour—back to the Huck Finns and the Pickwicks —Leacock 1943

Use of an apostrophe to form the plural of a name like *Mr. Chips* is considered by many to be an error. (There is a fuller treatment of proper nouns in *Merriam-Webster's Manual for Writers and Editors.*)

2. *Letters, numerals, symbols, and other oddities.* Older style recommended apostrophe plus *-s* to make the plurals of such things as *1, 1920,* and *&.* Newer style recommends just *-s.* Currently the older style and the newer style are used with about equal frequency. In the following example the author has chosen apostrophe plus *-s* to pluralize sounds spelled in ordinary letters:

We sprinkle our speech with nonverbal sound effects, snorts and mm's, sighs and tsk's —Mitchell 1979

See also APOSTROPHE 3.

plus The little four-letter word *plus* has prompted quite a bit of commentary in recent times. The two uses exciting the most interest are, grammatically, conjunctive and adverbial. Even though not a few commentators have mixed these together, we will treat them separately for clarity's sake.

1. *Conjunctive use. Plus* used as a conjunction springs directly from its earlier use as a preposition. There are two somewhat differing conjunctive uses which spring from two senses of the preposition. The first of these is found in the familiar "two plus two makes four." In this use *plus* means the same as *and* but demonstrates its prepositional character by not affecting the number of the verb. With *plus* used this way, the singular verb seems to be the standard in mathematics; there may be difficulties when non-mathematicians get involved, and these are explored at TWO AND TWO.

But *plus* does not limit itself to mathematical contexts. It has slipped out into general use. Ordinarily this use is acceptably prepositional; sometimes the prepositional character is emphasized when *plus* occurs between two noun phrases governing a verb:

This plus the old bitterness of Berliners . . . has made for a certain amount of ill-feeling —Walter Sullivan, *N.Y. Times,* 22 Mar. 1953

The partition of Germany, plus the Cold War, has cut off markets —Percy W. Bidwell, *Yale Rev.,* June 1953

. . . but fantasy plus fantasy adds up —Phoebe-Lou Adams, *Atlantic,* February 1972

As *plus* in its signification of "and" crept into general use, the likelihood increased that it would begin to be used like *and.* The first flares calling attention to this use were sent up by Theodore Bernstein. In Bernstein 1962 he exhibits this example:

This, plus a change in top management of the brewing company, are believed to be the factors responsible. . . .

He took the plural verb used here to mean that *plus* was being used as a conjunction, just like *and.* Perrin & Ebbitt 1972 has a similar example, perhaps a bit earlier:

The Smyth report, plus an idea and some knowledge of bureaucracy, were all I needed —Pat Frank, *Saturday Rev.,* 24 Dec. 1960

These examples show *plus* beginning to be apprehended as a conjunction between the parts of a compound subject of a sentence. It had in fact been used earlier as a conjunction in less obvious circumstances: in the two following examples, *plus* is a coordinating conjunction between adjectives and between prepositional phrases:

. . . a mere box-office success like *Kiss and Tell* and a box-office plus critical and artistic success like *Strange Interlude* —George Jean Nathan, *The Theatre Book of the Year, 1949–1950*

For some years, the Morrisons have lived quietly in a modest house in Eltham, a London suburb, plus in a sliver of an apartment in an old-fashioned small hotel —Mollie Panter-Downes, *New Yorker,* 31 Mar. 1951

This older conjunctive use of *plus* seems, then, to have originated around 1950, and to be primarily a written use. It cannot be called nonstandard, but it does not seem to be especially common.

The prepositional *plus* has another sense that means "besides." It seems to be only a little older than the first conjunctive *plus:*

And they swing awesomely. Plus which they avoid as much as possible using the Dixie standards that have been played to death —*Down Beat,* 20 Oct. 1950

Also, there is that Major Douglas bug he swallowed. Plus his conviction that he has

read American history —Archibald MacLeish, letter, 27 July 1943

Sometime in the 1960s this sense of *plus* began to turn up, primarily in speech, meaning "besides which" and introducing a clause rather than a noun or pronoun to which a clause is attached:

"I'm not a mere producer," he announced proudly. "I take the stills, plus I play a part in the film. . . ." —*New Yorker,* 23 July 1966

This is a danger to youngsters going to and from school, plus it cuts off many areas of the community from fire protection —letter to the editor, *Salt Lake Tribune,* 5 Aug. 1968

She'd give him some money, plus she'd go to bed with him —Robin Langston, quoted in Studs Terkel, *Hard Times,* 1970

This second, primarily spoken conjunctive *plus* appears to be rather more common than our earlier conjunctive use. But its areas of application, so far, are limited almost entirely to speech, advertising, and breezy prose:

If you want to make a superinvestment plus you don't happen to be rich —radio commercial, 22 Aug. 1973

. . . can emulate any standard HASP multileaving workstation in RJE mode, plus it can operate as a host to other workstations —advt., *Datamation,* December 1982

A fan gets to see new artists and new shows every year at Fan Fair, plus we get to see other fans —Loudilla Johnson, quoted in *People,* 27 June 1983

. . . once the hustling and shooting started up again, she couldn't manage without a nanny—plus there was the hefty expense —Robert Sawyer, *Metropolitan Home,* July 1984

This later conjunctive *plus* is much more prominent right now than the older one, and it has been the subject of considerable adverse comment. As a speech form it is impervious to such comment, but it shows no sign just now of elbowing its way into serious prose. You will probably not want to use it in writing except, perhaps, in your breeziest stuff.

2. *Adverbial use.* What we are calling the adverbial use of *plus* is in fact a third use of the conjunction. It is called adverbial by some commentators, however, probably because it is close in meaning to the adverb *besides.* It differs from the second conjunctive use primarily in being used to introduce a sentence rather than to connect two clauses. It too seems to date from the 1960s.

I would have liked to have written that ad myself. Plus, this is a free country —letter to the editor, *Saturday Rev.,* 9 July 1966

. . . I am impelled to add my own pet peeve. . . . It is "Plus you get," for "In addition you receive" —letter to the editor, *Saturday Rev.,* 9 July 1966

This use of *plus* appears in the same sorts of places as the second conjunctive use—speech, advertising, and informal prose—but it seems to be a bit more respectable in that it is found more often in informal prose than the second conjunctive use is.

Plus it's coming in with two times the level of sodium —George Cross, quoted in *New England Farmer,* November 1982

Plus, I get upset about this book she's writing —Patrick Anderson, *Cosmopolitan,* July 1976

You've got your comforts and you've got to be thankful for that these days, what with everything. Plus we like to plan a few improvements round the place —*Punch,* 14 Apr. 1976

Unlike most of us, David doesn't rumple. Plus, he's too rich —Douglas S. Looney, *People,* 31 Jan. 1983

Plus, he's relaxed enough to joke —Christopher Connelly, *Houston Post,* 2 Sept. 1984

To sum up, the first conjunctive *plus* has been in respectable use all along. The second conjunctive *plus* calls attention to itself, and it has little use in discursive prose. The third conjunctive or adverbial *plus* is a little more respectable than the second conjunction; you might want to use it occasionally in informal prose—many writers seem to do so these days. Neither of the latter two usages appears in formal surroundings.

p.m. See A.M., P.M.

podium The definition of *lectern* in Webster's Second reads like this:

1. A choir desk, or reading desk, in some churches, from which the lections, or Scripture Lessons, are chanted or read. 2. A reading or writing desk; an escritoire. *Chiefly Scot.*

This definition seems to have prompted several letters enquiring about the correct term for whatever it was that an ordinary lay lecturer placed his or her notes on before addressing an audience. Slips in our files show that for Webster's Third the editor who worked on *lectern* was instructed in no uncertain terms to define it in such a way as to reflect actual usage of the word.

We do not know if newspaper writers baffled by the churchly definition of *lectern* were the first to use *podium* for the lectern of the ordinary lecturer or not. At any rate some newspaper writers did begin using *podium* in that sense (and so did some lecturers), and the Webster's Third definer of *podium,* finding journalistic evidence, included a definition of *podium* meaning "lectern." For this attention to duty, Webster's Third has been rebuked by a usage commentator or two. One wonders whether they have ever looked up *lectern* in Webster's Second, their favorite large dictionary.

The "lectern" sense of *podium* is a favorite bugbear of the journalistic commentators. Several make jokes about a *New York Times* example reading

President Ayub, wearing a gray summer suit, white shirt and gray necktie, gripped the podium tightly as he answered questions —18 July 1961

by suggesting that the poor man must have been on hands and knees, or flat on his face.

What goes unmentioned by the commentators, however, is that the average reader has not been put off or misled one bit. So what we have here is not really a usage problem at all—no one is confused or misled—but a usage writer's in-joke.

Our current evidence shows that the "lectern" sense of *podium* (signaled by such words as *pound, at, behind*) is commonly found in standard journalistic sources:

. . . rushed up . . . and began pounding the podium —Ryan Lizza, *New Republic,* 28 Feb. 2000

. . . the beefy fellow standing behind the podium —Brian Kelly *Newsweek,* 10 Aug. 1992

Thurow shuffled lecture notes at the podium —Charles C. Mann, *Atlantic,* January 1990

At the podium an elderly man was delivering a harangue —Christopher Hitchins, *Harper's,* October 1992

. . . the podium that held the guest book —Camille Minichino, *The Lithium Murder,* 1999

The older sense of podium (signaled by *on, onto*) is just as common. But more of our citations use the word in such a way that the precise meaning is not obvious. You need not worry when you use it.

poetess *Poetess,* Evans 1957 says, "emphasizes the sex of the writer when the sex is largely irrelevant." That, of course, is a modern view. An 1873 citation in the OED informs us that Homer and Sappho were considered so preeminent among the ancients that Homer was referred to simply as "the poet" and Sappho as "the poetess." The word, is still associated with Sappho:

> The most famous of all poetesses, Sappho —Chester G. Starr, *A History of the Ancient World,* 1991

Copperud 1970, 1980 tells us that *poetess* has fallen into disuse; he is, without knowing it, repeating the opinion of Priestley in 1768, who pronounced it almost obsolete. Fitzedward Hall 1873, who dug out Priestley's comment, thought the word established.

Shaw 1987 observes that *poetess* and several other words ending in -*ess* were considered offensive "even before the women's lib movement." This is true, but the grounds on which they offended apparently had little to do with women's sensibilities. The attack seems to have been started by Edward S. Gould in 1867. His comments show him to have been offended by most compounds ending in -*ess,* which he seems to have considered neologisms (even though *poetess* has been in English since 1530). He had a number of other objections, none of them very concretely grounded, and thought we were in danger of being swamped with -*ess* coinages. Ayres 1881 quoted Gould with approbation and Bierce 1909 thought *poetess* "a foolish word." Richard Grant White 1870, on the other hand, found nothing especially objectionable about such words and considered the objections to be based on personal taste alone.

There is evidence that women have found the word objectionable. The OED has a 1748 citation from a Lady Luxborough, who calls *poetess* "a reproachful name," and in 1976 the scholar and teacher Helen Bevington was quoted in the *Saturday Review* as calling it "that mortifying word."

> She is a poet (she hates to be called a poetess) —*Time,* 17 Jan. 1955

Most of our evidence for *poetess* is neutral in tone. Some writers and reviewers seem to find it a handy way to identify sex and occupation in a single word:

> . . . the academic poetess who didn't receive tenure —Lewis H. Lapham, *Harper's,* August 1997

> . . . bizarre dialogue, in which a would-be poetess and a failed ballet dancer discuss "art" —James Campbell, *Times Literary Supp.,* 22 Aug. 1980

> The slim, shy poetess —John Updike, *Bech Is Back,* 1982

Occasionally we find a writer who assumes that *poet* designates males only:

> Among the poets and poetesses of the period —Donald C. Masters, *A Short History of Canada,* 1958

But in more cases it is used where there is no question about the sex of the writer:

> Fronted by the enigmatic punk poetess Polly Jane Harvey —Jeff Giles & Chris Mundy, *Rolling Stone,* 10–24 Dec. 1992

> She was a noted poetess and a famous beauty —Cornell H. Fleischer, *Bureaucrat & Intellectual in the Ottoman Empire,* 1986

> Anne Morrow Lindbergh, a poetess, philosopher and novelist —Donald Robinson, *Ladies' Home Jour.,* January 1971

It looks to us as though *poetess* is still alive, in spite of opinions to the contrary, is still associated with Sappho, and is still found useful by reviewers and other writers. It is clearly offensive to some women writers, but it generally seems in intention to be neutral. All the same, it does seem to be used at times when *poet* would work just as well.

See -ESS.

point in time Bureaucracy makes an easy target for criticism of many kinds, not excluding criticism of English usage. Harper 1975, 1985, for instance, has a whole entry devoted to *bureaucratic barbarism.* Part of this entry reads

> The tendency of bureaucrats to use two or three elaborate words or phrases when a simple word would suffice was never more in evidence than during the final months of the Nixon administration. . . . "At this (or that) point in time" became an instant cliché. . . .

Point in time (sometimes *point of time*) was indeed brought forcefully to public attention during the Senate Watergate hearings in 1973 and 1974, but it had been in use a long time before that. Arthur M. Schlesinger, Jr., mentioned the phrase as frequent among State Department people in the 1960s:

> . . . never said "at this time" but "at this point in time." —*A Thousand Days,* 1965 (in Nickles 1974)

But bureaucrats are hardly the only people to use the phrase. Usage commentators have been known to use it too:

> The first and obvious meaning is to put back to an earlier point of time —Harper 1975, 1985 (at *set back*)

> A locus of moods, impulses, ideas, behaviors, external forces, etc., at a given point in time and space —Thomas H. Middleton, *Saturday Rev.,* 4 Sept. 1976

Other writers on language and grammar have found it useful:

> The exact point in time has not yet been fixed —David Mellinkoff, *The Language of the Law*, 1963

> The other tenses, called perfect tenses, refer to time in a more complex way. They place an action or a statement in some relation to a specified point in time —Battles et al. 1982

> From a physical line not to be crossed, deadline evolved into a point in time not to be crossed —Craig M. Carver, *Atlantic*, November 1994

Many other writers use it:

> All of these men felt . . . that their life's work was, at each point in time, breaking against the shore of the moment —Donald Hall, *Goatfoot Milktongue Twinbird*, 1978

> At this point in time—1890—Independence was by no means the quaint little farming community —Margaret Truman, *Harry S. Truman*, 1972

> One has a strange propensity to fix upon some point of time from whence a better course of life may begin —James Boswell, *Journal of a Tour to the Hebrides*, 1785

> . . . sediments laid down at the so-called P-T boundary, the point in time between the Permian and Triassic periods —S. Perkins, *Science News*, 24 Feb. 2001

Bureaucrats can be blamed for a lot of things, but they cannot reasonably be blamed for *point in* (or *of*) *time*. The phrase can be shortened to *point* or *time* when the context is clear, but its use is a venial sin unless your space is limited.

point of view See STANDPOINT, VIEWPOINT.

politic, political Chambers 1985 distinguishes between *politic* and *political*. Actually *politic* is the earlier adjective used in reference to government and politics. *Political* has now superseded it in this use, except in the phrase *body politic*. *Politic* is now usually used to suggest shrewdness or tact:

> A punch in the nose is about as direct a statement as you can make, but it is not always politic —Red Smith, *N.Y. Times*, 6 Oct. 1980

politics *Politics* can take either a singular or a plural verb. When it means "a person's political opinions or sympathies," it is quite likely to be plural:

> Mr. Trumbo's politics were not mine —Richard Schickel, *Harper's*, March 1971

> . . . his somewhat doctrinaire radical politics offer a refreshing contrast —Gerald Jonas, *N.Y. Times Book Rev.*, 20 July 1975

Other senses may be either singular or plural:

> . . . politics is fully as sophisticated . . . as psychiatry —Arthur M. Schlesinger, Jr., *Saturday Rev.*, 7 Sept. 1974

> . . . Catholic politics in that period are one of Dr. Spadolini's special subjects —*Times Literary Supp.*, 16 July 1970

> Japanese politics on the surface also seems wild and confusing —Edwin O. Reischauer, *The Lamp*, Summer 1970

> . . . bedroom politics continue to be more tempestuous than national politics —N. Weber, *Harper's Weekly*, 23 Aug. 1976

poorly Handbooks from MacCracken & Sandison 1917 to Macmillan 1982 have denigrated the adjective *poorly* used as a predicate adjective to indicate poor health; they call it provincial, colloquial, or dialectal. Since we cannot be sure what these folks mean by *colloquial* we pass over that label, but provincial or dialectal *poorly* is not. Reader's Digest 1983 calls it standard but not very formal, which is accurate. The statement in the Oxford American Dictionary that careful speakers say "feeling poor" is fiction. *Poor* used as a modifier of animate nouns to indicate health or physical condition is applied chiefly to domestic animals; it is applied to human beings chiefly in dialect.

The OED speculates that the adjective *poorly* developed from the use of the adverb after verbs like *look*, which is now a linking verb and takes an adjective complement, but which in the 17th and 18th centuries was commonly followed by an adverb. The OED has a 16th-century example of adverbial *poorly* after *look*, followed by predicate adjective uses from the mid-18th century on.

Here are some examples:

> . . . poor little Cassy is grown extremely thin & looks poorly —Jane Austen, letter, 14 Oct. 1813

> She was rather poorly or troubled in mind, he thought —Norman Douglas, *South Wind*, 1917

> She is poorly and has been debating for several weeks whether she should take a dose of calomel —Flannery O'Connor, letter, 11 Oct. 1958

> He lost a stone in weight and became even more poorly after catching a chill —David Frith, *The Sunday Times Mag.* (London), 12 May 1974

pore, pour Some confusion in the use—or, actually, the spelling—of these two verbs was first noted by Evans 1957. A brief discussion of the problem, such as it is, can now be found in many usage books. The mistake that occasionally occurs is that *pour* is used when less familiar *pore*, "to read or study attentively," is called for:

> . . . had been spent pouring over constantly revised lists —*Northeast Horseman,* June 1982

> . . . couples and families pouring over the racks of home viewing choices —*Sunday Denver Post,* 16 Sept. 1984

This mistaken use of *pour* is a recent development that seems to be growing more common in less attentively edited publications.

portentious *Portentious* is an alteration of *portentous* that seems rather to show the effect of the adjective ending -*ious,* as in *pretentious,* than to be a true blend of *portentous* and *pretentious.* The earliest citations have the same meaning as the earliest sense of *portentous;* only the spelling has changed. The OED Supplement's earliest example, dated 1863, is spelled *portenteous* (the OED and Garner 1998 have *portentuous* too); Archibald MacLeish in 1918 used the spelling *portentious* in a letter. Partridge 1942 notes that *portentious* "is seldom written but often uttered"; here too we see the apparent attraction of the -*ious* ending over -*ous.* Partridge notes a similar tendency with *presumptuous;* it is often pronounced, he says, as if it were spelled *presumptious.* A more familiar example of -*ious* for -*ous* is *grevious* (see GRIEVOUS).

Although *portentious* is still quite rare in print, it does make occasional appearances in standard sources, and it has developed derivatives:

> The issues discussed in this fashion are not resolved so much as reframed, sometimes to show the shallowness of portentious debates —Richard Harvey Brown, *American Historical Rev.,* October 1987

> . . . no soundtrack narrator portentiously telling us what we should be seeing, how we should feel —Vincent Canby, *N.Y. Times,* 4 Oct. 1967

> Portentiousness—a sense that something grave and grand, though incomprehensible, is nigh —Benjamin DeMott, *N.Y. Times Mag.,* 23 Mar. 1969

The OED Supplement seems to be the only dictionary so far to try to account for *portentious* and its offspring. We do not know if it will ever establish itself, but currently it is not a word that we recommend using. See also PORTENTOUS.

portentous *Portentous* has as its earliest sense "relating to or being a portent." It can be a more neutral adjective than the similar *ominous,* which has come to indicate only bad things to come. Here we have a few examples:

> . . . the dreadful omens and portentous sights and sounds in the air —Washington Irving, "The Legend of Sleepy Hollow," 1820

> . . . the stillness in the Ritz bar was strange and portentous —F. Scott Fitzgerald, "Babylon Revisited," 1931

> What seem trivial details to others may be portentous symbols to him —Harry Levin, *James Joyce,* 1941

Almost concurrently with its first use in the 16th century, *portentous* developed a second sense that in effect reflected a different point of view of the same phenomenon. If the earliest sense is focused on the portent, the second sense is focused on the observers and what they think of the event. This sense removes consideration of the future and concentrates on the thing or event itself; it means "eliciting amazement or wonder; prodigious, marvelous, monstrous."

> . . . the portentous strength of the Black Knight forced his way inward in despite of De Bracy and his followers —Sir Walter Scott, *Ivanhoe,* 1819

> . . . my books and files for the last two years are beginning to assume a portentous size —Henry Adams, letter, 6 Mar. 1863

> The Secretary of Agriculture was the owner of a portentous power: within discretion . . . he could raise support prices to 90% of parity whenever he thought it desirable —*Time,* 31 Oct. 1949

Floating somewhere between these two senses were various uses of the word in which the notion of grave consequences or of weightiness or importance were uppermost:

> The assassination in itself was easy, for Caesar would take no precautions. So portentous an intention could not be kept entirely secret —J. A. Froude, *Caesar,* 1879

> . . . when Mrs. Bridgetower was talking about any subject less portentous than the Oriental plottings in the Kremlin, she was apt to be heavily ironical —Robertson Davies, *Tempest-tost,* 1951

> . . . and still more must his future be considered, a problem too portentous to grasp —Marcia Davenport, *My Brother's Keeper,* 1954

An editor of Webster's Second noticed that this sort of use was quite often applied to people, their actions, and their manner, and wrote a third definition "grave, solemn, significant" which was later refined to get across the idea that it often means "affectedly solemn, pompous." We are not quite sure when the new sense arose, but it was well attested before 1934:

> He paused, softly portentous, where he stood, and so he met Rosanna's eyes —Henry James, *The Ivory Tower,* 1917

> . . . a parliamentary candidate, very properly got up for the job and with the portentous seriousness that comes from having a mission —Harold J. Laski, letter, 1 Nov. 1920

> Troop, Peter held, regarded all these things with a portentous solemnity —H. G. Wells, *Joan and Peter,* 1918

> . . . and then the portentous thought, when it comes, turns out to be one of the commonplaces of modern scientific philosophy —Edmund Wilson, *Axel's Castle,* 1931

This third sense has become fully established—helped no doubt by frequent use in *Time* and the *New Yorker* in the 1950s—and is still in frequent use, especially in criticism:

> To be portentous, one ought to be deeper than that —Mary McCarthy, *N.Y. Times Book Rev.,* 22 Apr. 1984

> . . . relatively free of the portentous air and slick packaging that characterize the big networks' news shows —Thomas Whiteside, *New Yorker,* 3 June 1985

> **portend** sounds . . . portentous —Flesch 1964

possessed When *possessed* is used as a form of the verb *possess* meaning "to make or be the owner," it is used with *of:*

> . . . this delicacy at least was possessed of one advantage —Osbert Sitwell, *Noble Essences,* 1950

> . . . Second Lieutenant Charles Carter, who . . . wrongfully possessed himself of Lieutenant Day's side arm —James Gould Cozzens, *Guard of Honor,* 1948

> . . . he finds himself possessed of an immense spiritual and physical loneliness —Hollis Albert, *Saturday Rev.,* 27 Mar. 1954

When *possessed* is used as a past participle or an adjective meaning "influenced or controlled," it is used with *by:*

> Lawrence, then, possessed, or, if you care to put it the other way round, was possessed by, a gift—a gift to which he was unshakeably loyal —Aldous Huxley, *The Olive Tree,* 1937

> The scene was graceful and quietly amusing . . . sordid only if you were possessed by high morals —Peggy Bennett, *The Varmints,* 1947

> . . . a woman of remarkable energy and courage, possessed by a deep religious zeal —Peter Quennell, *N.Y. Times Book Rev.,* 29 Aug. 1954

Less frequently the adjective *possessed* is followed by *with:*

> . . . if Mr. Paul V. Carroll's priests were not so completely possessed with the idea of their immense importance —Thomas Halton, *Irish Digest,* April 1955

> There must be over 10,000 itchy Americans who are possessed . . . with the ambition to make a *Jules and Jim* —Daniel Talbot, *Evergreen,* August 1967

possessive See APOSTROPHE 2, 4; DOUBLE GENITIVE; GENITIVE; POSSESSIVE WITH GERUND; PRONOUN WITH POSSESSIVE ANTECEDENT.

possessive with gerund The gerund, or verbal noun, in English is the present participle of a verb used as a noun. Since at least the end of the 17th century, a construction involving the gerund and a preceding pronoun or noun has been part of the written language. Sometimes the pronoun or noun is in the possessive case:

> . . . in hopes of his being able to join me —Lewis Carroll, letter, 11 Mar. 1867

> I have consulted your father on the subject of your attending Mr. Godon's lectures —Thomas Jefferson, letter, 9 May 1809

> . . . in spite of . . . the company's not having any intention of issuing a new edition —Ian Ballantine, letter, 5 Aug. 1939

And sometimes the pronoun or noun is not in the possessive case:

> . . . however I suppose the music prevented any of it being heard —Lewis Carroll, letter, 11 Mar. 1867

> . . . I couldn't abide him being such a splendid man —Russell Baker, *Growing Up,* 1982

> . . . in spite of the book being out of print for many years —Ian Ballantine, letter, 5 Aug. 1939

The dates of these passages show you that one example of each construction comes from a single author in a single letter. One of the curious facts about this construction is that it is not at all uncommon for an author to use both forms and to use them close together.

From the middle of the 18th century to the present time, grammarians and other commentators have been baffled by the construction. They cannot parse it, they cannot explain it, they cannot decide whether the possessive is correct or not. The earliest commentators, including Lowth 1763, were distinctly hostile to the possessive case. Campbell 1776 thought the possessive ought not to be repudiated, Priestley in 1768 allowed either form, Murray 1795 favored the possessive, Noah Webster in *Dissertations on the English Language* (1789) prescribed the possessive as the true form of the idiom. But opposition to the possessive had not died; Goold Brown 1851 opposed it, and so, apparently, did some other 19th-century grammarians who objected to the possessive case being used with inanimate nouns.

The discussion continued right on into the 20th century. Fowler 1926 was a notable proponent of the virtue, even the necessity, of the possessive. (He labeled nonuse of the possessive the *fused participle*.) Otto Jespersen's profusely illustrated *S.P.E. Tract 25* (1926) was intended to overpower some of Fowler's contentions with a volley of quotations from literature. Hall 1917 treated the subject extensively, too, with lists and charts based on his investigations of literature. And so it has gone, down to the present time (Burchfield 1996 has many examples).

Almost the only really important information in the enormous amount of analysis and comment written about the construction is contained in the lists and quotations. These demonstrate beyond a doubt what our few examples at the beginning showed: the same authors commonly use both constructions. From this fact it should be obvious that the selection of the possessive or the selection of the "fused participle" is simply not a matter of right and wrong. But why, you may ask, would Boswell, George Eliot, Dickens, or Thackeray use one form one time and the other form another time?

The factors governing the choice between the possessive and the common (or objective or nominative) case in this construction appear to be rather complex. One of the factors appears to be a matter of what element is to be stressed.

> She approves of this one's being a girl —Flannery O'Connor, letter, 8 May 1955

In this example the object of *approves of* is a noun phrase *this one's being a girl*; the whole phrase is the object and there is no particular emphasis intended for the pronoun *one*.

> . . . but I can't see me letting Harold C. condense it —Flannery O'Connor, letter, 11 Dec. 1956

But in this second example additional emphasis is placed on the pronoun *me*; it serves as the direct object of the main verb and is followed by a complementizing phrase.

The same contrast can be found with nouns. In the first example below *protagonist's weaning* seems to be most important; in the second the writer is thinking about the person:

> . . . its episodes too neatly arranged to build to the quiet crescendo of the boy protagonist's weaning from his family —Tom Dowling, *San Francisco Examiner,* 19 Nov. 1985

> I keep thinking of Don Castro not smoking on the maiden voyage of that goddam zeppelin —James Thurber, letter, 18 July 1952

There seem to be a number of other considerations that may militate against using the possessive in particular situations. For instance, the noun or pronoun may be of such a form that it resists the genitive form.

> . . . to find out what is responsible for my feet swelling —Flannery O'Connor, letter, 30 Apr. 1960

> . . . I would certainly . . . insist on you all coming here —William Faulkner, letter, 1959

A noun ending in *-s* or a plural noun ending in *-s* sounds like the genitive and is consequently likely to be unmarked by an apostrophe:

> . . . without the parties having any choice —Samuel Johnson, in James Boswell, *Life of Samuel Johnson,* 1791

> The Grants showing a disposition to be friendly and sociable, gave great satisfaction —Jane Austen, *Mansfield Park,* 1814

> I was glad to hear of the bills being paid —Harry S. Truman, letter, 7 Sept. 1947

While our backing is not conclusive, we do have evidence of the possessive's not being used in speech of more recent vintage:

> I'll miss Moe screaming at me —Dan Issel, quoted in *Springfield* (Mass.) *Daily News,* 23 Jan. 1985

> . . . him getting that interception —Ronnie Lott, television interview, 29 Dec. 1984

> . . . the possibility of him being there —radio newscast, 23 Oct. 1985

But in writing the chances are that an ordinary personal pronoun will be in the possessive:

> . . . the possibility of my filling the vacancy —George Bernard Shaw, preface, *The Shaw–Terry Letters,* 1931

> . . . a performance I wouldn't mind your seeing —Alexander Woollcott, letter, 1 Apr. 1940

You don't know how much I appreciated your going to all the trouble —Harry S. Truman, letter, 4 Oct. 1957

My story of Houdini . . . begins with my meeting his widow —James Thurber, letter, 17 May 1961

. . . the danger of his dwindling into a employee —Gerald Weales, *Smithsonian*, December 1985

Let's recapitulate. This construction, both with and without the possessive, has been used in writing for about 300 years. Both forms have been used by standard authors. Both forms have been called incorrect, but neither is. Those observers who have examined real examples have reached the following general conclusions: 1. A personal pronoun before the gerund tends to be a possessive pronoun in writing (of course, with *her* you cannot tell the case). 2. The accusative pronoun is used when it is meant to be emphasized. 3. In speech the possessive pronoun may not predominate, but available evidence is inconclusive. 4. Both possessive and common-case (uninflected) nouns, including proper nouns, are used before the gerund. It is clear, however, that the possessive case does not predominate with nouns to the extent it does with personal pronouns. 5. Complicating factors such as modifying phrases tend to militate against use of the possessive form. 6. Plurals and other nouns ending in -*s* also are often unmarked for the possessive inflection. 7. Many writers use both forms of the construction. Clearly there are times when one or the other sounds more euphonious, is clearer, or otherwise suits the purpose better.

We suspect that this is one of those idiomatic usages that seldom give the native speaker trouble. It will trouble learners of English much more. We can only advise learners that the possessive will almost always be safe for pronouns and will probably work most of the time with nouns. But in doubtful cases, you may need to consult a native speaker.

possibility When the likelihood of something is being considered, we usually refer to the possibility of its occurrence or existence:

. . . a physiological study of the possibility of life on Mars —*Current Biography*, July 1966

. . . the possibility of reversal is questionable —Arthur M. Gompf, *Johns Hopkins Mag.*, Summer 1971

When *possibility* is used in the plural with a meaning close to "opportunities," it is idiomatically followed by *for*:

. . . additional possibilities for future growth —Leslie H. Warner, *Annual Report, General Telephone & Electronics*, 1970

. . . discussing the possibilities for the exchange of students —John Coyne, *Change*, March 1973

possible *Possible* is sometimes considered to be an absolute adjective. See ABSOLUTE ADJECTIVES.

possibly A number of commentators inform us that it is redundant to use *possibly* with the modal auxiliaries *may* and *might*. They say it might be all right in speech, but warn that it had better be omitted in writing. This is quite a new discovery in the promotion of better writing, having been discovered (or invented) only in the 1980s. Writers in the past didn't have the rule to guide them:

. . . Colds . . . which may possibly be spread by Contagion —Benjamin Franklin, letter, 14 July 1773

. . . could no longer afford . . . to lose one connection that might possibly assist her —Jane Austen, *Mansfield Park*, 1814

I might possibly be persuaded to give my vote for putting her on a farm —Robert Frost, letter, 27 July 1922

More recent writers have gotten along without the rule:

. . . the prediction that I might possibly someday learn to read but would never speak a word —Barbara Kingsolver, *The Poisonwood Bible*, 1998

The dust and firestorms produced by nuclear explosions may possibly shut off sunlight for a long enough period to complete the havoc of the war —Isaac Asimov, *TV Guide*, 1–7 June 1985

. . . allows that there might possibly be other beings whose forms of sensible awareness were totally different from ours —P. F. Strawson, *Times Literary Supp.*, 3 July 1992

Possibly is simply an intensifier of these modals; its use is common and harmless. You can avoid it if you want to.

pour See PORE, POUR.

practicable, practical *Practicable* has two basic senses, "feasible" and "usable." *Practical* has a much wider range of meaning, but the sense closest to those of *practicable* is "capable of being put into use, useful." These two words form a popular topic among usage writers, who advise against confusing them. The real issue would seem to be whether *practicable* can be used to mean "practical," since the meaning of *practical* subsumes that of *practicable*. Judging from the evidence we have, writers by and large successfully distinguish between *practicable* and *practical* where necessary. Here is a representative sampling of *practicable* citations:

> . . . the route was, where practicable, laid out on the southern exposures of hills to take the fullest advantage of solar heating to clear snow and wet pavement —Dan Cupper, *American Heritage,* May/June 1990

> . . . a marriage without love or respect is dead and should be legally buried as soon as practicable —Neil McKendrick, *N.Y. Times Book Rev.,* 4 Nov. 1990

> Loudspeaker systems had sufficiently advanced by this time to make the wiring of large theaters practicable —Peter Andrews, *Saturday Rev.,* 12 Nov. 1977

> . . . some easy, practicable strategies for achieving harmony on the job —Denise Fortino, *Harper's Bazaar,* August 1980

Some of our citations for *practicable* and *practical* supply a context in which either word could have been placed. We also have a few citations in which the meaning of *practicable* has been confused or blurred.

> . . . translating the feasible into the practicable —Forest Woody Horton, *Information World,* May 1980

However, such uses are quite uncommon and have not established a new sense of *practicable,* so the distinction between *practicable* and *practical* remains valid.

practically *Practically* has a second sense meaning "almost, nearly, virtually" that Bierce 1909 decided was a misuse (even though it had been in the language since 1748). Commentators as recently as the 1980s have been repeating Bierce's objection.

Now what is wrong with this sense? We are never given a clear explanation by any of the commentators; they simply see it as "loose" in relation to the original sense. The plain fact is, however, that a sense of a word that has been in everyday use for more than two centuries and comes naturally from the pens of reputable writers is entirely standard. Some examples follow:

> Under favorable conditions, practically everybody can be converted to practically anything —Aldous Huxley, *Brave New World Revisited,* 1958

> Who's wearing pants? Practically everybody —Amy Vanderbilt, *Ladies' Home Jour.,* January 1971

> . . . until Elizabeth's proclamation . . . in 1599 practically killed historical painting in England —*Times Literary Supp.,* 18 Dec. 1969

> . . . attracted practically no attention —John Fischer, *Harper's,* March 1971

practice, practise Here is what our files show about these words. The noun is almost always spelled *practice* in both British and American usage; we have British, Canadian, and American examples of *practise* as a noun, but not very many. The verb is regularly spelled *practise* in British usage; in American usage both *practice* and *practise* are used with considerable frequency.

precede, proceed Quite a few handbooks distinguish these words, lest you mix them up, but dictionaries do the job better. If you are in doubt, look in your dictionary. We believe, however, that problems with these words are more likely to be a matter of spelling than of semantics. Several books note that *precede* is occasionally misspelled *preceed.* This is true; we have several examples of the misspelling or typographical error. Be aware that this is a word prone to be misspelled. We have also seen *procede* a time or two.

precedence 1. *Precedence* is now usually followed by the preposition *over*:

> Henry began by demanding precedence over Francis —Francis Hackett, *Henry the Eighth,* 1929

> To give organizations precedence over persons is to subordinate ends to means —Aldous Huxley, *Brave New World Revisited,* 1958

> New exigencies began to take precedence over freedom —*New Yorker,* 10 Apr. 1971

Although we have no very recent evidence for the combination, *precedence* has also been used with *of*:

> . . . who hated her brother-in-law, and hated, still worse, his dead wife, who, as Queen-Dowager, had taken precedence of her —Edith Sitwell, *Fanfare for Elizabeth,* 1946

> . . . although weapons must in some instances take precedence of exports —Vera Micheles Dean, *Harper's,* December 1952

2. *Precedence, precedent(s).* From Vizetelly 1920 to Ebbitt & Ebbitt 1982 and Harper 1985 usage writers have warned against confusing *precedence* with *precedent.* Such confusion is only likely among those who pronounce *precedence* like *precedents.*

The Ebbitts cite a student paper with a sentence beginning "Now that precedence has been set . . ." where it was clear that *a precedent* was the meaning intended. The substitution of a mass noun for a count noun is most peculiar indeed, and the example is not an aberration—we ourselves have a little evidence of its occurrence in print:

> ... the United States Supreme Court where great precedence is going to be set —*Police,* September–October 1967

> If all goes well—and there is no precedence in these latitudes that it will —*Saturday Rev.,* 10 May 1964

We also have an example of *precedence* used for *precedent* (Garner 1998 has others). It must be considered a mistake.

> ... this incident sets a precedence —*Westfield* (Mass.) *Evening News,* 27 Feb. 1985

precedent 1. When the adjective *precedent* is used with a preposition, the preposition is usually *to:*

> Identification is a condition precedent to an inquest. It is a matter of law —Raymond Chandler, *The Simple Art of Murder,* 1950

> ... it most certainly is the condition precedent to any intelligent choice —Adlai E. Stevenson, *Speeches,* ed. Richard Harrity, 1952

> Croce has claimed the right to 'spiritualise' this primal vivacity which he makes precedent—not in time but in the spirit—to the moral choice —Cecil Sprigge, *Benedetto Croce,* 1952

Occasionally, *precedent* has been used with *of:*

> Therefore collective security is a condition precedent of all else —George Soule, *New Republic,* 14 June 1943

> ... a system ... that makes publication a condition precedent of advancement in a profession —*Times Literary Supp.,* 3 July 1969

From the evidence it appears that when the adjective is used postpositively, *condition* is very often the noun it follows.

2. When the noun *precedent* is used with a preposition, the preposition is most often *for:*

> I do not think there is any historical precedent for Israel's extraordinary success —Denis Healey, *New Republic,* 3 Jan. 1955

> There were, to be sure, precedents for crime in the Old World countries from which these immigrants came —Joseph Epstein, *Commentary,* January 1972

Precedent is also used with *of,* though somewhat less frequently:

> I shall hold you and your commanders criminally accountable under the rules and precedents of war —Douglas MacArthur, quoted in *Time,* 28 Aug. 1950

> ... the Republican Presidential contest of 1912, set an unhappy precedent of creative slander —Richard Reeves, *Harper's,* January 1972

Occasionally, *precedent* has been used with *against* or *to:*

> ... even in the Old Testament there is a dire precedent against registration —J. Carter Swaim, *Right and Wrong Ways to Use the Bible,* 1953

> ... the earlier discussions of his own ideas that were an essential precedent to the new concept —L. V. Berkner, *New Republic,* 12 June 1954

precipitate, precipitous Most usage commentators are insistent about keeping these adjectives distinct. *Precipitate,* they say, means "headlong," "abrupt," or "rash"; *precipitous* means only "steep." Such a clear distinction does not exist absolutely in actual usage, although *precipitate,* which formerly was sometimes used to mean "steep," does now appear to be used only in the senses approved by the critics:

> ... the precipitate withdrawal of the United Nations Emergency Force —*Saturday Rev.,* 8 July 1967

> ... causing him to appear precipitate, out of control —Aaron Latham, *New York,* 17 Nov. 1975

> ... her precipitate flight from the scene of the accident —Peter Taylor, *The Old Forest and Other Stories,* 1985

And *precipitous* does usually mean "steep":

> ... one of the less precipitous trails —Morten Lund, *Ski,* November 1971

> Precipitous mountain watersheds laced with energetic, fast-falling streams —Matt Herron, *Smithsonian,* December 1982

The problem is that *precipitous* and *precipitously* are also commonly used in contexts which, according to the critics, require *precipitate* and *precipitately:*

> I had intended to see you before leaving but at the last moment we go rather precipitously —Robert Frost, letter, 1915

> Cardinal Cushing's precipitous withdrawal of support —*Commonweal,* 23 Feb. 1968

> ... has not made precipitous changes in social welfare policy —Frances Fox Piven, *Columbia Forum,* Summer 1970

> ... protection against precipitous action by the military and other agencies —Harvey Wheeler, *Center Mag.,* January/February 1971

The black comedy . . . is too precipitously introduced —John Simon, *New York*, 22 Nov. 1971

. . . in view of its precipitous demobilization —George F. Kennan, *Atlantic*, November 1982

A mother can learn, perhaps, not to act precipitously —Carrie Carmichael, *N.Y. Times Book Rev.*, 25 Jan. 1987

The picture is further complicated by the common use of *precipitous* and *precipitously* in describing a sudden, sharp decline:

> . . . a precipitous decline in the number of Jews in the Soviet Government —*Newsweek*, 1 Sept. 1958

> . . . the performance . . . fell precipitously as their dosage of marijuana increased —Solomon H. Snyder, *Psychology Today*, May 1971

> His fall from power was even more precipitous —Geoffrey C. Ward, *N.Y. Times Book Rev.*, 1 Aug. 1982

> . . . the number of reported cases . . . fell precipitously —Nan Robertson, *N.Y. Times Mag.*, 19 Sept. 1982

These are really just straightforward figurative applications of the word's literal sense, "steep," but their connotations of suddenness and abruptness bear an obvious resemblance to those of *precipitate*. Most commentators will allow this figurative usage. A few, however, insist that *precipitous* should only be used to describe physical characteristics ("a precipitous cliff"). Such reasoning may play a part in persuading some writers to use the adverb *precipitately* in place of *precipitously* when describing a steep decline:

> . . . registration in Russian language courses dropped precipitately —William O. Douglas, *Freedom of the Mind*, 1962

> . . . childbearing has dropped precipitately in the United States since the end of the baby boom —Didi Moore, *N.Y. Times Mag.*, 18 Jan. 1981

Many commentators would regard this use of *precipitately* as an error.

Actual usage, then, is far more complicated than the commentators would like it to be. The objective truth is that *precipitate* and *precipitous* are similar words whose uses have had a tendency to overlap for centuries. Dictionaries, from Samuel Johnson in 1755 and Noah Webster in 1828, have always shown them to have synonymous senses. That is not to say, however, that the distinction favored by the critics has no basis. Evidence in the OED shows that in the 19th century "steep" became

the predominant sense of *precipitous*, with its other senses falling largely into disuse. Their revival in the early 20th century caught the attention of Fowler 1926, and the voices of criticism have been heard ever since. At this point, the criticized usage and the criticism itself are both alive and flourishing. So although almost all dictionaries show that *precipitous* has as one of its senses "precipitate" (and they are quite right to do so), you had better be prepared to defend yourself if you use it in that sense.

preclude When *preclude* is used with a preposition, it is usually *from*:

> Rover even attempted to preclude Lattimore's attorneys from opposing the affidavit of bias —Judge Luther W. Youngdahl, *New Republic*, 1 Nov. 1954

> . . . the discrimination that still precludes Catholics from senior . . . posts in civic and social life —Eric Bourne, *Christian Science Monitor*, 13 Sept. 1979

> . . . the pains Disney often took to preclude his cartoons and live-action films from consideration as serious art —Daniel Menaker, *N.Y. Times Book Rev.*, 28 Nov. 1976

Occasionally, *preclude* has been used with *to*:

> But there were many doors that he didn't open. Whole sections seemed precluded to him —Arturo Vivante, *New Yorker*, 11 May 1963

> He is not . . . an equally good novelist, though of course nothing is precluded to a man of his abilities —Stanley Kauffmann, *N.Y. Times Book Rev.*, 4 Apr. 1976

In another relation *preclude* may be followed with *by*:

> Monotony was precluded by the use of decorative pieces, color, and light —*American Guide Series: Michigan*, 1941

precondition "A modish but tautologous Lit Crit synonym for condition" is the evaluation of *precondition* pronounced by Howard 1980. On this side of the Atlantic, Safire 1986 worries about the word's redundancy. Garner 1998 finds it usually unnecessary.

Precondition had a literary beginning; it was introduced by Coleridge in 1825, and it was used by DeQuincey. But during the last forty years or so, it has been most frequently used in writing in social and political science and reporting on affairs of state, although it is by no means limited to such contexts. And it has a generous record of use, indicating that writers have found it a useful word.

If *precondition* were simply a tautologous synonym for *condition*, we should be able to use *condition* in its place wherever it occurs.

But we cannot. For instance, we find *precondition* used with the preposition *to*:

... a desire to obtain a favorable settlement of her dispute with Germany over the Saar Basin as a precondition to ratification of the EDC treaty —Omar N. Bradley, *Saturday Evening Post,* 10 Apr. 1951

... what the Thais regarded as unacceptable preconditions to the conference —Denis Warner, *The Reporter,* 26 Mar. 1964

... a necessary precondition to making the full emancipation of women a reality —Gerda Lerner, *Columbia Forum,* Fall 1970

Since we cannot put *condition* very comfortably into any of these examples, we must conclude that *condition* and *precondition* are not quite the same here.

We also find *precondition* with *of; condition* can also be used with *of,* so we should be able to substitute it without difficulty. But how many of these examples are unchanged by such substitution?

Weakness invites aggression. Now and in the future, strength is the precondition of peace —Dean Acheson, quoted in *The Pattern of Responsibility,* ed. McGeorge Bundy, 1951

The implication in such a pronouncement, emanating from the seat of government, is that religious faith is a *condition,* or even a *precondition,* of the democratic life —E. B. White, *New Yorker,* 18 Feb. 1956

... the biological preconditions of human speech —Philip Morrison, *Scientific American,* February 1978

... the classicizing sculptures ... which were a precondition of the development of a classicizing style in painting —*Times Literary Supp.,* 22 Oct. 1971

Finally we have *precondition* with *for.* Again, *condition* would seem to be usable in the same constructions. Test them.

... the precondition for woman's emancipation is the reform not of social institutions, but of ... —Dwight Macdonald, *The Reporter,* 14 Apr. 1953

... the precondition for existence at Daytop is truthfulness —Renata Adler, *New Yorker,* 15 Apr. 1967

Let us then assume that crises are a necessary precondition for the emergence of novel theories —Thomas S. Kuhn, *The Structure of Scientific Revolutions,* 2d ed., 1973

To insist on absolute answers as a precondition for any great undertaking is to deprive the future of its main source of intellectual energy —Norman Cousins, *Saturday Rev.,* 7 Aug. 1976

We think you will have found by now that *condition* does not satisfactorily replace *precondition* in many (if any) of the examples. The reason is simple: the *pre-* is not simply otiose. It focuses the mind of the reader (*condition* in Merriam-Webster's Collegiate Dictionary, Tenth Edition, has a dozen or more senses) and emphasizes the notion of "before." If you are going to spell out the notion of "before" contextually, you certainly do not need *precondition.* But the authors quoted here let the *pre-* take care of that part of the message. From our evidence we judge that *precondition* is not usually used redundantly.

predestine *Predestine* is often followed by the preposition *to*:

... for reasons which we cannot fathom, God predestines some to eternal life —Kenneth Scott Latourette, *A History of Christianity,* 1953

Who would expect a godfather to give a child a name that would predestine it to become a cruel person? —Kurt Lewent, *Modern Language Notes,* March 1957

Television is so beset by "new ideas"—generally predestined to disappear within weeks —Irving Kolodin, *Saturday Rev.,* 1 Nov. 1975

Predestine may also be used with *for*:

... adherence to socialist principles seemed to predestine him for a leading position in communist Hungary —*Times Literary Supp.,* 18 Dec. 1969

... to push the working class into the action for which history had predestined it —Alfred G. Meyer, *Marxism Since the Communist Manifesto,* 1961

predicate 1. The use of the verb *predicate* in the sense of "to base, found" with *on* or *upon* is an Americanism attested as early as 1766. The OED Supplement shows that this sense of *predicate* has entered British usage too. Here are a few examples from our collection:

Such a community predicates its operation upon the containment of various egoistic drives —Reinhold Niebuhr, *Yale Rev.,* Spring 1951

The grants are predicated on need —Horace Sutton, *Saturday Rev.,* August 1978

... their political success is predicated on disaster —Michael Straight, *New Republic,* 22 Nov. 1954

2. Older senses of *predicate*, when used in constructions requiring a preposition, take *of*:

> Many distinct ways in which a oneness predicated of the universe might make a difference —William James, *Pragmatism*, 1907

> And if we predicate simplicity of Hopkins. . . . —F. R. Leavis, *The Common Pursuit*, 1952

predominate, predominately Copperud 1964 sounded the clarion, calling *predominate* as an adjective an error, even though it can be found in the OED and all of Merriam-Webster's unabridged dictionaries. Copperud 1970 was still alone in objecting to *predominate* as an adjective, but his call would soon be heeded; Harper 1975, Bernstein 1977, Bremner 1980, and Johnson 1982 all denounce the use, as do a few college handbooks. Two other books, Watt 1967 and Perrin & Ebbitt 1972, recognize *predominate* as an adjective of some rarity, and recommend *predominant*.

Here is what the dictionaries know that most of the usage writers do not. *Predominate* has been an adjective in English since the end of the 16th century; it antedates the verb by a few years. It is first attested, according to the OED, in 1591 in the writings of Thomas Nashe, Elizabethan man of letters and controversialist. *Predominant* is slightly older, first attested in 1576; it was used in 1592 by William Shakespeare, a better-known and more influential Elizabethan man of letters. Most subsequent literary and general use has followed Shakespeare's lead rather than Nashe's.

The OED marked *predominate* and *predominately* "Rare," and so did Webster 1909 and Webster's Second. The editors of Webster's Second had a little bit of 20th-century evidence, so they moved both words from the pearl section—the small type at the foot of the page—where they had been in 1909 to the main word list. Between Webster's Second and Webster's Third more evidence accumulated, primarily from technical sources.

> Of predominate interest in chlorophylls are the locations of hydrogens which may be active in photoreduction —*Botanical Rev.*, December 1950

> . . . the predominate gonadal sex in cases of true hermaphroditism —*JAMA*, 9 Feb. 1952

> Throughout our analysis we attempt to conform to the predominate tendencies in the language —Eugene A. Nida, *Morphology*, 1946

Occasionally it could be found in general sources as well:

> His strong belief that patriotism should be one of the predominate principles of reli-

gion —*American Guide Series: Minnesota*, 1938

> Rieve's predominate strength is in New England —*New Republic*, 26 May 1952

The evidence for *predominately* from this period tended to be more general than technical:

> . . . the population is predominately native-born white —*American Guide Series: Texas*, 1940

> The poem gives a predominately creative expression —K. E. Cameron, *The Young Shelley*, 1950

> Blue light, which stimulates the rods predominately —Charles H. Best & Norman B. Taylor, *The Physiological Basis of Medical Practice*, 5th ed., 1950

Our most recent evidence shows that *predominately* is being used somewhat more frequently than *predominate* but that neither is likely to threaten the preeminent position of *predominant* and *predominantly*. Literary use has all along preferred the *-ant* form. But being less frequent does not make the *-ate* form wrong.

preface **1.** *Noun.* *Preface* is usually used with *to*:

> . . . Wilson explained in his preface to *Axel's Castle* —*Current Biography*, January 1964

> . . . we know that our defeat and dismay may be the preface to our successors' victory —T. S. Eliot, "Francis Herbert Bradley," in *Selected Essays*, 1932

Preface also has some use with *for*:

> Jean-Paul Sartre . . . wrote the preface for her second novel —*Current Biography*, June 1966

2. *Verb.* *Preface* may be used with *with*:

> The brief poems with which he prefaced and followed 'Al Aaraaf' —Daniel Hoffman, *Poe Poe Poe Poe Poe Poe Poe*, 1972

> Her cousin prefaced his speech with a solemn bow —Jane Austen, *Pride and Prejudice*, 1813

> . . . prefaces each section of his book with mystical epigraphs —Paul Zweig, *Saturday Rev.*, August 1978

> They prefaced their skating with dinner in a Spanish restaurant —Aurelia Levi, *Discovery*, March 1954

Preface often is found with *by*:

> . . . a forebuilding carrying two circular tempiettos at its ends and prefaced by an

open octagonal porch —John Summerson, *Heavenly Mansions,* 1948

The chapters on the historians are prefaced by chapters on Aristotle and Homer —*Times Literary Supp.,* 29 Aug. 1955

. . . the laws themselves should be prefaced by preambles of a "persuasive" sort —Glenn R. Morrow, *Philosophical Rev.,* April 1953

Infrequently, *preface* is followed by *to:*

. . . a note prefaced to the score —Edward Sackville-West & Desmond Shawe-Taylor, *The Record Year,* 1952

prefer *Prefer* is most often used in constructions that do not involve prepositions. However, when it is used to compare two things in the same sentence, the second, especially if it is a noun or pronoun, is usually introduced by *to:*

Movement is always to be preferred to inaction —Norman Mailer, *Advertisements for Myself,* 1959

. . . monarch butterflies, who prefer them to any other flower —Eleanor Perenyi, *Green Thoughts,* 1983

. . . he prefers sweaters and slacks to suits —*Current Biography,* July 1965

Sometimes other prepositions are used. The OED notes *above* and *before* as being used formerly (George Washington used *before*). *Over* is occasionally used:

. . . but who, nevertheless, are preferred over the A type or the D type —William J. Reilly, *Life Planning for College Students,* 1954

This construction is especially frequent in advertisements for products where doctors or housewives or members of some other group will be said to prefer one brand over all others.

Numerous commentators point out that when the two things compared are represented by infinitive phrases, there can arise a problem of too many *tos:* "prefers to eat to to starve." The solution hit upon by writers facing this problem has often been to use *rather than* in place of *to:*

. . . prefer to leave rather than to subvert their values —Shelly Halpern, *Change,* November–December 1969

Rather than is also used when the *to* or even the whole infinitive is understood:

. . . prefers to stand rather than sit —*Current Biography,* September 1964

. . . preferred to preach in it rather than in his mother tongue —*Dictionary of American Biography,* 1936

Only rarely do we find the *rather* omitted before the *than:*

. . . he would have preferred to fast than carry it —Margaret Drabble, *The Needle's Eye,* 1972

When the two things compared are expressed in gerunds (sometimes with the second -*ing* form deleted) we find both *to* and *rather than:*

He preferred living like a Grecian, to dying like a Roman —J. W. Croker, 20 July 1815, in *The Croker Papers,* 1884 (OED)

It seems we prefer reading magazines to books —John Barkham, *Saturday Rev.,* 13 Feb. 1954

. . . the rich preferred spending rather than investing —*Times Literary Supp.,* 2 July 1971

Beginning at least as early as Vizetelly 1906 there has been criticism of constructions with *than* and *rather than.* The critics have been far from unanimous in their opinions. Some condemn both *than* and *rather than;* some recommend *rather than* and condemn *than;* none give reasons for their opinions. Plain *than* seems to have no defenders and to be rarely used (the only genuine example besides our own that we have seen is in Reader's Digest 1983). And, to be truthful, plain *than* does sound awkward, perhaps simply from its unfamiliarity.

See also RATHER THAN 2.

preferable *Preferable* is sometimes considered to be an absolute adjective, so that its use with *more* is regarded as incorrect (Fowler 1926 calls it "an inexcusable pleonasm"). Our written evidence for *more preferable* is scanty.

. . . getting the word "hillbilly" taken off the label of his records, and therefore inspiring everyone else in the trade to replace it with the more preferable "country and western" —Bob Claypool, *Houston Post,* 8 Sept. 1984

See ABSOLUTE ADJECTIVES.

preference *Preference* is often followed by *for:*

Spinoza's preference for democracy —Morris R. Cohen, *The Faith of a Liberal,* 1946

Does the answer have something to do with a preference for superpower diplomacy? —Leslie H. Gelb & Morton H. Halperin, *Harper's,* November 1971

Preference is used with *to* when the object of the preposition is the thing not preferred. When *preference* is used in this way, it is often preceded by *in:*

. . . he chose Kentucky politics in preference to national affairs —*Dictionary of American Biography,* 1928

. . . a happy narcotic shrub widely grown in preference to food —Hal Lehrman, *N.Y. Times Book Rev.*, 15 Aug. 1954

When the object names the area within which preference is expressed rather than the specific thing preferred or not, *preference* also occurs with *in, of,* and *regarding*:

A German dialect is spoken generally, and German preferences in food prevail —*American Guide Series: Michigan,* 1941

. . . those preferences of sexual selection that go by the name of "love" —Edmund Wilson, *A Piece of My Mind,* 1956

Everyone has certain *preferences* regarding clothes —John E. Brewton et al., *Using Good English* (textbook), 1962

pregnant When *pregnant* is used with a preposition, it is usually *with*:

Every hour was pregnant with monotony and weariness —C. S. Forester, *The African Queen,* 1935

. . . create situations as pregnant with danger as with promise —Richard H. Rovere, *New Yorker,* 25 July 1953

The new physics is pregnant with revelations for everyone interested in the cosmos —Timothy Ferris, *N.Y. Times Book Rev.,* 20 Nov. 1983

Pregnant also occurs, although less often and in varying relations, with *by, for, in,* and *of*:

This time she's pregnant by a cad who won't marry her —John McCarten, *New Yorker,* 13 May 1950

. . . to see that the present is pregnant for the future, rather than a revolt against the past —Malcolm Bradbury, *Times Literary Supp.,* 25 Apr. 1968

. . . one of the indelible performances of my operatic experience, as rich in reality as it is pregnant in overtones —Claudia Cassidy, *Europe—On the Aisle,* 1954

Its five component essays are as pregnant of ideas as the leitmotif is of thematic metamorphoses —*Times Literary Supp.,* 23 May 1968

prejudice, prejudiced *Prejudice(d) against, in favor of, toward(s).* Given the generally negative meaning attached to *prejudice,* noun and verb, it is not surprising that the most frequently used preposition is *against*:

. . . some absurd prejudice against living on one's friends —Stella Gibbons, *Cold Comfort Farm,* 1932

. . . inner agreement with the prevailing prejudice against him —Eric Hoffer, *N.Y. Times Mag.,* 29 Nov. 1964

. . . the former middle-class prejudice against wearing second-hand clothing —Roy Lewis & Angus Maude, *The English Middle Classes,* 1950

In favor of is much less common.

. . . a definite prejudice in favor of low latitude living —William G. Byron, *Annals of the Association of American Geographers,* June 1952

Bander 1978 points out that *prejudice toward(s)* can be ambiguous, and indeed it can. Our few printed citations require quite a bit of context to make them clear, and we recommend that you avoid *toward(s).*

The verb (especially in the form of its past participle *prejudiced*) behaves just like the noun:

. . . is prejudiced against a lot of different kinds of people —Bob Beamon, quoted in *Sports Illustrated,* 15 July 1968

. . . no matter how prejudiced in favor of the men —Norman Mailer, *Harper's,* March 1971

prejudicial Usually *prejudicial* is followed by *to*:

. . . these are rarely useful to scholarship and are almost always prejudicial to teaching —Robert A. Nisbet, *Psychology Today,* March 1971

. . . information they considered irrelevant or prejudicial to the student's employability —Harold Perkin, *Times Literary Supp.,* 19 Mar. 1970

It has also been used with *of*:

His analysis was unfairly prejudicial of an administration superior to any previously known in the colony —*Australian Dictionary of Biography,* 1966

premier Gowers in Fowler 1965 and Flesch 1964 object to *premier* in the sense of "first, foremost," a sense it has had in English since the 15th century. There are no serious grounds for objection to uses like the ones quoted, even if advertisers like to use it hyperbolically at times.

. . . and thus Davis was first linked with the statesman whose mantle as the premier champion of states' rights he eventually assumed —Robert Penn Warren, *Jefferson Davis Gets His Citizenship Back,* 1980

. . . the nation's premier women's colleges —Diane Ravitch, *N.Y. Times Book Rev.,* 28 Oct. 1984

. . . and while King's Bench initially had greater prestige, in time Common Pleas became the premier central court —Norman F. Cantor, *Imagining the Law,* 1997

premiere The verb *premiere* is resoundingly rejected by the major usage panels, although most commentators take no notice of it and dictionaries treat it as standard. Garner 1998 agrees with the panelists that it is a noun misused as a verb. It is also a fairly new word, although not as new as some might suppose. We first encountered it in 1933, and by the 1940s it had established itself in regular use as both a transitive and intransitive verb:

> . . . the Paris Opéra plans to premiere an old work of Jean Cocteau and Arthur Honegger —*Modern Music,* November–December 1942

> The night Crosby premiered —*Newsweek,* 28 Oct. 1946

Its use continues to be common today:

> . . . Trollope will premiere on television in the midst of the latest squall in Anglo-American relations —Karl E. Meyer, *Saturday Rev.,* 22 Jan. 1977

> . . . when the play was premièred in 1889 —Ronald Hayman, *Times Literary Supp.,* 28 Jan. 1983

Anyone determined to avoid it will find that it has no exact synonym. *Open* can sometimes be used in place of the intransitive *premiere,* but it less strongly denotes a "first ever" public performance than does the longer word, and in many cases it is simply unidiomatic. In current English *premiere* is just another available verb, and we recommend that you regard it as such.

premises, premisses *Premises* is normally construed as a plural, even when used in the singular sense, "a building or part of a building":

> . . . a tenant may assign his lease or sublet the premises or any part of them —McKee Fisk & James C. Snapp, *Applied Business Law,* 8th ed., 1960

Usage commentators warn against treating *premises* in this sense as a singular, as by preceding it with the indefinite article *a*:

> The IRS padlocked a premises and was ordered to pay rent as the occupant —*Wall Street Jour.,* 2 June 1971

Such usage has a certain logic to it, but it is too uncommon to be considered standard.

A related topic is the correctness of the spelling *premisses.* Various commentators have described this spelling either as an error or as a variant sometimes used by the British to distinguish the plural of the "presupposition" sense of *premise* ("one of the premisses of his argument") from the "building" sense of *premises* ("was asked to leave the premises").

What it is, in fact, is the plural of *premiss,* a spelling variant of *premise* that is common in British English:

> What I object to is his basic premiss —John Higginbotham, *Times Literary Supp.,* 28 Dec. 1967

> . . . diameters, planets, terms, premisses —Howard 1977

Premiss is actually the original and etymologically more faithful spelling of this word, but it now survives only in Great Britain, and only in the senses of the word relating to logic and arguments. The spellings *premise* and *premises* are used for all senses in American English.

preoccupied *Preoccupied* is almost always used with *with*:

> . . . a society ever more preoccupied with leisure —William H. Whyte, Jr., *The Organization Man,* 1956

> . . . economic liberals are especially preoccupied with the free market and property rights —Kwame Anthony Appiah, *N.Y. Times Book Rev.,* 29 Oct. 2000

Although the verb almost always appears as a past participle when it is used with a preposition, once in a while an active use shows up:

> The children form a secret society which preoccupies itself with dares —*Times Literary Supp.,* 22 Oct. 1971

Preoccupied may also be followed by *about* or *by*:

> One has observed them so preoccupied about simultaneity of attack —Virgil Thomson, *The Musical Scene,* 1947

> Ignorant of life and of nature, she was, he has also supposed, preoccupied by love —Carol Ohmann, *College English,* May 1971

preparatory 1. When used with a preposition, *preparatory* is followed by *to*:

> . . . the transports were already taking in their cargoes preparatory to dropping down the Thames —W. M. Thackeray, *Vanity Fair,* 1848

> Van Helsing is lying down, having a rest preparatory to his journey —Bram Stoker, *Dracula,* 1897

> . . . his formal agenda is to make more progress in arms control, preparatory to the summit meeting —Elizabeth Drew, *New Yorker,* 19 Feb. 1990

2. A few commentators (Flesch 1964, Copperud 1964, 1970, 1980, Cook 1985, Garner 1998) consider *preparatory to* pretentious or wordy for *before.* Not every writer is willing to be limited to *before* in every case, however. If the examples above are not enough, here are four more. We are not persuaded that they sound pretentious or even that they mean just what they would mean if *before* were used:

> I sat it up on my desk for a while preparatory to rewrapping it —James Thurber, letter, 6 Sept. 1947

> He stopped, put the gears into reverse and twisted around in his seat preparatory to backing up —E. L. Doctorow, *Ragtime*, 1975

> For all I know, you are a spy, sent here by an alien race to study us, preparatory to invasion —Gore Vidal, "Visit to a Small Planet," 1955

> . . . a few years ago when I was shipping off stuff to Cornell preparatory to dying —E. B. White, letter, 9 Jan. 1970

See also PREVIOUS TO; PRIOR TO.

preposition 1. See PREPOSITION AT END.
2. The idiomatic preference for one preposition or another after certain verbs, adjectives, and nouns has been a subject for worry by grammarians since the 18th century. Lowth 1762 and Murray 1795, for instance, think it important to correct the prepositions selected by earlier 18th-century writers. Many modern handbooks, too, devote space to the problem. In this book such combinations are each treated separately, with examples of actual usage, the entry word being the verb, adjective, or noun.

preposition at end The question of the correctness of a preposition at the end of a sentence or clause is one which has been under discussion for more than three centuries. As is not the case with some of the other long-lived topics examined in this book, recent commentators—at least since Fowler 1926—are unanimous in their rejection of the notion that ending a sentence with a preposition is an error or an offense against propriety. Fowler terms the idea a "cherished superstition." And not only do the commentators reject the notion, but actual usage supports their rejection. So if everybody who is in the know agrees, there's no problem, right?

Wrong.

> Thank you for your reply to my questions but I find it extremely difficult to trust an opinion on grammar prepared by someone who ends a sentence with a preposition.

This is part of a letter received by one of our editors who had answered some questions for the writer. Members of the never-end-a-sentence-with-a-preposition school are still with us and are not reluctant to make themselves known:

> Some time ago I ended a column with the observation that sportscaster John Madden had better be respected "because he is too big to argue with." To my dismay, that sentence provoked at least a dozen reproachful letters saying that I had violated "one of the oldest rules" of good writing, and that I was providing a poor example to the young. Alas, I had ended a sentence with a preposition —Mary Pat Flaherty, *Pittsburgh Press*, 28 Apr. 1985

And, lest you think the true believers are made up only of the sort of people who write letters to the editor, a full twenty percent of the Harper 1975 usage panel—people who are professional writers—believed the preposition at the end was an error.

Where did this "cherished superstition" come from? It seems to have originated with the 17th-century English poet, playwright, and essayist John Dryden. In 1672 Dryden wrote a piece of criticism called "Defence of the Epilogue," the main purpose of which was to demonstrate that the English used by writers of Dryden's time was superior to that of an earlier generation of writers. The writers Dryden talks chiefly about are Shakespeare, Fletcher, and Jonson, and he chooses Jonson, who had the highest reputation of the three at the time, as the one from whom to take specific examples. The italic line is from Jonson's *Catiline* (1611); the comment on it is Dryden's:

> *The bodies that those souls were frighted from.*
> The Preposition in the end of the sentence; a common fault with him, and which I have but lately observ'd in my own writings.

Dryden at some time later in his career was supposed to have gone back over his own works and revised the final prepositions he found. We cannot be sure how Dryden developed the idea that the terminal preposition was an error, but Latin is probably involved. The construction does not exist in Latin, and Dryden claimed to have composed some of his pieces in Latin and then translated them into English—apparently for greater elegance or propriety of expression.

Almost a century later Bishop Lowth 1762 dealt with the problem. He may have had the episcopal tongue partly in the cheek:

> This is an idiom, which our language is strongly inclined to: it prevails in common conversation, and suits very well with the familiar style in writing: but the placing of the preposition before the relative, is more graceful, as well as more perspicuous; and agrees much better with the solemn and elevated style.

Lowth's approach is quite reasonable; clearly he cannot be blamed (as he is by Bryson 1984) for an absolutist approach to the matter. Hall 1917 says that Hugh Blair, author of a widely used book on rhetoric published in 1783, gave wide vogue to the notion that the terminal preposition must be avoided. If Blair did, then he may have passed the notion on to Lindley Murray 1795. Murray confected his very popular grammar from the works of several predecessors, including Lowth and Blair. Murray was notoriously strait-laced: he quoted Lowth's statement, but where Lowth said "which our language is strongly inclined to," Murray wrote "to which our language is strongly inclined." Even a bishop could not put a preposition at the end of a clause and satisfy Murray.

To Blair and Murray we may add Noah Webster. According to Baron 1982, Webster in his 1784 grammar strongly disapproved the terminal preposition. So the 19th century began with three widely used, standard school texts formidably opposing the preposition at the end of the sentence. The topic entered the general consciousness through schoolteachers, and, as we have seen, it persists there still.

Perhaps the construction was relatively new in Dryden's time, and he was reacting, as many do, to something new and obtrusive. But he did pick one out of Ben Jonson, and Shakespeare had used it too:

Thou hast no speculation in those eyes
Which thou dost glare with
               —*Macbeth,* 1606

We also have evidence that the postponed preposition was, in fact, a regular feature in some constructions in Old English. No feature of the language can be more firmly rooted than if it survives from Old English. Evidently the whole notion of its being wrong is Dryden's invention.

And what is curious is the fact that the first example Dryden picked to make his point about (the one quoted above) contains a construction in which the preposition must be put at the end—a relative clause introduced by *that.* Some recent commentators such as Burchfield 1981, 1996 have pointed out that there are a few constructions in which the postponed preposition is either mandatory or preferable. The restrictive clause introduced by *that* has required the postponing of the preposition since Old English. Here are some examples:

"Now," thought he, "I see the dangers that Mistrust and Timorous were driven back by." —John Bunyan, *Pilgrim's Progress,* 1678

Fanny could with difficulty give the smile that was here asked for —Jane Austen, *Mansfield Park,* 1814

. . . owing to the restrictions of space that Mr. Belloc has contented himself with —*Times Literary Supp.,* 20 Feb. 1937

. . . with whatever it is that good English is good for —James Sledd, in Greenbaum 1985

When the restrictive clause is a contact clause (with the relative pronoun omitted), the preposition also must come at the end:

These were some of the placid blessings I promised myself the enjoyment of —Samuel Johnson, *The Idler,* 10 June 1758

The University is one most people have heard of —Robert Frost, letter, 20 Jan. 1936

. . . to visit a guy I went to Ohio State with —James Thurber, letter, 1937

. . . something all of us can learn a thing or two from —Simon 1980

Clauses introduced by *what* require postponing the preposition:

I know what you are thinking of —Jane Austen, *Mansfield Park,* 1814

. . . what the small cars look like —*Young America Junior Reader,* 7 Mar. 1952

That's what the taxpayers provide our salaries and buildings for —John Summerskill, quoted in *Change,* October 1971

Wh- clauses in general tend to have the preposition at the end:

. . . the reception which this proposal met with —Henry Fielding, *Jonathan Wild,* 1743

. . . aspects of Army life which I delight in —Edward Weeks, *Atlantic,* December 1952

. . . people . . . whom you would like to dine with —Archibald MacLeish, letter, 13 Sept. 1954

. . . a pitch which the New York batter . . . swung at —E. L. Doctorow, *Ragtime,* 1975

Wh- questions usually have the preposition postponed:

. . . What else are they for? —Trimble 1975

"And what are they made of?" Alice asked —Lewis Carroll, *Alice's Adventures in Wonderland,* 1865

Whom is that literature about? —Earl Shorris, *N.Y. Times Book Rev.,* 1 July 1984

Infinitive clauses have the preposition at the end:

He had enough money to settle down on —James Joyce, *Dubliners,* 1914

. . . should have had a paragraph all to himself to die in —Leacock 1943

The peculiarities of legal English are often used as a stick to beat the official with —Gowers 1948

Burchfield also mentions two other constructions. One is the passive:

> None of them . . . has yet been heard of —*The Intimate Notebooks of George Jean Nathan,* 1932

The other is the exclamation: "What a shocking state you are in!" (example from Burchfield). And here are a few assorted inversions, passives, and other constructions in which the terminal preposition is idiomatic:

> Albania, indeed, I have seen more of than any Englishman —Lord Byron, letter, 3 May 1810

> . . . the Pretender had not gratified his enemies by getting himself put an end to —Henry Adams, letter, 3 Sept. 1863

> They probably know which shelf everything is on in the refrigerator —*And More by Andy Rooney,* 1982

> . . . shorts, size 36, which she spent the rest of the evening crawling in and out of —Russell Baker, *N.Y. Times Mag.,* 29 Jan. 1984

The preposition at the end has always been an idiomatic feature of English. It would be pointless to worry about the few who believe it is a mistake.

prerequisite, *noun* **1.** The noun *prerequisite* is usually followed by *for* or *to* when it takes a preposition:

> In other countries land reform is a prerequisite for democracy —Bruce Bliven, *New Republic,* 12 Nov. 1945

> . . . declaring that the prerequisite for destroying fascism was a socialist revolution in England —Irving Howe, *Harper's,* January 1969

> The pictures . . . were not notable for good draftsmanship—a prerequisite for surrealism —Anthony Burgess, *MF,* 1971

> A general background of content in liberal arts courses is a necessary prerequisite to professional training —*Catalogue: The College of William & Mary,* April 1952

> . . . he answered the questions put to him by the Senators as a prerequisite to his confirmation —*Current Biography 1949*

> . . . strengthening the bulwarks of academic freedom that . . . are an essential prerequisite to . . . your glorious future —Albert L. Nickerson, *University of Chicago Round Table,* 24 Jan. 1954

Sometimes *prerequisite* is used with *of*:

> . . . he possesses the prerequisite of an original poet—a percipience . . . exact and exhilarating —C. Day Lewis, *A Hope for Poetry,* 3d ed., 1936

> . . . the prerequisite of all German political parties, a daily newspaper in which to preach the party's gospels —William L. Shirer, *The Rise and Fall of the Third Reich,* 1960

2. See PERQUISITE, PREREQUISITE.

prerequisite, *adjective* The adjective *prerequisite* is usually followed by *to* when it takes a preposition:

> . . . contained most of the ingredients prerequisite to box-office success —*Current Biography,* May 1966

> The ability to perform that slight distortion of all the elements in the world of a play . . . which is prerequisite to great farce . . . —T. S. Eliot, "Philip Massinger," in *Selected Essays,* 1932

present The verb *present* is most commonly found with *to* or *with,* the former marking the receiver and the latter the thing presented:

> He had continually to be presenting to allies their supposed advantage —Hilaire Belloc, *Richelieu,* 1930

> The nature of the tasks presented to school administrators and teachers —James B. Conant, *Slums and Suburbs,* 1961

> . . . a mediocre man . . . whom, he thought, it would be positively humiliating to present to the Germans —William L. Shirer, *The Rise and Fall of the Third Reich,* 1960

> . . . the new instrument with which Einstein has presented the mathematicians —W. R. Inge, *The Church in the World,* 1928

> Both of these developments present us with the question: What are the potentialities of the human mind? —Margaret Mead, *The Lamp,* Summer 1963

> There was something mildly debonair, he thought pleasantly, in presenting your wife with a rose —William Styron, *Lie Down in Darkness,* 1951

Present is also used with *as, at,* or *for*:

> Reston presented himself and his staff as team players —Gay Talese, *Harper's,* January 1969

> Some of the photographers . . . presented their cameras at the Generals on the balcony as if they had been highwaymen —Eric Linklater, *Private Angelo,* 1946

Though not yet of legal age to practise, he was presented for the bar by Judah P. Benjamin —*Dictionary of American Biography,* 1929

presently An ill-founded notion, of fairly recent origin, holds that there is something wrong with the sense of *presently* that means "at present, now."

The "at present" sense of *presently* has been in use more or less continuously since 1485. According to the OED, it appears to have dropped out of literary English in the 17th century. It seems, however, to have continued in nonliterary use; the OED notes it as common in Scottish writers and "most other English dialects." Although 18th- and 19th-century citations are not numerous, the sense stayed in use. Thackeray knew it:

> I have been thinking over our conversation of yesterday, and it has not improved the gaiety of the work on w[hich] I am presently busy —letter, 4 Mar. 1862

The sense became more common in the 20th century. The OED cites a 1901 Leeds newspaper; here are a few examples from our files:

> I have no use for him presently —Lady Gregory, *Damer's Gold,* in *New Comedies,* 1913

> ... Professor Eric Walker—presently of the University of Capetown —*Times Literary Supp.,* 12 Sept. 1936

> ... for sheer theatrical ineptitude the once-esteemed Guild presently hasn't a rival this side of an Arkansas little theatre —George Jean Nathan, *Newsweek,* 10 Oct. 1938

> ... the diseases which presently afflict the South —*Saturday Rev.,* 28 Dec. 1940

> ... is presently chief editor at Chappell —Herbert Warren Wind, *New Yorker,* 17 Nov. 1951

> Lasser is presently fiddling around with ideas for a book —E. J. Kahn, Jr., *New Yorker,* 14 Mar. 1953

> ... but neither is presently able to engage in a sustained practical politics of its own —Irving Howe, *Partisan Rev.,* January–February 1954

Dictionary treatment of the "at present" sense has been somewhat spotty. Samuel Johnson, working with mostly literary material, had no citations for the sense more recent than the 16th and 17th centuries; he marked the sense obsolete. Noah Webster in 1828 followed Johnson and left it obsolete, as did Merriam-Webster dictionaries following Webster, right up through 1909. When the OED evidence for the sense became available in 1909, Webster 1909 had already been edited and the sense la-

beled *Obs.* The editors of the 1934 edition labeled the sense *Rare exc. dial.* and included the quotation from Lady Gregory above. The 1934 treatment brought us quite a bit of correspondence, some of it wondering if the quotation from Lady Gregory was meant to imply that the sense was of the Irish dialect, but most of it enclosing newspaper clippings and wondering why we thought it was rare. But most of our current evidence had been gathered after the book was published. Consequently in 1947 the entry was revised to show the sense as current; the sense has been treated as current in all our subsequent dictionaries.

Theodore Bernstein appears to have been the first usage writer to take a position against the sense: in *Winners & Sinners* (3 Feb. 1954) he states " 'Presently' means 'forthwith' or 'soon'; it does not mean 'at present.' " By 1958 when he collected his comments into a book, he softened the remark: " 'Presently' should be reserved for the meaning 'forthwith' or 'soon'; it should not be diluted to take in also 'at present.' " (He would retreat farther in his 1965 and 1977 books.)

Once Bernstein had let the genie out of the bottle, there was no getting it back, and numerous usage commentators have come forward to condemn the use, generally on the ground that it can be ambiguous. This observation is buttressed with a context-free example made up for the purpose. In actual use, the word is almost never ambiguous. Quirk et al. 1985 note that when *presently* means "at present," it is used in modern contexts with the present tense of a verb. (Quirk finds this more common in American than British English; Burchfield 1996 notes that Scots as well as Americans use it.) When it is used to mean "before long," it tends to go with a verb accompanied by a modal auxiliary or with a verb in the past tense.

If there is any restriction on the "at present" sense of *presently,* it is that it is used more often in business and political writing than in more literary or academic prose, but it is not infrequent in such writings either:

> The young Southern artist, fiction writer, and poet are presently hanging fire —Walker Percy, *Signposts in a Strange Land,* 1991

> ... the styles of volcanic activity which are presently observed or have occurred in the past —Lionel Wilson et al., *Nature,* 21–27 Apr. 1983

We close with a citation from a political writer:

> The fastest-rising welfare cost is Medicaid, presently paid by the states and cities —William Safire, *Springfield* (Mass.) *Morning Union,* 29 Jan. 1982

In his *New York Times Magazine* column of 14 Dec. 1980, Safire recommended avoiding the word entirely because of its ambiguity.

Conclusion: the sense of *presently* meaning "at present" has been in more or less continuous standard use since 1485. The commentators who warn against its use do so without good reason. There is nothing wrong with it.

present writer *The present writer* is a convention by which a reporter, reviewer, or author can put in personal observations or opinions without using the pronoun *I*. Copperud 1970, 1980, Bremner 1980, and Nickles 1974 express mild disapproval, but this is an innocuous convention.

The present writer once suggested to him . . . —F. Scott Fitzgerald, in *New Republic*, 22 Nov. 1954

The present writer too has wept over these —Virgil Thomson, *American Music Since 1910*, 1971

At last, the present writer, asked to say how he would go about it, . . . —Frederic G. Cassidy, Introduction to *Dictionary of American Regional English*, 1985

Burchfield 1996 lists several other combinations (such as *your reviewer, the author*) which are similarly used.

preside *Preside* is most commonly found with *over*:

. . . made one feel that the occasion was not a party over which he was presiding but a species of mixed smoker —Edmund Wilson, *Memoirs of Hecate County*, 1946

. . . met in Canterbury Cathedral to preside over the signing of the Channel Tunnel Treaty —William Grimes, *N.Y. Times Mag.*, 16 Sept. 1990

It is not the nature of the Mayor or the men around him to preside over the dismemberment of their empire —Dan Cordtz, *New York*, 22 Nov. 1971

. . . Berlin was always a place presided over by the camera —Stephen Spender, *N.Y. Times Mag.*, 30 Oct. 1977

Somewhat less frequently, *preside* is used with *at*:

Ella presided at the punch bowl —William Styron, *Lie Down in Darkness*, 1951

. . . will preside at a Judgment Day, when the saved will be winnowed from the damned —Edmund Wilson, *A Piece of My Mind*, 1956

As Council president, Impellitteri presided at its three or four meetings each month —*Current Biography 1951*

Preside is also sometimes used with *in*:

Carpetbaggers sat in every legislature, presided in every court, and ruled from every statehouse —Marshall Smelser & Harry W. Kirwin, *Conceived in Liberty*, 1955

. . . the mayor presides in council meetings in cities of Illinois —Frederic A. Ogg & P. Orman Ray, *Introduction to American Government*, 8th ed., 1945

prestigious It may come as a bit of a surprise to some readers to find that the only living sense of *prestigious* was aspersed by Follett 1966 and a panelist of Harper 1975 on the grounds of the word's etymological connection to *prestidigitation* and its early archaic sense relating to conjuring. The older sense has not been attested since the 1880s.

The current sense, as far as we know, was first used by Joseph Conrad in his novel *Chance* in 1913. How the word got from Conrad into American journalism we do not know, but here are our next two earliest citations:

. . . the most prestigious yearly salon of pictorial photography in America —*Carnegie Mag.*, March 1937

. . . starred in such prestigious successes as *Winterset* —*Time*, 3 Jan. 1938

Its frequent appearance in *Time* during the 1940s and 1950s undoubtedly helped popularize the new sense. It is in reputable use in spite of a few doubters; Burchfield 1996 notes it is part of the day-to-day vocabulary.

. . . journalistic awards more respectable but less prestigious than the Pulitzers —Simon 1980

A recommendation from the Philological Society . . . must be counted as one of Webster's more prestigious recommendations —E. Jennifer Monaghan, *A Common Heritage*, 1983

The change in the meaning of *prestigious* was influenced by a similar change in the meaning of *prestige* that took place in the 19th century.

presume See ASSUME, PRESUME.

presumptive, presumptuous Bryson 1984, Shaw 1975, 1987, the Oxford American Dictionary and Copperud 1970, 1980 warn us not to confuse *presumptive* with *presumptuous*. An old sense (1609) of *presumptive* does, in fact, mean "presumptuous." This sense, to judge from the example in Bryson 1984, is still found on rare occasions. It is not wrong, but it is rare enough to occasion surprise and perhaps confusion. We do not recommend your using it.

Here are a couple of mainstream uses of the words:

> The old indictment was now revised by the federal government to place him in a group of presumptive conspirators —Robert Penn Warren, *Jefferson Davis Gets His Citizenship Back,* 1980

> I don't even claim that the book is wholly purified of the sins it rails against with such presumptuous authority —Zinsser 1976

This is a question you can easily settle by using your desk dictionary.

Copperud 1980 and Garner 1998 note that *presumptuous* is sometimes misspelled *presumptious.* Actually, *presumptious* is an old spelling of the word; the OED has examples from about 1400 to 1815. Our files have a few examples. It is, however, a rare spelling that is better avoided.

pretense, pretence The usual spelling in American English is *pretense*; the usual spelling in British English is *pretence.* American writers have also used *pretence,* but we have no really recent examples and most of what we have dates from the 1940s or earlier. *Pretense* is very rare in British usage. We have Canadian examples of both spellings.

pretty The adverb *pretty,* used as a downtoning qualifier like *somewhat* or *rather,* has been used in literary English since 1565. And, at the same time, it has been used in speech and informal writing such as letters. Why it is a subject of discussion in more than twenty of our usage sources is something of a mystery. The fuss seems to start with Vizetelly 1906, who finds that it "lacks elegance and definitiveness." Later criticism adds nothing more substantial to this original criticism; time and time again we are told that *pretty* is established but it is overworked or it is colloquial or it is informal, etc. But such remarks might equally be made of *cat* or *dog* or *take* or *set. Pretty* is, in fact, widely used on all levels of discourse. The following examples will make our point. First some from informal sources:

> . . . a "northeast storm"—a little north of east, in case you are pretty definite —Emily Dickinson, letter, 8 June 1851

> I feel pretty sure —Lewis Carroll, letter, 27 May 1879

> . . . I am a pretty shrewd old boy for a countryman —Robert Frost, letter, 11 Oct. 1929

> Mother, however, looks pretty well —E. B. White, letter, 17 Oct. 1935

> . . . he did pretty well as a writer —William Faulkner, 20 May 1957, in *Faulkner in the University,* 1959

Some from literature of several kinds and from literary journalism:

> I must have felt pretty weird by that time —F. Scott Fitzgerald, *The Great Gatsby,* 1925

> My mother considered herself pretty well prepared in her kitchen and pantry for any emergency —Eudora Welty, in *The Contemporary Essay,* ed. Donald Hall, 1984

> . . . I'm being responsible in a pretty reckless way —William Stafford, *Writing the Australian Crawl,* 1978

> . . . even though their religious knowledge is often pretty exiguous —David Martin, *Times Literary Supp.,* 11 Dec. 1981

> . . . I could pretty much go wherever I felt a story led —Roy Blount, Jr., *N.Y. Times Book Rev.,* 9 Mar. 1986

And some from miscellaneous other writings:

> The unification of these two forces . . . is now pretty well accepted in the scientific community —James S. Trefil, *Science 81,* September 1981

> The word wed in all its forms as a substitute for marry, is pretty hard to bear —Bierce 1909

> The first round of the battle was fought over standards of usage and was pretty well finished by the late thirties —James Sledd, *A Short Introduction to English Grammar,* 1959

> . . . regards most of us as pretty irrevocably plunged in illusion —Iris Murdoch, *The Fire and the Sun,* 1977

The adverb *pretty* was entered in Johnson's 1755 Dictionary with eight quotations from the learned, pious, and elegant writers of the late 17th and early 18th centuries. It was acceptable to Samuel Johnson and it is acceptable today.

prevail *Prevail* is most often used with *upon* when it means "to use persuasion successfully":

> Knowing me to be under a promise that naught can prevail upon me to break —Rafael Sabatini, *Saint Martin's Summer,* 1924

> . . . Harney prevailed upon the men in the sloop to sail up the river again —Marjory Stoneman Douglas, *The Everglades: River of Grass,* 1947

> . . . the McCarthy advisers had been successful in prevailing upon the candidate —David Halberstam, *Harper's,* December 1968

Less frequently we find it with *on*:

> . . . could Wickham be prevailed on to marry his daughter —Jane Austen, *Pride and Prejudice*, 1813

> . . . the Mayor of Winsted . . . prevailed on Army engineers to spend a quarter of a million dollars —John Hersey, *New Yorker*, 17 Sept. 1955

This sense of *prevail* is also used sometimes with *with*:

> . . . 'I don't at all fear of prevailing with the young lady, if once I get her to the room.' —Fanny Burney, *Evelina*, 1778

> . . . they must also formulate policy and try to make it prevail with Congress —John McDonald, *Fortune*, July 1954

In its other senses, *prevail* is found quite often with *over* and *against*:

> . . . the rush of pity which always prevailed over every other sensation —Edith Wharton, *The Old Maid*, 1924

> . . . no matter how many troublesome Montgomerys there may be on his team, in the end he will prevail over them —Max Ascoli, *The Reporter*, 12 Jan. 1956

> Society may require that the squatter shall prevail over the swagman —William Power, *Yale Rev.*, Summer 1954

> Not until the slain father returns from heaven . . . in the form of his own statue, does he prevail against his slayer —George Bernard Shaw, *Man and Superman*, 1903

> . . . newly worked out moral truths can prevail against habit and prejudice —Robert M. Hutchins, *Center Mag.*, January 1968

prevent *Prevent* is used in several constructions that have received comment. The first of these is *prevent* + a noun or pronoun + *from* + an *-ing* form of a verb. This construction is prescribed as correct by both American and British usage books and is in fact the most common American construction represented in our files.

> It can't help you win, but it might prevent you from losing —Arthur Ashe, quoted in *Playboy*, May 1980

> . . . to prevent the President from establishing a military dictatorship —Francis D. Wormuth, "The Vietnam War: The President versus the Constitution," 1968

> . . . a slight defect in his spine prevented him from pursuing this ambition —*Current Biography*, July 1965

Prevent + an *-ing* form with no noun or pronoun turns up now and then:

> . . . obliged to cling, to prevent being washed

away —Captain Frederick Marryat, *Peter Simple*, 1834

> To prevent being misled —Melissa Ludtke, *Sports Illustrated*, 10 Apr. 1978

Barzun 1985 catches himself starting to use *prevent* + object + *to* + infinitive and then decides that it is an impossible construction. It is perhaps not possible for most writers, but we do find it once in a great while:

> . . . providing an excuse for preventing "foreign" blacks to settle in urban areas —*Times Literary Supp.*, 14 July 1966

> There is nothing to prevent what Congress has done today to be undone tomorrow —Arthur Markewich, quoted in *Springfield* (Mass.) *Union*, 30 Mar. 1967

preventative, preventive The critics have panned *preventative* for over a century, preferring its shorter synonym *preventive* in spite of the fact that both words have been around for over 300 years and both have had regular use by reputable writers. Here is the basic premise behind the objections: if two similar adjectives are derived from the same verb, then one of them must be in some way inferior to the other, and the likely culprit is the longer one. But the only real difference in status between these two words is that *preventative* is less common than *preventive*. If you decide you like the sound of that extra syllable and are willing to brave possible criticism for it, you may take heart from the example set by these writers:

> . . . send a preventative Medicine —Daniel Defoe, *A Journal of the Plague Year*, 1722 (OED)

> Wearing flannel next the skin is the best cure for, and preventative of the Rheumatism I ever tried —George Washington, *Writings*, 1793 (OED)

> Green onions are a mosquito preventative. In forty-four years he had yet to be bitten on the lips —Garrison Keillor, *Leaving Home*, 1987

> Fear is not a preventative of war —Frederic Wertham, *Johns Hopkins Mag.*, Summer 1971

> . . . which may or may not be particularly instructive and most certainly not preventative —Michael Stugrin, *Chaucer Rev.*, Fall 1980

There never has been a rational objection to *preventative*—unless you lack the breath or space for one extra two-letter syllable. The usual modern objection is that it is irregularly formed, but it is not; it is simply *prevent* + *-ative*, as *talkative* is *talk* + *-ative*. Still, *preventive* is more frequently used.

previous to   Back in 1770 Robert Baker objected to this compound preposition—he did not realize it was a preposition—because he detected something adverbial in the way it was used; he decided *previous* should be *previously*. His opinion resurfaced in the 19th century and commentators then and in the early 20th century recommended *previously to*. Subsequent comment became diffuse, different commentators making different suggestions. By the 1940s, *previously to*, which actually had a little 19th-century use, was dismissed as an error.

But usage commentators hate to let a subject go, and you can still find it disapproved for one reason or another. When one commentator calls it "commercialese" and another "highfalutin" you know that there is no substance to their objections. Our files show that *previous to* is simply an alternative to *before*. It does not seem to be used often enough to warrant the amount of criticism it has endured. It is standard and available to those who find it useful.

principal, principle   There is nothing that we can tell you about this spelling problem that innumerable handbooks (we have more than forty in our collection) and dictionaries from grammar-school level on up have not. But read it one more time: only *principal* is an adjective. *Principal* is also a noun, usually signifying either a person or money. *Principle* is only a noun, usually designating a law or rule. A quick check of any reputable dictionary will guide you in doubtful cases.

Ah, but even if you know the difference, it is still easy to goof by writing "the basic principal" or "their principle occupation." These errors seem to be the ones that are most common. And bear in mind that if you have a word processor, it will not help you here.

> I am even nervous about some words I should have mastered in grade school. I know when to use . . . "principle" not "principal," but I always pause just an instant to make sure —*And More by Andy Rooney,* 1982

Perhaps we should imitate Andy Rooney's pause. It could be the pause that refreshes the memory.

principle of proximity   See AGREEMENT, SUBJECT-VERB: THE PRINCIPLE OF PROXIMITY.

prioritize   *Prioritize* is a jargon word used in various specialized fields such as the military, business, the social sciences, and data processing. Here are three actual uses of the word:

> . . . consumers will want an on-line service to package the best sites and prioritize the jumble of Web services for a simple month-

ly rate —Jared Sandberg et al., *Wall Street Jour.,* 18 Jan. 1996

> We're having a great deal of difficulty in prioritizing our interests —Adm. Thomas B. Hayward, quoted in U.S. Naval Institute, *Proceedings,* August 1982

> . . . considers the paradoxes, tensions, and anxieties that inhere in the cultural prioritizing of the women in the Petrarchan and Neoplatonic systems of the Renaissance —Catherine Bates, *Notes and Queries,* June 1991

We bring up the question of actual use because our files indicate that this word almost never appears in general publications except in the form of comment on the word itself.

Unless you are working in a field where *prioritize* is commonly used (it may even be the technical approach to literature), you will probably never need the word or need to worry about it. We have no persuasive evidence that *prioritize* is moving out of specialized jargon into widespread general use.

See -IZE 2.

prior to   "Stilted," "affected," "formal," "incongruous," "stiff," and "clumsy" are among the adjectives that have been used by commentators to describe the use of *prior to,* with "formal" being the most common label. *Before* is the generally preferred substitute, "except in contexts involving a connexion between the two events more essential than the simple time relation," says Fowler 1926. Follett 1966 makes the same point more briefly: "*prior to* carries with it the idea of necessary precedence." This restricted use of *prior to* turns up in the following examples:

> If guards are to be used, arrangements must exist prior to the emergency —Mary Margaret Hughes, *Security World,* May 1968

> . . . her appointment would be terminated as of September 29, unless prior to that time she requested a hearing —*AAUP Bulletin,* September 1971

> . . . a final review of each death-penalty case prior to execution —William Saletan, *New Republic,* 21 Aug. 2000

However, such uses of *prior to* are in the minority in the Merriam-Webster citation files. We find that *prior to* used simply as a synonym of *before* is more common. The phrase most often appears in rather formal contexts:

> . . . only now do we understand that it's aliens who've been diddling us all these millennia. . . . But then why are there virtually no reports of flying saucers prior to 1947? —Carl Sagan, *The Demon-Haunted World,* 1996

Hawking has extrapolated Einstein's theory of gravity back to an epoch that was not simply prior to life but prior to atoms —Alan Lightman, in *World Treasury of Physics,* Timothy Ferris, ed., 1991

Reports can be previewed on screen prior to printing them out on paper —William F. Sharpe, *Linn's Stamp News,* 16 Mar. 1998

They had not been subject to Nazi rule or persecution prior to the war —William J. Vanden Heuvel, *American Heritage,* July/August 1999

. . . in the centuries prior to their descent on Britain the tribes of north-west Germany were continuously on the move —D. J. V. Fisher, *The Anglo-Saxon Age,* 1973

Although Reader's Digest 1983 says *prior to* is "now accepted at all levels of usage," we lack citations which show its use in informal or personal contexts. In a formal or impersonal context *prior to* is perfectly appropriate. See also PREPARATORY 2; PREVIOUS TO.

proceed 1. See PRECEDE, PROCEED.
2. *Proceed, procedure.* Note the spelling. A few commentators point out that the verb is sometimes misspelled *procede* (using the ending of *precede*) and the noun is misspelled *proceedure.* We have examples of both misspellings, so one needs to be alert.
3. Janis 1984 and Copperud 1964, 1970, 1980 seem to believe that *proceed* can mean only "to go forward." Where this notion originated, we have no idea. Look at any good desk dictionary, or an unabridged dictionary, or the OED to see the variety of meanings this word can have.

procure This word is pompous (or pretentious or formal) for *get,* say several commentators. A better description of many uses would be *literary*:

. . . felt grateful, as well she might, for the chance which had procured her such a friend —Jane Austen, *Northanger Abbey,* 1818

Some gifted spirit on our side procured (probably by larceny) a length of mine fuse —H. G. Wells, *Mr. Britling Sees It Through,* 1916

It is also used for official procurement, especially of such things as armaments:

. . . his program of building up the armed services and procuring arms for them —William L. Shirer, *The Rise and Fall of the Third Reich,* 1960

In less exalted contexts it suggests care and effort:

. . . the task of procuring men for the openings now available —Archibald MacLeish, letter, 9 May 1917

Unlike an agent, whose chief task is to procure acting roles —Nikki Grimes, *Essence,* March 1995

Procure is not an everyday substitute for *get* or *obtain,* but it has its uses and need not be consistently avoided.

prodigal 1. The adjective *prodigal* is frequently used with *of*:

. . . like a lovely woman graciously prodigal of her charm and beauty —W. Somerset Maugham, *The Moon and Sixpence,* 1919

Wildly prodigal of color, the new sun then sketched a wide band of throbbing red-gold —F. Van Wyck Mason, *Himalayan Assignment,* 1952

She had been prodigal of all her resources, money and energy and imaginative strategems —Katherine Anne Porter, *The Never-Ending Wrong,* 1977

Prodigal is also commonly followed by *with*:

He had always been prodigal with his whistle, tooting it for children's birthday parties —John Cheever, *The Wapshot Chronicle,* 1957

. . . excludes the debilitating habit of some state courts of being too prodigal with rehearing —Felix Frankfurter, in *Aspects of American Government,* ed. Sydney D. Bailey, 1950

It has also been used sometimes with *as to* or *in*:

Masterfully economical as to words, Mr. Saroyan is . . . almost recklessly prodigal as to feeling —Elizabeth Bowen, *New Republic,* 9 Mar. 1953

Nor will posterity censure the present age for having been too prodigal in its applause of this great man —Joseph Wood Krutch, *Samuel Johnson,* 1944

2. Bryson 1984 and Harper 1975, 1985 say that many people think *prodigal* means "wandering" or "tending to stray" because they associate it with the New Testament parable of the prodigal son who, having received his inheritance, "took his journey into a far country, and there wasted his substance with riotous living" (Luke 15:13, AV). The son returned, repentant, and was welcomed back by his father, who killed the fatted calf in celebration.
Our files do not show the adjective being used to mean "wandering." The usage, if it exists, may be primarily oral, or perhaps the idea has been oversimplified in the usage

books. The OED includes a sense under the noun *prodigal* that covers the many meanings the word can have when it is used in allusion to the parable. The examples there all reflect one aspect or another of the parable—especially that of the repentant sinner welcomed home. We have some recent allusive examples, but all are for the noun or for the adjective in the compounds *prodigal son* and *prodigal daughter*.

> . . . stared at the prodigal who had come home to her —Priscilla Johnson McMillan, excerpt in *Book Digest*, February 1978

> . . . she was received into her mother's household as a prodigal daughter —John Updike, *N.Y. Times Book Rev.*, 23 Feb. 1986

> . . . Spielberg has donned the hair shirt and paid his dues. It's time for Hollywood to embrace its prodigal son —Peter Travers, *Rolling Stone,* 24 Mar. 1994

These uses echo the parable and do not necessarily imply extravagance or wastefulness. Such use dates back to Shakespeare in 1596 and Ben Jonson in 1601 and, while apparently not especially common, would appear to be entirely legitimate. But it seems not to be the use Harper and Bryson are talking about.

productive When used with a preposition, *productive* is usually followed by *of*:

> Their knowledge and methods were enormously productive of new weapons and devices of war —James Phinney Baxter 3d, *Scientists Against Time*, 1946

> He is also aware that Congressional investigating committees have been productive of much good —Robert K. Carr, *N.Y. Times Book Rev.*, 27 Feb. 1955

proficient *Proficient,* when used with a preposition, usually takes *in* or *at*:

> While in college he was proficient in mathematics and philosophy —*Dictionary of American Biography*, 1929

> This captain must be an experienced person, trained and proficient in his job —F. Glen Nesbit, *Sperryscope*, Fourth Quarter 1954

> Jane began to type. It bored her, but she was fairly proficient at it —Rose Macaulay, *Potterism*, 1920

> Become proficient at lag putting and you may make a few —Dave Pelz, *Golf Mag.*, July 1996

Occasionally *proficient* is used with *on*:

> While he was a student he also became proficient on the guitar —*Current Biography*, July 1966

profit The verb *profit* is followed most often by *from* when it takes a prepositional-phrase complement:

> . . . his battle descriptions would sometimes have profited from consultation of the official records —Lynn Montross, *N.Y. Times Book Rev.*, 19 Sept. 1954

> . . . both Hawthorne and Thoreau profited more from their acquaintanceship than has been generally allowed —Earle Labor, *CEA Critic*, January 1971

Almost as frequently, *profit* is used with *by*:

> . . . whenever Miss Clark lets herself go her book profits by it —Sean O'Faolain, *Books of the Month*, April 1953

> . . . should get as much liberal education as he can intellectually absorb and profit by —Cormac Philip, *CEA Critic*, November 1954

prohibit A number of fairly recent books—Freeman 1983, Longman 1984, Copperud 1970, 1980—insist that *prohibit* should not be followed by *to* and an infinitive. This admonition goes back to Fowler 1926. The construction with *to* and the infinitive seems to be the original construction for *prohibit* in this particular sense. The OED, having no examples later than the middle of the 18th century, supposed the construction archaic. Actually it appears to be one of those banes of the lexicographer, the low-frequency item. It had not, in fact, quite disappeared:

> . . . they are prohibited to add new names —H. C. Burdick, *Sales Promotion by Mail*, 1916

H. W. Fowler 1926 culled two examples from British newspapers. Taking the OED's *archaic* label to be an absolute, he decided that his modern examples must, therefore, be violations of idiom. Fowler himself must have used the *prohibit from* followed by an *-ing* construction that he prescribed. This construction, which is the common one in present-day English, is only attested in the OED from about 1840.

> . . . prohibiting anyone working for the commission from having any financial interest in a strip mining operation —Marion Edey, *Not Man Apart*, July 1971

> . . . are prohibited from taking any job that involves contact or dealings with the government —Anthony Bailey, *New Yorker*, 20 Nov. 1971

Prohibit may also be followed by a noun or gerund direct object; no one has disputed these constructions:

... prohibited the employment of workers under 16 —*American Guide Series: North Carolina*, 1939

... family finances prohibited his going to college —*Current Biography 1953*

Prohibit from can also be followed by a noun:

... it should not be prohibited from prayer —George Bush, radio interview, 23 Aug. 1984

Prohibit to may still have an occasional user, but as Burchfield 1996 observes, it is probably obsolescent. *Prohibit from* followed by a gerund is the usual construction now.

prolegomenon, prolegomena *Prolegomenon* is the singular and *prolegomena* the plural form of this scholarly word, which means "prefatory remarks" or, more specifically, "a formal essay or critical discussion serving to introduce and interpret an extended work." It is also used in a broader sense to refer generally to something that serves as an introduction.

As is the case with its much commoner brethren *criterion* and *phenomenon*, the irregular plural form of *prolegomenon* may be mistaken for a singular by some English speakers. Another complicating factor is the meaning of the word, which simultaneously encompasses a singular and a plural notion, as you can see from the definitions above. The dual nature of the word is attributable to the use of *Prolegomena* in the title of noteworthy scholarly and philosophical works, such as Immanuel Kant's *Prolegomena to Any Future Metaphysics Which Will Be Able to Come Forth as Science* (1783), which not unnaturally came to be referred to as Kant's *Prolegomena*. People then started to think of *prolegomena* as denoting both a single work and the remarks included in it.

As a result, we find that when the context gives no clue to the singular or plural number of the word, *prolegomenon* and *prolegomena* are used with about equal frequency.

... it provides the best prolegomenon to *Comus* which any modern reader could have —T. S. Eliot, *Sewanee Rev.*, Spring 1948

... included the following passage in the prolegomenon to his treatise, *De Jure Belli ac Pacis*, written in 1625 —Jon M. Van Dyke, *Center Mag.*, July/August 1971

Study of the past should be prolegomena to understanding, engagement, and preparation for the future —Francis W. Nichols, *Commonweal*, 9 Apr. 1999

... whose *Art of Spiritual Harmony*, written in 1910, is the prolegomena to what ... I am

calling metaphysical painting —Herbert Read, *The Philosophy of Modern Art*, 1952

And while we do have citations in which *prolegomenon* is clearly construed as a singular and *prolegomena* is clearly construed as a plural, we also have a few examples in our files in which *prolegomena* is used in a singular construction.

... a valuable philosophical prolegomena to a sound theological understanding of the Christian faith —Theodore M. Greene, *Scientific Monthly*, May 1954

The book served as a stepping stone, or as Payne-Gaposchkin preferred to think of it, a prolegomena —Elske V. P. Smith, *Physics Today*, June 1980

We do not, by the way, have citations for *prolegomenon* used as a plural or for a plural form *prolegomenons*.

For other foreign plurals, see LATIN PLURALS.

promise Vizetelly 1906 objects to the verb *promise* in the sense of "assure." The same objection finds more recent voice in Shaw 1987 and Longman 1984.

The sense of *promise* under criticism here is pretty old—the OED dates it back to 1469. Shakespeare used it:

I do not like thy look, I promise thee —*Much Ado About Nothing*, 1599

The OED also has quotations from Addison, Fielding, and Thackeray. After Thackeray in 1862 there seems to be nothing. The OED suspected the sense to be archaic; so did the editors of Webster's Third. But Vizetelly must have seen or heard it somewhere, and so must Shaw and the editors of Longman 1984. But where?

The answer seems to be that the usage has receded into speech only, an assessment Burchfield 1996 shares. We have but a single modern example. It is taken from speech, that of a small-town American school superintendent:

She has promised me that the father is not a student —in *People*, 17 Jan. 1983

It appears, then, that instead of being archaic, this use still exists to a certain extent in British and American speech. Note that this sense of *promise* is not used in current ordinary discursive prose.

prone, supine Quite a few commentators insist on the distinction that *prone* means "face down" and *supine* means "face up." Harper 1975, for instance, says "It is impossible for a man to 'lie *prone* on his back.' *Prone* means 'face downward.' If he is lying on his back, he is *supine*." The first part of that assertion is somewhat dubious, as we shall see.

John Simon's pun that "when it comes to learning good English, most people are prone to be supine" (Simon 1980) points to one of the influences operating on the meanings of these words: the chief uses of both *prone* and *supine* have nothing to do with physical position. *Prone* is used chiefly in the sense of "having a tendency or inclination," as in "prone to worry" or "accident-prone." *Supine* is used chiefly in the sense of "mentally or morally slack." The senses that relate to physical position, then, are secondary.

Supine itself also complicates the situation. It is a relatively rare word: in Merriam-Webster files *prone* is nearly five times as frequent as *supine* and in the Brown University Corpus (Kučera & Francis, 1967) there are 14 *prone*'s to a single *supine*. It is clearly a less well known word, and it is more bookish or literary than *prone*.

A third factor is the use of *prone,* at least since the 18th century, with inanimate objects having no identifiable ventral surface, such as ancient towers or obelisks. In these uses *prone* contrasts with *upright* and simply means "lying flat"; the relative position on the ground is not a consideration:

> The third (obelisk) which had also lain prone for a thousand years —Emil Ludwig, *The Nile,* 1937

> I joyfully swish my feet through the prone golden autumn harvest of leaves —Michael P. O'Connor, *Irish Digest,* April 1955

A fourth factor is the pejorative overtones of the most frequently used sense of *supine.* One that is supine is usually looked down on in some fashion, as the Simon quotation suggests.

Given these four factors, it is not surprising that *prone* is used more loosely than some would wish in describing persons and objects having a discernible front and back.

Everybody seems to agree that *supine* means "lying face upward," but only a few writers actually use it in general or literary contexts:

> Foxy, in a . . . maternity swimsuit, lay supine on a smooth rock, eyes shut, smiling —John Updike, *Couples,* 1968

Prone is regularly distinguished from *supine* in medical and physiological writing, where the distinction is a very important one. *Prone* regularly means lying on one's belly to those who shoot guns and write about it, but *supine* appears to be unknown to them.

Outside these contexts, *prone* is sometimes used when the orientation of the body is uncertain, unknown, or unimportant:

> . . . I caught sight of the large prone figure in bed —D. H. Lawrence, *The White Peacock,* 1911

> I too have been prone on my couch this week, a victim of the common cold —Flannery O'Connor, letter, 20 Mar. 1961

It is even sometimes used when a human being is clearly flat on the back:

> He lies prone, his face to the sky, his hat rolling to the wall —James Joyce, *Ulysses,* 1922

When you consider all these uses, it is clear that in relation to physical position *prone* most often means flat on one's belly, quite often means merely flat or prostrate, and less frequently flat on one's back. It is possible that the choice of *prone* in this third case may be influenced by a desire to avoid the notion of passiveness connoted by *supine*; while such might have been the case with James Joyce, it is probable that nothing more than the relative rarity of *supine* works against its selection in other instances.

If you are about to use *prone* to describe physical position, you are unimpeachably safe if an animate object is face down, or if you are describing an inanimate object. If your prone person or animal is belly up, you might incur the wrath of some critic.

See also PROSTRATE.

pronoun agreement   See AGREEMENT, PRONOUN: NOUNS JOINED BY AND, OR.

pronounce   When *pronounce* is used with a preposition, generally it is found with *on* or *upon.* Both Raub 1897 and Bernstein 1965 (neither of whom mention *pronounce upon*) prescribe *on* with a thing; Bernstein allows only *against* with a person. Although *pronounce on* usually has a thing as its object, at times it does have a person. *Pronounce upon* occurs more often in British English than in American English.

> "What would uncle Egmont have said of Lawrence Leffert's pronouncing on anybody's social position? . . ." —Edith Wharton, *The Age of Innocence,* 1920

> . . . I found Sonia . . . pronouncing on various writers she knew —David Plante, *Difficult Women,* 1983

> Whatever he has pronounced himself upon—linguistics, genetics, . . . painting—his words have at once had the authority of holy writ —Malcolm Muggeridge, *Punch,* 11 Mar. 1953

> . . . his desire to influence others, to pronounce upon questions . . . of the day —Roy Jenkins, *The Times* (London), 19 Nov. 1973

Pronounce also occurs, though less frequently, with *in favor of* or its counterpart *against*:

> . . . when civil war seemed inevitable he pronounced himself decidedly in favor of the Union —*Dictionary of American Biography,* 1929

> . . . liberal platforms regularly pronounce in favor of more vigorous anti-trust enforcement —Carl Kaysen, *New Republic,* 22 Nov. 1954

> From his pinnacle of power . . . Nikita Krushchev . . . has pronounced against skyscrapers —Flora Lewis, *N.Y. Times Mag.,* 3 Apr. 1955

Pronounce is also found occasionally with *about*:

> . . . when my friends pronounce responsibly about the values of creative work —William Stafford, *Writing the Australian Crawl,* 1978

Although these uses of *pronounce* with various prepositions are usually intransitive, uses with a reflexive pronoun as direct object are found, the example from Muggeridge above being typical.

pronouns 1. English pronouns seem to be the source of many vexing usage problems. A few will be touched on here, but most of the ones that have generated considerable comment are treated in their own places. We refer you then to BETWEEN YOU AND I; BUT; I; IT'S ME; ME; MYSELF; ONE OF THOSE WHO; THAN; THAT; THEY, THEIR, THEM; WHO, WHOM; YOU; and to the several articles at AGREEMENT, many of which treat questions about pronouns.

2. It is sometimes useful to remember that we have several kinds of pronouns. People reminded of pronouns may think only of the personal pronouns, in their nominative, objective, and possessive forms, and maybe the reflexive pronouns based on the personal pronouns. But we also have relative pronouns, demonstrative pronouns, and indefinite pronouns. There are also interrogative pronouns, if you wish, although these are really just some of the relative pronouns doing extra duty.

Remembering the variety of pronouns will help keep you from making generalizations like "Every pronoun necessarily has an antecedent" (Barzun 1985). Barzun's statement (which, to be fair, is made in the context of an example that lacks a needed antecedent) is an overgeneralization. Indefinite pronouns, for instance, do not require an antecedent.

3. One of the favorite pastimes of writers on usage is to find examples of pronouns that are in the objective case when they should be in the nominative, or are in the nominative when

they should be in the objective. Sometimes a worried commentator will deduce from the frequency of such examples that the language is deteriorating or that illiteracy is about to overwhelm us or that our educational system is a complete failure. Beyond the likelihood that the educational system has failed to explain pronouns adequately to many people, the worries are without a sound basis. The use of object forms where subject forms belong, and vice versa, has been going on for hundreds of years.

It was, for instance, common in the 17th century to interchange the nominative and objective forms of the second person plural pronoun, *ye* and *you,* with the result that eventually the objective *you* replaced *ye* altogether. Interchange of nominative and objective forms of other pronouns was also anything but rare; Wyld 1920, for instance, gives this quotation from Sir John Suckling: "What have they to do with you and I?" You can find a good deal on the subject in historical grammars—Jespersen 1909–49, Henry Sweet's *A New English Grammar* (1892), and Wyld 1920, among others.

Quirk et al. 1985 notes that these interchanges of nominative and objective forms actually occur only in a limited number of constructions. The first of these is the use of the objective case where traditional normative grammar calls for the nominative after *be* or *as* and *than.* The rule calling for the nominative is based on analogy with Latin; the use of the objective comes from the influence of the rules of normal word order in English. In English, the nominative is required only in the subject position directly before the verb; the objective tends to be used everywhere else, as if the objective were the unmarked case form to be used everywhere there are no positive reasons for using the nominative. In this respect modern English is much like French. Besides those positions already mentioned, the objective form tends to be chosen in absolute and emphatic uses:

> Who said that? Me.

> Me—afraid of flying?

> Better them than us —Don Baylor, quoted in *Springfield* (Mass.) *Daily News,* 13 Oct. 1986

There is no question that these constructions, and "It's me" and the rest, would never have been anything but unexceptionable had not our earliest grammarians been so heavily influenced by Latin.

We next come to two separate constructions involving coordination, usually with *and.* The first is characteristic of non-mainstream varieties of English. This is the use of the objective case before the verb when the pronoun is co-ordinated with a noun or another pronoun:

> Me and my baby goes back and sleeps the day —anonymous speaker, quoted in Walt Wolfram, *Appalachian Speech,* 1976

Quirk says that the objective pronoun can even occur in the position next to the verb. Wolfram notes that the objective pronoun does not occur by itself in subject position, only in combination with another noun or pronoun.

The second coordinated pairing—which one of our correspondents has named "the Someone and I syndrome"—occurs in rather more educated varieties of English. Here we find a nominative pronoun coordinated with a noun or another pronoun and occurring in the object position after a preposition or after a verb. *I* is the most common pronoun in such pairs, but others such as *he* and *she* are also found:

> Now Margaret's curse is fall'n upon our heads,
> When she exclaimed on Hastings, you, and I . . .
> —Shakespeare, *Richard III,* 1593

> . . . invited my love and I —Lady Strafford, letter, 1734 (in Wyld 1920)

> It must all light upon Heartfree and I —Sir John Vanbrugh, *The Provok'd Wife,* 1697 (OED)

> . . . a most furious conflict between Sir W. Pen and I —Samuel Pepys, diary, 21 Feb. 1667

> . . . the poet, like you and I, dear reader —W. H. Auden, quoted in *Time,* 2 Feb. 1948

> According to both he and Sam, my donkey act . . . had quite an effect —Oliver North, quoted in *The Tower Commission Report,* 1987

In this construction, *someone and I* is treated as a polite fixed unit, to be used either in subject or object position. Several recent commentators ascribe this usage to hypercorrection—the overly cautious use of the nominative pronoun because it is prescribed in such constructions as "It is I." (See HYPERCORRECTION.) But the early appearance of the construction, with such 16th- and 17th-century exemplars as Shakespeare, Suckling, Pepys, and Vanbrugh, antedates the teaching of English grammar. (For a modern and more linguistically oriented explanation of *someone and I,* see the brief treatment of Chomsky's analysis at BETWEEN YOU AND I.)

Another linkage that produces case confusion is the pronoun in apposition to a noun. This combination frequently produces objec-

tive forms in subject positions where the pronoun is emphasized:

> Us Valley Girls have to endure a lot —letter to the editor, *People,* 13 Sept. 1982

It may be the influence of hypercorrection in avoiding the subjective *us girls* that leads to the nominative in apposition following a preposition:

> At last—a sherry for we Amontillado connoisseurs —advt., quoted in Howard 1978

> We ultimately commune with others of our own faith, and for we westerners, nature is an article out of another faith —Paul Gruchow, *Update* (Univ. of Minn.), October 1985

The last of the problem environments mentioned by Quirk et al. is the pronoun that seems to lie between two clauses; this pronoun is often drawn toward both the nominative and objective forms by reason of its different relationships to the preceding and following parts of the sentence. Usage is decidedly mixed:

> It was she (her?) John criticized —in Quirk et al.

> Everything comes to him who waits —English proverb

> Just as the ideal of even-handed justice for all can be somewhat tilted toward he who can afford to argue the rightness of his case —*Globe and Mail* (Toronto), 8 Oct. 1982, quoted in Greenbaum 1985

> I'm against whoever is in office —*And More by Andy Rooney,* 1982

> They can't decide where to fight or who to salute —*N.Y. Times,* 20 Feb. 1987

> But it were vain for you and I
> In single fight our strength to try.
> —William E. Aytoun, "Bothwell," 1856 (in Alford 1866)

> . . . the reporter whom Mr. Friendly said had been given the secret plan —*N.Y. Times,* 17 Feb. 1987

Some of these examples follow the dictates of traditional grammar, and others do not. But you can see how each of them is tugged in two directions at once.

pronoun with possessive antecedent Bernstein 1971 has an article under this heading in which he quotes from three books a rule applying to the construction; stated most baldly it goes "a pronoun cannot take as an antecedent a noun in the possessive case." Bernstein is not very impressed by the cogency of the rule, and he is right not to be, but it can be found enunciated in other handbooks—in

Barzun 1985, Simon 1980, and Ebbitt & Ebbitt 1982, for instance.

We have not discovered where this rule originated, but it is likely to have been with one of those 18th-century appliers of logic to language. We get a hint of this sort of origin from Barzun:

> . . . there can be no logical link between a proper name in the possessive case and a personal pronoun. "Wellington's victory at Waterloo made him the greatest name in Europe" is all askew, because there is in fact no person named for the *him* to refer to.

Right away you can see something missing from this analysis. In the first place, you have no trouble understanding the sentence; if it is illogical, at least its meaning is as plain as day. Second, you can see that the whole problem can easily be removed by changing *him* to *his* and greatly increasing the elegance of the sentence. But wait—isn't *his* a personal pronoun too? Yes, but at least it's in the possessive case and matches *Wellington's*. It must be all right for a possessive pronoun to refer to a possessive noun, proper or not:

> . . . Bob Tizzy . . . filed St. Boniface's nose smooth with his face —W. M. Thackeray, *The Book of Snobs*, 1846

> Your daughter's feet are nearly ruined by her shoes —Paula Fox, *A Servant's Tale*, 1984

Clearly the objection has to be to a pronoun in some other case referring to a noun in the possessive case. That can be viewed as illogical. But this sort of logic (which is only Latin grammar in disguise) does little more than impose an unnecessary burden on the writer. When the reader clearly understands what is written, what more logic is needed? The reader knows that Wellington is in the writer's mind even if, as Barzun contends, he is not technically there in the sentence. The reader ignores the technicalities, understands, and reads on.

Bernstein quotes the first of his three sources to the effect that the rule is little respected by writers. A little looking around shows that indeed it is not:

> It was Mr. Squeers's custom to call the boys together and make a sort of report, after every half-yearly visit to the metropolis, regarding the relations and friends he had seen —Charles Dickens, *Nicholas Nickleby*, 1839

> . . . shaking Snooks's hand cordially, we rush on to the pier, waving him a farewell —W. M. Thackeray, *The Book of Snobs*, 1846

> Strafford's enemies were in deadly earnest, because while he lived they and all they

strove for were in jeopardy —G. M. Trevelyan, *A Shortened History of England*, 1942

> My father tried valiantly to wrest Pittsburgh Phil's title from him —Frank Sullivan, *The Night the Old Nostalgia Burned Down*, 1953

> . . . played on Hull's mounting fear that he and his men would be cut off —James MacGregor Burns, *The Vineyard of Liberty*, 1981

> I just hope the people who make up the President's schedule don't arrange any more breakfast meetings for him —*And More by Andy Rooney*, 1982

Ebbitt & Ebbitt 1982 has an example of the construction in which the relative pronoun *who* refers to the possessive antecedent. The example is awkward indeed, to the point of sounding rather implausible. Yet we have a genuine example of the construction; it is old and similarly awkward-sounding, but still easily understandable.

> I do not at all mean to detract from Garrick's merit, who was a real genius in his way —Horace Walpole, letter, 1 Feb. 1779

Bernstein says the rule can be ignored where it does not interfere with sense. We agree. But we would not recommend Walpole's construction, which sounds awkward to the modern ear.

propellant, propellent The editors of the OED entered only the *-ent* spelling, but three-quarters of their citations were spelled *-ant*. The OED Supplement says the *-ant* spelling is now the most common for both adjective and noun. Our evidence shows that the word is much more often a noun than an adjective. The *-ant* spelling predominates. Our most recent evidence for the *-ent* spelling comes primarily from British sources; Burchfield 1996 says it is limited to the adjective.

prophecy, prophesy A surprising amount of ink has been used in a surprising number of handbooks to inform everyone that *prophecy* is a noun and *prophesy* is a verb—the very information carried in every dictionary. The common assertion is that the two words are confused—an assertion our files cannot confirm, even though we have a 1980 *prophecied* from the *Saturday Review*. The particular objection seems to be to the use of *prophesy* as a noun.

The OED shows that historically both spellings have been used for both functions. Webster's Second recognizes *-cy* for the verb and *-sy* for the noun as infrequent variants, and so does Webster's Third.

Most writers, then, follow the mainstream and use *prophecy* as a noun, and *prophesy* as a verb.

propitious *Propitious* is usually used with *for* or *to*. *For* is often followed by a gerund; *to* is often followed by an infinitive.

> Flora's fine eyes, that were so observant, noticed how propitious was this moment for their entry —Stella Gibbons, *Cold Comfort Farm*, 1932

> . . . when the environment was propitious for expanding the role of science and research —Eli Ginzberg, *Columbia Forum*, Fall 1970

> . . . the time might now be propitious for seeking an amelioration of the religious situation —Norman Cousins, *Saturday Rev.*, 30 Oct. 1971

> . . . those journalists who asserted, some years ago, that logical positivism was propitious to fascism —Alfred Jules Ayer, *Encounter*, April 1955

> . . . the French decided that the moment was propitious to declare Viet Nam completely independent —*Time*, 27 Sept. 1954

> . . . others might use their astrology . . . to note when the stars were propitious to overthrow the regime —Daniel J. Boorstin, *The Discoverers*, 1983

proportion There are two issues involving *proportion*. The first of these is an American newspaper tradition that seems to have begun with Bierce 1909, and is carried on by Bernstein 1958, 1965, and Bremner 1980. This is an objection to *proportion* used in the sense of "size, dimension." It is often plural in this sense. The reason for the objection is said to be that *proportion* expresses a relationship and has nothing to do with size. The argument may seem logical, but it is controverted by usage. The word has been used in the disputed sense at least since the 17th century.

The sense is, however, considered acceptable by several commentators and the usage panel of Heritage 1969. The sense has been standard all along, but it does not make up a very large part of our evidence for *proportion*. Here are some examples:

> He was fired as a security risk. . . . The anonymity of his discharge gave it oracular proportions —John Cheever, *The Wapshot Chronicle*, 1957

> Edith, in whom pride of blood was swollen to tumorous proportions, used to boast about the Plantagenet features of Osbert and herself —Richard Jenkyns, *New Republic*, 1 May 2000

> Popular obsession with the stock market has reached almost psychotic proportions —Robert J. Samuelson, *Newsweek*, 15 May 2000

> . . . hired . . . to disport her generous proportions around swimming pools —James Brady, *Saturday Rev.*, 30 Sept. 1978

The second issue was originally raised by Fowler 1926. He offers a long criticism of *proportion* in a sense meaning "share, part, portion"; his argument is based, apparently, on the same premise as Bierce's objection to the "size" sense—namely, that *proportion* properly expresses a relationship, a ratio. The reasoning is somewhat undermined by the OED, which shows the criticized meaning as the earliest sense in English. Later commentators—Partridge 1942, Flesch 1964, Copperud 1964, 1970, 1980—have repeated Fowler's objection while omitting his reasoning. This sense of the word has slightly more literary use than the first sense objected to.

> . . . traditionally gave their time and a good proportion of their possessions as a matter of course to those dependent upon them —Vita Sackville-West, *The Edwardians*, 1930

> . . . the greater proportion of these terms have never been taken up by the literary language —John Geipel, *The Viking Legacy*, 1971

> . . . a far smaller proportion were willing to emigrate —Samuel Eliot Morison, *Oxford History of the American People*, 1965

> At the stroke of any midnight in the year a far larger proportion of the population is awake in the United States than in any other place on earth —John Lear, *Saturday Rev.*, 15 Apr. 1972

Both of these uses are entirely standard.

proportional, proportionate, proportionable Dictionaries, Fowler 1926, and Copperud 1970, 1980 are in substantial agreement that *proportional* and *proportionate* mean the same thing. Copperud observes that *proportional* is the more common word, an observation confirmed by our citational evidence. *Proportional* is the more frequently used one in fixed technical combinations, such as *proportional counter, proportional dividers,* and *proportional representation.*

Proportionable is a rare word; Garner 1998 says it's an archaism. It has been seldom seen since the 19th century.

proposition 1. *Noun.* Sometime in the 1870s *proposition* acquired a new sense, meaning "something of an indicated kind." It originated in the United States and was a sense of broad application, applied variously to contrivances, situations, enterprises, or even people that one had to deal with. This use has been disparaged from 1881 down to Fowler 1926 (and his numerous followers into the

1980s). Burchfield 1996 reports that Fowler's objections went unheeded, and the disputed uses have established themselves as part of the ordinary language, in the U.K. as well as in the U.S.

> He was absorbed in his own dexterity and in the proposition of trying to deceive a fish with a bird's feather and a bit of hair —John Cheever, *The Wapshot Chronicle*, 1957

> The music hall is a worthless proposition economically —Paul Goldberger, *N.Y. Times*, 1 June 1979

> . . . getting a smile from her is a tough proposition —Barry McDermott, *Sports Illustrated*, 18 Jan. 1982

> Divorce . . . is a buy-now-pay-later proposition —Gael Greene, *Cosmopolitan*, July 1972

> The other book . . . is an altogether different proposition —Anatole Broyard, *N.Y. Times Book Rev.*, 24 Mar. 1985

2. The verb *proposition* is even newer than the noun sense just discussed, apparently having originated in the 1920s. Its presence seems to have been noticed in the 1930s, although none of our books mentions it before Bernstein 1958. Bernstein saw it in the *New York Times*, apparently in its later and more specific sense of suggesting sexual intercourse, and was so flabbergasted he didn't believe his eyes: "There's no such verb," he said. Copperud 1970, 1980 reports it as standard. It is certainly used without qualms:

> . . . was arrested as part of a vice detail's sweep of the area after he allegedly propositioned an undercover policewoman —*Sports Illustrated*, 28 Jan. 1985

The older and more general use of the verb has not received much mention in the handbooks. This sense too seems to have become entirely respectable:

> There hadn't been a box-office smash among them, and so the movie companies weren't propositioning Korty —Judith Crist, *New York*, 28 Jan. 1974

> . . . an English publisher propositioned me to write a life of Sainte-Beuve —John Russell, *N.Y. Times Book Rev.*, 23 Feb. 1975

Burchfield reports that these senses, like those of the noun above, are established as standard.

prostrate Some commentators say that *prostrate* should be confined to the meaning "lying face down." This same issue is frequently raised about *prone* (see PRONE, SUPINE) but less often about *prostrate*, which is just as well since *prostrate* often simply means "lying down." Like *prone*, it is sometimes used of

inanimate objects that have no faces to be up or down:

> He clambered over half-visible rocks, fell over prostrate trees —Willa Cather, *Death Comes for the Archbishop*, 1927

When used to describe the position of a person, *prostrate* implies "face down" only when the person is prostrate in adoration or submission. Otherwise the direction the person faces is unimportant—even in medical sources where terminology is precise.

> Prostrate in homage, on her face, silent —Gordon Bottomley, *King Lear's Wife*, 1915

> . . . it requires the patient . . . to assume the prostrate or horizontal position —Warren H. Cole & Robert Elman, *Textbook of General Surgery*, 6th ed., 1952

> . . . not even more brandy could revive the prostrate form of the vanquished boy —J. A. Maxtone Graham, *Sports Illustrated*, 15 July 1968

protagonist Fowler 1926 first made *protagonist* a usage issue. It was he who brought in the Greek roots of which the word is composed to deride plural use of the word as absurd, and it was he who suggested the influence of *pro-* "in favor of" in the development of the sense meaning "proponent, advocate." Thus we have two main lines of dispute, right down to the present time.

The first of these two disputed uses is the longer-lived one. Criticism of it is summed up reasonably succinctly here:

> Thus the worthy Irving Howe writes, on the front page of the *New York Times Book Review* (April 9, 1978), about "main protagonists." Now, the protagonist is the main actor in something and has, since Greek times, always been used in the singular. "Protagonists" is incorrect (unless you are referring to the protagonists of two or more dramas), and "main protagonists" (main main actors) is redundant to boot —Simon 1980

There are a few weaknesses in Simon's statement. To begin with, "always been used in the singular" is wrong: the earliest citation for the word in English is from Dryden (1671) and he uses it in the plural, meaning (in his words) "chief persons of the drama." And Simon has overgeneralized; the limitation to a single protagonist is true of Greek drama, but it is not therefore necessarily true in English literary tradition, as we have seen.

To understand how *protagonist* is used, we have to begin with 20th-century use. So if in ancient Greek drama the protagonist was the main character, in a modern work with more than one main character, there might be more than one protagonist. This is no more than taking the central notion of a word and stretching it to meet new conditions.

> ... you've made a grave mistake about the illustrator. . . . you ought to see the grey blurs he made of my beautiful protagonists —F. Scott Fitzgerald, letter, 25 June 1921

> *Badlands* has two protagonists and *Days of Heaven* four (though both movies are rich in colorful minor roles) —Richard Alleva, *Commonweal*, 12 Mar. 1999

> The end of the novel dissolves into a fantasia in which the narrator . . . places the protagonists on trial —*Times Literary Supp.*, 14 Nov. 1968

> The protagonists of Gordon's fiction are children who have been saddled with their parents' emotional bad debts —Judith Thurman, *New Yorker*, 12 Mar. 1990

Now let us suppose that we liken a real-life situation to a drama. Might not the central figure then be the protagonist? And if there were two central figures?

> ... the memoirs of the political and military protagonists, Mr. Churchill, General Eisenhower, Lord Cunningham —*Times Literary Supp.*, 4 Jan. 1952

> The chief losers in all this are the two original protagonists—Britain and Persia —Andrew Shonfield, *London Calling,* 7 Oct. 1954

> Ostensibly, this great medical row was about the correct treatment of the ailing Fuhrer, and the protagonists in it were Dr. Theodor Morell, Hitler's physician, and Dr. Karl Brandt, his surgeon —Hugh Trevor-Roper, *American Scholar*, Winter 1981/82

The unetymological sense "proponent, advocate, champion, supporter" was spotted by the OED in use as early as 1877. This sense is thought to have been influenced by *pro-* "in favor of." This sense seems to have become established in the 1920s:

> ... Raymond Poincaré, bitter anti-German, determined anti-bolshevist, protagonist of strict enforcement of the Treaty of Versailles —*The Nation*, 25 Jan. 1922

> The true university is the protagonist of liberty and tolerance —*Science,* 5 Mar. 1926

> Thoreau will be remembered . . . as a protagonist of man against the state —Henry Seidel Canby, *Thoreau,* 1939

> The most adamant opposition to my argument is likely to come from protagonists of secular reason —Glenn Finder, *Atlantic,* December 1989

> ... Sir Winston proclaimed himself a protagonist of high-level talks without agenda —*New Statesman & Nation,* 28 Nov. 1953

The loss of the notion of primacy is often signaled by the use of an adjective such as *chief* or *principal*:

> ... the chief protagonist of the Government in the Paris press —*Manchester Guardian Weekly,* 2 Sept. 1921

> ... the Socialists, who are the leading protagonists of the "Anschluss" movement —*N.Y. Herald Tribune,* 13 Nov. 1927

> Indeed he and Arnold Bennett were the chief protagonists in London of unusual evening shirts —Osbert Sitwell, *Noble Essences,* 1950

> ... the author's gross enthusiasm for the chief protagonists —*Times Literary Supp.,* 7 June 1996

These uses are all standard. The traditional bases for objection have been demolished by the evidence in the OED Supplement.

protect *Protect* is frequently found with *from* and a little less frequently (though still quite commonly) with *against*:

> ... the scanty vegetation was insufficient to protect the light soil from blustery winds —Ray Allen Billington, *Westward Expansion,* 1949

> Mark, being deaf, is protected from her interference —John Cheever, *The Wapshot Chronicle,* 1957

> To protect against such an eventuality the treaty contains a safeguarding clause —*Encyclopaedia of the Social Sciences,* 1933

> ... citizens need to be protected against thieves and murderers —Alexander B. Smith & Harriet Pollack, *Saturday Rev.,* 4 Dec. 1971

Protect is also used frequently with *by* to express a different relation:

> He blew hard on hands half protected by shabby woolen mittens —F. Van Wyck Mason, *The Winter at Valley Forge,* 1953

> I thought it would only be fair to protect the readers of the magazine I was editing by describing my own biases —Nicolas H. Charney, *Saturday Rev.,* 11 Dec. 1971

Protect with appears less often but is not rare either:

> ... the mind does not shy away from anything, it does not protect itself with any illusion —I. A. Richards, quoted in F. R. Leavis, *The Common Pursuit,* 1952

... protecting unimportant secrets with mystifying ritual —Frederic L. Paxson, *Pre-War Years 1913–1917,* 1936

protest, *noun* The noun *protest* is most often used with *against:*

... resigned from the government in protest against the backstage maneuvering —*Current Biography,* September 1964

And it would be bitterly ironic if a field that was founded upon a protest against exclusion should itself become fearful of pluralism —Henry Louis Gates, Jr., *N.Y. Times,* 4 Apr. 1998

... this was a kind of strategic protest against her husband's double life —Van Wyck Brooks, *Saturday Rev.,* 6 Mar. 1954

Protest is also followed by *at:*

He was also associated with the work of UNESCO, but resigned in protest at the admission of Franco's Spain —*Current Biography,* January 1964

... an immediate storm of public protest at the proposed use of park land for great buildings —*Dictionary of American Biography,* 1929

Occasionally *protest* is found with *of* or *to:*

... resigned from the "Voice of America" program in protest of this Kaghan discharge by ... the State Department's new security officer —T. R. B., *New Republic,* 8 June 1953

... have recalled their ambassadors in protest to the executions —radio news broadcast, 27 Sept. 1975

protest, *verb* *Protest,* when used with a preposition, usually appears with *against:*

He went here and there swearing and protesting against every delay —Sherwood Anderson, *Poor White,* 1920

... the number of people who were protesting against the morals of the time —Gilbert Seldes, *Saturday Rev.,* 13 Feb. 1954

In the next decades Cotter practised in various places and continued to protest against his dismissal —*Australian Dictionary of Biography,* 1966

Occasionally *protest* has appeared with *about, at,* or *over:*

I sent her off to her address in a taxi ... : she protested about the expense —Edmund Wilson, *Memoirs of Hecate County,* 1946

He protested at the usury laws of 1829 —*Australian Dictionary of Biography,* 1966

Here the poet seems to insist on, rather than protest over, her separation from the boy —Maxine Kumin, *To Make a Prairie,* 1979

While the use of intransitive *protest* with a preposition remains very common, this sense of *protest* used as a transitive verb without the preposition can be found about as often in the U.S. *Against* began to be omitted around the turn of the 20th century—some have said in order to save space in newspaper headlines—and *protest* used alone has become established in American English. British English normally still uses *protest against.* Although some usage commentators have warned that confusion may arise if *against* is not used, our evidence shows that this has not been the case:

She marched with the pickets, protesting atmospheric testing —Dick Kleiner, *Springfield* (Mass.) *Union,* 14 Mar. 1966

It has become customary for the Soviet Union to protest the seating of the delegates of the National Government of China —Philip C. Jessup, *The Reporter,* 6 July 1954

... she also became part of a politically oriented "gang of five" that protested Rostropovich —Martin Bernheimer, *N.Y. Times Book Rev.,* 23 Sept. 1984

protractor See INCOMPARABLE.

proved, proven A lot of ink has been devoted to questioning the propriety of *proven* versus *proved* since the controversy started in the 19th century (our earliest comment comes from 1829). *Proven* is historically the past participle of *preven,* in Middle English the usual spelling of what has become *prove. Proven* survived in and descends to us from Scottish English. It apparently first established itself in legal use and has been slowly working its way into literary and general use. Tennyson was one of its first frequent users in literature; he seems to have used it for metrical reasons.

Surveys forty or fifty years ago showed *proved* to be about four times as common as *proven.* But *proven* has caught up in the past twenty years; it is now nearly as common as *proved* as part of a verb phrase; it is more common than *proved* when used as an attributive adjective. You can use whichever form you like.

I should hate to see Ezra die ignominiously in that wretched place where he is for a crime which if proven couldn't have kept him all these years in prison —Robert Frost, letter, 24 June 1957

The Peace Corps has proven over the years that it can survive —Robert Shogan, *N.Y. Times Book Rev.,* 9 Feb. 1986

Coming up with a cure for this dreaded form of dementia has proven devilishly hard —Naomi Freundlich, *Business Week,* 11 June 2001

But I had proved I could make money if I put my mind to it —James Thurber, letter, 27 Dec. 1952

What artist had ever really proved a reliable guide to the meanings generated by his work? —Dan Hofstadter, *New Yorker,* 6 Jan. 1986

These injections have proved reasonably effective —*Women's Health,* Summer 1998

Although *proven* is more common as an attributive adjective. you can use *proved* too:

Richard Cork, a proven authority on the first machine age in its relation to British art —John Russell, *N.Y. Times Book Rev.,* 2 June 1985

. . . a perfect knowledge of their own past record and proved capabilities —Roger Angell, *New Yorker,* 9 Dec. 1985

Some writers use both:

. . . where they were known, where what they were did not have to be proved —E. L. Doctorow, *Loon Lake,* 1979

He had proven not the sturdiest member of the expedition —E. L. Doctorow, *Ragtime,* 1975

Both forms are standard now.

provide When *provide* is used intransitively, it is most often used with *for:*

. . . provide for the common defense —*Constitution of the United States,* 1787

And no sooner he's provided for than he turns on you —Joseph Conrad, *Chance,* 1913

. . . an Automobile Accident Compensation Board would provide for strict liability —Samuel H. Hofstadter, *N.Y. Times Mag.,* 21 Feb. 1954

The contract provided for increased wages, pensions, insurance —*Current Biography,* November 1965

When *provide* is used transitively to mean "to supply or make available," the recipient of the provision is frequently named in a prepositional phrase beginning with *for* or *to:*

. . . a discontent which has provided fertile soil for the agitator —L. S. B. Leakey, *Mau Mau and the Kikuyu,* 1952

A new Urban Service Corps providing public employment for unemployed youth —James B. Conant, *Slums and Suburbs,* 1961

. . . it will provide nearly eleven-million units of electricity to people in rural areas —*London Calling,* 18 Feb. 1954

Provide schools and teachers to all children and illiteracy goes down dramatically —Peter Rossi, *Trans-Action,* June 1967

But when *provide* is used transitively to mean "to make something available to," the thing being provided is usually named in a prepositional phrase introduced by *with:*

The bereaved woman was provided with a collection of gruesome anecdotes —Ellen Glasgow, *Barren Ground,* 1925

The route is well provided with signs —*American Guide Series: New Hampshire,* 1938

. . . a collection of short stories, like a sketch-book, may provide him with an ideal form —*Times Literary Supp.,* 23 Apr. 1970

When *provide* is used transitively to mean "to stipulate," it is often followed by a clause:

The next year the assembly provided that the fort be given to Abraham Wood for three years —*American Guide Series: Virginia,* 1941

. . . the Mutual Security Treaty, which provides that in June, 1970, either party may give notice —William O. Douglas, *Center Mag.,* March 1969

Provide is also used both transitively and intransitively with *against:*

. . . but can Congress predict, and provide against, every emergency in which quick action might be essential? —Elmer Davis, *But We Were Born Free,* 1954

. . . a cushion must sometimes be provided against too sudden deflation —Thurman W. Arnold, *The Bottlenecks of Business,* 1940

provided, providing Both *provided* and *providing* are in standard use as conjunctions, either alone or in combination with *that.* Both have been in use for about the same amount of time: *provided that* in the OED dates from 1460, *providing that* from 1423; *provided* alone from 1600, *providing* from 1632. You can use whichever sounds better to you. Our evidence shows that *provided* is used more often than *providing* and that *provided* has the greater literary backing.

Providing has been aspersed since Ayres 1881 decided on his own that the word was vulgar. His opposition to *providing* somehow found its way into the world of pedagogy, and *provided* has been insisted upon by teacher and commentator down through the years. The preponderance of recent opinion finds both words acceptable, and so do dictionaries.

> He would have offered better material for Dickens than Leigh Hunt or Landor, providing Dickens stuck to the text and curbed the spirit of caricature —*Times Literary Supp.*, 14 July 1950

> Already he was formulating the way he would let the news out, providing he decided not to keep it a secret —J. F. Powers, *Accent*, Winter 1946

> . . . there would be no reason to continue to hold him provided sensible arrangements for his care could be made —Archibald MacLeish, letter, 16 Oct. 1957

> ". . . I have nothing against mediocre people, provided I don't have to teach them anything." —John Updike, *Couples*, 1968

proximity See CLOSE PROXIMITY.

proximity, the principle of See AGREEMENT, SUBJECT-VERB: THE PRINCIPLE OF PROXIMITY.

publically *Publically* is an occasionally used variant spelling of *publicly*. It is either based on the obsolete *publiical* or, more likely, simply on analogy with many other *-ically* adverbs. Chambers 1985 considers it a misspelling. It is not really a misspelling—it is recognized in dictionaries like Webster's Third and the OED Supplement. You can use it if you like, but we do not really recommend it, because it will look unfamiliar to many who encounter it.

punish *Punish* is found most often with *for* and an object that names the offense:

> . . . with the terrible December wind punishing him for the ungodly hour —Larry L. King, *Harper's*, March 1969

> The gifted Don DeLillo is currently being punished for not writing "End Zone" again —Wilfrid Sheed, *N.Y. Times Book Rev.*, 3 June 1973

Less often *punish* is used with *by* or *with* and an object that names the punishment:

> . . . the wife whom he loved . . . who punished him with frenetic fits of "nerves" —Oscar Handlin, *Atlantic*, February 1955

> . . . the United States showed an inclination to punish Argentina by breaking off relations —Richard W. Van Alstyne, *Current History*, March 1953

purge *Purge* is most often used with *of*, and the object names what is gotten rid of:

> . . . whose minds were to be purged of all the natural decencies, of all the laboriously acquired inhibitions of traditional civilization —Aldous Huxley, *Brave New World*, 1932

> . . . the room had never quite been purged of the bad taste of preceding generations —Edmund Wilson, *Memoirs of Hecate County*, 1946

> . . . allowed even enemy aliens to purge themselves of the guilt of their emperors —Oscar Handlin, *The American People in the Twentieth Century*, 1954

> . . . it is severely purged of those autobiographical elements often germane to first novels —Francine Du Plessix Gray, *N.Y. Times Book Rev.*, 15 July 1979

Less often, *purge* is found with *from*, and here the object may name either what is removed or the environment from which it is removed:

> Pure economics, purged from the nationalistic virus, would work for free trade and peace —Albert Guérard, *Education of a Humanist*, 1949

> . . . religious dogmas were purged from public education —Rexford G. Tugwell, *Center Mag.*, January/February 1973

> The players themselves have had a spring in Florida or Arizona to purge the talk of tax shelters from their conversations —Daniel Okrent, *N.Y. Times Book Rev.*, 3 May 1981

Purge is sometimes used with *by* to show means:

> . . . he (Antony) purged his levies by executing a number of soldiers whose loyalty he distrusted —John Buchan, *Augustus*, 1937

> . . . he was sentenced to jail for refusing to hand over certain spending records . . . but later purged the sentence by handing over the documents —Stephen J. Sansweet, *Wall Street Jour.*, 28 Oct. 1976

purport Fowler 1926 started this hare. He discovered "an ugly recent development" in the use of *purport*: it was being used in the passive and also with a personal subject. His disapproval has been repeated by many later commentators.

Fowler thinks the passive use new, because he can only find one example in the OED, dated 1897. The OED shows that in the 19th century *purport* was undergoing changes in its idiomatic construction: the *purporting* recommended by Fowler in place of *purported* dates only from 1879 itself; *purport* appears with a personal subject in the meaning Fowler comments on only in 1884.

Purport came into English in the 16th century as a transitive verb with a noun or pronoun direct object, and by the very end of the 17th century could take a relative clause as object. In the 18th century it began to be followed by what some grammarians (for instance Quirk et al. 1985) call a "subjectless infinitive clause"—a clause with an understood subject in which the verb is an infinitive. The earliest example in the OED (1790) reads:

This epistle purports to be written after St. Paul had been at Corinth —William Paley, *Horae Paulinae, or the Truth of the Scripture History of St. Paul Evinced*

Here are modern examples of the same construction:

The regime adheres to a false philosophy which purports to offer freedom, security, and greater opportunity to mankind —Harry S. Truman, inaugural address, 20 Jan. 1949

This book purports to be a history of American imperialism —Arthur M. Schlesinger, Jr., *Saturday Rev.,* 5 Feb. 1972

This construction, with the infinitive complement, has now almost monopolized the verb; although the older transitive uses with noun or pronoun or clause still turn up, they are fairly rare.

Now a transitive verb can be made passive; for every "Man bites dog" there can be a "Dog is bitten by man." *Purport,* however, gives us no evidence of real passive use. And the predominant modern construction, with the infinitive complement, cannot be made passive. In "this book purports to be," *purport* is more like a copula, or linking verb, than a transitive.

But what about examples like these?

The second act brings the fairies with their military quartet to the castle, where each of the latter is set to woo the Beauty in what is whimsically purported to be his native fashion —George Jean Nathan, *Theatre Arts,* March 1953

. . . Cantelli introduced to this country a symphony, in C major, that was unearthed in Cremona after the war and is purported to have been written by Mozart at the age of fourteen —Douglas Watt, *New Yorker,* 21 Mar. 1953

. . . a scene of what is purported to have been passionate revenge —Ray B. West, Jr., *Sewanee Rev.,* 1949

These examples, like a couple of examples near the end of Fowler's exegesis, look like passives: they consist of a form of *be* followed by a past participle. But like the active *purport* with the infinitive complement, this construction too lacks its reciprocal: it has no active counterpart in which the subject of the pas-

sive verb becomes the direct object of the active verb. Thus they are not true passives. *Is purported* means and functions the same as *purports.* Most likely they are what Quirk calls a pseudo-passive, in which the *be* is not an auxiliary verb but is a copula.

And we have two more constructions to look at, as represented by these examples:

. . . when I smoked a cigarette purported to contain hashish and fainted dead away after two puffs —*New Yorker,* 12 Feb. 1949

. . . an undated instruction of the same period purported to have been sent to the Soviet Military Attaché —O. Edmund Clubb, *Annals of the American Academy of Political and Social Science,* September 1951

. . . a theory, purporting to come from a critic of high repute, that is worth mentioning —F. R. Leavis, *Revaluation,* 1947

. . . found to be carrying forged documents purporting to prove that Dr. Merida's moustache was not his own —*Punch,* 12 Sept. 1945

In these, the past and present participles are used much like postpositive adjectives with an infinitive complement, somewhat like *pleased* in "I'm pleased to meet you." Fowler lumped similar past participles in with his disapproved passives; the present participle in the same construction received his blessing.

That is a heavy dose of grammar, but it shows us that the older (and not quite dead) transitive *purport* has largely been supplanted by an active construction in which the verb is most like a copula, a construction that looks passive but is not, and a pair of constructions in which participles are used much like adjectives. So the grammatical objections of Fowler and his repeaters to the passive actually criticize a usage that does not exist.

There is one further observation to be made about *purports/is purported.* If we say "This book purports to be," we imply that what is asserted is overt—somehow, perhaps in a subtitle or in the preface, the book declares itself openly. In "This book is purported to be," however, may reside a suggestion that someone other than the book's author has discovered this undeclared purpose. The two constructions are likely not to be synonymous; perhaps here was a distinction aborning that Fowler, defender of distinctions, overlooked.

Fowler's other objection is to the use of a personal subject with *purport.* For Fowler's generation the usage was still fairly new (first attested in 1884); the OED called it rare. By Fowler's time it apparently was not so rare any more, and it is not at all rare today:

Most of the sequences in which Mr. Webb purports to be a Lothario of the silent screen are pretty funny —John McCarten, *New Yorker*, 2 Aug. 1952

. . . they purported to be too far from the sources of power . . . to be sure of the exact causes —Richard H. Rovere, *New Yorker*, 6 Aug. 1955

. . . interviewed someone who purported to be a member of their studio audience —Whitney Balliett, *New Yorker*, 24 Sept. 1973

None purports to have found a link between the quantum world and that of gravitation —Timothy Ferris, *N.Y. Times Mag.*, 26 Sept. 1982

Summary: *Purport* is most commonly used in these constructions: (1) active verb + infinitive complement; (2) *be + purported* + infinitive complement; (3) noun + *purporting* + infinitive complement; (4) noun + *purported* + infinitive complement. In addition the transitive use—*purport* + noun or pronoun or relative clause—is occasionally found. Of these the active verb is by far the most common and most commonly appears with an inanimate subject. All of these constructions, including the relatively rare transitive, are established in standard English.

These constructions, which Fowler distrusted, have stood the test of time—they are more common now than they were before 1926. The objection to *is purported* on the basis of grammar and a "passive meaning" (Fowler, Evans 1957, Garner 1998) we have found to be baseless because the construction is not grammatically passive. We have also noted that the active verb and the *is purported* construction seem to carry different connotations: the active verb connoting an overt claim, and *is purported* tending to suggest that somebody unnamed and perhaps unknown thinks so. Thus,

. . . publication of what is purported to be a semi-autobiographical novel —*N.Y. Times*, 14 Aug. 1976

suggests that the semi-autobiographical quality is alleged by somebody other than the author or publisher and not advertised on the front cover.

purposefully, purposely Distinguishing between *purposefully* and *purposely* is a concern of several fairly recent handbooks. It is not completely evident what the source of the sudden interest is; none of the commentators has brought forth a genuine example of confusion.

What is at work here may be the realization that the two adverbs can be used in similar situations. Here are a couple with *purposefully*:

. . . those who literally and often purposefully drank themselves to death —Herbert Hendin, *Columbia Forum*, Fall 1969

. . . at a New York address she has purposefully hidden from her father —Joshua Hammer, *People*, 27 Feb. 1984

In these contexts the writer might have used *purposely*, but with different meaning, for *purposely* is the simpler word, meaning merely "on purpose, not by accident," while *purposefully* is intended to suggest that the persons written about did what they did for a purpose. Here we have *purposely* used in similar surroundings:

If the Western Powers had selected their allies in the Lamarckian manner intelligently, purposely. and vitally —George Bernard Shaw, preface, *Back To Methuselah*, 1921

De Gaulle purposely arrived last and spoke first —Stephen E. Ambrose, *Johns Hopkins Mag.*, April 1966

Cases like these illustrate that there are contexts which will allow either word, and there is probably little to be gained by second-guessing the writer. You should, however, be aware of the distinction when you go to use either one yourself.

Purposefully is often used to describe a manner of locomotion:

. . . as I stride purposefully toward the children's department —Carol Eisen Rinzler, *New York*, 1 Nov. 1971

. . . the people in green were scurrying about purposefully —E. L. Doctorow, *Loon Lake*, 1979

Purposely is not used in this way.

These next examples are of contexts in which there is little likelihood of interchange:

His study should stimulate many teachers to think more purposefully about the books they use in the classroom —Janet Smith, *N.Y. Rev. of Books*, 2 Dec. 1971

. . . a basketball shoe covered, purposely, with graffiti —*Sports Illustrated*, 24 Feb. 1986

To sum up, then, there is no real evidence of widespread confusion of *purposefully* and *purposely*, but they are used in contexts where interchange is possible because the meaning of either word would make sense; in these contexts it is a good idea to remember the distinction between them—*purposefully* "for a purpose," *purposely* "on purpose." *Purposefully* and not *purposely* is used as an adverb to describe a style of performance.

pursuit When followed by a preposition, *pursuit* is used with *of*:

. . . the real founders of the typically English middle-class pursuit of branch banking

—Roy Lewis & Angus Maude, *The English Middle Classes,* 1950

. . . in pursuit of his objective to bring to America every bird mentioned in Shakespeare —Morris Gilbert, *N.Y. Times Mag.,* 19 Sept. 1954

Military action was not pursuit of a military solution but an argument by force that would bring Hanoi to an agreement —Barbara W. Tuchman, *N.Y. Times Book Rev.,* 11 Nov. 1979

Several publishers are bringing out books on Iran, in hot pursuit of the headlines —Herbert Mitgang, *N.Y. Times Book Rev.,* 17 Feb. 1980

pyjamas   See PAJAMAS, PYJAMAS.

qua   This Latinate preposition means "in the capacity or character of; as." It is not a word that most people use or recognize, but several usage writers have paid some attention to it. Fowler 1926 devoted a column to discussing what he regarded as its correct use. He believed it should be restricted to cases in which "a person or thing spoken of can be regarded from more than one point of view or as the holder of various coexistent functions, & a statement about him (or it) is to be limited to him in one of these aspects," as in "He was a good husband and father, but, qua businessman, he was a failure." Fowler disapproved its use in other contexts where the less "precise" *as* would be adequate. Later critics have simply regarded *qua* as a pretentious substitute for *as.*

Our evidence shows that *qua* is in fact used in a distinctive way, but not the one prescribed by Fowler. Consider the following passages:

> The novel, *qua* novel, is not really much at all —Sven Birkerts, *Harper's,* July 1989

> Not to teach students grammar qua grammar is as bad as teaching mathematics unmathematically —Simon 1980

> Since nearly every plot twist is stupidly motivated, the audience stops following the story qua story and is reduced to watching Stupid Human Tricks —Richard Alleva, *Commonweal,* 10 Apr. 1998

Most of our citations for *qua* show it being used in just this way, between repetitions of a noun. It seems to function in such contexts as a somewhat more emphatic synonym of *as.* If *as* were used instead, italics might very well be employed to signal the added emphasis the voice would provide in speech (" . . . the role of scientist *as* scientist"). When *qua* is used, the italics are not necessary (although *qua* is, in fact, sometimes italicized).

Qua does not always occur between repeated nouns, but its use in other contexts is a good deal less common:

> It cannot, qua film, have the scope of a long book —John Simon, *Esquire,* March 1974

> . . . in the "Washington" poem, great success qua stunt did not preclude reasonable success qua poetry —Douglas Hofstadter, *N.Y. Times Book Rev.,* 10 Mar.1996

If you choose to use the preposition *qua* as it is now most often used, you stand a small chance of being criticized by a disciple of Fowler. If you use it only as Fowler recommended, you still stand some chance of being called pretentious. In neither case should you be greatly concerned. A better reason for avoiding it—if you want one—is that most readers will find it a strange and unfamiliar word.

quandary   *Quandry* occasionally finds its way into print but is considered a misspelling of *quandary* that is based on pronunciation.

> . . . I still find myself in a quandry on this point —*Philosophical Rev.,* April 1953

> Such is the quandry of justice Harry Blackmun —*N.Y. Times Mag.,* 20 Feb. 1983

quantum jump, quantum leap   The phrase *quantum jump* (or *leap*) is derived from the world of physics, in which it has the meaning, "an abrupt transition (as of an electron, an atom, or a molecule) from one discrete energy state to another." Most people are more familiar with its extended use in the sense "an abrupt change, sudden increase, or dramatic advance." This sense has been common since the 1960s:

> . . . a quantum jump in the number of men considered qualified for the bench —*Time,* 21 Feb. 1955

> . . . the artistic quantum leap of our time —Donal Henahan, *N.Y. Times,* 7 July 1968

... we became friends in the late 50's, just as the United States was poised to make its quantum leap into the future —Maya Angelou, *N.Y. Times Book Rev.*, 20 Dec. 1987

In every election, the amount of press coverage of the early contests takes a quantum leap, compounding the distortion —Elizabeth Drew, *New Yorker*, 7 Mar. 1988

The program offers China and Brazil 3,000-pound satellites with high-resolution, widefield imagery in the visible and infrared bands of the spectrum—a technological quantum jump —Carl Posey, *Air & Space/Smithsonian*, November 1997

... we share a common view that the technological and biotechnical advances now under way can provide a unique opportunity for our race to make a quantum leap forward —*Emerge*, December/January 2000

Such usage has been criticized as voguish or jargonistic, but much recent commentary attacks it primarily on logical grounds, pointing out that in physics, a quantum jump is actually a very small change, not a large or dramatic one. But the criticized usage is now established as standard, and, as Garner 1998 points out, anyone using it to mean a sudden small change would probably be misunderstood. *Quantum leap* is currently more common than *quantum jump*.

quasi The pronunciation of *quasi*, which comes from a Latin form meaning "as if" and "as it were," perplexes many speakers. The clear front-runner in our file of attested pronunciations is \'kwā-ˌzī\ (rhyming with *day's eye*), a version not even mentioned in many discussions of this word, either as the pronunciation usually produced (but deprecated) or as the pronunciation to aim for. Following neck and neck at a respectful distance are \'kwä-ˌsī\ and \'kwä-zē\ (rhyming with *may sigh* and *Ozzie*). Trotting along companionably behind these are \'kwä-sē\ and \'kwä-ˌzī\, with \'kwä-ˌsī\ and \'kwä-zē\ bringing up the rear. A rule of thumb might be to say \'kwä-ˌzī\ if you want to sound like your neighbors, and \'kwä-sē\ if you want to sound like Caesar. All these pronunciations are in respectable use, however, and you might just prefer not to change the pronunciation you use now.

quasi-coordinators See AGREEMENT, SUBJECT-VERB: COMPOUND SUBJECTS 3; AS WELL AS.

query Several commentators have distinguished between the nouns *query* and *inquiry*, noting that *query* refers to a single question, while *inquiry* can also refer to a series of questions or an investigation. The implication is that *query* is sometimes misused in place of *in-*

quiry, but there is not much evidence of such misuse (Bernstein 1965 has an example and Garner 1998 has a couple more). Just about everyone uses *query* as the commentators says it should be:

A ... reader sends me a query about a word used by his great-grandfather —Ralph Whitlock, *Manchester Guardian Weekly*, 23 Feb. 1992

The word is very common in the context of computerized information systems:

... the actual software, which combs the index and looks for results that match a query —J. D. Biersdorfer, *N.Y. Times*, 27 Apr. 2000

question 1. When *question* is followed by a preposition, it is usually *of*:

A little honest thieving hurts no one, especially when it is a question of gold —Graham Greene, *Travels with My Aunt*, 1969

... President Lincoln privately raised ... the question of the franchise for a limited number of Negroes —John Hope Franklin, *Race and History*, 1989

The ubiquitous media coverage of the complex issues swirling around the question of who owns language —Andrea A. Lunsford et al., *College Composition and Communication*, October 1996

Flying has become as much a question of physical strength as of finesse —Sebastian Junger, *The Perfect Storm*, 1997

Question is also used, but much less frequently, with *about* and *as to*:

... after I'd later watched [the movie] on a plane flight, I e-mailed him a question about it —Wayne C. Booth, *College English*, September 1998

... the procedures ... are not easy and there is considerable question as to their value —James B. Conant, *Slums and Suburbs*, 1961

2. Preceded by a qualifier like *no* or *little*, *question* is often followed by a clause introduced by *but that, but what*, or simply *that*. Reader's Digest 1983 prefers *that*, though acknowledging the other conjunctions. All are standard.

There is no question but that these changes shift the civilian-military balance —Townsend Hoopes, *Yale Rev.*, December 1953

There is no question but what the national nominating convention is a faithful expression of the genius of the American people —Wilfred E. Binkley, *New Republic*, 1 Mar. 1954

... there seemed little question that it would be able to count on government support —*Collier's Year Book,* 1949

... there's no question that computers and the Internet are a substantial part of 21st-century life —*Psychology Today,* July/August 2001

Question may also be followed by a clause introduced by *whether* or *which*:

The move is an unusual admission in ... Silicon Valley, which may cause some to question whether Ms. Polese was pushed out —Kara Swisher, *Wall Street Jour.,* 26 July 2000

The President and the Prime Minister were both accustomed to holding the centre of the stage. In a sense, what the "first summit" was about was the question which would up-stage the other —*Times Literary Supp.,* 9 Apr. 1970

questionnaire This word is sometimes misspelled with only one *n*.

quick, quickly Use of *quick* as an adverb dates back to about 1300. It has a highly respectable pedigree, having occurred in the works of such authors as Shakespeare and Milton. This adverb is still correct and is commonly used, but it is now more likely to be encountered in speech ("Come quick!") than in writing, except when the writing is deliberately informal or includes dialogue:

He shook his head. "You could take her a cup of coffee pretty quick. . . ." —Walter Van Tilburg Clark, *Track Of The Cat,* 1949

With this guy I decided to end it quick —R. C. Padden, *Harper's,* February 1971

... I suppose the old lady was astounded at how quick I could get away on crutches —Flannery O'Connor, letter, 10 Nov. 1955

Its occurrence in less casual prose is relatively uncommon:

This lovely menace spreads unbelievably quick —Alan L. Otten, *Wall Street Jour.,* 19 June 1956

... he will probably die quicker —David Dempsey, *N.Y. Times Mag.,* 23 June 1974

The usual choice in such contexts—and the one recommended by usage commentators—is *quickly*:

A brilliant student, he moved quickly through his studies —*Current Biography,* March 1967

... he'd rise and walk quickly to Floral Hall —Edward Hoagland, *Harper's,* October 1970

Note that *quick* is also distinguished from *quickly* in that it almost always follows rather than precedes the verb it modifies ("They came quick," not "They quick came"; but "They came quickly" or "They quickly came"). See also FLAT ADVERBS.

quiet, quieten *Quieten,* a synonym of *quiet,* was considered a "superfluous word" by Fowler 1926. Despite Fowler's objections, *quieten* has persisted in British English.

When, at last, Lord Snowdon had quietened us —V. S. Pritchett, *New Yorker,* 24 June 1985

... she thought Roberta was quietening down —Doris Lessing, *The Good Terrorist,* 1985

In American English, the verb used is *quiet*:

... quieted the air like a summer Sunday morning —Zelda Fitzgerald, *Ladies' Home Jour.,* January 1971

... because, as one camp leader said, "They never quieted down." —Alfred Lubrano, *Plain Dealer* (Cleveland, Ohio), 27 July 1985

quite A number of recent commentators notice that *quite* is used in two almost antithetical senses, one approximately "fully, altogether, entirely" and the other approximately "to a considerable extent, moderately." In this respect, *quite* operates much like *rather* (see RATHER 2). There are actually three uses of *quite,* according to the OED and dictionaries that follow the OED analysis. The first use is a completive one originally used with verbs and participles to emphasize that an action is complete.

... an endeavour to recapture the treasure, which they were quite satisfied was hopeless —James Stephens, *The Crock of Gold,* 1912

He felt that the world he had loved had quite gone —Edmund Wilson, *N.Y. Times Book Rev.,* 20 July 1986

When used this way with adjectives and adverbs, *quite* emphasizes the fullest degree of the adjective or adverb. It functions as an intensive, emphasizing the meaning without changing it.

To-morrow I bury her, and then I shall be quite alone —Charles Lamb, letter, 12 May 1800

If you are quite sure you would have no use of them, I may as well destroy them —Lewis Carroll, letter, 21 June 1881

... bragged falsely of having made conquests of quite other girls —Renata Adler, *Pitch Dark,* 1983

From the intensive use a weaker, subtractive sense developed, a sense used not to intensify but to tone down. In the words of Fitzedward Hall 1873, it occupies "a place intermediate between 'altogether' and 'somewhat.' "

> As I came home through the woods with my string of fish, trailing my pole, it being now quite dark, I caught a glimpse of a woodchuck stealing across my path —Henry David Thoreau, *Walden*, 1854

Thoreau's *quite* is exemplary: it brings the adjective up just short of its full power.

By all accounts the subtractive sense is the prevalent one in current English, but in many particular instances it is hard to be certain that the subtractive sense rather than the intensive sense is intended:

> Her uncovered ears were quite white and very small —Aldous Huxley, *Those Barren Leaves*, 1925

> . . . and the weather in the main has been quite good —E. B. White, letter, 3 Mar. 1965

You would think that the coexistence of these two uses would lead to problems of ambiguity and confusion, but in practice this seems not often to be the case. For although the lexicographer must try to determine the exact meaning of each occurrence of a word, the reader is under no such constraint. The distinction between the two senses is not always crucial to a general understanding of the sentence; when it is, the reader has the larger context for help. And the writer can always use a negative with *quite* when he or she wants to emphasize a falling just short:

> In my opinion, my work . . . ain't quite good enough —William Faulkner, 13 May 1957, in *Faulkner in the University*, 1959

> He does not quite say that a propitious environment would create a population composed entirely of geniuses —John Butt, *English Literature in the Mid-Eighteenth Century*, edited & completed by Geoffrey Carnall, 1979

In the middle of the 19th century there was some reprehension of the use of *quite* before *a* and a noun. This is now a dead issue. *Quite a* is established, and is generally found in informal contexts.

> We decided, though, that he would be quite a swell guy sober —James Thurber, letter, April 1936

> Irene Franey, a little older than I, was quite a beauty —John O'Hara, letter, 30 Dec. 1963

These are established idioms, beyond cavil.

quondam See ERSTWHILE, QUONDAM, WHILOM.

quote   **1.** The noun *quote*, short for *quotation*, was first recorded in 1888:

> Stodgy 'quotes' from the ancients? —*Pall Mall Gazette*, 12 Dec. 1888 (OED)

One of its chief early uses was in the world of publishing to denote a passage of favorable criticism quoted as advertisement for a book:

> . . . three sentences that might have been framed specially to give the publisher an easy 'quote' —*Century Mag.*, February 1919

Its occurrence in general contexts was fairly rare until the 1940s, when we found it being used in a number of popular newspapers and magazines and very often without the distancing quotation marks of earlier years:

> With a quote from the *Troy Times* —Ben Lucien Burman, *Saturday Rev.*, 28 Dec. 1946

> . . . riddles his opposition with a salvo of quotes —Richard E. Lauterbach, *New Republic*, 11 Apr. 1949

> . . . some witty quotes picked from their own works —*Time*, 18 Apr. 1949

Its use since the 1940s has continued to be common and, for the most part, unremarkable. It occurs most often in writing that has a casual tone or, at least, is not highly formal:

> It was mighty thoughtful of you to send me that quote from dear old Sam Adams's letter —James Thurber, letter, 3 Dec. 1958

> It started with quotes taken out of context —Suzette Haden Elgin, *English Jour.*, November 1976

> Only after the sweat has dried comes the quote —Wilfrid Sheed, *Harper's*, February 1984

> A brief meditation on the stealing of books is mournfully vivid. One quote alone . . . is worth the price of admission —George Steiner, *New Yorker*, 17 Mar. 1997

This sense of *quote* has met with strong disapproval in some quarters. Such commentators as Bernstein 1965, Follett 1966, Shaw 1975, and Trimmer & McCrimmon 1988 have disparaged its use in writing, and the Heritage 1969, 1982 usage panel rejected it by a large majority (the 2000 panel has lightened up). Some other critics, however, have taken a more tolerant view. Harper 1985, for example, accepts its use in writing that has "a conversational tone," and Bremner 1980 calls it "standard in the publishing business."

The noun *quote* is now widely used in standard if mostly casual writing, as the above quotations show, but there are still times when it seems more appropriate to choose *quotation* instead. We recommend that you let your own judgment of the writing situation and your sense of idiom be your guide.

2. The noun *quote* is also used to mean "quotation mark," and it has also been criticized in this sense. Like the "quotation" sense, this "mark" sense is about 100 years old:

> The portion of this quotation which we have put within quotes —*Scottish Leader,* 2 Apr. 1891 (OED)

Its use in American English is well established:

> . . . quotes within quotes are often confusing, and unhinge the minds of thousands of poor copy-readers every year —H. L. Mencken, *The American Language, Supplement II,* 1948

The written contexts in which it appears are similar in tone to those in which the "quotation" sense of *quote* appears. Those critics who dislike the "quotation" sense tend naturally to dislike the "quotation mark" sense as well. Again, we recommend that you rely on your own judgment.

quoth *Quoth* is the past tense of an obsolete verb *quethen.* It is used in the first and third persons and is regularly followed by its subject. It is archaic as a regular verb form and is used nowadays in special contexts, such as when a writer of historical fiction tries to recreate the speech and atmosphere of an earlier time. It is also sometimes used in modern contexts for humorous or arch effect or simply to catch attention:

> "I don't want to say any more about it," quoth Jones —Rick Telander, *Sports Illustrated,* 19 Jan. 1987

> Then the mayor labored mightily and brought forth an "austerity" budget. Not good enough, quoth the bankers —Sidney Cohen, *Harper's Weekly,* 4 July 1975

R

rabbit, rarebit See WELSH RABBIT, WELSH RAREBIT.

rack, wrack The prescriptions of the critics are usually stated along the following lines: the verb *rack,* which is related to the noun designating an instrument of torture, properly means "strain" or "torment" and is the correct choice in *nerve-racking, rack one's brains,* and similar expressions; the verb *wrack* and noun *wrack,* on the other hand, are etymologically related to *wreck* and should therefore be used when wreckage or destruction is being described, as in *storm-wracked* and *wrack and ruin.*

The facts of actual usage are somewhat different. *Wrack* is commonly used as a verb synonymous with the figurative senses of *rack:*

> . . . if a society is wracked with internal conflicts —Kenneth E. Boulding, *Center Mag.,* May/June 1971

> . . . a world wracked by change —Harrison E. Salisbury, *N.Y. Times Book Rev.,* 6 Nov. 1966

> . . . wracking his brain for the next day's copy —William Irvin, *Saturday Rev.,* 24 Dec. 1955

Nerve-wracking is an established variant of *nerve-racking:*

> . . . a business more nerve-wracking and exhausting than reading a newspaper —H. L. Mencken, *Prejudices: Second Series,* 1920

> . . . this nerve-wracking chapter in so many American lives —Arthur M. Schlesinger, Jr., *Saturday Rev.,* 6 Jan. 1979

The noun *rack* is sometimes used as a synonym of *wrack,* especially in the phrase *rack and ruin:*

> . . . the Bank was going to rack and ruin without him —Rudyard Kipling, *Plain Tales from the Hills,* 1888

> . . . let the business go to rack and ruin —*Punch,* 15 June 1966

Wrack (verb) meaning *rack* was first recorded in 1553, *rack* (noun) meaning *wrack* was first recorded in 1599. The tendency among modern commentators is to regard *rack and ruin* as acceptable, but to persist in regarding such usage as "he wracked his brain" as incorrect. Why one should be acceptable and the other unacceptable is not easily discerned. Probably the most sensible attitude would be to ignore the etymologies of *rack* and *wrack* (which, of course, is exactly what most people do) and regard them simply as spelling variants of one word. If you choose to toe the line drawn by the commentators, however, you will want to write *nerve-racking, rack one's brains, storm-wracked,* and for good measure *wrack and ruin.* Then you will have nothing to worry about being criticized for—except, of course, for using too many clichés.

racket, racquet These spelling variants are both established in reputable use:

> . . . hoisted his racket to his shoulder like a baseball bat —John Updike, *Couples,* 1968

> . . . I grabbed a tennis racquet hanging in its press —E. L. Doctorow, *Loon Lake,* 1979

Racket is appreciably the more common of the two except when the reference is to the game racquets, which in American English is usually spelled as we have spelled it here:

> Racquets today is almost as aristocratic a game as court tennis —Dick Miller et al., *Town & Country,* May 1984

The British, however, prefer *rackets* for the name of the game:

> . . . recorded the double in the . . . tennis and rackets competitions at Manchester yesterday —*The Times* (London), 29 Oct. 1973

raise, rear The use of *raise* for bringing up children has been aspersed since the early 19th century. The Dictionary of American English says that *raise* used of children had some currency in British English at one time, but that it dropped out of use around 1800. It did not drop out of use in North America, and its use was criticized as provincial as early as 1818. Vizetelly attacked *raise* in his 1906 book. He says it is "often misapplied to the bringing up of human beings. One *rears* cattle, *raises* chickens, but *brings up* children. *Rear,* meaning 'to nurture and train,' may also be used of children." Many subsequent commentators and a great many schoolteachers have followed his prescription, although *bring up* is fairly often overlooked.

Raise, however, never dropped out of use despite the disapproval, and most modern commentators recognize that it is perfectly standard American. A few commentators, such as Kilpatrick 1984 and Jacques Barzun (quoted in Safire 1986), still follow the Vizetelly line. But as these examples show, *raise* is both perfectly respectable and still very common in the Southern U.S.

> . . . I was not trying to say, This is the sort of folks we raise in my part of Mississippi —William Faulkner, 15 May 1958, in *Faulkner in the University,* 1959

> I told my mother I'd changed my mind about wanting to succeed in the magazine business. "If you think I'm going to raise a good-for-nothing," she replied, "you've got another think coming." —Russell Baker, *Growing Up,* 1982

> . . . the town where I was born and raised —William Styron, *This Quiet Dust and Other Writings,* 1982

> Both parents are now more often engaged in active, day-to-day childraising —Elizabeth Janeway, in Harper 1985

> . . . she might at the same time be raising a family of her own —Peter Taylor, *The Old Forest and Other Stories,* 1985

> For Eliot, nonetheless, it was a very great advantage to have been raised in an atmosphere of evangelical piety —Irving Howe, *New Republic,* 18 Oct. 1954

> Every youngster as he grows up knows he was a darned sight smarter than his daddy was, and he has to get to be about forty before he finds out the old man was smart enough to raise him —Harry S. Truman, quoted in Merle Miller, *Plain Speaking,* 1973

Rear is still in common use too, and it varies freely with *raise* in the word-stock of some writers:

> She'd reared her children there —Russell Baker, *Growing Up,* 1982

> Born and reared in South Carolina —William Styron, *This Quiet Dust and Other Writings,* 1982

> . . . where Macon's grandfather, a factory owner, reared his four grandchildren —John Updike, *New Yorker,* 28 Oct. 1985

> She reared the kids and kept the house clean —Edwards Park, *Smithsonian,* February 1986

> Barkley kept looking at him and wondering if the gentleman could have been reared in Egypt —Harry S. Truman, letter, 28 Jan. 1952

raise, rise 1. *Verb.* It is an axiom of about twenty handbooks in our collection—mostly but not exclusively those aimed at a school and college audience—that *raise* is only transitive. A transitive *raise* and an intransitive *rise* make for a tidy world. Unfortunately the matter is a little more complicated than that. By and large *raise* and *rise* do form a transitive-intransitive pair; however, *raise* can also be an intransitive verb.

Intransitive *raise* has been objected to from as far back as Bache 1869, even though intransitive uses date to the 15th century in the works of Malory and Caxton. But it seems to have dropped out of mainstream British English before the end of the 18th century; the historian David Hume—and he was a Scot—is the last (1761) literary figure quoted in the

OED. It stayed alive, however, in dialectal use and in America:

> The Water having raised, . . . I could form no accurate judgment of the progress — George Washington, diary, 22 Sept. 1785 (in OED Supplement)

George Washington's use can still be found in American regional English:

> . . . and whenever there was much rain, and the river went to raising, I couldn't do my work —Elbert Herald, quoted in *Our Appalachia,* ed. Laurel Shackleford & Bill Weinberg, 1977

Our evidence shows four chief uses of the intransitive *raise.* They are not all regional, although the one which means "to get up out of bed" may be. It is found in the journals of Lewis and Clark in the early 19th century and also more recently:

> . . . Simon was beating the bottom of the dishpan with the spoon, hollering, "Raise up and get your four-o'clock coffee!" —William Faulkner, *Saturday Evening Post,* 5 Mar. 1955

There is also a use in which the intransitive is the semantic equivalent of a passive:

> He wants Britain's beet quota raising from 900,000 tons to 1,200,000 tons a year —*The Sun* (London), 22 Oct. 1974

> The flashlights momentarily converged on the dog, then raised —Erle Stanley Gardner, *The Case of the Negligent Nymph,* 1949

Another pattern finds *raise* used as if a reflexive pronoun object had been omitted from a transitive construction:

> At Bledsoe's defiance, he half raised from his seat and ejaculated, "The son of a bitch!" —Alexander Woollcott, letter, 23 Feb. 1933

> He periodically raised up on his elbows and fired —*N.Y. Times,* 24 Apr. 1970

> Uncle Jake was stirring unconsciously in the chair as he spoke, and I raised up from his lap and peered across the tablecloth into father's face —Peter Taylor, *The Old Forest and Other Stories,* 1985

And, finally, *raise* is simply used in place of various senses of *rise:*

> . . . perhaps it was the distraction of the drama which prevented him raising any higher on the moving staircase of public service —Laurence Irving, *Henry Irving: The Actor and His World,* 1952

> A blade [of a screwdriver] which tapers out from the tip . . . has a tendency to raise out

of the slot —General Motors Corp., *ABC's of Hand Tools,* 1945

The intransitive *raise* was labeled *obsolete* in some older dictionaries, but it is still alive in dialectal use and in some at least sporadic general use. It is not incorrect nor illiterate. It seems rather to be a little-used survival from the past.

2. *Noun.* Vizetelly 1906 and others of similar vintage objected to the noun *raise* used in the sense "an increase in pay." *Rise,* which is still the usual word in British English, was prescribed. The prescription survived long enough in some newspaper stylebooks to receive mention in Harper 1975, 1985. But *raise* is standard in this sense in America.

raising *Raising* is a term used by linguists for the idiomatic shifting of a subject or a negative from a subordinate clause to the "higher" clause it is dependent on (Bolinger 1980). The more important phenomenon, for usage writers (who do not use the term *raising*), is the one in which a negative is shifted.

Let's take an example:

> But I suppose I oughtn't to say that.

Does that seem a bit stiff and awkward? The most likely pattern in present-day English would show the negative shifted from *ought,* where it logically belongs, to the verb of the main clause:

> . . . but I don't suppose I ought to say that —Harry S. Truman, quoted in Merle Miller, *Plain Speaking,* 1973

Some of the most common expressions in which negative-raising is usual involve verbs like *think, suppose, believe,* and *seem.* The sentences "I don't think it will rain" and "I don't believe I'll go" were disapproved as solecisms by Vizetelly 1906. The objection was, of course, that the raised negatives are illogical. Illogical they may be, perhaps, but standard idioms nonetheless—especially in speech and relaxed writing. Flesch 1964 and Bolinger 1980 bother to defend them, so there evidently has been a fair amount of objection along Vizetelly's lines. Here are some examples of raising:

> I don't suppose there was a scarcer or more highly prized item in all of Belgium —*And More by Andy Rooney,* 1982

> "I don't suppose you remembered that bagel," Megan says —Jay McInerney, *Bright Lights, Big City,* 1984

> Well, I don't think the writer finds peace —William Faulkner, 13 Mar. 1958, in *Faulkner in the University,* 1959

> I don't think those things fall in the same category —Senator Lowell Weicker, radio interview, 28 Nov. 1975

... he says that he doesn't think he's going to like "your chapter on editing" —James Thurber, letter, 3 Dec. 1958

The roar of the traffic and continual street and building construction don't seem to faze the sidewalk cafe devotee —Barbara Gamarekian, *N.Y. Times,* 7 May 1978

... I went up to New York to see Meyer Wolfshiem; I couldn't seem to reach him any other way —F. Scott Fitzgerald, *The Great Gatsby,* 1925

Never is also raised sometimes. Vizetelly 1906 complains of one example, and Phythian 1979 corrects "I never expected to find it" to "I expected never to find it." But the raised position has long been established:

... though 'Gondibert' never appears to have been popular —Samuel Johnson, *Life of Dryden,* 1783 (in Fitzedward Hall 1873)

Objections to idioms like *I don't think* or *can't seem* are a waste of good indignation; English idiom simply defies the dictates of abstract logic at some points, and this is one of them.

See also CAN'T SEEM.

range   Bernstein 1965 states flatly that *range* (presumably the verb) takes the prepositions *through, with, along,* or *between.* Why he chooses to specify those four is unclear. Our evidence shows that *range* is idiomatically followed by a great many prepositions—so many, in fact, that to list and illustrate all of them would serve no useful purpose. Suffice it to say that you need not agonize over the choice of prepositions following *range.*

It may be worth noting that by far the most common preposition to follow *range* is one not included in Bernstein's list, namely *from:*

... ranging from lock-pickers through photographers to psychiatrists —*Times Literary Supp.,* 2 July 1971

... ranging from a whisper to a bray —Susan Braudy, *Ms.,* March 1973

rarefy, rarify   *Rarefy* is the usual spelling, but *rarify* has been in use as a variant since the 15th century. Examples of the *-i-* spelling in standard, edited prose are easy to find:

... by rarified philosophical speculation —*Times Literary Supp.,* 18 Dec. 1969

... a vocabulary from the rarified precincts of Princeton —Robert S. Boynton, *N.Y. Times Mag.,* 15 Sept. 1991

... interstellar gases are incredibly rarified —Jim Phillips, *Astronomy,* May 1998

... in the rarified ranks of Monday holidays —Todd S. Purdum, *N.Y. Times,* 19 Feb. 1995

Nevertheless, *rarify* is widely regarded as a spelling error, so if you want to avoid possible criticism, however mild, we recommend that you choose the more common spelling, *rarefy.*

rarely ever   *Rarely ever* is one of several intensive forms of the adverb *rarely.* Bryant 1962 calls it an established colloquial idiom, which agrees with our evidence. *Rarely ever* is used in both British and American English:

... and the thieves are rarely ever caught —magistrate, quoted in Ronald Blythe, *Akenfield,* 1969

I rarely ever think about the past —Edmund Wilson, *New Yorker,* 12 June 1971

The longer intensive forms of *rarely* include *rarely if at all* (cited in Bryant), *rarely or never* (Bryant and OED), and *rarely if ever,* the best-attested version in our files. It is used with or without commas:

In all the hullabaloo about Justice Douglas we rarely, if ever, told our readers . . . —Theodore Bernstein, *Winners & Sinners,* 30 Apr. 1970

... says it rarely if ever sees a repeat shoplifting offender —Glynn Mapes, *Security World,* May 1968

The criticism of *rarely ever* takes some strange forms. One critic calls it "wordy, unidiomatic." How a 300-year-old idiom can be unidiomatic he does not say. As to wordiness, this critic suggests you replace *rarely ever* with *hardly ever, rarely if ever,* or *rarely or never.*

Criticism of *rarely ever* can be ignored; Bryant has the right idea. In ordinary discursive prose, however, *rarely* is almost always used alone.

rarify   See RAREFY, RARIFY.

rather   1. See HAD RATHER.

2. *Rather* is used both as a mild intensifier and as a mild de-emphasizer. The intensifier:

He considers Pappy rather small potatoes —Harry S. Truman, diary, 10 Aug. 1945

The de-emphasizer:

... led a rather lonely but not altogether unhappy childhood —*Current Biography,* November 1965

In this respect *rather* operates much like *quite* (which see).

The use of *rather* in its diluting or softening function has drawn a smattering of criticism, but it appears to have no sound basis. Here are a few of our examples:

... and an occasional quarrel . . . was rather fun —Edward Seidensticker, *Low City, High City,* 1983

. . . would have looked down their aristocratic noses to see rather middle class men and women drinking sherry . . . in their rooms —Suzanne Wilding, *Town & Country,* June 1976

I read a little Samuel Pepys, rather like it —Renata Adler, *Pitch Dark,* 1983

The other stories in this volume are rather more cheerful —*Times Literary Supp.,* 16 Apr. 1970

I was becoming rather cross by this time —Graham Greene, *Travels with My Aunt,* 1969

You write rather well and if you are interested I think I can get you a job as a cub reporter —Groucho Marx, undated letter to Goodman Ace, in *The Groucho Letters,* 1967

3. *Rather a.* Phythian 1979 and Partridge 1942 offer some remarks on the proper employment of *rather a* before a noun. The concern here seems to be about the retention of the word order with the adverb before the article when an adjective intervenes between *rather a* and the noun. Both Partridge and Phythian accept *rather a* with no adjective:

. . . it was rather a relief when the narcotics testimony ended —Richard Dougherty, *Atlantic,* February 1972

They prescribe *a rather* when an adjective intervenes:

. . . inside a rather larger plastic fish tank —Charles Baptist-Smith, *Observer Mag.,* 3 Feb. 1974

Heritage 2000 notes that in *a rather* the *rather* modifies just the following noun. When the inverted order is used, the *rather* modifies the whole noun phrase:

. . . the French could make rather a good counter-argument —Stephen E. Ambrose, *Johns Hopkins Mag.,* April 1966

It was rather an unbelievable example of using excessive means —Hannah Arendt, *N.Y. Rev. of Books,* 18 Nov. 1971

He is rather a worried participant in the custom —Richard Poirier, *A World Elsewhere,* 1966

This, then, is not a matter of right and wrong; both orders are completely respectable. We suggest you make your choice with discretion; most of our examples follow the prescribed word order.

rather than 1. Commentators from Fowler 1926 to the mid-1980s worry themselves as to whether *rather than* functions as a conjunction or a preposition. It works both ways. As a preposition:

Rather than being so quick to knock an attempt at change, Mr. Rustin should extend it the same leeway . . . —Burrill L. Crohn, letter to the editor, *Harper's,* April 1970

Rather than argue for the overthrow of the entire system, the Colonists realized . . . that the basic values of British law were still valid —Daniel Sisson, *Center Mag.,* May 1969

It commonly is followed by a gerund:

Is there any chance of spring publication, rather than waiting till fall? —E. B. White, letter, 28 Jan. 1942

Rather than permitting us to imagine . . . , Lindblom forces us to consider . . . —*N.Y. Times Book Rev.,* 19 Feb. 1978

Burchfield 1996 and Garner 1998 note that *rather than* can be preceded by an infinitive with *to* and followed by the infinitive without *to*:

. . . they cause young people to think and reason rather than just sit and listen —Albert F. Eiss & Carolyn Mulford, *NEA Jour.,* November 1965

When parallel constructions appear on each side of *rather than,* it is a conjunction:

. . . implicating them, this time subtly rather than powerfully —J. I. M. Stewart, *Eight Modern Writers,* 1963

. . . speaking of her as a person rather than as an actress —*Current Biography,* September 1964

. . . for the sake of dramatic convenience rather than for motives that appeal to reason —John Butt, *English Literature in the Mid-Eighteenth Century,* edited & completed by Geoffrey Carnall, 1979

. . . I define the language by the literature in which it appears, rather than the literature by the language it employs —W. F. Bolton, *A Short History of Literary English,* 1967

Both of these uses are standard English.
2. Commentators from Partridge 1942 to Janis 1984 and Cook 1985 notice a curious construction in which a comparative that you would expect to be followed by *than* takes *rather than* instead. Here are two examples:

All this was new to him, his experience having made him more knowing about bookies rather than books —John Ferguson, *Death of Mr. Dodsley,* 1937 (in Partridge)

The group is more interested in the edible varieties and in experimenting with recipes rather than in pursuing rare specimens —*N.Y. Times,* 29 Dec. 1970 (in *Winners & Sinners,* 14 Jan. 1971)

Bernstein 1977 rejected these constructions on the basis of *rather*'s etymology—it is the comparative of an obsolete adverb—but etymology is not really the point. The reason for the awkwardness of the sentences is that the *more* in each sentence leads the reader to expect the usual *than*, but *rather than* turns up in its place. The existence of such sentences (which we advise you to avoid) is good evidence that *rather than* is perceived as a unit by many writers.

For the controversy over *rather than* after *prefer*, see PREFER.

ravage, ravish Both of these verbs are ultimately derived from the same Middle French verb, *ravir*, but their fundamental meanings are distinct. *Ravage* has the basic sense "to plunder or destroy":

> The war would ravage two particular reputations: Johnson's and McNamara's —David Halberstam, *Harper's,* February 1971

> . . . as the coal company's power shovels ravage the land around them —H. L. Van Brunt, *Saturday Rev.,* 8 Apr. 1972

Ravish has three primary senses—"to seize and carry away":

> The food was ravished by the semi-wild, emaciated cat —Dave Lee, *Cats Mag.,* July 1980

"to overcome with emotion (as joy or delight)":

> Bellow is ravished by Alexandra's exotic . . . celebrity —Richard Stern, *N.Y. Times Mag.,* 21 Nov. 1976

and "to rape":

> . . . brutally ravished her in a lower berth —*Time,* 3 Jan. 1955

As many commentators have noted, *ravage* and *ravish* are easily confused, although our evidence suggests that errors are rare in edited writing. We have only a few clear-cut examples:

> . . . coming whenever he wanted to ravage her —James T. Farrell, *What Time Collects,* 1964

> . . . a mountain torrent ravishes his potato field —*Saturday Rev.,* 29 Mar. 1952

If you feel uncertain about which word to use in a particular context, a quick look in the dictionary will clear things up.

It should be noted that *ravish* also has the rare sense "to plunder or rob."

> . . . slaves and concubines ravished from the Pecos people —Willa Cather, *Death Comes for the Archbishop,* 1927

> Buccaneer Henry Morgan, ravishing Panama of 400,000 pieces of eight in 1671 —*Time,* 24 Aug. 1953

Used in this sense, *ravish* resembles *ravage* closely enough that it may give the appearance of confusion even when none exists. That being so, you may well want to avoid this sense of *ravish*.

re This preposition was borrowed straight from Latin in the 18th century. It has some use in legal and business writing, but the usage books (for instance Harper 1975, 1985, Bernstein 1965, Flesch 1964, Copperud 1964, 1970, 1980, Irmscher 1976, Shaw 1975, 1987) tell everyone else to avoid it. Harper, for instance, calls it "pretentious in nonbusiness or nonlegal situations"; nonetheless, it is used in the book:

> (He voted "no" re writing.) —Harper 1985

The evidence in our files shows that *re* is not a high-frequency word but has more general use than the usage writers suppose:

> . . . fortunate or unfortunate enough to have something very like fanatical convictions re métier —Ezra Pound, *Polite Essays,* 1937

> I have no idea what Don Regan knows or does not know re my private U.S. operation —Oliver North, quoted in *The Tower Commission Report,* 1987

> . . . as low as you can get re fiction —Flannery O'Connor, letter, 31 May 1960

> Snow, who has come back to rendezvous with Abbott and Angel re a new musical —Martin Levin, *N.Y. Times Book Rev.,* 24 June 1973

It is only occasionally italicized in general contexts.

reaction There has been a considerable reaction against *reaction* used, as it often is in print and electronic journalism, as a sort of rough equivalent of *response, feeling,* or *opinion.* It usually turns up after something has been said, done, or produced:

> . . . the nature books . . . during the past three or four years have had a mixed reaction —Jude Bell, *N.Y. Times Book Rev.,* 19 Sept. 1976

> On the two evening news shows I watched, Mr. Ford got as much time as a local crime story; one station even filmed the reaction in a downtown tavern —Karl E. Meyer, *Saturday Rev.,* 20 Mar. 1976

> . . . asking for comments and reaction to the black students' criticisms —*Bowdoin Alumnus,* January 1971

. . . but I feel that using the score from a movie for the celebration of the Lord's supper borders on the profane. What is your reaction? —Amy Vanderbilt, *Ladies' Home Jour.,* September 1971

More than half the critics say something to the effect that *reaction* is a scientific word and should not be used of people, an opinion that conveniently overlooks nearly two centuries of use as a political term in such expressions as "the forces of progress and reaction." There is no reason to restrict its use to scientific contexts (in which, to be sure, it is frequently used), even if it becomes, at times, a tiresome cliché of the journalist. You can substitute some other word—*response, opinion, judgment, view,* or the like—if you think that *reaction* is overused. But the word has its own meaning and overtones, and it is not easily expendable in every circumstance.

Bremner 1980, Bryson 1984, and Burchfield 1996 prefer *reaction* restricted to an immediate response to the event. This is sensible, but we note that writers and interviewers often pay no attention to the thought.

read where   See WHERE 2.

real   The adverb *real,* which is used only as an intensifier, developed from a use of the adjective to modify compound noun phrases like *good turn.* By the 18th century the *real* was apprehended as an intensifier modifying *good* alone, and its independent use grew from then. It was a development that took place, apparently, outside of mainstream British English; the OED identifies it as chiefly Scottish and American, and we have some slight Irish evidence. It has been from the start primarily a spoken use.

Criticism of the adverbial *real* began as early as Ayres 1881, and it has not begun to drop off yet. Insofar as this criticism tells you that *real* is informal and more suitable to speech than to writing, it is fairly accurate. When it wanders from this line to insist that *real* is an adjective only, or that *real* is a substitute for *really,* it is wrong. It is potentially misleading to label *real* as an error for *really,* because *real* and *really* are not very often used in the same way. *Real* is a simple intensifier, more or less equivalent to *very*; it is used only with adjectives and adverbs. *Really* is a full-fledged adverb; it is only sometimes used in an intensive function, and even then is more likely to mean "truly, unquestionably" than simply "very." The difference can perhaps be suggested by this passage from an interview:

> You work at writing for a couple of years and you get to feeling real sociable. By the end of a day spent sitting in a room with a typewriter, you're really ready to meet and greet and go hang out with your friends

—Garrison Keillor, quoted in *Update* (Univ. of Minn.), Fall 1981

While it is still true that *real* is more likely to be encountered in speech than in writing, we notice that it has spread considerably in general writing—primarily that of newspapers and magazines—as a part of an informal, conversational style.

> A booth with a real different look was set up by a Los Gatos, Calif., shop —*Antiques and the Arts Weekly,* 3 Dec. 1982

> . . . he didn't follow politics real closely —Larry Pressler, *People,* 12 July 1982

> Also, armadillos are real special to Texans —Wayne King, *N.Y. Times,* 7 Dec. 1982

> . . . who will see viewers real soon —Guy D. Garcia, *Time,* 29 Oct. 1984

> . . . promising ourselves another visit real soon —Teresa Byrne-Dodge, *Houston Post Mag.,* 9 Sept. 1984

> . . . with the stereo turned up real loud —Jack McCallum, *Sports Illustrated,* 3 Nov. 1986

> On the first real warm day, you can sit on the back steps in your PJs —Garrison Keillor, *Lake Wobegon Days,* 1985

Although this is mainly an American usage, we do have just a bit of British evidence:

> I'm having a real good time —Ellen Terry, letter, 7 Dec. 1896

> The baddies were real bad, and the hero was intensely heroic —Benny Green, *Punch,* 4 May 1976

real facts   See TRUE FACTS.

Realtor   See JEWELRY.

rear   See RAISE, REAR.

reason is because   Bremner 1980 succinctly states two objections to *the reason is because*:

> The grammatical reason for the error in "The reason he failed is because he didn't study" is that *the reason is* calls for a nounal clause: "The reason he failed is that he didn't study." The adverbial conjunction *because* is correct in "He failed because he didn't study."
>
> A simpler reason is that *because* means "for the reason that" and therefore one would be saying, "The reason he failed is for the reason that . . . ," which is as redundant as saying "The because is because."

Bremner's first objection is a 20th-century one; the second is older. The grammatical objection that *because* can only introduce an adverbial clause qualifying a verb and hence is wrong introducing a noun clause synonymous with *reason* was presumably erected to buttress the older objection, but who first formulated it we do not know.

Evans 1957 offers the best treatment of the grammatical question. He notes that *because* in most cases introduces a clause that qualifies a verb and is therefore said to be an adverbial conjunction. He also notes that some grammarians claim that *because* cannot be used in any other way and especially that it cannot introduce a noun clause. But Evans disagrees:

> *Because* may certainly introduce a noun clause that is joined to *it, this,* or *that* by some form of the verb *to be,* as in *if you are hungry it is because you didn't eat.* This has been standard English for centuries and the very grammarians who condemn the use of *because* in a noun clause do not hesitate to write *this is because.*

One of those objecting grammarians was H. W. Fowler, and he indeed did use *because* after *is* to introduce a noun clause:

> There is indeed no mystery about why people go wrong; it is because, if the thing had to be said without the use of the verb *like, would* & not *should* is the form to use —Fowler 1926, s.v. *like,* v.

And if *because* can refer to a pronoun like *it, this,* or *that,* Evans continues, there is no reason it should not refer to a noun like *reason.*

In other words, the grammatical objection has no basis in principle. It is erected ad hoc to rationalize dislike of *the reason is because* and is not invoked in other cases where *because* introduces a noun clause.

So with the grammatical argument disposed of, the objectors must get along with the older charge of redundancy (as most of them do anyway). Bremner's summary is both succinct and apt, for he has used exactly the same test for redundancy that the original objector, Baker 1770, did: he defines *because* as "for the reason that" (Baker used "by Reason") and finds it redundant with the earlier *reason* in the sentence. Baker did not apply the term *redundant*; he merely said, "This Expression does not make Sense."

Any lexicographer can see the fault in that argument at once: *because* has been defined in such a way as to guarantee that it will be redundant or not make sense. Unless people actually write sentences like "The reason he failed is for the reason that . . ."—and in general they do not—there is no reason to assume that *because* has the meaning the critics assign it. Lexicographers have to define words *in situ,* not in the abstract, removed from context, and they know how easy it is to make hash of any sentence by deciding beforehand that a word in it means something other than what

the author intended. If, instead, you grant that *because* can have the meaning "the fact that" or simply be equivalent to the conjunction *that,* the phrase *the reason is because* makes quite clear sense and is not redundant.

So we conclude that there is no sufficient basis for either the 18th-century or the 20th-century objection. But there still remains a question of the kind of writing in which the construction is used. Is it relatively rare in literary use and found primarily in dialectal use or in the speech of the uneducated? We think these examples will answer:

> The Reason was, because the *Religion* of the Heathen, consisted rather in Rites and Ceremonies —Francis Bacon, *Essays,* 1625

> We may call them the weaker sex, but I think the true reason is because our Follies are stronger and our faults more prevailing —William Congreve, "Concerning Humour in Comedy," 1695

> The reason I tell you so is, because it was done by your parson —Jonathan Swift, *Journal to Stella,* 14 May 1711

> The reason is because it is of more importance . . . that innocence should be protected than it is that guilt should be punished —John Adams, final argument in defense of the British soldiers involved in the Boston Massacre, 1770

> If the fellow who wrote it seems to know more of my goings and comings than he could without complicity of mine, the reason is because he is a lovely old boy and quite took possession of me while I was in Boston —Robert Frost, letter, 22 Mar. 1915

> The reason every one now tries to avoid it, to deny that it is important, to make it seem vain to try to do it, is because it is so difficult —Ernest Hemingway, *Green Hills of Africa,* 1935

> One of the reasons so many found it difficult to understand Billy Mitchell was because the man was a stark realist —Eddie Rickenbacker, *Chicago Tribune Mag. of Books,* 28 Dec. 1952

> The reason such a job won't be done again is simply because nobody can afford it —William Morris, *College Composition and Communication,* October 1969

> The reason the story has never been made into a film is because I won't sign a contract —E. B. White, letter, 28 Oct. 1969

> The reason I live in Covington, Louisiana, is not because it was listed recently in *Money* as one of the best places in the United States to retire to —Walker Percy, *Signposts in a Strange Land,* 1991

The reason we know of this similarity is because DNA is a code written in a simple alphabet —Matt Ridley, *Genome*, 1999

Except for Adams, these examples are all from written sources, a good many of them literary, with some letters and journals. The phrase existed in 17th-century speech, and it exists in contemporary speech:

... I think the reason anyone writes is because it's fun —William Faulkner, 30 May 1957, in *Faulkner in the University*, 1959

You may have noticed that in the 20th-century examples, *reason* is often separated from the *because* clause by intervening matter, sometimes quite long. In the older examples *reason* is more frequently found right next to *is because*.

Reason and *because* are sometimes found in constructions where they are linked by *than*:

We settled in Hanover, New Hampshire, for no other reason than that it seemed an awfully nice place —Bill Bryson, *I'm a Stranger Here Myself*, 1999

Occasionally, I write out what I have said in verse, and generally for no better reason than because I remember that I have written no verse for a long time —*The Autobiography of William Butler Yeats*, 1953

In this construction, too, *because* introduces a noun clause.

No treatment of *the reason is because* would be complete without mention of the doubly "redundant" *the reason why is because* (see also REASON WHY). It is more common in older sources (it seems to have been a favorite construction of Swift's) than newer ones but is certainly not yet extinct:

Now, the Reason why those Antient Writers treated this Subject only by Types and Figures, was, because they durst not make open Attacks —Jonathan Swift, *A Tale of A Tub*, 1710

And perhaps the reason why common Criticks are inclin'd to prefer a judicious and methodical Genius to a great and fruitful one, is, because they find it easier for themselves. ... —Alexander Pope, preface to translation of the *Iliad*, Book III, 1715

He saw that the reason why witchcraft was ridiculed was, because it was a phase of the miraculous —W. E. H. Lecky, *History of Rationalism in Europe*, 1865 (in Hodgson 1889)

The reason why all we novelists . . . are abandoning novels and taking to writing motion-picture scenarii is because the latter are so infinitely the more simple —P. G. Wodehouse, *Something Fresh*, 1915

. . . one of the reasons why I am not particularly well read today is because I have spent so large a part of the last twenty years rereading Dickens and Jane Austen —Alexander Woollcott, letter, 15 Mar. 1932

The reason why his conclusion concerning Frege's argument seemed plausible at the time was because his propositional constituents are entities rather than the names of those entities —Ronald J. Butler, *Philosophical Rev.*, July 1954

. . . he clung to the literal truth of every word of the Bible, to the extent of believing that the reason why the Mastodons had become extinct . . . was because they were too big to get into the Ark —*Times Literary Supp.*, 19 Sept. 1968

Practically everything that we have shown you so far is from writing, although there are three instances of real speech (Adams, Faulkner, and Hemingway, who is quoting himself being interviewed). Bryant 1962 reports several studies showing *the reason is that*—the form prescribed by teachers of composition—occurs in edited prose about twice as often as *the reason is because*; the same studies show the proportion approximately reversed in speech. We have good evidence of the latter's currency in speech. In 1986 and 1987 we recorded it from a counsel at the Iran-Contra hearings, a local newscaster, television actor Edward Woodward, and such sports figures as Lee Trevino, Henry Aaron, Jim Palmer, and Billy Martin.

A few points made earlier in passing should be underlined. You will note, as Bryant did also, that *the reason is because* occurs more often than not with words intervening between *reason* and *is because*, especially in the 20th-century evidence. You will also note that the evidence is heavily literary; *the reason is because* is not a locution avoided by writers. We suspect, however, that its use is often a matter of habit. We have multiple examples from Francis Bacon, Jonathan Swift, Alexander Woollcott, Ernest Hemingway, and Groucho Marx—not bad company for a writer.

In conclusion, the locution *the reason is because* has been attested in literary use for about three and a half centuries. It has been the subject of denigration for more than two centuries. Both the literary use and the disapproval will doubtless continue unabated. *Reason* and *because* seem to go together, probably, as Bryant remarks, because "the natural connective stressing the idea of reason is *because*."

Our examination of the reasons for condemning the locution shows that they have little foundation, though this will not prevent their being repeated frequently (as recently as

1998). We are not advising you to use *the reason is because* just because many well-known writers have used it. If it is not your natural idiom, there is no reason for you to cultivate it. But if it is your natural idiom and you choose to continue with it, you will surely be in some very distinguished company.

reason why *Reason why* is denounced as a redundancy by American Heritage 1969, 1982, Shaw 1970, 1975, 1987, and Prentice Hall 1978; it is tolerated by Heritage 2000; it is defended by Evans 1957 and Bernstein 1971. Bernstein, in fact, finds instances when the *why* is required, and says that even when it is not required, it is never unidiomatic or wrong. Most other commentators who mention it are tolerant. Their tolerance is well taken, for many usage writers themselves use *reason why*. We have examples from Lounsbury 1908, Fowler 1926, Gowers 1948, Evans 1957, Phythian 1979, Johnson 1982, and Howard 1984.

The question of the propriety of *reason why* is an American one. We are not sure how it originated. Goold Brown 1851 expresses disapproval in a discussion of conjunctive adverbs. He does not single out *reason why* for disapproval; it is just one of several disapproved locutions. But the question must have been floating around in the 1920s; Frank Vizetelly called it correct in a 1929 issue of the *Literary Digest*. Leonard included it on his 1932 survey of usage, where it was considered established.

Tennyson has been given credit or blame for helping to propagate the phrase, but it dates back to 1225 and was well established long before Tennyson's time.

> The reason why a Poet is said, that hee ought to have all knowledges, is that . . . —Ben Jonson, *Timber: or. Discoveries,* before 1637

> I believe your Lordship will agree with me in the Reason, Why our Language is less Refined than those of Italy, Spain, or France —Jonathan Swift, *A Proposal for Correcting, Improving and Ascertaining the English Tongue,* 1712

> These observations will show the reason why the poem of *Hudibras* is almost forgotten —Samuel Johnson, *The Idler,* 2 June 1759

> I see no reason why you should't be heard from —Henry Adams, letter, 18 Dec. 1863

> . . . all reasons why he should avoid me —George Bernard Shaw, letter, 6 Sept. 1896

> . . . several reasons why I should like to see it get back —James Thurber, letter, 19 Nov. 1946

> . . . this was one reason why Romanized Britain fell so easy a prey to the invader —G. M. Trevelyan, *A Shortened History of Britain,* 1942

> . . . one of the many reasons why the passage . . . throws into relief . . . —Henry James, *The Art of the Novel,* 1934

Reason why is still current:

> This may have been the principal reason why he had refused the marquessate —Roy Jenkins, *Gladstone,* 1995

> This service is one of the reasons why so many of the largest libraries use the Library of Congress system —Nicholas Von Hoffman, *Civilization,* April/May 2000

Mary Vaiana Taylor's survey of university teaching assistants (*College English,* April 1974) discovered that 70 percent of them marked *reason why* as an error—making TAs more hostile to the phrase than even the Heritage usage panel. So if you are taking freshman English, you had perhaps best avoid offending with this usage. Anyone else can use *reason why* freely.

recipient Fowler 1926 scornfully cites several instances of inflated journalistic prose in which someone is said to have been "the recipient of a presentation" or "the recipient of congratulations." Such self-conscious formality is perhaps less popular among journalists than it once was; we, at least, have collected no further evidence of *recipient* used in such a stiffly unnatural way. Its most familiar use in current English is to denote a person to whom something desirable, such as an award or a diploma, has been formally presented:

> . . . is also the recipient of two honorary degrees —*Current Biography,* January 1967

> . . . would an Englishman rather be the recipient of the Victoria Cross or . . . —Herbert R. Mayes, *Saturday Rev.,* 4 Dec. 1971

The formality of the word is appropriate in these contexts.

reckon 1. When used with a preposition, *reckon* is most often followed by *with,* the phrase constituting an idiom meaning "to take into consideration":

> . . . a brilliant book that will have to be reckoned with by all informed students of American society —Richard Hofstadter, *N.Y. Times Book Rev.,* 27 Feb. 1955

> The assertion that man was always a killer . . . must reckon with these many alternative possibilities —Lewis Mumford, *American Scholar,* Winter 1966–67

. . . establishing the Christian right as an electoral force to be reckoned with —Christopher Buckley, *N.Y. Times Book Rev.*, 11 Feb. 1996

Although *reckon* is also followed by *without*, meaning "to fail to consider," this usage is not nearly so prevalent as is *reckon with*:

But the Georgia legislature had reckoned without the speculators and their friends —Sidney Warren, *Current History*, February 1952

Miss Hope reckoned without the genius of Feuer and Martin —Henry Hewes, *Saturday Rev.*, 16 Oct. 1954

Reckon is sometimes used with *on*:

The King scarcely knew on what members of his own cabinet he could reckon —T. B. Macaulay, *The History of England*, vol. I, 1849

The biggest surprise thus far has been the change in Bush as a candidate—something the Dukakis campaign certainly hadn't reckoned on —Elizabeth Drew, *New Yorker*, 10 Oct. 1988

Occasionally *reckon* is followed by *among, as, at, by, in*, or *upon*:

. . . he must be reckoned among the great mathematicians of our time —*Times Literary Supp.*, 21 May 1970

I pass to another field where the dominance of the method of sociology may be reckoned as assured —*Selected Writings of Benjamin N. Cardozo*, ed. Margaret E. Hall, 1947

These assets were reckoned at $1,250,000 —Marquis James, *The Texaco Story*, 1953

. . . each cutter's share . . . was reckoned only by the number of days he had worked —Joel Aronoff, *Psychology Today*, January 1971

. . . RCA's productivity as reckoned in sales per employee —Edgar H. Griffiths, *Annual Report, RCA*, 1977

There are many things in which I think I shall be wiser if I come back, but do not reckon upon it —*The Letters of Rachel Henning, Written between 1853 and 1882*, 1952

In American English, *reckon* may be found with *to*, but only infrequently. In British English, *reckon* followed by *to* and the infinitive is quite common:

. . . despite his astonishing anticipations of the painting of the end of the nineteenth century, it seems better to reckon him to

the old school —Frank Jewett Mather, Jr., *Modern Painting*, 1927

. . . up till then it had not reckoned to accept papers of living authors, even as gifts —Philip Larkin, *Required Writing*, 1983

. . . with gold in the $170 range, it is reckoned to be worthwhile having a look at the gold prospects —Leslie Parker, *Financial Times* (London), 17 Apr. 1974

. . . he reckons to spend about a year on a book —Anna Pavord, *Observer Mag.*, 14 Apr. 1974

In both American and British English, *reckon* is often followed by a clause:

"I reckon it would scare Senator Johns half to death. . . ." —John Dos Passos, *Number One*, 1943

". . . As for finishing the job, I reckon we'll all be there together. . . ." —Richard Llewellyn, *A Few Flowers for Shiner*, 1950

He doubtless reckoned, as almost everyone here reckons, that it was a mite better to uphold the courts —Richard H. Rovere, *New Yorker*, 5 Oct. 1957

We reckon that we have been hired to get results —*The Bookseller*, 18 May 1974

2. *"Reckon" in the sense of "suppose, think":*

. . . so I reckon Bernage is on very good foot when he goes to Spain —Jonathan Swift, *Journal to Stella*, 12 Feb. 1711

Howard 1977 notes this use of *reckon* as one of several standard 18th-century usages that survive in common use in British English but have dropped out of standard American use. Some examples from British English:

Our brickies reckon the house that Jack built in England would go up faster here —*8 O'Clock* (Auckland, N.Z.), 8 Feb. 1975

"If you reckon that paradise is a hamburger. . . ." —William Nagle, *Nation Rev.* (Melbourne), 1 May 1975

. . . I reckon they pinched the money —John Fowles, *The Collector*, 1963

Russia is one place Americans reckon they are unlikely to be victims of a terrorist attack —*The Economist*, 26 Apr. 1986

In American English this use is mostly dialectal; it may occasionally be used in informal or deliberately countrified contexts:

And I bought this one for $4.75. I was, oh I reckon, ten years old —William Faulkner, 7 Mar. 1957, in *Faulkner in the University*, 1959

I reckon he doesn't like to feel surrounded by females —Flannery O'Connor, letter, 20 Sept. 1951

. . . we fairly reckoned you'd be with us on one of the weekends —John O'Hara, letter, March 1931

I reckon if anybody wears a double-breasted suit properly it's Doug Fairbanks —G. Bruce Boyer, *Town & Country*, March 1983

More Americans would use *I guess* where these people use *I reckon.*

recollect, remember The distinction that can be made between these words is that *recollect* implies—or can imply—a conscious effort to recall something to the mind ("He tried to recollect the name of the street"), while *remember* more generally implies only having something available in one's memory ("He always remembered what she had said"). This distinction has been noted in dictionaries at least since Webster 1828, and in books on usage at least since Richard Grant White 1870. But the evidence shows that the distinction is not really a strong one. The "conscious effort" connotations of *recollect* certainly exist, and they come across clearly in some contexts:

". . . tried to recollect how you looked, but I have never been able to recall a single feature." —Douglas Southall Freeman, "General Lee at the Surrender," in *Worlds of Adventure* (textbook), ed. Matilda Bailey & Ullin Whitney Leavell, 1951

Wordsworth's phrase "emotion recollected in tranquillity"—still echoed occasionally—does not necessarily connote effort. So perhaps Burchfield 1996's definition "to succeed in remembering" is closer to reality. But Burchfield notes there is no absolute distinction; *recollect* often shares the meaning of *remember.* Our evidence bears out Burchfield's observation:

We may smile at such blatant exclusivism until we recollect that her attitude has been officially sanctioned by most of the Christian Church for most of the time —Felipe Fernández-Armesto & Derek Wilson, *Reformations,* 1996

Then he'll recollect I said I was coming. . . . He will recall that I have freinds who know him —B. J. Oliphant, *Dead in the Scrub,* 1990

. . . these essays . . . warmly crowded with recollected poems and literary friendships —Daria Donnelley, *Commonweal,* 24 Apr. 1998

You recollect the large stories we used to hear —James Clyman, *Journal of a Mountain Man,* 1984

. . . it offers some poignancy, if not poetry, to be recollected in whatever tranquillity

the post-vacation letdown affords —Mary Hood, *Gettysburg Rev.,* Winter 1998

In short, *recollect* can be distinguished from *remember* in some but not all of its uses.

reconcile Two prepositions are idiomatic after *reconcile*—*with* and *to*:

. . . to reconcile technology with human cussedness —Russell Lynes, *Harper's,* October 1968

. . . how could one reconcile this arrogant separatism with the goals of integration? —David Loye, *Psychology Today,* May 1971

. . . it temporarily reconciles us to that condition —Clifton Fadiman, *Center Mag.,* January/February 1971

Nothing can reconcile Nader to the time lag —Charles McCarry, *Saturday Rev.,* 12 Feb. 1972

Only *with* is possible when *reconcile* is being used as an intransitive verb:

. . . was estranged from her husband . . . but has since reconciled with him —*Springfield* (Mass.) *Union,* 24 May 1968

recrudescence *Recrudescence* in its literal sense is a medical word denoting a renewed outbreak of a disease:

. . . prompt use of penicillin in streptococcic pharyngitis . . . has eliminated recrudescences following such infections —*Therapeutic Notes,* Feburary 1951

In extended use, *recrudescence* typically describes a renewed occurrence or appearance of something undesirable or objectionable:

. . . he predicted that if matters went on in this way there would be a recrudescence of guerrilla warfare in the Lithuanian forests —Christopher Hitchens, *Harper's,* July 1990

It has also sometimes been used as a neutral term simply equivalent to *reappearance* or *revival*:

. . . dates from this recrudescence of the Italian theatre —Sacheverell Sitwell, *The Dance of the Quick and the Dead,* 1936

Contemporaries were fully aware that they were witnessing a continuation or recrudescence of the spiritual forces of the Reformation —Felipe Fernández-Armesto & Derek Wilson, *Reformations,* 1996

Such usage was first criticized in 1906 by the Fowler brothers, who argued that *recrudescence* should only be applied to the renewal of something unwelcome. H. W. Fowler repeated the criticism more strongly in 1926; Burchfield 1996 agrees. Evans 1957, however, asserted that in American usage *recrudescence* was applicable to any renewed outbreak, "good or bad."

This issue is not an important one for most writers. *Recrudescence* is a fairly uncommon word, and most writers are unlikely to use it. Our evidence suggests that *recrudescence* was in somewhat more common use during the first half of the 20th century than it is now, and most of our examples of the disputed use are from that period. Those who now use the word in extended applications, according to our evidence, mostly use it of something undesirable.

recur, recurrence, reoccur, reoccurrence
Of these two pairs, *recur* and *recurrence* are by far the more common. A couple of commentators criticize *reoccur* and *reoccurrence* as unnecessary, but they are distinguishable in some ways from *recur* and *recurrence*. *Reoccur* and *reoccurrence* are the more basic words: they simply tell you that something happened again. *Recur* and especially *recurrence* can suggest a periodic or frequent repetition as well as the simpler notion.

> Castillo was removed from the game after the third because of a muscle pull on the right side of his neck. Twins trainer Dick Martin said it was a reoccurrence of a previous injury —Tom Yantz, *Hartford* (Conn.) *Courant*, 20 May 1983

In this example, *reoccurrence* merely says that the muscle pull had happened before; if the trainer had used *recurrence*, it could have suggested that the player had had the same injury more than once before.

But such niceties aside, most writers make do with *recur* and *recurrence*:

> There was a recurrence of this after the cataract operation —James Thurber, letter, 18 Dec. 1950

> . . . institutions specifically created to prevent a recurrence of past fiscal problems —Felix G. Rohatyn, *The Twenty-Year Century*, 1983

> . . . the motifs have become so numerous . . . that the mind cannot hold them together. One can only enjoy them as they occur and recur —George Stade, *N.Y. Times Book Rev.*, 17 June 1979

redolent Follett 1966 did not like *redolent with*. He calls it "almost as uncouth as *smells with* would be." Bernstein 1965 says flatly that *redolent* takes the preposition *of*. And so it does:

> Unpacking my bag in a room redolent of hair oil —S. J. Perelman, *Baby, It's Cold Inside*, 1970

> . . . a style redolent of an earlier culture —Lawrence W. Levine, *The Unpredictable Past*, 1993

> . . . he sat in an office redolent of cigar smoke —Dan Barry, *N.Y. Times Mag.*, 6 Dec. 1998

But it also takes the preposition *with*, as a look in the OED clearly shows. *Redolent of* is the older and more common idiom, but *redolent with* has been in use since the early 19th century and is certainly standard:

> . . . the message . . . was redolent with the conferring of a benefit rather than a commitment to cooperation —Roy Jenkins, *Gladstone*, 1995

> . . . a London working-class shopping district . . . redolent with fried fish shops —C. S. Forester, *The African Queen*, 1935

> . . . the atmosphere had been redolent with sympathies —Angus Wilson, *Such Darling Dodos*, 1950

> . . . on a rocky shelf above the ocean, redolent with the smell of rotten eggs from its natural sulfur —Susan Spano, *N.Y. Times*, 30 Jan. 1994

redundancy Have you ever felt that when you were talking to someone you were not being listened to? That your message was being misunderstood, or only partially understood? We have all had that experience, surely. It could be described as transmitting a message over a noisy channel—the noise in this instance being whatever it is in the mind of our listener that distracts attention from what we are saying. It is analogous to the problem of sending a message by radio or telephone through a lot of static.

Every language, it seems, has built-in mechanisms for helping the spoken message penetrate the noise. These mechanisms are called *redundancy*, a sense of the term perhaps borrowed from information science, the mathematical study of the transmission of electronic messages. A useful definition of *redundancy* can be found in Todd & Hancock 1986:

> In linguistics, it refers to data which may be unnecessary but which may help our understanding. In a phrase such as:
> > *those two dogs*
> plurality is marked three times. Most speech contains redundancies and so we often understand utterances even if we miss part of what was said.

This redundancy is something that helps a speaker or a writer get a message across even when the hearer or reader has missed part of it through inattention or distraction. This, then, is a useful redundancy; it protects the message and it facilitates the reception of the information or the idea the speaker or writer is trying to communicate.

Repetition, in one way or another, is the most obvious form of useful redundancy; by repeating an idea or a whole message, the writer or speaker can ensure that the reader or hearer does not miss the point. But, as the information scientists point out, a price must be paid for this use of repetition. It is loss of transmission speed. If everything in the message were to be repeated, transmission speed would slow down to almost nothing. If the speaker repeats and repeats, communication is likely to be broken altogether; the hearer falls asleep or walks away. If the writer repeats and repeats, the reader closes the book.

This brings us to a second meaning of *redundancy* that Todd & Hancock mentions: the use of too many words, what we might call wordy redundancy. The whole question of redundancy for writers comes down to the identification of the fine line between useful redundancy and wordy redundancy. This is seldom a problem in conversation, unless you have the misfortune to be a long-winded bore, but it may be one for the public speaker. It is also not a problem for usage writers, almost all of whom fail to recognize that there is such a thing as useful redundancy, even though they employ it themselves.

Here are a number of examples of useful redundancy. We will depart from the usual style of our examples and italicize the redundancies. You will note that many of them involve adverbs and prepositions. There are also several examples with emphasizing adjectives.

These five passages have not been picked *out* because they are especially bad. . . . I number them so that I can refer *back* to them —George Orwell, "Politics and the English Language," 1946

. . . to see if the waters were abated from *off* the face of the ground —Genesis 8:8 (AV), 1611

And both return *back* to their chairs —Shakespeare, *Richard II,* 1596

. . . would also revert *back* to Panama —*Current Biography,* June 1968

concur . . . has three *different* meanings —Harper 1985

There is *also the additional* problem raised by the casting . . . —John Simon, *New York,* 5 Apr. 1976

. . . are usually *unnecessary* padding in a sentence —Little, Brown 1986

. . . marked for James the *final* end of his freedom —K. M. Elisabeth Murray, *Caught in the Web of Words,* 1977

. . . one's *past* history was going to be removed —Norman Mailer, *Harper's,* March 1971

. . . the process of starting *over again* —Leacock 1943

. . . let us begin with a *true and authentic* story —W. M. Thackeray, *The Book of Snobs,* 1846

. . . the unequal combat waged here nightly is replayed *again* —Robert E. Taylor, *Wall Street Jour.,* 11 Sept. 1980

. . . it commands our attention so much that we are never necessitated to repeat the same thing *over a second time* —Adam Smith, lecture, 14 Jan. 1763, in *Lectures on Rhetoric and Belles Lettres,* ed. John M. Lothian, 1971

None of these redundancies impedes the flow of information, not even the last and longest (taken from speech, where longer redundancies are more useful than they are in writing). They all belong to our first type of redundancy—the useful—or if not positively useful, at least harmless. It is interesting that the handbooks quoted here (especially Harper 1985 and Little, Brown 1986) devote considerable space to the denunciation of exactly these kinds of redundant combinations, as does the book written by John Simon (Simon 1980). And George Orwell, in the very article we have quoted, lays it down as a rule that we should cut all unnecesssary words out of our writing.

The notion that redundant words should be eliminated from writing goes back to the 18th century. Lindley Murray 1795 put it this way:

The first rule for promoting the strength of a sentence, is, to prune it of all redundant words and members.

Murray may have taken this rule from one of his sources. It is not much different from Orwell's:

If it is possible to cut a word out, always cut it out.

But it had been recognized by writers as early as Ben Jonson that too terse a style could be a fault, not a virtue:

. . . the Language is thinne, flagging, poore, starv'd; scarce covering the bone, and shewes like stones in a sack. Some men to avoid Redundancy, runne into that; and while they strive to have no ill blood, or Juyce, they loose their good —*Timber: or, Discoveries,* before 1637

Some recent commentators too, such as Evans 1957 and Bailey 1984, warn against being too concise.

To repeat, there are two kinds of redundancy—the desirable kind of the linguist and the undesirable wordy kind. Much that is written in usage books about redundancy mistakes the first for the second. The usual pronouncements about *refer back, final result, collaborate together, continue on, end result, past history, general consensus, personal friend, off of,* and many, many more should therefore be taken with a large grain of salt. This is not to say that you *must* use the redundant forms, but you should feel free to judge for yourself where they may be useful to communication or may simply sound better than the shorter alternatives. Remember that the sound and rhythm of a sentence are important in transmitting your message through the noise:

> . . . inside a sentence the mere sound, the mere number of syllables used, is sometimes more important than the bare meaning of the words. In writing, as in conversation, an economical use of words is not always what we want —Evans 1957

See also WORDINESS.

refer This verb is often used with *back*:

> . . . "Death in Venice" also refers back to Britten's earlier operas on nearly every page —Peter G. Davis, *N.Y. Times,* 13 Oct. 1974

Such usage has been the object of criticism at least since Krapp 1927 described it as "a crude pleonasm for *refer.*" Many recent commentators call *refer back* a redundancy. But Bernstein 1971 pooh-poohs such criticism, asserting that "The notion of *back* is not at all prominent or even necessarily present in the word *refer,* which has as its primary meaning to direct attention to." *Back* may seldom be necessary with *refer,* but the "backward" connotations of *refer* are usually not strong, and *back* can be useful in reinforcing them:

> Professor Dulles . . . has throughout referred back to the original sources —Owen Lattimore, *N.Y. Herald Tribune Book Rev.,* 2 June 1946

> I number them so that I can refer back to them when necessary —George Orwell, "Politics and the English Language," 1946

> I have to be careful with my own research. I put it down in black and white. People can refer back to it —John D. MacDonald, *TV Guide,* 24 Nov. 1979

> In one controversy after another, contenders refer back to the Founding Fathers —Pauline Maier, *N.Y. Times Book Rev.,* 31 Oct. 1999

If you tend to be especially sensitive to redundancy in writing, you may want to avoid *refer back* in your own. Many good writers find it useful, however.

referendums, referenda These two plurals are both common and standard. Garner 1998 finds *referendums* more common; our most recent evidence shows *referenda* in the lead. Take your pick.

No one seems to have any difficulty in recognizing *referenda* as a plural. For a list of foreign plurals which are sometimes used as singulars, see LATIN PLURALS.

reflexive pronouns For a discussion of the use of reflexive pronouns in place of nominative and especially objective forms, see MYSELF. See also HISSELF; THEIRSELVES; THEMSELF; YOURSELF, YOURSELVES.

refute *Refute* has two senses, both of which are in common use, but one of which is widely regarded as an error. Its original and uncontroversial sense is "to prove wrong; show to be false or erroneous":

> It is not necessary to refute such an argument point by point —Denis Goulet, *Center Mag.,* May 1969

> . . . his superior book . . . appears to refute that contention —*New Yorker,* 2 Oct. 1971

Its disputed sense is "to deny the truth or accuracy of":

> We refute these aspersions whether they come from our best friends or our worst foes —Sir Winston Churchill, address in House of Commons, 18 Jan. 1945, in *Voices of History 1945–46,* ed. Nathan Ausubel, 1946

> Prime Minister Michael Manley . . . yesterday again refuted allegations that Jamaica House interfered —*Jamaica Weekly Gleaner,* 13 Feb. 1974

This sense seems to have originated in the 20th century. Its common use has become apparent only in the past several decades, but criticism of it dates back as far as Utter 1916. Most usage commentators now routinely take note of it, and all that do consider it a mistake. It is, however, very common, and the contexts in which it occurs are standard. Its most frequent use is by journalists in reporting emphatic denials issued by those accused of wrongdoing.

regard 1. *In regard to, with regard to, as regards, regarding.* There is a mixed bag of opinion about these, in which we can discern two main lines of commentary. The first of these apparently began with Quiller-Couch 1916, who condemned *as regards* and *with regard to* as circumlocutory and jargonistic. Many modern handbooks, especially the college variety, express a similar judgment, often extending it to *in regard to* and *regarding* as well. The critics prefer such alternatives as *about, on,* and *concerning,* and in many contexts you will no doubt find them preferable yourself. But remember that the matter of wordiness is entirely secondary to the matter of how your sentence sounds. When longer phrases suit the rhythm of a sentence better than short ones, the longer ones are a better choice.

The second line of comment goes back at least as far as MacCracken & Sandison 1917, where *in regards to* used in place of *in regard to* is cited as an error. The adherents to this line are also numerous, but they are almost all American. The issue in this case appears to be largely a social one. *In regards to* seems to be an expression heard chiefly from those who speak H. L. Mencken's "vulgate."

Most of our citations were taken from unedited spoken English. We also have found it in print by this noted practitioner of the vulgate:

> . . . maybe boys and gals who wants to take up writing as their life work would be benefited if some person like I was to give them a few hints in regards to the technic of the short story —Ring Lardner, preface, *How to Write Short Stories,* 1924

Our evidence suggests that *in regards to* is usually an oral use not often found in edited prose.

In regard to, with regard to, as regards, and *regarding,* on the other hand, are all perfectly standard. Here are a few examples of the words at work:

> In regard to the work of an already famous or infamous author it decides . . . —Edgar Allan Poe, *The Literati,* 1850

> . . . conclusions I had reached with regard to Vietnam —Tip O'Neill with William Novak, *Man of the House,* 1987

> . . . adviser to Douglas of Cavers with regard to the annual distribution of alms —K. M. Elisabeth Murray, *Caught in the Web of Words,* 1977

> Indeed the similarity . . . is extraordinary, as regards the military methods of both sides —G. M. Trevelyan, *A Shortened History of England,* 1942

> As regards function, these centuries are those in which the ancient patterns of cumulative negation appear in the standard language —Strang 1970

> Regarding the four types of heart diseases . . . , the president of ABC said . . . —Winston Munnings, *Nassau* (Bahamas) *Guardian,* 3 Mar. 1984

> Miss Crawley was pleased at the notion of a gossip with her sister-in-law regarding the late Lady Crawley —W. M. Thackeray, *Vanity Fair,* 1848

2. A curious issue concerns the omission of *as* after *regard* in constructions where *as* would normally be expected ("was regarded a traitor" rather than "was regarded as a traitor"). This subject has troubled British commentators from Fowler 1907 to Longman 1988. The problem is this: *regard* is generally associated with verbs that take a direct object and a second complement introduced by a particle: *regard* (object) *as, describe* (object) *as, take* (object) *for, look upon* (object) *as,* and so forth. Since some time in the 19th century (the OED's earliest example is from 1836), *regard* has shown some movement in the direction of complex transitive verbs like *think,* which take an object and a complement with no intervening particle. *Consider,* the verb prescribed by Fowler to replace *regard* in his numerous examples, is strongly linked with the complex transitive verbs (though it is also used with *as* like *regard,* a usage decried by some American commentators).

The fact that Fowler 1926 has more than twice as many examples as Fowler 1907 suggests that this use of *regard* had a burst of popularity around the turn of the last century, which continued right up to 1926. Burchfield 1996 finds the construction no longer current, and our files pretty much agree. We have only a couple of examples. The first shows *regard* with an infinitive complement (Fowler's first objection):

> "You perceive that even if this Jehovah is not God he is nevertheless regarded to be in the enjoyment of considerable powers. . . ." —Henry Baerlein, *The House of the Fighting-Cocks,* 1880

And we have this complex transitive example:

> . . . treated in a manner calculated to make him feel that he is regarded a sinister figure —George F. Kennan, *New Republic,* 2 Feb. 1953

But this is all. Evidently the construction has become rare.

Objections to the use of *as* after other complex transitive verbs are noted at AS 5 and at CONSIDER 1.

regret When a preposition follows the noun *regret,* the usual choice is *for:*

> . . . his bitter regrets for past happiness —T. S. Eliot, "Shakespeare and the Stoicism of Seneca," in *Selected Essays,* 1932

> . . . regrets for past mistakes —*Times Literary Supp.,* 29 Apr. 1955

Note that in the Eliot citation "regrets for" means something like "regretful longings for," whereas in the second citation it means simply "regretful feelings for." The second citation illustrates the more common usage. Other prepositions that may occur after *regret* are *at* and *over*, neither of which would be idiomatic with the "regretful longings" sense, but both of which are possible with the "regretful feelings" sense.

regretful, regrettable, regretfully, regrettably Fowler 1926 was the first to observe that *regretful* is sometimes confused with *regrettable*. Many later commentators have also felt the need to explain the distinction between these words, although the emphasis in recent years has shifted more to the use of the adverbs, *regretfully* and *regrettably*. Fowler cited three passages, apparently gleaned from newspapers, in which *regretful* was used to mean "causing regret" rather than "feeling or showing regret." But we have no further evidence of *regretful* used in this way; apparently it is quite rare. The adverb *regretfully*, on the other hand, is beginning to show a tendency to be used as a synonym of *regrettably*, meaning "to a regrettable extent" or "in a manner that causes regret." Our first evidence of this use is from the mid-1960s, which is also when it was first criticized. It is possible that this use owes something to the similar use of *hopefully* (which see), which underwent a boom in popularity a few years earlier. *Regretfully* has never approached *hopefully* in frequency of use, however. We have only a few citations for the disputed sense of *regretfully*, including these:

> . . . seems to have been their last, and regretfully lost, chance to talk with Jenny —Mabel F. Hale, *New-England Galaxy*, Winter 1965

> . . . its regretfully pronounced tendency to obliterate distinctions —Maurice Friedberg, *Saturday Rev.*, 10 Jan. 1970

> Personalized items are regretfully nonreturnable —advt., *Home Decorators Collection*, Autumn 1998

> Regretfully, . . . all innovation, passion and energy lie with the adversaries of secular, democratic society —Chris Hedges, *N.Y. Times Book Rev.*, 26 Mar. 2000

Regrettably is still much the more common choice in such contexts:

> . . . and shows, regrettably, that he is still under their influence —John Kenneth Galbraith, *Saturday Rev.*, 6 Nov. 1971

> None of my uncles, regrettably, was French —S. J. Perelman, *N.Y. Times Mag.*, 15 Jan. 1978

> . . . which I regrettably missed —Simon 1980

Note that *regrettably* functions in these passages as a sentence modifier (see SENTENCE ADVERB), more or less equivalent to "I regret to say." *Regretfully* in the passage from *N.Y. Times Book Review* functions in the same way.

reign, rein The triumph of the automobile is revealed in our loss of awareness of words associated with the horse. *Rein* is a case in point. Once an everyday household word, it has been driven into relative obscurity by the automobile. Several idiomatic expressions with *rein* continue in general use, but since the word is not nearly as common as it once was, writers and keyboarders tend to confuse it with its homophone *reign*. Copperud 1980 takes note of *in full reign* and *turn over the reigns*. Our files have *free reign* and *takes the reigns*. The computer's spelling checker won't help you here; you'll need a dictionary.

reiterate This verb has attracted commentary because it has a kind of built-in redundancy; there is a rarely used verb *iterate* (from the Latin *iterum*, "again") that itself means "to say or do again," so that it seems as if *reiterate* ought to mean something like "to re-say or re-do again," or "to say or do over and over." Some commentators disapprove its use in describing a first repetition, but other commentators recognize that such a nice distinction hardly exists in actual usage. Both *iterate* and *reiterate* are used essentially as synonyms, with the chief distinction between them being that *reiterate* is the far more common word.

rejoice The next time something makes you feel like rejoicing, feel free to rejoice either *in* it or *at* it. *In* is the more common choice, but *at* is also idiomatic and far from rare:

> We do not, I suspect, rejoice in force more than other nations —Stringfellow Barr, *Center Mag.*, May 1968

> . . . the young people who rejoice in such language —Franklin L. Ford, *Harvard Today*, Autumn 1968

> A layman can only rejoice at the legal subtlety and boldness —Robert Lekachman, *New Republic*, 29 Nov. 1954

Rejoice in is sometimes used to mean simply "have or possess":

> One of the characters . . . rejoices in the name of Sherlock Feldman —Bennett Cerf, *Saturday Rev.*, 22 May 1954

> The higher parts of the mountains rejoice in an average annual rainfall of thirty inches —Oliver La Farge, *N.Y. Times Mag.*, 15 Aug. 1954

Another preposition that occasionally occurs after *rejoice* is *over*:

> I wish you to rejoice with me over the consummation of this great gift —Ira Remsen, quoted in *Johns Hopkins Mag.*, April 1966

relate The sense of intransitive *relate* that means "to have or establish a relationship, interact" seems to have had its origins in the jargon or shoptalk of psychology and sociology. It established itself in general use during the 1960s as something of a vogue word. It has received unflattering notice from numerous commentators. A few of these find it a tad more tolerable when *relate* is followed by a *to* phrase. It occurs both without and with such a phrase:

> . . . she herself had been the kind of child to grow up incapable of relating: insecure, cold, undeveloped, guilt-ridden —Margaret Drabble, *The Needle's Eye*, 1972

> "They (teen-age salespeople) know what you want and they can relate," says Karen Rascon as she thumbs through Contempo's racks —Bonnie Gangelhoff, *Houston Post*, 2 Sept. 1984

> "You can't just come in off the street and make them," Mr. [Bob] Raspanti said emphatically. "You have to understand the dough in order to relate to it." —*New Yorker*, 4 Oct. 1982

> I really don't relate to football like I do baseball —Joe Falls, *Sporting News*, 25 Oct. 1982

In this last example *relate* means roughly "respond favorably," a sense that has grown out of the popularized psychological one. The commentators—and you—may find these uses a bit tiresome, but they are established in speech and general writing.

relation 1. *Relation, relative.* It is not exactly clear why these words are to be found in so many usage books when almost the only useful things to be said about them are that they are synonymous in the sense "a person to whom one is related" and that they are frequently plural in that sense. The commentators differ from one another in trivial and inconsequential ways. We can say with certainty that both *relation* and *relative* are in common current use:

> I grew up in a house where the only regular guests were my relations. On a certain day, enormous families of relatives would visit us —Richard Rodriguez, in *The Bedford Reader*, ed. X. J. Kennedy & Dorothy M. Kennedy, 1985

Garner 1998 finds *relative* more common.

2. *Relation* is usually used with *of* in the sense of "relative" and sometimes in other senses:

> . . . a polar explorer and a relation of Butler's first wife —*Current Biography*, September 1964

> . . . she stood in the relation of a chaperone and sponsor to Elfine —Stella Gibbons, *Cold Comfort Farm*, 1932

But *to* is more common with most senses and with most of the idiomatic expressions:

> While his relations to women were self-serving —Anatole Broyard, *N.Y. Times Book Rev.*, 9 May 1982

> He has expressed his views on Africa and its relation to the rest of the world —*Current Biography*, March 1966

> . . . bears no relation to what I'm saying —Stephen Vizinczey, letter to the editor, *Times Literary Supp.*, 5 June 1969

> Stanza two presents her mind and body in relation to her soul —John T. Shawcross, *Hartford Studies in Literature*, vol. 2, no. 1, 1969

> . . . their comfortable and complacent lives bear little relation to the ideology they proclaim —*Times Literary Supp.*, 7 Mar. 1968

In other senses, *with* and *between* (occasionally *among*) are used:

> . . . their relation with their slaves rested on injustice and violence —Eugene D. Genovese, *N.Y. Times Book Rev.*, 20 July 1986

> Relations between the United States and Spain —*Current Biography*, November 1965

> . . . the cultivation of relations among people for the improvement of society —Dale B. Harris, in *Automation, Education, and Human Values*, ed. W. W. Brickman & S. Lehrer, 1966

relative See RELATION 1.

relatively *Relatively* has been subjected to the same strictures as *comparatively* has been—namely, that it should not be used to modify an adjective when no comparison is stated or implied—and by essentially the same commentators. The first to state the proposition seems to have been Gowers 1948, who later added it to Fowler 1965.

The OED definition at *relatively* makes no mention at all of comparisons, either stated or implied. The OED examples show that the usage Gowers dislikes has been established since the earliest uses of the adverb to modify adjectives.

In current practice, both uses of *relatively*—without an explicit comparison and with an explicit comparison—are common, and there is no valid reason for you to bother yourself about which way you use the word. Here are a few examples of both:

> I had a talk with Armstrong, who was looking quite spick and span in relatively new clothes —*The Journals of Arnold Bennett,* ed. Frank Swinnerton, 1954

> It apparently made relatively slow progress at the start, but after a couple of years it was in wide and indeed almost general use —H. L. Mencken, *The American Language, Supplement I,* 1945

> An atomic problem is not absolutely insoluble.... A problem is only relatively insoluble; insoluble with given tools —W. W. Sawyer, *Prelude to Mathematics,* 1955

> Yes, men were relatively fragile —Norman Mailer, *Harper's,* March 1971

> The relatively few American leaders who understood the military absurdity of this exercise were quickly cowed —Chester Bowles, *Saturday Rev.,* 6 Nov. 1971

> Those who are worried about their status discover in the use of textbook English a relatively easy way to assert their superiority to the masses —Barnard 1979

> By comparison the progress of Leonid Brezhnev . . . seems relatively modest —Geoffrey Hosking, *Times Literary Supp.,* 15 Aug. 1980

relative pronouns See THAT; WHAT; WHICH; WHO, WHOM; WHOSE.

relevant A number of commentators warn against the metathesized pronunciation and spelling *revelant.* It sometimes turns up in surprising places:

> . . . furnishes references where revelant to STC —*Times Literary Supp.,* 15 Oct. 1964

See METATHESIS.

reliable Lounsbury 1908 commented that the controversy over *reliable* was then a century or more old (he did not say who started it, unfortunately) and showed no signs of dying out. The issue was etymology: since *reliable* means "able to be relied *on*" rather than "able to rely," it was held to have been improperly formed. Its critics were many, some of whom wrongly criticized it as an Americanism. In spite of Lounsbury's feeling that the issue would not die soon, it did. There is no usage problem with *reliable* anymore.

relish When the noun *relish* is followed by a preposition, the preposition may be either *of* or *for. For* is the more common choice:

> . . . a certain relish for debate —Bell Gale Chevigny, *Village Voice,* 28 Feb. 1968

> . . . the reader must have a relish for suspense —Catherine Meyer, *Harper's,* May 1971

But *of* is also standard:

> She had tremendous earthy relish of concrete manifestations of place and people —Ruth Suckow, *College English,* March 1953

> . . . a relish of the trivia of the private lives of public persons —J. H. Plumb, *Saturday Rev.,* 28 June 1969

remand Critics from 1958 to 1991 caution against what they consider the redundant use of *back* with *remand.* Their warnings may be unnecessary in this case; *remand back* hardly ever occurs except in legal writing and usage books.

See also REDUNDANCY.

remediable, remedial Several commentators distinguish between these words, but only two of them explicitly state that *remediable* and *remedial* are confused. Follett 1966 cites an instance in which *remedial,* which means "serving or intended as a remedy," is used in place of *remediable,* which means "capable of being remedied." Our files contain no other examples of such misuse. The OED shows that the original meaning of *remediable* was, in fact, "remedial," but the most recent evidence of *remediable* in this obsolete sense is from 1596. What we conclude from all of this is that these two words are rarely confused. Here are a few examples of typical current use:

> He noted the various remedial proposals that have been made —*Center Mag.,* November 1969

> . . . he had begun this remedial reading with the firmest male prejudice of them all —Norman Mailer, *Harper's,* March 1971

> Happily, my problem was remediable —Carll Tucker, *Saturday Rev.,* 18 Mar. 1978

> . . . at least partly remediable social wrongs —Irving Howe, *N.Y. Times Book Rev.,* 18 Apr. 1982

remedy When used with a preposition, *remedy* is often followed by *for*:

> Work was generally deplored as too drastic a remedy for our unemployment —Cyril Connolly, *The Condemned Playground,* 1946

> . . . we applied the human remedy, the remedy my family had found in Saskatchewan for any unwanted life —Wallace Stegner, *Blair & Ketchum's Country Jour.,* December 1979

Less frequently, it is found with *against* or *to*:

> ... the people's remedy against the abuse of government —Morris R. Cohen, *The Faith of a Liberal,* 1946

> ... to wait with growing impatience for the remedies against tyranny —*Times Literary Supp.,* June 1969

> ... controls offer no real remedy to inflation, but merely serve as a tranquilizer —Leif H. Olson, quoted in *Barron's,* 8 May 1972

> ... endorsed the plan ... as a remedy to the deep stagnation which engulfed Germany —Fritz Karl Mann, *Annals of the American Academy of Political and Social Science,* January 1950

remember   See RECOLLECT, REMEMBER.

renowned   A couple of commentators say that *renown* is sometimes misused as an adjective equivalent to *renowned.* We have a little evidence of this error in our files:

> ... a world-renown authority on peregrines —*Massachusetts Audubon News Letter,* April 1971

> ... a renown clinical psychologist —*Cats Mag.,* December 1985

Remember that *renown* is not established as an adjective in standard English. Use *renowned* instead.

The same commentators also mention the misspellings *reknown* and *reknowned.* These are both attested in our files and should be avoided.

reoccur, reoccurrence   See RECUR, RECURRENCE, REOCCUR, REOCCURRENCE.

repeat again   Jensen 1935, Copperud 1980, Shaw 1987, and Garner 1998 consider *repeat again* redundant for *repeat.* But look at this example:

> A theme was repeated again and again. In the middle of frills, grace-notes, runs and catches it recurred with a strange, almost holy, solemnity —James Stephens, *The Crock of Gold,* 1912

This is a perfect example of useful redundancy, for a discussion of which see REDUNDANCY.

repel   See REPULSE, REPEL.

repetition   See REDUNDANCY.

replete   There is a sense of *replete* which some critics regard as nonexistent. The problem has to do with the use of *replete* as a synonym of *complete.* The OED, which treats this sense of *replete* as standard, shows that it has been used—although only rarely—since 1601,

when it occurred in Shakespeare's *All's Well That Ends Well.* Its use became more frequent in the 20th century. The first to criticize it was Fowler 1926, whose opinion has been more or less repeated by several later commentators. The distinction they draw between *replete* and *complete* begins from a valid observation, that *replete* normally indicates fullness or abundance. To describe a book as "complete with illustrations" is to simply say that it has illustrations, but to describe it as "replete with illustrations" is to say that it has illustrations in abundance. As far as the critics are concerned, that is where the story ends, but in fact *replete* is also not uncommonly used in standard writing to mean "complete":

> ... the Chevy Suburban that Arizona Cardinal Eric Swann recently ordered, replete with two TV screens, a Super Nintendo system, a VCR and a video camera —Robert L. Simison et al., *Wall Street Jour.,* 11 Dec. 1998

> Her host's staff had made Sandi Golden over into a suburban mom, replete with contact lenses and molded coiffure —Randall Sullivan, *Rolling Stone,* 14–28 July 1994

> ... the restored raw-timbered barn that, replete with a giant fireplace and a cozy bar, functions as the lounge —Jack Beatty, *Atlantic,* September 1989

> ... a postmodern merman replete with scaly fishtail —*Vanity Fair,* October 1996

> ... a traditional Pomeranian wedding ceremony, replete with carriages and champagne, elaborate banquets and dancing —Mary Nolan, *N.Y. Times Book Rev.,* 1 Sept. 1991

Sometimes *replete* has been chosen because it has connotations of abundance and opulence, but sometimes this does not seem to have been a consideration.

replica   *Replica* is used in the fine arts with the narrow meaning of a copy or reproduction of a work of art made by or under the supervision of the original artist. Fowler 1926, 1965, Bernstein 1958, 1965, 1977, and Shaw 1975, 1987 believe this to be the only proper sense; Kilpatrick 1984 knows it is not but wishes it were. The evidence in the OED suggests, however, that the word has been applied loosely since the middle of the 19th century, when it was first introduced into English. In present-day use it more often refers to a reproduction of some artifact than to a work of art and frequently is used of a miniaturized copy. It is also used figuratively. Some examples:

> At the moment, a replica of the Mayflower —or, rather, what purports to be a replica, for nobody knows exactly what the ship

looked like—is being built in England —E. J. Kahn, Jr., *New Yorker*, 1 Oct. 1955

The Langley Research Center has designed, constructed, and tested a 1/5-scale replica model of the Saturn SA-1 launch vehicle —Harry L. Runyan & Robert W. Leonard, *Structures for Space Operations*, December 1962

. . . chemists learned how to make laboratory replicas of increasingly complex natural products —Barry Commoner, *New Yorker*, 2 Oct. 1971

. . . building a bridge that was said to be an exact replica of one of the bridges that Caesar built across the Rhine —Merle Miller, *Plain Speaking*, 1973

. . . transforming some of the shore and lake country of southern Maine . . . into replicas of suburban shopping malls —Morgan McGinley, *N.Y. Times*, 12 Aug. 1984

Intensifying adjectives such as *exact, authentic,* and *perfect* are sometimes used with *replica* to stress fidelity of detail. They are harmless, and at any rate are more common in advertising matter than in other contexts.

reprisal Bernstein 1965 notes that *reprisal* "takes preposition *for* (an act); *against* or *upon* (the perpetrator)," but actual usage is less clear-cut. The most common preposition following *reprisal* seems to be *against*, and while it is true that a reprisal is usually *against* a "perpetrator," we also have evidence for its occasional use when an "act" is involved:

The seizure may have been a reprisal against the action of the Privy Council in London —Theodore Hsi-en Chen, *Current History*, November 1952

In "All Quiet" waggish reprisals against noncoms were still possible —Frederic Morton, *Saturday Rev.*, 22 May 1954

. . . any terrorist act by any Arab or Jew can properly be the occasion for a reprisal against any Jew or Arab —Noam Chomsky, *Columbia Forum*, Winter 1969

. . . I think we can say that *Bech*, at least in part, represents a reprisal, and a healthy one, against the literary establishment —L. E. Sissman, *Atlantic*, August 1970

Upon seems to occur with *reprisal* very seldom now, but *on* does have some use. It occurs in the same contexts as *against*, but less frequently:

. . . lest Mr. Raycie's mysterious faculty of hearing what was said behind his back should bring sudden reprisals on the venerable lady —Edith Wharton, *False Dawn*, 1924

. . . had considered it a peculiarly unfortunate feature of Jackson's proposal for reprisal on French shipping —Francis D. Wormuth, "The Vietnam War: The President versus the Constitution," 1968

Reprisal is also used with *for* in the way noted by Bernstein:

. . . in reprisal for maltreatment of an American naval lieutenant —Francis D. Wormuth, "The Vietnam War: The President versus the Constitution," 1968

repugnance When *repugnance* is used with a preposition, it is usually *to*:

. . . her instinctive dignity and repugnance to any show of emotion —George Eliot, *Silas Marner*, 1861

. . . a deep-seated repugnance to monopoly in almost any form —Neil J. Curry, *Atlantic*, December 1955

Other prepositions sometimes used with *repugnance* are *for, toward,* or *towards*:

. . . they headed for a place prostrated by war which also shared their repugnance for arms —George Weller, *Saturday Evening Post*, 1 Sept. 1956

. . . without at the same time restraining her repugnance toward the political philosophy of the Fascist states —Maurice Halperin, *Foreign Affairs*, October 1940

. . . having so far overcome his repugnance towards the language employed in their theoretical writings —*Times Literary Supp.*, 8 Oct. 1954

Repugnance was also once used with *against*, as the OED shows, but we have no evidence that such usage still occurs.

repulse, repel Quite a few commentators—Evans 1957, Bernstein 1962, 1965, Bremner 1980, Copperud 1970, 1980, Shaw 1975, 1987, Bryson 1984, Freeman 1983—insist on a distinction between the figurative uses of *repel* and *repulse*. What this distinction amounts to is disapproval of the sense of *repulse* that means "to cause repulsion in." Bernstein illustrates the desired distinction with this sentence:

She repulsed the suitor because he repelled her.

Here *repulse* means basically "to drive off or turn away," which is its oldest sense (and which, incidentally, is also a sense of *repel*). *Repulse* is often used in this sense, as Bernstein suggests, and *repel* is often used to mean "to cause repulsion in":

. . . she had learned to be on the watch and to repulse advances that were disagreeable —Ellen Glasgow, *Barren Ground*, 1925

. . . the inevitable promiscuity attached to a sexual search repelled him —Norman Mailer, *Harper's,* March 1971

. . . he was personally repelled by some of the racial policies of the Metropolitan Club in Washington —Gay Talese, *Harper's,* January 1969

But *repulse* is also used like *repel,* as in these examples:

. . . Malone sat trembling on the edge of the table, repulsed by his own weakness and distress —Carson McCullers, *Botteghe Oscure,* Quaderno XI, 1953

Hoarding repulses Mr. Risolo, the barber —Philip Hawkins, *Wall Street Jour.,* 5 Oct. 1966

People who had been repulsed by his wartime pamphleteering were eager to forget him —John W. Aldridge, *Saturday Rev.,* 7 Aug. 1976

The suggestion in Copperud and Evans that it is an error to associate *repulse* with *repulsion* has no foundation; both words are derived from the same Latin word, and there is no logical reason they should not share senses.

You will, of course, feel free to observe the distinction between *repulse* and *repel* urged by the commentators if you find it useful to do so. The distinction itself does not seem to be an especially helpful one. The context in all our citations for *repulse* makes it clear which sense is being used. *Repel* is, however, far more common in the disputed sense than is *repulse.* The choice is yours.

request A number of British commentators, from Fowler 1926 to Longman 1988, and one American, Bernstein 1958, 1965, have objected to the use of *for* after the verb *request.* Here is Bernstein's example:

The President has requested Congress for both these powers —*N.Y. Times,* 28 Feb. 1957

The opinion of all the commentators is that this construction is based on analogy with *ask,* common in the same construction, and that it is unidiomatic (or incorrect). Another influence may be the noun *request,* which is common with *for*:

. . . the request for the release of Archbishop Slipyi —Norman Cousins, *Saturday Rev.,* 30 Oct. 1971

At any rate, the construction appears to be rare in print. We have only one example besides those given by Fowler and Bernstein:

. . . Prime Minister Attlee has requested President Truman for renewed American efforts —*Current History,* November 1951

Such usage should not be confused with the use of *request* with *for* in a construction like the following, in which *request* has an impersonal object:

Indian officials requested the area for Indian families —*American Guide Series: Minnesota,* 1938

The impersonal object can also be followed by *of*:

. . . the machine could begin to request specific things of the child —*Johns Hopkins Mag.,* April 1966

resemblance When *resemblance* is followed by a preposition, the preposition is usually *to*:

. . . a resemblance to one of his own targets —Phoebe-Lou Adams, *Atlantic,* February 1972

He bears little resemblance to the characters he has portrayed —Claire Safran, *Redbook,* July 1974

In another common construction, *between* follows *resemblance*:

. . . to discover any resemblance between the two situations —Edith Wharton, *The Age of Innocence,* 1920

. . . the resemblance between this correspondence and the epistolary novel —*Times Literary Supp.,* 19 Feb. 1971

Bernstein 1965 indicates that *resemblance* is also followed by *among*:

The first two grape varieties . . . produce some of the finest reds of California and Australia, and it's no surprise that there is a family resemblance among them —Alexis Bespaloff, *Elk,* October 1990

resentment *Resentment* is not very particular about the prepositions that follow it. We have evidence for more than a half-dozen, the most common of which are *at, of,* and *against*:

She felt no resentment at this miscarriage of her preparations —John Cheever, *The Wapshot Chronicle,* 1957

. . . to gratify an old man's resentment of skepticism —Anthony Boucher, *Far and Away,* 1955

. . . resentment against other poets' prizes —Martin Green, *N.Y. Times Book Rev.,* 19 Dec. 1976

Other possibilities are *toward* (or *towards*) and, much less often, *over* and *for*:

. . . a great deal of children's resentment toward school in general —Bruno Bettelheim, *Ladies' Home Jour.,* September 1971

. . . French resentment over Secretary Dulles' recent speech —Roscoe Drummond, *Town Jour.,* January 1954

... not because of resentment for his hard youth —Sherwood Anderson, *Poor White,* 1920

reside For a usage issue of low intellectual content, you have to look no farther than the century-long disparagement of *reside* as pretentious for *live.* It is a word used in legal contexts, in rules, in constitutions (including the U.S. Constitution), and in other such writings. In more general works, it is used in books of brief biographies and similar works of reference, whose authors surely need an occasional change from *live*:

... was born on March 31, 1912, in Chicago, where his brother and three sisters still reside —*Current Biography,* July 1967

It is also used in contexts where *live* would be inappropriate:

The sensitive corporate data that reside on intranets —Alison L. Sprout, *Fortune,* 27 Nov. 1995

... the temporal lobes . . . of the brain, where memory and feelings reside —Natalie Angier, *N.Y. Times,* 12 Oct. 1993

These uses are perfectly acceptable.

respect *Respect* occurs in a few idiomatic phrases that have been involved in one usage issue or another over the years. For instance, Bierce 1909 objected to *respect* in the sense "way, matter," which is used in such phrases as *in that respect.* Such phrases are, of course, perfectly standard:

More representative in this respect was Lord Chesterfield —John Butt, *English Literature in the Mid-Eighteenth Century,* edited & completed by Geoffrey Carnall, 1979

In one other respect Johnson proposed to improve upon his predecessors —John Butt, *English Literature in the Mid-Eighteenth Century,* edited & completed by Geoffrey Carnall, 1979

And Quiller-Couch 1916 objected to *in respect of* as jargonish. *Respect* occurs in three such phrases: *in respect of, in respect to,* and *with respect to.* For a discussion of these phrases, see IN RESPECT OF, IN RESPECT TO, WITH RESPECT TO.

respective, respectively There is quite a bit of opinion about *respective* and *respectively* in print, and it all concerns the familiar use of the two words in matching sets of things in the correct order.

... we will continue to use the conventional symbols NP, VP, AP, and PP for the maximal projections of N, V, A, and P, respectively —Noam Chomsky, *Knowledge of Language,* 1986

Respective and *respectively* also have a distributive function that assigns separate things to members of a group referred to by a plural noun:

... blows up an atomic energy plant during dedication ceremonies, respectively killing and injuring the daughters of two Supreme Court justices —*Publishers Weekly,* 17 June 1983

The gist of the commentary is that *respective* and *respectively* are often used where not strictly necessary (does Chomsky really need *respectively* to help you match *NP* with *N,* etc.?) and, even when correctly used, should be avoided because they tend to slow down the progress of the reader.

The points made by the critics are worth remembering, but so is the point that there are times when a writer wants to slow readers down to make sure they are paying attention.

The uses in the three examples that follow are all of the kind that would be called unnecessary by the commentators. The first two are harmless, mere reminders of individuality. The third is surely otiose, a classic example of omissible *respectively.*

... the . . . result of this arrangement is, that such men as have female companions with them pass their time in prowling about the precincts of the "ladies' apartment"; while their respective ladies pop their heads first out of one door and then out of another —Fanny Kemble, *Journal of a Residence on a Georgian Plantation in 1838–1839,* 1863

She analyzes CDs, stocks, bonds, options, mutual funds, U.S. Savings Bonds, tax-free investments, collectibles, and partnerships as to their suitability in an IRA. . . . She also "forecasts" their respective suitability should the new tax law affect them —Steven J. Mayover, *Library Jour.,* August 1986

... a harshly funny and effective study of Nazi self-delusion and atrocity respectively, presenting them in terms of elaborate fantasy —*Times Literary Supp.,* 14 Nov. 1968

responsibility A person is usually said to have a responsibility *for* something and *to* someone:

The responsibility for engineering the line of cars which in 1908 evolved the immortal Model T —John Kenneth Galbraith, *N.Y. Times Book Rev.,* 28 Feb. 1954

... Joachim not only assumed personal responsibility for his future study but became his part-time teacher —*Current Biography,* February 1966

A great soprano has a responsibility to her public —Robert Evett, *Atlantic,* September 1970

. . . Landau's piece, examining the fan's, and the journalist's responsibility to rock stars —Lawrence Dietz, *Los Angeles Times Book Rev.,* 23 May 1971

Responsibility is also frequently followed by *of,* which occurs in the same contexts as *for:*

. . . he determined to take upon his own shoulders the responsibility of organizing some amusements —Thomas Hardy, *The Mayor of Casterbridge,* 1886

The banks had the responsibility of the amalgamation of industries —*The Autobiography of William Allen White,* 1946

Other prepositions that sometimes occur with *responsibility* include *about, in,* and *toward* (or *towards*):

Things you've had to take responsibility about really should have been mine —Angus Wilson, *The Middle Age of Mrs. Eliot,* 1958

. . . federal responsibility in civil rights shifted from the Department of Justice to a broad government base —*Current Biography,* February 1965

Anthony Burton had once said that this was your responsibility toward society —John P. Marquand, *Atlantic,* November 1947

The idea that he has any responsibility towards Amy or should feel any affection for their son —*Times Literary Supp.,* 29 June 1967

restaurateur, restauranteur The word *restaurateur* was borrowed into English from French at the end of the 18th century. Several decades later, according to written evidence, *restaurant* was similarly borrowed. In the years since, *restaurant* has become an extremely common English word, but *restaurateur* has remained far less common. This difference in frequency of use has given rise to the variant form *restauranteur.* Our first written evidence of *restauranteur* is from the 1920s:

The individual restauranteur is helpless —*New Yorker,* 20 Feb. 1926

It still turns up sporadically in print:

. . . respected cooking teacher, cookbook author and restauranteur —*Publishers Weekly,* 17 Sept. 1982

. . . a 19-year-old who lives with her 62-year-old restauranteur boyfriend —Margy Rochlin, *Elle,* September 1992

Restaurateur is the usual written form, especially in writing that has passed under a copy editor's eye, but *restauranteur* is a standard secondary variant.

restive The "impatient, fidgety" sense of *restive,* recorded in Merriam-Webster dictionaries, has upset commentators since 1870. The first spate of criticism, which died out after 1909, was concerned with the preservation of an earlier sense. A second spate followed World War II, these critics finding fault with the meaning because it was synonymous with *restless* (it's not defined that way in our dictionaries, but critics sometimes don't read dictionaries closely). While *restive* can come close to *restless* in meaning, it more typically connotes impatience:

They were all becoming restive under the monotonous persistence of the missionary —Willa Cather, *Death Comes for the Archbishop,* 1927

Often it suggests a hostile or surly impatience:

. . . a stubborn President, a restive party and Congress, a mounting opposition—something had to give —James MacGregor Burns, *The Vineyard of Liberty,* 1981

This criticism is now more than a century and a quarter old, and is as baseless now as it was in 1870.

restrictive appositives See APPOSITIVES.

reticent, reticence *Reticent* has recently developed a new sense, and usage watchers are not keeping quiet about it. In its older, better established uses, *reticent* can mean "inclined to be silent":

An extremely reticent man, Morris does not like to talk about his experience in personal terms —Helen Dudar, *N.Y. Times Mag.,* 30 Oct. 1977

or "restrained in expression or appearance":

. . . two or three rather reticent abstract paintings —Jay Jacobs, *Gourmet,* January 1979

In its disputed sense, *reticent* is synonymous with *reluctant* or *hesitant.* This use seems to have developed in the 1950s:

. . . its sponsors, not reticent to affirm their aspiration —*Annual Report of the Librarian of Congress,* 1952

This use is generally marked by *to* and an infinitive following *reticent:*

Foreign sovereigns were not reticent to receive "gifts" from the Chinese emperor —Daniel J. Boorstin, *The Discoverers,* 1983

. . . taxpayers have been reticent to put up the money —Connie Chung, television news broadcast, 24 Aug. 1985

The Cupertino-based company has been reticent to publicly detail its cutback plan —Nancy Ryan, *Chicago Tribune,* 9 June 1991

. . . cigar merchants have been reticent to continue the service —James Suckling, *Wine Spectator,* 15 Feb. 1992

We find it in British English too:

. . . his friends and associates are conspicuously reticent to discuss him in public —Martin Flanagan, *Manchester Guardian Weekly,* 29 Dec. 1991

The same extension of meaning has occurred with the noun *reticence*:

. . . criticized the reticence of West European governments to support American sanctions —*N.Y. Times,* 19 Mar. 1980

Arafat's reticence to talk is understandable —Peter Carlson, *People,* 1 Aug. 1983

This use has been with us for a half century, and is established as standard, but it is still a minority use. Many commentators (and others) still regard it as an error.

return back This is another verb phrase that is sometimes cited (by Shaw 1987, for example) as redundant. *Back* is, of course, not needed with *return*; it is simply a little reinforcement that is occasionally added to make sure the reader or hearer does not miss the point. The combination is an old one:

. . . the bill must be sent to Murry, accepted by him, and then returned back —Jonathan Swift, *Journal to Stella,* 7 June 1711

. . . when that's done, 'twill be time to return back to the parlour fire-side, where we left my uncle *Toby* in the middle of his sentence —Laurence Sterne, *Tristram Shandy,* 1760

. . . I shall return back to Venice in a few days —Lord Byron, letter, 12 May 1817

See REDUNDANCY.

Rev. See REVEREND, REV.

revel Bernstein 1965 says that *revel* is used with the preposition *in,* and most of the time it is:

. . . revelling in its barber shop quavers —Eugene O'Neill, *The Great God Brown,* 1926

. . . I fairly revelled in reminiscent sympathy with him —Max Beerbohm, *Seven Men,* 1920

. . . a woman . . . reveling in the violent surge of her blood —William Styron, *Lie Down in Darkness,* 1951

. . . it revels in name-calling —Daniels 1983

Once in a while *revel* can be found with *at, around, on,* or *with.* Of these only *at* is used like *in,* to connect the verb with the object of revelry.

. . . they reveled at his cockiness —A. H. Raskin, *N.Y. Times Mag.,* 7 Nov. 1976

. . . a brilliant scapegrace who had . . . revelled around Europe for years —Herman Wouk, *Marjorie Morningstar,* 1955

. . . was revelling on the fat of the land in Philadelphia —Samuel Eliot Morison & Henry Steele Commager, *The Growth of the American Republic,* 3d ed., 1942

. . . a school teacher afraid life is passing her by, revels with Arthur O'Connell —*N.Y. Times Mag.,* 25 Dec. 1955

revenge 1. See AVENGE, REVENGE.
2. The noun *revenge* is often followed by *on, against,* or *for.* The first two of these prepositions mark the object of the revenge, the last its motive.

. . . an act of revenge on their greatness —David Denby, *Atlantic,* September 1971

It often takes revenge on civilians —Max Clos, *N.Y. Times Mag.,* 10 Jan. 1965

. . . thirsting for revenge against his "friend and successor" —William L. Shirer, *The Rise and Fall of the Third Reich,* 1960

Is this some kind of revenge for what happened to your sister? —John Masters, *Fandango Rock,* 1959

Reverend, Rev. Concern over the proper use of *Reverend* and its abbreviation *Rev.* in addressing American Protestant clergymen goes back at least to Richard Grant White 1870; it has continued unabated in usage books, etiquette books, and the public prints ever since. The usual prescriptions can be easily summed up: *Reverend* is an adjective; it is not a title; it should be preceded by *the*; it should be followed by a surname or a title such as *Dr.* or *Mr.*; therefore, it is wrong to address a clergyman, as President Reagan did in 1981, as "Reverend Moomaw."

A few usage books, such as Reader's Digest 1983, Copperud 1980, and Harper 1975, 1985, acknowledge that these prescriptions do not reflect actual usage and that many American Protestant denominations do not follow them. (The prescriptions reflect primarily the practice of the Church of England and American Episcopalians.) The prescriptions have a couple of other weaknesses, for *Reverend* is in fact used as a title, and it is also used as a noun (and has been since the 17th century). This is primarily an American problem because of history: the forms prescribed now did not come into use in England until the 18th century, and early English settlers in this country brought the older prevailing practice—in which *the* was omitted regularly and the surname omitted at least some of the time. So early American Protestant practice continued forms that later went out of style in England.

There seems to be considerably greater acceptance of such forms as "Reverend Moomaw" than most authorities recognize. The Harper usage panel, for instance, gave 50 percent acceptance to the omission of *the*, 45 percent acceptance to the omission of the surname, and 40 percent acceptance to *Reverend* by itself as a form of address. Reader's Digest says many churches freely use those forms.

If you are trying to be really careful, then, you will need to learn the preferred or accepted forms for the church in question, perhaps by, as Reader's Digest suggests, asking your own clergyman. In a pinch you can probably make do with the old prescribed forms.

The abbreviation *Rev.* is subjected to the same restrictions as *Reverend* by most of the usage books. But as these three examples show, heterodox usage is as well entrenched for the abbreviation as it is for *Reverend*:

> Rev. John Hayes of Salem or Rev. W. Wolcott of this city will answer questions with regard to me —Robert Frost, letter, 11 Sept. 1897

> . . . Rev. Harris was Chaplain for the Senate when I was V.P. —Harry S. Truman, diary, 8 Feb. 1948

> The release of Rev. Jenco did little to mitigate their unhappiness —*The Tower Commission Report*, 1987

There is, clearly, acceptable usage other than that prescribed in most of the stylebooks, handbooks, and etiquette books. Again, this is really a matter of etiquette more than linguistic propriety, and the preference of the clergy involved should be taken into account if it can be determined.

revert   Although *revert back* is frequently cited as a redundancy (see REDUNDANCY), its occurrence in edited writing is not rare:

> . . . would also revert back to Panama after a specified time —*Current Biography*, June 1968

> . . . if they wanted to sell it, they had to sell it to another black family or the rights would revert back to the Nedeeds —Gloria Naylor, *Linden Hills*, 1985

> Left to itself, the neutral silver atom . . . is unstable and will eventually . . . revert back to an ion —Tony Hey et al., *The Quantum Universe*, 1987

But our evidence does show that *revert* by itself occurs far more often.

review, revue   *Review* has many meanings, but *revue* has only one: "a theatrical production consisting typically of satirical skits, songs, and dances." That also happens to be one of the meanings of *review*:

> His opportunity to appear in a Broadway musical review —*Current Biography 1953*

> . . . the Shanghai Theatre . . . with three blue films which were shown in the intervals of a nude review —Graham Greene, *Travels with My Aunt*, 1969

Review acquired this sense from *revue*, which was the name given these shows when they first became popular in Paris during the 19th century. The French word simply means "review." Perhaps because of this etymological connection, usage commentators are generally tolerant toward the use of *review* as a synonym of *revue*. A few think *revue* the only proper spelling; it is appreciably more common than *review* in this sense.

reward   The usual idiom with this verb calls for your being rewarded *for* something done, *with* or sometimes *by* something desirable, and *by* an agent, which need not be human. Thus the *by* construction can either indicate the reward or its giver. Both *by* uses do not, of course, occur in the same sentence.

> . . . rewarded them for outstanding work —Harry Levinson, *Think*, May–June 1967

> . . . individuals who, while not technically public servants, are rewarded . . . with public money for performing a public service —Roy Lewis & Angus Maude, *The English Middle Classes*, 1950

> . . . made a mild pun involving Latin and was rewarded with an immediate laugh —Jacques Barzun, *Atlantic*, December 1953

> . . . books whose theme was that if the poor are virtuous, they are always rewarded by wealth and honor —*Collier's Year Book*, 1949

> . . . was never rewarded by the least glimpse of the celebrated Lady Paignton —J. D. Beresford, *Jacob Stahl*, 1911

> . . . portrait painting applauded & rewarded by the rich & great —William Blake, Annotations to Sir Joshua Reynolds' *Works*, ca. 1808

> . . . you will be well rewarded by a visit to the Marine Historical Association's unique museum —Dana Burnet, *New England Journeys*, No. 2, 1954

rhinoceros   The plural of *rhinoceros* seems to have vexed a great many writers, to judge from the wide variety of plurals shown in the

OED. The variety has boiled down to three in present-day use: *rhinoceroses,* the most common, and *rhinoceros* and *rhinoceri. Rhinoceri* has occasionally been disapproved, apparently because of its irregular formation, but has been used at least occasionally since the end of the 18th century.

> . . . the African giants—elephants, rhinoceroses, hippopotamuses —Barbara Ford, *Saturday Rev.,* 5 Aug. 1972

> . . . land-based creatures that have since disappeared: elephants, buffalo, rhinoceros —Frederic V. Grunfeld, *The Reporter,* 14 July 1966

> . . . the perissodactyls, dwindled to a few tapirs and myopic rhinoceri in my own era —John Updike, *New Yorker,* 14 Aug. 1971

rich When used with a preposition, *rich* is most often found with *in*:

> . . . a dog rich in leisure and in meditation —Sinclair Lewis, *Babbitt,* 1922

> . . . Beecham's "Capriccio Italien," if not so rich in sound, is richer in spirit —Irving Kolodin, *Saturday Rev.,* 26 June 1954

> Retrospective wisdom (in which we're all rich) —Irving Howe, *N.Y. Times Book Rev.,* 7 Nov. 1976

It is also found less frequently with *with*:

> . . . life . . . in all its manifold complexity, rich with its unnoticed and unrecorded little happenings —Thomas Wolfe, *You Can't Go Home Again,* 1940

> Life for her was rich with promise. She was to see herself fulfilled —D. H. Lawrence, *Sons and Lovers,* 1913

rid *Rid* is now almost always used with *of*:

> . . . I set out to rid myself of a sneaky city prose style —Garrison Keillor, *New Yorker,* 18 Sept. 1971

> . . . distinguished people who simply could not rid themselves of the notion that Europe was the home of the arts —Edmund Wilson, *A Piece of My Mind,* 1956

> . . . had not yet completely rid itself of the stillness of night —Hamilton Basso, *The View from Pompey's Head,* 1954

The past participle is common in the idiomatic phrases *get rid of* and *be rid of*:

> . . . a desire of serfs to get rid of the feudalism that has held them in a vise —William O. Douglas, *Saturday Rev.,* 23 Apr. 1955

> The liberals wished to get rid of sectarian injustices —Conor Cruise O'Brien, *N.Y. Rev. of Books,* 6 Nov. 1969

> . . . were willing to sacrifice everything in order to be rid of slavery —Henry Seidel Canby, *Walt Whitman,* 1943

> . . . desired nothing in the world so much as to be rid of us —Katherine Anne Porter, *The Never-Ending Wrong,* 1977

At one time *rid* was commonly used with *from,* but this combination now seldom occurs:

> . . . the most effective combinations for ridding sandflies from houses —*Experiment Station Record,* August 1939

In this context, *rid* essentially means "to remove completely." The more likely construction in current English would be "ridding houses of sandflies," where *rid* means "to make free; relieve."

right **1.** This old and homely adverb (many of its senses go back to the time of King Alfred the Great) has bothered commentators—primarily American commentators—for about a century and a half.

Much of the attention given to adverbial *right* has concerned its use as an intensifier. This intensive use is old, too; the OED dates it from about 1200. It has a long literary pedigree:

> I am right glad that he's so out of hope —Shakespeare, *The Tempest,* 1612

> . . . those illustrious and right eloquent Penmen, the Modern Travellers —Jonathan Swift, "A Discourse Concerning the Mechanical Operation of the Spirit," 1710

> Of his person and stature was the King
> A man right manly strong
> —Dante Gabriel Rossetti (in Hall 1917)

But its range of use has shrunk considerably. British observers note it is much more informal in British English than it formerly was. In American English the most noticeable shrinkage has been in geographical spread. It appears to have been pretty widely used:

> . . . a right merry letter it was too —Emily Dickinson, letter, 21 Oct. 1847

> I should like right well to make a longer excursion on foot —Henry David Thoreau, *A Yankee in Canada,* 1866 (OED)

> . . . enabled him to carry himself in right royal fashion —Jack London, *The Call of the Wild,* 1903

But recently most of our evidence is from the Southern and Midland speech areas:

> I did not feel right comfortable for some time afterward —Mark Twain, *Innocents Abroad,* 1869 (*A Mark Twain Lexicon,* 1938)

He was a man for detail, and he did a right competent job of stage management —*The Autobiography of William Allen White*, 1946

I am right embarassed to think every story is the best —Flannery O'Connor, letter, 6 Mar. 1959

I know I whine right regularly over things about our town that are no more —Celestine Sibley, *Atlanta Jour.-Constitution*, 19 Sept. 1984

And, of course, *right* is sometimes used, like *ain't* and *allow as how*, in a deliberately casual or pseudo-dialectal style:

He moved nimbly among the delegates, chanting: "Peanuts, popcorn, chewing gum, cigars, cigarettes!" He did right well for a lad of 11 —*Newsweek*, 18 June 1956

. . . a defender of the language—you remember, he defended it right profitably in his earlier *Strictly Speaking* —William Cole, *Saturday Rev.*, 13 Nov. 1976

Oh no, they came out of the box right smartly —Paul Zimmerman, *Sports Illustrated*, 12 Nov. 1983

Clearly we do not know everything there is to know about the intensive *right*. That it is in some respects a regionalism is evident, but no simple label seems adequate to describe the range of its common use. In practical terms, if the intensive *right* is part of your native dialect, you should of course feel free to use it without qualm when it seems appropriate. Our evidence shows that it is fairly common in current writing, especially in writing that has a light and informal style.

2. *Right, rightly.* See WRONG, WRONGLY.

ring, rang, rung   The usual past tense of *ring* is *rang*:

His voice rang around in the girdered heights of the gymnasium —Paul Horgan, *Ladies' Home Jour.*, January 1971

Josef rang for cold drinks —Irving Stone, *McCall's*, March 1971

The past participle of *ring* is *rung*:

. . . as many as 479,001,600 changes can be rung —Lois I. Woodville, *Christian Science Monitor*, 1 Oct. 1954

". . . She told me that you'd rung her. . . ." —*Sunday Mirror* (London), 3 Mar. 1968

Rung was also formerly in common use as an alternative past tense of *ring*:

The Heav'ns and all the Constellations rung —John Milton, *Paradise Lost*, 1667 (OED)

One with whose name the world rung —Benjamin Disraeli, *Venetia*, 1837 (OED)

But this use of *rung* is now extremely rare in writing. Dialect studies such as E. Bagby Atwood's *A Survey of Verb Forms in the Eastern United States* (1953) have found *rung* continuing in reputable spoken use as a past tense, especially in parts of New England. Atwood describes this use of *rung* as "old-fashioned," however.

rise   See RAISE, RISE.

rob   **1.** *Rob* is used most often with *of*, when a prepositional phrase follows:

"Yes, it was wonderful," she said, but robbed the phrase of its full effect by adding: "I didn't imagine I *could* be so glad to see him again. . . ." —Aldous Huxley, *Point Counter Point*, 1928

At funerals his mien of settled woe somehow robbed the chief mourners of their proper eminence —Robertson Davies, *Tempest-tost*, 1951

His friends say that the history profession robbed the stage of one of its most gifted mimes —C. Vann Woodward, *N.Y. Rev. of Books*, 3 Dec. 1970

Once in a great while, *rob* occurs with *from*:

Concave surfaces are troublesome in that they tend to focus sound in some spots and rob sound energy from others —James F. Nickerson, *Education Digest*, March 1953

One red or green bulb . . . will not rob color from your fish —Virginia Carlson, *All Pets*, July 1962

2. *Rob*, as used figuratively in the last two examples above, sometimes has as its object what is stolen, as *steal* would. This use is quite old, going back to the 13th century. It is not uncommon in earlier literature:

. . . They themselves contrive
To rob the Honey and subvert the Hive.
              —John Dryden, *Virgil's Georgics*,
                                          1697 (OED)

The OED describes the use as *now rare*. It is not, indeed, nearly as common as the other uses, and it is sometimes considered wrong, or archaic, by commentators no longer familiar with it. We have collected evidence of it from news broadcasts and newspaper reports.

. . . set it afire on Sunday, then robbed $100 after the clerk fled the flames —*Springfield* (Mass.) *Morning Union*, 24 Feb. 1986

This is not really a misuse, since it is a continuation of an old standard sense. Still, we find it occurring only in news reports. It does not appear to be used at present in other writing, except for the rare figurative use, and we cannot recommend its cultivation.

robbery   See BURGLARY, ROBBERY.

round, around See AROUND 2.

royal *we* See WE 1.

ruddy See BLOODY.

rules There exists in the folk memory a set of facetious grammatical rules that pop up in various places and in various forms from time to time. They are to be found in Harper 1985 and Einstein 1985, for example, and in each instance the rules are ascribed to some old newspaper editor of beloved memory. The order may change, the phraseology may vary, but the essential idea is always the same. The rules we show here are taken from an article by George W. Feinstein in *College English*, April 1960. We will give only the first fifteen of his twenty rules, because they are the ones that seem to turn up most often.

1. Each pronoun agrees with their antecedent.
2. Just between you and I, case is important.
3. Verbs has to agree with their subjects.
4. Watch out for irregular verbs which has crope into our language.
5. Don't use no double negatives.
6. A writer mustn't shift your point of view.
7. When dangling, don't use participles.
8. Join clauses good, like a conjunction should.
9. Don't write a run-on sentence you got to punctuate it.
10. About sentence fragments.
11. In letters themes reports articles and stuff like that we use commas to keep a string of items apart.
12. Don't use commas, which aren't necessary.
13. It's important to use apostrophe's right.
14. Don't abbrev.
15. Check to see if you any words out.

The beauty of rules like these is that almost anybody can come up with the same or similar ones and believe that they are original creations. Mr. Feinstein's set is the earliest we have found in print, but similar sets have undoubtedly been around for many years.

In the realm of language, *rule* is a word that the wise tend not to bandy about. Many observers from the 18th century to the present have pointed out the limitations of rules as a guide to good writing:

> Rules may obviate faults, but can never confer beauties —Samuel Johnson, *The Idler*, 19 May 1759

> I think the following rules will cover most cases: . . . (vi) Break any of these rules sooner than say anything outright barbarous —George Orwell, "Politics and the English Language," 1946

We ought not to get so straitjacketed in "rules" that we sacrifice vigor and clarity to form —James J. Kilpatrick, *Portland Oregonian* (syndicated column), 2 Nov. 1985

run Funny things happen to our verbs. *Run* results from the coming together in Middle English of two older verbs, an intransitive *rinnan* and a causative *irnan*. The first of these produced the past *ran* and the second produced the past *run*. If everything had developed according to theory, we would now have, according to Lamberts 1972, a verb *rin* with a past singular *ran*, a past plural *run*, and a past participle *run* or *runnen*, in the same class of irregular verbs as *ring, swim*, and *begin*. But things went awry in early modern English: *run* replaced *rin* sometime around the 16th century (Lamberts says *rin* still survives in Scottish and Irish folk speech). So instead of developing into *rin, ran, run*, the verb developed into two patterns, *run, ran, run* and *run, run, run*. (If you look into the OED, you will see the full story is much more complex than this brief sketch reveals.)

In terms of current usage, the problem with this verb centers on the past *run*. It appears in literature from the 16th to the 19th centuries; Jespersen 1909–49 (volume 6) lists Shakespeare, Bunyan, Defoe, Swift, Fielding, and Goldsmith as using it. Modern dialectologists, such as Michael I. Miller (*American Speech*, Summer 1984), attest its currency in speech in both southern England and in parts of the U.S. But *ran* is now virtually the only form used in writing. Modern practice may be partly attributable to Johnson's Dictionary (1755), where only *ran* is listed for the past. Lowth 1762 attacked past *run*, and the tradition in school grammars ever since has been to insist on *ran*. Noah Webster 1828 gave *ran* or *run*, departing from Johnson, and his successors through 1909 followed suit. Webster's Second, however, called *run* dialectal, and Webster's Third calls it nonstandard. Miller feels this treatment misrepresents the usage of past *run*, and perhaps it does to some extent. But dictionaries find it hard to devise a short descriptor that will mean "used in speech in southern England and in the southern U.S. and New England, especially by older people, and used formerly in literature."

In any case, there is no denying that past *run* is now considered nonstandard by many people, if not by dialectologists. The surveys of Leonard 1932 and Crisp 1971 indicate as much. If it is part of your natural speech, you should not avoid it. But you will want to use *ran* in writing, as just about everyone now does.

run-on sentences See COMMA FAULT.

S

sacrilegious This word is sometimes misspelled *sacreligious* and (according to Garner 1998) *sacriligious*. The first misspelling shows the influence of *religious,* but the two words are not related etymologically. *Sacrilegious* is the adjective formed from *sacrilege.*

Sahara, Sahara desert Because the Arabic word *sahara* (or *sahra*) means literally "desert," several commentators have criticized *Sahara desert* as a redundancy. If English and Arabic were one language, the critics might have a good argument, but the fact is that *Sahara* in English is no more a synonym for *desert* (except in figurative use) than are *Gobi* and *Mojave*; it is, instead, the specific name of a specific desert, one that is commonly and idiomatically called both "the Sahara" and "the Sahara desert." Some writers do omit *desert* after *Sahara,* but many others do not, and there is no reason why you should feel compelled to.

> . . . so the Sahara desert had to form —David Attenborough, TV broadcast, 2 Nov. 1987

> Blowing dusts could mark a barren land, like the Sahara Desert —Joseph A. Amato, *Dust,* 2000

It is interesting to note that the Mongolian word *gobi* means literally "waterless place," so that the same logic that finds redundancy in *Sahara desert* should also find it in *Gobi desert.* As far as we know, however, no one has ever called *Gobi desert* redundant.

For similar problems with words borrowed from foreign languages, see HOI POLLOI and SIERRA.

said All commentators agree that use of *said* as an adjective synonymous with *aforementioned* is appropriate only in legal and business contexts, and it is certainly true that it now appears far more commonly in those contexts than in any other:

> . . . fixed sinking fund requirements and final maturity amount on the said bonds —*Annual Report, Armco Steel Corp.,* 1970

> . . . an order rescinding the supplemental agreement referred to in said Note —*Annual Report, R. J. Reynolds Industries, Inc.,* 1970

Said has been favored in legal writing for centuries, but its use in general contexts was also unremarkable once:

> The said article is so very mild and sentimental —Lord Byron, letter, 22 Aug. 1813

> . . . attending them to their carriage after the said dinner visit —Jane Austen, *Mansfield Park,* 1814

> And so you don't agree with my view as to said photographer? —Lewis Carroll, letter, 1 Apr. 1887

Such usage still occurs, but the legalistic connotations of *said* have long been so familiar that those who employ it in other contexts typically do so for deliberate effect, often humorous:

> He was also an extremely vain man who would keep said mustache at the proper rakish tilt with the aid of paper clips —Richard Freedman, *N.Y. Times Book Rev.,* 28 Mar. 1976

sake Fowler 1926 and Evans 1957 both regard the apostrophe as optional in *for goodness' sake, for conscience' sake,* and similar expressions in which the word preceding *sake* ends in an *s* or *z* sound. They both consider it incorrect to add an apostrophe plus -*s.* Our evidence indicates that the apostrophe is rarely omitted in such expressions, and that the apostrophe plus -*s* is only avoided when the \s\ sound is never added in speech, as when the expression is a fixed idiom (as *for goodness' sake* and *for conscience' sake* are), or when the word in question is multisyllabic (as in *for convenience' sake*) so that pronouncing the -*s* would be especially awkward. When the word is short and no fixed idiom is involved, the -*s* is likely to be pronounced and the apostrophe plus -*s* is likely to be written: *for peace's sake, for the human race's sake.*

salad days Shakespeare coined this term in *Antony and Cleopatra* (1607), wherein Cleopatra dismisses her former love of Caesar as having occurred in "My salad days, when I was green in judgment. . . ." Modern writers have taken up the figure of speech, and *salad days* is often now used to mean "a time of youthful inexperience":

> . . . I am not writing French but American, and, specifically, the American in vogue on

the newspapers of my native Baltimore in my salad days as a journalist —H. L. Mencken, *Newspaper Days,* 1941

I suffer from a wonky system of values, acquired in my Paris salad days and still with me —Mordecai Richler, *GQ,* November 1997

In recent years, it has developed a new sense, "an early flourishing period; heyday":

. . . was McGwire's teammate in the Oakland A's salad days of the late 1980s —George F. Will, *Newsweek,* 26 Apr. 1999

. . . courtly and distinguished, young in the eyes, and full of fond memories of salad days in Araby —Robert D. Kaplan, *The Arabists,* 1993

Those were Sahl's salad days, when The New Yorker did a worshipful profile —Jean Shepherd, *N.Y. Times Book Rev.,* 3 Oct. 1976

A few usage commentators have objected to *salad days,* even finding it growing quaint and disused. But it remains in common and reputable use.

same The use of *same* as a pronoun, often with *the,* has attracted criticism from many commentators from 1906 to 1998. The use of *same* as a substitute for *it, this, that,* and *them* is typically described as unliterary business jargon, if not as an out-and-out error. But a look at the long history and current use of the pronoun *same* shows clearly that the judgment of the critics is undeservedly harsh. *Same* has been in continuous use as a pronoun since the 14th century. It was well known to the Shakespearean businessman:

And in the instant that I met with you
He had of me a chain. At five o'clock
I shall receive the money for the same.
—Shakespeare, *The Comedy of Errors,* 1593

But its use has never been limited to the world of business. Here are some further examples, old and new, to counter the dismissal of pronominal *same* as mere business jargon:

Each house shall keep a journal of *its* proceedings, and from time to time publish the same —*Constitution of the United States,* 1787

It then transpired that Old Crockford was a village, and, from the appearance of the team on the day of battle, the Old Crockfordians seemed to be composed exclusively of the riff-raff of same —P. G. Wodehouse, *Tales of St Austin's,* 1903

You said you wanted a picture of me and I enclose same —Flannery O'Connor, letter, 16 Nov. 1961

. . . the letters he wrote were revealing and full of immense feeling and the joy of life and the terror of same —E. B. White, letter, 21 June 1967

The rich had clothes made by couturiers, tailors, or designers, and the masses wore knockoffs of same —Tom Wolfe, *Esquire,* December 1979

. . . have brought rejoicing to millions who have now seen opera live in their homes and who can look forward to more of the same next winter —Irving Kolodin, *Saturday Rev.,* 8 July 1978

He also discusses the wisdom, or lack of same, of candor —Genevieve Stuttaford, *Publishers Weekly,* 7 Sept. 1984

The pronoun *same* may sound wooden in an awkwardly written business letter, but in the hands of a competent writer it is often simply a mark of an informal style.

same as Several usage books, dating back to Krapp 1927, have warned against using *the same as* as an adverbial phrase in place of *as* or *just as* ("He acts the same as he used to" instead of " . . . just as he used to"). No particular reasons are given for the warnings, but they are presumably attributable to the elliptical and somewhat informal quality of adverbial *the same as*:

Black folks have a right to hate white folks the same as white folks have a right to hate us —Dick Gregory, *Avant Garde,* January 1969

Writers were at each other's throats in the thirties the same as they are today —Granville Hicks, *American Scholar,* Summer 1966

As and *just as* are more common in writing than *the same as,* but *the same as* is not incorrect. Note that it is actually more flexible in its application than is *just as,* in that the *same* in the phrase can be qualified:

. . . function much the same as they did five hundred centuries ago —David R. Reuben, M.D., *McCall's,* March 1971

sanguinary See BLOODY.

sans This French preposition meaning "without" was borrowed into English in the 14th century and occurs fairly commonly today, but it has never entirely lost its Frenchness. It might have passed into disuse long ago were it not for the influence of Shakespeare, who used it in many of his plays, most memorably in *As You Like It* (1600):

Last scene of all,
That ends this strange eventful history,
Is second childishness and mere oblivion,
Sans teeth, sans eyes, sans taste, sans everything.

Modern writers still occasionally echo this famous passage:

I had forgotten . . that this was wartime; sans Salts, sans fish, sans nets, sans sails, sans everything —Gladys Bronwyn Stern, *Trumpet Voluntary,* 1944

But *sans* also frequently occurs when no allusion to Shakespeare is being made.

"Cynic" commonly suggests a detached pessimism, a pessimism sans bitterness —Cynthia Ozick, *N.Y. Times Book Rev.,* 1 Jan. 1995

. . . our hero wakes up in a crypt in a Mexican border town, sans money, credit cards —Richard Alleva, *Commonweal,* 10 Oct. 1997

You can now get a decent . . . PC for $700 or $800, sans monitor —Walter S. Mossberg, *Wall Street Jour.,* 26 Mar. 1998

Its French appearance makes *sans* a word that calls attention to itself. It occurs much more commonly in writing than in speech, but if you do have occasion to say it, its usual pronunciation in English is \'sanz\.

sartorial *Sartorial* was scorned by Fowler 1926 as "pedantic humor." While Burchfield 1996 allows it has both facetious and straightforward use, we have little evidence of facetiousness in our most recent examples. It is a word that has no synonym, and hence is the only word to use in some contexts.

I use the tie to push me over the edge when I am at my sartorial greatest —E. B. White, letter, 9 Jan. 1967

He swears the new look . . . wasn't a sartorial signal of his Internet ambitions —Johnnie L. Roberts, *Newsweek,* 24 Jan. 2000

Their sartorial style harks back to neo-Edwardian British dandyism of the 1960s —Bruce Boyer, *Forbes,* 9 Mar. 1998

. . . something sadly lacking in our sartorially challenged, dress-down Friday society —Michael Walsh, *Playboy,* February 1997

. . . shed her sartorially lackluster image and transformed into a sex symbol —Amy Fine Collins, *Vanity Fair,* March 1998

. . . a sartorially impressive figure —Robert Penn Warren, *Jefferson Davis Gets His Citizenship Back,* 1980

sated, satiated Both *sated* and *satiated* are idiomatically followed by *with:*

. . . tend to be quickly sated with tales involving fame or wealth —Norman Cousins, *Saturday Rev.,* 24 June 1978

. . . went and went again, never satiated with the theme —Robert Morss Lovett, *All Our Years,* 1948

saturate When *saturate* is followed by a preposition, the usual choice is *with:*

. . . Soviet trading missions abroad were so saturated with intelligence agents . . . —Hedrick Smith, *Atlantic,* December 1974

. . . have an easy time saturating the marketplace with their potboilers —Norman Cousins, *Saturday Rev.,* 24 June 1978

. . . his books . . . are saturated with politics —Irving Howe, *N.Y. Times Book Rev.,* 24 Oct. 1982

Other prepositions that occasionally occur after *saturate* are *by* and *in:*

. . . saturated by prejudice and emotion —William J. Reilly, *Life Planning for College Students,* 1954

. . . children are so saturated by television —Michele Murray, *Children's House,* Summer 1970

A moment ago, he was saturated in sunniness —Liz Smith, *Cosmopolitan,* May 1975

. . . are they not . . . saturated in Christian cosmology? —John Updike, *N.Y. Times Book Rev.,* 23 May 1976

When the object of *saturate* is a reflexive pronoun, the preposition that follows is *in:*

. . . saturated himself in literature about, and photographs of, Nijinsky —Walter Terry, *Saturday Rev.,* 13 Nov. 1976

. . . will allow athletic types to saturate themselves in basketball, volleyball, and skating —Richard F. Shepard, *N.Y. Times,* 10 Dec. 1976

saving, savings The usage problems for *savings* arise when it is used as a singular noun with the sense "an act or instance of economizing" or "reduction in cost." We first recorded this use in the 1940s, and we have found it frequently in the decades since:

. . . resulting in an *actual cash savings* on your taxes —*N.Y. Herald Tribune Book Rev.,* 15 Dec. 1946

. . . a savings which can be passed on to you —advt., *N.Y. Times Mag.,* 27 Sept. 1964

. . . up to a 25 minute time savings on each inbound trip —John D. Caplan, *Annual Report, General Motors Corp.,* 1971

A savings of space becomes a savings in money —Steve Lambert, *Apple Computer Publication,* July 1984

... a savings of as much as $5 billion —*Wall Street Jour.,* 3 Dec. 1997

A few usage commentators (notably Bernstein 1965 and Safire 1986) disapprove this use of *savings,* and the usage panelists of Heritage 1969, 1982 and of Harper 1975, 1985 reject it in writing. Nevertheless, it is extremely common and has clearly established itself as idiomatic in American English. If you feel inclined to avoid it, you can always use *saving* instead:

... a saving of approximately $60,000,000 a year —*Current Biography,* January 1965

... can be purchased at a saving of up to 60% —Caleb Pirtle III, *Southern Living,* November 1971

A related concern is the use of *savings* in *daylight savings time.* The original term, and the usual term in writing, is *daylight saving time,* but *daylight savings time* (or often just *daylight savings*) is very common in speech, and it does occasionally make its way into print:

He called this idea Daylight Savings Time —Joseph M. Oxenhorn et al., *Pathways in Science* (textbook), 1982

... if you're headed for the Navajo Nation in the north of the state, be advised, the Navajos are going along with most of the U.S. and using Daylight Savings Time —*Historic Traveler,* June 1996

Usage commentators who take up this subject regard *daylight savings time* as an error.

scan The case of *scan* is a bit unusual. In the 20th century it developed a new sense which—on the face of it—seems directly contradictory to one of its older senses, but almost no one seems to mind. The older sense is "to examine thoroughly and carefully." It was first recorded in about 1800, and continues in use today:

Conscious of handwritings now, she scanned Eden's carefully —Herman Wouk, *Marjorie Morningstar,* 1955

The newer, and now more common, sense of *scan* is "to look over or glance through quickly," which was first recorded in the 1920s:

I scanned the story rapidly and felt a little better —Russell Baker, *Growing Up,* 1982

Scan in its "look over quickly" sense has been criticized by some British commentators. American commentators, including Evans 1957, Bernstein 1971, and Garner 1998, note its ambiguity with the older sense, but regard it as established and acceptable nevertheless. Heritage 1969 suggests that care should be taken to assure that the context makes clear which sense is intended. This is usually accomplished by the use of adverbs, such as *carefully* and *rapidly* in the passages quoted above.

scarcely 1. *Scarce, scarcely.* Several commentators have disparaged as an affectation the use of the old flat adverb *scarce* in modern contexts where *scarcely* would also do. The flat adverb was once common:

... the gentlemen of the next age will scarce have learning enough to claim the benefit of the clergy —Thomas Shadwell, *The Virtuoso,* 1676

... allow his surgeon scarce time sufficient to dress his wound —Laurence Sterne, *Tristram Shandy,* 1759

But it is now relatively rare. The extent to which it is an affectation in a particular context can only be judged subjectively. These examples do not seem to be affected:

Store money was predicated on handling the products of the community, something scarce any store does nowadays —John Gould, *Christian Science Monitor,* 19 Nov. 1976

Patton sent some pumpers to put water on it, but they had scarce begun when they were forced to flee —John McPhee, *New Yorker,* 22 Feb. 1988

See FLAT ADVERBS.

2. *Scarcely* is lumped with *hardly* (which see) in quite a few usage books as a negative, and its use with a preceding negative is disparaged as a double negative. There are two points to be made concerning this issue. First, *scarcely* is not a negative. Obviously "I scarcely studied" and "I didn't study" do not mean the same thing; the second is a negative, the first only somewhat like a negative. Second, the criticized construction seems to be rare in present-day English. Here is a late 19th-century example:

... it wa'n't scarcely fair to keep it all to myself —H. N. Westcott, "The Horse Trader," 1898, in *The Mirth of a Nation,* ed. Walter Blair & Raven I. McDavid, Jr., 1983

Our files do not hold recent examples of this sort of construction, and we suspect that it is not nearly as common as similar constructions with *hardly,* for which we have abundant evidence.

On the other hand, *scarcely* is commonly followed by some sort of negative construction:

... there was scarcely an old family in New England which ... did not profit from the slave trade —Chester Bowles, *N.Y. Times Mag.,* 7 Feb. 1954

There is scarcely a peroration or passage . . . which does not contain a gibe —Richard M. Weaver, *The Ethics of Rhetoric*, 1953

No one objects to these standard constructions.

scarcely . . . than The sequence *scarcely . . . when* is considered impeccable by all commentators:

Scarcely had Ida May recovered . . . when she heard a loud, bumptious knocking at her door —Katherine Anne Porter, *Ladies' Home Jour.*, August 1971

David had scarcely rung the bell when the door flew open —Agnes Sligh Turnbull, *The Gown of Glory*, 1951

This sequence means about the same as *no sooner . . . than*. The combining of *no sooner . . . than* with *scarcely . . . when* produces the syntactic blend *scarcely . . . than*, which has been denounced as an error since at least the 1880s (see SYNTACTIC BLEND). Hodgson 1889 has several examples, including these:

Scarcely had she gone, than Clodius and several of his gay companions broke in upon him —Edward Bulwer-Lytton, *The Last Days of Pompeii*, 1834

But, as it happened, scarcely had Phoebe's eyes rested again on the judge's countenance than all its ugly sternness vanished —Nathaniel Hawthorne, *The House of the Seven Gables*, 1851

If the examples in Hodgson are a reliable guide, *scarcely . . . than* was quite common in the 19th century. We have discovered that it was habitual with Edgar Rice Burroughs:

Scarcely had the search commenced than the overturned cauldron was discovered —Edgar Rice Burroughs, *Tarzan of the Apes*, 1914

Fowler 1926 has one example, and Bryant 1962 has another, from 1940. Our files contain nothing more recent than Burroughs. Apparently this construction is no longer a part of written standard English.

See HARDLY . . . THAN for a similar syntactic blend.

scared When used with a preposition, *scared* is most often followed by *of*:

I am scared of rats —Graham Greene, *Another Mexico*, 1939

He tells us as much about the Presidency as he does about the C.I.A., and he leaves me scared stiff of both —John le Carré, *N.Y. Times Book Rev.*, 14 Oct. 1979

". . . I think he was scared of what you'd say to him, that's why he took off." —John Updike, *New Yorker*, 28 Dec. 1981

It is also used quite commonly with *about, at,* and *by*:

. . . a weak government allows bigger wage increases than it ought to; then it gets scared about them —*The Economist*, in *Atlas*, December 1969

Many Democrats were scared stiff at the prospect of being out of step with the mood of the country —Tip O'Neill with William Novak, *Man of the House*, 1987

. . . obviously scared by the prestige and the mass base the Communists built up during the war —Alfred Kazin, *Partisan Rev.*, May 1948

Scared is also followed by *to* and the infinitive:

What they said to him was that he was a country boy in the city, scared to go out on the street —Peter Taylor, *The Old Forest and Other Stories*, 1985

scarify *Scarify* is really two words, the older of which, first attested in 1541, has the basic meaning "to make scratches or cuts in." It has several literal applications:

. . . burning over or scarifying the ground, then planting seedlings —John J. Putnam, *National Geographic*, April 1974

Men and women have been beautifying, scarifying and mutilating their bodies . . . since the dawn of time —Matilda Traherne, *Times Literary Supp.*, 7 Mar. 1980

And it is sometimes used figuratively:

. . . this is the Nixon . . . that Garry Wills (in his fascinating book) scarifies as a human being —William F. Buckley, Jr., *National Rev.*, 26 Jan. 1971

The newer *scarify*, meaning "scare" or "frighten," was first recorded in 1794. But we don't find it again until the end of the 19th century, and it is only in the past 50 years or so that this new *scarify* has begun to appear commonly in print. It occurs most often in the form of the present participle, *scarifying*, used as an adjective. Our files contain enough examples to show that the newer *scarify* is now in widespread, standard use. Here are some of those examples:

. . . vivid snapshots of the Paris barricades . . . and a few scarifying pictures of both sides' firing squads —*Times Literary Supp.*, 30 Sept. 1965

. . . with two bullet holes in his car and a scarifying tale to go with them —Peter Goldman, *Newsweek*, 15 July 1968

. . . dire, scarifying illustrations of what can happen to kids who have the habit —Arthur Knight, *Saturday Rev.,* 2 Oct. 1971

It is scarifying in the opposite way from a nightmare —Paul Theroux, *N.Y. Times Book Rev.,* 16 Nov. 1975

. . . in the two weeks following Black Monday, as the Dow careened down a scarifying herky-jerky course —Gerald Parshall, *U.S. News & World Report,* 9 Nov. 1987

A couple of usage commentators reject it, saying in effect that there is no *scare* in *scarify.* Whether they like it or not, however, the *scare* is there, and it is probably there to stay.

scenario *Scenario* first attracted attention as a vogue word in the late 1960s, not long after it had crept out of theater and visual arts parlance into use by politicians and government officials and by the journalists who report what politicians and governmental officials say and do. We first encountered it in 1967:

His scenario for a settlement envisages the eventual reunification of Vietnam —Selig S. Harrison, *New Republic,* 25 Nov. 1967

Here *scenario* means an imagined or postulated sequence of events. This is the primary new use of the word.

The use attracted some negative criticism in the 1970s and 1980s, especially after the Watergate hearings brought it to wide public attention. Nevertheless, its use continues to be popular.

The worst-case scenario would be a flood that ripped through the lab building and washed uranium or plutonium downstream —Mark Hosenball, *Newsweek,* 31 July 2000

Our whole budget plan, I told them, depended on the accuracy of "Rosy Scenario," the five-year economic forecast we had fashioned in February —David A. Stockman, *Newsweek,* 28 Apr. 1986

scene The most recent extended senses of *scene* have been the object of some disparagement from usage commentators. Our files show that the vogue for these senses in the middle 1970s has fallen off considerably, but they can still be found:

. . . the local police are powerless to control the drug scene that flourishes in this part of the village —Kim Waller, *Town & Country,* September 1983

The MBAs don't fit seamlessly into the Valley scene —Eryn Brown, *Fortune,* 27 Sept. 1999

. . . time went on and Sovietology became an established feature of the academic scene —Abraham Brumberg, *The Nation,* 23–30 Aug. 1999

As the vogue for these uses passes and they become a settled part of the vocabulary, they are likely to draw less critical attention. They are certainly standard in general writing.

scotch When Shakespeare wrote in *Macbeth,* "We have scotch'd the snake, not kill'd it," he was using *scotch* to mean "to disable by wounding," a sense of the verb that is now archaic. The current meaning of *scotch* is "to put an end to."

But if the king's suspicions of Roger of Salisbury were justified, he did well to scotch the danger while he was still strong —Frank Barlow, *The Feudal Kingdom of England 1042–1216,* 3d ed., 1972

In the process they scotch many a fable —Timothy Ferris, *N.Y. Times Book Rev.,* 31 July 1983

The plan was scotched in the White House —*Business Week,* 5 Aug. 1985

. . . questions about allocation of tobacco-related liabilities scotch the deal —Stephanie Strom, *N.Y. Times,* 12 July 1994

Fowler 1926 made the modern use of *scotch* an issue when he attributed it to the carelessness of journalists, and a few recent commentators have followed him by continuing to insist that the disused sense is the only correct one. But the cause is lost. The current sense of *scotch* is unquestionably standard. Burchfield 1996 points out, interestingly, that the *scotch'd* in *Macbeth* is an 18th-century emendation; Shakespeare may not actually have intended the word.

Scotch, Scottish, Scots Chambers 1985, which, having been published in Scotland, would seem to be a reasonable source for accurate and up-to-date information on this subject, says that *Scottish* is the normal adjective:

The revival of Scottish literature —John Butt, *English Literature in the Mid-Eighteenth Century,* edited & completed by Geoffrey Carnall, 1979

In most Scottish schools —K. M. Elisabeth Murray, *Caught in the Web of Words,* 1977

Scotch is used chiefly in familiar compounds for well-known things like Scotch broth, Scotch whisky, Scotch salmon, the Scotch pine and the Scotch terrier. *Scots,* too, is restricted in application, referring mostly to law or language.

But as a child he started writing down the Scots words and phrases —Howard 1984

These are essentially the usages preferred by the Scots (Burchfield 1996 points out that these are middle-class preferences; the working class apparently use *Scotch*), and these preferences have evolved over about the last century. Earlier usage is different, as the admirably detailed historical sketch in the OED shows. *Scotch* dates only from the end of the 16th century, but was the predominant adjective in the 18th and 19th centuries; it was used by such writers as Boswell, James Beattie, Robert Burns, and Sir Walter Scott. It was likewise used by more recent Scots, including James A. H. Murray, the OED editor.

Non-Scottish use has never quite conformed to Scottish preferences. In North America *Scotch* is the prevailing adjective, at least partly because the earlier immigrants to this continent from Scotland left that country when *Scotch* was still prevalent there.

> My first two books were published in England by the Scotch and English —Robert Frost, letter, 26 July 1942

> . . . a difference of opinion as to who was superior. The Scotch believed, I have always thought rightly, that they were —John Kenneth Galbraith, *The Scotch,* 1964

> William Panton and his Scotch partners were loyalists —Jerrell H. Shofner, *American Historical Rev.,* April 1987

If you live in the United Kingdom, you are aware of Scottish preferences. If you live in North America, you are likely to use *Scotch* automatically, especially when Scottish susceptibilities are not a consideration. There is no harm, of course, in following the Scottish preferences—*Scottish* is, after all, the old word, and both *Scotch* and *Scots* are derived from it. There is another rule of thumb that works fairly well for the American who does not want to offend but does not know or want to know the finer points of Scottish practice: use *Scottish* for people and *Scotch* for things.

sculp, sculpt, sculpture About half a century ago, dictionaries such as the OED and Webster's Second 1934 were calling the verbs *sculp* and *sculpt* "jocular" and "humorous." The evidence on which those labels were based must have been primarily oral, as written evidence from that period is scanty. It was not until the 1940s and 1950s that we began to find *sculp* and, in particular, *sculpt* in widespread written use, very little of which was humorous:

> . . . Mussolini's sculpted horses —Irwin Shaw, *Yale Rev.,* Summer 1944

> Moore, who sculpts and draws mostly figures —*Newsweek,* 11 Mar. 1946

> . . . sculpted works which themselves implied the conquest of space —*Horizon,* December 1946

> . . . was one of the fifty artists chosen . . . to paint or sculp her portrait —Robert Gibbings, *Trumpets from Montparnasse,* 1955

Citations such as these made it clear that the old labels were no longer appropriate, and they have since been dropped. *Sculp* and *sculpt* are now established as standard synonyms of *sculpture.*

search When used with a preposition, the noun *search* is usually followed by *for,* except in the phrase *in search of*:

> . . . the requisite search for knowledge —Robert A. Nisbet, *Psychology Today,* March 1971

> . . . the growers worked hard in search of new markets —A. V. Krebs, Jr., *Commonweal,* 9 Oct. 1970

Shaw 1970 says that *in search for* is also common, but that *in search of* is preferred. Our evidence shows that *in search for* is pretty rare in edited prose. We have few examples of it.

> . . . while in search for a title for his first book of poems —*Time,* 15 Feb. 1954

seasonable, seasonal Whereas *seasonable* means "suitable to the season" (seasonable temperatures) and "opportune" (a seasonable time for discussion), *seasonal* means "of or relating to a season; occurring in a particular season" (seasonal migration, seasonal employment). So say the usage writers, and, according to our evidence, they are right. We do have some evidence of *seasonable* being used where *seasonal* would be expected, but it is rare and not standard.

Seasonal is sometimes used to mean "seasonable" as well, but this use is also nonstandard.

Also to be considered are the words *unseasonable* and *unseasonal,* which, as it happens, are synonyms. *Unseasonable* is the more common word by far, and it means just what you would expect it to, "not seasonable." *Unseasonal,* however, seems never to have meant "not seasonal." All of our evidence shows *unseasonal* being used to mean "not seasonable":

> . . . adjourned happily into the unseasonal Long Island sunshine —*Time,* 17 Jan. 1949

> . . . in which to store potatoes, cotton, tobacco and the few unseasonal clothes —Max Steele, *Discovery,* March 1954

> During the worst of this unseasonal heat wave —Jeff MacGregor, *Sports Illustrated,* 8 Nov. 1999

But *unseasonal* is a very rare word.

secondly Used with some frequency in a series after *first* or *in the first place*—by Charles

Lamb and Samuel Johnson, to name just two. See FIRSTLY.

see, seed, seen The standard past tense of *see* is *saw*. American dialectologists say that the past forms *see* and *seed* are nonstandard and regionally restricted. Both of them were commonly used by the American dialect humorists of the 19th century, and *seed* was additionally listed as a Cockneyism as far back as 1807.

Seen as the past tense seems to be widespread but nonstandard. There are at least two explanations for its low status. Margaret Shaklee in Shopen & Williams 1980 says that it was a southern regionalism brought into the north and midwest around the end of the 19th century by southerners who migrated north looking for work. This explanation is given some support as to chronology by our earliest evidence for the correction of *seen,* in Vizetelly 1906. Mencken 1963 (abridged), on the other hand, associates *seen* with the immigration of the Irish to the United States in the 1840s. His explanation is supported by the English Dialect Dictionary, which calls past tense *seen* chiefly Irish. In either case we see that a regional speech characteristic has turned into a social rather than a regional marker.

Past *seen,* then, is a speech characteristic associated with the less educated and is used in writing chiefly to mark characters as being such. An example:

> We had a visitor the other day, an old man, who said he wouldn't go to Europe if they gave it to him. Said a feller went over there and set down on some steps he seen in front of a church . . . —Flannery O'Connor, letter, 1953

seeing, seeing as, seeing as how, seeing that *Seeing* has long been used as a conjunction meaning "inasmuch as; in view of the fact that":

> They all wanted to know why—seeing I had the same genes as Tracy—I couldn't swim as fast as she could —Amy Caulkins, quoted in *Sports Illustrated,* 20 Apr. 1981

This conjunction has been in use since the 16th century, but it does not now appear very frequently in writing. It originally appeared as part of a compound in *seeing that,* which is still used, and it also appears in the compound forms *seeing as* and *seeing as how.*

Seeing as and *seeing as how* are both attested in American and British English. They are primarily spoken forms, but they are appearing fairly often in print in casual or informal edited prose.

> And seeing as he gets good gas mileage, he drives himself to film locations —Amy Lumet, *Seventeen,* February 1994

> It sounds like the theme song from Charlie's Angels, which is just fine, seeing as we are all in a retro mood —Jay Nordlinger, *National Rev.,* 6 Dec. 1999

> . . . understands the suspicion, seeing as how chemotherapy is not thought to be performance-enhancing —Richard Hoffer, *Sports Illustrated,* 26 July 1999

> . . . an excuse that is hard to swallow, seeing as how Hoover was the F.B.I. —Robert Sherrill, *N.Y. Times Book Rev.,* 13 Sept. 1987

Seeing that is the best attested of all four forms in writing:

> Seeing that Ireland is among the most fertile and rainy countries in Europe, the Great Famine beggars belief —*Globe and Mail* (Toronto), 28 June 1995

> There seemed to be quite a crowd in the corridor, seeing that it was nearly ten-thirty on a Monday night —T. Coraghessan Boyle, *The Road to Wellville,* 1993

> . . . making great headway as the lingua franca of the whole country, a not surprising development seeing that it is of Indonesian stock —W. B. Lockwood, *A Panorama of Indo-European Languages,* 1972

These have been used by literary figures of the past, but seem to have little current literary use except in fictional speech. They are not nonstandard, but you will not want to use them in your most dressed-up prose.

seek The verb *seek* is frequently used with *after* or *for. After* tends to occur most often with the past participle *sought* in an idiomatic passive, but active use also occurs. *For* is common with all tenses and voices.

> . . . Namath was the one collegiate player most sought after by professional teams —*Current Biography,* December 1966

> ". . . If the *effect* of his behaviour does not justify him with you, we had better not seek after the cause." —Jane Austen, *Northanger Abbey,* 1818

> These differences are by no means so evident to (or so sought for by) a majority of peoples of non-European origin —Weston La Barre, *The Human Animal,* 1954

> Now he learns to talk and thereby joins the Republic of Learning, a republic composed of men who seek for meaning —Stringfellow Barr, *Center Mag.,* March 1968

Seek is also commonly followed by *to* and an infinitive:

> We can seek to perpetuate the myths or to focus on the real issues —Leslie H. Gelb &

Morton H. Halperin, *Harper's*, November 1971

seem See CAN'T SEEM.

see where *See where* is disparaged in many usage books, most of which identify it as a speech form. *Where* is also used to introduce clauses that are the objects of other verbs than *see*. See WHERE 2.

seldom ever, seldom if ever, seldom or ever, seldom or never All of these idioms are intensive forms of *seldom* that have attracted comment and vilification from usage writers since the 1860s. *Seldom ever* and *seldom or ever* have borne the brunt of the complaints. *Seldom ever,* according to the OED, has been around since about 1000; it is a well-aged idiom. Since we have in our files more complaints about it than examples of its use in print, we suspect that it may be more frequently a feature of speech than of writing. Here is one of our few written examples:

> . . . consideration of curriculum is frequently postponed to some future date which seldom ever arrives —Dayton Benjamin, *American School Board Jour.,* June 1968

Seldom or ever is not attested until the 18th century. This undated example is probably older than the first citation in the OED:

> We seldom or ever see those forsaken who trust in God —Francis Atterbury (in Raub 1897)

The phrase seems to have been quite common during the 19th century.

> Those who walk in their sleep have seldom or ever the most distant recollection that they have been dreaming —Sydney Smith, *Moral Philosophy,* 1850 (in Hodgson 1889)

> Seldom or ever could I detect any approach to a labial —Alexander Ellis, *Transactions of the Philological Society* (in Jespersen 1917)

We have no recent 20th-century examples; it may, as Burchfield 1996 suggests, have dropped out of use.

Seldom or never dates back to 1398 and it is still in use:

> My interest is always in the subjective event, seldom or never in the objective event —H. L. Mencken, letter, 23 Apr. 1911

> . . . elementary school, where home assignments are seldom or never given —Betty M. Shaw, *NEA Jour.,* February 1965

> Seldom or never does one encounter a TV network nabob who confesses that his net-

work might bore you —Clark Secrest, *Denver Post,* 20 Sept. 1984

Seldom if ever is well attested in 20th-century use. It seems to be a bit more frequent than *seldom or never.*

> But the women at work in the shipyards and other war plants were seldom if ever called *ladies* —H. L. Mencken, *The American Language, Supplement I,* 1945

> . . . and seldom if ever is he aware of the eternally problematic character of his concepts —Albert Einstein, Foreword, *Concepts of Space,* 1954

> Seldom, if ever, has that august group . . . been accused of progressive thinking —Austin Murphy, *Sports Illustrated,* 20 Feb. 1989

> He also rejects the view that throwing money at problems seldom if ever helps —Andrew Hacker, *N.Y. Times Book Rev.,* 6 Oct. 1991

self Several commentators have disparaged *self* used like *myself* for *I* or *me*. Such use dates back to the 18th century, but we have little evidence of its occurrence in modern edited prose. Here is one example:

> Self and coworkers . . . have shown that hornworms . . . —B. C. Akehurst, *Tobacco,* 1968

This use of *self* is not an error, but it will not win you any awards as a prose stylist.

A good deal more attention has been paid to *myself* and other reflexive pronouns used in this way. See MYSELF.

self-confessed *Self-confessed* has been regarded by a few critics as a tautological substitute for *confessed.* Note, however, that in typical usage the meaning of *self-confessed* is closer to *admitted* or *avowed* than it is to *confessed* and *confessed* will not always substitute for it comfortably:

> . . . a man old enough to be my father, and a self-confessed master of English prose —Ernest Hemingway, "African Journal," 1956

> That was the fate of . . . Eugene McCarthy, a self-confessed poet —E. L. Doctorow, *N.Y. Times,* 11 Apr. 1976

> Books that are self-confessed verbal constructions simply need more earnest and witty inventing —Roger Sale, *On Not Being Good Enough,* 1979

> Where did exposure to the torment of East Germany leave a self-confessed Germanophobe? —Robert Darnton, *Wilson Quarterly,* Summer 1991

... agent Arn Tellem, self-confessed inspiration for the HBO series Arli$$ —Steve Rushin, *Sports Illustrated,* 10 July 2000

self-defeating See COUNTERPRODUCTIVE, SELF-DEFEATING.

self-deprecating, self-deprecatory These adjectives are apparently of quite recent formation. They are occasionally dragged into the dispute about *deprecate* and *depreciate,* to the obfuscation of that issue. The earliest citation we know of for *self-deprecatory* is included—without a date—in Fowler 1907, in which it is treated as a misuse of *deprecate:*

In the present self-deprecatory mood in which the English people find themselves —*Spectator*

The Fowlers prescribed *self-depreciatory,* but *self-depreciatory* is a word that no one seems ever to have actually used.

Self-deprecating is more recent, first recorded in 1952. In its place, *self-depreciating* has been recommended. *Self-depreciating* actually does have a few users outside of those who prescribe it, but it is not common. *Self-deprecating* is the most frequently used.

Some kind of embarrassment about her own intentions, though, has made her trim her novel with that self-deprecating humour lady columnists in Sunday newspapers use to protect themselves —*Times Literary Supp.,* 2 Oct. 1969

His . . . patter, with a good dose of self-deprecating humor, always goes down well —Jonathan Freedland, *New Republic,* 10 Jan. 2000

. . . a bracing sort of person with a self-deprecating wit —Gwen Kinkead, *N.Y. Times Mag.,* 10 Apr. 1994

. . . cultivate a flat, unrhetorical style to convey a self-deprecatory impression —*Times Literary Supp.* 14 Nov. 1968

Mr. Krauss is self-deprecatory about his own academic goals and achievements —Greg Denig, *N.Y. Times Book Rev.,* 5 Mar. 1989

See also DEPRECATE, DEPRECIATE; DEPRECATING, DEPRECATORY, DEPRECIATORY; SELF-DEPRECIATION, SELF-DEPRECATION.

self-depreciation, self-deprecation *Self-depreciation* is attested in our files as early as 1917. It appears at first to have indicated a lack of self-esteem:

. . . the self-depreciation that made him powerless before her mother's reproaches —*Hearst's Mag.,* March 1917

This sense has not been lost:

. . . an increase in group solidarity, a lessening of self-depreciation, a feeling of potential strength —Gerda Lerner, *Columbia Forum,* Fall 1970

The word is also used for a conscious downplaying or undervaluing of oneself, usually for the purpose of conveying a real or assumed modesty:

. . . owes her nationwide popularity largely to her mastery of satirical self-depreciation —*Current Biography,* July 1967

In this use, it is a noun clearly parallel to the adjectives *self-deprecating* and *self-deprecatory* (see SELF-DEPRECATING, SELF-DEPRECATORY).

In recent years—only since 1971 in our files—*self-deprecation* has sprung up as a synonymous rival to *self-depreciation.* It is used in the same ways:

One pollyannish anecdote after another illustrates each phase—anecdotes that will plunge any experienced mother into feelings of inadequacy and self-deprecation —Margaret O'Brien Steinfels, *N.Y. Times Book Rev.,* 7 Nov. 1976

. . . they use self-deprecation as a way of making themselves attractive, and it is as aggressive as ordinary boasting —David Denby, *Atlantic,* April 1971

He proved everything by his self-deprecation, his sighs, his lachrymose pauses —E. L. Doctorow, *Loon Lake,* 1979

. . . the way in which the poet in a mood of ironic self-deprecation sets forth the way in which he feels he must appear to the world —Cleanth Brooks, *American Scholar,* Spring 1989

Self-deprecation makes a better match with the adjectives *self-deprecating* and *self-deprecatory* than does the older *self-depreciation,* and it is not unlikely that the influence of the adjectives has promoted the use of the newer word. While our evidence may not be conclusive, it shows that the use of *self-depreciation* began to decline just about the time *self-deprecation* came into use. *Self-deprecation* is now the more common word.

self-destruct See DESTRUCT, SELF-DESTRUCT.

senior See IMPLICIT COMPARATIVE.

sensible In a range of senses having to do with awareness and sensitivity rather than good sense, *sensible* may take a prepositional phrase complement, usually beginning with *of:*

"If my children are silly, I must hope to be always sensible of it." —Jane Austen, *Pride and Prejudice*, 1813

". . . For my part. though deeply sensible of its influence, I cannot seize it." —Nathaniel Hawthorne, *The Marble Faun*, 1860

. . . he had been to a certain extent sensible of having been noticed in a quiet manner by the father —Joseph Conrad, *Chance*, 1913

. . . Hooker, like Burke, is sensible of the force of circumstances —A. S. P. Woodhouse, *Philosophical Rev.*, October 1952

Sensible is used less often with *to*:

. . . quickly become sensible to slight changes of temperature —Samuel Eliot Morison, *Admiral of the Ocean Sea*, 1942

Sensible to these favors, he resisted the temptation —Noel F. Busch, *My Unconsidered Judgment*, 1944

To judge from the evidence that has been collected for the Merriam-Webster files over the last thirty or forty years, *sensible* is now being used less often in these constructions than it formerly was.

sensitive When *sensitive* is complemented by a prepositional phrase, the preposition is often *to*:

Madame Defarge being sensitive to cold, was wrapped in fur —Charles Dickens, *A Tale of Two Cities*, 1859

Lawrence is as sensitive to falsity as the True Princess was to the pea —Eudora Welty, *Atlantic*, March 1949

. . . became sensitive to the rights and special needs of the handicapped —Ronald Reagan, *Abortion and the Conscience of the Nation*, 1984

The next most common preposition is *about*, followed by *of* and *on*:

. . . the Nationalist Government today is probably more sensitive about its face —Peggy Durdin, *N.Y. Times Mag.*, 23 Jan. 1955

I'm sorry. I'm somewhat sensitive about it —Leonard Bernstein, *Atlantic*, April 1955

. . . be sensitive of the rights of the Opposition —Clement Attlee, Speech on the King's Address, 16 Aug. 1945, in *Voices of History 1945–46*, ed. Nathan Ausobel, 1946

". . . This affair is too damned serious to be sensitive on etiquette. . . ." —Van Wyck Mason, *The Shanghai Bund Murders*, 1933

Very occasionally, *sensitive* has also been used with *as to*, *for*, *in*, or *over*:

. . . was sensitive as to its rights and jealous of its constitutional prerogatives —*Dictionary of American Biography*, 1928

. . . a little frightened, big-eyed and simple, sensitive for himself in a way that bordered on the humble —Francis Hackett, *Henry The Eighth*, 1929

The Russians are notoriously sensitive in keeping all observers from their border areas —*New Republic*, 9 July 1951

. . . sensitive over the affliction of growing deafness —*Dictionary of American Biography*, 1929

sensual, sensuous *Sensuous* was coined by John Milton in 1641 in order to avoid "certain associations"—to use the OED's phrase—of the much older word *sensual*. *Sensuous* seems to have existed only in Milton's works until Coleridge unearthed it in the early 19th century. Once it had been set in circulation, it became used quite commonly, and since its meaning was not far removed from some meanings of *sensual*, it began after a time to attract attention in usage books, many of which now distinguish between the two words. The consensus of the commentators, from Vizetelly 1906 to the present, is that *sensuous* emphasizes aesthetic pleasure while *sensual* emphasizes gratification or indulgence of the physical appetites.

The distinction is true enough within one range of meanings, and it is worth remembering. The difficulty is that both words have more than one sense, and they tend often to occur in contexts where the distinction between them is not as clear-cut as the commentators would like it to be. Here are a few examples showing typical uses of *sensual* and *sensuous*, in some of which the prescribed distinction is clear, but in others of which it is not clear at all:

You or I will feel a poem sensuously: your Frenchman will receive sensuous pleasure from the fact that he has comprehended a poem intellectually —Archibald MacLeish, letter, March 1925

You would not believe it Lucinda, but I was very sensual.
I believe it.
No, you're smiling. But I was, I really was. I lived in such an altered state that even the daylight sifting through a cloud would give me enormous shuddering response
                    —E. L. Doctorow, *Loon Lake*, 1979

Yet in the work of Ernest Hemingway our sharpest memories are of sensuous experiences—primarily visual, though also at times involving hearing and smell and taste and touch —Barnard 1979

Having placed in my mouth sufficient bread for three minutes' chewing, I withdrew my powers of sensual perception and retired into the privacy of my mind —Flann O'Brien, *At Swim-Two-Birds,* 1939

Both men said that all sensuous qualities are mere appearances that result from different arrangements of the atoms —Morris Kline, *Mathematics and the Search for Knowledge,* 1985

. . . a fluffy zabaglione, that sensual blend of Marsala, egg yolks, and sugar —Geri Trotta, *Gourmet,* July 1982

. . . the delicacy and sensuously creamy qualities of Italian sweets at their best —C. P. Reynolds, *Gourmet,* April 1982

Refinishing furniture was a minor occupation but a major pleasure of Eliza's. She had a sensual feeling for wood, for its smooth unvarnished touch —Alice Adams, *Listening to Billie,* 1977

As long as the beat people abandon themselves to all sensual satisfactions, on principle, you can't take them for anything but false mystics —Flannery O'Connor, letter, 21 June 1959

It is her creed she is pronouncing, of feverish enjoyment, without distinction between sensuous delight and sensual pleasure —Mary McCarthy, *Occasional Prose,* 1985

If you feel doubt about which word to choose in a particular context, we recommend consulting a dictionary, particularly one which devotes itself to, or includes within its apparatus, discrimination of the meanings of closely related words.

sentence adjective *Sentence adjective* is a term used in the OED Supplement to describe the use of *important* in constructions like this:

More important, a majority of public school students come from a poverty subculture —Susan Jacoby, *Saturday Rev.,* 18 Nov. 1967

Quirk et al. 1985 indicates that sentence-modifying adjectives are quite a bit less common than adverbs in the same function. You can find the controversy over *(more) important* and *(more) importantly* at IMPORTANT 1.

See also SENTENCE ADVERB.

sentence adverb The sentence adverb is an adverb or adverbial phrase that is connected with a whole sentence rather than with a single word or phrase in the sentence. Sentence adverbs are a common feature of present-day English, and they go by many names. You will

find them called *dangling adverbs, floating adverbs, adverbial disjuncts,* and probably other things as well.

The chief virtue of the sentence adverb is its compactness: it permits the writer or speaker to express in a single word or short phrase what would otherwise take a much longer form. Consider this example:

Luckily I never mentioned having asked —Henry Adams, letter, 23 Nov. 1859

That one *luckily* replaces some longer expression like "It's lucky for me that. . . ." Here is another one:

Strictly, when *because of* is right, *due to* is wrong —Johnson 1982

Strictly could be replaced here by the popular *strictly speaking,* but that too is a variety of sentence adverb. If the adverb were not available, it would be necessary to write something like "From the standpoint of strict grammatical correctness. . . ." So you can see the appeal of the sentence adverb.

The most common use of the sentence adverb is to enable the writer or speaker to express an opinion or attitude directly to the reader or hearer (Quirk et al. 1985 call this adverb a disjunct):

Clearly we have found that violence is no answer —W. E. Brock, *AAUP Bulletin,* September 1969

Strangely, people who write and think like that insist that they are champions of what they have named "humanistic" education —Mitchell 1979

Hopefully, The Bluebird, when it is finished, will turn out to be a bluebird and not a turkey —Art Evans, *Edmonton Jour.,* 22 May 1975

Curiously enough, I met Hartman for the first time last night —H. L. Mencken, letter, 24 Oct. 1924

Luckily the strength of the piece did not depend upon him —Jane Austen, *Mansfield Park,* 1814

Oddly, though, over the years *scan* also has developed an opposite meaning —Michael Gartner, *Advertising Age,* 17 Oct. 1985

Amusingly, they had widely divergent attitudes toward corrections in their copy —Simon 1980

A great many of these disjunct adverbs are also used as adverbs of manner, as *frankly* is used here:

He frankly admits his fondness for the wealth and fame —*Current Biography,* December 1965

This duality of function is one of the reasons advanced by commentators in objection to a few specific sentence adverbs (in particular, *hopefully,* which see). They also purport not to understand who is expressing the attitude, although it is perfectly plain that it is the writer or speaker.

Note that sentence-modifying adverbs do not necessarily stand first in a sentence:

> This is one of the words that turn up, predictably, in the sports pages —Harper 1985

> Matters complicate, unsurprisingly —Stanley Kauffmann, *Before My Eyes,* 1980

separate, separately, separation Note the spelling, especially the sequence *-par-.* The substitution *-per-* is well attested:

> It is of singular use to *Princes,* if they take the Opinions of their *Counsell,* both Seperately, and Together —Francis Bacon, *Essays,* 1625

But Francis Bacon had the advantage of writing before the invention of spelling books. His spelling is no longer considered acceptable.

sequence of tenses Although this is not a subject to stir strong feelings, a great deal has been written about it in usage books (Fowler 1926, 1965, Bernstein 1965, Bremner 1980, Copperud 1980, Cook 1985, and many college handbooks). One problem commonly discussed under this heading (there are others) concerns the tense of the verb in a subordinate clause pointing to present or future time. When the present or future tense is used without reference to the verb in the superordinate clause, we have what Roberts 1954 calls the "natural sequence of tenses," as in a sentence like "Novak said that she is going tomorrow." When the verb in the subordinate clause is made past to agree with the first verb, we have the "attracted sequence of tenses": "Novak said that she was going tomorrow." Roberts says that the attracted sequence is normal in what he calls "Choice" English. Most of the discussions in usage books relate to problems with the attracted sequence.

For instance, there is the problem of the "continuing or timeless fact"—as in "Crime doesn't pay." If we make this a subordinate clause with a main clause in the past tense, the commentators would have us follow natural sequence: "The Lone Ranger said that crime doesn't pay." Most writers probably do just that, but what of the earnest seeker after Choice English who makes it past? "The Lone Ranger said that crime didn't pay." We suspect that such usage in an ordinary context would pass unnoticed by the average reader: ". . . and then the Lone Ranger said that crime didn't pay, and he and Tonto rode off into the sunset."

This subject has been discussed in usage books since the 18th century. The evidence in Murray 1795 suggests that the early commentators were at great pains to correct such locutions as "The Lord hath given and the Lord hath taken away." We suggest you will be a lot happier if you simply do not worry about them.

See also WOULD HAVE.

service Many commentators disparage the use of the verb *service* in contexts where *serve* is also possible. They favor restricting *service* to those senses which are uniquely its own, especially "to repair or provide maintenance for," as in "service a car." This verb is not an old one in any of its senses. Its first recorded use was by Robert Louis Stevenson:

> If I am to service ye the way that you propose, I'll lose my lifelihood —Robert Louis Stevenson, *Catriona,* 1893 (OED Supplement)

Stevenson used *service* in this one instance as a synonym of *serve.* There is no further evidence of *service* as a verb until the 1920s, when the "repair or maintain" sense began to appear commonly in print:

> Here we serviced the ship, as we had been out two hours and forty-five minutes —*Aero Digest,* August 1924

H. L. Mencken, in *The American Language* (4th ed., 1936), says that this sense was first used around 1910, when "American garages began *servicing* cars." Almost certainly it was a new coinage, unrelated to Stevenson's *service.* Further written evidence of the "serve" sense did not appear until the 1940s:

> . . . any town serviced by Greyhound bus —*Esquire's Jazz Book,* ed. Paul E. Miller, 1944

> Airports are so far from the cities they supposedly service —John Steinbeck, *Russian Journal,* 1948 (OED Supplement)

Critics such as Copperud 1964, Bernstein 1965, Gowers in Fowler 1965, Shaw 1975, Phythian 1979, Bryson 1984, Janis 1984, and Garner 1998 would presumably have advised Steinbeck to use *serve* instead. Nevertheless, the disapproved sense of *service* continues to be fairly common:

> . . . remote areas serviced only by helicopter —David Fisher, *Hard Evidence,* 1995

> Many of those not in the energy business are also doing very nicely by servicing it —Tom Curtis, *Town & Country,* September 1979

> . . . and bordellos that serviced high-rollers and pigeons alike —Michelle Cottle, *New Republic,* 15 Mar. 1999

set, sit Originally *set* was the causative verb corresponding to the intransitive *sit* and meant "to cause to sit." But as early as the early 14th century *set* began to be used as an intransitive equivalent to *sit*. *Sit* itself later took on the sense of "to cause to sit" from *set*. Given that these interchanges between the two words had several centuries' head start on the lexicographers, grammarians, and teachers who have since tried to disentangle them, it is a wonder that things are as relatively simple as they are today.

The intransitive sense of *set* meaning "to be seated" is at the present time considered dialectal or uneducated; it is in general a socially marked usage. Dr. Johnson in his 1755 Dictionary said that *set* meaning "to sit" was "commonly used in conversation" and "though undoubtedly barbarous, is sometimes found in authors." Some other 18th-century commentators (including Webster in 1790) commented on the usage. Yet the OED quotes Thomas Jefferson using it in 1788:

> It is very possible that the President and the new Congress may be setting at New York.

Noah Webster, whose 1828 dictionary made heavy use of Johnson, simply omitted Johnson's sense. The battle was left to the teachers, textbooks, and handbooks. Textbooks, especially: Malmstrom 1964, which compares the findings of the linguistic atlases with textbooks, reports 170 textbooks that treat *set* and *sit* from nine different viewpoints.

The linguistic atlas researchers found *set* "to sit" in the speech of high school graduates and some college graduates in large areas along the Atlantic seaboard; these findings (along with British evidence) are the basis for calling the usage dialectal. It is presumably this oral use that Pyles 1979 notes as having been heard during the Army–McCarthy hearings in 1954:

> Actually, members of this Committee set in a semijudicial capacity —Senator Charles E. Potter, Michigan

> You've let them set there and testify day after day —Senator John McClellan, Arkansas

But *set* "to sit" is also typical of less educated and more rural people. English writers of the 19th century—Dickens and Thackeray are cited in the OED—put *set* in the mouths of their more countrified and less educated characters. American writers have done the same:

> I had set next to him at so many Speakers Tables, at banquets —Will Rogers, *The Illiterate Digest*, 1924

> This is a great big yard with a whole lot of benches strewed round it, but you can't set on them in the daytime —Ring Lardner, *The Big Town*, 1921

> We had a visitor the other day, an old man, who said he wouldn't go to Europe if they gave it to him. Said a feller went over there and set down on some steps he seen in front of a church. Another feller came along and held out his hand. First one said, What for now? Feller holding out his hand said, Step rent —Flannery O'Connor, letter, 1953

Baker 1770 disapproved the transitive use of *sit*: "*I'll sit you down—He sat her down—They sat us down—* are not proper." The use is fully standard today:

> She sat me in a claw-foot tub and gave me a bath —E. L. Doctorow, *Loon Lake*, 1979

> I got Loretta on the train and sat her down by a stern-looking man —Flannery O'Connor, letter, July 1952

The transitive *sit* is, in fact, so standard that the original transitive *set* is felt to be dialectal in this use. The character speaking here is a Southerner:

> . . . I turned just as two men arrived at the table. "Set yourself down!" Red greeted them —E. L. Doctorow, *Loon Lake*, 1979

In summary, *set* for *sit* is primarily a spoken use; it is considered dialectal or uneducated; it is generally not used in writing except to represent the speech of characters who would use it naturally. Some intransitive uses of *set* have become fully standard: the sun sets, a hen sets, and so do jelly, plaster, and concrete; clothes may set or sit on the wearer. The transitive *sit* is also fully standard.

sexism The women's movement has in recent years drawn considerable attention to the problems of masculine bias in the language. The issues here are social rather than linguistic, but like earlier social issues they will probably leave a mark on the language.

Ebbitt & Ebbitt 1982 sensibly points out that the hard choices in word selection with respect to sexism have to be made by middle-of-the-roaders; the partisans—the militant feminists and the entrenched elderly males—have already made up their minds and are seldom in doubt. The areas where the thoughtful in-betweener will want to be alert concern nouns and pronouns.

1. *Nouns.* Occupational titles that incorporate the word *man*, such as *fireman, policeman, salesman,* and *mailman,* are frequently replaced by gender-neutral terms such as *firefighter, police officer, sales representative,* and *letter carrier.* There are several influences at work here. One is that more women are now employed in many of these occupations than were formerly. Some changing of nomenclature has also been mandated by government agencies, and some by voluntary associations to which both men and women belong. It seems likely that many of the new terms will stick, especially if schoolchildren grow up familiar with them from their textbooks, in which nonsexist language has been mandated.

It should be noted that a few traditional female occupational designations are also in transition. *Stewardess,* for instance, is being replaced by *flight attendant.* Such changes are again attributable in part to the fact that both men and women are now commonly employed in jobs that were formerly reserved for one sex or the other. Harper 1985 lists some of the new occupational names taken from various sources. A few—like *private household cleaners* for *maids* and *servants*—look more like euphemisms to disguise menial jobs than new descriptors to avoid sexual bias.

Some years ago there was considerable interest in finding a substitute suffix for *-man* in a number of compounds like *spokesman, chairman, congressman,* and *draftsman.* The combining form *-one* was a failure; compounds like *chairone* simply looked too mysterious to be useful. The form *-person* has had more, but limited, success. Although loudly decried by some, such combinations as *spokesperson, chairperson,* and *anchorperson* have received wide enough currency to gain at least marginal dictionary recognition (see PERSON 2). *Draftsperson* can be found in the want ads. *Chairperson* and *anchorperson* are in competition with the simpler and equally neutral *chair* and *anchor.*

The *-person* compounds have also been somewhat retarded in their general adoption by some women who reject feminine and neutral forms for the older masculine forms, such as *chairman* and *spokesman.* And in some areas of endeavor, indeed, the existing masculine forms seem to be used simply as a matter of course; in women's basketball, for instance, no one seems chary of playing an aggressive man-to-man defense.

The status of nouns ending in *-ess* is an older but related topic. Their use was urged by at least one 19th-century feminist and disparaged by several 19th-century male commentators (they were particularly hard on *authoress* and *poetess*). In recent years, there has been some changing of positions. This subject is treated in more detail at -ESS.

2. *Pronouns.* The issue here concerns pronoun reference to an indefinite pronoun or singular noun used generically. Feminists have merely given new emphasis to an old problem (see the articles on pronoun reference at AGREEMENT, and THEY, THEIR, THEM 1) in attacking the routine use of the masculine singular pronoun in all instances. Handbooks examin-

ing the question of the generic masculine from a nonsexist point of view generally recommend several approaches to a solution. Let us make up an example to demonstrate those approaches:

> Each student must send his references with his application.

In order not to seem to exclude women, this could be revised using the old expedient *his or her:*

> Each student must send his or her references with his or her application.

If this seems wordy or "legalistic" (a term several commentators apply to *his or her*), you can try omitting the pronoun or substituting an article:

> Each student must send references with the application.

Another commonly suggested solution is to rephrase in the plural:

> Students must send their references with their applications.

Generally not recommended is the use of such obviously manufactured forms as *(s)he* and *his/her,* chiefly on the grounds that they are distracting. Not recommended on the same grounds is the alternation of masculine and feminine pronouns. A few authors have used the generic feminine pronoun ("Each student must send her references with her application"), but this too seems to be more distracting than useful.

The folk, of course, have had a solution to this impasse for many centuries—one of stunning simplicity: they simply use the plural pronouns *they, their, them.* The folk solution exists more commonly in speech than in writing, and is probably more acceptable in references to indefinite pronouns such as *anyone, someone,* and *everyone* than to generic nouns such as the *student* of our made-up example.

Since the 19th century, theorists have proposed remedying the lack of a gender-neutral singular pronoun with any number of invented forms, some of which make confections like *s/he* look almost sensible. There is a list of such forms at EPICENE PRONOUNS.

In conclusion, all we can offer as a general recommendation is that, being a thoughtful writer, you give some consideration to the question of careless or unconscious sexual bias in the language you use and, where you find it, seek a solution that makes sense in the immediate context.

shall, will *Shall* and *will* have attracted a great deal of attention from usage commentators. Let us begin with a clear expression of present-day American use:

The old distinction between these words is no longer observed by most people. *Shall,* which was once considered the only correct form for the expression of the simple future in the first person, has been replaced by *will* in the speech and writing of most people. . . . In a few expressions *shall* is the only form ever used and so presents no usage problem: *Shall* we go? *Shall* I help you? To use *will* in these expressions would change the meaning. With the exception of these special uses, *will* is as correct as *shall* —Warriner 1986

And let us contrast that with the traditional rule, as expressed in a British usage book:

In its simplest form, the rule governing the use of *shall* and *will* is as follows: to express a simple future tense, use *shall* with *I* or *we, will* with *you, he, they,* etc.; to express permission, obligation, determination, compulsion, etc., use *will* with *I* and *we, shall* elsewhere —Chambers 1985

Chambers goes on to note that there are "many exceptions" to this rule, especially in American, Scottish, and Irish English (as distinguished from the English of England itself).

The reason that things have come to this pass is history. The traditional rule given by Chambers was first set down in the 17th century by John Wallis, a bishop and a well-known mathematician. Wallis's grammar was written in Latin for the edification of foreigners; modern commentators assume it was a sort of learner's grammar. Wallis's rules were probably simplified. Strang says they do not reflect the practice of the preceding century, and thinks they might have been closer to the actual usage of Wallis's own time than that of any other. A few randomly collected examples of 17th-century usage cast doubt even on that cautious assessment; sometimes usages match the rules and sometimes they do not. A good part of the problem is in interpretation—both of the terms used by the grammarians to make the distinctions and of the intentions of old writers. With this warning, here are some 17th-century examples:

If a man will begin with certainties, he shall end in doubts —Francis Bacon, *The Advancement of Learning,* 1605

. . . I shall speak when I have spoken of the Passions —Thomas Hobbes, *Of Speech,* 1651

. . . I hope I shall not be thought arrogant —John Dryden, "Defence of the Epilogue," 1672

. . . I will only add this in defence of our present Writers —John Dryden, "Defence of the Epilogue," 1672

"He that will have a May Pole shall have a May Pole." This is a maxim with them —William Congreve, "Concerning Humour in Comedy," 1695

. . . the two great Seminaries we have, are without comparison the *Greatest,* I won't say the *Best* in the World —Daniel Defoe, *Of Academies,* 1697

These examples seem to us to follow the theory sometimes and sometimes not. If the usage of Wallis's own century was not exactly uniform, you can well imagine that over time the rules came to match actual usage even less.

By the 18th century, grammarians were finding Wallis's rules too simple. Lowth 1762 added rules for interrogatives, and later grammarians elaborated even further. But William Cobbett 1823 did not bother with rules; he told his son, to whom his grammar was addressed, that the uses of the auxiliaries, "various as they are, are as well known to us all as the uses of our teeth and noses." He had nothing more to say about *shall* and *will,* relying instead on the native speaker's instinct. Such reliance was not uncommon in the 19th century. Alford 1864 commented that he never heard an Englishman who misused *shall* and *will* but had never heard an Irishman or Scotchman who did not misuse them sometimes. On this side of the Atlantic, Richard Grant White 1870 was employing the same method to distinguish the "correct" New England use from that of the provincial folk and immigrants (mostly Irish at that time). A somewhat similar attitude can be found in Fowler 1926, in which a distinction is made between those "to the manner born"—in this case, the English—and those not so lucky.

Fowler listed several pages of what he regarded as misuses culled from British newspapers, but his faith in the English English rules never wavered, perhaps because of his belief that the British press was controlled by Scots. Had he looked to literary rather than journalistic sources, however, he could have found plenty of variation among non-Scots:

If you procure the young gentleman in the library to write out . . . , I will send to Mr. Prince the bookseller to pay him —Samuel Johnson, letter, 7 Aug. 1755

If I come to live at Oxford, I shall take up my abode at Trinity —Samuel Johnson, 1754, quoted by Thomas Warton, in James Boswell, *Life of Samuel Johnson,* 1791

I have no desire to return to England, nor shall I, unless compelled —Lord Byron, letter, 12 Nov. 1809

I will write when I can —Lord Byron, letter, 12 Nov. 1809

As plainly as I behold what happened, I will try to write it down —Charles Dickens, *David Copperfield*, 1850

His French author I never saw, but have read fifty in the same strain, and shall read no more —Thomas Gray, letter, 18 Aug. 1758

. . . as soon as I am settled there, I will propose a day for fetching my newest little friend —Lewis Carroll, letter, 1 July 1892

Notice how easily first person *will* slips in when it is part of a contraction:

I'll send her book from Oxford —Lewis Carroll, letter, 9 June 1892

Well, I won't talk about myself, it is not a healthy topic —Lewis Carroll, letter. 29 July 1885

Notice too that *will* and *would* can be used with second and third persons to give directions or to show determination:

You will therefore retain the manuscript in your own care —Lord Byron, letter, 23 Aug. 1811

. . . he would carve a fowl, which he did very ill favordly, because 'we did not know how indispensible it was for a Barrister to do all those sort of things well . . .' —Charles Lamb, letter, 24 May 1830

Fowler dismissed the use of *shall* and *will* in the same construction as "elegant variation." We have seen two or three examples of such usage from the 17th century already. Here is one from the 19th century:

. . . I shall delay it till it can be made in person, and then I will shorten it as much as I can —Lord Byron, letter, 29 Feb. 1816

It is clear that even in the English of England there has always been some deviance from Wallis's (and Fowler's) norm.

In America, of course, there has been considerable straying from the Wallis rules. *Will* has by no means entirely supplanted *shall* for marking simple futurity, but *will* and *would* are certainly fully established as standard with the first person:

I have no idea on what continent I will be in September —Alexander Woollcott, letter, 8 Jan. 1936

We would all like it if the bards would make themselves plain, or we think we would —E. B. White, in *The Practical Cogitator*, ed. Charles P. Curtis, Jr., & Ferris Greenslet. 1945

The mechanics . . . were perfect, I would say —Philip Hamburger, *New Yorker*, 12 Aug. 1950

Tomorrow morning I will wake up in this first-class hotel suite . . . and I will appreciate its elegance —Tennessee Williams, *Story*, Spring 1948

Tell Stan I have a textbook out, on English usage and style, and will send him a copy —E. B. White, letter, 16 June 1959

. . . since I will be seeing you in a fortnight, we can then talk until the cows come home —Groucho Marx, letter, 16 Sept. 1960

I know beforehand what I will not like about Jane later (she'll be too thin, of course. . . . What will I find to talk to her about? . . .) —Joseph Heller, *Something Happened*, 1974

As for *shall*, it has become a bit fashionable in recent years to disparage its use in American English. Its critics allow that it is entrenched in legal usage and in the questions mentioned at the beginning of the article, but in other uses they tend to regard it as affected or precious. Some allowance is made for the expression of determination or resolve, in which it is used with pronouns of all persons:

I shall return —General Douglas MacArthur, on leaving the Philippines, 11 Mar. 1942

I can't approve of such goings on and I shall never approve it —Harry S. Truman, letter, 18 Aug. 1948

. . . those who frustrate communication and threaten identity by insisting that everybody else shall speak and write as they themselves do —James Sledd, in Greenbaum 1985

Shall and *should* are also used in more ordinary functions, however, by those Americans to whom they are natural (some of whom also use *will* and *would* in the same ways).

So I've sent Hopkins to Moscow and Davies to London. We shall see what we shall see —Harry S. Truman, diary, 22 May 1945

Perhaps I shall get down in January —Flannery O'Connor, letter, 15 Dec. 1948

We shall call *I, we, he, she,* and *they* the subject forms —Roberts 1962

I shall always remember two sentences he handed me —James Thurber, letter, 21 May 1954

. . . and "I did not think to tell them"—I should use in conversation without a second thought —Barnard 1979

. . . I shall be embarrassed by the check —Archibald MacLeish, letter, March 1972

. . . I should love to settle myself uncomfortably into a chair by Josef Hoffmann but

I can't afford it —William J. Gass, *N.Y. Times Book Rev.*, 3 Aug. 1986

Our conclusion is that the traditional rules about *shall* and *will* do not appear to have described real usage of these words very precisely at any time, although there is no question that they do describe the usage of some people some of the time and that they are more applicable in England than elsewhere. In current American English, *shall* and *should*, *will* and *would* are pretty much interchangeable, with the second pair more common. There is perhaps only one thing to concern the learner of English, and that is the business of questions mentioned by Warriner. Consider these two examples:

. . . shall I be compassionate or shall I be uncompassionate? —William Faulkner, 25 Feb. 1957, in *Faulkner in the University*, 1959

Shall we be relativists, and leave everybody's language alone . . . ? —James Sledd, *American Speech*, Fall 1978

Both of these ask for an opinion, a preference, a decision. What do we want to do? If *will* replaces *shall*, the meaning changes. A prediction is asked for. What is going to happen? *Shall* also occurs in an interjected question of fixed rhetorical form. No answer is expected, and *will* is simply not used:

He was 6 foot 2. I was somewhat shorter, shall I say, and from the city —Stephen A. Howard, quoted in Wallace Terry, *Bloods*, 1984

See also SHOULD, WOULD.

shambles *Shambles* is both an old word and a new one—old in that most of its senses had developed by the end of the 16th century, new in that the senses in which it is now commonly (and almost exclusively) used date only from the 1920s. It had originally meant "a stool" and "a money changer's table." Later it acquired the additional meaning "a table for the exhibition of meat for sale," which in turn gave rise in the early 15th century to a use of the plural with the meaning "a meat market." A further extension of meaning in the 16th century produced the sense "a slaughterhouse," from which quickly developed the figurative use of *shambles* to refer to a place of terrible slaughter or bloodshed. In the 20th century, another extension of meaning took place; *shambles* acquired the senses "a scene or state of great destruction" and "a scene or state of great disorder and confusion; a mess." These senses were first recorded in the 1920s. Some critics objected, but the new senses of *shambles* have become standard. They are far and away the most common senses of the word:

The apartment was usually in disorder, except on the day the maid came in, when it became a shambles —S. J. Perelman, *New Yorker*, 23 Apr. 1955

. . . saved the evening from becoming an utter shambles —Robert Shaplen, *New Yorker*, 10 Nov. 1956

He was a shambles of a man, an embarrassment —T. Coraghessan Boyle, *The Road to Wellville*, 1993

. . . The Cuban economy is in shambles — *Wilson Quarterly*, Autumn 1990

. . . the shambles of my high school French vocabulary —Stephen King, *Playboy*, January 1982

. . . had not the city itself been a shambles of torn-up streets —Eleanor Perenyi, *Atlantic*, February 1982

The courtyard of the U.S. Embassy was a shambles —Evan Thomas, *Newsweek*, 1 May 2000

Shambles, you will note, is regularly treated as a singular noun in modern English. Sometimes, especially in the phrase *in shambles*, it is used much like *tatters*.

shame The basic sense of the noun *shame* can be followed by *at* or *for*; you can feel shame *at* or *for* something, or you can feel shame *for* someone *at* something. *Over* and *about* also have some use following *shame*:

. . . shame at wanting or enjoying sex —Harriet La Barre, *Ladies' Home Jour.*, August 1971

. . . shame for having chosen to marry someone who falls short of their expectations —Elizabeth Janeway, *Atlantic*, March 1970

. . . he feeling shame for her at the unease with which she read —Norman Mailer, *Advertisements for Myself*, 1959

. . . shame over wasted time and talents —Elizabeth Janeway, *Atlantic*, March 1970

There is a shame about advertising yourself —Norman Mailer, *Advertisements for Myself*, 1959

shan't *Shan't* is a standard contraction of *shall not*. It came into use sometime during the 17th century, along with such other negative contractions as *an't*, *don't*, *han't*, and *won't*, most of which displeased commentators in the 18th and 19th centuries, and some of which are still usage issues. The forms *shan't*, which is still predominant, and *sha'n't* have both been used from the 17th century on.

The few American commentators who mention *shan't* agree that it is more common in British English than in American English. Our evidence confirms their observation. Here are some American examples, two older and two newer.

I sha'n't apologize for the Whitmanesque —Robert Frost, letter, 19 Dec. 1911

I shan't pretend to be full of jollity —Alexander Woollcott, letter, 12 Jan. 1918

The last time I was seasick was when I was thirteen. But that is no guarantee that I shan't be seasick tomorrow —William F. Buckley, Jr., *New Yorker,* 9 Feb. 1987

. . . the next year in which outlays shan't exceed the receipts —Vermont Royster, *Wall Street Jour.,* 4 Aug. 1982

See also SHALL, WILL.

she   A few commentators take note of the conventional usage in which *she* and *her* are used to refer to certain things as if personified—nations, ships, mechanical devices, nature, and so forth. The origin of the practice is obscure. The OED has evidence from the 14th and 15th centuries, some of which is translated material, and it is not known if the gender markers in the original had any influence on the translators' practice. The conventions are still observed:

It was a good furnace all last winter . . . ; it ran real quiet and when they turned up the thermostat early Sunday morning, she went from fifty to seventy in about an hour flat —Garrison Keillor, *Lake Wobegon Days,* 1985

In 1841 Steers designed the *William G. Hagstaff* for the Jersey pilots, and she regularly beat the New York boats —Robert H. Boyle, *Sports Illustrated,* 30 June 1986

England, therefore, was not so feudal as Gaul. But she was probably developing in the same direction —Frank Barlow, *The Feudal Kingdom of England 1042–1216,* 3d ed., 1972

Nature has come through again—she always does —Stephen Jay Gould, *The Flamingo's Smile,* 1985

Copperud 1964, 1970, 1980 and Flesch 1964 prefer *it* when the reference is to a nation. Reader's Digest 1983 says that many women object to the feminine pronouns. To the extent that this is so, they seem to be viewed as relatively minor problems in comparison with other aspects of sexism in language.

See also SEXISM 2.

s/he, (s)he   These conspicuously created forms are among the more recent proposed solutions to the problem of the missing gen-

der-neutral (but not quite so neutral as *it*) third person singular pronoun in English. They will probably not be the last of these suggestions (a list of some of the older ones can be found at EPICENE PRONOUNS).

Unlike most of the earlier artificial pronouns, both *s/he* and *(s)he* have actually appeared in otherwise relatively commonplace prose. Frequent use so far, however, does seem to be limited chiefly to specialized journals (most of them in the fields of English language and linguistics). But how do you pronounce *s/he* and *(s)he?* The unpronounceability of these invented forms is a major problem for anyone who advocates their use.

See also SEXISM 2; THEY, THEIR, THEM 1.

sherbert, sherbet   We have had a few inquiries in recent years about the *sherbert* spelling of *sherbet,* which Merriam-Webster dictionaries recognize as a standard variant, but which many other people regard as a misspelling. The basis for their opinion is that the second *r* is unetymological, the word being derived from Turkish or Persian words without it.

The word was imported into English—along with the drink it named—in the 17th century. Derived from an exotic language with an exotic alphabet, it naturally had numerous spellings as an English word. Among fourteen shown in the OED (for the 17th century) are *sherbet* and *sherbert,* the only two in use today (not counting *sorbet,* which came from the same source through Italian). *Sherbet* became the established spelling in the 18th century. *Sherbert* staged its comeback in the 20th century. Its resurgence seems to parallel the more widespread use of the word in a new sense, "a flavored ice," which is now far and away the usual sense in American English.

Curiously, our earliest evidence for *sherbert* is American, and our most recent evidence is heavily British. We leave you with two examples from British fiction. The first is English, and the compound terms are favorite sweets of schoolchildren. The second is Australian, and the *sherbert* there probably means "beer."

. . . Rose had promised either twopenny sherbert fountains with liquorice suckers, or sherbert dabs —Margaret Drabble, *The Needle's Eye,* 1972

We run down Bourke Street with McCarthy a balloon pumped up with sherberts —Barry Oakley, *A Salute to the Great McCarthy,* 1970

Sherbet is still the usual spelling. Probably more common than the *sherbert* spelling is the pronunciation it represents, \'shər-bərt\, which is also sometimes cited as an error, though it can be heard from educated speakers of English.

shibboleth A story in the Bible tells how the pronunciation of the word *shibboleth* was used by the Gileadites to distinguish between the soldiers of their own army and those of their enemy, the Ephraimites, who were attempting to escape after being routed in battle. *Shibboleth* in the realm of grammar and usage denotes a word or a use of language that is supposed to distinguish the members of one group—usually the anointed, the educated, the elite—from another group—usually the illiterate, the uneducated, the rabble:

Still, "ain't" . . . is the shibboleth that divides the saved from the damned —Barnard 1979

. . . another great Shibboleth of English syntax, the split infinitive —Howard 1984

It is apparently a fact that many of these traditional usages no longer work very well as shibboleths. Some of the people who devise aptitude tests for college-bound students have discovered that poor students were better at spotting many of the traditional shibboleths than good students were. Since the tests are supposed to help identify good students, those likely to be successful in college, the testers have removed many of the traditional shibboleths, including the famous split infinitive.

Longman 1988 and Burchfield 1996 note that *shibboleth* has also become a term for some entrenched or mindlessly repeated dogma or opinion. That use of *shibboleth* looks like this:

. . . sees himself as an anarchist, a rebel, a one-man opposition party to fashionable shibboleths and slogans —Michael Billington, *N.Y. Times,* 17 Jan. 1982

Nor does the book address the current shibboleth that technological advances are diminishing the relevance of terrain in warfare —*Publishers Weekly,* 12 Oct. 1998

It may seem a liberal shibboleth, but last week's clash proved once again that the NRA is a powerful force on Capitol Hill —Matt Bai, *Newsweek,* 28 June 1999

shine *Shine* is a verb that has had competing strong and weak principal parts since the 16th century. Samuel Johnson in his 1755 Dictionary gave *shone* as the primary past tense and past participle with *shined* as the secondary past and past participle. But a century later, Fitzedward Hall 1873 thought *shined* was then only used by the uneducated, although he noted that it had once been in more elevated use. The OED (1914) more or less confirmed Hall's opinion, terming *shined* "now chiefly *dial*[ectal] and *arch*[aic]," but the OED also showed that *shined* was usual for the sense "polish."

Evans 1957, on the other hand, found *shined*

to be standard—indeed, literary—in transitive uses generally, and not just in the "polish" sense. It seems clear, in fact, that *shined* has never lost currency in American English to the extent that it has in British English.

We regularly find *shined* meaning "polished":

He was having his shoes shined —*And More by Andy Rooney,* 1982

American English also uses *shined* for the transitive sense "to direct the light of":

. . . shined his flashlight into the den —Adele Conover, *Smithsonian,* April 1983

British English uses *shone:*

. . . and shone his torch down to give him some light —Ann Bale, *Maratoto Gold,* 1971

Intransitive uses tend to be *shone* in both varieties:

For the first time, light shone on a possibility —Russell Baker, *Growing Up,* 1982

The long, toothy face, with the big ears on either side, simply shone with enthusiasm —Roald Dahl, *Someone Like You,* 1953

. . . that hard fierce light of publicity which everybody hates shone on everything he did —William Faulkner, 16 May 1957, in *Faulkner in the University,* 1959

But we also occasionally find intransitive *shined* in American English:

The California sun shined on the ninth annual . . . show —*Southwest Art,* July 1985

These uses of *shined* are standard in American English.

should, would

I need not dwell here on the uses of *will, shall, may, might, should, would, can, could,* and *must:* which uses, various as they are, are as well known to us all as the uses of our teeth and our noses —Cobbett 1823

It is very tempting to adopt Cobbett's attitude and let *should* and *would* go, but they have unfortunately been dragged into the rules propounded originally in the 17th century for *shall* and *will.* We need not go into detail here (all you need to know is at SHALL, WILL), but it does seem worthwhile to point out the typical ways in which *should* and *would* are actually used.

The reason *should* and *would* are mentioned with *shall* and *will* is that they function as the past tenses of those verbs. They turn up in this function in the indirect reporting of speech:

She banged on the door and said we should be late —Basil Boothroyd, *Punch,* 30 Oct. 1974

. . . asked in a commanding voice if I wouldn't turn to my third choice —Warren Bennis, *Atlantic,* April 1971

No doubt the woman in the first example said, "We shall be late." An American describing this scene might not be so accurate as Booth-royd and might very well write *would* even though *shall* had been said. In the second example the speaker might have said either *will* (i.e., *won't* in this case) or *would,* which is often used in place of *will* because it is felt to be more polite.

In conditional sentences both *should* and *would* are used:

. . . I should not be bothering you with this letter if I thought the trouble at all likely to end where it is today —Joseph Alsop, *N.Y. Times Mag.,* 14 Dec. 1975

We . . . would be glad to have three or four more machines if you could send them to us —E. B. White, letter, 9 Aug. 1922

If Eastbourne was only a mile off from Scarborough, I would come and see you tomorrow —Lewis Carroll, letter, 14 July 1877

. . . had we been continued in office we would have quickly overcome the depression —Herbert Hoover, quoted in *Time,* 5 May 1952

Would is used with pronouns of all persons to express habitual action:

In the semicircular portico of the National Library we would meet every morning —Oliver St. John Gogarty, *It Isn't This Time of Year At All!,* 1954

He would eat hot soup and drink whiskey and sweat —Aristides, *American Scholar,* Winter 1981/82

You are not the kind of guy who would be at a place like this at this time of the morning —Jay McInerney, *Bright Lights, Big City,* 1984

Would is also used as a finite verb to express a wish. It is used with or without a subject:

I would God you two were the tender apple blossom and could be shipped here in a sachet bag —James Thurber, letter, October 1936

It does not. Would that it did —Margaret Drabble, letter to the editor, *Times Literary Supp.,* 4 Oct. 1985

. . . would that I'd kept all my charts! —John Gardner, *N.Y. Times Book Rev.,* 30 Jan. 1983

Should is used in the sense of "ought to":

. . . the necessity of accomplishing something in less time than should truly be al-

lowed for its doing —Ernest Hemingway, *Green Hills of Africa,* 1935

The third recommendation was that the fleet should be ordered to move north —Dean Acheson, quoted in Merle Miller, *Plain Speaking,* 1973

His French vocabulary was drawn from conversations with his mother and aunt, and should have been full of tenderness —Mavis Gallant, *New Yorker,* 8 July 1985

Should also has a few idiomatic uses all to itself:

My own feeling about this, if I may put it in slang, is "I should worry." —Leacock 1943

"He should live so long I'd make him such a price. . . ." —Mordecai Richler, *The Apprenticeship of Duddy Kravitz,* 1959

Jimmy should be so lucky as to get liverwurst —Jean Gonick, *Northeast Mag.,* 13 Jan. 1985

The point to be remembered here is this: the uses of *should* and *would* are more varied than those of *shall* and *will,* and the traditional rules, shaky as they are for *shall* and *will,* tell us even less about *should* and *would.* And we have not even tried to examine all the uses of *should* and *would* (you can find these recorded in a good dictionary). Native speakers of English mostly handle these words with Cobbett's attitude—they do what comes naturally and do not worry. Learners have more of a problem, but they should follow the practice of native speakers and not become ensnared in artificial distinctions.

should of This is a transcription of the contracted form *should've* of *should have.* Sometimes it is used intentionally for a special effect—for instance, by Ring Lardner—but most writers will want *should have* or *should've.* See OF 2.

should ought See OUGHT 3.

show *Showed, shown.* The usual past participle of *show* is *shown:*

. . . the Vatican has shown itself ready —Irving R. Levine, *Atlantic,* September 1970

Showed can also be used as a past participle:

. . . had showed their willingness to compromise —*Book Previews,* November 1950

. . . there had never been a moment when he had showed any meanness of spirit —Mario Puzo, *The Sicilian,* 1984

Such usage is entirely correct; the past participle *shewed* dates from the 14th century, *showed* from the 15th century. *Showed* occurs too frequently to be considered rare but is less common than *shown*. Usage commentators generally acknowledge that *showed* as a past participle is standard, but they recommend using *shown* instead.

show up *Show up* in its chief transitive and intransitive senses has been labeled a colloquialism in college handbooks from Woolley & Scott 1926 and Jensen 1935 to Prentice Hall 1978 and Bell & Cohn 1981. The label is, it seems, a bit of a tradition in such works. Our evidence shows wide use in general prose and occasional use in more formal contexts. Some examples:

> The good thing about the intelligent anti-intellectual is that he scents with appropriate alarm the dangers of committing himself to abstract attitudes that a later or rougher or rounder experience would show up —Robert Fitzgerald, *New Republic*, 25 Apr. 1949

> ... American ships showed up now and then to continue the blockade —C. S. Forester, *The Barbary Pirates*, 1953

> The virus, which first showed up in the Far East, contaminates 32-bit executable files —Stephen E. Brier, *N.Y. Times*, 30 July 1998

> ... whereupon he was shown up as hollow, his character feeble —Hugh Trevor-Roper, *Times Literary Supp.*, 12 Feb. 1993

> ... you could show up on registration day without advance notice —Tom Wicker, *Change*, September 1971

> The first inkling of that collision has recently showed up in increased radio and x-ray emission —*Astronomy*, May 1997

shrink According to our evidence, in written use the usual past tense of *shrink* is *shrank*:

> ... he shrank from forcing the decision —Henry F. Graff, *N.Y. Times Book Rev.*, 20 May 1979

> Families shrank partly because . . . —Christopher Jencks, *N.Y. Times Book Rev.*, 10 Apr. 1983

Shrunk also occurs as the past tense of *shrink*. In fact, in linguistic surveys conducted in the eastern and midwestern U.S. several decades ago more than 80 percent of the people polled used *shrunk* in preference to *shrank*. The past tense *shrunk* is undoubtedly standard, but it is not especially frequent in print:

> After the 1968 season, officials also shrunk the strike zone —Murray Chass, *N.Y. Times*, 22 May 1994

> . . . I shrunk self-consciously in my seat —Stringfellow Barr, *Center Mag.*, May 1968

> ... Waterstone's shrunk one of its 20,000-sq.-ft. megastores into 1,500 square feet

—Judith Rosen, *Publishers Weekly*, 13 Mar. 2000

Shrunk and *shrunken* are both used as the past participle of *shrink*. *Shrunk* is the usual choice when the participle is functioning as a verb:

> ... the lake has shrunk to a mirage of shimmering blue —William Kittredge, *Fiction*, vol. 1, no. 3, 1973

> Or had they only shrunk? —Wilfrid Sheed, *The Good Word and Other Words*, 1978

Shrunken is the usual choice when the participle is functioning as an adjective:

> ... a somewhat shrunken functionary, barely worth a book —Wilfrid Sheed, *The Good Word and Other Words*, 1978

> ... a frail and shrunken fragment of the old dream —Mavis Gallant, *N.Y. Times Book Rev.*, 11 May 1983

shy A person can be said to be shy *of* or *about* doing something:

> ". . . Mr. Fox could not be afraid of Dr. Johnson; yet he certainly was very shy of saying any thing in Dr. Johnson's presence." —Edward Gibbon, quoted in James Boswell, *The Life of Samuel Johnson*, 1791

> ... one may well be rather shy of reverting to topics that are not, perhaps, yet exhausted —F. R. Leavis, *Revaluation*, 1947

> ... I should have been more shy about questioning such a suggestion —F. R. Leavis, *The Common Pursuit*, 1952

> Miss Mori did not, as expected, produce printed furs. However, she wasn't shy about lavender or mauve dyed minks —Angela Taylor, *N.Y. Times*, 17 May 1980

Shy can also be followed by *to* and the infinitive:

> Authors even then were not shy to take liberties with the English language —*Times Literary Supp.*, 2 Oct. 1969

> Although shy to call himself a collector, Mr. Coady means business about handcrafted furniture —Stephen Drucker, *N.Y. Times*, 21 Oct. 1982

When *shy* has the sense "showing a lack" or "short," it is followed by *of*:

> . . . a fat man shy of natural quickness —Larry L. King, *New Times*, 21 Feb. 1975

> The entire tree is just shy of eight feet tall —*Early American Life*, August 1980

sibling *Sibling* is to *brother* and *sister* more or less as *spouse* is to *husband* and *wife*: a formal word that is sometimes useful in contexts where either of the sexually specific words would be inappropriate. *Sibling* most often occurs in scientific writing:

> . . . the genetic changes undergone by one or both siblings during the period of separation —Peter Matthiessen, *New Yorker,* 27 May 1967

> . . . how dependent these children are on their parents or siblings —Jerome L. Singer, *Psychology Today,* April 1968

It sometimes shows up in general writing as well:

> . . . a small fee to reward the older sibling for serving as a sitter —Letty Cottin Pogrebin, *Ladies' Home Jour.,* September 1971

In recent years figurative uses have become increasingly popular:

> Pocket Books is a sibling of Simon & Schuster's many divisions —Ray Walters, *N.Y. Times Book Rev.* 14 Oct. 1979

> The sun has its starry sibling: Alpha Centauri —Philip Morrison, *Scientific American,* February 1978

sic   *Sic,* usually enclosed in brackets, is a word editors use in the reproduction of someone else's speech or writing to indicate that an unexpected form exactly reproduces the original and is not a copier's mistake. In the three typical uses here, *sic* is used to show a word spoken with an extra syllable, an unusual spelling, and a misspelling.

> "I'm a conservationalist [sic]," she replies —Judy Klemesrud, *N.Y. Times,* 1 Dec. 1974

> . . . the Phenix [sic] Society —Albert H. Johnston, *Publishers Weekly,* 6 Feb. 1978

> . . . we beleive [sic] it to be worth the risk —*The Tower Commission Report,* 1987

Several commentators remind us that it is bad manners to use a [*sic*] to needlessly call attention to someone's error or to deride the language of a less educated person.

Sierra   The literal meaning of *sierra* in Spanish is "saw," from which arose its extended sense, "a jagged mountain range." This sense has some use in English as well as in Spanish:

> . . . invasions that have taken place in the Peruvian sierra in recent years —Norman Gall, *N.Y. Rev. of Books,* 20 May 1971

But *sierra* is far less well known to most English speakers as a generic noun than as a part of the proper names of several mountain ranges—especially, for Americans, the Sierra Nevada of eastern California, also commonly known as the Sierra Nevada range, the Sierra Nevada mountains, the Sierra mountains, the Sierra Nevadas, the Sierras, and the Sierra. This plurality of names leads to a familiar problem: the same people who find redundancy in *Sahara desert* (because *sahara* means "desert" in Arabic) are also likely to find it in *Sierra Nevada range, Sierra Nevada mountains,* and *Sierra mountains.* In addition, some critics have objected to *the Sierras,* arguing that *sierras* can only mean "the mountain ranges" since the singular *sierra* denotes an entire range rather than a single mountain. What this means in practical terms is that if you want to be absolutely sure of offending no one, you will have to write either *the Sierra Nevada* or *the Sierra* when referring to the Sierra Nevada mountains. If, on the other hand, you can accept the idea that the *Sierra* of *Sierra Nevada* is actually a proper name, not a generic noun, and that English and Spanish are two different languages, you will feel entitled to refer to those mountains in whatever way seems natural and idiomatic to you.

See also SAHARA, SAHARA DESERT.

sight   See CITE, SITE, SIGHT.

simple reason   This common phrase has attracted surprisingly strong criticism from several commentators (Bernstein 1958, 1965, Copperud 1970, 1980, and Shaw 1975, 1987) who regard it as verbose and patronizing. The second of these objections seems to be a subjective one. We find nothing particularly patronizing in our evidence. The patronizing tone, to judge from printed evidence, must exist mainly in the eye of the beholder.

The wordiness objection is based on the assumption that the phrase *for the simple reason that* can be replaced by *because.* This is true, but the evidence we have shows that quite often writers do not choose to express themselves in the smallest number of words. For instance, we find the aspersed phrase in usage books:

> There was no such thing as a split infinitive in Latin for the simple reason that each Latin infinitive was a single word —*Harper* 1985

And in letters:

> . . . I think I had better come next Tuesday, instead of tomorrow, for the simple reason that if I come tomorrow you will certainly drive the car and risk your back again —Virginia Woolf, letter, 27 Aug. 1932

And we find it in books and in journalism:

> The limas I don't even dry, for the simple reason that there are never enough. We eat them all —Eleanor Perenyi, *Green Thoughts,* 1983

... the character ... feels like a wholly original conception, for the simple reason that he isn't a professional investigator —Terrence Rafferty, *New Yorker*, 25 Oct. 1995

It should be noted that *simple reason* occurs in other constructions than the aspersed five-word phrase:

A creative craze is spreading for a simple reason: The staff works —Michael Bamberger, *Sports Illustrated*, 20 Apr. 1998

The markets are hypersensitive to these wayward signals for one simple reason. The government has furnished them with nothing more substantial to believe in —*The Economist*, 29 Apr.–5 May 1989

And there aren't any Russian products in the stores either. ... There is a simple reason for this. The Russian stuff is no good —P. J. O'Rourke, *Rolling Stone*, 19 Sept. 1996

Simple reason has been in use since at least the 1750s. You can use it or avoid it. It's your choice.

simplistic *Simplistic* is usually a denigrating word that means "oversimplified." However, it is occasionally used with the neutral meaning "simple," a fact that causes some prescriptivists to start prescribing. There is probably some cause for complaint here, for in some citations the meaning is potentially confusing:

... to show variety of Hindu thought from simplistic tales to sophisticated speculations —Callie Kingsbury, *English Jour.*, January 1975

... the simplistic murals ... still circumnavigated the upper reaches of a dining room distinguished by the mellowness of its patina —Jay Jacobs, *Gourmet*, April 1980

Many people who think of *simplistic* as a word with negative connotations, as they are entitled to from the dominant use, will be taken aback by such neutral uses and may even misunderstand them.

Shaw 1975 and Ebbitt & Ebbitt 1982 call *simplistic* a vogue word, and indeed the bulk of our evidence for *simplistic* is from the past two or three decades. We see no reason to disdain a word just because other people happen to find it useful, but we do counsel using this one as a pejorative rather than a neutrally descriptive term.

since 1. If you have already read many articles in this book, you will have noticed times change and language habits with them. Not long ago a correspondent wrote to us inquiring if it is "incorrect to begin a sentence with *because*." He admitted to preferring to replace *because* with *since* whenever possible. His attitude represents quite a turnabout; Bernstein 1971 and Copperud 1970, 1980 point out that at one time there was a notion current that *since* could not be used as a causal conjunction. Our old books do not shed much light on this notion, but Sellers 1975, the work of a British newspaperman, censures *since* for *because* as an unacceptable Americanism. We are not sure whether this is simply an idiosyncrasy or whether British newspapermen traditionally reject the usage of Shakespeare; Bernstein 1971, an American newspaperman, quotes two instances from Shakespeare:

Since mine own doors refuse to entertain me, I'll knock elsewhere —*The Comedy of Errors*, 1593

Since it is as it is, mend it for your own good —*Othello*, 1605

Some other commentators (Kilpatrick 1984, Freeman 1983, Johnson 1982) prefer *because* to *since*, finding it more emphatic.

Clearly *since* can be used to mean "because," though it may be a bit less emphatic than *because*. It can, however, cause readers to stumble if both its causal and temporal senses are meaningful in the same context. It is not necessarily preferable to *because*, as our correspondent perhaps hoped we would tell him.

2. *Since, ago.* There are three different issues concerning *since* and *ago*, all of them pretty ancient. First we have the flat condemnation of *since* meaning "ago"; it appears in Bierce 1909, and a usage note in Webster 1909 testifying to the dislike of some critics suggests there were others besides Bierce. But the editors of Webster's Second deleted the 1909 note, and there seems to have been no basis for the objection. The sense is old, going back, according to the OED, to about 1489; Shakespeare used it, and many subsequent authors, including this well-known American of some years since:

I received, some time since, your *Dissertations on the English Language* —Benjamin Franklin, letter to Noah Webster, 26 Dec. 1789

This particular usage appears to be rather uncommon, and perhaps old-fashioned sounding, in current American English. It still is active in British English. It has currency in both British and American English in the phrase *long since*:

I should have done it long since —Veronica Milligan, *Observer Mag.*, 18 Nov. 1973

... I have long since learned to divide them into two classes —John Barkham, *Saturday Rev.*, 13 Feb. 1954

Note that this is interchangeable with *long ago* when the present perfect tense is used:

. . . would long ago have retired him —*Current Biography,* July 1964

But with other past tenses, *long ago* tends to be used rather than *long since*:

> Moscow long ago had to accept the Yugoslav heresy —Arthur M. Schlesinger, Jr., *Harper's,* March 1969

The affinity of *since* for the present perfect tense is also noted in Bryson 1984 and Bernstein 1965 (among others).

The second issue also concerns the same meaning. Here the use is not condemned, but instead the commentators limit *since* to time recently past and *ago* to time long past. Among these commentators were Vizetelly 1906, the synonymist of Webster 1909 (John Livingston Lowes), Whipple 1924, and Lurie 1927. Utter disagreed. The issue appears to have died.

Fowler 1926 raised the third issue in objecting to the tautology of employing *ago* and *since* in the same sentence:

> It is barely 150 years ago since it was introduced —example in Fowler 1926

His objection goes back to Baker 1770 ("*It is three years ago since his Father died.*—These Expressions don't make sense. . . .") and has been repeated as recently as Freeman 1983. Fowler calls the mistake very common, but the Merriam-Webster files do not bear that out, having added but a single example since Fowler was published:

> It is just a hundred years ago since there was published in Britain a famous report —Professor K. C. Wheare, *London Calling,* 16 Sept. 1954

Since this too is British, it is possible that the usage itself is chiefly British. *Ago* is certainly expendable in these examples, but its inclusion does not seem to be a problem of great moment.

sing Usage commentators dating back to Richard Grant White 1870 have agreed that *sang* is the usual past tense of sing. White regarded the past tense *sung* as an error, and a few more recent commentators have taken the same line, but most recognize that both *sang* and *sung* have had reputable use as the past tense of *sing*.

In current English, the past tense *sung* is not so much wrong as simply old-fashioned. Samuel Johnson in his 1755 Dictionary listed the past tense as *sung* or *sang*, but over the intervening two centuries, *sang* has come to predominate. Here are a few older examples with *sung*:

> Mrs. Bland sung it in boy's clothes the first time I heard it —Charles Lamb, letter, 2 Jan. 1810

> . . . Huldy was just like a bee: she always sung when she was workin —Harriet Beecher Stowe, "The Minister's Housekeeper," 1871, in *The Mirth of a Nation,* ed. Walter Blair & Raven I. McDavid, Jr., 1983

> Once M'Cola, in the dark . . . sung out a stream of what sounded like curses —Ernest Hemingway, *Green Hills of Africa,* 1935

sink Both *sank* and *sunk* are used for the past tense of *sink. Sank* is used more often, but *sunk* is neither rare nor dialectal as a past tense, though it is usually a past participle.

> He sank himself word by word into the literature —Robert Penn Warren, *Jefferson Davis Gets His Citizenship Back,* 1980

> Then I sunk back never again to blaze perhaps —Robert Frost, letter, 8 July 1935

> . . . when I saw that program listing my heart sank —Edith Oliver, *New Yorker,* 20 Nov. 1971

> . . . the squall that sunk the Pride of Baltimore —M. Murray, *Science News,* 2 Aug. 1986

sit See SET, SIT.

site See CITE, SITE, SIGHT.

situated Watt 1967 finds *situated* often used as padding, and *Winners & Sinners,* 21 Apr. 1988, elaborates upon the same theme. Here are two examples from the latter publication:

> . . . the centers are often situated in poor neighborhoods —*N.Y. Times,* 8 Mar. 1988

> The hall is situated on the college's campus —*N.Y. Times,* 21 Mar. 1988

The *Winners & Sinners* editor says that *situated* should have been omitted from both of these because it adds no information. But the question that should be asked is whether the sentence is improved by dropping the word. Some writers' ears for English prose will tell them immediately that in those examples something more readily stressed than a preposition is needed in the place where *situated* appears. Here is a similar *situated* from an essay; we doubt that the author would view with much favor a suggestion that he strike the word.

> The city, situated above the rapids and its clumps of vivid green islands . . . —William Styron, *This Quiet Dust and Other Writings,* 1982

Situated may be omissible in some contexts, but in others it serves a useful purpose. Remember: you need not delete words unless deletion improves the sentence. (The same objection has been raised against *locate,* which see).

situation The *situation* situation is a major concern in British usage circles, but not so much of a cause for comment by Americans. Criticism of *situation*, particularly in phrases like *emergency situation* and *strike situation* used in place of *emergency* and *strike*, appears to be a sort of post-World War II tradition in Britain; the topic begins with Gowers 1948 and receives more space in each of his succeeding editions (1954 and 1973); it is found in Fowler 1965 (which Gowers edited), Phythian 1979, Burchfield 1981, 1996, Bryson 1984, Longman 1988, and Amis 1998; it is discussed by J. Enoch Powell in Michaels & Ricks 1980 and by Robert F. Ilson in Greenbaum 1985. The criticized uses of *situation* have also been satirized in the British magazine *Private Eye*, in which particularly bad examples have appeared in a regular column headed "Ongoing Situations." (The phrase *ongoing situation*, for which we have almost no evidence, is especially notorious among the British. They also dislike *ongoing* by itself. See ONGOING.)

Most of what little American comment there has been on *situation* can be found in college handbooks, in which it is typically dismissed as padding. The jargonistic usage appears to be rare in American English. Here is a tongue-in-cheek sentence from a British commentator to give you a better idea of its quality:

> Clearly 'clearly' is in an ongoing perspicuity situation as a transparently vacuous vogue word —Howard 1980

Ilson in Greenbaum 1985 comments thoughtfully on two compounds—*crisis situation* and *no-win situation*—listed as objectionable by Burchfield. Ilson points out that a crisis situation is likely not to be quite the same as a crisis, and that *no-win situation* is a short way to express a fairly complex idea. These combinations are both found in American English:

> . . . the family doctor, . . . now being recast in a modern role as a specialist in comprehensive, continuing medicine, with as much emphasis on prevention as on crisis situations —Dodi Schultz, *Ladies' Home Jour.*, August 1971

> . . . the ingenious Mr. Jeffries juggles his plot so that the murderer is faced with a no-win situation —Newgate Callendar, *N.Y. Times Book Rev.*, 8 Jan. 1984

Neither of these combinations has attracted much criticism from American commentators. *No-win situation*, in particular, is established as a common idiom and is inoffensive to American ears. Other American uses of *situation* with a noun attributive modifier seem also to differ somewhat from those disliked by the British:

> Not necessarily the man for a heart-to-heart, but indispensable in a party situation —Jay McInerney, *Bright Lights, Big City*, 1984

> . . . to get the hostage situation out of the way —Charles Allen, quoted in *The Tower Commission Report*, 1987

We conclude that the British use of *situation*, especially in official jargon, is a bit different from American use. The jargon of the bureaucrat is, in any case, rather of an eddy along the mainstream of English. Its faults and virtues are essentially unchanging, and it seems to have little effect on general usage. *Situation* is one of those vague words that is useful when precision is not wanted. No doubt it can be and is used unnecessarily, but in American English, at least, there seems to be no reason to go out of your way to avoid it.

slate As a verb, *slate* has very different meanings in American and British English. In American English it commonly means "to schedule or designate":

> . . . how many employees are slated to be taken off the payroll —Maria Shao & Bill Paul, *Wall Street Jour.*, 28 June 1982

> . . . on Monday he's slated to appear in Kansas City —Curry Kirkpatrick, *Sports Illustrated*, 14 Feb. 1983

The meaning of the British *slate* is "to criticize severely":

> . . . she slated me like a fishwife for being a lazy slacker —Richard Hull, *The Murder of My Aunt*, 1934

> . . . a national weekly transport magazine which slates the use of the word "Transit" as an "Americanism" —*Evening Gazette* (Middlesbrough, England), 31 May 1974

The American *slate* and the British *slate* are two entirely different words. The American verb is derived from the familiar noun *slate*, while the British verb is thought to be derived from the little-used verb *slat*, which has among its senses "to hurl or throw smartly" and "to strike or pummel." Burchfield 1996 thinks that the use of *slate* in brief contexts like headlines (Summit Meeting Slated) might be ambiguous. But an American seeing it in an American newspaper would be unaware of the British interpretation.

slave In literal use, the noun *slave* usually takes *of* when it needs a prepositional-phrase complement:

> . . . a Nazi-ruled Europe . . . whose people would be made slaves of the German master race —William L. Shirer, *The Rise and Fall of the Third Reich*, 1960

Of also occurs with *slave* in figurative use, but *to* is more common:

> . . . much too functional as an accompaniment for a visual medium of which it is the slave —Otis L. Guernsey, Jr., *N.Y. Herald Tribune Book Rev.,* 7 Nov. 1954

> All his life he had been a slave to the land —Ellen Glasgow, *Barren Ground,* 1925

> . . . a habitual bird-watcher, a canoe addict, and a slave to the camping-out habit —Dwight Macdonald, *New Yorker,* 18 July 1953

slay The surviving and normal past tense of *slay* is *slew* (for an inkling of the huge variety of alternatives that once was, see the OED), and the past participle *slain.*

> . . . he slew twenty-nine adversaries in his lifetime —Robert Penn Warren, *Jefferson Davis Gets His Citizenship Back,* 1980

> . . . the Japanese swordsmen who are indifferent to getting slain —Flannery O'Connor, letter, 25 Nov. 1960

There is also a regular form *slayed.* It is sparsely attested as a dialectal form in the American Dialect Dictionary. Roberts 1954 and Longman 1988 note, and our evidence confirms, that it is usual with the showbiz sense "to be a great hit with" (stodgily defined in dictionaries as "overwhelm"):

> . . . it turns out *Harold and Maude* just slayed 'em in Japan —Ruth Gordon, quoted in *People,* 13 Oct. 1980

Slayed as the past tense for the "kill" sense seems to occur occasionally in speech. It is also sparsely attested in print. We have few examples; Garner 1998 has a few more. But *slayed* cannot be considered established in such use. Whether it eventually becomes established remains to be seen.

slow, slowly The controversy over whether *slow* is a proper adverb seems to have come in with the automobile, which brought with it the "GO SLOW" and "DRIVE SLOW" signs. We find comment on the subject as far back as 1917. The automotive aspect of the question is still sometimes mentioned:

> The adverb *slow* is used mainly by highway police, who order us to *go slow.* Careful writers prefer the adverb *slowly* —Oxford American Dictionary 1980

But restriction of adverbial *slow* to the vocabulary of policemen is simply uninformed. *Slow* is an old adverb, and it has had many users other than highway police:

> I pray you have a continent forbearance till the speed of his rage goes slower —Shakespeare, *King Lear,* 1606

> Faith this letter goes on but slow; it is a week old —Jonathan Swift, *Journal to Stella,* 16 Feb. 1711

> The war moves slow if it moves at all —Robert Frost, letter, 7 Mar. 1944

> He drives slower, staring ahead for the slightest clues of road —Garrison Keillor, *Lake Wobegon Days,* 1985

Slow, however, has a rather restricted range of application. Except in exclamatory expressions (". . . how slow they walk"), *slow* regularly follows the verb it modifies, and the verb is regularly one of action or motion. *Slowly* is more generally applicable. It can precede the verb:

> . . . a test, it is true, which can only be slowly and cautiously applied —T. S. Eliot, "Tradition and the Individual Talent," 1917, in *American Harvest,* ed. Allen Tate & John Peale Bishop, 1942

> It was almost as if something . . . were slowly circling the tent —Arthur C. Clarke, *Boy's Life,* August 1967

It can follow the same sort of verbs *slow* can:

> . . . because, she said, I drove too slowly —David Plante, *Difficult Women,* 1983

> . . . I tried to walk as slowly as I could —Ernest Hemingway, *Green Hills of Africa,* 1935

It appears in contexts where *slow* would not be idiomatic:

> . . . the leadership turned slowly toward bombing as a means of striking back —David Halberstam, *Harper's,* February 1971

> . . . grain by grain, as the pigeon said when he picked up the bushel of corn slowly —Edward Lear, letter, 29 May 1862

> . . . I did an abrupt about-face . . . and started walking slowly away —James Jones, *Harper's,* February 1971

Slowly also modifies participial adjectives:

> . . . the slowly accumulated intimacy on which Mrs. Wharton places such redeeming value —Richard Poirier, *A World Elsewhere,* 1966

> . . . stares gravely out over lines of slowly moving cars —Irwin Shaw, *Harper's,* September 1970

Slow is not used with past participles, but it can form compounds (usually hyphenated) with some present participles, including *moving:*

> . . . slow-moving shell-encrusted survivors from an earlier epoch —John Fischer, *Harper's,* February 1971

Slow and *slowly* should really present no usage problem. They each have their proper place, and good writers keep them there.

See also FLAT ADVERBS.

smell 1. In British English either *smelt* or *smelled* may be used as the past tense of this verb, while *smelled* is usual in the U.S.:

> I smelt the sooty reek of the oil flames —Benedict Allen, *Who Goes Out in the Midday Sun?*, 1986

> ". . . I smelt beer on the breath of a young lad. . . ." —Frank Palmer, *Daily Mirror* (London), 21 Nov. 1974

> . . . even the noblest in the land must have smelled a long way off —Hunter Davies, *Sunday Times Mag.* (London), 14 Apr. 1974

> I turned toward her and smelled that she'd brushed her teeth —John Irving, *The Hotel New Hampshire*, 1981

> As a boxing contest and as vaudeville, it smelled —Red Smith, *N.Y. Times,* 4 Oct. 1976

2. The question of whether the intransitive *smell* must be followed by an adjective or whether it may be followed by an adverb is discussed by a few commentators. *Smell* is one of those verbs, linking verbs often, that are used with both adjectives and adverbs. When a writer is describing the quality of a smell, an adjective is usual:

> . . . the soil of America smelled so good to them —Russell Lord, *Behold Our Land,* 1938

> On this score, Dante and Milton . . . don't smell neutral to us —Peter Viereck, *New Republic,* 7 June 1954

> . . . the smaller places usually smelt so awful that you wouldn't have noticed the preparation of a complete Tandoori meal —Barry Took, *Punch,* 13 Jan. 1976

But *smell* can also be used with an adverb of manner. Longman 1988 and Burchfield 1996 point out that adverbs are more likely to be used when *smell* means "stink":

> Abdullah wrinkled the edge of his flat nose and shook his head. They really smelled abominably —Ernest Hemingway, *Green Hills of Africa,* 1935

Smell is also frequently followed by a prepositional phrase introduced by *of.* In this construction, an adverb of manner is quite common:

> . . . smelt very powerfully of the fish they spent most of their lives catching —John Davies, *Annabel,* July 1974

> . . . who smelled quite as richly of class privilege as their British counterparts —John le Carré, *N.Y. Times Book Rev.,* 14 Oct. 1979

sneak, snuck *Sneak* is a word of mysterious origin. It first turns up around the end of the 16th century; John Lyly used it in a 1594 play called *Mother Bombie,* and Shakespeare used it in *Measure for Measure* (1605). It seems to have no sure antecedents. There is a possible source in Old English—a verb *snīcan,* of similar meaning. But Old English strong verbs of the class that *snīcan* belongs to came into modern English with *-ike* (as *strike* from *strīcan*), and there is no evidence extant in Middle English to connect *sneak* with *snīcan.* The original past and past participle of *sneak* were regular, *sneaked.* But sometime in the late 19th century a variant irregular form, *snuck,* began to appear in the United States.

> . . . an' den snuck home —*The Lantern* (New Orleans), 17 Dec. 1887

The *Lantern* citation is the earliest yet uncovered. The American Dialect Society turned up a few examples from around the turn of the century. The earliest printed citation in the Merriam-Webster files dates from 1902:

> Dock Knowital he Snuck Out the room an' Disappeared —Frank W. Sage, D.D.S., *Dental Digest,* November 1902

A decade later, *snuck* appeared in the stories of Ring Lardner:

> . . . I snuck off down the street and got something to eat —Ring Lardner, *You Know Me Al,* 1916

From these sparse pieces of evidence it appears that the few authors who had heard *snuck* considered it typical of the speech of rural and not overly educated Americans and they used it in generally humorous contexts. The members of the American Dialect Society who began collecting examples early in this century clearly assumed *snuck* to be a dialectal form. Novelists did too. From the 1930s on, *snuck* turns up in novels set in such various places as Tennessee, Ohio, and New England, often around the Civil War period. From the evidence we now have, use of *snuck* in a mid-19th-century setting would appear to be anachronistic.

Eventually *snuck* began to appear in contexts with a different purpose—not representing the comical speech of a bumpkin or the supposed dialect of a fictional character in the past, but in journalistic prose where it seems to be used for a lightening or humorous effect:

> . . . photographers snuck up and took pictures of the inventor sound asleep and snoring in the middle of the day —*N.Y. Herald Tribune Book Rev.,* 22 Jan. 1939

. . . I attended a fashion show the other day. I snuck in like a sneak —Vincent X. Flaherty, *Los Angeles Examiner,* 6 Apr. 1952

From such uses, it shortly began to appear in other kinds of contexts:

He snuck the Hearst collection away from Macy's, you know —an unnamed Gimbel's executive, quoted in *New Yorker,* 17 Feb. 1951

. . . I really hammed it up. I snuck an extra blanket under my bedspread, making sure I'd sweat plenty —William Goldman, *Temple of Gold,* 1957

Since the 1950s, *snuck* has appeared with increasing frequency in newspapers and magazines, primarily in straightforward contexts without humorous overtones. Two language surveys in the 1970s, one in Canada and one in the United States, revealed the use of *snuck* to be widespread—not restricted geographically—and to be more common among younger informants. If we assume that the younger informants will continue to use it as they grow older, it would seem that *snuck* stands a good chance to become the dominant form of the past and past participle. The results of these surveys corroborate the evidence in the Merriam-Webster files.

Usage commentators were slow to discover *snuck.* There seems to be little comment until the 1970s when a few critics offer remarks indicating they were aware of the way the word was being used in Ring Lardner's time. Some more recent commentators are aware of *snuck*'s increasing use in standard contexts, but they are still diffident.

In summary we can say that in about a century *snuck* has gone from an obscure and probably dialectal variant of the past and past participle to a standard, widely used variant that is almost as common as the older *sneaked.* Some evidence suggests it may become the predominant form in North American English. Occurrence in British English is rare but not unknown. Perhaps there is no better illustration of the rise of *snuck* to respectability than a comparison of Dr. Sage's 1902 use quoted early in this article with more recent ones:

Entitlements is a word that snuck into the political lexicon with few considering what it meant —*Wall Street Jour.,* 27 Mar. 1981

The ingredients of logic such as predicate, agreement, and proposition, and the compositional machinery to handle them, have to be snuck back in to get a model to do mindlike things —Steven Pinker, *How the Mind Works,* 1997

. . . in the nineteen-thirties, when "runner cars" snuck illegal whiskey past watchful

sheriffs —Nicole LaPorte, *New Yorker,* 20 Mar. 2000

Ever since Passover snuck in like a lamb last March —Joshua J. Hammerman, *Jewish Week,* 2–8 Sept. 1994

But, again, Ruddock has snuck his unexpected and modern signature into these rooms —Carol Vogel, *N.Y. Times Mag..* 15 Apr. 1984

so, *adverb* The use of *so* as an intensifier has been subject to criticism in usage books since at least MacCracken & Sandison 1917. Here is a succinct version of the usual warning:

Avoid, in writing, the use of *so* as an intensifier: "so good"; "so warm"; "so delightful." —Strunk & White 1959

But some commentators (notably Bryant 1962) have observed that the usage of intensive *so,* considered in its full range, is not quite as simple as these examples suggest. *So* is regularly used as an indefinite adverb of degree with the degree indicated by a following clause:

. . . and so frightened Mark Twain that he died —James Thurber, letter, 2 May 1946

It had gone so simply and easily that he thought it might be worthless —Ernest Hemingway, "An African Betrayal," in *Sports Illustrated,* 5 May 1986

When there is no following clause, *so* becomes more of an intensifier. Nevertheless, it may sometimes be rooted in material that went before in the context:

I cannot be so patient with the White House —David A. Stockman, *Newsweek,* 28 Apr. 1986

I don't know why it got on my nerves so —Peter Taylor, *The Old Forest and Other Stories,* 1985

And in another intensive use—never criticized—*so* indicates a definite degree that is implied rather than specified:

Many thanks for sending me so truly welcome a piece of news —Lewis Carroll, letter, 17 June 1893

. . . the kind of sterile over-ingenuity which afflicts so many academic efforts —*Times Literary Supp.,* 2 Oct. 1969

This use is frequently found in negative contexts:

. . . the word ballet was not so well known then —G. B. L. Wilson, *Dance News,* May 1982

What we are not so keen on is getting the truth —Anthony Quinton, *N.Y. Times Book Rev.,* 15 July 1984

The criticized use of the intensive *so* occurs when it means "to a large and indefinite extent or degree" and functions much like *very, exceedingly,* or *extremely.* In general, the written contexts in which this *so* appears are informal; since the use is common in speech, it naturally gravitates to contexts that are close to speech. A few commentators call it a feminine use, and we do, of course, have evidence of its use by women:

> ... how am I to read these books? What is the right way to get about it? They are so many and so various. My appetite is so fitful and so capricious —Virginia Woolf, "How Should One Read a Book?" 1926, in *Yale Review Anthology,* 1942

Robin Lakoff, in *Language and Woman's Place* (1975), agrees that this intensive *so* is more common in women's language than men's, "though certainly men can use it." Indeed, they can and do:

> ... on the ground under the shelf were little orange and magnolia trees. It looked so pretty —Mark Twain, letter, 1 June 1857

> ... she chose a little red one from high on the vine, wiped it on her dress, and bit off half of it. It was so good, and then the bright sunshine made her sneeze —Garrison Keillor, *Lake Wobegon Days,* 1985

> ... I'm dreadfully sorry to hear about all the pains and colds and everything, it is so discouraging —E. B. White, letter, 4 Feb. 1942

> I appreciate your sending the sporting magazines and the Book Reviews ever so much —Ernest Hemingway, letter, 20 Mar. 1925

> This is me, Winston Churchill, speaking himself to you, and I am so glad to be able to thank you in this remarkable way —quoted in *Time,* 1 Apr. 1946

We can see that men are not afraid of the usage, at least in their letters.

Clearly the intensive *so* is well established (the OED traces it back to Old English), and in spite of the adjurations of the commentators it is not avoided in speech or in informal writing. In its less noticeable varieties it can even appear in more formally edited prose. You may, however, want to avoid its baldest form— where it modifies an otherwise unadorned adjective ("The scenery was *so* beautiful!") —in your most serious writing.

so, *conjunction*   Except for the repeated complaint in schoolbooks and college handbooks that *so* is overused as a connective, opinion about conjunctional *so* is divided. Some critics tell us that *so that* should be used instead of *so* in both clauses of result and clauses of purpose; others think *so* is all right to introduce

clauses of result but *so that* should be used for clauses of purpose; and still others find *so* all right in both uses but *so that* more formal.

In spite of what the usage books say about *so that* being the more appropriate in formal prose, however, we do not find much difference in level of formality between *so* and *so that* in our evidence. You can judge their relative formality in the following examples (in which you will also note that the clause introduced by *so* may be a separate sentence). First, clauses of result:

> Rarely here is one more than a few miles from a great brackish tideland stream ... , so that what is specifically Southern becomes commingled with the waterborne, the maritime —William Styron, *This Quiet Dust and Other Writings,* 1982

> It was a convention of each periodical that the work was directed by a projector ... whose imaginary personality was adopted by each contributor. So Boswell's essays were written by The Hypochondriack —John Butt, *English Literature in the Mid-Eighteenth Century,* edited & completed by Geoffrey Carnall, 1979

> One of the actors fumbled every line and kept saying "Balls," so that fifteen speeches ended with this word —James Thurber, letter, Summer 1950

> "Realistic" politicians have prided themselves on understanding that "the people" are concerned only with ... bread-and-butter issues—taxes, inflation, and the like. So they have been frequently surprised —Elizabeth Drew, *New Yorker,* 3 May 1982

And clauses of purpose:

> ... some overtures to be made to what were described as more moderate elements within the Iranian Government, and it was related to establishing a relationship so that we would have some influence in the future —Edwin Meese 3d, quoted in *The Tower Commission Report,* 1987

> ... about to lose his fight to save his "Garden of Eden" from city officials who want to bulldoze it so low-income housing can be constructed —*New Yorker,* 8 July 1985

> Just be sure you've got the guts. So that if you have to steal or take a sap to someone's head for a meal, you'll be able to —E. L. Doctorow, *Loon Lake,* 1979

> ... and half the citizens don't know or care where they were born just so they can get somewhere fast —Robert Penn Warren, *Jefferson Davis Gets His Citizenship Back,* 1980

Conjunctive *so* can also introduce clauses other than clauses of purpose and result:

The American League East is a demanding division, I said, but with their pitching the O's could not lose many games in a row. . . . And so the season has started, and Baltimore, at this writing, is at four and twelve, and dead last —Roger Angell, *New Yorker*, 7 May 1984

. . . could get baskets full of horror stories about teaching. So who would they surprise? —Ken Donelson, *English Jour.*, November 1982

There does not seem to be much reason for you to fret over the choice between *so* and *so that*. We see little difference between *so* and *so that* in level of formality at present.

so . . . as See AS . . . AS 1.

so-called Several commentators find fault with using quotation marks to enclose a term or terms following *so-called*, as in "you and your so-called 'friends.' " Their advice is to omit either the quotation marks or the *so-called*: "you and your so-called friends" or "you and your 'friends.' " Our evidence shows that in edited writing quotation marks are in fact more often than not omitted after *so-called*:

The so-called gender gap . . . —Nancy J. Walker, *N.Y. Times Book Rev.*, 11 Mar. 1984

These so-called Watergate Babies . . . —Tip O'Neill with William Novak, *Man of the House*, 1987

But their use is not at all rare:

. . . their so-called "news value" . . . —Orville Schell, *N.Y. Times Book Rev.*, 11 May 1983

. . . the so-called "Fifth Generation" of computers . . . —Paul Delany, *N.Y. Times Book Rev.*, 18 Mar. 1984

The use of quotation marks following *so-called* is a matter of choice, but they are just as easily and sensibly omitted.

so far as See AS FAR AS, SO FAR AS.

solicitous It is possible to be solicitous *about, for*, or *of* something:

. . . as if he were shy and solicitous about it, and wanted to protect it from us —Edmund Wilson, *Axel's Castle*, 1931

Contracts . . . are the objects about which the constitution is solicitous —John Marshall, *Dartmouth College* v. *Woodward*, 1819

. . . what naturalist with a microscope in his pocket, what scholar solicitous for the changing shapes of language —Virginia Woolf, *The Second Common Reader*, 1932

. . . no one solicitous for the future of American culture —Jacques Barzun, *Saturday Rev.*, 9 Mar. 1940

. . . if only Pamela would try to be a little less solicitous of my welfare —Roald Dahl, *Someone Like You*, 1953

. . . parents solicitous of the moral welfare of their progeny —George Jean Nathan, *Encyclopaedia of the Theatre*, 1940

Much less commonly, *solicitous* is followed by *toward*:

For its part, the All England made sincere attempts to be more solicitous toward its athletic minions —Frank Deford, *Sports Illustrated*, 12 July 1982

And it has had some use with *to* and the infinitive:

. . . an opinion which he had seemed solicitous to give —Jane Austen, *Persuasion*, 1818

. . . Middleton is solicitous to please his audience —T. S. Eliot, "Thomas Middleton," in *Selected Essays*, 1932

solon *Solon*, the name of a wise lawgiver of ancient Athens, has been used figuratively as an English word for many centuries, but it has never been remarkably common or widespread. Most of its figurative uses have had a strongly ironic quality. Its greatest popularity has been among 20th-century American journalists, who have employed it as an occasional—somethimes sneering—synonym for *legislator*:

. . . in the U.S. Senate 35 years ago, when the solons were debating the Civil Rights Act —Dan Seligman, *Forbes*, 20 Sept. 1999

. . . many solons were already poised to ratchet down further the reimbursement rates —Ann Reilly Dowd, *Fortune*, 14 Nov. 1994

It is occasionally used for a presumed wise man:

That's the question that has the movie solons tugging at their gray beards and wondering —Richard Corliss, *Time*, 23 Nov. 1998

Solon in its current use has been criticized as journalese by several commentators. You probably won't need the word.

solution When used with a preposition, *solution* is usually followed by *of* or *to*:

. . . the solution of the mystery of existence —Sherwood Anderson, *Poor White*, 1920

. . . the intervention of government for the solution of problems that cannot be solved by private enterprise —*Current Biography*, July 1967

. . . has tried to find a peaceful solution to the Cyprus crisis —*Current Biography,* September 1964

. . . presumably his solution to the problem will carry some weight —J. D. O'Hara, *Saturday Rev.,* 20 May 1972

Occasionally *solution* is followed by *for*:

. . . the population [was] too backward for political independence to be considered as a current solution for their problems —*Collier's Year Book,* 1949

some, *adjective*   Like the adverb (see SOME, *adverb* 3), adjective *some* is used as an intensive, but its appearance usually draws no stronger reprobation from the commentators who notice it than the label colloquial or informal. It is, in fact, always found in casual surroundings and more often in speech than in writing of any kind. Here are a few examples:

You'd be some kind of hitter if you took a wider stance —Willie Mays, quoted in *Sporting News,* 25 Mar. 1966

MacLeish looks a little like Doctor Devol, and he is some smooth poet —E. B. White, letter, 31 Jan. 1942

. . . that was some sustained drive —Arnold Dean, radio broadcast of football game, 21 Sept. 1974

. . . it had taken her some doing to get it —Liz Smith, *Cosmopolitan,* February 1972

some, *pronoun*   The indefinite pronoun *some* is governed by notional agreement and may take either a singular or plural verb. *Some of* followed by a plural noun or pronoun takes a plural verb:

. . . demonstrated that some of the new particles were slow to decay —*Current Biography,* February 1966

And some of them are saying that . . . —Margaret Mead, *Barnard Alumnae,* Winter 1971

When a singular mass or collective noun follows *some of,* a singular verb is usual:

Some of the biggest news in knits this year is being made at home —Nora O'Leary, *Ladies' Home Jour.,* August 1971

Some of the office staff was there —E. L. Doctorow, *Ragtime,* 1975

When *some* stands by itself, the source of the notional agreement will be only in the writer's mind or in more distant context, but it will still prevail. This *some* usually takes a plural verb when it means "some people":

It may be, as some argue, that . . . —Amos Elon, *New Yorker,* 29 July 1985

Some feel we are not treating other people in the world fairly —W. E. Brock, *AAUP Bulletin,* September 1969

The use of a singular verb with this sense, as in a recent newspaper headline which read "Should Meals Be Included in Education Budget? Some Thinks So," is distinctly odd-sounding. But when *some* stands for part of a mass, a singular verb is usual:

The text . . . is rather uneven. Much is summary and factual. . . . Some has undertones of . . . —*Times Literary Supp.,* 24 Nov. 1966

See also AGREEMENT, INDEFINITE PRONOUNS; NOTIONAL AGREEMENT, NOTIONAL CONCORD.

some, *adverb*   **1.** When *some* is used to modify a number, it has the force of *about* and is almost always tacked onto a round number:

. . . would by now have collected some $500 billion from the tax —Felix G. Rohatyn, *The Twenty-Year Century,* 1983

. . . ordered the slaughter of some 20,000 of his brother's followers in Rome —Robert Payne, *Saturday Rev.,* 18 Mar. 1972

There has been occasional objection (Bernstein 1958, 1965, 1977, Copperud 1970, 1980) to *some* used with numbers that are not approximate. Such usage seems to take two forms. First, with dates: since years and centuries are equivalent more or less to round numbers, *some* usually retains its meaning of "about":

Some fifteen years ago, a gentleman representing an exclusive and expensive special-editions club came to the office —James Thurber, letter, August 1947

. . . a point in time some fourteen centuries before the earliest authentic example —*Times Literary Supp.,* 19 Feb. 1971

The second example also suggests the second use of *some* with numbers that are not approximate: as a mild intensifier, used as if to elicit "Wow! That many?" from the reader. Bernstein has a perfect example:

Some 35,683 attended the races at Aqueduct —Bernstein 1958, 1965

And here is one from our own files:

An expert parachutist, he has some 115 jumps to his credit —*Current Biography,* July 1965

Some is certainly omissible in such contexts, but it does provide an emphasis which would otherwise be lacking. It is also good to keep in mind that a unit that seems quite precise to you may not be so precise to someone accustomed to smaller units. It would be overfastidious, for instance, to object to *some* in a context like this one:

> . . . had, collectively, improved the boat's upwind speed by some six seconds a mile in winds of 18 knots and up —Sarah Ballard, *Sports Illustrated,* 26 Jan. 1987

2. A favorite with usage writers for more than a century has been the subject of the use of *some* in the sense "somewhat." It can be found as early as 1869 and as recently as 1988, and probably even more recently. Evidence in the OED suggests that the usage has two sources. As the modifier of a comparative ("some better"), it seems to have belonged originally to Scots or northern English dialect. As the postpositive modifier of a verb ("has grown some"), it is apparently not dialectal. Both uses were imported to America from Great Britain, and the outbreak of comment in the later 19th century was apparently in reaction to popular 19th-century spoken American usage.

Commentary on this subject has varied little over the years. The repeated prescription has been to use *somewhat* in place of *some,* which was called dialectal and provincial in Vizetelly 1906 but has more recently been labeled informal, colloquial, or nonstandard. The basic prescription is, however, more than a little oversimplified. The only use in which *somewhat* is virtually certain to substitute smoothly is the one where *some* precedes a comparative:

> She does feel some better, and is able to take short walks —E. B. White, letter, 14 Feb. 1963

Our most recent evidence shows very few examples of this construction in writing, in spite of its being mentioned in almost every usage book since Bache 1869.

And our recent evidence shows that *some* following the verb is the usual construction. When *some* is itself followed by *more,* you certainly would not want to use *somewhat* instead:

> Here in Newport, both Southern Cross and Courageous practiced some more —William N. Wallace, *N.Y. Times,* 10 Sept. 1974

But in what is by far the most common construction in our evidence *some* stands alone after the verb. It can sometimes be replaced by *somewhat,* but it also occurs commonly in contexts where *somewhat* is not idiomatic:

> But I've been brooding some about it —E. B. White, letter, 4 Feb. 1942

> She wept some, and tried to retract —William Faulkner, "Centaur in Brass," in

The Collected Stories of William Faulkner, 1950

> I know him some, not well —*And More by Andy Rooney,* 1982

> . . . was slowing down some, now that he'd reached middle age —Andrew H. Malcolm, *N.Y. Times Mag.,* 23 Mar. 1986

> He also helped out some at Ben & Jerry's —Calvin Trillin, *New Yorker,* 8 July 1985

> She may be oversimplifying some —Jay Cocks, *Time,* 19 Mar. 1984

The evidence shows, in short, that the adverbial *some,* in the senses "in some degree; to some extent; a little; somewhat," is a well-established American idiom. It is freely used in edited prose, although it seems not to be found in prose of the highest formality. You need not (and sometimes cannot) automatically replace it with *somewhat* when it is used in constructions like those illustrated above.

3. There is also an intensive adverbial *some,* best known, perhaps, in the combinations *going some* and *go some:*

> I still retain my pure English, even when I lose my temper, which is going some —Kenneth McGaffey, *The Sorrows of a Show Girl,* 1908 (in A Dictionary of Americanisms 1951)

> . . . will have to go some to surpass the April program —Robert J. Armbruster, *Johns Hopkins Mag.,* June 1970

This sense is attested as modifying a following adjective, too. Our most recent examples associate it with the state of Maine:

> I knew one thing: With that eye he looked some funny —Oscar Cronk, Jr. (identified as a Maine trapper), quoted in *Sports Illustrated,* 24 Jan. 1983

> The salmon preparation . . . was, in the argot of Maine and Long Island lobstermen, some good —Jay Jacobs, *Gourmet,* April 1985

Earlier it had use outside of Maine:

> Husky young fellow, nice voice, steady, clear eyes, kinda proud, I thought, an' some handsome —Zane Grey, *Desert Gold,* 1913

M. H. Scargill, in *A Short History of Canadian English* (1977), mentions *some hot* "really hot" as existing in Canadian English. Editors of the Dictionary of American Regional English tell us that this use is currently attested in Hawaii, Texas, and New Jersey, as well as Maine (and elsewhere in northern New England). It also exists in British dialect. It looks to us like a form that was once rather widespread but has survived in speech only in scattered places.

somebody, someone 1. *Somebody* and *someone* are two of those curious indefinite pronouns that take a singular verb but are often referred to by the plural pronouns *they, their,* and *them.* A number of commentators are on record as insisting on grounds of logical consistency that singular pronouns be used. The governing principle in the choice of pronouns is notional agreement, and when the speaker or writer has more than one person in mind, or a very indefinite somebody, the plural pronoun tends to be used:

"Somebody told me they thought he killed a man once." —F. Scott Fitzgerald, *The Great Gatsby,* 1925

You talk to someone like Dore Schary, and they say, 'Miss Cornell, wouldn't you be interested in making a picture?' —Katherine Cornell, quoted in *Time,* 20 Apr. 1953

. . . if he finds someone who needs help . . . he should tell them where they can get it or offer to pass on their name —*Times Literary Supp.,* 4 Apr. 1968

. . . too nice a man to decline when someone says they want him to show up at one of their functions so they can honor him —*And More by Andy Rooney,* 1982

Then someone suggested knocking off early and getting some beer and they even offered to chip in for a bottle of Chivas Regal for Manny —Joseph Wambaugh, *Lines and Shadows,* 1984

You will note that in some of these examples the choice of *they, their, them* contrasts usefully with another pronoun which is third person singular.

When a singular pronoun is used to refer to *somebody* or *someone,* the speaker or writer often seems to have someone specific in mind (or in Alice's case, in sight):

"I see somebody now!" she exclaimed at last. "But he's coming very slowly. . . ." —Lewis Carroll, *Through the Looking-Glass,* 1871

. . . till somebody happened to note it as the only case he had met . . . —Henry James, "The Turn of the Screw," 1898

. . . it was a bit risky to bring him home as eventualities might possibly ensue (somebody having a temper of her own sometimes) —James Joyce, *Ulysses,* 1922

But the singular pronoun is also used when the *someone* or *somebody* is not specific:

If someone doesn't carry any money, the chances are he's loaded. I'm not sure about rich women, but I know rich men don't usually have a nickel with them —*And More by Andy Rooney,* 1982

See also AGREEMENT: INDEFINITE PRONOUNS; NOTIONAL AGREEMENT, NOTIONAL CONCORD; THEY, THEIR, THEM.

2. Copperud 1980 has a curious note to the effect that it is a superstition that *someone* is preferable to *somebody,* and Shaw 1987 mentions it too. *Somebody* and *someone* are of the same age, according to the OED, and when the OED came out, *somebody* was much better attested. In the 20th century, however, *someone* has come on strong, and we have more evidence now for *someone* than for *somebody.* But both, of course, are equally standard; use whichever one you think sounds better in a given context.

somebody else's See ELSE 1.

someone See SOMEBODY, SOMEONE.

someplace *Someplace* is like *anyplace,* an adverb that has become standard in American English during the 20th century. A few commentators still call it an informal word and discourage its written use in favor of *somewhere,* but our evidence shows that *someplace* has been common in general and even academic writing since at least the 1940s:

. . . which we fear because someplace therein lurks a terror, the beast, which we cannot see —William Van O'Connor, *Sense and Sensibility in Modern Poetry,* 1948

If the Government is going to raise the same amount of revenue with a flat rate tax system as it raises under the present system, it is going to have to get the money from someplace —Daniel Q. Posin, *Federal Income Taxation of Individuals,* 1983

Members of this group tend to be located someplace other than Japan —James Fallows, *Atlantic,* August 1989

Note that you will want *someplace* if your next word is *where*:

A gifted reporter can write a memorable book about someplace where nothing much is happening —Geoffrey Wheatcroft, *N.Y. Times Book Rev.,* 25 Nov. 1990

See also ANYPLACE; EVERYPLACE; NOPLACE.

something The adverb *something,* synonymous with *somewhat,* is now something less of an adverb than it once was. In previous centuries, it was used in ways that made its adverbial nature unmistakable:

There is one Bill ordered to be brought in of a something new nature —Andrew Marvell, letter, 1666 (OED)

"Answer for thyself, Friar," said King Richard, something sternly —Sir Walter Scott, *Ivanhoe,* 1819

Now, however, it prefers to keep a low profile. The OED notes that it "chiefly survives in contexts which admit of the word being felt as a noun." Here are some examples of typical current use:

... have to pay nonresidence entrance fees, averaging something over $300 —Frank J. Taylor, *Saturday Evening Post,* 24 May 1958

The critical response . . . was something less than enthusiastic —*Current Biography,* May 1966

Something more than two centuries later —Gorham Munson, *Southern Rev.,* April 1970

Another use of the adverb *something* is as an intensive modifying an adjective like *awful, fierce,* and *terrible* when the adjective is being used adverbially. A bit confusing, perhaps, but here is an example of what we are talking about:

... they cried and took on something terrible until I removed my wig —Bob Hope, *Saturday Evening Post,* 10 Apr. 1951

The main function of *something* in such a context seems to be to give adverbial force to the adjective, so that "something terrible" is really just another way of saying "terribly." This use of *something* is rare in writing.

sometime 1. The adverb is written as a single word: "He arrived sometime last night." A phrase combining the adjective *some* and the noun *time* is written as two words: "He needed some time to think"; "We haven't seen them for some time." The difference is easy to see in these examples, but it is not always so clear. Consider the sentence "He arrived some time ago." The difference between *sometime last night* and *some time ago* may not be instantly apparent, since both phrases have an adverbial function. In *some time ago,* however, *some* and *time* still function within the phrase itself as an adjective and a noun, like *five* and *minutes* in the phrase *five minutes ago.* An easy way to tell if *some* and *time* should be written as one word or two in most contexts is to insert *quite* before *some* and see if the passage still makes sense. If it does, *some* and *time* should be written separately: "We haven't seen them for quite some time"; "He arrived quite some time ago." If it does not, *sometime* is the correct choice.
2. The adjective *sometime* has two meanings, the older of which is "former":

... a sometime Communist . . . refuses to say whether he is a Communist now —*National Rev.,* 30 June 1970

... a sometime English professor turned administrator —Bruce Dearing, *CEA Forum,* April 1971

In its newer sense, *sometime* is essentially equivalent to *occasional.* This sense was first attested in the 1930s. It appears to have originated in the southern U.S., but in recent decades it has worked its way into the mainstream of American English:

... was a sometime participant in the international activities of Dada after the First World War —Roger Shattuck, *N.Y. Rev. of Books,* 12 Mar. 1970

It is for this sometime shrillness of tone that one criticizes Mr. Brackman —Edmund Fuller, *Wall Street Jour.,* 8 Sept. 1980

... was the confidant, adviser and sometime agent of Presidents from Franklin D. Roosevelt to Lyndon B. Johnson —William V. Shannon, *N.Y. Times Book Rev.,* 28 Oct. 1984

It often occurs in the phrase *a sometime thing,* where its meaning may tend toward "unreliable" or "transient":

... feel that the health care in pro football is a sometime thing —William Barry Furlong, *N.Y. Times Mag.,* 30 Nov. 1980

It turned out in later years that Mr. Frank's liberalism was no sometime thing —Suzanne Garment, *Wall Street Jour.,* 27 Feb. 1981

someway, someways The adverb *someway,* synonymous with *somehow,* is recognized by dictionaries as standard in American English, but its standing among usage commentators is less certain. Our evidence shows that *someway* occurs at all levels of writing, but is not especially common at any of them. It sometimes shows up in representations of dialectal speech:

I hate the hawks eatin' the quail, but I don't someway mind the 'coons eatin' the grapes —Marjorie Kinnan Rawlings, *The Yearling,* 1938 (OED Supplement)

But it also appears in much more formal contexts:

Someway, somehow, we must let the peoples of the world know that. We must reach behind the façade of ministers and cabinets and commissions —William O. Douglas, *Being an American,* 1948

The variant *someways* is rare. Its use in writing is limited to representations of speech:

"Oh, it's a good morning. I someways like a day just like this. . . ." —Elizabeth Madox Roberts, *My Heart and My Flesh,* 1927

somewhat See SOME, *adverb* 2.

somewheres *Somewheres* is, like *anywheres* and *nowheres,* a dialectal Americanism that is not used in standard writing. Its written use is limited almost entirely to dialogue:

> A police man come and said, . . . you all git on somewheres else so I won't have to run you in —Robert Penn Warren, in *New Directions,* 1947

> "Oughta be a lamp somewheres around the place. . . ." —Burt Arthur, *The Buckaroo,* 1947

See also ANYWHERES; NOWHERES.

sooner See NO SOONER.

sort, sort of, sort of a See KIND 1; KIND OF, SORT OF; KIND OF A, SORT OF A.

so that See SO, *conjunction.*

sparing *Sparing* is generally followed by *in* or *of* when it is complemented by a prepositional phrase:

> The English, for instance, are sparing in their use of it —David Abercrombie, *English Language Teaching,* October–December 1954

> . . . again the music critics were sparing in their praise —*Current Biography,* February 1966

> He was lavish of encouragement, sparing of negation —Samuel Hopkins Adams, *Incredible Era,* 1939

> Miss Foley's foreword . . . is notably sparing of generalizations —Milton Crane, *Saturday Rev.,* 5 Sept. 1953

Occasionally, *sparing* is found with *with*:

> Unfortunately, however, Ellison is too sparing with this gift of characterization —*American Mercury,* June 1952

spay, spayed, spade, spaded *Spay* is a transitive verb meaning "to remove the ovaries of (a female animal)." Its most familiar use is in the form of the past participle, *spayed*:

> . . . their jittery spayed terrier —John Updike, *Couples,* 1968

> . . . found in spayed females —Susan L. Mathews, *Cats Mag.,* September 1984

A synonymous verb is *spade,* which was first recorded in 1611, and which undoubtedly originated from a misunderstanding of *spayed.* The OED labels *spade* obsolete as a synonym of *spay,* but we find that its use is now fairly common (quite possibly, its modern use represents a recoinage rather than a continued use of the old verb). It seems to be mostly a speech

form. Our only modern written evidence is from classified advertisements:

> LOST German shepard [sic] spaded dog —classified advt., *Springfield* (Mass.) *Union,* 30 June 1953

Spade also sometimes appears as a misspelling of *spayed*:

> OLD ENGLISH Sheep Dog, spade —classified advt., *Denver Post,* 20 Sept. 1984

special, specially, especial, especially These words are etymologically the same, so they might be expected to be synonymous. That they are essentially synonymous is at least historically true, but in present-day English they are not synonymous very often. When they are, it is usually *special* and *specially* that are used like *especial* and *especially* rather than the other way around.

Special is the older and more widely used of the adjectives. It has all the fixed phrases, like *special delivery, special effects,* and *special interest,* and all the euphemistic uses, like *special needs, special education,* and *special children. Especial,* as the less usual word, is therefore somewhat more emphatic:

> . . . dissected in minute detail but with especial glee —Tony Palmer. *Observer Mag.,* 16 Dec. 1973

> In fact Mexicanness is concentrated with especial flair in this small provincial capital —Jan Morris, *Locations,* 1992

Special would not work as well in either of those contexts. But a present-day writer would most likely use *special* for Jane Austen's *especial* here:

> . . . I must wait till there is an especial assembly for the representation of younger sons —*Mansfield Park,* 1814

The adverbs, however, are much different. While *especially* is apparently much the more common word in general, *specially* has typical uses that *especially* lacks:

> . . . treats his friends very specially —Samuel G. Freedman, *N.Y. Times Mag.,* 21 Apr. 1985

> The plants have been specially selected to associate well —Roy Hay, *The Times* (London), 17 Nov. 1973

> The breeder who has a range of specially constructed kennels —Roy Genders, *Greyhounds,* 1960

Especially would not be used in any of those contexts. It typically is found in constructions like the following:

> . . . even thereafter the older use survived, especially in fixed phrases like 'I know not'

—W. F. Bolton, *A Short History of Literary English,* 1967

It is an especially British condition, I think —Jan Morris, *N.Y. Times Mag.,* 2 Feb. 1975

. . . seems to have been built especially for developmental research —Gary Blonston, *Science 84,* March 1984

Specially is sometimes used in the same constructions. It has a somewhat more informal quality:

. . . the history of the American South, specially that of the state of Virginia —Douglas Tallack, *British Book News,* April 1984

. . . euphemism, which is an effort to make something sound specially nice —Robert M. Adams, *N.Y. Times Book Rev.,* 31 Mar. 1985

An appropriate bread is baked specially for the dinner —Caroline Bates, *Gourmet,* October 1981

Specially seems to be a stronger competitor of *especially* in the construction of the third example—modifying a preceding verb—than in those of the first two. It is much less likely to be used in constructions like these:

Especially did she disagree with the observation that social stability is not a precondition for the writing of a novel —Norman Cousins, *Saturday Rev.,* 24 June 1978

. . . there was nothing especially radical in the notion —Stanley Karnow, *N.Y. Times Mag.,* 15 Jan. 1978

species, specie The word *species* has the same form both in the singular and the plural:

. . . it ranks as a new species —Norman Myers, *Natural History,* February 1985

There are about thirty thousand species of spiders throughout the world —Katherine W. Moseley, *Massachusetts Audubon,* June 1971

That final *s* looks like a plural ending, however, and it fools some people into thinking that the singular form must be *specie.* This is scarcely a modern corruption, as the OED's first record of *specie* as the singular of *species* is from 1711, and they have half a dozen more citations from the 18th and 19th centuries. Our own files provide a number of 20th-century examples:

Working in a studio where . . . 75 to 100 Dall sheep are mounted annually, I have become extremely familiar with this specie —Robert Holshouser, *Breakthrough,* September 1986

. . . some new specie appears that is difficult to classify —John P. Marquand, *New England Journeys,* 1953

Some people think God made the universe in six days and personally handcrafted each plant and animal specie —Sanford Berman, *Library Jour.,* 15 Oct. 1985

The evidence we have accumulated in recent decades shows that this use of *specie* is not yet sufficiently widespread to be considered standard. The standard use of *specie* in current English is as a noun meaning "money in coin":

With a limited amount of specie in the country, . . . the American monetary system was uniquely ill-qualified to cope with financial "panics" —Martin Mayer, *The Bankers,* 1974

. . . where money was necessary and specie scarce —Arthur M. Schlesinger, Jr., *The Age of Jackson,* 1945

spell Not long ago one of our correspondents asking for information used these words in her letter:

. . . how words with variant spellings will be spelt in our publication.

This gave us some recent evidence that *spelt,* which is much more common in British English, is still occasionally used in American English. Here are two British examples:

. . . culture is spelt with a small "c" —Michael Watkins, *The Guardian,* 27 Oct. 1973

Misspelt names bring newspapers into disrepute. They should be spelt out, spelt back, and re-checked —Sellers 1975

Americans generally use *spelled*:

These jolly buccaneers knew that rum spelled "gold" —Marilyn Kayter, *American Way,* December 1971

The ability to convert a field goal spelled the difference —*Sporting News,* 27 Dec. 1972

The past tense of the unrelated *spell* "to relieve for a time" always is *spelled*:

For the next seven hours, several planes spelled each other —Michael McRae, *Outside,* December 1985

spelling Ernest Hemingway, in a letter to F. Scott Fitzgerald, made this remark in his first paragraph:

You write a swell letter. Glad somebody spells worse than I do —24 Dec. 1925

Fitzgerald was notorious for his bad spelling, although one of his editors says in his defense that his spelling seemed worse than it really was because he consistently misspelled certain words. Hemingway, on the other hand, was an inconsistent misspeller; he could spell a word both right and wrong in the same letter.

It does not seem the least bit strange to talk about someone's misspelling words. We do it all the time, and quite a few usage commentators have been fond of belittling their correspondents (the ones who disagree with them) and others on the basis of bad spelling. But bad spelling is a flimsy basis for belittling anyone; you can see that the literary reputations of Fitzgerald and Hemingway have not suffered noticeably by their personal difficulties with English orthography. Nor is it easy to think of any writer who made a considerable reputation on the basis of slick spelling alone.

Wilson 1987 makes the interesting observation that "spelling is mostly a neuromuscular skill in the development of which practice helps, but for which certain innate equipment is the main requirement." In this respect it is rather like swinging a golf club or hitting a tennis ball. You know you can improve by practice, but you also know that Tiger Woods will putt better and Andre Agassi will serve better than you, no matter how much practicing you do. Aptitude for spelling is no more evenly distributed in the population than is aptitude for golf or tennis. We all have to make the best of the ability we have. Those whose innate ability to spell is not especially high can take heart by remembering that there are various devices—dictionaries and computer spelling checkers, for instance—that can be more useful to a bad speller than a new putter is to a bad golfer.

The idea of bad spelling is a relatively new one. If Ben Jonson had corresponded familiarly with William Shakespeare, he would not have made the sort of wisecrack that Hemingway made to Fitzgerald. In Shakespeare's time there were no rules for spelling English, a situation which troubled some reformers. Thomas Smith, John Hart, and William Bullokar, from about the mid-1560s to the 1580s, separately published works advocating phonetic spelling systems. Perhaps they were reacting to the Latin-based tinkering with English spelling that was going on at about the same time, in which a number of words were remodeled according to their real or supposed ultimate classical source. Many of these tinkerings have come down to us. For instance, *avance* became *advance; faucon, falcon; parfit, perfect; dette, debt; doutte, doubt; vittles, victuals*; and *savacion, salvation* (these particular examples are drawn from McKnight 1928 and Strang 1970). Some of these tinkerings were downright erroneous: the *s* in *island,* for one, has no business being there; the word is not related to *isle* (from early French) but comes from Old English *igland* or *iegland*. The *c* in *scissors* and *scythe* is a similar intruder. But we live with them all today.

The conventional spelling of today was arrived at only gradually. The two primary influences in its development were printers and dictionaries. Printers began the trend toward consistency in the 17th century. When large dictionaries became available in the 18th century, the trend toward uniformity increased.

Greater uniformity of spelling meant that the number of acceptable variant spellings was greatly reduced. But more survive in dictionaries than many people realize. Their recognition is not as consistent as you might expect, but lexicographers have no simple objective test by which to judge the acceptability of a variant spelling. Almost any reasonable spelling will be found to have some historical precedent, given the history of our present-day spelling; what is given dictionary recognition, therefore, is often a matter of precedent in earlier editions and individual decisions made by editors.

Our present-day spelling, then, is a mishmash of archaism, reform, error, and accident, and it is unsurprising that not everyone who is heir to the tradition can handle it perfectly. Even so, with all the aids available to the poor speller, including computer spelling checkers, you might think there would be very few misspellings found in print.

But the opposite is true, to judge from ordinary observation and from published comment. There seem to be several factors bearing on this. First, there seems to be a noticeably smaller population of proofreaders and copy editors in the publishing business than there once was. Taking the place of proofreaders in some cases is the electronic device for checking spelling. Most such devices are very good at finding mechanical errors: if you intend "sly as a fox" but instead keyboard in "sgy as a ofx," the machine will catch the errors. But if you enter "shy as a fox" or "sly as a box," the chances are the machine will not find anything wrong, for both *shy* and *box* are real words. It has been conjectured, perhaps without basis, that overreliance on such machines may account for the frequency with which garbled homophones—*they're* for *their, reign* for *rein, tow* for *toe, diffuse* for *defuse, sight* for *site,* and so forth—can be found in print, not infrequently in rather tony publications.

Many of the words that commentators feel to be frequently misspelled are separate entries in this book. See also SPELLING REFORM.

spelling reform The inadequacies of English spelling were apparent to some observers as early as the middle of the 16th century—long before our present traditional but inconsistent system was established. Three such observers were Thomas Smith, John Hart, and William Bullokar. Each of them was interested in phonetics and was aware that there were more sounds in English than there were letters in the alphabet—then counted as 24 letters, with *i* and *j* and *u* and *v* being used as variant forms rather than as one distinct vowel and one distinct consonant. And each of them devised an extended alphabet to remedy the problem. All of the new alphabets were failures, but one radical suggestion from both Smith and Hart—that *i* and *u* be used exclusively as vowels and *j* and *v* as consonants—did bear fruit after a couple of centuries.

The hope of these early reformers was to institute a more phonetic system of spelling. (Bullokar was a teacher, and he may have been the first to go on record with the complaint that it was hard to teach children to read with the current method of spelling. The same complaint resulted in the Initial Teaching Alphabet of the mid-20th century). The hope of almost every subsequent spelling reformer has been the same: to bring the spelling of English more in line with its pronunciation.

Opposing the reformers have been those who have felt that a strictly phonetic system would obscure the etymological background of words. The conflict of opposing sets of reformers and etymology preservers in the end produced almost no change of a theoretical sort in English spelling.

Probably the most successful spelling reformer was Noah Webster. His reading books, spellers, and dictionaries from about 1787 through 1828 succeeded in instituting most of the major systematic differences between American and British spelling. That we spell *honor, music,* and *theater* the way we do is largely his achievement. Webster was not initially a spelling reformer, but in 1786 he met Benjamin Franklin, an ardent spelling reformer (Franklin, too, devised an improved alphabet). Franklin seems to have won Webster over to the side of reform, for by 1787 Webster was directing his printer to use the spellings *honor, music,* and *theater,* then usually spelled *honour, musick,* and *theatre.*

The reformed Webster was an adherent of phonetic spelling, although his system was not as radical as several proposed by such contemporaries as Franklin, because he more or less restricted himself to the regular alphabet. It is interesting to note that where he can be said to have been successful—as in the three words above—the spellings he promoted were not outright inventions, but alternative forms that had been in occasional use all along. His more phonetic innovations, such as *iz* (for *is*), *improovment, yeer, ritten,* and *reezon,* did not catch on at all. Although Webster put what we might call his simplified spellings—*honor, music, ax, plow*—in his dictionaries, he forebore from including his phonetic inventions. This was probably no more than a matter of

good business, as there was considerable controversy about the reformed spellings.

Although phonetic systems and new alphabets—some of them very elaborate—continued to be proposed during the 19th century (and are still being proposed today), the next high tide of spelling reform concerned itself less with the implementation of a whole system of spelling than with the simplification, chiefly through the omission of silent letters, of the spelling of particular words. This movement, which was better organized and better financed than previous ones, began in the 1880s and lasted into the first decades of the 20th century. It involved leading scholars, writers, journalists, lexicographers, and politicians on both sides of the Atlantic, and several professional organizations as well. Around the turn of the century the participants in this crusade had high hopes of success; some newspapers and some of the writers associated with the movement actually began using the new forms. President Theodore Roosevelt was convinced of the rightness of the movement, and in 1906 he issued an executive order directing the Government Printing Office to use a list of 300 simplified spellings suggested by the Simplified Spelling Board. But the GPO resisted, and eventually the order was withdrawn.

In spite of the involvement and approval of many prominent figures, the simplified spelling movement eventually petered out, leaving behind only a few accepted forms—*catalog, analog, tho, thru*—which have had varying degrees of success. The *Chicago Tribune* adopted many simplified spellings and stuck with them longer than anyone else, but finally threw in the towel in 1975.

So four hundred years and more of proposals for spelling reform have left a few tracks in our spelling, but have had no systematic effect at all. You can see two obvious reasons for the failure. First, if a phonetic spelling scheme were adopted, we would be further from a consistent spelling than we are now, for the language is not pronounced consistently. The more accurate the phonetic system, the more varied would be the resulting spellings. Our present system has at least the virtue of having one traditional spelling that can serve as the visual equivalent of any number of variant pronunciations. The second reason is the considerable investment in time and effort every literate user of English has made in learning the present system. Few of us would be willing to throw that away and learn a new system, no matter how efficient it was.

spill   In American English the usual past tense and past participle of *spill* is *spilled:*

> Gasoline lines spilled onto freeways —*N.Y. Times,* 12 May 1979

. . . could sop up 1,000 barrels of spilled oil —*Dun's,* October 1971

The variant *spilt* is common in British English, especially as the past participle:

. . . too much blood has been spilt —*Times Literary Supp.,* 28 May 1971

Far more American blood has been spilt in Asia —Alistair Buchan, *The Listener,* 13 Dec. 1973

When the past participle is used as an attributive adjective (as in the proverb, "There's no use crying over spilt milk"), *spilt* also occurs occasionally in American English:

. . . began wondering where all the spilt oil went —Warren R. Young, *Smithsonian,* November 1970

spit The common verb *spit* has as its past tense and past participle either *spat* or *spit.* The British prefer *spat,* but both forms are widespread in American English:

I spit the beer out, and with it came a long, thin brown roach —Dennis Smith, *Report from Engine Co. 82,* 1972

. . . the Jamaican mountains that were spit from the sea —Caleb Pirtle III, *Southern Living,* November 1971

A computer spat out this list in June —*Fortune,* September 1981

. . . I'd have thought she'd inwardly cursed or spat —Kenneth Roberts, *Oliver Wiswell,* 1940

Nonstandard variants are *spitted* and *spitten:*

. . . like someone had spitten tobacco into it —Dave Godfrey, in *Canadian Short Stories, Second Series,* ed. Robert Weaver, 1968

In the helicopter one of [them] spitted in this lieutenant's face —Richard J. Ford III, quoted in Wallace Terry, *Bloods,* 1984

The unrelated verb *spit* meaning "to skewer or impale on a spit" consistently becomes *spitted* in the past tense and past participle:

Juma cooked the birds spitted on a stick —Ernest Hemingway, "An African Betrayal," in *Sports Illustrated,* 5 May 1986

spitting image The original phrase was *spit and image,* derived from the use of *spit* to mean "the exact likeness." The phrase *spit and image* dates from the late 19th century. *Spitting image* was first recorded in 1901. *Spitting image* was once commonly cited as an error, in dictionaries and elsewhere, but it has now established itself as the usual form:

. . . the spitting image of her mom —Nancy Anderson, *US,* 28 Mar. 1983

I could swear it's the spitting image of the house I saw —David M. Schwartz, *Smithsonian,* November 1985

Spit and image may continue in occasional use, but our evidence suggests that it is rare.

split infinitive *Split infinitive* is the name given to a syntactical construction in which an adverbial modifier comes between *to* and the infinitive itself. The term is first attested in 1897, when the construction had already been under discussion for about half a century. But the term is actually a misnomer, as *to* is only an appurtenance of the infinitive, which is the uninflected form of the verb. In many constructions the infinitive is used alone or with some other word such as *and* preceding it.

Burchfield 1996 gives a compendious historical sketch of the split infinitive. He notes that the evidence in Visser 1963–73 shows the split infinitive as far back as the 13th century. It was only occasionally in use from the 13th to the 16th centuries, then dropped out of sight until the end of the 18th century. Burchfield has examples that certainly look like the construction was consciously avoided during that period. After the split infinitive came back into favor at the end of the 18th century it came into frequent enough use to draw the unfavorable attention of 19th-century commentators like Alford 1866. Since then it has become a staple of the usage industry. Here are a few 20th-century examples of the construction:

In a quarter of an hour the movement began to noticeably slacken —James Stephens, *The Crock of Gold,* 1912

But I would come back to where it pleased me to live; to really live —Ernest Hemingway, *Green Hills of Africa,* 1935

And then when the time came to really bury the silver, it was too late —*The Collected Stories of William Faulkner,* 1950

. . . I got a brief note from [Harold] Ross splitting an infinitive as follows: "Tell Sayre to damn well and soon return those proofs." —James Thurber, letter, 13 Dec. 1950

We would like to make one point often mentioned by other commentators: ambiguity can result by avoiding the split. This example will illustrate:

. . . the authorities would be required correctly to anticipate their requirements for at least ten days ahead —W. Manning Dacey, *The British Banking Mechanism,* 1951

In the sequence "required correctly to anticipate" the adverb *correctly* can be construed as modifying either *required* or *to anticipate.* In spoken English there would be no ambiguity, and if the author had certainly intended *cor-*

rectly to mean "as they should be" he could have made that clear by setting the adverb off with commas. But as it appears on the printed page, there is just a slight opportunity for doubt. The sequence "required to correctly anticipate" would remove that doubt, without changing the intended meaning of the sentence. The adverb can also be placed after *anticipate,* but doing this would have the effect of emphasizing the adverb rather than the verb. Had the author intended *correctly* to be the focus, he probably would have written "required to anticipate their requirements correctly." Some commentators have advised routinely repairing split infinitives by placing the adverb after the infinitive, but note that this has the effect of altering the emphasis of the sentence.

Sometime between Alford 1866 and the end of the 19th century, the split infinitive seems to have established itself in that subculture of usage existing in the popular press and in folk belief. Almost every commentator from then on, in the course of giving a more measured opinion, has said that the split infinitive is roundly condemned by grammarians, or, sometimes, by purists. We know it is firmly established in the popular mind.

Critical opinion as expressed in usage books has generally settled on a wary compromise. The commentators recognize that there is nothing grammatically wrong with the split infinitive, but they are loath to abandon a subject that is so dear to the public at large. Therefore, they tell us to avoid split infinitives except when splitting one improves clarity. Since improved clarity is very often the purpose and result of using a split infinitive, the advice does not amount to much. The upshot is that you can split them when you need to.

If the split infinitive fascinates you, you can find extensive treatments in Burchfield, Visser, Lounsbury 1908, and Curme 1931. Fowler 1926 investigates the subtleties of the construction, and Garner 1998 updates Fowler's treatment.

spoil, spoiled, spoilt In American English *spoiled* is usual for both verbal and adjectival use, although we have some evidence for *spoilt* as an adjective. In British English both *spoiled* and *spoilt* are used. Longman 1988 and Burchfield 1996 say *spoilt* and *spoiled* are equally common in British use.

> . . . spoiled rotten and considerably less than innocent —Newgate Callendar, *N.Y. Times Book Rev.,* 6 Feb. 1983

> . . . behave like a spoilt hysteric —*Time,* 5 Mar. 1984

> . . . spoiled Notre Dame's unbeaten season —*Oxford Companion to Sports and Games,* ed. John Arlott, 1975

This comedy, although it is spoilt in places by some childish farce —James Sutherland, *English Literature of the Late Seventeenth Century,* 1969

> You have hitherto been a spoiled child —William Hazlitt, letter, March 1822

> . . . grew up into a stuttering, spoilt brat —Harold Beaver, *Times Literary Supp.,* 4 July 1980

spokesperson See PERSON 2.

spoonful This word has two plural forms: *spoonfuls* and *spoonsful. Spoonfuls* is by far the more common of the two and is the form preferred by usage commentators. See -FUL.

spouse The advantage that *spouse* has over *wife* and *husband* is that it is not limited to a particular sex. This makes it a useful word in contexts such as legal documents and income tax forms, where the person referred to may be either male or female. Its use outside such contexts has been advised against by several commentators, who generally regard it as too formal a word to be used in ordinary speech and writing for anything other than pseudo-elegant humor. Our evidence shows that these remarks are out of date. *Spouse* is commonly used in ordinary contexts where the writer simply chooses not to specify husband or wife, even when considerations of sex are not an issue:

> . . . she was our Princess Di, bravely blonde spouse of a swine of a husband —Noemie Emery, *National Rev.,* 17 July 2000

> . . . vivid evidence of the wife's ability to follow the twists and turns of her husband's innermost character, to take her spouse in —John Updike, *New Republic,* 21 Feb. 2000

> Yet the vocations of spouse and parent simply do not wait while I "work things out" —Richard R. Gaillardetz, *Commonweal,* 8 Sept. 2000

> . . . the vertiginous spate of memoirs that have appeared recently, with their derigueur regimens of child, spouse, and substance abuse —Andre Aciman, *New Yorker,* 21 Dec. 1998

> Jenny Walker, the much younger spouse of a famous nature writer, has left New England in the hope that a change of climate will work its magic on her increasingly distant, preoccupied husband —Francine Prose, *N.Y. Times Book Rev.,* 12 July 1998

spring The past tense of the verb *spring* can be either *sprang* or *sprung. Sprang* is the more common form, but *sprung* is not at all rare:

> The parents sprang into action —Susan Edmiston, *Woman's Day,* October 1971

Dufour . . . sprung up the rocks like a cat —Jeremy Bernstein, *N.Y. Times Mag.*, 28 May 1978

. . . none of these problems sprung into being overnight —Norman Cousins, *Saturday Rev.*, June 1980

Self-help computer clubs sprung up around the country —Paul Freiberger, *Infoworld*, 28 Nov. 1983

Sprung also serves as the past participle of *spring*:

The new Avery Fisher Hall, which has sprung from the skeleton of the old one —Harold C. Schonberg, *N.Y. Times*, 20 Oct. 1976

squeeze, squoze When the President of the United States uses a dialectal past tense of a verb at a news conference, people notice. Ronald Reagan in August 1985 was commenting on a small skin cancer that had been removed from his nose. He had thought it a pimple:

I picked at it and I squoze it and so forth and messed myself up a little.

Squoze is apparently the most common of a number of dialectal variants of the past tense of *squeeze*. It is attested in both British and American dialect: the OED Supplement shows it in American English since 1844. Our most recent evidence apart from President Reagan happens to associate it with orange-growing areas, but older evidence shows *squoze* to be more widespread.

The form used in writing is consistently *squeezed. Squoze*, so far, is oral and dialectal.

squinting modifier, squinting construction The squinting modifier resides chiefly in college-level handbooks. The term is used of an adverb or phrase that stands between two sentence elements and can be taken to modify either what precedes or what follows.

Let us look at an example sent to us by a correspondent from Korea:

The store that had the big sale recently went bankrupt.

Here *recently* can be interpreted as modifying either the preceding or following part. But the content of the sentence suggests it is a learner's sentence; a native speaker would not be likely to convey the information in such a flat and unspecific manner.

The examples of the squinting modifier shown in college handbooks are comparable to the one we have used here, and they seem pretty unlikely to occur in actual writing. This degree of improbability, along with the dearth of examples in our own files, suggests to us that the squinting modifier is more of a theoretical

possibility than a real problem. It would seem most likely to occur when a split infinitive is being carefully avoided by putting the would-be splitting adverb ahead of the infinitive, as in

. . . authorities would be required correctly to anticipate their requirements —W. Manning Dacey, *The British Banking Mechanism*, 1951

stadium Some people, mindful of the Latin origins of *stadium*, prefer to give it a Latin plural, *stadia*, while others are content to treat it as a normal English word with a normal English plural, *stadiums*. Both plural forms are standard and correct. *Stadiums* is usual when the word is being used in its most familiar sense:

. . . addressing huge audiences—some of them in stadiums —*N.Y. Times Book Rev.*, 11 Apr. 1982

Stadia is much less common than *stadiums* in this sense, but we do have evidence of its written use:

Most American of all, I suspect, are the shopping-mall stadia that went up . . . in the sixties and early seventies: Atlanta, Busch, Three Rivers —Roger Angell, *New Yorker*, 21 May 1990

Most of the other, less common senses of *stadium*, such as "an ancient Greek unit of length," hark back more clearly to the classical origins of the word and are usually pluralized as *stadia*:

. . . Aristotle even quoted an estimate that the distance around the earth was 400,000 stadia —Stephen W. Hawking, *A Brief History of Time*, 1988

For other foreign plurals, see LATIN PLURALS.

stamp See STOMP, STAMP.

stanch, staunch Fowler 1926 observed that the verb is usually spelled *stanch* and the adjective *staunch*. That observation still holds true today. The two spelling variants have been in reputable use for centuries, and they are standard both for the verb and for the adjective. *Stanch* is the much more common spelling of the verb:

. . . the icy cold . . . had stanched the flow of blood —Brock Brower, *Holiday*, February 1966

. . . has stanched a dangerous cash hemorrhage —Ralph E. Winter, *Wall Street Jour.*, 11 Aug. 1981

But *staunch* is not rare:

Proposition 10 may staunch the wounds —*Wall Street Jour.*, 27 May 1980

For the adjective, *staunch* is by far the more common spelling, but *stanch* is also in widespread use:

. . . animal lovers who have been zoos' staunchest supporters —Jon Luoma, *Audubon Mag.*, November 1982

. . . even now many programmers are staunch holdouts —Steve Olson, *Science 84*, January/February 1984

. . . a stanch foe of the Vietnam war —Philip B. Kurland, *N.Y. Times Book Rev.*, 14 Oct. 1973

standard, standard English *Standard English* is of necessity defined in somewhat general terms in dictionaries. We would like to point out three of its characteristics from the definition in Merriam-Webster's Collegiate Dictionary, Tenth Edition. It is "substantially uniform," "well-established" in the "speech and writing of the educated," and "widely recognized as acceptable." There is room for a lot of variation within those limits, with the result that there can be substantial disagreement about the propriety of perfectly standard words and constructions.

It is quite common for usage commentators to use *standard English* in a highly personal way to stand for the particular brand of English that they are expounding. We need only one example to make the point:

At about. This wordy phrase should be avoided in standard English —Shaw 1970

Now compare Shaw's opinion with this use of *at about*:

Two of your stories, "The Boarding-House" and "A Little Cloud" are in the May Smart Set; I am having two copies of the number sent to you by this post. We were unable to take more because the American publisher of "Dubliners," Mr. B. W. Huebsch, of 225 Fifth Avenue, New York, planned to bring out the book at about this time —H. L. Mencken, letter to James Joyce, 20 Apr. 1915

Mencken's letter is plainly written in standard English, so we conclude that Shaw's *standard English* has a very personal meaning.

We can use Mencken's letter to make another point. Standard English is the language of business, literature, and journalism. It has evolved over the centuries as the means by which speakers of diverse dialects of English can communicate effectively with each other. It is an economic necessity in a world where English is the most widely recognized language and is not likely to disappear any time soon, whatever reports of its death may come your way.

See also NONSTANDARD; SUBSTANDARD.

standpoint *Standpoint* came into English in the first half of the 19th century as a translation of or a coinage on the model of German *standpunkt*. American commentators began to disparage it as early as 1870. It was subsequently criticized by several commentators in the late 19th and early 20th centuries.

The problem was simply that it was a new and popular word. As it has continued to be popular but has ceased to be new, the old antagonism toward it has gradually died out.

See also VIEWPOINT.

stanza See VERSE, STANZA.

state Commentators from 1870 to 1998 have repeatedly condemned what they regard as the pretentious misuse of *state* in place of *say*. The frequent criticism suggests that the problem is widespread, but our files actually contain little evidence of this use of *state*. Most commonly, *state* is used to imply a formal, precise, or emphatic declaration or report:

. . . being able to state clearly a technological problem or define a technological need —Hubert H. Humphrey, in *Automation, Education, and Human Values*, ed. W. W. Brickman & S. Lehrer, 1966

Richard Nixon, who had often stated he would never be the first American President to lose a war —Goodman Ace, *Saturday Rev.*, 20 Nov. 1971

Say is a far more common and widely applied word. It is the word that is normally used in reporting ordinary remarks ("He said he'd be a little late" seems more natural than "He stated he'd be a little late"). *State* can, however, be appropriately used where *say* might be expected as a way to underscore the emphatic nature of what might otherwise seem to be an ordinary remark:

"I like you, Alice," he stated. "You are a really sincere person. . . ." —Doris Lessing, *The Good Terrorist*, 1985

state of the art Here is another term from technical literature that has moved into the general consciousness and into general use. Although it is not as well known to or as widely disliked by the critics as *parameter* or *interface* (which see), it has attracted some disapproval.

In general use *state of the art* more often functions as a hyphenated adjective than as a noun. As a general adjective it is not much more than a snappy version of *up-to-date* with pleasant overtones of technical know-how. Here are a few general uses of the adjective:

. . . the main concern was to retain money in the hospital to buy state-of-the-art equipment —Milt Freudenheim, *N.Y. Times*, 31 Oct. 1999

. . . spend thousands of dollars building the fastest, most state-of-the-art soap-box-derby cars —Melanie Warner, *Fortune,* 6 Dec. 1999

. . . a good bet to remain in San Antonio now that the city will start construction on a state-of-the-art arena —L. Jon Wertheim, *Sports Illustrated,* 13 Dec. 1999

Use as a noun is less common in general prose, but not at all rare:

. . . Petersen's film is traveling the highest plane of the state of the art —Jesse Cagle, *Time,* 3 July 2000

Hobbyist-inventors can and do forward the state of the art —Tom Atwood, *Games,* June 1994

This popularized technicality has been censured as salesman's jargon, and while it is used in promotional writing, most of our evidence shows it to be used in straightforward contexts. There is no reason to avoid using it.

stationary, stationery The adjective that means "not moving" is *stationary*; the noun that means "paper for writing letters" is *stationery*. These two words look like prime candidates for being misspelled, but our evidence shows that they rarely are, at least in edited prose. The usual advice for remembering the distinction is to associate the *er* in *stationery* with the *er* in *letter* or *paper.*

statistic The singular *statistic* is derived from *statistics,* which in its oldest sense refers to a field of study, like *economics,* and which is itself often construed as a singular:

To reach a better understanding of how statistics functions, and of its limitations, weaknesses and dangers —Darrell Huff, *Think,* January 1963

This sense of *statistics* dates back to the late 18th century. The earliest recorded use of *statistics* as a plural occurred not long afterward:

. . . the few who love statistics for the sake of what they indicate —Harriet Martineau, *Society in America,* 1837 (OED)

Statistics here denotes not a field of study, but numerical data that have been collected for study. Derivation of the singular *statistic* from this plural use was almost inevitable.

There is not a statistic wanting. It is as succinct as an invoice —Mark Twain, *A Tramp Abroad,* 1880 (OED Supplement)

Statistic has at times been criticized (as by Follett 1966) on the theory that if there is no plural word *statistics,* there can be no singular *statistic.* However, the plural *statistics* does

exist and has for more than 150 years. The singular *statistic* is now completely standard.

staunch See STANCH, STAUNCH.

stave The verb meaning "to break or crush inward" has as its past tense and past participle either *staved* or *stove.* It usually takes the adverb *in:*

. . . that had stove in the planks of the wheelhouse —Alistair MacLean, *Saturday Evening Post,* 23 Sept. 1956

. . . a massive gold-processing plant . . . , its peaked front all staved in —James Traub, *Smithsonian,* November 1984

Stave off, meaning "to ward or fend off," regularly becomes *staved off* in the past tense:

. . . it staved off its possible demise by signing a new labor contract —*Wall Street Jour.,* 18 Dec. 1981

still and all This adverbial phrase is not well-loved by several critics who regard its last two words as illogical and superfluous—mere excess baggage adding nothing to the meaning of *still.* Its frequent appearance in print is a fairly recent development, but the phrase itself is not new: the OED Supplement dates it from 1829. The attractions it holds for the writers who use it are probably that it is less formal than the starchy *nevertheless* and less abrupt than the monosyllabic *still.* It has a casual, conversational quality which is consistent with the informal tone of much modern prose:

Still and all, Homerdome or away, the critical ingredient may have been the calm manner of Kelly —Tom Callahan, *Time,* 26 Oct. 1987

Still and all, the crowd had a good time —Steve Wulf, *Sports Illustrated,* 20 Aug. 1990

But, still and all, Monaco remains a jewel of a playground —Barry Tarshis, *Town & Country,* April 1980

Still and all, there may be more laughs than blood spilled this summer at the local cineplexes as comedies outnumber action adventures two to one —*Vibe,* June/July 1994

Still and all, there is no manual or handbook for the creation of a perfect translation —Gregory Rabassa, *American Scholar,* Winter 1974/75

stink, stank, stunk Both *stank* and *stunk* are used as the past tense of *stink. Stank* is more common in edited prose. Both are standard:

. . . Arthur Levitt thought the idea stank —Byron Klapper, *Wall Street Jour.,* 15 Dec. 1975

. . . will tell you that in 1979 business stank —Marc Kirkeby, *Rolling Stone*, 24 July 1980

. . . although I stunk at algebra, Zock pushed me through —William Goldman, *Temple of Gold*, 1957

When the verb is followed by *of*, the past tense is almost invariably *stank*:

The room stank of cigar smoke —Walter Wager, *Telefon*, 1975

. . . for whom both stank of corruption —Peter Schjeldahl, *N.Y. Times Book Rev.*, 15 Feb. 1976

The past participle of *stink* is always *stunk*.

stomp, stamp *Stomp* originated in American English as a dialectal variant of *stamp* in the early 19th century. The passing years have seen it gain steadily in respectability. Its status in current English is that of a standard synonym of *stamp* in several of its senses, all having to do, literally or figuratively, with bringing the foot down heavily:

. . . she angrily stomped out of the office —*Current Biography*, December 1966

. . . resist the temptation to stomp on him when he's down —Norman Cousins, *Saturday Rev.*, 14 Oct. 1978

. . . I heard the horses stomping in the stable —E. L. Doctorow, *Loon Lake*, 1979

On national television, he stomped a folding chair and verbally abused players —Alexander Wolff, *Sports Illustrated*, 3 Feb. 1986

stomping ground, stamping ground Both of these are in standard respectable use. *Stamping ground* is apparently preferred in British English, but is also common in American writing.

. . . the ideal stomping ground for big, predatory gamefish —Pete Bodo, *N.Y. Times*, 27 June 1999

Athletes from the poorest neighborhoods once sought to escape their old stomping grounds —Mark Starr et al., *Newsweek*, 29 May 2000

. . . the stuffy Ivy Club, a stamping ground for sherry-drinking good old boys —Ruth Shalit, *New Republic*, 12 June 1995

. . . next door to many of Rome's best-known tourist stamping grounds —William Murray, *New Yorker*, 22 Aug. 1988

stop The use of *stop* to mean "stay" was much criticized in the late 19th and early 20th centuries. American commentators no longer bother with the subject, but a few British observers (as Longman 1984) still fret over it. Burchfield 1996 identifies the usage (stopping with friends, stop for a week) with 19th-

century fiction, and notes that it has much receded since. It still has some 20th-century use:

. . . when he was in New York he usually stopped at the Windsor House —John Kobler, *New Yorker*, 25 Feb. 1956

"You must not sleep alone at Hampstead," said Godfrey. "Call on Lisa Brooke and ask her to stop with you for a few days. . . ." —Muriel Spark, *Memento Mori*, 1959

Stay is more common in such contexts.

straight, strait A few commentators, most of them British, warn against the confusion of *straight* and *strait*. Actual confusion seems unlikely, since the words are used in rather different senses, but they are homophones and hence can be muddled in spelling:

The framework it provided was literally too strait and narrow —Harriet Ritvo, *The Platypus and the Mermaid*, 1997

If you are in doubt, check your dictionary,

straitened The adjective that means "distressed" or "deprived" ("straitened circumstances") is actually the past participle of the verb *straiten* and has no relation to either *straight* or *straighten*. Despite that fact, the spelling error is still fairly easy to make in a moment of inattention:

. . . in the Chinese farmer's straightened circumstances —*N.Y. Times Book Rev.*, 12 Dec. 1948

. . . living perhaps in some straightened home or lonely cottage —*Time*, 8 Oct. 1951

straitjacket, straitlaced, straightjacket, straightlaced The original and still the usual spellings are *straitjacket* and *straitlaced*:

. . . this would put a straitjacket on industrial progress —*Times Literary Supp.*, 23 June 1972

. . . he's inclined to be rather straitlaced —Rosemary Brown, *Ladies' Home Jour.*, September 1971

But *straightjacket* and *straightlaced* are also in common use:

. . . loosening a few strings of the economic straightjacket —John Fischer, *Harper's*, July 1972

. . . showed up at a straight-laced . . . church —Dennis Farney, *Wall Street Jour.*, 12 Nov. 1981

The *straight-* spellings originated as errors, and they are still regarded as errors by many people. Because of their common occurrence in reputable publications, however, they are recognized as standard variants in almost all current dictionaries.

strata, stratum *Strata* is a Latin plural with ambitions to become an English singular. The Latin *stratum*, which means literally "something spread or laid down," was first used in English at the end of the 16th century. As an English word it has become common in several senses, all of which share the basic meaning "layer" or "level." The Latin plural has been retained as the usual plural in English:

> . . . an omnibus organization that attracted all strata of society —Michael T. Kaufman, *N.Y. Times Mag.,* 23 Mar. 1980

A variant plural, *stratums*, is rare in writing:

> . . . must learn to move in the various stratums of society —Lou Richter, *Annual Report, Peace Officers Training School,* August 1952

In addition to its plural use, *strata* has seen occasional use as a singular since the 18th century. It occurs most often in the sense "a social level":

> There was a strata of Paris which mere criticism of books fails to get hold of —Ezra Pound, *Polite Essays,* 1937

> . . . interviewing every strata, from Prime Minister to shepherd —Christine Papp, *Grand Tour,* Fall/Winter 1997–98

Its plural is *stratas*:

> . . . to support the various other stratas of society —Carl Waldman, *Atlas of the North American Indian,* 1985

Our evidence does not show the singular *strata* to be common, but it does seem to be persistent. Usage commentators will not tolerate it, and you are well advised to avoid it. When the sense is singular, use *stratum*; when plural, *strata*.
Strata, with a plural *stratas*, is also used of a sandwich.
For other foreign plurals, see LATIN PLURALS.

strike, struck, stricken *Struck* is the past tense of *strike* ("The clock struck twelve"), and in most contexts it also functions as its past participle ("The tree was struck by lightning"). The alternative participle *stricken* is used when *strike* has the sense "to afflict suddenly":

> . . . was stricken with ileitis in June 1956 —*Current Biography,* April 1968

> . . . with so much devilry having stricken the life of Mrs. MacNeil —Keith S. Felton, *Los Angeles Times Book Rev.,* 23 May 1971

It is also common for the sense "to cancel or delete":

> . . . have certain of their remarks modified or stricken from the record —Andy Logan, *New Yorker,* 30 Oct. 1971

> . . . the term "false alarm" has been stricken from the vocabulary —*Harper's,* June 1972

And *stricken* has several familiar adjectival uses as well:

> With several stricken faces looking at him —Nancy Milford, *Harper's,* January 1969

> . . . blew up two 100,000-barrel oil storage tanks. . . . The two stricken tanks were 15 per cent full —Lawrence Mosher, *National Observer,* 28 Apr. 1973

Other uses of *stricken* are rare, and they tend to have an unidiomatic ring:

> I am still stricken by McComb's and Mangin's classic City Hall and its calm exterior —Gilbert Millstein, *N.Y. Times Mag.,* 30 Nov. 1975

strive *Strive* is most often followed by *to* and the infinitive:

> . . . they strove to establish the sense of their identity —Oscar Handlin, *The American People in the Twentieth Century,* 1954

> . . . perhaps it is for them that he has so rigorously strived "to be exact" —John Irving, *N.Y. Times Book Rev.,* 12 Aug. 1979

> . . . the limitations of background that, subconsciously rather than consciously perhaps, he had striven to overcome —Norman Cousins, *Saturday Rev.,* 6 Apr. 1974

Once in a while, *to* is followed by a noun object:

> . . . women have either borne the moral burden, or shared it, or striven, through the self-love Trilling denies them, to the autonomous condition that might redeem the earth —Carolyn Heilbrun, *Saturday Rev.,* 29 Jan. 1972

Strive is also frequently used with *for:*

> With all his will Venters strove for calmness —Zane Grey, *Riders of the Purple Sage,* 1912

> . . . each national group, striving for greater freedom, has the support of its neighbors —Henry C. Atyeo, *Current History,* November 1952

> We have strived for reform of the chaotic and unworkable welfare system —John Gardner, *Common Cause,* 9 Jan. 1973

Other prepositions used with *strive* include *after, against, at, in, into, toward, towards, with,* and *within:*

> . . . apartments that have exceeded mere functionalism and now strive after taste —Anthony Austin, *N.Y. Times Mag.,* 9 Mar. 1980

". . . Though we strive against butchers, let us not wet our hands in butchery. . . ." —Irwin Shaw, *The Young Lions,* 1948

. . . he strove at his seemingly endless task —*American Guide Series: Texas,* 1940

The San Francisco 49ers and Oakland Raiders have striven mightily in football, without success —*Springfield* (Mass.) *Union,* 23 Oct. 1972

. . . the farmers roll from their bunks, strive into their jeans, and fall out for morning roll-call —*Century Mag.,* April 1919

. . . two sentences which state beautifully what many educators have been striving toward —Sim O. Wilde, Jr., *Center Mag.,* May 1969

. . . some curious region where the spirit strives towards an unseen God —Virginia Woolf, *The Second Common Reader,* 1932

. . . a figure that had striven with the generations who found Chicago a swamp mudhole and saw it made into an audacious metropolis —*Dictionary of American Biography,* 1936

He guessed at the grief and perplexity that must strive within her —Anne Douglas Sedgwick, *The Little French Girl,* 1924

subject 1. *Noun.* When the noun *subject* is followed by a preposition, it is usually *of*:

. . . it's our fighting men . . . that make the proper subject of American fiction —James Purdy, *Cabot Wright Begins,* 1964

. . . the exercise of power is the great subject of history —*Times Literary Supp.,* June 1969

. . . became a subject of violent controversy —William L. Shirer, *The Rise and Fall of the Third Reich,* 1960

Subject is sometimes also used with *for*:

The subject for Milton's "Paradise Lost" is, as Bradley says, the fall of man —John Dewey, *Art as Experience,* 1934

It was so long since the sculptress had regarded sex as anything but a subject for conversation —Angus Wilson, *Anglo-Saxon Attitudes,* 1956

When *subject* is used to mean "victim," it has also been used with *to*:

. . . one would never have guessed that William James was the subject to a heart ailment —Sidney Lovett, *Yale Rev.,* Summer 1954

2. *Adjective.* The adjective *subject* is usually used with *to*:

. . . the party convicted [after impeachment] shall, nevertheless, be liable and subject to

indictment, trial, judgment, and punishment —*Constitution of the United States,* 1787

Paul was rather a delicate boy, subject to bronchitis —D. H. Lawrence, *Sons and Lovers,* 1913

. . . they proved that the society is no longer as subject to that "relentless tide of ups and downs" which Marx was among the first to chart —Michael Harrington, *Center Mag.,* September 1969

3. *Verb.* The verb *subject* is usually used with *to*:

My partners in St. Louis have been subjected to several attempts to stop the flight —Charles A. Lindbergh, *The Spirit of St. Louis,* 1953

. . . she had never subjected herself to the discipline of continuousness —John Cheever, *The Wapshot Chronicle,* 1957

He writes of them in their own right, without attempting to subject them to general concepts —*Times Literary Supp.,* 26 Mar. 1970

Uncle Harold was often subjected to these small humiliations —Russell Baker, *Growing Up,* 1982

subject-verb agreement See the several articles at AGREEMENT, SUBJECT-VERB.

subjunctive

Fading into the sunset, probably forever, is that splendid old mood we have known as the subjunctive —Richard L. Tobin, *Righting Words,* May/June 1988

Another writer, it seems, has discovered the disappearing subjunctive; observers of the language have been reading obsequies for the subjunctive for a century or more. As long ago as 1907 the brothers Fowler were quoting "an experienced word-actuary" who put the subjunctive's life expectancy at a generation. The word-actuary was Henry Bradley, one of the OED editors, and he made the statement in a book, *The Making of English,* published in 1904.

But even Bradley was not breaking new ground. Ayres 1881 paraphrased three unnamed grammarians who thought the subjunctive more or less defunct. One of them was probably William Dwight Whitney, who is quoted in Finegan 1980 as remarking in an 1877 grammar that "the subjunctive, as a separate mode, is almost lost and out of mind in our language." Even earlier, at the end of the 18th century, Noah Webster was either regretting or welcoming the loss of the subjunctive (he took different views in different works).

And even before that Priestley—we assume from our 1798 edition that it was in his 1768 book—observed that the subjunctive (he called it *conjunctive*, after the practice of Samuel Johnson) was "much neglected by many of our best writers." The 18th-century grammarians had barely discovered the subjunctive, so apparently it was in decline as soon as it was recognized. The historical grammarians show that it has, in fact, been in decline since Old English, when the modal auxiliaries began to take over some of its functions.

But the subjunctive has not disappeared. H. L. Mencken, who had declared the subjunctive "virtually extinct in the vulgar tongue" in *The American Language* (4th ed., 1936), commented in his second supplement (1948):

> On higher levels, of course, the subjunctive shows more life, and there is ground for questioning the conclusion of Bradley, Krapp, Vizetelly, Fowler and other authorities that it is on its way out.

Mencken made the distinction between the written and spoken language that many other commentators have overlooked. Our evidence, mostly written, bears out Mencken's observation.

The subjunctive in modern English is, however, an all but invisible verb form. Its chief characteristic for most verbs is a lack of inflection, and so it is only noticeable when it turns up in a context calling for an inflection. The present subjunctive of the verb *think*, for instance, is *think*, and you really only notice that it is a subjunctive when it appears with a subject that would ordinarily require *thinks*. The verb whose subjunctive forms are most noticeable is *be*, with *be* in the present, which contrasts with all the indicative forms (*am, are, is*), and *were* in the past, which frequently (as we shall see) contrasts with *was*. It is this latter contrast, especially in various conditional clauses, that has stirred the most controversy. First let us take note of two uncontroversial uses of the subjunctive which are seldom considered in notices of its death.

The subjunctive is preserved like a fossil in a number of fixed formulas—*so be it, be that as it may, Heaven forbid, come what may, suffice it to say,* and so forth—that are used every day without much thought about their peculiarity. An example or two of some others:

> . . . willing to make digressions and, if need be, to get nowhere —Leacock 1943

> ". . . and far be it from me to throw any fanciful impediment in the way. . . ." —Jane Austen, *Mansfield Park*, 1814

> . . . the randomness and drift, the sheer, as it were, deadness —Wilfrid Sheed, *The Good Word and Other Words*, 1978

These phrases excite no controversy.

Also uncontroversial is the so-called mandative subjunctive—a highfalutin term for the subjunctive found in the common parliamentary formula "I move that the meeting be adjourned." This subjunctive occurs in clauses following such verbs as *ask, demand, recommend, suggest, insist* and such phrases as *it is advisable* and *it is necessary*.

> . . . it was recommended that the President not inform Congress —Edwin Meese 3d, quoted in *The Tower Commission Report*, 1987

> . . . when to recommend that a student seek help —Nancy S. Prichard, *College Composition and Communication*, February 1970

> Mrs. Clark suggested that the class learn some simple first-aid and health rules —Matilda Bailey et al., *Our English Language*, 3d ed., 1963 (6th-grade text)

This use of the subjunctive is regular.

The controversial uses of the subjunctive occur with verbs of wishing and in contrary-to-fact conditional clauses, almost always in contexts involving the contrast of the subjunctive *were* with the indicative *was*. Here are some examples of the subjunctive in such contexts:

> . . . although I wish that Ralph Mooney's sweet-and-sad singing steel guitar were a bit more up-front —Tony Glover, *Rolling Stone*, 18 July 1974

> If I were younger and could see anything at all I would appear or let someone make a film —James Thurber, letter, 15 Aug. 1959

> . . . brings it down gently on the driver's shoulder, as if he were bestowing knighthood —Jay McInerney, *Bright Lights, Big City*, 1984

> . . . minutely scrutinizes the novels along with the writer, as though she were inviting us to watch her take an extremely rare watch to pieces and put it together again —Mollie Panter-Downes, *New Yorker*, 4 Nov. 1985

> Today it is snowing here & were I not confined to my bed taking two-toned pills I would be painting a snow scene —Flannery O'Connor, letter, March 1960

> Were a war to break out —Kosta Tsipsis, *Discover*, April 1987

From these examples it can be seen that the subjunctive is likely to be found after the verb *wish* (and perhaps in other expressions of a wish), after *if, as if,* and *as though,* and at the beginning of a clause or sentence stating something contrary to fact or hypothetical.

Hall 1917 and Jespersen 1909–49 (vol. 4) observe that *was* began to compete with *were* in these contexts sometime around the end of the 16th century, but it apparently did not become frequent in this use until around the end of the 17th century.

Some examples:

I wish my cold hand was in the warmest place about you —Jonathan Swift, *Journal to Stella,* 5 Feb. 1711

I wish H. was not quite so fat —Lord Byron, letter, 8 Dec. 1811

I wish it was Elinor and I seeing you about now instead of them two irresponsible wastrels our son and daughter —Robert Frost, letter, 1 Nov. 1927

I wish I was six feet tall and I wouldn't mind if I was handsome —*And More by Andy Rooney,* 1982

Was is likewise common after *if, as if,* and *as though*:

The situation in the Middle East . . . might be very different if there was an international left with a strong base —Noam Chomsky, *Columbia Forum,* Winter 1969

Why do I grin when I see her, as if I was delighted? —W. M. Thackeray, *The Book of Snobs,* 1846

. . . and the women can all carry me in their arms as though I was a baby —Henry Adams, letter, 9 Oct. 1890

It may seem that *was* is crowding out subjunctive *were* in informal contexts, such as the letters and journals among our examples here. But not necessarily:

. . . if you were allowed to cut your finger with it, once a week —Lewis Carroll, letter, 23 Jan. 1862

If I were ten years younger I might have tackled one of these assignments —Groucho Marx, letter, 5 July 1961

. . . I should feel as if I were flirting with my aunt —Henry Adams, letter, 23 Nov. 1859

Jespersen observes that subjunctive *were* is least likely to be displaced in the constructions without a conjunction in which it begins a clause or sentence. But even here he found a few examples with *was,* like this one:

Was I Diogenes, I would not move out of a kilderkin into a hogshead —Charles Lamb, letter, 29 Mar. 1809

One of the curiosities of the *was–were* competition is the tendency of many writers to use both, often very close together. even in the same sentence. The tendency was noted as

early as the 18th century. Here are a couple of examples we have found:

. . . and all staring, gravely, as if it were a funeral, at me as if I was the coffin —Henry Adams, letter, 15 May 1859

I wish I was a dog and Ronald Reagan were a Jelly Bean tree —Reinhold Aman, *Maledicta,* Summer/Winter 1982

It should be remarked that *if* and *as if* do not always introduce an unreal condition and therefore *if* and *as if* do not necessarily call for a subjunctive:

If he was to marry the queen, the power of the nobles was such that he would have first to gain their approbation —John Butt, *English Literature in the Mid-Eighteenth Century,* edited & completed by Geoffrey Carnall, 1979

. . . Freud felt as if he was being observed; raising his eyes he found some children staring down at him —E. L. Doctorow, *Ragtime,* 1975

. . . asked Dick if there was any way that he could get us to meet before the 3 Nov. meeting —Oliver North, quoted in *The Tower Commission Report,* 1987

Sometimes the subjunctive *were* is actually used when there is no unreal or hypothetical condition; it is probably triggered somewhat automatically by a preceding *if*:

He was asked if he were apprehensive —*N.Y. Times,* 16 Jan. 1972

I do not even know if she *were* actually a War Widow —Richard Cobb, *Still Life,* 1983

It could have been then; if it weren't, it was certainly the next day —Donald Regan, testifying at the Iran-Contra hearings, 1987

This use is considered hypercorrect by the few who notice it.

To repeat, we do not really know why, three or four hundred years ago, *was* began to compete with the older subjunctive *were* in wishes and hypothetical and other unreal statements. It simply happened. The success that the indicative form has had since then has probably been abetted by the near invisibility of the subjunctive. We do not have any distinctive subjunctive forms in modern English; every one we can identify as a subjunctive is simply an indicative form doing double duty. The subjunctive as an entity, then, has very little support in the grammar, and much of the time the subjunctive and indicative are identical:

And here in Missouri we don't charge our kinfolks with fees like we would do if they were strangers —Luther Burrus, quoted in Merle Miller, *Plain Speaking,* 1973

Little wonder, then, that the subjunctive has so little impact on the general consciousness.

But the old forms die hard. If it is generally true, as commentators have been saying for a century, that the subjunctive is dying out of the common speech (as distinct from writing), there are still signs that it is not yet extinct. A colleague reports hearing this subjunctive in the chatter of two children on a Chicago subway train:

If I were fat like you, I wouldn't. . . .

And clearly the subjunctive is not gone from writing, no matter how many commentators say that it is not as common now as it was a century ago. You will doubtless find many uses for it in your own writing, whether you are aware of them or not.

See also IF 3.

subsequent, subsequently, subsequent to
Some relatively mild criticism has been directed at these terms by a few commentators who regard them as little more than stuffy substitutes for such words as *following, later,* and *after.* It is certainly true that informality is not their strong point:

As subsequent sections of this memorandum seek to make plain, this kind of multiple activity is not necessarily incompatible with good teaching —Hazen Foundation Committee on Undergraduate Teaching, *The Importance of Teaching,* 1968

. . . this notification was subsequently rescinded through a compromise that gave Dr. Gibbs a temporary research assignment —*AAUP Bulletin,* December 1967

My acquaintance with him was subsequent to the heart affliction, which must have necessarily precluded bodily exercise —Sidney Lovett, *Yale Rev.,* Summer 1954

Our evidence indicates that use of these terms is generally restricted to writing in which one is deliberately aiming at a formal tone. Formality is not their only distinctive feature, however. To describe something as "later" is usually just to establish its relative place in time, but to describe it as "subsequent" may also imply that it not only follows but in some way grows out of or is otherwise closely connected with what precedes it:

. . . the reviews we saw were favorable and looked forward to the subsequent books in the series —Leo Bergson & Robert McMahon, *The Writer,* October 1968

The report, and its authors' subsequent prodding, moved the faculty last spring to agree —Larry A. Van Dyne, *Change,* November–December 1969

substandard The label *substandard* is widely used in usage books. In dictionaries—and in this book—it signifies no more than that the word or construction so labeled is normally used within a speech community by a group other than the one with prestige. This tends to suggest use by the least educated. Hence *substandard* contrasts with *nonstandard* (which see), which is applied to words and constructions that are not characteristic of the usage of educated native speakers but may be employed by them at times—for example, a strictly local term or a slang expression. In much writing about usage, however, *substandard* tends to mean only that the word or construction so labeled does not accord with the commentator's own notions of good English.

substitute In its oldest and still most common transitive sense, *substitute* means "to put or use in place of another":

. . . echoes of a more spontaneous life before the Puritan middle class had substituted asceticism for beauty . . . —Vernon Louis Parrington, *Main Currents in American Thought,* 1930

Such logic encourages the state to substitute its vision . . . for the religious views of the Amish —Stephen Arons, *Saturday Rev.,* 15 Jan. 1972

However, the OED shows that *substitute* has also been used since the 17th century to mean "to take the place of; replace":

Good brandy was being substituted by vile whiskey —Catherine C. Hopley, *Life in the South,* 1863 (OED)

The OED said in 1915 that this use was "now regarded as incorrect." Fowler 1926 was strong in his objection to this newer sense, which he found to be increasingly common and which he regarded as a serious threat to the older meaning of the word. Several later commentators have repeated Fowler's criticism.

Despite this criticism, there is ample evidence showing *substitute* being used in this sense in standard writing on both sides of the Atlantic:

. . . at least substitute conjecture with facts —Maurice Friedberg, *Saturday Rev.,* 4 Dec. 1971

. . . concludes that British Rail's proposals to compensate . . . at rates of four, five, and six per cent. are inadequate and substitutes them with levels of five, 7½, and 10 per cent. —*Daily Telegraph,* 25 July 1974 (OED Supplement)

. . . first-rate criminals were substituted by hi-jackers, hostage-takers, and other blackmailers —George Mikes, *Punch,* 1 Jan. 1975

... the pungent pines ... have been substituted by filling stations, Pizza Huts, and shoddy motels —Suzanne Wilding, *Town & Country*, August 1976

Given its use in general writing and its presence in the language for more than 300 years, we see no reason to dismiss this use of *substitute* as an error, and it has been recognized as standard in Merriam-Webster dictionaries since Webster's Second (1934).

If you want to avoid this sense of *substitute*, note that the choice of preposition makes the meaning clear. The older sense of *substitute* is used with *for* ("substitute a new version for the old one"); the "replace" sense is used with *by* or *with* ("substitute the old version with (or by) a new one").

succeed A person may fail *to do* something or succeed *in doing* it:

> ... the little man had succeeded in disturbing the boy —Roald Dahl, *Someone Like You*, 1953

> ... may well succeed in carrying the day —*Times Literary Supp.*, 19 Feb. 1970

Fowler 1926 cited as an error a passage in which *succeed* was followed by an infinitive rather than by *in* plus a gerund. A few later commentators have also observed that the infinitive after *succeed* is not idiomatic. Our evidence supports that observation.

such 1. *Pronoun.* There has been much discussion of *such* as a pronoun. Most commentators agree only in criticizing it; otherwise, their comments are divergent. One calls it formal, another informal if not substandard, another stilted, another literary. Some just call it wrong:

> May one say, correctly, "Of *such* I want no part"? Not in the opinion of most authorities. In that example, *such* is acting as a pronoun, a part of speech to which it does not belong, even though the Bible says ". . . of such is the kingdom of God." —Freeman 1983

But the OED shows that *such* has been a pronoun since the time of King Alfred the Great, a millennium ago. It is still in use, and it is used in standard English, no matter how the commentators label it. Many of its uses are actually uncontroversial. It is most likely to attract criticism when it occurs in contexts where it can be replaced by common alternatives like *it, them, this,* and *these,* as in a sentence such as "If you retained a receipt, please enclose such." *Such* may not be the best-chosen word in such a context, but it is not an error. To give you a better idea of the respectability and range of pronominal *such,* here is a sampling of usage:

> . . . Suffer little children to come unto me, and forbid them not: for of such is the Kingdom of God —Luke 18:16 (AV), 1611

> Edmund did not wonder that such should be his father's feelings —Jane Austen, *Mansfield Park*, 1814

> . . . my last two books have been clipbooks, and I have been hoping that before publishing another such I could produce an Original Work —E. B. White, letter, 19 Aug. 1940

> . . . the wives will be free to have their say to such as Lord Redmayne —*The Times* (London), 16 Apr. 1974

> She was looking for . . . an unfamiliar movement, one that was out of place in her world. Had she seen such, she would have disappeared back into the burrow —Lawrence Wishner, *Smithsonian*, October 1982

> Locke envisaged clean and decent residential training centres. Few such existed —*Times Literary Supp.*, 5 Mar. 1970

> . . . a token nonacademic or two; one such was Courtenay Stone —Steve Lohr, *N.Y. Times,* 12 Mar. 1980

Such is often followed by a clause that explains or expands. The clause is usually introduced by *as*:

> . . . were such as made him seem not even quite an Englishman —Edmund Wilson, *New Yorker,* 18 Sept. 1971

> . . . an easy lack of fearsomeness such as is weirdly charming —Christopher Ricks, *N.Y. Rev. of Books,* 9 Mar. 1972

If the clause following *such* shows a result, it is usually introduced by *that*:

> . . . a container such that when rations were dropped from airplanes to ground troops there would be no breaking or crumbling of Saltines —Renata Adler, *Pitch Dark*, 1983

> . . . Anderson's medical knowledge is such that it's surprising to learn she's never worked in a hospital —*Publishers Weekly,* 24 May 1985

Such is also used as part of a tag that suggests an indefinite number of the same sort; the common forms are *and such, or such,* and *or some such.* These uses of *such* seem to attract a fair amount of criticism, but our evidence shows them to be respectable:

> When the story begins, fourteen daughters of doctors, bankers, lawyers, and such are graduating from the local Female College —Mona Simpson, *Vogue,* July 1984

> . . . excellent Alsatian wine (the noble Riesling, the flowery Gewürztraminer, or such)

—Colman Andrews, *Metropolitan Home,* November 1983

. . . by a calculus of his own devising, the letters in the word "love" added up to sixteen, or fifty-four, or some such —*New Yorker,* 19 Mar. 1984

Evans 1957 observes that in speech some of the pronominal uses of *such*—not the tag lines—tend to be replaced by other pronouns or by other constructions. In other words, *such* as a pronoun tends to be more likely in writing than in speech.

2. *Adverb.* Back in the 18th and 19th centuries a few commentators managed to puzzle themselves about the word order in constructions like these:

. . . said that he never remembered such a severe winter as this —Jane Austen, letter, 17 Jan. 1809

. . . but such a dismal Sight I never saw —Daniel Defoe, *Robinson Crusoe,* 1719

They convinced themselves that *such* in this construction must be a misuse for *so.* They were wrong and nobody believes it is a misuse any more, but since the subject had been started, almost nobody was willing to forget it, which they should have. The 20th-century focus was on the use of *such* as an intensive, as in "He's such a nice boy" and "She has such beautiful manners." The assertion is that this use of *such* is informal and not to be used in formal writing. And of course it is, because informal examples have been brought forth to make the point. But real usage is not necessarily informal:

In such an immense intellectual and linguistic exercise, many defects will eventually be apparent —Francis Steegmuller, *Times Literary Supp.,* 3 Dec. 1993

. . . congratulated Kinsey for handling himself so well in the face of such venomous criticism —David Halberstam, *American Heritage,* May/June 1993

The tortured reasoning of the 18th- and 19th-century pundits was irrelevant, and the 20th-century concerns are unnecessary. You need not worry about adverbial *such* at all.

such as See LIKE, SUCH AS.

suffer A few sources of usage comment, Copperud 1970, 1980 and Heritage 1969 among them, say that *suffer* should be used with *from* rather than *with* when referring to a condition of health. Longman 1984 says "One *suffers from* a disease . . . but *suffer with* is often used where actual pain is involved. . . ." The evidence in our files shows that *suffer* is almost always used with *from*:

About 5,000 people worldwide suffer from Fabry disease —*USA Today,* 10 Oct. 2000

Some writers suffer from depressive doubt —Geoffrey Wheatcroft. *Atlantic,* September 2000

Suffer with may be mostly confined to speech; it is rare in print:

Babies with a Chiari anomaly often suffer with hydrocephalus —Bruce H. Dobkin, M.D., *N.Y. Times Mag.,* 27 Nov. 1988

When *with* accompanies *suffer,* it usually means "along with":

For we suffer with them, we partake of their affliction —Ken Follett, *The Man from St. Petersburg,* 1982

suitable The usual preposition after *suitable* is *for*:

. . . subjects regarded as suitable for college work —James B. Conant, *Slums and Suburbs,* 1961

. . . more suitable for a boy than a girl —*Current Biography,* October 1967

To is also used, but less commonly:

Apparently no words were suitable to this strange pilgrimage —Lloyd C. Douglas, *The Big Fisherman,* 1948

. . . arable land . . . suitable to vegetables and flowers —Marion Wilhelm, *Americas,* July 1954

superior See IMPLICIT COMPARATIVE; INFERIOR, SUPERIOR.

superlative of two The notion, so beloved of modern commentators, that the superlative degree should not be used of only two seems to have had its origin in the 18th century. Joseph Priestley was one of the earliest to express it (Leonard 1929 cites a 1769 edition), but he only gave one example of the superlative of two and concluded, "This is a very pardonable oversight." Campbell 1776 was the next to take it up. He did so speculatively, allowing both "the weaker of the two" and "the weakest of the two," but preferring the comparative to the superlative on "the most general principles of analogy," which principles he did not explain. Lindley Murray 1795 took his discussion of the superlative straight from Campbell, but in later editions he eliminated any element of doubt. "The weaker of the two" became "the regular mode of expression, because there are only two things compared." Campbell's speculation had become a rule.

Evidently Murray's formulation of the question was picked up by a great many grammarians in the 19th century. Goold Brown 1851 provided a long list of them, side by side with examples of the superlative of two drawn from their own works. The rule did not impress Goold Brown:

> The common assertion of the grammarians, that the superlative degree is not applicable to *two* objects, is not only unsupported by any reason in the nature of things, but is contradicted in practice by almost every man who affirms it.

But Goold Brown's opinion seems to have had no influence on the school books, and both grammarians and rhetoricians clung steadfastly for a time to Murray's rule. Around the turn of the century, according to Hall 1917, the attitude of some grammarians began to soften. But the rhetoricians of the time held fast. The same division of opinion exists today. The grammarians are more latitudinarian: even school grammars allow the superlative of two in everyday or informal circumstances. The hard-line commentators of today, however, continue to insist that the superlative of two is an error.

Two things should be noted about the rule. First, as Lamberts 1972 points out, it makes no difference from the standpoint of communication whether you use the comparative or the superlative of two. The rule serves no useful purpose at all. It is therefore a perfect shibboleth, serving no practical function except to separate those who observe the rule from those who do not.

The second thing is that the rule has never reflected actual usage. From the examples collected by Otto Jespersen and other historical investigators, it is plain that many of our best writers have used either the comparative or superlative of two, as suited their fancy at the time. Among the writers who found the superlative appropriate for two are Shakespeare, Milton, Defoe, Addison, Goldsmith, Dr. Johnson, Chesterfield, Austen, Byron, Scott, Irving, Hawthorne, Thackeray, Disraeli, Ruskin, Emerson, Stevenson, Thoreau, and James Russell Lowell. There is clearly a strong literary tradition for the practice. Here are some examples from our collection:

> Here am I brought to a very pretty dilemma; I must commit murder or commit matrimony! Which is best, now? —George Farquhar, *The Constant Couple,* 1699

> However, I was condemned to be beheaded, or burnt, as the king pleased; and he was graciously pleased, from the great remains of his love, to choose the mildest sentence —Henry Fielding, *A Journey from This World to the Next,* 1743

We cannot agree as to which is the eldest of the two Miss Plumbtrees —Jane Austen, letter, 31 May 1811

dinghy, dingey. The first is best —Fowler 1926

> Crane wrote two fine stories. *The Open Boat* and *The Blue Hotel.* The last one is the best —Ernest Hemingway, *Green Hills of Africa,* 1935

> . . . there was once a contest between Athena and the god Poseidon for the possession of the Acropolis. Athena came off best —H. D. F. Kitto, *The Greeks,* rev. ed., 1957

It is not rare to find the comparative and superlative cheek by jowl:

> Warburton has the most general, most scholastic learning; Lowth is the more correct scholar. I do not know which of them calls names best —Samuel Johnson, in James Boswell, *Life of Samuel Johnson,* 1791

> . . . it usually turns out that not the better man but the least tired man wins —Aristides, *American Scholar,* Autumn 1981

It seems clear from our experience in gathering examples of the superlative of two for this book that they are plentiful and can be readily found by anyone who is interested enough to look for them.

We conclude that the superlative of two is alive and well in current English. The rule requiring the comparative has a dubious basis in theory and no basis in practice, and it serves no useful communicative purpose. Because it does have a fair number of devoted adherents, however, you may well want to follow it in your most dignified or elevated writing.

In speech, we recommend that you simply follow your instincts—the native speaker is not likely to go wrong. There are more traps for the learner, however. If you are a learner you must look out for the fixed phrases: it is always *lower lip* and *best foot forward.* It is always the comparative in a construction with *than* following: "I am taller than Jim." The superlative seems to be most likely when the judgment, measurement, or characteristic denoted by the adjective or adverb is the primary point being considered. Thus Fowler's "the first is best." He is not interested in comparing the two spellings as such; he is recommending that you use the first one.

supersede, supercede *Supercede* has a long history of occasional use as a spelling variant of *supersede*; or, to put it another way, people have been misspelling *supersede* for centuries. It all depends on your point of view. Both spellings can be etymologically justified: the original Latin verb was spelled *supersedere,* but the derivative verb in Old French, by way of which the word came into English, was first spelled *superceder* and only later *superseder,* according to the OED. The earliest record of this word in English (1491) shows it spelled with a *c*. Most other early citations, however, are for the *s* spelling, and there is no doubt that the *s* spelling has always been the dominant one in English and it continues to be widely regarded as the only correct spelling of this word. *Supercede,* on the other hand, continues to turn up in standard, edited prose:

> . . . Henry James is about to supercede Jane Austen as Hollywood's hottest author —Rachel King, *Arts & Antiques,* January 1997

> They were superceded early in the twentieth century by publicly owned corporations —Webster Schott, *Saturday Rev.,* 29 Apr. 1978

> . . . has since been superceded by the Ferber decision —Howard Fields, *Publishers Weekly,* 4 May 1990

> . . . had been superceded by more modern values —Eric Foner, *N.Y. Times Book Rev.,* 23 May 1982

supine   See PRONE, SUPINE.

supposed to   *Supposed to* is indistinguishable in speech from *suppose to*—the *d* is not pronounced. For this reason the unwary sometimes omit it in writing as well. Many commentators warn against this error, but it does turn up in print:

> . . . a practice known as "scarfing," which is suppose to heighten orgasm —Peter Pringle, *Playboy,* December 1994

> . . . a VCR that does what it's suppose to do —Len Feldman, *Video Rev.,* May 1990

> Americans are suppose to have a deep distrust of cities —Kurt Anderson et al., *Time,* 23 Nov. 1987

We also find the *d* was deliberately omitted to suggest nonstandard speech (somewhat pointlessly, since *suppose to* and *supposed to* sound alike when spoken).

> ". . . All I can say is that I'm suppose to be at the U of Chicago hospital at eight. . . ." —Garrison Keillor, *Leaving Home,* 1987

See also USED TO, USE TO.

supreme   *Supreme* is sometimes considered to be an absolute adjective. See ABSOLUTE ADJECTIVES.

surcease   This word still occurs fairly often as a literary or old-fashioned synonym of *cessation, relief,* or *respite*:

> . . . come to the park every day to gain surcease from the stifling heat of their apartment —Wayne King, *N.Y. Times,* 20 Aug. 1991

> What is the prayer for surcease from dentistry? —Peter Freundlich, *Harper's,* September 1987

> Notepaper condolences, no matter how awkwardly expressed, offer more surcease than printed cards —Edmund Morris, *New Yorker,* 16 Jan. 1995

Several usage commentators, dating back to Fowler 1926, have found *surcease* to be archaic and have discouraged its use as an affectation. Burchfield 1996 notes that its continuing use is mainly confined to American English.

sure, surely   The adverbs *sure* and *surely* are both reasonably old; *surely* is about a century earlier than *sure.* The OED evidence of early use shows both words occurring in the same senses, but over the centuries they have diverged. For instance, one of the chief uses of *surely* is persuasive; it is used with a statement that the speaker or writer is trying to get the hearer or reader to agree with. As recently as the 18th century, both adverbs could be used in this way:

> Surely nothing is more reproachful to a being endowed with reason, than to resign its powers to the influence of the air —Samuel Johnson, *The Idler,* 24 June 1758

> . . . the most undeserving people in the world must sure have the vanity to wish somebody had a regard for them —Thomas Gray, letter, 20 Dec. 1735

And both adverbs were also once used in the sense "without doubt, certainly," as by John Milton:

> . . . but he shall surely be put to death —*Eikonoklastes,* 1649

> God sure esteems the growth and completing of one virtuous person —*Areopagitica,* 1644

But during the 19th and 20th centuries the use of adverbial *sure* dropped off in mainstream British English, except in a few fixed phrases like *sure enough* and *as sure as. Sure* continued in use in the outlying forms of English, such as Scottish English, Irish English, and American English. In Irish English, *sure* and *surely* seem to have remained more or less interchangeable into the 20th century. Here is James Stephens, for instance:

> "I never ate cheese," said Seumas. "Is it good?"
> "Surely it is," replied Pan
>   —*The Crock of Gold,* 1912

> "Let me sit here for a while and play with the little dog, sir," said she, "sure the roads do be lonesome. . . ." —*The Crock of Gold,* 1912

In American English adverbial *sure* came under attack around the end of the 19th century. The assault has continued vigorously in the years since, especially in schoolbooks and college handbooks.

But the long-continued attack on *sure* has not driven it out of use; to the contrary, adverbial *sure* is probably now better established in speech and in general writing than ever. Its uses are, however, clearly differentiated from those of *surely. Sure* is used in less formal contexts, on the whole, than *surely.* It is used as a simple intensifier, primarily of verbs rather than adjectives.

> A Time gal phoned me to see if I still stuck to a quote of mine she found in the Time clips. . . . I told her I sure did stick to it —James Thurber, letter, 9 July 1959

> You ought to write an article on Iris Murdoch. . . . I sure wish you would —Flannery O'Connor, letter, 27 May 1961

> I can never know how much I bored her, but, be certain, she sure amused me —Norman Mailer, *N.Y. Times Mag.,* 18 Apr. 1982

Sure is used in affirmation:

> Q. Do you just take it from what you read? A. Sure, you can get a lot of it. That's a very good way to learn the craft of writing —William Faulkner, 6 May 1957, in *Faulkner in the University,* 1959

> Sure, it's escape music, and what's wrong with that? —Nat Hentoff, *Cosmopolitan,* April 1976

As a strong intensifier, *sure* is used when the writer or speaker expects the reader or hearer to agree:

> 'Images' sure don't *reflect!* —George Wald, in Harper 1975, 1985

> Well, he's sure not following out your orders, if that's the case —John Erlichman, 17 Apr. 1973, quoted in *The Presidential Transcripts,* 1974

> The Iranians sure have a way of bringing out the worst in us —Meg Greenfield, *Newsweek,* 29 Dec. 1986

And *sure* is regularly used in the same phrases that survive in British English—*sure enough, as sure as, sure as*:

> . . . I said, 'That son of a bitch is gonna run against me,' and sure enough I was right —Harry S. Truman, quoted in Merle Miller, *Plain Speaking,* 1973

> I knew it was for me as sure as I knew my own face in the mirror —E. L. Doctorow, *Loon Lake,* 1979

> It's a moot point whether politicians are less venal than in Twain's day. But they're sure as the devil more intrusive —Alan Abelson, *Barron's,* 8 May 1972

> But we all looked like that. I sure as hell did —Maurice Sendak, *N.Y. Times Book Rev.,* 8 May 1983

Surely, in American English, tends to be used in somewhat more elevated styles than *sure.* It too can be used as an intensive:

> I surely don't want to leave the impression that I had an unhappy childhood —Edward C. Welsh, quoted in *Current Biography,* January 1967

> I don't want you to get the wrong impression and I'm surely not talking about a sick cat or kitten —Susie Page, *Cats Mag.,* October 1983

Surely is less positive, more diffident, or more neutral than *sure.* Its use suggests that the writer or speaker is not altogether confident that the reader or hearer will agree:

> . . . it would surely be possible, within a few years, to program a computer to construct a grammar from a large corpus of data —Noam Chomsky, *Columbia Forum,* Spring 1968

> . . . the worst sort of empty rant, all the more so because Wolfe himself surely knew better —William Styron, *This Quiet Dust and Other Writings,* 1982

> As my reader has surely heard if he is tuned in to literary events —Mary McCarthy, *Occasional Prose,* 1985

> Webster's 10th Collegiate surely will include it —James J. Kilpatrick, *Mayville* (Ky.) *Ledger-Independent,* 25 Aug. 1984

> Surely if they have any real bona fides they can get a visa in Tehran —Robert C. McFarlane, quoted in *The Tower Commission Report,* 1987

In present-day American English, then, adverbial *sure* and *surely* are not used in quite the same contexts or for quite the same purposes, even though they share the same meanings.

sure and　For constructions like *be sure and,* see TRY AND.

surely　See SURE, SURELY.

surprised　The prepositions that occur after *surprised* are *at* and *by. By* is the choice when *surprised* means "taken unawares":

> At dawn the household was surprised by a sudden Indian attack —*American Guide Series: New Hampshire,* 1938

Both *at* and *by* are possible when *surprised* means "struck with wonder" or "taken aback":

I am surprised at this evidence —Eric Larrabee, *CEA Critic,* October 1954

. . . have been myself continually surprised . . . by the abrupt and vast changes that I have seen —S. P. B. Mais, *The English Scene To-day,* 2d ed., 1949

suspected When used with a preposition, *suspected* ordinarily takes *of*:

. . . expel from the Army all officers suspected of complicity in the plot against him —William L. Shirer, *The Rise and Fall of the Third Reich,* 1960

. . . spent with the bravado of a man who suspected himself of infallibility —Israel Shenker, *Smithsonian,* September 1979

The 1998 Tour de France was a bust. Seven people . . . were suspected of using or providing riders with a synthetic version of erythropoietin —N. Seppa, *Science News,* 17 June 2000

suspicion An issue about which there is some comment but no real controversy is the use of *suspicion* as a verb meaning "to suspect." In modern English the verb *suspicion* has been chiefly a feature of uneducated or dialectal speech. It occurs in writing primarily in representations or imitations of such speech:

Anybody would suspicion us that saw us —Mark Twain, *Tom Sawyer,* 1876

Everybody knowed them Newton boys wasn't no 'count and was rustling cattle, but nobody would have suspicioned them of killing a man —J. Frank Dobie, *Coronado's Children,* 1931

Our nineteen-year-old son, which he's home from Yale . . . and don't suspicion that his folks are rifting —S. J. Perelman, *New Yorker,* 5 Jan. 1946 (OED Supplement)

It does not appear in formal writing.

sustain *Sustain* is an old verb with many senses, most of which have been in use for centuries. Among them is the sense "to suffer or undergo," as in "sustain an injury" and "sustain losses," which was first attested in the early 1400s. Samuel Johnson included this sense without stigma in his dictionary, illustrating its use with quotations from Shakespeare and Milton. Noah Webster also regarded it as a standard sense, and it continues to be treated as one in current dictionaries. Usage commentators, however, have found various reasons for disliking it, beginning in 1866 and continuing to at least 1998.

The criticism is simply beside the point. The usage is not diluted English, pretentious, flossy, nor officialese. It is simply a word used in straightforward reportage:

. . . the company sustained operating losses totalling more than $30 million —Richard A. Lester, *New Republic,* 27 June 1955

. . . the result of wounds sustained in action in 1916 —Martin Gilbert, *The First World War,* 1994

. . . mentioned the "neglect and destruction" Jerusalem had sustained "during its more-or-less recent history" —Katharine Kuh, *Saturday Rev.,* 24 Jan. 1976

. . . sat out the third period with a slight groin pull sustained in warmups —Michael Farber, *Sports Illustrated,* 20 Mar. 2000

. . . sustained a career-threatening leg injury in a flag football game —*N.Y. Times,* 5 Sept. 1999

swap, swop *Swap* is the usual spelling in American English, and, according to British dictionaries, it is also preferred in British English. *Swop* is not common in American English (except perhaps in that corner of New England where *Yankee Magazine* is edited), but we have evidence of its use by British writers:

. . . language change in the twentieth century seemed to be much less of a developmental process than a swopping one —Robert Burchfield, *The English Language,* 1985

. . . just swopping old cigarette cards and comics —*This England,* Autumn 1983

Back in 1918, the editors of the OED considered *swap* slang or colloquial, but our evidence clearly shows that the OED's assessment is no longer valid. *Swap* is in use in all but the most formal writing and is now unremarkable:

. . . a $200 million swap of floating assets for fixed-rate ones —Keith Sill, *Business Rev.,* January/February 1997

. . . in him the scholar, the linguist and the storyteller swap hats —Jason Goodwin, *N.Y. Times Book Rev.,* 2 Apr. 2000

. . . we don't have a designated bed but have to swap bunks in order to sleep always on the windward side of the boat —Liz Price, *The Times* (London), 30 Nov. 2000

. . . chromosomes swap pieces of DNA each time a sex cell is formed by meiosis —Josie Glausiusz, *Discover,* June 1995

. . . was acquired from the Yankees in a minor-league-level swap last year —Roger Angell, *New Yorker,* 29 Nov. 1982

swell This verb has two past participles in standard usage—*swelled* and *swollen*. The principal distinction that can be made between them is that *swollen* is the one used frequently as an attributive adjective:

> . . . does not have to kowtow to some swollen bureaucracy —Ted Williams, *Massachusetts Wildlife*, November–December 1975

> . . . battle of avarice and swollen ego —Anson Mount, *Playboy*, August 1977

Swelled is used attributively only in the idiom *swelled head*, as far as our citations indicate:

> . . . where isolation too often breeds swelled heads in legislators and administrators —*Round Table*, March 1939

Otherwise, the two forms are more or less interchangeable, although, as Longman 1984 notes, *swollen* is more likely in describing a harmful or undesirable swelling:

> The area becomes inflamed and swollen —Claude A. Villee et al., *General Zoology*, 3d ed., 1968

> . . . his vanity had swollen to monstrous proportions —Malcolm Muggeridge, *Esquire*, December 1971

Swelled also occurs in such contexts:

> Their feet had swelled up with infection —Raymond A. Sokolov, *Fading Feast*, 1981

But more often *swelled* tends to be used in a neutral or positive way, especially in describing an increase in numbers:

> From 105 attorneys . . . , the firm has now swelled to 120 —Paul Hoffman, *New York*, 26 Apr. 1971

> . . . the student body has swelled to 500 —Hank Hersch, *Sports Illustrated*, 19 Nov. 1986

The past and past participle *swole* is apparently dialectal in American English:

> "How's your arm this morning?" Collins drawed a deep breath. "Swole plumb to a strut, Doc," says he —Oakley St. John, July 1921, in Vance Randolph, *Pissing in the Snow & Other Ozark Folktales*, 1986

It seems to have a little British use as well:

> . . . my uncle blew and bugled and swole —Dylan Thomas, *Quite Early One Morning*, 1954

swim, swam, swum In current English, the standard past tense of *swim* is *swam*, and the standard past participle is *swum*:

> . . . the moon swam palely in the pale blue daylight sky —Graham Greene, *Travels with My Aunt*, 1969

> . . . and we have swum naked in cold country ponds —John Cheever, *N.Y. Times Book Rev.*, 28 Aug. 1983

Evidence in the OED shows that *swam* was also once in reputable use as a past participle:

> Who, being shipwrecked, had swam naked to land —Samuel Johnson, *The Rambler*, 1750 (OED)

However, we have no 20th-century evidence of such use in writing. More complex is the history of *swum* in the past tense. It was used by Tennyson:

> Who turn'd half-round to Psyche as she sprang
> To meet it, with an eye that swum in thanks
> —Alfred, Lord Tennyson, *The Princess*, 1847 (OED)

Burchfield 1996 doesn't find it after the 19th century. American dialect studies have shown that *swum* as the past of *swim* was common in certain areas of the U.S.—particularly New England—until fairly recently. E. Bagby Atwood, in *A Survey of Verb Forms in the Eastern United States* (1953), noted that *swum* then appeared to be passing into disuse. Whatever its present status in speech, *swum* has never been commonly used in writing as the past tense of *swim*.

swop See SWAP, SWOP.

syntactic blend A syntactic blend is an unconscious combination of two (or perhaps more) phrases to produce a new one, such as *equally as good* from *just as good* and *equally good* (example from Bolinger 1980). A few syntactic blends recur often enough to become the subject of discussion in usage books (including the present one)—*equally as, accused with, hardly . . . than, scarcely . . . than*, for instance—and some may eventually become well enough established to be counted as idioms. A few are probably conscious combinations used as slang.

But most syntactic blends are accidents of speech and are probably not repeated except by chance. Gerald Cohen, who produces the journal *Comments on Etymology*, has been presenting lists of syntactic blends on a regular basis since 1975; his number 3–4 of 1981 contains almost a hundred of them, a great many taken from people talking on television. The bulk of these could be more accurately described as malapropisms. Some of Cohen's examples include *bet your bottom boots*, from *bet your boots* and *bet your bottom dollar; couldn't give a damn less*, from *couldn't care less* and *don't give a damn*; and *out of skelter*, from *out of kilter* and *helter-skelter*.

Once in a while such blends will crop up in print. Here are a few we have found:

> . . . though perhaps not quite to the degree as was believed at the time

This seems to be from *to the degree that* and *to such a degree as*.

> Quite a lot of more falling bodies

This must be from *quite a lot of* and *a lot more of*.

> . . . probably alongside with the legends which the author has tried to destroy

This seems to be from *along with* and *alongside (of)*.

Part of Gerald Cohen's interest in syntactic blends stems from the fact that current theories of language do not account for them very well. So keep an ear and eye open for syntactic blends. They can show you how the language works when it is not hitting on all cylinders.

See also MALAPROPISM; MIXED METAPHOR.

T

tablespoonful, teaspoonful These words are usually pluralized *tablespoonfuls* and *teaspoonfuls*, although *tablespoonsful* and *teaspoonsful* also occur as occasional variants. Most people successfully avoid having to choose between these plurals by using the plurals *tablespoons* and *teaspoons* instead.

See -FUL.

take 1. For a discussion of point of view in relation to the use of *bring* and *take*, see BRING 1.
2. *Take*, a verb of Scandinavian origin, is a model strong verb with a past tense *took* and a past participle *taken*. Lamberts 1972 notes that there has long been some leveling of the past and past participle—going back at least to the 16th century. Mencken 1963 notes the same in his discussion of the vulgate, and *taken* as a past and *took* as a past participle are apparently not rare in the folk speech of many areas.

> He hesitated a second and then he taken that whiskey glass and put it up to his face —William Wister Haines, *High Tension,* 1938

> . . . leaving their half-took drinks behind —Flann O'Brien, *At-Swim-Two-Birds,* 1939

> Old Eagle had done already took off —William Faulkner, *Saturday Evening Post,* 5 Mar. 1955

In ordinary prose, of course, the standard forms are used.

take and *Take and* is used in essentially an intensive function before another verb in much the same way as *go and* (as in "Go and leave me if you want to"). Our evidence of the construction is not as full as we would like, but what we have suggests that it was quite common in the 19th century. Mark Twain used it often:

> ". . . Well, when pap's full, you might take and belt him over the head with a church and you couldn't phase him. . . ." —*Tom Sawyer,* 1876

> So she took and dusted us both with the hickry —*Huckleberry Finn,* 1884

It persists in 20th-century American English, too:

> Homer was courting a second time to get him a good wife and a home-keeper for his children, when he took and fell off the church-house roof —Maristan Chapman, *The Happy Mountain,* 1928

> You might as well take and trim the rim off an old soft hat —William Carlos Williams, *Life Along the Passaic River,* 1938

And it also occurs in Irish English:

> Look at Matt Finn, the coffin-maker, put his hand on a cage the circus brought, and the lion took and tore it —Lady Gregory, *The Full Moon,* in *New Comedies,* 1913

Wentworth's American Dialect Dictionary carries a report that *take and* was "exceedingly common" in the mid-1930s. Our recent evidence of it in print is slight, but we suppose that the criticism of *take and* in Shaw 1975, 1987 and Prentice Hall 1978 attests to its continued vitality in speech.

Take and is one of those speech constructions that mark the language of the common people—H. L. Mencken's "vulgate." Its primary use in writing is to re-create that speech. It does not occur in ordinary prose.

See also GO AND.

take exception to See EXCEPTION.

talented

I regret to see that vile and barbarous vocable *talented,* stealing out of the newspapers into the leading reviews and most respectable publications of the day —Samuel Taylor Coleridge, *Table-Talk,* 8 July 1832 (OED)

It may seem hard to believe now, but *talented* was in fact once regarded by more than a few people as "vile and barbarous." Their objection to it was based on the mistaken notion that an adjective could not properly be formed by adding -*ed* to a noun. *Talented* was unacceptable as an adjective. in this view, because there was no such verb as *talent;* according to Bierce 1909, "If Nature did not talent a person the person is not talented." It follows from the same reasoning that if nature did not wing a bird, a bird is not winged. The fact is that many English adjectives have been formed by adding -*ed* to a noun; for example, *bigoted, crested, dogged, moneyed, skilled, spotted,* and *tenured.* The criticism of *talented* was entirely groundless. The issue died a quiet death in the early 20th century.

target

Several commentators have aimed their guns at the figurative use of *target* to mean "an objective or goal to be achieved." This sense of *target* seems to have originated in World War II. Its most characteristic use relates to industrial production:

The 1942 production targets set by the government home timber production department were exceeded —*Britannica Book of the Year 1944*

. . . the failure of plants to reach their target —John Baker White, *Atlantic,* April 1949

. . . the production of cloth. cement. sugar and coal has exceeded the targets —Adlai E. Stevenson, *Look,* 14 July 1953

Production targets had to be cut back again and again —*Newsweek,* 11 Jan. 1954

Criticism, mostly British, concentrated on the incongruity of verbs like *reach, pursue,* and *exceed* with the literal notion of a target. This was merely mixed-metaphor fun and games; the Brits had a lot of fun with *bottleneck* around that time too. The critics missed the point that the incongruous verbs were evidence that the figurative *target* was no longer a metaphor but had become a new sense of the word. There is nothing for you to worry about here.

tautology

Although a few commentators treat *tautology* as a term to be distinguished from *pleonasm,* most American commentators use both of them as synonyms for *redundancy.* They are referring, in general, to things that are discussed at REDUNDANCY.

tax

When the verb *tax* means "charge, accuse," it is idiomatically followed by *with:*

. . . suddenly taxed the little clergyman with being the sole author —H. L. Morrow, *Irish Digest,* November 1953

. . . but they will not be taxed with sin —Eugene Kennedy, *N.Y. Times Mag.,* 5 Aug. 1979

The less common sense "censure" is followed by *for:*

. . . taxes science for being unable . . . to give us moral directives —Bernard Rosenberg, *American Scholar,* Spring 1953

. . . one would not tax a man for such becoming modesty —Richard Schickel, *Harper's,* April 1971

teaspoonful

See TABLESPOONFUL, TEASPOONFUL.

temperature

A few critics have gotten hot under the collar about the use of *temperature* to mean "fever," as in "You look like you're running a temperature." This sense of *temperature* is common in speech but not common in edited prose. Its first use is recorded in the OED as from near the end of the 19th century. This sense of *temperature* is usually used with *run* and *have.* It can be found in articles about animals and in fiction:

Brian's mother never touches his cheek except to see if he has a temperature —Garrison Keillor, *Leaving Home,* 1987

The critical blather about illogicality is irrelevant. This is an established standard sense, but it is still primarily spoken.

tenant, tenet

Kilpatrick 1984 cites a newspaper article in which *tenant,* "occupant, landholder," is mistakenly used in place of *tenet,* "principle, doctrine." This does not seem to be a common error, but we find an example of it now and then:

One of the ancient tenants of the Buddist [sic] belief is, "He who sits still, wins" —*Police,* January/February 1968

Bolinger 1980 has seen the same error; he associates it with jargonistic writing. Here is his example:

Indeed this has been stated as an explicit tenant by Chomsky —Charles Goodwin, "The Interactive Construction of the Sentence Within the Turn at Talk in Natural Conversation," 1975

Garner 1998 has some journalistic examples. While you probably won't make this mistake, if you do, your computer spelling checker won't notice it.

tend The use of *tend* as an intransitive verb meaning "to pay attention; attend" is standard in American English:

> We should tend to our business—which is to teach the young —Milton Friedman, reprinted column, 1969

> . . . tends to the worldwide oil empire his late father built up —Susan Sheehan, *McCall's,* October 1971

> . . . the administrations have tended to the more general matters of institutional survival —George W. Bonham, *Change,* April 1972

This sense of *tend* is extremely old, dating back to the 14th century. It originated as a short form of *attend,* as did the transitive *tend* of "tend the fire" and "tend the sick." The intransitive *tend* appears to have fallen out of written use in the 1600s, but it survived in spoken dialect thereafter and has experienced an impressive revival in writing during the past 100 years. Recent decades have seen a gradual increase in its respectability, and it now occurs regularly in standard contexts. Burchfield 1996 notes that it has begun to have some standard British use as well.

tendency A tendency may be either *to* or *toward* (or *towards*) something:

> . . . an endearing tendency to wild exaggeration —*Times Literary Supp.,* 22 Oct. 1971

> . . . Arlene, with her tendency toward guile —Edith-Jane Bahr, *Ladies' Home Jour.,* October 1971

> . . . a tendency towards maintaining the status quo —Calvin H. Plimpton, *Amherst College Bulletin,* November 1967

In medical writing, *to* is preferred:

> . . . a family in which there is a tendency to diabetes —Morris Fishbein, *The Popular Medical Encyclopedia,* 1946

tendinitis, tendonitis The common health problem that keeps runners from running and pitchers from pitching can be spelled either *tendinitis* or *tendonitis. Tendinitis* is much more common, especially in medical publications, although *tendonitis* seems to prevail in veterinary contexts:

> It is unusual for the pain of supraspinatus tendinitis to persist for as long as five years —John L. Skosey, *JAMA,* 4 Jan. 1980

> Wind-puffs usually do not cause lameness, however, unless accompanied by arthritis, bursitis or tendonitis —Heather Smith Thomas, *Chronicle of the Horse,* 3 May 1985

tenet See TENANT, TENET.

tenses See SEQUENCE OF TENSES.

terminal preposition See PREPOSITION AT END.

terminate *Terminate,* a long word, has been criticized now and again as an overused substitute for *end, finish,* or *stop,* short ones. Nevertheless, writers seem to find *terminate* a useful word. When both words are possible in a particular context, *terminate* is more likely to be used if the ending described has an official or a legal nature:

> If the insured wishes to terminate his insurance coverage, he may surrender his policy —Nelda W. Roueche, *Business Mathematics,* 1969

> . . . the Congressional vote to terminate action in Cambodia —Barbara W. Tuchman, *N.Y. Times Book Rev.,* 11 Nov. 1979

> The anthropology department . . . voted to terminate his candidacy for the Ph.D. —Richard Bernstein, *N.Y. Times Book Rev.,* 30 Oct. 1983

terms See IN TERMS OF.

terrible, terribly Much of the terror has gone out of these words. The frequent use of *terrible* in the sense "extremely bad" is often cited as a colloquialism, or at least as something to be avoided in formal writing. This sense has long been established in ordinary speech, and our evidence shows that its occurrence in ordinary writing is also now common:

> . . . though the book is hard to classify, it is not hard to evaluate. It is terrible —Dwight Macdonald, *New Yorker,* 22 May 1954

> She could not have known that her terrible luck would stick like gum on a running shoe —Brian Cazeneuve, *Sports Illustrated,* 1 May 2000

> . . . unrest in Pakistan is aggravated by terrible living conditions —Robert D. Kaplan, *Atlantic,* September 2000

> As could easily have been predicted, the song is terrible —Newman 1974

The adverb *terribly* is an issue primarily because of its use as an intensive equivalent to *very* or *extremely.* Such usage dates back to the 19th century. The critics feel, again, that the intensive *terribly* is inappropriate in formal writing, and the evidence shows, again, that it occurs commonly in ordinary discursive prose.

> . . . our conviction that we were doing something *terribly* important —Russell Baker, *The Good Times,* 1989

> . . . he kept thinking there was something terribly wrong with him —Martin Amis, *New Yorker,* 24 June & 1 July 1996

. . . were certainly not terribly cultured by European standards —Neal Gabler, *Life: the Movie,* 1998

They were, in the main, extremely talented, terribly hard workers —John Chancellor, *N.Y. Times Book Rev.,* 27 May 1984

See also AWFUL, AWFULLY.

than 1. A dispute over whether *than* is a preposition or a conjunction has been going on now for more than two centuries. Although some commentators hold that the traditional view is that *than* is a conjunction, there were two sides to the question right from the beginning. Lowth 1762 held *than* to be a conjunction, and the case of a following pronoun to be determined by its relation to a verb understood. Thus, "thou art wiser than I [am]" and "you love him more than [you love] me." Since the second construction is fairly infrequent, Lowth's analysis was essentially a prescription for *than* plus the nominative. Priestley, at least as early as the 1769 edition cited by Leonard 1929, considered *than* a preposition and thought the objective case proper. He suspected that others' preference for the nominative was based not on English, but on a dubious analogy with Latin. Most grammarians, however, chose to follow Lowth.

Lowth's prescription for the nominative had one important exception: he held *than whom* to be correct. His explanation for this single exception—that *who* has reference only to its antecedent and not to an understood verb or preposition—is grammatically unimpressive, but the real reason may have been the authority of Milton's use of *than whom* in *Paradise Lost* (1667), which he quotes:

Which when Beëlzebub perceived—
than whom,
Satan except, none higher sat—with grave
Aspect he rose. . . .

(Milton, however, did not originate *than whom*; the OED and Hall 1917 have earlier examples.) Murray 1795 accepted Lowth's defense of *than whom,* as have many succeeding generations of grammarians and commentators. As a result, the consensus of the critics has reached these inconsistent conclusions: *than* is a conjunction and in ordinary comparisons must be followed by the nominative case of the pronoun, but *than whom* is standard.

It is hard to avoid the conclusion, however, that if *than whom* is indeed standard, *than* must be a preposition as well as a conjunction. And if it is indeed a preposition, why may it not be followed by *me* or *him* or *her* or *us* or *them,* where the grammar of the sentence calls for the objective case, as well as by *whom*? No amount of tortuous reasoning can answer this question satisfactorily, for there really is no reason.

Leonard 1929 mentions a grammarian named William Ward who in 1765 had the answer to the whole problem. He allowed *than* to be both a conjunction and a preposition. Ward's explanation covered actual usage perfectly, but it was too commonsensical to prevail.

Than has been a conjunction since Old English, but it has only been a preposition since the 16th century. From the 16th century on, writers have used it as a preposition when it suited their fancy. Shakespeare did:

A man no mightier than thyself or me
In personal action, yet prodigious grown
And fearful, as these strange eruptions are.
—*Julius Caesar,* 1600

So the preposition had some two centuries of at least occasional use behind it before the 18th-century grammarians began their wrangling. Here are a few 18th-century examples:

No man had ever more discernment than him, in finding out the ridiculous —Samuel Johnson, *A Dissertation on the Greek Comedy* (in Hall 1873)

A woman does not complain that her brother, who is younger than her, gets their common father's estate —James Boswell, *Life of Samuel Johnson,* 1791 (in Jespersen 1909–49, vol. 7)

And here are some more recent examples:

Though he was thirty years or so older than us, he tolerated our company —Oliver St. John Gogarty, *It Isn't This Time of Year At All!,* 1954

Our consul general here is a Columbus man named Streeper, about two years younger than me —James Thurber, letter, 1 June 1954

Why should a man be better than me because he's richer than me —William Faulkner, 7 Mar. 1957, in *Faulkner in the University,* 1959

Macmillan was nine or ten years older than me —Lord Butler of Saffron Walden, BBC interview, 8 Aug. 1966

. . . but I was a better Senator McCarthy than him —Garrison Keillor, *Lake Wobegon Days,* 1985

LoPresti, who was a few years older than me —Tip O'Neill with William Novak, *Man of the House,* 1987

The *than whom* construction, against which only Baker 1770 seems to have objected, has continued beyond Milton's time:

I was on Montmartre not long ago with my dear Walter Duranty, than whom no one can have a warmer spot in my foolish heart —Alexander Woollcott, letter, 5 Sept. 1918

T. S. Eliot, than whom nobody could have been more insularly English —Anthony Burgess, *Saturday Rev.,* 28 Apr. 1979

And reflexive pronouns (see MYSELF) have also been used after *than:*

... a man who we know was last year no better than ourselves —Samuel Johnson, in James Boswell, *Life of Samuel Johnson,* 1791

... Mr. Rushworth could hardly be more impatient for the marriage than herself —Jane Austen, *Mansfield Park,* 1814

The conjunction, however, is more common than the preposition, at least in print, and is not at all uncommon even in such informal contexts as letters:

... so you are no better off than I —Emily Dickinson, letter, 6 Nov. 1847

... someone else who can take it less seriously than I —Robert Frost, letter, 2 Feb. 1920

... he is twenty years younger than I —John O'Hara, letter, 8 Nov. 1962

... Uncle Etch's oldest son, much older than I —Russell Baker, *Growing Up,* 1982

... others might be affected even more than he —Garrison Keillor, *Lake Wobegon Days,* 1985

Even Lowth's conjunction with the objective turns up once in a while:

My experience is larger, and my comment says more about me than them —James Baldwin, quoted in *N.Y. Times Book Rev.,* 27 May 1984

To conclude: William Ward had it right in 1765. *Than* is both a preposition and a conjunction. In spite of much opinion to the contrary, the preposition has never been wrong. In current usage *than* is more often a conjunction than a preposition; *than whom* is pretty much limited to writing; *me* after the preposition is more common than the other objective-case pronouns; and the preposition is more common in speech than in edited prose. You have the same choice Shakespeare did—you can use *than* either way. But the closer your writing is to speech, the more likely you are to choose the preposition.

2. There are a number of syntactic blends involving *than,* some of which are separately treated in this book: see AS GOOD OR BETTER THAN; HARDLY . . . THAN; SCARCELY . . .

THAN. Priestley 1798 has an example of *scarcely . . . than* from Smollett, which makes that construction older than it would appear from OED evidence.

See SYNTACTIC BLEND.

3. *Than, then.* A number of handbooks are at pains to point out that *than* and *then* are different words. This is simply a spelling problem. Actually, *then* was occasionally used as a variant spelling of *than* in centuries past:

... there are fewe Universities that have lesse faultes then Oxford —John Lyly, *Euphues. The Anatomy of Wit,* 1578

Our composition must bee more accurate in the beginning and end, then in the midst —Ben Jonson, *Timber: or, Discoveries,* before 1637

This spelling is no longer acceptable.

than any See ANY 3.

thankfully The adverb *thankfully,* used as a sentence modifier ("thankfully, it didn't rain"), is at once less popular and less unpopular than the sentence-modifying *hopefully* ("Hopefully, it won't rain"). Its use is sufficiently common to have drawn some critical attention, but not so common as to have attracted the kind of sustained and vitriolic abuse that has been heaped on *hopefully.*

Our earliest evidence for the sentence-modifying *thankfully* is from 1963, which is about the time when *hopefully* was beginning to become an infamous word among language watchers.

Thankfully, the publishers have reproduced many of the canvases in detail —*Saturday Rev.,* 16 Feb. 1963

The disjunctive *thankfully* is simply the correlative of *hopefully:* while *hopefully* expresses hope that something will turn out as desired, *thankfully* expresses thanks that it turned out as it did. While the commentators continue to express their ill-founded objections, our evidence shows that the sentence-modifying *thankfully* occurs in both British and American general writing in contexts that are entirely reputable. It is the predominant use of the word in our most recent files.

Garton, thankfully, is perfectly English —*The Observer,* 6 Jan. 1974

Thankfully, Without Walls has returned to the basic pleasures of the intellectual forum —Sean Macaulay, *Punch,* 5–11 Feb. 1992

Thankfully, evolution has softened their monstrous image, leaving us with cardinals and chickadees instead of a yard full of Velociraptors —John Noble Wilford, *N.Y. Times Book Rev.,* 25 Jan. 1998

Greek art, thankfully, is not obsessed by either death-demons or ghosts —John Boardman, *Times Literary Supp.*, 25 Jan. 1980

That book, thankfully, has arrived —Jay Nordlinger, *National Rev.*, 22 May 2000

. . . the odor had thankfully diminished —Michael Baughman, *Sports Illustrated,* 22 Nov. 1982

. . . one bomb hung on the rack just long enough to obliterate one of the bunkers, thankfully empty —Tom Clancy, *Without Remorse,* 1994

Thankfully, those opinions are advanced with graceful prose —Ken Auletta, *N.Y. Times Book Rev.,* 28 July 1985

For more detailed consideration of sentence-modifying adverbs, see HOPEFULLY and SENTENCE ADVERB.

thanking you in advance Many commentators strongly denigrate the use of this phrase in correspondence, finding in it such faults as triteness, a presumption that the favor being asked will be done, and an implication that the writer will not take the trouble to express appreciation later when the favor actually *has* been done. The writers who use it, we suspect, are really just trying to be polite, but its reputation is bad enough to make it a poor choice for politeness. Inoffensive alternatives are not hard to come by; for example, "Any help that you may give me will be appreciated" or simply "Your help will be appreciated."

than whom See THAN 1.

that 1. *"That," "which" introducing restrictive and nonrestrictive clauses. That* is our oldest relative pronoun. According to McKnight 1928 *that* was prevalent in early Middle English, *which* began to be used as a relative pronoun in the 14th century, and *who* and *whom* in the 15th. *That* was used not only to introduce restrictive clauses, but also nonrestrictive ones:

Fleance his son, that keeps him company —Shakespeare, *Macbeth,* 1606

By the early 17th century, *which* and *that* were being used pretty much interchangeably. Evans 1957 quotes this passage from the Authorized (King James) Version (1611) of the Bible:

Render therefore unto Caesar the things which are Caesar's; and unto God the things that are God's.

During the later 17th century, Evans tells us, *that* fell into disuse, at least in literary English. It went into such an eclipse that its reappearance in the early 18th century was noticed and

satirized by Joseph Addison in *The Spectator* (30 May 1711) in a piece entitled "Humble Petition of *Who* and *Which* against the upstart Jack Sprat *That*." *That* had returned, and although it could still be used to introduce a nonrestrictive clause,

Age, that lessens the enjoyment of life, increases our desire of living —Oliver Goldsmith (quoted in Lurie 1927)

this function was much reduced. Its nonrestrictive function continued to diminish, and although it was still so used in 19th-century literature, by the early 20th century such use seemed anomalous enough that Fowler 1907 singled out these examples (and others) for censure:

And with my own little stock of money besides, that Mrs. Hoggarty's card-parties had lessened by a good five-and-twenty shillings, I calculated . . . —Thackeray

How to keep the proper balance between these two testy old wranglers, that rarely pull the right way together, is as much . . . —George Meredith

The brothers Fowler may have been prompted to find nonrestrictive *that* anomalous by the opinions some grammarians expressed around the turn of the century. Hall 1917 cited several of these, who seem to have felt that nonrestrictive *that* had always been rare or had become so lately. Hall thought the grammarians had not looked very hard at English literature; he did, and listed some 115 authors who used nonrestrictive *that* (in some 1100 passages). About half of his authors are from the 19th century. Hall made one important point that no one else seems to: poets are the heaviest users of nonrestrictive *that*. The reason is fairly obvious: *that* flourishes in unstressed positions where *which* will not fit comfortably. Grammarians and usage commentators tend to look at prose. It may well be that the historical tendency of *that* to be less often used in introducing nonrestrictive clauses has always been more marked in prose than in poetry and speech. At any rate, Virginia McDavid in *American Speech* (Spring–Summer 1977) reports a study showing *that* introduces only restrictive clauses in mid-20th-century edited prose.

The finding of 1977 should satisfy you if you are writing prose. No one seems to have considered poetry since Hall in 1917. The nonrestrictive *that* is not entirely dead, however; Evans 1957 hinted at its continuing use, but his two unidentified examples may be from poetry (or even older prose). We do find the use occasionally in represented speech and in speechlike prose (as, for instance, a chatty letter not intended for publication):

"I mean little Sid Mercer, that rides for me. He's the duke of them all when he lays off the liquor. . . ." —Ring Lardner, *The Big Town,* 1921

". . . Take while I'm in an offering mood. I'm not the Red Cross that you can call at any emergency." —Mordecai Richler, *The Apprenticeship of Duddy Kravitz,* 1959

When I was in the hospital even the nurses' aides that didn't have sense enough to do anything but empty the ice-water were full of that chatter —Flannery O'Connor, letter, April 1956

And in January 1969 Theodore Bernstein in *Winners & Sinners* took time to censure two instances of nonrestrictive *that* that had appeared in the *New York Times* earlier in the month. He said that he had not had to mention such a use for years. The evidence seems to indicate, however, that nonrestrictive *that* is still natural to some people, even though it is not used in edited prose.

The examples Fowler 1907 gives of nonrestrictive *that* show that commentators and grammarians were then well aware of its diminishing range. And if *that* was being confined to introducing restrictive clauses, might it not be useful (as well as symmetrical) to confine *which* to nonrestrictive clauses? The Fowler brothers thought so, as perhaps some of their predecessors had (such as Ayres 1881 and Bierce 1909). Fowler 1926 put the proposition succinctly:

. . . if writers would agree to regard *that* as the defining relative pronoun, & *which* as the non-defining, there would be much gain both in lucidity & in ease. Some there are who follow this principle now; but it would be idle to pretend that it is the practice either of most or of the best writers.

Evans 1957 responds: "What is not the practice of most, or of the best, is not part of our common language."

Evans's commonsensical observation did not occur to, or did not impress, most subsequent usage writers, who remember only Fowler's first sentence. The general recommendation of the majority is to follow Fowler's wish, although many of them hedge the recommendation round with exceptions, caveats, and appeals to euphony or formality.

But *which* is as firmly entrenched in its restrictive function as in its nonrestrictive one. Joseph M. Williams in *College Composition and Communications* (May 1981) points out that even some of those who recommend using *that* instead of *which* in restrictive function use *which* themselves unawares. For instance, Jacques Barzun, in *Simple & Direct* (1975), says this in the middle of one page:

In conclusion, I recommend using *that* with defining clauses, except when stylistic reasons interpose. [The stylistic reasons discussed refer to a succession of *that*s.]

And this to open the first paragraph on the next page:

Next is a typical situation which a practiced writer corrects "for style" virtually by reflex action: . . .

Williams also cites the discussion of *which* and *that* from Strunk & White 1959, which recommends "which-hunting," and then quotes White's own usage:

. . . the premature expiration of a pig is, I soon discovered, a departure which the community marks solemnly on its calendar —E. B. White, "Death of a Pig"

If the discussions in many of the handbooks are complex and burdened with exceptions, the facts of usage are quite simple. Virginia McDavid's 1977 study shows that about 75 percent of the instances of *which* in edited prose introduce restrictive clauses; about 25 percent, nonrestrictive ones.

We conclude that the usage of *which* and *that*—at least in prose—has pretty much settled down. You can use either *which* or *that* to introduce a restrictive clause and *which* to introduce a nonrestrictive clause.

2. *"That," "which," "who"—what may they refer to? That* is our most general relative pronoun, as well as our oldest. It was regularly used to refer to persons as well as to things in earlier literature:

Ah, great God that art so good —*Noah's Flood,* prob. written before 1425, in *Everyman and Medieval Miracle Plays,* ed. A. C. Cawley, 1959 (spelling modernized)

By heaven, I'll make a ghost of him that lets me —Shakespeare, *Hamlet,* 1601

When *that* came back into literary use around the beginning of the 18th century after falling out of favor during the 17th, it was noticed with some disapproval (see section 1 above) by such writers as Joseph Addison. Jespersen 1905 points out that the expressed preference for *who* and *which* may have come partly from their conforming to the Latin relative pronouns (*that* having no Latin correlative). Jespersen also notes that when Addison edited *The Spectator* to appear in book form, he changed many of his own uses of *that* to *who* or *which.* The 18th century also marks the first appearance of works devoted to the correction of English usage; some, naturally, discussed relative pronouns. McKnight 1928 cites an anonymous 1752 *Observations upon the English Language* (George Harris wrote it, says Leonard 1929), which condemned the use of *that* and prescribed *who* as "the only proper Word to be used in Relation to Persons and Animals" and *which* "in Relation to Things." It may be that some carryover from the 18th-century general dislike of *that* produced the apparently common, yet unfounded, notion that *that* may be used to refer only to things. Bernstein 1971 and Simon 1980 mention receiving letters objecting to the use of *that* in reference to persons. The notion persists: William Safire in the *New York Times Magazine* (8 June 1980) panned an ad beginning "We seek a managing editor that can. . . ." *That* has applied to persons since its 18th-century revival just as it did before its 17th-century eclipse. Evans 1957 records an 1885 translation of the Bible that began "The Lord's Prayer" with

> Our Father that art in heaven

using the same *that* used in Wycliffe's version of 1389.   A few other examples:

> In a letter dated Aug. 16, 1776, Horace Walpole wrote the Countess of Upper Ossory, "This world is a comedy to those that think, a tragedy to those that feel." One might add, "And a put-on to those that neither think nor feel. . . ." —Vincent Canby, *N.Y. Times,* 27 June 1976

> . . . being filled with one of my rolls, gave the other two to a woman and her child that came down the river in the boat with us —Benjamin Franklin, *Autobiography,* 1788

> The woman who kissed him and—pinched his poke—was the lady that's known as Lou —Robert W. Service, "The Shooting of Dan McGrew," 1907

> Ben Lucien Burman: "I would like to unmirandize any person that uses the word. . . ." —Harper 1985

In the past *which* was also used of persons as well as things:

> Our Father which art in heaven —Matthew 6:9 (AV), 1611

> Caroline, Anna, and I have just been devouring some cold souse, and it would be difficult to say which enjoyed it most —Jane Austen, letter, 14 Jan. 1796

It has now been replaced by *who* and *that* in this function, and is usually limited to things:

> . . . that curious access of tenderness which may bring tears to the eyes —C. E. Montague, *A Writer's Notes on His Trade,* 1930

> . . . that voice which was such a strange amalgam of fog and frog —William Styron, *This Quiet Dust and Other Writings,* 1982

Which may still be used of one considered somewhat less than human:

> A banshee which has long stationed itself outside my office, and who devilishly calls Pell "Mel" —Safire 1984

Which may also be used of persons in conscious echoing of an older style:

> Beware of the scribes, which love to go in long clothing, and love salutations in the marketplaces —Howard 1980 (echoing Luke 20:46 (AV), 1611)

Who and *whom* are not very controversial, save in relation to their case forms (see WHO, WHOM 1). The prescription of our anonymous 18th-century critic that *who* "is the only proper word to be used in Relation to Persons and Animals" seems fairly descriptive of actual use of *who*:

> Our Father who art in heaven —Matthew 6:9 (RSV), 1946

> . . . a strapping, loud woman named Doris, whom Ronda Ray fervently called a slut —John Irving, *The Hotel New Hampshire,* 1981

> . . . snapshots she had taken . . . of the hamster who had died —John Updike, *Couples,* 1968

> Tonto is his cat, whom he walks on a leash —Stanley Kauffmann, *Before My Eyes,* 1980

Who also refers to words for entities that consist of people:

> There is a very good literary society whom it would be well worth while to know —Henry Adams, letter, 23 Nov. 1859

> Texaco, who is proud to present. . . . —cited in Simon 1980

Summary: In current usage, *that* refers to persons or things, *which* chiefly to things and rarely to subhuman entities, *who* chiefly to persons and sometimes to animals. *That* is definitely standard when used of persons. Because *that* has no genitive form or construction, *of which* or *whose* must be substituted for it in contexts that call for the genitive. See WHOSE 1.

3. *Omission of "that."* See CONTACT CLAUSE.

4. *"That" repeated. That* is sometimes unnecessarily doubled, Copperud 1970 tells us; it happens when an interrupting element delays the rest of the clause. Watt 1967 concurs: "Because *that* is such a natural, unobtrusive connective, a writer sometimes forgets that he has used it. . . ." Robert Baker made the same discovery back in 1770, citing this sentence:

I expected that, when I told him the News, that he would be more surprised at it than he really was.

"This is nonsense," says Baker bluntly. However, he does excuse the practice when enough words intervene "that it may be supposed the Reader or Hearer has so far forgot it."

5. *"That" as an adverb.* Sometime in the second half of the 19th century the propriety of *that* as an adverb was called into question. Hall 1917 cites Alford 1866 as calling it "quite indefensible." Vizetelly 1906 calls it "wholly inexcusable" and "an unpardonable vulgarism." The condemnation is repeated in various handbooks and grammars from the turn of the century through the 1920s and 1930s. Bryant 1962 and Harper 1975, 1985, however, find this use standard.

Prentice Hall 1978 labels adverbial *that* colloquial and gives two example sentences: "She's that poor she can't buy food" and "I didn't like the book that much." These two examples are really different uses. In Prentice Hall's first sentence *that* qualifies an adjective completed by a clause. Hall 1917 cites "I am *that* sick I can hardly stand up" as a common locution in his part of Virginia. The American Dialect Dictionary cites many examples from various parts of the country, including one from Edith Wharton, in a novel set in New England, one from an Uncle Remus story, and one from a 1941 radio broadcast of Lowell Thomas. The OED dates this adverbial use from the 15th century and labels its survival Scottish and dialectal. Webster's Third labels it dialectal, Bryant 1962 colloquial.

The second use of *that* as an adverb is much more common and widespread. The OED dates it back to the 17th century; Thomas Jefferson and Harriet Beecher Stowe, among others, are cited. The OED identifies the adverb as being used chiefly with adjectives to express quantity and ascribes its use in preference to *so* to its being more precise. Usually the amount or degree which *that* refers to is specified earlier in the text:

The Altgeld Gardens project is now considered unpoliceable. Before the Cabrini Green project became that bad, headquarters saturated the area —Gail Sheehy, *McCall's*, March 1971

. . . makes pronouncements about corruption in the courts, ambitious judges, plea-bargainings for the rich, lock-up pens for the poor. The only stereotype left out is police brutality, it's that clichéd a novel —Genevieve Stuttaford, *Publishers Weekly*, 11 Aug. 1975

The most common current use, however, is in negative statements in which *that* is reduced more or less to an intensifier:

He said to Ratliff: "This town aint that big. Why hasn't Flem caught them?" —William Faulkner, *The Town,* 1957

. . . I often forget myself and remind them of their futures as parents. It is not that easy —Thomas J. Cottle, *Saturday Rev.,* 1 Feb. 1969

The movie *is* different, but not *that* different —Pauline Kael, in *The Film,* 1968

McNamara was rather casual about it at first. He did not think that they were that close to a treaty —David Halberstam, *Harper's,* February 1971

This use in negative constructions is frequently found with the intensifier *all* added. See ALL THAT.

Summary: *that* has essentially two adverbial uses, both of some longevity. In the first of these, it modifies an adjective that is followed by a clause. This use seems to be chiefly dialectal. In the second, *that* modifies an adjective (or occasionally an adverb). In positive constructions this *that* cannot usually be replaced by *so*. In negative constructions, *that* is closer to being a simple intensifier. Both aspects of the second use are standard in general prose.

6. For the use of pronominal *that* to refer to preceding ideas, topics, sentences, or paragraphs, see THIS 1.

that there See THIS HERE, THAT THERE.

thee See THOU.

their **1.** *Their, there, they're.* It is not unusual to see these common words interchanged in casual or poorly edited writing. Haste and inattention to detail probably have more to do with most such errors than does actual confusion about which word is which. However, for the record, *their* is a possessive pronoun ("Their house is down the street"); *there* has various uses as an adjective ("that man there"), a noun ("take it from there"), a pronoun ("There shall come a time"), and, chiefly, an adverb ("stop right there"); and *they're* is a contraction of *they are* ("They're coming tomorrow").

2. See THEY, THEIR, THEM.

theirs Like *its, ours,* and *yours, theirs* is spelled without an apostrophe in present-day English. Editors and proofreaders are undoubtedly well aware of this fact, but in casual writing the apostrophe can sneak in fairly easily, and it sometimes even succeeds in making its way into print:

. . . Exxon gas stations have the best I've seen and their's is free —letter to the editor, *Harper's Weekly,* 1 Dec. 1975

theirselves *Theirselves* is, like *hisself,* a logically formed pronoun of impressive age that now occurs only in substandard speech and representations thereof. In form it is analogous to *myself, yourself, herself,* and *ourselves,* but logic and analogy are as nothing compared to usage, and usage decrees that the word favored in standard English is *themselves.* In centuries past, *theirselves* did appear from time to time in reputable writing, but the only writing it now shows up in is imitative of rustic speech:

> They was talking and bawling amongst theirselves, but . . . the ones I heard was more scairt than hurt —William Wister Haines, *High Tension,* 1938

See also HISSELF.

them 1. See IT'S ME; THEY, THEIR, THEM.
2. *Demonstrative pronoun.*

A century ago New York Mayor "Boss" Tweed, smarting from Thomas Nast's cartoons, exclaimed, "I don't care what they print about me, but stop them damn cartoons!" —Peter Bates, *Bostonia Mag.,* March 1984

Boss Tweed's *them* is a demonstrative pronoun with a mysterious history. In its modern form, it is attested only since the end of the 16th century. But many observers have been tantalized by the possibility that modern English *them* is a survival of Old English *þæm (thæm),* the masculine and neuter dative of the definite article. The theory is an attractive one, but it has one serious defect—the missing Middle English link. All examples of *them* found in Middle English so far are of the personal pronoun, not the demonstrative. In Middle English the Old English dative seems to have weakened and the final *-m* become *-n* or simply disappeared. If there was a demonstrative *them* that survived in Middle English, it has not been discovered yet.

From the early examples in the OED and in Jespersen 1909–49 (vol. 2), it would appear that demonstrative *them* enjoyed about a century of unnoticed use. Many of its early occurrences were in works of piety, of which John Bunyan's *Grace Abounding to the Chief of Sinners* (1666) is probably the closest approach to literature. There seem to have been no truly literary uses of the word until the 19th century, when it began to occur in fictitious speech.

The demonstrative *them* seems to have first attracted commentary at about the beginning of the 19th century. It reached usage books in 1869, and from that point on it has come in for regular criticism in schoolbooks.

Perhaps because of the efforts of two centuries worth of schoolmasters, the demonstrative *them* is now largely restricted to the speech of the uneducated and to the familiar

speech of others. It has been in use for about four centuries, and has still not reached respectability. In writing, then, you can expect to find it in the same places you would find words of similar status: in reported speech, in fictitious speech (especially of little-educated characters), and, especially in the 20th century, in the familiar usage of educated people when they are being humorous. Here are some of our examples:

> . . . he bars the doctors. He'd die roarin' before he'd let them boys put a finger on him —Myles na gCopaleen (Flann O'Brien), *The Best of Myles,* 1968

> Can I afford to let Etta clean up those dishes in the sink and get them biscuits baked . . . ? —Robert Benchley, *The Benchley Round Up,* 1954

> She never really had liked them big droopy things —Garrison Keillor, *Lake Wobegon Days,* 1985

> You mustn't fake articles any more. Not even in details. Them's orders —Robert Frost, letter, 18 Mar. 1913

> I aim to read Cicero, Caesar, Tacitus and any other of them boys that I can think of —Flannery O'Connor, letter, 7 Apr. 1956

> You remember Chesterton's slogan—"My mother, drunk or sober!" Well, them's my sentiments toward you, old thing —Alexander Woollcott, letter, 15 Nov. 1920

themself According to the OED, *themself* was the normal form of the third person plural reflexive pronoun until about 1540, when it was superseded by *themselfs* and, ultimately, *themselves.* The OED says that *themself* "disappeared" by about 1570, but we have evidence of its use persisting in familiar use (by Emily Dickinson and F. Scott Fitzgerald, among others) into the 20th century. Since the 1970s or so it has been revived as a gender-neutral singular reflexive pronoun, taking the place of *himself or herself.* This use of *themself* is similar to the use of *they, their,* and *them* in reference to singular terms and indefinite pronouns (see THEY, THEIR, THEM).

> Walking through Pilsen, the casual observer might easily think themself back in 1945 —*The Times* (London), 7 May 1990

> With the unselfconscious absorption of someone working something out for themself —J. Hoberman, *Village Voice,* 15 Oct. 1991

Such use of *they, their,* and *them* is old and well established. Similar use of *themself,* however, is not very well established but appears to be on the increase.

then 1. A couple of critics have disapproved *then* as an adjective, but the few other commentators who have taken note of it consider it to be a useful and concise word. It is an old one, certainly, first recorded in 1584. Among the authors who have used it are Johnson, Boswell, Coleridge, Poe, Tennyson, and Henry James. In recent years some people attach *then* to the word it modifies by means of a hyphen:

> . . . aimed at Reagan, the then-Governor of California —Jess Nierenberg, *Maledicta 1983*

But it is usually treated as a separate adjective:

> . . . to the then prominent engraver, John Farley —Barry Moser, *Publishers Weekly,* 6 July 1984

> . . . the then editor of the Merriam dictionaries —Harper 1985

See also NOW.
2. See THAN 3.

thence See FROM WHENCE, FROM THENCE, FROM HENCE.

theorize As an intransitive verb, *theorize* is usually used with *about*:

> . . . a great mass of theorising about adolescence is flooding the book shops —Margaret Mead, *Coming of Age in Samoa,* 1928

> Sheed theorized about, and deplored, what he called a "Guiness Book of World Records" approach to book reviewing —John Leonard, *N.Y. Times Book Rev.,* 10 June 1973

It also occurs with *on*:

> There are few subjects on which people, informed or less informed, are more willing to theorize than the history of Russia —*Times Literary Supp.,* 22 Oct. 1971

there See THEIR 1; THERE IS, THERE ARE.

therefor, therefore *Therefor* and *therefore* were originally variant spellings of the same adverb. Each came eventually to have a distinct meaning and a distinct pronunciation, however, and they are now regarded as separate words. *Therefor,* which is pronounced with the principal stress on the second syllable, almost always means "for that" or "in return for that." It is not a word that is now commonly used, except, perhaps, by accountants:

> . . . so far as they relate to accountancy and to managerial responsibility therefor —*Jour. of Accountancy,* April 1940

> . . . any expenditure or liability incurred therefor which creates an asset —Wayne K. Goettsche, *Arthur Young Jour.,* Autumn 1967

Therefore is pronounced with the principal stress on the first syllable. It is, of course, an extremely common word, whose basic meaning is "for that reason; consequently":

> . . . providing a constantly renewed source of food for the larger forms of marine life, which therefore abound —Edward P. Lanning, *Peru Before the Incas,* 1967

Therefor has also been occasionally used as a synonym of *therefore*:

> . . . it would not, therefor, be a morpheme —Dwight L. Bolinger, *Word,* April 1948

> . . . the frog test for pregnancy is probably therefor based on the excess of the luteinizing hormones —*Biological Abstracts,* January 1943

When used in this way, *therefor* is pronounced in the same way as *therefore*. Most readers will undoubtedly regard it simply as a misspelling or typographical error, and it seems safer to keep the two words distinct in spelling.

there is, there are When *there* is a "dummy" or anticipatory subject, the number of the verb is determined by the number of the true subject following:

> There is no more grasping man within the four walls of the world —Lady Gregory, *Damer's Gold,* in *New Comedies,* 1913

> "There are whiskers on it," said he soberly —James Stephens, *The Crock of Gold,* 1912

Simple enough, isn't it? A singular verb followed by a singular noun, a plural verb followed by a plural noun. That is the way things are supposed to work and often do, but there are complications.

For instance, when a compound subject follows the verb and the first element is singular, we find mixed usage—the verb may either be singular or plural. Jespersen 1909–49 (vol. 2) explains the singular verb as a case of attraction of the verb to the first subject, and illustrates it with this from Shakespeare:

> There comes an old man, and his three sons —*As You Like It,* 1600

Perrin & Ebbitt 1972 also suggests that many writers feel the plural verb is awkward before a singular noun, and Bryant 1962 cites studies that show the singular verb is much more common in standard English.

> So long as there's rain and salamanders on Henry Street, Winston will be there too —Elizabeth Frey, *Springfield* (Mass.) *Morning Union,* 1 Apr. 1987

> . . . there's a touch pad pointing device, a USB port, a Fast IR port, dual speakers . . .

and a PC/Card bay —Cade Metz, *PC Mag.*, 21 Oct. 1997

There's road rage, sky rage and work rage —*Playboy*, February 2000

Some writers, however, follow formal agreement and use a plural verb:

. . . there were perplexity and agitation —Jane Austen, *Mansfield Park*, 1814

. . . where there were a white beach and an amusement park —John Cheever, *The Wapshot Chronicle*, 1957

We also find mixed usage when a collective noun that is the formal subject is followed by a prepositional phrase with a plural noun as the object. A correspondent in 1984 complained of the lack of agreement in this sentence:

There's been a lot of highway traffic problems.

The verb in a construction like this is governed by notional agreement. When the speaker or writer has the collective in mind, a singular verb is used:

There is a handful of other caves —*Geographical Mag.*, May 1984

. . . she suddenly perceives, feels, that there is an extraordinary number of handsome young men —Alice Adams, *Listening to Billie*, 1977

And when the plural noun is in mind, a plural verb is used:

. . . there are a new variety of potatoes — unidentified woman on television, 9 Feb. 1983

. . . there were a passel of Italian movie producers shooting Westerns in the Israeli desert —Daniel B. Drooz, *N.Y. Times*, 1 July 1973

Harder to explain, perhaps, is a long-standing propensity for *there is* or *there's* in every case, even when the following subject is clearly plural and there are no complications to cloud our minds. Jespersen finds the same construction in Danish, Russian, and Italian, and dates it back in English to the 15th century. It certainly has been common:

Honey, and milk, and sugar: there is three —Shakespeare, *Love's Labour's Lost*, 1595

How many is there of 'em, Scrub? —George Farquhar, *The Beaux Stratagem*, 1707

. . . but there is in nature, I fear, too many tendencies to envy and jealousy —Charles Lamb, letter, 13 June 1797

. . . if there's several ways you can use something before or after the verb, we'll use two

sample sentences —Stuart Berg Flexner, quoted in *Righting Words*, July/August 1987

Jespersen has a theory that *there is* or *there's* is often out—in speech or on paper—before the whole sentence is formulated. Early choice of the verb before the number of the subject is actually decided would also explain the occasional instance of the plural verb with a singular subject:

There were one group you did not mention —Daniel Schorr, speaking on television, 27 Jan. 1981

Jespersen notes that the invariable singular occurs mostly in the colloquial style—speech and speechlike prose—and is generally avoided in the literary style. That observation accords with our evidence. In the more complex constructions, you are best guided by your own sense of what sounds right in the particular context to avoid awkwardness and maintain the smooth flow of the sentence.

the same as   See SAME AS.

these kind of, these sort of   See KIND 1.

they   1. For *they* used to refer to a singular noun or pronoun, see THEY, THEIR, THEM.
2. *They* used as an indefinite subject is sometimes objected to, primarily on the assumption that every pronoun should have an antecedent. Lamberts 1972 calls that assumption shaky, as indeed it is, since many pronouns do not require antecedents. Perrin & Ebbitt 1972 reports that indefinite *they* occurs in all varieties of usage. It is standard. Here is a sample of its uses:

In Lagos, they were sleeping in the streets —John Updike, *Bech Is Back*, 1982

In seventh grade they were always assigning you to write about things like farm produce —Russell Baker, *Growing Up*, 1982

They're tearing down a nine-story building just outside my office window —*And More by Andy Rooney*, 1982

3. *They* as a pronunciation spelling of *there* goes back as far as 1799 (the earliest occurrence we have seen is in a citation for *an't* in the Dictionary of American English). In this century it has been used chiefly to represent dialectal or uneducated speech:

They's also a ballroom and a couple card rooms —Ring Lardner, *The Big Town*, 1921

they, their, them   The question of the propriety of using *they, their, them* to refer to indefinite pronouns and singular nouns has two aspects that are distinct but often overlap. Both relate to perceived gaps in the language. The first, and most often discussed, is the lack of a common-gender third person singular pronoun. The second aspect of the question is what Jespersen 1909–49 (vol. 2) refers to as a lack of common number or neutral number, a form of number that is neither definitely singular nor definitely plural. Jespersen says that "the lack of a common-number (and common-sex) pronoun leads to the frequent use of *they* and *their* in referring to an indefinite pronoun (or similar expression) in the singular." We shall examine these problematic aspects of the use of *they, their, them* separately.

1. *Common-gender pronoun.* Although the lack of a common-gender third person singular pronoun has received much attention in recent years from those concerned with women's issues, the problem, as felt by writers, is much older; the plural pronouns have been pressed into use to supply the missing form since Middle English:

And whoso fyndeth hym out of swich
    blame,
They wol come up . . .
—Chaucer, "The Pardoner's Prologue," ca.
1395 (in Jespersen)

The use of the plural pronouns to refer to indefinite pronouns—*anyone, each, everyone, nobody, somebody,* etc.—results from the concurrence of two forces: notional agreement (the indefinite pronouns are usually plural in implication) and the lack of sexual identification that indefinite pronouns share with *they, their, them.* You will find many examples of this reference at the entries in this book under AGREEMENT and at those for the individual indefinite pronouns. We add only a few examples here:

And every one to rest themselves betake
—Shakespeare, *The Rape of Lucrece*, 1594

. . . if ye from your hearts forgive not every one his brother their trespasses —Matthew 18:35 (AV), 1611

Nobody here seems to look into an Author, ancient or modern, if they can avoid it —Lord Byron, letter, 12 Nov. 1805

I would have everybody marry if they can do it properly —Jane Austen, *Mansfield Park*, 1814

. . . it is too hideous for anyone in their senses to buy —W. H. Auden, *Encounter*, February 1955

. . . the detachment and sympathy of someone approaching their own death —Alan Moorehead, *The Blue Nile*, 1962

Each designs to get sole possession of the treasure, but they only succeed in killing one another —Sir Paul Harvey, *The Oxford Companion to English Literature*, 4th ed., 1967

The relative pronoun *who* is also unmarked as to sex, and the plural pronoun is used in reference to it:

Who makes you their confidant? —Jane Austen, *Emma*, 1815 (in Jespersen)

. . . who ever thought of sparing their grandmother worry? —Edith Wharton, *The Age of Innocence*, 1920

A second kind of reference connects *they, their, them* to singular nouns that can apply to either sex or to noun phrases that apply to both sexes. Again, we can see that the practice has a long history:

. . . every fool can do as they're bid —Jonathan Swift, *Polite Conversation*, 1738 (in Jespersen)

Every person . . . now recovered their liberty —Oliver Goldsmith, *The History of England*, 1771 (OED)

A person can't help their birth —W. M. Thackeray, *Vanity Fair*, 1848 (OED)

. . . unless a person takes a deal of exercise, they may soon eat more than does them good —Herbert Spencer, *Autobiography*, 1904 (in Jespersen)

We can only know an actual person by observing their [sic] behaviour in a variety of different situations —George Orwell, as quoted by Edward Crankshaw, *Times Literary Supp.*, 26 Dec. 1980

I had to decide: Is this person being irrational or is he right? Of course, they were often right —Robert Burchfield, in *U.S. News & World Report*, 11 Aug. 1986

As most commentators note, the traditional pronoun for each of these cases is the masculine third person singular, *he, his, him.* This tradition goes back to the 18th-century grammarians, who boxed themselves into the position by first deciding that the indefinite pronouns must always be singular. They then had to decide between the masculine and feminine singular pronouns for use in reference to the indefinites, and they chose the masculine (they were, of course, all men). Naturally there is plenty of evidence for the masculine pronoun used in this way:

Nobody attains reality for my mother until he eats —Flannery O'Connor, letter, 28 June 1956

Now, a writer is entitled to have Roget on his desk —Barzun 1985

. . . everyone allegedly being entitled to his ignorance —Simon 1980

In my book, everyone has his book, everyone blows his nose, and everybody goes his way —Kilpatrick 1984

But the insistence on the masculine singular has its limitations. Sometimes its results are downright silly:

> . . . everyone will be able to decide for himself whether or not to have an abortion —Albert Bleumenthal, N.Y. State Assembly (cited in Longman 1984)

Reader's Digest 1983 also points out that the masculine pronoun is awkward at best used in reference to antecedents of both sexes:

> She and Louis had a game—who could find the ugliest photograph of himself —Joseph P. Lash, *Eleanor and Franklin* (in Reader's Digest)
>
> . . . the ideal that every boy and girl should be so equipped that he shall not be handicapped in his struggle for social progress —C. C. Fries, *American English Grammar*, 1940 (in Reader's Digest)

It is an arguable point whether a phrase like "every boy and girl" is singular or plural. But note how much more natural and sensible the plural pronoun sounds:

> . . . the liberty of every father and mother to educate their children as they desire —Robert A. Taft, quoted in *Time*, 20 Sept. 1948

Some commentators recommend *he or she, his or her, him or her* to avoid the sex bias of the masculine and the presumed solecism of the plural. Bolinger 1980 points out that this solution, too, is old, going back to the 18th century, but that many commentators are also hostile to the forms as unwieldy (see HE, HE OR SHE). Even the *he or she* formula can lead the unwary into trouble, as in this instance where it is used to refer to a plural pronoun:

> Those who have been paid for the oil on his or her property —Lucia Mouat, *Christian Science Monitor*, 4 Aug. 1983 (cited by Allan Metcalf, *American Speech*, Fall 1984)

One more point needs to be made. Simon 1980 writes:

> . . . I bristle at Miller and Swift's advocacy of *they, their,* etc., as singular pronouns because "reputable writers and speakers" have used them with indefinite antecedents. . . . But the lapses of great ones do not make a wrong right. . . .

The examples here of the "great ones" from Chaucer to the present are not lapses. They are uses following a normal pattern in English that was established four centuries before the 18th-century grammarians invented the sole-

cism. The plural pronoun is one solution devised by native speakers of English to a grammatical problem inherent in that language— and it is by no means the worst solution.

2. *Common-number pronoun.* The examples involving nouns like *person* cited in the preceding section might have equally well been set down here, because they illustrate the use of *they, their, them* to refer to singular nouns used in such a way that the singular stands for and includes any or all. Examples of this use are very old, and they include many cases where sex is perfectly obvious:

> The righteous man . . . that taketh not their life in vain —*Pearl*, ca. 1380 (spelling modernized)
>
> 'Tis meet that some more audience than a mother,
> Since nature makes them partial, should o'erhear
> The speech
>   —Shakespeare, *Hamlet*, 1601
>
> No man goes to battle to be killed.—But they do get killed —George Bernard Shaw, *Three Plays for Puritans*, 1901 (in Jespersen)
>
> The GI in Britain feels that the papers . . . are ungrateful for their "sacrifices" and contemptuous of their society and country —Jean Rikhoff Hills, *New Republic*, 23 Aug. 1954

We even find *they, their, them* used in reference to inanimate nouns (although we have no literary evidence for this practice):

> Do you wear a chain belt? If not, you may be out of the run of fashion in Ireland, for they are gaining a widespread popularity —*Irish Digest*, July 1953
>
> Your usual store should have their Autumn stocks in now —advt., *Punch*, 30 Sept. 1953
>
> Oh, we have an argument now and then, but they never carry over —Lessa Nanney, quoted in *Bluegrass Unlimited*, February 1981

In addition, we find *they, their, them* used in reference to singular nouns modified by a distributive (such as *every*) which imparts a notional plurality:

> . . . every man went to their lodging —Lord Berners, translation of Froissart's *Chronicles*, 1523 (in McKnight)
>
> . . . every horse had been groomed with as much rigour as if they belonged to a private gentleman —Thomas De Quincey, *The English Mail Coach*, 1849 (in McKnight)

They, their, them are used in both literature and general writing to refer to singular nouns, when those nouns have some notion of plurality about them. All the cases in this section, and a good many of those in the first section, illustrate this operation of notional agreement. Look again at the example from Shaw above. It would be a violation of English idiom to use a singular pronoun in the second sentence (But he does get killed) on the assumption that because *no man* is singular in form and governs a singular verb, it must take a singular pronoun in reference. Notional agreement is in control, and its dictates must be followed.

3. See also THEY 2, 3.

they're See THEIR 1.

think The use of *think* with *to* and an infinitive (as in "We didn't think to ask him") was called an illiteracy by Fowler 1926, but it has now won general acceptance. Evans 1957 found the construction to be standard in American English when the sense of *think* was "remember" but archaic when the sense was "plan" or "expect." Our evidence shows, however, that *think to* meaning "expect or intend to" continues in good use:

> ... and I thought to succeed as they did, and as rapidly —*The Autobiography of William Butler Yeats*, 1953

> What other actor would think to achieve rampant movie fame by playing a Soviet spy and two baseball fanatics? —Richard Corliss et al., *Time*, 26 June 1989

> Martin thinks to make a case for Whitman as a model —Robert Boyers, *Times Literary Supp.*, 30 May 1980

thinking man *Thinking man* and similar expressions are sometimes used as a way of discouraging disagreement:

> Equally, no thinking person can fail to recognize the individual and, even, the occasional corporate courage and wisdom —letter to the editor, *Center Mag.*, May/June 1971

The implication—that anyone who disagrees with what the writer is asserting must be an idiot—is bound to cause a certain amount of irritation, as Fowler 1926, Flesch 1964, and Burchfield 1996 have noted. But *thinking man* has other uses which are entirely inoffensive:

> Mr. Ustinov is a thinking man with a satiric mind —Haskel Frankel, *Saturday Rev.*, 13 Nov. 1971

> ... he is a thinking man's spy—reflective, historically aware —Michael Malone, *N.Y. Times Book Rev.*, 12 Jan. 1986

this 1. *Pronoun.* The use of pronominal *this* (and *that, which,* and *it* as well) to refer broadly to a preceding idea, topic, sentence, or paragraph, was under severe attack in usage books years ago, but nowadays the usage, which is often convenient, is considered quite respectable. College handbooks still include this subject (see Little, Brown 1980 and Macmillan 1982, for example), but they are now content with simply advising the student writer to make the reference clear. Here are some examples of the usage:

> But language is the expression of the human psyche, and this is something that nobody has yet been able, except in the crudest way, to measure —Barnard 1979

> I decided a good idea might be to drive along the road in the car, watching for kudu, and hunt any likely-looking clearings. We went back to the car and did this —Ernest Hemingway, *Green Hills of Africa*, 1935

Now that *this* is no longer an issue when referring to a preceding clause or sentence, a few commentators have switched their objections to *this* when it refers to a preceding noun and another pronoun could possibly be used instead. The underlying reason for the criticism in this case is probably that the construction is more typical of speech than writing.

> And I listened to him talk for a half hour or so . . . to evaluate what kind of person this was —Robert C. McFarlane, quoted in *The Tower Commission Report*, 1987

> . . . an old man . . . sent I am sure by the Lord to be a plague to the penwomen. This was a poet, and he had his poems in a paper bag —Flannery O'Connor, letter, 9 Aug. 1957

The use of constructions typical of speech is not a particularly heinous fault in writing, unless you are aiming to produce highly formal prose.

See also WHICH 2.

2. *Adjective.* It is not rare in speech for *this* to be used for emphasis in place of the indefinite article, as in "This guy said to me. . . ." Use of the emphatic *this* in writing has sometimes been discouraged, but our evidence shows that it is neither rare nor inappropriate in writing of a conversational tone. You can get a good sense of its quality from these examples:

> From the beginning of the show, Stanley makes a real pain in the neck of himself as this farmer who wants a ride in an airplane —Alan Loncto, quoted in *New Yorker*, 27 Aug. 1984

> Strange, even to me, that I haven't become a cynic after all I've been through, that I am still this sucker for the Land of Opportunity —Philip Roth, *Atlantic*, April 1981

. . . is comic-book stuff that reads as though he snapped it off on a free afternoon with his favorite word processor. There's this retired C.I.A. hit man —Newgate Callendar, *N.Y. Times Book Rev.,* 10 Apr. 1983

He pictured himself as this hard, lonely man —Wilfrid Sheed, *People Will Always Be Kind,* 1973

See also THIS HERE, THAT THERE.

this here, that there The frequency with which admonitions against the use of *this here* and *that there* are included in handbooks on writing suggests that students everywhere are composing essays in some sort of backwoods idiom: "Well, now, this here Captain Ahab fella gets hisself all riled up agin that there whale. . . ." For all we know they might be, but our evidence from published sources shows that writers in general have no need to be told that *this here* and *that there* are something less than standard English. The use of *here* and *there* for emphasis following a demonstrative adjective is a characteristic of dialectal and uneducated speech. It does not occur in writing except when such speech is being recorded, evoked, or imitated:

Brush, brush, brush, that there brush kept on swearing through its teeth, proper savage, it was —Richard Llewellyn, *None But the Lonely Heart,* 1943

"My back's nearbout broke and I ain't able to do another lick. This here kitchen looks like a hog sty." —Margaret Long, *Louisville Saturday,* 1950

See also THIS 2.

thither See HITHER 1.

thitherto See HITHERTO.

tho *Tho* has seen occasional use as a spelling variant of *though* for many centuries:

For tho' we allow every man something of his own and a peculiar Humour —William Congreve, "Concerning Humour in Comedy," 1695

Attempts by 19th- and 20th-century spelling reformers to encourage the use of *tho* have not met with widespread success, but in its heyday *tho* did appear in some widely circulated periodicals:

Even then this was said partly in earnest —*Better Homes and Gardens,* August 1946

. . . tho the average speed dictated by its rule makes the drivers go fast enough —*Road and Track,* December 1951

It has little current use. For more information about the history and current status of simplified spellings, see SPELLING REFORM; THRU.

those kind of, those sort of See KIND 1.

thou *Thou* was once the common form of the second person singular pronoun. In other words, it was once normal to address another person as "thou." In the period of Middle English, however, *thou* (and the related forms *thee, thy,* and *thine*) was gradually replaced by the plural *you* (and *your*), first in addressing a person of high social rank (as in "your majesty") and later in addressing a social equal. *Thou* was used only in speaking to a person of inferior social position, such as a servant, and it was eventually superseded by *you* even in this use. In Modern English, *thou* has been most familiar as a formal alternative to *you* in prayers and poetry:

Thou still unravag'd bride of quietness,
Thou foster-child of silence and slow time
    —John Keats, "Ode on a Grecian Urn," 1819

Thou has also persisted in more general use in some dialects—most notably, perhaps, in the language of the Friends (that is, the Quakers). An interesting feature of some dialectal usage, including that of the Friends, is that the accusative form *thee* ("I shall teach thee") occurs in place of the nominative *thou* ("Thou shalt learn from me") and is used with verbs inflected in the third person singular, so that instead of saying, "Thou hast forgotten" a Friend will say, "Thee has forgotten."

I remember in court when they were going to indict a Norwegian Quaker . . . his wife said, "Simon, thee must go to jail." —Harry Terrell, quoted in Studs Terkel, *Hard Times,* 1970

Exactly how this nominative use of *thee* developed is not known.

though See ALTHOUGH, THOUGH.

thrill As an intransitive verb meaning "to become thrilled," *thrill* is idiomatically followed by either *at* or *to*:

Alice thrilled at the suggestion —Patrick J. Costello, *Irish Digest,* April 1954

. . . was taken to it by two maiden aunts who, I dare say, thrilled to it —John Simon, *New York,* 30 Aug. 1971

thronged *Thronged* is usually used with *with:*

. . . his mind must have been thronged with feelings of being unwanted —John Cheever, *New Yorker,* 26 Sept. 1953

. . . on a cold Sunday, when the galleries were thronged with out-of-towners —Jean Stafford, *Children Are Bored on Sunday,* 1953

... my head became thronged with ideas for books —Edmund Wilson, *New Yorker,* 5 June 1971

Sometimes it occurs with *by:*

... always much covered by newspapers and television, and thronged by over two hundred thousand visitors —Libby Purves, *British Airways High Life,* May 1982

Thronged in season by hunters and fishermen —*American Guide Series: California,* 1939

through The use of *through* as an adjective meaning "finished" was disparaged by many American commentators in the early 20th century; Bierce 1909 was perhaps the first. The "finished" sense of *through* was still fairly new at the time, having originated in American English during the late 1800s:

He ... scrawled a dash underneath. 'There! I'm through!' he said —*Scribner's Mag.,* May 1887 (OED Supplement)

What may be most noteworthy about the criticism of *through* in this sense is that it did not last. Most commentators have abandoned the subject altogether, and both American and British dictionaries now routinely treat the "finished" sense as standard. Its two principal applications in current English are in describing the completion of an activity:

... the hour when he expected to be through with his day's writing —Irving Wallace, *The Writer,* November 1968

And in describing a person who is washed-up:

... he had believed the 1950s would bring him to greatness. Now they were almost at an end and he was through —Paul Nelson, *Rolling Stone,* 14 Sept. 1972

See also DONE 1; FINISHED.

thru A high-school English teacher wrote to us not long ago about the spelling *thru,* which she had apparently met with in a school memorandum and which she found in some way offensive. She wanted to know our reason for treating *thru* as an unstigmatized variant of *through* in a recent edition of Merriam-Webster's Collegiate Dictionary.

The OED shows that *thru* dates back to the 14th century, but our modern use is due primarily to the spelling reform movement of the late 19th and early 20th centuries (see SPELLING REFORM). *Thru* was on the first list of reformed spellings issued by the American Philological Association in 1876 and on the list issued by the National Education Association in 1898, as well as on the lists published by the Simplified Spelling Board in the early 20th century. It was also one of the reformed

spellings used by the *Chicago Tribune* from 1935 to 1975. In the heyday of the reformed spelling movement *thru* was widely used in newspapers and magazines:

Experience has shown thru ever reoccurring instances —*Catholic School Jour.,* March 1927

... borrowed thru a public library —*Library Jour.,* 1 Dec. 1925

... this stem went thru vegetation —*American Botanist,* August 1923

Poisonous tides from the mother's blood swept thru my foetal heart —*JAMA,* 14 Aug. 1926

... pressed on thru the novel —*The Bookman,* September 1925

As the organized interest in spelling reform waned, however, the use of *thru* in publications also shrank, although in the 1940s it could still be found in such periodicals as *Better Homes and Gardens* and the *New Republic.* We have evidence that the NEA was still using *thru* in their publications as late as 1944, even though they had withdrawn their endorsement of the reformed spelling movement in 1921.

Moreover, our evidence shows that *thru* is still in use, primarily in technical journals, and in places like catalogs and programs where compactness is a virtue. We have no recent evidence of its use in literature, and very little evidence of its use in any kind of book. *Thru* is showing some signs of vitality in combination: we are beginning to find examples like *feedthru* and *thruput* (*thruway,* of course, is well established). It undoubtedly continues to flourish as a spelling of convenience in letters and notes:

After we got thru our conversation —Harry S. Truman, appointment sheet, 19 May 1945

... leaves ... with the sun coming thru them —Randall Jarrell, letter, 6 May 1952

Thru has never been less than standard, but it remains a distant second choice in print. In the Brown University million-word corpus, which is composed of edited English texts published in 1961, there are 969 examples of *through* to just 10 of *thru* (Kučera & Francis 1967). It is an available spelling, but not many writers avail themselves of it when they are writing for publication.

See also THO.

thusly Few words have a worse reputation among the arbiters of correct usage than *thusly.* Bernstein 1965 is relatively kind in his characterization of it: he calls it "superfluous." Most other critics have shown less leniency, typically describing it as nonstandard or illiterate. Garner 1998 characterizes it as "a serious lapse."

The first recorded use of *thusly* is from 1865:

It happened, as J. Billings would say, 'thusly' —*Harper's,* December 1865 (OED Supplement)

The "J. Billings" referred to is undoubtedly Josh Billings, an American humorist who became famous after the Civil War for his illogical, ungrammatical, and misspelled comic essays. The *Harper's* citation suggests that *thusly* was either coined by Billings for comic effect or was used by him in imitation of actual rustic speech. Other sources in our file indicate—although without substantiating evidence—that the word originated with Artemus Ward, another popular American humorist of the 19th century. It seems clear, in any case, that *thusly* as originally used was not a word to be taken seriously.

The process by which *thusly* arose from its comic origins to an established, if not exalted, place in the vocabulary of English is not easily traced. There are a few citations from the late 1800s which show the word being used in what seems to be a straightforward way, but written evidence through the early decades of the 20th century is scanty. The first usage commentator to take note of it was Krapp 1927, who called it "facetious." H. L. Mencken, in *The American Language, Supplement II* (1948), also regarded *thusly* as a chiefly humorous word, although he noted an instance of its serious use in the *Congressional Record* in 1943. Citational evidence from the late 1940s and early 1950s shows that *thusly* was beginning then to appear more frequently in standard writing. In current English, *thusly* is probably still more likely to occur in speech than in writing, but its written use is by no means rare.

One reason *thusly* has gradually been able to gain a secure foothold in the language is undoubtedly that it is used primarily in ways that are, to some degree, distinct from the principal uses of *thus*. As in the original *Harper's* citation, *thusly* almost always follows the verb it modifies:

I have the vision of a little old man . . . who gives himself silent chuckles by seating people thusly —William F. Buckley, Jr., *Esquire,* September 1974

. . . she is still ranked No. 1 and seeded thusly here —John Walters, *Sports Illustrated,* 3 July 2000

Its most frequent use is as an introductory word preceeding a quotation or other passage set off by a colon:

. . . the syllogism would apparently turn thusly: The United Nations is the sole bul-

wark of world peace. There can't be a United Nations with the Soviet Union —Vermont Royster, *Wall Street Jour.,* 7 Dec. 1964

He also defends Chaplin's routine use of the camera and even those locomotive wheels, the former thusly: "Chaplin . . . obviously believes that. . . ." —Dwight Macdonald, *Esquire,* April 1965

When asked about his statements questioning whether the Holocaust occurred, David Duke "explained" thusly: "I believe there are certainly atrocities in war" —George F. Will, *Springfield* (Mass.) *Union-News,* 16 Mar. 1989

. . the revolutionary watch-word, which John Adams translates thusly: "Nip the shoots of arbitary power in the bud" —Walter Karp, *Harper's,* May 1988

. . . a bachelor deals with a filthy house thusly: He moves to a new one —Mike Nichols, *Life and Other Ways,* 1988

Of course, it is also possible to use *thus* in this way:

The experimental psychologist generalizes thus: "Interest in religion. . . ." —F. Ernest Johnson, *Annals of the American Academy of Political and Social Science,* March 1953

But such use, while not rare, is relatively uncommon in American English. *Thusly* appears to be appreciably more common than *thus* when the adverb follows the verb and precedes a colon. On the other hand, *thusly* is rarely used in contexts where *thus* would normally be expected. When such use does occur, *thusly* may indeed seem badly out of place:

It's often possible to pull boards thusly fastened off the house with your hands —Jim Locke, *The Apple Corps Guide to the Well-Built House,* 1988

. . . should occupy no more than 4000 cubic inches and thusly fit into a standard large suitcase —Gene Miller with Barbara Mackle, *Ladies' Home Jour.,* May 1971

What these facts indicate is that, whatever its origins, *thusly* is not now merely an ignorant or comic substitute for *thus:* it is a distinct adverb that is used in a distinct way in standard speech and writing. Knowledge of the subtleties of its use may give you the courage to face down its critics, but if discretion, prudence, or faintheartedness compels you to shun it (or if you just dislike it), our advice is not to replace it automatically with *thus* but to consider instead a more natural-sounding phrase such as "in this way" or "as follows."

thyself See MYSELF.

tight, tightly *Tight* is usually an adjective, but it is also commonly used as an adverb. Some of its adverbial uses overlap with those of *tightly*:

> "Hold him tight," said the sergeant —James Stephens, *The Crock of Gold,* 1912

> Liz had closed her apartment tight —Van Siller, *Cosmopolitan,* March 1972

> "My baby," she said, holding Marilee tightly —Paul Horgan, *Ladies' Home Jour.,* January 1971

> . . . houses and shops which survived plundering are still closed tightly —*Time,* 2 Sept. 1946

By and large, however, the two words are used in distinct ways. *Tight* almost always follows the verb it modifies. It occurs especially in such idioms as *freeze tight, sit tight,* and *sleep tight,* as well as with such verbs as *hold, close, squeeze,* and *shut. Tightly* is a somewhat more common word which is used both before and after the verb or participle it modifies:

> . . . a tightly woven cycle of mutually dependent events —Barry Commoner, *Columbia Forum,* Spring 1968

> His argument is tightly reasoned —John Fischer, *Harper's,* March 1971

> . . . that green baseball cap clamped tightly on his head —Caleb Pirtle III, *Southern Living,* June 1972

> . . . thinking that is focused tightly on human problems —*Christian Science Monitor,* 13 Feb. 1980

See also FLAT ADVERBS.

till, until, 'til *Till* and *until* are both venerable words, and are both highly respectable. The notion that *till* is a short form of *until* is erroneous: *till* is actually the older word. Most handbooks discuss these words, and find, to no one's surprise, that they are both acceptable. *Until* is usually pronounced somewhat more formal, and more likely to be used at the beginning of a sentence. In general, our evidence supports those observations. Note, however, that *till* can still be perfectly at home in serious writing and at the beginning of a sentence:

> . . . initiate change instead of responding to pressures, or waiting till revolution has destroyed the seam of its structure —Calvin H. Plimpton, *Amherst College Bulletin,* November 1967

> . . . 25 chapters cover the whole period from the arrival of the Portuguese explorers till today —Thomas Pakenham, *N.Y. Times Book Rev.,* 21 June 1998

> Till she got through, he would have to hide his face —Conrad Richter, *The Trees,* 1940

> Till the end of his life Truman insisted that he had suffered no agonies of regret over his decision to bomb Hiroshima and Nagasaki —Thomas Powers, *Atlantic,* July 1993

The real purpose of these handbook discussions is to asperse the form *'til,* about which some silly things have been said, including that it is used in poetry for metrical purposes. (How does *'til* differ metrically from *till?*) *'Til,* as Burchfield 1996 notes, is a 20th-century contraction of *until,* and is appropriate in informal contexts:

> . . . the Yankees still won the Series and the Brooklyn Dodgers had to "Wait 'til next year," as always —George Vecsey, *N.Y. Times,* 23 Oct. 1994

> . . . not counting the replays MSNBC will roll from midnight 'til 6 or 7 a.m. —Bob Woods, *Sports Illustrated,* 18 Sept. 2000

The form *'till* was in use in the 18th century (by George Washington, among others) but is rarely found in edited prose today.

time period This phrase has been cited for redundancy by several commentators.

> One dashing man in an ornate uniform . . . seemed at once properly matched to the time period and also somehow out of place —Cullen Murphy, *Atlantic,* August 1997

Usage writers themselves sometimes use the phrase:

> Now and then, an extremely conservative grammarian will suggest that *since* should be used only to indicate a time period —Patricia T. O'Conner, *Woes Is I,* 1996

Like most redundant phrases, this one is idiomatic. You can easily avoid it, if you are inclined to, by deleting either word. See also POINT IN TIME.

times Back in 1926 a note from a University of Missouri professor expressed surprise at finding "seven times less" in a book written by a prominent London physician. He said that he had heard "this error" from the lips of students, but did not expect to find it in a serious and well-written book. It did not occur to the professor that he might be looking at an idiom rather than an error. It is a long-established idiom:

> . . . but now I am resolved to drink ten times less than before —Jonathan Swift, *Journal to Stella,* 30 July 1711

The question about "times less" eventually reached usage commentators. They also discovered "times more" and disapproved both on dubious mathematical grounds. One even convinced himself—or a correspondent convinced him—that "five times greater" actually meant "six times as much," a conclusion that no person with a normal understanding of English would have reached.

The mathematical muddle we may leave to the commentators. The idiomatic uses we find clearly not misunderstood; they are quite common in published edited prose, often in articles dealing with scientific matters:

> . . . comets are about 10 times less likely to hit our planet than asteroids —Kelly Beatty, *Air and Space/Smithsonian*, June/July 1989

> The cause of lupus is unknown, but it affects women about nine to ten times more often than men —Arthur Grayzel, M.D., *Newsweek*, 8 Nov. 1993

> Though dying in a plane is, notoriously, twenty times less likely than dying in a car, every single airline crash is front-page news —Pico Iyer, *Harper's*, August 1995

> . . . charged one large corporate client an annual rate of 90% . . . three times more than a year ago —*Wall Street Jour.*, 30 Aug. 1998

There is no evidence that anyone is confused by these usages. They are standard idiomatic English.

For *times* in formulas like *two times two*, see TWO AND TWO.

tinker When used with a preposition, *tinker* is most often found with *with*:

> . . . loved to tinker with what he considered infelicities in Keats's poems —Amy Lowell, *John Keats*, 1925

> Parliaments and synods may tinker as much as they please with their codes and creeds —George Bernard Shaw, *Man and Superman*, 1903

> He was still tinkering with the engine when recess ended —Russell Baker, *Growing Up*, 1982

> The idea is to tinker with MAO inhibitors so a patient doesn't have to follow a special diet —Judy Foreman, *Boston Globe*, 15 Mar. 1999

A number of usage books of the early 20th century prescribed *tinker at*, treating *tinker with* as an error based on faulty analogy with *tamper with*. The earliest evidence of *tinker with* in the OED, however, is from 1658, while *tinker at* is not attested until the 19th century. It may be that *tinker at* was the usual idiom at one time, but it now occurs extremely infrequently.

> He began to tinker at the wound in rather a clumsy way —Stephen Crane, *The Red Badge of Courage*, 1895

> . . . of course, I was always tinkering at verse —*The Autobiography of William Allen White*, 1946

tired The usual preposition after *tired* is *of*:

> . . . the mood of the media seemed against him, tired of him —Gay Talese, *Harper's*, January 1969

> I'm tired of being squashed in with other people —Marjorie Holmes, *Woman's Day*, October 1971

Much less commonly, *with* follows *tired*:

> The tourist tired with *Baedeker* and his latter-day substitutes may turn . . . —*Times Literary Supp.*, 2 Mar. 1967

Both *of* and *with* are standard. *With* never occurs when the object of the preposition is a gerund, as in the Holmes example.

to **1.** The use of *to* in place of *at* has occasionally been cited as an error by American commentators since Ayres 1881. The issue primarily involves the use of *to* following a form of the verb *to be*, as in "She was to church yesterday." Such usage occurs only in nonstandard idiom when the verb is in the past tense, *was* or *were*.

> We was to the breakfast-table a talkin' it over —Marietta Holley, "A Pleasure Exertion," in *Mark Twain's Library of Humor*, 1888

Ayres also considered *to* erroneous following the present perfect tense of *to be*, "She has been to church." Such usage is now recognized as standard, however, and is actually quite distinct from the "was to church" construction. The verb *be* in "She has been to church" is almost synonymous with *go*, although its connotations are somewhat different: "She has gone to church" may mean that she is still there, but "She has been to church" strongly suggests that she is there no longer. The essential point, in any case, is that *to* does not mean "at" when it follows *has been, have been*, or *had been*, and it is not at all erroneous:

> I have been to the mountaintop —Martin Luther King, speech, 1968

2. It is unlikely that anyone reading this book needs help in distinguishing *to, too*, and *two*, but these words are often inadvertently misspelled, and you may want to keep an especially sharp eye out for possible errors when you proofread your own (or anyone else's) writing. Mistakes can be embarrassing:

The Needlenose tape shows the wreckage of that one two —*Pleasure Boating,* February 1984

to a degree See DEGREE.

to all intents and purposes Several commentators have found fault with this phrase and its relatives (like *for all intents and purposes*), mostly finding it either wordy or hackneyed. It is an old phrase, apparently originating in the language of 16th-century English law. Writers have long found it useful, in spite of what the critics have said.

> Most of the essential policies . . . were, to all intents and purposes, those of a British colonial premier —H. L. Mencken, *Prejudices: Second Series,* 1920

> For all intents and purposes, they may as well be nouns —Patricia T. O'Connor, *Woe Is I,* 1996

> His courteous response was, to all intents and purposes, no response —Philip Roth, *N.Y. Times Book Rev.,* 15 Feb. 1976

There is no compelling reason to avoid these phrases. If you prefer a shorter alternative, however, the best one is usually *in effect.* Garner 1998 has evidence of a garbled version in which *intensive* replaces *intents and.* It would be good to avoid it.

together *Together* is sometimes cited as a redundancy when it occurs following such verbs as *join, gather, assemble,* and *connect.* See REDUNDANCY.

together with A number of books, including Bryson 1984, Heritage 1982, and Guth 1985, insist that *together with* is not equivalent to *and,* so that when *together with* tacks on another noun to a singular noun that is the subject of a sentence, the verb remains singular, as in this example:

> The Corporation, together with Noranda Mines Limited, holds approximately 60% voting control —*Annual Report, The Mead Corp.,* 1970

This is acceptable theory, and it usually works where the segment introduced by *together with* is clearly perceived as parenthetical. When it is not so perceived, as Scott, Foresman 1981 points out, usage is mixed.

The only examples of additive *together with* that bear on this question are ones where the noun to which it is attached is singular and the verb is in the present or present perfect tense; in all others agreement does not reveal itself. As you might expect, revealing examples are not especially numerous. Examples with plural verbs are few, but we do have a few:

That realism, together with music's human appeal, are all that ever interested me artistically —Barry Laurence Scherer, *Opera News,* April 1999

During the year that the Arbuckle case, together with several other movieland scandals . . . , were headline fodder —J. Hoberman, *Village Voice,* 13 Sept. 1994

The prescribed use appears to be the most generally used.

See also AGREEMENT, SUBJECT-VERB: COMPOUND SUBJECTS 3.

token The idiomatic phrase *by the same token* has been the object of sporadic criticism, sometimes because it is thought to be archaic. Archaic it certainly is not. The evidence in our files shows clearly that *by the same token* occurs commonly and idiomatically in current English. Its meaning is usually close to "for the same reason," "at the same time," or "in the same way":

> We are so self-conscious . . . that we not only generate critical prophesies, but by the same token defy them or undo them by discussing and examining them to death —Robert Coles, *Trans-Action,* May 1968

> New York was the pleasure capital. . . . But by the same token it was unreal, a mirage, and distinctly treacherous —Alfred Kazin, *Harper's,* December 1968

No serious objection can be made to these uses of the phrase. What you may want to avoid, however, is relying too heavily on *by the same token* to connect statements whose logical association may not be immediately clear:

> Physicians dominate medical licensing and examining boards. By the same token, a leading intellectual is a person whom other leading intellectuals consider a leading intellectual —*Change,* March 1972

tolerance, tolerant The noun *tolerance* may be followed by any of several prepositions. *Tolerance of* usually means "willingness to tolerate":

> . . . has acquired a tolerance of viewpoints not his own —Milton S. Eisenhower, *Johns Hopkins Mag.,* February 1966

> . . . there is no tolerance of dissent —William G. Mather, in *Automation, Education, and Human Values,* ed. W. W. Brickman & S. Lehrer, 1966

Tolerance to is most likely to occur where it has the meaning "ability to tolerate":

> . . . what happens when a person becomes addicted to heroin is that his tolerance to the drug is increased —*Nature,* 14 Apr. 1972

. . . is said to have had a low tolerance to alcohol —John Corry, *N.Y. Times,* 27 Mar. 1976

A plant that possesses only tolerance to insect attack —A. N. Kishaba & G. R. Manglitz, *Jour. of Economic Entomology,* June 1965

Tolerance of is also sometimes used to mean "ability," and *tolerance to* is sometimes used to mean "willingness." *Tolerance for* is commonly used to mean both "willingness" and "ability":

. . . the society's decreasing tolerance for hardship —Richard Todd, *Atlantic,* September 1970

. . . his body develops a *tolerance* for the drug —James H. Otto & Albert Towle, *Modern Biology,* 1973

An uncommon variant, *tolerance toward* (or *towards*) is used only to mean "willingness":

. . . he should develop . . . tolerance toward the opinions of others —*Bates College Bulletin,* 1 Jan. 1952

The adjective *tolerant* is most often followed by *of*:

. . . could be argued that the chronic smoker is tolerant of marijuana —Solomon H. Snyder, *Psychology Today,* May 1971

. . . he seemed more tolerant of them than some of the other local men —Edward Hoagland, *Harper's,* October 1970

Tolerant to is limited to scientific contexts:

Mice that were rendered tolerant to denatured DNA —*Science,* 5 Oct. 1973

Tolerant is never followed by *for. Toward* occurs about as frequently after *tolerant* as it does after *tolerance*:

. . . he had grown more tolerant toward literature —Robertson Davies, *Tempest-tost,* 1951

tome   In its original sense, *tome* is a synonym for *volume;* that is, "a book forming part of a larger work." The use in which *tome* has become established as a familiar word, however, is as a synonym for *book.* It commonly suggests great size or detailed and often tedious scholarship:

I waded conscientiously through many formidable tomes —W. Somerset Maugham, *The Summing Up,* 1938

The authors' opinions make it livelier than the ordinary academic tome —Rod Nordell, *Christian Science Monitor,* 5 Sept. 1957

. . . a 2097-page tome hailed by its advocates as the channeled wisdom of celestial beings

—Genevieve Stuttaford, *Publishers Weekly,* 6 Mar. 1995

. . . this seven-hundred-page tome could have used some intensive editing —*New Yorker,* 20 Mar. 2000

You will note that the notions of large size or dullness are given in the context. Without such suggestions, *tome* is simply a synonym of *book:*

This outstanding Elvis tome is an album of pictures —Ray Olson, *Booklist,* 15 May 1991

This lovely tome is chock-full of helpful hints —Marcia Colish, *Commonweal,* 4 Dec. 1998

. . . about the only new thing in the suspiciously sourced tome the reader can trust —Andrew Sullivan, *N.Y. Times Book Rev.,* 5 Oct. 1997

Ludmilla took out library books on basketball, including how-to-play tomes by Wilt Chamberlain and Bob Cousy —*Hartford Courant,* 3 Mar. 1999

too   **1.** *Too* is like *very*—an adverb used only to modify adjectives ("too large") and other adverbs ("too far"). When a verb is being modified, an additional adverb, such as *much,* is required ("You talk too much"). The use of *too* in modifying the past participles of verbs ("We were too interested to leave") is analogous to the use of *very* with past participles, and though relatively few commentators have taken note of it, it raises similar questions. For a discussion of the aspects of such usage, and of the opinions concerning it, see VERY 1.
2. *Too,* meaning "also," sometimes occurs at the beginning of a sentence:

Too, the Dutch emerged from the oil crisis with their heads high —Gordon F. Sander, *N.Y. Times Mag.,* 22 Aug. 1976

Too, it probably calls for the same kind of gas as today's small cars —Charles E. Dole, *Christian Science Monitor,* 29 Apr. 1980

Too, the agencies have increasingly pushed banks into the market —Susan Lee, *Wall Street Jour.,* 11 July 1983

Moreover, besides, in addition, and *also* are more common in such contexts, but *too* is not incorrect. The OED indicated in 1913 that *too* was "rarely, now never, used at the beginning of a clause," but the OED Supplement shows that such usage was revived in the 20th century, originally in American English, then in British English as well. No grammatical objection can be made to it, and the practice is clearly standard. Whatever problems it causes have to do with idiom—which is to say that, because of its relative rarity, it sounds peculiar to some people. Several usage handbooks therefore discourage the use of *too* at the beginning of a sentence. We suggest that the best guide in matters such as this is your own sense of idiom.

tormented The preposition that usually occurs after *tormented* is *by*:

> . . . was also obviously tormented by doubts and misgivings —Thomas Wolfe, *You Can't Go Home Again,* 1940

> . . . at times tormented by voluptuous visions —Rebecca West, *The Thinking Reed,* 1936

> . . . tormented by a lust for the pleasures and knowledge of this world —Robert E. Herzstein, *N.Y. University Bulletin,* Spring 1967

With is also used after *tormented,* but much less commonly than *by*:

> . . . though tormented with a bitter sense of failure —Jerome Stone, *Saturday Rev.,* 8 Jan. 1955

> . . . tormented with hunger and thirst —Nevil Shute, *Most Secret,* 1945

tortuous, torturous Commentators routinely warn against confusing these two words. The distinction to be made between them is that *tortuous* means chiefly "winding or twisted" and that *torturous* means "causing torture; excruciating." The main concern of the critics is that *torturous* should not be used in place of *tortuous* in such phrases as *a tortuous path.* Our evidence shows that such usage is rare in edited prose, but we do find *torturous* used in contexts where either it or *tortuous* may have been intended:

> Ahead of the racers lay 1,946 miles of torturous mountain roads —*Time,* 1 Dec. 1952

> . . . headed deep into the countryside on a torturous, kidney-jarring dirt road —Bob Shacochis, *Harper's,* February 1995

Tortuous is, in general, a more common word than *torturous.* It is especially common in extended uses, in most of which it can be defined as "exceedingly complex or involved" or "deviously indirect or tricky":

> . . . pursued a tortuous policy in his testimony, disclosing this piece of evidence and withholding that —Rebecca West, *Atlantic,* June 1952

> . . . tortuous intrigues had at last brought him to the highest office —William L. Shirer, *The Rise and Fall of the Third Reich,* 1960

> . . . the ways of the Legislature are slow and tortuous —John Deedy, *Commonweal,* 30 Jan. 1970

We do find the more common *tortuous* substituted for *torturous*:

> . . . the few shade trees that gave the party some relief from the tortuous heat —Mirella Tenderini et al., *The Duke of the Abruzzi,* 1997

> After a tortuous childhood and an early life of crime —Shelby Steele, *New Republic,* 21 Dec. 1992

Sometimes the notion of complexity can carry a connotation of torture:

> . . . the tortuous procedures that make up our criminal-justice system —John Sansing, *The Washingtonian,* October 1978

> . . . the tortuous equations of quantum chromodynamics —Gary Taubes, *Science,* 13 Sept. 1996

And *torturous* can have connotations of extreme complexity:

> . . . today's dazzling landscape of higher education, with its vast mushroom fields of crowded campuses, its torturous selection processes, its maniacal pressures on the tender young —Tom Wicker, *Change,* September 1971

What this means is that the two words can and do appear in similar contexts. Our evidence shows, however, that the basic distinction in their meanings favored by the critics is in fact observed by most writers. Here are a few more examples of *tortuous* and *torturous* in their distinct senses:

> But the Avon . . . is difficult to navigate; a narrow, tortuous stream —Samuel Eliot Morison, *The European Discovery of America,* 1971

> Weary and depressed after his torturous afternoon —Paul Zimmerman, *Sports Illustrated,* 31 Jan. 1983

> . . . on the tortuous, corkscrew roads —Ronald Sullivan, *N.Y. Times,* 8 Jan. 1984

> . . . found the strength and courage to survive torturous inquisitions —*Booklist,* 1 Nov. 1984

to the manner (manor) born See MANNER.

toward, towards Many commentators have observed that *toward* is the more common choice in American English, while the preference in British English is for *towards.* Our evidence confirms that such is indeed the case. Both words are commonly used in the U.S., but *toward* is undoubtedly prevalent:

> . . . looked down across sloping cornfields toward a small village —Russell Baker, *Growing Up,* 1982

His later development . . . was toward the occult —Arthur Miller, *N.Y. Times Book Rev.,* 6 Jan. 1985

. . . a strong tendency towards ethical idealism —Peter Green, *New Republic,* 20 Mar. 2000

The British strongly favor *towards*:

There was . . . some jolly singing as they bowled down the A22 towards Bexhill-on-Sea —Will Self, *Cock & Bull,* 1992

. . . edging slowly towards social democracy —Graham Greene, *Getting to Know the General,* 1984

to wit   *To wit* has occasionally been criticized as an inappropriately legalistic synonym for *namely.* While the phrase may be most at home in legal contexts, it is by no means a rarity in general edited prose:

. . . let's look at megagreedy winners. To wit, the folks who are already loaded to the eyeballs with stock in their own companies but take stock options as part of their pay package —Allan Sloan, *Newsweek,* 15 Mar. 1999

. . . as meticulous craftsmen searched for a most unlikely 16th-century building material: to wit, hazelnut shells —Hugh Pope, *Wall Street Jour.,* 11 Dec. 1997

track, tract   Confusion of these words is warned against by Copperud 1980 and Garner 1998. We have some evidence of it in our files:

SCCAP skirted those obstacles by buying tracks of undeveloped land —*New Spirit,* October 1979

For the record, however, the word called for in this context is *tract,* meaning "an area of land." Garner also has evidence of *tract* used in place of *track.*

tragedy   In the world of literature, a tragedy is a highly serious work that typically describes the downfall of a great or heroic figure. Several commentators, with the literary sense in mind, have disapproved extended uses of *tragedy* to describe real events or circumstances of a somewhat less than earth-shaking nature. The use most likely to be criticized is in such contexts as the following:

The tragedy of marriage is not that it fails to assure woman the promised happiness —H. M. Parshley, translation of Simone de Beauvoir, *The Second Sex,* 1952

It would be a genuine tragedy if liberals lost all sense of proportion —*Commonweal,* 11 Apr. 1969

The meaning of *tragedy* in such contexts is "something to be deeply regretted; a great misfortune." This sense of the word is common and well established, but it can at times have a needlessly hyperbolic quality. We recommend that you use it thoughtfully.

transcendent, transcendental   Some distinctions between these adjectives have been noted by several commentators, the primary one being that *transcendent* is preferred in the sense "surpassing" (as in "an issue of transcendent importance"). Our evidence supports this distinction, although it should be noted that *transcendental* is not incorrect when used to mean "surpassing":

. . . produced a series of objects of transcendental monstrosity —Osbert Lancaster, *All Done From Memory,* 1953

It has had this sense since the 18th century. Its primary senses, however, relate to philosophy and especially metaphysics.

transmute   When this somewhat bookish verb is followed by a preposition, the preposition is almost always *into*:

. . . took the national anguish . . . and transmuted it into wildly successful comedy —Richard Grenier, *Cosmopolitan,* October 1976

. . . Melville transmutes the lowly fact . . . into a meditation on mankind —John Updike, *New Yorker,* 10 May 1982

A much less common preposition after *transmute* is *to*:

. . . such a star transmutes lighter elements to heavier ones —Dietrick E. Thomsen, *Science News,* 10 Aug. 1985

transpire   The use of *transpire* to mean "to come to pass, occur, happen" has been disparaged since at least 1870. Some of its critics have rather shortchanged this interesting word, saying that *transpire* can mean only "to leak out, become known." They pass over its earlier technical senses, which we still find in use, most often in botanical contexts.

Transpire was born as a technical word in the 17th century. In its literal senses, *transpire* describes the passing of a vapor through the pores of a membrane, such as the surface of a leaf. The word began to be used figuratively sometime in the first half of the century (the earliest figurative citation in the OED is from 1741). Samuel Johnson's 1755 Dictionary is the first to record the new sense, albeit disapprovingly. Johnson defined the sense as "To escape from secrecy to notice" and appended this comment: "a sense lately innovated from *France,* without necessity." He gave no example of its use. In James Boswell's *Life of Samuel Johnson* (1791), the Earl of Marchmont tells Boswell that Johnson's dislike of *transpire* was actually owing to its having first been used by Lord Bolingbroke, with whom Johnson had deep political differences. Here are a few examples of its use in English:

> ... certainly, it would be next to a miracle that a fact of this kind should be known to a whole parish, and not transpire any farther —Henry Fielding, *Tom Jones,* 1749

> You ask me if any thing transpires here on the subject of S. America? Not a word —Thomas Jefferson, letter, 13 Nov. 1787

> No more news has transpired of that Wanderer —Charles Lamb, letter, 1 Feb. 1806

> ... it had just transpired that he had left gaming debts behind him to a very considerable amount —Jane Austen, *Pride and Prejudice,* 1813

> Manning had a long interview with Pius IX ... Precisely what passed on that occasion never transpired —Lytton Strachey, *Eminent Victorians,* 1918

This particular use is no longer very common, according to our evidence. In present-day general English *transpire* most often occurs in an impersonal construction with *it.* The construction may have developed from uses like Jane Austen's above. In this impersonal construction *it transpired* ranges in meaning from "it was learned" to "it turned out." Here are several examples:

> It transpired after a confused five minutes that the man had heard Gatsby's name around his office —F. Scott Fitzgerald, *The Great Gatsby,* 1925

> It transpired that the ghost had communicated with Yeats through automatic writing —Oliver St. John Gogarty, *As I Was Going Down Sackville Street,* 1937

> ... but when they get there, it transpires that this is not the point of departure of their ship —James Thurber, *Thurber Country,* 1953

> ... therefore it was not resented by anybody when it transpired that indeed they did —William F. Buckley, Jr., quoted in *Harper's,* January 1986

> On to the Nutty Boys, who are no longer boys, or, it transpires, particularly nutty —Caroline Sullivan, *Manchester Guardian Weekly,* 23 Aug. 1992

The newest sense of *transpire,* "to take place; occur; happen," originated obscurely, probably in the late 18th century. Noah Webster in his 1828 Dictionary was the first to record the new meaning, which may be of American origin. It seems likely that it developed by misinterpretation of the earlier figurative sense in ambiguous contexts. For instance, the Dictionary of Americanisms and the OED Supplement both give this quotation as the first example of the new sense:

> There is nothing new transpired since I wrote you last —Abigail Adams, letter, 31 July 1775

With just this much context given, however, the example is ambiguous: *transpired* might mean "has come out" or "has happened." We think it not unlikely that the new sense came from people's hearing *transpire* in such an ambiguous context, taking it to mean "happen," and then using it to mean "happen." At any rate, *transpire* was clearly used to mean "happen" as early as 1804 in a fugitive publication from Hartford, Connecticut.

This early example of the "happen" sense was probably journalistic, and it was journalistic use that after some sixty years resulted in controversy. The first two critics were Richard Grant White 1870 and John Stuart Mill in *A System of Logic* (whether first in the 1866 or the 1872 edition we do not know).

Mill dismissed the new sense as a vulgarism, and White buttressed his censure by reference to etymology. Many subsequent commentators have disapproved the use, including Fowler 1926, some carrying on White's etymological objections, and others finding the use undesirable for various other reasons. The tenor of the argument against the new sense of *transpire* has not changed much since the 1870s. Here are some examples of the disputed use:

> Few changes—hardly any—have transpired among his ship's company —Charles Dickens, *Dombey and Son,* 1848 (OED)

> All memorable events, I should say, transpire in morning time and in a morning atmosphere —Henry David Thoreau, *Walden,* 1854

> In 1884 the chancellor published a new edition of his commentaries, in which he adds some notes of what had transpired on the question since 1826 —Abraham Lincoln, speech in Congress, 20 June 1848

> Several other stirring events transpired at the session of 1820 — *The Autobiography of Martin Van Buren,* begun 1854

> ... yet paleontology holds a coroner's inquest here in the fifth geologic period on an "unpleasantness" which transpired in the quaternary, and calmly lays it on the MAN —Mark Twain, *Brief Lectures on Science,* October 1871

> The stage, of course, was the dream. All that transpired there is now a memory —Charles A. Lindbergh, *The Spirit of St. Louis,* 1953

... most agreed that I gave an honest account of what transpired —James A. Michener, *Saturday Rev.*, 1 May 1954

The advertised purpose of the gathering was to recast the long twilight struggle against the "totalitarian" foe, but what actually transpired was a two-day confrontation between neoconservatism and itself —Christopher Hitchens, *Harper's*, July 1990

I did not learn much of what transpired until the next day —William L. Shirer, *The Nightmare Years*, 1984

Much of *The Changeling* (1622) transpires in Alibius's mad-house —Douglas Bruster, *Notes and Queries*, June 1993

... and even now, after all that had transpired, he still didn't think the boy had had an active hand in it —T. Coraghessan Boyle, *The Road to Wellville*, 1993

In summary, *transpire* has two uses in general publications today. It is used in an impersonal construction, usually *it transpired that*, which means approximately "it turned out that" or "it developed that." And it is used to mean "to take place, occur, happen." In both uses it is a somewhat formal word. In both uses it is firmly established as standard. The use of *transpire* to mean "happen" has attracted criticism for more than a century and will perhaps continue to attract criticism for many years to come, but it is extremely common, can be found in the works of excellent writers, and is in no sense an error.

treat When used as an intransitive verb meaning "negotiate," *treat* is idiomatically followed by *with*:

... to provide France with a competent representative to treat with President Eisenhower —Lansing Warren, *N.Y. Times*, 7 June 1953

... a Sioux Indian coming to treat with yet another cavalry general —Lewis H. Lapham, *Harper's*, May 1971

In less-typical constructions, this sense of *treat* is followed by *for* and *on*:

... delegates were reported as leaving Berlin to treat for an armistice —Elizabeth Madox Roberts, *He Sent Forth a Raven*, 1935

... the commissioners sent to Hartford to treat on the Connecticut boundary —*Dictionary of American Biography*, 1936

When used to mean "to deal with a matter in writing," *treat* is followed by *of*:

Mr. Robson treats of Kipling's middle rather than late stories —*Times Literary Supp.*, 2 Apr. 1964

The first volume ... treated of the seminal thinkers —Theodore M. Avery, Jr., *Library Jour.*, 1 Apr. 1966

Several critics have called the use of *on* or *with* after this sense of *treat* an error. There is no evidence of such usage in the Merriam-Webster files. If it occurs, it probably represents a mental blending of *treat* with such combinations as *expound on* or *deal with*.

treble See TRIPLE, TREBLE.

trek *Trek* is derived ultimately from the Middle Dutch verb *trecken*, "to pull, haul, migrate." The English word was borrowed in the 19th century from the Boers of South Africa. As used by the Boers, *trek* referred specifically to large-scale migrations over land by means of ox-drawn wagons. That was also its original reference in English, both as a noun and as a verb, but in the 20th century it came to be used more broadly.

In actual usage, *trek* generally retains at least some suggestion of arduousness, distance, or slow progress, even when being used hyperbolically.

I tell myself that making the trek is good for my body, hiking uphill on Riverside Drive —Richard Robin, *Atlantic*, July 1996

... twice a year trekking down to Bloomingdale's —Carol Eisen Rinzler, *New York*, 1 Nov. 1971

... endured a dangerous, punishing trek through the jungle before reaching the Liawep village —Francine Prose, *N.Y. Times Book Rev.*, 7 Dec. 1997

... thousands of prospectors trekked north on the Alaska Gold Rush —Maria Wilhelm, *People*, 30 Aug. 1982

Pioneer 11 ... completed a two-year trek to Jupiter in December —James S. Kunen, *New Times*, 4 Apr. 1975

From cautious saver to citizen speculator in just a decade—that's quite a trek across the spectrum of financial risk —Bernard Wysocki, Jr., *Wall Street Jour.*, 3 Aug. 1999

Garner 1998 notes that the word is occasionally misspelled *treck*.

triple, treble Some distinctions in the use of these two basically synonymous words have been discussed by several commentators, beginning with Fowler 1926. He observed that *treble* was the more common verb and noun, that *triple* was the more common adjective, and that, as an adjective, *treble* was more likely to mean "multiplied by three" and *triple* to mean "having three parts or elements." His observations, based on British usage, have been repeated by Garner 1998. Other American commentators, such as Evans 1957 and Shaw 1975, have found that *triple* is much more common in the U.S. than *treble* in all their synonymous senses. Our evidence indicates that *triple* is in fact the usual choice in American English, except that the verb *treble* is sometimes favored in business and legal contexts, and the adjective *treble* is common in the legal term *treble damages*:

> . . . a total of $543,000 in damages, which was trebled as stipulated by federal antitrust law —Lester Munson, *Sports Illustrated*, 21 Sept. 1992

> . . . the $66 billion used to purchase stocks . . . could instead have more than trebled our acquisition of new . . . equipment —Alfred E. Kahn, *N.Y. Times Book Rev.*, 12 Dec. 1982

> . . . is seeking $1.05 billion from the defendants, or treble damages, for alleged violations —*Wall Street Jour.*, 26 Nov. 1982

Treble also occurs—and is certainly standard—in general writing, but *triple* predominates. Excluding the musical senses of *treble* and the baseball sense of *triple*, neither word is commonly used as a noun.

triumphal, triumphant Fowler 1926 observes a distinction in the meanings of these words, and a few later commentators have followed suit. The basic idea is that *triumphal* should be used with the meaning "ceremonially celebrating or commemorating a victory," as in "a triumphal procession" and "a triumphal arch," and that *triumphant* should be used in all other cases, as with the meanings "having triumphed" ("a triumphant army"), "rejoicing for victory" ("a triumphant shout"), and "notably successful" ("a triumphant performance"). By and large, that is exactly how *triumphal* and *triumphant* are in fact used, except that *triumphal* occasionally occurs when *triumphant* might be expected:

> . . . two certainties remain after last night's triumphal success —Virgil Thomson, *The Musical Scene*, 1947

> . . . during the Toronto Symphony's triumphal visit to London —*Current Biography*, February 1968

Such usage was first recorded in 1513, but it seems never to have been common.

trivia *Trivia* is much like *data*—an English word that has the form of the Latin plural that is its source but that is used as both a plural and a singular noun. *Trivia* was first used in this sense in the early 20th century:

> . . . induces them to publish trivia of a peculiarly ephemeral character —*N.Y. Times*, 26 Dec. 1927

Such usage drew some early criticism on etymological grounds, but the small controversy concerning it never caught on among usage commentators. A more persistent issue has been the use of *trivia* as a singular mass noun. Various commentators have disapproved this use (as recently as Freeman 1990). Our evidence shows both singular and plural use, but most of our examples occur in contexts in which number is not revealed.

> Celebrity trivia is useless; family trivia is vital —James Bishop, *Smithsonian*, May 1993

> They cram their heads with so much trivia that they cannot see the wood for the trees —Matt Ridley, *Genome*, 1999

> . . . she tends to revel in trivia for its own sake —Michael Kammen, *N.Y. Times Book Rev.*, 6 Nov. 1988

> Trivia go alongside glcom in Cukor's book —*Punch*, 23 Dec. 1975

> The trivia of life aboard the Calypso are made to seem just as important —Laurence Wylie, *N.Y. Times Book Rev.*, 8 Mar. 1987

Current dictionaries recognize that the singular use of *trivia* is now standard. For other foreign plurals used as singulars, see LATIN PLURALS.

trooper, trouper A state policeman who can be counted on to do his job when the going gets rough is not only a good trooper (that is, a good state policeman), he is also a good trouper. *Trouper* is used figuratively to describe a person who carries on gamely through good times and bad. Such use owes its origin to the theatrical world of the 19th century, when *troupe* was first used in English to mean "a company of performers" and *trouper* to mean "a member of a troupe." In the 20th century, *trouper* came to be applied to anyone who recognizes that the show must go on:

> Gary Hart came to Houston Thursday in the role of the good Democratic trouper . . . chipping in a good word or two on behalf of Walter Mondale, the man who edged him out for the Democratic presidential nomination —Jim Simmon, *Houston Post*, 7 Sept. 1984

Trooper is a more common word than *trouper*, with various meanings that relate primarily to the military and the police. The two words are close etymological relatives (both derived ultimately from the Middle French *troupe*, meaning "company, herd"). It is not surprising that the more familiar *trooper* is sometimes used in place of *trouper*:

... real troopers in cultured places have turned out to be pills in the wild —John Heminway, *Town & Country,* July 1983

... I didn't want to be consoled or patted on my head or told what a great trooper I was —Linda Ellerbee, *"And So It Goes,"* 1986

During the Bush years, Dole was a loyal trooper, helping to pass Poppy's budgets and his tax increases —Matthew Cooper, *New Republic,* 3 June 1996

This use of *trooper* is treated as standard in the OED Supplement and Merriam-Webster's Collegiate Dictionary, Tenth Edition. Most of the usage writers who take up this subject consider it an error.

truculent This adjective is ultimately derived from the Latin *trux,* meaning "fierce, savage." Its oldest use is in fact as a synonym of *savage*:

His aspect . . . was fierce, truculent, and fearful —Edward Topsell, *The Historie of Foure-Footed Beastes,* 1607 (OED)

In current usage, however, it has lost much of its etymological fierceness. It now chiefly serves to describe speech or writing that is notably harsh or a person who is notably self-assertive and belligerent:

... she had debated Norman Mailer in a truculent disputation at Town Hall in New York —Margaret Talbot, *New Republic,* 31 May 1999

... the IRS has started taking a truculent tone with foreign multinationals —*Wall Street Jour.,* 28 July 1992

... the death of William II had relieved the States Party and Amsterdam in particular of their most truculent antagonist —Simon Schama, *The Embarrassment of Riches,* 1988

Challenged to a fight by a truculent layabout —Wole Soyinka, *Isara,* 1989

The "harsh" sense of *truculent* was first recorded in 1850; the "belligerent, surly" sense is a development of the 20th century.

The extended meanings of *truculent* have been occasionally questioned by critics, but they are established, and are the most common uses in current English.

true When *true* means "faithful," it is followed by *to*:

... reaps all the advantage there is in being true to a particular piece of earth —Mark Van Doren, *N.Y. Times Book Rev.,* 21 Mar. 1954

True to form, I store it in the icebox, ready for unexpected guests —M. F. K. Fisher, *New Yorker,* 26 Apr. 1969

In other senses, *true* occurs commonly with *for* or *of*:

... black men are more likely to hold the doctorate than black women in the sample, and the same is true for whites —David M. Rafky, *Change,* October 1971

... it is not an age when the same event can be said to be true for faith but untrue for science —W. R. Inge, *The Church in the World,* 1928

This, I shall maintain, is necessarily true of any form of externality —Bertrand Russell, *Foundations of Geometry,* 1897

... even this, it seems, was truer of the Ivy League schools than of most others —Richard H. Rovere, *New Yorker,* 18 Nov. 1972

true facts The phrase *true facts* is cited as a redundancy by many commentators, who argue that all facts are, by definition, true. Against this argument it may be pointed out that many statements that are presented as facts turn out on closer examination to be less than entirely true. The phrase *true facts,* like *real facts* and *actual facts,* serves to emphasize that the truth of the facts in question is beyond doubt. *True facts* is especially likely to occur, and is most appropriately used, when there is reason to be suspicious of some of the "facts":

I flung it aside after fifty pages and laid hold of *Mrs. Phillips,* where I expected to find at least probable, if not true, facts —Lady Mary Wortley Montagu, letter, 16 Feb. 1752

Each entry gives the fact as falsely known plus the true facts, and frequently adds an interesting story behind the myth —*Science News,* 7 July 1984

It's only now that the true facts are coming out, almost a hundred years, and it's a pity it took so long —Harry S. Truman, in Merle Miller, *Plain Speaking,* 1973

trust The prepositions *in* and *to* both occur after the verb *trust*:

... hope for the best, and trust in God —Sydney Smith, *Lady Holland's Memoir,* 1855

Some of them, trusting to common sense —Aldous Huxley, *The Olive Tree,* 1937

The noun *trust* is usually followed by *in*:

... do not confuse trust in the students with sentimentality about them —Charles E. Silberman, *Atlantic,* August 1970

trustee, trusty Several commentators observe the distinction between these nouns: *trustee* denotes someone to whom property is legally committed in trust (or, more broadly, someone who has been entrusted with something); *trusty* denotes a prisoner who is considered trustworthy and is given special privileges. This distinction is observed by most writers, but *trustee* does turn up from time to time in the sense of *trusty*:

> The city government used trustee convicts from State Prison Camp 22 —*N.Y. Times,* 28 Aug. 1967

This use of *trustee* is not common, and people who pride themselves on their spelling will undoubtedly call it an error. We recommend that you use *trusty* instead.

Note that the noun *trusty* is pronounced both \'trəs-tē\ and \ˌtrəs-'tē\. The pronunciation with the primary stress on the second syllable is analogous to the *trustee* spelling, but it occurs much more commonly than the spelling and, so far as we know, has never been criticized.

try and The use of *try and* in contexts where *try to* would be possible has been subject to criticism since the 19th century. The issue continues to enjoy great popularity, although a number of usage commentators, including Fowler 1926, Evans 1957, and Follett 1966, are on record as recognizing that *try and* is an established standard idiom.

The basis for objecting to *try and* is usually the notion that *try* is to be followed by the infinitive combined with the assumption that an infinitive requires *to.* This is the same mistaken assumption that has caused so much trouble over the so-called split infinitive (which see). In spite of what these critics believe, however, infinitives are used in many constructions without *to,* and some of those constructions use *and.*

The use of *and* between two verbs where *to* might be expected is an old one in English. The OED has examples back to the 16th century; the Middle English Dictionary has examples as far back as the 13th. The verbs most often used in this construction in past centuries were *begin, go, take,* and *come*—the last three of which are still so used. *Try* did not appear as *try and* until the 17th century, when our familiar sense of the word was first established. Interestingly, the earliest example for the "make an attempt" sense in the OED involves the *try and* construction, so *try and* may actually be older than *try to.*

The oldest example of *try to* in the OED, in fact, is an inverted construction:

> To repair his Strength he tries —John Dryden, *Virgil's Georgics,* 1697

Try and could not be used in an inverted construction. *Try and,* in fact, is not capable of much in the way of variation; it is almost always used in the fixed form *try and* followed by an infinitive. If you inflect *try,* insert an adverb, or invert the construction, you will use *try to.* In this example, notice how Herbert Read has had to switch constructions in order to use *trying:*

> . . . to try and keep it alive by State patronage is like trying to keep the dodo alive in a zoo —Herbert Read, *The Philosophy of Modern Art,* 1952

And Henry Adams, not averse to *try and* (as a later example will demonstrate), has to use *try to* when he slips in an adverb:

> . . . I like the girls and try always to be polite —Henry Adams, letter, 7 June 1859

A negative may precede *try and,* but if a negative follows *try, to* is used:

> . . . when you are on your moorings, don't try and get into her —Peter Heaton, *Cruising,* 1952

> Not to try and keep either a diary or careful income tax records —*And More by Andy Rooney,* 1982

> Try not to take her out shopping —nurse, quoted in *McCall's,* March 1971

These restrictions give native speakers no problem whatever, but if you are a learner of English, you will want to keep them in mind and maybe stick to the simpler *try to.*

A popular misconception among those who disparage *try and* is that the construction has only recently become widespread:

> "I'll try and see" is now universal in the spoken language, and is now spreading into print —Patrick Brogan, *Encounter,* February 1975

But *try and* has actually been common in print for about a century and a half, as the following examples show. You will observe that many of the examples are not from highly formal styles, but many of our more recent ones come from standard general prose:

> Now I will try and write of something else —Jane Austen, letter, 29 Jan. 1813

> The unfortunate creature has a child still every year, and her constant hypocrisy is to try and make her girls believe that their father is a respectable man —W. M. Thackeray, *The Book of Snobs,* 1846

> . . . to try and soften his father's anger — George Eliot, *Silas Marner,* 1861 (in Hall 1917)

> Do try and send me a little news —Henry Adams, letter, 18 Dec. 1863

> I'm going to try and see him today —E. B. White, letter, August 1936

I am glad of the opportunity to try and get this point cleared up —William Empson, *Essays in Criticism,* July 1953

He always dressed rapidly, so as to try and conserve his night warmth till the sun rose —Doris Lessing, reprinted in *Literature Lives* (9th-grade text), ed. Hanna Beate Haupt et al., 1975

. . . and Issy who has to try and outwit his own electronic burglar alarm system when he wants to raid the refrigerator in the middle of the night —David Lodge, *Times Literary Supp.,* 26 Sept. 1980

He had the idea that at the top of this mountain there would be a certain butterfly. . . . We set off to try and get it —Donald Hall, *N.Y. Times,* 23 Aug. 1981

As an encouragement to them to widen their scope, to try and do justice to the diversity of literature —Anatole Broyard, *N.Y. Times Book Rev.,* 9 Nov. 1986

. . . assigning executives from soundly run thrifts to try and clean up the mess —L. J. Davis, *Harper's,* September 1990

. . . Hunt volunteered . . . to fly to Milwaukee and try and break into the apartment —Seymour M. Hersh, *New Yorker,* 14 Dec. 1992

It takes a brave taxpayer these days to try and fill out anything more than the short form —Dody Tsiantar, *Newsweek,* 14 Mar. 1994

Try and conceptualize the virtual life that is now being so eagerly sold and promoted —Christopher Hitchens, *Times Literary Supp.,* 10 May 1996

. . . Minor became truly remorseful for what he had done, and resolved to try and make some kind of amends —Simon Winchester, *The Professor and the Madman,* 1998

We need binoculars to even try and catch a glimpse of the sixty-foot swimming pool —Margaret Talbot, *New Republic,* 20 Oct. 1997

. . . joining Rep. Gary Condit's . . . camp to try and make lemonade out of a multiplying pile of lemons —Paul Farhi, *Washington Post,* 20 July 2000

These examples show that *try and* has been socially acceptable for these two centuries but that it is not used in an elevated style.

Quite a few commentators lump *try and* with other constructions in which *and* replaces a possible *to. Go and* is the oldest of these, dating back to the 13th century. It has always been respectable in speech and casual writing:

But I sought after George Psalmanazar the most. I used to go and sit with him at an alehouse in the city —Samuel Johnson, in James Boswell, *Life of Samuel Johnson,* 1791

There! I may now finish my letter and go and hang myself —Jane Austen, letter, 24 Dec. 1798

I must go and see him again —Lord Byron, journal entry, 1 Dec. 1813

I have been leaving Franconia, New Hampshire . . . to go and live in South Shaftsbury, Vermont —Robert Frost, letter, 10 Oct. 1920

Come and is also old, and equally respectable:

. . . desired I would come and see her —Jonathan Swift, *Journal to Stella,* 2 Feb. 1711

I was meditating to come and see you —Charles Lamb, letter, 4 Mar. 1830

. . . I would come and see you tomorrow —Lewis Carroll, letter, 14 July 1877

Be sure and is also frequently encountered:

And be sure and get tested for sheep blast —James Thurber, letter, 1937

You've got to get every Protestant in this outfit to be sure and be there at that mass —Harry S. Truman, quoted in Merle Miller, *Plain Speaking,* 1973

There are a few other verbs that turn up with *and* where *to* could have been used:

He didn't have to stop and think about his answer —Elmer Davis, *But We Were Born Free,* 1954

And you can tell your daddy that someday I'll be President of this country. You watch and see —Lyndon B. Johnson, quoted in Sam Houston Johnson, *My Brother Lyndon,* 1970

If you want to write, start and write down your thoughts —Leacock 1943

About the only thing that can be held against any of these combinations is that they seem not to be typical of high-toned writing, but clearly they are not out of place in informal and general prose. The judgment of *try and* in Fowler 1926 remains eminently sensible today:

It is an idiom that should be not discountenanced, but used when it comes natural.

turbid, turgid Some words seem to have been specially created to encourage the use of dictionaries. *Turbid* and *turgid* are two such words. Not only do they look alike and sound alike, but they tend to be used in similar ways.

Compounding the difficulty is their unfamiliarity: few people other than scientists and book reviewers have frequent occasion to describe anything as "turbid" or "turgid." All things considered, it is not surprising that these two words are sometimes confused. The distinction in their literal senses is that *turbid* means "muddy, clouded," and *turgid* means "swollen, distended." In their figurative senses, *turbid* means "unclear, confused, obscure," and *turgid* means "overblown, grandiloquent." These characteristics can occur side by side, so it is sometimes difficult to tell exactly what is meant by *turbid* and *turgid*:

> . . . they seem to share a certain turbid homogeneity of thought and phrase which perhaps explains their popularity —Wilfrid Sheed, *The Good Word and Other Words*, 1978

> . . . the Pentagon study is long, the documents turgid, and the summer had already begun —Peter Schrag, *Saturday Rev.*, 13 Nov. 1971

Chances are excellent that *turbid* and *turgid* are being used in their time-honored senses in these passages, but the context does not make their meanings obvious. Sometimes one word is clearly being used when the other is called for. The tendency is to replace *turbid* with *turgid*, which is relatively the more common word:

> The background is laid in the murky, turgid England of Roger Bacon —*Time*, 29 Oct. 1945

> The turgid water is pumped over the top of the bed. The water percolates through the bed, and the solids are retained in the sand —*McGraw-Hill Encyclopedia of Science & Technology*, 1960

The best way to avoid such mishaps is to keep a dictionary handy.

two and two Several people have written to us in recent years to ask whether the common arithmetical formulas *two and two, two times two, two plus two,* and the like take singular or plural verbs. The question is an old one that has been examined by various commentators who reached different conclusions. Historical grammarians have looked into the problem too, without coming to complete agreement.

A survey of American math texts in our library reveals universal use of the singular, as here:

> What number plus nine equals fifteen? —Edwina Deans et al., *Basic Mathematics*, Book D, 1977

> 36 plus 12 times n is 48 —Max A. Sabel et al., *Essentials of Mathematics*, Book 1, 1977

None of these books, however, use the common formula with *and*. Older literature, on the other hand, runs heavily to the plural verb with *and*, especially when the verb is *make*:

> We do in our Consciences believe two and two make four —Joseph Addison, *The Spectator*, No. 126, 1711 (OED)

> O Ireland! O my country! . . . when will you acknowledge that two and two make four . . . ? —W. M. Thackeray, *The Book of Snobs*, 1846

> How much do one and one make? —Robert Frost, letter, 26 Mar. 1915

Charles Lamb, however, used the singular:

> Reason is only counting, two and two makes four —letter, 1830

We conclude that unless you are writing a mathematics text, you have the option to use either a singular or a plural verb. The plural is more likely with *and* than with other constructions, although our evidence of plural use in print now shows its age.

type, -type, type of Objection has been made to the use of *type* in the sense of "sort" as an attributive modifier of another noun, as in this example:

> . . . the one big impression I got was that the game hasn't changed. It's the same as it was when I played. I see the same type pitchers, the same type hitters —Ted Williams & John Underwood, *The Science of Hitting*, 1971

The concern is an American one that seems to have first surfaced in the 1950s. The gist of the objection appears to be that *type* is a noun and should not be used as an adjective. The usual suggestion is to use *type of* instead of *type* alone. Attributive nouns (such as *apple* in *apple pie*) are a commonplace in English, however, and there is no grammatical reason why *type* should not be used attributively. It may be that the criticism actually has some more subtle basis. A number of critics mark the use socially, associating it with lower-class people or with business, technical, and advertising usage.

Our evidence suggests that the usage has not established itself strongly in edited prose. It turns up occasionally in trade publications, but only seldom in more general writing. A sample:

> . . . many breeders both new and old are searching for a smaller, meaty type rabbit —Rusty Schultz, *Rabbits*, September–October 1986

> . . . reported to be interested in this type product —Richard C. Sizemore, *Women's Wear Daily*, 14 Jan. 1974

. . . the Supervisor in charge of this type office —Arthur S. Aubry, Jr., *Police,* January–February 1968

Examples from speech show a somewhat wider spread of usage:

After an NSC meeting or an NSC type meeting . . . , a few of us were asked to gather in the Oval Office —Edwin Meese 3d, quoted in *The Tower Commission Report,* 1987

I do a warm-up about local Buffalo things, and there's a champagne party afterward. It's really a family-type thing —Mark Russell, quoted in *TV Guide,* 23 June 1978

Notice the hyphen in the last example. Mark Russell obviously did not pronounce it; a writer or editor put it in. For some mysterious reason this hyphen removes much of the stigma from the usage: many commentators excuse the hyphenated use in technical contexts, and Copperud 1980 says it is "verging on respectability" in other contexts as well. A couple of examples:

. . . a field jacket-type parka would have cost in the neighborhood of $250 —Kent Mitchell, *Atlanta Jour.-Constitution,* 19 Sept. 1984

One of my trenchcoat-type coats has two buttons missing —*And More by Andy Rooney,* 1982

Type is frequently used to make compound modifiers as needed in this way. It is fairly common with technical terms:

. . . tetracycline-type antibiotic —*Annual Report, Pfizer,* 1970

It's not practical to shrink this conveyor-type dishwasher down —William H. Dennler, quoted in *General Electric Investor,* Winter 1970

And many writers attach *-type* to proper names:

. . . an adult Western with an Othello-type plot —*Current Biography,* June 1965

It was a Scottie Pippen-type shot —Grant Wahl, *Sports Illustrated,* 6 Mar. 2000

While a majority of commentators prescribe *type of* in place of attributive *type,* a minority—mostly college handbooks—disparage *type of* as frequently unnecessary. *Type of* is, indeed, deadwood in some uses. Here are a couple of examples where it could have been cut with no loss:

. . . is all business—in a friendly type of way —Julie Gilbert, *Houston Post,* 3 Sept. 1984

The most flagrant type of misuse is to say something like: 'They *decimated* almost half the enemy.' —Howard 1977

U

unaware, unawares *Unaware* is common as an adjective and uncommon as an adverb. The usual adverb is *unawares.* Either adverb is most likely to occur following *catch* or *take*:

The out-break of the *intifada* in December 1987 once again caught the Israelis unawares —Bernard Wasserstein, *Times Literary Supp.,* 26 Apr. 1991

But it may work even better if it takes you unawares —Pauline Kael, *New Yorker,* 18 Apr. 1988

. . . the students' responses could be symptomatic of a proliferation of honorary societies that caught Phi Beta Kappa unaware —*Key Reporter,* Spring 1995

. . . consumers could be taken unaware if an otherwise safe food was genetically endowed with an allergen —Jane E. Brody, *N.Y. Times,* 5 Dec. 2000

Unaware used as an adverb is so rare as to be thought a mistake by some, even though it is standard.

unbeknown, unbeknownst The history of *unbeknown* and *unbeknownst* is relatively straightforward. *Unbeknown* was first recorded in 1636, *unbeknownst* in 1849 (exactly how the *-st* came to be added is not understood). The OED labeled *unbeknownst* colloquial and dialectal, but the OED Supplement notes that it is "now of much wider currency than in the 19th. cent." According to our evidence, both *unbeknown* and *unbeknownst* are now in widespread standard use and have been for many years.

Both forms and especially *unbeknowst* have been the subject of critical commentary from about 1869 at least until 1980. These comments are muddled, contradictory, and entirely irrelevant to present-day English. *Unbeknownst* is the more common in American English:

. . . quite unbeknownst to her —E. B. White, *New Yorker,* 7 Apr. 1956

Unbeknownst to them —Garrison Keillor, *Lake Wobegon Days,* 1985

. . . prevents advertisers from collecting detailed information unbeknownst to users —Jennifer Tanaka, *Newsweek,* 5 July 1999

Unbeknownst to us, the physical world throbs with infrasonic noise —Yvonne Baskin, *Discover,* April 1992

Unbeknown is less common (but far from rare) in American English and seems to be the preferred form in British English:

Meanwhile, unbeknown to either of them, Sarah is being stalked by yet another lawyer —Marilyn Stasio, *N.Y. Times Book Rev.,* 10 Mar. 1991

. . . computer viruses (programs that destroy other programs unbeknown to the computer user) —Igor Alesander, *Nature,* 17 Nov. 1988

Unbeknown even to some of his close associates, he was already an alcoholic —Frank Rich, *N.Y. Times Book Rev.,* 24 Oct. 1982

uncomparable adjectives See ABSOLUTE ADJECTIVES.

underhanded, underhand *Underhanded* was strongly criticized in the 19th century as a vulgarism for *underhand.* The 19th-century criticism enjoyed little popularity in the 20th century, and no commentator since Partridge 1942 has repeated it. *Underhanded* continues to be used commonly as both an adjective and an adverb. As an adjective meaning "marked by secrecy and deception," it has almost entirely replaced *underhand* in American English:

. . . the term *lobbyist* sets up an unpleasant image of someone prowling the halls of political power, using underhanded methods —A. W. Godfrey, *Commonweal,* 11 Feb. 2000

The British, however, continue to use *underhand* in this sense:

. . . as unquieting and ambivalent and underhand in intention as he found them —Margaret Drabble, *The Needle's Eye,* 1972

When a method of throwing or striking a ball is being described, the adjective is usually *underhand* ("an underhand toss"), but the adverb can be either *underhand* or *underhanded*:

Why won't Shaq try shooting them underhanded? —Michael Farber, *Sports Illustrated,* 29 Nov. 1999

. . . and then tried to show Steffi Graf by serving underhand —*Sports Illustrated,* 5 July 1999

under the circumstances See CIRCUMSTANCES.

under way, under weigh The original expression is *under way,* probably adapted from the Dutch *onderweg,* "on the way." It is a nautical expression describing a vessel that is moving through the water or is not lying at anchor or aground. The first written record of *under way* is from 1743. *Under weigh* first appeared in print not long afterward, in 1777. No doubt the substitution of *weigh* for *way* was influenced by the use of the verb *weigh* to mean "lift" in "weigh anchor." Neither *under way* nor *under weigh* makes much literal sense, but *under weigh* at least has the advantage of looking nautical. For whatever reason, many prominent authors in the past have preferred *under weigh* to *under way*:

She got under weigh with very little fuss —Richard Henry Dana, *Two Years Before the Mast,* 1840 (OED)

. . . no profane songs would be allowed on board the Pequod, particularly in getting under weigh —Herman Melville, *Moby Dick,* 1851 (in Reader's Digest 1983)

Under weigh was first called a mistake in 1869. Various 20th-century commentators have also favored *under way,* although several acknowledge that *under weigh* has a history of respectable use. The OED treats both *under way* and *under weigh* as standard. Our evidence indicates, however, that *under weigh* is now much rarer than it was during the 19th century. It has probably fallen into disuse because *under way* has come to be used so widely in general contexts:

. . . a welcoming gala is about to get under way at the convention center —Michelle Cottle, *New Republic,* 14 Aug. 2000

There is an increasing tendency (encouraged by Garner 1998) in recent years to write *under way* as a solid word, *underway*:

Work is already underway on a new East River tunnel —Bruce Kovner, *New York,* 7 Feb. 1972

. . . as the expected wave of mergers gets underway —Michael Hirsh, *Newsweek,* 1 Nov. 1999

It is quite possible that this solid form will eventually predominate over the two-word form, but at present *under way* is still quite a bit more common.

underwhelm This word was coined in the 1940s, but we're not sure by whom. Our earliest record of it is from the *New Yorker* in 1944, when it was used by Howard Brubaker in the form of the participial adjective *underwhelm-*

ing. We first found it used as a transitive verb in 1949:

> . . . leaves me, in the words of Abner Dean, utterly underwhelmed —Philip Wylie, letter to the editor, *Atlantic,* April 1949

A few American critics call the word tired, but Burchfield 1996 calls it successful. It seems to be:

> Baseball needs ambassadors to sell the game to an increasingly uninterested audience and an equally underwhelmed advertising community —Tom Verducci, *Sports Illustrated,* 3 May 1993

> . . . rather wooden turn as the righteous Robin left critics and many moviegoers a bit underwhelmed —Alan Rickman, *Entertainment Weekly,* 9 Aug. 1991

> The game was every bit as underwhelming as it had promised to be, and the miseries continued to mount for the Washington Redskins —Mark Maske, *Washington Post,* 16 Oct. 2001

undoubtedly   See DOUBTLESS, NO DOUBT, UNDOUBTEDLY.

uneatable   See INEDIBLE, UNEATABLE.

unequal   *Unequal* is idiomatically followed by *to*:

> Perhaps it is of the very essence of gratitude that it should feel itself unequal to the task —Ralph Barton Perry, *Atlantic,* October 1946

> . . . they too have proved unequal to controlling the Mekong —*The Lamp,* Summer 1963

> . . . we are unequal to the task —Peter F. Drucker, *Harper's,* January 1972

Fowler 1926 encountered at least one instance of *for* used in place of *to,* and he cited it as an error. A few later critics have followed suit, but this appears to be a nonissue; aside from the single citation in Fowler, we have no evidence of *for* used with *unequal.*

unequivocably, unequivocally   The standard word is *unequivocally*:

> . . . went on to state unequivocally that no other author had collaborated on the work —Gay Talese, *Harper's,* January 1969

> . . . should speak out more unequivocally than it has —Samuel Krislov, *AAUP Bulletin,* September 1970

The nonstandard equivalent that occasionally shows up in reputable writing is *unequivocably*:

> . . . only in adequately controlled studies can improvement following EMDR treat-

ment be unequivocably attributed to the treatment itself —Scott O. Lilienfeld, *Skeptical Inquirer,* January/February 1996

> The results . . . unequivocably demonstrate the demise of fatalism —Edwin S. Shneidman, *Psychology Today,* June 1971

unexceptionable, unexceptional   Commentators beginning with Fowler have made the following distinction: *unexceptionable* means "not open to objection or criticism," and *unexceptional* means "not out of the ordinary; not exceptional." The use of *unexceptional* to mean "not open to objection or criticism; unexceptionable" is regarded by all as incorrect.

The first recorded use of *unexceptional* was in 1775, when Madame D'Arblay (Fanny Burney) wrote "She bears an unexceptional character." The meaning of *unexceptional* here, as defined in the OED, is "unexceptionable." The OED includes two other citations for this sense of *unexceptional,* one from 1806 and one from 1877. The OED treats this sense as standard.

In current usage, however, *unexceptional* nearly always means what the critics say it should mean:

> . . . his thoughts . . . are realistically stated, but unexceptional —Henry J. Steck, *Library Jour.,* 15 Jan. 1966

> . . . moments and details in routine days of mostly unexceptional lives —Robert Kiely, *N.Y. Times Book Rev.,* 1 July 1979

> . . . make unexceptional pizza all but irresistible —Gwen Kinkead, *Fortune,* 26 July 1982

> . . . unexceptional intellect, limited education and incompatible social background —Robert Craft, *N.Y. Times Book Rev.,* 29 Apr. 1984

The stigmatized sense of the word is now extremely rare:

> . . . it was only the unexceptional work of the aircraft and engine manufacturers . . . which enabled the Expedition to take place that spring —*World Today,* September 1934

> Although they were both in good health and of unexceptional figure, Tony and Brenda were on a diet —Evelyn Waugh, *A Handful of Dust,* 1934

The exact meaning of *unexceptional* in the Evelyn Waugh quotation is questionable, but the context seems to call for "not open to criticism" rather than "not exceptional."

Unexceptionable is an older word, first attested in 1664. Typical current usage is illustrated by the following citations:

> . . . is an entirely legitimate and unexceptionable principle —Charles Yost, *Saturday Rev.,* 3 Apr. 1976

And Engel's principal thesis . . . is, if unoriginal, unexceptionable —Benjamin DeMott, *N.Y. Times Book Rev.,* 10 Oct. 1976

As for slang, I'm all for it! . . . there are thousands of now unexceptionable English words such as "clever" . . . that began life as slang —Steven Pinker, *New Republic,* 31 Jan. 1994

Although *unexceptionable* can sometimes be a highly complimentary word, it is normally a term of lukewarm praise. *Unexceptional,* on the other hand, is normally a term of lukewarm criticism. The use of *unexceptional* in its original sense as a synonym for *unexceptionable* has been almost entirely superseded by its use as the negative of *exceptional.* The distinction favored by the critics is in this case observed by almost all writers.

See also EXCEPTIONABLE, EXCEPTIONAL.

unhuman, inhuman *Inhuman* is the older of these two words and by far the more common. Both were originally used to mean "lacking pity, kindness, or mercy"—*inhuman* in the 15th century and *unhuman* in the middle of the 16th. That sense of *inhuman* is still in frequent use, but since the late 1800s *unhuman* has primarily served simply as the negative of *human*:

. . . the bodies looked as limp and unhuman as bags of grain —Norman Mailer, *The Naked and the Dead,* 1948

Inhuman is also used to mean "not human" with no implication of moral judgment. It is, in fact, more common in this sense than *unhuman*:

. . . saw a strangeness in the daylight, and loved inhuman nature —John Updike, *N.Y. Times Book Rev.,* 14 Nov. 1976

. . . a timeless and abiding (and inhuman) reality reasserts itself in the surrounding wilderness —Joyce Carol Oates, *N.Y. Times Book Rev.,* 13 Feb. 1983

uninterest See DISINTEREST, DISINTERESTEDNESS, UNINTEREST.

uninterested See DISINTERESTED, UNINTERESTED.

unique The law has been laid down time and time again: *unique* is an absolute adjective (see ABSOLUTE ADJECTIVES); it cannot be modified by such adverbs of degree as *more, most, somewhat,* and *very*; a thing is either unique or it isn't. These observations are accepted as gospel by many people, and no one who adheres to them is likely to be persuaded not to, but let it be noted anyway that they are not entirely true.

The French word *unique* was first borrowed into English in the early 17th century with two

senses, "being the only one; sole" and "having no like or equal." It did not come into widespread use until about the middle of the 19th century.

Words that are in widespread use have a tendency to take on extended meanings. *Unique,* used to describe something that was unlike anything else, also came to be used more broadly to describe something that was, simply, unusual or rare. (A similar extension of meaning has occurred with *singular.*) It began to be used more broadly at almost the time that it became a common word:

A very unique child, thought I —Charlotte Brontë (in Fowler 1907)

. . . the great G.B. & the greater L.M.A. did the "Morning Call" in a very unique manner, Sir Edward being got up in a red velvet hunting suit & a surprising wig —Louisa May Alcott, letter, 13 Feb. 1859

. . . these summer guests found themselves defrauded of their uniquest recreations —*Harper's,* April 1885 (OED)

It was not long, however, before such usage began to be criticized. Loud and persistent voices of protest were raised after the turn of the century—earlier criticism seems to have been a bit fuzzy. But by 1906 the present lines of criticism were laid down. They have not been much changed since, but neither has the actual usage of *unique.*

In current English, *unique* has four principal senses, the least common of which is its original sense, "being the only one; sole, single":

"But what about your wife typing it out? I can't walk away with a unique copy. Suppose I lost it? . . ." —Kingsley Amis, *Antaeus,* Spring 1975

The other misconception held man to be the unique toolmaker among animals —*Current Biography,* November 1967

Fowler 1926 disliked this use of *unique,* and Evans 1957 asserted that *unique* "can no longer be used in this sense." No other commentator has noticed it.

The use of *unique* approved by the critics is its second sense, "having no like or equal":

These fresh enemies are unique. Each has its own name and a capacity to cause its own kind of fear —Joseph A. Amato, *Dust,* 2000

. . . he could stare at the flames, each one new, violent, unique —Robert Coover, *Harper's,* January 1972

Like every other integer, 1,001 can be factored into a unique set of prime numbers —Martin Gardner, *Scientific American,* August 1998

. . . a one-time phenomenon, unique in its time —James A. Michener, *N.Y. Times Book Rev.,* 27 Feb. 1977

Use of this sense is widespread and shows no sign of dying out. As several commentators have noted, *unique* in this sense can be modified by such adverbs as *almost, nearly,* and *practically:*

. . . a curious, almost unique turn of affairs —Roger Angell, *New Yorker,* 15 Aug. 1983

In a related and equally common sense, *unique* is used with *to* and has the meaning "distinctively characteristic; peculiar":

The chapels I discovered on several recent visits are unique to this part of Piedmont —Corby Kummer, *Atlantic,* August 2000

. . . a common degenerative dental disease unique to cats —Drew Weigner, D.V.M., *Cat Fancy,* August 1998

Fowler also disliked this use of *unique,* although he stopped short of calling it incorrect. Howard 1980 takes exception to it as well.

The controversial sense of *unique* can be variously defined. It sometimes equals *unusual,* sometimes *rare,* and sometimes *distinctive.* It is generally used to imply excellence and is therefore popular with writers of advertising copy (doubtless one reason why the critics are hostile to it):

A very unique ball point pen —advt., *Wall Street Jour.,* 21 May 1975

The most unique fabric stores in the country —advt., *New Yorker,* 13 Apr. 1987

But copywriters are by no means the only ones to make use of this sense:

. . . nothing quite so unique in literature as these solemn admonitory poems —Edith Hamilton, *The Greek Way to Western Civilization,* 1930

The more we study him, the less unique he seems —Harry Levin, *James Joyce,* 1941

. . . isn't into boring, run-of-the mill exercise programs; her motto is: the more unique, the better —Janet Di Lauro, *Soap Opera Weekly,* 27 Oct. 1998

She's the most unique person I ever met —Arthur Miller, quoted in *Theatre Arts,* November 1956

. . . I do think Jimmy Carter was very unique —Hedley Donovan, *Time,* 6 May 1985

He was the most unique of men —Frank Deford, *Sports Illustrated,* 30 Apr. 1984

An extremely unique enzyme —Richard Fitzhugh, *US,* 10 Sept. 1984

Wiesbaden town and spa must have been fairly unique in the Germany of that post-war period —Sybille Bedford, *New Yorker,* 20 Feb. 1989

This sense is most noticeable when it occurs with a modifying adverb, as in the above quotations, but its use without a modifier is equally common:

. . . the unique camaraderie of career servicemen —Malcolm S. Forbes, *Forbes,* 1 Dec. 1970

. . . is in a unique position to evaluate them both —*Times Literary Supp.,* 22 Oct. 1971

. . . a unique breed of woman—independent, daring, cool-headed —Margaret Cronin Fisk, *Cosmopolitan,* October 1976

Those who sell gourmet foods say buyers must be convinced that the products are unique and high-quality but not intimidating —Janet Guyon, *Wall Street Jour.,* 6 May 1982

. . . his unique combination of touch and power led to tournament wins in Madrid —Barry Lorge, *Sport,* September 1983

What, then, is the intelligent writer to make of *unique?* The evidence allows several definite conclusions. Those who insist that *unique* cannot be modified by such adverbs as *more, most,* and *very* are clearly wrong: our evidence shows that it can be and frequently is modified by such adverbs. Those who believe that the use of such modifiers threatens to weaken (or has already weakened) the "having no like or equal" sense of *unique* are also wrong: our evidence shows that the "having no like or equal" sense is flourishing. And those who regard the use of *unique* to mean "unusual" or "distinctive" as a modern corruption are wrong: *unique* has been used with those meanings for well over a hundred years. Should you therefore use the disputed sense of *unique* with utter disregard for possible criticism? Maybe not. The reasons people have for disliking such usage may not be especially sound, but they are cherished nonetheless, and they are widely promoted. You will have to make your own choice based on your knowledge.

United States In current American usage, *United States* takes a singular verb when it is the subject of a sentence. (Our meager British evidence shows the plural verb preferred.) But the verb was always plural once:

I think it a great misfortune that the United States are in the department of the former —Thomas Jefferson, letter, 30 Jan. 1787

Sometime between 1787 and now *United States* went from being considered a plural noun to being considered a singular one. Obviously during those two centuries the perception of the United States as a single entity established itself. Do we have any idea when?

We have theories but no conclusive evidence. The first is from an undated and unidentified newspaper clipping in which General John W. Foster, who was Secretary of State under Benjamin Harrison, replies to criticism of his use of the singular in a book he published in 1900. According to Foster, Andrew Jackson was the first president to adopt the singular, and every president from Lincoln to McKinley regularly used it. Two more recent commentators, W. V. Quine, *Quiddities,* 1987, and Gary Wills, *Lincoln at Gettysburg,* 1992, point to the Civil War as the time when plural use gave way to singular, Wills pinpointing the Gettysburg address.

These are interesting theories, but they are hard to prove. We don't know what Andrew Jackson used, but his second vice president and successor, Martin Van Buren, wrote in his autobiography (around 1854):

> . . . the dignity and immense power that the United States have acquired since that day . . .

And if Lincoln changed the outlook (and usage) of most Americans, he didn't change his own usage:

> . . . the United States must hold themselves at liberty to increase their naval armament upon the lakes —annual message to Congress, December 1864

And it seems likely that those who grew up using the plural didn't change:

> . . . the United States inherit by far their most precious possession —Walt Whitman, *North American Rev.,* vol. 141, 1885, reprinted in Bolton & Crystal 1969

Actual usage seems to have been most markedly changing around the turn of the century, when General Foster's singular was questioned and commentators like Bierce 1909 (against the singular) and Utter 1916 (noting the increasing use of the singular) were writing. About the only vestige of plural use we have left today is the expression "these United States."

unless and until Criticized by many commentators as wordy and redundant, this somewhat legalistic-sounding phrase seems to occur rarely in edited prose. It serves, when used, to give added emphasis to a conditional statement when a simple *unless* or *until* is felt to be inadequate.

unlike The use of *unlike* as a conjunction is less common than the conjunctive use of *like* and, while criticized, is not as common a subject of censure. The conjunctive *unlike* almost always introduces a prepositional phrase. Its meaning is "not as" or "as is not the case":

> . . . in American movies, unlike in Oliver Goldsmith's famous poem, dog is even more sacred than mom —John Simon, *National Rev.,* 28 Feb. 1998

> Unlike in baseball, the length of the ban is not determined by the severity of the offence —Pete Davies, *Twenty-two Foreigners in Funny Shorts,* 1994

In spite of criticism, conjunctive *unlike* is well established in both American and British usage.

Sometimes the preposition following the conjunctive *unlike* is inadvertently dropped, with results like the following:

> . . . unlike most boats the rounded end is the front —W. E. Swinton, *The Corridor of Life,* 1948

> So many fine men were outside the charmed circle that, unlike most colleges, there was no disgrace in not being a "club man" —John Reed, *New Republic,* 22 Nov. 1954

Such constructions, sometimes known as false comparisons, are best avoided.

See also FALSE COMPARISON; LIKE, AS, AS IF 1.

unreadable See ILLEGIBLE, UNREADABLE.

unsanitary, insanitary These synonyms were both coined at about the same time: *unsanitary* was first recorded in 1871, *insanitary* in 1874. In the early part of the 20th century, *unsanitary* was regarded as somehow improper (many objectors had failed to find it when it was entered in Webster 1909), but no one objects any more. Garner 1998 says *insanitary* has stronger negative connotations than *unsanitary,* but our evidence shows them both used in about the same way. *Unsanitary* is more common.

> Apparently the privacy advocates believe hepatitis is not too high a price to pay for preserving the dignity of unsanitary hash slingers —Joseph R. Garber, *Forbes,* 20 Oct. 1997

> . . . forcing its employees to work in unsafe conditions and live in unsanitary housing trailers —N.Y. Times, 20 May 1997

> . . . passed through immigration and sat himself in the insanitary lounge —John le Carré, *A Perfect Spy,* 1986

> In Lower Mesopotamia heat and insanitary camps led to much dysentery, malaria and heat stroke —John Laffin, *Combat Surgeons,* 1970

unsatisfied　See DISSATISFIED, UNSATISFIED.

unseasonable, unseasonal　See SEASON-
ABLE, SEASONAL.

until　See TILL, UNTIL, 'TIL; UNLESS AND
UNTIL.

up, *adverb*　This tiny adverb is one that no
native speaker of English ordinarily misuses,
yet handbook compilers and other commentators by the dozen seem determined to legislate
it out of use. In its reprehended function it
serves to connote the completion of the action
of a verb, as in *burn up, end up, divide up,* or to
intensify the verb, as in *hurry up,* or to indicate
direction, as *climb up.* These are all natural idiomatic uses, but our commentators would
have us believe *up* is superfluous, redundant.
Its elimination would result in a minute saving
of two letters and one space, hardly enough to
warrant the waste in paper and ink that has
been spent on trying to eliminate it and mess
up normal idiom. Such advice has no intellectual content, and the completive adverb is so
insidiously useful that commentators use it
without even thinking:

> But in a sentence such as 'He climbed up the
> ladder', the *up* does nothing but take up
> space —Bryson 1984

Our recommendation is just the opposite: always use *up* when it occurs naturally.

up, *verb*　**1.** While a few commentators are
dubious about *up* meaning "raise" or "increase," it is standard but not especially formal:

> . . . China initially said six villagers choked
> or burned to death, and later upped the
> number to 56 —Adam Cohen, *Time,* 7 June
> 1999

> Advertisers have upped the creative ante
> —Dottie Enrico, *TV Guide,* 20 July 1996

2. Some usage books and schoolbooks view
the phrase *up and* with the same distaste they
direct at *take and, go and,* and *try and* (which
see). *Up and* is no bucolic idiom redolent of
our frontier past, however; it is current on
both sides of the Atlantic, and is used in general publications, often by writers of more
than ordinary sophistication. It, too, is not
highly formal:

> He upped and offed to the gents —Will Self,
> *Cock & Bull,* 1992

> You up and run away from home —Alan
> Coren, *Punch,* 12 Mar. 1975

> . . . I think all biographers subconsciously
> hope their man will up and die, clearing the
> boards and making everything a whole lot
> simpler —E. B. White, letter, 20 Sept. 1968

> . . . the Caribbean has seen a steady hemor-
> rhage of talent to New York and Miami. . . .
> The best and the brightest have just upped
> and left —Michael Elliott, *Newsweek,* 18
> July 1994

upcoming　The adjective *upcoming* was
formed in just the same way as *oncoming,
forthcoming, incoming,* and *outgoing.* It differs
from them in only one respect: it is relatively
new. It was coined in the early 1940s and did
not come into frequent use until after World
War II. By the 1950s it had established itself as
a common word, and it continues to be one
today.

> This will make some sizable "bunching" for
> the upcoming holidays —Bosley Crowther,
> *N.Y. Times,* 15 Dec. 1957

> . . . they have only to look at the coverage of
> the upcoming political conventions —*New
> Republic,* 31 July 2000

> . . . a crowded thoroughfare where
> billboards flack upcoming spectacles
> —Michael H. Martin, *Fortune,* 9 June 1997

Upcoming has been denigrated as "journalese" by a few commentators, who recommend substituting *coming, forthcoming,* or *approaching* in its place. It does in fact occur
most often in journalistic use, but that is hardly surprising considering that journalists are
frequently called upon to write about events,
occasions, and ceremonies that are coming up.
Upcoming is a standard and reputable word,
recognized as such by current dictionaries.
Disapproval of it has never been especially
widespread, and recent evidence suggests that
it has become less so. You have little to worry
about if you choose to use *upcoming.*

upon　See ON 1.

upward, upwards　The adjective is *upward*:

> She shifted her bill to a slightly upward
> angle —Josephine & Gilbert Fernandez,
> *Massachusetts Audubon,* June 1968

The adverb may be either *upward* or, less commonly, *upwards.* Both are standard:

> . . . the electric door groans and rattles up-
> ward —Frank Conroy, *Harper's,* November
> 1970

> . . . its small flame will flicker upward
> —Laurence Leamer, *Harper's,* December
> 1971

Both *upward* and *upwards* are used with *of*
to mean "more than; in excess of." *Upwards of*
is more common than *upward of*:

> . . . East Timor, where upwards of a quarter
> of the territory's 850,000 people were on the

run —Jeffrey Bartholet, *Newsweek,* 20 Sept. 1999

. . . had won upwards of $7 million but had squandered that fortune —William Nack, *Sports Illustrated,* 23 July 1984

. . . statistics now indicate that women represent upward of 60 percent of adventure travelers —Holly Morris, *Ms.,* May/June 1998

Such usage, which was first recorded in the early 18th century, was disliked by Alfred Ayres in 1881 and by Ambrose Bierce in 1909, but is now recognized as perfectly reputable.

us Like the other personal pronouns, *us* turns up in contexts where the schoolbooks have long said it does not belong. As might be expected, it occurs after the verb *be:*

This is this year, and we are us —Paul Horgan, *Ladies' Home Jour.,* January 1971

And it is common in an emphatic position at the beginning of a statement:

Us kids at Concord school in Mr. Thompson's reading class are studying dictionaries —letter from a schoolgirl in Pennsylvania, March 1980

. . . a sense of departmental loyalty: us against them —Jay McInerney, *Bright Lights, Big City,* 1984

A little harder to explain are the other appearances in subject position:

This is not what us journalists call a "happy beat" —Hunter S. Thompson, *Rolling Stone,* 2 Mar. 1972

. . . wherein us romantics are supposed to accept Ava Gardner as Omar Sharif's royal mama —Judith Crist, *TV Guide,* 27 July 1973

These vexing usages and kindred problems concerning personal pronouns are discussed and illustrated at various places in this book. We suggest that you start with IT'S ME and PRONOUNS. These will lead you to other points of interest.

usage It is inevitable, we suppose, that a number of usage commentators comment on the word *usage.* What they say, by and large, is that *usage* should not be employed simply as a synonym of *use* in contexts like "the use/usage of public lands" and "increased use/usage of electricity." This issue seems to have originated with Gowers 1954 and has continued as recently as Garner 1998.

A look in almost any dictionary shows, however, that *usage* does mean "act of using or being used; use; employment." Evidence in the OED establishes that *usage* has had this sense since the 14th century. It has occurred in the works of such writers as Geoffrey Chaucer, Joseph Priestley, and Alfred, Lord Tennyson. Here are some 20th-century examples from our files:

. . . his blue eyes dimmed with time and usage —Claude G. Bowers, *The Young Jefferson, 1743–1789,* 1945

The book you sent back for more signs and marks of usage, having now been through another campaign, looks to me in as ideal a condition for your purposes as you could expect —Robert Frost, letter, 4 Aug. 1953

. . . ending credit card usage altogether —Guy Halverson, *Christian Science Monitor,* 10 Apr. 1980

. . . a squat, ladder-back chair whose short legs had the look of being worn away through long usage —Peter Taylor, *The Old Forest and Other Stories,* 1985

It is accurate to say that *use* is more common than *usage* in this sense, but it is not accurate to say that *usage* in this sense is therefore an error. *Usage* meaning "use" is standard English.

used to, use to *Use* was once commonly employed as an intransitive verb meaning "to be in the habit or custom; be wont":

I did this night give the waterman who uses to carry me 10*s.* —Samuel Pepys, diary, 24 Mar. 1667

He does not use to be the last on these occasions —George Lillo, *London Merchant,* 1731

But this sense of *use* now occurs only in the past tense with *to:*

. . . the passion this issue used to ignite in the State Department —Henry Brandon, *Atlantic,* March 1970

Used to is extremely common in both speech and writing. Such problems as arise with it have to do with the *d* of *used.* Because the *d* is not pronounced, *used to* is indistinguishable in speech from *use to.* It may be, in fact, that many people actually say *use to* rather than *used to,* but since the pronunciations are essentially identical, it makes no difference. In writing, however, *use to* in place of *used to* is an error.

The problem becomes a little trickier in constructions with *did.* The form considered correct following *did,* at least in American English, is *use to.* Just as we say "Did he want to?" rather than "Did he wanted to?," so we say "Did he use to?" rather than "Did he used to?" Here again, it may be that some people actually say "did . . . used to," but the question is moot in speech. Only in writing does it become an issue. Our evidence shows that most writers do remember to drop the *d* of *used* following *did*:

"Didn't he use to go with Laura?" she asked —Irwin Shaw, *The Young Lions,* 1948

". . . It didn't use to be like that." —James Jones, *From Here to Eternity,* 1951

I believe Polk did use to be a town —Eudora Welty, *The Ponder Heart,* 1954

Didn't half-mast use to represent mourning? —Lois Long, *New Yorker,* 21 Oct. 1967

But the spelling "did . . . used to" does sometimes find its way into print:

"Did you used to walk with them?" he asked Concetta —Constantine FitzGibbon, *The Holiday,* 1953

He told me, "Today orchestras announce auditions, which they didn't used to do. . . ." —James Lincoln Collier, *Village Voice,* 28 Feb. 1968

Some commentators call such usage an error, but others find it acceptable. Quirk et al. 1985 says that the spelling *did . . . used to* is often regarded as nonstandard on both sides of the Atlantic, but Garner 1998 insists on it. According to our evidence, the usual form in American English is *didn't use to.*

See also SUPPOSED TO.

used to could Admonitions against the use of this phrase have appeared in a number of handbooks and usage books. They decry it as nonstandard or semiliterate, but it is regional. It is a double modal, and double modals are a characteristic of Southern speech. The linguist Raven I. McDavid, Jr., observed in 1963 (in his abridgement of Mencken's *The American Language*) that in his experience *used to could* (or *use to could,* as he wrote it) was not limited to those of little education but was common in the casual speech of educated Southerners. It seldom occurs in writing except when reporting speech or when used for deliberate effect:

. . . we'll no longer be able to read good prose like we used to could —James Thurber, letter, 15 Aug. 1959

useful Something is said to be useful *to* somebody:

Information and guidelines . . . are most useful to the beginner —Bill Scott, *Media & Materials,* February 1970

. . . literary criticism, useful to all of us who remember the books of our childhood —Clara Claiborne Park, *Saturday Rev.,* December 1978

When the way in which something is useful is being described, either *in* or *for* may be used:

. . . the book is useful in recording the details of several rare editions —*Times Literary Supp.,* 2 Oct. 1970

. . . a low-power . . . microscope will be found useful for examining material such as the larger insect larvae —W. H. Dowdeswell, *Animal Ecology,* 2d ed., 1959

It was then we found our sea-slugs useful for turning on our opponent —Gerald Durrell, *My Family and Other Animals,* 1956

utilize Usage writers dislike *utilize* because they regard it as a needlessly long and pretentious substitute for *use.* They generally recommend either that it be disdained altogether or that it be used only when it has the meaning "to turn to practical use or account." That is, in fact, usually the meaning of *utilize* in actual usage:

. . . the race to utilize nuclear fission for military purposes —Seymour Mauskopf, *Science,* 11 Apr. 1997

Displays with backlighting also use a reflector to shine the light source through the display to utilize as much of the light produced as possible —Catherine Greenman, *N.Y. Times,* 30 July 1998

. . . women who want to work at jobs that utilize their full potential —Bella S. Abzug, *Saturday Rev.,* 7 Aug. 1976

Utilize is a distinct word having distinct implications. More than *use,* it suggests a deliberate decision or effort to employ something (or someone) for a practical purpose. It is commonly used and is standard.

V

variant spellings See MILLENNIUM; SPELLING.

various *Various* is a pronoun produced by functional shift from the adjective—the same way the pronouns *certain, few, many,* and *several* were formed—when it is followed by *of*:

> Various of the men, then Clark, and finally Lewis fell ill —Bernard De Voto, *Minority Report,* 1940, in *The Practical Cogitator,* ed. Charles P. Curtis, Jr., & Ferris Greenslet, 1945

This use was first recorded in Bartlett's *Dictionary of Americanisms* (4th ed., 1877), which included a quotation from a correspondent in the *New York Times*: "I talked for an hour with various of them.' The OED made no mention of this use in 1916, but by 1926 it was widespread enough for Fowler to discover and censure it. Fowler included seven examples, all presumably drawn from British newspapers. Sir Ernest Gowers' 1965 revision of Fowler replaced the original seven examples with four new ones. Sir Ernest thought that *various* might force its way into the company of those similarly formed pronouns. But somehow this evidence never reached the OED editors, for the second edition of the OED still has no entry for the pronoun. And, curiously, Burchfield 1996, the most recent reviser of Fowler, says *various* is now used idiomatically as a pronoun in British English, although he does show American examples. To finish this strange tale, an electronic search of the OED turns up four citations for *various of* hidden in other entries. Two of these are British. One is the earliest example yet found:

> . . . apologies for various of the great doctrines of the faith —John Henry Newman, 1850, in *Certain Difficulties Felt by Anglicans in Catholic Teaching Considered,* 1864

The other is a note at *evolve* written by Henry Bradley, editor of the E volume of the OED: "in various of the above senses." Evidently the pronoun *various* was once idiomatic in British English, even if it is not now, as Burchfield claims. The pronoun is standard, but not frequent, in American English:

> I showed Mr. Shawn various of these creations —Jeremy Bernstein, *American Scholar,* Winter 1987

> . . . how a given economy will behave if various of its factors change —Jane Jacobs, *Cities and the Wealth of Nations,* 1984

See also NUMEROUS.

various and sundry This is a common fixed phrase which has been criticized as a redundancy. It need not be despised as such, but if you like your prose to be lean, you will probably want to avoid it.

various different This phrase has been criticized as redundant by those who do not recognize that its meaning is "a number of different," not "different different." Other critics have contended that it is incorrect to use *various* in this way to mean "of an indefinite number greater than one." Such use is actually well established and is certainly standard:

> The boy dreamed of saving the various nickels which he earned by hours of lawnmowing —Sinclair Lewis, Introduction to *Four Days on the Webutuck River,* 1925

> . . . the various press representatives were forced to share a single radio teletypewriter —*Current Biography,* December 1964

Even so, you may wish to steer clear of *various different.* It has the appearance of redundancy, and our evidence shows that does not often occur in edited prose.

vary One thing or group of things is said to vary *from* another:

> . . . the relative spaces allotted vary greatly from the norm —*Philosophical Rev.,* October 1953

> . . . these numbers vary inversely . . . from the corresponding given numbers —Ethel L. Grove et al., *Basic Mathematics,* Book 1, 1961

When a range of variation is being described, *vary* is followed by a prepositional phrase beginning with either *from* or *between. From* is more common:

> . . . his weight varies from about 138 to 145 pounds —*Current Biography,* July 1965

> . . . webs that vary from the loosely tangled web of the house spider to the work of art of the garden spider —Katherine W. Moseley, *Massachusetts Audubon,* June 1971

The temperature . . . varies between 120 and 140 degrees Fahrenheit —Gerald S. Craig & Margaret Oldroyd Hyde, *New Ideas in Science,* 1950

vastly The use of *vastly* to mean "to a great degree" in contexts not involving measurement or comparison was disapproved by Fowler 1926. Burchfield 1996 says the use was common in the 19th and 18th centuries, but is now restricted in British English. Such use is common and idiomatic in American English:

> . . . pot stirrers can be vastly amusing as long as they're stirring someone else's pot —Andrew Ferguson, *Time,* 28 Dec. 1998

> . . . the most eclectic—yet also vastly entertaining—evening of dance I have seen —Rita Felciano, *San Francisco Bay Guardian,* 1 Sept. 1993

And it also occurs in British English:

> . . . because the existence of God would make them vastly probable —Stephen Clark, *Times Literary Supp.,* 25 Jan. 1980

> . . . the ways of life of their inhabitants were vastly different —Christopher Hibbert, *Redcoats and Rebels,* 1990

vast majority See MAJORITY 3.

vehement See VEHICLE.

vehicle For a long time, dictionaries recommended sounding the \h\ in *vehicle,* and similarly in *vehement.* But we have evidence back to the early 17th century that the \h\ was often dropped in these words. *Annihilate* \ə-'nī-ə-ˌlāt\ also shows this dropping of \h\ when it would fall after the stress and between vowels. The resulting vocalic hiatus (two vowels occurring next to each other without a consonant in between) is often simplified to a single vowel: again, we have early evidence for two-syllable pronunciations \'vē-kəl\ and \'vē-mənt\. A similar simplification may be observed in the very common current American pronunciations of *diamond* and *diaper:* \'dī-mənd\ and \'dī-pər\.

Today, the usual (and the recommended) pronunciation of *vehicle* is without \h\: \'vē-ə-kəl\ or \'vē-ˌik-əl\. In the United States, a pronunciation with \h\ is also widespread: \'vē-hik-əl\ or \'vē-ˌhik-əl\. It is considered especially characteristic of the South, though it is not universal there and may also be heard throughout the rest of the country. For reasons that are not entirely clear, \'vē-ˌhik-əl\ suffers from an unjust stigma as a yokel's pronunciation. Various suggestions have been put forward for the tenacity of the \h\: influence of the spelling, of the adjective *vehicular* where \h\ is normally sounded, and of the special cadences of Armed Services speech.

We are also warned, in usage sources, against giving primary stress to the second syllable of *vehicle.* This pronunciation is far less common than any of the variants with initial stress. Our pronunciation files include only three citations for \(ˈ)vē-'hik-əl\, although one of them is from a university president.

See also H.

venal, venial *Venal,* which means "open to or characterized by corruption," is sometimes confused with *venial,* which means "pardonable":

> I'm a . . . sinner! Venal, mortal, carnal, major, minor—however you want to call it —Hunter S. Thompson, *Fear and Loathing in Las Vegas,* 1972

> . . . the venial, inefficient trading community —Peter Forster, *London Calling,* 17 Mar. 1955

These mistakes are not common in edited writing, but they are easily made in a moment of inattention.

verbal, oral The first definition of *verbal* in Johnson's Dictionary (1755) is "Spoken; not written." Noah Webster also made this the first sense in his *American Dictionary of the English Language* (1828): "Spoken; expressed to the ear in words; not written; as a *verbal* message; a *verbal* contract, *verbal* testimony." The earliest citation for this sense of *verbal* in the OED dates from 1591. (The earliest citation for the synonymous sense of *oral,* on the other hand, is from 1628.) There is no indication from Johnson, Webster, or the OED that this sense of *verbal* is anything other than standard English.

Why, then, has it been singled out for criticism by commentators on usage? The trouble seems to have started in the late 19th century. Hodgson 1881, who knew the etymologies of *verbal* (from Latin *verbum* "word") and *oral* (from Latin *os* "mouth"), declared that the correct meaning of *verbal* was "couched in words" (which is, in fact, one of the many senses of *verbal,* first attested in 1530). Hodgson dismissed the "spoken rather than written" sense as a "blunder," albeit a common one made by "writers of standing" such as Anthony Trollope, Henry Kingsley, and Henry Fielding:

> The captain returned a verbal answer to a long letter —Henry Fielding, *Journal of a Voyage to Lisbon,* 1755

He might also have added Samuel Pepys, Jonathan Swift, and Charles Dickens:

> "I would not consent to your being charged with any written answer, but perhaps you will take a verbal one?" —Charles Dickens, *A Tale of Two Cities,* 1859

Since Hodgson's time, disapproval of this sense of *verbal* has been widespread among usage commentators, most of whom clearly regard it as a recent development. Some commentators now concede that it is standard, but nearly all express a preference for *oral,* arguing that the multiple meanings of *verbal* could cause confusion. The truth is that the context almost always makes the meaning clear, and the only serious confusion appears to be in the minds of the commentators themselves.

The use of *verbal* to mean "spoken rather than written" occurs commonly and unambiguously with such words as *agreement, commitment,* and *contract.* Very often it is contrasted with the adjective *written* in contexts that make its meaning unmistakable:

> The Italian word also had the extended sense "a volley against an enemy" which English adopted too . . . and has further extended to mean "a forceful verbal or written assault" —Craig M. Carver, *Atlantic,* July 1994

> . . . far fewer written, recorded discussions, far more private, verbal discussions —Warren Bennis, *Saturday Rev.,* 6 Mar. 1976

The adverb *verbally* is also common in this sense:

> . . . have already expressed to me in a letter (as well as verbally) their desire to produce a faithful adaptation —E. B. White, letter, 24 May 1967

> Whilst Bode was able to communicate verbally his feelings . . . , he failed when it came to putting pen to paper —*Times Literary Supp.,* 2 May 1968

> . . . but Freeman says she'd already verbally accepted a CNN offer —*TV Guide,* 31 May 1985

There is no ambiguity in these passages. Of course, if you do see a chance of ambiguity in a particular context, you can always use *oral* instead.

verbal nouns See POSSESSIVE WITH GERUND.

verbiage *Verbiage* in its original and usual sense denotes an excess of words. It is similar to *wordiness,* except that it stresses more the superfluous words themselves than the quality that produces them; that is, a writer with a fondness for *verbiage* might be accused of *wordiness.*

> . . . designed to decode the verbiage of experts —Judith Appelbaum, *N.Y. Times Book Rev.,* 9 Jan. 1983

> As an artist, I find much of the verbiage of art commentators insufferable —Gertrude Myrrh Reagan, letter to the editor, *Science News,* 17 May 1986

Verbiage has also been used since the early 19th century as a synonym of *wording* or *diction*:

> The language of the dialogue is as familiar as the verbiage of the parlour fireside —*The New British Theatre,* 1814 (OED)

> In musical verbiage a phrase is a portion of a melody that is performed without a pause —Albert E. Weir, *The Piano,* 1940

> . . . Washington verbiage equated any non-Communist group with the "free" nations —Barbara W. Tuchman, *The March of Folly,* 1984

Such usage is treated as standard in the OED and in many current dictionaries, including our own, but some people continue to regard it as an error, insisting that *verbiage* should always imply excess. Those same people are also likely to find fault with such phrases as *excess verbiage* and *excessive verbiage,* in which they detect redundancy. The evidence shows, however, that the meaning of *verbiage* is often underscored in standard writing by an appropriate adjective:

> . . . stoically subdues his indignation, wrapping his feelings in a protective layer of bland verbiage —Sam Roberts, *N.Y. Times Mag.,* 7 Apr. 1991

> . . . English men. Charm the knickers off you with their mellow vowels and frivolous verbiage —Margaret Atwood, *NewYorker,* 5 Mar. 1990

> The senator later pruned the excess verbiage for newspaper "reports" —George F. Will, *N.Y. Times Book Rev.,* 30 June 1991

> The cotton padding of this jacket, called bombast (the source of the term for inflated verbiage) —John Tierney, *N.Y. Times,* 21 Jan. 1999

verbified nouns See NOUNS AS VERBS.

verse, stanza In prosody, *verse* means "a line of metrical writing," *stanza* means "a division of a poem consisting of a series of lines arranged together in a usually recurrent pattern of meter and rhyme." In the great world outside of prosody, *verse* is often used to mean "stanza," especially with reference to the lyrics of a song. Use of *verse* to mean "a line of metrical writing" is rare in general prose; the word of choice for most people is, simply, *line.*

very 1. *"Very" and the past participle.* The propriety of using *very* to modify a participle adjective, as in "very pleased" or "very flattering" has been the subject of considerable speculation since the 1870s. *Very* as an intensifier does not modify verbs, and it was therefore a matter of dispute whether *very* could modify participles. However, the question is not one of propriety, but of grammar. Participles have been moving into the class of adjectives since at least the 17th century. And one of the surest signs that a participle is established as an adjective is its being comfortably modified by *very*. The transition from verb form to adjective is a gradual one, and at any given time there will be participles that will sound right with *very* to some people and wrong to others. So you will have to trust your ear and use *very* where it sounds right and *very much* or *quite* or something else where *very* sounds wrong.

We leave you with a few typical examples:

She has become very attached to the house mother and is a "big sister" to the other boys and girls —Mary-Lou Weisman, *Atlantic,* July 1994

Catherine Gladstone was passionately engaged with the success and wellbeing of her husband, but not very interested in either politics or the intricacies of religious doctrine —Roy Jenkins, *Gladstone,* 1995

Now, I won't be satisfied, in fact I'll be very dissatisfied, if you are not one of the sponsors —Robert Frost, letter, 20 Jan. 1947

I am very pleased to know that I can get a quart of mouse milk for under ten dollars —E. B. White, letter, 10 Nov. 1966

2. From the numerous warnings in usage books against overuse or even any use of *very* in writing, you might think that no writer of reputation would actually use "this colorless, exhausted word" (McMahan & Day 1980) as an intensifier. But, of course, many writers do:

The Philosopher was very hungry, and he looked about on all sides to see if there was anything he might eat —James Stephens, *The Crock of Gold,* 1912

David had worked very hard for four days —Ernest Hemingway, "An African Betrayal," in *Sports Illustrated,* 5 May 1986

The hero is a computer expert with a very pregnant wife —Newgate Callendar, *N.Y. Times Book Rev.,* 18 Dec. 1983

It's going to be very interesting, you think, to look at these many objects from olden days —Garrison Keillor, *Lake Wobegon Days,* 1985

. . . very representative of Washington this winter. It is a seething turmoil of glumness —Russell Baker, *N.Y. Times Mag.,* 15 Feb. 1976

The important thing is to consider carefully how you use the intensifier. It is even possible to achieve emphasis by using a string of *verys,* as in this example:

It was a day of very white clouds, and very blue skies, and very dark green spruces —E. B. White, letter, 27 June 1922

But you are more likely to make effective use of the word if you use it—or any intensifier—sparingly in your writing. Use it where it will count the most.

vest An abstract possession, such as a power or right, is vested *in* a person or institution, but a person or institution is vested *with* an abstract possession. Both these uses of the transitive verb *vest* are common and correct:

The United States Constitution vested all harbor rights and responsibilities in the Federal Government —*Dictionary of American History,* 1940

The framers of the system of 1875 intended to vest the President with some measure of independent power —Ernest Barker, *Essays on Government,* 1945

via The English preposition *via* was taken directly from Latin in the late 18th century. It was used to mean "by way of; by a route passing through" and was usually italicized until the 20th century, when it began to be treated more as a native word and used with extended meanings. Webster 1934 covered these with a second sense labeled colloquial and illustrated by a somewhat jocular example. Many things have changed since 1934, but not the mindsets of a number of critics, one of whom still disapproves "send a message via the milkman." Milkman indeed:

The signal travels via satellite to onshore listening posts —Sebastian Junger, *Outside,* October 1994

. . . a 20-city road show that was organized largely via e-mail —Walter Kim, *Time,* 24 Apr. 2000

. . . an executive committee of the board heard the evidence, via a conference call —John J. Miller, *National Rev.,* 6 Dec. 1999

. . . information so quickly and extensively disseminated via the Internet —Daniel Kadlec, *Time,* 24 Apr. 2000

Not everything is electronic:

Since the 1890s, malaria has been understood to be spread not person to person but via mosquitoes —Wayne Biddle, *A Field Guide To Germs,* 1995

This use is very common in writing on scientific and technical subjects, but is by no means limited to them:

. . she is a hack writer in urgent need of financial rescue via bestsellerdom —Cynthia Ozick, *N.Y. Times Book Rev.,* 1 Jan. 1995

. . . a deer can't move anywhere in this community without having its whereabouts flashed via the grapevine —E. B. White, *New Yorker,* 24 Dec. 1955

I want to thank the officials and judges of the American Book Awards via whom this honor has come to me —John Updike, quoted in *Publishers Weekly,* 14 May 1982

. . . he was never able to rid himself of the thought that suicide via jumping from the nineteenth floor was a religious act —Norman Mailer, *Harper's,* March 1971

This use is entirely standard.

viable This adjective, which literally means "capable of living" (as in "a viable fetus"), has been much criticized as a vogue word that is imprecisely used in place of such established alternatives as *workable, feasible,* or *practical.* It is not a new word; the OED shows that it has been used in both literal and figurative senses since the middle of the 19th century. Its use, however, has become common only since the 1940s:

. . . the chances of a viable international order —Max Lerner, *New Republic,* 7 July 1941

A viable society is one in which those who have qualified themselves to see indicate the goals to be aimed at —Aldous Huxley, *The Perennial Philosophy,* 1945

By the 1950s it had become a common word, and it was soon to attract unfavorable attention, from Flesch 1964 and Gowers in Fowler 1965, among others. It has continued to receive unfavorable attention, right up to Garner 1998 and Amis 1998. The repeated criticism has had no apparent effect on the word's popularity:

Is it possible that feminist concerns . . . are no longer viable as subjects for serious fiction? —Joyce Carol Oates, *N.Y. Times Book Rev.,* 21 Nov. 1976

Eggs of elephants, baleen whales, and tortoises remain viable for at least 60 years —Jared Diamond, *Discover,* July 1996

If . . . performing arts and cultural programs on TV become commercially viable —Peter Caranicas, *Saturday Rev.,* January 1981

. . . gives Cleveland something few other Eastern Conference teams can boast: a viable center —Mark Bechtel, *Sports Illustrated,* 1 Nov. 1999

. . . cameralism, which held that the state . . . could create a viable national economy —Thomas W. Laqueur, *New Republic,* 5 June 2000

Dictionaries recognize these uses of *viable* as standard, and so should you, but you may also want to approach this word with some caution, as it is heavily used and as some common combinations, such as *viable alternative,* may be considered clichés.

vice, vise In American English, the "moral fault" is spelled *vice* while the "clamping tool" is spelled *vise.* In British English, *vice* is the preferred spelling for both the fault and the tool.

victual This word, which is pronounced \\'vit-ᵊl\\, provides a good example of the confusion that can result from artificial tampering with the language. It was originally borrowed from Middle French in the 14th century as *vitaille* (with many variant spellings). The present spelling resulted from the efforts of 16th-century grammarians to restore the word to a form more closely resembling its Latin ancestor, *victualia.* They succeeded in establishing the new spelling, but the old pronunciation remained unchanged.

The noun *victual* is almost always used in the plural. It is regarded as a rustic or homely synonym for *food:*

. . . I was putting away a heaping plate of down-home victuals —Tom Wicker, *N.Y. Times,* 24 Dec. 1976

But it is also often used without a hint of rusticity:

. . . parents wonder whether . . . the government-issued victuals in the national school lunch program are fit for consumption —Jessica Portner, *Education Week,* 24 Sept. 1997

There seem to have been no cooking facilities; the crew lived on cold victuals —Samuel Eliot Morison, *The European Discovery of America,* 1971

The variant *vittles* is standard, and is consistent with the word's pronunciation:

You will find no listings for Cajun food in Boston or neutered cowboy vittles in New York —Jane & Michael Stern, *Cook's,* September/October 1986

. . . the vittles famed for keeping buckaroos feisty—Rocky Mountain Oysters —Carole Tonkinson, *Elle,* September 1990

So Taco Cabana of San Antonio makes sure its vittles are the freshest Tex-Mex north of the Rio Grande —Richard S. Teitelbaum, *Fortune,* 22 Feb. 1993

Vittles has the rustic and especially western flavor that *victuals* does not necessarily carry. It is also used in representations or transcriptions of speech.

Victual is also used as a verb, usually meaning either "to supply with food" or "to lay in provisions." The verb has rustic connotations:

... his cart and two horses lost in the king's service while victualling the castle —article from *Irish Echo,* reprinted in *Irish Digest,* November 1953

... American whalers who victualled at the port —*Australian Dictionary of Biography,* 1966

vie *Vie* is typically used with the prepositions *with* and *for:* competitors vie *with* each other *for* something desired.

... we have lately been vying with the Russians in an ostrich-like and naïve absurdity —Edmund Wilson, *A Piece of My Mind,* 1956

Welsh literature vies with Irish in antiquity —Simeon Potter, *Language in the Modern World,* 1960

... hosts of other social and civilian programs are vying for the federal budget dollar —*Forbes,* 1 Dec. 1970

Diverse objects, both contemporary and antique, vie for attention —Monica Meenan, *Town & Country,* July 1980

Vie against has been called a mistake; what it is, however, is very rare:

In the real world, interest groups vie against one another for resources —Louis Menand, *Harper's,* December 1991

You will most likely want *with* in such a context.

view The phrase *with a view* usually takes the preposition *to:*

... treating patients ... with a view to bringing about benefit, if not cure —Morris Fishbein, *The Popular Medical Encyclopedia,* 1946

... began acquiring Monhegan's wildlands ... with a view to preserving them in their natural state —Eleanor Sterling, *Yankee,* July 1968

Alternative prepositions are *toward* and *of,* both of which occur much less frequently than *to:*

... studying the structure of the Federal Government, with a view toward reorganizing the executive branch —*Current Biography 1947*

... prompted the boy to turn back ... with a view of asking Miss Eustacia Vye to let her servant accompany him home —Thomas Hardy, *The Return of the Native,* 1878

When the phrase is *with the view* rather than *with a view, of* is almost invariably the preposition that follows:

... accepted a second term as governor with the view of winning the United States senatorship —*Dictionary of American Biography,* 1928

The OED treats *with a view of* (for which the earliest evidence is from 1723), *with a view to* (1728), and *with the view of* (1827) as standard phrases. Fowler's preference in 1926 was for *with a view to,* although he also found *with the view of* acceptable. He considered *with a view of* to be a mistake, but it is not clear why he thought so. Some later commentators have followed Fowler's lead in prescribing against *with a view of,* but this is not an issue that stirs deep feelings.

Fowler also disliked the use of the infinitive following *with a view to,* as in "with a view to preserve" rather than "... to preserving" or "... to preservation." Burchfield 1996 notes that this construction has fallen out of common use, though it was common in the 18th and 19th centuries.

viewpoint A few critical brickbats have been directed at *viewpoint* since it was coined in the mid-19th century. Most modern commentators who take note of this word regard it as a useful alternative to *point of view.* Simon 1980 is almost alone when he says "centuries of sound tradition have hallowed *point of view* as preferable to the Teutonism *viewpoint.*" The evidence does not support him. Garner 1998 points out that *viewpoint* says in one word what *point of view* says in three. In any case, both are certainly standard:

... it probably produces more variety of age and viewpoint —Kingman Brewster, Jr., *Yale University: Report of President 1967–68*

... he'd eventually come around to the opposite viewpoint from the one he'd previously advocated —Irvine Welsh, *Trainspotting,* 1993

... the book features shifting narrative points of view —A. O. Scott, *N.Y. Times Book Rev.,* 5 Mar. 2000

Her point-of-view and how, or if, it differs from the viewpoints of others —Susan Jacoby, *N.Y. Times Book Rev.,* 10 Oct. 1982

See also STANDPOINT.

view with alarm *View with alarm* is sometimes called a cliché that is a typical bit of political bombast, but the most conspicuous thing about the phrase may be its rarity. William Safire mentions it in *Safire's Political Dictionary* (1978) but has no examples of its use, and H. L. Mencken (*The American Language, Supplement I,* 1945) notes that it is missing from the Dictionary of American English and the Dictionary of Americanisms.

Our evidence of the phrase is slim, but shows that it can be used straightforwardly and unbombastically:

... many health experts view with alarm the possibility of casual overuse or misuse of these nonprescription drugs —Melva Weber, *Vogue,* March 1985

And it's not just the pierced and tattooed variety of youth that makes them cringe— even young children are viewed with alarm —Cheryl Russell, *Demographics,* November 1997

Its being considered a cliché may discourage writers from using *view with alarm.*

vigilant When *vigilant* is used with a preposition, the choice is most often *against, in,* or *to:*

. . . we should be eternally vigilant against attempts to check the expression of opinions that we loathe —Oliver Wendell Holmes d. 1935, *Abrams et al.* v. *United States,* 1919

All of us . . . must be vigilant in preserving our birthright —Adlai E. Stevenson, *Speeches,* ed. Richard Harrity, 1952

We must be eternally vigilant to prevent that —Peter P. Muirhead, quoted in *Change,* October 1971

Occasionally, *vigilant* may be followed by *about* or *for:*

. . . has always been cannily vigilant about the moneys coming in —Robert Lewis Taylor, *New Yorker,* 28 Apr. 1956

The saints at table, ever vigilant for propriety, are uneasy —William Laurence Sullivan, *Epigrams and Criticisms in Miniature,* 1936

violoncello It is logical to suppose that the beginning of this word is spelled like *violin,* and in fact the spelling *violincello* has turned up in respectable surroundings on occasion:

Mr. Skimpole could play on the piano and the violincello —Charles Dickens, *Bleak House,* 1852 (OED)

Nevertheless, the original and accepted spelling is *violoncello.*

vis-à-vis The literal meaning of *vis-à-vis* in French is "face to face," and it has had some use in English (as in French) as a preposition meaning "face to face with":

His master dived down to him, leaving me *vis-à-vis* the ruffianly bitch —Emily Brontë, *Wuthering Heights,* 1847 (OED)

But *vis-à-vis* is far more familiar in its two extended senses, "in relation to" and "in comparison with," both of which it also has in French, and both of which have been in use in English since the 18th century. They now occur fairly commonly in writing:

The percent of intact black families vis-à-vis white families was much higher in 1950

—Robert Staples, in *Lure and Loathing,* Gerald Early, ed., 1993

. . . reappraises . . . the contemporary role of Alanbrooke vis-à-vis Churchill —Edward N. Luttwak, *Times Literary Supp.,* 29 Jan. 1993

A standoff will have been achieved vis-à-vis the Russians —Mary McCarthy, *N.Y. Times Book Rev.,* 9 Feb. 1986

. . . the militia called Amal . . . , which still stands for moderation vis-à-vis more militant Shiites —Mary Catherine Bateson, *N.Y. Times Book Rev.,* 25 May 1986

These standard uses of *vis-à-vis* are largely uncontroversial even though frequently remarked in usage books.

vise See VICE, VISE.

visit, visit with A few British critics unfamiliar with American idiom have misunderstood the phrase *visit with* as a needlessly wordy alternative to *visit.* Most Americans, however, will instantly recognize that to "visit with someone" is not the same as to "visit someone." "Visit with" is actually a typical American use of *visit* as an intransitive verb meaning "chat" or "converse." It is usually followed by *with:*

We visited with him for two hours —*The Autobiography of William Allen White,* 1946

As her son sat to visit with her in the late 1970s, she was beyond explaining what he wanted to know about the world she reared him in —Russell Baker, *Wall Street Jour.,* 4 Nov. 1982

. . . where in the late afternoon neighbors visit with neighbors —Marian Burros, *N.Y. Times,* 7 Oct. 1987

visitation A few commentators are concerned that *visitation* should not be used interchangeably with *visit.* They would be reassured to see our citational evidence, which confirms that the two words are used in distinct ways. *Visit* is, of course, the more general and widely applicable word. *Visitation* normally connotes a visit that is in some way out of the ordinary, as in having a formal or official nature or a supernatural dimension, or as in representing a kind of benefaction:

. . . invited to make a three-month lecture tour of the States. This visitation was so well received that it was extended to seven months —Kenneth Harris, *N.Y. Times Book Rev.,* 31 Aug. 1997

When the assessor arrives on his annual visitation —Jonathan Evan Maslow, *Saturday Rev.,* 16 Sept. 1978

The last satanic visitation was in Easter Week, 1994 —Anne Campbell Dixon, *Daily Telegraph* (London), 27 Mar. 1999

. . . the rare visitations of evening grosbeaks and bluebirds that make one feel, quite unjustifiably, like one of the chosen —Eleanor Perenyi, *Green Thoughts*, 1983

Visit would be possible in any of the above passages, but it lacks the connotations that make the longer word especially apt there. *Visitation* also has several distinct uses for which *visit* is not possible:

The town suffered severely from a visitation of the plague in the 17th century —*The Encyclopedia Americana*, 1943

. . . serious people who study reports of supposed alien visitation —Patrick J. Lyons, *N.Y. Times*, 30 June 1997

. . . said she would help her own adopted children seek their biological parents when they reach the age of majority. But she objected to visitation rights before that time —Nadine Brozan, *N.Y. Times*, 23 Jan. 1978

Memorial services at 11 a.m. Monday, May 22, 2000, preceded by visitation after 10 a.m. at Broadmoor United Methodist Church —*Advocate* (Baton Rouge, La.), 17 May 2000

visual *Visual* is sometimes used to mean "visible":

. . . finding a visual equivalent for feelings which enrich experience —Michael Kitson, *Encounter*, February 1955

This sense of *visual* is not new. It was used in 1756 by Edmund Burke, who wrote of "visual beauty" and "perceptions and judgments on visual objects." Such usage is standard but uncommon. It is most likely to occur in contexts where the writer is distinguishing that which can be seen from that which is perceived by the other senses—contexts, in other words, where the emphasis is on the sense of vision rather than the specific object of vision. It does not occur in contexts such as "The horizon became visible as the fog cleared" or "His distress was clearly visible."

vittles See VICTUAL.

viva voce See HYPERFOREIGNISMS.

vocal chords, vocal cords See CHORD, CORD.

voice The use of *voice* as a verb meaning "to express in words" (as in "voice a complaint") has attracted sporadic criticism since before 1917. Recently it has been termed pompous and wordy. Our evidence shows that *voice* has distinct connotations that make it a useful and appropriate verb in many contexts. It usually implies not simply expressing something, but expressing it publicly or openly:

"There's no passion inside the campaign," says one Gore loyalist, voicing a common complaint —Dana Milbank, *New Republic*, 29 Nov. 1999

While voicing disapproval of all the above-mentioned vices, the respondents were also indulging in them —Roy Porter, *Times Literary Supp.*, 16–22 Feb. 1990

. . . part of a new proposal voiced by Ellen Sulzberger Straus, a leader in the volunteer movement —*McCall's*, March 1971

The response was usually sour; teachers voiced anger at having been deceived —Joseph Pilcher et al., *People*, 20 Dec. 1982

void When the adjective *void* is followed by a preposition, the preposition is *of*:

. . . a drama which . . . is really void of sexual interest —George Bernard Shaw, preface to *Man and Superman*, 1903

. . . a force directly opposed to him and void of love —Norman Mailer, *Harper's*, March 1971

The OED includes two citations showing *void* used with *in*, but we have no modern evidence of such use.

vulnerable *Vulnerable* is often followed by the preposition *to*:

". . . you're less vulnerable to whatever horrors happen in life." —Herman Wouk, *Marjorie Morningstar*, 1955

This timetable was, of course, terribly vulnerable to bad weather —John Kenneth Galbraith, *The Scotch*, 1964

. . . those institutions most vulnerable to government pressure —Daniel P. Moynihan, *Atlantic*, August 1968

W

waive, wave The usual meaning of *waive* is "to relinquish" or "to refrain from enforcing," as in "to waive a right" or "to waive a rule." It is also sometimes used in a sense synonymous with *wave*:

> . . . concrete troubles and evils remain. They are not magically waived out of existence —John Dewey, *Reconstruction in Philosophy*, 1920

> He would waive the whole business aside —Oliver St. John Gogarty, *It Isn't This Time of Year at All!*, 1954

> . . . said "no,"
> And waived them off
> —Edgar Lee Masters, "Finding of the Body," *Domesday Book*, 1920

This sense of *waive* was first attested in 1832. It undoubtedly arose from confusion with *wave*, and it is widely regarded as an error. The prudent thing to do is to use *wave* instead.

wake, waken We had a phone call not long ago from a concerned grandmother who was disturbed by her grandson's use of the past participle *woken*. She knew only *waked* and was surprised to find that *woken* was recognized as legitimate in the dictionary. *Wake* is a verb whose usage changed in the 20th century, and it may continue to change. *Waken* is included here only by way of contrast: its principal parts are regular—*wakened, wakening*—and have not changed at all.

The ferment noticeable in the past and past participle of *wake* comes from its origin. In the beginning there were two separate verbs, one intransitive with irregular principal parts and the other causative or transitive with regular principal parts. These coalesced in Middle English, and our modern muddle of inflected forms is the result.

The OED tells us that the strong forms *woke* and *woken* are not found in Shakespeare, the 1611 Bible, or Milton's verse. The strong forms were, however, in use by other writers around the same time.

Woken was described as perhaps "obsolescent" in the OED in 1921; Fowler 1926 thought *woke* and *woken* both rare. But both forms, *woke* especially as the past tense, underwent a revival in the 20th century, and are at the present time the dominant forms.

For the past tense, *woke* is usual:

> The porter woke by himself —James Thurber, letter, 4 Sept. 1944

> . . . he woke once with the moonlight on his face —Ernest Hemingway, "An African Betrayal," in *Sports Illustrated*, 5 May 1986

> Every morning you woke to the smell of bread from the bakery downstairs —Jay McInerney, *Bright Lights, Big City*, 1984

> Last night my daughter woke up at 4 a.m. —Garrison Keillor, *Time*, 6 Sept. 1999

Waked was more common formerly than it is now, but it has not disappeared from use:

> She waked on earth, not in heaven —Dorothy West, *The Wedding*, 1995

> . . . and only just waked up in time to dress for breakfast —*New Yorker*, 28 Nov. 1970

For the past participle, *woken* is the predominant form in British English:

> I have just been woken up from my summer sleep by the first rugger practices —Robert Graves, letter, 11 Sept. 1918

> In the mornings he was woken by his butler —Julian Huxley, *Memories*, 1970

> . . . one night he was woken by someone coming into the bedroom —Graham Greene, *Getting to Know the General*, 1984

In American English *woken* and *waked* are both used for the past participle:

> Woken by a flashlight held close to her face —*New Yorker*, 9 Aug. 1982

> He was woken by his wife —John Cheever, *New Yorker*, 12 Aug. 1991

> . . . I knew this was one time he would not mind being woken up —Harrison E. Salisbury, *N.Y. Times Mag.*, 17 Apr. 1983

> During the night he has waked up sweating —Mary McCarthy, *Occasional Prose*, 1985

> . . . is waked this morning by the whistling of the 7:18 —John Cheever, *The Wapshot Chronicle*, 1957

> . . . and had waked from dreams —John Townsley, *New England Monthly*, July 1990

Woke as the past participle is less frequent:

> . . . it must have woke him up —Ted Williams & John Underwood, *The Science of Hitting,* 1971

See also AWAKE, AWAKEN.

wangle, wrangle *Wangle* and *wrangle* are easily distinguished in most of their uses. *Wangle* has the basic sense, "to accomplish something in a scheming or indirect way," while *wrangle* basically means "to argue or engage in controversy." The distinction in most cases is clear, but not when the two verbs occur in such contexts as the following:

> . . . he had to wangle independent financing —Hollis Alpert, *Saturday Rev.,* 16 Nov. 1974

> And when Jacob wrangled from his brother, Esau, the rights of the firstborn —Robert Farrar Capon, *N.Y. Times Mag.,* 4 Oct. 1992

> . . . delivering luxury yachts to distant ports and wangling . . . cushy deals —Ray Kennedy, *Sports Illustrated,* 14 May 1984

> Rebuked by Mayor Koch in his attempt to wrangle a multimillion tax abatement and zoning exemptions —*Newsweek,* 29 June 1987

This may look like a simple case of one verb being confused for the other, but the matter is not quite as straightforward as that. Both *wangle* and *wrangle* appear to have developed the sense "to obtain" independently. The OED shows that *wrangle* was used to mean "to obtain by wrangling" (that is, by arguing or bargaining) as far back as 1624:

> We wrangled out of the King ten quarters of Corne for a copper Kettell —Captain John Smith, *The Generall Historie of Virginia,* 1624 (OED)

Wangle, a 19th-century verb of American origin, has been used in the sense "to obtain by wangling" (that is, by slyly using one's influence or powers of persuasion) since at least the early 20th century:

> . . . and when in home waters had 'wangled' a few days' leave —*Bulletin,* 28 Dec. 1917 (OED)

The "obtain" sense of *wrangle* was labeled "obsolete or rare" by the OED in 1928, but recent decades have seen its revival. Chances are that its renewed use is due in part to the success of *wangle* in its own "obtain" sense—and may in fact be mainly the result of confusion about which word is which. Nevertheless, the "obtain" sense of *wrangle* is established in reputable use, and is treated as standard by current dictionaries. The "obtain" sense of *wangle* is also standard, of course, and is appreciably more common than that of *wrangle.*

want A few informal idioms with *want* are commonly cited with disapproval in usage handbooks. The most frequent admonitions are against the use of such a construction as "I want for you to do this" instead of "I want you to do this." This "want for" construction appears to be limited to informal speech; we do not find it in published sources. It should not be confused with the use of *want for* to mean "lack," which is standard (Burchfield 1996 believes it to be receding in use):

> They do not want for customers —Richard Rhodes, *The Inland Ground,* 1991

> No one in the movie wants for anything but love —Pauline Kael, *New Yorker,* 3 Feb. 1973

Also standard, as Heritage 2000 points out, are such constructions as "What I want is for you to do this" and "I want very much for you to do this," in which the clause introduced by *for* does not follow immediately after *want:*

> . . . she very much wanted, we all did, for him to succeed —Mary Jane Truman, quoted in Merle Miller, *Plain Speaking,* 1973

A related issue concerns the use of *want* with a clause introduced by *that* as its object:

> They wanted that the debts due them should be paid, or payable, in gold —Mark Sullivan, *Our Times,* vol. 6, 1935

Again, such usage appears to be limited almost entirely to speech. The normal written construction would be "They wanted the debts due them to be paid. " As with the "want for" construction, however, the use of *want* with a *that* clause is standard when the clause does not immediately follow the verb; for example, "What they wanted was that the debts due them should be paid."

See also WANT IN, WANT OUT.

want in, want out The use of *want* in the elliptical sense "to desire to come. go, or be" (as in "the cat wants in") is generally regarded by usage commentators as a colloquialism to be avoided in writing. Its popularity in the U.S. seems to have formerly been somewhat localized, being confined primarily to the Midwest and to the Appalachians, but it has grown increasingly widespread over the years and is no longer strongly associated with any particular region.

The elliptical *want* is especially common in the phrases *want in* and *want out,* both of which now occur frequently not only in speech but also in writing. Written use tends to be figurative:

> Now everyone wants in on the act —*ESPN,* 23 Aug. 1999

As can be imagined, a lot of people wanted in on the action —William Kittridge, *Harper's*, October 1988

. . . shareholders wanted out of the merger —Don L. Burroughs, *U.S. News & World Report*, 16 May 1994

But he wanted out, and we agreed to take care of him —Daniel P. Moynihan, *N.Y. Times Book Rev*, 17 Feb. 1985

The informal quality of *want in* and *want out* is evident, but that informality can be useful in expressing a sense of urgency or determination that may not be communicated as well by a more formal alternative. The same holds true for other uses of *want* in its elliptical sense:

. . . airline pilots all wanted back in the Air Force —*Newsweek*, 20 Dec. 1948

. . . will want off at the second floor —Bill Harrison, *Saturday Evening Post*, 11 Dec. 1954

ESPN badly wants into the NFL —William Taaffe, *Sports Illustrated*, 29 Sept. 1986

wary *Wary* is often followed by *of*:

. . . the White House seemed wary of greater U.S. involvement —Michael Isikoff et al., *Newsweek*, 3 Apr. 2000

The rector was a large man and . . . not at all wary of clerical black —John Cheever, *New Yorker*, 16 Apr. 1955

He did, however, seem wary of reporters —Trevor Armbrister, *Saturday Evening Post*, 12 Feb. 1966

A less common preposition following *wary* is *in*. It obviously could not be used in any of the above quotations, but it does occur when a cautious or hesitant approach toward *doing* something is described or advocated:

. . . leads the student to be wary in giving his trust to the professor —W. David Maxwell, *AAUP Bulletin*, September 1969

. . . he must be wary in offering assurances neither he nor a successor may be able to keep —William Colby, *N.Y. Times Book Rev.*, 5 June 1988

Of could certainly be used in such contexts, but its use would result in a slight change of meaning. To be wary *in* doing something is to do something warily, while to be wary *of* doing something is usually to avoid doing it at all:

We should always be wary of relying on government —*Newsweek*, 23 Aug. 1999

. . . voters are wary of changing this way of doing business —Charles Lane, *New Republic*, 13 & 20 Sept. 1999

Another possible preposition after *wary* is *about*. It occurs in the same contexts as *of*, but less often:

. . . scientists . . . are wary about possible side-effects —Elyse Tanouye, *Wall Street Jour.*, 2 Aug. 1995

was, were See SUBJUNCTIVE.

wave See WAIVE, WAVE.

wax The verb *wax*, in the sense "to grow or become," is uncommon enough in present-day English for some writers to feel quite uncertain about how to use it. Copperud 1980 cites a passage in which "TV commentators" are said to have "waxed authoritatively." We have evidence in our files of a similar error:

. . . he does not wax enthusiastically over combining rock and symphonic music —*Philharmonic Hall*, December 1970

Standard English requires "wax enthusiastic." The reason for the confusion is presumably that such phrases as *wax authoritative* and *wax enthusiastic* normally relate to speech or writing, so that *wax enthusiastic* is almost equivalent in meaning to *speak enthusiastically*. Writers who follow *wax* with an adverb apparently understand it as meaning "to speak or hold forth," but that meaning is not established. For the phrase *wax wroth*, see WRATH, WRATHFUL, WROTH.

ways Those commentators (and there are plenty) who think *ways* is an error in American English are out of touch with reality:

We went along a canyon a ways and stopped within sight of an eagle nest —Ian Frazier, *New Yorker*, 27 Feb. 1989

. . . the downturn still has a ways to go —Alan Abelson, *Barron's*, 24 July 1972

. . . media-age writers may have a ways to go before they can compete with the average Civil War infantryman or Victorian diarist —Neal Stephenson, *New Republic*, 13 Sept. 1993

Casey's idea of fund-raising was quite a ways from mine —Wilfrid Sheed, *People Will Always Be Kind*, 1973

While I was on the moon, there was a wave of realization . . . of us being a long ways away —Buzz Aldrin, *Discover*, July 1994

He ran a little ways down the ravine —Garrison Keillor, *Lake Wobegon Days*, 1985

Such usage is standard in American English. In British English it's a different story. *Ways* was in reputable, even literary, use through the 19th century. But its use and status fell off in the 20th century; Burchfield 1996 says it is now only dialectal in British English. *Way* occurs more commonly.

we **1.** The use of *we* to mean "I" is very old in English. The OED dates such use by sovereigns, sometimes called the "royal *we*," back to the time of Beowulf, and includes citations from Henry VI, James I, and Charles I. Burchfield 1996 says the royal *we* is dropping out of use.

Just as old—or perhaps a bit older—is the use known nowadays as the "editorial *we*," which the OED also traces back to before 1000. The editorial *we* gets its name from its use in newspaper editorials, in which it is meant to imply that a collective rather than an individual opinion is being expressed. More generally, it typically serves to give a less personal tone to the writing in which it occurs. The casual editorial *we* is well known to readers of the *New Yorker* magazine, in which it was long ago adopted as a stylistic mannerism.

> An hour later, when we were in the front seat of a cab heading crosstown and Matt and his cello were riding in the back, we turned around and asked if he could tell us about his instrument —*New Yorker,* 2 May 1988

We can also indicate that the speaker or writer identifies himself or herself with a group (in this example, referred to by a generic singular, *architect*):

> ... his view of how an architect works is more romantic than accurate. He thinks we jump out of bed in the morning and design any pretty building that happens to enter our heads —The Duke of Gloucester, quoted in *New Yorker,* 2 May 1988

There are in addition a couple of oral uses of *we*—not much found in writing—that receive occasional mention by commentators. These are characterized by Perrin & Ebbitt 1972 as "the kindergarten *we* (We won't lose our mittens, will we?)" and "the hospital *we* (How are we feeling this morning?)."

These various uses of *we* should not be cause for concern. Consider that the *New Yorker* has been using *we* for a half century or better, and making it sound sophisticated. All you really need worry about is its appropriateness to the piece you are writing; there is nothing wrong in the *we* itself.

2. The OED, with typical thoroughness, devotes a whole numbered sense of *we* to its uses in place of *us*; the earliest example comes from the dawn of the 16th century. The OED assures us that *we* for *us* is now heard only from the uneducated. It is certainly to be found in the speech of the fictional uneducated:

> What makes we New Yorkers sore is to think they should try and wish a law like

that on us —Ring Lardner, *The Big Town,* 1921

But we also have some evidence of its use by the educated. The writer of the next example is noted on our citation as the literary editor of a prestigious British newspaper:

> ... at that time in the faculty of English was J. R. R. Tolkien; he was equally at the disposal of we cadets —Anthony Curtis, *British Book News,* June 1977

Note that in these examples *we* turns up hard by an appositive ("we New Yorkers"). Most of our evidence for the accusative *we* shows it occurring with appositives.

wean A peculiar extension in the meaning of *wean* occurred in the 20th century. The word means, in its literal sense, "to accustom (a child) to take food other than by nursing," and, in an established figurative sense, "to detach from a cause of dependence or preoccupation":

> Despite gallant efforts to wean the populace from the tube —Carll Tucker, *Saturday Rev.,* 15 Sept. 1979

Increasingly common, however, is the use of *wean* (usually with *on*) as a figurative synonym of *raise* or *rear*. Our earliest evidence of this use is from the letters of Fred Allen:

> Babies are being weaned on aspirin to fortify them for the economic headaches they will certainly face —Fred Allen, letter, 6 May 1931

No doubt other people besides Allen were using *wean* in this way in the 1930s (and perhaps earlier), but, curiously, we have no further evidence of such usage until 1958:

> Boswell, who happens to come from a line of English coach builders and who was weaned on timber, so to speak —Ernest O. Hauser, *Saturday Evening Post,* 9 Aug. 1958

The new use of *wean* was noticed and criticized by Bernstein 1965 and several later commentators. We find it in a wide range of publications:

> They are loathe to admit that a small child, born of love, weaned on innocence, and nurtured with such gentleness could frustrate them —Erma Bombeck, *The Best of Bombeck,* 1965

> ... a handsome Conservative MP who can be said to have been weaned in the television studios —Hardcastle, *Punch,* 2 Oct. 1974

The young Baby Boomers, though weaned on TV, became a faithful teenage movie audience —Douglas Gomery, *Wilson Quarterly*, Summer 1991

. . . State Department veterans weaned on the notion that good will can be measured in dollars given away —*Wall Street Jour.*, 27 Aug. 1982

Musicians weaned on the free jazz of the sixties —Gary Giddins, *Atlantic*, November 1982

Weaned on the microcomputer, . . . these pubescent youngsters have been hailed . . . —Frank Rose, *Science 82*, November 1982

. . . speak as if they were weaned on Twinings English Breakfast Tea —Jay McInerney, *Bright Lights, Big City*, 1984

. . . a public weaned on the professional image-promotion of its heroes —Woody Allen, *N.Y. Times*, 8 Oct. 2000

Although we are not sure how this sense developed, it has become well established in general reputable prose.

weave   When *weave* is used in its literal senses ("weave cloth," "weave a basket"), its usual past tense and past participle are *wove* and *woven*:

. . . people who wove their homespun clothes —*American Guide Series: North Carolina*, 1939

The nest was woven of grass tucked into a slight depression —Dr. Henry Marion Hall, *Massachusetts Audubon*, June 1968

The same inflected forms are normally used in straightforward figurative applications of *weave*:

Choreographers . . . wove dance into the fabric of musicals —Celia Wren, *Commonweal*, 9 Apr. 1999

. . . values and perceptions long woven into the fabric of society —Osborn Elliot, *One Nation Divisible* (published speech), November 1969

But when *weave* describes a winding course of movement the form that usually serves as both its past tense and past participle is *weaved*:

. . . sat in the backseat of a courtesy car as it weaved through the streets of Melbourne —Tim Layden, *Sports Illustrated*, 8 Feb. 1999

. . . Russian and U.S. delegates . . . have weaved through a maze of procedural and technical arguments —*Time*, 17 Mar. 1947

These patterns are usual and are prescribed by several commentators. However, Burchfield

1996 notes that the two uses are also interchanged:

. . . I weaved an elaborate fantasy —Nick Hornby, *Fever Pitch*, 1992

. . . two cars, older, jacked-up Chevies, that wove back and forth in front —Don Wallace, *Harper's*, June 1997

I wove my way through the crowd —Richard Zabel, *Atlantic*, May 1996

wed   *Wed* is an old Anglo-Saxon word that has been largely displaced in its literal sense by *marry*, a word derived from French. The literal sense of *wed* is now most likely to occur in special contexts, including popular songs ("Oh, how we danced on the night we were wed") and in the marriage ceremony itself:

With this Ring I thee wed —*The Book of Common Prayer*, 1789

As has been noted by several commentators, the literal sense of *wed* is also used in newspaper headlines, where its brevity gives it an advantage over *marry*. Its use in general contexts is relatively uncommon, but it does occur:

. . . the public announcement, on three successive Sundays, of intention to wed —Andrea Sachs, *Time*, 19 Apr. 1999

. . . sports stars who wedded pinups —*Sports Illustrated*, 30 Nov. 1998

. . . whose mom, Hannah, wed the director in 1973 —*People*, 7 Dec. 1998

. . . after just a few months of courtship, Penny and Paul were wed —Kennedy Fraser, *New Yorker*, 13 May 1991

The past and past participle of *wed* is usually *wedded*, but the form *wed* occurs as a secondary variant both for the literal uses above and for figurative use:

It may seem . . . that we are wed to our test tubes —Peter Benchley, in *Cosmopolitan*, July 1974

. . . a program in which dancing and skating are inextricably wed —Chip Greenwood, *Rolling Stone*, 7 Feb. 1980

weep   The past tense and past participle of *weep* is *wept*:

. . . when winter wept its damp upon the panes —Virginia Woolf, *Between the Acts*, 1941

Some wept; some were stoic —Amy E. Turnbull, *Sunday Star-News* (Wilmington, N.C.), 8 Aug. 1999

A variant form, *weeped*, shows up once in a great while in reputable writing:

All the way in she weeped and wailed —Flannery O'Connor, letter, 24 Feb. 1962

He talked of how his brother . . . had weeped over his loss —Michael Goodwin, *N.Y. Times,* 4 Oct. 1982

Weeped, however, is far too rare to be judged a standard variant. Use *wept.*

weird   *Weird* is one of a number of words that give the lie to the old chant, "*i* before *e* except after *c* or when sounded as *a,* as in *neighbor* and *weigh.*" There is no *c* in *weird,* and no *a* sound either, but the *e* comes before the *i* just the same. Other words that break the "rule" are *either, neither, foreign, forfeit, height, leisure, seize,* and *seizure.*

For a discussion of the vagaries of English spelling, see SPELLING.

welch   See WELSH, WELCH.

well   There are those who will criticize your "do good" and your "feel badly," but you are safe no matter how you use *well. Well* has been both an adjective and an adverb since the time of King Alfred the Great, and you can use it with impunity after a linking verb:

> . . . I imagined it might be well to publish the articles —Benjamin Franklin, *Autobiography,* 1788

> We had a very neat chaise from Devises; it looked almost as well as a gentleman's —Jane Austen, letter, 5 May 1801

> . . . if I couldn't think well of Clara, I'd turn my mind from her —E. L. Doctorow, *Loon Lake,* 1979

> . . . it is well to preserve a distinction —Harper 1985

See also GOOD; FEEL BAD, FEEL BADLY.

well-nigh   The adjective *well-nigh* has been variously called "antique" (Fowler 1926, 1965), "a cliché" (Partridge 1942), "rustic or comic" (Evans 1957), and "medieval" (Flesch 1964). None of these characterizations is given much support by the evidence in our files. Burchfield 1996 observes that it tends to be found in literary contexts and is somewhat receding in use. It is not especially frequent, but is certainly standard.

> . . . the Vienna Philharmonic had been playing one or other of the programs well-nigh every day —Andrew Porter, *New Yorker,* 12 Oct. 1987

> . . . the pressures for conformity . . . have been well-nigh overwhelming —Martin Kilson, *N.Y. Times Mag.,* 2 Sept. 1973

> . . . found it well-nigh impossible to enjoy a work of art he found morally distasteful

—Terry Eagleton, *Times Literary Supp.,* 18 Dec. 1992

> . . . was actually a well-nigh total edulcoration of the novel —John Simon, *Atlantic,* April 1982

welsh, welch   The proper noun and the proper adjective which refer to the people, things, and language of Wales are almost always spelled *Welsh. Welch* is an established but uncommon variant. The verb meaning "to avoid payment" or "to break one's word" is also usually spelled *welsh,* but the variant *welch* is widely used. Whatever its spelling, the verb is typically followed by *on:*

> . . . the Devil has never tried to welsh on a deal —Peter Andrews, *N.Y. Times Book Rev.,* 1 Aug. 1982

> . . . did not want Linda to think that he'd welsh on a promise —Mordecai Richler, *The Apprenticeship of Duddy Kravitz,* 1959

> . . . would accuse the networks of welshing on some vital public responsibility —Ron Powers, *Inside Sports,* August 1982

> . . . state officials welched on the deal —John Fischer, *Harper's,* December 1970

The etymology of the verb, which many Welsh find insulting, has never been conclusively established.

Welsh rabbit, Welsh rarebit   The dish that goes by the name *Welsh rabbit* or *Welsh rarebit* has no rabbit in it, is not especially rare, and may not even be originally Welsh. It consists essentially of melted cheese with a few well-chosen additions (such as beer, mustard, and red pepper) served over toast or crackers. The name *Welsh rabbit* was first given to this humble dish during or some time before the early 18th century, presumably by the same kind of wag as those who later gave the name *Cape Cod turkey* to codfish and *Arkansas T-bone* to bacon. The earliest written evidence for *Welsh rabbit* is from 1725. When Francis Grose defined *Welsh rabbit* in *A Classical Dictionary of the Vulgar Tongue* in 1785, he mistakenly indicated that *rabbit* was a corruption of "rare bit." It is not certain that this erroneous idea originated with Grose, or even that his book had much to do with spreading it, but before long *Welsh rarebit* had become established as a synonym of *Welsh rabbit. Welsh rarebit*—sometimes shortened to just *rarebit*—is now the more common name, although *Welsh rabbit* is also frequently used.

what   As a plain relative, meaning "who, that, which," *what* has largely dropped out of mainstream English and has retreated to mostly oral use in rural areas. Our present evidence shows that relative *what* survives in the United

States primarily in Midland and Southern speech areas and is used chiefly by the little educated. It was in use up into the 19th century:

... so that in getting Baker the nomination, I shall be "fixed" a good deal like the fellow who is made groomsman to the man what has cut him out —Abraham Lincoln, letter, 24 Mar. 1843

Dialect humorists used it:

"Well, when we got there I went to the basket what had the vittles in it. . . ." —William C. Hall, "How Sally Hooter Got Snakebit," 1850, in *The Mirth of a Nation,* ed. Walter Blair & Raven I. McDavid, Jr., 1983

. . . Miss Watson, what's the sourest old Maid in the city —Frank W. Sage, D.D.S., *Dental Digest,* November 1902

And it still crops up in print in quoted speech, sometimes in fixed phrases:

You're looking at a man what ain't straining —George C. Wallace, quoted in *N.Y. Times,* 30 Mar. 1975

. . . dance with the ones what brung me —Representative Philip Gramm, quoted in *People,* 24 Jan. 1983

It also occurs, of course, in fictional dialogue:

". . . Boy, the guy what thought it up sure was a smart one. . . ." —Garrison Keillor, *Lake Wobegon Days,* 1985

what-clauses See AGREEMENT, SUBJECT-VERB: WHAT-CLAUSES.

whatever 1. Fowler 1926 was certain that when *whatever* was used to start a question, it should be written as two words. The reasoning behind that opinion is straightforward: the *ever* was originally an intensive adverb added to *what* for emphasis. Most subsequent commentators who mention the issue favor the two-word styling, and our evidence shows that the two-word styling is the norm:

What ever happened to honor among thieves? —Katha Pollitt, *New Republic,* 7 June 1999

What ever happened to the rock & roll mama . . . ? —Jim Farber, *Entertainment Weekly,* 15 May 1998

The OED shows that *whatever* has been used as an interrogative pronoun by some writers since the 14th century. Some still use it:

Whatever happened to the Sunday stroll through the woods? —Chet Raymo, *AMC Outdoors,* May 1999

Dictionaries list the one-word form as standard, but more writers or editors prefer two words.

2. Fowler 1926 also warned against following *whatever* with *that,* as in "He dismisses whatever arguments that have been made against him." In such a sentence, *whatever* is being used as a synonym for *any.* There is some historical precedent for such usage, and we suspect that its occurrence in speech may be fairly common, but our evidence shows that it is extremely rare in edited writing. We think you would be well advised to omit *that.*

when, where A substantial number of recent usage books and schoolbooks object to the use of *is when* or *is where* in framing definitions, which use is often described as childish or immature. Bryant 1962 finds the objection (going back to Goold Brown 1851) to be founded on the theory that it is improper to have a clause introduced by *where* or *when* follow the verb *be.* The usual argument runs that such clauses are adverbial and either a noun construction is needed after *be* or a verb (such as *occur*) that can take an adverb clause. (For another usage problem that is argued similarly, see REASON IS BECAUSE.) Bryant's cited studies show, however, that *when* and *where* clauses are commonly used after *be* in standard writing:

It is when states have rising caseloads and falling resources that a "race to the bottom" may ensue —*N.Y. Times,* 30 Dec. 1997

Experiences were many. Perhaps the most exciting was when the driving, sleety snowstorms came on winter nights —Willa Cather, *The Old Beauty,* 1948 (in Bryant)

That was when life went from unpleasant to unbearable —Samantha Power, *New Republic,* 9 Aug. 1999

This was where Jefferson learned to read and write —Garry Wills, *Atlantic,* January 1993

. . . Harlem was where the action was —Ishmael Reed, *N.Y. Times Book Rev.,* 29 Aug. 1976

This is where I say that I don't believe in scientists —James Thurber, letter, 6 Oct. 1937

. . . it's not smug to point out that anguish is where some artists need to live —Stanley Kauffmann, *Saturday Rev.,* 1 Nov. 1975

Most recent commentators do not object to standard uses like these. Their objection is to definitions. These are not rare:

. . . a bear market is when stocks go down and down and down —Allan Sloan, *Newsweek,* 22 Apr. 1996

What is humor? Humor is when you laugh —Earl Rovit, *American Scholar,* Spring 1967

. . . a half-volley is when the ball is kicked just after it has bounced —*N.Y. Times*, 12 June 1994

. . . "framing" is when one site takes content directly from another site but surrounds it with its own Web page —Martha L. Stone, *Editor & Publisher*, 12 Dec. 1998

A holiday is when you don't have to go to work —Robert Carver, *Times Literary Supp.*, 4 June 1993

Leonard 1929 tells us that the *is when, is where* definition was freely utilized throughout the 18th century, and he gives short examples from the grammarians Greenwood (who originally published in 1711) and Lowth (who originally published in 1762). Goold Brown had a large number of definitions from grammar books; here are two of them:

A Solecism is when the rules of Syntax are transgressed —Alexander Adam, *Latin and English Grammar*, 1772

A Proper Diphthong is where both the Vowels are sounded together; as *oi* in *Voice* —A. Fischer, *Grammar*, 1753

Evidence scattered throughout the OED shows that *is when* definitions have appeared in a wide variety of reference books. Most of these are specialized glossaries of such subjects as medicine, law, falconry, heraldry, music, and seamanship. But the construction was also used in standard encyclopedias and dictionaries:

3. In elections, a *plurality of votes* is when one candidate has more votes than any other, but *less than half* —Webster 1828

This formerly standard pattern of defining has dropped out of use in present-day lexicography, but it continues to flourish in less formal surroundings, as those shown above, and in speech:

I've always said that power is when people think you have power —Tip O'Neill with William Novak, *Man of the House*, 1987

when and if   See IF AND WHEN.

whence   See FROM WHENCE, FROM THENCE, FROM HENCE.

where   1. See WHERE . . . AT.
2. A number of schoolbooks and college handbooks are concerned about the use of *where* in the sense "that" after the verbs *see* and *read*. The schoolbooks prohibit the use; the college handbooks find it informal. No reason is set forth to explain why *where* should be avoided in these contexts. Our evidence shows that it is not avoided:

In the Bible we don't find the word "maybe" so much, or read where God says "On the other hand. . . ." —Garrison Keillor, *Leaving Home*, 1987

The music got on her nerves, and he could see where it would —John Cheever, *The Brigadier and the Golf Widow*, 1964

You read where Pres. Reagan supports a move to repeal the 22nd Amendment, which limits the president to two four-year terms? —Herb Caen, *San Francisco Chronicle*, 5 Aug. 1986

. . . I don't see where he's lost anything —Jay Greenberg, *Sports Illustrated*, 10 Sept. 1990

How about burying them in the sand up to their chins and leaving them out in the hot sun? I've read where they do it that way in some Middle Eastern countries —Andy Rooney, *Pieces of My Mind*, 1982

The construction gets used in fictional dialogue too:

I have nothing against Mr. Jones personally, but I can't see where he's fitted to be President —Frank Sullivan, *A Rock in Every Snowball*, 1946

I can see where bribing might be excusable if the consulship was the prize, but quaestor? Never! —Colleen McCullough, *The First Man in Rome*, 1990

He . . . cackled maliciously, "I suppose you saw where Forward Press folded up. . . ." —James A. Michener, *The Fires of Spring*, 1949

The criticism of this use in the handbooks is legitimate only insofar as it draws your attention, as do most of our examples, to the fact that this use is typically found in less formal kinds of writing.

whereabouts   The final *-s* in the noun *whereabouts* may look like a plural ending, but it isn't one. The noun is derived from the adverb *whereabouts*, and the *-s* is actually an adverbial suffix—one that also occurs in such words as *hereabouts, thereabouts*, and *towards*. The adverbial origins of that final *-s* have persuaded a few critics that the noun *whereabouts* should only be construed as singular, but both singular and plural verbs are standard. The plural is more common:

. . . she got rid of it, and its whereabouts is unknown —Calvin Tomkins, *New Yorker*, 4 Apr. 1988

The whereabouts of the Cartier necklace is currently unknown —John Steele Gordon, *American Heritage*, May/June 1989

. . . was taken out of Estonia to another mental institution, whose whereabouts were not known —David K. Shipler, *New Yorker,* 18 Sept. 1989

The painting's whereabouts were unknown until last summer —Phil Patton, *Smithsonian,* March 1991

. . . war criminals whose whereabouts have not yet been discovered —Ronald Sanders, *N.Y. Times Book Rev.,* 13 May 1990

where . . . at The use of *at* following *where* was first noted in 1859 by Bartlett, who observed in his *Dictionary of Americanisms* that it was "often used superfluously in the South and West, as in the question 'Where is he *at*?' " Such usage first drew the attention of critics at about the turn of the century, and they have routinely prescribed against it since. Although fairly common in speech (the *at* provides a convenient final word to receive stress at the end of a sentence), this construction rarely occurred in writing until the 1960s, when the idiomatic phrases *where it's at* and *where one is at* came into widespread use:

Harvey and I are going through this dynamic right now and it's kinda where I'm at —Cyra McFadden, *The Serial,* 1977

. . . grab them by the collar and tell them where it's at —Paul Mazursky, quoted in *Christian Science Monitor,* 22 Aug. 1980

. . . they realized vocals were where it's at —Charles M. Young, *Rolling Stone,* 29 Nov. 1979

. . . make sure you know just exactly where it's at —Hunter S. Thompson, *Rolling Stone,* 6 Jan. 1972

These phrases continue to be used today, although they have some of the passé quality of old slang. They are most likely to occur when the language and attitudes of the 1960s and early 1970s are being deliberately evoked or mimicked. Other than in these phrases, *at* almost never occurs after *where* in writing from standard sources. See also AT.

whereby, wherein Criticized by several commentators as archaic or excessively formal, these words continue nevertheless to be in widespread use as conjunctions in general as well as in more elevated prose:

. . . the system whereby corn, beans and squash are planted in the same hole —Francesca Bray, *Scientific American,* July 1994

. . . a program whereby foreign-service officers will serve —David FitzHugh, *Saturday Rev.,* 18 Oct. 1975

. . . electronic tickets, whereby the "ticket" is only a record in the airline's computer system —Betsy Wade, *N.Y. Times,* 21 June 1998

. . . chivalric fable wherein the heroine suffers and dies —John Seelye, *New York,* 15 Feb. 1971

. . . the strange phenomenon wherein the family home manifests an eerie affinity for lightning —Lewis Nordan, *Publishers Weekly,* 10 Mar. 1997

As an interrogative adverb (as in Shakespeare's "Whereby hangs a tale, sir?"), *whereby* is obsolete. *Wherein* continues to be used as an interrogative adverb, but only rarely:

Wherein lies the success of the coot? —Kenneth Brower, *Smithsonian,* December 1998

wherefore When Juliet asks, "O Romeo, Romeo! wherefore art thou Romeo?" she is not trying to find out if her true love is hiding in the bushes beneath her window. *Wherefore* means "why," not "where." The frequent use of the line "wherefore art thou" has resulted in *wherefore*'s being understood as "where":

. . . wherefore Art Howe, Romeo? If this is Sunday, then Art Howe is in Chicago —Steve Rushin, *Sports Illustrated,* 24 Aug. 1992

Wherefore is now rarely used except as a noun meaning "reason":

. . . good to know the whys, hows, and wherefores of what you are seeing —Elin Schoen, *American Way,* December 1971

Whether or not to explain to the author the why and wherefore of rejection —James Thurber, quoted in *N.Y. Times Book Rev.,* 4 Dec. 1988

. . . the whys and wherefores of depression among the elderly —Stanley Jacobson, *Atlantic,* April 1995

Note that *why* also means "reason" in such contexts, so that the alliterative phrase *whys and wherefores* could, it seems, be called redundant. In truth, however, to know the whys and wherefores is not simply to know the reasons, but to know *all* the reasons. The seemingly redundant phrase has an added meaning of its own.

wherein See WHEREBY, WHEREIN.

wherever See WHATEVER 1.

whether See IF 1.

whether or not Numerous commentators have pointed out that *or not* is not always necessary after *whether,* as in "We don't know whether or not they'll come." They naturally recommend that *or not* should be omitted whenever possible, on the usual assumption that fewer words make better prose. It should be noted, however, that this use of *or not* is more than 300 years old and is common among educated speakers and writers. It is, in short, perfectly good, idiomatic English:

> . . . will you go and see it and tell me whether they murder it or not —George Bernard Shaw, letter, 28 Nov. 1895

> . . . never knew whether or not to insert the names of his parents —John Updike, *Couples*, 1968

> . . . trying to determine whether or not she is wearing a bra —Jay McInerney, *Bright Lights, Big City*, 1984

> I don't know whether or not you are a writer of gobbledygook —Bailey 1984

The option of omitting *or not* only exists when the clause introduced by *whether* serves as the subject of the sentence or as the object of a preposition or verb, as in the above quotations. When the clause has an adverbial function, *or not* must be retained:

> Whether or not one agrees with Vidal's judgments, there are some trenchant formulations —Simon 1980

> . . . adhere to some kind of . . . methodology, whether or not it works —Daniels 1983

Of course, the simplest way to determine whether the *or not* can be omitted is to see if the sentence still makes sense without it.

An alternative to *whether or not* is *whether or no*, which is discussed at NO 3.

which 1. For a discussion of *which* in restrictive and nonrestrictive clauses, and of what it, along with *who* and *that*, may refer to, see THAT 1, 2.

2. The use of *which* to refer to a whole sentence or clause, or as the OED puts it, to a fact, circumstance, or statement, was at one time considered a mistake. The argument was that *which* should refer to a specific antecedent. This is a specious argument because the clause or sentence is clearly the antecedent. Most modern commentators find it acceptable. Here are a few examples of the construction:

> It was decided . . . that the hotel glass should be returned to me, which it was —James Thurber, letter, 6 Oct. 1937

> We are to be at Astley's to-night, which I am glad of —Jane Austen, letter, August 1796

> . . . but nobody really wanted to hear him speak. They wanted to see him grin and show his teeth, which he did —Harry S. Truman, quoted in Merle Miller, *Plain Speaking*, 1973

> "I don't want to be a teacher," Father said quietly, which meant he was angry again —John Irving, *The Hotel New Hampshire*, 1981

> You don't want to be talking to this bald girl, or even listening to her, which is all you are doing —Jay McInerney, *Bright Lights, Big City*, 1984

> The cultural positioning of a work of art is often helpful, but, which is too often forgotten, it is quite distinct from esthetic judgment —Stanley Kauffmann, *Before My Eyes*, 1980

See also THIS 1.

while The earliest meanings of *while* are temporal, but senses unrelated to time have been established in English since Shakespeare's time. American commentators decided that such use was questionable early in the 20th century, and they have continued to express doubts about it in the years since. Here are a few examples:

> While it looks innocent enough, the white sand is a cause of miners' silicosis —Laurence Leamer, *Harper's*, December 1971

> The hit shows are always sold out, and while there may be an occasional gem being ignored, most of what's left is third rate —*And More by Andy Rooney*, 1982

> . . . the Yanks did most of the heavy military lifting, while the Brits did most of the bellicose threatening —Nicholas von Hoffman, *Civilization*, October/November 1999

> . . . seemed to have been over-cleaned in restoration, while other pictures, which were gummy and dark, seemed to need restoration —Sanford Schwartz, *New Yorker*, 16 Sept. 1985

These uses are established and standard. They are also extremely common.

A number of commentators raise the specter of ambiguity with respect to nontemporal uses of *while*. It is not very difficult to work up a sentence in which *while* can be understood in more than one way, but real examples are hard to find. Ambiguity is not an inherent problem in these uses of *while*.

whilom See ERSTWHILE, QUONDAM, WHILOM.

whiskey, whisky The spelling *whiskey* is used by Irish and American distillers; *whisky* is preferred by their counterparts in Britain and Canada. Both spellings are used by Americans in general contexts, but *whiskey* is more common:

> . . . he had been arrested and tried for making whiskey —William Faulkner, *Knight's Gambit*, 1949

... walking to the filing cabinet for the hidden whiskey —James Jones, *From Here To Eternity,* 1951

... produced bootleg whisky —Nicholas Pileggi, *New York,* 24 July 1972

... a glass of whiskey beside the typewriter —Arthur M. Schlesinger, Jr., *Saturday Rev.,* 29 Oct. 1977

Some writers make a point of omitting the *e* when referring specifically to whiskey distilled in Britain (that is, Scotland) or Canada.

whither See HITHER 1.

who, whom 1. It may seem that the use of these interrogative and relative pronouns should be simple enough: *who* is the nominative ("Who is it?") and *whom* is the objective ("the man whom we had met"). As is generally recognized, however, there is a certain disparity between the way *who* and *whom* are supposed to be used and the way they are actually used. Let us begin with a little lesson in Shakespeare.

> LAUNCE. Can nothing speak? Master, shall I strike?
> PROTEUS. Who wouldst thou strike?
> LAUNCE. Nothing.
> —*The Two Gentlemen of Verona,* 1595

> BOYET. Now, madam, summon up your dearest spirits.
> Consider who the King your father sends,
> To whom he sends, and what's his embassy
> —*Love's Labour's Lost,* 1595

> MACBETH. ... For certain friends that are both his and mine,
> Whose loves I may not drop, but wail his fall
> Who I myself struck down.
> —*Macbeth,* 1606

> ALBANY. Run, run, O, run!
> EDGAR. To who, my lord? Who has the office?
> —*King Lear,* 1606

> POLONIUS. ... I'll speak to him again.— What do you read, my lord?
> HAMLET. Words, words, words.
> POLONIUS. What is the matter, my lord?
> HAMLET. Between who?
> POLONIUS. I mean, the matter that you read, my lord.
> —*Hamlet,* 1601

> IAGO. Not this hour, Lieutenant; 'tis not yet ten o'th'clock. Our general cast us thus early for the love of his Desdemona; who let us not therefore blame.
> —*Othello,* 1605

These examples to show that Shakespeare was not at all averse to using *who* in places where

the strict grammarians—who were still a century and a half away when Shakespeare wrote—would prescribe *whom.* They show, in addition, that he sometimes used both *who* and *whom* in the fashion later to be prescribed. Shakespeare's use does not in fact appear to be substantially different from present-day use; *who* for *whom* is most usual at the beginning of an utterance ("Who wouldst thou strike?"), but it sometimes occurs after a preposition or verb ("To who, my lord?"). And it should be noted that most of the speakers represented here are from the upper orders of society; these speakers are not louts or clowns. Nor was Shakespeare an innovator with these uses. Flesch 1983 notes that *who* had been substituted for *whom* in constructions like these as far back as the 14th century.

The anomaly of finding both *who* and *whom* used for objective functions did not escape the attention of the 18th-century grammarians. Lowth 1762 came out foursquare for strict construction, insisting on (for example) "Whom is this for?" rather than "Who is this for?" Only the considerable prestige of Milton's *Paradise Lost* dented Lowth's orthodoxy; he allowed *than whom* as an exception (see THAN 1). Priestley, at least as early as the 1769 edition cited by Leonard 1929, disagreed with Lowth, favoring "Who is this for?" as the more natural way of speaking. Leonard mentions several other grammarians of the age, each disagreeing with one point or another urged by some other grammarian, or introducing some new analogy. Noah Webster managed to write himself, through successive editions and works, from Lowth's position around to Priestley's.

The 19th-century grammarians seem not to have added anything of substance to the dispute. But Richard Grant White 1870 did sound a new note when he predicted the demise of *whom*:

> One of the pronoun cases is visibly disappearing—the objective case *whom.*

Since White's solemn pronouncement, quite a few commentators have made the same observation. Here is a sampling:

> *Whom* is fast vanishing from Standard American —Mencken, *The American Language,* 1936

> If ... we lose the accusative case *whom*—and we are in great danger of losing it —Simon 1980

> *Whom* is dying out in England, where "Whom did you see?" sounds affected —Anthony Burgess, *N.Y. Times Book Rev.,* 20 July 1980

The first question that needs to be asked, then, is whether *whom* is truly in danger of disappearing. *Whom* seems to be rare in ordinary speech, which is what Mencken and Burgess were paying attention to. But it does not seem to be disappearing from written English. It is worth pointing out, though we will not take the space to illustrate at length, that the Merriam-Webster files are rich in examples of the prescribed uses of *whom*. Beyond that, persistence of *whom* in constructions such as "a person whom everybody admits is successful"—where in fact normative grammar prescribes *who*—gave Fowler 1926 considerable concern. He found an abundance of evidence in British newspapers and feared the use might become a "sturdy indefensible." Bryant 1962 devotes some space to these constructions, which she calls "hypercorrect" and in which she says *whom* is "mistakenly" used as the subject.

Jespersen 1909–49 (vol. 3) has a fairly long treatment of the "hypercorrect" *whom*. After discussing Fowler's interpretation, he goes on to list a large number of examples and to examine in some detail the reasons for the use of *whom*. His judgment is quite the opposite of Fowler's; he concludes that *whom* is natural and correct in such constructions and that *who* represents either the historical trend of avoiding *whom* or is the result of schoolmastering.

It is distinctly possible, then, that subject *whom* need not be hypercorrect. Let us return to Shakespeare, before hypercorrectness or even simple correctness was a concern, for some examples:

PROSPERO. . . . They now are in my pow'r;
And in these fits I leave them, while I visit
Young Ferdinand, whom they suppose is drown'd,
And his and mine lov'd darling.
—The Tempest, 1612

TIMON. . . . Spare not the babe
Whose dimpled smiles from fools exhaust their mercy.
Think it a bastard whom the oracle
Hath doubtfully pronounc'd thy throat shall cut,
And mince it sans remorse.
—Timon of Athens, 1608

BASTARD. . . . And others more, going to seek the grave
Of Arthur, whom they say is kill'd to-night
On your suggestion.
—King John, 1597

HELENA. . . . But such a one, thy vassal, whom I know
Is free for me to ask, thee to bestow.
—All's Well That Ends Well, 1603

ELBOW. My wife, sir, whom I detest before heaven and your honour—

ESCALUS. How? thy wife?
ELBOW. Ay, sir; whom I thank heaven is an honest woman.
—Measure for Measure, 1605

The grammatical point at issue can be illustrated by Elbow's two *whom*s. In the first, "My wife . . . whom I detest," the relative pronoun is the object of *I detest*. But in ". . . whom I thank heaven is an honest woman," the *I thank heaven* is parenthetical, and the relative is actually the subject of *is an honest woman*. The two constructions are otherwise similar, however, and *whom* has been produced for both. According to Jespersen, it is something about the tightness of such constructions that elicits *whom*. When the parenthetical insertion is clearly set off by a pause or a pause is indicated by punctuation, *who* then becomes much more likely than *whom*. Jespersen has numerous examples, of which we append two here:

MARK ANTONY. . . . I should do Brutus wrong, and Cassius wrong,
Who, you all know, are honourable men.
—Shakespeare, Julius Caesar, 1600

There was one H———, who, I learned in after days, was seen expiating some maturer offence in the hulks —Charles Lamb, *Essays of Elia*, 1823

When *who* is affixed without pause to the parenthetical insertion, Jespersen lays it to the historical trend away from *whom* and the effect of schoolmastering. He provides examples, including Fielding, from before schoolmastering, and Dickens, after schoolmastering. He also notes that some writers have used both *who* and *whom* as subject—Benjamin Franklin and James Boswell among them.

To repeat, our evidence shows that present-day uses of *who* and *whom* are in kind just about the same as they were in Shakespeare's day. What sets us apart from Shakespeare is greater self-consciousness: the 18th-century grammarians have intervened and given a reason to watch our *who*s and *whom*s. Self-consciousness turns up at least as early as Dickens:

'Think of who?' inquired Mrs. Squeers; who (as she often remarked) was no grammarian, thank God —*Nicholas Nickleby*, 1839

And later:

"It's not what you know," we say, "but who you know." And I don't mean "whom." —W. Allen, *Western Folklore*, January 1954

"By whom?" I said. When I was serious my English was good —Robert B. Parker, *The Widening Gyre*, 1983

And sometimes self-consciousness becomes an unfortunate self-doubt:

> Mr. Beeston said he was asked to step down, although it is not known exactly who or whom asked him —*Redding* (Conn.) *Pilot*, in *New Yorker*, 31 May 1982

But this greater self-consciousness appears to have changed actual usage very little. The following examples show just about the same kinds of uses found in Shakespeare:

> They become leaders. It doesn't matter who they lead —Ernest Hemingway, *Green Hills of Africa*, 1935

> And he said, Well, haven't you got any opinion at all about them? and I said, About who? —William Faulkner, 18 May 1957, in *Faulkner in the University*, 1959

> . . . which social group we identify with . . . , and who we are talking to —Margaret Shaklee, in Shopen & Williams 1980

> . . . his three cousins from Minneapolis . . . who he left because he was nervous being around them —Garrison Keillor, *Lake Wobegon Days*, 1985

> Let tomorrow's people decide who they want to be their President —William Safire, *N.Y. Times Mag.*, 11 Oct. 1987

> Colombo, 48 years old, whom law enforcement officials have said is the head of a Mafia family in Brooklyn —*N.Y. Times*, 5 July 1971

> "My roommate and I sat up half the night talking about it," said one student, whom, I suspect, has never before read anything he wasn't forced to —John Medelman, *Esquire*, January 1974

> In preparing to make a speech, the speaker gives some thought to whom his audience is —Linda Costigan Lederman, *New Dimensions*, 1977

> . . . the Blair family, whom Safire says were the Kennedys of their time —Trish Todd, *Publishers Weekly*, 29 May 1987

> Aikman will always have a chilly relationship with coach Barry Switzer, whom Aikman believes is too soft when it comes to player discipline —Peter King, *Sports Illustrated*, 7 Apr. 1997

> . . . you'd have to give Nelson a plus for being a Vietnam veteran. Who else would you want to lead a team into battle? —Mike Purkey, *Golf Mag.*, February 1996

All that remains to be said is that objective *who* and nominative *whom* are much less commonly met in print than nominative *who* and objective *whom*. In speech, you rarely need to worry about either one. In writing, however, you may choose to be a bit more punctilious, unless you are writing loose and easy, speechlike prose. Our files show that objective *whom* is in no danger of extinction, at least in writing.

2. For a discussion of *who (whom), that,* and *which* in reference to persons or things, see THAT 2.

who else's See ELSE 1.

whoever, whomever These words are much less common than *who* and *whom*, and the problems of case attendant upon them are not substantially different in kind from those that beset *who* and *whom*. For a discussion of such problems, see WHO, WHOM 1.

whom See WHO, WHOM.

who's, whose See WHOSE 2.

whose **1.** *Whose, of which.* Since English is not blessed with a genitive form for *that* or *which, whose* has been used to supply the missing forms since sometime in the 14th century. No one seems to have thought the use worthy of notice until the 18th century, when such grammarians as Lowth, Priestley, and Lindley Murray worried about it. They seemed not to like it, but knew writers of note had used it.

After Lowth and Priestley had let the genie of disapproval out of the bottle, however tentatively, there was no putting it back. Many other 18th- and 19th-century grammarians disapproved. Even Henry Bradley in the OED says that *whose* is "usually replaced by *of which*, except where the latter would produce an intolerably clumsy form."

Hall 1917, somewhat to his surprise, found *whose* used of inanimate things in some 140 authors, in more than 1,000 passages, from the 15th century to the early 20th. Once again we find the peculiar situation of usage commentary: the grammarians are very attentive to one another's opinions, and the standard authors pay them no attention at all.

The force that has always worked against acceptance of *whose* used of inanimate things is its inevitable association with *who*. The force that has always worked in its favor was suggested by Murray: it provides not only a shorter but a smoother and more graceful transition than the alternative "the . . . of which." In prose as well as poetry, the value of gracefulness (or, at least, the value of avoiding awkwardness) is generally recognized by good writers. As a result, this is one disputed usage that is perhaps more likely to occur in the works of good writers than bad ones:

> . . . villages and farms whose inhabitants reflect the various cultures —Norman Douglas, *Siren Land*, 1911

... house in one of whose rooms was a striker wounded by Adkin's men —Sinclair Lewis, *Cheap and Contented Labor,* 1929

... a world whose values were becoming totally materialist —Stephen Spender, *New Republic,* 20 July 1953

... a wonderful book ... whose author is the German poet Rainer Maria Rilke —e e cummings, *New Republic,* 2 Nov. 1953

... a precaution whose necessity was demonstrated a while back —Lewis Mumford, *New Yorker,* 6 Apr. 1957

... a word whose sources have been explained and reexplained over the centuries —Baron 1986

I can see its lights through my window, whose sash rattles —John Updike, *New Yorker,* 23 Jan. 1989

In the last half of the 20th century the subject of *whose* and *of which* was discussed in most books, but not one of them finds *whose* anything but standard.

The notion that *whose* may not properly be used of anything except persons is a superstition; it has been used by innumerable standard authors from Wycliffe to Updike, and is entirely standard as an alternative to *of which the* in all varieties of discourse.

2. *Whose, who's.* Nearly every handbook right down to the level of the fifth grade or so is at pains to distinguish *whose*, possessive pronoun, from *who's*, contraction of *who is, who has.* Since they are pronounced the same, however, people do muddle the two spellings:

Teaching Reading and Writing Skills: Whose Responsible —brochure for a New England educational conference, reprinted in *New Yorker,* 21 Mar. 1983

... somebody else whose got nine jillion dollars —*Town & Country,* May 1976

When others are called for cross-checking, who's timing is always right? —advt., cited in Simon 1980

These are errors of inattention and should be avoided.

whys and wherefores See WHEREFORE.

will See SHALL, WILL.

-wise The suffix *-wise* has been attached to nouns to make adverbs since at least the 1670s (Bunyan used *Dialogue-wise* in *Pilgrim's Progress* in 1678). Sometime during the 1930s, *-wise* developed a new meaning "with regard to; in respect of." Presumably this new use developed mainly from its original "in the manner of" sense of *-wise,* which has often been

tacked onto nouns to form convenient nonce words:

... his hands clasped Buddha-wise before him —Celestine Sibley, *Saturday Evening Post,* 27 Dec. 1958

Such adaptability is also one of the most noteworthy features of *-wise* meaning "with regard to." Our earliest evidence for the new sense of *-wise* is from 1938, when *Fortune* magazine was using it in the word *percentagewise*:

... industrial sales remained more or less level percentagewise —*Fortune,* February 1938

The new use attracted some notice; this letter to publisher H. R. Luce makes fun of it:

I too think Fortune is in good shape organization-wise though understaffed as always good-writer-wise —Archibald MacLeish, letter, 20 July 1938

The rapid success of the new *-wise* is easily explained: it provided a simpler and shorter way to say things. It was not discovered by writers on usage until the 1950s. E. B. White, for instance, added a warning against it to the collection of misused words in his 1959 edition of *Elements of Style.* Such warnings, of course, are for other people:

This has been the summer of the great discontent and widespread confusion, weatherwise, healthwise, and otherwisewise —E. B. White, letter, 4 Sept. 1959

Since the '50s, the subject has become a staple of college handbooks. Their strictures seem to have had little effect. *-Wise* is just too handy to be stamped out. Writers use it when they're being humorous:

Have a safe week, sexwise and otherwise —Herb Caen, *San Francisco Chronicle,* 31 Aug. 1987

Gentle, nonaggressive and stoned out of his mind, he'd struck Kate as slightly off balance yin-and-yangwise —Cyra McFadden, *The Serial,* 1977

And they use it when they're serious:

... the *triskelion,* a heraldic device consisting of three legs radiating swastika-wise from a hub —W. V. Quine, *Quiddities,* 1987

... no longer needing to impose himself Prospero-wise on the world —Theodore Weiss, *Triquarterly,* Fall 1988

This is an established standard use. Note, however, that the adverbs formed this way are nonce formations, intended to serve a particular purpose, and are seldom heard of again.

wish *Wish* is commonly used as a transitive verb meaning "to want" or "to desire," usually with an infinitive or clause as its object:

... a man who sincerely wished he could do more —*New Yorker,* 28 Mar. 1994

It is not that they wish to pretend that they are busy —Oliver St. John Gogarty, *It Isn't This Time of Year at All!,* 1954

... the clergy of the Diocese of Manchester, whom Ruskin wished to terrify —Tim Hilton, *Times Literary Supp.,* 28 Dec. 1990–3 Jan. 1991

... they wished that they could direct the domestic and foreign policies of the nation —John L. Recchiuti, *N.Y. Times Book Rev.,* 16 June 1991

In another typical construction, the object is a proper name or personal pronoun followed by an infinitive:

I wished Foster to go away —Robert McAlmon, *There Was a Rustle of Black Silk Stockings,* 1963

These uses of *wish* are not controversial, although a couple commentators express a general preference for *want.* The real point of dispute is whether the transitive *wish* should be used with a simple noun object. Several commentators have criticized such usage as a genteelism, typically offering some such sentence as "Do you wish some more coffee?" as an example of what not to say. The OED shows that the use of *wish* with a simple noun object dates back to Old English, but called it dialectal in 1933. Our evidence shows the construction standard but not common:

... a majority of employees wished a union shop —*Current Biography 1948*

When a visitor ... wishes a license to operate a rented car —Bert Pierce, *N.Y. Times,* 14 Mar. 1954

It is perhaps most often found with a direct and indirect object or in a passive construction:

... then wished Gordon luck —Jeremy Mindich, *Village Voice,* 3 May 1994

I wished her Godspeed and turned on the TV —Lawrence Block, *American Heritage,* April 1990

To be feared, however—that is the consummation most devoutly to be wished —Anthony Holden, *Big Deal,* 1990

... pretend that the competition between the two concerns could be wished away —Alan Tonelson, *N.Y. Times Book Rev.,* 4 Feb. 1990

with *With* used to join two nouns (as what Quirk et al. 1985 calls a quasi-coordinator) has attracted some attention among usage commentators. A few maintain that a singular noun coordinated with another singular noun by *with* should take a singular verb; others, quoting authoritative works on syntax, believe either a singular or plural verb may be used, depending on notional agreement. Surveyed opinion (Leonard 1932, Crisp 1971) holds the use of a plural verb to be disputable. Here is one example of such use:

Pichon was, indeed, glowering. He with Roosevelt were the representatives of republics —Mark Sullivan, *Our Times,* vol. 4, 1932

For more on this topic, see AGREEMENT, SUBJECT-VERB: COMPOUND SUBJECTS 3.

with a view, with the view See VIEW.

without The use of *without* as a conjunction meaning "unless" was once perfectly respectable:

A very reverent body. Ay, such a one as a man may not speak of without he say 'sir-reverence' —Shakespeare, *The Comedy of Errors,* 1593

That any laud to me thereof should grow, Without my plumes from others' wings I take

—Sir Philip Sidney, *Astrophel and Stella,* 1591

By the 18th century, however, it had fallen far enough from grace for Samuel Johnson to note in his 1755 Dictionary that it was "not in use." Since the late 19th century, this conjunction has occurred rarely in print except in representations of uneducated or dialectal speech:

You don't know about me without you have read a book by the name of *The Adventures of Tom Sawyer* —Mark Twain, *Huckleberry Finn,* 1884

"... There ain't none in the oil-shed, that I do know—without there might be a bit in the wash'us—but it'll have been there a long time," she concluded dubiously —Dorothy L. Sayers, *Busman's Honeymoon,* 1937

"Doctor'll be here soon, without the snow holds him up ..." —H. E. Bates, *Selected Stories,* 1957

without hardly See HARDLY.

with regard to See REGARD 1.

with respect to See IN RESPECT OF, IN RESPECT TO, WITH RESPECT TO.

with the exception of This phrase is commonly used as a synonym for *except* or *except for:*

. . . accepted by the legislatures of all the territories concerned with the exception of British Guiana and the Virgin Islands —*The Americana Annual 1953*

. . . with the exception of cases of deliberate, premeditated theft —Glynn Mapes, *Security World,* May 1968

An emphatic adjective is sometimes added before *exception:*

He was a very bad influence over all his friends, with the single exception of myself —Oscar Wilde, *The Picture of Dorian Gray,* 1891

This is a venerable phrase, first attested in the early 17th century, when it was written *with exception of.* In recent years it has been criticized by some for wordiness, but it continues to be in good use. You should avoid it only if you count yourself among those who believe that you can never be too terse.

See also EXCEPTION.

with the hope of, with the hope that See HOPE 2.

woman See LADY.

won't *Won't* is one of the most irregular-looking of the negative contractions that came into popular use during the 17th century and into print around the 1660s. *Won't* was shortened from earlier *wonnot,* which in turn was formed from *woll* (or *wol*), a variant form of *will,* and *not.* It appeared in various forms in Restoration comedies:

No, no, that won't do —Thomas Shadwell, *The Sullen Lovers,* 1668

We'll thrust you out, if you wo'not —William Wycherly, *The Country Wife,* 1675

But wo't thou really marry her? —Aphra Behn, *The Dutch Lover,* 1673

Why, you wont baulk the Frollick? —William Congreve, *The Double-Dealer,* 1694

Won't was among the contracted and truncated forms that Joseph Addison attacked in *The Spectator* on 4 August 1711. It seems to have been under something of a cloud, as far as the right-thinkers were concerned, for more than a century afterward. This did not, of course, interfere with its employment, and it was common enough to enjoy the distinction of being damned in the same breath as *ain't* in an address delivered before the Newburyport (Mass.) Female High School in December 1846, as reported by Shirley Brice Heath in Shopen & Williams 1980. The speaker termed both "absolutely vulgar." How *won't* eventually escaped the odium that still

clings to *ain't* is a mystery, but today it is entirely acceptable.

See also AIN'T.

wordiness You might tend to think or opine that *wordiness* would refer to the use and/or utilization of many more extra words, terms, phrases, and locutions than are absolutely required, needed, or necessary for writing, saying, or otherwise expressing your ideas, thoughts, theses, or opinions. In theory it is. In practice, it is not. Usage writers are nearly unanimous in condemning as wordy the ordinary, short, idiomatic phrases of spoken discourse, such as *climb up, as to, consensus of opinion, for free, have got to, meet up with, refer back, what for, able to, would like to, who is, advance planning, ask a question, at about, continue on, but that, but what, the field of, where . . . at, first began, off of,* and *inside of,* to name a few. Many commentators are also pretty severe on the old formal phrases of business correspondence and on long formulas like *in view of the fact that, somewhere in the neighborhood of,* and *the question as to whether,* which are sometimes used to rescue a writer from a desperate construction. Nearly all of the commentators would heartily subscribe to Professor Strunk's Rule 13 (see Strunk & White 1959): "Omit needless words."

In actual practice, of course, writers—even usage writers—do not omit all needless words:

. . . remember that *due to the fact that* is a wordy way of saying the short and simple word *since* —Shaw 1970

What does "the short and simple word" add to the statement?

Certain other *in* phrases are nothing but padding and can be omitted entirely —Little, Brown 1986

Couldn't this be boiled down to "Other *in* phrases may simply be omitted"? And here is Bernstein 1965 on *climb up:*

But here we have tautology aggravated by wastefulness. The writer who values terseness will usually omit the *up.*

The writer who really values terseness could omit everything but the last three words.

But this is too easy a game to be helpful. What we see in these examples are writers who have warmed to their subject and who are trying to make their point, heedless of their own prescriptions. No good writer writes to rule. James Sledd has demonstrated persuasively (in Greenbaum 1985) that E. B. White contravened his own rules of composition in the very act of composing Strunk & White 1959.

Conciseness is a virtue in writing, but it is not the only virtue. If you use the forms that are natural to speech, you will often get your point across better—or at least more easily. The conscious avoidance of the natural expressions of speech can sometimes lead you to stray into jargon (see JARGON).

See also REDUNDANCY.

wordy See WORDINESS.

worser See DOUBLE COMPARISON.

worst comes to worst The idiomatic phrase *if worst comes to worst* has many variants. It was first recorded in 1597 as *if the worst come to the worst*. As is the case with many idioms, the phrase seems nonsensical if its parts are examined individually. Presumably it was the desire to make the phrase more logical that gave rise to the variant *if the worse comes to the worst*, which was first recorded in 1719, when it was used (in the past tense) by Daniel Defoe in *Robinson Crusoe*. Some examples:

> If worst comes to worst, I was told that the only practical final recourse is through a small-claims court —*ITN,* May 1995

> When worse comes to worst—when a dangerous pest starts an infestation —Erik Larson, *Smithsonian,* June 1987

> If worst came to worst I could always get by —James Norman Hall, *Atlantic,* October 1952

> If worse came to worst she could telephone Nick —Daphne du Maurier, *Ladies' Home Jour.,* August 1971

> If the worst comes to the worst, you may have to cut it out using another tool —A. Fyffe & I. Peter, *The Handbook of Climbing,* 1990

The forms which are most commonly used are *if worst comes to worst* and *if worse comes to worst*. The definite articles are now omitted more often than not in American use; our little British evidence shows them usually retained.

worst way The adverbial phrase *the worst way* originated in American speech during the 19th century. It is basically equivalent to *very much*, but it has forceful connotations all its own. To want something very much is not quite the same as to want it the worst way. *The worst way,* now often used with *in,* typically implies an intense, almost desperate longing:

> . . . he wanted to be a football star in the worst way —*Time,* 13 Aug. 1956

> And the canons hated Vivian. They wanted him out in the worst way —Herb Kessler, quoted by Tristan Davies, *Hopkins Arts & Sciences,* Spring 1992

The use of this phrase in writing has occasionally been discouraged in handbooks on usage,

from 1917 to 1990. Our evidence shows that it is not common in edited prose and tends to be used in contexts having an informal or conversational tone.

worthwhile This adjective originated as a two-word phrase, *worth while,* which was essentially a short way of saying "worth one's while" and which functioned strictly as a predicate adjective (as in "the experience was worth while"). In the early 20th century, it first began to appear as an attributive adjective, in which use it was hyphenated (as in "a worth-while experience"). Eventually the hyphenated form was largely superseded by the solid form, *worthwhile,* which became so well established in time that it grew to be the favored form even in the predicate ("The experience was worthwhile"). In current English, the hyphenated and two-word forms are still in use:

> . . . identifying himself as a worth-while citizen —Virgil M. Rogers, in *Automation, Education, and Human Values,* ed. W. W. Brickman & S. Lehrer, 1966

> . . . is better off than when he started—which tells him that his gamble was worth while —*National Rev.,* 22 Dec. 1997

But the solid form is by far the usual choice in all contexts:

> If microgravity turns out to be worthwhile in the long run, so much the better —Fenella Saunders, *Discover,* May 1997

> . . . we looked for a worthwhile lesson we could draw — *Time,* 2 Aug. 1999

Burchfield 1996 regrets the popularity of the solid form, but Garner 1998 prescribes it.

would See SHALL, WILL; SHOULD, WOULD.

would have The use of *would have* in place of *had* in the protasis of a conditional sentence (as in "If they would have come earlier, we could have left on time") has been cited as an error in books on usage since at least 1924. Such usage appears to be a characteristic of informal speech, in which it may often occur in a contracted form ("If they'd have come earlier . . ."). Our evidence indicates that it does not often find its way into print in edited text, but it is notorious in student writing and therefore a staple of college handbooks even today.

See also PLUPLUPERFECT.

would of This phrase is a transcription of the contracted form *would've* of *would have*. It is sometimes used intentionally—for instance, by Ring Lardner. Except for very special purposes you will want *would have* or *would've*. See OF 2.

would rather See HAD RATHER.

wrack See RACK, WRACK.

wrangle See WANGLE, WRANGLE.

wrath, wrathful, wroth These related words have had overlapping uses in centuries past, but they are now easily distinguished. *Wrath* is the noun:

> But it is by no means only physicists that are the objects of his wrath —David L. Goodstein, *Science,* 30 Oct. 1998

Wrathful is the usual adjective:

> . . . appealing to both wrathful social conservatives and resentful working-class Americans —David Corn, *The Nation,* 26 June 1995

And *wroth* is an adjective synonymous with *wrathful* that is mostly found in the phrase *wax wroth*:

> My plan was to wax wroth today about gasoline prices being raised —Russell Baker, *Springfield* (Mass.) *Union-News,* 9 Aug. 1990

Fowler 1926 proposed as a further distinction that *wrathful* be considered the attributive adjective and *wroth* the predicative adjective. His proposal is generally followed, except that *wrathful* is also occasionally used as a predicate adjective:

> Was he formidable, was he wrathful, . . . was he emotional? —Antonia Byatt, *New Yorker,* 12 Jan. 1987

Fowler also preferred \'rōth\ (rhyming with *both*) as the pronunciation of *wroth,* but the pronunciation now favored in both American and British English is \'róth\ (rhyming with *cloth*).

wreak, wreck Havoc is usually said to be wreaked:

> Nor is this feisty crew beyond wreaking havoc among themselves —James Atlas, *N.Y. Times Book Rev.,* 13 Sept. 1981

But it is sometimes said to be wrecked:

> . . . the isolationists wrecked their havoc by boldly asserting that economic and military assistance were two entirely different and separate things —*New Republic,* 10 Sept. 1951

Wreak havoc is the original expression and is regarded by many people as the only correct one. Those same people regard \'rēk\ as the only correct pronunciation of *wreak,* but \'rek\ also occurs as a secondary variant (so it is not always possible to determine whether the person saying \'rek\ would write *wreak* or *wreck*).

Other verbs are also used with *havoc;* the most common are *play, create,* and *cause*:

> . . . could play havoc with the electronics —Andrew Lawler, *Science,* 6 Nov. 1998

> Their little delinquents run up and down the aisles, creating havoc —S. B. Canyon, *Upside,* January 2000

> . . . in order to cause havoc behind the front line —Martin Gilbert, *The First World War,* 1994

After *wreak,* by far the most popular choice, these last three verbs outnumber the rest (including *raise, work, wreck, wrought*) in our most recently collected evidence. Usage commentators variously warn against *wreck, work,* and *wrought.* In spite of these warnings, *wreck* and *wrought* turn up, although not with great frequency:

> . . . wrecking havoc with your body —Mary Ann Marshall, *Cosmopolitan,* August 2000

> . . . could have wrought havoc with the model shots —Ron Magid, *American Cinematographer,* June 1995

We have very little recent evidence for *raise* or *work.*

write The standard surviving principal parts are past tense *wrote* and past participle *written.* Lamberts 1972 notes that *write* and *bite* are in the same class, but when their old four-part inflection was reduced to our modern three-part one, *write* kept its singular preterite *wrote,* with plural *writ* dwindling into dialectal use, while *bite* kept the plural preterite *bit.*

For the past participle, *wrote* was acceptable well into the 18th century:

> . . . he had wrote to hinder it on some pretence or other —Thomas Gray, letter, 12 Sept. 1756

But it has long since dropped out of mainstream use. Another old past participle, *writ,* probably derived from the even older *ywritte,* is kept alive by the phrase *writ large* and by writers who use it when being deliberately or playfully literary or dialectal:

> For two months, dear Bang, I have rotted a dry rot. I have read nothing, writ nothing, dreamed nothing —Archibald MacLeish, letter, 30 July 1915

> Write me what you want writ in them and I will write it —Flannery O'Connor, letter, 1 Mar. 1960

> (And, yes, Little Eva, the foregoing sentence was writ deliberate.) —Kilpatrick 1984

wrong, wrongly *Wrong* is a versatile word. It can be used as an adjective, noun, or verb, and as an adverb synonymous with *wrongly.*

Some commentators have observed that *wrong* is preferred to *wrongly* when the adverb occurs after the verb it modifies, while *wrongly* is used when the adverb precedes the verb. This observation accords with usage in most respects, but it leaves out several important complications.

The adverb *wrong* occurs most frequently with the verbs *do, get, have,* and especially *go.* With each of these verbs it forms set phrases in which *wrongly* cannot be idiomatically substituted:

> . . . none of them had done anything wrong —Anna Quindlen, *Newsweek,* 13 Mar. 2000

> Don't get me wrong. I'm no bluenose —Guy Trebay, *N.Y. Times Mag.,* 11 Jan. 1998

> . . . figures you can't go wrong relying on the ignorance of the average juror —Graham Button, *Forbes,* 21 Oct. 1996

Wrong is also used with other verbs. It usually follows immediately after the verb, often at the end of a sentence or clause:

> After all, one could guess wrong —Stan Sauerhaft, *Dun's,* March 1972

> The costs had been figured wrong —Martin Mayer, *Change,* March 1972

Wrongly occurs in such contexts, but it is less common than *wrong.*

When the adverb precedes the verb or participle that is being modified, *wrongly* is indeed the only possible choice:

> . . . the innocence of wrongly accused inmates —James Ryerson, *Lingua Franca,* September 2000

> . . . the unattached or wrongly attached participle —Amis 1998

> . . . restored him to a position which has wrongly been denied him —Maurice Edelman, *Books of the Month,* April 1953

Note, however, that it is still necessary to use *wrongly* in these sentences even if it were to follow the verb. In contexts where unfairness or error is suggested, *wrongly* is the right adverb.

> . . . imparts misinformation, as when he says wrongly that the Blackfriars Gate-house mortgage deed has been lost —S. Schoenbaum, *Shakespeare's Lives,* 1991

> . . . reckoning wrongly every multiplication that he attempted —Richard Preston, *New Yorker,* 2 Mar. 1992

The best way to choose between *wrong* and *wrongly* is to rely on your own grasp of English idiom. The one that *sounds* correct *is* correct. If they both sound correct, then either one may be used.

These general observations also hold true for the analogous adverbs *right* and *rightly.*

wroth See WRATH, WRATHFUL, WROTH.

X

Xmas *Xmas* has been used as a short form of *Christmas* since the 16th century. The *X* is derived from the Greek letter chi (X), which is the first letter in Χρι τος, "Christos." *X, Xp,* and *Xt,* all derived from the Greek name, have been used to stand for *Christ-* in other words besides *Xmas.* There is evidence in the OED and the OED Supplement for *Xpen* (1485), *Xpian* (1598), and *Xtian* (1845, 1915, 1940), all meaning "Christian," and for *Xpofer* (1573), "Christopher," *Xstened* (1685–86), "christened," and *Xtianity* (1634, 1811, 1966), "Christianity." Most of the recent evidence for these words comes from the letters of educated Englishmen who know their Greek. *Xmas* also has shown a tendency to turn up in the letters of the well-educated:

> . . . but if you won't come here before Xmas, I very much fear we shall not meet *here* at all —Lord Byron, letter, 9 Sept. 1811

> . . . which I hope to get published before Xmas —Lewis Carroll, letter, 10 June 1864

> I expect about Xmas a visit —Oliver Wendell Holmes d. 1935, letter, 11 Oct. 1923

By and large, however, *Xmas* is limited in current usage to advertisements, headlines, and banners, where its brevity is an advantage. When read aloud, it is pronounced either \'kris-məs\ or \'ek-sməs\. Some people dislike it because it displaces the *Christ-* in *Christmas.* Its association with the world of advertising has also done nothing for its reputation.

Y

yclept This peculiar-looking word is actually the past participle of the archaic verb *clepe*, which means "to call or name." Its strange spelling gives it a certain appeal, as does the fact that many people have no idea what it means, and the occasional writer still enjoys using it as a playful synonym of *called* or *named*:

> These folks include the gargantuan Neanderthal proprietor, yclept Thor —Judith Crist, *Saturday Rev.*, 29 May 1976

> . . . a monstrous big sloop, yclept the Concorde —William F. Buckley, Jr., *N.Y. Times Mag.*, 9 Oct. 1983

> . . . the crane's-nest-style beard attached to the aptly yclept . . . Henry N. Beard, Esq. —Bruce McCall, *Esquire*, September 1990

If you are willing to risk puzzling your readers, you may find some use for *yclept* yourself. But before you start singing about "A Boy Yclept Sue," be warned that Fowler classed *yclept* as "worn-out humor" back in 1926, and several subsequent commentators (Evans 1957, Flesch 1964, and Bernstein 1965) have also failed to be amused.

ye, *pronoun* *Ye* was originally the nominative form of the second person plural pronoun. It contrasted with *you*, the oblique (accusative and dative) form. Around the middle of the 16th century the contrast began to break down, and the two forms became interchangeable. Wyld 1920 says that in the 16th century nominative *you* was much more frequent than *ye* as an accusative or dative. But in the 17th century *ye* was much more often found in object positions:

> All of ye —Thomas Shadwell, *The Sullen Lovers*, 1668

> . . . I'll be judge between ye —Aphra Behn, *The Dutch Lover*, 1673

It was also used in a reduced form—just a representation of the vowel, tacked to the end of another word:

> Paints de'e say? —William Congreve, *The Double Dealer*, 1694

> Hark'ee, Oriana —George Farquhar, *The Inconstant*, 1702

Attached to the end of words like *hark* and *thank*, a remnant of *ye* has survived in various spellings. *Ye* by itself has survived, too, primarily as a dialectal variant of *you*:

> ". . . every damn man of ye. . . ." —James Stephens, *The Crock of Gold*, 1912

> . . . if a man is going to pay you he'll pay ye without too much dunning —Dock Franklin, quoted in *Our Appalachia*, ed. Laurel Shackelford & Bill Weinberg, 1977

> Straight man [at a Scottish music-hall performance]: "Why didn't ye cut him doun?" —Israel Shenker, *N.Y. Times*, 20 Oct. 1974

It is quite common in fictional Scots and Irish dialogue.

Strang 1970 points out, in addition, that in the 18th century, as *you* took over as the usual second person pronoun in all functions, *ye* continued in elevated literary use. Some of the elevated use was liturgical and ceremonial, and survives:

> Hark ye, O, King Solomon, and all ye who hear me —*Adoptive Rite Ritual—Eastern Star*, rev. ed., 1952

It also occurs in a few fixed contexts:

> Avast, Ye Pirates!. . . . Music belongs to artists and their labels —*Newsweek*, 8 May 2000

> Oh, Andy, we hardly knew ye —Walter Goodman, *N.Y. Times*, 11 Mar. 1990

See also YOU 3.

ye, *article* Students of English spelling are aware that part of its oddity derives from the fact that the earliest printers were working with manuscripts in which the spelling at least in part represented pronunciations that were no longer in use. These printers had to work with European types, whose letters were those in general European use. Not in use on the continent were some of the runic characters still being used in Middle English. One such was the thorn (þ), a character which stood for what the continental alphabets less efficiently spelled *th*.

In 14th-century manuscripts, some scribes were writing a form of the thorn that was all but indistinguishable in shape from the letter *y*, and one of its most common uses was in the short forms of *the, that, they, them*, and the like, that the scribes used to save themselves writer's cramp. Early printers set these abbreviated forms as they found them, with *y* for the thorn.

So this early rendition of scribal *the* has given us the alternate form *ye*, typically used nowadays because of its conspicuous antiquarian flavor with *olde* in the quaint-sounding names of various business establishments ("Ye Olde Antique Shoppe").

It would seem that few things could be less important than a disquisition upon the pronunciation of antiquarian *ye*, but a fair number of commentators have troubled themselves to remark upon the subject, and they have disagreed. Some have insisted that *ye* should be pronounced like *the*, others have noted and accepted that its far more common pronunciation is \yē\. This is not a matter to be taken seriously. We think you can safely judge for yourself how *ye* is to be pronounced in such facetious uses as still occur:

You are in ye olde desperate straits —Kathy Crafts & Brenda Hauther, *Surviving the Undergraduate Jungle*, 1976

. . . when ye olde faithful hoste, Alistair Cooke, introduces the author —Arthur Unger, *Christian Science Monitor*, 19 Nov. 1980

yearn People who yearn usually yearn *for* something:

He yearned for a drink —William Styron, *Lie Down in Darkness*, 1951

. . . the man yearns for companionship —Daphne du Maurier, *Ladies' Home Jour.*, August 1971

Less common prepositions following *yearn* are *after*, *toward* (or *towards*), and *over*:

. . . who yearned after the social and economic setup of the nineteenth century —*Collier's Year Book*, 1949

He yearns toward the European grand-prix circuits —*Newsweek*, 22 Mar. 1954

. . . and the new . . . hand-sewing machines the Indian women yearned over —Marjory Stoneman Douglas, *The Everglades: River of Grass*, 1947

yet The use of *yet* with a verb in the plain past tense with *did* ("Did he leave yet?" rather than "Has he left yet?") has sometimes been criticized. Such use is common and unobjectionable in ordinary speech. Its occurrence in writing, according to our evidence, is rare except in transcriptions of speech and fictional dialogue:

Asked about the verdict, he said only, "I did not study it yet" —Hanna Rosin, *New Republic*, 13 Mar. 2000

"Did it come down yet?" —Joseph Wambaugh, *The Secrets of Harry Bright*, 1985

you 1. You may have noticed that the editors of this book have often used *you* in addressing you, the reader, directly. Our reason for doing so is well described in this comment:

Bernstein and Copperud agree that the use of you to address the reader . . . conduces to informality and directness —Copperud 1970

Quite a number of commentators also remark that you can use *one* instead of *you* when you want to be more formal, distant, and impersonal. They sensibly warn, however, that you should be careful not to mix the formal *one* with the more informal *you*.

2. The history of the pronoun *you* provides a good example of the effect social forces can have on the language. *You* began as the accusative and dative form of the second person plural pronoun. The nominative plural was *ye*. The form used to address one person in centuries past was *thou* (*thee* was the accusative and dative form of the singular).

As far back as the 14th century, the plural forms *ye* and *you* began to be used to address one person—usually a superior—as a mark of deference and respect. And the use of the polite plural gradually grew: Strang 1970 points out that such a use once begun must grow, since people would rather be polite than risk giving offense in cases of doubt. So as the use of the plural increased, the singular became the special use, the limited form. By about the beginning of the 17th century, *thou* and *thee* marked an intimate or personal relationship, or a superior to inferior relationship.

Then by about the middle of the 16th century the contrast in function between *ye* and *you* began breaking down. Henry Sweet, in his *New English Grammar* (1892), attributed part of the breakdown to sound: there seems to have been a tendency to push *ye* into uses that matched the rhyming *thee* and *you* into those that matched the rhyming (then) *thou*. Ben Jonson's early-17th-century Grammar listed *you* and *ye* as simple variants, while *thou* and *thee* retained their traditional functions. Wyld 1920 observes that the first Queen Elizabeth seems to have used only *you* in writing; a user of her prestige must surely have given *you* a boost. Wyld also says that in 16th-century usage there was much more use of *you* as a nominative than of *ye* as an accusative or dative—in other words, *you* was expanding its range at the expense of *ye*. This process has continued, although *ye* has not disappeared entirely (see YE, *pronoun*).

The loss of a singular pronoun for everyday use was noticed in the common speech and gave rise to various remedies. The first was to make the distinction between singular *you* and plural *you* by verb agreement; *you was* for the singular continued in polite if informal use well into the 18th century before it lost respectability. Special plural forms were later contrived to hold *you* chiefly to singular use; these include such formations as *you-all* (see YOU-ALL), *you-uns*, *yez*, and *youse*. None of these save *you-all* has enjoyed much success or much prestige.

So the simple social drive of good manners has in a few centuries completely remade the second person pronoun. No doubt the social pressures of today will work changes in the language as well. (For examples of changes that may be taking place, see PERSON 2 and THEY, THEIR, THEM 1.) The chances are, however, that most changes they bring about will not be rapid.

you-all The debate over *you-all* (and its contraction, *y'all*) has to do with whether Southerners use it strictly as a plural of *you* or sometimes use it as a singular as well. An entertaining history of the dispute, which dates back to the end of the 19th century, can be found in H. L. Mencken, *The American Language, Supplement II* (1948). In brief, Southerners themselves have for the most part insisted that *you-all* is only a plural and that its use as a singular occurs only among Northerners doing a poor imitation of Southern speech, while contentious Northerners and a few renegade Southerners have argued that singular use is not unheard of among Southerners themselves. Just about everyone agrees, at least, that *you-all* does usually function as a plural. Even when only one person is being addressed, *you-all* normally implies the inclusion of another or others whom the single person is understood to represent. However, the evidence, most of which is testimonial, does indicate that *you-all* has also been used as a singular in the South, although such usage is certainly atypical and is not regarded with approval by a great many Southerners.

your, you're The possessive pronoun is *your*: "Your spelling is atrocious." The contraction of *you are* is *you're*: "You're an atrocious speller."

yours It is true that the *-s* in *yours* is a genitive ending, and it is true that the genitive *-s* is normally preceded by an apostrophe, but it is not true that there is an apostrophe in *yours*. Do not be too hard on yourself if you mistakenly include one, however. It could happen to almost anyone:

> ... if you will do your's by repeating the French Grammar —Jane Austen, letter, 12 Nov. 1800

> Believe me, Mr. Terry, your's Truly —Lord Byron, letter, 12 Nov. 1805

> Your's of the 28th. ult. came to hand by our last post —Thomas Jefferson, letter, 9 May 1809

Actually, *your's* was standard in the 18th century, and it was an acceptable variant in the early 19th century, although it was appreciably less common than *yours*. Today, however, *yours* is the only acceptable form.

See also HERS.

yourself yourselves The use of the reflexive pronouns *yourself*, singular, and *yourselves*, plural, in constructions where they are not reflexive or intensive has been criticized since at least 1917, chiefly by the same commentators who have attacked *myself*. The criticism has been somewhat perfunctory for the most part. Nothing particularly baneful has been seen in either *yourself* or *yourselves*, and in general the unpleasant name-calling of the *myself* issue has not been repeated (see MYSELF).

The most insightful commentary about these pronouns can be found in Jespersen 1909–49 (vol. 2) and Evans 1957. Both point out that *yourself* and *yourselves* preserve the distinction between singular and plural that has been lost from *you*, and they further suggest that *yourself* and *yourselves* are sometimes used in place of *you* for the purpose of making number explicit.

The OED shows *yourself* in uses neither reflexive nor emphatic from the 15th century on; the same uses for *yourselves*, a less common word, start in the 16th century. Here are some examples of ours:

> I remark a considerable payment made to yourself on this Third of December —Robert Browning, *Pippa Passes*, 1841

> I have read you; that is a favour few authors can boast of having received from me besides yourself —Samuel Johnson, *The Idler*, 10 June 1758

> ... I shall be as much benefited by it as yourselves —Jane Austen, *Sense and Sensibility*, 1811

> In our days there is scarcely an instance of a learned or unlearned man who has written gracefully, excepting your friend Goldsmith and (if your modesty will admit my approaches) yourself —Walter Savage Landor, *Imaginary Conversations*, 1848

> Get me some good left-handers like yourself and Robinson —Robert Frost, letter, 23 Jan. 1921

In all this I look to nothing but the happiness of yourself, Mr. Randolph, and the dear children —Thomas Jefferson, letter, 27 Feb. 1809

Those who, like yourself, know what they are about —Walter W. Skeat, letter, in K. M. Elisabeth Murray, *Caught in the Web of Words*, 1977

. . . you once told me about sighting a sea serpent—either yourself or a friend of yours saw it —James Thurber, letter, 4 Aug. 1955

The respectability of these uses is obviously above reproach. Evans finds them acceptable but is doubtful of their literary standing. We think these examples show a modest connection with literary usage.

Z

zeal One may either have zeal *for doing* something or zeal *to do* something:

Wilson's zeal for converting the world to American virtues —Milton Viorst, *Interplay*, February 1969

. . . has allowed his zeal for overlooking no one to lead him into being inconclusive —*Saturday Rev.*, 19 Dec. 1953

In its zeal to protect itself from liability —John C. Burton, *Arthur Young Jour.*, Winter/Spring 1971

. . . and genuine zeal to throw off colonialism —Jon Stewart, *Mother Jones*, June 1979

Where the object is a noun rather than a verbal, *for* is the usual preposition after *zeal*:

. . . confessed that Chinese youth lack zeal for the Revolution —Alex Campbell, *New Republic*, 2 Apr. 1966

. . . there was no widespread zeal for the idea —Ben Harte, *The Lamp*, Spring 1972

zealous 1. See JEALOUS 1.
2. When it is followed by a preposition, *zealous* usually occurs with *for*:

. . . its industry, eager for markets, and its bankers, zealous for investments, developed new techniques of economic imperialism —Allan Nevins & Henry Steele Commager, *The Pocket History of the U.S.*, 1942

Lewis, zealous even to bigotry for the doctrines of the Church of Rome —T. B. Macaulay, *The History of England*, vol. I, 1849

It has occasionally occurred with *about*:

. . . those who are more zealous about the triumph of their righteous cause —Morris R. Cohen, *The Faith of a Liberal*, 1946

And it also occurs with *to* plus an infinitive:

. . . Swinburne stops thinking just at the moment when we are most zealous to go on —T. S. Eliot, *The Sacred Wood*, 1920

zoology The traditional and recommended pronunciation of this word is \zō-'äl-ə-jē\. Gowers in Fowler 1965 calls \zü-'äl-ə-jē\ a "very common vulgarism," due probably to the influence of *zoo*. Another possible reason for the rise of this variant is the fact that, in relaxed speech, the first pronunciation tends to come out as \zə-'wäl-ə-jē\, which could easily be apprehended as a reduced or relaxed form of \zü-'äl-ə-jē\. (A similar interplay between stressed and unstressed versions of a single word led historically to the differentiation of *of* and *off*.)

An analogous state of affairs obtains for *zoological*: traditionally \ˌzō-ə-'läj-i-kəl\, now also \ˌzü-ə-'läj-i-kəl\.

Condemnation of the newer variant is sociolinguistically problematic, since the people to whom one might be inclined to allow the last word, namely zoologists themselves, not uncommonly use the \zü-\ version. We even find the traditional disyllabic \ˌzō-ə-\ being reduced in the speech of scientists to a monosyllabic \ˌzü-\. Our pronunciation files show these bargain-basement variants for a couple of fifty-dollar words: *zoonoses* pronounced \ˌzü-'nō-ˌsēz\ by a university veterinarian, and *zooxanthellae* turned to \ˌzü-ˌzan-'thel-ē\ in the mouth of a biologist.

zoom Usage commentators get strange ideas. Since sometime in the 1950s some of them have asserted that it is not possible to zoom in any direction but up. This notion seems to have originated with airplanes. But the origins of *zoom* actually have nothing to do with airplanes. The word is onomatopoeic, like *zap*, *zing*, and *zip*. The earliest evidence of its use dates to the 1880s and was meant to suggest the sound of something moving at a high speed. Other early citations for *zoom* have to do with sounds produced by bees and by musical instruments. The airplane sense of *zoom* had to wait until the early 20th century. If you think of the sound of the engines in those old airplanes, you'll understand how the use developed from the buzzing sense.

But as popular as airplanes became, the aeronautical *zoom* never drove the older meaning out of use. It has persisted especially in describing something or someone moving at great speed, regardless of direction:

> . . . two of the 143 roaring racers zoomed off the road —*Time*, 18 Apr. 1938

> . . . zooming sixty-five yards to a touchdown —*Kansas City Star*, 2 Jan. 1943

> . . . Bold Ruler went zooming along alone, passing the six-furlong pole —Audax Minor, *New Yorker*, 22 June 1957

> . . . a rocket sled zooming on rails down an incline —*Science News Letter*, 19 Dec. 1964

After a couple of decades it dawned on the commentators that *zoom* was not being used in the prescribed directional way, and a couple of them, Shaw 1975, 1987 and Freeman 1990, deigned to permit level movement, but both find downward movement nonstandard. They are out of touch with reality:

> . . . peels off, zooming down in a 60-degree power dive —Byron Kennerly, *Harper's*, July 1941

> . . . government planes zoomed down to bomb tanks and strafe street fighters —*Time*, 1 Aug. 1949

> . . . she zoomed recklessly down ski slopes —*People*, 3 Jan. 1983

> . . . a cutback, in which you zoom down on the steep, smooth face of the wave —Jonathan Sale, *Manchester Guardian Weekly*, 22 Dec. 1991

Zoom often tends to suggest great speed with the direction indicated by an adverb:

> . . . teenage boys . . . zoom around on motorcycles —Stan Sesser, *New Yorker*, 20 Aug. 1990

> . . . fired a tracer from the right face-off circle that zoomed past goalie Dominik Hasek —Michael Farber, *Sports Illustrated*, 24 Apr. 2000

> . . . a beat-up Oldsmobile . . . zoomed across in front of the van —Joseph Wambaugh, *Finnegan's Week*, 1994

The "upward" connotations of *zoom* are also strongly established, especially in the figurative sense "to increase rapidly":

> The popularity of her novels has zoomed —Ray Walters, *N.Y. Times Book Rev.*, 6 Nov. 1977

> His estimated income zoomed to $18.4 million in '99 —David Hume Kennerly, *Newsweek*, 21 June 1999

And *zoom* is also commonly used in computers and photography, without connotations of either speed or upward movement:

> . . . you can click on anyplace on the Global Relief Map, zoom in and out of several levels of magnification —Roger Blake, *New Age Jour.*, December 1994

> . . . when the KTTV camera zoomed in on George and Crazy Ed —Joe Eszterhas, *Rolling Stone*, 14 Sept. 1972

All of these uses are standard.

Bibliography

This list consists primarily of works—books of commentary on English usage, grammars, college handbooks, dictionaries, and a few miscellaneous items—that have been referred to in the body and front matter of the present book.

A few additional works have also been included even though they are not referred to specifically elsewhere in the book. Some were consulted for general orientation during the course of work; others are simply important books on such topics as the history of English and the American variety of the language that are of general interest.

A uniform style is followed throughout this bibliography, except that no attempt is made to give a publisher for books published before 1900.

Cross-references leading to appropriate entries in the bibliography are supplied when text references to a work do not match the name or title under which the work is listed here or when an editor's name may be more familiar than the title of a work.

Alford, Henry. 1866. *A Plea for the Queen's English.* London and New York.

Algeo, John. 1977. "Grammatical Usage: Modern Shibboleths." In *James B. McMillan: Essays in Linguistics by His Friends and Colleagues.* Ed. James C. Raymond and I. Willis Russell. University: Univ. of Alabama Press.

_____. 1983. "Usage." In *Needed Research in American English.* Publication of the American Dialect Society No. 71.

American Dialect Dictionary. See Wentworth, Harold.

American Heritage Dictionary of the English Language. 1969. Ed. William Morris. Boston: Houghton Mifflin.

American Heritage Dictionary of the English Language. 1982. 2d College ed. Boston: Houghton Mifflin.

American Heritage Dictionary of the English Language. 2000. 4th ed. Boston, New York: Houghton Mifflin.

Amis, Kingsley. 1998. *The King's English.* New York: St. Martin's Press.

Ayres, Alfred. 1881. *The Verbalist.* New York.

[Bache, Richard Meade.] 1869. *Vulgarisms and Other Errors of Speech.* 2d ed. Philadelphia.

Bailey, Edward P., Jr. 1984. *Writing Clearly: A Contemporary Approach.* Columbus: Charles E. Merrill.

Baker, Josephine Turck. 1927. *The Correct Word: How to Use It.* Evanston, Ill.: Correct English.

[Baker, Robert.] 1770. *Reflections on the English Language.* London.

_____. 1779. *Remarks on the English Language.* London.

Baker, Sheridan. 1981. *The Practical Stylist.* 5th ed. New York: Harper and Row.

_____. 1984. *The Complete Stylist and Handbook.* 3d ed. New York: Harper and Row.

Ball, F. K. 1923. *Constructive English.* Boston: Ginn.

Bander, Robert G. 1978. *American English Rhetoric.* 2d ed. New York: Holt, Rinehart & Winston.

Bardeen, C. W. 1883. *Verbal Pitfalls.* Syracuse.

Barnard, Ellsworth. 1979. *English for Everybody.* Amherst, Mass.: Dinosaur.

Baron, Dennis E. 1982. *Grammar and Good Taste.* New Haven: Yale Univ. Press.

_____. 1986. *Grammar and Gender.* New Haven: Yale Univ. Press.

Barzun, Jacques. 1985. *Simple & Direct.* Rev. ed. New York: Harper and Row.

Battles, H. K., et al. 1982. *Words and Sentences, Book 2.* Lexington, Mass.: Ginn.

Baugh, Albert C., and Thomas A. Cable. 1978. *A History of the English Language.* 3d ed. Englewood Cliffs, N.J.: Prentice Hall.

Belanoff, Pat, et al. 1986. *The Right Handbook.* Upper Montclair, N.J.: Boynton/Cook.

Bell, James K., and Adrian A. Cohn. 1981. *Bell & Cohn's Handbook of Grammar, Style, and Usage.* 3d ed. New York: Macmillan.

Bernstein, Theodore. 1958. *Watch Your Language.* Great Neck, N.Y.: Channel.

_____. 1962. *More Language That Needs Watching.* Manhasset, N.Y.: Channel.

_____. 1965. *The Careful Writer.* New York: Atheneum.

_____. 1971. *Miss Thistlebottom's Hobgoblins.* New York: Farrar, Straus and Giroux.

_____. 1977. *Do's, Don'ts & Maybes of English Usage.* New York: Times Books.

Bierce, Ambrose. 1909. *Write It Right.* New York: Union Library Assoc., 1937.

Bolinger, Dwight L. 1980. *Language—The Loaded Weapon.* London: Longman.

Bolton, W. F. 1966. *The English Language.* Cambridge, England: Cambridge Univ. Press.

Bolton, W. F., and D. Crystal. 1969. *The English Language.* Vol. 2. Cambridge, England: Cambridge Univ. Press.

Bremner, John B. 1980. *Words on Words.* New York: Columbia Univ. Press.

Bridges, Robert. 1919. *On English Homo-*

phones. S.P.E. (Society for Pure English): Tract No. 2. London: Oxford Univ. Press.

Brown, Goold. 1851, 1880. *The Grammar of English Grammars*. New York.

Brown, Ivor. 1945. *A Word in Your Ear and Just Another Word*. New York: E. P. Dutton.

Brown University Corpus. *See* Kučera, Henry; Francis, W. Nelson.

Bryant, Margaret M. 1962. *Current American Usage*. New York: Funk & Wagnalls.

Bryant, William Cullen. 1877. *Index Expurgatorius*. Reprinted in Bernstein 1971.

Bryson, Bill. 1984. *The Facts on File Dictionary of Troublesome Words*. New York: Facts on File.

Building English Skills. Orange Level (9th grade). 1982. Rev. ed. Ed. Joy Littell et al. Evanston, Ill.: McDougal, Littell.

Burchfield, Robert. 1981. *The Spoken Word*. New York: Oxford Univ. Press.

Burchfield 1996. *See* Fowler 1996.

Campbell, George. 1776. *The Philosophy of Rhetoric*. Edinburgh.

Canby, Henry Seidel, and John B. Opdyke. 1918. *Good English*. New York: Macmillan.

Century Collegiate Handbook. See Greever, Garland.

Century Dictionary. 1889–91. Ed. William Dwight Whitney. New York.

Chambers Pocket Guide to Good English. 1985. Ed. George W. Davidson. Edinburgh: W & R Chambers.

Clark, Thomas L., et al. 1981. *Language: Structure And Use*. Glenview, Ill.: Scott, Foresman.

Cobbett, William. 1823. *A Grammar of the English Language*. Oxford.

Colter, Rob. 1981. *Grammar to Go*. Rev. ed. Toronto: Anansi.

Compton, Alfred G. 1898. *Some Common Errors of Speech*. New York.

Cook, Claire Kehrwald. 1985. *Line by Line*. Boston: Houghton Mifflin.

Copperud, Roy H. 1960. *Words on Paper*. New York: Hawthorn.

_____. 1964. *Webster's Dictionary of Usage and Style*. New York: Avenal.

_____. 1970. *American Usage: The Consensus*. New York: Van Nostrand Reinhold.

_____. 1980. *American Usage and Style: The Consensus*. New York: Van Nostrand Reinhold.

Corder, Jim W. 1981. *Handbook of Current English*. 6th ed. Glenview, Ill.: Scott, Foresman.

Creswell, Thomas J. 1974. *Usage in Dictionaries and Dictionaries of Usage*. Diss. U. of Chicago. Publication of the American Dialect Society Nos. 63–64. 1975.

Crisp, Raymond Dwight. 1971. *Changes in Attitudes Toward English Usage*. Diss. U. of Illinois. Ann Arbor: University Microfilms International, 1980. 72–12,126.

Curme, George O. 1931. *Syntax*. Boston: D. C. Heath. Vol. 3 of *A Grammar of the English Language*. 2 vols. 1931–1935.

_____. 1935. *Parts of Speech and Accidence*.

Boston: D. C. Heath. Vol. 2 of *A Grammar of the English Language*. 2 vols. 1931–1935.

Daniels, Harvey A. 1983. *Famous Last Words*. Carbondale, Ill.: Southern Illinois. Univ. Press.

A Dictionary of American English. 1938–44. Ed. Sir William A. Craigie and James R. Hulbert. 4 vols. Chicago: Univ. of Chicago Press.

A Dictionary of Americanisms. 1951. Ed. Mitford M. Mathews. 2 vols. Chicago: Univ. of Chicago Press.

Dictionary of American Regional English. 1985– . Vol. 1 Ed. Frederic G. Cassidy, Vol. 2 Ed. Frederic G. Cassidy and Joan Houston Hall, Vol. 3 Ed. Frederic G. Cassidy and Joan Houston Hall. Cambridge, Mass.: Harvard Univ. Press.

Dillard, J. L. 1976. *American Talk*. New York: Random House.

Ebbitt, Wilma R., and David R. Ebbitt. 1982. *Writer's Guide and Index to English*. 7th ed. Glenview, Ill.: Scott, Foresman.

Einstein, Charles. 1985. *How to Communicate*. New York: McGraw-Hill.

Evans, Bergen. 1962. *Comfortable Words*. New York: Random House.

Evans, Bergen, and Cornelia Evans. 1957. *A Dictionary of Contemporary American Usage*. New York: Random House.

Fennell, Francis L. 1980. *Writing Now: A College Handbook*. Chicago: Science Research Associates, Inc.

Fernald, James C. 1946. *English Grammar Simplified*. New York: Funk and Wagnalls.

Finegan, Edward. 1980. *Attitudes toward English Usage*. New York: Teachers College Press.

Flesch, Rudolf. 1964. *The ABC of Style*. New York: Harper and Row.

Fisher, James A. 1996. *Talking Correctly for Success*. Cincinnati, Ohio: Avant Publishing Co.

_____. 1983. *Lite English*. New York: Crown.

Follett, Wilson. 1966. *Modern American Usage*. Ed. and completed by Jacques Barzun. New York: Hill and Wang.

Foster, Brian. 1968. *The Changing English Language*. London: Macmillan.

Fowler, Henry W. 1926. *A Dictionary of Modern English Usage*. Oxford: Clarendon Press.

_____. 1965. *A Dictionary of Modern English Usage*. 2d ed. Ed. Sir Ernest Gowers. Oxford: Clarendon Press.

_____. 1996. *The New Fowler's Modern English Usage*. 3d ed. Ed. R. W. Burchfield. Oxford: Clarendon Press.

Fowler, Henry W., and Francis George Fowler. 1907. *The King's English*. Oxford: Clarendon Press.

Francis, W. Nelson. 1958. *The Structure of American English*. New York: Ronald.

Francis, W. Nelson, and Henry Kučera. 1982. *Frequency Analysis of English Usage*. Boston: Houghton Mifflin.

Freeman, Morton S. 1983. *A Treasury for Word Lovers*. Philadelphia: ISI Press.

_____. 1990. *The Wordwatcher's Guide to Good Writing & Grammar.* Cincinnati, Ohio: Writer's Digest Books.

Fries, Charles Carpenter. 1927. *The Teaching of the English Language.* New York: Thomas Nelson.

_____. 1940. *American English Grammar.* New York: D. Appleton-Century.

Funk & Wagnalls New Standard Dictionary of the English Language. 1913.

Garner, Bryan A. 1998. *A Dictionary of Modern American Usage.* New York, Oxford: Oxford Univ. Press.

Goldstein, Miriam B. 1966. *The Teaching of Language in Our Schools.* Urbana, Ill.: National Council of Teachers of English.

Goold Brown. *See* Brown, Goold.

Gould, Edward S. 1867. *Good English.* New York.

Gowers, Sir Ernest. 1948. *Plain Words.* London: His Majesty's Stationery Office.

_____. 1954. *Complete Plain Words.* London: Her Majesty's Stationery Office. Reprinted 1962 as *Plain Words: Their ABC.* New York: Alfred A. Knopf.

_____. 1973. *Complete Plain Words.* Ed. Sir Bruce Fraser. 2d ed. London: Her Majesty's Stationery Office.

Greenbaum, Sidney. 1984. "Good English." Inaugural Lecture. University College London. 14 March.

_____, ed. 1985. *The English Language Today.* Oxford: Pergamon Press.

Greenbaum, Sidney, and Janet Whitcut. 1988. *Longman Guide to English Usage.* Harlow, Eng.: Longman.

Greenough, James B., and George L. Kittredge. 1901. *Words and Their Ways in English Speech.* New York: Macmillan.

Greever, Garland, and Easley S. Jones. 1924. *The Century Collegiate Handbook.* New York: Century.

Guth, Hans P. 1980. *American English Today.* 3d ed. New York: McGraw-Hill.

_____. 1985. *New English Handbook.* 2d ed. Belmont, Calif.: Wadsworth.

Hall, Fitzedward. 1872. *Recent Exemplifications of False Philology.* New York.

_____. 1873. *Modern English.* New York.

Hall, J. Lesslie. 1917. *English Usage.* Chicago: Scott, Foresman.

Harper Dictionary of Contemporary Usage. See Morris, William.

Heritage. See American Heritage Dictionary of the English Language.

Hiatt, Mary. 1977. *The Way Women Write.* New York: Teachers College Press.

Hill, Adams Sherman. 1895. *The Principles of Rhetoric.* New York.

Hill, Archibald A. 1965. "The Tainted Ain't Once More." *College English* Jan.: 298–303.

_____. 1979. "Bad Words, Good Words, Misused Words." In *Studies in English Linguistics.* Ed. Sidney Greenbaum et al. London: Longman.

Himstreet, William C., and Wayne Murlin Baty. 1977. *Business Communications.* 5th ed. Belmont, Calif.: Wadsworth.

Hodges, John C., and Mary E. Whitten. 1984. *The Harbrace College Handbook.* 9th ed. New York: Harcourt Brace Jovanovich.

Hodgson, William B. 1889. *Errors in the Use of English.* Edinburgh.

Howard, Philip. 1977. *New Words for Old.* New York: Oxford Univ. Press.

_____. 1978. *Weasel Words.* New York: Oxford Univ. Press.

_____. 1980. *Words Fail Me.* New York: Oxford Univ. Press.

_____. 1983. *A Word in Your Ear.* New York: Oxford Univ. Press.

_____. 1984. *The State of the Language.* New York: Oxford Univ. Press.

Hyde, G. M. 1926. *Handbook for Newspaper Workers.* Enlarged ed. New York: Appleton.

Irmscher, William F. 1976. *The Holt Guide to English.* 2d ed. New York: Holt, Rinehart and Winston.

Janis, J. Harold. 1984. *Modern Business Language and Usage in Dictionary Form.* Garden City, N.Y.: Doubleday.

Jensen, Dana O., et al. 1935. *Modern Composition and Rhetoric.* Boston: Houghton Mifflin.

Jespersen, Otto. 1909–49. *A Modern Grammar on Historical Principles.* 7 vols. Heidelberg: Carl Winter.

_____. 1917. *Negation in English and Other Languages.* Copenhagen: Ejnar Munksgaard.

_____. 1924. *Philosophy of Grammar.* New York: Holt.

_____. 1946. *Mankind, Nation and Individual.* Bloomington, Ind.: Indiana Univ. Press.

_____. 1948. *Growth and Structure of the English Language.* 9th ed. New York: Macmillan.

Johnson, Edward D. 1982. *The Handbook of Good English.* New York: Facts on File.

Johnson, Samuel. 1755. *A Dictionary of the English Language.* London.

Jonson, Ben. 1640. *The English Grammar.* London. Ed. with introduction and notes by Alice V. Waite. New York: Sturgis and Walton, 1909.

Joos, Martin. 1967. *The Five Clocks.* New York: Harcourt Brace Jovanovich.

Kilpatrick, James J. 1984. *The Writer's Art.* Kansas City: Andrews, McMeel & Parker.

Krapp, George Philip. 1909. *Modern English: Its Growth and Present Use.* New York: Scribners.

_____. 1925. *The English Language in America.* 2 vols. New York: Ungar, 1960.

_____. 1927. *A Comprehensive Guide to Good English.* Chicago: Rand McNally.

Kučera, Henry, and W. Nelson Francis. 1967. *Computational Analysis of Present-Day American English.* Providence, R.I.: Brown Univ. Press.

Kurath, Hans. *See Middle English Dictionary.*

Lakoff, Robin. 1975. *Language and Woman's Place.* New York: Harper and Row.

Lamberts, J. J. 1972. *A Short Introduction to English Usage.* New York: McGraw-Hill.

Language 8. 1981. Ginn Language Program. Lexington, Mass.: Ginn.

Language: Structure and Use. See Clark, Thomas L.

Leacock, Stephen. 1943. *How to Write.* New York: Dodd, Mead.

Leonard, Sterling A. 1929. *The Doctrine of Correctness in English Usage, 1700–1800.* Madison: University of Wisconsin Studies in Language and Literature: No. 25.

———. 1932. *Current English Usage.* English Monograph No. 1. Chicago: National Council of Teachers of English.

The Lincoln Library of Essential Information. 1924. Buffalo, N.Y.: Frontier Press.

Lindley Murray. See Murray, Lindley.

The Little, Brown Handbook. 1980. Ed. H. Ramsey Fowler et al. Boston: Little, Brown.

The Little, Brown Handbook. 1986. Ed. H. Ramsey Fowler et al. 3d ed. Boston: Little, Brown.

Long, J. H. 1888. *Slips of Tongue and Pen.* New York.

Longman Dictionary of the English Language. 1984. London: Longman.

Longman Guide to English Usage. See Greenbaum, Sidney.

Lounsbury, Thomas R. 1908. *The Standard of Usage in English.* New York: Harper.

Lowth, Robert. 1762. *A Short Introduction to English Grammar.* London.

———. 1763. *A Short Introduction to English Grammar.* 2d ed., corrected. London.

———. 1775. *A Short Introduction to English Grammar.* Philadelphia.

Lurie, Charles N. 1927. *How to Say It.* New York: G. P. Putnam's.

Lynes, Russell. 1970. "Usage, precise and otherwise." *Harper's* April: 6 +.

MacCracken, H. N., and Helen E. Sandison. 1917. *Manual of Good English.* New York: Macmillan.

McKnight, George H. 1928. *Modern English in the Making.* New York: Appleton.

McMahan, Elizabeth, and Susan Day. 1980. *The Writer's Rhetoric and Handbook.* New York: McGraw-Hill.

———. 1984. *The Writer's Rhetoric and Handbook.* 2d ed. New York: McGraw-Hill.

The Macmillan Handbook of English. 1982. Ed. Robert F. Willson, Jr., et al. 7th ed. New York: Macmillan.

Maggio, Rosalie. 1987. *The Nonsexist Word Finder.* Phoenix: Oryx.

Malmstrom, Jean. 1964. "Linguistics Atlas Findings *vs.* Textbook Pronouncements on Current American Usage." In Harold Allen, ed. *Readings in Applied English Linguistics.* New York: Appleton-Century-Crofts.

Marckwardt, Albert H. 1958. *American English.* New York: Oxford Univ. Press.

Marckwardt, Albert H., and Fred Walcott.

1938. *Facts About Current English Usage.* New York: Appleton-Century.

A Mark Twain Lexicon. See Ramsay, Robert L.

Marsh, George Perkins. 1859. *Lectures on the English Language.* New York.

Martin, Phyllis. 1977. *Word Watcher's Handbook.* New York: David McKay.

Mathews, Mitford M. 1931. *The Beginnings of American English.* Chicago: Univ. of Chicago Press.

Matthews, Brander. 1901. *Parts of Speech.* New York: Charles Scribner's.

Mencken, H. L. 1919. *The American Language.* New York: Knopf.

———. 1936. *The American Language.* 4th ed. New York: Knopf.

———. 1945. *The American Language, Supplement I.* New York: Knopf.

———. 1948. *The American Language, Supplement II.* New York: Knopf.

———. 1963. *The American Language.* 4th ed. and two supplements. Abridged by Raven I. McDavid. New York: Knopf.

Meredith, L. P. 1879. *Every-Day Errors of Speech.* Philadelphia: J. B. Lippincott & Co.

Merriam-Webster's Collegiate Dictionary, Tenth Edition. 1993. Ed. Frederick C. Mish. Springfield, Mass.: Merriam-Webster

Michaels, Leonard, and Christopher Ricks, eds. 1980. *The State of the Language.* Berkeley: Univ. of California Press.

Middle English Dictionary. 1954– . Ed. Hans Kurath et al. Ann Arbor, Mich.: Univ. of Michigan Press.

Miller, Casey, and Kate Smith. 1976. *Words and Women.* Garden City, N.Y.: Doubleday.

———. 1980. *The Handbook of Nonsexist Writing.* New York: Lippincott.

Mitchell, Richard. 1979. *Less Than Words Can Say.* Boston: Little, Brown.

Mittins, W. H., et al. 1970. *Attitudes to English Usage.* London: Oxford Univ. Press.

Montgomery, Michael, and John Stratton. 1981. *The Writer's Hotline Handbook.* New York: New American Library.

Moon, George Washington. 1865. *The Dean's English.* 4th ed. New York.

Morris, William, and Mary Morris. 1975. *Harper Dictionary of Contemporary Usage.* New York: Harper and Row.

———. 1985. *Harper Dictionary of Contemporary Usage.* 2d ed. New York: Harper and Row.

Murray, Lindley. 1795. *English Grammar Adapted to the Different Classes of Learners.* York.

———. 1847. *English Grammar, Adapted to the Different Classes of Learners.* 55th ed. London.

Newman, Edwin. 1974. *Strictly Speaking.* Indianapolis: Bobbs-Merrill.

Nicholson, Margaret. 1957. *A Dictionary of American-English Usage.* New York: Oxford Univ. Press.

Nickles, Harry G. 1974. *Dictionary of Do's and*

Don'ts for Writers and Speakers. New York: Greenwich House.

O'Connor, Patricia T. 1996. *Woe Is I.* New York: G. P. Putnam's Sons.

Opdyke, John B. 1935. *Get It Right.* New York: Funk and Wagnalls.

_____. 1939. *Don't Say It.* New York: Funk and Wagnalls.

Oxford American Dictionary. 1980. New York: Oxford Univ. Press.

Oxford English Dictionary. 1884–1933. Ed. James A. H. Murray et al. 13 vols. Oxford: Clarendon.

Oxford English Dictionary, Supplement. 1972–1986. Ed. Robert W. Burchfield. 4 vols. Oxford: Clarendon.

Oxford English Dictionary, Second Edition. 1989. Ed. J. A. Simpson and E. S. C. Weiner. Oxford: Clarendon.

Partridge, Eric. 1942. *Usage and Abusage.* New York: Harper.

Perrin, Porter G., and Wilma R. Ebbitt. 1972. *Writer's Guide and Index to English.* 5th ed. Glenview, Ill.: Scott, Foresman.

Phythian, B. A. 1979. *A Concise Dictionary of Correct English.* Totowa, N.J.: Littlefield, Adams.

Pooley, Robert C. 1974. *The Teaching of English Usage.* Urbana, Ill.: National Council of Teachers of English.

Post, Emily. 1927. *Etiquette.* New and enlarged ed. New York: Funk and Wagnalls.

_____. 1945. *Etiquette.* New ed. New York: Funk and Wagnalls.

Poutsma, H. 1904–26. *A Grammar of Late Modern English.* Groningen, Netherlands: P. Noordhoff.

Powell, John A. 1925. *How to Write Business Letters.* Chicago: Univ. of Chicago Press.

Prentice Hall Handbook for Writers. 1978. Ed. Glenn Leggett et al. 7th ed. Englewood Cliffs, N.J.: Prentice Hall.

Prentice Hall Handbook for Writers. 1988. Ed. Glenn Leggett et al. 10th ed. Englewood Cliffs, N.J.: Prentice Hall.

Priestley, Joseph. 1761. *The Rudiments of English Grammar.* London.

_____. 1798. *The Rudiments of English Grammar.* A New Edition Corrected. London.

Pyles, Thomas. 1952. *Words and Ways of American English.* New York: Random House.

_____. 1979. *Selected Essays on English Usage.* Ed. John Algeo. Gainesville, Fla.: Univ. of Florida Presses.

_____. 1982. *Origin and Development of the English Language.* 3d ed. New York: Harcourt Brace Jovanovich.

Pyles, Thomas, and John Algeo. 1970. *English.* New York: Harcourt, Brace and World.

Quiller-Couch, Sir Arthur. 1916. *On the Art of Writing.* New York: G. P. Putnam's.

Quinn, Jim. 1980. *American Tongue and Cheek.* New York: Pantheon.

Quirk, Randolph, et al. 1985. *A Comprehensive Grammar of the English Language.* London: Longman.

Ramsay, Robert L., and Frances Guthrie Emerson. 1938. *A Mark Twain Lexicon.* University of Missouri Studies: Vol. 13, No. 1. Columbia, Mo.: University of Missouri.

Randall, Bernice. 1988. *Webster's New World Guide to Current American Usage.* New York: Simon & Schuster.

The Random House Dictionary of the English Language. 1966. Ed. Jess Stein. New York: Random House.

The Random House Dictionary of the English Language. 1987. 2d ed. Ed. Stuart Berg Flexner. New York: Random House.

Raub, Robert N. 1897. *Helps in the Use of Good English.* Philadelphia.

Reader's Digest. *See Success with Words.*

Richard Grant White. *See* White, Richard Grant.

The Right Handbook. See Belanoff, Pat.

Roberts, Paul. 1954. *Understanding Grammar.* New York: Harper and Row.

_____. 1962. *English Sentences.* New York: Harcourt, Brace and World.

Safire, William. 1980. *On Language.* New York: Times Books.

_____. 1982. *What's the Good Word?* New York: Times Books.

_____. 1984. *I Stand Corrected.* New York: Times Books.

_____. 1986. *Take My Word for It.* New York: Times Books.

_____. 1988. *You Could Look It Up.* New York: Times Books.

_____. 2001. *Let a Simile Be Your Umbrella.* New York: Crown.

Scargill, M. H., et al. 1974. *Modern Canadian English Usage.* Toronto: McClelland and Stuart.

Schele de Vere, M. 1872. *Americanisms: The English of the New World.* New York.

Scott, Foresman. *See* Clark, Thomas L.

Sellers, Leslie. 1975. *Keeping Up the Style.* London: Pitman.

Shaw, Harry. 1970. *Errors in English.* 2d ed. New York: Barnes and Noble.

_____. 1975. *Dictionary of Problem Words and Expressions.* New York: McGraw-Hill.

_____. 1987. *Dictionary of Problem Words and Expressions.* Rev. ed. New York: McGraw-Hill.

Shopen, Timothy, and Joseph M. Williams. 1980. *Standards and Dialects in English.* Cambridge, Mass.: Winthrop.

Simon, John. 1980. *Paradigms Lost: Reflections on Literacy and Its Decline.* New York: Clarkson N. Potter.

Sledd, James. 1959. *A Short Introduction to English Grammar.* Chicago: Scott, Foresman.

Sledd, James, and Wilma R. Ebbitt, ed. 1962. *Dictionaries and THAT Dictionary.* Chicago: Scott, Foresman.

Strang, Barbara M. H. 1970. *A History of English.* London: Methuen.

Strunk, William F., Jr., and E. B. White. 1959. *The Elements of Style.* New York: Macmillan.
_____. 1972. *The Elements of Style.* 2d ed. New York: Macmillan.
_____. 1979. *The Elements of Style.* 3d ed. New York: Macmillan.
Success with Words. 1983. Ed. Peter Davies. Pleasantville, N.Y.: Reader's Digest Association.
Sundby, Bertil, et al. 1991. *A Dictionary of English Normative Grammar 1700–1800.* Amsterdam: John Benjamins.
Swan, Michael. 1980. *Practical English Usage.* Oxford: Oxford Univ. Press.
Sweet, Henry. 1892–98. *A New English Grammar.* 2 vols. Oxford.
Thornton, Richard H. 1912. *An American Glossary.* Vols. 1 and 2. London: St. Francis.
_____. 1939. *An American Glossary.* Vol. 3. Ed. Louise Hanley. Madison, Wisc.: American Dialect Society.
Todd, Loreto, and Ian Hancock. 1986. *International English Usage.* London: Croom Helm.
Treble, H. A., and G. H. Vallins. 1937. *An A.B.C. of English Usage.* New York: Oxford Univ. Press.
Trimble, John R. 1975. *Writing with Style.* Englewood Cliffs, N.J.: Prentice Hall.
Trimmer, Joseph F., and James M. McCrimmon. 1988. *Writing with a Purpose.* 9th ed. Boston: Houghton Mifflin.
Tucker, Susie I. 1967. *Protean Shape: A Study in Eighteenth-Century Vocabulary and Usage.* London: Athlone Press.
Utter, Robert Palfrey. 1916. *Everyday Words and Their Uses.* New York: Harper.
Venolia, Jan. 1982. *Write Right!* Berkeley, Calif.: Ten Speed Press.
Vere, M. Schele de. *See* Schele de Vere, M.
Visser, F. T. 1963–73. *An Historical Syntax of the English Language.* 4 vols. Leiden, Netherlands: Brill.
Vizetelly, Frank. 1906. *A Desk-Book of Errors in English.* New York: Funk and Wagnalls.
_____. 1920. *Mend Your Speech.* New York: Funk and Wagnalls.
_____. 1922. *S.O.S.: Slips of Speech.* New York: Funk and Wagnalls.
Warriner, John E. 1986. *English Grammar and Composition: Complete Course.* Orlando, Fla.: Harcourt Brace Jovanovich.
Watt, William. 1967. *A Short Guide to English Usage.* Cleveland: World.
Webster, Noah. 1800. *A Grammatical Institute of the English Language. . . . Part Second. Containing a Plain and Comprehensive Grammar. . . .* 6th Connecticut ed. Hartford.
_____. 1806. *A Compendious Dictionary of the English Language.* Hartford.
_____. 1828. *An American Dictionary of the English Language.* New York.
_____. 1841. *An American Dictionary of the English Language.* Rev. ed. New York.
_____. 1847. *An American Dictionary of the English Language.* Ed. Chauncey Goodrich. Rev. and enlarged. Springfield, Mass.
_____. 1864. *An American Dictionary of the English Language.* Ed. Noah Porter. Royal Quarto ed. Springfield, Mass.
Webster's International Dictionary. 1890. Ed. Noah Porter. Springfield, Mass.
Webster's New Dictionary of Synonyms. 1968. Springfield, Mass.: G. & C. Merriam.
Webster's New International Dictionary. 1909. Ed. William Torrey Harris. Springfield, Mass.: G. & C. Merriam.
Webster's New International Dictionary. 1934. Ed. William Allan Neilson. 2d ed. Springfield Mass.: G. & C. Merriam.
Webster's New World Dictionary. 1980. Ed. David B. Guralnik. 2d College ed. New York: Simon and Schuster.
Webster's New World Guide to Current American Usage. See Randall, Bernice.
Webster's Ninth New Collegiate Dictionary. 1983. Ed. Frederick C. Mish. Springfield, Mass.: Merriam-Webster.
Webster's Standard American Style Manual. 1985. Springfield, Mass.: Merriam-Webster.
Webster's Tenth. See Merriam-Webster's *Collegiate Dictionary, Tenth Edition.*
Webster's Third New International Dictionary. 1961. Ed. Philip B. Gove. Springfield, Mass.: G. & C. Merriam.
Wentworth, Harold. 1944. *American Dialect Dictionary.* New York: Thomas Y. Crowell.
Weseen, Maurice H. 1928. *Crowell's Dictionary of English Grammar.* New York: Thomas Y. Crowell.
Whipple, T. H. Bailey. 1924. *Principles of Business Writing.* East Pittsburgh, Pa.: Westinghouse Technical Night School Press.
White, Richard Grant. 1870. *Words and Their Uses, Past and Present.* New York.
Whitford, Robert C., and James R. Foster. 1937. *American Standards of Writing.* New York: Farrar & Rinehart.
Williams, Ralph Olmstead. 1897. *Some Questions of Good English.* New York.
Wilson, Kenneth G. 1987. *Van Winkle's Return.* Hanover, N.H.: Published for the Univ. of Conn. by the Univ. Presses of New England.
Winners & Sinners: A Bulletin of Second-Guessing Issued Occasionally from the Newsroom of the New York Times. 1951– .
Woolley, Edwin C. 1920. *Handbook of Composition.* Rev. ed. Boston: D. C. Heath.
Woolley, Edwin C., and Franklin W. Scott. 1926. *New Handbook of Composition.* Boston: D. C. Heath.
Wyld, H. C. 1920. *A History of Modern Colloquial English.* London: T. Allen Unwin.
Zinsser, William. 1976. *On Writing Well.* New York: Harper and Row.